THE HISTORIANS'
HISTORY
OF THE WORLD

MICHELET

The Historians' History of the World

of the World

A comprehensive narrative of the rise and development of nations as record: ed by over two thousand of the great writers of all ages : edited, with the assistance of a distinguished board of advisers and contributors

by

Henry · Smith · Williams · LL.D ·

in twenty-five volumes · Volume XVI :
Scandinavia, Switzerland to 1715

The History Association
London and New York

PRIUS
PLACENDUM
QUAM
DOCENDUM

19   07

TITLE-PAGE DESIGNED AND ENGRAVED

CONTENTS

VOLUME XVI

SCANDINAVIA

CHAPTER IV

Permanent settlement of Iceland by the Norwegians, 121. The political organisation of Iceland, 123. The promulgator of the law, 124. The introduction of Christianity, 125. Trial by battle, 127. Icelandic language and literature, 128. The Sagas; the Elder Edda, 129.

CHAPTER V

Harthacnut and Magnus, 133. Svend and the new dynasty, 136. The church under Knud the Saint, 139. The Guilds, 141. The rise of the bourgeoisie, 143. Church and State, 144. Eric III, Niels, Eric IV, and Eric the Lamb, 145. The division of the kingdom, 148. Valdemar (I) the Great subdues Rügen, 150. Absalon and the Skånians, 153. The death of Valdemar; his laws, 154. Knud VI, 155. Absalon's good works and death, 157. Valdemar II at variance with the emperor, 158. The conquest of Esthonia, 160. The king's captivity, 162. Peace is bought at a high price, 164. Rise of the Hanseatic League and its power in the Baltic, 166. The decline of Denmark in the thirteenth century, 168. The sons of Valdemar the Victorious, 169. Abel the Fratricide is murdered, 171. Christopher I and Eric Glipping, 172. The disintegration of Denmark, 176. Valdemar Atterdag, the restorer of the kingdom, 181. The reunion of the Skånian provinces, 183. Valdemar's reign closes in losses, 184.

CHAPTER VI

Valdemar I begins a new dynasty, 190. Sweden, Norway and Denmark are united under Margaret, 197. Saint Bridget of Sweden, 197. Spread of the order of Saint Bridget; Vadstena Convent, 198.

CHAPTER VII

Events leading up to the Kalmar Union, 201. The consummation of the union, 203. The Holstein War, 205. The union is shaken; Eric resigns his crown, 207. The three countries accept Christopher, 208. Sweden and Denmark separate under Christopher's successor, Charles Knutsson, 209. Under Christian the three kingdoms are again united, 210. The last conflicts of Christian's reign, 214. The stormy reign of Hans, 219. The campaign in Ditmarsh, 225. Christian (II) the tyrant, 229. The carnage of Stockholm, 231. Further atrocities, 234. Gustavus Vasa, 236. Christian aids his own downfall, 239. Frederick I, 243. Christian reappears, and is cast into prison, 247. Pontoppidan tells the story of the reformation in Denmark, 250. Coarseness and ignorance of the clergy, 250. The Odense recess and its results, 252. The death of Frederick, 254. Interregnum, 255. The Count's War, 258. The accession of Christian III, 259. The diet of Copenhagen, 262. Norway and Protestantism, 265. The death of Christian III, 268. Pontoppidan's estimate of Christian III, 268.

CHAPTER VIII

CHAPTER IX

CHAPTER X

CHAPTER XI

CHAPTER XII

CHAPTER XIII

CHAPTER XIV

SWITZERLAND

CONTENTS

CHAPTER IV

PAGE

PART XIX

THE HISTORY OF SCANDINAVIA

BASED CHIEFLY UPON THE FOLLOWING AUTHORITIES

ADAM OF BREMEN, A. AHNFELDT, C. F. ALLEN, G. BINDER, K. BLASENDORFF,
G. P. BLOM, H. L. BRÆKSTED, J. P. W. CATTEAU-CALLEVILLE, O. CELSIUS,
A. CRICHTON, O. DALIN, O. H. DUMRATH, S. A. DUNHAM, A. FRYXELL,
C. A. GOSCH, E. G. GEIJER, G. F. VON JENSSEN-TUSCH, S. LAING,
S. LAGERBRING, K. LUNDBLAD, P. H. MALLET, O. MONTELIUS, F. C. K. H. MÜN-
TER, W. ONCKEN, C. P. PALUDAN-MÜLLER, O. PETRI, E. PONTOPPIDAN,
K. VON SCHLÖZER, P. C. SINDING, SNORRE STURLESON,
H. VON TREITSCHKE, H. WHEATON

WITH ADDITIONAL CITATIONS FROM

ALFRED THE GREAT, ANONYMOUS, J. ARCKENHOLTZ, ARNOLD OF LÜBECK,
R. N. BAIN, J. W. BARDILI, E. DE BEAUMONT-VASSY, J. L. F. BERTRAND,
BIOGRAPHICAL DICTIONARY, C. L. VON BUCH, CHARLES XII, G. DROYSEN,
THE YOUNGER EDDA, THE ELDER EDDA, ENCYCLOPÆDIA BRITAN-
NICA, A. DE FLAUX, ABBÉ FLEURY, E. W. GOSSE, P. F. A.
HAMMERICH, O. HENNE-AM RHYN, HERVARAR SAGA, A. HVITFELDT, JOHAN-
NES MAGNUS, C. R. MARKHAM, J. N. MIDDLETON, H. R. MILL, LORD
MOLESWORTH, OSCAR II, E. L. POSSELT, A. RAMBAUD, O. RUDBECK,
SAXO GRAMMATICUS, THE SAXON CHRONICLE, D. SCHÄFER, F. C.
SCHLOSSER, SIR WALTER SCOTT, J. SIME, TACITUS, H. DE
TERLON, B. THORPE, A. VANDAL

CHAPTER I

THE LEGENDARY PERIOD OF SCANDINAVIAN HISTORY

MONTELIUS ON THE ORIGIN OF THE SCANDINAVIANS

"Concerning the point of time when northern and Gothic lands received their first inhabitants," says Lagerbring,[b] "we know absolutely nothing, and this ignorance we share with all other European countries. Our legends do not go back so far, and even assuming that they had preserved to us the record of a memorable event of such remote antiquity, we could not put faith in them. Johannes Magnus[c] was quite at liberty to assure us that Magog, the grandson of Noah, was pleased to set a term to his wanderings in Sweden; but we are likewise at liberty not to believe him."

After showing how Dr. Bäng, a disciple of Rudbeck,[d] by way of demonstrating his patriotic zeal, prevailed upon our common ancestor Adam to settle in Sweden, Lagerbring continues: "Our own times have lost this fine taste for antiquity, and we now think that our history will not suffer hurt if we make it a few centuries older or younger." Geijer concurs in Lagerbring's opinion that the Jotes [Jotuners or Jotuns], the aboriginal inhabitants of Sweden, were a Lapp or Finnish tribe, but seeks to prove that two other tribes distinct from each other, though closely akin by religion and origin, subsequently migrated thither. First came the Götar [Goths], and after them (probably a short time before the birth of Christ) the Svear [Swedes], under the leadership of Odin.

About the middle of the nineteenth century two Norwegian historians,

Keyser and Munch, propounded another theory concerning the immigration, which attracted much attention for a time, and was as follows:

In the dim backward of time, more than three or four hundred years at least before Christ, the Germans started on their wanderings from the ancient primitive home of their race, about the upper Volga and its tributaries, in the heart of Russia. Several tribes migrated into Germany across the Baltic and the south of Sweden, and we still see a remnant of them in the Gothic population of Sweden and Denmark. Further north the Svear took their way, and migrated into Middle Sweden by way of the Åland Islands. Further north still went the Northmen, either round the bay of Bothnia or by the maritime route from the White Sea. Their oldest settlements are consequently in Halogaland, far to the north, and thence they spread southward over Norway.

The views respecting the immigration of northern tribes which we have here mentioned are based upon the scanty information that can be gathered from historical records. But these records all date from a period when our forefathers were already settled in the north, and the oldest native writings which tell us anything about the immigration were chronicled several thousand years after the event. Under the circumstances any attempt to resolve the question by these methods must be barren of result, every answer must be open to doubt.

The possibility of finding a satisfactory answer only came into view with the discovery of monuments which date from primitive times, and may possibly be referred to the immigration period. About half a century ago it was incontrovertibly demonstrated that both the stationary and movable antiquities which were then attracting more general attention than before dated from periods very remote from one another, that the most ancient go back to the first settlement of the country, and that the inhabitants of northern lands had passed through three great stages of development before the full light of history begins to shine upon the north with the introduction of Christianity.

Since we have as little cause for assuming an immigration *en masse* at the beginning or during the course of the Bronze Age as at the beginning of the Iron Age, it follows that at the end of the age of Stone Scandinavian lands were peopled by the same race as was settled there in the Iron Age; or, in other words, that our Germanic forefathers had already migrated into the country in the Stone Age. What we know of the conditions of the Stone Age, or more correctly speaking of the last portion of that period, does not militate against this theory. We possess a not inconsiderable number of human skulls, found in the graves of that period, which supply us with important particulars concerning the population of the country at the time. Most of these skulls are elongated in form and bear a strong resemblance to those of the present inhabitants of Scandinavia. Professor Virchow, who has examined the skulls from the Scandinavian graves of the Stone Age, says that he inclines to the opinion that the forefathers of the present inhabitants of the country were actually living there in the Stone Age.

Besides these long skulls, others, comparatively short, have been found in the same graves. They are distinct from those of the Scandinavian race and remind us rather of the Finnish tribes. They have been supposed, probably not without reason, to belong to the aboriginal inhabitants of Scandinavia, the people that possessed the land before the immigration of our Germanic forefathers. And although there seem to be no grounds for regarding these aborigines as the ancestors of the Lapps, who have now been driven into the extreme north of the Scandinavian peninsula, that does not preclude the possibility that they belonged to the same group as the Lapps and Finns of to-day.

We cannot, however, come to any definite conclusion as to the race to which these aboriginal inhabitants belong until we discover graves dating back to that part of the Stone Age which preceded the immigration of our own forefathers. That probably took place at the beginning of the so-called Neolithic Age, that is to say the period to which the dolmens, chamber tombs, and other megalithic graves belong. Up to this time not a single grave can be referred to the so-called *Kjökkenmödding* or Paleolithic Age in Scandinavia, and we therefore know absolutely nothing of the skull conformation of the population of that date.

If the views here set forth are correct, our forefathers came to this country at a time when the use of metals was then unknown. This does not imply that they were on the level of " savages." It is most probable that even at the time of their immigration they possessed all our common domesticated animals, as they certainly did long before the end of the Stone Age, and in all likelihood they were not ignorant of agriculture.

It was long supposed that the results of philological research were incompatible with the theory that our Germanic ancestors separated themselves from other Indo-Germanic races as early as the Stone Age, and appeared in the north at so remote a period. Philologists fancied that they had discovered that the use of metals was known before the migration of the Indo-European tribes. Recent research has now shown that this view is incorrect, and that the separation had taken place before metals and the uses of metal were known. The theory that our forefathers migrated to this country during the Stone Age meets with no contravention from the philological point of view.

Any attempt to determine the exact time at which our forefathers first appeared in this country must always be compassed with great difficulties. As far as we can tell at present, the Stone Age of the north ended about the second half of the second millennium B.C. The large number of graves and other monuments dating from the Neolithic Age which are still to be seen after the lapse of thousands of years proves that the duration of the period was so long that we may assume without hesitation that it began, at latest, in the third millennium B.C. I, for my part, see nothing to prevent us from supposing that it goes back even farther; and according to that view our forefathers would have migrated hither more than four thousand years ago.

The Route of the Invaders

Of the route by which they came we can say no more than that, in all probability, they started from the regions about the Black Sea and the lower Danube, and advanced to the northwest through countries that were peopled by Germanic tribes in the very dawn of history. On reaching the Baltic they took possession of the Cimbric peninsula and the Danish islands. Thence, as we learn from their graves and the various forms in which they were made, they first crossed to Kåne, and pressed forward along the west coast into Vestergötland, where the extensive plains were of great value to them. After that they continued to spread; some by way of Dal and southwestern Vermland, and the forest-clad region of southern Vestergötland, to which the great water course of the west coast afforded them an easy means of access; some by way of Blekinge, Småland, and the western portion of Östergötland.

It is worthy of note that while the west coast of Sweden is extremely rich in graves of the Stone Age, there is a great paucity of such remains on the east coast; and in both Öland and Gotland we find fewer memorials of this period than might have been expected, considering the great importance of these two islands in later civilisations. The Svealand districts, which are likewise not rich in monuments of the Stone Age, were settled very much later, and in all likelihood from Vestergötland. Thousands of years later the way from Denmark and Skåne to the lowlands of Mälar lay through Vestergötland; and the first railway which connected Stockholm with the Sound took the same route. In Norrland monuments of the Stone Age corresponding to those found in other parts of Sweden are so rare that there can have been nothing but isolated settlements there. One colony of this sort certainly lay far back to the north, on the Byske Elf, near the present Skellefteå. And it is possible that these monuments of the Stone Age in northern Sweden date from a period when bronze was in use in the south of the country. In Norrland, as in northern Norway, many Lapp remains dating from the Stone Age have been found, which go to prove that at one period this race occupied a far larger portion of the country than it does at present.

The notion that our forefathers came to this country from the East, through Russia, gains no support from the more exact knowledge of prehistoric conditions which we now possess. Such vestiges of Germanic habitation as are met with in Russia may unhesitatingly be explained either by the emigration of Germanic hordes from the southern shores of the Baltic into what are now the Baltic provinces and the districts bordering on them, or by colonies from Sweden which certainly came into existence long before the days of Rurik. The conclusion to which archæological research on the subject of the immigration of our forefathers has led is in accord with the usual assumption of historians — namely, that our Gothic ancestors were settled in the north from time immemorial. When we read in Johannes Magnus *c* that King Sven ruled over the Goths (Götar) in Sweden shortly before the Flood we can hardly repress a smile. Yet the fugitive archbishop was probably less mistaken than many people have supposed. By his reckoning the Flood took place about 2304 B.C. We have shown that, in all probability, our forefathers migrated to the north quite as long before our era as that, even if they had not long been dwelling here by that time.*e*

THE EARLIEST INHABITANTS

That the original inhabitants differed widely from the Gothic conquerors, in language, manners, religion, and character, is certain. The earliest poems of the latter — those traditionary relics of a far more ancient age — are filled with allusions to this distinction. They represent the Finns and Lapps as magicians, as invested with uncontrollable authority over the elements; and the Jotuns as at once giants and magicians. But the warriors of Odin arrogated to themselves no such powers, though their priests might. Legend, indeed, records some instances in which these powers were communicated to fortunate Gothic heroes; but the old inhabitants were the teachers, and what knowledge they imparted — which was always grudgingly imparted — was little in comparison with that which they retained. In the old Sagas, in the collection of Snorre Sturleson,*f* in Saxo Grammaticus,*g* and even in later authorities, we everywhere discover a marked antipathy between the victors and the vanquished. It originated in a two-fold cause — in the difference of religion no less than that of race; and it was embittered in the same degree that it was perpetuated by mutual hostilities. The Finn, indeed, was unable to cope with the powerful Goth; but this sense of inferiority sharpened his invention, and made his hostility to be dreaded in proportion to its secrecy. The blow was struck in darkness; and the Goth, who had a sovereign contempt for the valour of his foe, was led to attribute it to supernatural rather than to human agency.

What ancient history really informs us concerning the people of the north may be comprised in a few lines. They were split into tribes; and of these the Suiones (the Svear) were the most conspicuous. They were a rich and powerful maritime nation; and, if Tacitus [h] is to be credited, their kings were despotic. Lest they should turn against one another, or, what was worse, against their rulers, their arms were taken from them, and kept by the royal slaves. They were, no doubt, a tribe which inhabited Sweden. In the same region were the Guttones, or Goths, another tribe, probably, of more ancient arrival. As the lands of the two were con-

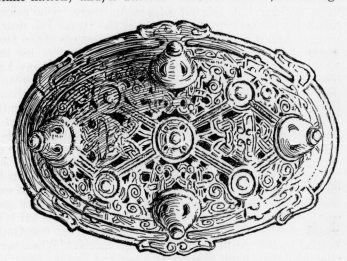

OLD SCANDINAVIAN BUCKLE

terminous, the Suiones must have often called on their king for weapons, unless, indeed, their enemies, too, had been disarmed. But this alleged disarming [says Dunham [k]] is pure fable. The Dankiones — probably the Danskir or Danes — bordered on the Guttones. If, by Cadononia, Tacitus really means the peninsula, the Teutones were also there. In regard to the Fenni, who are manifestly the Finns, he doubts whether he should call them a Teutonic or a Sarmatian tribe. Ptolemy locates them in western Lithuania; Tacitus, more to the north. For many centuries after Tacitus no great additions were made to the history of the north. In the fifth we learn that between the Elbe and the Baltic — no doubt, too, on both sides of that river, to some extent — were Angles, Jutes, and Saxons. Of these the first had no other seat. The second were doubtless a bastard colony from the more northern parts of the peninsula; and the last were an offset from the great Saxon confederation. The Jutes were the fewest in number; yet they were the progenitors of the men of Kent and the Isle of Wight, and of a tribe among the West Saxons. The rest of the Saxons — West, East, and South — were derived from the Saxon division of the colonists. The Angles gave their name to the people who bore it (the East Angles and Middle Angles) and likewise to the Mercians and Northumbrians. Such, according to that venerable authority the *Saxon Chronicle*,[l] was the connection between these people and the island of Great Britain. But, reverting to the state of northern Europe after the time of Tacitus, yet before geography made us well acquainted with it, King Alfred,[i] in his epitome of Orosius, adds some particulars which he had learned from his own inquiries. These particulars he derived from Ottar, a Norwegian, and Wulfstan, a Danish seaman. The former said that he lived north of all the Northmen, in Halogaland, opposite to the west sea; that north of him there was an immense waste land, some parts of it, however, being visited by the Finns for hunting in summer and fishing in winter; that he had once sailed round the North Cape to the White Sea, and on the coast had found a people called Beormas, who spoke a kindred language with the Finns. "This Ottar," says the king, "was a rich man, according to the opinion of his own country; he had six hundred tame deer, and six decoy ones, whose value in catching the wild deer was incalculable, hence these decoy deer were much esteemed by the Finns." But this Norwegian captain had not above twenty head of horned cattle, and as many sheep and swine. The Finns paid rent in skin, feathers, whalebone, and ropes for shipping. (The proprietors of these lands were evidently Goths, the conquering tribe.) Ottar further said that the country of the Northmen (Norway) was long and narrow, cultivated on the sea coast but to the east overlooked by wild barren mountains. Yet Finns inhabited them even in the ninth century — a proof that they were tributary to these Goths, especially as we may infer from this Norwegian's account that they were the only people that paid rent: the dominant race were freeholders. Opposite to this country of the Northmen, in the south, was Swevland, or Sweden; and to the north, the country opposite was Quenland, or that portion of the region between the gulf of Bothnia and Mount Sevo. "These Quens," says Ottar, "frequently assailed the Northmen, and the Northmen were no less inclined to pass the mountains against the Quens. From Halogaland [where Ottar dwelt] to the north of the land inhabited by the Northmen is a great distance — so great that no one could reach it by sea in a month." To be brief, the whole course of the navigation, from the extremity of Norway to the south of Jutland, is so minutely described as to render it impossible for anyone to mistake the localities intended, or to refuse credit to the relation of this old Norwegian navigator.

"The followers of the historic Odin," says Wheaton,[j] "were the Svear, known unto Tacitus under the name of Suiones; and the inhabitants whom they found in the country were another tribe of Goths, who had emigrated thither at a remote period, veiled from the eye of history. The primitive people by whom it was occupied, were the Jotnar [Jotuns] and Dwarfs; the Fenni of Tacitus; the Skrithfiuni of Procopius, and the Quens and Finnas mentioned by the Norwegian navigator to King Alfred. They were gradually expelled, and driven further north, towards the arctic circle, by the Goths and Svear, with whom they maintained perpetual war, embittered by religious rancour, often represented, in the fictions of the northern age, under the allegory of a contest between the celestial deities and the giants or evil genii." But of this subject more hereafter, when we come to the exploits and policy of Odin.

The Heroes of Tradition

Of the Scandinavians, prior to the arrival of Odin, and, indeed, for centuries after that event, little, as far as regards their domestic history, is known. Rejecting wholly, as fabulous, the boast of native writers that they had monarchs centuries before the foundation of Rome, we may, however, admit that they had kings — or, if the reader pleases, local judges — in time of peace, and military chieftains in war. There is reason to think that their chieftains, who assumed the regal title, were at one period, and, indeed, generally, exceedingly numerous. "At this time," says a chronicler, speaking of the age following the birth of Christ, " there were many kings in the north." Sweden had a dozen of them; Norway no fewer than eighteen; Jutland had usually two; and the various islands composing the rest of the Danish monarchy had each one. As in the heroic age of Greece, so in that of Scandinavia the same condition of society produced the same form of government. Of these *reguli* some were probably hereditary, some elective; some were certainly principal, others tributary. This distinction was the result, first, of some fancied superiority in the family of certain princes, but in a greater degree of their superior success. In Norway, for instance, the Finnish family of Fornjoter (Forniot) was esteemed the most ancient, and was that to which all the princes of that country referred their origin.

But let us not forget that little dependence is to be placed on the alleged progenitors of these reguli, or the names of the reguli themselves, or their respective order of succession, or on the deeds attributed to them. All is darkness, uncertainty, contradiction. In the history of Norway, for instance, we are referred to Swedish kings as contemporary, whom the history of the latter kingdom places many generations before or after the alleged period. This is more strikingly the case in regard to the Danish and Swedish kings. In the history of the one we are referred to that of the other; yet the latter, in a majority of cases, have not one syllable on the subject. Names and events, on which the destinies of each country seem to turn, are mentioned by one class of historians and passed over by another as having had no existence. But if so little reliance is to be placed on these regal successions, we must not lose sight of the fact that were they and the events ascribed to them wholly fabulous (yet wholly fabulous they are not, since tradition does not so much create as amplify and distort), they would still demand our attention. Reject them, and nine-tenths of northern history must be rejected with them. And these traditionary songs, which form the entire history of the north, deserve our notice in another respect — they supply us with the best, the only picture of national manners. For this reason we shall cast a hasty glance at the more remarkable events which Saxo *g* represents as prior to the Odinic times, but which, in fact, were subsequent.

Of the Swedish and Norwegian history during this fabulous or mythologic, or at best doubtful period, we have little information beyond what is afforded us by the historian of Denmark, and he only mentions them incidentally. Not so in regard to the Danish themselves, which, thanks to his romantic bias and untiring industry, are sufficiently well known to us.

Prior to the reign of Dan, the son of Humble, Denmark, like the whole of the north, was subject to chiefs — whether hereditary or elective we need not inquire. But such a form of government had its evils. A hundred tyrants were more galling than one; and Dan, who gave his name to the nation, was invested with an authority superior to the other chiefs, and with the regal title. On his death, the sceptre passed by election, and not by inheritance, into the hands of his son Humble; but the people found that monarchy, too, has its curses, though they are neither so numerous nor so great as those inseparable from an aristocracy. Lother, the brother of Humble, revolted, was victorious, and enabled to usurp the regal dignity. As he had been a rebellious subject, so he made a tyrannical king. The most illustrious of the Danes he deprived of property or life, until a conspiracy served him as he had served so many others.

Skiold, the son of Lother, was raised to the vacant dignity, a proof (always supposing the traditionary guides of Saxo to be worthy of credit) that the hereditary principle has great force even in the most ancient forms of society; indeed, the application of this principle to the chief magistracy of the state is the natural and almost inevitable result of the patriarchal system — a system which we all know to be coëval with the existence of the world. Skiold was the Hercules of his age; and at a time when wild beasts disputed with man the empire of the forest, he was a greater benefactor than if he were merely a warrior. Even in his youth he was a prodigy; he would seize and fetter the most savage bear, leaving to his followers the less noble task of despatching the monster. Yet he frequently struggled with the bravest of his own species; no wrestler of Scandinavia could withstand him; in a single combat, he overthrew the duke of the Alamanni or Swabians, his army and that of his enemy being spectators; reduced that people to the condition of tributaries, and returned home in triumph, accompanied by the daughter of the duke, the beautiful Awilda, whom he made the partner of his throne. Nor was he less distinguished for wisdom than for valour. He was a legislator: bad laws he abolished, and enacted such as were required by an improved state of society. He was a great friend to the poor and the afflicted; the debts of others he often paid from his own treasury; the spoils taken in battle he uniformly abandoned to his followers; and it was one of his noble sayings that, while money was the reward of the soldier, glory was enough for the general. So much esteemed, indeed, was this prince that his posterity were glad to derive additional distinction from his name; and the Skioldungs, or the descendants of Skiold, were long dear to Denmark.

Gram, the son of Skiold, and the fifth king, was endowed with equal strength and equal enterprise, and his life was more romantic. His first consort was the daughter of his tutor or governor, a grim old chief; but thinking this lady beneath him, or, more probably, anxious to reward his brother-in-arms, Bessus, he soon bestowed her upon that hero. The dearer the gift, the greater the merit of the action; nor are similar instances of liberality wanting in other pagan heroes of the north. Probably Gram undervalued a conquest so easy as the wife he thus presented to his friend; and his ambition was roused by the hope of obtaining a lady whom nothing short of the highest courage could win. Gro, the daughter of Sigtrug, king of the Swedes, had been affianced to a giant, *viz.* a Jotun or a Finn. Indignant at this prostitution of royal blood and virgin modesty, the Danish monarch, attended by his never-failing companion, Bessus, passed into Sweden, killed the relatives of Gro, subdued the country, and brought away the princess in triumph.

But, with all his valour, Gram was inconstant. Leading his army against the king of the Finns, he was so struck with the beauty of that monarch's daughter that he was speedily converted from an enemy into a suitor; and he obtained a promise of her hand on the condition of repudiating Gro. Scarcely, however, had he left the Finnish territory when a Saxon duke arrived, courted the lady, and the nuptial day was appointed. But he was not of a temper to bear this insult. Leaving his troops, he repaired silently and quickly into Finland, assumed a mean disguise, entered the royal palace, and took a humble seat. Being asked what brought him there, he replied his profession as leech — a character held sacred in all ancient communities, and sure of access to every house. As he had expected, the assembled guests were soon steeped in drunkenness. According to the manner of the times, he sung his own exploits, beheaded the unsuspecting bridegroom, prostrated many of the attendants to the earth, and bore away the princess to his vessel, which awaited him on the coast. But his end was fatal. By Swibdager, king of Norway, he was deprived of empire and of life; his dominions became the prize of the victor; and his two infant sons, Guthrum and Hadding, were secretly carried to Sweden, and confided to the charge of two giants.

Here Saxo is careful to explain what he means by the word "giant." There were, he assures us, three species. First, there were the vulgar giants, those who excelled all mankind in bodily stature. Next, were the wise men, who were as much inferior to the former in bulk as they were superior in knowledge: these penetrated into the secret workings of nature, and were enemies of the monster giants, whom they subdued. Like the Persian magi, they struggled for and obtained the chief power of the state wherever they settled, and arrogated to themselves a divine no less than a regal authority; in short, they were expert magicians, able to delude all mankind by their prestiges. Next, we have the third class of giants, who were the offspring of the two preceding, and were inferior to one parent in magnitude of body, to the other in knowledge; yet, in both respects, they were above the ordinary standard of our nature, and were thought, by their deluded admirers, to inherit some portion of divinity. After this sage distinction, the Danish ecclesiastic observes that we ought not to be surprised at the credulity of the Northmen, for were not the Romans, though the wisest of men, equally credulous? Whatever may be thought of that distinction, or of the personages whom he has drawn from everlasting obscurity, of the existence of this credulity we have abundant evidence; and it furnishes one of the best comments on the manners and opinions of the times.

Swibdager, the conqueror of Gram, and the sixth king of Denmark, found the weight of three crowns too much for one brow. At the entreaty, therefore, of Gro, the divorced queen of Gram, he recalled her son Guthrum from exile, and placed him, as a vassal, on the throne. This prince was naturally despised as the slave of a foreign prince. Not so his brother Hadding, who, preferring liberty to a dependent court, and the hope of avenging his father's death to the smiles of that father's murderer, remained in exile, and with him were the hearts of Denmark. Of all the ancient heroes of the monarchy, this is, perhaps, the most celebrated. Wondrous, indeed, were his actions. While a youth, he inflamed the heart of Hardgrip, the giant daughter of his giant foster-father, who urged him to make a corresponding return. How could he love a giantess? Was he — whom she could, almost, enclose in one of her hands — a fit match for her? The thing was impossible. "By no means," was the reply. "We of the superhuman breed can change, at pleasure, our forms, and even our substances; in short, we can reach the clouds, or reduce ourselves to your size." The royal youth consented; and never had man a more useful or more faithful companion. Her magical knowledge was of more avail to him than her valour, for in that he could equal her; but she could furnish him with superior weapons, defend him from unseen danger, and cure his wounds where human aid would have been useless.

At length, perceiving that he yearned to revisit his native country, she resolved to accompany him. On their journey, they one night arrived at a house where a corpse was duly laid out, until the mournful funeral rites were celebrated. Here was an opportunity of consulting the will of the gods, and the magic giantess availed herself of it. Producing a piece of wood on which certain verses of might, in Runic characters, were inscribed,[1] she caused it to be placed by Hadding under the tongue of the deceased. The effect was instantaneous: the corpse began to speak, and to utter the direst anathemas on her who had disturbed the repose of the dead. It predicted her immediate destruction in a neighbouring wood. No sooner, indeed, had they reached the wood, and erected their tent for the night, than a huge hand was seen to move around them. The terrified Hadding called on his companion for help; and she, dilating her body to a great extent, was able to seize the hand, and present it for amputation to the prince. From the wound issued more venom than blood. But the victory was dearly purchased; the gigantic witch was torn to pieces by the irritated powers of darkness. "Neither her supernatural condition," says Saxo, "nor her vast bulk availed her."

Hadding, however, did not much suffer by the event: a wise old man with one eye, pitying his disconsolate situation, provided him with a brother-in-arms, a celebrated pirate, and both entered into what was considered the holiest of compacts in the manner of the times, *viz.* each besmeared the footsteps of the other with his own blood. The two heroes being conquered by a chief on whom they made war, the same old man took Hadding on horseback to his own mysterious seat, and both renovated and prodigiously fortified him by a magic drink. At the same time a metrical prophecy told him how he was to escape from the captivity which impended over him. Who was this unknown benefactor? On his return to the place whence he was taken, he could perceive, through the folds of his mantle, that he was conveyed over the sea. The horse which bore him was evidently a demon, obedient to Odin, the god of the north.

After some great exploits in the east, to which his ardour, no less than his fear of Swibdager, bore him, Hadding returned to Scandinavia. In a sea-fight he defeated and slew his enemy, and thus became sovereign of Denmark, or, we should say, of the Danish islands — for Jutland and Skåne obeyed different princes. Asmund, the son of Swibdager, he thus transformed into a foe, and a foe, too, greatly to be dreaded. In a battle which ensued, finding that the tide of success was against him, he silently invoked the aid of the wizard giant Wagnoft, the father of his deceased mistress, Hardgrip. Wagnoft obeyed the spell, and was immediately by his side. Asmund lost the battle, and fell; but in his last moments he had the satisfaction of knowing that he had rendered Hadding lame for life. And he had another kind of joy, dear enough to a pagan: his wife Gunhilda, disdaining to survive him, slew herself with his sword, and was laid in the same grave with him. An invasion of his own country by Uffo, the son of Asmund, prevented Hadding from pursuing his advantage; but the following spring he again invaded Sweden; but his ranks were thinned alike by famine and disease. His men were obliged to feed on their horses; next, on their dogs; and, lastly, on each other. To increase their consternation, a

[1] In the Scandinavian superstition every rune was consecrated to some deity. Nearly all the magic of the north consisted in runes. They could raise or allay tempests; they could change times, and they could bring the most distant objects together. They could produce good or bad seasons; they could raise the dead; in short, they were omnipotent over all nature, —the invisible no less than the visible world.

nocturnal voice assured them of great evils. The following night, even, another unknown voice threatened the Swedes with destruction. Both armies, therefore, were alarmed; each had a supernatural enemy, while each was perhaps unconscious that it had, also, a supernatural friend. That same night the two armies engaged; when, behold! two aged men, of a form larger than the human, were seen by the light of the stars in the battle, — one for the Swedes, the other for the Danes. The latter were subdued, and their king was glad to flee to his own country.

But misfortune pursued him. One day, as he was cooling his limbs in the waters of the sea, he perceived a fish different from any that he had ever seen; as it was near the shore, he killed it, and it was taken to his camp. But what was his consternation when a sea-nymph appeared, and denounced direct vengeance on his head! He had killed one of the gods under the form of a fish. Henceforth the elements should be hostile to him; if he ventured on the deep, his vessel should be wrecked by the fury of the tempest; on land, the house which received him should, by a tempest, also be levelled with the ground; his flocks should perish in the fields; every place which he visited should be cursed for his sake: and this dreadful doom was to remain in force until he had propitiated the divine wrath by frequent sacrifices. The mandate was not to be despised; during the course of a year altars perpetually smoked with oxen immolated to Fro, the awful deity of the winds.

The life of Hadding was full of portents and marvels. Scarcely had he rescued the princess Regnilda of Norway from the obligation of marrying a giant, by killing the monster and making her his bride, when a most wonderful adventure befell him. One winter evening, as he was supping with his bride, a woman like a culler of simples was seen to raise her head from the ground close by the hearth; she inquired whether the king did not wish to know where such herbs grew at that season of the year. He replied that he should very much wish to know. Hearing this, she enveloped him in his own mantle, and sank with him into the ground. What they saw in this subterranean journey bears some resemblance to the descriptions which have been given us of the Scandinavian world of spirits. They first entered a dark path, worn out by the feet of many travellers, and here they perceived some great ones of the earth — some in purple and gold — whose doom appeared to consist in their indefinite windings. Passing them, they entered a region of some fertility, whence the woman had derived her simples. Further still, they reached a river of precipitate course and black waters, which rolled along the weapons of many heroes, and over which a bridge conducted them to a different region. One of the first objects that met their eyes was two armies engaged in deadly strife. "Who are these?" demanded Hadding. "These," replied the sorceress, "are they who fell in battle; and it is their delight in this world continually to imitate their martial deeds in the other." At length they reached a high wall, totally impassable. The woman, indeed, made no attempt to scale it; but, twisting off the head of a cock which she had brought with her, she threw it over; when, behold! the cock began to crow as if nothing had been done to it! Unable to proceed further, the adventurous travellers returned to the palace.

The rest of this monarch's life must be hastily despatched. He triumphed over Uffo, who fell in battle, and bestowed the vacant throne of Sweden on Hunding, brother of the deceased monarch. His last days were embittered by the unnatural conduct of his daughter Ulwilda, who, with her husband, planned his destruction. Though he escaped all the snares of his enemies, at length he laid violent hands upon himself, leaving the throne of Denmark, and the superiority over that of Sweden, to his eldest son, Frode I.

Frode I was also a great warrior, and he carried his depredations from Russia to the British islands, on which, unfortunately for the natives, he made a longer stay than kings, whose sole object was plunder, were accustomed to make. If there were any truth in the Danish account of this period, Scotland and South Britain were in frequent intercourse with the northern kingdom — sometimes for war and sometimes for peace. But these accounts are all to be distrusted. Events which happen at a much later period have been removed to the one before us; and the basis has been so much overlaid by fable that no ingenuity can separate the true from the false. When Frode commenced his reign, he found the treasury empty. How replenish it? By an expedient frequently to be found in Scandinavian legends. On a solitary island, a dragon, formidable alike for size and venom, brooded over immense riches. The youthful monarch hastened to the spot, entered the cave, fought and killed the serpent, and brought away the golden hoard. Whether there be any meaning in this and similar fables has been much disputed: probably, however, it had a foundation, and the dragon may have been some terrible pirate whom Frode destroyed, and whose subterraneous riches he seized. This unexpected supply, we are told, enabled him to pursue his expeditions on various coasts of Europe. But we have no inclination to follow him. We may, however, allude to the way in which he gained possession of London; because the same expedient is often to be found in northern writers. Despairing of the reduction of a place so well defended, he caused a report to be spread that he had suddenly died in his tent. Permission was asked to bury him in one of the temples of the city, and was granted. On the day appointed, the pretended corpse was borne through the gates; a great number of Danes attended to do honour to their monarch; but, under the garb of mourning, they hid their weapons of war; and, on a signal being given, they threw off the mockery of woe, assailed the Britons, and took the city by surprise.

Of the immediate successors of this monarch little is known. Haldan, his son, was a great warrior, who put his own brother to death, and was hated by the people. Roe, the son of Haldan, was a quiet prince, mean in stature, but with a mind whose care it was to make his subjects happy. Helge,[1] his brother and successor, with whom, during his own life, he had shared the throne, was also a prince of great qualities; but his vices were still greater. "Whether his lust or his tyranny were more intolerable," says the historian, "is very doubtful." His amours are too disgusting to be recorded. At length, seeing the execration in which he was held, he bade adieu to his country; and it proved a final adieu. According to report, he fell on his own sword. In the reigns of these princes, we have no mention of the Norwegian sovereigns; but those of Sweden — let us not forget that it is a Dane who writes — are represented as still dependent on Denmark. Rolf (or Rollo) succeeded his father, and was much beloved by his subjects.[2] He fell through the treachery of a brother-in-law, who was excited to the deed by the sister of Rolf. Daughters conspiring against fathers, sisters against brothers, wives against husbands are among the common events of Scandi-

[1] Both Roe and Helge reigned some centuries after the time fixed by Saxo — as recently as the fifth century of the Christian era.

[2] Whether there was any other Rolf than the celebrated Rolf Krake, who is thought to have reigned in the sixth century after Christ, is doubtful. The best northern writers admit of no other.

navian history.   As this prince died without issue, the Danish states elected
for their monarch Hoder, a descendant of the famous Hadding, who had been
educated by Gewar, a king of Norway.   As it is in the reign of this latter
monarch that Odin is again introduced on the stage of northern history —
his first appearance being referred by Saxo to the time of Hadding — we can
no longer refuse to notice what antiquity records with respect to him.   In
this, as in other parts of this introduction, the reader may admit or reject
what he pleases.

According to Saxo, this personage was a mortal, king of the Hellespont,
who laid claim to the honours of divinity, and was actually worshipped by
most of Europe.   His profound knowledge of magic procured him the character.   His ordinary residence was Byzantium; but he held Upsala, which
he frequently visited, in much esteem.   Anxious to testify their respect for
this new deity, the kings of the north cast a golden statue in his honour,
adorned it with bracelets and other costly ornaments, and sent it to Byzantium.   It was received by Odin with great joy, and placed in the temple of
the gods.   But Frigg, the wife of Odin, whom Saxo judges to be quite
worthy of such a husband, stripped the statue of its ornaments to adorn
herself.   The incensed deity hung the mechanics who acted by her orders;
and, for greater security, placed the image on a high pedestal, and by his
wonderful art rendered it vocal to human touch.   But when was female
vanity cured?   To secure the aid of a domestic of the temple, Frigg did not
hesitate to grant him the last favour; and by his aid, the gold, being again
abstracted, again adorned her person.

This two-fold injury was too much for a god to withstand; and Odin
left the country for a season, until the public discourse, like a nine days'
wonder, had evaporated itself into empty air.   During his absence, several
persons — probably priests of his own temple — arrogated to themselves the
attributes of divinity.   These, on his return, he forced not only to lay down
their borrowed honours but to flee from the country.   Among them one is
mentioned whose case affords a curious illustration of popular superstition.
Mitothin was a great magician, and had long enjoyed the favour of the gods.
But they were incensed with his impiety, while he no longer paid them the
slightest homage.   On the return of Odin he fled to Fünen, and was killed
by the inhabitants.   In his tomb, however, he was amply revenged: he introduced into the whole region various kinds of plague; he destroyed multitudes
of the inhabitants, until they, one day, opened his sepulchre, exhumed his
body, cut off his head, and drove a stake through the corpse: then the mysterious visitation was at an end.   He is, probably, the first vampire on
record.

The account of Snorre Sturleson,*j* who followed Norwegian, not Danish
authorities, differs in many respects from the preceding.*k*   It may best be
given in his own words:

SNORRE STURLESON'S ACCOUNT OF ODIN

The country east of the Tanaquisl in Asia was called Asaland, or Asaheim,
and the chief city in that land was called Asgard.[1]   In that city was a chief
called Odin, and it was a great place for sacrifice.   It was the custom there

---

[1] Asgard is supposed by those who look for historical fact in mythological tales to be the
present Assor; others that it is Chasgar in the Caucasian ridge, called by Strabo Aspurgum —
the Asburg or castle of Aas; which word Aas still remains in the northern languages, signifying a ridge of high land.*q*

that twelve temple godars[1] should both direct the sacrifices and also judge the people. They were called Diars, or Drotners, and all the people served and obeyed them. Odin was a great and very far-travelled warrior, who conquered many kingdoms, and so successful was he that in every battle the victory was on his side. It was the belief of his people that victory belonged to him in every battle. It was his custom when he sent his men into battle, or on any expedition, that he first laid his hand upon their heads, and called down a blessing upon them; and then they believed their undertaking would be successful. His people also were accustomed, whenever they fell into danger by land or sea, to call upon his name; and they thought that always they got comfort and aid by it, for where he was they thought help was near. Often he went away so long that he passed many seasons on his journeys.

HELSINGBORG'S KÄRNA

Odin had two brothers, the one called Ve, the other Vitir, and they governed the kingdom when he was absent. It happened once, when Odin had gone to a great distance, and had been so long away that the people of Asa doubted if he would ever return home, that his two brothers took it upon themselves to divide his estate; but both of them took his wife Frigg to themselves. Odin soon after returned home, and took his wife back.

Odin went out with a great army against the Vanaland people; but they were well prepared, and defended their land, so that victory was changeable, and they ravaged the lands of each other, and did great damage. They tired of this at last, and on both sides appointed a meeting for establishing peace, made a truce, and exchanged hostages. The Vanaland people sent their best men, Njörd the Rich, and his son Frey. The people of Asaland sent a man called Hæner, whom they thought well suited to be a chief,[2] as he was a stout and very handsome man, and with him they sent a man of great understanding called Mimir; and on the other side the Vanaland people sent the wisest man in their community, who was called Quaser. Now, when Hæner came to Vanaheim he was immediately made a chief, and Mimir came to him with good counsel on all occasions. But when Hæner stood in the Things or other meetings, if Mimir was not near him, and any difficult matter was laid before him, he always answered in one way, "Now let others give their advice"; so that the Vanaland people got a suspicion that the Asaland people had deceived them in the exchange of men. They took Mimir, therefore, and beheaded him, and sent his head to the Asaland people.

Odin took the head, smeared it with herbs so that it should not rot, and sang incantations over it. Thereby he gave it the power that it spoke to him, and discovered to him many secrets. Odin placed Njörd and Frey as

[1] Hof godars, whose office of priests and judges continued hereditary in Scandinavia. q

[2] These exchanges appear not to have been of hostages, but of chiefs to be incorporated with the people to whom they were sent, and thus to preserve peace. q

priests of the sacrifices, and they became deities of the Asaland people. Njörd's daughter Freya was priestess of the sacrifices, and first taught the Asaland people the magic art, as it was in use and fashion among the Vanaland people. While Njörd was with the Vanaland people he had taken his own sister in marriage, for that was allowed by their law; and their children were Freyn and Freya. But among the Asaland people it was forbidden to come together in so near relationship.

There goes a great mountain barrier from northeast to southwest, which divides the Greater Sweden from other kingdoms. South of this mountain ridge it is not far to Turkland, where Odin had great possessions. But Odin having foreknowledge and magic-sight, knew that his posterity would come to settle and dwell in the northern half of the world. In these times the Roman chiefs went wide around in the world, subduing to themselves all people; and on this account many chiefs fled from their domains. Odin set his brothers Ve and Vitir over Asgard; and he himself, with all the gods and a great many other people, wandered out, first westward to Gardarige [Russia], and then south to Saxland [Germany]. He had many sons; and after having subdued an extensive kingdom in Saxland he set his sons to defend the country. He himself went northwards to the sea, and took up his abode in an island which is called Odinsö in Fünen. Then he sent Gefion across the sound to the north, to discover new countries; and she came to king Gylfe, who gave her a ploughgate of land. Then she went to Jötunheim, and bore four sons to a giant, and transformed them into a yoke of oxen, and yoked them to a plough, and broke out the land into the ocean right opposite to Odinsö, which land was called Zealand, where she afterwards settled and dwelt. Skiold, a son of Odin, married her, and they dwelt at Leidre.[1] Where the ploughed land was is a lake or sea called Laage. In the Swedish land the fiords of Laage correspond to the nesses in Zealand. Brage the Old sings thus of it:[2]

> Gefion from Gylfe drove away,
> To add new land to Denmark's sway, —
> Blythe Gefion ploughing in the smoke
> That steamed up from her oxen-yoke:
> Four heads, eight forehead stars had they
> Bright gleaming, as she ploughed away;
> Dragging new lands from the deep main
> To join them to the sweet isle's plain.

Now when Odin heard that things were in a prosperous condition in the land to the east beside Gylfe, he went thither, and Gylfe made a peace with him, for Gylfe thought he had no strength to oppose the people of Asaland. Odin and Gylfe had many tricks and enchantments against each other; but the Asaland people had always the superiority. Odin took up his residence at the Mälar Lake, at the place now called Sigtuna. There he erected a large temple, where there were sacrifices according to the customs of the Asaland people. He appropriated to himself the whole of that district of country, and called it Sigtuna. To the temple gods he gave also domains. Njörd dwelt in Noatun, Frey in Upsala, Heimdall in Himinbjörg, Thor in Thrudvong, Baldur in Breidablik; to all of them he gave good domains.

When Odin of Asaland came to the north, and the gods with him, he began

---

[1] Leidre, or Hleidre, or Leire, at the end of Isafiord, in the county of Lithraborg, is considered the oldest royal seat in Denmark. *q*

[2] This fable is possibly the echo of some tradition of a convulsion in which the ocean broke into the Baltic through the Sound and Belts, or in which the island of Zealand was raised from the deep. *q*

to exercise and teach others the arts which the people long afterwards have practised. Odin was the cleverest of all, and from him all the others learned their magic arts; and he knew them first, and knew many more than other people. But now, to tell why he is held in such high respect, we must mention various causes that contributed to it. When sitting among his friends his countenance was so beautiful and friendly that the spirits of all were exhilarated by it; but when he was in war he appeared fierce and dreadful. This arose from his being able to change his colour and form in any way he liked. Another cause was that he conversed so cleverly and smoothly that all who heard were persuaded. He spoke everything in rhyme, such as now composed, and which we call scald-craft. He and his temple gods were called song-smiths, for from them came that art of song into the northern countries. Odin could make his enemies in battle blind, or deaf, or terror-struck, and their weapons so blunt that they could no more cut than a willow twig; on the other hand, his men rushed forwards without armour, were as mad as dogs or wolves, bit their shields, and were strong as bears or wild bulls, and killed people at a blow, and neither fire nor iron told upon them. These were called bersærkers. [1]

Odin could transform his shape: his body would lie as if dead, or asleep; but then he would be in shape of a fish, or worm, or bird, or beast, and be off in a twinkling to distant lands upon his own or other people's business. With words alone he could quench fire, still the ocean in tempest, and turn the wind to any quarter he pleased. Odin had a ship which was called *Skidbladner*, in which he sailed over wide seas, and which he could roll up like a cloth.[2] Odin carried with him Mimir's head, which told him all the news of other countries. Sometimes even he called the dead out of the earth, or set himself beside the burial-mounds; whence he was called the ghost-sovereign, and lord of the mounds. He had two ravens, to whom he had taught the speech of man; and they flew far and wide through the land, and brought him the news. In all such things he was pre-eminently wise. He taught all these arts in runes, and songs which are called incantations, and therefore the Asaland people are called incantation-smiths.

Odin understood also the art in which the greatest power is lodged, and which he himself practised; namely, what is called magic. By means of this he could know beforehand the predestined fate [3] of men, or their not yet completed lot; and also bring on the death, ill luck, or bad health of people, and take the strength or wit from one person and give it to another. But after such witchcraft followed such weakness and anxiety that it was not thought respectable for men to practise it; and therefore the priestesses were brought up in this art. Odin knew finely where all missing cattle were concealed under the earth, and understood the songs by which the earth, the hills, the stones, and mounds were opened to him; and he bound those who dwell in them by the power of his word, and went in and took what he pleased. From these arts he became very celebrated. His enemies dreaded him; his friends put their trust in him, and relied on his power and on himself. He taught the most of his arts to his priests of the sacrifices, and they came nearest

---

[1] Bersærker — so called from *ber*, bare; and *serkr*, shirt; that is, bare of any shirt of mail, as they fought without armour. The bersærkers appear to have gone into battle intoxicated with opium, or some exciting drug; as the reaction after their bersærker gang was over, and their lassitude and exhaustion, prove the use of some stimulant previously to a great excess. *q*

[2] This possibly refers to boats covered with skin or leather — the coracle of the Welsh and Irish. *q*

[3] Orlög — the original law, the primæval law fixed from the beginning. It is curious that this idea of a predestination existed in the religion of Odin. *q*

to himself in all wisdom and witch-knowledge.   Many others, however, occupied themselves much with it; and from that time witchcraft spread far and wide, and continued long.   People sacrificed to Odin, and the twelve chiefs from Asaland — called them their gods, and believed in them long after. From Odin's name came the name Audun, which people gave to his sons; and from Thor's name comes Thorer, also Thorarinn; and also it is sometimes augmented by other additions, as Steenthor, or Hafthor, and many kinds of alterations.

Odin established the same law in his land that had been in force in Asaland.   Thus he established by law that all dead men should be burned, and their property laid with them upon the pile, and the ashes be cast into the sea or buried in the earth.   Thus, said he, everyone will come to Valhalla with the riches he had with him upon the pile; and he would also enjoy whatever he himself had buried in the earth.   For men of consequence a mound should be raised to their memory, and for all other warriors who had been distinguished for manhood a standing stone; which custom remained long after Odin's time.   Towards winter there should be blood-sacrifice for a good year, and in the middle of winter for a good crop; and the third sacrifice should be in summer, for victory in battle.   Over all Sweden the people paid Odin a *scatt* or tax — so much on each head; but he had to defend the country from enemy or disturbance, and pay the expense of the sacrifice feasts towards winter for a good year.

Njörd took a wife called Skadi; but she would not live with him, but married afterwards Odin, and had many sons by him, of whom one was called Sæming; and of this Eyvind Skaldaspiller sings thus:

> To Asa's son Queen Skadi bore
> Sæming, who dyed his shield in gore, —
> The giant-queen of rock and snow,
> Who loves to dwell on earth below,
> The iron pine-tree's daughter, she
> Sprung from the rocks that rib the sea,
> To Odin bore full many a son,
> Heroes of many a battle won.

To Sæming Earl Hakon the Great reckoned up his pedigree.   This Sweden they called Mannheim, but the Great Sweden they called Godheim; and of Godheim great wonders and novelties were related.

Odin died in his bed in Sweden; and when he was near his death he made himself be marked with the point of a spear, and said he was going to Godheim, and would give a welcome there to all his friends, and all brave warriors should be dedicated to him; and the Swedes believed that he was gone to the ancient Asgard, and would live there eternally.   Then began the belief in Odin, and the calling upon him.   The Swedes believed that he often showed himself to them before any great battle.   To some he gave victory; others he invited to himself; and they reckoned both of these to be well off in their fate.   Odin was burned, and at his pile there was great splendour.   It was their faith that the higher the smoke arose in the air, the higher he would be raised whose pile it was; and the richer he would be, the more the property that was consumed with him.*f*

HISTORY PARTIALLY RECONCILED TO TRADITION

The qualities of this extraordinary man are the favourite theme of the Swedish and Norwegian chroniclers.   Whether Odin ever existed — whether himself and his alleged Asiatics are not mere creatures of the imagination —

whether they are not purely mythologic, and referrible to an Asiatic source, at a period lost in the depths of antiquity, have long exercised the ingenuity of writers. In matters of pure history it is certainly better to err on the side of scepticism than of credulity; but in the present instance we cannot discover sufficient grounds for the former opinion. That he existed, and at no distant period antecedent to the invasion of England by the Saxons, is affirmed, alike by written testimony and tradition. According to that venerable and most inestimable relic of antiquity, the *Saxon Chronicle*,[l] all the princes of the nation derived their origin from the deified hero; and the number of generations between him and the reigning king are minutely recorded. Thus, from Odin to Cerdic, 495 A.D., are ten generations; from Odin to Ida, 547 A.D., the same number; from Odin to Ælla, 560 A.D., twelve; from Odin to Ceolwulf, 597 A.D., thirteen; from Odin to Penda, 626 A.D., twelve; from Odin to Offa, 755 A.D., sixteen; from Odin to Æthelwulf, 854 A.D., twenty-three generations. In all these lists the intervening chain, from the wizard king to his Saxon descendant, are carefully specified.

In the same manner the series of northern kings, from the sons of Odin, who were placed by him over the thrones of Denmark, Sweden, and Norway, is progressively detailed. Thus, in Denmark, the generations from Skiold, the son of Odin, to Ragnar Lodbrok, 794 A.D., are twenty-five. In Sweden, from Njörd (the adopted son, perhaps, of Odin) to Olaf, 630 A.D., are twenty-three generations. In Norway, the succession of kings from the same Njörd, to Harold Harfagr, the first "monarch" of that country, 934 A.D., are twenty-eight. We think that these genealogical series, so carefully, so minutely particularised, afford a presumption, at least, that the pontiff king of the north both lived and reigned at a period not very far distant from the birth of Christ. Not that the subject is without its difficulties. The events ascribed to Odin's times have, by many writers, been deemed inapplicable to any century within the known history of the world. Hence, some have removed him to the age immediately following the flood; some, to the seventh century after that event; some, to the age of Darius Hystaspes; others, to that of Philip, king of Macedon; others, to less than two centuries before Christ; while another party contends that he was more recent still, and that Ariovistus, whom Cæsar conquered, was one of his sons. Where so much contradiction, so much absurdity abound, our only guide, in the absence of positive evidence, is reason; and this confirms the generally received opinion that this personage is of far less antiquity than was formerly supposed. Not that many of his rites, many of his notions, many, perhaps, of his alleged actions, are not more ancient. There is, indeed, some reason to infer that they were known in Asiatic Scythia, a thousand years before his time. But this fate is not peculiar to Odin; it has been that of all celebrated men. Whoever has entered profoundly into the history of tradition must be aware that legends which were formerly applicable to the most ancient characters were applied to comparatively modern ones, when the latter had been dead long enough to permit the imagination to invest them with new attributes. Thus many which have been related of Charlemagne's heroes — of Charlemagne himself — of the crusaders, especially of Cœur de Lion's age, were once the glory of pagans, and were derived from a northern or an oriental source, before Normans, Franks, or Angles were known.

So much for direct and positive evidence, which is strongly confirmed by inference. The Goths, like all the Scythians, were accustomed to deify their deceased heroes. This is expressly affirmed by several writers, especially by Adam of Bremen;[m] and heroes are mentioned, who, we find, were deified.

Thus, Arminius, or Hermann, the courageous supporter of Germanic independence against the Romans, was worshipped as a god; and his famous idol, which was called, after his name, Irminsul, drew multitudes of pagans to the Isle of Rügen: it was, indeed, regarded as the palladium of Germanic liberty. The facility with which kings and heroes were deified is still more strikingly illustrated in the life of St. Anskar, the apostle of the Scandinavians. Alarmed at the success which attended the preaching of that admirable missionary (this was about the middle of the ninth century), the priests of the Odinian worship had recourse to a bold imposture. By their contrivance a man suddenly appeared in the Swedish capital, who affirmed that he had just attended a general meeting of the gods, and that he was bearer of a communication from them to King Olaf and his people. The substance of it was that the ancient deities had always been most indulgent to the Swedes; that, hitherto, they had found no reason to complain of an ungrateful return from their worshippers; that now, however, there was a sad decline in the sacrifices and other proofs of devotion; and that their wrath was especially excited by the introduction of a new deity, of one peculiarly hostile to the gods of the kingdom. "If," added they, "you Swedes really wish to increase the number of gods, we will readily admit your departed king, Eric, to the honours of deification."

That the proposal was accepted, that a temple was immediately erected to Eric, that his altars perpetually smoked with sacrifices — are among the most indubitable facts of history. Hence, there is nothing unreasonable in the deification of Odin; indeed, he could not have avoided the honour. One so celebrated as he was — a great warrior, a great legislator, the founder of a new empire and of a new religion — assuredly could not fail to be invested with the same honours as an Arminius or an Eric. Indeed, as it was the obvious policy of the Asiatic followers of Odin to represent the authority of their pontiff king and his successors as founded on divine, not on human sanction, as that authority was avowedly theocratic — he must, of necessity, have been regarded as a god, if not in his lifetime, immediately after his decease. The temporal no less than the spiritual government of Odin, and the social superiority of his immediate followers over the inhabitants he found in Sweden, drew our attention in former pages. Our opinions on this subject are strongly confirmed by Münter [n] as follows:

Odin founded the empire of the Svear, which was originally confined to a small territory around the Mälar Lake, in the present Swedish province of Upland, called the lesser Svíthjód, in contrast to the greater Svíthjód, or Scythia, whence they migrated, and Mannaheim, or the Home of Man, in contrast to the celestial abode of Asgard. By degrees the Svear, as the leading tribe governed by the pontiff kings, the immediate descendants of Odin, and having the custody of the great temple at Sigtun, the principal seat of the new superstition, acquired an ascendancy over the Goths, who possessed the more southern tract of country called Gautland, Gotland, or Göto-rike. This precedence of the Svear over the Goths is established by the express terms of the ancient fundamental law of their joint empire, according to which the "king was elected by the national assembly of all the Swedes (å Ting allra Svia), at the Mora-Stone, in the plain near Upsala, and the assembly of all the Goths (Ting allra Göta) shall re-elect or confirm him." This distinction between the two tribes is constantly preserved in the traditions and annals of the Middle Ages, and the division between the Svea and Göta-rike is strongly marked by a chain of mountains running between Södermanland and Östergötland.

One of the ancient documents which throws the most light upon the history of the heroic age in the north is the Eddaic poem, called *Rigs-mál*. The prince of that name is said to have been the son of Skiold, and, according to the chronology of Suhm, reigned in Skåne about the end of the second century of the Christian era. This poem contains a minute classification of the different orders of society, personified as the children of King Rig, who is supposed to have divided them into distinct castes, assigning to each its respective rank in the social scale. As a literary composition, it resembles the Anglo-Saxon poem of Beowulf, and all other genuine traditionary poems or romances of uncivilised nations, in its unpretending and Homeric simplicity of style and incidents. In this respect it has been justly called one of the most curious and interesting "manners-painting strains" that have been preserved and handed down to posterity. The effects of the original Gothic migration and conquest in Scandinavia are here distinctly marked in the features of the slave caste, descended from the aboriginal Finns, and distinguished from their conquerors by black hair and complexion, as well as the squalid poverty and misery in which they were compelled to live. The caste of freemen and free-holders — lords of the soil which they cultivated, and descended from the Gothic conquerors, with their reddish hair, fair complexion, and all the traits which peculiarly mark that famous race — is in like manner personified in a vivid description of a single family. Then comes the caste of the illustrious Jarls and the Herser, earls and barons, who are distinguished from the others by their still fairer hair and skin, by their noble employments and manners, from whom descend the kingly race, skilled in runic science, in manly exercises, and the military art.

We have, here, the early history of the Scandinavians traced in a few lines; but these are strongly marked, and confirmed by all the traditions of the ancient north, respecting the different races of men by which the country was successively occupied. The first Gothic emigrants subdued the Celto-Finnish tribes, who were the primitive inhabitants of the country, and reduced them to servitude, or drove them, first to the mountains, and then to the desert wilds and fastnesses of Norrland, Lapland, and Finland. Here the Jötuners or Jötnar, as they were called by their Gothic invaders, continued to adhere to the grovelling superstition of their fathers, which was that form of polytheism which has been called fetichism, or the adoration of beasts and birds, of stocks and stones, all the animate and inanimate works of creation. The antipathy between these two races, so continually alluded to in the songs and sagas of the mythic and heroic age, is significantly expressed in the legend of Njörd, who dwelt by the sea-side, and Skadi, a mountain-nymph of the rival race of the Jötuner, whom he had espoused. She very naturally prefers her native abode on the Alpine heights, whilst he insists on dwelling where he can hear the roar of the ocean billows. At last, they compromise this matrimonial dissension by agreeing to pass nine nights alternately among the mountains, and three on the sea-shore. But Njörd soon tires of this compact, and vents his dissatisfaction in a lay to this effect: "How do I hate the mountain wilds! I have only passed nine nights there; but how long and tedious did they seem! There one hears nothing but the howling of wolves, instead of the sweet notes of the swan." To which Skadi extemporises this response: "How can I rest on the sandy sea-shore, where my slumbers are every morning broken by the hideous screaming of the seagulls?" The result is that she deserts her husband and returns to the mountains, where her father dwells: there, snatching up her bow, and fastening on her snow-skates, she bounds over the hills in pursuit of the wild beasts.

The Svear, who migrated with the historic Odin, achieved no forcible conquest over their national brethren of the Gothic tribe, by whom they had been preceded. The ascendancy of Odin and his followers over their predecessors was acquired and maintained by superstition, and their supposed superiority in magic and the other arts which win the confidence or influence the fears of a barbarous nation. The older worship of the primitive inhabitants, and of their conquerors, was modified by this new prophet, who, taking advantage of the pre-existing belief in the doctrine of the transmigration of souls, and the incarnation of divine spirits, so widely diffused among the ancient people of the earth, pretended to be the former Odin, who had again descended among his faithful Goths.[1] His worship thus soon supplanted that of the more ancient Odin, and the attributes and actions of both were gradually confounded together in the apprehension of the Scandinavians. But it did not supplant that of Thor, whom the primitive people of the north regarded as the elder and most beneficent of the deities. In him they worshipped the goodly elements of nature — the light, the heat, and especially the thunder, shaking and purifying the atmosphere. This deity was principally revered in Norway; and, after its discovery and settlement, in Iceland: but he maintained his recognised equality with the other superior gods even in the great temple of Upsala, the principal seat of the northern superstition. His votaries formed a distinct sect, who were often engaged in deadly strife with the peculiar worshippers of Odin.

The next deity in the Scandinavian hierarchy was Frey, who represented the prolific powers of Nature, and, with his sister Freya, the Venus of this mythology, was principally revered in Sweden, Norway, and Iceland; whilst Odin and his son, Baldur, were adored both at Upsala and Leidre as the peculiar national deities of the Gothic Danes and Svear. The religion of the north, as it was at last modified by this new dispensation, in the conjoint adoration of Thor, Odin, and Frey, bore a strong family likeness to the three principles of Shamanism, or the faith professed by the votaries of the Dalai Lama in central Asia. This correspondence points most significantly to its origin; and the filiation of religious creeds and forms of worship thus combines with that of language to trace the present people of the north to the remotest regions of the East. [n]

The temporal government established by Odin was perpetuated through his sons. Thus Heimdall was placed over Skåne, the original seat of the Danes. Sæming had Norway. From another son sprung the Ynglingar, who reigned for many centuries in Sweden and Norway. Skiold, a fourth son, led a colony into Zealand, which became the seat of a different kingdom; hence the Skioldungs, or the regal family of Denmark. And as to Baldur, he was the king of the Angles, if any faith is to be placed in the *Saxon Chronicle.*[l] Thus, according to tradition, as embodied in the Icelandic and Norwegian sagas, and in other monuments of antiquity, Odin was the progenitor of all the great dynasties of the north. But in regard to some parts of Norway we must not forget the family of Nor — the mythologic, or rather mythic Nor, whose fame was so widely spread, and from whom the whole country derived its name. Doubtless the native chiefs, those who descended from ancestors long antecedent to Odin's arrival, were proud enough of their descent, and too much attached to their ancient religion — more ancient than Odin's — to care for either the Asiatic conqueror or his attendant Drotner. But the kings of the Æsir, or

---

[1] To this opinion, says Dunham, [k] we do not subscribe. We have no proof of the existence of two Odins.

divine race, whose chief deity was this very Odin, boasted of a spiritual pre-eminence, superior, by far, to their temporal.

THE LEGEND OF BALDUR

But, reverting to the narrative of Saxo, *g* and the alleged succession of the Danish kings, Hödur, whom (as we have before observed) Gewar, a king in Norway, had educated, won the heart of Nanna, the daughter of his bene-factor. She had, however, the misfortune to influence a divine lover, Baldur, the son of Odin, who, like David, had seen her in the bath. As he knew of her attachment to Hödur, he resolved to remove that person by violence; but the latter had friends powerful as those of his enemy. One day, while hunting in the mountains, Hödur entered a cloud, and suddenly beheld a number of virgins, who, though bearing some resemblance to the maids of Norway, were in reality the fatal sisters. They accosted him by name, told him that his beloved Nanna had smitten the heart of Baldur, but warned him not to attempt the life of the demi-god. They informed him that they were present, unseen, in all battles — that they were the arbiters of good and evil — and that they often assisted their mortal friends when assistance was most required. Saying this, they disappeared so quickly that his eye could not follow them.

On his return, he related to Gewar what he had seen, and besought the hand of Nanna. The old king had no objection to the match; but he dreaded the wrath of Baldur, on whose charmed body mortal weapon could have no effect. He added, however — for he was a great magician — that there was a sword kept by Mimring, a satyr of the woods, with virtue enough to slay the demi-god. The same being had bracelets, of efficacy so wonderful as greatly to increase the bodily strength of the possessor. But how obtain these miraculous gifts? The abode of the satyr was amidst rocks and snows, and almost inaccessible to man. Hödur was, however, to take his sledge and reindeer; to reach the alpine solitudes; to pitch his tent, so that the shadow of the satyr's grove might fall upon it; and to watch day and night, with untiring patience, for the appearance of the mysterious occupant. The prince did as he was commanded; he fasted and watched, until one night, feigning to be asleep, he perceived the satyr attentively observing his tent. In a moment, he struck the monster, bound it with fetters, and threatened to kill it if it did not surrender the sword and bracelets. His life was dearer than those treasures. Hödur gained his object, and returned in triumph to the court of Gewar. The value of the treasure, indeed, was too great not to raise up rivals for its possession; and one king (Gelder, who has left his name to a well-known Dutch province), sailed with a powerful armament against him; but if it excited envy, it also aided its owner, and Hödur was victorious.

In the mean time, Baldur, terrible in arms, entered the dominions to obtain the fair Nanna by force, should entreaties be ineffectual. But she was deaf to the most honied flattery. Without betraying her attachment for Hödur, which would only place him in greater jeopardy, she represented in strong colours the inequality of the proposed marriage. "The chain which bound a god to a mortal," she observed, "could not be a lasting chain. When the fervour of passion had subsided, the superior being, despising his ill-assorted choice, would at once dissolve it." Baldur had recourse to arms; and he was joined by the army of the gods, at the head of which were Odin and Thor. Here were fearful odds; but Hödur was not discouraged. His magic bracelets rendered him impenetrable to steel; and though the hammer of Thor crushed everything on which it fell, he had the courage to meet the Scandinavian thunderer. With his wonderful sword he cut off the handle of the all-destructive weapon, so as to render it useless; and the gods, deprived of their great support, took refuge in flight.

The victory was complete; the allies of the gods were destroyed; their bodies cast by the waves on the shores; and the victor performed the last rites to their manes. "Strange," concludes Saxo, "that gods could be thus routed by mortals!" But he accounts for the circumstance by gravely observing that they were deities in human estimation only, and not in reality. He evidently regards them merely as magicians and priests; wise, indeed, far beyond human wisdom, but still mortal. His religion, his profession, compelled him thus to regard them; and often, when he employs the term god, he adds the saving clause which we have just noticed. As the reward of his victory, Hödur obtained the hand of Nanna, with the throne of one part of Sweden; but he was shortly afterwards vanquished by Baldur, and he lost the crown of Denmark. He and Baldur were dreadful rivals. Through his love for Nanna, the latter wasted gradually away. To procure a greater share of the divine favour, he offered human sacrifices to Fro, and the fatal precedent was but too well imitated by succeeding ages. In the next battle, he was again the victor, and his rival was compelled to seek an asylum in an obscure village of Jutland. Here, unattended and discouraged, Hödur felt the more deeply the contrast of situations. From Jutland, he passed into Sweden, privately assembled his staunch adherents, and represented to them the hopelessness of his prospects — that he was alike weary of empire and life. Compelled, indeed, to consult his safety by wandering from forest to forest, from one cavern to another, he exhibited a remarkable example of the instability of fortune, in a region where such vicissitudes were more frequent than in any other part of the world.

In this emergency, while sojourning amidst woods never trod by man, he one day entered a cave, in which he found the weird sisters. Being asked what had brought him to their solitudes, he replied, "Misfortune in war." He bewailed his hard fate, and asserted that their predictions had not been verified, but had been contradicted by the event. They contended, however, that if he had been twice put to flight, he had inflicted as great an injury on the enemy as the enemy had inflicted on him. But Baldur was on the throne of Denmark; what consolation, therefore, could he receive? He was, indeed, told that if he could only discover and appropriate to himself a certain species of food, which was every day served to his rival, and which increased that rival's strength in a prodigious manner, he should become the victor. How discover it? But, whatever his fate, it could not be more disastrous than the present; and he again sought Baldur in arms.

The first day's fight was indecisive. At night, he lay in his tent; but sleep refusing to visit him, he arose and went towards the enemy's camp. There he saw three virgins (the purveyors of Baldur's table) leave that prince's tent. He accosted them; and being asked who he was, replied, "A harper" — a character always sacred in the north. As he was really expert in the use of the instrument, he was really believed, and he was allowed to see what the mysterious substance was which had such miraculous effect on the body of his rival: it was the venom of three snakes which the virgins daily or nightly extracted from the mouths of the reptiles, and which they mixed with the more solid food of Baldur. One of the maidens wished to give some of the food to Hödur, but the eldest forbade her. All, however, were so pleased with his minstrelsy that they presented him with a belt, which would ensure him the victory over all his enemies. The prophecy was soon fulfilled. Possessed of this belt, in addition to his other magical treasures, he met his enemy and gave him a mortal wound. Like a true northern hero, Baldur, being resolved to die on the field of battle, was carried in a litter into the heart of Hödur's army; but he soon breathed his last sigh. Over his body a huge mound was erected by his troops. That treasures of inestimable value were buried with him was the unanimous opinion of posterity. In the time of Saxo some youths one night hastened to the spot, and endeavoured to open it; but their ears being assailed by terrific noises, they desisted, and fled. All this, says the historian, was unreal; it was merely the illusion of magic.

Respecting the death and interment of Baldur, we have in the latter Edda⁰ many details wholly omitted by Saxo, and more which are entirely dissimilar from his. One night, this Balᴅur had a dream, which was thought to be portentous of his fate. With the consent of the gods his mother, Freya or Frigg, called on fire, water, earth, stones, iron, and other metals, trees, animals, birds, reptiles, poison, and all diseases, to renounce all power over him; and they took an oath to that effect. To try the efficacy of the engagement, some of the gods threw darts and stones at him, while some assailed him with other weapons: in vain; no one could injure him. Seeing this, Loki, the genius of evil, assumed the disguise of an old woman, went to the palace of Frigg, and informed her what the gods were doing. "Let them try as long as they please," was the reply; "all living things have promised to respect my son." "What!" rejoined Loki, whose purpose is evident enough, "have all substances, without exception, thus promised?" "All," was the reply, except one insignificant plant, called mistletoe, which grows on the western side of Valhalla, and from which, such is its feebleness, I exacted no oath."

This was enough for Loki: he went to the place where the mistletoe grew, plucked it up by the roots, and returned to the assembly of the gods, who were still occupied in the same diversion. According to this account, Hödur was present; but he was not a deity, he was merely a blind old man. "Why dost thou not join in the exercise?" demanded Loki. "Because I am blind." "Take this trifling reed, and throw it; I will guide thine hand; meet it is for us all to honour Baldur!" The missile flew, and the hero fell to rise no more. The gods were in sad consternation at this event; the more so as the evil was irreparable. All that the afflicted father could now do was to pay due honours to his remains. His body was borne to the sea coast; it was placed in the famous ship of the deceased, which was one of the largest in the world; but neither Odin nor all the gods assembled could move the vessel into the waters. In this emergency, they had recourse to a famous sorceress of the giant race, and she obeyed the call. She arrived on the back of a wild beast, having serpents for reins. So dreadful was this animal, that it required four giants to hold it after she had dismounted. At one push, Gyges sent the ship into the sea; and so great was its velocity that the earth trembled. The funeral pile was then erected by command of Odin, and the body of Baldur's wife, whom grief brought to the grave, laid on it, close by his.

Who was she? The Edda expressly calls her Nanna, but assigns her another father than Gewar. There can, however, be no doubt that the beautiful confusion so prevalent in everything connected with Scandinavian characters and events, is doubly apparent in this case — that the wife of Hödur and Baldur is one and the same Nanna, however the tradition in regard to her may have been distorted. Yet, there is no greater confusion respecting this lady than there is respecting Hödur himself in the different relations of Saxo and Snorre, the compiler of the prose Edda. In the one case, as we have seen, he was a vigorous young prince; in the other, a blind, feeble, and apparently old one. This diversity of narrative arises from the diversity of sources consulted by the two historians — the one confining himself to the national songs of Denmark, the other consulting the old Norwegian, or rather Icelandic traditions, which the Skalds had transmitted to posterity. During the Middle Ages, especially anterior to the fourteenth century, there was a vast body of legendary lore respecting Odin, his family, and his sacerdotal companions — lore from which different Skalds took what they judged most interesting to their hearers. But, reverting to the funeral of Baldur, Thor furnished the consecrated fire: the horse of the deceased hero was placed on the pyre; and Odin added his golden ring, which had the miraculous virtue of producing eight other rings every ninth night. Thus, in the presence of all the gods, satyrs, nymphs, and cyclops, was the conflagration effected.

According to the same venerable authority, namely, the Edda o of Snorre, an attempt was made to recover the soul of Baldur from the empire of Hel, or death. Who would undertake the perilous mission? It was Hermod, another son of Odin, that, at the entreaty of his mother, saddled Sleipnir, the famous black steed, mounted him, and plunged into the subterranean paths which led to the abodes of the dead. This Sleipnir has a reputation never before enjoyed by a quadruped. During the frequent contests between the gods and the giants — that is, between the Goths and the Jotuns — the former were not always victorious; nor were they always sure of impunity within their fortress, well guarded as it was. One day an architect appeared before them and proposed to build them such a city that all the power of Jötunheim should fail against it. For this service, however, he must have his reward; and a splendid one it was — the goddess Freya to wife, with the sun and moon as her dowry. They agreed to his terms, provided he did what no doubt they believed impossible, viz. execute the work himself, within the space of a single winter; and they were liberal enough to allow him the use of his horse. In a short time the gods had reason to be alarmed; for the horse not only drew stones of vast magnitude, but did more of the architectural work than the master.

Within three days of the completion of winter nothing remained but the hanging of the gates. In great consternation the gods assembled to consult by what means the ruin impending might be averted. As the covenant between them and the architect had been advised by Loki, they menaced him with death unless he discovered some expedient to save them. Loki, who has sometimes been called the Scandinavian devil, was fond of mischief: but he was fonder still of his life: and that very night he caused a mare to issue from a forest and neigh amorously. Sleipnir, hearing the sound, left the work to pursue the mare, while the architect followed to recover his horse. Thus the whole night was lost. The architect now perceived that he must trust to himself. He assumed his natural size, and there he stood, a veritable giant — the everlasting enemy of the gods! They did not allow him to finish the work; but, regardless of their oaths, which in their opinion were not binding when made to a giant, they called on Thor to dash out his brains with the awful mallet. In the meantime the mysterious horse remained with the mare, and the issue of the connection was Sleipnir with eight feet — the most excellent of all the animals ever possessed by gods or men.

Such was the animal on which Hermod descended to the regions of Hel. The description of his journey is highly poetical. During nine days and as many nights, he travelled down the precipitous way — often abrupt — along the sides of yawning gulfs — through rugged valleys; and everything was involved in so great a darkness that he was obliged to grope, or trust to the instinct of his wondrous beast. At length he reached a river, the bridge of which was kept by a virgin called Modguder. She inquired his name, his race, his family; and expressed her surprise at his weight. "But yesterday," she observed, "and three legions of dead rode over this bridge; yet all together did not shake it as much as thou alone. But thou hast not the look of one dead. What brings thee here?" He replied, "I am in search of my brother Baldur; hast thou seen him pass?" "I have: he rode over the bridge: the path to Hecate's dark abode is still downwards, towards the north!"

On he rode until he came to the gates of hell, which were closed to all but the dead. But he was not discouraged; plunging his spurs into his wondrous horse, he cleared the gate, and proceeded into a hall of vast extent. Here he perceived his brother, who filled the most honourable place. But far less honourable was it than the meanest in Valhalla, which Baldur could not enter because it had not been his good fortune to die in battle. It is, however, some consolation for us, poor mortals, to perceive that hospitality is not forgotten in the gloomy regions below. Hermod remained the whole night; and the next morning he acquainted Hel with the anxiety of the gods, of men, of all nature, for the return of Baldur, and besought her to permit it. She seemed to doubt whether the mourning for the hero was so universal as he had represented; but, to place the matter beyond dispute, she replied that if all objects, inanimate no less than animate, would weep for him, the request of the gods should be granted. Hermod accordingly rose to depart. By Nanna he was intrusted with several presents for Frigg, his mother: from Baldur he was the bearer of a ring (no doubt the one which had been placed in the funeral pile!) to their father Odin. He was then escorted to the outer gate as if he had been a favoured guest just leaving the palace of an earthly sovereign. On reaching Asgard, where Odin then was, he acquainted the gods with the message of Hel. By their advice agents were sent through all creation, praying everything to weep for Baldur. By everything was the mandate obeyed, except by one old sorceress, who refused to weep, and said that Hel must keep her prey.

But in the elder or poetical Edda — that erroneously attributed to Sæmund the Wise, which in compilation is antecedent a full century to Snorre's — the journey to the shades is attributed to Odin himself. When it was undertaken, Baldur was yet alive, but dreams and portents afflicted him; and, after consulting the fates, Odin mounted his steed, Sleipnir, and descended in darkness towards the abode of Hel, where a celebrated prophetess had been long interred. He met the terrible dog which the Greeks preserved in their mythology, and which, with bloody jaws, barked loudly as he passed along. Downwards he went, the earth trembling beneath his steed, until he reached the lofty hall of Hel. From the eastern gate he proceeded to the spot where he knew the tomb of the prophetess was to be found. Turning himself towards the north, he then commenced the fatal incantation, and placed in order the mystic rhymes. Many were the words of might which he uttered, until he forced the unwilling prophetess to raise her head, and to speak in the language of men.

"What unknown mortal is he who has thus disturbed my repose? Bleached by the snow, beaten by the winds, drenched by the rains, have I long remained — long here I have been in the arms of death." "Vegtam is my name, the son of Valtam.[1] Tell me the secrets of hell, and I will tell thee what passes on earth. For whom are these costly benches, for whom these golden couches prepared?" "This tempered mead, this liquid nectar awaits the arrival of Baldur. Sorrowful are the sons of heaven. Unwillingly have I spoken; now my lips shall be closed." "Listen, prophetess, for I must know the whole. Whose hand shall deprive Odin's son of life?" "That of Hödur: he the bruiser shall be of Odin's son, the spoiler of Baldur's life! Unwillingly have I spoken; now my lips shall be closed."

"Listen, prophetess, for I must know the whole. Who shall revenge on Hödur the death of the hero — who shall bear the smiter of Baldur to the funeral pyre?" "Rinda, a virgin of the west, shall bear a son by Odin; he, when only one night old, shall slay the murderer. His hands he shall not wash, nor his head shall he comb, until he bears to the funeral pyre the enemy of Baldur. Unwillingly have I spoken; now my lips shall be closed." "Listen, prophetess, for I must know the whole. Who are these damsels that weep at pleasure and raise their covered heads on high?[2] Say this only, and thou mayest sleep." "Ah! no wandering spoiler art thou, as I have hitherto believed: well do I know thee for Odin, the preserver of nations!" "And thou art not Vala; no prophetess art thou; but the mother of the three infernal furies!" "Odin, ride back to thine house, and there command! Never again will I be consulted by the living until Loki shall break loose from his fetters, and the dreaded twilight of the gods arrive!" Such is the dark poetical legend which the genius of the poet Gray has immortalised. It is among the most imaginative efforts of the Scandinavian muse.

THE RULE AND WORSHIP OF ODIN

According to Saxo,[g] it was not the mystic Vala, but Rostiof, king of the Finns, who foretold that Odin's son, by Rinda, should avenge the death of Baldur. That Odin, who was esteemed chief of the gods, should be less prescient than a Finnish king, may appear strange; but this term god frequently means no more than Goth, and the chief of the gods means only the head of the pontifical college established, first in Asia, and next in Sweden. And we must remember that the Finns were expressly declared to be unrivalled in magic, at least in that dark magic which sought the injury of mankind. Yet Odin was equally malignant. He could not rest until he had discovered the maiden whose offspring was thus predestined to accomplish his purpose. This Rinda was a princess, and, consequently, demanded more attention than one of humbler birth. The disguises which he successively assumed at her father's court; his frequent repulses by her; his numerous stratagems, and his ultimate triumph under the character of a physician are gravely related by the venerable historian of Denmark. His conduct on these occasions was so unworthy of a god that his colleagues at Byzantium (or we should rather suppose Asgard) removed him for a time from their society, deprived him of his supernatural powers, degraded him to the level of mortals, and sentenced

---

[1] The names are mythologic, or rather abstract : Vegtam, the Spoiler; Valtam, Slaughter.

[2] *Hveriar ro maeyiar*
Ær at muni grata
Ok a himin Verpa
Halsa Skautvm?

The passage is a dark one. It probably alludes to the custom of the northern women, who uncovered their heads to mourn. These damsels did not uncover ; they could weep at pleasure, that is, they were not afflicted. Were they the fatal sisters, who cannot be expected to feel sympathy for mortals? And was Vala their mother?

him to exile — a doom which he, therefore, suffered a second time, though on the former occasion it had been self-imposed.

All this, in plain English, means that he was expelled from the college of priests. This natural explanation is confirmed by the statement that, in ten years, the gods, pitying his sufferings, or perhaps bribed by flattery and costly gifts, restored him to all his former privileges. Lest the public worship should sustain any injury, his place had been supplied by one Oller, a priest so expert in magic that he could cross the seas on a bone; but this usurper was slain by the Swedes, just as Mitothin had been slain. In the mean time Bo, the issue of Odin's connection with Rinda, grew up, and was entrusted by the father with the sacred task of revenge. Accordingly he advanced against the Danish king. Hödur foresaw his doom; and, in an assembly of chiefs, he prevailed on them to elect his son, Runi, for his successor. In the battle which followed destiny was fulfilled: he fell by the hand of Bo; but the victor also received a mortal wound and died the following day.

All that we have further to say respecting Odin, in this place, may be despatched in a few words. Perceiving his end approach, he marked his body with a sword, probably to denote the advantage of dying by that weapon; and declared that he was going to Godheim or paradise, where he should joyfully receive his people. The Swedes were persuaded that he was returned to Asgard to enjoy eternal life; and in this belief his worship was renewed and enlarged. In time of war, and before great battles, he often appeared to them, promising victory to some, inviting others to his hall — in both respects the harbinger of good. After death he was placed on the funeral pyre, and burned with exceeding pomp. His followers believed the higher the smoke ascended the higher would be his place among the gods; and that the more abundant the riches consumed with him the richer he would be in the other world.

From the concurrent testimony of Snorre, Saxo Grammaticus, and the two Eddas, little doubt can be entertained in regard to the true character of Odin. He was evidently a conqueror, a king, a priest, a lawgiver, and an adept in the superstitious practices of his age. Endued with commanding talents and an unmeasured ambition, he was enabled to take advantage of circumstances in a degree seldom attained by mortals. Perceiving the success which attended his views, and the veneration in which his wisdom was held, he did not hesitate to ascribe both to the peculiar favour of the gods, from whom, like most of the Scythian princes, he boasted of his descent. As he was of divine race, why should he not participate in the privileges of divinity? Short, indeed, is the transition from veneration to actual worship; and there can be little doubt that, even in his lifetime, this artful pontiff king had altars smoking in his honour. But it is worthy of remark that he was often regarded as a mortal, not merely in his own age but in subsequent ages; that the words giants and gods are to be understood of the original possessors of the soil, the invading Goths, the dominant caste which arrogated to itself the sacerdotal and regal functions, and thus preserved its empire over the barbarous, enslaved population.

It was some time after his death before his worship was general in the north; and never would it have been general had he not been esteemed the god of war, the deity above all others dear to the ferocious Northmen. Even as it is, he did not hold the highest rank in the worship of all the Scandinavian nations. The Norwegians held him inferior to Thor. Still he is by far the most remarkable person that ever took advantage of human credulity. Over a considerable portion of Europe his worship was extended; and it was not a transitory worship: for it prevailed, in Germany, far into the ninth century; in Denmark and Sweden, a century later; and in some parts of Norway it was not extinct in the twelfth. Of the religion which, however, he founded, or which he incorporated with the superstition already subsisting on his arrival in the north, we shall speak in a future chapter.

THE HAMLET OF HISTORY: DIFFICULTIES OF CHRONOLOGY

On the death of Hödur, the sceptre of Denmark, or rather of a portion of Denmark, passed into the hands of his son Rörik. The name of this prince is interesting from the fact that the alleged events on which the tragedy of *Hamlet* is founded happened in his reign. According to Saxo,[g] Hamlet [or Amleth] was not the son of a Danish king. His father was Horvendill, governor of Jutland, a famous pirate and vassal of Rörik; but the authority was not undivided: it was shared by Fengo, brother of Horvendill. Fengo did nothing to merit the favour of Rörik; but Horvendill was so valiant and able that he was honoured with the hand of Gerutha, or Gertrude, daughter of the Danish king. From this marriage sprung Amleth, whose history is so famous in the traditions of Denmark. Fengo could not, without envy, behold the good fortune of his brother: envy led to hatred, and hatred to fratricide. After this deed he married the widowed Gerutha, and succeeded to the whole government of Jutland.

Amleth was no inattentive observer of these events. As a pagan, his first duty was to revenge his father's death: a duty to the force of which his uncle was fully alive, and watchful to frustrate it. Spies being set on all his actions, he feigned madness; he painted his face, put on a strange garb, and uttered the most ridiculous things. Frequently was he to be seen on the hearth, seated among the ashes and making wooden hooks, which he hardened by the heat. His madness, however, had method in it; and some of his replies, ridiculous as they seemed, made the experienced doubt whether he should be classed among the wisest or the most foolish of mankind. "For what purpose are these hooks?" was one day demanded of him. "For the revenge of my father!" was the answer. As nobody could see how they could effect that purpose, he was ridiculed by all but the discerning, who supposed that beneath this ostentatious display of insanity a profound object was concealed. Among these was Jarl Fengo, who, wishing to prove whether the suspicions were well or ill-founded, had recourse to an expedient. The disposition of the prince was exceedingly amatory; and it was thought that, if a young handsome female were sent to him, he would betray himself. The meeting was to be effected in a wood, and spies were to be placed near him.

On the day appointed, he was commanded to ride into a forest. As usual, he mounted with his face to the tail, which he held in lieu of a bridle. There he found the woman; and would have immediately betrayed himself, had not his foster-brother obscurely hinted that he should beware. The way in which this intimation was communicated, like many other parts of Saxo's narrative, is too gross for translation. Enough to know that Amleth was made to understand the danger of his situation. Among his virtues, chastity was not to be reckoned; and though the instances of its violation cannot be recorded in these times, we may observe that, even on the occasion before us, he indulged his propensity, and was cunning enough to conceal it. Fengo, therefore, was disappointed; but by the advice of a friend he had recourse to another expedient. Under the pretext of a long absence on affairs of moment, he left the palace, and provided that Amleth should be brought into the mother's presence, while a spy, unknown to both, should be near them, to hear every word that he should utter. If he had any reason left, it was not doubted he would be communicative with one whom he loved, and who he knew would never betray him. At the time appointed, the courtier hastened to the apartment, where mother and son were to meet, and hid himself under a heap of straw that accidentally lay there — a curious illustration of domestic economy in that age. Immediately afterwards, Amleth and Gerutha arrived; but the former was too much aware of the dangers which involved him to indulge in rational conversation with his mother, until he had examined the locality. Imitating the crowing of a cock — an imitation in which he was singularly successful — and waving his arms as if they were wings, he leaped on the straw, and was immediately sensible that something lay beneath. With his sword he despatched the intruder. After this act, while his mother was bewailing his supposed insanity, he fiercely upbraided her for her incestuous marriage with the murderer of her first husband. This double crime he did not assail exactly in the manner represented in the drama, but in one more conformable with the barbarism of the age, that is, in one of exceeding coarseness.

His remonstrances are said to have kindled the sparks of virtue in her heart; but the sequel ill corresponded with this moral intention, or with the refined character which the dramatist has given him. The man whom he had killed he cut in pieces, boiled the members, and threw them into the sewer to be eaten by the swine. When Fengo returned, great was his surprise to find that his courtier had disappeared — that not the slightest trace of him could be discovered. One day Amleth, who was regarded as no more than a motley fool, and to whom questions were put for amusement only, being asked what had become of his uncle's friend, replied, "He fell into the common sewer, and being unable to extricate himself, was found, and eaten by the swine!" His reply furnished some amusement to the hearers, who regarded it as a good motley invention. They did not know that on all occasions, whether grave or trivial, Amleth spoke the truth.

But if the multitude were thus deluded, Fengo was not. For his own safety he felt that the youth must be removed; but to effect this some management was required. He would not exasperate his wife, still less the sovereign of Denmark, by openly executing the prince. The deed must be secret, and done by other than native hands — namely, by those of the English king, who, we are gravely assured, was a tributary of Denmark. Before Amleth's departure, he privately desired his mother, in one year from that time, to celebrate his funeral obsequies; assuring her, however, that he would in one year return. Two creatures of Fengo were his companions. One night, while they were buried in sleep, he examined their baggage, and found, carved on wood, the mandate to the English king. With his usual cunning, he erased a portion of the characters; and so altered the rest, that the foreign king was to put his two companions to death, but to show every possible kindness towards himself, and even to give him the hand of an English princess. On their arrival in England, they presented their wooden mandate, which they were unable to read; and were invited, with much parade of hospitality, to the royal table. But while the two messengers were thus deluded, Amleth was received with much respect. The more curious reader may consult the venerable authority before us for an account of what passed at the English court — an account as minute as it is romantic.

To be brief: the two messengers were executed; and Amleth, whose wisdom was so much admired, obtained the hand of the monarch's daughter.

He pretended, however, to be much affected by the death of his companions; and, to pacify him, the king gave him a considerable quantity of gold, which he melted and inclosed in the hollow of two walking sticks. At the expiration of the year, he obtained leave to revisit his native country; but, of all his riches, he took only the staves which contained the gold. On reaching Jutland, he assumed his own motley garb, and reached the house of his uncle at the very time his funeral rites were performed. At first, his sudden appearance terrified the domestics and guests; but terror yielded to mirth when they saw him resume his motley character. "Where are your two companions?" demanded they. "Here they are!" was his reply, as he produced his two sticks. Soon he joined the cup-bearers; and as his long flowing garments interfered with his activity, he girt his sword round him, but it had no scabbard; and to impress all the guests with a stronger notion of his insanity, he frequently grasped the blade until the blood flowed from his fingers. Little did they suspect his object in thus descending to the meanest occupation: it was to make all of them drunk, and then to exact his revenge. So well did he succeed in the first intention, that most of them, being unable to stagger from the apartment, were compelled to remain all night in the hall of entertainment.

At length, all being buried in sleep, he cut off the cords which supported a huge curtain that occupied the whole room: as it fell on the drunken sleepers, by his wooden hooks he fastened it in many places to the ground; and drawing the cords over the curtain, so bound them by knots and hooks as to bid defiance to the efforts of drunken men. Startled by the weight no less than by the sudden difficulty of breathing, they strove to raise the curtain, but in vain; it was too well secured to be moved. In this state they were soon enveloped in flames, which consumed them and the palace. Fengo retired to his bedroom, and fell asleep: he was awakened by Amleth, who, after upbraiding him for his various crimes, put him to death. He then flew to a safe retreat to watch the progress of events. Great was the surprise of the Jutes at this disaster; but, as Fengo was a tyrant, the majority were not displeased. Amleth, therefore, reappeared; surrounded himself with those whom he knew to be attached to the interests of his family; sought the public assembly; and, by his eloquence, so wrought on the people, that they unanimously declared him the successor of Fengo.

In the remaining adventures of Amleth — all equally wonderful with the preceding — we cannot enter. Whoever may wish to read his subsequent visit to Britain; his marriage with a second wife, the queen of Scotland; his quarrel with the British king, the father of his first wife; his domestic life with both in his hereditary government of Jutland; his war with Vikletus, king of Denmark, the successor of his grandfather, Rörik; his death in battle; and the facility with which the idol of his heart, his second wife, passed into the arms of the victor, must consult the venerable Saxo.

We have no wish to pursue farther the list of Danish kings, who, according to Saxo, reigned prior to the birth of Christ. Some of them, probably, never reigned at all. Others, certainly, reigned after that event. Others, again, ruled at the same time, over different provinces of the kingdom. The reigns of many whom Saxo places before the Christian era are identical with those which the best Danish writers regard as posterior; and the actions attributed to both are substantially the same. All writers admit that Denmark had no monarch before Skiold, the son of Odin; indeed, it had none for some generations afterwards: for there is room to believe that even his authority was more of a sacerdotal than of a temporal character. In virtue of this character he might, and probably did, claim a twofold sovereignty over the peninsula and islands; but that sovereignty was never virtually exercised — it was one merely nominal.

Several of the islands had their separate governors, whom Saxo calls kings; and Jutland, as we have seen in the sketch of Amleth's life, had them also. The men whom personal qualities elevated above the rest became chiefs; and when one chief had others subject to him, he assumed the regal title. There were kings of various kinds. We read of petty kings (*sma-konungur*, or *fylke-konungur*); of sea kings, island kings, and cape kings. The name of the last may require an explanation. They were neither more nor less than the pirate chiefs, who lived in caverns or in huts near the promontories, ready, at any moment, to sally forth and seize the unsuspecting mariner. Thus there were kings enough scattered over the seas, the forests, the mountains, the maritime coasts of the north. Probably all those in the Danish islands might yield a nominal homage, at least, to the one that reigned in Skåne in Zealand. But no dependence whatever can be placed on the list of Danish kings prior to what we now call the historic times — that is, to about the eighth century of our era.

But later writers have made sad work with this list. They contend that some of the names are altogether fabulous; that Skiold reigned only forty years before Christ; Frode I, thirty-five years after Christ; Wermund, one hundred and fifty; Roe and Helge, in the fifth century of our era. The truth, however, is that, while no dependence is to be placed on the genealogical series of the former, very little is due to the latter. The whole, prior to the eighth century, is one mass of confusion. If the names of many princes are to be found, not merely in the earliest writers of the north, but on runic inscriptions, no power of criticism can fix the period in which they reigned. All is pure conjecture; and one system is preferable to another only so far as it is more reconcilable to common sense. Yet, while we thus reject some of the ancient sovereigns whom Saxo and the elder chroniclers have handed down to us, we are not so sceptical as to reject the majority. If, prior to Odin's arrival, the north had no monarchs, it had kings or, if the reader pleases, chiefs, whose office was sometimes hereditary, sometimes elective. It would, perhaps, be more accurate to say that, while they succeeded by hereditary right to the domains of their predecessors, as generals and judges, they were elected by the free-born warriors. Of these some were, beyond all doubt, elevated into monarchs by tradition; from tradition they passed into the songs of the skalds; and from these songs their memory was perpetuated by the old chroniclers.[k]

CHAPTER II

THE AGE OF THE VIKINGS

[To 1050 A.D.]

THE ANCIENT KINGS OF SWEDEN

AFTER briefly relating the legend of Odin, the *Ynglinga Saga*[b] proceeds to deduce the history of the dynasty of that name in Sweden, during the first seven centuries of the Christian era. Of the sovereigns descended from Magog who are alleged to have reigned before that epoch, no record worthy of credit has been preserved, nor of the events that took place prior to the death of Gylfe, when the crown was transferred to the sacred line of the Ynglings. We shall therefore entirely discard those lists of primeval monarchs, who could only be local chiefs, or petty rulers, alternately the conquerors and the vassals of each other, and adopt the theory of commencing from the arrival of Odin, as accredited by the most judicious and enlightened of the old Northern annalists—our only guides through a long period of darkness and fable.[1] The following table represents the names and number of the kings, in the order of their succession, who reigned at Upsala until the beginning of the tenth century:

[1] Our authorities, besides the *Ynglinga Saga*, for the order and chronology of these ancient kings, are Torfæus, Suhm, Geijer, and the Langfedgatal in the *Scriptores Rerum Danicarum Medii Ævi*, etc., a Jocobo Langebek, 8 tom. *Hafniæ*, 1772, et seq. In this valuable collection of Scandinavian antiquities, above twenty different catalogues of ancient kings are given, whose genealogies are traced back "*fra Noa till varra konunga*," a *Noacho ad reges nostros.*

TRADITIONAL LIST OF THE ANCIENT KINGS OF SWEDEN — THE YNGLINGS

Odin arrived in the North	. . B.C.	70
Njörd	died "	20
Frey-Yngve . . .	. A.D.	10
Fiolner	.	14
Svegdir	.	34
Vanland or Valland .	.	48
Visbur	.	98
Domald	.	130
Domar	.	162
Dyggve	.	190
Dag-Spaka, the Wise .	.	220
Agne	.	260
Alrek and Eric .	.	280
Yngve and Alf .	.	300
Hugleik	.	302
Jorunder and Eric .	.	312
Aun hinn Gamle (the Old)	.	448
Egill Tunnadolgi .	.	456
Ottar Vendilkraka .	.	460
Adils	.	505
Eystein	.	531
Yngvar	.	545

Braut-Onund . . .	died A.D.	565
Ingiald Illrada .	.	623
Olaf Trætelia . .	exiled about	630

Accession of the Skioldungs

Ivar Vidfadme .	died A.D.	647
Harold Hildetand .	.	735
Sigurd Ring .	.	750
Ragnar Lodbrok .	.	794
Björn Ironside .	.	804
Eric Bjornson .	.	808
Eric Ræfillson .	.	820
Emund and Björn .	.	859
Eric Emundson .	.	873
Björn Erickson .	.	923
Eric the Victorious .	.	993
Eric Arsæll .	.	1001
Olaf the Lap-King .	.	1026
Anund Kolbrenner .	.	1051
Edmund Slemme .	.	1056
Stenkil . .	raised to the throne	1056

The annals of these pontiff-kings possess little historical interest. From the reverence in which the immediate descendants of Odin were held, as vested with the sacerdotal character, and from the superstitious belief that ascribed to them those blessings of peace and abundance which made their reign the golden age of the North, the first princes of this sacred line were raised to divine honours; and their names hold a distinguished place in the Scandinavian Pantheon. Frey removed his capital from Sigtuna to Upsala, where he is said to have built a palace and a magnificent temple, which he surrounded with a chain of gold, and endowed with considerable wealth in lands and other revenues. He adopted the surname of Yngve, and hence the sacred race of Ynglings derived their historical appellation. Dyggve is alleged to have been the first that assumed the regal title, his predecessors being merely called *drottar* or lord, and their queens *drottingar*.

At the death of Agne, the kingdom, which had hitherto remained entire, was shared between his two sons, Alrek and Eric — an unwise policy, which had the effect of dividing the prerogatives as well as the dominions of the crown among a multitude of provincial chiefs, who assumed an independent authority. From this circumstance, and from the occasional conquests of the neighbouring kings in Denmark and Norway, whose usurpations often extended beyond their own territory, has arisen much of the confusion that perplexes the order and chronology of the several dynasties which fill up this era of Scandinavian history;[1] one royal chronicle differing from another, and sometimes representing the same monarch as ruling in each of the three countries. The Swedes, however, still adhered to the sacred race, and expelled every foreign intruder. Adils was involved in a protracted quarrel with the Norwegians, which was at length terminated in his favour by a pitched battle on Lake Venern, the two armies being drawn up on its frozen

[1] According to the *Ynglinga Saga*,[b] Hugleik was driven from his throne by Hakon, a Norwegian pirate. Aun was twice expelled; once by Halfdan I of Denmark, who reigned at Upsala twenty-five years, and again by Ali hinn Frækni, or Ole the Active, son of Fridlief III. Egill derived his surname from slaying a rebel, called Tunni, who had defeated him in eight battles. Ottar fell in a naval action with Frode IV, in the Limfjord, after ravaging the district of Vendila, or Vendsyssel. Eystein was burned in his own palace by Solvi, a king of Jutland, who usurped the crown for several years.

surface. The hereditary occupant of the throne at Upsala continued to enjoy a pre-eminence in dignity and power until the fatal reign of Ingiald Illrada, when the hallowed sceptre was transferred from the line of the Ynglings to that of the Skioldungs, in the earlier part of the seventh century.

That prince, when young, is said to have been of a gentle disposition, but being vanquished in some juvenile contest, such as the sons of the nobility were then accustomed to display at their annual festivals, the Saga relates that in order to alter his temper he was fed with wolves' hearts. Judging from his future actions, this regimen appears to have had the desired effect. His reign, from its commencement to its close, was a series of cruel and lawless atrocities. It was the ancient custom at the royal inauguration, which always took place at the funeral of the deceased prince, for the next heir to seat himself on the lowest step of the vacant throne, in the midst of the grandees, until presented with a huge ox-horn filled with wine; after taking the usual oaths, he drank off the liquor, mounted the chair of state, and was proclaimed amidst the shouts of the people. This initiatory rite Ingiald accompanied with the additional ceremony of swearing, before draining the mystic cup, that he would either double the extent of his kingdom, or perish in the attempt. The fulfilment of his vow led to those acts of treachery and murder which procured him the name of Illrada (the deceitful), and ultimately occasioned his own destruction.

Fire and sword were employed to exterminate the chiefs and nobles, many of whom were consumed in the flames of the palace where they had been hospitably entertained by their perfidious sovereign. Twelve petty princes in Sweden fell victims to the rapacity of the tyrant, who seized their possessions and added them to the dominions of the crown. But a just retribution awaited the perpetration of his crimes. His daughter Asa had been given in marriage to Gudrod, the Gothic king of Skåne; at her instigation he assassinated his brother, Halfdan III of Denmark, and was afterwards himself cut off in a plot, by the artifices of his own wife. Having sacrificed her husband, she fled to the court of Upsala, where she became an accomplice in the death of her father. Ivar Vidfadme, son of Halfdan, had invaded Sweden with a powerful host, to avenge the murder of his kindred. His ravages filled the guilty Ingiald with terror and despair. As the victorious foe approached, he was entertaining his courtiers at a grand banquet; when, finding it impossible to resist or make his escape, he resolved, with the aid and advice of his daughter, to terminate his life by setting fire to the hall. Olaf, his son, unable to repel the invaders, was driven into exile; passing to the westward of the Venern Lake, he settled, with the few companions that still adhered to his standard, in the province of Vermland; there he hewed down the immense forests (hence his name of Trætelia, the tree-cutter), and laid the basis of a new kingdom, where, in a short time, the star of the Ynglings rose again with more than its ancient splendour, in the person of Harold Harfagr (or Fairhair), founder of the Norwegian monarchy.

The habits and actions of this venerated race appear to have been often singularly inconsistent with their pretensions to a celestial descent. Some of them died of excessive intoxication; others from the intrigues of their wives or courtiers. Fiolner was drowned in a large vat of mead, into which he had stumbled while under the dominion of liquor; his three immediate successors perished by violent means; the fourth, Domald, was slain by the advice of his councillors, under the superstitious idea that a severe famine which afflicted the country could only be removed by sprinkling the altars of the offended deities at Upsala with the blood of their king. War was the principal occupation of their reign, and numerous bloody battles were fought in repressing the incessant piracies of the neighbouring nations. Yet several of them were distinguished for their encouragement of civilisation and social improvement. Onund received the name of Braut (the road-maker), from his exertions in draining marshes, extending cultivation, and opening up channels of intercourse to every province in the kingdom.

The name of Ivar Vidfadme has been omitted by some historians in the list of Swedish kings; while others more worthy of credit not only assign him that honour, but rank him among the most distinguished warriors of antiquity. The Saga, in adverting to his military exploits, says that "he conquered all Sweden (allt Sviaveldi), and united it with all Denmark (allt Danaveldi); and a great part of Saxland, the whole of Estland (Esthonia), and a fifth part of England.[1] From him, henceforth, descend the supreme kings of the Danes and the Swedes." The throne and extensive dominions of Ivar were inherited by his grandson, Harold Hildetand; from him they descended to Sigurd Ring and Ragnar Lodbrok — all of whom swayed the Danish sceptre in the eighth century.

The latter prince bestowed the Swedish crown, as a distinct possession, on one of his sons, Björn Jarnasida (Ironside), in whose grandson's reign (Björn II) it is generally admitted that the light of the Gospel first dawned in the North; although it did not become the established religion until the accession of Olaf the Lap-King (Skotkonung), who was baptized with his whole family in the year 1001, and exerted himself with great enthusiasm to propagate the true faith. His father Eric is said to have carried his zeal for Christianity so far as to cause the magnificent heathen temple at Upsala, with its idols and images, to be destroyed, and the ancient sacrifices to be interdicted, under the severest corporal inflictions; but this imprudent mandate cost him his life, as he was murdered in a tumult of the people, enraged at the demolition of their pagan worship.

The conversions under Olaf would have been more expeditious, had not his zeal been restrained by the diet, who decided for full liberty of conscience; hence the strange mixture both in doctrine and rites, which long prevailed, and the incoherent association of the sacred characters in Scripture with the gods and goddesses of the Scandinavian mythology. This prince was more successful as a warrior than a reformer. He made a temporary conquest of Norway, and having annexed Gothland inalienably to his own dominions, he assumed the title of king of Sweden; his predecessors being merely styled sovereigns of Upsala. His son, Anund Jacob, contributed so much to the progress of divine truth among his subjects as to obtain the designation of "most christian majesty."[2] A severe law, which procured him the name of Kolbrenner (the coal-burner), enacted that, if any man injured his neighbor, his effects, to the same value, should be consumed with fire.

His successor became involved in a dispute with the Danes, about adjusting the frontiers of the two kingdoms, and fell at the head of an army which he had levied for recovering the ceded province of Skåne. Indignant at the surrender of that valuable district, the Swedes raised Stenkil to the throne,

[1] The part of England subdued by Ivar Vidfadme is more explicitly marked in the *Hervarar Saga* as Northumbria, which is said to have descended to Ivar's grandson, Harold Hildetand. The Anglo-Saxon annals make no mention of these earlier conquests of the Scandinavians; but as they are generally silent respecting the transactions in the north of England at this period, no inference is to be drawn against the credibility of the Icelandic accounts from this circumstance.

[2] Olaf was baptised by Sigefroy, an English monk, whom King Æthelred had sent to Sweden.

[40 B.C.–270 A.D.]

who founded a new dynasty, to the exclusion of the race of Lodbrok. The Goths, who likewise claimed the right of election, chose Hakon the Red as their king; but the rival monarchs came to an amicable arrangement, by stipulating that the latter should enjoy the regal dignity for life, on condition that, at his demise, Gothland should revert inseparably to Sweden.

THE STATES OF DENMARK

The small states forming the kingdom of Denmark, which next claim our attention, continued three or four centuries under the sway of various petty princes, the chief of whom were the Skioldungs, that branch of the family of Odin which established the seat of their authority at Leidre, in Zealand. Skiold, the founder of this dynasty, reigned, according to Suhm's chronology, about forty years before the Christian era. The series of kings who derived from him their name and pedigree is given in the following order:

TRADITIONAL LIST OF THE ANCIENT KINGS OF DENMARK — THE SKIOLDUNGS

Odin arrived in the North	B.C. 70	Frode VI	died A.D.	510
Skiold	died " 40	Rolf Krake		522
Fridlief I	23	Frode VII		548
Frode I	A.D. 35	Halfdan III		580
Fridlief II	47	Rörik Slyngebaud		588
Havar	59	Ivar Vidfadme		647
Frode II	87	Harold Hildetand		735
Vermund the Sage	140	Sigurd Ring		750
Olaf the Mild	190	Ragnar Lodbrok		794
Dan Mykillati	270	Sigurd Snogoje		803
Frode III the Pacific	310	Harde-Knud		850
Halfdan I	324	Eric I		854
Fridlief III	348	Eric II		883
Frode IV	407	Gorm the Old		941
Ingild	456	Harold Blaatand		991
Halfdan II	447	Sweyn Splitbeard		1014
Frode V	460	Canute the Great		1035
Helge and Roe	494	Harthacanut		1044

Tradition has ascribed to Skiold the usual qualities of the heroic ages — great bodily strength, and the most indomitable courage. Among his other military exploits, he is said to have conquered the Saxons, and subjected them to the payment of an annual tribute. Of his immediate successors the native chroniclers have preserved few details worthy of being recorded. Frode I enjoyed the reputation of unrivalled prowess as a warrior, having carried his victorious arms into Sweden, Germany, Hungary, England, and Ireland. So strict was the administration of justice in his own dominions, and so promptly were the laws against robbery and pillage enforced, that, if we may credit the northern legends, bags of gold might have been safely exposed on the highways. It is alleged, perhaps with more truth, that he compiled a civil and military code, which Saxo states to have been extant in his times.

The first that united the Danish provinces (except Jutland, which formed a separate monarchy) under one government was Dan Mykillati, the Magnanimous, king of Skåne, a descendant of Heimdall, and married to a daughter of Olaf, sovereign of Zealand, and sixth in descent from Skiold. He reduced the whole country, with the smaller islands, to subjection; and is alleged to have given his name to the new kingdom of which he was the founder, although at a subsequent period it was again dismembered, and broken down into several independent principalities. The union of his sister with Dyggve of Sweden is reckoned the earliest matrimonial alliance that was formed between the two crowns. Wars and other events of no importance fill up the history of his successors for ten or twelve generations. Halfdan I subdued Sweden; he defeated Aun in many battles, and having driven him from the throne he fixed his residence in Upsala, where he died, after possessing the government twenty-five years.

The dominions of Halfdan II were inherited by his sons Roe and Helge, who agreed to divide the sovereignty between them; the former is said to have built the city of Roeskilde, but he exchanged his patrimony in the North for the Danish possessions in Northumberland, where he fixed his residence, and conquered several provinces from the Anglo-Saxons. His brother invaded the Swedish territory, defeated Adils, plundered the palace at Upsala, and carried off the queen, a Saxon princess named Yrsa. The lady, from being his prisoner, became his wife, and the mother of the celebrated hero Rolf Krake, one of the brightest ornaments of the throne. His stature was gigantic and his strength extraordinary; but we must leave the historians of the times to relate his numerous feats, and the princely virtues by which he won the universal esteem of his subjects. Having perished childless, by the treachery of a nobleman on whom he had bestowed his daughter in marriage, the crown became the prize of contending factions, until the kingdom was again united under one sceptre by Ivar Vidfadme, who, as already stated, transmitted it to his grandson, Harold Hildetand.[1]

This latter monarch appears to have raised Denmark to an unprecedented height of power. Not content with chastising the neighbouring states, he made frequent incursions into Germany, took the Vandals under his protection, reduced several nations on the Rhine, invaded the coasts of France, and overran part of Britain, which, according to Saxo, had withdrawn its allegiance from the Danish kings since the death of Frode III. Whatever truth there may be in these achievements, the naval resources of Harold were certainly great. His fleets are described as covering the Sound, and, like those of Xerxes, bridging over the northern Hellespont from shore to shore; but his life and reign terminated at the fatal battle of Bravalla, fought on the coast of Skåne, against his nephew, Sigurd Ring, in consequence of his attempt to expel him from the throne.

At this famous engagement all the petty kings and maritime forces of the North, including most of the nations around the Baltic, were assembled. Chieftains and pirates rushed to this scene of carnage with their champions. The ships of Sigurd were reckoned at two thousand five hundred; the hosts of Sweden, Gothland, and Norway, headed by their most renowned warriors, composed his army. The party of his antagonist was joined by the Livonians, Saxons, Frisians, Vandals, and other German tribes. Besides common soldiers, whose numbers are not stated, it comprehended about thirty thousand nobility, three celebrated Amazons, and all the court poets. The leaders, amongst the bravest of whom were Ubbo, a famous viking, and Starkadder the Scandinavian Hercules, fought hand to hand in single combat. The heroic Harold, old, blind, and infirm, was seated in his battle-car; but after a long and sanguinary contest, he perished on the field, with fifteen other royal chieftains in his train. The body was discovered amidst heaps of slain, and burned by order of Sigurd on a magnificent funeral-pile, with

---

[1] Harold was the son of Rörik Slyngebaud and Audur, daughter of Ivar Vidfadme. His surname of Hildetand or Golden Teeth is thus accounted for: *Hildetanni cognomen obtinuit ab Hilde, quæ Dea belli perhibetur, seu septentrionis Bellona, et dentibus aureis.*

his armour, chariot, and war-horse. The fortune of the day was decided by the Norwegian archers from Tellemark; and the skalds, who have sung this truly Homeric combat, not satisfied with the martial energies by which the victory was obtained, have introduced Odin himself as taking part against the Danes, and perfidiously despatching their aged monarch with his resistless war-club. The lays of the poets have commemorated the exploits and immortalised the names of the principal warriors engaged in the fray. In this "great and terrible fight," according to the northern muse, "the sun was darkened with the immense multitude of darts and stones, and the smoke of human gore."

The Danish throne fell to the possession of Sigurd, who, like other kings of his time, embarked in sea-roving expeditions, to keep alive the military enthusiasm of his people. He recovered the English province of Northumberland, conquered by Ivar Vidfadme, which had asserted its independence; and at his death he left the crown to his son, the famous Ragnar Lodbrok.

RAGNAR LODBROK AND HIS HEIRS

The remarkable history of this Scandinavian adventurer has been so obscured by conflicting traditions and poetical embellishments as to create considerable difficulty in reconciling the chronology and other circumstances of his life with the accounts given in the Frankish and Anglo-Saxon annals. The anachronism is generally explained by supposing two piratical chiefs of the same name, although this seems hardly consistent with the Sagas and other ancient Icelandic writings. All the northern chronicles agree in the main particulars related of the prince who reigned in Denmark and Sweden in the latter part of the eighth century, and who could not, therefore, be the formidable invader that infested France and England about the middle of the ninth. It is not improbable, however, that the chieftain whose exploits have been confounded with those of the more ancient Ragnar, was a prince of Jutland, whose real name was Ragenfrid, or Regnier, who became a sea-king on being expelled from his dominions in the time of Harold Klak (827 A.D.), and subsequently invaded France under the reign of Louis le Débonnaire.

Without venturing to narrate the wars and piracies of this redoubted monarch, or the extraordinary feats of courage ascribed to him by Saxo we may record what tradition states as to the cause and singular manner of his death. While ruling his dominions in peace, his jealousy was excited by rumours of the daring achievements of his sons in various regions of Europe; and he determined to undertake an expedition that should rival their fame. Two vessels were built of immense size, such as had never before been seen in the North. "The arrow," the signal of war, was sent through all his kingdoms, to summon his champions to arms. With this apparently inadequate force he set sail, contrary to the advice of his queen, Aslauga, who presented him with a magical garment to ward off danger.

After suffering from storms and shipwreck, he landed on the coast of Northumberland, which had been so often ravaged by his predecessors. Ælla, the Saxon king of that country, collected his forces to repel the invader. A battle ensued, wherein the valiant Dane, clothed in his enchanted robe, and wielding the huge spear with which he had slain the guardian serpent of the princess Thora, four times pierced the enemy's ranks, dealing death on every side, whilst his own person was invulnerable. But the contest was unequal; his warriors fell one by one around him, until he was at last taken prisoner, stripped of his miraculous vest, and thrown alive (as the Saga relates), by order of Ælla, into a dungeon full of serpents, in the midst of which he expired with a laugh of defiance, chanting the famous death-song called the *Lodbrokar-quida,* or *Biarka-mal,* which he is alleged to have composed in that horrible prison.

This ancient lay mentions his ravaging the coast of Scotland, and his battle with three kings of Erin at Lindis Eiri. The English chronicles also allude to the same invasion, when they relate that the monastery of St. Cuthbert, in the isle of Lindisfarne (Holy Island), was plundered in 793 by a band of pagan rovers from Denmark and Norway; and that their leader was taken the following year, and put to death in a cruel manner by the natives. The life of this hero is represented as an uninterrupted course of wise measures, noble actions, and glorious victories; for not only did the British Isles quail at the terror of h's name — the prowess of his arms was also felt by the Saxons, Russians, and Greeks on the distant Hellespont.

At the time when the father perished, the sons were engaged in foreign piracies; and the first news of his tragical fate they received after their return, while feasting in their hall, from the messengers sent by Ælla to propitiate their anger. The Saga-men have carefully preserved their names, and the pastimes in which they were engaged. Sigurd Snogoje (Snake-eye) played at chess with Huitserk the Brave, whilst Björn Ironside polished the handle of his spear. Ivar diligently inquired what kind of death Ragnar had suffered; and when the deputies narrated the dreadful story, and mentioned the words of the expiring king, "how the young cubs would rage when they learned their sire's fate," the youths ceased their amusements, and vowed instant revenge. An expedition, led by eight crowned heads and twenty jarls, and composed of the various Scandinavian tribes, was again directed against England. In a battle which took place at York, the Anglo-Saxons were entirely routed; Ælla, being made prisoner, was subjected to the most barbarous treatment. According to a strange and savage custom of the vikings, the sons of Lodbrok ordered the figure of an eagle to be cut in the fleshy part of his back, the ribs to be severed from the spine, and the lungs extracted through the aperture. After this victory Northumbria appears no more as a Saxon kingdom; Ivar took possession of the sovereignty, while the rest of the Northmen wasted and conquered the country as far as the mouth of the Thames.

Sigurd Snake-eye inherited the Danish crown, but was slain in a battle with the Franks (803 A.D.), after extending his sway over all Jutland, Skåne, Halland, and part of Norway. Björn was placed on the throne of Sweden; and a third brother Göttrik (Gudrod or Godefrid), became king of Jutland, which again asserted its independence. The latter prince, by attempting to expel a troublesome colony of the Abodriti, planted on the Elbe by Charlemagne, involved himself in a quarrel with that powerful emperor, who was then carrying on a bloody war of extermination against the pagan Saxons, for refusing to be converted to Christianity. Göttrik for some time harassed his imperial adversary; and appearing with a fleet of two hundred barks on the coast of Friesland, he landed at three different points, dispersed the natives, slew their duke, Rurik, and levied an assessment of 100 pounds weight of silver, which the Frisians brought to his treasury and threw into a copper basin in his presence. Judging from the sound that the tribute-money was debased with alloy, he ordered every coin to be confiscated that did not ring to his satisfaction.

This daring marauder even attempted to take the emperor by surprise, in his palace at Aix-la-Chapelle; but he was himself cut off in the midst of his designs (810 A.D.) by the hand of an assassin. Charlemagne entered into a treaty with Hemming, the nephew and successor of Göttrik (813 A.D.), which stipulated that the Eider should form the boundary between Denmark and the Frankish Empire — the Danes thus abandoning all their conquests southward of that limit.

Harde-Knud, the heir of Sigurd, being young at the time of his father's death, was left to the guardianship of his uncle Göttrik, regent of the kingdom. During the prince's minority, grievous commotions had arisen. Jutland threw off its allegiance, and the sovereignty was fiercely contested between the sons of Göttrik and Harold Klak, a petty king of Schleswig, and father of Rurik, who had taken violent possession of Friesland. He was repeatedly driven from his dominions, and his flight became remarkable as the means of shedding the first rays of Christianity over the pagan darkness of the North. In the peace which Charlemagne had concluded with Hemming, that politic conqueror did not attempt to impose his religion upon the Danes, which would have been rejected by them as a badge of slavery. However anxious to reclaim them from their wild and barbarous habits, he was unwilling to excite a spirit of hostility that might have spread to the bordering nations, by interfering with their obstinate attachment to idolatry.

The achievement of this desirable object was reserved for his son and successor, Louis le Débonnaire, whose court at Ingelheim, on the Rhine, was visited (826 A.D.), by the exiled prince of Jutland, accompanied with his queen, his sons, and a numerous retinue, in a fleet of a hundred galleys. Here the solicitations of the emperor and his prelates induced Harold to renounce the errors of paganism. His wife and children, and many of his followers, were baptised, having solemnly abjured, according to a rude formula still extant, "the works and words of the devil, of Thor, and Woden, and Saxon Odin, with all the evil spirits, their confederates." After the ceremony, the royal convert proceeded in his white garments to the imperial palace, where he received rich baptismal presents of mantles, jewels, armour, and other gifts. The day was ended with a magnificent festival, in which every effort was made to impress the Danes with a lively idea of the pomp and splendour of the Romish religion, as well as the wealth and power of the Franks.[d]

HOLGER DANSKE AND MISSIONS IN THE NORTH

There are other instances of the conversion of Danes and Norwegians at this period. Amongst them is included the famous Holger Danske, the favourite hero of Danish legend and renowned in mediæval romance as Ogier le Danois. His story probably owed its origin to those of two real personages. One of these was a Northman who, in 851 appeared with a fleet of two hundred vessels on the coast of Friesland. Some years before he had pillaged Rouen, and now his followers advancing far inland carried fire and sword to Ghent, Aix-la-Chapelle, Treves, and Cologne. The leader of this terrible invasion has been confounded with a certain Othgar or Ottokar who fought with the Lombards against Charlemagne in 773, and being defeated by the Frankish emperor became his vassal and one of his generals. Thus in the romances Ogier le Danois figures as a paladin of Charlemagne.

A legend similar to that told in Germany of Frederick Barbarossa is related by the Danes of Holger Danske. In a cavern under the castle of Kronborg at Elsinore the hero and his followers are sleeping, seated round a stone table. Once a condemned criminal, having been promised his life if he would explore the underground passages beneath the castle, penetrated to the vault; as he entered Holger rose, but he had sat there so long that his beard had grown into the table, and as he wrenched it out the table itself burst asunder. Holger commanded the intruder to give him his hand, when the man prudently held out an iron bar, and Holger, whose sight appears to have become somewhat impaired during his long sleep, grasped the metal. So hard was his grip that the iron retained the impression of his fingers; the hero, doubtless amazed to meet with no shrinking, observed as he let go that he was glad to find there were still men in Denmark.*a*

In order to carry forward the good work so auspiciously begun, Louis determined to send Anskar as a missionary to the North. This intrepid monk, with a brother from the same convent of Corvei, readily undertook the holy enterprise, and on their arrival in South Jutland, in 827, they commenced their labours under the patronage and protection of Harold. They purchased some heathen children (probably captives taken in war), and founded a school for their instruction in the elementary principles of the new faith; but their progress was interrupted by the civil strife which still raged with unabated fury between the factions competing for the throne. In a great battle near Flensburg, Harold, whose change of religion had inflamed the popular indignation against him, was finally defeated (828 A.D.), and compelled to take refuge in Oldenburg, one of the possessions which Louis had assigned him by way of indemnity. The missionaries followed his retreat, and abandoned their proselytes to the vengeance of the heathen.

Meantime an opportunity occurred for advancing the standard of truth further into the benighted regions of Scandinavia. Ambassadors from Björn II of Sweden had visited the imperial court, imploring that missionaries might be sent into that country. Anskar offered to accompany them on their return, and joined a caravan of merchants travelling to the annual fair at Sigtuna. On their passage across the Baltic they were attacked by pirates, and plundered of nearly all their effects, including forty volumes of sacred literature. At Upsala, the zealous preacher was received in the most friendly manner by the king; and during his short residence he converted and baptised many of the Svear, among whom were some of the highest rank.

The success of this mission induced Louis to establish an archbishopric at Hamburg, from which as a common centre the Catholic emissaries might superintend the spiritual concerns of the North. Anskar was raised to the newly elected see, and received the confirmation of Pope Gregory IV, in a bull declaring him the papal legate in Denmark, Norway, and Sweden. This border-post served him as a convenient station for watching the glimmerings of the light which he had borne, at the hazard of his life, to the centre of Scandinavia. He founded schools for the education of young missionaries, built cloisters and hospitals, and laboured with unremitting efforts to kindle in others the same fervid enthusiasm with which his own breast was inspired. He made a second journey to Sweden, where he availed himself of the toleration granted by the diet to propagate the Christian doctrines.

The lawless habits of the Danes, and their invincible attachment to the ancient idolatry, presented formidable obstacles to their conversion. In a popular commotion some of the clergy were murdered, and others were compelled to flee from persecution. A fleet of sea-rovers, commanded by Eric I,

[845-941 A.D.]

called the Usurper, who had seized the crowns of Jutland and Fünen, sailed up the Elbe (845 A.D.), and laid Hamburg in ashes. Anskar saw his church burned, his library destroyed, and himself obliged to seek safety in flight. After that prince had become, by the death of Harde-Knud (850 A.D.), king of all Denmark, he extended his favour to the missionaries; but it was revoked by his successor, Eric I, under whom the nobility, jealous lest their power should be overthrown, stirred up the people against the Christians, by representing them as the cause of all the calamities that had fallen upon the land. Anskar contrived, however, to ingratiate himself once more with the court; and he was again earnestly invited to visit Jutland, where he continued to the close of his life (865 A.D.), engaged in the sacred task of converting the heathen, and acquiring a stock of personal sanctity by those acts of self-mortification which in that age were considered so meritorious. He was canonized by the papal authority; festivals were instituted in honour of his memory and churches built to perpetuate his name. He continued to be worshipped as the tutelar saint of the North until the period of the Reformation, and still merits the gratitude of the Scandinavian nations, not merely as their deliverer from a barbarous superstition, but as a benefactor who opened to them the career of civilisation.

It was at this epoch that a revolution occurred in Denmark, similar to those which happened about the same time in the two neighbouring kingdoms. Gorm, the son of Harde-Knud, surnamed the Old, from the length of his reign, had distinguished himself in early youth by his piratical excursions. Profiting by the absence of many of the jarls and chiefs in distant predatory expeditions, he subdued Jutland, and put an end to the ascendancy of those petty kings who had grown formidable only through the negligence of the sons or grandsons of Ragnar Lodbrok, who took greater delight in attacking the dominions of others than in ruling peacefully over their own. Other conquests followed, until he succeeded in uniting into one state the territories which now constitute the Danish monarchy, including the Swedish provinces of Skåne and Halland. He had espoused the beautiful Thyra Dannebod (Ornament of Denmark), daughter of Harold Klak, who had been baptised when a child in France. A deep cloud of obscurity hangs over this long and important reign, which the diligence of the native historians has not entirely removed.[d]

GORM THE OLD, HAROLD BLUETOOTH, AND SWEYN

Gorm the Old is chiefly to be remembered for collecting all the small provinces into one body. At that time the Danish kingdom comprised Zealand (Själland), with the adjacent islands, Jutland and South Jutland (now Schleswig), where the Eider river was the limit towards the south, and Skåne, Halland, and Blekinge, in southern Sweden. But, though these parts were now thus united, they preserved for a long space of time their popular peculiarities, each part having its own laws, and the king receiving his homage separately in each province. We are not able to detail many facts of the reign of Gorm the Old, but we know, however, that he was a bitter enemy to the Christians, whom he persecuted in every quarter, demolishing their churches and banishing their clergy. Amongst other sacred buildings, he totally destroyed the famous cathedral in Schleswig, and ordered the pagan idols to be erected wherever they had formerly stood.

While his two sons, Knud and Harold — twins by birth, and rivals in glory — were gathering laurels abroad, Gorm took arms against the Saxons, with a view to oblige them to renounce Christianity, but the emperor, Henry the Fowler, soon came to the relief of the Saxons, defeated Gorm, and forced him to permit Christianity to be preached in Denmark. Gorm's queen has rendered herself distinguished by founding Dannevirke (a great wall of earth and stones across Schleswig, strongly fortified by moats and tower bastions), to protect the country against inroads of the Germans. Already Göttrik had erected a like fortification, called Kurvirke, but the irruption of Henry the Fowler had proved that the country needed a stronger bulwark, wherefore the queen founded that famous Dannevirke, remnants of which are yet to be seen. Gorm, loving his son Knud, generally called Danaast (the Splendor of the Danes), more than Harold, declared, dreading the death of his dearly beloved son, of whom he for a great while had received no intelligence, that whosoever might tell him of his son's death should lose his life. Finally, notice was given of his death on a Viking expedition in England. The queen, not risking to tell it to the king, made the courtiers observe an unusual silence at the table, and had the apartment covered with black cloth. Guessing the reason, Gorm cried out: "Surely Knud, my dear son, is dead, for all Denmark is mourning!" "Thou sayest so, not I," answered the queen; upon which the king sickened with grief, and died in a good old age (941).

Harold Bluetooth (Blaatand), his son, was immediately elected king, but he refused to accept the crown until he had first performed his father's obsequies with all the magnificence becoming his high rank. One of the earliest acts of Harold's reign was, as we shall see, the conquest of Norway which became a province of Denmark. After Harold Bluetooth had settled this affair, he sailed against the Wends, who committed horrible depredations on all the coasts of the Baltic, but he attacked them with such vigour that he reduced and plundered all their strongholds, and, among the rest, the rich and important city of Wollin, built on an island of the same name, which is formed by two branches of the river Oder. But he had scarce rid his hands of this war when his aid and protection were solicited by Styrbear, king of Sweden, who was driven out of his own dominions by Eric the Victory-blest. To enforce his request Styrbear had brought along with him Gyntha, his sister, a lady of admirable beauty. The stratagem had the intended effect; Harold Bluetooth became enamored of her, married her, and promised the brother all the assistance in his power. Nevertheless Styrbear was defeated by Eric, the Victory-blest, at Fyrisval, near Upsala.

The progress of Christianity, which Gorm the Old had resisted and disregarded, began now to attract the notice of the ruling power, and was, during the whole reign of Harold Bluetooth, vigorously promoted by Adeldag, who now was invested with the archiepiscopal see of Hamburg. In the days of Anskar two churches had been erected in Schleswig and Ribe, and a third was now built in Aarhvus, situated on the eastern coast of Jutland, and bishoprics were established in those cities. But, although in favour of the new doctrine, the king would not comply with the exorbitant and undue claims which the German emperor, Otto I [936-973] arrogated to himself. The German kings claimed, by virtue of their dignity as Roman emperors, to be acknowledged as secular heads of the whole Christian world, as the popes were of the ecclesiastical; this claim Otto I realised by giving to the bishoprics above mentioned immunity and property in Denmark.

His successor, Otto II, claiming the same, excited the resentment of Harold Bluetooth, who collected all his forces (974), and pitched his camp on the narrow neck of land at Schleswig, to intercept Otto, but was defeated, the mighty emperor demolishing the famous fortification, Dannevirke, and making his way through the country right up to the Limfjord. A treaty of peace was made, and the king received baptism from Bishop Poppo — Otto, the emperor, being sponsor — and the same ceremony was performed for his son, Sweyn. Bishoprics were now also established in Odense and in Roeskilde, where Harold Bluetooth erected a splendid church. Odinkar Hvide, a native Dane, now began to preach Christianity and to annihilate the pagan worship; all of which excited the resentment of the heathen party, in front of which went the king's own son, Sweyn, and his master-in-arms, Palnatoke, a mighty chief from the Danish island, Fünen, who in his heart inclined to heathenism, and besides that believed himself to have several personal offences to be avenged upon the king. Harold Bluetooth, however, raised an army and gave battle to his son, who aspired to his father's crown (991). But the king was defeated, and shot by the hand of Palnatoke, while he was walking in a grove near his camp. Before leaving Harold Bluetooth, it ought to be noticed that he removed the royal residence from Leidre to Roeskilde, where the Danish kings resided for about five centuries, till, during the reign of Christopher of Bavaria, Copenhagen was made the capital.

Harold Bluetooth was succeeded by his son Sweyn, or Sveand (991-1014), generally called Sweyn Splitbeard, from some peculiarity observed about his beard. He is also sometimes called Sweyn Otto, after his godfather, the emperor. Nearly all his time was spent in making expeditions to Norway, Germany, and England. Notwithstanding Sweyn Splitbeard and the mighty chief, Palnatoke, above mentioned, had been on a very intimate footing, their good understanding soon ceased; for the murder committed by Palnatoke on Sweyn's father, Harold Bluetooth, required vengeance of blood. Palnatoke resorted to Jomsburg, a fortress on the island of Wollin, on the coast of Pomerania, founded by Harold Bluetooth to maintain the Danish dominion in these regions. Here Palnatoke established a band of northern vikings, who, by severe laws, preserved the ancient warfaring life and manners, and under the name of Jomsvikings, for a long time struck the whole North with fear.

Palnatoke's institutions tended to instil into his vikings the contempt of life. "A man," says the chronicle of Iceland, "in order to acquire glory for bravery, should attack a single enemy, defend himself against two, and not yield to three, but might, without disgrace, fly from four," and it was, on the whole, glorious to seek every opportunity of encountering death. Some instances of their savage heroism are recorded which almost exceed belief. In an irruption made by the Jomsburgers into Norway, the invaders were defeated and a few were taken prisoners. They were sentenced to be beheaded, and this intelligence they received with every demonstration of joy. One said: "I suffer death with the greatest pleasure; I only request that you will cut off my head as quickly as possible. We have often disputed," said he, "at Jomsburg, whether life remained for any time after the head was cut off: now I shall decide the question. But remember, if so, I shall aim a blow at you with this knife which I hold in my hand. Despatch," said he, "but do not abuse my long hair, for it is very beautiful." Not till the eleventh century was this piratical stronghold destroyed by Magnus the Good. The following chief of Jomsburg, the designing Sigvald, by stratagem made Sweyn Splitbeard, who had taken up arms against him, a prisoner, and compelled him to acknowledge the independence of Jomsburg and all the provinces along the Baltic; and Sweyn was only set at liberty on promising to pay a ransom of twice his own weight, when full armed, in pure gold. The ransom was settled at three payments, but the king's person was confined till the last payment was made, which was raised by the generosity of the Danish ladies, who sold their jewels for this purpose. Upon his return he, therefore, ordained that the women should inherit the half of all estates, real and personal.

Sweyn Splitbeard, thirsting for vengeance, induced Sigvald, at a wassail-bout, to undertake a very hazardous expedition against the mighty Hakon Jarl, in Norway, who had shown the same unwillingness to pay tribute to Denmark as his predecessor, Harold Graafeld; Sweyn himself making a vow to wage war against England, which some years before had thrown off her subjection to the throne of Denmark. The elsewhere almost indomitable Jomsvikings were totally defeated at Hjórringebay (994); Sigvald himself had to make his escape, and Norway was not subdued. Sweyn Splitbeard was more successful in his expedition against England. The impotent Anglo-Saxon king, Æthelred II, also called Æthelred the Unready, held at this time the supreme authority in that kingdom. Putting all to the fire and sword, wherever he went, and treating England with the utmost severity, Sweyn obliged the English king to acknowledge his superiority, and to get rid of the Danes by paying a large sum of money, called Danegeld.

But an important event took place now in the North. The Norwegian prince, Olaf Tryggvason, who had been allied with Sweyn in England, left him treacherously for Norway, the throne of which he ascended, after the death of Hakon Jarl, without taking any oath of allegiance to Sweyn; and the misunderstanding increased when Olaf, without Sweyn's consent, married the latter's sister, Thyra, who had fled from her husband, Burislief, of Wendland (Pomerania).

Sweyn Splitbeard, Olaf the Lap King of Sweden, and Eric Jarl, a Norwegian prince, who lived at the Danish court, attacked Olaf Tryggvason, who, with his fleet had gone through the sound to Wendland in order to claim his wife's property. A sea battle took place near Swalder, September 9th, 1000, on the Pomeranian coast. Seldom has a more memorable naval engagement been fought. Olaf Tryggvason was defeated after a most heroic resistance, and his fleet totally dispersed. Escaping out of the battle with a few ships, he was so closely pursued that, to avoid the disgrace of being taken prisoner, he precipitated himself into the sea and was drowned. The most renowned heroes of Norway shared in this battle, and the heroic songs of Einar Tambarskelver, the great archer, Ulf the Red, and Thorgeir, who all fought as madmen, resound yet among the rocks of old Norway, which was now divided between the three victors, and had to submit to the conditions which they dictated. But while Sweyn was occupied with the affairs of Norway, Æthelred II had taken advantage of Sweyn's absence to perform a dreadful carnage among the Danes in England (1002). Informed of it, Sweyn immediately appeared in England with a powerful army of the most valiant soldiers, was everywhere victorious, expelled Æthelred, who had to flee to Normandy; and Sweyn Splitbeard was at his death undisputed sovereign of the whole of England (1014). In the beginning of his reign, he persecuted Christianity; but, before he expired, he began to perceive the folly he had committed in opposing the faith in which he had been baptised and instructed. Afterwards, in prevailing upon the people to receive the light of the Gospel, he was aided by Poppo, a German bishop of great piety and eloquence, who, by dint of example and persuasion, brought about what the king's authority could not effect. Several miracles are related of this prelate; and, indeed, he was possessed of the happy talent of impressing the people with whatever notions he thought fit; in which alone, of course, consisted his supernatural powers. A see was

[1014–1018 A.D.]

given to Poppo, with power to preside over the Danish clergy; while at the same time he was suffragan of Adeldag, archbishop of Hamburg.

CANUTE, AND THE DAWN OF DISCOVERY

Sweyn Splitbeard had two sons, Harold and Canute or Knud; and the Danish historian, Meursius, says that "Harold, by right of primogeniture, succeeded his father on the throne of Denmark, while Canute, who at Sweyn's death was living in England, was elected king of the Danes there." But the English taking advantage of Canute's youth, threw off the subjection they had promised his father, Sweyn Splitbeard, and called the fugitive Æthelred II back from Normandy, and a general insurrection broke out. After having ordered the tongues and ears of the English hostages to be cut off, and, on the whole, shown an inflexible severity, Canute repaired to Denmark, where he brought together a numerous host of brave soldiers, and a well-manned fleet, with which he went back to England, accompanied by Eric Jarl, from Norway, Thorkel the High, and Ulf Jarl, who afterwards married Canute's sister, Estrith. He met with the English fleet, commanded by King Æthelred in person, whom he defeated after a sharp engagement. The valiant Eadmund Ironside, who succeeded his father Æthelred on the throne of England [in April, 1016], was forced to yield the half of England to Canute. But a month after, Eadmund Ironside was treacherously killed by his brother-in-law, Edric Streon, whereupon Canute was acknowledged king of the whole of England.

The first measure of Canute was now to seize Eadmund's two sons, whom he sent to his ally, the king of Sweden, Anund Jacob, with the request that they might be put to death. Humanity, however, induced the Swedish monarch to spare their lives and send them into Hungary. Canute, now ruler of England, tried to make himself both beloved and esteemed there; he reigned with great judiciousness, paid respect to the privileges of the people of the country, and raised them to the highest offices; advanced commerce and literature, and courted, in a particular manner, the favour of the church by munificent donations and by presenting monasteries with rich gifts; and he has, indeed, much better title to saintship than many of those who adorn the Roman calendar. To make himself yet more popular, he married the virtuous Emma of Normandy, the queen-dowager of Æthelred, whom the English people loved dearly. But while he thus tried to make himself popular, and provide for the welfare of the state, his despotism and cruelty were often insupportable, and those whose influence seemed pernicious to him he was not unscrupulous in putting out of the way. Thus he caused Edric Streon and Thorkel the High to be killed; the first of whom had been invested with Mercia, the latter with East Anglia, as absolute fiefs. To confirm his power, and perform the conquests he had in view, he established a standing army, called the Thingmannalid, consisting of the most famous warriors; and, on account of the sumptuous armour they had to wear, containing only the richest and most prominent. To this army he gave a peculiar law, called the Vitherlagslaw, which for a long time enjoyed great credit in Europe.

His brother Harold, king of Denmark, died after a reign of four years (1018). Weak from his infancy, he was little able to rule, and his profligacy and entire contempt of decency and morality rendered him odious to his subjects. Nothing need be said of him but that he reigned four years; whereupon Canute, generally called Canute the Great, was unanimously chosen to

succeed him on the Danish throne.   Thus, after an interval of only four years,
Denmark was reunited with England; which, superior to Denmark in refine-
ment, arts, trade, and agriculture, long exercised a beneficial influence upon
the Danish kingdom.   It is to Canute the Great that Denmark has to ascribe
the complete introduction of Christianity; for under him the last vestiges of
the pagan worship were destroyed, its idols overthrown, its altars demolished,
and its temples closed.   Many English clergy migrated in this period to Denmark.   The Danish bishoprics were generally bestowed on Englishmen; and,
on the whole, Canute considered England the principal realm, and resided
there.   But he deserved well, also, of Denmark, by bringing a great portion
of the Wendland under subjection, and subduing the formidable Wendish
pirates.   About the same time Christianity was introduced into Sweden,
under Olaf the Lap King, who was baptised by an English monk, Sigefroy;
and into Norway, under St. Olaf.

Before relating Canute's last expedition to Norway, his exploits there,
and his end, it may be noticed that he, like most royal persons in the period
under consideration, made a pilgrimage to Rome, to pay, in that sacred city,
his devotion to the relics of some deceased saint, and obtain from the pope
remission of his sins (1026).   While in Rome he established, by assent of the
pope, a caravansary for Scandinavian pilgrims; procuring his subjects, also,
on the same occasion, several commercial privileges.   Upon his journey to
Rome he chanced to meet with the German emperor, Conrad II, whom he
induced to renounce his claims to the Danish mark (Schleswig), founded by
Henry the Fowler, and a marriage was agreed on between Canute's daughter,
Gunhilda, and Conrad's son, Henry.

About this time, or a little before, the Scandinavians began to make discoveries in the north and west.   The Faroe Islands had been discovered at
the latter end of the ninth century, by some Scandinavian pirates, and soon
after this Iceland was colonized by the Norwegians.   [From Iceland, towards
the close of the tenth century, Jarl Eric the Red, who had been banished
from the island, led the first colony to Greenland, which had been discovered
about a hundred years before.]   The settlement made in Greenland, though
comprising only a small population, seems to have been very prosperous in
mercantile affairs.   It had bishops and priests from Europe, and paid the
pope, as an annual tribute, 2,600 pounds of walrus teeth as tithe and Peter's
pence.   But the art of navigation must have been at a very low pitch, for the
voyage from Greenland to Iceland and Norway, and back again, consumed
five years; and upon one occasion the government of Norway did not hear
of the death of the bishop of Greenland until six years after it had occurred.[e]

This colony in Greenland continued in a flourishing condition down to the
fourteenth century when it suffered severely from two terrible scourges, the
Black Death and the attacks of the natives.   In the fifteenth century all intercourse between the Scandinavian colony in Greenland and the civilised world
entirely ceased.   Modern investigation has resulted in the discovery of the
ruins of buildings and of the graves of the old colonists, but their descendants,
if not entirely wiped out, appear to have been absorbed by the Esquimaux
population.

For Lief, son of Eric the Red, is claimed a far greater achievement than his
father's.   The account of a country far to the southwest which had been
sighted by an Icelander in the year 1001, prompted Lief to undertake a voyage
in search of it and to plant, in a country which he called Vinland, a colony that
subsisted for many years.   The details of this expedition as given in the old
sagas have furnished data for a theory which places Vinland on a portion of the

United States in the vicinity of Rhode Island, and thus gives to Lief Ericsson the glory of being the first discoverer of America.*a*

To return to Canute the Great : While he tarried in Rome St. Olaf of Norway and Anund Jacob of Sweden availed themselves of Canute's absence to fall upon Denmark, both of them fearing his increasing power, and being angry because Norwegian mutineers had found an asylum at the Danish court. The united kings making great progress, Ulf Jarl, who was married as we have seen to Estrith, a sister to Canute, and who had been appointed lieutenant-governor under the king's absence, deemed it necessary for the country to have a head, and prevailed upon the people to elect the crown prince, Harthacnut [Hardi Canute] king. Canute, informed of this, hastened home, but though highly incensed against Ulf, he delayed his vengeance till the enemies were driven away. A battle was fought near Helgebrook in Skåne, where Canute himself would have perished, had it not been for Ulf's aid (1027).

But even this could not appease the exasperated king, who, under pretence of friendship, invited him to a drinking-bout in Roeskilde. They played at chess together. The king, making a wrong move, wished to correct it, but Ulf Jarl upset the chess-board, and left in anger. "Dost thou now fly, thou cowardly Ulf?" cried the king. "Thou didst not call me cowardly," answered Ulf, "when the Danes, at Helgebrook, took to their heels like dogs, and I saved thy life." The king, yet more irritated at this reply, caused Ulf to be killed in the cathedral of Roeskilde, to which he afterwards gave a whole canton as a propitiatory sacrifice for his crime.*e*

The ambition of Canute was not satisfied with the possession of two crowns; he pretended to have some claims upon Norway through his father Sweyn, who had formerly ruled over a portion of that country. Its reduction, which was accomplished (1028) without much difficulty, and its temporary annexation to his other dominions make it necessary that we now revert to that portion of Scandinavian history.

EARLY NORWEGIAN KINGS

The early Norwegian annals, geographical and political, have been critically analyzed and minutely detailed by Torfæus. Tradition, as already mentioned, placed Sæming, a son of Odin, on the throne of that country, and from him descended a race of pontiff-kings of whom nothing but their names is recorded. The first mortal alleged by the native legends to have worn the crown was a chief called Nor, sprung from the ancient Finnish family of the Fornjoter, who established himself at Trondhjem, and subdued the neighboring territories about the beginning of the fourth century. It is evident, however, that the old chronicle (*Fundinn Noregr*, or *Norway Discovered*) containing this account is entitled to no credit whatever. Nor is altogether a mythic personage; his supposed ancestor Fornjoter, with his three sons, the rulers of the air, earth, and sea, are considered to be merely the Scandinavian antitypes of Noah, and the patriarchs Shem, Ham, and Japhet. Among other progenitors that adorn his genealogy, we find Frostius, Snær, and Drifa (frost, snow, and drift), which are obviously symbols of the climate, rather than names of chiefs or petty kings. This part of the national records must therefore be viewed as an allegory, merely intended to give lustre to the pedigree of the Norwegian monarchs.

The several branches of Nor's posterity were dignified with the regal title, and are said to have reigned over the districts of Thrandia, Naumdal, Raumsdal, Guldbransdal, Rogaland, Hordaland, Ringarike, Raumarike, and other provinces, which are supposed to derive from them their modern appellations. It belongs to mythology rather than history to narrate their wars, and exhibit their feats of incredible strength and their wonderful skill in sorcery and incantation. The princes or chiefs of a less fabulous origin, who held sway over these sterile mountains, it would be superfluous to enumerate, as there is no reason to believe that any considerable portion of Norway was ever united under a single monarch prior to the era of Harold Harfagr, who first combined the various tribes among whom it was divided into one nation, by reducing their kings or jarls to a state of vassalage in the latter part of the ninth century.

This famous conqueror was a scion of the ancient Ynglings. The last of that sacred dynasty, Olaf Trætelia, when driven from the Swedish throne, as already stated, laid the foundation of a new government in Vermland, which gradually extended across the frontier, until it embraced wholly or partially the adjacent districts of Vestjold, Vingulmarken, Raumarike, Hordaland, and Hedemarken. The crown descended to five princes in succession, the last of whom, Halfdan Svart (the Black), was father to Harold. In the following table, the names and reigns of the Norwegian sovereigns are given in order, down to the important epoch when Christianity was established under Olaf the Saint:

TRADITIONAL LIST OF ANCIENT KINGS OF NORWAY

Olaf Trætelia . . . died A.D. 640	Eric Blodæxe . . . died A.D. 940
Halfdan Huitben 700	Hakon the Good 963
Eystein 730	Harold Graafeld 977
Halfdan Millde 784	Hakon Jarl 995
Gudrod Mikillati 824	Olaf Tryggvason 1000
Olaf Geirstada 840	Olaf the Saint 1030
Halfdan Svart 863	Svend Knudson 1035
Harold Harfagr 934	Magnus the Good 1047

Every circumstance connected with the genealogy and youth of Harold has been carefully preserved by his countrymen. His mother was Ragnhilda, daughter of Harold Golden-Beard, who ruled over the district of Sogne, near Bergen. Dreams and prodigies augured his future greatness; the giant Dofre taught him the military art, and at the age of ten, when he lost his father (863), he had the reputation of surpassing all his contemporaries in beauty, courage, wisdom and warlike accomplishments. During his minority, the regency of his paternal dominions was committed to his uncle Guttorm, whose prompt interference kept in awe the rebellious vassals. At the age of twelve, the young prince is said to have formed the resolution of subduing all Norway. His first achievement was the conquest of Thrandia (Trondhjem), whose eight kings or chiefs he defeated in as many battles. These victories were followed by the subjugation of the whole western coast, from Finmarken to the Naze. Hordaland, Telemarken, and Vermland were also reduced to subjection; whilst the famous naval engagement in the bay of Hafurs Fjord, now called Stavanger Fjord, fought (875) with the confederated princes of Rogaland and other southern districts, made him master of the entire kingdom in the short space of ten years. Most of the jarls and hereditary nobles being either slain or dispersed, Harold, ere he had reached the prime of manhood, thus saw himself in possession of a monarchy more extensive than had yet been enjoyed by any other northern potentate.

Triumphant at home, his arms were no less successful in the expeditions which he undertook to exterminate the pirates and refractory chieftains, who had escaped his vengeance at Hafurs Fjord by seeking refuge in the Scottish isles. The Scandinavian historians claim for him the reduction of Shetland, the Orkneys, the Hebrides, and the whole country north of the Grampians. They even allege that the Isle of Man, where a Norman dynasty had long been established, and part of Ireland, including Dublin, were added to his dominions. The government of these foreign possessions he entrusted to chiefs or relations of his own, under the title of earls, with a feudal dependence on his crown; but their authority was little respected by the turbulent and lawless inhabitants.

Threatened with civil broils and dissensions in his own family, he adopted the unwise policy of dividing the kingdom among his numerous sons, to each of whom he assigned the administration of a province, with the title and prerogatives of royalty. This expedient having increased rather than diminished the evil, his next resource was to abdicate in favour of Eric, which was done with the consent of the remaining brothers, eight of whom had then perished in battle. Harold survived this event only three years, and died in 934; leaving by his five wives a numerous progeny, male and female, from whom genealogists have computed the descent of most of the royal families in Europe. He had the reputation of being a brave and generous prince, of a handsome form, robust constitution, and majestic stature. Iceland and the Faroe Isles of whose discovery we have spoken, were colonised during his reign, and Normandy was conquered by daring adventurers under the celebrated Rolf Ganger (afterwards Duke Rollo), who had fled to avoid death or servitude under his rigorous administration.

Though a barbarian, Harold possessed the lofty spirit of that heroic age, and even aspired to civilise and legislate. His own interest, combined with motives of policy, induced him to adopt measures for the entire suppression of private feuds, of marauding expeditions by land and piracy on the seas. The *strandhug*, or impressment of provisions, which the depredators were in the practice of exercising, by seizing the cattle of the unprotected peasantry, he prohibited under the severest penalties. These he found to be the greatest obstacles to social order and improvement, and at the same time the principal means of keeping alive the embers of insubordination and resistance to his authority.

It has been supposed that his conduct in these beneficial arrangements was in some degree influenced by the example of the English king Æthelstan, who had visited Norway in his youth. An intercourse of friendship and courtesy is said to have commenced between them at that early period, in virtue of which Harold sent his son Hakon to be educated at the Anglo-Saxon court, with a present of a magnificent ship, the sails of which were purple and the beak gold; the whole deck being surrounded with shields, gilt in the inside, and curiously ornamented. Æthelstan gave his pupil in return a sword with a golden hilt and a blade of wonderful temper, which he kept till the day of his death. Besides studying the manners of the nation, the young prince was converted to the Christian faith, and received the ordinance of baptism — an event which afterwards gave occasion to the first planting of the seeds of the Gospel in his native land.[1]

Eric, after spending his youth as a sea-rover, had been elevated to the throne before his father's death; but the rest of his brothers, who claimed an equal title to the sovereignty, refused to acknowledge his supremacy, or pay

---

[1] Snorre's narrative of Harold's intercourse with Æthelstan differs from that given above (*Saga ens Harfagra*, c. 41, 43), but the account given by the old Norwegian chronicler Thiodrek seems most credible, *viz.* that Hakon was sent to England to be taught the manners of the nation.

their annual tribute to the crown. The seeds of internal dissension thus planted soon ripened into acts of cruelty and bloodshed. In the domestic strife that ensued, several of the refractory princes were put to death by him, and hence the name of Blodæxe, or Bloody-axe, was entailed on the relentless fratricide. Weary of the oppressions under which they had groaned for several years, the people at length shook off the yoke of the sanguinary tyrant, and unanimously called Hakon to the throne, who, though educated in a foreign land, and in a religion unknown to their country, was received with joy as their king and deliverer. The principal jarls, and especially Sigurd, his uncle on the mother's side, who had been his godfather when he was sprinkled with water after the heathen fashion in his infancy, espoused his cause.

Eric, unable to cope with the superior fortunes of his younger brother, fled with his adherents to the Orkney Isles, where he became a sea-king, and exercised his depredations on the British shores. Æthelstan soon after conferred upon him the kingdom of Northumbria, then peopled with Danes, upon condition that he and his followers should abstain from molesting Norway, embrace Christianity, and protect the English coasts against the piratical incursions of the Northmen. But the habits of this barbarian were inveterate; and resuming his old practices, with a band of his former associates, he invaded Northumbria, from which he had been expelled by the Anglo-Saxons. Edred, son of Eadward the Elder, marched an army to oppose him, and the contest was finally decided in a great battle, wherein Eric, with five other sea-kings, was slain. Notwithstanding the alleged conversion of this prince, he is represented in one of the last strains of the heathen skalds as invited to take his seat among the kings and heroes deemed worthy to inherit the joys of Valhalla.

Relieved from the apprehension of foreign invasion, the first care of Hakon was to suppress the robbers and pirates that infested his kingdom. The Danes he also chastised for certain depredations they had committed; and to retaliate their injuries he made an incursion into Zealand, where, without meeting opposition, he collected immense spoil, and obliged many of the inhabitants to ransom their lives by paying heavy pecuniary fines. Seeing peace re-established within his dominions, his subjects happy, and his revenue flourishing, he next turned his attention to the framing of salutary laws, and the substitution of the faith in which he had been educated for the superstitious rites of paganism. On his return from the court of Æthelstan, he had brought with him some Christian priests, and openly announced his resolution to protect and encourage them in their missionary labours. A national assembly of the people was convened at Trondhjem, in which he stood up and declared his will and desire that all present, "rich as well as poor, noble, peasant, and serf, young and old, man and woman, should be baptised, and believe in one true God, the Son of Mary (laying aside the vain worship of the heathen deities), fast every Friday, and rest every seventh day." To this proposition none were inclined to listen; murmurs arose against it from all parties, when Asbiorn, a rich and popular landholder, addressed the sovereign in a strain of firm remonstrance, expressing surprise and regret that he who had been the restorer of their lost freedom should endeavour to fasten upon them a new and more intolerable yoke of slavery. "As to what thou now wouldst require of us, and insist upon with such obstinate zeal, as if thou wouldst constrain us by violence, know, O king! that we are all resolved to abandon thee and choose another sovereign, who will suffer us peacefully to enjoy our liberties, and that religion which is dear to our hearts."

The sentiments of the people found utterance in the voice of the speaker, and they manifested their approbation with tumultuous applause. When silence was restored, Sigurd Jarl stood forth and explained to the multitude that it was not the wish or intention of the king to compel them to change their religion, or to dissolve the bonds that united them in friendship and affection. To ascertain the sincerity of this declaration, the assembly expressed their unanimous desire that Hakon should offer for them the usual solemn sacrifices, or Yule-feasts, for peace and for fruitful seasons, as had been the custom of his forefathers. Perceiving the danger of urging the matter further, Sigurd advised the king to forego his purpose in the meantime, and the convention quietly dispersed. But, on the approach of Christmas, agitation recommenced with greater violence, and the people renewed their demand that the king should either preside at the yearly festival, after the ancient manner, or abdicate the throne.

The wary jarl endeavoured to assuage their angry passions, and promised that the feast, which always took place after the sacrifice, should be honoured with the royal presence. This pledge was faithfully kept, when Sigurd, in virtue of his pontifical office, the duties of which he performed in the palace, took the drinking-horn, and having consecrated it to Odin, offered it to the king. This seemed the critical moment when Hakon must openly proclaim his choice between the Pagan and the Christian religion. He attempted to evade the difficulty by consecrating the horn anew with the sign of the cross, before applying it to his lips; but this movement was observed by the people, who gave vent to their feelings in terms of strong indignation, until their wrath was again pacified by the assurance of Sigurd that they had entirely mistaken the nature of the offensive emblem, which was not the sign of the cross but of the mallet; so that the sacred liquor had in reality been dedicated to Thor, according to the ceremonies of the national faith. With this ingenious explanation the multitude was satisfied, and the jarl obtained the reputation of being "the wisest man in Norway."

Notwithstanding this prudence and moderation in avoiding a collision between two hostile factions, a secret conspiracy was soon afterwards formed among eight of the most distinguished pontiff-chiefs against the king and his religious innovations. The destruction of the Christian edifices, which he had built in the northern provinces, was their first object; their next was to compel him to renounce entirely and forever the form of worship he was so anxious to introduce. Four of the confederates repaired to the district of Mære, which had a famous temple dedicated to Thor; and having burned the churches to the ground, they slew the Anglo-Saxon priests whom Hakon had brought from England. The king himself, having arrived in the same place to attend the great festival that was about to be celebrated, was menaced with personal violence by the congregated crowd, at the instigation of the conspirators, who had determined that he should sacrifice, without evasion or reserve, to the ancient deities of the nation.

Resistance was impossible, his train of courtiers being too small to offer opposition. Yielding to the entreaties and advice of his friendly counsellor Sigurd, he at length consented to humour the idolatrous prejudices of his subjects by eating the liver of a horse which had been sacrificed, and afterwards emptying three drinking-horns successively, consecrated to Odin, Thor, and Bragi; without violating the heathen rites as he had formerly done, by substituting the Christian symbol.[1] But instead of abandoning his favourite

---

[1] The eating of horse flesh was customary amongst the old Scandinavians at their religious festivals, and hence considered a proof of paganism. The practice was afterwards punished by St. Olaf with death or mutilation; and the insurrection which drove him from the throne was partly

project, this constrained apostasy only inflamed his resentment against his superstitious countrymen, and set him on devising means to punish what he deemed an insolent act of rebellion against his authority

The threatening storm of civil and religious war was now suspended over the kingdom; but, fortunately for Hakon, the gathering clouds were dissipated by the news of the arrival of the sons of Eric by his queen Gunhilda on the coast, with a powerful armament which Harold king of Denmark had equipped to aid them in recovering the crown of Norway. Intestine feuds were forgotten in the common danger, and all parties, even the confederated chiefs, united in defence of their native land and their national liberties. The Norwegian fleet obtained a signal victory over that of the exiled princes, who escaped to their former refuge at the Danish court.

After repelling this invasion, he revived, with new sanctions, the ancient law by which the whole territory of the state was divided into a certain number of maritime districts, called *skip-reidor*, which extended into the country as far up the rivers as the salmon ascended. Each of these was bound to furnish a certain number of vessels and men for the common defence; and, to give effect to this ordinance, stations were appointed on the principal mountains and heights along the coast, so that, on the approach of an enemy, the alarm could speedily be conveyed from the northern point of Helgeland (now included in Norrland) to the Naze.

Notwithstanding these wise precautions, and the devoted attachment of his countrymen, Hakon at last fell a victim to the insatiable ambition of Gunhilda and her sons, who made a second attempt on the crown, with the assistance of a fleet from Denmark. The king, who happened to be in a remote part of the country, was taken by surprise before he could collect his forces, and mortally wounded in the first assault of the enemy. Before his death he sent messengers to his brother's sons, declaring them his successors in the kingdom, as he had no children except one daughter named Thora, and entreating them to spare his relations. He expressed his desire, in the event of surviving, to leave his dominions, and retire to a Christian land, where he might expiate his sins and confirm his faith. When his friends inquired if he would not be sent to England for interment according to the rites of that Church, he replied, "As a heathen have I lived, as a heathen, and not as a Christian, must I be buried." His untimely fate was deeply and universally lamented; and the epithet of the Good, by which his contemporaries designated him, has been confirmed by the judgment of a milder and more enlightened age. His memory was celebrated in the songs of the skalds, and especially in a lay called the *Hakonar-mal*, composed by the celebrated poet Eyvind Skaldaspiller, where the two nymphs of war, Skogul and Gondul, conduct the pious king in triumph into the heaven of Odin, there "to quaff ale with the gods in the happy society of heroes."

The sceptre of Norway now fell into the hands of Harold II, called Graafeld or Gray Mantle, the eldest son of Eric and Gunhilda. This prince bore the name of his fair-haired grandfather, who had himself sprinkled him with water at his birth (930) after the heathen manner. He was educated at the Danish court, and having become a sea-rover at an early age he signalized his prowess in the Baltic by various piratical exploits, which were recorded by the skald Glum Geirison in an ode dedicated to his praise. His sovereignty

occasioned by his cruelties towards those who were accused or suspected of using this food, and consequently of having relapsed into heathenism. The Icelanders refused to adopt Christianity, unless St. Olaf allowed them to use horse flesh as formerly. — LAING'S *Residence in Norway.*]

as a king was merely nominal; for such was the loosely compacted structure of society in that barbarous age and country that not only was the regal authority shared with him by his brothers, but two other chieftains ruled with irresponsible power over their respective local districts.   Tryggve and Gudrod, grandsons of Harold Harfagr, held separate governments; the former the prefecture of Vika or Vigen, the latter that of Vestfjold.

From elements so discordant it was hardly to be expected that union or harmony could be produced; accordingly, as a first step towards securing the entire monarchy of Norway in her own family, the ambitious Gunhilda instigated her sons to murder the aged Sigurd Jarl, who still retained an independent jurisdiction over the province of Trondhjem.   Tryggve and Gudrod were the next victims to the intriguing widow of Eric; they were both assassinated, and their families compelled to seek refuge in Sweden.   The attachment of the inhabitants of Trondhjem to their late governor, and their election of his son Hakon Jarl to succeed him, involved the distracted kingdom in a civil war; and after many bloody conflicts between the rival princes, a perpetual truce was at last concluded, by the terms of which Hakon was to rule over the territories possessed by his father, whilst the remaining dominions were to continue under the sovereignty of the brother kings.

This treaty of partition was soon broken, and the competitors for power once more appealed to the sword.   Harold Graafeld perished in a plot contrived by Hakon, who, in his turn, sought the aid of Harold Bluetooth; but the Danish monarch, instead of an auxiliary, was hailed as a deliverer by the Norwegians, weary of internal dissension and domestic tyranny.   Gunhilda fled with her two surviving sons, Gudrod and Regnford, to the Orkney Islands, where she ended her days by a violent death; leaving behind her the character of a haughty, cruel, and insidious woman, and the proud title of "mother of kings."   Harold invested the jarl with the viceroyalty of seven provinces, upon condition that as his vassal he should pay a yearly tribute of sixty falcons and fifty marks of gold.   The rest of the kingdom he divided between his own son Sweyn, and Harold Gränske son of Gudrod, reserving to himself the paramount sovereignty of all Norway.

The ambitious Hakon soon manifested a disposition to assert his independence.   He exacted a tribute from the colonies in the Scottish isles, and endeavoured by every art of popularity to extend his influence at home.   But he was not yet prepared to throw off his allegiance; and to cover his designs he did not hesitate to obey the call of his liege lord, when summoned to his assistance against the invasion with which Denmark was threatened by the emperor Otto III.   After an obstinate battle with the imperial army at the Dannevirke, peace was concluded with Harold, in terms of which Hakon with his followers was constrained to submit to the ceremony of baptism, and to receive on board his fleet a company of priests as missionaries for the conversion of his countrymen.   But the crafty jarl, taking advantage of a favourable wind to escape through the Sound, set the monks on shore, and steered to the coast of Gotland, where he landed, and offered sacrifice to the gods as a propitiation for his apostasy.   The flight of two ravens, the birds of Odin, which passed at the moment, was interpreted by him as a favourable omen.   Accordingly, having burned his ships, and pursuing his way through Sweden, which he laid waste with fire and sword, he reached Norway in the hope of surprising the Danish squadron, which had been despatched with an additional supply of missionaries; but, on advancing to the port, he discovered that the fleet had departed in safety.

The two princes now became implacable enemies.   Hakon refused to pay the stipulated tribute, and declared himself independent, but without assuming the regal title. A rebellion of the Danes, in which their king was slain, might have relieved him from a formidable antagonist, had not Sweyn, who succeeded to the throne, inherited his father's resentment against the Norwegians, whom he attacked with a numerous squadron. The invaders, however, were entirely routed in the bay of Bergen, those who escaped the sword having perished in the waves.[1] The victorious jarl was soon afterwards delivered, by the death of Harold Gränske, from the only remaining competitor for the sovereignty.

The reign of this prince was distinguished by the restoration and triumph of the heathen superstitions; he was himself a zealous votary of the national deities, and by his command the pagan temples were rebuilt, and the accustomed sacrifices renewed. The country had been afflicted with a desolating famine, but peace and plenty returned under his administration, which the grateful people did not fail to attribute to the favour of the gods, appeased by the revival of their ancient worship. They even conferred upon their king the title of the Good — an appellation which he forfeited by his subsequent conduct. His court displayed a style of rude and barbaric grandeur; but he excited the general indignation of his countrymen by the unrestrained gratification of his licentious passions, which he did not scruple to indulge at the expense of the honour of their wives and daughters. This last indignity, to which even a people born to servitude will not submit with patience, at length roused the Norwegians to take arms against the tyrant, who was compelled to seek in flight a refuge from their vengeance.

The final catastrophe of his eventful life is closely linked with the romantic story of Olaf Tryggvason, his next successor on the throne. Tryggve, the father of this prince, having been cut off, as already mentioned, by the artifices of Gunhilda, Astrid his widow, then pregnant, fled to a small sequestered island in a lake on the western coast of Norway, where Olaf was born and received the name of his grandfather, one of the sons of Harold Harfagr. After wandering some time in poverty and disguise, Astrid found an asylum in the hall of the aged Hakon, a Swedish jarl; but the vengeance of Gunhilda, who pursued her in every retreat, induced her to seek a more distant concealment in Russia, where her brother Sigurd had risen to great distinction. The fugitives were captured by the Esthonian pirates, amongst whom Olaf had lived six years as a slave, until he was discovered and ransomed by his uncle, whilst collecting the tribute due to the Russian crown, and carried to the court of Vladimir at Novgorod, where he resided nine years. Here he distinguished himself by his proficiency in all manly exercises, as they were practised in that age and country; and being remarkable for beauty as well as strength and courage, he won the affections of the queen, and incurred the hatred of the courtiers, who beheld with jealousy the rising power of a foreign adventurer.

Having procured a small fleet of Russian pirates, he quitted the service of Vladimir, and at the age of nineteen became a sea-rover in the Baltic. In one of his excursions, being driven into a port in Wendland, (Pomerania), he espoused Geira, daughter of Burisleif, prince of that country, and with him joined the final expedition of the emperor Otto against Denmark; after which, returning with his father-in-law, he resided under his roof until the

---

[1] The Danish expedition was commanded by Sigvald Jarl, chief of the Jomsvikings; and their defeat is ascribed to Hakon's having sacrificed his son to the family goddess, Thorgerda Horgabrud, whom he consulted during one of the pauses in the battle, and who would promise victory on no other terms.

VIKINGS MAKING A LANDING

(Painted for the Historians' History of the World by Thure de Thulstrup)

death of his wife, when he resumed the habits of a freebooter. For a considerable time he cruised on the coasts of Scotland, England, Ireland, and France; the Hebrides, the Isle of Man, Northumberland, Cumberland, and Wales all suffered from his depredations. He entered the Thames, and although repelled in his attack upon London, his forbearance was purchased with a heavy tribute and rich presents; in return for which he solemnly promised never more to invade the country. On arriving at the Scilly Islands, he was converted to Christianity by a solitary monk or hermit, who had won his esteem in the character of a prophet; but it is probable he had before acquired some notion of that religion, as it was understood and practised in those barbarous times in Russia; and both the English and Norman chronicles assure us that he was solemnly baptised in London, while residing at the court of Æthelred, and afterwards at Rouen. Perhaps, like most of the northern adventurers in those days, he might not be unwilling to give repeated proofs in different countries, and at separate times, of his determination to renounce the errors of paganism, and adopt a faith which had then established itself in almost every kingdom of Europe. During his stay in England, he married Gyda, the widow of a powerful nobleman, and sister to a Scandinavian prince who reigned in Dublin.[1]

The fame of Olaf's distant exploits reached the ear of Hakon in Norway, at the time when his indignant subjects were preparing to release their country from the yoke of the tyrant. Hearing with dismay that there was a youthful hero of the race of Harfagr still surviving, who might challenge his claim to the sceptre, he despatched one of his subtlest agents, Thorer Klack, to Dublin, to discover and circumvent his rival by some plausible stratagem. This artful emissary, who had visited Ireland both as a merchant and a sea-rover, represented himself to Olaf as one of the victims of Hakon's cruelty, and described his countrymen as ready to receive the descendant of the renowned Harold with open arms, as their deliverer from a tyranny which had become insupportable. Encouraged by these solicitations, the confiding prince set sail for Norway, accompanied by his pretended friend, and on their arrival they discovered that the greater part of the chiefs and the people were in arms against their king.

Thorer was confounded on perceiving that his deceitful message had actually been realised during his absence. His first anxiety was to communicate with Hakon, but this was rendered impossible, as the tyrant had fled before the rising storm to a distant part of the kingdom, and sought refuge with a woman of illustrious birth named Thora, who had been one of his concubines, and who provided him with a secret grotto, where he remained concealed from his enemies. Returning to the fleet, the disappointed miscreant resolved on a second act of treachery to accomplish his object, by advising Olaf to land and take advantage of the popular excitement. His intention, however, was to betray the young prince, and thus consummate his villany by adding to it the crime of murder; but the design was revealed, and frustrated by the death of the traitor.

Meantime the insurrection had become general. Hakon, who had con-

---

[1] Very little sincerity appears to have accompanied the conversions of some of these Scandinavian pirates. On one occasion, as we learn from a monkish chronicler of the times, so many Northmen presented themselves to be baptised that there was not time enough to prepare a sufficient number of white robes, such as were worn by the neophytes; they were consequently obliged to use such coarse garments as could be found in the emergency. A chieftain who presented himself to receive the holy rite exclaimed, as they offered him such a dress, "This is the twentieth time I have been baptised, and I have always received a fine white robe; such a sack is more fit for a base hind than for a warrior like me."

trived to elude the search of his enemies by lying concealed in a subterranean excavation, over which was spread a dunghill, with a herd of swine feeding upon it, was at length assassinated by one of his domestics, named Kark, the only companion of his dreary abode. Tidings of this catastrophe were brought to Olaf, who commanded the faithless slave to be instantly put to death for having basely slain his master. The licentious conduct of this prince left a stigma on his memory, and obliterated the good opinion which his subjects formed of him at an earlier period of his reign; whilst the triumph of the adverse party, and the ascendency of the new religion, confirmed the epithet of the Bad, which the indignant people finally associated with his detested name.

The Norwegians immediately elected Olaf Tryggvason to fill the vacant throne. The first measure undertaken by the youthful monarch was the establishment of Christianity in his new dominions.[d] In the Heimskringla[b] we are given many interesting details of his method and results in this direction, as well as in various others. Some of these are worth transcribing.[a]

SNORRE STURLESON ON KING OLAF TRYGGVASON

When King Olaf Tryggvason had been two years king of Norway [Snorre[b] tells us], there was a Saxon priest in his house who was called Thangbrand, a passionate, ungovernable man, and a great man-slayer; but he was a good scholar and a clever man. The king would not have him in his house upon account of his misdeeds; but gave him the errand to go to Iceland, and bring that land to the Christian faith. The king gave him a merchant vessel; and, as far as we know of this voyage of his, he landed first in Iceland at Ostfjord, in the southern Alftafjord, and passed the winter in the house of Hall of Sidu. Thangbrand proclaimed Christianity in Iceland, and on his persuasion Hall and all his house-people, and many other chiefs, allowed themselves to be baptised; but there were many more who spoke against it. Thorvald Veile and Veterlid the skald composed a satire about Thangbrand; but he killed them both outright. Thangbrand was two years in Iceland, and was the death of three men before he left it.

There was a man called Sigurd, and another called Hauk, both of Halogaland, who often made merchant voyages. One summer they had made a voyage westward to England; and when they came back to Norway they sailed northwards along the coast, and at North Möre they met King Olaf's people. When it was told the king that some Halogaland people were come who were heathen, he ordered the steersmen to be brought to him, and he asked them if they would consent to be baptised; to which they replied, No. The king spoke with them in many ways, but to no purpose. He then threatened them with death and torture; but they would not allow themselves to be moved. He then had them laid in irons, and kept them in chains in his house for some time, and often conversed with them, but in vain. At last one night they disappeared, without any man being able to conjecture how they got away. But about harvest they came north to Harek of Thiottö, who received them kindly, and with whom they stopped all winter, and were hospitably entertained.

It happened one good-weather day in spring that Harek was at home in his house with only few people, and time hung heavy on his hands. Sigurd asked him if he would row a little for amusement. Harek was willing; and they went to the shore, and drew down a six-oared skiff; and Sigurd took the mast and rigging belonging to the boat out of the boat-house, for they often used to sail when they went for amusement on the water. Harek went out into the boat to hang the rudder. The brothers Sigurd and Hauk, who were very strong men, were fully armed, as they were used to go about at home among the peasants. Before they went out to the boat they threw into her some butter-kits and a bread-chest, and carried between them a great keg of ale. When they had rowed a short way from the island the brothers hoisted the sail, while Harek was seated at the helm; and they sailed away from the island. Then the two brothers went aft to where Harek the bonder was sitting; and Sigurd said to him, " Now thou must choose one of these conditions: first, that we brothers direct this voyage; or, if not, that we bind thee fast and take the command; or, third, that we kill thee."

Harek saw how matters stood with him. As a single man, he was not better than one of those brothers, even if he had been as well armed; so it appeared to him wisest to let them determine the course to steer, and bound himself by oath to abide by this condition. On this Sigurd took the helm, and steered south along the land, the brothers taking particular care that they did not encounter people. The wind was very favourable; and they held on sailing along until they came south to Trondhjem and to Nidaros, where they found the king. Then the king called Harek to him, and in a conference desired him to be baptised. Harek made objections; and although the king and Harek talked over it many times, sometimes in the presence of other people, and sometimes alone, they could not agree upon it. At last the king said to Harek, " Now thou mayst return home, and I will do thee no injury; partly because we are related together, and partly that thou mayst not have it to say that I caught thee by a trick: but know for certain that I intend to come north next summer to visit you Haloga-landers, and ye shall then see if I am not able to punish those who reject Christianity." Harek was well pleased to get away as fast as he could. King Olaf gave Harek a good boat of ten or twelve pair of oars, and let it be fitted out with the best of everything needful; and besides he gave Harek thirty men, all lads of mettle, and well appointed.

Harek of Thiottö went away from the town as fast as he could; but Hauk and Sigurd remained in the king's house, and both took baptism. Harek pursued his voyage until he came to Thiottö. He sent immediately a message to his friend Eyvind Kinnrif, with the word that he had been with King Olaf; but would not let himself be cowed down to accept Christianity. The message at the same time informed him that King Olaf intended coming to the north in summer against them, and they must be at their posts to defend themselves; it also begged Eyvind to come and visit him, the sooner the better. When this message was delivered to Eyvind, he saw how very necessary it was to devise some counsel to avoid falling into the king's hands. He set out, therefore, in a light vessel with a few hands as fast as he could. When he came to Thiottö he was received by Harek in the most friendly way, and they immediately entered into conversation with each other behind the house. When they had spoken together but a short time, King Olaf's men, who had secretly followed Harek to the north, came up, and took Eyvind prisoner, and carried him away to their ship.

They did not halt on their voyage until they came to Trondhjem, and presented themselves to King Olaf at Nidaros. Then Eyvind was brought up to a conference with the king, who asked him to allow himself to be baptised, like other people; but Eyvind decidedly answered he would not.

The king still, with persuasive words, urged him to accept Christianity, and both he and the bishop used many suitable arguments; but Eyvind would not allow himself to be moved. The king offered him gifts and great fiefs, but Eyvind refused all. Then the king threatened him with tortures and death, but Eyvind was steadfast. Then the king ordered a pan of glowing coals to be placed upon Eyvind's belly, which burst asunder. Eyvind cried, "Take away the pan, and I will say something before I die," which also was done. The king said, "Wilt thou now, Eyvind, believe in Christ?" "No," said Eyvind, "I can take no baptism; for I am an evil spirit put into a man's body by Lapland sorcery, because in no other way could my father and mother have a child." With that died Eyvind, who had been one of the greatest sorcerers.

The spring after, King Olaf fitted out and manned his ships, and commanded himself his ship the *Crane*. He had many and smart people with him; and when he was ready, he sailed northwards with his fleet past Byrd Isle, and to Halogaland. Wheresoever he came to the land, or to the islands, he held a Thing, and told the people to accept the right faith, and to be baptised. No man dared to say anything against it, and the whole country he passed through was made Christian. King Olaf was a guest in the house of Harek of Thiottö, who was baptised with all his people. At parting the king gave Harek good presents; and he entered into the king's service, and got fiefs, and the privileges of lendsman from the king.

There was a bonder, by name Raud the Strong, who dwelt in Godö Isle in Saltenfjord. Raud was a very rich man, who had many house servants; and likewise was a powerful man, who had many Laplanders in his service when he wanted them. Raud was a great idolater, and very skilful in witchcraft, and was a great friend of Thorer Hiort. Both were great chiefs. Now when they heard that King Olaf was coming with a great force from the south to Halogaland, they gathered together an army, ordered out ships, and they too had a great force on foot. Raud had a large ship, with a gilded head formed like a dragon, which ship had thirty rowing benches, and even for that kind of ship was very large. Thorer Hiort had also a large ship. These men sailed southwards with their ships against King Olaf, and as soon as they met gave battle. A great battle there was, and a great fall of men; but principally on the side of the Halogalanders, whose ships were cleared of men, so that a great terror came upon them. Raud rowed with his dragon out to sea, and set sail. Raud had always a fair wind wheresoever he wished to sail, which came from his arts of witchcraft; and, to make a short story, he came home to Godö Isle.

Thorer Hiort fled from the ships up to the land; but King Olaf landed people, followed those who fled, and killed them. Usually the king was the foremost in such skirmishes, and was so now. When the king saw where Thorer Hiort, who was quicker on foot than any man, was running to, he ran after him with his dog Vig. The king said, "Vig! Vig! catch Hiorten."[1] Vig ran straight in upon him; on which Thorer halted, and the king threw a spear at him. Thorer struck with his sword at the dog, and gave him a great wound; but at the same moment the king's spear flew under Thorer's arm, and went through and through him, and came out at his other side. There Thorer left his life; but Vig was carried wounded to the ships.

King Olaf gave life and freedom to all the men who asked it and agreed to become Christian. King Olaf sailed with his fleet northwards along the

---

[1] Hiorten signifies the deer or hart.[k]

[995-1000 A.D.]

coast, and baptised all the people among whom he came; and when he came north to Saltenfjord,[1] he intended to sail into it to look for Raud, but a dreadful tempest and storm was raging in the fjord. They lay there a whole week, in which the same weather was raging within the fjord; while without there was a fine brisk wind only, fair for proceeding north along the land. Then the king continued his voyage north to Omd, in Hind Island, where all the people submitted to Christianity. Then the king turned about and sailed to the south again; but when he came to the north side of Saltenfjord, the same tempest was blowing, and the sea ran high out from the fjord, and the same kind of storm prevailed for several days while the king was lying there. Then the king applied to Bishop Sigurd, and asked him if he knew any counsel about it; and the bishop said he would try if God would give him power to conquer these arts of the devil.

Bishop Sigurd took all his mass robes and went forward to the bow of the king's ship; ordered tapers lighted, and incense to be brought out. Then he set the crucifix upon the stem of the vessel, read the Evangelist and many prayers, besprinkled the whole ship with holy water, and then ordered the ship tent to be stowed away, and to row into the fjord. The king ordered all the other ships to follow him. Now when all was ready on board the *Crane* to row, she went into the fjord without the rowers finding any wind; and the sea was curled about their keel track like as in a calm, so quiet and still was the water; yet on each side of them the waves were lashing up so high that they hid the sight of the mountains. And so the one ship followed the other in the smooth sea track; and they proceeded this way the whole day and night, until they reached Godö Isle.

Now when they came to Raud's house his great ship, the *Dragon*, was afloat close to the land. King Olaf went up to the house immediately with his people; made an attack on the loft in which Raud was sleeping, and broke it open. The men rushed in: Raud was taken and bound, and of the people with him some were killed and some made prisoners. Then the king's men went to a lodging in which Raud's house servants slept, and killed some, bound others, and beat others. Then the king ordered Raud to be brought before him, and offered him baptism. "And," said the king, "I will not take thy property from thee, but rather be thy friend, if thou wilt make thyself worthy to be so." Raud exclaimed with all his might against the proposal, saying he would never believe in Christ, and making his scoff of God. Then the king was wroth, and said Raud should die the worst of deaths. And the king ordered him to be bound to a beam of wood, with his face uppermost, and a round pin of wood to be set between his teeth to force his mouth open. Then the king ordered an adder to be stuck into the mouth of him; but the serpent would not go into his mouth, but shrunk back when Raud breathed against it. Now the king ordered a hollow branch of an angelica root to be stuck into Raud's mouth; others say the king put his horn into his mouth, and forced the serpent to go in by holding a red-hot iron before the opening. So the serpent crept into the mouth of Raud and down his throat, and gnawed its way out of his side; and thus Raud perished.

---

[1] The Saltenfjord is more celebrated in the north of Norway, and more dreaded, than the famous Maelstrom. It is a large fjord within; but the throat through which the vast mass of water has to run in and out at flood and ebb is so narrow, that it makes a very heavy and dangerous race or roost for many miles out in the sea, especially in ebb, when the whole body of water is returning to the ocean. The stream can only be crossed during a few minutes at still water, when flood or ebb has not begun to run, unless at a great distance from the jaws of this singular gulf.[k]

King Olaf took here much gold and silver, and other property of weapons, and many sorts of precious effects; and all the men who were with Raud he either had baptised, or if they refused had them killed or tortured. Then the king took the dragon-ship which Raud had owned, and steered it himself; for it was a much larger and handsomer vessel than the *Crane*. In front it had a dragon's head, and aft a crook, which turned up, and ended with the figure of the dragon's tail. The carved work on each side of the stem and stern was gilded. This ship the king called the *Serpent*. When the sails were hoisted they represented, as it were, the dragon's wings; and the ship was the handsomest in all Norway. The islands on which Raud dwelt were called Gilling and Hæring; but the whole islands together were called Godö Isles, and the current between the isles and the mainland the Godö Stream. King Olaf baptised all the people of the fjord, and then sailed southwards along the land; and on this voyage happened much and various things, which are set down in tales and sagas — namely, how witches and evil spirits tormented his men, and sometimes himself; but we will rather write about what occurred when King Olaf made Norway Christian, or in the other countries in which he advanced Christianity. The same autumn Olaf with his fleet returned to Trondhjem and landed at Nidaros, where he took up his winter abode. What I am now going to write about concerns the Icelanders.

Kiartan Olafsson, a son's son of Hoskuld, and a daughter's son of Egil Skalagrimson, came the same autumn from Iceland to Nidaros and he was considered to be the most agreeable and hopeful man of any born in Iceland. There was also Haldor a son of Gudmund of Modrovald; and Kolbein a son of Thord, Frey's godar and a brother's son of Brenno-Flose; together with Swerting a son of the godar Runolf. All these were heathens; and besides them there were many more — some men of power others common men of no property. There came also from Iceland a considerable people, who, by Thangbrand's help had been made Christians; namely, Gissur White, a son of Teit Retilbiornson; and his mother was Alöfa, daughter of Herse Bodvar who was the viking Kare's son. Bodvar's brother was Sigurd, father of Eric Biodascalla, whose daughter Astrid was King Olaf's mother. Hialte Skeggiason was the name of another Iceland man, who was married to Vilborg, Gissur White's daughter. Hialte was also a Christian; and King Olaf was very friendly to his relations Gissur and Hialte, who lived with him. But the Iceland men who directed the ships, and were heathens, tried to sail away as soon as the king came to the town of Nidaros, for they were told the king forced all men to become Christians; but the wind came stiff against them, and drove them back to Nidarholm. They who directed the ships were Thorarin Nefiulsson, the skald Halfred Ottarson, Brand the Generous, and Thorleik Brand's son.

It was told the king that there were Icelanders with ships there, and all were heathen, and wanted to fly from a meeting with the king. Then the king sent them a message forbidding them to sail, and ordering them to bring their ships up to the town, which they did, but without discharging the cargoes. They carried on their dealings and held a market at the king's pier. In spring they tried three times to slip away, but never succeeded; so they continued lying at the king's pier. It happened one fine day that many set out to swim for amusement, and among them was a man who distinguished himself above the others in all bodily exercises. Kiartan challenged Halfred Vandrædaskald to try himself in swimming against this man, but he declined it. "Then will I make a trial," said Kiartan, casting off his clothes, and springing into the water. Then he set after the man, seized

[995-1000 A.D.]

hold of his foot, and dived with him under water. They came up again, and without speaking a word dived again, and were much longer under water than the first time. They came up again, and without saying a word dived a third time, until Kiartan thought it was time to come up again, which, however, he could in no way accomplish, which showed sufficiently the difference in their strength. They were under water so long that Kiartan was almost drowned. They then came up, and swam to land. This Northman asked what the Icelander's name was. Kiartan told his name.

He said, "Thou art a good swimmer; but art thou expert also in other exercises?" Kiartan replied that such expertness was of no great value.

The Northman asked, "Why dost thou not inquire of me such things as I have asked thee about?" Kiartan replied, "It is all one to me who thou art, or what thy name is."

"Then will I," says he, "tell thee: I am Olaf Tryggvason." He asked Kiartan much about Iceland, which he answered generally, and wanted to withdraw as hastily as he could; but the king said, "Here is a cloak which I will give thee, Kiartan." And Kiartan took the cloak with many thanks.

When Michaelmas came, the king had high mass sung with great splendour. The Icelanders went there, and listened to the fine singing and the sound of the bells; and when they came back to their ships every man told his opinion of the Christian man's worship. Kiartan expressed his pleasure at it, but most of the others scoffed at it; and it went according to the proverb, "The king has many ears," for this was told to the king. He sent immediately that very day a message to Kiartan to come to him. Kiartan went to the king with some men, and the king received him kindly. Kiartan was a very stout and handsome man, and of ready and agreeable speech. After the king and Kiartan had conversed a little, the king asked him to adopt Christianity. Kiartan replied that he would not say No to that, if he thereby obtained the king's friendship; and as the king promised him the fullest friendship, they were soon agreed. The next day Kiartan was baptised, together with his relation Bolle Thorleikson, and all their fellow travellers. Kiartan and Bolle were the king's guests as long as they were in their white baptismal clothes, and the king had much kindness for them. Wherever they came they were looked upon as people of distinction.

As King Olaf one day was walking in the street some men met him, and he who went the foremost saluted the king. The king asked the man his name, and he called himself Halfred. "Art thou the skald?" said the king. "I can compose poetry," replied he. "Wilt thou then adopt Christianity, and come into my service?" asked the king. "If I am baptised," replied he, "it must be on one condition — that thou thyself art my godfather; for no other will I have." The king replied, "That I will do." And Halfred was baptised, the king holding him during the baptism.

Afterwards the king said, "Wilt thou enter into my service?" Halfred replied, "I was formerly in Jarl Hakon's court; but now I will neither enter into thine nor into any other service, unless thou promise me it shall never be my lot to be driven away from thee."

"It has been reported to me," said the king, "that thou are neither so prudent nor so obedient as to fulfil my commands." "In that case," replied Halfred, "put me to death." "Thou art a skald who composes difficulties," said the king; "but into my service, Halfred, thou shalt be received."

Halfred said, "If I am to be named the composer of difficulties,[1] what dost

---

[1] Vandrædascald — the despair of skalds, or the difficult skald. *k*

thou give me, king, on my name-day?" The king gave him a sword without a scabbard, and said, "Now compose me a song upon this sword, and let the word sword be in every line of the verses." Halfred sang thus:

> This sword of swords is my reward.
> For him who knows to wield a sword,
> And with his sword to serve his lord,
> Yet wants a sword, his lot is hard.
> I would I had my good lord's leave
> For this good sword a sheath to choose :
> I'm worth three swords where men swords use,
> But for the sword-sheath now I grieve.

Then the king gave him the scabbard, observing that the word sword was wanting in one line of his strophe. "But there are three swords at least in two other lines," says Halfred. "So it is," replies the king.[1] Out of Halfred's lays we have taken the most of the true and faithful accounts that are here related about Olaf Tryggvason.

The same harvest Thangbrand the priest came back from Iceland to King Olaf, and told the ill success of his journey — namely, that the Icelanders had made lampoons about him; and that some even sought to kill him, and there was little hope of that country ever being made Christian. King Olaf was so enraged at this that he ordered all the Icelanders to be assembled by sound of horn, and was going to kill all who were in the town; but Kiartan, Gissur, and Hialte, with the other Icelanders who had become Christians, went to him, and said, "King, thou must not fall from thy word — that however much any man may irritate thee, thou wilt forgive him if he turn from heathenism and become Christian. All the Icelanders here are willing to be baptised; and through them we may find means to bring Christianity into Iceland: for there are many amongst them, sons of considerable people in Iceland, whose friends can advance the cause; but the priest Thangbrand proceeded there as he did here in the court, with violence and manslaughter, and such conduct the people there would not submit to." The king hearkened to these remonstrances; and all the Iceland men who were there were baptised.

King Olaf was more expert in all exercises than any man in Norway whose memory is preserved to us in sagas; and he was stronger and more agile than most men, and many stories are written down about it. One is, that he ascended the Smalsor Horn[2] and fixed his shield upon the very peak. Another is that one of his followers had climbed up the peak after him, until he came to where he could neither get up nor down; but the king came to his help, climbed up to him, took him under his arm, and bore him to the flat ground. King Olaf could run across the oars outside of the vessel while his men were rowing the Serpent. He could play with three daggers, so that one was always in the air, and he took the one falling by the handle. He could walk all around upon the ship's rails, could strike and cut equally well with both hands, and could cast two spears at once. King Olaf

---

[1] From this dialogue, which we may fairly take as a true representation of the tone of conversation, and very likely of the words, between a king and a man of literature or skald in the tenth century, it may be inferred that there was a considerable taste for the compositions of skalds, and for intellectual effort ; but that this taste was gratified by the art of verse-making — by the reproduction of words, letters, metres, in difficult technical circumstances — much more than by the spirit of poetry. It is likely that in all ages, and even among individuals, the taste for the simple and natural in poetry is the last, not the first developed taste. It is the savage who loves frippery in dress, and in what addresses itself to taste. *k*

[2] Now called Hornelen — an inaccessible peak or needle on the summit of a mountain in Bremanger. *k*

[995–1000 A.D.]

was a very merry, frolicsome man; gay and social; had great taste in everything; was very generous; was very finical in his dress, but in battle he exceeded all in bravery. He was distinguished for cruelty when he was enraged, and tortured many of his enemies. Some he burned in fire; some he had torn in pieces by mad dogs; some he had mutilated, or cast down from high precipices. On this account his friends were attached to him warmly, and his enemies feared him greatly; and thus he made such a fortunate advance in his undertakings, for some obeyed his will out of the friendliest zeal, and others out of dread.

Leif, a son of Eric Rode, who first settled in Greenland, came this summer from Greenland to Norway; and as he met king Olaf he adopted Christianity, and passed the winter with the king. Gudrod, a son of Eric Blodaexe and Gunhilda the "mother of kings," had been ravaging in the western countries ever since he fled from Norway before the Jarl Hakon. But the summer before mentioned, when King Olaf Tryggvason had ruled four years over Norway, Gudrod came to the country, and had many ships of war with him. He had sailed from England; and when he thought himself near to the Norway coast, he steered south along the land, to the quarter where it was least likely King Olaf would be. Gudrod sailed in this way south to Viken; and as soon as he came to the land began to plunder, to subject the people to him, and to demand that they should accept of him as king.

Now as the country people saw that a great army was come upon them, they desired peace and terms. They offered King Gudrod to send a Thing-message over all the country, and to accept of him at the Thing as king, rather than suffer from his army; but they desired delay until a fixed day, while the token of the Thing's assembling was going round through the land. The king demanded maintenance during the time this delay lasted. The bonders preferred entertaining the king as a guest, by turns, as long as he required it; and the king accepted of the proposal to go about with some of his men as a guest from place to place in the land, while others of his men remained to guard the ships. When King Olaf's relations, Hyrning and Thorgeir, heard of this, they gathered men, fitted out ships, and went northwards to Viken. They came in the night with their men to a place at which King Gudrod was living as a guest, and attacked him with fire and weapons; and there King Gudrod fell, and most of his followers. Of those who were with his ships some were killed, some slipped away and fled to great distances; and now were all the sons of Eric and Gunhilda dead.

The winter after King Olaf came from Halogaland, he had a great vessel built at Ladehammer,[1] which was larger than any ship in the country, and of which the beam-knees are still to be seen. The length of keel that rested upon the grass was seventy-four ells. Thorberg Skafting was the man's name who was the master builder of the ship; but there were many others besides — some to fell wood, some to shape it, some to make nails, some to carry timber;[2] and all that was used was of the best. The ship was both long and broad and high-sided, and strongly timbered.

While they were planking the ship, it happened that Thorberg had to go

---

[1] Ladehammar — the knob or point of land below the house of Lade, still known by the same name. Lade is close to Trondhjem. k

[2] This division of labour and trades, and this building of a vessel equal in length to a frigate of forty guns, give a curious peep at the civilisation of these pagans in the tenth century, and of the state of the useful arts among them. We need not be surprised that a people who had master-carpenters among them had skalds — the useful and the fine arts keep some kind of pace together. k

[995–1000 A.D.]

home to his farm upon some urgent business; and as he remained there a long time, the ship was planked up on both sides when he came back. In the evening the king went out, and Thorberg with him, to see how the vessel looked, and everybody said that never was seen so large and so beautiful a ship of war. Then the king returned to the town. Early next morning the king returned again to the ship, and Thorberg with him. The carpenters were there before them, but all were standing idle with their arms across. The king asked what was the matter. They said the ship was destroyed; for somebody had gone from stem to stern, and cut one deep notch after the other down the one side of the planking. When the king came nearer he saw it was so, and said, with an oath, "The man shall die who has thus destroyed the vessel out of envy, if he can be discovered, and I shall bestow a great reward on whoever finds him out."

"I can tell you, king," said Thorberg, "who has done this piece of work." "I don't think," replied the king, "that anyone is so likely to find it out as thou art." Thorberg said, "I will tell you, king, who did it. I did it myself." The king said, "Thou must restore it all to the same condition as before, or thy life shall pay for it."

Then Thorberg went and chipped the planks until the deep notches were all smoothed and made even with the rest; and the king and all present declared that the ship was much handsomer on the side of the hull which Thorberg had chipped, and bade him shape the other side in the same way, and gave him great thanks for the improvement. Afterwards Thorberg was the master builder of the ship until she was entirely finished. The ship was a dragon, built after the one the king had captured in Halogaland; but this ship was far larger, and more carefully put together in all her parts. The king called this ship *Serpent the Long*, and the other *Serpent the Short*. The long Serpent had thirty-four benches for rowers. The head and the arched tail were both gilt, and the bulwarks were as high as in sea-going ships. This ship was the best and most costly ship ever made in Norway.[b]

OLAF AT WAR WITH SWEYN

The fame of Olaf spread over all the countries of the North, and when he demanded the fair hand of Sigrid the Proud, a Swedish princess who had rejected with disdain many a suitor of princely birth, his overtures were favourably received. A treaty of marriage was on the eve of being concluded, when it was broken off on the point of religion; the king insisting upon a renunciation of the errors of idolatry, whilst the haughty bride scouted the proposal with contempt. The match was as scornfully declined on the part of the royal lover, who declared, in most uncourteous terms, that he would "never consent to live with an old heathen hag." To crown the insult, he struck his obstinate mistress with his glove, who, in her turn, predicted that this unmannerly outrage should cost him his throne and his life. Sigrid became the wife of Sweyn king of Denmark, and through her machinations the vindictive prophecy was soon fulfilled.

This monarch had a sister named Thyra, married to Burisleif, the same Wend prince whose daughter Olaf had formerly espoused. Being dissatisfied with her husband, and not daring to return to her native country, she sought a refuge in Norway, where she was immediately honoured with the hand of the sovereign, in violation of the most sacred precepts of that religion which he had laboured to inculcate on others with fire and sword.

This conduct furnished a brand to kindle the train already laid by jealousy and insulted pride. A pretext for open hostilities was opportunely afforded by the expedition which the Norwegian king had despatched to Pomerania, to recover the dowry and other property left by his queen in that country.

As the fleet was equipped, and had passed without asking the consent of Sweyn through the seas over which Denmark, even in that early age, claimed a sort of feudal jurisdiction, the enemies of Olaf were thus supplied with an ostensible cause of war, which his own imprudence seemed to justify. In the confederacy against him, Sigrid employed the agency of the piratical chief of Jomsburg, Sigvald Jarl, who contrived, by his intrigues and mis-representations, to engage in the quarrel both the king of Sweden and the exiled Eric (son of Hakon Jarl), who sojourned at that court, and was easily persuaded to join an enterprise which encouraged the hope of regaining his patrimonial dominions.

Whilst the three allied princes were maturing their arrangements, and had actually put to sea, the suspicions of Olaf were lulled to sleep by the artful protestations of the treacherous Sigvald, who even carried his perfidy so far as to offer him the aid of his own valiant band, in case of sudden attack; and having undertaken to pilot the fleet back to Norway, through the passages between the small islands scattered along the southern coasts of the Baltic, he basely conducted the whole squadron into the midst of the enemy, who lay concealed near the present city of Stralsund. Perceiving their danger, the king's friends advised him to retreat, or to form a junction with the main division, which had already reached the open sea, and which composed the greater part of his effective force; but he indignantly rejected their counsel, declaring that he had never yet turned his back upon the foe, and should scorn to save his life by flight.

The royal ship, called the *Long Serpent*, led the van, from which the cour-ageous monarch could observe and direct every movement of the battle.[d] Let Snorre[b] tell the issue of this notable conflict:

Snorre Sturleson on the Great Sea Fight

King Olaf stood on the *Serpent's* quarterdeck, high over the others. He had a gilt shield, and a helmet inlaid with gold; over his armour he had a short red coat, and was easy to be distinguished from other men. When King Olaf saw that the scattered forces of the enemy gathered themselves together under the banners of their ships, he asked, "Who is the chief of the force right opposite to us?" He was answered that it was King Sweyn with the Danish army.

The king replied, "We are not afraid of these soft Danes, for there is no bravery in them; but who are the troops on the right of the Danes?" He was answered that it was King Olaf with the Swedish forces.

"Better it were," says King Olaf, "for these Swedes to be sitting at home killing their sacrifices, than to be venturing under our weapons from the *Long Serpent*. But who owns the large ships on the larboard side of the Danes?" "That is Jarl Eric Hakonson," said they. The king replied, "He, methinks, has good reason for meeting us; and we may expect the sharp-est conflict with these men, for they are Northmen like ourselves."

The kings now laid out their oars, and prepared to attack. King Sweyn laid his ship against the *Long Serpent*. Outside of him Olaf the Swede laid himself, and set his ship's stem against the outermost ship of King Olaf's line; and on the other side lay Jarl Eric. Then a hard combat began. Jarl Sig-

vald held back with the oars on his ships, and did not join the fray.　So says
Skule Thorsteinson, who at that time was with Jarl Eric:

> I followed Sigvald in my youth,
> And gallant Eric ; and in truth,
> Tho' now I am grown stiff and old,
> In the spear-song I once was bold.
> Where arrows whistled on the shore
> Of Swalder fjord my shield I bore,
> And stood amidst the loudest clash
> When swords on shields made fearful crash.

And Halfred also sings thus:

> In truth, I think the gallant king,
> Midst such a foemen's gathering,
> Would be the better of some score
> Of his tight Trondhjem lads, or more ;
> For many a chief has run away,
> And left our brave king in the fray,
> Two great king's power to withstand,
> And one great jarl's, with his small band.
> The king who dares such mighty deed
> A hero for his skald would need.[k]

This battle was one of the severest told of, and many were the people
slain.　The forecastle men of the *Long Serpent*, the *Little Serpent*, and the
Crane threw grapplings and stem chains into King Sweyn's ship, and used
their weapons well against the people standing below them, for they cleared
the decks of all the ships they could lay fast hold of; and King Sweyn, and
all the men who escaped, fled to other vessels, and laid themselves out of
bow-shot.　It went with this force just as King Olaf Tryggvason had foreseen.　Then King Olaf the Swede laid himself in their place; but when he
came near the great ships it went with him as with them, for he lost many
men and some ships, and was obliged to get away.　But Jarl Eric laid the
Iron Beard side by side with the outermost of King Olaf's ships, thinned it of
men, cut the cables, and let it drive.　Then he laid alongside of the next,
and fought until he had cleared it of men also.　Now all the people who were
in the smaller ships began to run into the larger, and the jarl cut them loose
as fast as he cleared them of men.　The Danes and Swedes laid themselves
now out of shooting distance all around Olaf's ship; but Jarl Eric lay always
close alongside of the ships, and used his swords and battle-axes, and as fast
as people fell in his vessel others, Danes and Swedes, came in their place.
So says Haldor:

> Sharp was the clang of shield and sword,
> And shrill the song of spears on board,
> And whistling arrows thickly flew
> Against the *Serpent's* gallant crew.
> And still fresh foemen it is said,
> Jarl Eric to her long side led ;
> Whole armies of his Danes and Swedes,
> Wielding on high their blue sword-blades.

Then the fight became most severe, and many people fell.　But at last it
came to this, that all King Olaf Tryggvason's ships were cleared of men
except the *Long Serpent*, on board of which all who could still carry their

arms were gathered. Then *Iron Beard* lay side by side with the *Serpent*, and the fight went on with battle-axe and sword. So says Haldor:

> Hard pressed on every side by foes,
> The *Serpent* reels beneath the blows;
> Crash go the shields around the bow!
> Breast-plates and breasts pierced thro' and thro'!
> In the sword-storm the *Holm* beside,
> The *Iron Beard* lay alongside
> The king's *Long Serpent* of the sea—
> Fate gave the jarl the victory.

Jarl Eric was in the forehold of his ship, where a cover of shields[1] had been set up. In the fight, both hewing weapons, sword and axe, and the thrust of spears had been used; and all that could be used as weapon for casting was cast. Some used bows, some threw spears with the hand. So many weapons were cast into the *Serpent*, and so thick flew spears and arrows, that the shields could scarcely receive them; for on all sides the *Serpent* was surrounded by war ships. Then King Olaf's men became so mad with rage that they ran on board of the enemies' ships, to get at the people with stroke of sword and kill them; but many did not lay themselves so near the *Serpent*, in order to escape the close encounter with battle-axe or sword; and thus the most of Olaf's men went overboard and sank under their weapons, thinking they were fighting on plain ground. So says Halfred:

> The daring lads shrink not from death,—
> O'erboard they leap, and sink beneath
> The *Serpent's* keel, all armed they leap,
> And down they sink five fathoms deep.
> The foe was daunted at their cheers;
> The king, who still the *Serpent* steers,
> In such a strait—beset with foes—
> Wanted but some more lads like those.

Einar Tambarskelver, one of the sharpest of bowshooters, stood by the mast, and shot with his bow. Einar shot an arrow at Jarl Eric, which hit the tiller-end just above the jarl's head so hard that it entered the wood up to the arrow-shaft. The jarl looked that way, and asked if they knew who had shot; and at the same moment another arrow flew between his hand and his side, and into the stuffing of the chief's stool, so that the barb stood far out on the other side. Then said the jarl to a man called Fin — but some say he was of Finn (Laplander) race, and was a superior archer — "Shoot that tall man by the mast." Fin shot; and the arrow hit the middle of Einar's bow just at the moment that Einar was drawing it, and the bow was split in two parts.

"What is that," cried King Olaf, "that broke with such a noise?" "Norway, king, from thy hands," cried Einar. "No! not quite so much as that," said the king; "take my bow, and shoot," flinging the bow to him.

Einar took the bow, and drew it over the head of the arrow. "Too weak, too weak," said he, "for the bow of a mighty king!" and, throwing the bow aside, he took sword and shield, and fought valiantly.

The king stood on the gangways of the *Long Serpent*, and shot the greater part of the day; sometimes with the bow, sometimes with the spear, and always throwing two spears at once. He looked down over the ship's side,

---

[1] Both in land and sea fights the commanders appear to have been protected from missile weapons — stones, arrows, spears — by a shieldburg; that is, by a party of men bearing shields surrounding them in such a way that the shields were a parapet, covering those within the circle. The Romans had a similar military arrangement of shields in sieges — the testudo.

and saw that his men struck briskly with their swords, and yet wounded but seldom. Then he called aloud, "Why do ye strike so gently that ye seldom cut?" One among the people answered, "The swords are blunt and full of notches." Then the king went down into the forehold, opened the chest under the throne, and took out many sharp swords, which he handed to his men; but as he stretched down his right hand with them, some observed that blood was running down under his steel glove, but no one knew where he was wounded.

Desperate was the defence in the *Serpent*, and there was the heaviest destruction of men done by the forecastle crew, and those of the forehold, for in both places the men were chosen men, and the ship was highest; but in the middle of the ship the people were thinned. Now when the Jarl Eric saw there were but few people remaining beside the ship's mast, he determined to board; and he entered the *Serpent* with four others. Then came Hyrning, the king's brother-in-law, and some others against him, and there was the most severe combat; and at last the jarl was forced to leap back on board the *Iron Beard* again, and some who had accompanied him were killed, and others wounded. Thord Kolbeinsson alludes to this:

> On Odin's deck, all wet with blood,
> The helm-adorned hero stood;
> And gallant Hyrning honour gained,
> Clearing all round with sword deep stained.
> The high Fielde peaks shall fall,
> Ere men forget this to recall.

Now the fight became hot indeed, and many men fell on board the *Serpent;* and the men on board of her began to be thinned off, and the defence to be weaker. The jarl resolved to board the *Serpent* again, and again he met with a warm reception. When the forecastle men of the *Serpent* saw what he was doing, they went aft and made a desperate fight; but so many men of the *Serpent* had fallen that the ship's sides were in many places quite bare of defenders; and the jarl's men poured in all around into the vessel, and all the men who were still able to defend the ship crowded aft to the king, and arrayed themselves for his defence. So says Haldor the Unchristian:

> Eric cheers on his men,—
> 'On to the charge again!"
> The gallant few
> Of Olaf's crew
> Must refuge take
> On the quarterdeck.
> Around the king
> They stand in ring;
> Their shields enclose
> The king from foes,
> And the few who still remain
> Fight madly, but in vain.
> Eric cheers on his men—
> On to the charge again!

Kolbiorn the marshal, who had on clothes and arms like the king's, and was a remarkably stout and handsome man, went up to the king on the quarterdeck. The battle was still going on fiercely even in the forehold.[1]

---

[1] From the occasional descriptions of vessels in this and other battles, it may be inferred that even the *Long Serpent*, described in chapter XCV as of 150 feet of keel, was only decked fore and aft; the thirty-four benches for rowers occupying the open area in the middle, and probably gangways running along the sides for communicating from the quarterdeck to the forecastle.

But as many of the jarl's men had now got into the *Serpent* as could find room, and his ships lay all round her, and few were the people left in the *Serpent* for defence against so great a force; and in a short time most of the *Serpent's* men fell, brave and stout though they were. King Olaf and Kolbiorn the marshal both sprang overboard, each on his own side of the ship; but the jarl's men had laid out boats around the *Serpent*, and killed those who leaped overboard. Now when the king had sprung overboard, they tried to seize him with their hands, and bring him to Jarl Eric; but King Olaf threw his shield over his head, and sank beneath the waters. Kolbiorn held his shield behind him to protect himself from the spears cast at him from the ships which lay round the *Serpent*, and he fell so upon his shield that it came under him, so that he could not sink so quickly. He was thus taken and brought into a boat, and they supposed he was the king. He was brought before the jarl; and when the jarl saw it was Kolbiorn, and not the king, he gave him his life. At the same moment all of King Olaf's men who were in life sprang overboard from the *Serpent;* and Thorkel Nefia, the king's brother, was the last of all the men who sprang overboard. It is thus told concerning the king by Halfred:

> The *Serpent* and the *Crane*
> Lay wrecks upon the main.
> On his sword he cast a glance, —
> With it he saw no chance.
> To his marshal, who of yore
> Many a war-chance had come o'er,
> He spoke a word — then drew in breath,
> And sprang to his deep-sea death.

Jarl Sigvald, as before related, came from Wendland, in company with King Olaf, with ten ships; but the eleventh ship was manned with the men of Astrid, the king's daughter, the wife of Jarl Sigvald. Now when King Olaf sprang overboard, the whole army raised a shout of victory; and then Jarl Sigvald and his men put their oars in the water and rowed towards the battle. Haldor the Unchristian tells of it thus:

> Then first the Wendland vessels came
> Into the fight with little fame ;
> The fight still lingered on the wave,
> Tho' hope was gone with Olaf brave.
> War, like a full-fed ravenous beast,
> Still oped her grim jaws for the feast.
> The few who stood now quickly fled,
> When the shout told — Olaf is dead !

But the Wendland cutter, in which Astrid's men were, rowed back to Wendland; and the report went immediately abroad, and was told by many that King Olaf had cast off his coat of mail under water, and had swum, diving under the long-ships, until he came to the Wendland cutter, and that Astrid's men had conveyed him to Wendland: and many tales have been made since about the adventures of Olaf the king. Halfred speaks thus about it:

> Does Olaf live? or is he dead?
> Has he the hungry ravens fed ?
> I scarcely know what I should say,
> For many tell the tale each way.
> This I can say, nor fear to lie,
> That he was wounded grievously, —
> So wounded in this bloody strife,
> He scarce could come away with life.

[1000 A.D.]

But, however this may have been, King Olaf Tryggvason never came back again to his kingdom of Norway.[b]

THE DISAPPEARANCE OF OLAF TRYGGVASON: OLAF OF NORWAY

The romantic incidents in the chequered life of this warlike prince have perhaps too much alloy in their composition to abide the scrupulous test of history. It was a tradition long cherished by his countrymen that, like the famous Dom Sebastian of Portugal, he disappeared in the midst of battle, and never returned to his own country. But according to the legend of his biographers, Gunnlaug and Oddur, he saved his life by swimming, proceeded in the disguise of a palmer to Rome, and afterwards to the Holy Land where he became an anchorite, and was said to be still living in the reign of Magnus, his fourth successor on the throne of Norway.[1] The northern chronicles represent him as the most distinguished hero of his times. In bodily strength and agility he surpassed all his contemporaries; he could climb the steepest rocks, and walk along the oar when the ship was impelled by the rowers; he used both hands with equal dexterity and would amuse himself with twirling three sharp swords in the air at once, catching each in its turn by the hilt. His taste for the liberal and useful arts had been improved by his widely-extended travels both in the East and the West. He was a munificent patron of the skalds, although it might be supposed that their connection with the ancient heathen faith would have excited his prejudice against them. He greatly encouraged the art of ship-building; and the advantages of commerce and civilisation, which he witnessed in his youth in foreign countries, induced him to become the founder of a city, at the mouth of the river Nid, called, from its position, Nidaros, and afterwards Trondhjem, from the name of the province of which it is still the capital, to serve as a dépôt or granary for that part of the kingdom so often exposed to the scourge of famine.

On the death or disappearance of Olaf, his dominions became the spoil of the confederated victors. The kings of Denmark and Sweden claimed such portions of territory as suited their convenience, leaving the rest to Eric and Svend, the sons of Hakon Jarl. The latter princes endeavoured to obliterate from the minds of their countrymen the recollection of the violent means which had raised them to power, by exercising it in the mildest and gentlest form; and although professing Christianity themselves, they wisely refused to persecute the adherents of the ancient national faith. The Danish monarch, Canute the Great, was for a time too much occupied in subduing England, and securing the dubious inheritance of a foreign crown, to turn his attention to Norway; but so soon as the reduction of the Anglo-Saxons to a state of tolerable order had allowed him an opportunity of revisiting his native land, he urged his pretensions to the sceptre of that kingdom in right of his father, who had been instrumental in wresting it from the hands of Tryggvason.

The Norwegians, however, had previously chosen and acknowledged as their sovereign a lineal descendant of Harfagr, named Olaf [called Dick, or the Thick], the son of Harold Gränske. This youthful prince had been educated by Sigurd Syr, the chief of an upland district, who had espoused Olaf's

---

[1] Gunnlaug and Oddur, two Icelandic monks of the twelfth century, wrote each a separate Saga or Life of Olaf, which were used by Snorre Sturleson among other original materials in the compilation of this part of the Heimskringla. The different relations tending to corroborate the account of Olaf's escape by swimming, are carefully collected in Olaf's *Tryggvasonar Saga*, published by the Society of Northern Antiquaries at Copenhagen.

{1000 A.D.}

widowed mother. In his twelfth year he was entrusted with a piratical expedition to the British coasts, where he assisted the Anglo-Saxons in opposing the Danes; and at the age of sixteen he had been engaged in nine great battles.[d]

The following is Snorre's[b] account of this expedition so far as concerns England: When Æthelred, the king of the English, heard in Flanders that Sweyn was dead, he returned directly to England; and no sooner was he come back, than he sent an invitation to all the men who would enter into his pay, to join him in recovering the country. Then many people flocked to him; and among others, came King Olaf with a great troop of Northmen to his aid. They steered first to London, and sailed into the Thames with their fleet; but the Danes had a castle within. On the other side of the river is a great trading place, which is called Sudrviki (Southwark). There the Danes had raised a great work, dug large ditches, and within had built a bulwark of stone, timber, and turf, where they had stationed a strong army. King Æthelred ordered a great assault; but the Danes defended themselves bravely, and King Æthelred could make nothing of it. Between the castle[1] and Southwark there was a bridge, so broad that two wagons could pass each other upon it. On the bridge were raised barricades, both towers and wooden parapets, in the direction of the river, which were nearly breast high; and under the bridge were piles driven into the bottom of the river. Now when the attack was made the troops stood on the bridge everywhere, and defended themselves. King Æthelred was very anxious to get possession of the bridge, and he called together all the chiefs to consult how they should get the bridge broken down. Then said King Olaf he would attempt to lay his fleet alongside of it, if the other ships would do the same. It was then determined in this council that they should lay their war forces under the bridge; and each made himself ready with ships and men.

King Olaf ordered great platforms of floating wood to be tied together with hazel bands, and for this he took down old houses; and with these as a roof he covered over his ships so widely that it reached over the ships' sides. Under this screen he set pillars so high and stout that there was room for swinging their swords, and the roofs were strong enough to withstand the stones cast down upon them. Now, when the fleet and men were ready they rowed up along the river; but when they came near the bridge, there were cast down upon them so many stones and missile weapons, such as arrows and spears, that neither helmet nor shield could hold out against it; and the ships themselves were so greatly damaged that many retreated out of it. But King Olaf, and the Northmen's fleet with him, rowed quite up under the bridge, laid their cables around the piles which supported it, and then rowed off with all the ships as hard as they could down the stream. The piles were thus shaken in the bottom, and were loosened under the bridge.

Now, as the armed troops stood thick of men upon the bridge, and there were likewise many heaps of stones and other weapons upon it, and the piles under it being loosened and broken, the bridge gave way; and a great part of the men upon it fell into the river, and all the others fled, some into the castle, some into Southwark. Thereafter Southwark was stormed and taken. Now, when the people in the castle saw that the river Thames was mastered, and that they could not hinder the passage of ships up into the country, they became afraid, surrendered the tower, and took Æthelred to be their king.

---

[1] On the site, probably, of the Tower of London. [k]

So says Ottar Swarte:

> London Bridge is broken down, —
> Gold is worn, and bright renown
>   Shields resounding,
>   War-horns sounding,
> Hildur shouting in the din !
>   Arrows singing,
>   Mail-coats ringing—
> Odin makes our Olaf win !

And he also composed these:

> King Æthelred has found a friend :
> Brave Olaf will his throne defend —
>   In bloody fight
>   Maintain his right,
>   Win back his land
>   With blood-red hand,
> And Eadmund's son upon his throne replace—·
> Eadmund, the star of every royal race !

Sigvat also relates as follows:

> At London Bridge stout Olaf gave
> Odin's law to his war-men brave —
>   "To win or die ! "
>   And their foemen fly.
> Some by the dyke-side refuge gain —
> Some in their tents on Southwark plain !
>   This sixth attack
>   Brought victory back.

King Olaf passed all the winter with King Æthelred, and had a great battle at Hringmara heath[1] in Ulfkel's land, the domain which Ulfkel Snelling at that time held; and here again the king was victorious. So says Sigvald the skald:

> To Ulfkel's land came Olaf bold,
> A seventh sword-thing he would hold.
> The race of Ælla filled the plain—
> Few of them slept at home again
>   Hringmara heath
>   Was a bed of death :
>   Harfagr's heir
>   Dealt slaughter there.

And Ottar sings of this battle thus:

> From Hringmar field
>   The chime of war,
> Sword striking shield,
>   Rings from afar.
>   The living fly ;
>   The dead piled high
>   The moor enrich :
>   Red runs the ditch.

The country far around was then brought in subjection to King Æthelred; but the Thing-men[2] and the Danes held many castles, besides a great part of the country.

[1] This is an unknown place, Hringmaraheidi ; but must be in East Angeln, as it is called Ulfkel Snelling's land, and he appears to have been chief of the part of England called East Angeln occupied by the Danes. Ashdown in Kent, and Assington in Essex, have each been taken by antiquaries for this battle-field. *k*

[2] Thing-men were hired men-at-arms ; called Thing-men probably from being men above the class of thralls or unfree men, and entitled to appear at Things, as being udal born to land

King Olaf was commander of all the forces when they went against Canterbury; and they fought there until they took the town, killing many people and burning the castle. So says Ottar Swarte:

> All in the grey of morn
>   Broad Canterbury's forced.
> Black smoke from house-roofs borne
>   Hides fire that does its worst;
> And many a man laid low
> By the battle-axe's blow,
> Waked by the Norsemen's cries,
> Scarce had time to rub his eyes.

Sigvald reckons this King Olaf's eighth battle. At this time King Olaf was intrusted with the whole land defence of England, and he sailed round the land with his ships of war. He laid his ships at land at Nyamode,[1] where the troops of the Thing-men were, and gave them battle and gained the victory. So says Sigvald the skald:

> The youthful king stained red the hair
> Of Angeln men, and dyed his spear
> At Newport in their hearts' dark blood;
> And where the Danes the thickest stood —
> Where the shrill storm round Olaf's head
> Of spear and arrow thickest fled,
> There thickest lay the Thing-men dead!
> Nine battles now of Olaf bold,
> Battle by battle, I have told.

King Olaf then scoured all over the country, taking scatt of the people, and plundering where it was refused. So says Ottar:

> The English race could not resist thee,
> With money thou madest them assist thee,
> Unsparingly thou madest them pay
> A scatt to thee in every way:
> Money, if money could be got —
> Goods, cattle, household gear, if not.
> Thy gathered spoil, borne to the strand,
> Was the best wealth of English land.

Olaf remained here for three years. The third year King Æthelred died, and his sons Eadmund and Edward took the government.[b] Then Olaf sailed southwards out to sea. During two years he infested the shores of France and Spain; and subsequently took advantage of the absence of Eric, son of Hakon Jarl, then fighting under the banner of Canute in England, to assert his claim to the throne of his ancestors. He was joyfully received by his countrymen, and especially by the Christian party, to whom he was attached from infancy, having been baptised in his third year. But his zeal, like that of his godfather Olaf Tryggvason, led him to persecute the refractory heathen with fire and sword. Not content with burning their temples, and erecting churches on their ruins, he marched through the country with armed bands, for the purpose of converting his subjects and rooting out the last vestige of pagan superstition.

at home. They appear to have hired themselves out as hird-men; that is, court-men, or the bodyguard of the kings. The Varangians at the court of Constantinople were of this description. The victories of King Sweyn and of Canute the Great have been ascribed to the superiority of these men, who formed bodies of standing troops, over levies of peasantry. *k*

[1] Nyamode is supposed to be Newport in the Isle of Wight; more likely New Romney, the river-mouth of the Rother in Kent. *k*

While thus occupied in forcibly establishing the new religion, Canute landed with a powerful armament at Trondhjem, and met with little opposition on the part of his rival, now abandoned by the principal chieftains, some of whom were disgusted with his severities, whilst others were seduced by the promises and rich presents of the invader. The majority of the people followed the example of their leaders, and submitted to the authority of the Danish king. Olaf fled, with his infant son Magnus, to the Russian court, where he was hospitably received by his brother-in-law Yaroslav, a prince of the house of Rurik. Here he sojourned during the regency of Hakon, son of Eric Jarl, whom Canute had appointed his lieutenant in Norway. On the death of the viceroy, he returned to Sweden, where obtaining suitable assistance he made a desperate effort to recover the crown; but he was defeated and slain in a battle fought (August 31st, 1030) at Stiklestad, near the city of Trondhjem. His body was discovered and secretly buried by one of his faithful adherents, but afterwards disinterred and conveyed to Trondhjem, where it was deposited in the magnificent cathedral which rose upon the ruins of the temple of Thor. The recollection of his cruelties was forgotten, and such was the reverence paid to him as a hero and a martyr that he might almost be said to have filled the place of the ancient idols in the affections of the nation. Churches and shrines were erected in honour of the royal saint, not only in Norway but in Denmark, Sweden, Russia, England, and even by his countrymen at Constantinople.[d]

The Sainthood of King Olaf

Pilgrims journeyed in crowds to St. Olaf's shrine, and legends of cripples who had there recovered the use of their limbs, and of other miracles, soon became numberless. St. Olaf's shrine of silver, inlaid with gold and precious stones, was on solemn occasions, such as the saint's yearly festival or the election of a king, borne in procession by sixty men, and was an abundant source of revenue to the clergy and the cathedral.

When the Swedes in 1564 had taken possession of Trondhjem, they found nothing remaining of St. Olaf's treasures except his helmet, spurs, and the wooden chest that had contained his body. The helmet and spurs they took with them to Sweden, where they were preserved in the church of St. Nicholas at Stockholm; but the chest they left behind in a church, after having drawn out the silver nails, which had been left by the Danes. After the expulsion of the Swedes, St. Olaf's body and chest were, with great solemnity, carried back to the cathedral, where, a contemporary bears witness, the body was found entire in a grave of masonry in 1567, and "his blood is seen to this day in a barn, and can never be washed out by water or human hands." In the following year St. Olaf's body was by a royal ordinance covered with earth.

St. Olaf's sanctity is no more thought of, even his last resting-place is forgotten; but his name still lives, as is proved by the numerous traditions still fresh in the memory of the Norwegian people. Throughout the land are to be found traces of St. Olaf's deeds and miraculous power. Fountains sprang forth when he thirsted, and acquired salutary virtue when he drank; rocks were rent at his bidding, and sounds (sunde) were formed at his nod; churches were raised, and trolls found in St. Olaf a foe as formidable as they had formerly had in the mighty Thor, whose red beard even was inherited by St. Olaf. In many places trolls are still shown, who were turned into stone at St. Olaf's command.

[1035 A.D.]

What heathenism attributed to the gods of Valhalla and to the mighty Thor, the Catholic ecclesiastics, with their earliest converts, no doubt transferred to the powerful suppressor of the Asa faith, St. Olaf, whose axe supplanted Thor's Miölnir, and whose steed, renowned in tradition, the goats of the Thunder-god. The numerous representations, which in the days of Catholicism were no doubt to be found in many of the churches dedicated to St. Olaf, are now for the most part destroyed; but from the notices which we have of them, the hero was generally represented with a battle-axe in his hand, and treading on a troll or a dragon.*i*

SVEND IS SUCCEEDED BY MAGNUS; THE DEATH OF CANUTE

The death of the viceroy Hakon had made way for the accession to the throne of Norway of Svend, son of Canute and his first wife Alfifa. But Svend rendered himself odious by his severe laws and his impolitic government, and was soon obliged to surrender the rule when a powerful party of malcontents sent for Magnus the Good, son of St. Olaf. Thus the great empire, whose elements had not been united by intimate ties but only by the strength and wisdom of Canute, began to disintegrate even during the lifetime of that prince. Soon after, in 1035, died, at the age of forty years, the most powerful king who had reigned in the north.

Gifted with a pleasing countenance, he had the appearance of good health, a clear complexion, beautiful long hair, and an aquiline nose. He had shunned no means, even the most unjust, which were potent to accomplish his purposes, and his memory is soiled by more than one murder, but we cannot refuse to recognise, in the sovereign who knew how to unite and maintain such great territories, either an eminent talent for rule or a rare ability for mastering events and turning them to his own advantage.*g*

THE PRESERVATION OF THE SAGAS

The fierce and barbarous elements in the character of the Northmen have been sufficiently displayed in the foregoing pages; it will therefore be some relief to turn to the other side of the picture and see how far these same wild peoples had already advanced in the useful arts of civilisation and even in literature.*a* This body of literature, produced by the Scandinavians of the viking age, is remarkably distinguished from that of any other people of the same period by being composed entirely in the native national tongue, and intended to instruct or amuse an audience of the people; and not in a dead language, and intended merely for the perusal of an educated class in the monasteries.

It may be said that the influence of sagas or songs, of the literature, such as it may be, upon the spirit and character of a people, is overstated, and that it is but a fond exaggeration, at any rate, to dignify with the title of a national influential literature the rude traditionary tales and ballads of a barbarous pagan population. But a nation's literature is its breath of life, without which a nation has no existence, is but a congregation of individuals. However low the literature may be in its intellectual merit, it will nationalise the living materials of a population into a mass animated with common feeling. During the five centuries in which the Northmen were riding over the seas, and conquering wheresoever they landed, the literature of the people they overcame was locked up in a dead language, and within the walls of monasteries. But the Northmen had a literature of their own, rude as it was; and the Anglo-Saxon race had none — none at least belonging to the people. In the five centuries between the days of the Venerable Bede and those of Matthew Paris, that is from the ninth to the end of the thirteenth century, the northern branch of the common race was not destitute of intellectuality, notwithstanding all their paganism and barbarism, and they had a literature adapted to their national spirit, and wonderfully extensive.

It does not appear that any saga manuscript now existing has been written before the fourteenth century, however old the saga itself may be. The Flatö manuscript is of 1395. Those supposed to have been written in the thirteenth century are not ascertained to be so on better data than the appearance and handwriting. It is known that in the twelfth century Are Frode, Sæmund, and others began to take the sagas out of the traditionary state, and fix them in writing; but none of the original skins appear to have come down to our times, but only some of the numerous copies of them. Bishop Müller shows good reasons for supposing that before Are Frode's time, and in the eleventh century, sagas were committed to writing; but if we consider the scarcity of the material in that age — parchment of the classics, even in Italy, being often deleted, to be used by the monks for their writings — these must have been very few. No well-authenticated saga of ancient date in runic is extant, if such ever existed; although runic letters occur in Gothic, and even in Anglo-Saxon manuscripts, mixed with the other characters.

The writings of Are, who lived about the year 1117 and first committed to writing the Icelandic compositions, and of Sæmund, who flourished about the year 1083 and had studied at universities in Germany and France, and of Oddo the Monk, who flourished in the twelfth century, are almost entirely lost. Kolskegg, a contemporary of Are, and, like him, distinguished by the surname of Frode — the wise, or the much-knowing — Brandus, who lived about the year 1163, Eiric, the son of Oddo, and his contemporary Karl, abbot of the monastery of Thringö, in the north of Iceland, and several others, appear to have been collectors, transcribers, and partly continuators of preceding chronicles; and all these flourished between the time of Bede in the end of the seventh and beginning of the eighth century, when the devastations of these piratical vikings were at the worst, and the time of Snorre Sturleson in the middle of the thirteenth century, when the viking life was given up, invasions of Northmen even under their kings had ceased, and the influence of Christianity and its establishments was diffused.

This body of literature may surely be called a national literature; for, on looking over the subjects it treats of, it will be found to consist almost entirely of historical events, or of the achievements of individuals, which, whether real or fabulous, were calculated to sustain a national spirit among the people for whom they were composed; and scarcely any of it consists of the legends of saints, of homilies, or theological treatises, which constitute the greater proportion of the literature of other countries during the same ages, and which were evidently composed only for the public of the cloisters. It is distinguished also from any contemporary literature, and indeed from any known body of literature, by the peculiar circumstance of its having been for many centuries, and until the beginning of the twelfth century, or within 120 years of Snorre Sturleson's own times, an oral not a written literature, and composed and transmitted from generation to generation by word of mouth and by memory, not by pen, ink, and parchment.

[—1050 A.D.]

The early history of every people can only have been preserved by traditionary stories, songs, ballads, until the age when they were fixed by writing. Snorre Sturleson has done for the history of the Northmen what Livy did for the history of the Romans. Moreover, the sagas have been preserved among the Northmen, or at least have not perished so entirely but that the sources from which their historian Snorre drew his information may be examined. If we consider the scarcity of the material — parchment — in the Middle Ages, even in the oldest Christianised countries of Europe, and the still greater scarcity of scribes and men of learning and leisure, who would bestow their time and material on any subjects but monastic legends in the Latin language, we must wonder that so many of these historical tales had been committed to writing in Iceland; not that so many which once were extant in the traditionary state have not been preserved.

THE SKALDS

Who were the original authors of these compositions; and what was the condition of the class of men, the skalds, who composed them? What were the peculiar circumstances in the social condition of the Northmen in those ages, by which such a class as the skalds was kept in bread, and in constant employment and exertion among them, and even with great social consideration; while among the Anglo-Saxons, the equivalent class of the bards, troubadours, minstrels, minnesingers was either extinct, or of no more social influence than that of the court jesters or the *jongleurs?*

Before the introduction or general diffusion of writing it is evident that a class of men whose sole occupation it was to commit to memory and preserve the laws, usages, precedents, and details of all civil affairs and rights, and to whose fidelity in relating former transactions implicit confidence could be given, must of necessity have existed in society — must have been in every locality; and from the vast number and variety of details in every district, and the great interests of every community, must have been esteemed and recompensed in proportion to their importance in such a social state. This class was formed of the skalds — the men who were the living books, to be referred to in every case of law or property in which the past had to be applied to the present. Before the introduction of Christianity, and with Christianity the introduction of the use of written documents, and the diffusion, by the church establishment, of writing in every locality, the skald must have been among the pagan landowners what the parish priest and his written record were in the older Christianised countries of Europe. In these all civil affairs were in written record either of the priest or the lawyer; and the skalds, in these Christianised countries, were merely a class of wandering troubadours, poets, story-tellers, minnesingers, entertained, like the dwarfs, court-jesters, or jugglers, by the great barons at their castles, for the entertainment which their songs, music, stories, or practical jokes might afford. Here, in this pagan country, they were a necessary and most important element in the social structure.

They were the registrars of events affecting property, and filled the place and duty of the lawyer and scribe in a society in which law was very complicated; the succession to property, through affinity and family connection, very intricate, from the want of family surnames, and the equal rights of all children; and in which a priesthood acquainted more or less with letters, the art of writing, and law, was totally wanting. The skalds of the north disappeared at once when Christian priests were established through the country. They were superseded in their utility by men of education, who knew the art of writing; and the country had no feudal barons to maintain such a class for amusement only. We hear little of the skalds after the first half of the twelfth century; and they are not quoted at all in the portion of Magnus Erlingsson's reign given by Snorre Sturleson within the twelfth century.

Besides the payment of scatt, and the maintenance of the king's household in the royal progresses, the whole body of the landowners were bound to attend the king in arms and with ships, whenever they were called upon to serve him either at home or abroad. The king appears, in fact, not only not to have wanted any prerogative that feudal sovereigns of the same times possessed, but to have had much more power than the monarchs of other countries. The middle link in the feudal system — a nobility of great crown vassals, with their sub-vassals subservient to them as their immediate superiors, not to the crown — was wanting in the social structure of the Northmen. The kingly power working directly on the people was more efficient; and the kings, and all who had a satisfactory claim to the royal power, had no difficulty in calling out the people for war expeditions. These expeditions, often merely predatory in their object, consisted either of general levies, in which all able-bodied men, and all ships, great and small, had to follow the king; or of certain quota of men, ships, and provisions, furnished by certain districts according to fixed law. All the country along the coasts of Norway, and as far back into the land "as the salmon swims up the rivers," was divided into ship-districts or ship-rathes; and each district had to furnish ships of a certain size, a certain number of men, and a certain equipment, according to its capability; and other inland districts had to furnish cattle and other provision in fixed numbers.

This arrangement was made by Harold Harfagr's successor, Hakon, who reigned between 933 and 961; and as Hakon was the foster-son of Æthelstan of England, and was bred up to manhood in his court, it is not improbable that this arrangement may have been borrowed from the similar arrangement made by King Alfred for the defence of the English coast against the Northmen; unless we take the still more probable conjecture that Alfred himself borrowed it from them, as they were certainly in all naval and military affairs superior to his own people in that age. It is to be observed that, for the Northmen, these levies for predatory expeditions were by no means unpopular or onerous. "To gather property" by plundering the coasts of cattle, meal, malt, wool, slaves, was a favourite summer occupation. When the crops were in the ground in spring, the whole population, which was seafaring as well as agricultural in its habits, was altogether idle until harvest; and the great success in amassing booty, as vikings, on the coasts, made the *leding*, as it was called, a favourite service during many reigns: and it appears that the service might be commuted sometimes into a war tax, when it was inconvenient to go on the levy. Every man, it is to be observed, who went upon these expeditions, was udal born to some portion of land at home; that is, had certain udal rights of succession, or of purchase, or of partition, connected with the little estate of the family of which he was a member.

All these complicated rights and interests connecting people settled in Northumberland, East Anglia, Normandy, or Iceland, with landed property situated in the valleys of Norway, required a body of men, like the skalds, whose sole occupation was to record in their stories trustworthy accounts, not only of the historical events, but of the deaths, intermarriages, pedigrees, and other family circumstances of every person of any note engaged in them. We find, accordingly, that the sagas are, as justly observed by Pinkerton, rather memoirs of individuals than history. They give the most careful heraldic tracing of every man's kin they speak of, because he was kin to landowners at home, or they were kin to him. In such a social state we may believe that the class of skalds were not, as we generally suppose, merely a class of story-tellers, poets, or harpers, going about with gossip, song, and music; but were interwoven with the social institutions of the country, and had a footing in the material interests of the people.

To take an interest in the long-past events of history is an acquired intellectual taste, and not at all the natural taste of the unlettered man. When we are told of the Norman baron in his castle-hall, or the Iceland peasant's family around their winter fireside in their turf-built huts, sitting down in the tenth or the eleventh century to listen to, get by heart, and transmit to the rising generation the accounts of historical events of the eighth or ninth century in Norway, England, or Denmark, we feel that, however pleasing this picture may be to the fancy, it is not true to nature —not consistent with the human mind in a rude illiterate social state. But when we consider the nature of the peculiar udal principle by which land or other property was transmitted through the social body of these Northmen, we see at once a sufficient foundation in the material interests, both of the baron and the peasant, for the support of a class of traditionary relators of past events. Every person in every expedition was udal born to something at home — to the kingdom, or to a little farm; and this class were the recorders of the vested rights of individuals, and of family alliances, feuds, or other interests, when written record was not known. For many generations after the first Northmen settled in England or Normandy, it must, from the uncertain issue of their hostilities with the indigenous inhabitants, have been matter of deep interest to every individual to know how it stood with the branch of the family in possession of the piece of udal land in the mother-country to which he also was udal born, that is, had certain eventual rights of succession; and whether to return and claim their share of any succession which may have opened up to them in Norway must have been a question with settlers in Northumberland, Normandy, or Iceland, which could only be solved by the information derived from such a class as the skalds.

Before the clergy by their superior learning extinguished the vocation of this class among the Northmen, the skalds appear to have been frequently employed also as confidential messengers or ambassadors; as, for instance, in the proposal of a marriage between Olaf king of Norway and the daughter of King Olaf of Sweden, and of a peace between the two countries to be established by this alliance. The skalds, by their profession, could go from court to court without suspicion, and in comparative safety; because, being generally natives of Iceland, they had no hereditary family feuds with the people of the land, no private vengeance for family injuries to apprehend; and being usually rewarded by gifts of rings, chains, goblets, and such trinkets, they could, without exciting suspicion, carry with them the tokens by which, before the art of writing was common in courts, the messenger who had a private errand to unfold was accredited. When kings or great people met in those ages they exchanged gifts or presents with each other, and do so still in the East; and the original object of this custom was that each should have tokens known to the other, by which any bearer afterwards should be accredited to the original owner of the article sent with him in token, and even the amount of confidence to be reposed in him denoted.

We, with writing at command, can scarcely perhaps conceive the shifts people must have been put to when even the most simple communication or order had to be delivered *vivâ voce* to some agent who was to carry it, and who had to produce some credential or token that he was to be believed. Every act of importance between distant parties had to be transacted by tokens. Our wonder and incredulity cease when we consider that such a class of men as those who composed and transmitted this great mass of saga literature were evidently a necessary element in the social arrangements of the time and people, and, together with their literature or traditional songs and stories, were intimately connected with the material interests of all, and especially of those who had property and power. They were not merely a class of wandering poets, troubadours, or story-tellers, living by the amusement they afforded to a people in a state too rude to support any class for their intellectual amusement only. The skalds, who appear to have been divided into two classes — poets, who composed or remembered verses in which events were related, or chiefs and their deeds commemorated; and saga-men, who related historical accounts of transactions past or present — were usually, it may be said exclusively, of Iceland.[h]

Several of the kings of Sweden entertained Icelandic skalds, but it was at the courts of Norwegian monarchs that they found the most hospitable reception and liberal patronage. Thus Harold Harfagr had always in his service four principal skalds, who were the intimate companions of his leisure hours, and with whom he even counselled upon his most serious and important affairs. He assigned them the highest seats at the royal board, and gave them precedence over all his other courtiers. St. Olaf, king of Norway — whose zeal against the pagan religion induced him to include the songs of the skalds among the other inventions of the demon, and of whom the skald Sigvat said, "He was unwilling to listen to any lay" — deprived them of their accustomed precedence at his court. But such was the force of ancient feelings and prejudice that this monarch continued to give them much of his confidence, and frequently employed them on the most important public missions.

Nor could he suppress the wish that his own name might live in song, and he was accompanied to the field in the last fatal battle, which terminated his life and reign, by three of the most celebrated Icelandic skalds of the time, to whom he assigned in the midst of his bravest champions a conspicuous post, where they might be able distinctly to see and hear, and afterwards relate the events of the day. Thormod, one of these skalds, dictated a lay, which the whole army sung after him, and which is still extant. Two of them fell dead by the king's side, and Thormod, though mortally wounded by an arrow, would not desert him, but still continued to chant the praises of the saintly king until he expired.[i]

THE SOCIAL CONDITION OF THE NORTHMEN

If the historical sagas tell us little concerning the religion and religious establishments of the pagan Northmen, they give us incidentally a great deal of curious and valuable information about their social condition and institutions. The following observations are picked up from the sagas.

The lowest class in the community were the *thraell* (thralls, slaves). They were the prisoners captured by the vikings at sea on piratical cruises, or carried off from the coasts of foreign countries in marauding expeditions. These captives were, if not ransomed by their friends, bought and sold at regular slave markets. The owners could kill them without any fine, mulct, or manbod to the king, as in the case of the murder or manslaughter of a free man. King Olaf Tryggvason, in his childhood, his mother Astrid, and his foster-father Thorolf, were captured by an Esthonian viking, as they were crossing the sea from Sweden on their way to Novgorod, and were divided among the crew, and sold. An Esthonian man called Klerkon got Olaf and Thorolf as his share of the booty; but Astrid was separated from her son Olaf, then only three years of age. Klerkon thought Thorolf too old for a slave, and that no work would be got out of him to repay his food, and therefore killed him; but sold the boy to a man called Klærk for a goat.

A peasant called Reas bought him from Klærk for a good cloak; and he remained in slavery until he was accidentally recognised by his uncle, who was in the service of the Russian king, and was by him taken to the court of Novgorod, where he grew up. His mother, Astrid, apparently long afterwards, was recognised by a Norwegian merchant called Lodin at a slave market to which she had been brought for sale. Lodin offered to purchase her, and carry her home to Norway, if she would accept of him in marriage, which she joyfully agreed to; Lodin being a man of good birth, who sometimes went on expeditions as a merchant, and sometimes on viking cruises. On her return to Norway her friends approved of the match as suitable; and when her son, King Olaf Tryggvason, came to the throne, Lodin and his sons by Astrid were in high favour. This account of the capturing, selling, and buying slaves, and killing one worn out, is related as an ordinary matter. In Norway this class appears to have been better treated than on the south side of the Baltic, and to have had some rights. Lodin had to ask his slave Astrid to accept of him in marriage.

We find them also in the first half of the eleventh century, at least under some masters, considered capable of acquiring and holding property of their own. When Asbiorn came from Halogaland in the north of Norway to purchase a cargo of meal and malt, of which articles King Olaf the Saint, fearing a scarcity, had prohibited the exportation from the south of Norway, he went to his relation Erling Skialgsson, a peasant or bondi, who was married to a sister of the late King Olaf Tryggvason, and was a man of great power. Erling told Asbiorn that in consequence of the law he could not supply him, but that his thralls or slaves could probably sell him as much as he required for loading his vessel; adding the remarkable observation that they, the slaves, are not bound by the law and country regulations like other men — evidently from the notion that they were not parties, like other men, to the making of the law in the Thing.

It is told of this Erling, who was one of the most considerable men in the country, and brother-in-law of King Olaf Tryggvason, although of the bonder or peasant class, that he had always ninety free-born men in his house, and two hundred or more when Jarl Hakon, then regent of the country, came into the neighbourhood; that he had a ship of thirty-two banks of oars; and when he went on a viking cruise, or in a levy with the king, had two hundred men at least with him. He had always on his farm thirty slaves, besides other workpeople; and he gave them a certain task as a day's work to do, and gave them leave to work for themselves in the twilight, or in the night. He also gave them land to sow, and gave them the benefit of their own crops; and he put upon them a certain value, so that they could redeem themselves from slavery, which some could do the first or second year, and "all who had any luck could do it in the third year." With this money Erling bought new slaves, and he settled those who had thus obtained their freedom on his newly cleared land, and found employment for them in useful trades, or in the herring fishery, for which he furnished them with nets and salt. The same course of management is ascribed in the Saga of St. Olaf to his stepfather, Sigurd Syr, who is celebrated for his prudence, and wisdom, and skill in husbandry; and it has probably been general among the slaveholders. The slaves who had thus obtained their freedom would belong to what appears to have been a distinct class from the peasants or bonders on the one hand, or the slaves on the other — the class of unfree men.

This class — the unfree — appears to have consisted of those who, not being udal born to any land in the country, so as to be connected with and have an interest in the succession to any family estate, were not free of the Things; were not entitled to appear and deliberate in those assemblies; were not Thingsmen. This class of unfree is frequently mentioned in general levies for repelling invasion, when all men, free and unfree, are summoned to appear in arms; and the term unfree evidently refers to men who had personal freedom, and were not thralls, as the latter could only be collected to a levy by their masters. This class would include all the cottars on the land paying a rent in work upon the farm to the peasant, who was udal born proprietor; and, under the name of housemen, this class of labourers in husbandry still exists on every farm in Norway. It would include also, the house-carls, or free-born indoor men, of whom Erling, we see, always kept ninety about him. They were, in fact, his bodyguard and garrison, the equivalent to the troop maintained by the feudal baron of Germany in his castle; and they followed the *bondi* or peasant in his summer excursions of piracy, or on the levy when called out by the king. They appear to have been free to serve whom they pleased.

We find many of the class of bonders who kept a suite of eighty or ninety men—as Erling, Harek of Thiottö, and others. Sweyn, of the little isle of Gairsay in Orkney, kept, we are told in the Orkneyinga Saga, eighty men all winter; and as we see the owner of this farm, which could not produce bread for one-fourth of that number, trusting for many years to his success in piracy for subsisting his retainers, we must conclude that they formed a numerous class of the community. This class would also include workpeople, labourers, fishermen, tradesmen, and others about towns and farms, or rural townships, who, although personally free and free-born, not slaves, were unfree in respect of the rights possessed by the class of bonders, landowners, or peasants, in the Things. They had the protection and civil rights imparted by laws, but not the right to a voice in the enactment of the laws, or regulation of public affairs in the Things of the country. They were, in their rights, in the condition of the German population at the present day.

Bondi

The class above the unfree in civil rights, the free peasant-proprietors, or bonder class, were the most important and influential in the community. We have no word in English, or in any other modern language, exactly equivalent to the word *bondi*, because the class itself never existed among us. Peasant does not express it; because we associate with the word peasant the idea of inferior social importance to the feudal nobility, gentry, and landed proprietors of a country, and this bonder class was itself the highest class in the country. Yeoman, or, in Cumberland, statesman, expresses their condition only relatively to the portions of land owned by them; not their social position as the highest class of landowners. If the Americans had a word to express the class of small landholders in their old settled states who live on their little properties, have the highest social influence in the country, and are its highest class, and, although without family aggrandisement by primogeniture succession, retain family distinction and descent, and even family pride, but divide their properties on the udal principle among their children, it would express more justly what the bonder class were than the words landholder, yeoman, statesman, peasant-proprietor, or peasant. In the translation of the Heimskringla, where the word peasant is used for the word *bondi*,[1] the reader will have to carry in mind that these peasants were, in fact, an hereditary aristocracy, comprehending the great mass of the population, holding their little estates by a far more independent tenure than the feudal nobility of other countries, and having their land strictly entailed on their own families and kin, and with much family pride, and much regard for and record of their family descent and alliances, because each little estate was entailed on each peasant's whole family and kin.

Udal right was, and is to this day in Norway, a species of entail, in realty, in the family that is udal born to it. The udal land could not be alienated by sale, gift to the church, escheat to a superior, forfeiture, or by any other casualty, from the kindred who were udal born to it; and they had, however distantly connected, an eventual right of succession vested in them superior to any right a stranger in blood could acquire. The udal born to a piece of land could evict any other possessor, and, until a very late period, even without any repayment of what the new possessor having no udal right may have paid for it, or laid out upon it; and at the present day a right of redemption within a certain number of years, is competent to those udal born to an estate which has been sold out of a family. The right to the crown of Norway itself was udal born right in a certain family or race, traced from Odin down to Harold Harfagr through the Yngling dynasty, as a matter of religious faith; but from Harold Harfagr as a fixed legal and historical point. All who were of his blood were udal born to the Norwegian crown, and with equal rights of succession in equal degrees of propinquity. The eldest son had no exclusive right, either by law or in public opinion, to the whole succession, and the kingdom was more than once divided equally among all the sons.

This principle of equal succession appears to have been so rooted in the social arrangement and public mind that, notwithstanding all the evils it produced in the succession to the crown by internal warfare between brothers, it seems never to have been shaken as a principle of right; and the kings who had laboured the most to unite the whole country into one sovereignty, as Harold Harfagr, were the first to divide it again among their sons. One cause of this may have been the impossibility, among all classes, from

---

[1] *Bondi* (in the plural *bœnder*) does not suit the English ear, and there is no reasoning with the ear in matters of language. Bonder, although it be plural, is therefore used singularly; and bonders, although it be a double plural, to express more than one of the bondi. The word itself, *bondi* or *buandir*, seems derived from *bu*, a country dwelling, signifying also the stock, wealth, affairs, and all that belongs to husbandry. The word *bu* is still retained in Orkney and Shetland, to express the principal farm and farm-house of a small township or property, the residence of the proprietor; and is used in Denmark and Norway to express stock, or farm stock and substance.

the king to the peasant, of providing otherwise for the younger branches of a family than by giving them a portion of the land itself, or of the products of the land paid instead of money taxes to the crown. Legitimacy of birth was held of little account, owing probably to marriage not being among the Odin-worshippers a religious as well as a civil act; for we find all the children, illegitimate as well as legitimate, esteemed equal in udal-born right even to the throne itself; and although high descent on the mother's side also appears to have been esteemed, it was no obstacle even to the succession to the crown that the mother, as in the case of Magnus the Good, had been a slave.

This was the consequence of polygamy, in which, as in the East, the kings indulged. Harold Harfagr had nine wives at once, and many concubines; and every king, even King Olaf the Saint, had concubines as well as wives; and we find polygamy indulged in down to about 1130, when Sigurd the Crusader's marriage with Cecilia, at the time his queen was alive and not divorced, was opposed by the Bishop of Bergen, who would not celebrate it; but nevertheless the priest of Stavanger performed the ceremony, on the king's duly paying the church for the indulgence. Polygamy appears not to have been confined to kings and great men; for we find in the old Icelandic law book, called the *Grey Goose*, that, in determining the mutual rights of succession of persons born in either country, Norway or Iceland, in the other country, it is provided that children born in Norway in bigamy should have equal right as legitimate children — which also proves that in Iceland civilisation was advanced so much further than in Norway that bigamy was not lawful there, and its offspring not held legitimate. Each little estate was the kingdom in miniature, sometimes divided among children, and again reunited by succession of single successors by udal-born right vesting it in one. These landowners, with their entailed estates, old families, and extensive kin or clanship, might be called the nobility of the country, but that, from their great numbers and small properties, the tendency of the equal succession to land being to prevent the concentration of it into great estates, they were the peasantry.

In social influence they had no class, like the aristocracy of feudal countries, above them. All the legislation, and the administration of law also, was in their hands. They alone conferred the crown at their Things. No man, however clear and undisputed his right of succession, ventured to assume the kingly title, dignity, and power, but by the vote and concurrence of a Thing. He was proposed by a bonder; his right explained; and he was received by the Thing before he could levy subsistence, or men and aid, or exert any act of kingly power within the jurisdiction of the Thing. After being received and proclaimed at the Ore Thing held at Trondhjem as the general or sole king of Norway, the upper king — which that Thing alone had the right to do — he had still to present himself to each of the other district Things, of which there were four, to entitle him to exercise royal authority, or enjoy the rights of royalty within their districts.

The bonders of the district, who had voice and influence in those Things by family connection and personal merit, were the first men in the country. Their social importance is illustrated by the remarkable fact that established kings — as, for instance, King Olaf Tryggvason — married their sisters and daughters to powerful bonders, while others of their sisters and daughters were married to the kings of Sweden and Denmark. Erling the bonder refused the title of jarl when he married Estrith, the king's sister. Lodin married the widow of a king, and the mother of King Olaf Tryggvason.

[—1050 a.d.]

There was no idea of disparagement, or inferiority, in such alliances; which shows how important and influential this class was in the community.

The Absence of a Feudal Aristocracy

It would be a curious inquiry for the political philosopher to examine the causes which produced, in the tenth century, such a difference in the social condition of the Northmen and of the cognate Anglo-Saxon branch in England and Germany. Physical causes connected with the nature of the country and climate, as well as the conventional causes of udal right, and the exclusion of inheritance by primogeniture, prevented the accumulation of land into large estates, and the rise of a feudal nobility like that of Germany. The following physical causes appear not only to have operated directly in preventing the growth of the feudal system in the country of the Northmen, but to have produced some of the conventional causes also which concurred to prevent it.

The Scandinavian peninsula consists of a vast table of mountain land, too elevated in general for cultivation, or even for the pasturage of large herds or flocks together in any one locality; and although sloping gently towards the Baltic or the Sound on the Swedish side, and there susceptible of the same inhabitation and husbandry as other countries, in as far as clime and soil will allow, on the other side — the proper country of the Northmen — throwing out towards the sea all round huge prongs of rocky and lofty ridges, either totally bare of soil or covered with pine forests, growing apparently out of the very rock, and with no useful soil beneath them. The valleys and deep glens between these ridges, which shoot up into lofty pinnacles, precipices, and mountains, are filled at the lower end by the ocean, forming fjords, as these inlets of the sea are called, which run far up into the land, in some cases a hundred miles or more; yet so narrow that the stones, it is said, rolling down from the mountain slope on one side of such a fjord, are often projected from the steep overhanging precipice, in which the slope half-way down ends, across to the opposite shore. These fjords in general, however, are fine expanses or inland lakes of the ocean, — calm, deep, pure blue; and shut in on every side by black precipices and green forests, and with fair wooded islets sleeping on the bosom of the water.

These fjords are the peculiar and characteristic feature of Norwegian scenery. Rivers of great volume of water, but generally of short and rapid course, pour into the fjords from the Fielde, or high table-land behind, which forms the body or mass of the country. It is on the flat spots of arable land on the borders of these fjords, rivers, and the lakes into which the rivers expand, that the population lives. In some of these river-valleys and sea-valleys a single farm of a few acres of land is only found here and there in many miles of country, the bare rock dipping at once into the blue deep water, and leaving no margin for cultivation. In others, narrow slips of inhabitable arable land extend some way, but are hemmed in behind, on the land side, by the rocky ridges which form the valley; and they are seldom broad enough to admit of two rows of little farms, or even of two large fields, in the breadth between the hill-foot and the water; and in the length are often interrupted by some bare prong of rock jutting from the side-ridge into the slip of arable level land, and dividing it from such another slip. All the land capable of cultivation, either with spade or plough, has been cultivated from the most remote times; and there is little room for improvement, because it is the ground-rock destitute of soil, not merely trees or loose rocks encumbering the soil, that opposes human industry. The little estates, not averaging perhaps fifty acres each of arable land, are densely inhabited; because the seasons for preparing the ground, sowing, and reaping, are so brief that all husbandry work must be performed in the shortest possible time, and consequently at the expense of supporting, all the year, a great many hands on the farm to perform it. And the fishing in the fjord, river, or lake, the summer pasturage for cattle in the distant fielde-glens attached to each little estate in the inhabited country, and a little wood-cutting in the forest afford subsistence to many more people than the little farm itself would require for its cultivation in a better clime, or could support from its own produce. The extent of every little property has been settled for ages, and want of soil and space prevents any alteration in the extent, and keeps it within the unchangeable boundaries of rock and water.

It is highly interesting to look at these original little family estates of the men who, in the ninth and tenth centuries, played so important a part in the finest countries of Europe — who were the origin of the men and events we see at this day, and whose descendants are now seated on the thrones and in the palaces of Europe, and in the West have made a new world of social arrangements for themselves. The sites, and even the names, of the little estates or gaards on which these men were born remain unchanged, in many instances, to this day; and the posterity of the original proprietors of the ninth century may reasonably be supposed, in a country in which the land is entailed by udal right upon the family, to be at this day the possessors — engaged, however, now in cutting wood for the French or Newcastle market, instead of in conquering Normandy and Northumberland.

Some of the great English nobility and gentry leave their own splendid seats, parks, and estates in England, to enjoy shooting and fishing in Norway for a few weeks. They are little aware that they are perhaps passing by the very estates which their own ancestors once ploughed — sleeping on the same spot of this earth on which their forefathers, a thousand years ago, slept, and were at home; men, too, as proud then of their high birth, of their descent, through some seven-and-twenty generations, from Odin, or his followers, the Götar, as their posterity are now of having " come in with or before the Conqueror." The common traveller visiting this land destitute of architectural remains of former magnificence, without the temples and classical ruins of Italy, or the cathedrals and giant castles of Germany, will yet feel here that the memorials of former generations may be materially insignificant, yet morally grand. These little farms and houses, as they stand at this day, were the homes of men whose rude, but just and firm sense of their civil and political rights in society, is, in the present times, radiating from the spark of it they kindled in England, and working out in every country the emancipation of mankind from the thraldom of the institutions which grew up under the Roman Empire, and still cover Italy and Germany, along with the decaying ruins of the splendour, taste, magnificence, power, and oppression of their rulers. Europe holds no memorials of ancient historical events which have been attended by such great results in our times as some rude excavations in the shore-banks of the island of Vigerö,[1] in Möre — which are pointed out by the finger of tradition as the dry docks in which the vessels of Rolf Ganger, from whom the fifth in descent was our William the Conqueror, were drawn up in winter, and from whence he launched them, and set out from Norway on the expedition in which he conquered Normandy.

[1] Vigerö, the isle of Viger, is situated in Haram parish, in the bailiwick of Soud Mör.

[—1050 A.D.]

The philosopher might seat himself beside the historian amidst the ruins of the Capitol, and with Rome and all the monuments of Roman power and magnificence under his eye might venture to ask whether they, magnificent and imposing as they are, suggest ideas of greater social interest — are connected with grander moral results on the condition, well-being, and civilisation of the human race in every land, than these rude excavations in the isle of Viger, which once held Rolf Ganger's vessels.

It is evident that such a country in such a climate never could have afforded a rent, either in money or in natural products, for the use of the land, to a class of feudal nobility possessing it in great estates, although it may afford a subsistence to a class of small working landowners, like the bonders, giving their own labour to the cultivation, and helping out their agricultural means of living with the earnings of their labour in other occupations — in piracy and pillage on the coasts of other countries in the ninth century, and in the nineteenth with the cod fishery, the herring fishery, the wood trade, and other peaceful occupations of industry. On account of these physical circumstances — of a soil and climate which afford no surplus produce from land, after maintaining the needful labourers, to go as rent to a landlord — no powerful body of feudal nobility could grow up in Norway, as in other countries in the Middle Ages; and, from the same causes, now in modern times, during the four hundred years previous to 1814 in which Denmark had held Norway, all the encouragement that could be given by the Danish government to raising a class of nobility in Norway was unavailing.

Slavery even could not exist in any country in which the labour of the slave would barely produce the subsistence of the slave, and would leave no surplus gain from his labour for a master; still less could a nobility, or body of great landowners drawing rent, subsist where land can barely produce subsistence for the labour which, in consequence of the shortness of the seasons, is required in very large quantity, in proportion to the area, for its cultivation. We find, accordingly, that when the viking trade, the occupation of piracy and pillage, was extinguished by the influence of Christianity, the progress of civilisation, the rise of the Hanseatic League and of its establishments, which in Norway itself both repressed piracy and gave beneficial occupation in the fisheries to the surplus population formerly occupied in piracy and warfare, that class of people which had formerly been engaged all summer and autumn in marauding expeditions fell back upon husbandry and ordinary occupations; and the class of slaves, the thralls, was necessarily superseded in their utility by people living at home all the year. The last piratical expeditions were about the end of the twelfth century, and in the following century thraldom, or slavery, was, it is understood, abolished by law by Magnus the Law Improver. The labour of the slave was no longer needed at home, and would not pay the cost of his subsistence.

The Things

Physical circumstances also, and not conventional or accidental circumstances, evidently moulded the other social arrangements of the Northmen into a shape different from the feudal. The Things or assemblies of the people, which kings had to respect and refer to, may be deduced much more reasonably from natural causes similar to those which prevented the rise of a feudal class of nobles in Norway, than from political institutions or principles of social arrangement carried down from the ancient Germans in a natural state of liberty in remote ages. In every age and country, there are but two ways in which the governing class of a community can issue their laws, commands, or will, to the governed. One is through writing and by the arts of writing and reading being so generally diffused that in every locality one individual at least, the civil functionary or the parish priest, is able to communicate the law, command, or will of the governing to that small group of the governed over which he is placed.

The other way, and the only way where, from the nature of the soil and climate, the governed are widely scattered, and writing and reading are rarely attained, and such civil or clerical arrangement not efficient, was to convene Things or general assemblies of the people, at which the law, command, or will of the governing could be made known to the governed. There could be no other way, in poor, thinly inhabited countries especially, by which the governing, however despotic, could get their law, command, or will done; for these must be made known to be executed or obeyed, whether they were for a levy of men or of money, for war or for peace, for rewarding and honouring, or for punishing and disgracing — the law, command, or will must be promulgated.

The concurrence of a few great nobles could not here give effect to the royal command, law, or will; because the few, the intermediate link of a powerful aristocracy, were from physical causes — the poverty of the soil — totally wanting among the Northmen, and the kings had to deal direct with the people in great general assemblies or Things. The necessity of holding such general meetings or Things for announcing to the people the levies of men, ships, and provisions required of them, and for all public business, and the check given by the Things to all measures not approved of by the public judgment, appear in every page of the Heimskringla, and constitute its great value, in fact, to us, as a record of the state of social arrangement among our ancestors. The necessity of assembling the people was so well established that we find no public act whatsoever undertaken without the deliberation of a Thing; and the principle was so engrafted in the spirit of the people that even the attack of an enemy, the course to be taken in dangerous circumstances, to retreat or advance, were laid before a Thing of all the people in the fleet or army; and they often referred it to the king's own judgment — that is, the king took authority from the Thing to act in the emergency on his own plan and judgment.

A reference to the people in all that concerned them was interwoven with the daily life of the Northmen, in peace and in war. We read of "house Things," of "court Things," of "district Things," for administering law, of Things for consultation of all engaged in an expedition; and in all matters, and on all occasions, in which men were embarked with common interests, a reference to themselves, a universal spirit of self-government in society, was established. King Sverri, who reigned from 1177 to 1203, although taking his own way in his military enterprises, appears in a saga of his reign never to have omitted calling a Thing, and bringing it round by his speeches, which are often very characteristic, to his own opinion and plans.

So essential were Things considered, wheresoever men were acting with a common stake and interest, that in war expeditions the call to a Thing on the war-horn or trumpet appears to have been a settled signal-call known to all men — like the call to arms, or the call to attack; and each kind of Thing, whether it was a general Thing that was summoned, or a house Thing of the king's counsellors, or a herd Thing of the court, or of the leaders of the troops, appears to have had its distinct peculiar call on the war-horn known to all

Things with any power. The kings themselves appear to have been but Thingmen at a Thing.

THE LACK OF BUILDING MATERIALS

Two circumstances, which may be called accidental, concurred with the physical circumstances of the country, soil, and clime, to prevent the rise of a feudal nobility in Norway at the period, the ninth century, when feudality was establishing itself over the rest of Europe. One was the colonisation of

INTERIOR OF RADA CHURCH, VERMLAND

Iceland by that class which in other countries became feudal lords; the other was the conquests in England and in France by leaders who drew off all of the same class of more warlike habits than the settlers in Iceland, and opened a more promising field for their ambition abroad in those expeditions than in struggling at home against the supremacy of Harold Harfagr. In his successful attempt to reduce all the small kings, or district kings, under his authority, he was necessarily thrown upon the people for support, and their influence would be naturally increased by the suppression through their aid of the small independent kings.

This struggle was renewed at intervals until the introduction of Christianity by King Olaf the Saint; and the two parties appear to have supported the two different religions: the small kings and their party adhering to the old religion of Odin, under which the small kings, as godars, united the offices of judge and priest, and levied certain dues, and presided at the sacrificial meetings as judges as well as priests; and the other party, which included the mass of the people, supported Christianity, and the supremacy of King Olaf, because it relieved them from the exactions of the local kings and from internal war and pillage. The influence of the people, and of their Things, gained by the removal to other countries of that class which at home would have grown probably into a feudal aristocracy. In Iceland an aristocratic republic was at first established, and in Normandy and Northumberland all that was aristocratic in Norway found an outlet for its activity.

A physical circumstance also almost peculiar to Norway, and apparently very little connected with the social state of a people, was of great influence, in concurrence with those two accidental circumstances, in preventing the rise of an aristocracy. The stone of the peninsula in general, and of Norway in particular, is gneiss, or other hard primary rock, which is worked with difficulty, and breaks up in rough shapeless lumps, or in thin schistose plates; and walls cannot be constructed of such building materials without great labour, time, and command of cement. Limestone is not found in abundance in Norway, and is rare in situations in which it can be made and easily transported; and even clay, which is used as a bedding or cement in some countries for rough lumps of stone in thick walls, is scarce in Norway. Wood has of necessity, in all times and with all classes, been the only building material. This circumstance has been of great influence in the Middle Ages on the social condition of the Northmen. Castles of nobles or kings, commanding the country round, and secure from sudden assault by the strength of the building, could not be constructed, and never existed in Norway. The huge fragments and ruins of baronial castles and strongholds, so characteristic of the state of society in the Middle Ages in the feudal countries of Europe, and so ornamental in the landscape now, are wanting in Norway. The noble had nothing to fall back upon but his war-ship, the king nothing but the support of the people. In the reign of the English king Stephen, when England was covered with the fortified castles of the nobility, to the number, it is somewhere stated, of fifteen hundred, and was laid waste by their exactions and private wars, the sons of Harold Gille — the kings Sigurd, Inge, and Eystein — were referring their claims and disputes to the decision of Things of the people.

In Normandy and England the Northmen and their descendants felt the want in their mother-country of secure fortresses for their power; and the first and natural object of the alien landholders was to build castles, and lodge themselves in safety by stone walls against sudden assaults, and above all against the firebrand of the midnight assailant. In the mother-country, to be surprised and burned by night within the wooden structures in which even kings had to reside was a fate so common that some of the kings appeared to have lived on board ships principally, or on islands on the coast.

This physical circumstance of wanting the building material of which the feudal castles of other countries were constructed, and by which structures the feudal system itself was mainly supported, had its social as well as political influences on the people. The different classes were not separated from each other, in society, by the important distinction of a difference in the magnitude or splendour of their dwellings. The peasant at the corner of the forest could, with his time, material, and labour of his family at command, lodge himself as magnificently as the king — and did so. The mansions of kings and great chiefs were no better than the ordinary dwellings of the bonders. Lade, near Trondhjem — the seat of kings before the city of Trondhjem, or Nidaros, was founded by King Olaf Tryggvason, and which was the mansion of Jarl Hakon the Great, and of many distinguished men who were jarls of Lade — was, and is, a wooden structure of the ordinary dimensions of the houses of the opulent bonders in the district. Egge — the seat of Kalf Arneson, who led the bonder army against King Olaf which defeated and slew him at the battle of Stiklestad, and who was a man of great note and social importance in his day — is, and always has been, such a farm-house of logs as may be seen on every ordinary farm estate of the same size. The foundation of a few loose stones, on which the lower tier of logs is laid to raise it from the earth, remains always the same, although all the superstructure of wood may have been often renewed; but these show the extent on the ground of the old houses. The equality of all ranks in these circumstances of lodging, food, clothing, fuel, furniture, which form great social distinctions among people of other countries, must have nourished a feeling of independence of external circumstances — a feeling, also, of their own worth, rights, and importance among the bonders — and must have raised their habits, character, and ideas to a nearer level to those of the highest. The kings, having no royal residences, were lodged, with their court attendants on the royal progresses, habitually by the bonders, and entertained by them in regular turn; and even this kind of intercourse must have kept alive a high feeling of their own importance in the bonder class, in the times when, from the want of the machinery of a lettered functionary class, civil or clerical, all public business had to be transacted directly with them in their Things.

The lendermen, or tacksmen of the king's farms and revenues, could scarcely be called a class. They were temporary functionaries, not hereditary nobles; and had no feudal rights or jurisdiction, but had to plead in the Things like other bonders. As individuals they appear to have obtained power and influence, but not as a class; and they never transmitted it to their posterity.

Jarls, Churchmen, and Thingmen

The jarls or earls were still less than the lendermen a body of nobility approaching to the feudal barons of other lands. The title appears to have been altogether personal — not connected with property in land, or any feudal rights or jurisdiction. The jarls of Orkney — of the family of Rognvald jarl of Möre, the friend of Harold Harfagr, and father of Rolf Ganger — appear to have been the only family of hereditary nobles under the Norwegian crown exercising a kind of feudal power. The jarls of Möre appear to have been only functionaries or lendermen collecting the king's taxes, managing the royal lands in the district, and retaining a part for their remuneration. The jarls of Orkney, however, of the first line, appear to have grown independent, and to have paid only military service, and a nominal quit-rent, and only when forced to do so. This line appears to have been broken in upon in 1129, when Kala, the son of Koll, was made jarl, under the name of Jarl Rognvald. His father Koll was married to the sister of Jarl Magnus the Saint; but the direct male descendants of the old line, the sons of Jarl Magnus' brothers, appear not to have been extinct. In Norway, from the time of Jarl Hakon of Lade, who was regent or viceroy for the Danish kings when they expelled the Norwegian descendants of Harfagr, there appears to have been a jealousy of conferring the title of jarl, as it probably implied some of Jarl Hakon's power in the opinion of the people. Harold Harfagr had appointed sixteen jarls, one for each district, when he suppressed the small kings; but they appear to have been merely collectors of his rents.

The churchmen were not a numerous or powerful class until after the first half of the twelfth century. They were at first strangers, and many of them English. Nicholas Breakspear, the son, Matthew Paris tells us, of a peasant employed about the Benedictine monastery of St. Albans in Hertfordshire, and educated by the monks there, was the first priest who obtained any political or social influence in Norway. He was sent there, when cardinal, on a mission to settle the church; and afterwards, when elected pope, 1154, under the title of Adrian IV, he was friendly to the Norwegian people. His influence when in Norway was beneficialy exerted in preventing the carrying of arms, or engaging in private feuds, during certain periods of truce proclaimed by the church. The body of priests in the peninsula until the end of the twelfth century being small, and mostly foreigners from England, both in Sweden and in Norway, shows the want of education in Latin and in the use of letters among the pagan Northmen; and shows also the identity or similarity of the language of a great portion at least of England with that of the Scandinavian peninsula.

Several of the smaller institutions in society, which were transplanted into England by the Northmen or their successors, may perhaps be traced to the mode of living which the physical circumstances of the mother-country had produced. The kings having, in fact, no safe resting place but on board ship, being in perpetual danger, during their progresses for subsistence on shore, of being surprised and burned in their quarters by any trifling force, had no reluctance at all to such expeditions against England, the Hebrides, or the Orkney Islands, as they frequently undertook; and when on shore, and from necessity subsisting in guest-quarters in inland districts, we see the first rudiments of the institution of a standing army, or bodyguard, or body of hired men-at-arms. The kings, from the earliest times, appear to have kept a *herd*, as it was called, or court. The *herdmen* were paid men-at-arms; and it appears incidentally from several passages in the sagas that they regularly mounted guard — posted sentries round the king's quarters — and had patrols on horseback, night and day, at some distance, to bring notice of any hostile advance. We find that Olaf Kyrre, or the Quiet, kept a body of 120 herdmen, 60 giesters, and 60 house-carls, for doing such work as might be required. The standing armed force, or bodyguard, appears to have consisted of two classes of people. The herdmen were apparently of the class udal born to land, and consequently entitled to sit in Things at home; for they are called Thingmen, which appears to have been a title of distinction. The giester appears to have been a soldier of the unfree class; that is, not of those udal born to land, and free of or qualified to sit in the Things. They appear to have been the common seamen, soldiers, and followers; for we do not find any mention of slaves ever employed under arms in any way, or in any war expeditions. The giesters appear to have been inferior to the Thingmen or herdmen, as we find them employed in inferior offices, such as executing criminals or prisoners.

The victories of Sweyn, and Canute the Great, are ascribed to the superiority of the hired bands of thingmen in their pay. The massacre of the Danes in 1002, by Æthelred, appears to have been of the regular bands of thingmen who were quartered in the towns, and who were attacked while unarmed and attending a church festival. The herdmen appear not only to have been disciplined and paid troops, but to have been clothed uniformly. Red was always the national colour of the Northmen, and continues still in Denmark and England the distinctive colour of their military dress. It was so of the herdmen and people of distinction in Norway, as appears from several parts of the sagas, in the eleventh century.

Olaf Kyrre, or the Quiet, appears to have introduced, in this century, some court ceremonies or observances not used before. For each guest at the royal table he appointed a torch-bearer, to hold the candle. The butler stood in front of the king's table to fill the cups, which, we are told, before his time were of deer's horns. The court-marshals had a table, opposite to the king's, for entertaining guests of inferior dignity. The drinking was either by measure, or without measure; that is, in e ch horn or cup there was a perpendicular row of studs a⁺ qual distances, and each guest when the cup or horn was passed to him drank down to the stud or mark below. At night, and on particular occasions, the drinking was without measure, each taking what he pleased; and to be drunk at night appears to have been common even for the kings. Such cups with studs are still preserved in museums, and in families of the bonders. The kings appear to have wanted no external ceremonial belonging to their dignity. They were addressed in forms, still preserved in the northern languages, of peculiar respect; their personal attendants were of the highest people, and were considered as holding places of great honour. Jarl Magnus the Saint was, in his youth, one of those who carried in the dishes to the royal table; and torch-bearers, herdmen, and all who belonged to the court were in great consideration; and it appears to have been held of importance, and of great advantage, to be enrolled among the king's herdmen.

We may assume from the above observations, derived from the facts and circumstances stated in various parts of the *Heimskringla*, that the intellectual and political condition of this branch of the Saxon race, while it was pagan, was not very inferior to although very different from that of the Anglo-Saxon branch which had been Christianised five hundred years before, and had among them the learning and organisation of the church of Rome. They had a literature of their own; a language common to all, and in which that literature was composed; laws, institutions, political arrangements, in which public opinion was powerful; and had the elements of freedom and constitutional government. What may have been the comparative diffusion of the useful arts in the two branches in those ages? The test of the civilisation of a people, next to their intellectual and civil condition, is the state of the useful arts among them.

ARCHITECTURE AND THE BUILDING OF SHIPS

The architectural remains of public buildings in a country — of churches, monasteries, castles — as they are the most visible and lasting monuments, are often taken as the only measure of the useful arts in former times. Yet a class of builders, or stone-masons, wandering from country to country, like our civil engineers and railroad contractors at the present day, may have constructed these edifices; and a people or a nobility sunk in ignorance, superstition, and sloth may have paid for the construction, without any diffusion of the useful arts, or of combined industry, in the inert mass of population around. Gothic architecture in both its branches, Saxon and Norman, has evidently sprung from a seafaring people. The nave of the Gothic cathedral with its round or pointed arches, is the inside of a vessel with its timbers, and merely raised upon posts, and reversed. No working model for a Gothic fabric could be given that would not be a ship turned upside down, and raised on pillars.

The name of the main body of the Gothic church — the nave, navis, or "ship" of the building, as it is called in all the northern languages of Gothic root — shows that the wooden structure of the shipbuilder has given the idea and principles to the architect, who has only translated the wood work into stone, and reversed it, and raised it to be the roof instead of the bottom of a fabric. The Northmen, however, can lay no claim to any attainment in architecture. The material and skill have been equally wanting among them. From the pagan times nothing in stone and lime exists of any importance or merit as a building; and the principal structure of an early age connected with Christianity, the cathedral of Trondhjem, erected in the last half of the twelfth century, cannot certainly be considered equal to the great ecclesiastical structures of Durham, York, or other English cathedrals, scarcely even to that of the same period erected in Orkney — the cathedral of St. Magnus. We have, however, a less equivocal test of the progress and diffusion of the useful arts among the Northmen than the church-building of their Saxon contemporaries, for which they wanted the material. When we read of bands of ferocious, ignorant, pagan barbarians, landing on the coasts of England or France, let us apply a little consideration to the accounts of them, and endeavour to recollect how many of the useful arts must be in operation, and in a very advanced state too, and very generally diffused in a country, in order to fit out even a single vessel to cross the high seas, much more numerous squadrons filled with bands of fighting men. Legs, arms, and courage, the soldier and his sword, can do nothing here.

We can understand multitudes of ignorant, ferocious barbarians, pressing in by land upon the Roman Empire, overwhelming countries like a cloud of locusts, subsisting, as they march along, upon the grain and cattle of the inhabitants they exterminate, and settling, with their wives and children, in new homes; but the moment we come to the sea we come to a check. Ferocity, ignorance, and courage will not bring men across the ocean. Food, water, fuel, clothes, arms, as well as men, have to be provided, collected, transported; and be the ships ever so rude, wood-work, iron-work, rope-work, cloth-work, cooper-work, in short almost all the useful arts, must be in full operation among a people, before even a hundred men could be transported, in any way, from the shores of Norway or Denmark to the coasts of England or France.

Fixed social arrangements too, combinations of industry working for a common purpose, laws and security of person and property, military organisation and discipline, must have been established and understood, in a way and to an extent not at all necessary to be presupposed in the case of a tumultuous crowd migrating by land to new settlements. Do the architectural remains, or the history of the Anglo-Saxon people, or of any other, in the eighth or ninth century, and down to the thirteenth, give us any reasonable ground for supposing among them so wide a diffusion of the arts of working in wood and iron, of raising or procuring by commerce flax or hemp, of the arts of making ropes, spinning, and weaving sailcloth, preserving provisions, coopering water casks, and all the other combinations of the primary arts of civilised life, implied in the building and fitting out of vessels to carry three or four hundred men across the ocean, and to be their resting place, refuge, and home for many weeks, months, and on some of their viking cruises even for years? There is more of civilisation, and of a diffusion of the useful arts on which civilisation rests, implied in the social state of a people who could do this, than can be justly inferred from a people quarrying stones, and bringing them to the hands of a master builder to be put together in the shape of a church or castle.[h]

THE VIKINGS

But however great the progress which the Northmen may have attained in the arts of civilisation, they were at this time themselves the terror of the whole of the civilised west.*a* As the bellicose tendencies with which their religion was impregnated were a product of the national spirit, so a doctrine which proclaimed personal valour as the highest of virtues, and cowardice as the most shameful of vices must in return contribute powerfully to nourish the inherent taste for war and make it take root. The thirst for glory and the hope of booty were the two strongest passions which animated the people of the North, and to satisfy them they shrank neither from difficulties nor perils. Danger, on the contrary, stimulated their courage, since the greater the peril the greater the glory, and he who succumbed covered with honourable wounds enjoyed, in Valhalla, the greatest happiness it were possible to imagine, and his memory was perpetuated on earth in the songs of the skalds. To die on a bed of sickness was the greatest misfortune that could fall to the lot of a Scandinavian hero, for this kind of death was dishonourable and shut him out

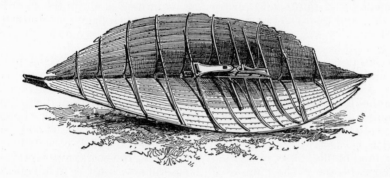

REMAINS OF VIKING SHIP FOUND IN NORWAY

from the joys of Valhalla. It was, therefore, not unusual that an old warrior, after having vainly sought death in battle, would pray one of his friends to run him through with his sword, or by some kind of a violent death end an existence which no longer had any charm.

This contempt for life was so strongly rooted in the Northern spirit that the mother herself silenced her solicitude for her children rather than to assure their welfare at the price of the slightest dishonour. There is a tale of a northern chief who consulted his mother to know whether it were not better to retire before a much stronger enemy. She replied: "If I had thought that thou wouldst live forever, I would have had thee swathed in wool. Know that life depends on destiny; it were better to die with honour than to live in shame."

Accustomed from childhood to a rude mode of life and a nutriment which developed their strength, they were in a condition to support easily the hardships of war, while the consciousness of their own valour made them brave every peril of land and sea. The limits of the fatherland were often too narrow for youth, eager for glory and perilous adventure, and therefore they sought in foreign countries a more extensive area for their wild exploits. Their ruling idea did not, moreover, allow any honourable man to remain inactive at home; if he would gain the esteem of his fellows and the love of women he must scour the world and acquire reputation and wealth abroad.

Besides this the northern countries were poor and sterile, producing barely enough for the needs of their people; so necessity and inclination joined to develop the barbaric custom of piracy, which made the Northmen so dreaded and at the same time so famous. Each spring numerous bands left the shores of the fatherland and cruised in every sea, pillaging merchant ships and ravaging the coasts. These terrible vikings spared nothing; if a captive escaped death, he found himself reduced to slavery, and his property was considered legitimate spoil. Yet all vikings were not alike — some made a profession of piracy and spent almost their whole life upon the sea with no dwelling on shore except perhaps some tiny fortress by the sea, as a safe place of deposit for their loot. It is of these that it has been said, "They never slept under a smoke-blacked roof, nor ate and drank at any hearth." Their mode of life and their manners were as savage as their profession was cruel, if we are to believe what the sagas recount of some of them — that they drank blood and ate raw meat; but there were also vikings of another kind, who, instead of disturbing the peaceful merchant, protected him and sought glory in pursuing and fighting the fierce pirates — asking of the merchant only what they and their companions absolutely stood in need of, after which they went their way in peace. Hjalmar, the viking, declares for example: "I shall never take from the merchant or the peasant more than what I need to maintain my crew, and then shall pay its value. I shall never let a woman be robbed, however rich she may be, and if one of my men does violence to a woman or brings her on shipboard against her will, he shall pay for it with his life, be he of high or low degree."

The vikings did not confine themselves to northern parts, but at an early date ventured into more distant seas, penetrating even to the countries of southern Europe which attracted them by their fertility and wealth, and whose inhabitants, more civilised, but less hardy, were able to offer but feeble resistance to the impetuous bravery of the Northmen. England, where social order, commerce and agriculture had been developed at an early date and had spread prosperity and wealth among the inhabitants, was the first to be exposed to the incursions and ravages of the Danes; while Scotland and Ireland were principally visited by the Norwegians who, under the name of "Eastmen," established separate kingdoms in these lands and later on extended their dominion over the north of Great Britain. But the Normans (as the southerners called all the vikings that came from northern latitudes, whether they were Danes, Norwegians, or Swedes) spread the terror of their name into countries still farther south. All the south and west coasts of Europe, Flanders, France, Portugal, Spain, Italy, and Greece were ravaged and pillaged by the terrible Normans. Even the sunburnt peoples of Africa learned to know the power of the North. At one time almost the whole of France was conquered by them; from the south, west, and north they ascended in their shallow vessels the great water-courses and joined their forces in the centre of the country. The city of Paris was taken, plundered, and sacked; and the capital of Christendom, Rome, barely escaped the same fate.

The people of these lands, too weak to repel the foreign invaders by the sword, in their distress sought with gold and silver to make them withdraw; but this only encouraged the rapacious bands to return very soon. Foreign chroniclers of this age have left terrible descriptions of the cruelties and horrors which the Normans perpetrated during their expeditions. The river valleys and the most beautiful and fertile tracts of country were changed into deserts where one could travel great distances without meeting a single living being. Children and old people were massacred in cold blood or thrown living into the flames of their burning homes. Women were maltreated and men put to death or reduced to slavery. But it was principally the churches, cloisters, and other sacred edifices, with their inmates, the nuns, monks, and priests, which were the object of the fury, insults, and outrages of the still pagan Normans, whose natural cruelty was mixed with hatred of religion. During the ninth and tenth centuries these piratical excursions increased in so astounding a manner that it seemed as if the entire South would inevitably become the prey of the innumerable viking bands which poured out of the North as if a great migratory movement were taking place by sea. The reason for this increase was in part the demoralised condition the Frankish Empire had then reached owing to dissensions among the worthless successors of Charlemagne. It was therefore an easy thing for the bold Normans to make great progress, and after some of them were established in a place new bands were soon drawn thither in the hope of meeting with equal success.

To this reason must be added an important change which the North was at that time undergoing. During these same centuries the numerous little kingdoms of Denmark, as well as Norway and Sweden, were being united into great states, and Christianity began to be propagated throughout these lands and to supplant the old religions. Many chiefs lost their possessions, and there were besides numbers of discontented ones who, sincerely attached to the religion of their fathers and the old customs, could not accommodate themselves to the new order of things. They preferred, therefore, to abandon their fatherland rather than their religion and the unrestrained freedom to which they were accustomed. By their emigration they augmented the already numerous bands of the vikings. The expeditions now assumed a different character. The Normans no longer sought only to plunder and pillage, they hoped also to establish permanent settlements to replace the fatherland they had lost. It was not until after Norman states had been set up in Normandy, Italy, Russia, and elsewhere, and after the union of the petty kingdoms and the introduction of Christianity had somewhat dried up the flow by bringing peace and order to the north — it was not until then that the movement began to abate, and Europe was delivered from the scourge which, for centuries, had desolated its fairest lands.*g*

CHAPTER III

NORWAY TO THE UNION OF KALMAR

[1050–1397 A.D.]

MAGNUS I TO THE DIVISION OF THE KINGDOM

MAGNUS, whom the Norwegians had called to the throne in place of the unpopular Svend, was a bastard son of that odd saint Olaf by his concubine Alfhilda. He accompanied his father in the exile to Holmgard, and there he remained during that father's unfortunate expedition to Norway. Left an orphan, he was well entertained by his host, the grand prince of Russia. Here he received intelligence of the unpopularity of Svend, and of the anxiety with which his return was expected. Proceeding to Sweden, he was honourably received by the Swedish monarch; and a small but resolute band of armed men accompanied him into Norway. As he passed the mountains into Trondhjem, the adherents of Svend fled in great alarm towards the southern provinces; and Svend himself followed the example. In his progress, Magnus received many evidences of the popular good will. At the capital, his reception was enthusiastic. To the Thing assembled on the occasion flocked a multitude of men friendly to his cause; and there he was solemnly elected king.

The first care of Magnus I was to reward his followers by conferring on them the governments which had been held by Svend's adherents. His next was to collect troops and march against his rival. To assert his rights, the latter, who was then in Hadaland, sent out the arrow of war in every direction; and many hastened to his summons. In the midst of the assembly, he asked whether they were ready to join him in resisting Magnus. Some expressed their consent; some openly refused; the greater number hesitated: but disaffection to his cause was so evident in the great body that he declared his resolution of seeking more faithful defenders. Leaving Norway, he repaired to Denmark, where, that very year, he died. Harthacnut son of Canute the Great claimed the crown of Norway; but hostilities were closed by the singular compact that if either died without children, he should succeed to the states of the other.

Astrida, the widow of St. Olaf, had accompanied Magnus into Norway; and such had been the aid she had procured him that he gratefully settled her in his palace, showing her the utmost honour. But, at the same time, he sent for his mother Alfhilda, whom he treated with more affection but with less honour. Indignant at this distinction, she insisted on more than an equality, which Astrida being unwilling to grant, the two ladies could no longer reside in the same house. In his kingdom Magnus had more influence than in his palace; he effectually restored tranquillity, and became popular. Of his deceased father miracles were reported. The mere report was enough: he pretended to believe it; he well knew what honour would be his through his descent from a saint; and he caused the relics of the royal martyr to be placed in a magnificent casket, and displayed for the veneration of the faithful.

On the death of Harthacnut, Magnus, in accordance with the compact which had been made between them, proceeded in Denmark, to take possession of the throne. His claim was admitted by his new subjects.c But he had to contend with two enemies, Svend, nephew of Canute the Great, and Harolda Hardrada, his own cousin. The history of his wars and agreements with these two princes will be related in connection with the history of Denmark.a

The demise of Magnus immediately followed his successful expedition in Denmark to avenge a rebellion of Svend. The son of a saint could scarcely leave the world without some manifestation of divine favour. In a dream his father Olaf appeared to him, and ordered him to make his choice between two proposals — either to die and join the deceased king in heaven, or to live the most powerful of monarchs yet commit some crime for which he could hardly expect the divine forgiveness. He instantly chose the former alternative; and was immediately afflicted with a disease the result of which, to the great sorrow of his people, was fatal. He was a great and good prince; as much superior to his father in intellect and moral worth as one man can be to another. That he was not without ambition is evident; and as the heir of the Danish throne, by his compact with Harthacnut, king of England and Denmark, he claimed, after that monarch's death, all the states of the great Canute. Edward the Confessor returned a spirited reply, the justice of which he acknowledged by his inactivity.

By the death of Magnus the Good (1047) Harold Hardrada was the undisputed king of Norway. He aspired also to the throne of Denmark, from which he endeavoured to unseat his former ally Svend. But in 1064 peace was made, no permanent advantage having been gained by either.

On the death of Edward the Confessor (1066), and the accession of Harold the son of Earl Godwin, the Norwegian monarch led an armament against the English sovereign. The ambition which could prompt him to such an undertaking was not very measured; but it was characteristic of this king, whose early familiarity with danger and whose wild adventures in the East and North had rendered him confident of success. If the English were not favourable to Earl Godwin's son, they could scarcely be so to the king of Norway, and the hope of conquest, when so valiant a competitor as William of Normandy was entering the field, would have appeared futile to any less desperate man. The result is known to every reader of English history: at Stamford Bridge Harold Hardrada found a grave.

From the fatal shores of England Olaf III (Kyrre the Quiet), the son of Harold, returned to Norway (1066), and with his brother Magnus II was elected to the government. The former had the eastern, the latter the northern provinces of the kingdom. In three years Magnus paid the common debt, and Olaf became monarch of the whole (1069). The reign of Olaf was pacific; and he applied his efforts to the civilisation of his kingdom. He first introduced chimneys and glass windows into houses: he established a commercial emporium at Bergen; and to him we must ascribe the introduction of guilds or mercantile fraternities, after the model of those existing in Germany and England. He must be praised, too, for his humanity to the servile class: he carried in the national Thing a law that in every district throughout Norway a serf should be annually enfranchised. To the church he was a munificent patron. At Trondhjem he began to build a stone cathedral destined to receive the hallowed relics of his ancestor. "This city," says Adam of Bremen [b] the contemporary of Olaf Kyrre, "is the capital of the Northmen. It is adorned with churches, and frequented by a great concourse of people. Here lies the body of the holy king and martyr Olaf, at whose tomb miracles are daily wrought: here, from the most distant nations, pilgrims flock to his shrine to share in his blessed merits. Hitherto there are no fixed limits to the dioceses in Norway and Sweden. Any bishop, when desired by the king and people, may build a church in any district, and govern those whom he converts to the day of his death." These regionary bishops, as they are called, moved from place to place, baptising and preaching as they went along.

Magnus III, surnamed Barfod, or the Barefoot, succeeded his father Olaf III (1093). At first, he was acknowledged by the southern provinces: in the northern was opposed to him Hakon, nephew of the late king. Though death soon rid him of that rival, an army only could induce those provinces to receive him. This was the first Norwegian monarch after St. Olaf that visited the Orkneys. He went to punish the jarls of those islands, which had thrown off their allegiance to the yoke of Norway. These jarls were Erling and Paul, whom he took and sent prisoners to his kingdom. Leaving his son Sigurd in the government, with fit councillors, he laid waste Sutherland, which was a portion of the jarldom, and feudally dependent on the Scotch crown. Proceeding to the Hebrides, he reduced them also. Very different was his conduct at Iona from that which had been pursued by his pagan ancestors. He showed great veneration for the memory of St. Columba, and great affability to the inhabitants of all the islands that submitted. Islay was next reduced, then Kintyre.

These successes were followed by depredations on both the Irish and Scottish coasts. Most places offered little resistance, but the conquest of Anglesea could not be effected without a battle. Two Welsh chieftains, both named Hugh, fought stoutly for their independence. One, Hugh the Magnanimous, was so encased in armour that his two eyes only were visible: Magnus shot an arrow into one eye, a Norwegian warrior wounded the other; after a valiant struggle victory declared for the Northmen. The whole island, we are told, acknowledged the king; but this statement will obtain little credit with any reader. The truth seems to be that he made some of the chiefs do homage for their respective domains; but they reasserted their independence the moment he had left the shores. There is more probability in another statement of the northern chroniclers that he forced Malcolm of Scotland to cede to him the sovereignty over all the islands, from the Orkneys to Man. From this expedition he returned in 1099. Its results were valuable: the Hebrides and the Orkneys were now his. The possession of the former indeed was short-lived and precarious; but the latter were long subject to his successors.

The next war of this restless prince was with his neighbour Yngve, king of Sweden. It arose from a dispute as to the boundary, and raged for two years with varied success until, through the mediation of Eric king of Denmark, peace was restored. On this occasion, Magnus married the princess Margaret, daughter of Yngve (1101). Within a year from this pacification, Magnus, whose enterprise was excited by his late successes, again sailed for Ireland, with the design of subjugating, if not the native kings, those who were of Scandinavian origin. At this period the island contained several of these principalities. Landing on the coast of Connaught, the king of which, Murdoch, was his acquaintance and ally, he effected a junction with that chief, and subdued the kingdom of Dublin. The following winter he spent in Connaught; and when spring arrived he embarked to return.

As he slowly passed along the Ulster coast, he sent a party of his followers in search of provisions, that is, of plunder. Their stay being much longer than he had expected, he landed with a small body, and with difficulty made his way through the marshes. Being at length joined by the foragers, he was returning to his ships, when he fell into an ambush prepared for him by the natives. He was easily known by his shining helmet and breastplate, and by the golden lion on the red shield — the device of the Norwegian kings. Ordering one of his chiefs with a body of archers to clear the marsh, and from the other side to gall the enemy with their arrows, so as to cover his passage also, he fought with desperation. Unfortunately, the chief on whom he thus relied fled, and was followed by the rest. Magnus, therefore, with a mere handful of men, had to sustain the hostile assaults of a multitude. All that valour could do was effected by him; but the contest was too unequal; and, after receiving several wounds, he fell. His followers retreated, leaving his corpse in the hands of the enemy. Thus perished a monarch whose valour and constancy rendered him equal to the ancient heroes of the North. By the warlike he was beloved; but with the people at large, whom he taxed heavily to defray the expenses of his frequent expeditions, he was no favourite. His character may be best conceived from the reply which he gave to his courtiers, who expressed their apprehension lest his continued wars should prove fatal to him — " It is better for a people to have a brave than an old king."

THE KINGDOM IS DIVIDED; THE EXPLOITS OF SIGURD I

On the death of Magnus III (1103), Norway was divided between his three sons. Sigurd had the southern provinces, with the Scottish islands, which he governed by his jarls. Eystein I reigned over the North. Olaf IV had the central and eastern provinces. All were children at their accession: the eldest, Eystein, was but fifteen; and Olaf was so young that for some years his portion of the monarchy was administered by his elder brothers.

Of these kings, two may be dismissed with little notice. Eystein was distinguished for prudence, and for the useful structures with which he adorned his portion of the kingdom. He erected stone churches and palaces, which were novelties in the North. He was well versed in history and

the laws, and was the patron of literary men, especially of the skalds.   Olaf
was the best beloved of the three; but he died in 1116, and his dominions
were divided by his brothers.   Eystein was never at open war with Sigurd
but the two brothers could scarcely be warm friends; and while we read of
their disputes, we are surprised that there should have existed so much
tranquillity in the realm.   In 1122 he breathed his last, and Sigurd was monarch of Norway.

The name of Sigurd I is celebrated in the annals of the North alike for
his pilgrimage to Jerusalem [which won him the name of Jorsallafari], and
his exploits during the voyage.   To aid in the recovery of the holy places
from the hands of the infidels might enrich an adventurous monarch, and
would surely open to him the gates of heaven.   Influenced by this two-fold
advantage, and by the hope of booty on the passage, Sigurd, with sixty
ships, sailed from the North.   During the first winter he remained in England, and was hospitably entertained by Henry I.   The second winter, at
least the greater part of it, he passed near the shrine of Santiago in Galicia:
he was a pilgrim, no less than a champion of the cross.   On his way to Lisbon, he captured some infidel privateers, and destroyed several Moorish
settlements on the coast, especially one at Cintra.   All who refused baptism
he put to the sword.   Lisbon, according to the Northern chroniclers, was
divided into two parts, one inhabited by the Moors, the other by the Christians.   The former he assailed, took it, and with much booty proceeded
through the straits of Gibraltar in quest of new adventures.   Having passed
these straits, he conquered a whole fleet of the infidels, and this was the fifth
battle since he left Norway.   In vain did the Mohammedan pirates on the
African coast resist him: his valour overcame everything.

Landing in Sicily, he was magnificently entertained by Roger, sovereign
of the island, who had expelled the Saracens.   Roger was of Norman descent:
he remembered the land of his sires; and so far did he carry his good will
as to insist on serving Sigurd at table.   Continuing his voyage, he landed at
Acre, and proceeded to Jerusalem, where the offer of his sword was most
welcome to Baldwin.   From that king he received what he thought a valuable treasure — a fragment of the true cross, which he promised to deposit
in the shrine of St. Olaf.   He promised too, at the instance of his new friends,
to establish an archi-episcopal see in Norway, to build churches, and to
enforce the payment of tithe.   His last exploit in these regions was to join
in the siege of Sidon; and when that city was taken half the booty became
his.   On his return through Constantinople, his reception by the Greek
emperor was a noble one; but much of what the northern annalists relate
bears the marks of invention.   Such are the opening of the golden gate; the
carpeting of the streets; the three large presents made him by Alexius, with
their immediate distribution among the followers of Sigurd; and the gift by
the latter of his sixty ships to Alexius.   Such fables may gratify a northern
imagination; but history can only say that in 1111 the king arrived in Norway after an absence of four years.

That this remarkable expedition redounded greatly to the honour of
Sigurd is certain: he was thenceforth much venerated throughout the North.
He married, and attended to the duties of government, especially to the
extirpation of idolatry.   His expedition (undertaken at the request of the
Danish king) against the inhabitants of the isle of Småland, was one con-
genial to his feelings.   They had received Christianity, but, like many
other portions of the Scandinavian population, had returned to idolatry.
Great was the punishment inflicted by Sigurd and his ally Nicholas on the

pagans whom they had vanquished; but mercy to infidels, and still less to apostates, formed no portion of their creed.

In his latter days, Sigurd seems to have occasionally lost the use of his reason, or perhaps he was visited by some bodily infirmity which gave him the appearance of insanity. But he never relinquished the duties of royalty. One of his last cares was to fortify Konghella on the river Göta, to ornament it with a fine Gothic church, and to place in that sacred edifice some of the pictures which he had brought from the East. But with all his attachment to the church, he was not without his delinquencies. Of these one of the most noted was his dismissal of his queen to make room for a concubine, Cecilia by name, whom he resolved to marry. A great entertainment was provided for the occasion, and many were the guests assembled at Bergen. The bishop of the district, hearing of the intention, hastened to the town, and expostulated with the king on the guilt of dismissing one wife to take another, when there was no charge against the former, and consequently no way of annulling the marriage. Great was the wrath of Sigurd, who held a drawn sword in his hand, and who, at one moment, seemed disposed to use it on the neck of the prelate. If he so far restrained his passion as to walk away, he persevered in his design, and the union was celebrated. The truth is that his heart was so fixed on the maiden that no earthly consideration could induce him to abandon her.

Some time afterwards he was afflicted with his last illness, which was regarded by many as the judgment of heaven on his crime. His courtiers urged him to dismiss her; and she, out of regard for him — to save him from renewed guilt — really wished to leave him. Such was the attachment he bore her that he could not give his consent to the separation. She departed, however, and with her departed the only solace which had been left him. In a few days he was no more. Previously to his death, he had caused his son Magnus to be recognised as his successor, and had prevailed on the states to swear that they would obey him.

THE ANARCHY OF THE TWELFTH CENTURY

From the death of Sigurd I (1130) to the union of Norway with Denmark, there is little in the history of the former country to interest us. During the whole of the twelfth century we perceive nothing but anarchy and bloodshed occasioned by disputes for the throne. In a country where illegitimacy was no bar to the succession, and where partition of the sovereign power was frequent, there could not fail to be numerous candidates. Sigurd I was succeeded by his son Magnus IV, to whom, as we have related, the estates of the realm had sworn fealty before the death of Sigurd.

How little dependence could be placed on such a guarantee soon appeared. In the reign of the preceding monarch, an adventurer, Harold Gilchrist, or Gille, had asserted — probably with justice — that he was a natural son of King Magnus Barfod. As he could produce no satisfactory proof of that connection, recourse was had to the decision of heaven, and he was made to pass over nine red-hot ploughshares. This ordeal, merely to prove his parentage, was thought to be severe; but he shrank not from it, and led by two bishops he sustained it unhurt. To resist the divine pleasure was impossible, and Harold's claim was allowed even by Sigurd, on the condition that he would not insist on the advantage to which his relationship entitled him, before the death of his son Magnus IV. Scarcely, however, had this Magnus succeeded to the throne, than Harold came forward to assert his right; and from the number no less than the influence of those who espoused his interests (among them were the kings of Denmark and Sweden), he had everything to hope from a civil war. In this emergency, Magnus consented to a division of the kingdom, the very year of his accession.

Harold IV (1130–1152) was very different in character and manners from his colleague Magnus. He was mild as the latter was severe, and generous as the latter was penurious. He therefore became the favourite of the people. This circumstance probably roused the jealousy of Magnus, who at the head of many followers marched against him, conquered him, and compelled him to forsake the realm. Repairing to the court of Eric Emun, king of Denmark, he was well received by that monarch, "because they were brothers-in-arms." With the supply of money and men furnished him by his generous host, he returned to Denmark, and surprised rather than defeated Magnus, whom he consigned to a monastery and deprived of eyesight (1134). He was now therefore monarch of Norway. But his reign was of short duration. The town of Konghella which Sigurd had fortified, and adorned with so magnificent a church, was taken by the Wend pirates: it was completely sacked, and the inhabitants were led into captivity. For this disaster, Harold was censured: he was accused of inactivity in repelling the invaders; and was even forsaken by the great body of his supporters. In this condition he was assassinated. A melancholy illustration of the spirit of the times is afforded by the fact that the assassin, Sigurd,[1] also claimed Magnus Barfod for his father. From this deed of blood he derived no advantage. The nation would not admit his claim, but proclaimed two sons of the murdered king, Sigurd II (1136–1155) and Inge I (1136–1161).

Both, however, were children; and their inability to defend themselves led to civil war. Sigurd, their reputed uncle, the assassin of their father, raised troops and laid waste the country. To strengthen his party he formed an alliance with Magnus the Blind, whom he drew from the monastery; but he was defeated and compelled to flee. Both soon obtained the aid of the Danish king Eric; but fortune was still unfavourable: in battle, Magnus lost his life; and the restless Sigurd too was made prisoner, and subsequently executed. Though two enemies were thus removed, the royal brothers, Sigurd and Inge, were often at discord; and a third firebrand was soon added in Eystein II (1142–1157), a younger brother, who, returning from Scotland in 1142, was invested with a third portion of the realm. There was not, nor could there be, any tranquillity in the country. Complaints, recriminations, quarrels, treachery, bloodshed succeeded each other, when the arrival of a papal legate, the cardinal Albano, suspended for a time the sanguinary proceedings of these princes.

The Mission of Nicholas Breakspear; Renewed Warrings

This legate was Nicholas Breakspear, an Englishman, who subsequently ascended the pontifical throne as Adrian IV. His mission was two-fold — to restore peace between the unnatural brothers, and to establish an archbishopric. The Norwegian monarchs had long demanded a primate of their own, instead of being dependent on the archbishops of Lund. In both objects he was successful. The three kings laid down their arms; united in showing the highest deference to the legate; and beheld with joy the creation of a metropolitan see at Trondhjem, with a jurisdiction, not over

[1 The story of Sigurd forms the subject of one of Björnsen's plays, the trilogy, Sigund Slemve.

Norway merely, but Iceland, Greenland, the Faroe Islands, the Shetlands, the Orkneys, the Hebrides, and Man. In return, the chiefs and people readily agreed to pay the tribute of Peter's Pence.

Many were the reforms which this well-meaning dignitary endeavoured to carry out. He introduced more decorum into the public worship; he enjoined the clergy to attend more to their proper functions, and to interfere less in secular matters; and impressed on the new archbishop the necessity of a rigorous control over the morals of his flock. In attempting to enforce clerical celibacy, he did not meet with so ready an acquiescence; but no one dared openly to resist him. To another of his measures we must award a much higher meed of praise. Seeing that bloodshed had for many reigns stained the proceedings of the Landsthing, or provincial assembly, he prevailed on the chiefs to promise that they would not in future attend with arms. Even the king was to be accompanied only by twelve armed men — an exception conceded less to his dignity than to the necessity under which he lay of enforcing the judicial sentences. "In several other respects," observes Snorre [speaking of the legate], "he reformed the customs and manners of the people during his stay; so that never did stranger come to the land more honoured or more beloved by the princes and their subjects."

If the ascendency of the cardinal had restored peace, his departure was immediately followed by new struggles between two of the brothers. Eystein had no share in them, because he absented himself on a piratical expedition. He is said to have ravaged the eastern coasts of Great Britain, from the Orkneys to the Humber. Soon after his return, he entered into a plot with Sigurd to remove their brother Inge. In 1155, Sigurd and Inge met in the Thing held at Bergen, and though they could not fight, for want of arms, both they and their followers regarded one another with deadly hatred. Scarcely was the assembly dissolved, when Inge, who had heard of the plot for removing him, determined to prevent it by assailing Sigurd, and after a sharp contest the latter fell. The following year Inge and Eystein, who were still hostile, met to agree on conditions of peace; but it was a truce rather than a peace, and in a few months it was broken by both parties. They marched towards each other with the resolution of deciding their quarrel by the sword; but Eystein, who was unpopular, was deserted by most of his followers, and compelled to seek an asylum in the mountains of Vikia. Thither he was pursued by Inge, was betrayed in a forest, and put to death by one of his brother's myrmidons.

By this deed therefore Inge was the monarch of the country. But he had soon a competitor in Hakon III, son of Sigurd II, whom the party of Eystein proclaimed king (1157). The four succeeding years were years of civil war. Hakon, a mere child, was driven into Gothland. The following season he returned and besieged Konghella; but he was again defeated and forced to re-enter Sweden. Yet early in 1159 he arrived at Trondhjem, where he found adherents. With thirty vessels he laid waste the coasts which held for Inge; but in a great naval battle he was defeated by that king, though not without considerable loss to the victor. Repairing into Trondhjem, where he passed the winter, he prepared for the next campaign. It was not decisive; but in 1161 Inge, betrayed by his own followers, fell in battle with Hakon.

By this event Hakon, it might be expected, would be left undisputed sovereign of Norway. But the Norwegians at this period seem to have had little wish for a monarchy; and Magnus V (1162-1186) was raised by the party of the deceased Inge to the throne of the North. Magnus was the grandson of Sigurd I, and one of his duties in the opinion of the times was to revenge the murder of his kindred. As, however, he was but a child, the government was administered by his father Erling. Erling was, by marriage, a kinsman of the Danish monarch, from whom he obtained aid to resist the hostility of Hakon. Through that aid he was victor; Hakon fell (1162), and consequently Magnus was the only king left. A rival indeed, Sigurd a son of Sigurd II, was opposed to him; but in little more than a year that rival was crushed by the indefatigable Erling.

To confirm the authority of his son by religious sanction, Erling requested the primate to crown him. The archbishop consented on the condition that Norway should be regarded as a fief of St. Olaf; that on the death of every monarch the crown was to be formally offered to the saint in the cathedral; that the saint's representative, the archbishop of the time, should receive it; that from each diocese the bishop, the abbots, and twelve chiefs, should assemble to nominate a successor, and that the sanction of the primate should be necessary before anyone could be lawful king of Norway. That a considerable reduction in the number of electors was politic cannot be disputed; and probably this was one of the reasons that induced the archbishop to introduce so extraordinary an innovation. But a greater no doubt, was the superiority which the church would thereby acquire over the state. The proposal was accepted; and Magnus, then only eight years of age, was solemnly crowned by Eystein in presence of the papal legate (1164).

The aid furnished by the Danish king was not gratuitous. In return for it Erling had promised the province of Vikia (Vigen), and Valdemar (the first of that name) now demanded the fulfilment of that pledge. His position was a critical one. He had not power to transfer that province, and if he attempted that transfer, his own destruction and that of his son must be the result. Yet if he did nothing, he must expect an encounter with that formidable monarch. To escape from this dilemma, he convoked the states, and laid before them the proposition of Valdemar: they indignantly refused to receive the Danish yoke. Open war followed, but through the policy of Erling it was soon succeeded by peace. He secretly engaged to hold Vikia with the title of jarl as a fief of Denmark; and, in the event of a failure of issue in his son, to subject the whole kingdom to the same crown.

Neither the sanction of the church, nor the vigour of his father, nor even his own virtues could except Magnus from the common lot of Norwegian kings — open rebellion and rivalry for the throne. The next who troubled his tranquillity was Olaf, a grandson of Eystein II. Proclaimed king by the Uplanders, Olaf had the glory to defeat the regent; but in his turn he was defeated, and compelled to flee into Denmark, where he died the following year (1169).

The next was a more formidable rival, in the person of Eystein, a prince of the same family. Placing himself at the head of the discontented, the banished, the proscribed, this prince became a bandit chief, and laid waste the provinces on the borders of Sweden. As the number of his followers increased, so did his boldness, until with a small fleet he sailed for Trondhjem which he subdued. Here he persuaded or forced the people to elect him king (1176). The following year he penetrated into the central provinces, which had the option of either doing homage or of experiencing all the evils of desolation. In 1177, four years after the commencement of his adventurous career, he met Magnus in the field, and was defeated. His followers hastened into Sweden, the eastern provinces of which were still pagan, and but loosely connected with the crown. He was less fortunate: he was slain in his flight.

Sverri's Conquest and Rule

Of a different character from either of the preceding, and more successful in his object, was the next adventurer, Sverri, whose career is one of romance. His mother, Alfhilda, had been the concubine of Sigurd II; and he was the issue of the connection. After Sigurd's death, she became the wife of a smith — a business of high repute in the North — and removed, with her husband and son, to the Faroe Isles. Young Sverri was designed for the church, and on reaching the age of twenty-five he entered into holy orders. Now, for the first time, his mother acquainted him with the secret of his birth.

Far more wisely would she have acted by keeping it in her own bosom; for no sooner did the young priest know it, than he indulged in dreams of ambition. As our sleeping are but the images of our waking thoughts, he had a dream which seemed to prognosticate his future greatness. He mentioned it to a friend, who promised him the archbishopric of Trondhjem. But he had no relish for the ecclesiastical state; and he mentally interpreted it in a different way. Urged by ambition, he left the obscure isles in which he had been so long imprisoned, and repaired to the court of Magnus. His learning and his martial appearance made a favourable impression on the regent Erling; and he too so admired the vigorous administration of that chief, that in despair of effecting a revolution, he withdrew into the Swedish province of Vermland. Probably his design was to subsist by plunder, in the service of one of those predatory bands, so frequent on the confines of the two kingdoms. At first, however, his prospects were gloomy; and in his restlessness, he had resolved to go on a pilgrimage to Jerusalem, when the band which Eystein had commanded solicited him to become their chief. After some hesitation he consented, was invested with the royal title, and enabled to take the field.

The early efforts of this adventurer were bold but unsuccessful. In an expedition through the southern provinces he was indeed joined by some hundreds of followers, mostly bandits; but when he proceeded towards the north, where Magnus and Erling had their seat of government, he was abandoned by most of his adherents: the enterprise was too desperate even for them. With great difficulty did he save himself by penetrating through the mountain passes into Vermland. To escape the pursuit of his enemies, no less than to recruit his numbers, the following spring he plunged into the vast forests of the modern Dalecarlia, then called Jarnberaland, or the Iron-being land. The inhabitants knew little of Swedish kings, or of the rest of the world, or of Christianity; but they knew the value of freedom; and in the apprehension that he came to deprive them of it, they prepared a stout resistance. He had no difficulty, however, in persuading those sons of the forest, the mountain, and the river, that he had no design against them — that he wanted hospitality, guides, and troops. Of the last he seems to have obtained none; but he was well entertained, and conducted into Jämtland, where this little band was recruited. The hardships which he underwent in this expedition — cold, hunger, fatigue — made him resolve to attempt some enterprise, the success of which would rescue him from this wretched mode of life. Appearing suddenly before Trondhjem, he hoped to surprise the place; but he was repulsed, and again forced to seek a refuge in the mountains.

His next object was to increase the number of his followers; and as he, or some about him, were well acquainted with the haunts of the banditti in the trackless forest, and the inaccessible cavern, he obtained a considerable accession. But a hardy band of peasant archers from Telemarken was his most valuable acquisition. Reappearing before the gates of the capital, he defeated the little army of Magnus, and captured the banner of St. Olaf. As both king and regent were at Bergen, their usual place of residence, he pushed his way into the city, assembled the inhabitants of the province, and was proclaimed king! His task, however, was not half accomplished. A numerous party, including all the churchmen, adhered to Magnus; and he was soon expelled from Trondhjem, to seek a shelter in his mountain fastnesses. But with these revolutions he was now familiar: he knew how to recruit his forces — to advance when there was a prospect of victory — retreat when the danger was evident. During two years the civil war raged with violence, and the alternations of triumph and defeat succeeded each other with rapidity.

At length Sverri suddenly descended from the mountains, and defeated the regent and his son, leaving the former dead on the field. Magnus fled, but only to return with another army. The second battle, however, was not more fortunate than the first; his army was annihilated or dispersed, and he was glad to seek a refuge in Denmark, while the archbishop fled to England. By the Danish monarch Magnus was supplied with an armament, with which he again contended for the throne, but with no better success. A second time he repaired to that country for aid, and again he fought with the usurper. As on the two former occasions, victory declared for Sverri: his rival fled, and perished in the waves. He was not one of those savage chieftains in whom ancient Norway rejoiced, and whom some of her modern sons would have us mention with respect. If his soul had not been much improved by religion, it had been humanised by education. To the followers of Magnus he exhibited great clemency. He caused the fallen monarch to be magnificently interred in the cathedral of Trondhjem; and he himself, in conformity with ancient custom, pronounced the funeral oration of the deceased, to whose virtues, now that he had no reason to fear them, he paid the sincere homage of praise.

Sverri (1186–1202) thus obtained the object of his ambition; but he could not expect to hold it in peace. In fact, the whole of his reign was a struggle to preserve what he had so painfully gained. From England Archbishop Eystein hurled the thunders of the church at the head of the apostate priest; but the promise of the king, that he would lay his case before the pope, and submit to such penance as his holiness might impose, induced the primate to return and resume his metropolitan functions. Much of his attention was employed on the enlargement and improvement of his cathedral, which he wished to vie with the most splendid Gothic edifices in Europe. From the king he derived considerable aid towards this end; but he lived only to finish the choir. The rest was completed by Archbishop Sigurd, in 1248. It was then a very respectable structure. The high altar, which was adorned with a costly silver shrine containing the relics of St. Olaf, and which was visited by pilgrims from all parts of the North, had a splendid appearance. Sverri no doubt expected that by his liberality on this occasion he should win over to his government the great body of the clergy; but he refused to hold the crown as a feudatory of St. Olaf, that is, of the primate; and this rebellion cancelled all his other merits. Aware of the influence which the primate exercised over the people, he endeavoured, on the death of Eystein, to obtain the election of a successor favourable to his views; but in defiance of his influence, that successor was one of his enemies, Eric bishop of Stavanger, who had been the warm friend of Erling and Magnus.

[1186–1202 A.D.]

From the hands of the new primate he solicited the ceremony of the coronation; but Eric refused, and for so doing he has been severely censured. It should, however, be remembered that he could not crown an excommunicated prince. That penalty Sverri had incurred by various crimes — by forsaking the altar without the leave of his diocesan, by the shedding of blood at the head of banditti, by assuming the crown without secularisation, and by taking a wife. No bishop, no metropolitan could absolve him: the pope only was competent to dispense with the authority of the canons. In revenge for this refusal, Sverri endeavoured to curtail the revenues and patronage of the church. He insisted that its claim to the pecuniary fine in case of homicide should be abolished, and that the fine should revert to the crown. He also attempted to usurp the patronage of the church. Eric supported with firmness the rights of the church, and by so doing incurred the royal displeasure to such a degree that he was compelled to flee into Denmark. From thence he appealed to the pope, who threatened to place the kingdom under an interdict, unless satisfaction were made to the church. In vain did Sverri endeavour to prove that the pope had no right to interfere in such cases: the canons, he well knew, taught a different doctrine. In vain did he attempt to make the multitude believe that the blindness with which the archbishop was visited during the dispute was owing to the wrath of heaven. The people had more confidence in the primate and in the pope than they had in a monarch whose early career had not been the most edifying.

Convinced by experience how little was to be gained by struggling with the formidable power which humbled the greatest monarchs, Sverri now applied to the pope for absolution and pardon. He was directed, in the first instance, to make his peace with the archbishop, who alone could intercede for him. Incensed at the reply, and fearful lest the people should desert him because he had not been crowned, he convoked his bishops, and prevailed on one of them — a mere court tool — to perform the ceremony. To anoint an apostate priest would not have been within the bounds even of papal authority: penance and absolution were previously indispensable; but neither was exacted, and if they had been the censure could only have been removed by the supreme pontiff. The bishop who performed a ceremony in its very nature null was excommunicated; and the king's own excommunication was confirmed. In this emergency, Sverri convoked an Althing at Bergen, where a resolution was passed to send deputies to Rome to procure his absolution. On their return they all died in Denmark — no doubt through poison. They brought no absolution; but a confirmation of the former sentence. For this instrument the king, who was capable of any act, substituted another, which contained a plenary remission, and which he declared was the one brought from the head of the church. To account for the death of his messengers, he asserted that they had been poisoned by his enemies lest the papal absolution should reach him. The benefits of this deception he could not long hope to enjoy. The pope charged him with both the forgery and the murder, and placed the whole kingdom under an interdict. Even the bishop, Nicholas, who had crowned him, now escaped into Denmark, to join the metropolitan; and both were nobly entertained by Archbishop Absalon, primate and minister of that kingdom.

During these transactions with the church, Sverri was twice compelled to enter the field against claimants for the crown. The first was Sigurd, son of Magnus V, who had taken refuge in the Orkneys. Accompanied by a band of adventurers, Sigurd landed in Norway, and was joined by many of the peasantry. But Sverri had a body of men whose valour was unequalled, and whose fidelity was above all suspicion — men whom he had commanded before his accession, to whom he was indebted for the throne, and whom he had transformed from robbers into good soldiers. With them he triumphed over Sigurd, whose corpse rested on the field. The next adventurer was supported by Bishop Nicholas, who was anxious to ingratiate himself with his metropolitan and the pope, by exhibiting uncommon zeal in the destruction of the king. His name was Inge, and he was represented by his patron as a son of that same Magnus. When he and the bishop landed, they were joined by a considerable number of the discontented; but the king, who had obtained archers from England, was better prepared than even on the former occasion to defend his authority. Still the struggle was a desperate one; several battles were fought, and two or three victories were necessary to humble the hopes of the assailants.

In the midst of these struggles, after a whole life passed in fomenting rebellion or crushing it, Sverri breathed his last at the age of fifty-one. That he was a man of great genius and of commanding character is evident from his unparalleled success. Whether he was really the son of a Norwegian king is extremely doubtful; but, even if he were, he had none of the advantages which the relationship generally ensures. His fortune was the result of his own enterprising powers. Few indeed are the characters in history who have risen from so obscure to so high a station against obstacles so great; fewer still who, in the midst of perpetual dangers, have been able to maintain themselves in that station. In both respects he is almost unequalled. On the whole, he may safely be pronounced one of the most extraordinary men of the Middle Ages.

Before the death of his father, Hakon IV (1202-1204) had been saluted as heir of the monarchy; and he ascended the throne without opposition. One of his first acts was to recall the primate, the rest of the bishops, and all whom his father had exiled. In return the interdict was removed from the realm; and prosperity was returning to a country so long harassed by civil wars when the young king died.

THE DYNASTY IS CONTINUED UNDER HAKON V

Guthrum (1204-1205), a grandson of Sverri, was next raised to the throne; but his reign was only a year, and there seems to be little doubt that he was removed by poison, through the contrivance of a faction which hoped to restore the ancient line of kings. In consequence of this event, Inge II (1205-1207), a grandson, on the female side, of Sigurd II, acceded; but in two years he too descended to the tomb, whether violently or in the order of nature is unknown. The death of four princes in five years is a melancholy illustration of the times.

There now remained only one male descendant of this dynasty — Hakon, a natural son of Sverri. After his father's death, and during the struggles between the old and the new dynasty for the supreme power, this prince was secreted in the mountains. Fortunately for him, the companions of his father, the devoted Birkebeinar, the bandit soldiers, still remained: they espoused his cause, and procured his election to the throne. Before the church, however, would ratify the election, the mother, Inga, was required to undergo the ordeal of hot iron, in proof of her having truly sworn to the paternity of her son. She consented; was shut up in a church to prepare by fasting and prayer for the trial; was guarded night and day by twelve armed men; and the burning-iron left no wound on her fair hand. Whoever doubted that the ordeal was a fair one, that Hakon was the offspring of Sverri, was menaced with excommunication.

Hakon V, who bears in history the surname of "the Old," was thus the recognised monarch of the country; but he had still to sustain the hostility of the faction which adhered to the former dynasty. The most inveterate as well as the most powerful of his enemies was Skule the jarl, half-brother of Inge II. To pacify this ambitious noble, he was admitted to a share in the government; and his daughter became a wife of Hakon. This union, in effecting which the church had a great share, was expected to combine the hearts of both factions. But the hope was vain: other pretenders to the legitimate or illegitimate honour of royal descent appeared in succession to claim a portion of their birthright. So distracted was the country by these conflicting claims that a great council of the nation was convoked at Bergen. The decision was that Hakon was the only lawful king. Yet through the advice of the primate, whose object was evidently to avert a civil war, the northern provinces were confided to Skule; and by the king he was soon adorned with the ducal title — a title which had been in disuse ever since the ninth century.

But this ambitious noble was not to be silenced by benefits. On a memorable day (1240) he convoked the states of his own government to assemble in the cathedral: his descent from the martyr Olaf was then attested by oath on the relics of that saint; and by his party, amidst the silence of the spectators, he was declared the lawful heir to the crown, as the successor of Inge II. Constrained by the example, the rest did homage to him after he had sworn to administer the laws in righteousness, as his holy predecessor had administered them. Thus the northern provinces were again dissevered from the monarchy. But Hakon was true to his own rights and the interests of his people. Assembling his faithful Birkebeinar, and all who valued the interests of his order, he marched towards Trondjhem. At his approach, the usurper fled into the interior, but only to collect new forces, with which he obtained some advantages over those of Hakon. When spring returned, however, and the latter marched against the rebels, fortune declared for him. Skule was signally defeated, compelled to flee, overtaken, and killed.[1]

Released from the scourge of civil war, Hakon now applied his attention to the internal government of his kingdom. He made new treaties of commerce with the neighbouring powers: he fortified his sea-ports; he improved the laws; he made salutary changes in the local administration. But he was not yet fully at peace with the church; and he requested Innocent IV to mediate between them, and to cause the crown to be placed on his brow. Innocent despatched a legate, the cardinal bishop of Sabina, for this purpose. At first the king was desired to comply with the law of his predecessor Magnus V — that Norway should hereafter be regarded as a fief of St. Olaf: but he had the patriotism to refuse: he would protect, he observed, the just rights of the church, but he would never sanction this domination of the ecclesiastical over the secular state. His firmness was respected, and at the cardinal's instance he was crowned without subscribing to the obnoxious compact. He had gratified that churchman by promising to go on the crusade; but though he made preparations circumstances prevented his departure. His kingdom indeed could not safely be left at such a crisis.

[1] It is this early period of Hakon's history which Ibsen has celebrated in the drama translated into English under the name of *The Pretenders*.

His frontiers were still subject to ravage from the licentious bands who infested the western provinces of Sweden, and who took refuge in either territory when pursued by the injured inhabitants of the other. Without a cordial union between the two governments, there could be no hope of extirpating these predatory bands. Fortunately Birger, the regent of Sweden, concurred with him in his object.

To create a good understanding between the two countries, a marriage was negotiated between the daughter of Birger, whose son was on the throne of Sweden, and Magnus, the eldest son of Hakon. But this union was never effected: the subsequent conduct of Birger was not agreeable to the monarch; and Magnus married the daughter of Christopher, king of Denmark. The clemency of Hakon led to this connection. He had many causes of complaint against Denmark; and he did not resort to hostilities until he had long and vainly sued for redress. He soon reduced Christopher to long for peace; but with a generosity of which there are few records among kings, he forgot his wrongs in sympathy for his brother monarch, and became the friend of the man whom he had left Norway to chastise.

The last and by far the most memorable expedition of Hakon was against the Scots. The chief incentive to this war was the attempt of Alexander III to recover the Hebrides, which, as we have before observed, had been subdued by Magnus Barfod. Not that they were then subdued for the first time. The truth is that they had frequently been reduced to the Norwegian yoke as far back as the ninth century, and from that time had, at intervals, paid tribute to that power. More frequently, however, they had asserted their independence. Colonies, too, from the mother-countries, had assisted to people those islands, which Harold Harfagr and his successors had regarded as no less a dependency than the Shetlands or the Orkneys. In the time of Magnus the number of those colonists increased; and there were not a few nobles of the isles who could trace their pedigree to the royal line of Norway.

But their position drew them into the sphere of Scottish influence: to Scotland, and not to the distant North, they must look for allies in their frequent wars with one another; and the eagerness of the Scottish monarchs to establish their feudal superiority over them brought the two parties into continual communication. In 1244, two bishops arrived in Norway to induce Hakon to renounce all claim to the Hebrides. They told him that he could have no just right to them, since Magnus Barfod had only gained possession of them by violence — by forcibly wresting them from Malcolm Canmore. The king replied with more truth that Magnus had not wrested them from the Scottish king, but from the Norwegian Gudred, who had thrown off the allegiance due to the mother country. Defeated in their historical arguments, they had recourse to one which with a poor monarch they hoped would be more convincing — the pecuniary argument. They besought him to say what sum he would demand for their entire cession. "I am not so poor that I will sell my birthright!" was the reply, and the prelates returned. Alexander III, however, would not abandon the hope of annexing these islands to his crown; and he commenced a series of intrigues among the Highland chieftains. The vassals of Hakon began to complain of the vexatious hostilities to which they were subject, especially from the thane of Ross, and to beg immediate aid. The atrocities which they detailed we should scarcely expect to find in a Christian people and in the thirteenth century: we should rather assign them to the period when the pagan Northmen ravaged the coasts of these islands. In great anger Hakon convened a diet at Bergen, and it resolved that the aid required should be immediately furnished.

Leaving his son, prince Magnus, regent of the kingdom, Hakon sailed for the Hebrides (1263). In the Orkneys he was joined by the jarls and by the king of Man. On the western coast of Scotland, many of the Highland chieftains submitted to his arms. But though he took Arran and Bute, and laid waste many of the western districts of the continent with fire and sword, his expedition was a disastrous one. At the mouth of the Clyde, while landing his troops, a tempest arose and forced him from the shore; and those who were landed were overpowered by the superior number of the enemy.[1] In vain did Hakon endeavour to lead the rest of his forces with the view of saving the brave men who were thus overwhelmed: the storm was too powerful for him; some of his ships were lost; more were dispersed; and in great anguish of mind he repaired to the Orkneys where he intended to winter, and invade Scotland the ensuing spring.

That spring he was never to see. A fever, the result of anxiety no less than of fatigue, laid him on the bed from which he was no more to rise. The activity of his mind, however, was not arrested even by fatal disease; he caused the Bible and the old sagas to be read to him night and day. When convinced that there was no hope of his recovery, he dictated his last instructions to his son; made liberal presents to his followers; confessed and received the sacrament; and "at midnight Almighty God called him from this world, to the exceeding grief of all present and of all who heard of his death." His body was first interred in the cathedral of St. Magnus, Kirkwall, but subsequently removed to Bergen, and laid with those of his royal ancestors.

MAGNUS VI (1263–1280 A.D.)

Magnus VI (1263-1280), who had been crowned during his father's life, now ascended the throne. He had the wisdom to make peace with the Scots, by ceding to them all the islands off their coast except the Orkneys, but not in full sovereignty. For these he was to receive 4,000 marks, and an annual tribute of 100 marks. At the same time Margaret, the daughter of Alexander, was betrothed to the son of Magnus. The islands ceded had never produced any benefit to the crown: to maintain them would have entailed a ruinous expenditure of money and blood. But the Orkneys, though frequently independent, had been so long connected with the mother country, and lay so much nearer, that though their preservation might bring no great advantage they were useful as nurseries for seamen. In the reign of Magnus, too, Iceland became thoroughly dependent on the Norwegian crown.

Internally, the reign of this prince exhibits considerable improvement. One of his most serious objects, (which had also been his father's) was to establish, on fixed principles, the succession to the throne. As in other European countries, that succession was now made to depend on the law of primogeniture, in the male line only. To this regulation the bishops gave their assent; and, in accordance with it, they not merely recognised Eric as the successor of Magnus, but crowned that prince. Hence they no longer insisted on the obnoxious compact between Magnus V and the primate of that day. It is indeed true that in return for their sanction of this new and fundamental law of succession, they obtained some favours; but most of them related

---

[1 There is considerable difference between the Scotch and Scandinavian accounts of this battle, and the loss sustained is variously computed. By the Scots it was remembered under the name of the battle of Largs as a glorious victory won by a sovereign to whose reign they looked back with pride and regret from the stormy years of civil war which followed.]

to their own matters. They were excepted, for instance, from the secular tribunals; but so they were in every other country in communion with Rome. But when each prelate claimed the right of coining money, and of maintaining a body-guard of forty men-at-arms, he surely forgot his spiritual character, and remembered only that he was a temporal baron.

This reign, too, witnessed some other changes. The allodial proprietors became vassals: the old jarls and hersers were replaced by dukes and barons and knights; feudal usages were introduced in lieu of the ancient national customs. As a necessary consequence the small landed proprietors began to disappear, and to be replaced by farmers. Still in the national character there was that which prevented the worse evils of feudality. If the peasant had no longer a voice, or we should rather say a vote, in the assembly of the estates, except by representation, he yet continued to be free, and to bear arms. In the cities and towns of the kingdom there was also a modification of the old system. In proportion to the increase of commerce, and to the prosperity of the great dépôts, was that of municipal rights. These rights were, as much as possible, assimilated to those of the German towns. For the two important cities of Bergen and Trondhjem, Magnus himself drew up a code of regulations, to define the rights of the guilds and of the different classes of burghers. And for the defence of the coasts he revived the ancient act of division of the maritime districts, each of which was to furnish a certain number of ships, and to maintain its beacon fire, so that intelligence of an invasion might speedily fly throughout the country. But the fame of this monarch chiefly rests on his legislative talents: hence his surname of Lagabætr, or "law-mender." He compiled from the centenary observances of the four Norwegian provinces a code which he designed for general use throughout his dominions.

ERIC II (1280–1299 A.D.)

Eric II, while yet a minor, succeeded his father without opposition; but his reign (1280-1299) was not one of peace. His first disputes were with the church. At his coronation, he promised rather to amplify than to curtail its privileges. In virtue of this promise, the archbishop of Trondhjem drew up a list of offences against the canon laws, and claimed for the clerical tribunals the pecuniary mulcts demanded on such occasions. These mulcts were considered the right of the crown, and as such were claimed by royal councillors, on behalf of the king. So far the conciliations were justifiable; but when they persuaded him to revoke all the privileges which his father had conceded, they wantonly perilled the tranquillity of the kingdom. They were excommunicated by the primate, who in his turn was banished. Both parties appealed to Rome; but the pope seems to have been a moderate man; and, though not disposed to surrender any rights which the church universal possessed, he doubtless saw that the Norwegian branch of it had usurped some that were inconsistent with civil government. The successor of the primate consented to abandon one or two of the more obnoxious claims, and to become the liege vassal of Eric. The king too was embroiled with Denmark, through the protection which he afforded to the assassins of Eric Glipping. Long and disastrous was the war which raged between the two countries. At length, both opened negotiations for peace; but it was not signed during the life of Eric.

These disputes with the church and his royal neighbour prevented Eric from engaging in another war for which he might have urged a better reason.

In conformity with the treaty between his father and Alexander III, he married Margaret of Scotland. The issue was a daughter, who, on the death of her grandfather, in 1289 (her mother was no more), was undoubted heiress to the throne of that kingdom. The English king, Edward I, proposed a marriage between his son and the Maid of Norway. The proposal was readily accepted by Eric; but before it could be carried into effect, the princess died in the Orkneys. If Eric exposed himself to ridicule in claiming the Scottish crown in her right, he had an indisputable claim to his queen's dowry, most of which had never been paid. For this cause he might have troubled the kingdom; and he had another reason for interference. His second wife was Isabel, daughter or sister of Robert Bruce, whose pretensions he might have supported against those of Baliol. But he declared for neither party — a degree of moderation, as we have intimated, attributable rather to his disputes with the church and with Denmark, than to any other cause.

HAKON VI (1299–1319 A.D.)

As Eric the Priest-hater left no heirs male, he was succeeded by his brother Hakon VI (1299-1319), whom he had created duke of Norway, and who had been admitted to some share in the government. One of his first objects was to resume the negotiations with Denmark; but through the intrigues of the men who were implicated in the murder of Eric Glipping, the signature of the treaty was delayed until 1308. His transactions with Sweden are more important, since they led to a temporary union between the two crowns. His daughter Ingeburga became the wife of Eric, brother of Birger, king of Sweden. When Eric was barbarously murdered by his own brother, Hakon armed to revenge the death of his son-in-law. After a war of some duration, Birger was compelled to abdicate, and Magnus the son of Ingeburga, was elected in his place. As Hakon had no heirs male, and females could not inherit, Magnus became the heir of the Norwegian throne, to which he succeeded on the death of Hakon.

Under this prince, who died in 1319, Norway was not so powerful as it had been under his father: just as in his father's time it was not to be compared with what it had been under the domination of Hakon V. With this monarch indeed ended the greatness of the kingdom: from his time to the union of the crown with that of Denmark, there was a continued decline in the national prosperity. One reason is to be found in the wars between the kingdom and Denmark — wars which thinned the population, diminished the national revenues, and aimed a fatal blow at the national industry. A second is the monopoly of trade by the Hanse Towns. The vessels of that league had long frequented the coasts of Norway; Sverri had favoured them; Hakon V in 1250 had conferred upon them exclusive privileges; Magnus VI had established the foreign merchants in his dominions, especially at Bergen. Hakon also exempted them from many of the imposts to which they were subject in other countries.

These avaricious strangers did not benefit the country. The advantage was entirely in favour of these foreigners, who absorbed a traffic which ought to have been divided into many channels, and by their monopoly excluded the natives from other markets. In this respect, we must condemn the short-sighted policy of Hakon, or rather perhaps the engrossing disposition of the league. But another reason may also be assigned for the decline of the national prosperity — the increase of luxury — the creation of artificial wants. The cardinal bishop of Sabina had expressed surprise at the condition of the people: he had found not merely the comforts but the luxuries of life. After the visit of that dignitary, the evil was not mended. The monarchs were fond of displaying a splendour which richer and more extensive kingdoms could not well support; and as the example of the court is sure to be followed by all who visit it, we may form some notion of the progress which luxury made amongst the people.

On the death of Hakon, as we have already intimated, the throne of Norway fell to his grandson Magnus VII (1319-1343), king of Sweden. In 1343 Magnus resigned the Norwegian sceptre to his son Hakon VII (1343-1380). This prince, as we have before observed, married Margaret, the daughter of Valdemar IV, king of Denmark, and died in 1380. He was succeeded in both thrones by his infant son Olaf (the fifth of Norway, the third of Denmark), on whose death both Denmark and Norway were ruled by Queen Margaret.

At this period the close connection of the three northern kingdoms can be explained only by reverting to the history of Sweden.c But meantime this is a convenient place to glance at the affairs of that interesting dependency of Norway, the uniquely situated little territory of Iceland.a

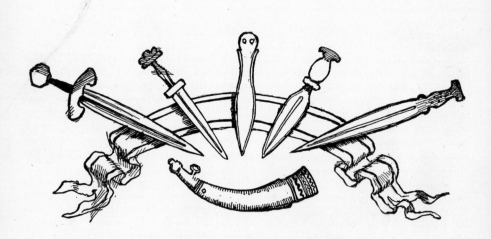

CHAPTER IV

ICELAND

[874–1275 A.D.]

PERMANENT SETTLEMENT OF ICELAND BY THE NORWEGIANS

Ingolf, the first settler of Iceland had found a refuge there in 874; he was followed by other illustrious exiles from Norway, who found in the enjoyment of liberty and independence a full compensation for the toils and hardships they were compelled to endure. The habitable parts of the island thus became in a few years entirely peopled by a Norwegian colony, among whom were several of the descendants of the Ynglings or ancient kings of Norway and Sweden, supposed to be the posterity of Odin. The manner in which this new society was formed and organised may be best illustrated by the story of a single individual.

We have selected for this purpose that of Rolf, or Thorolf, as it is told in the *Eyrbyggja*[b] and other sagas. This chieftain resided in the northern parts of Norway, and, like all the other petty kings and chiefs of the country, was the pontiff of religion as well as the patriarchal head of his clan. Rolf presided in the great temple of Thor, the peculiar national deity of Norway, in the island of Mostur, and wore a long beard, from which he was called Thorolf-Mostrar-skegg. Thorolf had incurred the resentment of king Harold Harfagr, by giving an asylum to Björn, one of Thorolf's relations, who was persecuted by that monarch. Harold held an assize or *Thing*, and proclaimed Thorolf an outlaw, unless he surrendered himself with Björn into the king's hands, within a limited period. Thorolf offered a great sacrifice to his tutelary deity, and consulted the oracle of Thor, whether he should surrender himself to the king or migrate to Iceland, which had been settled by Ingolf ten years before. The response of the oracle determined him to seek an asylum in this remote and sequestered island.

He set sail, carrying with him the earth upon which the throne of Thor had been placed, the image of the god, and the greater part of the wooden work of his temple. He took also his goods, his slaves and his family. Many friends followed him. When the vessel approached the southwestern coast of Iceland, and entered the Maxe-Fjord, the adventurer cast into the sea the columns of the sanctuary, on which the image of the god was carved, intending to land wherever they should be carried by the winds and waves. He followed them to the northward round the promontory of Snæfellsness, and entered the bay on the other side, to which, from its extreme breadth, he gave the name of Breidi Fjord. Here Thorolf landed, and took formal possession of that part of the coast in the ancient accustomed manner, by walking with a burning firebrand in his hand round the lands he intended to occupy, and marking the boundaries by setting fire to the grass. He then built a large dwelling-house on the shores of what was afterwards called the Hofs-vog, or Temple Bay, and erected a spacious temple to Thor, having an entrance door on each side, and towards the inner end were erected the sacred columns of the former temple, in which the *regin-naglar*, or nails of the divinity, were fastened. Within these columns was a sanctuary, on which was placed a silver ring, two ounces in weight, which was used in the ministration of every solemn oath, and adorned the person of the pontiff-chieftain in every public assembly of the people. The basin for receiving the blood of the sacrifices was placed by the side of the altar, with the instrument of sprinkling, and around it stood, in separate niches, the images of the other deities worshipped by the people of the North.

The assize, or *Herjar-thing*,[1] of the infant community was held in the open air near this temple, and the oaths of the jurors and witnesses were sanctioned amidst the blood of sacrifice, by a solemn appeal to the national deities: "So help me Freyr, Njord, and the all-mighty As [that is, Odin]!" The site of the temple and the place of popular assembly were both considered consecrated ground, not to be defiled with blood, nor polluted with any of the baser necessities of nature. A tribute was established and collected by Thorolf from all the members of his little community, to defray the expenses of the temple and the worship there maintained.

The infant settlement thus commenced was soon strengthened by the arrival of Björn the fugitive outlaw, on whose account Thorolf was compelled to leave his native country. Each freely chose his several habitation according to his own pleasure, and the new colony soon became divided into three separate districts, each of which at first acknowledged the authority of Thorolf as supreme pontiff. At last dissensions broke out among the inhabitants, and the sacred spot was polluted with blood shed in their feuds, which were prosecuted with deadly fury. But it is unnecessary to pursue the narrative any further, as sufficient has been stated to enable the reader to form a general notion how these little communities were founded, with their public institutions partaking at once of a patriarchal, pontifical, and popular form of government, but not extending beyond the limits of the narrow valley in which they were established, and but imperfectly adapted to secure the blessings of public order.

In the space of about sixty years the habitable parts of this great island were occupied by settlers from Norway, notwithstanding that King Harold

---

[1] *Thing* signifies in the ancient language of the North a popular assembly, court of justice, or assize : *Al-thing*, a general meeting of that kind, and *Alls-herjar-thing*, the general convention of chiefs, nobles, or lords. The diet of Norway is called to this day the *Stor-thing*, a great assembly.

had endeavoured to discourage the spirit of emigration by imposing a severe penalty upon those who left his dominions for this purpose. They brought with them both the religious and the civil institutions of their native land. The chieftains, who led each successive company, were, like Thorolf, the patriarchal rulers, and the religious pontiffs of their tribe. They brought with them not only their families and domestic slaves but a numerous retinue of dependents. These may more properly be called clients than vassals, since their relation to their chieftains was more like that of the Roman plebeian to his patron than of the feudal vassal to his lord. The followers were elevated far above the class of slaves by the possession of personal freedom and property, but they resorted to the protection of the aristocracy, as the natural judges of their controversies in peace and their leaders in war.

The chieftains who bore the principal part of the expense of these expeditions naturally appropriated to themselves the lands, which they afterwards granted out to the poorer colonists, upon the payment of a perpetual rent and a sort of tithes for the maintenance of religious rites. To this was sometimes superadded a hereditary personal jurisdiction over the client and his posterity, which partook somewhat more of the feudal relation. The chieftains who thus formed this patriarchal aristocracy were called *godar* or *hof-godar*, because they performed the public offices of religion, as well as the functions of civil magistracy. And it is very remarkable that, even after the introduction of Christianity into the island, the bishops continued for some time to exercise civil jurisdiction under the sacred name of godar — such is the force of habit over the minds of a rude people in the union of secular and ecclesiastical authority.

THE POLITICAL ORGANISATION OF ICELAND

The pontiff-chieftains of the various little communities, among which the island was divided, had at first no common umpire, and the evils growing out of their dissensions and the animosities engendered between so many rival tribes or clans rendered it at last imperiously necessary to combine these separate societies by some kind of fundamental law. On this occasion the Icelanders, like the people of the ancient Greek republics, resorted to the wisdom of a single legislator, and confided to him the task of providing a remedy for the disorders of their infant state. Ulfljot, who was the object of their choice, undertook a voyage to Norway, in his sixtieth year, to acquire a more perfect knowledge of the legal customs and institutions of the parent country (925). Here he sat for three years at the feet of Thorleif the Wise, famous for his skill in the laws; and, on his return to his native island, with the assistance of another chieftain of great influence and sagacity, Grim Geitskor, framed a code which was accepted by the people in a general national assembly (928).

The Icelandic legislators, following the indications pointed out by nature, divided the whole island into four great quarters, called, in the Icelandic tongue, *Fjerdingar*. In each of these they established a chief magistrate, who was chosen by the free voice of the people, and whose office very much resembled that of the *godi* before mentioned. These quarters were again divided into smaller districts, in which all the freemen possessed of landed property had a voice in the public assembly. The great national assembly, or assize of the island, at which all the freeholders had a right to participate, by themselves or their delegates, was held annually, and was called the

Al-thing. It bore a strong family likeness to the national assemblies of the parent country and of the other Scandinavian nations, and some similitude to the Witenagemot of the Anglo-Saxons and the Fields of March and May of the primitive Franks. The place of meeting was situated on a level plain on the shores of the lake of Thing-valle, and was called Lög-bergit, or the Law-Mount. It is at this early day a wild and dreary scene, the surrounding country having been convulsed and torn to pieces by volcanic eruptions; but it must always have presented a striking picture, suited to the solemnity of the occasion which brought together the assembled people of Iceland.

The Promulgator of the Law

The national assembly continued to be held at this place for eight centuries, until it was removed about a century ago, to a more convenient spot, but one less hallowed in popular opinion by its venerable antiquity and historical associations. The president of this assembly was chosen for life, and was called *lögsögomadr*, or promulgator of the law. His functions were both legislative and judicial, and in the latter respect were similar to those of the *lagman* of the Gothic institutions. Indeed, he afterwards received the same name. After the introduction of book-writing, the book of the law was deposited in his hands, and he naturally became its most authoritative expounder. For nearly two centuries after their enactment, the laws of Ulfljot were preserved by tradition only, being for that purpose recited annually by the lögsögomadr in the national assembly; from which we may readily infer how extremely simple they must have been in their details, and how great the latitude of interpretation indulged by this magistrate. Like all other systems of unwritten law, and this was literally such, it attributed great weight to the authority of precedents, which also were preserved in the same manner as the original laws themselves — by oral tradition. The forms of action and of pleading, which were very exactly observed by the Northmen, even of this earlier age, were also expounded by the promulgator of the law in the public assembly, so that they might be known to the people, and invariably observed in the assizes of the local districts. When the laws came afterwards to be reduced to a written text, those precedents, which had acquired the force of law, were incorporated into the code.

Ulfljot was the first citizen raised to that high office by his grateful countrymen. It was afterwards filled by the celebrated Snorre Sturleson, and the degree of importance attached to it is strikingly illustrated by the circumstance that time was computed by the Icelanders from the periods during which this magistracy was occupied by different individuals, the anniversary of their election serving to mark a distinct chronological epoch in the national annals.

As the laws of Ulfljot nowhere exist at the present day in a perfect form, it is impossible to form anything like an adequate notion of the precise nature of these institutions. In general we may conclude that they were framed after the model of the customary law of the parent country, with an adaption to the special circumstances and local condition of Iceland. Indeed, a system of original legislation, departing entirely from historical antecedents, and unaccommodated to the prejudices and usages of the people, would have been unhesitatingly rejected by them. Thorleif the Wise, who was consulted by Ulfljot in the compilation of his laws, was afterwards employed by King Hakon the Good in the formation of the Norwegian law, called the Gule-thing law. But as this latter code no longer exists in its original form, and as we have only scattered fragments of the laws of Ulfljot, the two systems of jurisprudence cannot be compared together. Doubtless both of them were collections of the immemorial usages and customs already sanctioned by popular acceptances, rather than systematic codes of civil and criminal jurisprudence. The political part of Ulfljot's institutions formed the basis of the government of Iceland during the three centuries of the republic. If they secured the blessings of social order in an imperfect degree only, the same may be said of the constitutional code of every other country in Europe during the Middle Ages. The Icelandic commonwealth was torn with civil dissensions of the most implacable character, resembling at once the factions of the Italian republics and the anarchy of the feudal law. But the great body of the people was never reduced to the condition of feudal serfs. They nourished a proud spirit of personal independence, which, if partaking of the barbarous character of the age, became the parent of adventurous enterprise, at first in brilliant feats of arms and afterwards in those arts which adorn and embellish human life.

THE INTRODUCTION OF CHRISTIANITY

The introduction of Christianity into Iceland is the most remarkable epoch in its subsequent history. Some of its inhabitants had always refused to worship the new gods originally introduced into the parent country from the East. Others refused to sacrifice to the peculiar national deities. Every family had its private faith and worship. Thorkill, the grandson of the first settler Ingolf, as he felt the near approach of death, requested to be carried out into the open air, where he might see the cheering light of the sun, and commend his parting spirit to the God who had created both sun and stars. Many of the Icelanders, in their voyages to Denmark and England, and in their military service with the Varangians at Constantinople, had received the initiating rites of Christianity, as then administered in those countries; but on their return to Iceland did not scruple to sacrifice to Thor as the local tutelary deity of the island.

The first Christian missionary was brought to Iceland by Thorwald, son of Kodran, a sea-rover, who, having been baptised on the banks of the Elbe by a German priest named Frederick, persuaded his instructor to accompany him to his native country, one hundred years after the first settlement, and during the chief magistracy of the lagman Thorkel Mani. His exertions were not wholly fruitless, and were afterwards seconded by other missionaries sent by Olaf Tryggvason, king of Norway, who, having established the new religion in that country, was anxious to propagate the faith among the various Norwegian colonies in the western seas. Among these missionaries were Gissur the White, and Hjalti, both Icelandic converts, who had been banished by the heathen party on account of their zeal for Christianity.

On the arrival of these exiles in the island (1,000), they found the national assembly of the Al-thing in session at Thing-valle, and immediately proceeded thither for the purpose of rallying the Christian party. Being joined by their friends, they boldly marched to the Lög-berg, or Mount of the Law, in solemn procession, carrying crosses in their hands. Whilst the whole assembly were awed with this extraordinary scene, Hjalti offered incense, and Gissur expounded to the multitude the truths of Christianity with such fervid eloquence that a large portion of his audience broke off from the assembly and avowed their determination to embrace the new religion. Whilst they were engaged in this discussion, news arrived that an eruption of lava had broken out with great fury in a neighbouring mountain. "It is the effect of the wrath of our offended deities," exclaimed the worshippers of Thor and Odin. "And what excited their wrath," answered Snorre Gode, a distinguished pontiff-chieftain, "what excited their wrath when these rocks of lava, which we ourselves tread, were themselves a glowing torrent?" This answer effectually silenced the advocates of the ancient religion, at least for the time; for these lava rocks were universally known to have been there before the country was inhabited. But the genius of heathenism was still stubbornly bent on resistance to this innovation. The heathen party determined to offer two human beings from each quarter of the island as a sacrifice to appease the wrath of the gods, and stay the further progress of what they deemed this moral pestilence. On which, the Christian missionaries, determined not to be outstripped in zeal, convened a meeting of their friends, and proposed that an equal number of the Christian party should seal with their blood the truth of the religion for which they so strenuously contended.

The next day, Thorgeir, who was the lagman of the time, convened the assembly, with the avowed determination to put an end to the controversy which thus threatened to kindle a civil war, and to deluge the island with blood. With this view, he addressed them as follows: "Hear me, ye wise men, and listen to my words, ye people! The ruin of that state is at hand, when all the citizens do not obey the same law and follow the same customs. Division and hate prevail among us; these must soon give rise to civil war, which will destroy our resources, lay waste our isle, and reduce it to a barren wilderness. As union and concord strengthen the weak, so disunion and discord weaken the strong. Let us then strive with all our might, lest our internal peace be destroyed by a divided rule. Reflect then upon what ye well know, without having need to be reminded of the fact — how the kings of Denmark and Norway have become enfeebled by the destructive wars waged on the dispute of religion, until at last their subjects and counsellors have been reduced to the necessity of making peace without their consent. These monarchs have thus come to feel the healing virtue of peace and friendship, and laying aside their bitter hate have become, to the great joy of their subjects, the best of friends. And though we, magistrates and chieftains of this island, cannot pretend to compare ourselves with these kings in power, or with their counsellors in wisdom, still we may laudably imitate whatever is praiseworthy in their public conduct. We should then endeavour to pursue a course by which all may be reconciled, and adopt the same laws and customs; otherwise nothing is more certain than that our peace is gone forever."

This speech was received with approbation by the assembly, who referred to the decision of the lagman, who promulgated a decree purporting that all the inhabitants of the island should be baptised, the idols and temples destroyed, no man to worship the ancient deities publicly upon the penalty of banishment; but private worship, the exposition of infants, the eating of horseflesh, and other practices not inconsistent with the precepts of Christianity, to be still tolerated. This law was ratified by the assembly, all the heathens suffered themselves to be signed with the cross, and some were baptised in the hot-water baths of Langerdal and Reikdal. The apprehensions of famine, from abolishing the practice of exposing their infant children and the eating of horseflesh, soon subsided, and these last remnants of heathenism were suppressed in consequence of the earnest remonstrance of St. Olaf, king of Norway (1016).

ICELAND

TRIAL BY BATTLE

The introduction of Christianity was followed by the abolition of trial by battle, a mode of procedure recognised by the early laws of all the northern nations, and growing out of their warlike habits and wild spirit of independence, which made every individual the arbiter of his own wrongs. This mode of trial derived its name (*holmgánga*) from the ancient usage among the northern warriors of retiring to a solitary island, there to decide their deadly feuds in single combat. The *holmgánga* was abolished in Iceland in 1011. The laws of the island still remained in oral tradition until more than a century afterwards, when they were revised and reduced to a written text in 1117, under the superintendence of Bergthor Rafni, then lagman of the republic, and Haflidi Mauri, another distinguished chieftain, who were assisted in this recompilation by experienced lawyers of the time.

This code, afterwards called the Grágás, was adopted by the national assembly of the Al-thing in the following year, 1118, and preserved the force of law until the year 1275, when Iceland became subject to the kings of Norway. The loss of national independence was followed by the introduction of the Norwegian collection of laws, called Jonsbok in 1280, which still continues to be the basis of the Icelandic legislation. The Grágás code was not, as has commonly been supposed, borrowed from the law of the same name, introduced into Norway by King Magnus the Good. It was founded mainly on the primitive laws of Ulfljot, and the revision of 1118; but in the form in which the Grágás now exists, it is intermingled with precedents of judicial decisions and the glosses of different commentators which have been incorporated into the original text. This code abounds with many examples of that spirit of litigation and legal subtlety which has ever marked the character of the Northmen.

These laws contain the same provisions for the satisfaction of penal offences by pecuniary mulcts, which are adjusted by a minute scale, according to the nature of the crime and the rank of the offender. They also contain the rude elements of the trial by jury, of which there are many traces to be found in the ancient annals of the North. In the saga of the famous chieftain Egill, son of Skallagrim, there is a curious and picturesque account of a civil trial in Norway, in the reign of King Eric Blodæxe, respecting an inheritance claimed by that chieftain. Soon after the battle of Brunanburh, in which Egill had aided King Æthelstan with a band of vikings and other northern adventurers, his wife's father died in Norway, and his brother-in-law Bergaumund took possession of the entire inheritance, of which Egill claimed a part, in right of his wife, which circumstance compelled Egill to make a voyage from Iceland to the parent country. On his arrival in Norway he brought a suit against Bergaumund, who was protected by the interest of King Eric and his queen Gunhilda. The suit was tried at the Gule-thing assizes, where the parties appeared, attended by numerous bands of followers and friends.

In the midst of a large field a ring was stretched out, with hazel twigs bound together with a cord, called a sacred band (*vebönd*). Within this circle sat the judges, twelve from the district called Fjordefylke, twelve from Sognefylke, and twelve from Hördafylke; these three districts being thus united into what may be called one circuit for the administration of justice. The pleadings commenced in due form, and Bergaumund asserted that Egill's wife could not, as the child of a slave, inherit the property in question. But Egill's friend Arinbicern maintained, with twelve witnesses or compurgators, that she was of ingenuous birth; and as the judges were about to pronounce sentence, Queen Gunhilda, the old enemy of Egill, fearing the result might be favourable to him, instigated her kinsmen to cut the sacred cord, by which the assizes were broken up in confusion.   Thereupon Egill defied his adversary to single combat in a desert isle (*holmgánga*) in order to decide their controversy by battle, and denounced vengeance against all who should interfere.   King Eric was sorely incensed; but as nobody, not even the king and his champions, was allowed to come armed to the assizes, Egill made his escape to the sea shore.   Here his faithful friend Arinbiœrn informed him that he was declared an outlaw in all Norway, and presented him with a bark and thirty men to pass the seas.

But Egill could not forego his vengeance, even for a season; and returned to the shore, where he lurked until he found an opportunity to slay not only his adversary Bergaumund, but King Eric's son Ragnvold, a youth of only eleven years, whom he accidentally encountered at a convivial meeting in the neighbourhood.   Before Egill set sail again for Iceland, he took one of the oars of his ship, upon which he stuck a horse's head, and as he raised it aloft, exclaimed: "Here I set up the rod of vengeance, and direct this curse against King Eric and Queen Gunhilda!"   He then turned the horse's head towards the land, and cried aloud: "I direct this curse against the tutelary deities who built this land that they shall forever wander, and find no rest nor abiding place, until they have expelled from the land King Eric and Queen Gunhilda." He then carved this singular formula of imprecation in runic characters upon the oar, and fixed it in a cleft of the rock, where he left it standing.

ICELANDIC LANGUAGE AND LITERATURE

Under the protection of a form of government which might, however, more properly be called a patriarchal aristocracy than a republic, the Icelanders cherished and cultivated the language and literature of their ancestors with remarkable success.   The cultivation of these was favoured by their adherence to the ancient religion for some time after all the other countries of the North had yielded to the progress of Christianity.   The early dawn of literature in Europe was almost everywhere else marked by an awkward attempt to copy the classical models of Greece and Rome.   In Iceland [as we have seen] an independent literature grew up, flourished, and was brought to a certain degree of perfection, before the revival of learning in the south of Europe.   This island was not converted to Christianity until the end of the tenth century, when the national literature, which still remained in oral tradition, was full blown and ready to be committed to a written form.

With the Christian religion, Latin letters were introduced; but instead of being used, as elsewhere, to write a dead language, they were adapted by the learned men of Iceland to mark the sounds which had been before expressed by the runic characters.   The ancient language of the North was thus preserved in Iceland, whilst it ceased to be cultivated as a written and soon became extinct as a spoken language in the parent countries of Scandinavia. The popular superstitions, with which the mythology and poetry of the North are interwoven, continued still to linger in the sequestered glens of this remote island.   The language, which gave expression to the thoughts and feelings connected with this mythology and this poetry, rivals in copiousness, flexibility, and energy every modern tongue.

Thus we perceive how the flowers of poetry sprung up and bloomed amidst eternal ice and snows.   The arts of peace were successfully cultivated by the free and independent Icelanders.   Their arctic isle was not warmed by a Grecian sun, but their hearts glowed with the fire of freedom.   The natural divisions of the country by icebergs and lava streams insulated the people from each other, and the inhabitants of each valley and each hamlet formed, as it were, an independent community.   These were again reunited in the general national assembly of the Al-thing, which might not be unaptly likened to the Amphictyonic council or Olympic games, where all the tribes of the nation convened to offer the common rites of their religion, to decide their mutual differences, and to listen to the lays of the skald, which commemorated the exploits of their ancestors.   Their pastoral life was diversified by the occupation of fishing.   Like the Greeks, too, the sea was their element, but even their shortest voyages bore them much further from their native shores than the boasted expedition of the Argonauts.   Their familiarity with the perils of the ocean and with the diversified manners and customs of foreign lands stamped their national character with bold and original features, which distinguished them from every other people.   The countries from which this branch of the great northern family had migrated were marked by equally striking moral and physical peculiarities.

The wild beauty of the northern scenery struck the poetic soul of Alfieri, as it must that of every other traveller of genius and sensibility.   He was moved by the magnificent splendour of its winter nights, and, above all, by the rapid transition from the rudeness of that season to the mild bloom of spring.

This and the other distinctive qualities of the northern climate and modes of life act powerfully on the being of man; and, as has been beautifully observed by the distinguished living historian of Sweden, "draw the attention of man to nature, and create a closer relation to her and to her mysteries. To this cause may also be attributed that peculiarly deep and comprehensive perception of nature which forms a fundamental principle in distinguished northern minds — a tendency which, even in the earliest mythology and poetry of the North, expresses itself by dark images and tones, and in later times, purified by cultivation, has been principally developed in sciences and art."

The Sagas; The Elder Edda

The ancient literature of the North was not confined to the poetical art. The skald recited the praises of kings and heroes in verse, whilst the Saga-man recalled the memory of the past in prose narratives.   The talent for storytelling, as well as that of poetical invention, was cultivated and highly improved by practice.   The prince's hall, the assembly of the people, the solemn feasts of sacrifice, all presented occasions for the exercise of this delightful art.   The memory of past transactions was thus handed down from age to age in an unbroken chain of tradition, and the ancient songs and sagas were preserved until the introduction of book-writing gave them a fixed and durable record.   A young Icelander, Thorstein Frode, was entertained at the court of Harold Hardrada as a saga-man or story-teller, and often amused the king and his courtiers in this manner.   As the great Yule festival, or Christmas, approached, the king, observing him to become serious and melancholy, apprehended that his stock of stories might be nearly exhausted.   On being asked the question, Thorstein confessed that he had indeed but a single story left, and that one he did not like to tell, because it related to the deeds of the king himself in foreign lands.　Being encouraged by Harold, he at last narrated the story to the great satisfaction of the king, who asked him where he had learned it.　Thorstein answered that he had been in the constant habit of attending the Al-thing, or annual national assembly of Iceland, where he had heard different parts of this saga at different times, until he had firmly imprinted it on his memory.　The original narrator was one Haldor, an Icelander who had accompanied King Harold in all his travels and expeditions to Russia, Greece, Asia, Sicily, and Palestine, and on his return to his native isle had spread the fame of the king's achievements among his countrymen.

These recitations were embellished with poetical extracts from the "works" of different skalds, if such an expression may be used for literary compositions before the art of book-writing was known, and quoted by the narrator as apt to the purpose of illuminating some remarkable passage in the life and exploits of the hero whose adventures he was relating.　Story and song were thus united, and the memory was strengthened by this constant cultivation, so as to be the safe depository of the national history and poetry.　A striking example of the degree to which this faculty was cultivated is given in the saga of a famous Icelandic skald, who sang before King Harold Sigurdson sixty different lays in one evening, and, being asked if he knew any more, declared that these were only the half of what he could sing.

The power of oral tradition, in thus transmitting, through a succession of ages, poetical or prose compositions of considerable length, may appear almost incredible to civilised nations accustomed to the art of writing.　But it is well known that, even after the Homeric poems had been reduced to writing, the rhapsodists who had been accustomed to recite them could readily repeat any passage desired; and we have, in our own times, among the Servians, Calmucks, and other barbarous and semi-barbarous nations, examples of heroic and popular poems of great length thus preserved and handed down to posterity.　This is more especially the case where there is a perpetual order of men whose exclusive employment it is to learn and repeat, whose faculty of memory is thus improved and carried to the highest pitch of perfection, and who are relied upon as historiographers to preserve the national annals. The interesting scene presented to this day in every Icelandic family, in the long nights of winter, is a living proof of the existence of this ancient custom. No sooner does the day close, than the whole patriarchal family, domestics and all, are seated on their couches in the principal apartment, from the ceiling of which the reading and working lamp is suspended; and one of the family selected for that purpose, takes his seat near the lamp, and begins to read some favourite saga, or it may be the works of Klopstock and Milton (for these have been translated into Icelandic), whilst all the rest attentively listen, and are at the same time engaged in their respective occupations.　From the scarcity of printed books in this poor and sequestered country, in some families the sagas are recited by those who have committed them to memory, and there are still instances of itinerant orators of this sort, who gain a livelihood during the winter by going about from house to house repeating the stories they have thus learned by heart.

About two centuries and a half after the first settlement of Iceland by the Norwegians, the learned men of that remote island began to collect and reduce to writing these traditional poems and histories.　Sæmund Sigfussen, an ecclesiastic, who was born in Iceland in 1056, and pursued his classical studies in the universities of Germany and France, first collected and arranged the book of songs relating to the mythology and history of the ancient North

which is called the poetic, or elder *Edda*. Various and contradictory opinions
have been maintained as to the manner in which this collection was made by
Sæmund, who first gave it to the world. Some suppose that he merely
gathered together the runic manuscripts of the different poems, and trans-
scribed them in Latin characters. Others maintain that he took them from
the mouths of different skalds, living in his day, and first reduced them to
writing, they having been previously preserved and handed down by oral
tradition merely. But the most probable conjecture seems to be that he
collected some of this fragmentary poetry from contemporary skalds and other
parts from manuscripts written after the introduction of Christianity and
Latin letters into Iceland, which have since been lost, and merely added one
song of his own composition, the *Sólar Ljód*, or Carmen-Solare, of a moral and
Christian religious tendency, so as thereby to consecrate and leaven, as it
were, the whole mass of paganism.

He thus performed for these ancient poems the same office which, according
to the theory proposed by Wolf and Heyne, was performed by the ancient
Greek rhapsodist (whoever he was) who first collected and arranged the songs
of his predecessors, and reduced them to one continuous poem, which bears
the name of Homer's *Iliad*. It should, however, be observed that the different
lays contained in Sæmund's *Edda* are not, in general, connected as one continuous poem in point of subject and composition, but consist of different
pieces of ancient fragmentary poetry, relating to the characters and exploits
of the northern deities and heroes. There is abundant internal evidence that
the work, with the exception just mentioned, was not of his own composition
or that of any other Christian writer; and that the poems contained in it
could not have been collected by him, or by anybody else, from runic manuscripts, will be evident from the following considerations.

The runic alphabet consists properly of sixteen letters, which are Phœni-
cian in their origin. The northern traditions, sagas, and songs attribute their
introduction to Odin. They were probably brought by him into Scandinavia,
but they have no resemblance to any of the alphabets of central Asia. All
the ancient inscriptions to be found on the rocks and stone monuments in the
countries of the North, and which exist in the greatest number near old
Sigtuna and Upsala, in Sweden, the former the residence of Odin, and the latter
of his successors, and the principal seat of the superstition introduced by him,
are written in the Icelandic or ancient Scandinavian language, but in runic
characters. Saxo Grammaticus, who wrote in the twelfth century, asserts
that the ancient Danes engraved verses upon rocks and stones, containing
accounts of the exploits of their ancestors. But he does not pretend to cite
any runic inscriptions of the sort; and though he speaks of the rock on which
King Harold Hildetand had caused the achievements of his heroic father to
be inscribed, he admits that when Valdemar I endeavoured to copy this lapidary inscription it was found for the most part effaced and illegible.

It is probable that the zeal of the first converts to Christianity was
employed in destroying these monuments, which they considered rather as
the works of the demon than as contributing to illustrate the exploits of their
pagan ancestors, whose fame was far from being held in honour by them.
The runic characters were also used for inscriptions on arms, trinkets, amulets,
utensils, and buildings, and occasionally on the bark of trees or wooden tablets
for the purpose of memorials or epistolary correspondence. Thus Venantius
Fortunatus, a Latin poet of the sixth century, asks his friend Flavius, if he is
tired of the Latin, to write him in Hebrew, Persian, Greek, or even runic
characters.

Barbara fraxineis pingatur Runa tabellis,
Quodque papyrus ait, virgula plana valet;
Pagina vel redeat perscripta dolatile charta,
Quod relegi poterit, fructus amantis erit.

And the biographer of St. Anskar, the great apostle of the North, speaks of a letter written in the ninth century in runic characters, by a king of Sweden, to the emperor Louis le Débonnaire. These characters were also used for purposes connected with the pretended art of magic, and their efficacy in this respect is inculcated by Odin in several passages of the fragmentary poetry collected by Sæmund. Saxo Grammaticus speaks of magical songs carved on wooden tablets, and in the saga of the famous skald and hero Egill it is related how he was so deeply afflicted by the death of his beloved son that he resolved to starve himself to death, when he was diverted from his fatal purpose by his daughter persuading him to dictate an elegiac lay to his son's memory, which she offered to carve in wood *pä Kafle*. But the runic characters were principally used for lapidary inscriptions, and for the other purposes already mentioned, and there is no evidence that any such thing as "books," properly so called, existed among the Scandinavian nations before the introduction of the religion and language of the Roman church. The oldest manuscript book in the runic characters now existing is a digest of the customary laws of Skåne, written in the thirteenth or fourteenth century, which is preserved in the library of the university of Copenhagen.[c]

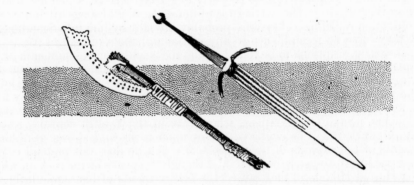

CHAPTER V

DENMARK UNDER THE KNUDS AND VALDEMARS

[1050–1375 A.D.]

HARTHACNUT AND MAGNUS (1035–1042 A.D.)

By his father's death, Harthacnut, the heir of Denmark, was equally so of England; and he was preparing to pass over into that kingdom when intelligence reached him of Harold's usurpation. But that usurpation was not sudden, nor complete; and had he hastened with a few thousand followers to claim the crown, he would have triumphed. But he had little energy of character; and while he remained irresolute, the period favourable for his hopes passed away. Fortunately Harold's reign was short; and in 1040 he was called by the English themselves to ascend the throne. On his arrival he committed an act of impotent vengeance against the memory of his brother, whose bones he caused to be disinterred and cast into the Thames. They were, however, reburied.

In his government of England, Harthacnut seems to have committed only one reprehensible act, and for that he had provocation. A tax levied for the support of the Danish soldiery was condemned by the English, and at Worcester resisted by the murder of the two collectors. To vindicate his authority, he resorted to severe measures. The ringleaders were executed, the city pillaged and partly burned. In other respects he was not unpopular. His kindness to the family of Æthelred did him great honour. To Emma he confided a share in the administration; and to Prince Edward, the youngest son of Æthelred, afterwards named the Confessor, whom he recalled from Normandy, he gave a splendid establishment. As he died without issue, with him ended the Danish dynasty in England.

Of Harthacnut's government in Denmark we have few records. He was negligent and intemperate; and his father's memory, more than his own

133

qualities, secured him on the throne. His transactions with Norway deserve especial consideration. Svend, the son of Canute, having been expelled from that kingdom by Magnus the Good as narrated in a former chapter, took refuge with his nearest brother in Denmark, and died soon after. If the Danish king was feeble, he was not without ambition. He knew that he should succeed to the English throne; and as, after that event, he should be the sole heir of Canute's extensive empire, he urged his claim to the crown of Norway. Finding Magnus too powerful for him, he met that prince, and as we have related, concluded a treaty singular in its nature and in its results important. If either king died without issue, the other was to inherit his dominions. This convention was guaranteed by the chief nobles and prelates of the two countries. Harthacnut did die without issue, and the throne of Denmark accordingly fell to Magnus (1042–1047).

On the arrival of this prince in Denmark, he was received with open arms. He was the son of a saint, with whose miracles the North resounded; and his own virtues (much less questionable than his father's) justified the expectation of a happy reign. To few princes, indeed, can history accord more virtues than to Magnus; yet he was not deficient in the active duties of his station. The Jomsburg pirates who had revolted, and whose ferocity was the dread of the North, he speedily reduced, and their capital he laid in ashes. This was a service both to the Danes and the Norwegians for which they could not be too grateful.

But the former, influenced by fickleness or by attachment to their old line of kings, or by mortification at receiving a sovereign from a country which they had twice conquered, soon cast their eyes on Svend, son of Jarl Ulf and of Estrith, sister of Canute the Great. After his father's murder, this prince had sought refuge at the court of the Swedish king. As he approached man's estate, he grew weary of inactivity, and having something to hope from the generosity of Magnus, he repaired to that monarch in Norway. He did not ask for any portion of Canute's vast possessions: he wanted employment merely under so generous a monarch; and his request was immediately granted. His talents, his lofty mien, his deportment, and above all his skilful flattery won the confidence of the Norwegian, who made him first minister, and next his lieutenant in Denmark. There was much imprudence in confiding to one so ambitious and so nearly connected with the throne a trust of this nature; but judging of other men's hearts by his own, Magnus thought that such a trust would forever bind Svend to his interests, and be agreeable to the Danes. On the relics of St. Olaf the young prince swore fidelity to the monarch, and was well received by the people. To deepen this favourable sentiment was his constant care; and by his affability, his attention to his duties, and his liberalities, he completely succeeded. When secure of their affection, he openly revolted. Magnus assembled an armament, proceeded to Denmark, defeated and expelled the usurper, who again sought refuge at the Swedish court.

No sooner was this enemy vanquished, than another appeared in the pagan bands which occupied all the eastern shores of the Baltic, that are now comprised in the Russian monarchy. These men, scarcely less ferocious than their allies the Jomsburg pirates, invaded Schleswig, wasting everything with fire and sword. Magnus flew to oppose them, and after a severe struggle triumphed. During his absence, Svend returned from Sweden, reduced Skåne, and passing into Zealand and Fünen was again acknowledged by the people. Victory, in two or three successive actions, still declared for the monarch. Yet the cause of Svend was not destroyed. In the assistance of the Swedish king, in the adventurers on all the maritime coasts of the Baltic, and still more in the attachment of the Danes, he had resources which even the power of Magnus was not able wholly to destroy.

A third enemy now appeared in Harold, surnamed Hardrada, or the Stern, the son of Sigurd, and the half-brother of St. Olaf. If there be any truth in the ancient sagas, his adventures were most extraordinary. He was present at the last fatal scene of Olaf's life; and from Norway he fled to the court of the Russian duke Yaroslav, whose service he entered. Of Elisif, daughter of Yaroslav, he became deeply enamoured; but, his suit being unsuccessful, he repaired to Constantinople, and was admitted amongst the Varangian guard of the emperors. By his valour and his birth he obtained at length the command of that formidable though small body, and by his exploits invested his name with much lustre. Heading an expedition against the pirates of the African coast, he was the victor in several battles, and the owner of immense booty, a portion of which he sent to his friends in Russia. He was afterwards employed in Sicily, in Italy, and in a journey to the Holy Land. In all this there is no great improbability; but what follows is too romantic to be credited: As the reward of his services, Harold had demanded the hand of a princess of the imperial family, and had been refused.

"Those Varangians (Væringjar)," says Snorre,[c] "who were in Miklagard, and received rewards for their services during the war, have said since their return home to the North that they were told in Greece by wise and grave men of that country that Queen Zoe herself wished for Harold as her husband, and that this in truth was the cause of her resentment, and of his wishing to leave Miklagard, though other reports were spread among the people. For these reasons the king Constantine Monomachus, who ruled the empire jointly with Queen Zoe, ordered Harold to be cast into prison. On his way thither, St. Olaf appeared to him, and promised him protection; and on that same street a chapel has been since erected, which is standing at this day. Here was Harold imprisoned with Halldór and Ulfr his men. The following night there came a noble lady, with two attendants, who let down a cord into the dungeon, and drew up the prisoners. This lady had been before healed by St. Olaf, the king, who revealed to her that she should relieve his brother from captivity. This being done, Harold immediately went to the Varangians, who all rose up at his approach and received him with joy. They seized their arms, and went to the chamber where the king slept and put out his eyes. The same night, Harold went, with his companions, to the chamber in which Maria slept, and carried her away by force. They afterwards proceeded to the place where the galleys of the Varangians were kept, and, seizing two vessels, rowed into the Bosporus (Sœvidar-sund). When they came to the iron chains which are drawn across the sound, Harold ordered all his men who were not employed in rowing to crowd to the stern with their baggage, and when the galleys struck upon the chains, to rush forward to the prow, so as to impel the galleys over the chains. The galley in which Harold embarked was carried quite over on to the other side, but the other vessel struck upon the chains and was lost. Some of her crew perished in the water, but others were saved. In this manner, Harold escaped from Miklagard, and entered the Black Sea, where he set the virgin on shore, with some attendants, to accompany her back to Miklagard, requesting her to tell her cousin, Queen Zoe, how little her power could have availed to prevent his carrying off the virgin, if he had been so minded."

The anxiety of Harold was occasioned by the intelligence that his nephew Magnus had ascended the thrones of Norway and Denmark. Proceeding through Russia, he married the daughter of Yaroslav; and with her returned to Norway through Sweden. On reaching Sweden, where the fame of his riches had preceded him, he entered into a league with Svend. The objects of this league are not very clearly defined; but we may infer that one of them was to place Harold on the Norwegian, Svend on the Danish throne. The wealth of Harold hired numerous adventurers; and by the two princes the coasts of Denmark were ravaged.

Again Magnus prepared an armament to oppose them; but his surer recourse was policy. To detach the celebrated Varangian chief from the cause of the Dane, he offered him half of the Norwegian kingdom (and also no doubt the eventual succession), on the condition of Harold's allowing in like manner a division of his treasure. The latter eagerly accepted the proposal; he forsook Svend, repaired to Norway, divided the treasure, the amount of which is described as wonderfully large, and was admitted to a share in the administration. Contrary to the usual experience of rulers so placed in regard to each other, they lived in harmony until the death of Magnus in the following year. By this defection, or rather by this conversion of an ally into an enemy, Svend was compelled to retire. But he had his partisans in Denmark, and Magnus, at his death, had the generosity to declare him his successor in that kingdom. To Harold was left the Norwegian throne. Thus the two adventurers became kings, in little more than a year after the arrival of Harold in the North.

The surname of Harold the Good sufficiently establishes his character. He was indeed an admirable king and a virtuous man. Much praise is awarded to a code of laws which he compiled; but they no longer exist in their original form.

SVEND AND THE NEW DYNASTY (1047–1076 A.D.)

As with Harthacnut had ended the ancient male line of Denmark — a line that traced itself to Odin — Svend II may be called the founder of a new dynasty. That dynasty occupied the throne until the extinction of its male line in Valdemar IV, when it was succeeded by the house of Oldenburg.

Scarcely was Svend invested with the dignity, when he found an enemy as powerful as Magnus, and less generous, in Harold Hardrada, who claimed the Danish crown. The assertion of this claim led to many years of warfare, ruinous to both kingdoms, but especially to Denmark, the coasts of which were often ravaged. In general the advantage rested with the Norwegian monarch, who, in 1064, obtained a great victory over the Danish fleet at the mouth of the Nissa. With great difficulty Svend escaped into Zealand, and began to collect a new armament. Fortunately the mind of Harold was now disposed to peace. Sixteen years of hostilities had brought him little advantage; the fortune of war was dubious; and the Danes, like their king, were averse to a foreign yoke. The two monarchs met, and entered into a treaty, which left affairs just as they had been at the death of Magnus.

These were not the only hostilities in which they were engaged. Both undertook predatory expeditions to the English coast; but they could obtain no advantage over the vigilant and intrepid monarch (William I), who now swayed the sceptre of that kingdom. Svend too had the mortification to see his own coasts (those of Holstein) ravaged by the Wend pirates, who laid both Schleswig and Hamburg in ashes. Before he could reach them they retired. Subsequently he was persuaded to march against the Saxons, then at war with the emperor; but his troops having no inclination to exasperate a people with whom they had long been on terms of amity, he desisted from the undertaking.

Svend showed much favour to the church. He built many places of worship, which he endowed with liberality; and he founded four new bishoprics: of these two were in Skåne, *viz.* Lund and Dalby, which were subsequently united; and two in Jutland, *viz.* Viborg and Borglum. Yet this liberality did not preserve him from quarrelling with it. His chief vice was incontinence. Numerous were his mistresses, and numerous his offspring: thirteen sons are mentioned, of whom five succeeded him; but the number of his daughters was much inferior; two only appear in history. His queen was a Swedish princess within the prohibited degrees of kindred. When Adalbert, archbishop of Bremen, heard of the union, he angrily condemned it, and by his messengers threatened the king with excommunication if he did not separate from the princess. The king resisted, and even threatened to lay Bremen (the legate's residence) in ashes; but the power of the church was too great even for him to resist, and in the end he dismissed his wife.

Svend was a man of strong passions, and of irritable temperament. In a festival which he gave to his chief nobles in the city of Roeskilde, some of the guests, heated by wine, indulged themselves in imprudent though perhaps true remarks on his conduct. The following morning some officious talebearers acquainted him with the circumstance; and in the rage of the moment he ordered them to be put to death, though they were then at mass in the cathedral — that very cathedral which had been the scene of his own father's murder. When, on the day following this tragical event, he proceeded to the church, he was met by the bishop, who, elevating the crosier, commanded him to retire, and not to pollute by his presence the house of God — that house which he had already desecrated by blood. His attendants drew their swords, but he forbade them to exercise any degree of violence towards a man who in the discharge of his duty defied even kings. Retiring mournfully to his palace, he assumed the garb of penance, wept and prayed, and lamented his crime during three days. He then presented himself, in the same mean apparel, before the gates of the cathedral. The bishop was in the midst of the service; the *Kyrie Eleison* had been chaunted, and the *Gloria* about to commence, when he was informed that the royal penitent was outside the gates. Leaving the altar, he repaired to the spot, raised the suppliant monarch, and greeted him with the kiss of peace. Bringing him into the church, he heard his confession, removed the excommunication, and allowed him to join in the service. Soon afterwards, in the same cathedral, the king made a public confession of his crime, asked pardon alike of God and man, was allowed to resume his royal apparel, and solemnly absolved. But he had yet to make satisfaction to the kindred of the deceased in conformity with the law; and to mitigate the canonical penance he presented one of his domains to the church. This prelate was an Anglo-Saxon ecclesiastic, William, whom the archbishop of Bremen had nominated to that dignity, and who had previously been the secretary of Canute the Great. During the long period that he had governed the diocese of Roeskilde, he had won the esteem of all men alike by his talents and his virtues. For the latter he had the reputation of a saint, and for the former that of a wizard. It is no disparagement to the honour of this apostolic churchman that he had previously been the intimate friend of the monarch; nor any to that of Svend, that after this event he honoured this bishop more than he had done before.

From this time to his death, Svend practised with much zeal the observances of the Roman Catholic church. By his excessive liberalities he injured his revenues; and by his austerities, perhaps, his health. A faithful portrait is given of him and of his people by one who knew him well, Adam of Bremen.[d] This ecclesiastic, hearing so much in favour of the royal Dane, proceeded to his court, and, like all other strangers, was graciously received.[b] "Svend," says the canon,[d] "is not only liberal towards foreigners, but well versed in literature; and he directs with much ability the missions which he has established in Sweden, Norway, and the isles; from his own mouth have I received most of the facts contained in this history." In his reign the pagans of Bornholm were first converted to Christianity by bishop Egin. The image of Frigg, which they had been so long accustomed to venerate, they demolished with contempt. Another proof of their sincerity appeared from their offer of their most valuable effects to the bishop. This, unlike most churchmen of the age, he refused to accept; and advised them to expend it in two noble ways — in the foundation of churches, and the redemption of the Christian captives. "The king," proceeds Adam,[d] "has no vice but incontinence."

The canon speaks of Denmark as consisting almost wholly of islands. "Of them Zealand is the largest and richest, and its inhabitants are the most warlike." Leidre had been, but Roeskilde was then the capital. Next to Zealand in importance was Fünen, which was very fertile, but its coasts were exposed to the ravages of the pirates. The capital, Odense, was a large city. To cross from island to island was perilous, not only from the stormy sea that rolled between them but from the pirates. Jutland had a barren soil except on the banks of the rivers, the only parts cultivated: the rest of the country consisted of forests, marshes, and wastes, and was hardly passable. The chief towns lay near the narrow bays on the coast. Skåne, always geographically, now politically included in Sweden, is represented as fertile, as very populous, and full of churches. Nowhere, indeed, had Denmark much lack of these structures; Fünen, Adam assures us, had 100; Zealand, 150. "Skåne is almost an island, and separated from Gothland by large forests and rugged mountains. Here is the city of Lund, where the robbers of the deep laid their treasures. These robbers paid tribute to the Danish king, on the condition of being allowed to exercise their vocation against the barbarians." Among the Danes, Adam perceives many other things contrary to justice: he sees little indeed to praise beyond the custom of selling into slavery such women as dishonoured themselves. So proud were the men that they preferred death to stripes; and they marched to the place of execution not only with an undaunted but with a triumphant air. Tears and groans they held to be unmanly; and they mourned neither for their wives nor for their dearest connections.

As Svend left no legitimate offspring, the only claim that could be made was from his numerous bastards. Harold was the eldest; but then, as he was of a quiet, gentle nature, he was not very agreeable to a fierce people. On the other hand, Knud, the next brother, had distinguished himself greatly in the wars against the pagans of Livonia. There was, accordingly, a dispute when the states assembled, most declaring for Harold, but all Skåne for Knud; and a civil war must have been the result; but for the bribes of two chiefs, who prevailed on the electors of that province to confirm the choice of Harold. After this decision, Knud refused to remain in Denmark, and passed the rest of his brother's life in his old occupation.

The short reign of Harold (1076–1080) affords no materials for history. Silent, reserved, timid, averse to the shedding of blood, even for judicial delinquencies, he was little esteemed. Yet few periods were more happy than that which witnessed his administration. He made new laws, which have been praised and condemned. According to Saxo, whose means of information cannot be disputed, he abolished the judicial combat, and substituted purgation by oath — a change which led to frequent perjury. But if the testimony of Elnoth be admissible, he enacted other laws which were long valued by the people — so valued that they made every new monarch swear to observe them.[b]

THE CHURCH UNDER KNUD THE SAINT

After the death of Harold (1080) his brother Knud the Saint succeeded him without opposition. Although he possessed many fine qualities, he was beloved neither by the people nor the nobles, and from the very beginning of his reign had difficulties with the inhabitants of Halland and Skåne because they refused to respond to the numerous statute duties he imposed upon them. But he knew how to bring them to obedience by threatening to exclude them, some from the great oak forests where their pigs found food, others from the Sound fishing grounds; for he claimed that the forests and pasturing grounds, the gulfs and straits belonged to the king. Although Christianity had long been established in Denmark, many of the people still practised piracy, especially in isolated localities. A remarkable type of corsair was the powerful chief Egil-Ragnarsen of Bornholm, usually called Blod-Egil, because in the heat of battle he quenched his thirst with the blood of the wounded. Knud the Saint, who was now resolved to put an end to this barbarous practice of piracy, had warned Egil several times; and as the latter was not willing to give up his old habits, the king went to Bornholm, seized Egil, and hanged him.

This severity, while just, greatly incensed that portion of the people which was still animated by the spirit of paganism, and could not see anything wrong in piracy — but especially Egil's numerous and powerful friends and relatives became sworn enemies of the king. Knud's efforts tended principally to soften the manners of the Danes and to spread order and a higher civilisation throughout Denmark. He also showed much concern towards foreigners who made homes in the kingdom, and worked zealously to suppress slavery, which was a relic of paganism. The cessation of the piracy, which had provided the country with slaves, paved the way for the abolition of slavery; but this happy result was due above everything else to the influence of Christianity, which taught the equality of men, and the more the Christian spirit filtered down through the people the more it obliterated their degrading heritage of paganism.

While Knud was at loggerheads with the people and the chiefs because he found himself compelled to restrain the ancient liberties of the one and to bring the license of the others within the limits of order, he upheld with all his might the influence of the clergy, and sought in them a support against the other classes. He was himself of a very pious nature, rigidly observing days of abstinence, fasting frequently, and devoting himself to severe exercises of penance; sometimes he even went so far as to undergo flagellation from his chaplains.

He gave proof of a royal generosity with regard to the poor, the churches, and the priests, and it was the magnificent cathedral built in his reign that received the greatest marks of this. In the epoch when the church was governed by the energetic Gregory VII, she attained throughout Europe a high degree of power, not only spiritual but temporal as well, before which people and kings were compelled to bow. In Denmark, the clergy had struggled for more than a century and a half before they were even tolerated, but their strength and power increased rapidly when Christianity was universally established, and their pretention to enjoy in the North the same privileges as in the rest of Europe seemed to be equally just and natural. In the midst of the license which prevailed during the centuries of barbarism, the people felt the need of some protection against arbitrary power and threw themselves into the arms of the church, which upheld justice against force and gave the oppressed a refuge against the persecutions of violence. Through auricular confession the clergy became masters of the conscience, and by excluding recalcitrants from divine service and from the communion they had a means of coercion which was especially efficacious in an age of devotion.

Generosity towards the church and respect for the clergy became articles of faith, and were considered the highest mark of piety, even as disobedience to the clerical orders was the greatest sin. It is not, therefore, to be wondered at that people and kings rivalled one another in generosity towards the church and her religious establishments, and showered on them privileges which brought them at the same time riches and consideration. Thus favoured by the spirit of the age and the force of circumstances, the church obtained a degree of pre-eminence over the state which worked for good as long as the latter remained in a low state of development, and had power neither to protect civilisation nor maintain the law, but which became harmful as soon as the state could stand by itself.

Svend Estridsen raised the power of the church upon the foundations laid by Canute the Great, but under Knud the Saint the theocracy attained the apogee of its development, it made the clergy the first order of the state by giving bishops the rank of the greatest lords, dukes, and lay princes; it exempted ecclesiastics from the reach of ordinary jurisdiction in religious matters, and under King Niels the privilege was further extended to include every cause, so that in no event could the clergy be cited before a secular tribunal; and even at a later period laymen were amenable to clerical jurisdiction in certain pretended ecclesiastical matters, such as adultery, perjury, usury, etc. The ecclesiastics obtained, moreover, the right of "forfeit" for condemnations pronounced within their jurisdiction, a most important source of revenue in an age where the majority of punishments consisted in pecuniary reparation. Finally Knud tried to introduce the tithe system — one third of the revenue thus obtained to go to the bishop, one third to the parish priest, and the remainder to the maintenance of the church and the needs of public worship; but this experiment failed on account of the open resistance the people opposed to so onerous an innovation, and it finally cost the king his life.

In the impoverished country of Wendsyssel, north of Limfjord, open rebellion broke out and spread quickly over the whole of Jutland. Knud fled to Fünen, but the insurgents pursued and overtook him at Odense, where he shut himself up in the church of St. Alban with the men who had remained faithful to him. Knud would make no resistance and threw himself in prayer before the altar, but his brothers, Eric and Benedict, defended him with the most splendid bravery. The rebels attacked the sanctuary crying, "Where is Knud the Accursed? Let him show himself. Where is he hiding? He has betrayed the Danes long enough, and it must cease." Others exclaimed in meting out blows to the king's defenders, "Take this for my cow, King Knud; take this for my ox; take this for my horse." They finally broke into the sanctuary. Knud the Saint was assassinated before the altar,

Benedict perished in the fight, but Eric fought his way out through the assailants (1086).

Knud the Saint is the sole Danish king to meet death in a general uprising. He was the victim of resistance to a new order of things that was beginning to creep into Denmark, but which he attempted to make prevail with too much violence and thoughtless zeal. After Knud's death, an embassy was sent to Flanders to bring back Olaf [the brother of Knud, whom the latter had sent thither in chains as a punishment for exciting a rebellion against him] but he was not set at liberty until his brother Niels was sent as a hostage in pledge for 10,000 silver marks of ransom, which could not be furnished just at the moment.

Olaf reigned nine years, but his reign is only noteworthy for a great famine, whence came his surname of "Hunger." Although scarcity and high prices prevailed over all Europe at the time, the clergy did not fail to represent the calamity as a divine punishment for the murder of Saint Knud. The same rumours of miracles at his tomb began to be circulated, but it took a long time to make the people believe in the sanctity of this detested king.

THE GUILDS

The canonisation of Saint Knud had important consequences in giving rise to the foundation of brotherhoods or guilds, founded in his honour and placed under his protection.   They were institutions whose object was mutual assistance in misery and in danger, common defence, and the maintenance of order and morality in an age of license. These brotherhoods were composed of men and women, and governed by elders (oldermænd) according to the *Skraa* or particular statutes which the members engaged themselves by oath to observe; and these laws had without any doubt their origin in the frequent social reunions or guilds of antiquity. That explains the identity of the name, as well as the custom, practised also by the members of the later guilds, of coming together for purposes of banqueting and amusement. But it was only through the influence of Christianity that the guilds assumed their special character of half religious and half worldly associations.

The oldest guilds existed merely for religious purposes — such as saying prayers and holding services, subscribing donations to churches and monasteries, helping the poor and the pilgrims, or nursing the sick. But on account of the necessities and requirements of the age, brotherhoods were soon formed which held in view also the material welfare and safety of their members. Although of a more worldly nature, these societies, nevertheless, always kept their religious character, and continued to hold relations with the church; they were under the protection of a saint whose name they took; at the death of a brother the members kept vigil, that is to say they passed the night in singing hymns and saying prayers; masses were said for the repose of the dead man's soul; and the members were constantly making offerings, especially tapers, to the church dedicated to the patron saint of the brotherhood.   Guilds may have been introduced into Denmark at the time of the country's union with England — one of the oldest homes of these associations; but it is also quite possible that they arose spontaneously from circumstances and necessities similar to those which developed the guilds elsewhere: in any case, it cannot be shown with certainty that guilds existed in Denmark before the canonisation of Saint Knud.

The secular guilds instituted on this occasion — and which are called royal because they were dedicated to Saint Knud, and later to Duke Knud Lavard and King Eric Plovpenning, who, without being canonised was honoured in Denmark as one of the blessed — soon became famous and spread rapidly. Their distinguishing feature was the protection their members promised one to the others. When a brother was killed by a non-member it became the members' duty to force the murderer to pay the price of blood; and if he refused he became the object of the brotherhood's vengeance, against which he could preserve neither power nor rank: and so inevitable was this that even a king (Niels) was unable to escape it. The guild exercised extensive jurisdiction over its members, and differences which arose among the latter were settled by its own tribunal. When, on the contrary, a member was dragged by a non-member into the ordinary courts, his brothers were bound to appear with him, and to sustain him with their oath and their testimony, which latter was so respected that the word of one was worth that of three others. The danger which might thus result to justice in general was in part attenuated by the fact that the brotherhoods admitted none but persons of good character, and expelled all who were guilty of dishonourable actions. By these regulations, and by the discipline and order which ruled in the assemblies, the guilds exercised in that barbaric age a beneficial influence, and served as one of the pillars of morality as long as they themselves retained their primitive purity.

While not enjoying quite the same privileges as the royal ones, the petty guilds were nevertheless extremely important. They were composed of artisans and merchants, who met at certain times in a specified place to eat, drink, and consider their common interests. Each member had to pay a share of the expense incurred in the festivals, and as their cost was somewhat high, only the most affluent and prominent burghers could belong to them. Although these petty guilds did not have so extended a jurisdiction as the royal ones, yet the majority of disputes concerning trade and industry were judged by the tribunal of the corporation before being taken into the ordinary courts. Those guilds known as the *Calendars*, because their members met on the first day of every month (Kalends), were composed for the most part of priests, and other ecclesiastics, and only concerned themselves with religious questions.

The character and organisation of the guilds will become still clearer if we cite the most important articles of their rules. " If a member causes the death of one of his fellow members, he shall pay 40 marks to his victim's heirs, or be excluded from the brotherhood as a felon. If on the other hand a member of the guild kill a non-member, his brethren, if they be present, shall aid in saving their fellow's life; if it happen on the sea they shall procure him a ship with oars, an instrument for baling, a steel and flint, and an axe; after that he must defend himself as he can. If he has need of a horse they shall accompany him to the pasture grounds and procure for him free a horse for one day and one night. Members who have witnessed the killing of a fellow without going to his defence are expelled from the guild as felons.

" If a member lose his money a collection shall be taken for his benefit at the next banquet, and each of his *confrères* shall give what he thinks is right. Each member shall give three pieces of money to the brother whose house has been burned, or whose ship has been wrecked, or who is about to set out on a pilgrimage. Members shall not try to do each other harm by act or conduct whether in competition or any other fashion. Members shall watch two by two at the bedside of a sick comrade who has need of their aid, and shall continue to do so until he is well. At a member's death four comrades shall guard the corpse, and all share the funeral expenses, accompany the body and bear it to the tomb."

There are numberless other regulations with the object of preventing insults, quarrels, drunkenness, and other unpleasantnesses that would disturb the meetings. The oldest guilds mentioned are those of Odense, Schleswig, Ribe, Flensburg, Malmö, Lund, and Skanör; but they were soon to be found in every town of the kingdom. Their relation with the church, and the need of protection against the rampant license and immorality, facilitated their extension. When social order was established and laws were better respected, the guilds became not only superfluous but positively harmful, in their quality of little states within the state. To which it must be added that they slowly degenerated and became centres of quarrels, drunkenness, debauchery, and all sorts of violence — the very things which it had originally been their object to prevent. And so the kings were compelled gradually to reduce and suppress them; Valdemar Atterdag and his daughter Margaret worked to this end at the close of the fourteenth century, and their successors pursued the same aim. The Reformation, which abolished the cult of saints and masses for the dead, accomplished the complete dissolution of the guilds, which transformed themselves into simple corporations, armourers' companies, fire insurance companies, etc.

THE RISE OF THE BOURGEOISIE

The guilds were a powerful element in the development of the burgher class, in that they taught the burghers self-respect, and awoke them to a consciousness of their own strength, and showed them how to unite in common efforts to defend their rights. Although there had been since ancient times, various towns, not without importance, yet their number was not great, and the origin of the majority of Danish towns may be assigned to the eleventh and twelfth centuries. Commerce and the trades made considerable progress; new sources of industry were opened up and the population of the towns began to be differentiated more and more from that of the country, by its occupations, its manner of life, and its organisation. The majority of the towns situated on the sea or inland waters took their origin from fortresses, built here and there on the coast for protection against pirates and as shelters during the winter to the ships drawn up on the sands. Merchants and fishermen, artisans and labourers, established themselves in proximity to these secure places, where there was, besides, a chance of profit; others were constantly coming in, until a whole town was formed whose origin is revealed by the termination "borg" like Aalborg, Vordingborg, Faaborg, etc., and their inhabitants were called *borgere* (burghers). A sufficiently large number of towns owe their origin to the foundation of monasteries and other religious institutions.

The construction of these edifices drew thither a crowd of masons, carpenters, and smiths, who established themselves in the neighbourhood with their families; where they were soon joined by others in the hope of sharing in the work and the profit always to be found around the rich religious establishments. In this manner were born the towns of Nestved, Sorö, Præstö, Maribo, Mariager, Nykjöbing, on the island of Mors, and several others. A safe harbour, good fishing grounds, and a situation favourable for commerce and navigation were sure to lead to the foundation of towns, which accordingly bore the termination *kjöbing* (place for trade), like Ring-kjöbing, Stubbekjöbing, Rudkjöbing, Kjöbenhavn (Copenhagen); or the ending ör when they were situated on a point of land, like Korsör, Helsingör (Elsinore), Skanör, etc. The artisans and merchants who first settled these towns were those engaged in preparing and selling the necessaries of life — as bakers, brewers, butchers, inn-keepers, shoe-makers, tanners, smiths, masons, carpenters, etc. In the beginning the towns had the same tribunals as the surroundng country; but as the difference grew between villages and towns the latter obtained special tribunals, their own legislation, and very liberal charters under elective magistrates. But while these changes had begun to take place in this age they were not fully brought about until the following, when the burghers took their place for the first time among the orders of the state.

CHURCH AND STATE

The creation of a special metropolitan see in the North, so long meditated and planned, was finally realised. An apostolic legate came on this occasion to Denmark, and chose for the residence of the future archbishop the city of Lund, already the seat of an important diocese, and well situated to be the ecclesiastical metropolis of the three northern kingdoms.

The bishop of Lund, Adser, nephew of Queen Bothilde, wife of Eric Eiegod, was the first called to that office (1104). By the institution of a national archbishopric the kings no longer had the inconvenience of dealing with a foreign prelate, often imperious and not readily to be conciliated; but they did not gain much by the change, for the archbishops of Lund meddled much more with the affairs of the state than the archbishops of Hamburg had been able to do, and as natives they had family relations with the powerful men of the land, which still further increased their influence.

The state then had two heads, one civil and the other religious, whose opposing interests occasioned perpetual strife. The archbishops, thanks to their great revenue, important domains, and the influence they enjoyed as primates of the North, were soon in a position to defy the king and shake his throne with rebellion and civil war. The establishment of the archdiocese of Lund gave the clergy a point of support, heretofore lacking, which permitted them henceforth to take a firmer attitude towards the state.

The archbishop of Lund's jurisdiction extended over the churches of Norway and Sweden; but under Eskil, Adser's successor, each of these two kingdoms recovered its own archbishop; while the archbishops of Lund received, with the title of apostolic legate and primate of Sweden, a sort of supremacy over the whole northern clergy. This was rather an honorary than a real distinction, for the Norwegian and Swedish archbishops watched jealously over their rights and opposed every encroachment of the Danish primate. When the North had been provided with a special ecclesiastical chief, the sovereign pontiff thought to complete the separation of church and state by introducing the celibacy of the priesthood, which for nearly half a century had existed in the majority of European countries. As a result of the first Lateran council (1123) the Danish priests were enjoined to repudiate their wives and to live a celibate life; but it was a long time before the prescription was observed.

Archbishop Eskil was himself married, and the priests were sustained by the people in their resistance to the new regulation. In vain did the energetic archbishop Absalon work for the suppression of marriage in the priesthood; the people, already irritated by the tithes and other vexatious burdens, showed their opposition by a revolt in Skåne, where the peasants cried, "Down with the bishop. We will keep our priests, but only on condition that they are married." Denmark, however, could not escape a regulation so vigorously applied throughout the whole Catholic world, and after more than a century's struggle the Danish clergy were compelled to renounce their obstinate resistance.

The apostolic nuncio, Gregory, who came to Denmark in 1222, caused the marriage of priests to be once more forbidden in the council of Schleswig, and pronounced civil punishments for offenders. Even some priests in Jutland, who had had the courage to appeal to a general council as higher than the pope, could do nothing further. It was thus that the celibacy of the clergy was introduced little by little, but not without great detriment to their morals, for the ministers of religion henceforth kept concubines and scandalised their flocks by most irregular lives.

HAMRA CHURCH, GOTLAND

(Built in the twelfth century)

The church did not suppress this notorious evil, but shut her eyes to vice under a mask. In forbidding marriage to the priests, she broke the last link that held them to their fellow citizens, and ranged herself opposite the state as a separate and often hostile society.[e]

ERIC III, NIELS, ERIC IV, AND ERIC THE LAMB

Eric III, called Eiegod or the Ever-good, was the fourth son of Svend II, and from the jarldom of Jutland was raised by the estates to the throne of that kingdom [on the death of Olaf Hunger, 1095]. As the next harvest was one of abundance, the people were again contented, and he obtained credit for the abundance with the same injustice as his brother had been condemned for the famine. More active than his predecessor, he administered the laws with vigour; and he destroyed Jomsburg, the stronghold of the pirates, who had again reared their heads during the preceding reign. To keep them in continued subjection, he erected fortresses in their country, and garrisoned them well. The most remarkable event of this monarch's reign is the erection of Lund into an archbishopric.

The cause of a pilgrimage which Eric undertook in 1103, and from which he was destined never to return, is not well known; but it was probably to expiate a homicidal act which he had perpetrated in a fit of anger or of drunkenness. Whatever the case, he resolved to visit the Holy Land, and that too in opposition to the prayers and tears of his people, by whom he was cherished. Passing through Rome, where he obtained the erection of Lund into a metropolitan see, he repaired to Constantinople. By Alexius Comnenus he was received with much distinction; though for some time he was narrowly watched, lest, with all his piety, he should place himself at the head of the Varangian guard, and become troublesome to his host. His manners soon dispelled this diffidence, and he was splendidly entertained. Being supplied not only with provisions and vessels but with a liberal store of gold, he sailed for Palestine; but, landing in the isle of Cyprus, he fell a victim to a pestilential disease.

After Eric's death there was an interregnum of two years. He had left his son Harold governor of the realm during his absence; but the conduct of that prince was so unpopular that when the states assembled they excluded him and his brothers, and resolved to choose one of his uncles. The eldest, named Svend, died before he could be elected. Ubbo, the next prince, refused the dignity, which then descended to Niels, the next in age.

The long reign of this monarch (1105–1134) was one of calamities, occasioned chiefly by his jealousy of his nephew Knud [called Lavard, that is, lord], second son of the late king. Henry king of the Abodriti, a Wend people who dwelt on the Baltic coast from Mecklenburg to Pomerania, was nearly connected with the royal house of Denmark, his mother being Sigritha, daughter of Svend II. As the Abodriti had been subdued by at least two Danish kings, and forced to embrace Christianity, they were regarded in the light of vassals. But Henry, more powerful than any of his predecessors, since he had reduced other Wend tribes to his yoke, would be no vassal to Denmark, though he was certainly one to Germany. He first demanded his mother's dowry, which he asserted had never been paid; and, when it was refused, invaded the southern part of Jutland. Niels marched against him, and was defeated.

To arrest the career of the invader was reserved for Knud, who had been invested by his father with the ducal fief of Schleswig [then known as South Jutland]. This prince not only cleared the duchy of its invaders, but carried the war into the country of the Abodriti. Henry now sued for peace, and was thenceforth the friend of his nephew. Knud had saved Denmark from many evils; and his conduct now showed that he was no less excellent a governor than he had been a general. He exterminated the banditti, restored the empire of the laws, and caused the arts of life to flourish. His reputation gave much umbrage to the king; nor was that feeling diminished when, after the death of Henry, he was presented by the emperor Lothair with the vacant regal fief. With this augmented power he maintained tranquillity the more easily, not in his ducal fief only but in the whole of Denmark. His eldest brother Harold, whose vices had excluded him from the throne, made many hostile irruptions into Jutland; but Eric, his next brother, was no less ready than he to protect that kingdom.

The contrast between the conduct of Niels and of Knud made a deep impression on the Danes. On two of them, the king and his son, it was no

less painful than it was deep. To hasten Knud's destruction was the object
of both. The first attempt was to accuse him of some crime in the assembly
of the estates; but he defended himself so powerfully that he was unanimously
absolved. Disappointed in this aim, Magnus requested an interview with
Knud, under the pretext of settling all differences amicably; and, while unsuspicious of danger, assassinated him. All Denmark was in instant commotion. The kindred of the victim hastened to the meeting of the estates, and
displaying his bloody garments called for vengeance on the murderers. To
escape the popular indignation, Magnus fled into Sweden; but Niels, who
relied on the support of a party, endeavoured to brave the storm. He was,
however, solemnly deposed, and Eric, the brother of Knud, elected in his
stead. But he refused to comply with the decree. He collected troops,
and took the field against his rival, who exhibited no less activity in his own
behalf. In the civil war which followed the bishops took part, and fought
like the temporal nobles. Knud had been the vassal of Lothair, and had
demanded the assistance of the empire; and that monarch collecting a small
army, marched into Jutland to co-operate with Eric in avenging the death
of Knud. Seeing that the junction of the emperor and Eric must be fatal to
his cause, Niels withdrew the former from the alliance by the offer of a large
sum of money, and by consenting to hold Denmark as a fief of the empire.
Lothair then returned, leaving the fortune of war to decide between the
two kings.

The retreat of the Germans was the signal for renewed and more fierce
hostilities between the rivals. With his usual perversity Harold forsook the
cause of his brother Eric, to fight for Niels; and Magnus, who had powerful
armies in Sweden, brought reinforcements to the war. Success was varied:
on the deep Magnus was defeated; on the land, Eric. But some acts of
more than usual barbarity perpetrated by Niels and Harold at Roeskilde,
diminished the number of their supporters. Still they were enabled to make
another stand on the coast near the gulf of Fodvig in Skåne. Victory
declared for Eric: Magnus fell in the battle; and Niels with much difficulty
escaped into Jutland. Among the slain were five bishops and sixty priests.
As Magnus was dead, Niels declared Harold, the brother of Eric, his successor — a declaration which did no good to his own cause. To escape the
pursuit of his rival, he threw himself into Schleswig, which was better fortified
than any city in the North. But this was an imprudent act: in that city
the memory of Knud was idolised; and there he was massacred by some
members of a fraternity of which the deceased prince had been the head
(1135). Thus fell a monarch who in the early part of his reign had afforded
his subjects reason to hope that he would prove a blessing to the realm, but
whose subsequent conduct had covered him with universal odium.

In the reign of Eric IV, surnamed Emun, who on the death of his rival
succeeded to the government of the whole kingdom, there is little for history. One of his first exploits was to put to death his brother Harold, and
eleven sons of that prince. There was a twelfth, Olaf, who escaped into
Sweden, and became in the sequel king of Denmark. He next pursued the
Wend pirates into their stronghold of Arkona, which he took and destroyed.
On his return, he applied himself with zeal to the administration of justice;
and was assassinated by a Jutland chief, whose father or brother he had
judicially condemned to death. This tragedy took place in the midst not
merely of his court but of his people, while presiding over an assembly of
the Jutland states (1137).

There were candidates for the crown — (1) Knud the son of Magnus, and consequently grandson of Niels; (2) Svend, a natural son of Eric IV; (3) Valdemar, the son of Knud king of the Abodriti, who had been murdered by Magnus, and who in 1170 was canonised, like the martyr of that name who had ruled over Denmark. The bias of the assembly was evidently in favour of Valdemar; but as both he and the two other candidates were of tender years, the choice fell on Eric, called the Lamb, whose mother was a daughter of Eric Eiegod.

The surname of this king will sufficiently explain his character. He was indeed one of the most pacific of men. Yet he was compelled to fight for his crown; for Olaf, the only son of Harold that had escaped the bloody proscriptions of Eric Emun, appeared at the head of a considerable force and claimed it. That, if hereditary right only was to be consulted, the claim was a valid one is certain, for he was the only representative of his father, the eldest son of Eric Eiegod. But the Danish throne was elective; and though the claim was confined to one family, little regard was paid to primogeniture. After many alternations of fortune, Olaf was vanquished and slain (1143). But Eric himself was conquered by the Wend pirates of the Baltic, who, though so frequently humbled (if any credit is to be placed in the national historians), soon re-appeared in numbers formidable enough to alarm the kingdom. This check and the consequent decline of his reputation in the eyes of a warlike people induced him soon afterwards to resign the crown, and to profess as monk in the cloister of Odense.

On the retirement of Eric the Lamb (1147), the three princes who had before been rejected on account of their youth were again candidates. Valdemar being deemed still too young, the choice was restricted to the other two. Unfortunately for the interests of order both were elected — Svend by the Landsthing of Skåne and Zealand, Knud by the people of Jutland.

THE DIVISION OF THE KINGDOM

That the division of the sovereignty would inevitably lead to civil war might have been foreseen by the blindest. It was a long and a bloody one, which, though suspended for a time through the efforts of the pope, who wished all Christendom to arm against the infidels, burst out with renewed fury. Adser, archbishop of Lund, led the Danish host against the pagans of the Baltic; but the expedition was inglorious, and the remnant which returned from it embraced one of the two parties. The fortunes of both varied; but when Valdemar, the favourite of the nation, joined Svend, the advantage was on the side of that king, who gained at least three battles over his rival. At one time Knud was driven from the realm, and forced to seek shelter at the court of the emperor Conrad III. But tranquillity was not the result of his retirement. The Wend pirates, not satisfied with having defeated the archbishop, and incited by the agitated state of the public mind, ravaged the coasts both of Jutland and of the isles. Finding their king and nobles unable to protect them, the people entered into armed fraternities, which were consecrated by religion. They not only defended their own coasts, but equipped vessels to cruise in the Baltic, and to surprise such of the pagan ships as they might find detached from the rest. In a few years twenty-two of these vessels took above eighty of the enemy's. Still these were partial, isolated effects, which had little influence over the general mass of misery. When Knud returned as the vassal of the empire, the civil war again raged. Frederick Barbarossa, as the lord paramount, now interfered, and meeting the two parties, decreed that while the title of king of Denmark should be left to the victorious Svend, Knud should reign over Zealand as a fief of the Danish crown.   This award satisfied neither party, and least of all the nation, which was indignant with both of them for sacrificing its independence to the emperor.   Svend refused to cede Zealand to his rival; and the civil war was about to recommence, when Valdemar, to whose valour Svend owed everything, prevailed on the one to give and the other to accept, in lieu of that island, certain domains in Jutland and Skåne. Peace therefore was procured for the moment; but it was a hollow peace, which the accident of an hour might break.

The advantage which Svend had gained by the aid of Valdemar he lost by his misconduct.   He adopted the German costume; imitated the German manners; expressed much contempt for everything Danish as in the highest degree barbarous; seldom appeared at the national Thing; restored the old judicial ordeal of duel; became luxurious; and levied high contributions on his people.   A disastrous expedition into Sweden made him despised as well as hated; and on his return into Skåne, he was assailed by the yellings of the infuriated populace.   Something worse than this result would have been experienced by him, had not a chief, named Tycho, one of the most influential in the province, rescued him from his position.

When at liberty, he allowed his licentious followers to plunder the inhabitants.   Many he put to death; and among them was the brave man who had saved him from their fury.   This atrocious ingratitude lost him the favour of Valdemar, who passed over to the side of Knud, and cemented the alliance by marrying the sister of that prince.   It was now the object of Svend to seize both princes, either openly or by stratagem; but they were on their guard; and each was always surrounded by armed attendants.   At length he was vanquished, and forced to seek a temporary asylum in Saxony. But he obtained succour from the duke of that province, and from the archbishop of Bremen, who could never forgive the Danes for forcing the abolition of his jurisdiction over the North, and allied himself with the Wend pirates, who were always ready to join any party that offered them plunder. At the head of these forces he returned, and compelled the people to receive him as their king.   Again Valdemar and Knud marched against him; but the former, pitying the sufferings of the people, offered his mediation, and tranquillity was for the moment re-established.   The chief condition of this treaty was that the kingdom should be divided into three sovereignties; that Svend should have Skåne, Knud the isles, and Valdemar Jutland, in addition to his duchy of Schleswig.   The whole people abandoned themselves to joy, and Svend, pretending to join in it, gave a magnificent entertainment to his brother kings in the castle of Roeskilde.   But at that very festival he ordered both to be assassinated.   Knud fell; but Valdemar, who defended himself courageously, escaped into Jutland.

The reputation of Valdemar, and above all his words, easily induced the people to espouse his cause.   Pursued by his active enemy, he was constrained to fight before his preparations were completed.   The result, however, was indecisive.   In a subsequent and more general action, near Viborg, Svend was defeated and compelled to flee.   He was eagerly pursued by the victors, who overtook him in a morass, from which the weight of his armour prevented him from emerging; and he was immediately beheaded.   Never did the Danes suffer more than under this unworthy prince.   Enfeebled at home, degraded abroad, without government or security for either person or substance, they were sunk even in their own estimation.   But for these disasters they could only blame themselves; they were the inevitable results of their own folly in dividing the monarchy.*b*

VALDEMAR (I) THE GREAT SUBDUES RÜGEN

When peace was restored in the interior of the kingdom, Valdemar, who had already shown evidence of a generous and lofty soul, strove to give it the security and glory it had formerly enjoyed. The Wends were always its cruellest foes. These barbarians never ceased making irruptions into Jutland, where, in some of the Danish isles, and sometimes in several places at once when not opposed with prompt resistance, they left horrible traces of their rage. This gave another reason for attacking these undisciplined people, whom Valdemar regarded, not unjustly, as rebellious subjects over whom he could reassume the authority which Knud Lavard, his father, had exercised as their king. Moreover the desire to assemble them again under the standard of the faith made of this expedition a holy enterprise and one agreeable to the clergy, and this motive filled with fresh ardour all those who were destined to take part in it. Absalon was one of the leaders in whom Valdemar had the most confidence. He came of an illustrious Danish family and united bravery with prudence, wisdom and fidelity with ambition and a passion for arms. The see of Roeskilde being vacant in the time of which we speak, and the clergy and people not being able to agree on the choice of a prelate, two factions were formed which nearly came to blows, and which the king had some trouble in appeasing. Then, without having in any way touched on the liberty of the voters, he had the pleasure of seeing his favourite, Absalon, elected, who while he was invested with this dignity was not less zealous in peace than in war.

The Wends of Rügen, knowing the king to be occupied in Norway, had recommenced their incursions, and driven away the Danes, for whom they bore a hatred inspired by long wars, customs, and a different language and religion. Always sure of finding in Arkona, which they regarded as impregnable, a retreat where they with their plunder could brave the conqueror's anger, they abandoned to him without regret the badly cultivated fields, hoping, not without reason, to glean richer harvests in those of their enemies. Valdemar resolved to make every effort to demolish this fortress, and with it the last support of such obstinate ferocity. He prepared a formidable force, to which Duke Henry the Lion, Pribislaw who had become his vassal and prince of the Abodriti, Kasimir and Bogislaw, dukes of Pomerania, joined bodies of their troops. Having made a descent on the isle of Rügen, he marched without stopping as far as Arkona, which he immediately invested. Arkona, of which to-day only traces remain, was then the most considerable town of all Wendland. It was situated at the northern extremity of the isle of Rügen on a very protruding cape, and was defended on the east, south, and north by high and steep rocks. The western side was guarded by an extremely strong and high rampart.

Christianity had been preached to the people of Rügen long before. The monks of Corvei had even made several conversions there under Ludwig the German, and built a church in honour of St. Wit their patron. But as these people were the most ferocious and unconquerable of all the Slavs, they did not long suffer the Christian yoke. The missionaries were driven away, and there remained no trace of their work, save worship rendered to St. Wit, of whom these barbarians made an idol whom they soon adored under the name of Swanto-Wit as the supreme deity. Thus it is dangerous,

[1168 A.D.]

justly says a learned ecclesiastic, to preach the worship of saints before teaching the knowledge of the true God.

This idol had its chief temple in Arkona, a temple which was as remarkable for its size as for its statue of the pretended divinity.   The gigantic idol was topped by four heads; its right hand held a horn which the high priest filled with wine every year; from the more or less quick evaporation of this, the fertility of the season was foretold.   The other hand held a bow.   Divers offerings were at its feet.   Each year after harvest people hastened from every quarter to offer sacrifices, but nothing was more acceptable than a Christian.   This festival was held every year.   The priest who presided was more respected than even the princes.   He interpreted the oracles and the decrees of the god, who gave through him most absolute orders.   He alone had the right of entering into the enclosure where the idol dwelt.   He dared not breathe in this sanctuary, and for fear an impure breath should offend a present divinity, he went outside to draw breath each time he had need. On the festive day, all the people being assembled before the temple door, he took the horn from the idol's hand and examined it attentively.   If he found the wine had evaporated much he threatened an approaching drought and advised them to store their grain.   If the contrary, he permitted them to sell superfluous stores.   Several other auguries of this kind prolonged a ceremony which was ended by an exhortation from the priest to lavish sacrifices on the god.   The assembly ended in feasts and wild debauchery, these being regarded as proofs of zeal for the idol.

This temple contained great riches, from tribute levied by the cunning of priests over the credulity of the people.   All the nations of Wends scattered on the southern coasts had to make annual offerings.   Some sent the spoils of their enemies, others the third part of the booty taken in their sea voyages.   Princes sent presents to gain favourable answers from the god when they questioned him concerning the future, or when they formed some enterprise which needed his help.   Three hundred military horsemen were specially dedicated to him and only plundered on his behalf.   The sovereign pontiff also kept a white horse which he alone might approach, and on which the god rode when he went forth to combat enemies to the faith.   Often this horse might be seen early in the morning covered with sweat caused by night rides.   Favourable predictions were also drawn from the manner in which the animal ran.   Neighbouring countries were filled with reports of such great marvels that the people of Rügen came to be regarded as the happiest and most formidable of all the Slav nations.

In reality, this people — animated and emboldened by the situation of their isle, by the enthusiasm inspired by the presence of the Swanto-Wit, by the riches they had collected on their journeys, by those sent from nations tributary to the pretended divinity, and by those moreover drawn from the abundant herring fishery on their coasts — was, as one might say, the root and trunk of the pagan Slav leagues, and as long as this trunk rested whole it was in vain that at great expense certain branches, always ready to give forth fresh shoots, were lopped off.

Thus all eyes were turned on Valdemar, awaiting with impatience the success of an enterprise wherein two nations and two religions combatted for their greatest interest.   The Danes, animated by such powerful motives and by the presence of their king, attacked Arkona with the greatest valour, building battering rams to demolish the rampart.   They lodged themselves in several advantageous posts and burned the principal tower.   The fire, which spread by degrees to the combustibles which entered into the composition of these ancient ramparts, seconded the efforts made by the Danes to overthrow them. At last the besieged, tired of warring against iron and fire, decided to capitulate. The king, who could flatter himself with the knowledge of being able to take the town by assault, and whose soldiers, greedy for rich plunder, besought him to sack it, yet yielded to the remonstrances of Bishop Absalon and Archbishop Eskil, who with a moderation very rare in a religious war advised him not to heed the plea of his soldiers, but to avoid bloodshed, and not reduce the besieged to despair. It was then agreed that the people of Rügen should deliver to the king the idol, Swanto-Wit, with all treasure in the temple; that all Christian slaves should be set at liberty without ransom; and that they should, for the future, all embrace and profess the Christian religion. All land assigned for the maintenance of their priests should be given to the church. Service in the Danish army when necessity arose was also demanded, and an annual tribute.

The hostages who were exacted as surety for the fulfilment of promises having been delivered, Esbern and Sunon, two prominent officers in the army, were ordered to go and overthrow the idol Swanto-Wit. They were obliged to knock down the colossus with precaution, for fear its fall should cause some accident, and give the people of Rügen grounds for saying that it avenged itself in perishing. In reality, the pagans had gathered in crowds to witness the sight, hoping to behold punishment of such sacrilege. But when the idol had fallen, and hurt no one, and they saw pieces of it quietly cut into firewood amid cheers from the Danes, the greater part saw their own simplicity and conceived more respect for the Divinity of their conquerors than for their own.

The temple, as well as the idol, was burned, after the treasure had been removed to a safe place. From Arkona Bishop Absalon, who directed the war under the king's orders, went to receive the submission of six thousand of the people of Rügen who composed the garrison of another fortress, named Karentz. He had burned three temples dedicated to three colossal and monstrous statues of other pretended gods tutelary of the nation. The ease with which these gods allowed themselves to be reduced to cinders prepared the minds of their worshippers to embrace the new religion which Absalon was authorised in one of the articles of capitulation to offer them. He substituted churches for their temples, in the country as in the towns, to the number of twelve, after which he took back hostages and seven large coffers full of money to the king.

After having subdued and pacified the people, and after the Rügen princes, Tetistas and Jarimar, had solemnly acknowledged themselves tributaries to the Danish crown, Valdemar, glorious and content, recrossed the sea with his army. Absalon, whom the cares of war could not distract from those of the episcopate, sent soon after to Rügen zealous priests to complete by persuasion conversions begun by force. Prince Jarimar, who was really converted, heartily seconded the efforts of these missionaries. Absalon did not neglect for this the interests of the see he occupied. Valdemar caused the conquests the church had made by arms to be made known to Pope Alexander III. Alexander loaded him with praise, and in the same bull ordered, in conformity with Absalon's desires, that the isle of Rügen should thenceforth form part of the diocese of Roeskilde. Other letters of the same pontiff, accorded two years after in answer to the insistence of the king, granted the canonisation of Knud. This was celebrated at Ringsted with great pomp, in presence of an infinite number of Danish prelates and strangers and other spectators. The inhabitants of Zealand had conceived such esteem for

Knud that, not having been able as they desired to have him for an earthly king, they would thenceforth take him for patron saint in heaven.

ABSALON, AND THE SKÅNIANS

A short time after, Archbishop Eskil resolved to end his days in retirement, renouncing those dignities which seemed as heavy in old age as they had been worthy of envy before he had attained them. Vainly they tried to turn him from his object. He had vowed on the hand of the famous St. Bernard, abbot of Clairvaux, who had great love for him, as may be seen in his letters. In his quality as legate, Eskil had the right of naming his successor. But for fear of depriving the church of rights which he himself had defended with so much zeal, he remitted his power to the assembly, which ordinarily made the election. Then the king, speaking in the name of this assembly, nominated Absalon bishop of Roeskilde, his choice being approved by general acclamations.

But whether, as Absalon declared, he found the burden too heavy, or whether he secretly desired to become primate and archbishop, without ceasing to be bishop of Roeskilde, it is known that he persisted in refusing the offered dignity. The assembly and the king being equally obstinate on their side in refusing to make another choice, this seeming conflict of interests and wills had every promise of ending in a serious quarrel. Saxo even relates that certain men trying forcibly to seat Absalon on the archiepiscopal chair met with such resistance that several were thrown down. At last it was agreed to send an account of this singular difference to the pope for decision, and to that end deputies from either side were despatched. Doubtless this was just what Absalon wished. Alexander III crowned Absalon's secret satisfaction by the verdict given. He was permitted by the legate sent into Denmark to retain his bishopric and was threatened with excommunication if he refused the archbishopric of Lund. After this threat resistance would have been a crime, and nothing remained but to make a virtue of docility. Absalon then submitted and undertook his part in uniting in his person the two highest ecclesiastical dignities of the kingdom, with the offices of generalissimo, admiral, first minister, and senator.

The revolt of the Skånians was an event more remarkable when one sees what motives influenced the inhabitants of this province. They wished permission for their priests to marry, and pretended that their ministry was sufficient without the service of bishops. It might have been thought that these priests were the secret authors of the rebellion, if the Skånians had not at the same time refused to pay the ecclesiastical tenth and exacted that thenceforth only governors of their country should be sent to them.

In spite of his eloquence, his worth, and his power, Absalon could not stay the progress of this outbreak. He was even constrained to take refuge in Zealand; and, far from the threats of the king having any effect, the rebels were so irritated by them that they resolved to pay no more taxes, and forced the priests to take wives.

Valdemar, seeing the danger of suffering such disorders any longer, went to Skåne, followed by Absalon and a small army. He was received by a deputation of the principal men of the province, who promised to return to obedience if the king would recall Absalon and the foreign officials to whom the country had been given in charge. As this good prince always inclined to moderation, he obliged Absalon to retire again to Zealand and then followed him. In the hope that this condescension would satisfy the malcontents, the king even consented to examine their grievances against his minister, conjointly with deputies they might name. But these deputies, gained over or intimidated, subscribed to everything in Zealand, and retracted everything in Skåne. Revolt broke out with renewed force and everyone flew to arms, while the archbishop on his side did not spare his diocesans his ecclesiastical thunders, and Valdemar raised an army capable of dealing even more effectual blows.

The king's setting out was the signal for war. But he flattered himself with the hope of being able to reduce them by fear alone, for repugnance to shed the blood of his subjects made him wish to avoid resorting to extreme measures. But the rebels forced his hand by defending a bridge over which he had to cross to get to them. In the efforts made by the soldiers of either side the battle became more deadly and sanguinary. Absalon, however, turned the scale in the king's favour by the skill with which he managed his cavalry, causing them to fall suddenly on the Skånians, and throwing many of them into the river. Help which came shortly afterwards only served to render their defeat more complete, so that, their troops being dispersed or destroyed, they could only ask for peace. Valdemar willingly granted this, receiving their hostages and submissions. But he found them so obstinate on the subject of the tithes that, for fear of renewing the bloody tragedies which a similar cause had evoked under King Knud IV, he obliged Archbishop Absalon to desist from his claim if only for a time. Thus the sedition was appeased, but we shall see afterwards that peace could only last as long as the clergy found it served their own interests. It was as little durable as their disinterestedness was sincere.

THE DEATH OF VALDEMAR; HIS LAWS

Valdemar was preparing to repress fresh incursions of the Wends when an illness detained him at Vordingborg, a town in Zealand; a short time afterwards he died of the results of this illness, or rather from the ignorance of a Skånian abbot who boasted of possessing great knowledge of medicine. The king was found dead immediately after having taken from these imprudent hands the drink which was meant to cure him. He was only forty-eight, and had reigned twenty-five years. His premature death was sincerely mourned by the people. It has been remarked that, when his body was taken to Ringsted for burial, the country people flocked weeping from all parts, crying that in him they had lost a father and a liberator to whom they owed the happiness of no longer fearing brigands and the barbarities of pirates. In truth this prince had united the principal virtues which make a king loved and esteemed. He understood how to conquer and how to pardon, to make his enemies fear him by being good to his people, and to re-establish peace and good order in his kingdom by increasing its consideration and influence abroad.

It was he who edited and published the code called *The Skånian Laws* and the *Law of Zealand*, as well as the *Ecclesiastical Rights* of these two provinces. The ecclesiastical laws of Skåne, composed of twenty-five articles, were published in 1162, the civil laws in the year following. The laws of Zealand appeared in 1171. These laws, conjointly with the *Jutland Code* published by Valdemar II, are the source of those which Denmark is to-day justly proud of possessing. They are simple, clear, concise, and generally adapted to assure liberty and property to citizens. Good sense is shown in him who dictated them, as in the style in which they are couched. There is no flourish of rhetoric, no vain ostentation of grandeur and authority, such as marks the début of so many other laws — as if the authors wanted to show the people that the pleasure of commanding them, not the care of rendering them happy, was uppermost. Brilliant centuries and nations famous for learning and spirit might envy the wise simplicity which governed these two codes.*

KNUD VI (1182–1202 A.D.)

Knud had been crowned in his father's lifetime, and from his fourteenth year had been admitted to a share in the government. His accession therefore to the undivided sovereignty was expected to pass without opposition. But the people of Skåne elected another sovereign — Harold, a grandson of Prince Magnus. The contest, however, was short-lived; they were reduced, and their ruler was compelled to flee into Sweden.

The reign of this monarch was one of conquest and of prosperity. Soon after his accession, Absalon led an armament against Bogislaw, duke of Pomerania, who exhibited ill-will to Denmark and her vassals, and obtained a complete victory over the enemy.

SLEIGH OF AXEL OXENSTIERNA

(In State Historical Museum)

During the following two years the warlike operations continued, and Bogislaw at length was compelled to throw himself on the royal mercy. Besides offering a large quantity of gold, he did homage for all his possessions to Knud. The two dukes of Mecklenburg were also reduced, and acknowledged fealty to him. The submission of two such provinces, which had been dependent on Henry the Lion [duke of Bavaria and Saxony], and had subsequently acknowledged the superiority of the empire, filled the king with so much pleasure, that he assumed the title of king of the Wends.

To assume the feudal supremacy over these regions was a blow struck at the authority of the emperor Frederick Barbarossa. Between these potentates there was a misunderstanding from the very commencement of Knud's reign. Frederick invited him to his court under the pretext of drawing more closely the amicable bonds which had been formed between him and Valdemar; but as the king suspected that this was only a lure to enforce the payment of homage, he evaded compliance. It soon appeared that such was indeed the intention; for he was formally summoned to visit the diet for that purpose. A second refusal to attend so exasperated Frederick that he threatened to confer the fief of Denmark on some other vassal. The king replied that before he could give it he must first take it. All negotiation being useless, the emperor offered the greatest insult to the majesty of Denmark by sending back to her own country the sister of Knud, who had been betrothed to his second son, the duke of Swabia. From this moment the breach was irreparable; and the king turned with more zeal to the cause of his father-in-law, Henry the Lion.*b*

After the capture of Jerusalem by Saladin in 1187 messengers arrived [in Denmark] with letters from Pope Clement III, in which that pontiff exhorted the Danes to go on crusade like the faithful of other countries to try to recover the Holy City. The emperor himself went on crusade and, being obliged to be reconciled with his enemies, used the pope's favour to get Knud to make an agreement with him in which that king engaged not to trouble the peace of the empire during the absence of its head; and, effectually to do away with all sorts of discontents, he also revoked the proscription he had issued against Duke Henry the Lion, whose disgrace had embittered the greater part of the princes, and in particular the king of Denmark, his son-in-law, and the king of England, his father-in-law. Reading the papal letters made a great impression on the Danish nobility. Esbern, brother of the archbishop, himself supported the exhortations they contained with all the force of his eloquence. Fifteen of the principal lords of the assembly solemnly took crusader's vows, but only five kept their resolutions.

The king had the wisdom not to take any part. The five crusaders having enrolled those who presented themselves, went in their vessels to Norway, where they were joined by two hundred crusaders of that kingdom. But their journey was thenceforward made apart, and the Norwegians alone arrived in Syria. The Danes were shipwrecked on the coast of Friesland, where they sold their ships. Thence they went by land to Venice, where they embarked afresh, and at last arrived in the Holy Land. This long and painful voyage had no result. The Christians had just made peace with the Saracens, so they returned to their own land without having unsheathed their swords. There were also many Danes in the fleet of fifty-three ships which the Frisians and Flemish sent to sea. Frederick took the land route with his army to go into Palestine. An ancient historian tells us that a relation of the king was among them, with several great lords and about four hundred Danes.*f*

The tranquillity of Denmark was further disturbed by a bishop and a member of the royal family. This was Valdemar, a bastard son of Knud V, who held the see of Schleswig. The king had also conferred on this bishop the government of the duchy until that other Valdemar, the king's brother, for whom the fief was destined, reached an age fit to govern. When that age arrived the prince was knighted, and at the same time invested with the duchy, of which he hastened to take possession. The bishop had tasted the sweets of power, and he was deeply hurt at its withdrawal: from that moment he became the enemy of the king.

Determined on revenge, he entered into alliance with all whom he knew to be hostile to Knud, and, among others, with Adolf of Schauenburg, count of Holstein. When his preparations were matured, he threw off the mask, declaring that his right to the Danish throne was as good as the king's, and demanding a share of the sovereignty. Passing into Norway, which at that time was not on friendly terms with Denmark, he obtained supplies, returned to the latter kingdom, and assumed the royal title. At the same period another army, led by the count of Holstein, marched towards the Eider to support his views. To Knud it was evident that their operations could not be long sustained; that the invaders would soon be in want of provisions, and disperse of themselves. Instead therefore of risking an action he quietly watched the motions of the bishop. The result justified his policy: the treasures of Valdemar were speedily exhausted; his mercenaries disappeared; he threw himself on the royal mercy, but was conducted a close prisoner to a strong fortress in Zealand (1194). Adolf yet remained; the king marched against him, and forced him to sue for peace. But that peace was of short duration. The count, being required to do homage to Knud for some of the domains which he had obtained by the deposition of Henry the Lion, refused to acknowledge any other superior than the emperor; and to fortify himself against the vengeance of the king he entered into an alliance with the markgraf of Brandenburg, whose territory adjoined the Wend dominions of the Dane, and who had an interest in preventing any further augmentation in that quarter. To assail both, Knud sent an armament to the northern coast of the Baltic; and as the venerable Absalon was now too old and too infirm for active warfare, the bishop of Roeskilde was invested with the command.

The result was not very favourable to the king. Two years afterwards however, he took the field in person, and forced Adolf to accept terms of peace: the chief were that Ditmarsh, with the strong fortress of Ratzeburg, should be ceded to Denmark (1200). But in this, as on the former occasion, tranquillity was of short duration. Adolf again quarrelled with his ally; and Valdemar, the king's brother, invaded Holstein. The result was favourable to the Danish arms: Adolf, who had thrown himself into Hamburg, was compelled to leave it, and to witness the fall of Lübeck, which was feudally subject to him. Most of Holstein was now reduced; and the duke having, in the king's name, received the homage of the towns and nobles, returned to Schleswig. No sooner had he left the province than the count reappeared; but it was only to be made prisoner and conveyed in triumph to one of the Danish fortresses. The king himself soon appeared amidst his new subjects; and at Lübeck he received the homage of the great vassals of Holstein, Ditmarsh, Stormarn, Ratzeburg, Schwerin, and other lordships, which were now subject to him, but which he could not incorporate with the monarchy, because they were dependencies of the empire and for them he must himself do homage to the chief of that empire. This was a proud day for Denmark; but that pride was much alloyed by the sudden death of Knud in the very flower of his age.

The flourishing state of Denmark under this prince is well described by Arnold of Lübeck.[g] He alludes to its vast commerce, to its ceaseless activity, to its constantly increasing wealth, to its improvements in the arts of life, to its military reputation, to its zeal for learning. Many Danish youths, he informs us, were annually sent to study at Paris, where they distinguished themselves in philosophy, law, and theology. Many became admirable canonists; many subtle didacticians. The visits of young Danes to the capital of France may be explained by the union of Ingeborg, sister of Knud, with Philip Augustus.

Absalon's Good Works and Death

Towards the close of Knud's reign died Archbishop Absalon, who had held the see of Roeskilde since 1158, and the primacy since 1178.[b] Absalon, whom nature had formed to occupy a great position, came from an illustrious Danish family, and was brought up with King Valdemar I, who, through discernment as much as friendship, never undertook anything without consulting him. He was elected bishop of Roeskilde in 1158, and archbishop

of Lund in 1178.   One might have seen without being scandalised the prelates
of these days pass their lives in camp or at sea, if all those who left the pastoral
staff for the sword had had, like Absalon, not only zeal for their country but
qualities necessary to serve it.   He was a great general and seaman, yet he
did not neglect the government of his two dioceses, the propagation of the
faith in countries he conquered, or the maintenance of religion in the interior
of the kingdom.   It was he who introduced uniformity in the celebration of
divine service, in which the first missionaries sent into different countries
had made changes.

Like all ministers who have been high-minded and loved true greatness,
he was familiar with men of letters, encouraging them as a wise friend and a
protector both zealous and powerful.   By this the great Absalon rendered
his nation services which were perhaps unknown or despised by contemporaries, but from which to-day she draws more satisfaction and glory than
from the most signal victories he won.   In reality it is to him she owes that
elegant and poetical work of Saxo Grammaticus, a true wonder in a century
wherein barbarism triumphed.   Absalon, fearing that the history of past
times would rest in oblivion, and future history would share the same fate,
sought to remedy such past and present evil by charging Saxo and Sveno
Aggonis (Svend Aagesen) to write a history of Denmark down to their own
times, and by founding a monastery at Sorö where men could be entertained
who would undertake to transmit remarkable events to posterity.

But of these projects, so worthy of the author, only the first was executed.
Saxo wrote an entire history of Denmark, but one may say that not the least
important light on history issued from the Sorö monastery, so that after the
death of these two men the history of Denmark was found sterile and lacking
in monuments and memoirs of all kinds.*

VALDEMAR II AT VARIANCE WITH THE EMPEROR (1202–1241 A.D.)

In 1202 Knud VI died; and as he was without heirs male, the choice of
the states fell on his brother Valdemar, duke of Schleswig, who, as we have
related, had given some proofs of military talent [and who bears the surname
of Seir, or the Victorious].

Like his predecessor, the new king repaired to Lübeck to receive the homage
of the conquered inhabitants; and there he assumed the titles, "king of the
Wends" and "lord of Nordalbingia."   In the midst of his triumph he offered
to release Count Adolf, provided the latter would forever renounce all pretension to Holstein with his other domains north of the Elbe, and engage
not to make war, either personally or through his allies, on the king of Denmark.   The conditions were accepted; and hostages being given for their execution, the count was released.   Imprisonment seemed to have sobered him;
for he passed the rest of his days in tranquillity.

Having fomented the troubles of Norway in revenge for the aid given to
Bishop Valdemar, and exacted an annual tribute from Erling, whom he had
supported against rival sovereigns, the Danish king departed on a more
distant expedition — against the pagans of Livonia.   It was attended, however, with no great success: the best that can be said of it is that it was not
disastrous.   A subsequent expedition into Sweden was more unfortunate:
he was signally defeated; but peace was made on terms sufficiently honourable.   About the same time the national arms regained their former lustre
by the conquest of Eastern Pomerania, the duke of which did homage to
Valdemar.

From the prison to which he had been consigned by Knud VI the bishop of Schleswig was no inattentive spectator of events. He longed for revenge; but he must first recover his liberty. In this view he applied to the pope, to the archbishop of Lund, to many prelates of Denmark, and even to the queen, and interested them so far in his behalf that Valdemar, at their intercession, agreed to release him, on the condition of his never again entering Denmark, or any other place where he might give umbrage to the state.[b]

Germany was, at this time, in a state of special ferment. There were vacillations, broken pledges, weakness, and anger on all sides. Otto IV, the new emperor, was no sooner in tranquil possession of the throne than a friendship he had formerly professed for Valdemar, not being now so necessary to his plans, gave place to jealousy excited by the conquests of a neighbour — jealousy made stronger by the fact that Valdemar was sovereign over the very provinces once held by the emperor's father, Henry the Lion. Thus, when the see of Bremen was again empty, the emperor quietly allowed Bernhard, duke of Saxony, to put Bishop Valdemar in possession of the archbishopric, although through a remnant of regard for the king he would not appear to take part in the affair. But a short time after, having become less circumspect, he allied himself against the king with Albert, markgraf of Brandenburg, who sought unceasingly to gain ground on the Wend side at the Dane's expense.

Valdemar easily discovered in this conduct a project to get Nordalbingia away from him, and authorised by Otto's example entered into alliance with Frederick II, son of Henry VI, emperor and king of Sicily. Valdemar recognised him as emperor, united with him, and as reward for such great services obtained the absolute cession of all the provinces he held in Germany, so that these were actually united to the Danish crown, and cut off from the empire. Letters patent from the emperor are dated May, 1214.

It is easy to understand to what degree this alliance of Valdemar and Frederick irritated the emperor Otto, who made several vain efforts to regain his footing. He then leagued himself against the king with his brother Henry, count palatine of the Rhine, and Albert, markgraf of Brandenburg, who continued his ordinary hostilities in Wendland; and with the help of these allies Otto made an irruption into Holstein, resolved to revive the rights which his ancestors, the two dukes of Saxony, had held over this province. He first took Hamburg without meeting any resistance. This was not all: to weaken still more the credit of the king in Germany the confederates openly took the part of Bishop Valdemar, who was still occupying the see of Bremen, and who had aided them in the siege of Hamburg.

But the king no sooner learned of the reddition of this town than he appeared in Holstein at the head of a formidable army. The league and its hopes vanished at the approach of this force. Otto hastily recrossed the Elbe; Hamburg held out, but the king and Count Albert, his nephew, having closed it in with two forts which they caused to be built at the gates of the town, it was obliged to surrender. Otto, abandoned by nearly all the German princes, and excommunicated by the pope, could do nothing but make several fruitless incursions into the diocese of Bremen.

Bishop Valdemar, struck with the same storm, was driven from that country. He was obliged to yield the see to Gerhard, bishop of Osnabrück, whom the pope protected, and was reduced to entering a cloister, where eighteen years after he ended a life that had only been used to the unhappiness of his fellows and himself.

THE CONQUEST OF ESTHONIA (1219 A.D.)

In the midst of these troubles certain religious dissensions in Livonia had passed unnoticed. In a period of about twenty years Riga had been founded, peopled, and fortified so as to be able to resist the repeated attacks of barbarians. Christians had multiplied on the coast, and with them forts, churches, and monasteries. A new order of knights, named the brotherhood of Christ's Soldiers [or Brothers of the Sword], was formed during this crusade, less celebrated than those of the Holy Land, and more lasting in its effects. Princes of these countries even saw themselves obliged to declare themselves its vassals, and to receive as a benefit their own states from these strangers. One party of the Livonians had seriously abjured the errors which had drawn on them so many anxieties and wars. New churches had been founded; the inhabitants of Esthonia, that is northern Livonia, in their provinces along the gulf of Finland, were yet independent and would have to be conquered and christianised. These men, proud and jealous of their liberty, gloried in having always rendered useless the efforts which the Danes, Swedes, and Christians in Riga had made at various times to convert them. Sworn enemies of their new hosts, they held them in continual alarm because their numerous and warlike hordes were often joined by Russian neighbours; these latter, being attached to the Greek ritual, seemed only Christianised that they might hate the Latins.

In this conflict of opposed passions, and forces nearly equal, it was necessary in order that one side might gain a decided advantage that a powerful and warlike prince should intervene. There was none whom personal qualities, resources, and reputation, combined with the situation of his states, made more fit to settle the quarrel than the king of Denmark. It was to him that the strongest appeals were made. They had already produced some effect by 1205, but the success of these first efforts had not been such as was expected from a great king. Valdemar had then determined to make new efforts, when his nephew, Count Albert, returning from Livonia, told him that the Russians, leagued with the Esthonians, were threatening the new church of Riga. "Thereupon he solemnly engaged," says a contemporary author, who witnessed the greater part of what he writes, "to pass the following year in Esthonia, as much for the honour of the Virgin Mary as for the remission of his sins."

Motives of this kind give birth to capabilities for the greatest achievements. The king began by rendering the German frontiers safe by leaving there good garrisons in well fortified strongholds. He also ordered that as many ships as possible should be manned for war in every port. Historians of that day tell us that never before was there seen in the North such a large fleet as the one destined for this expedition. It was composed of fourteen hundred vessels of various sizes, but it appears that he used only a thousand, the others remaining in Denmark for the safety of the kingdom. Of these thousand there were five hundred small ones, none of which carried, beside rowers to the number of twelve, more than one cuirassier and one archer. The other five hundred, called long ships, contained each 120 men. From which one may judge that the armament of Valdemar was really the largest that had been seen in any country. A crowd of ecclesiastics and young warriors, illustrious by birth or exploits, hastened to take part in the glory and merit of this holy expedition. Among the number one distinguishes Andrew, archbishop of Lund; Nicholas, bishop of Schleswig; Peter, bishop of Roeskilde; and the chancellor, Theodoric, bishop designate of a country neither yet converted or conquered; a Wend prince named Wenceslas or Vitzlas, with a corps of his troops; and many German generals and soldiers.

On their side the Esthonians were able promptly to raise armies as formidable for numbers as for the fury which animated them. Surprised, however, at the sight of so prodigious an armament as that of the Danes, they could not hinder its descent nor prevent the ruin of one of their fortresses, or the erection of another at the same place, which the Danes called Revel, that being the name of the province. The Esthonians even pretended to have no other resource than the clemency of Valdemar, and while reassembling their forces sent their chiefs to sue for peace.

The king, not sufficiently on his guard, granted it joyfully; bishops baptised them; they were sent back loaded with presents: but three days afterward a swarm of armed horsemen burst on the camp towards nightfall, attacked it at five different points, and drove back the Danes, who were scattered and for the most part disarmed, with such vigour that their defeat seemed inevitable. But Wenceslas, posted farther afield, had time to range his men in battle array and come to their aid. Then the aspect of affairs quickly changed. The Danes rallied, the Germans joined them, and, uniting their efforts, they soon quenched the impetuosity of the Esthonians. These, little accustomed to fight against regular troops, disbanded, and fleeing precipitately left a thousand of their men on the field of battle.

Such are the real facts of a combat concerning which there are many accounts full of exaggeration and marvels. It has been written a thousand times that the Danes, having lost their standard in the thickest of the fight, had begun to give way when there fell from heaven another — red, with a white cross in the centre; and, re-animated at the sight of this wonder, they gained a victory over their enemies. Afterwards a standard was said to have been sent by the pope, as was a custom in religious wars, but neither this deed nor that conjecture is supported by any authority, and an anonymous contemporary who was personally at Esthonia, and gives us all the circumstances of this fight, never mentions it. If then the standard named Dannebrog owes its origin to this war, it was some other event which gave rise to it.[1]

After this victory all the province of Revel was subdued. The town of this name had its bishop, the building of the new fortress was finished, and the king departed leaving a strong garrison, generals, and many bishops who were to work in concert to advance his interests and those of the church, in a country whose uncultivated and wild state could not hide natural fertility.

But these Danish designs were too strongly opposed to the bishop of Riga's views for him to allow them to pass without contradiction. This prelate claimed the greater part of Esthonia as a conquest effected by pilgrims devoted to the church, and by the Brothers of the Sword, or Soldiers of Christ, his vassals. He had given the bishopric of Esthonia to his brother, and sent missionaries there, trying to win as many neophytes as he could from his rival, and carrying on the "Danish baptism," by detachments of the Revel garrison. Animosity concerning baptism was carried to such a pitch that an Esthonian chief was hanged by the Danes for receiving baptism from their enemies, and probably the Riga Christians showed no more moderation. The

[1] Mallet's naïve refutation of the miracle of the Dannebrog needs no addition ; but it is interesting to note the further marvel related of this battle, in which legend assigns to Andrew, archbishop of Lund, the part of Moses at Rephidim. Fortune, so ran the story, favoured the Danes, as long as the archbishop held his arms raised, but when from weariness he let them fall, she deserted his countrymen. Finally his companions lent their support in keeping the old man's hands in the attitude of blessing till the victory of Valdemar was complete.]

Esthonian barbarians began to think that the God of the Danes was not that of the Germans.

Albert, bishop of Riga, went personally to Rome to claim protection from the head of the church. But the favor in which Valdemar and his envoys were held by the pope rendered these solicitations useless. It was the same at the court of the emperor Frederick, who was too politic not to keep on good terms with a king who, better than all others, could cross his plans of weakening the Guelfs. So the bishop, seeing that he could receive no help from Germany either, since Valdemar, master of Lübeck, had closed the gates of that city to Livonian crusaders, resolved to yield, and trust to the king's clemency. Thereupon Valdemar, having equipped a large fleet, landed on the isle of Ösel, and after defeating and bringing the inhabitants to submission opened a conference at which the bishop of Riga and the master of the Brothers of the Sword assisted. It was there that, touched by the prayers of the bishop, who brought him to see that his claims on Livonia caused trouble and prejudice to religion, the king recognised the prelate's rights over the province. The king also severed portions of the lands he reserved for himself and gave them to the Brothers of the Sword, on condition that they should render him homage and hold themselves always ready to furnish help against the Russians or heathen. Osel was also assigned to the king, but the natives of this island were not yet disposed to leave him in peaceful possession of the conquest.

THE KING'S CAPTIVITY

By all these conquests Valdemar had brought the Danish monarchy to a degree of glory and power it had never yet attained to. There were few kings in Europe who reigned over such a large extent of country, few who had added so many provinces to their heritage and had had such sustained and brilliant success at the head of their armies, or could put fleets so numerous and formidable to sea. But that mysterious power which seems to play with all fixed plans of men, and take pleasure in eternal vicissitude, had marked this high degree of prosperity as the term of a new period wherein we shall see this same kingdom fall from disgrace to disgrace, torn by intestine war, a prey to foreigners, and sometimes touching on total ruin — an event the more striking because it was from the feeblest of her enemies that this powerful monarchy received her rudest blow.

A count of Schwerin, named Henry, cherished in profound secrecy an implacable hatred which became fatal to Valdemar. Schwerin had been constrained to receive his states from the king's hands, and to do him homage for them. In thus investing him, Valdemar had demanded the count's sister for his natural son, named Nicholas, count of northern Halland, with the half of the Schwerin castellany and its dependencies. Probably Henry had refused to fulfil these conditions after the marriage celebrations, and Valdemar, irritated by this refusal, had forcibly compelled him to be faithful to his engagements, and had taken away a part of his states to give to Nicholas.

Henry, in desperation, had recourse to the vengeance of the weak. He went to Valdemar's court and sought to regain his confidence by an appearance of great zeal. The king, too generous not to show favour to so submissive and repentant a subject, allowed him great familiarity. One day, when they had both been hunting in a little isle named Lyö on the southern coast of Fünen, the king invited Henry to sup with himself, his son, and a small number of courtiers, passing the evening without precaution or fear. Soon the fumes of wine, joined to the fatigues of hunting, plunged the king into a deep sleep. The count, who had waited impatiently for this, called his people, who were posted at some distance, seized Valdemar and his son, loaded them with chains, took them forcibly into a forest near the sea, and finally carried them on board a vessel with which he sailed through manifold dangers, and took them to the opposite coast of Mecklenburg. His illustrious and unhappy prisoners were first taken to the castle of his ally, the count of Danneberg, then to his Schwerin castle, where they were condemned to remain in irons.

All Europe experienced the greatest surprise on hearing of an insult committed with so much audacity on the person of so great a king, and that by one of his weakest vassals. But this news, which plunged Denmark herself into extreme consternation, roused the hopes of her enemies and armed those whom fear alone had held in obedience. The first care of the senate at this juncture was to have recourse to the emperor's good offices. But sentiments quite opposed to compassion and justice animated Frederick II. Although he maintained a firm aspect, it was plain that in spite of the lapse of years he wished Germany to see renewed the drama of Leopold of Austria and Richard king of England.

The pope himself, who seemed to have taken Valdemar's cause in hand with a zeal worthy of the head of Christendom, yet demanded a high price for his services. He said in his letter to the archbishop of Cologne that he was obliged to take Valdemar's part, among other reasons because Denmark was tributary to the papacy. This new claim opposed itself to that of the emperor, but both were equally without foundation. What could be thought of a Roman emperor who had been driven from Rome, and a bishop of Rome, rarely master of that city, who thus disputed at the other end of Europe as to who had bestowed a crown or counted kings among his vassals?

However, day by day the kingdom felt the disadvantage of being deprived of its head. The rumour of the king's captivity was no sooner spread in Livonia than the Brothers of the Sword and the bishop of Riga seized a part of Esthonia and the isle of Ösel, whilst for his part, William of Savoy, bishop of Sabine and papal legate in these northern regions, adjudged to the holy see lands which were in litigation between the Danes and Germans, thus conquering by ecclesiastical warnings and censures that which the others had bought at the price of much bloodshed. In the other conquests of the king a like defection seemed near.*j*

In Denmark itself reigned distrust and discouragement. Count Adolf the Younger, supported by all the princes of the north of Germany, returned to Holstein and took possession of his paternal estates. Bishop Valdemar himself, now eighty years old, left the solitude of the cloister as soon as he heard of the king's captivity, and crossed the frontiers of Denmark to slake his hatred against the king. Finally the brave Albert of Orlamünde, who had been appointed regent, collected an army; but he wished first to see what he could obtain by negotiations. The enemy demanded that Valdemar should pay 50,000 marks of silver for his ransom, that he should abandon his Slav and Wend possessions and what he had conquered south of the Elbe, that Holstein should be ceded to Albert of Orlamünde as a fief of Germany, and that Valdemar should acknowledge himself the emperor's vassal for Denmark. Although these terms were advantageous to the regent he rejected them as dishonouring to the king and country. The difference could be settled only by the sword. Unfortunately Albert lost the battle of Mölln (January, 1225), after a fight which lasted from dawn to nightfall; the conquered general went to join his sovereign, not as liberator but as a companion in captivity. The city of Hamburg then submitted to Adolf, and Lübeck gave herself up to Germany. Valdemar was compelled to submit to the hard conditions which his enemies imposed on him.[e]

PEACE IS BOUGHT AT A HIGH PRICE

In a convention which still exists, Valdemar promised to pay the count, for his own and his son's ransom, 45,000 fine silver marks, all the gold the queen used in her ornaments excepting her crown, and complete habiliments for a hundred knights.

When he left prison he was to be replaced by forty Danes chosen by the court, among which number were to be included two of Valdemar's sons, to remain as hostages until the entire fulfilment of the treaty (1225). Valdemar ceded to the empire all he possessed between the Elbe and the Eider, and all the Wend countries, except the principality of Rügen. He had also to swear not to aid Count Orlamünde, his nephew, in recovering Nordalbingia, with which he had invested him. The king had also to cede to Count Adolf of Holstein the fortress of Rendsburg and to hold the count of Schwerin free and exempt from all rights he had had over him.

These were the most important articles of the convention. The king, the princes his sons, the bishops, and the chief gentlemen of Denmark had to swear to observe them faithfully. Of the release of the count of Orlamünde there is no mention in the treaty, which confirms what we learn elsewhere about the count of Schwerin and his allies not being willing to let him go at any price, doubtless fearing that he would only too well aid and abet the king in a plan to reconquer the provinces he had held in fief. Such were the conditions in which the king and his son found themselves at the end of their captivity — a captivity as singular in its accomplishment as it was rigorous during the three years it lasted, and whose long and miserable consequences were fatal to the nation. It has been said that one hardly knows what to wonder at most, in these events — the audacity of the plot formed by the count of Schwerin, or the courage and success with which he carried it out, or the feebleness of the efforts made by the Danes to avenge their king.

On his return to his realm the king's first care was to send ambassadors to Pope Honorius III, begging him to summon the count of Schwerin to return the hostages and free him from the extorted oath. The pope did not think success impossible, and a private motive, moreover, urged him to lend his intervention. Valdemar had given him to understand that if he could recover the hostages without paying the rest of the stipulated sum he would himself lead an army to help the crusaders. In this hope the pope wrote threatening letters to the count and charged the bishop of Verden to summon Henry under pain of excommunication to restore Valdemar his hostages and release him from all other engagements. Results show how the count answered these letters. He returned neither money nor hostages, save Prince Valdemar, who, according to the terms of the convention, was to be set free a short time after his father. But although three of his sons and other hostages were still in his enemy's power, Valdemar did not fear to recommence war, to enter fully armed into Nordalbingia, surprise Rendsburg, and to reduce Ditmarsh, in spite of resistance from the inhabitants.

On his side Count Schwerin was still aided by his accomplices in usurpation — Adolf of Schauenburg, newly possessed of Holstein, the heritage of his ancestors; the archbishop of Bremen; the town of Lübeck; Albert, duke of Saxony; and Henry Burwin, prince of Werle. These confederates, having learned of the irruption of Valdemar into Holstein and the progress he was making there, went to meet him and encountered him near Bornhöved at some distance from Segeberg. The two armies did not face each other long before having recourse to arms. Animated by the remembrance of a grand past, by insults and losses, and embittered by the presence of his perfidious enemy, Valdemar marched towards him impetuously and fought him with most obstinate valour. But all his efforts were useless. The Ditmarshians who composed a part of his army vilely betrayed him in a moment when bravery could have given victory to his side. They turned their arms against the Danes, who, seeing themselves assailed on all sides, gave up hope after a long resistance. The king lost an eye in this fight, was thrown off his horse, and barely escaped from the enemy. Many Danes were made prisoners, among them three bishops and the king's nephew.

We have observed that the people of Lübeck had part in this victory. Already they had profited from the downfall of Valdemar to regain their liberty. The preceding year they had secretly bought the favour and protection of the emperor, who liberally promised them favours and gave them privileges. Their confidence increased with the king's misfortunes, and they soon dared to seize the citadel which that prince had built to hold them in check. A stratagem made them masters of it, and thenceforth, supported by Denmark's enemies, favoured by their situation, animated by the courage and ardour inspired by growing liberty, they asserted their independence and formed the first and most powerful of the Hanse Towns, soon seeing themselves able to rule the northern seas by their numerous fleets. While all this was passing, the count of Orlamünde, losing all hope of being succoured by the king or escaping from the chains in which the count of Schwerin still held him, was at last obliged to yield as his ransom the important fortress of Luxemburg, which Valdemar in happier times had given him for his own as the best gift with which a warrior's services could be rewarded.

So unhappy a war, far from restoring the kingdom to its early splendour, only served to increase its weakness and make the decline every day more apparent. Finally Valdemar showed some desire to be reconciled to his enemies. The celebration of the wedding of his son Valdemar having drawn many foreign lords to Ribe, an effort was made through their intervention to conclude a treaty between the king and the count of Holstein. It was agreed that the count should keep the states which his father had possessed north of the Elbe, and which he had reconquered, that is Holstein, Stormarn, and Wagrien. Then the king was reconciled with Albert, duke of Saxony, who took the title of lord of Nordalbingia; and Valdemar after that did not touch it. The same duke obliged Quncelin, count of Schwerin, his new vassal, to set the king's sons, Eric, Abel, and Christopher, at liberty, along with the remaining hostages; also to take 7,000 silver marks, instead of the 17,000 which remained to be paid, as ransom for the king and his eldest son.

Such was the price by which the Danes bought a long-absent peace and which for that reason alone seemed advantageous. In reality they lost by these treaties Holstein, Mecklenburg, and the towns of Hamburg and Lübeck.*j* Of all the conquests under former reigns there remained to them besides the principality of Rügen only some parts of Mecklenburg, Prussia, and Esthonia, together with the title of King of the Wends.

During the rest of his life, the unfortunate Valdemar prudently applied himself to the internal administration of the affairs of his kingdom. He died in 1241 A.D.

RISE OF THE HANSEATIC LEAGUE AND ITS POWER IN THE BALTIC

Amongst the misfortunes of the reign of Valdemar the Victorious, the separation of Lübeck from Denmark was wide reaching in its consequences. She was now free to devote all her force and enterprise to strengthening and developing the formidable organisation of which she became the head.[a]

About the middle of the thirteenth century there began to form upon the southern shores of the Baltic a power which was a true scourge for Denmark. The Valdemars had put an end to the bloody incursions of the Wends, but the latter were replaced by the invasions, usually more pacific but none the less harmful, of the Hanse Towns. The great Hanseatic League which came to play so important a rôle, not only in Denmark but in all history, had very modest beginnings. At first it included but a few north German towns which united to carry out great commercial enterprises in concert or to arm, at the common expense, ships of war to protect their merchant fleets against the pirates who, throughout the whole of the Middle Ages infested the northern seas. During the thirteenth century the allied towns numbered but ten or twelve, and their sole aim was peaceful commerce. They were not yet seeking ruling power — only toleration. Their number increased little by little by the accession of new towns, and the somewhat loose union developed in time into a closely woven society which was subject to its own laws and tribunals, and in its assemblies took decisions that were binding upon all the towns. Nearly a century passed, however, before the league became fully conscious of its strength; but once aroused it went forward with giant strides. The united towns were now about eighty in number, and they dominated the seas with a power of which no other example can be found except in England's maritime empire of our own day. Their envoys were received like kings; they laid down the law to nations and decided war and peace. The North Sea and the Atlantic Ocean were covered with their fleets and even England had to bend before them. But the principal seat of their power was the Baltic where they appropriated, to the exclusion of all other maritime nations, the commerce of Denmark, Norway, Sweden, Poland, and Russia.

In order to explain how a handful of German merchants could thus make themselves masters of the North, it must be remembered that the formation of the Hanseatic League falls just between 1240 and 1340 — a period in which Denmark was afflicted with almost all the misfortunes and reverses that any country could experience — and that at the end of it she was not far from complete dissolution. While Denmark's strength was being consumed in deadly contests between royalty, the clergy, nobility and peasantry, in the eternal struggles with the dukes of Schleswig and the counts of Holstein, and in the maritime wars with Norway, during which half the towns in the country were destroyed, neither was Sweden spared, and Norway's power was undermined by internal civil war. Moreover, in consequence of the change in the manner of conducting war, the kings occupied themselves only with the land armies and let their fleets fall into ruin, whereas the Hanse Towns kept up their sea power, which gave them a decided advantage in their wars with the northern kingdoms. To which must be added the statement that the kings of that day were lacking in the simplest notions with regard to commerce, did not trouble themselves whether trade was in the hands of their subjects or of foreigners, and often granted the Hanse Towns the most ruinous privileges in return for some temporary advantage.

What most attracted the merchants of these towns to Denmark were the important herring fisheries off the coast of Skåne. This fish at one time abounded off the shores of Rügen, but migrated to Skåne about the beginning of the thirteenth century. The herring must then, according to an old account, have quitted the Sound at the beginning of the fifteenth century (1425) and found its habitat on the coasts of Norway, Scotland, and England; but it is also certain that the herring fishery in the Sound was still extraordinarily abundant and lucrative in the first part of the sixteenth century. Trade followed the migrations of the herring. In the early years of the thirteenth century, even before the Hanseatic League was formed, vessels from the north of Germany, and especially from Lübeck, came in large numbers into the Sound to fish for herring. At the same time Lübeck became a Danish city through Valdemar II's conquests, and that monarch sought to conciliate his new subjects by granting them important privileges (1203). They not only obtained the right to the fisheries without any other restriction than the obligation of paying the ordinary duties, but landing places were given them on the coast where they could prepare and salt their herring. The fish was then sent to all the markets of Europe, and the Skånian herring was preferred to all others on account of its superior quality.

The merchants had, moreover, the right of choosing a syndic from among their compatriots to settle their differences, and no Dane could establish himself or ply a trade in their marts without consent. No foreigner was ever allowed to engage in retail trade in Denmark, but the Lübeckers could no longer be considered aliens, and therefore they could import, sell cloth, linen, and everything that could be measured by the yard, as well as everything that could be weighed by the pound. Later, when they ceased to be subjects of Denmark (1226), they should have lost their privileges; but once established in the country it was difficult to get rid of them, and the dissensions that followed were favourable to their remaining. During the civil wars between Abel and Eric Plovpenning [which we shall treat later] they took side with the former, and on his accession were recompensed by new privileges which were likewise extended to Wismar, Rostock, Stralsund, and Hamburg; but Lübeck continued nevertheless to play the principal rôle. These towns with Luneburg formed a close union within the Hanseatic League and were known as the Six Wend towns. Under Eric Glipping, less than half a century after Valdemar the Victorious, who had been able to put on the sea a fleet of a thousand ships, Denmark found herself reduced to borrowing thirty vessels from the Hanseatic League with which to defend the Sound against Norwegian pirates, and a few years later at the demand of the league she was compelled to forbid her subjects to engage in any trade with Norway. Eric Menved's many expeditions into Mecklenburg and Pomerania favoured the extension of Lübeck's commerce; for, still holding friendly relations with the king, the privilege the merchants had obtained from Valdemar II of carrying on trade at Falsterbo and Skanör was extended to all Danish towns in which they might be pleased to establish themselves.

It stands to reason that a country thus delivered over to the rapacity of foreign merchants must become exhausted and impoverished, and that energy and the spirit of enterprise must disappear from the towns. Denmark, in spite of its fortunate position for trade, had almost no merchant ships or even merchants. The Hanse Towns took advantage of the country to the detriment of the natives; and although the country supplied a quantity of products suitable for manufacture, there were no factories, and the body of artisans was impoverished and discouraged, for the Germans imported almost all the commodities of which the people stood in need. Corn purchased in Denmark came back in the form of flour; Danish beer brewed with sweet gale (*myrica gale*), which formerly had been the ordinary and preferred drink, had to give way to the strong German beer brewed with hops. Even the simplest and commonest objects, as shoes, clothing, furniture, etc., were imported from Germany. The fisheries, once a most important industry, declined more and more, until the natives had to buy from abroad the fish that abounded on their shores. For not only were other maritime nations excluded from the fisheries of Skåne, but Danish subjects themselves suffered from the power and influence of the Hanseat·c League. Even the king of Denmark could permit fishing and salting for his own court on certain days only.

This fatal monopoly of the Hanse Towns makes us realize why the Danish burghers, favoured as they were in many points, played during the Middle Ages only a mediocre rôle in the state. Without trade, without industry, and without capital, they necessarily lost all importance.[e]

THE DECLINE OF DENMARK IN THE THIRTEENTH CENTURY

During the thirteenth century the power of Denmark steadily declined. Towards the fifties we find the German army in the heart of the country. Odense was burnt down; Copenhagen, then scarcely built, was rased to the ground by the men of Lübeck, as was also its citadel. The very excess of power which the little country had displayed, carried within itself the germ of decay. In order to have always at command a host of men accustomed to and delighting in war, the institution of a feudal nobility had been encouraged in Denmark. The members of this nobility soon acquired large estates, and gradually robbed the free peasant class, upon which the strength of the country had once been founded, of all political and military significance; and the peasants sought in vain by violent and sanguinary insurrections to repudiate the unwonted oppression and to win back their old status. To this was added another abuse, that of endowing the younger or the natural sons of the king with large appanages, which soon began to assume a hereditary character — a dangerous custom for a country which from of old had been liable to civil dissension and peasant wars, for there was seldom any lack of ambitious kings' sons. It is noteworthy that of Valdemar's sons and grandsons not one died a natural death. Conflicts with the grasping archbishops and clergy, extending over long periods, still further increased the civil disorder.

The most important factor in Denmark's development during this century was, however, the duchy of Schleswig and its gradual separation from the united kingdom. It had long been the custom to hand over the government of this particular portion of the country to the younger princes, some of whom — as Knud Lavard — had brought the district under their administration into a very self-reliant attitude. In the year 1232 it was given to Abel, the second surviving son of Valdemar the Conqueror.

"He degraded the kingdom, with the help of the Germans, more than his father ever raised it," said Detmar; and, in fact, his marriage with Mechthild, the daughter of Adolf IV of Holstein, was the cause of Schleswig's remaining in that family for over two hundred years and being finally completely incorporated with Holstein; it was, moreover the cause of the Danish kingdom itself appearing to remain for a time under the influence of Holstein.

It is not entirely without reason that a very patriotic contemporary, the annalist of Ruhkloster in Schleswig, dates the misfortunes of Denmark from this circumstance, and from the death of Valdemar the Victorious in 1241.

"For, from that day forward, civil war in Denmark between the kings and the dukes never ceased stimulating the counts, who ever sought the destruction of Denmark. With the death of Valdemar the crown fell in fact from the Danish head. For since his time the Danes, having fallen a prey to civil war wherein they mutually destroyed one another, have become a laughing stock to other nations."

The alliance of the dukes of Schleswig with the Holstein counts procured for the latter unfailing assistance in the satisfaction of their lust for independence, and for the former — by dint of extending their borders — a desirable protection against Danish attack. Schleswig inclined more and more to the Holsteiners and the Germans, the bishop of Schleswig allowing himself to be consecrated by the archbishop of Bremen. The fact that the duchy, being partly populated by Germans, was now a country with two languages, gave this proceeding a certain justification; it is, indeed, the only explanation, at all acceptable, of the strength and duration of the tie, at that time quite recent, which bound these provinces to the neighbouring German territory.[h]

UPSALA CATHEDRAL

THE SONS OF VALDEMAR THE VICTORIOUS (1241–1259 A.D.)

Valdemar II had associated with him in the government his eldest son, under the title of Valdemar III; and when that prince was killed in hunting (1231), Eric, duke of Schleswig, the next son, took his place. Eric, therefore, had been crowned, and had had an active share in the government ten years before the death of his father. When he was thus associated in the regal power, he relinquished the duchy of Schleswig in favour of his next brother, Abel, while Christopher and other brothers had extensive domains conferred on them in different parts of the kingdom. Nothing could be more unwise than such feudal concessions: they were sure to engender quarrels, and eventually civil wars.

Scarcely was Eric on the throne, when he had a deadly quarrel with Abel, duke of Schleswig, his next brother. He wished to recover some of the territories which his father had been forced to cede, especially Holstein: Abel, who was the guardian of the count of Holstein's children, resisted, on the specious plea that he was bound to defend their interests; but his real motive, as we shall soon perceive, was a very different one. The two brothers flew to arms; but an apparent reconciliation was effected between them through the interference of German and Danish friends. Abel resigned the guardian-ship, and therefore ceased to be responsible for the result. But he evidently nursed a vindictive feeling towards Eric, and could not long refrain from exhibiting it. He refused to do homage for Holstein, which he determined to hold in full sovereignty. Again the sword was drawn; and though it was for a time returned to the scabbard, the feeling of hatred rankled in the duke's heart. During this short suspension of hostilities, Eric endeavoured to regain Lübeck, and sent an armament into the river Trave; but a fleet from Sweden, which country had a great interest in the protection of that city, compelled him to raise the siege. The coasts of his kingdom were now ravaged by the combined Swedes and citizens; and at the same time, through the influence of his perverse brother, the count of Holstein and the archbishop of Bremen became his open enemies. Allured by the successful example of Abel, the other brothers also refused to do homage. Seeing that the very existence of the monarchy was at stake, Eric took the field. Numerous as were his enemies, he created more, and those more formidable than the rest — his own bishops, who naturally threw themselves into the party of Abel. The ravages committed in the fraternal war were dreadful. At length, the city of Schles-wig being taken by surprise, Abel fled to his allies; and when he could effect nothing by arms, had recourse to stratagem. He received with eagerness the proposals of a pacification from the duke of Saxony and the markgraf of Brandenburg, who were connected with the regal family of Denmark. The brothers met, swore friendship, and separated.

Freed from that dreadful scourge, civil war, Eric now projected an expedi-tion into Livonia, to recover the territories which his father had ceded. To defray the expenses, a tax of a silver penny was laid on every plough in the kingdom [whence Eric's surname of Plovpenning, or Plough-penny]. With much difficulty he obtained the sanction of the estates to this impost; with still more difficulty it was collected, at least in Skåne. The inhabitants of that province were fond of rebellion: they rebelled on the present occasion; but as usual they were subdued, punished, and made to contribute like the rest of the Danes. The expedition arrived in Esthonia, but its details are very imperfectly recorded in the national chronicles. They merely tell us that the Teutonic knights acknowledged the king's right to what he held, and to what he might hereafter conquer from the pagans. He certainly made no conquests; and probably his troops were defeated by St. Alexander Nevski, governor of Novgorod.

Eric, on his return, engaged in war with the count of Holstein, who, conjointly with the archbishop of Bremen and the bishop of Paderborn, laid siege to Rendsburg. To relieve it, the king advanced at the head of a con-siderable force. But his doom was at hand. Near Schleswig he was met by Abel, who treated him with the utmost deference, with the most obsequious respect; and so disarmed him, that in the joy of his heart he accepted an invitation to one of the duke's country palaces, in the immediate vicinity of Schleswig. From that palace he was forcibly dragged on board a boat in the Schlei, taken to a solitary part of that river, landed, allowed to make his confession, and beheaded. Heavy chains were then fastened to his corpse, and it was thrown into the deepest part of the river. The news was spread that he had perished by accident in the river; but the monks who had admin-istered to him the last offices of religion declared that he had been murdered — by whose contrivance was unknown. The body, which was afterwards found by some fishermen, confirmed that declaration. It was buried in the church of the monastery (1250). The brethren even asserted that miracles were wrought at his tomb, and they were believed.   Some years after his death he was canonised; and is the fifth Danish prince who has been thus deified.

Abel, the Fratricide, is Murdered

To obtain the reward of this fratricide, Abel sent his creatures to the assembly of the estates, convoked for the election of a new king.   As there was only suspicion, he was permitted to purge himself by his own oath, and by the oath of twenty-four nobles, that he was innocent of the deed.   That he could find this number of men to take such an oath, may surprise us; but we must remember that the tenor of it was that "to the best of their belief" the accused party was not guilty of the crime.   He was therefore elected and crowned by the archbishop.   By lavish gifts to the clergy and to the nobles who adhered to him, and by confirming his brethren (from whom he had the most to fear) in their respective fiefs, he stifled all murmurs.   To avert war, too, which he well knew would lead to his ruin, he surrendered to the count of Holstein the domains which his brother had occupied, and to the Teutonic knights most of what he yet held in Livonia.   These concessions did no harm to Denmark; and some of his other measures were decidedly good.   He restored the wisest parts of the Danish constitution, especially the annual meeting of the estates; he improved the laws; and began to redeem the crown lands, which during the late reigns had been pledged.   In short, like all usurpers, he sacrificed to popularity, and succeeded so well that he was enabled to raise an extraordinary impost to complete his work of redemption. In the western parts of Schleswig, however, the collectors met with opposition, and Abel marched with a body of troops to punish the disobedience.   He penetrated into a country always marshy, and now rendered more so by the rains.   Surprised by a strong party of the inhabitants, he fled, and fell into a morass, from which the weight of his armour made it impossible for him to emerge.   In this helpless situation he was discovered and slain.

The mutilated corpse of Abel was left in the marsh where it remained for some time, and, if tradition be true, to the great annoyance of the whole country.   Abel was too great a sinner to lie peacefully in his grave.   He became a wandering spirit.   Supernatural voices had so terrified the people that they were glad to deliver the corpse to the canons of Bremen, who honoured it with the rites of sepulture.   But they too had soon reason to regret the contiguity of the vampire.   He was frequently seen out of his tomb; and at length the corpse was disinterred, and buried in a solitary marsh a few leagues from Gottorp.   Still there was no respite; and the inhabitants nearest to the place removed to a distance.   To this day the superstition has been perpetuated that the murderer may sometimes be seen on a dingy horse, followed by demon hounds, amidst the echoing of the magic horn.

Abel left three sons, the eldest of whom, Valdemar, was designed to be his successor; but the young prince, returning from the university of Paris, was seized by the archbishop of Cologne, and detained in prison until a ransom of 6000 silver marks was paid.   Probably this act was done at the instigation of Christopher, a brother of the late king, who knew that he alone was to be dreaded, since he had been already recognised by the estates and his brothers were too young for the duties of government.   Besides, the dislike of Abel's posterity was general; and Christopher might well aspire to a throne which, after their exclusion, became his of right.   Nor was he disappointed: he was immediately elected by the estates.

CHRISTOPHER I AND ERIC GLIPPING

The reign of this prince was even more troubled than that of his predecessors. Fearing a popular reaction in favour of Abel's sons, who were minors, he claimed the guardianship. The claim was resisted by the house of Holstein; and to decide the contest both parties resorted to arms. The king was defeated; and though he soon collected a larger force, he found the number of his enemies increased. The people of Lübeck, always hostile to Denmark, as we have seen, and for that same reason always the allies of the counts of Holstein, ravaged the coasts, while those nobles reduced Schleswig. The two markgrafs of Brandenburg also complained that one of them had not received the dowry promised with his wife, Sophia, daughter of Valdemar II; and they joined the common league.

Nor was this all: during Abel's reign there had been some disputes with Sweden and Norway; and to allay them a conference had been covenanted between the three kings. The death of Abel had prevented the pacification; and Christopher, engrossed by other troubles, was unable to give them the satisfaction required. In revenge, the Norwegians arrived with a great armament, while five thousand Swedes penetrated into the heart of the country. Never had the situation of Denmark appeared so critical; but strange to say, its safety lay in the number of its enemies, who became jealous of one another, and of the advantages which each might secure. In this disposition, the offer of mediators was accepted, and conditions of peace between Christopher and his nephews were at length sanctioned. He agreed to invest these nephews, on their reaching their majority, with the duchy of Schleswig; and they, in return, were to renounce all pretensions to the crown. In conformity with this treaty, Valdemar, the eldest son of Abel, was released from prison at Cologne, and invested with the government of the duchy. The markgraf of Brandenburg was appeased by the pledge of two fortresses until the dowry could be paid. Thus there remained only Norway and Sweden to be pacified; and though hostilities existed for some time, they were desultory and were terminated by a reconciliation. An interview with Birger, regent of Sweden, easily led to that result; and when Hakon of Norway, who had again arrived with a formidable armament, saw that Christopher was sincerely desirous of satisfying him, he accepted the will for the deed, and became the friend of the monarch.

But the chief troubles of Christopher arose from his own prelates. Jacob Erlandsen, bishop of Roeskilde, a personal friend of Innocent IV, had imbibed the highest notions of clerical privileges. He condemned the influence of the crown in the election of bishops, which was certainly an evil, since royal favourites only were appointed to the rich sees. Acting on his own principle, that bishops had no earthly superior except the pope, he refused, when elected by the chapter of Lund to the primacy, either to allow royal influence any weight in the election, or to accept of confirmation at the royal hands. He next condemned some of the provisions in the ecclesiastical law which Valdemar I had promulgated in Skåne; and when opposed by the king he intrigued with the royal enemies. Erlandsen was summoned before the estates at Viborg. In reply he convoked a national council to be held at Veile, a town in the diocese of Ribe in Jutland. In that assembly it was decreed that if any Danish bishop were taken and mutilated, or afflicted with any other atrocious injury, by the order or with the connivance of the king or any noble, the kingdom should be laid under an interdict and the divine service suspended. If the same violence were committed by any foreign prince or noble, and there were reason to infer that it was done at the instigation of the king or any of his council, in the diocese of that bishop there should be a *cessatio a divinis*, and the king during a month should be bound to see justice done: if he refused, the interdict was to be extended over the whole kingdom. After it was laid, no ecclesiastic, under pain of excommunication, was to celebrate any office of religion in the royal presence. The decree was sent to Rome, and confirmed by the pope in October, 1257.

The wrath of the king and of his nobles was roused by this bold act. But the primate was of an intrepid temper and quite prepared to share, if necessary, the fate of Thomas à Becket. In the next diet a number of frivolous and two or three substantial charges were made against him; and he begged time until the next meeting of the estates to prepare his answers. In the interim efforts were made to reconcile the two; and they sometimes met. But Erlandsen, by excommunicating a lady of Skåne, a favourite of the king, rekindled the half-smothered wrath of Christopher. Repairing to Lund, the latter held his tribunal, invited all who had any complaint against the archbishop to appear before him, and summoned the archbishop himself to appear and answer whatever might be urged against him. As ecclesiastics were, by a regulation of some standing, amenable to their own laws alone, the churchman denied the competency of the tribunal. In revenge the king revoked the concessions of privileges, immunities, and even of domains, made by his ancestors to the cathedral of Lund. The officer who served the act of revocation was excommunicated by the primate, who had the people also on his side. Two or three of the bishops were gained by the court; the rest adhered to their spiritual head. Every day widened the breach between the two chief personages in the nation. The estates being convoked at Odense to swear allegiance to Eric, eldest son of the king, Erlandsen refused to appear, and commanded his suffragans also to refuse. The rage of the king was unbounded. From the estates, which he now convoked at Copenhagen, he obtained permission to seize the primate with the other bishops and imprison them. A brother of the primate's was the instrument of his apprehension, and he was conveyed to a fortress in Fünen. The dean and archdeacon of Lund, with the bishop of Ribe, were next secured; but the two spiritual peers of Odense and Roeskilde had time to flee from the realm.

In his captivity the primate was treated with much rigour. What his proud spirit could least bear was insult: if it be true that he was forced to wear a cap made from a fox's skin, we may smile at what called forth the bitter resentment of himself and the pope. The king was soon made to repent his violence. In virtue of the ordinance of the national council at Veile, the fugitive bishops laid an interdict on the kingdom; the pope espoused the cause of his church; and Jarimar, prince of Rügen, to whose hospitality the bishop of Roeskilde had fled, was persuaded by both to arm in behalf of the altar. Great was the wrath of Christopher to see the interdict so well observed, and to hear the murmurs of his people. How could he, alone, resist a power which had proved fatal to so many emperors and so many kings, and compared with which his was that of the meanest vassal in his dominions? He appealed to Rome. Yet at the same time he endeavoured to dispose his royal neighbours of Sweden and Norway in his favour. They, too, had bishops, and the cause of one was the cause of all: it was a struggle, he observed, between the rights of kings and the insolence of their subjects. They promised to assist him in this war alike on the pope and on his own clergy, whom he was about to deprive of their temporalities; and had already powerful armaments in motion when intelligence reached them that he was no more.

Whether this monarch died naturally, or through poison, is doubtful. The evidence, however, is rather indicative of a tragical end, though the causes and the circumstances must forever rest a mystery.

Eric, the eldest son of the king, was elected by the estates; and as he was only ten years of age at his father's death, the regency devolved on his mother, Margaret, daughter of Sambir, duke of Pomerania. That princess had great courage and great prudence, and both were required in the peculiarly difficult circumstances in which she was placed. Some of the bishops were exiles, some in prison, but all protected by the pope and venerated by the people. Eric, the son of Abel, supported by the counts of Holstein, by the prince of Rügen, and by the exiled prelates, aspired to the throne. The interdict still remained, and consequently the discontent of the people. And now Jarimar, prince of Rügen, and the duke of Schleswig, accompanied by the bishop of Roeskilde, made a descent on the coast of Zealand with a formidable army. Margaret collected what troops she could, and hastened to meet the enemy. The battle was disastrous to the royal party, ten thousand being left on the field.

The consequences were still more disastrous — the occupation of Zealand and the destruction of several towns (among others Copenhagen, which had recently been invested with municipal rights) by the victors. Bornholm was next reduced, then Skåne, which remembered its primate with gratitude; and the whole kingdom must have been subjugated by the Slav prince had not a tragical death arrested him in his career. This was a heavy loss to the ecclesiastical party; but the bishop of Roeskilde confirmed the censure and denied Christian burial to the dead of the royal party. Jutland only remained faithful to the latter. Yet Margaret was not dismayed: notwithstanding the interdict and the absolute prohibition issued alike by the primate and the bishop of Roeskilde, she caused her son to be crowned. To soothe in some degree the animosity of the former, she released him and all the churchmen; but he would not compromise what he deemed his duty; he refused all overtures from her, and retired into Sweden to await the decision of Rome.

Urban IV [who became pope in 1261], took cognizance of the cause. He condemned the primate, and ordered him to resign his archbishopric into the hands of two ecclesiastical commissioners whom he nominated for that purpose. Erlandsen obeyed; but, hearing that Clement IV had succeeded to Urban (1264), he hastened to Rome to plead for himself. Clement did not confirm the judgment of his predecessor; he took up the case *de novo*, and sent a legate to examine on the spot into the circumstances of the dispute. Erecting his tribunal at Schleswig, the papal functionary cited the king and the queen-mother to appear before him; but they refused on the plea that Schleswig was unfavourable to them. Apprehensive for their safety in a city which depended on the king, the legate and the bishops repaired to Lübeck, whence they excommunicated Eric, his mother, and all who had refused to obey the citation. The primate retired to Rome, where he remained about seven years; and during that period the interdict remained in full force.

While these events were passing, others occurred of still greater moment to the queen and her son. On the death (1257) of Valdemar, eldest son of Abel, without issue, the succession was claimed by Eric, the next brother. Christopher, who then reigned, had refused to invest him, and he had therefore thrown himself into the arms of his kinsmen, the counts of Holstein, and by their aid had entered on the administration of the duchy. Unable to dispossess him, Margaret proposed to recognise him, provided he would acknowledge that he held the fief by the pure favour of the crown, and not by any right of inheritance. But Eric refused, and to chastise him, the queen and her son marched towards the south; but on the plains of Schleswig they were signally defeated. Flight did not save them from the power of their enemies: they were overtaken and consigned to imprisonment. There both might have remained to the close of life had not Albert of Anhalt, who had married the princess Mechtilda, sister of the king, interfered in their behalf. The queen was soon released (1263), and enabled to resume the administration: the king was confided to the guardianship of John, markgraf of Brandenburg, also connected by ties of blood with the royal family. It was at length agreed that he should be released, on the condition of his marrying Agnes, daughter of the markgraf, whose dowry 6,000 marks, was to be placed against his ransom. Returning to his capital (1264), he was now old enough to assume the reins of government.

In 1272 Eric, duke of Schleswig, died — an event which again disturbed the tranquillity of the country. He left two sons, Valdemar and Eric, both minors. To the guardianship a claim was put in by the king, and another by the counts of Holstein. Both parties flew to arms, and at first the counts had the advantage; but seeing the royal forces augmented, they consented to resign the trust into the royal hands, on the condition of the king's investing the eldest, when arrived at due age, with the duchy. Eric now celebrated his marriage with Agnes of Brandenburg; and he had also the satisfaction to see the convocation of a general council (that of Lyons, 1274), destined to remove the interdict from his kingdom. He was, however, enjoined not merely to receive the primate into his friendship, but to pay him 15,000 marks by way of indemnification. The following year (1275), a national council held at Lund finished the work of reconciling the king with the church.

But if Eric was thus at peace with his spiritual, he was often in dispute with his temporal, barons, on whose rights he was always ready to encroach. Notwithstanding his treaty with the counts of Holstein, he endeavoured to evade the investiture of Schleswig in favour of Valdemar. Both parties, however, were equally to blame; for when Valdemar was invested he claimed other domains. When these were refused, he leagued himself with the enemies of Denmark; the plot was discovered, and he was imprisoned. But his detention was of short duration; and at the intercession of his allies, he was released, after subscribing some conditions which more clearly established the authority of the crown over the fief. Still, if one enemy was vanquished, others remained, and to some of them, or rather to his own vices, the king fell a victim. To the count of Halland he had been oppressive: he had deprived him of his domains, and if report is true, dishonoured the wife during the husband's absence. Revenge was sworn, and the oath was kept. One night, after hunting, he was murdered while asleep at a rural village in Jutland. The king's chamberlain was privy to the design, and it was he who guided the assassins (all in masks) to the bed.

Thus ended a reign of troubles, most of which cannot with any justice be imputed to the monarch. Yet his own vices added greatly to his misfortunes. After his peace with the church, when moderation might have been expected from him, he frequently seized the church tithes, and applied to his own use the produce arising from the monastic domains. With his nobles he was no less severe; and more than once (especially in 1262) he was in danger of being driven from the realm by their united arms. Eric promulgated the code called *Birkerett*.

THE DISINTEGRATION OF DENMARK

At his father's death, Eric surnamed Menved,[1] was only twelve years of age. A guardian and regent was therefore necessary; and the post was demanded by Valdemar, duke of Schleswig, the nearest male kinsman of Eric. The queen-mother, Agnes of Brandenburg, unwilling but afraid to refuse, at length recognised his claim. There could not have been a better choice: he forgot the wrongs of his family in his new duties. In the first assembly which he convoked he called for vengeance on the murderers of the late king. They were in alarm; and to escape the consequences, they entered into a plot, the object of which was to seize the young king, and detain him as a hostage until their pardon should be declared by the estates. That plot did not escape the vigilance of the regent, who took measures to disconcert it, and at the same time caused a commission to be appointed, with power to inquire into the circumstances of Eric Glipping's death. That commission consisted of Otto of Brandenburg, brother of the queen-mother, of the prince of Rügen, the counts of Holstein, and twenty-seven Danish nobles. The result was a verdict of wilful murder against James, count of Halland, Stig, marshal of the court, and seven others.

Condemned to perpetual banishment, they repaired to the court of the Norwegian king, then at war with Denmark, by whom they were hospitably received. Assisted by him they were enabled to visit the northern parts of their fief, and to commit, during many years, considerable depredations. That the Norwegian monarch should thus become the ally of murderers — the murderers, too, of a brother king — might surprise us, if we did not remember that he and his father had long applied, but applied in vain, for satisfaction on points the justice of which had never been denied. One of them was that the dowry of his mother, Ingeborg, a Danish princess, had never been paid. At the head of a considerable fleet, he himself soon followed the regicides, and devastated the coasts. He would listen to no proposals of peace unless the regicides were pardoned — for such was his engagement with them. This war raged until 1308, when peace was restored in the Treaty of Copenhagen. The chief condition was that, in compensation for his mother's dowry, the Norwegian monarch should hold northern Halland as a fief from Eric of Denmark. In regard to the regicides, it was stipulated that some should be allowed to return and enjoy their property, but that the more guilty should never revisit the realm. Yet, even to them a permission during three years was given to dispose of their lands and personal substance.

This long war was not Eric's only trouble. Like his two predecessors, he was embroiled with the church. To Grandt, a dignitary of Roeskilde, he was hostile, apparently for reasons which had no foundation. When that dignitary was elected to the see of Lund, he refused, like Erlandsen, either to solicit or to accept the royal confirmation; and he hastened to Rome to obtain that of the pope. On his return he was arrested by Christopher, the king's brother, and treated with remarkable severity. His property was seized; he was made to exchange his pontifical robes for the meanest rags; he was fastened to the back of a worn-out horse; and in this state led, amidst the jeers of the royal dependants, to the fortress of Helsingborg. He was soon transferred to the castle of Soeburg, where an unwholesome dungeon, heavy fetters, and meagre fare awaited him. The same treatment was inflicted on Lange, another dignitary of Lund; but he had the good fortune to escape and to

---

[1] So called from his frequent use of the word *mœn — certainly*.

reach Boniface VIII at Avignon (1295). Some time afterwards, Grandt himself was so lucky as to escape and repair to Bornholm, where he was received as a martyr. He too arrived at Avignon, and was welcomed by the pope, who observed, with much truth, that there were many saints who had suffered less for the church than archbishop Grandt. The dispute between the king and the church was examined at Rome, by a commission of cardinals. The award was a severe one for the king: it sentenced him to pay the archbishop, by way of indemnification, 49,000 silver marks; and until the money was paid, not only was his kingdom to remain under an interdict (it had been subject to one ever since the archbishop was seized), but the king himself was to be excommunicated, and also his brother Christopher, the instrument of that arrest. When the king evinced no disposition to pay the money, the papal legate who had been dispatched to Denmark for the occasion, sequestered a portion of the royal revenues in Skåne. This measure Eric could feel; and he threw himself on the mercy of the pope. Boniface so far relaxed from his severity as to allow the archbishop to resign his see of Lund, and to abate the indemnification to 10,000 marks. Grandt subsequently became archbishop of Bremen, while the papal legate succeeded to the primacy of Denmark.

But the whole of Eric's reign was not disastrous. Lübeck and the baron of Rostock sued for his protection, and paid him for it: he obtained from the latter some augmentation of his territory, and from other German powers a large sum of money. Tranquillity, however, for any long period, he was not to enjoy. One of his worst domestic enemies was his brother Christopher, who leagued himself with the kings of Sweden and Norway, and other enemies of the realm. As a punishment, seeing that leniency had no result, Eric occupied his brother's domains. Christopher fled to Wratislaw, duke of Pomerania, who espoused his cause; so did the counts of Holstein and some other princes. In 1317 peace was made, but Christopher was not restored. Two years afterwards the king paid the debt of nature, leaving his kingdom plunged in debt occasioned by his efforts to contend with his misfortunes. He had more discernment than some of his predecessors. He encouraged the rising municipalities, to some of which he granted charters analogous to those which existed in Germany. To commerce he was a benefactor; and he was useful to the judicial administration by the compilation of a code (in six books), called the *Law of Zealand*. He did more; he made a collection [*Congesta Menvedi*] of such public acts as might throw light on the national history. Of his offspring none survived him; one at least, on whom his hopes were placed, met a tragical but accidental death; and grief led his queen to the cloister, where she died a few months before him. There was nobody, therefore, to succeed him but his turbulent brother Christopher, then in Sweden, whom he advised the estates to remove from the succession.

But Christopher was not to be so easily deprived of what he regarded as his birthright; and when he heard that he should have a rival in Eric, duke of Schleswig, he commenced his intrigues and pushed his warlike preparations with a vigour that showed his determination to attain his object. The promises which he made to the nobles, the clergy, and the municipalities, were exceedingly lavish, and they answered his purpose, for he was elected by the estates, and at the same time his eldest son Eric was joined with him in the government.

Though Christopher was thus placed on the throne, he soon found that to maintain himself on it, while an active rival was striving to unseat him, was no easy matter. He therefore began to lavish grants on his nobles so as to plunge the crown in new difficulties and to threaten the dismemberment of the monarchy. To the church he showed great deference: he bore, without complaint, the postponement of his coronation until it suited the convenience of the primate to return from abroad; and he engaged never to violate the privileges which had been usurped.

But he had also need of foreign allies, and to procure them he evinced the same disregard of the public interests. To Wratislaw of Rügen he confirmed the investiture of that fief, with some other domains. To Henry of Mecklenburg, who held Rostock in pledge, in consideration of money advanced to the late king, he granted that territory in perpetuity, as a fief of the Danish crown. With Gerhard [or Geert] count of Holstein (then count of Rendsburg), he entered into a closer treaty, by which each engaged to assist the other, whenever required, with all the disposable force at his command. The cession of so many fiefs within and without Denmark proper, could not but have fatal consequences. Not less fatal was the custom of assigning, until payment was made, whole islands and provinces, in return either for personal services or advances of money.

What all men might have foreseen soon arrived. Though Christopher was never to impose any tax without the consent of the nobles, and never, in any circumstances, to require a tax from the church, his necessities were so great that he soon laid a new and extraordinary impost on both orders. The nobles were to pay one tenth of their annual revenues; the clergy in an equal proportion; the people still more. Suddenly one universal cry of resistance arose from every part of the kingdom. The archbishop boldly declared that he would resist to the last; that if the king did not keep the promises made at his accession, no more would the church or the nobles keep theirs; and that they should consider themselves absolved from their allegiance. Christopher bent to the influence which he could not resist; but he had already exasperated his people, and his relinquishment of the impost did not restore them to good humour. His next measure was to recover by force of arms the islands, provinces, and domains, which had been pledged, without paying any portion of the debt. The whole of Skåne, nearly one third of the kingdom, was thus held by one noble. The creditors thus deprived of their rights naturally combined to obtain justice by force. They were aided by all that were discontented, and by not a few who had no cause for dissatisfaction, but who hoped to benefit by a change. Skåne and Zealand were laid waste by fire and sword. From two of his enemies, the archbishop of Lund and Eric duke of Schleswig, he was released by death; but the latter event, from which he expected so much advantage, had baneful consequences. Eric left a young son, Valdemar. Who was to be the guardian? To obtain the post, Christopher invaded Schleswig. But he found a competitor in the very ally on whom he had so much relied, Gerhard of Holstein, who has been styled the Great, and who, as the maternal uncle of Valdemar, had equal right to the trust. In the midst of his successes, after reducing most of the duchy, he was defeated by this count and compelled to retire.

Many of Christopher's disaffected subjects had been silent through fear; now that he was vanquished, he was assailed by one universal complaint. The nobles demanded their fiefs, the creditors their money, the people a removal of taxation, and all bitterly complained of his breach of faith. Revolt became general; and when the estates met he was solemnly deposed, the reason assigned for this measure being "the intolerable abuse which he had made of his authority." When Christopher received this intelligence he was in Zealand with his son; at the same time he learned that Count Gerhard was advancing. Eric marched with the disposable troops to repel the invader;

but he was defeated, betrayed into the hands of his enemies, and consigned to a dungeon.   With the loss of that son, his colleague on the throne, Christopher lost all hope of present resistance; and with two younger sons he precipitately left the kingdom.   At Rostock he procured aid from Henry of Mecklenburg and some Wend princes, and returned to struggle for his rights.   He reduced a fortress, but this success did not render the estates more favourable; they persisted in their resolution to elect another sovereign.   Besieged and taken by Gerhard, he was allowed to retire into Germany.   He made another attempt, with equal want of success, was again taken, and again set free, on the condition of his retiring to Rostock.

The estates assembled at Nyborg to elect a king made choice of Valdemar, duke of Schleswig, still a minor — the chief cause, no doubt, of his election, since there must be a regency and the most powerful might hope to participate in the public spoils.   Gerhard was the head of the regency; half a dozen other nobles were joined with him, and all were eager to derive the utmost advantage from a tenure of dignity which must evidently be brief.   Gerhard obtained the duchy of Schleswig in perpetuity.   Count John of Holstein was invested with the islands of Laaland, Falster, and Femern.   Knud Porse, who by Christopher had been created duke of North Halland, and who yet had been one of the first to desert that unfortunate king, was confirmed in the fief in addition to South Halland: it was no longer to be revocable, but to descend to his posterity.   The archbishop of Lund obtained Bornholm; another noble had Kolding and Ribe; a third, Langeland and Æröe; in short, the whole country was parcelled out into petty principalities, which, though feudally subject to the crown, would be virtually so many sovereignties. These measures could not fail to displease all who had any love for their country: a dozen tyrants were more tyrannical, more rapacious, than one; and pity began to be felt for the absent Christopher.   That prince was not inactive in his retirement at Rostock.   By the most lavish promises he obtained succours of men and money from some of his allies; and many of his own nobles, among whom were the primate and the bishops, engaged to join him as soon as he landed in Denmark.   He did land, and was joined by the bishops of Aarhus and Ribe and by many nobles, and was enabled to obtain some advantages over the regents.   But he had not learned wisdom by adversity.   One of his allies, Count John of Holstein, he converted into a deadly enemy; and he offended the church by arresting the bishop of Borglum.   The prelate escaped by corrupting his guard, and hastened to Rome to add the pope to the other enemies of Christopher.   The kingdom was immediately placed under an interdict.

In this emergency Christopher endeavoured to prevent his expulsion from the realm by resorting to the same means of bribery that he had before adopted.   To pacify Count John, he ceded to him Zealand and part of Skåne, in addition to Laaland and Falster, which he still held.   By grants equally prodigal and equally ruinous to the state, he endeavoured to secure the aid of other nobles.   So well did he succeed that Gerhard, abandoned by many supporters, sued for peace.   The articles were signed at Ribe in 1330.   Valdemar was sent back to Schleswig; but the reversion to the duchy was secured to Gerhard in the event of Valdemar's dying without heirs male.   As this was merely a future and contingent advantage, Fünen was placed in his hands until Schleswig should become his by inheritance; and for that island he was to become the vassal of the Danish crown.   Nor was this all: he was to hold the whole of Jutland by way of pledge until reimbursed for the expenses of the war, which he estimated at forty thousand marks.

This tranquillity was of short duration. The two counts, Gerhard and John, quarrelled; and Christopher, instead of remaining neuter, espoused the cause of the latter. He was defeated by Gerhard, and the greater part of Jutland withdrew from him to swell the cause of the victor. His only resource was now to throw himself on the generosity of the other, who professed his willingness to make peace in return for one hundred thousand marks; and until that sum (immense for those days) was paid, he was to hold Jutland. The two counts also treated with each other, John surrendering to Gerhard one half of the debt on Fünen; and they agreed to guarantee each other in the acquisitions which they had made, that is, in the dismemberment of the realm.

At the same time Skåne escaped for a season from the sceptre of the Danish kings. That province had passed into the hands of John, count of Holstein, through the inability of the crown to discharge the loans which had been borrowed on it. Holstein collectors therefore overran it, to collect the revenues claimed by the representative of the creditors. They were even more unpopular than those of the king had been; and the natives not unfrequently arose to massacre them. Three hundred were at one time put to death in the cathedral of Lund. To escape chastisement the inhabitants looked, not to Christopher, who was helpless as an infant, and whom they distrusted, but to Magnus king of Sweden. Him they proposed to recognise as their sovereign, on the condition of his defending them against the counts of Holstein. It is almost needless to add that Magnus joyfully availed himself of the opportunity of obtaining a province which was geographically within the limits of his kingdom, and which had always been an object of desire to his predecessors. He received the homage of the whole country, and sent forces to defend it. Instead of drawing the sword to recover it, John sold his interest in it and all claim to its government or revenues, for thirty-four thousand marks — a sum which Magnus readily paid him. The latter had now a double right to the province — that of voluntary submission and that of purchase.

In the last year of Christopher's life two of his nobles, with the view of obtaining the favour of the Holstein family, entered into a plot for his assassination. They set fire to his house, seized him as he was escaping, and bore him to a fortress in the isle of Laaland, which belonged to Count John. That nobleman, however, no longer feared a prince who had fallen into universal contempt, and whose cause was hopeless. He therefore ordered him to be released. The following year Christopher died a natural death, after the most disastrous reign in the annals of the kingdom.

By his wife Euphemia, daughter of Bogislaw, duke of Pomerania, he had three sons and three daughters. Eric, the eldest, preceded him to the tomb; Otto ultimately became a knight of the Teutonic order; Valdemar, after a short interregnum, succeeded him. Of his daughters two died in youth; but the eldest, Margaret, was married to Ludwig of Brandenburg, son of the emperor Ludwig of Bavaria.

The two counts of Holstein, who had thus partitioned the kingdom between them, consulted how they might perpetuate their usurpation. The best mode was to delay as long as possible the election of a new monarch; to exclude the two sons of the late king from the succession; and, when an election could no longer be avoided, to procure the union of the suffrages in favour of some prince whom they might control. In any case, as their sway might and probably must be brief, their interest lay in deriving the utmost advantage in the shortest possible time from their position. Hence their rapacity, which their armies enabled them to exercise with impunity.

Under no circumstances would the domination of strangers have been long borne without execration: that of rapacious strangers was doubly galling. The murmurs which arose on every side emboldened the two sons of Christopher to strive for his inheritance. But they entered the field before their preparations were sufficiently matured. Otto, with a handful of troops supplied by his brother-in-law the markgraf of Brandenburg, landed in Jutland. He was vanquished and committed to close confinement. To avert another invasion by excluding the sons from all hope of succession, Gerhard turned towards Valdemar, duke of Schleswig, who had been placed on the throne during Christopher's exile. If the duke succeeded, the duchy became the inheritance of Count Gerhard; but he would not wait for probabilities. In return for his promised aid, Valdemar, in a solemn treaty, agreed to surrender that province immediately; and if he did not obtain the object of his ambition, he was to receive Jutland in lieu of it. The rights of Gerhard over that peninsula, in virtue of the one hundred thousand marks which he claimed from the crown, have been mentioned: these rights therefore he might transfer. In the midst of the negotiation Prince Valdemar prepared to return and conquer, or to share the fate of his brother Otto. The people were almost universally favourable to him; and his arrival was expected with impatience. When the Jutlanders heard of the treaty which consigned them to Valdemar of Schleswig, they no longer waited for their prince, but openly revolted. Gerhard was compelled to retreat, but only to return with ten thousand German auxiliaries; and with these he laid waste the peninsula. His fate, however, was at hand. A Jutland noble, with fifty accomplices only, resolved to rid his country of a tyrant. Hastening to Randers, where the count lay with four thousand men, at midnight, he disarmed the guard, penetrated into the bedchamber of the regent, murdered him, and escaped before the army was aware of the deed (1340).

Thus perished Gerhard, surnamed the Great, a prince of great talents and of greater ambition. With him perished the grandeur of his house. His sons had not his personal qualities, and they could not maintain themselves in the position in which he left them. Emboldened by the event, the estates met, and declared the absent Valdemar, the third son of Christopher (Otto was still in confinement), heir to the throne. The act of election was sent to that prince in spite of the care taken by the counts of Holstein to prevent all intercourse between the country and the exile. Valdemar received it at the court of the emperor Ludwig of Bavaria. Under the imperial sanction there was a conference at Spandau. It was there agreed that Otto should receive his liberty on the condition of his resigning all claims to the crown. The new king engaged to marry Hedwige, sister of Valdemar, duke of Schleswig, whose dowry of 24,000 marks was to be deducted from the 100,000 claimed by the sons of Count Gerhard. Until the rest was paid, Fünen and a part of Jutland were to remain in the hands of the counts. The king was not to protect the murderers of the late count. There were some other conditions of much less moment — all dictated by the necessity of sacrificing much to obtain a greater advantage.[b]

VALDEMAR ATTERDAG, THE RESTORER OF THE KINGDOM (1340–1375 A.D.)

When the most important questions had been settled in this manner Valdemar proceeded to Jutland and was solemnly pronounced king in the assembly of Viborg (1340), after which he promulgated, in place of capitulation, an act of armistice towards all those who had passed through the disaster of the preceding years.

The end of all his efforts was to bring together the scattered portions of the Danish Kingdom, but this was not accomplished until after many cruel years, filled with hardships, struggles, and perils. He was, moreover, none too scrupulous in the choice of means, and did not hesitate to regain by trickery what had been taken from him by force. He began with Zealand, and — now by purchase and treaty, now by violence and bloody struggles in which he was assisted by the exasperated inhabitants who attacked and massacred the Holsteiners whenever they could be found — he succeeded at last, but only after five years of effort, in recovering the whole of that important division of the kingdom. Laaland and Falster came next, and he purchased at this time, or shortly after, a large part of north Jutland. He then turned his attention to the island of Fünen, which the Holsteiners were holding as guaranty for a debt of 41,000 marks. By making a skilful use of circumstances and by resorting to the sword where prudence and diplomacy failed, he succeeded in obtaining from the courts of Holstein, by the Treaty of Nebbegaard (1348), half of Fünen, and at the same time in getting other favourable conditions which gave him the hope of shortly recovering the other half of that island. But questions arose later as to the interpretation of these conditions, and the remainder of Fünen was the cause of a bloody conflict, in which the king was sometimes beaten but again won brilliant victories, as at the battle fought near the castle of Gamborg in the northwest district of the island.

The great expenditures which Valdemar had to make, both in prosecuting the war and in buying up fiefs and castles, compelled him to levy heavy contributions from his subjects ; and to forestall popular discontent, he called all the orders of the kingdom to a diet at Ringsted (1349), when he gave account of all the money he had received. The people, recognising the good use of the public funds, were all the more ready to make new sacrifices. Another means which he employed to procure necessary funds was to sell Esthonia. This he disposed of to the Teutonic Knights for 19,000 marks which went to redeem more important parts of the kingdom. His most ardent desire was to recover the Skånian provinces, but as circumstances at the beginning of his reign did not favour this plan, he deferred it for a time and confirmed even the grant made to Magnus Smek, who in return paid Valdemar a sum of money. But he never lost sight of his plan, and always kept one eye on affairs in Sweden, where things were in very bad shape and gave this prudent monarch hope of finding an opportunity of fulfilling his ambitions with even more advantage.

The reconstitution of the realm would have been accomplished with more rapidity if his subjects had been loyal, which was not always the case. Intelligent and thoughtful men well understood that Valdemar rightly deserved the throne, but there remained many malcontents, especially in the nobility, and notably among that of Jutland. During the preceding period of disorganisation the aristocracy had grown accustomed to violence and arbitrary action, but it could not so easily accommodate itself to the rigorous equity with which Valdemar the Restorer applied the law to high and low. He was accused of tyranny because he reunited to the crown and applied to the good of the country the numerous domains which the nobility had appropriated during the troubles. In many localities the peasants joined the rebellious nobles because they found insupportable the taxes and duties exacted by the king. They came to forget, little by little, the disasters from which Valdemar had delivered the realm, and felt only the weight of the actual burden which was the necessary consequence of preceding misfortunes.

After several years of strife, generally victorious, the king finished by concluding a peace with his foreign enemies (1360), and at the same time an arrangement with his subjects which held for some years. The latter was confirmed at the diet of Kallundborg (1360), where an ordinance was adopted with a view to defining the rights of the king and his subjects and establishing peace and order in the land. In this document the king promised to maintain the ancient laws and customs as well as the recognised rights of the nobility, clergy, burghers, and peasantry. All present agreed to pursue the brigands and incendiaries who were harassing the country, and to do their best to ensure that crimes against the king and crown of Denmark should be judged and punished. When the king or his officers prosecuted law-breakers, resentment was not to be cherished against them as though they pursued this course through personal hatred or enmity; on the other hand, the king was not to hold in abhorrence or persecute those who sought in the law a protection against injustices committed by him or his officials. The ordinance has been called a capitulation, and if it must be so regarded, it is to be wished that all capitulations were conceived in the same spirit; for it prescribed the duties not only of the king but of the orders as well, and did not, like preceding and subsequent documents, contain a particular enumeration of the privileges of nobles and clergy, but only a general confirmation of these rights, together with those of the burghers and peasants. In consequence of its character, it was not only signed by the king, but by all the bishops; and a large proportion of the nobles present were obliged, by hand and seal, to endorse its terms. This is one great proof of the prudence and strength with which Valdemar the Restorer, in difficult and troublesome times, knew how to maintain the royal prerogatives, as well as the rights of the weaker orders, against the clergy and powerful nobility.

THE REUNION OF THE SKÅNIAN PROVINCES

Valdemar was getting nearer and nearer to the end he had long been seeking — the reunion of the Skånian provinces to the Danish crown. King Magnus Smek was in constant strife with the unruly nobles of his realm, including his own son and co-ruler, Eric. In his need he asked help of the king of Denmark, who showed himself disposed to give it, but only for a large return from the simple Magnus Smek. The latter, in company with Queen Blanca and his son Hakon, visited Valdemar at Copenhagen (1359), where he had to promise to release the Skånian provinces before Valdemar would assist him against his rebellious subjects and son. The malicious Blanca hated her son Eric, and sought Valdemar's protection for her favourite, Bengt Algotsson. It was she especially who managed all the negotiations. The alliance of the two kings was sealed by the betrothal of Valdemar's seven-year old daughter Margaret to Magnus' son Hakon, then twenty years of age, and as pliant and docile to his father as his brother Eric was headstrong and hostile.

The following year (1360), Valdemar passed into Skåne, occupied the whole country, and forced Magnus Smek to surrender the documents which attested Sweden's right to the provinces — Count John's deed of purchase and the homage which the inhabitants of Skåne, Halland, and Blekinge had given the Swedish crown. According to a tale scarcely worthy of credit, Valdemar was no sooner in possession of these documents than he hastened to burn them. After succeeding so well in Skåne, the Danish king armed himself for an expedition to Visby, in the island of Gotland — one of the richest cities in all Europe and the principal trading station of the Hanseatic League on the Baltic. As excuse for this attack on Visby, some satirical songs about the king, which the inhabitants had sung, are usually alleged; but it is more probable that the king was seeking opportunity to deal a blow to the commerce of the Hanse Towns and to make himself master of Visby's wealth. The town was taken, the walls rased, and an immense booty seized (1361). From this day Visby's fame declined. A portion of its trade betook itself to the henceforth flourishing Copenhagen, and it remained but the spectre of its former greatness.

VALDEMAR'S REIGN CLOSES IN LOSSES

After the conquest of Gotland, Valdemar took the title "king of the Goths" *(de Göters Konge)*, but the destruction of Visby and the occupation of the Skånian provinces woke to action all his former enemies. The Swedish nation compelled Magnus Smek to break the marriage agreement between his son and Margaret and to declare war against Valdemar. The counts of Holstein, whose sister Elizabeth, daughter of Gerhard the Great, was now promised to Hakon; the duke Valdemar of Schleswig; and a little later Duke Albert the Elder of Mecklenburg, allied themselves with the Hanse Towns against Valdemar the Restorer. Seventy-seven of these towns sent at one time as many declarations of war, but the king laughed at their number, comparing them to a flock of cackling geese; and before long, as much by force as by ruse, he destroyed the powerful coalition. In the naval war which broke out, we hear for the first time after a long period of silence of a Danish fleet; and it fought with glory against that of the Hanse Towns, so long accustomed to victory.

The latter met such great reverses that its admiral, a Lübeck burgomaster, was put to death on his return home. After these disasters, some of the Hanse Towns first of all, sought an armistice with Denmark, which determined the others to conclude one of those so-called perpetual peaces. While these events were taking place, the princess Elizabeth left Holstein, late in the autumn, to marry King Hakon in Norway, but was wrecked in a storm on the Danish coast. Valdemar received her with the greatest courtesy, but under various pretexts and an appearance of solicitude for her safety, he would not allow her to set out on the sea in so stormy a season. Meantime he sent messages to Hakon and Magnus Smek, who came at once; and the marriage of Hakon and Margaret was celebrated (1363), although the latter had not yet completed her eleventh year. When, a short time after, Valdemar's son Christopher died of wounds received in battle with the Hanse fleet, this marriage assumed a special importance in opening a way for a union between Denmark and Norway, over which Hakon was king. The unfortunate princess of Holstein exchanged the throne to which she had been destined for a cloister cell.

If Valdemar's enemies had been thoroughly exasperated with him, they were now all the more so on account of this transaction. The Swedes excluded Prince Hakon from the succession, deposed Magnus Smek, and made his nephew Albert of Mecklenburg, son of Albert the Elder, king; and, indeed, a short time after the arrangement of the above-mentioned "perpetual peace," the Hanse Towns made a new alliance with Holstein, Mecklenburg, and Sweden. For some years Valdemar succeeded in controlling his own destiny, and forced several of his enemies to peace; but in 1368 a large number of the most powerful noble families of Jutland revolted and entered into formal alliance with the foreign enemies of the realm, and the king was forced to leave his country and seek help abroad. The situation in Denmark became terrible; the counts of Holstein invaded Jutland; Albert attacked Skåne; the Hanse Towns ravaged the shores and islands—the allies, in fact, made such progress that they were beginning to think of dividing the Danish provinces among themselves. However, the able Henning Podbusk, whom Valdemar had left as regent in his absence, succeeded in detaching his most dangerous enemies, the Hanse Towns, from the coalition, though at enormous sacrifice. By the Treaty of Stralsund (1370) the Hanseatic League obtained the right to trade, wholesale and retail, throughout the whole of Denmark, the right to establish all sorts of foreign workmen in the cities granted to it, and to import, free of duty, whatever material they needed. The Sound dues were entirely abolished on fish, and reduced to almost nothing on ships and articles of merchandise. Finally all the maritime towns of Skåne, with the townships and cantons dependent on them, were leased to the league for fifteen years. Henning Podbusk and the other members of the royal council had to assent to another demand of the haughty merchants; namely, that after Valdemar's death, the Hanse Towns should have a voice in the election of the king, and that Valdemar should not re-enter the kingdom without ratifying the treaty.

After much hesitation, Valdemar accepted this peace, and returned, in 1372, to his country, where the results of thirty years' work had been almost totally destroyed. The king succeeded, however, during the last three years of his life, thanks to his great skill and indefatigable energy, in re-establishing order in the kingdom and healing the most grievous wounds of the war. He had enough strength left in 1374 to invade North Friesland and chastise the inhabitants, who refused to pay their taxes. By coming to terms with one after another of the factions in Schleswig, he worked unceasingly to reunite that country to the kingdom; and when in 1375 Duke Henry, the last of the house of Abel, died childless, the outlook seemed brighter than ever. Just before or immediately after this death, the king had taken prudent measures to assure himself of the possession of Schleswig by occupying Hadersleben, Apenrade, Tondern, and Alsen with Sonderburg and Norburg, and placing royal officials in these towns and castles. But the counts of Holstein, who after the treaty of Ribe (1330) thought themselves entitled to some claim on Schleswig, armed themselves, and a serious war seemed on the point of breaking out, when Valdemar was surprised by death, that same year 1375, at the castle of Gurre.

Valdemar III has received the surname Atterdag (New Day Restorer) — perhaps because, owing to his great qualities, under his reign daylight began to pierce the gloom in which Denmark had long been plunged; or perhaps, as others explain it, because he loved to repeat the proverb, *I Morgen er det Atter Dag* (Daylight will reappear to-morrow), when his plans met with unexpected obstacles and, instead of giving them up, he postponed them for a more favourable occasion. His ungrateful people called him Valdemar Onde (the Bad), because this prince, strict himself in the performance of his royal duties, exacted work and sacrifices from his subjects, and because the situation of the kingdom forced him to impose heavy taxes

on them.[1] Some old annals written by a contemporary ecclesiastic complain bitterly of this monarch's severity.

"In Valdemar's day," we may read in them, "the good customs were abolished in Denmark; nor soldier, nor burgher, nor merchant had any rest; no one had time to eat, sleep, or rest, but all were forced to ceaseless weary labour, under pain of incurring the king's displeasure." Nevertheless, Denmark has had few kings who so well deserved to rule the country as Valdemar Atterdag. With his huge task of reconstructing the state entirely afresh and ceaselessly combating rebellious subjects and enemies abroad, he found time to undertake the internal improvement of the country. He built roads, dug canals, cultivated wasted districts, built dykes, erected watermills and a large number of castles and fortresses. He was constantly travelling over the whole kingdom, rendering justice in the assemblies and looking to the execution of the law. He lifted the Danish fleet from its decline, and employed a certain number of professional sailors who were lodged at Vordingborg. A proof of this great king's energy is that, without neglecting the administration of his kingdom, he made a number of journeys to foreign parts, where he was always well received on account of his rare talents as negotiator and mediator. He went several times to Germany, visited the pope in the south of France, and even made a rapid pilgrimage to distant Palestine.

Under the reign of Valdemar Atterdag, there raged in Denmark that deadly epidemic known as the Black Death (*den Sorte Død*). It made such havoc in neighbouring districts that in Lübeck, for example, it was said to have carried off two thousand five hundred people in twenty-four hours, and ninety thousand in a single summer, but the latter figure must be much exaggerated. In Denmark also, whither it was brought by a crewless ship which came ashore in the Vendsyssel, it was so violent a scourge that according to some reports, perhaps exaggerated, there did not remain, in some localities, one inhabitant out of a hundred.*e*

[[1] In tradition Valdemar Atterdag figures as the flying huntsman who was compelled to ride nightly accompanied by his dogs, from Burre to Gurre, in punishment for having declared that God might keep heaven so he might only hunt in Gurre wood.]

CHAPTER VI

SWEDEN TO THE UNION OF KALMAR

[1056–1389 A.D.]

In Swedish history the chronological difficulties of which we have already had so much reason to complain, are scarcely fewer even in the eleventh century. Most writers give different lists of kings down to the twelfth century. The reason of this difference is two-fold: there were sometimes two kings reigning at the same time, the one over the Goths, the other over the Swedes; and sometimes each of these peoples had two. On the death of Edmund Slemme in 1056, the Swedes and the Goths, who were often hostile to each other, disagreed about the succession and, as we saw in a former chapter, the Swedes raised Stenkil to the throne, while the Goths chose Hakon the Red as their king. Thus there were two kingdoms, two courts— the one reigning over the eastern, the other over the western and southern provinces.

The Goths and the Swedes had never perfectly amalgamated, from the period when Odin had led the latter into Sweden and driven the former from the coast into the interior of the country. But, on the other hand, experience had taught both of them the destructive effects of disunion; and on the present occasion, now that Christianity had made so considerable a progress among them (more however in Sweden than in Gothland), they felt more sensibly the impolicy of their conduct. The heads of the two peoples met together, and agreed that Hakon should continue to rule over the Goths, but that on his death his kingdom should cease to have a separate existence and be re-merged into that of Sweden. We shall, however, see that the same moderation did not always govern the two parties; and that double elections continued to agitate the common-weal long after this period. But this circumstance does not detract from the merit of the men who sanctioned the present agreement. In thirteen years Hakon paid the debt of nature, and in conformity with the agreement his crown reverted to the prince of the Swedes.

Of Stenkil the national historians speak with praise. Of gigantic size, unrivalled strength, and indomitable courage, he was yet one of the mildest

187

princes of his age. Over Svend II, king of Denmark, he is said by the Swedish historians to have frequently triumphed; but of such triumphs we have no record in the historians of the rival nation. Equal honour is accorded to his successor Inge I, surnamed the Good. In his wars this prince is said to have exhibited great valour; but he was more distinguished for his attachment to Christianity, and for the zeal with which he extirpated paganism. In this great work he probably evinced more ardour than discretion, if it be true that he was murdered in his bed by his idolatrous subjects. Halstan, the brother and successor of Inge, if indeed they did not reign conjointly over different parts of the kingdom, had the same mild virtues. Philip and Inge II were equally worthy of the diadem. Distinguished alike for his piety and for the rigour with which he punished the banditti who infested his western provinces, and the pirates who ravaged his coasts, Inge, in particular, reigned in the hearts of his people, except those whose ill deeds he punished. To the hatred of a faction he became a victim. That faction raised to the throne Rognerald, a chief of gigantic dimensions and of fiercer qualities. His yoke was soon felt to be intolerable: he was removed by violence; and a double election followed — the Swedes choosing a chieftain named Kol; the Goths, Magnus, son of Niels king of Denmark. The former soon perished in battle; the latter, a great tyrant, reigned seven years only (1148), when the suffrages of the people fell on one who had neither birth nor connections to recommend him, but who had the great qualities becoming the dignity. This was Swerker I. It is worthy of remark that Hakon the Red and Rognerald, and Kol and Magnus, are not usually classed amongst the Swedish kings — at least by modern historians.

The reign of Swerker was pacific and admirably adapted to the interests of the kingdom. He was a wise and patriotic monarch. But he had one grievous fault — blindness to the vices of his son. Never, if contemporary chroniclers are to be credited, did a youth so richly merit the curses of the people. At the head of a licentious gang, he violated the persons of the noblest virgins and matrons; he was addicted to every species of riot; and the insolence of his manners gave a more odious shade to his vices. In vain were remonstrances made to the father, whose first duty, as the people thought, was to insist that his own family should set the first example of obedience to the laws. Indignant at this guilty toleration, the people arose and murdered the prince. Swerker's own end was tragical; but whether he died through the influence of the same conspirators, or through the avarice of a domestic, is doubtful.

On his death (1155), the same ruinous division took place as in the preceding century: the Goths elected Charles, another son of Swerker; the Swedes made choice of St. Eric, who had married the daughter of Inge the Good — a name dear to the people. As civil war was so much to be deprecated, the heads of both parties met and agreed to this compromise — that Eric I should retain both crowns during his life, and on his death both should be inherited by Charles. But what was to become of the rights of their children? To prevent future disputes, the descendants of each were to rule alternately, without prejudice, however, to the elective suffrage of the people. It would have been impossible to devise any expedient better adapted to produce the contrary of what was intended.

The reign of Eric was one of vigour. The Finns, who had declared themselves independent, he reduced to subjection; and he also forced them, we are told, to forsake idolatry for Christianity. We may, however, doubt whether his efforts in this respect were so general as the chroniclers would have us believe; certainly, they were not very permanent. Probably they did as most barbarians do in similar circumstances — they submitted while the victor was near them, but reverted to their ancient superstitions when he had left. That he had idolaters nearer to him than Finland, and more immediately subject to his sway, is evident from the distinction he was accused of making between the worshippers of Odin and those of Christ. The former he deprived of the rights which the law conferred upon them. For this conduct he naturally incurred their indignation, and he also made enemies of another party — the licentious, the disturbers of the public tranquillity, who were scarcely less numerous. Both conspired against him; and as their own strength was inadequate to the object, they invoked the aid of the Danish king, offering, as it appears, the crown of Sweden to the son of that monarch. A Danish army arrived, and being joined by the malcontents marched towards Upsala. They were soon met by Eric, who, though he performed prodigies of valour, was defeated and slain (1160). His tragical death was one of the causes that led to his canonisation. Another was the zeal which he showed in the extirpation of idolaters, whom he pursued with fire and sword. Add that he was the founder of monasteries and churches, and we have reasons enough for his deification. By most readers he will be valued, less for his unenlightened devotion than for his compilation of a code of laws — *St. Eric's Lag.* Yet the provisions which it contains are deeply impressed by his dominant characteristics. Against pagans they are sanguinary; and they visit offences against the Christian religion and the Christian worship with stern severity.

Charles, the son of Swerker, was now monarch of the whole country. But he had some difficulty in expelling the invaders, who had proclaimed the son of the Danish king. He, too, was much attached to the church, to which he was more generous than even his predecessor. If tradition be true (there is no contemporary authority for the statement), he embarrassed his affairs by his immoderate liberality. As he obtained from the pope the erection of an archbishopric — that of Upsala — he was expected to endow it. From his munificence in this respect may have originated the report in question. His reign was not exempt from trouble. The adherents of the rival dynasty were his enemies, from a suspicion (apparently ill-founded) that he had been one of the conspirators against St. Eric. Though in conformity with the agreement which we have mentioned he nominated Knud, the son of Eric, his successor, that prince would not remain in the kingdom, under the pretence that his life was in danger. In a few years he returned into Sweden, at the head of a considerable Norwegian force, was joined by the partisans of his house, and enabled to triumph over his rival, whom he captured and beheaded. This act he justified by appealing to the untimely end of his father, which he represented as the work of Charles.

The reign of Knud was disturbed by two invasions: the first by the Danes, who had armed to revenge the death of the late king, or rather under that plea to profit by the disasters of a rival country (the Goths, who loved the memory of Charles, immediately joined it, but the king was victorious); the second was an irruption of the Esthonian pirates, who laid Sigtuna in ashes, slew the archbishop of Upsala, and carried away many prisoners before the king could overtake them.

Swerker II, the son of Charles, was the next king (1195-1210), in virtue of the compact between the Goths and the Swedes. But every day more clearly evinced the dangers resulting from that compact: it daily widened the breach, not merely between the two royal families but between the two great tribes which constituted the nation. Blood had been openly or treacherously spilt by both parties; and the deadly feud had descended to the chiefs of both. It was, from the first, the object of Swerker to exterminate the family of his rival; but one prince — Eric, the only son of the late king — escaped into Norway. For some years he governed with moderation; but when he became tyrannical, the people of Upland invited the exile to return. Eric obeyed the call, was joined by most of the nobles, and enabled to triumph over Swerker, though the latter was supported by a Danish army. The king was expelled, and though he subsequently twice returned to renew the contest, twice he was defeated, and on the latter occasion his own corpse was among the slain.

The reign of Eric II (1210–1220) commenced more judiciously than could have been anticipated from preceding events. To pacify the rival faction, he declared Prince John, the son of Swerker, his successor. To conciliate the Danes, who had so warmly espoused the cause of his rivals, he obtained the hand of a Danish princess, the sister of Valdemar II. His reign was pacific, but too short for the interests of his people. John I (1220–1222) ascended without opposition the united thrones of the Swedes and the Goths; but his reign was still shorter — a misfortune the more keenly felt from his admirable conduct. If he was less fortunate in two or three military expeditions (so obscure, however, as scarcely to deserve notice) than was hoped from the justice of his cause, his civil government was one of great success. He was succeeded without opposition by the son of his predecessor, Eric II, named after the father.

Eric III, surnamed the Halt and the Lisper (1222–1250), had a reign less peaceful than those which immediately preceded it. There was a family in the realm too powerful for obedience — that of the Folkungar — the chiefs of which, by their wealth and their numerous connections, evidently aspired to the throne. To bind them to his interests, he married two of his sisters to nobles of that house, while he himself took to wife a lady of that family. But these alliances, as might indeed have been expected, only gave a new impulse to ambition. To wrest the crown from him, the whole family or tribe, the chiefs of which must have been connected with the royal line of either the Goths or the Swedes, broke out into rebellion — one noble only, the jarl Birger, remaining faithful to him. In the first battle Eric was defeated and compelled to flee; but he raised an army in Denmark, returned to Sweden, vanquished the usurper Svend, and was again acknowledged by the whole realm. In the last year of his reign, he sent an expedition against the Finns, who had reverted to idolatry. It was commanded by Birger Jarl, on whom he had conferred the hand of his youngest sister. The cruelty of the general, who probably acted in obedience to the royal orders, equalled that of the former military apostle, St. Eric.

VALDEMAR I BEGINS A NEW DYNASTY

The death of Eric the Lisper (1250) was followed by a violation of the compact which had established the alternate order of succession. The Folkungar nobles no longer concealed their intention of aspiring to the throne. Through the intrigues of a dependent, when the diet met for a new election the choice fell on Valdemar I, the son of Birger Jarl by the sister of the late king. On the part of the electors, this was an attempt to combine the interests of two great families. But Birger was dissatisfied: he had expected the crown himself; and he objected to the impolicy of choosing a child like his son. His design was to obtain the regency, and he succeeded (1251).

However censurable the means by which Birger arrived at power, he had qualities worthy of the post. He founded Stockholm, which he also fortified: he revised and greatly improved the *Landslag*, or written laws of the kingdom; he conferred on the cities and towns privileges similar to those contained in the charters of later ages; he improved the internal administration in other respects, while he defended the coasts against the ravages of the pirates. Such indeed was the prosperity which he introduced that the diet requested the king to confer on him the ducal title — a title previously unknown in Sweden. But the success of his administration and the power held by his family incurred first the jealousy and soon the hatred of a faction, or rather of several factions who united to oppose him. A civil war followed, which was indecisive; and it was ended by a pacification, but a pacification dictated by deceit. After Birger had solemnly sworn to it, and the heads of the other party repaired in unsuspecting confidence to his camp, he caused them to be put to death. One noble only escaped — Charles, who fled to the Teutonic knights, became a member of the order, and left a heroic name behind him. This perfidious act is a sad stain on the glory of his regency. Another was his excessive love of power, which induced him to retain the reins of government long after his son had arrived at manhood, and even after that son had married Sophia, daughter of Eric Plovpenning, king of Denmark. Death alone caused him to release his grasp (1266).

The reign of Valdemar was one of trouble. Whether through the persuasion of the diet, or through fraternal attachment, he tolerated if he did not himself establish the independence of his brothers. Magnus duke of Södermanland, Eric prince of Småland, and Benvit duke of Finland, had separate courts, and exercised a sovereign authority in their respective jurisdictions. Magnus, the eldest, was formed for a monarch. He was learned, courteous, generous, and highly accomplished in all military sciences. So popular did he become that his palace was more frequented than the king's. Of his popularity Valdemar soon became jealous; yet he could do no other than leave the regency to Magnus during his pilgrimage to Rome. The motive of this pilgrimage was to expiate a criminal connection, of many years' standing, with Jutta, sister of his queen. The severity of the penance was owing to the fact of Jutta's being a nun, who had precipitately fled from the convent of Roeskilde, and the pope would not give him absolution until he had visited the Holy Land. Jutta was condemned to perpetual seclusion.

In 1276, after an absence of nearly three years, the royal penitent returned and accused Magnus of intriguing for the throne. Whether there was any truth in the charge cannot well be ascertained; but that suspicion should arise in his mind was inevitable. He was jealous, not of Magnus only, but of all his brothers. On this occasion, Benvit, the youngest, exhibited a proof of magnanimity which may well obtain the praise of history: to consolidate the royal power, he resigned his duchy, took holy orders, and subsequently became bishop of Linköping. The elder brothers, far from imitating the example, united themselves closely with the Danes, and a civil war followed. Valdemar was surprised, pursued, and captured. To end these disorders, the diet met and divided the kingdom between the two brothers. To Valdemar were conceded the two Gothlands (East and West) with Småland and Dalecarlia: the rest fell to Magnus.

This peace was of short continuance. Magnus did not pay his Danish auxiliaries, by whose aid he had triumphed. In revenge the Danish king [Eric Glipping] ravaged the Swedish provinces, and entered into a treaty with Valdemar to restore him to the undivided throne. At the head of a Danish army, Valdemar marched against Magnus, but was defeated.   To repair this disaster, Eric of Denmark took the field with a large army — so large that Magnus would not risk an action.   But the Swedish prince obtained by policy the advantage which arms could not give him.   He drew the invaders into the heart of the kingdom; cut off all supplies; and awaited the approach of winter to effect their destruction.   But through the mediation of the chiefs on both sides peace was restored.   As Magnus had not the money due to Eric, he pledged one of his maritime towns.   In return, he obtained not merely a friend but his recognition as monarch of Sweden.   Valdemar, thus sacrificed, was made to renounce his claim to the whole country, and to pass the remainder of his days in Denmark, on one of the domains which he had received with his queen.

Magnus I at his accession (1279) assumed the title "king of the Swedes and the Goths," to denote his superiority over the whole kingdom.   But the title was more pompous than the power.   He was soon accused of undue partiality towards the people of Holstein, who in virtue of his marriage with Hedwige, daughter of the count Gerhard, flocked to Sweden in great numbers. The remonstrance did not weaken his attachment to these foreigners, whom he loaded with honours.   To the great families, especially that of the Folkungar, this preference was gall; and a conspiracy was formed to extirpate the odious strangers.   An opportunity for the execution of this plot soon arrived. Escorted by a considerable number of Holsteiners, the queen proceeded to Skara, a town of Gothland, to meet her father.   The conspirators followed, and massacred the guard, including even the brother-in-law of the king. Nor was this all: they threw the count of Holstein into a dungeon; and they certainly would have laid their hands on the queen, had she not contrived to escape to a monastery.   Knowing the power of the family which had instigated these excesses, and fearing that they were supported by foreign alliances, the king dissimulated, and made use of the most conciliating language, until he had obtained the release of the count.   He then summoned a diet, charged the unsuspicious Folkungar with high treason, sent them to Stockholm, and beheaded all of them except one, who was allowed to be ransomed.   From this time that ambitious family ceased to have much influence over the realm. To establish his throne still more solidly, he entered into a double matrimonial alliance with Denmark.   His son Birger, still a child, was affianced to a daughter of the Danish king, and as she too was a child, she was taken, in conformity with the custom of the times, to the Swedish court to be educated.   And soon afterwards Ingeborg, daughter of Magnus, became the wife of Eric Menved.

The tranquillity obtained through these measures enabled Magnus to devote his whole time to the internal administration.   Prior to his reign, the local nobles had not hesitated to levy contributions on the peasants.   He decreed that whoever took anything from a poor man without paying the value should be visited with rigorous penalties [and thus he earned the name of Ladu-laas, or Barnlock, because he protected the contents of the peasant's barn].   From his brother Valdemar he sustained some trouble; but he crushed the seeds of rebellion by imprisoning that restless prince.   To support with greater magnificence, the regal state, he obtained, from the gratitude of his people, a considerable augmentation of his resources.   This augmentation consisted in certain returns from the mines and from the great lakes of Sweden.   Well did he merit this liberality; for never had the country a greater king.

Birger, the son of Magnus, being only eleven years old at his father's death, the regency devolved on Torkel, a noble Swede. Nothing can better illustrate the merit of Magnus than this choice. At home and abroad Torkel evinced his talents and his patriotism. His expeditions against the Finns, the Karelians, and the Ingrians were crowned with success. But his great object was to render the people happy. [He introduced a law prohibiting the sale of slaves, and in 1295 a codification amendment of the law of Upland was made.] Having reason to fear the interruption of the social tranquillity, Torkel arrested the sons of the late king Valdemar, who could not forget their claims to the throne. But as Birger grew to manhood, he had still more cause of apprehension from Eric and Valdemar, brothers of the sovereign. Both evidently aspired to distinct governments. To strengthen his interests, the former married Ingeborg, daughter of Hakon VI, king of Norway. Seeing that he and Valdemar were acting more openly in pursuit of their treasonable object, yet unwilling to adopt extreme measures, Birger, with the advice of his minister, obtained from them a written pledge never to leave the kingdom, or approach the royal residence without permission; never to conspire against the government; never to maintain more than a given number of armed men; and always to obey the commands of their sovereign.

The princes still continued to plot; and to escape imprisonment, they fled into Denmark. The Danish king, however, being persuaded to abandon them, they took refuge in Norway, were hospitably received by Hakon, and enabled, from their new fiefs of Nydborg and Konghella, to lay waste the neighbouring provinces with fire and sword. A body of troops sent by Birger to repulse them was defeated. A second army was raised, and the king marched in person to chastise his brothers. They were, however, at the head of a large force, not of their own partisans merely but of the Norwegians; and to avoid the effusion of blood a pacification was recommended. They were received into favour on the condition of their swearing obedience to the king; in return he conferred on Duke Eric the fief of Varberg. The next feature of this transaction was the sacrifice of the able and patriotic Torkel. The brothers could not forgive him for thwarting them in their rebellion; and Birger was made to believe the vilest calumnies respecting him. The aged minister was sent to Stockholm and beheaded (1306). At the same time his daughter, the wife of Valdemar, was repudiated. Thus was a long course of public service rewarded.

By this criminal weakness, Birger was righteously left to the intrigues of his brothers. By them he was surprised and made prisoner, together with his wife and children, and forced to resign the crown in favour of Eric. His eldest son, Magnus, escaped, and fled to Denmark, the king of which armed for the restoration of his sister's husband. From this period to the close of Birger's reign there was war, alternated by hollow peace. In 1307 he obtained his liberty, on the condition of his kingdom being dismembered in favour of his brother. To revoke this dangerous act he renewed his alliance with Denmark, and again obtained help; but his proceedings were not decisive, and a new pacification followed, on conditions similar to the preceding, except that Birger was now regarded as the liege superior of his brothers, who did homage to him for their fiefs. Unable to reduce them by force, he had recourse to the usual acts of the base. He pretended great affection for them, and sent them many presents. At length, alluring them to his court at Nyköping, he arrested them in bed, and consigned them to dungeons, with expression of triumphant insult more galling than the perfidy itself. One died of the wounds which he had received in the effort to escape: the other was starved to death.

But from this deed of blood the king derived no advantage. The bodies of the murdered princes, being exposed to the public, roused the wrath of the very numerous party hostile to his government. The civil war was now renewed by Mats Ketilmundsson in behalf of Duke Eric's son. Since the death of Torkel the king had become rapacious, tyrannical, and consequently unpopular. The people, who lamented the fate of the murdered princes, favoured the cause which Ketilmundsson had espoused: the fortresses that still held for the king were soon reduced: Magnus, his son, was made prisoner; and he himself was compelled to seek a refuge in Denmark, where he was coldly received.

Fate had not yet done its worst for this exiled prince. A diet was assembled to choose a successor. Such was the hatred borne towards him and his line that his son Magnus was beheaded. The suffrages of the electors united in favour of Duke Eric's son, a child three years old. Grief the following year (1320) brought Birger to the tomb. Whatever good signalised his reign must be attributed to his able and virtuous minister: his own conduct was dictated by odious vices.

During the long minority of Magnus II, the regency was exercised by Ketilmundsson, who had contributed so largely to the expulsion of Birger and the execution of the blameless Magnus, the son of Birger. His administration, which continued eighteen years, is mentioned with respect; but it was signalised by no great exploit deserving the attention of history. Both his policy and that of his sovereign, in respect to Skåne, has been related. In the administration of justice and the maintenance of the public tranquillity he was successful. On his demise, Magnus assumed the reins of government; but did not give so much satisfaction as his minister. He undertook an expedition against the western provinces of Russia (then subject to their own princes), influenced only by a wild ambition. The result was not glorious. The taxes which he levied on the people for its support gave rise to complaint. The pope, too, complained that he had appropriated to his own use the money which, in virtue of Olaf the Lap-King's act, should have gone to the Roman treasury. Still his necessities increased: the purchase of Skåne was another channel of expenditure; and though he pledged some of the royal domains, he had still to exact more from his people, including the clergy, than their patience would support. For this cause he was excommunicated by the pope.

Regardless of murmurs, he proceeded in his course: he was distinguished alike for rashness, feebleness, and irresolution. Governed by young favourites, and still more by his queen, who persuaded him that he might do whatever he pleased with impunity, and anxious to place a third crown on his brow (he had inherited Norway in right of his mother), he exhibited at once his silly ambition and his incapacity by embroiling himself with Denmark. So far from obtaining that crown, he lost his own. The diet insisted that he should resign Norway to Hakon, and Sweden to Eric, his two sons. He fled into Skåne; implored the aid of Valdemar Atterdag, and in return ceded that province to the Danish crown. He was enabled by this means and by the support of a party, to carry on a war with Eric. Its ravages were deeply felt; its issue was dubious; and a diet was convoked at Jönköping to avert by a pacification the ruin of the monarchy. Under the mediation of two princes connected with the royal family, it was decreed that the country should be divided between the father and the son: to the former were assigned Upland, the two Gothlands, Vermland, Dalecarlia, with the northern portion of Halland and the isle of Öland; to the latter, Finland, Småland, the southern portion of Halland, and Skåne.

The indiscretions of Magnus had lost him the hearts of his people, which turned with ardour to Eric IV. This circumstance roused his jealousy and that of his queen, and they are said to have conspired against the life of Eric. Whether he was removed by poison administered to him by his mother, or by the violence of conspirators, or by lawless banditti, or, finally, by natural causes, must forever rest unknown, since ancient annals say nothing on the subject. The only fact that is certain is that Eric died, and that Magnus profited by the event, since it restored him to the monarchy.

It was impossible for this weak and unscrupulous prince to win the esteem of the Swedes. He hated them because they had deposed him; and to be revenged on them he entered into a close alliance with Valdemar of Denmark. Valdemar, to whom he ceded Skåne, became, as we have before related, the willing instrument of that vengeance in the sack of Visby and in other depredations. This was not the way to acquire popularity: he and the whole Danish nation were soon detested; nor was the feeling diminished when the secret transpired of a projected union between the king's son, Hakon, of Norway, and Margaret, the daughter of Valdemar. To prevent this obnoxious alliance, the nobles arose, imprisoned Magnus in the fortress of Kalmar, called on Hakon to assume the administration, and made him promise not only that he would renounce all connection with Denmark but that he would marry Elizabeth, sister of Henry, count of Holstein. Though Hakon II (the sixth of Norway) engaged to fulfil the wishes of the diet, neither he nor his father, who was soon released, had the least intention of doing so. On the contrary, they renewed their connection still more closely with the obnoxious Valdemar. The manner in which Elizabeth was deluded by that monarch, until the marriage of his daughter with Hakon was celebrated, has been already described.

Nothing could exceed the anger of the Swedes, or rather of a considerable faction (for the majority were passive) when they heard of this marriage. Determined to exclude both father and son they invited Henry of Holstein, who was connected with the royal line, to ascend the throne. But Henry was an old man; and he would not risk his tranquillity for an object that he could not long enjoy. He recommended the electors to make choice of Albert duke of Mecklenburg, whose mother was the sister of Magnus. But the duke had no wish to rule a divided, turbulent people; nor did he wish his eldest son to undertake the perilous charge. He had, however, a second son, also named Albert, who had nothing to lose, and whom he recommended to the suffrages of the electors.

Albert arrived at Stockholm early in 1364. That city was in the interests of Magnus, and for a time it resisted; but he forced or persuaded it to capitulate. There he was joined by most of the nobles who were discontented with Magnus. Their first act was to renew the deposition of the one; their next, to confirm the election of the other. Hakon, then in Norway, prepared to invade the kingdom; and Magnus, who had still a party, effected a junction with him. Their army being augmented by a considerable number of Danes, they penetrated into Upland. But Albert, on his side, hastened to oppose them; and in a battle of some magnitude, victory the most decisive inclined to his standard: Magnus was taken prisoner; Hakon was wounded and compelled to retreat with expedition into his own kingdom (1365). The fortresses which held for the two princes were next reduced; two or three of them only made a vigorous defence. But Valdemar of Denmark, whose interests lay in disturbing the kingdom, sent, from time to time, supplies of troops, which harassed the king.

Peace with that formidable rival was felt to be necessary for the repose of the realm, and it was purchased by the cession of some domains. Among them was the isle of Gothland with Visby the capital. That these cessions were unwillingly made may be easily conceived; and to procure their restoration Albert entered into a close league with the enemies of Denmark. The war was consequently renewed. While his allies assailed other parts of Denmark, he invaded Skåne, a portion of which he reduced. But little time was left him for exultation. Hakon of Norway invaded Sweden, defeated him, and compelled him to throw himself into Stockholm, which was closely invested. In this extremity he proposed an interview, in which the conditions of peace were agreed on. Magnus was enlarged for a ransom of 12,000 marks; and in return for his cession of the Swedish crown, he received as fiefs

QUEEN MARGARET OF DENMARK, NORWAY,
AND SWEDEN
(1353-1412)

Vestergötland, Vermland, and Dalecarlia (1371). He was, however, to have no share in the administration of these provinces, but merely to receive the revenues with the title of governor; and the rest of his days he was to pass in Norway. Lest he should break this, with as much levity as he had broken all his former engagements, sixty gentlemen of his party were to surrender themselves prisoners to Albert if he should again disturb the peace of the realm. He did not disturb it, because he was soon afterwards drowned in crossing a ford (1374).

For some years after this pacification Albert enjoyed comparative security. But he was not popular: he brought over many Germans to share in the spoils of the kingdom; and exhibited in their favour a partiality so gross as much to indispose the nation against him. Insecure as was his possession of Sweden, he raised troops to support the claims of his nephew, Albert of Mecklenburg, to the Danish throne, in opposition to Olaf, the son of Margaret and Hakon. The enterprise failed: the armament that was sent against the Danes was mostly destroyed by a storm; and there was no disposition to renew the contest.

The gross partiality of Albert for his foreign mercenaries was not the only fault he committed. Having a high notion of the kingly prerogative, he endeavoured to rule without the control of the diet. For his attempt to restrain the privileges of the nobles he would deserve our praise, were not his motives of the most selfish character. The people had still more reason to complain. Not only were they subject to a tyranny odious as that of the nobles, but they were ground to the earth by new imposts, and, what was still more mortifying, for the enrichment of avaricious foreigners. In this state of the public mind, he convoked a diet at Stockholm (1386) and demanded an augmentation of his income. It was not, he observed, adequate to the decent support of royalty; and he solicited one third of the whole revenue, civil and ecclesiastical. Nothing could equal the indignant surprise of the diet at this extraordinary demand. They replied that former kings had found the usual revenues enough, not merely for comfort but for splendour; and intimated that if he was straitened the cause lay in the number of foreigners whom he enriched. This intimation might have been expected to produce some good effect; but it had none on this imprudent king except to exasperate him, and to make him resolve that he would wrest by force what had been refused to his solicitations and plunge the kingdom into a ruinous civil war.

SWEDEN, NORWAY AND DENMARK ARE UNITED UNDER MARGARET

At this time Margaret, who had succeeded her son Olaf (1387), was sovereign of Denmark and Norway. To her the malcontents applied for aid, which she would not afford them, unless they acknowledged her for their queen. The condition was accepted: an army of Danes marched into Sweden and was immediately joined by many of the nobles and clergy. The lower classes of the population were indifferent to the result, or if they had any bias it was in favour of Albert — not from any attachment to him but from dislike of the nobles. At Falköping, in Vestergötland, however, a good stand was made by his army, consisting not merely of Swedes but of Germans and many adventurers whom the offer of large pay and the hope of plunder had drawn to his standard. But after a desperate conflict, he was defeated and captured, together with his son (1389). Both were committed to a fortress, where, notwithstanding the efforts of their German allies and those of their own party, they remained above six years; nor did they obtain their release without a solemn renunciation of the Swedish crown. With Margaret, sovereign of three kingdoms, begins a new era in northern history.[b]

ST. BRIDGET OF SWEDEN

Amongst the conspicuous figures belonging to the age which had just closed, a character of a species widely different from most of those which have passed before us claims attention — both from its intrinsic interest and the European influence which it exerted, and from the fact that the foundation which was the starting-point of that influence played an important part in the life of Sweden for two hundred years. The fame and influence of St. Bridget of Sweden extended far beyond her own country and century. A typical mediæval saint in the ecstatic simplicity of her faith and her belief in her own visions, she was equally distinguished for the benevolence towards her fellows that found a practical vent in the charities which were continued by the order she founded. Vadstena, the chief convent of that order, became the centre of a whole cycle of legendary and historic story, and its history is closely interwoven with that of the Swedish nation. The following brief epitome of Bridget's life is by a Catholic historian : [a]

In the month of July (1370) St. Bridget of Sweden came to Montefiascone to present herself to the pope. She was born about 1302 of one of the noblest families of Sweden, and was named Birgitta (Bridget). She was married at thirteen to a young nobleman named Ulf Gudmarson, by whom she had eight children. They made together the pilgrimage to the shrine of Sant Jago in Galicia, and on their return home both resolved to enter religion. Ulf died before he could carry out his plan. Bridget, finding herself a widow, redoubled her austerities and her charities, and a short time after, that is to say about the year 1344, she founded a monastery for sixty nuns and twenty-five brothers of the order of St. Augustine, at Vadstena, in the diocese of

Linköping. She made certain provisions for it, and named it the monastery of the Holy Saviour.

Such was Bridget when she came to seek Pope Urban V and ask his approval of her work. This she obtained. Then she sent word to the pope by Count Nicholas of Nole that if he retired he would commit a great folly and would not finish his journey. Furthermore she declared to Cardinal Beaufort, afterwards pope, in the presence of Alfonso, bishop of Jaen, that when she was at Rome the Holy Virgin revealed to her the following message: "It is God's will that the pope should not leave Italy, but that he should remain until his death at Rome or elsewhere. But if he return to Avignon he will die at once, and render an account to God of his conduct. Bridget told the cardinal of this revelation so that he might send it secretly to the pope in writing; but the cardinal dared not do this, and the sainted widow gave it herself to the pope, written in Alfonso's hand." [The incident gave Bridget the reputation of a prophetess, for Urban returned to Avignon two months later and died in December of the same year.]

After St. Bridget had obtained the confirmation of her order from the pope, she went on to Naples and then to Sicily. On returning to Rome she believed herself to have had a revelation to go to Jerusalem, and although sixty-nine years old she set out with her daughter Catherine. Arriving in the Holy Land she visited all the holy places, among which was always reckoned that of the Annunciation, the house at Nazareth. Bridget returned to Rome and died there in the odour of sanctity, July 23rd, 1373, at the convent of the nuns of St. Clara. The following year her body was taken back to Sweden through her daughter's efforts, and placed in the monastery of Vadstena which Bridget had founded.[c]

Bridget's name is attached to various writings of a religious character, the principal of which are her *Uppenbarelser* or *Revelations*, which reflect the ecstatic mysticism of her religious standpoint, while the practical side of her character is represented by the recognition voiced in them of the urgent need of reformation in the church. This book was denounced by the French theologian Gerson, a younger contemporary of Bridget, but was recognised by the council of Bâle, forty years after her formal canonisation.[a]

Spread of the Order of Saint Bridget; Vadstena Convent

The order of St. Bridget soon spread itself throughout all the countries of Europe, until finally there were about seventy convents of the order, in which day and night brothers and sisters sang the praises of the immaculate Virgin. The Reformation and freedom of spirit at the end of the preceding and beginning of this century reduced the Birgittine order in number; and of the once widely ramified order there now exist only the religious houses of Altomünster in Upper Bavaria, the "Refuge of Mary" and "Mary's Heart" in the Netherlands, and the "Lion House" at Spetisburg in England. None of these four religious houses has any longer priests of the order.

That which chiefly gave importance to the order was the religious awakening it called forth among the nobles of the North — the Swedes, the Norwegians, and the Danes. Bridget understood how to evoke enthusiasm in her equals in station. Even princesses and members of the imperial council let themselves be initiated and were glad to serve as sisters or brothers in the convents. Vadstena and the other Birgittine convents worked beneficially in the three northern kingdoms, by their care of the poor, by scientific research, and by encouraging upright conduct among the inhabitants. The revival of mental life is reflected in many books which proceeded from the silence of the convents. The convent of Vadstena was a small highschool. Partly by buying, partly by diligent copying, and partly by presents the library there increased, and in the year 1490 the monks set up a printing press. Theology was the principal study; but philosophy, history, geography, astronomy, medicine, music, painting, and sculpture also received attention. Sisters as well as brothers studied Latin, and also the use of the mother tongue. Many of the brothers sought to extend their education by travelling abroad, especially in Rome, so as later to become teachers in the Vadstena schools. As in Vadstena so in all the Birgittine convents there reigned an active literary life. But Vadstena remained the most important among them. For two centuries it formed the centre of religious life in Sweden.

King Albert of Mecklenburg spent great sums in endowing the convents. In them the children and grandchildren of St. Bridget also found their last resting place. The relics of the great saint were held in high honour as long as the Catholic faith blossomed. In 1403 a costly reliquary was made in Stockholm, for which alone 420 marks of pure silver were used; and there was no place of pilgrimage throughout the whole North that could compare with the Birgittine convent, where the most distinguished of every nation contended with foreign pilgrims in showing honour to Bridget. In the year 1403 Queen Margaret knelt at the tomb of the saint, and the year 1406 saw a Scotch bishop of Skeninge come to Vad-

ENTRANCE TO VADSTENA CHURCH (1563)

stena through ell-deep snow. Queen Margaret joined the Birgittine sisterhood; she was followed by the high nobles of the North, who considered it a blessing to hold spiritual relations with the brothers and sisters of St. Bridget.

The old convent church still stands, with its wide porch, its high columns, its five arches gray with age as they were built at the end of the fourteenth century. It is built of Omberger chalkstone, and in the north is known under the name of "Bluestone church." In Catholic times the inside of the church was furnished with thirteen altars for the thirteen priests, of which the high altar, contrary to custom, lay to the west. It had three doors — "the door of forgiveness," by which the faithful entered the church, the "door of atonement" by which the brethren entered, and the "door of mercy" by which the sisters went into the choir. The chief building of the nuns was towards the north and extended from east to west ; the monks lived on the south side of the church. Rich donations fell to the convent. Free from taxation and burdens, richly endowed by all the Swedish provinces south of the Dal-Elf, the foundation enjoyed a considerable income. One residence after the other arose around the convent, so that soon there was an entire city. Among the inhabitants of the convent, besides learned men, there were architects, mechanicians, painters, sculptors, and artisans of every kind. Of its monks one became an archbishop, another a bishop.

The fame of the convent rose to its highest when, after the canonisation of Bridget's daughter Catherine, her remains, which until then had rested in consecrated ground, were raised. The celebration took place in 1489. With all honour the sacred treasure was raised and placed on the altar where it remained till the beginning of the Reformation. The convent was at its zenith, and this day was one of the last great days it witnessed. In 1513 the shrine of St. Catherine was almost completed; the work was, however, never finished, as King Gustavus Vasa used the silver of which it was to be made, and robbed the monks of much more for the needs of the country. It was the first step towards the destruction of the convent of St. Bridget. The year afterward the nuns received an order from King Gustavus to send some monks to Lapland, to convert the people to the Christian faith; in reality he wished to weaken the convent. From 1528 to 1541 we find no entries noted in the records of Vadstena; it was desired that the convent of itself should cease to exist through a want of brothers and sisters. In 1540 the Catholic service was done away with in Vadstena, the archives of the convent and the treasures were removed, and in 1543 the monks were forbidden to wear the dress of the order. At the diet of Söderköping in 1593 the suppression of the time-honoured convent was decreed. The costly shrines containing the remains of St. Bridget and St. Catherine, as well as of St. Eric, were torn down from the altars, and the relics of the saints buried in an unknown place. The nuns were no longer allowed to dwell there; for some time the convent had had no monks. Then the last abbess, Carin Olofsdotter, with seven of her faithful sisters, fled to the convent of their order in Poland. Thus fell this monastery, an honour to the country, and the northern church, the residence of true piety and knowledge; after a famous existence of 240 years the work of the great Saint of Scandinavia was destroyed.[e]

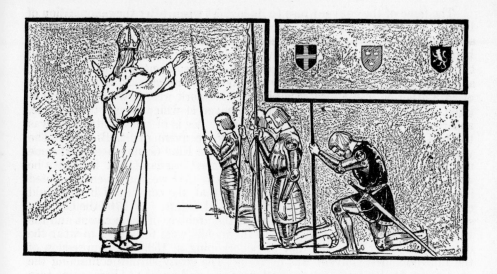

CHAPTER VII

THE UNION OF KALMAR

[1397–1523 A.D.]

EVENTS LEADING UP TO THE KALMAR UNION

MARGARET possessed masculine keenness of intellect, and subtlety tempered with kindliness, together with all the accomplishments of her sex. She was of a dark complexion and masculine in appearance, but pleasing withal, and as well disposed to love as to ambition. She gladly availed herself of any means to weaken the powerful nobility, at the same time ingratiating herself with the clergy by that liberality which has ever been the road to absolute power. She loved Denmark better than Sweden, as the sequel will abundantly show. But she nevertheless strove anxiously to lay the foundations of her power more firmly in this kingdom—the more so as she saw her rule thereby extended over the whole North, from Ladoga and Russia to the northern islands hard by Scotland, and from the uttermost pole southwards to Holstein. In the year 1389, being then in Malmö, she issued, at the request of both archbishops, an admonitory letter to the Laplanders, exhorting them to be converted to the Christian faith, whereof the principal articles were enumerated in the same letter. The abbey of Vadstena had been reduced to ashes in the troublous days of the war. The queen, who had loved the abbess from her childhood up, took the abbey under her protection, and thereafter bestowed many benefits upon it. In temporal matters she proved herself no less vigilant, but in all such things she had at first very great difficulties to contend with.[b]

The Scandinavian union, usually called after the place where it was instituted the "Kalmar Union," owes its existence to the following causes:

When in 1375 King Valdemar of Denmark died without leaving any male heirs to the throne, his son-in-law Hakon VII ruled in Norway. His wife was Princess Margaret of Denmark, at that time twenty-two years of age, who four years earlier presented him with a son, Olaf. Clever Queen Margaret successfully used the controversy about votes which soon after raged in Denmark to get Prince Olaf acknowledged king, as early as 1376, and herself appointed his guardian during the time of his minority. Olaf died in his twelfth year, however, and as meanwhile Hakon had also died, Queen Margaret found herself in possession of both the Danish and Norwegian royal crowns.

In all these proceedings the young and enterprising princess had discovered a most active co-operator in the Hansa—the burgomaster of Lübeck, Heinrich Westhof, was her steadfast admirer—and Lübeck had at that time very considerable influence in all decisions upon northern affairs. The great influence which, since the Peace of the Hanse Towns, Stralsund had possessed over the Danish crown had in 1376 been turned to considerable account in Margaret's interests in the following manner:

LÜBECK TOWNHALL

Olaf was, as we have stated, acknowledged king by the Hansa, in pursuance of the old right to the franchise, and therefore the election (at the beginning very uncertain) was decided according to the wishes of his mother. The Hansa proved itself not less useful when it was a question of checking the plague of the Baltic pirates, who again had been long troubling all the waters of the Baltic Sea. Margaret had applied to the Hansa in this difficulty; and in 1384 made a pilgrimage on foot to Stralsund, and received from the Hanse Towns a promise of strong measures against the pirates, whilst she and the leaders in her kingdom could only pledge themselves to provide nine weakly-manned vessels. In the spring of the same year, about Whitsuntide, the ships of the Hansa engaged the pirates and frightened them away from their haunts, so that trade on the Baltic could be carried on the summer through without fear of disturbance. This was no doubt greatly to the advantage of the whole northern world of commerce, but particularly to Denmark, and was not accomplished without a serious sacrifice on the part of the Hansa. Accordingly, when in 1385 the treaty expired which for fifty years had controlled and protected the north German towns, King Olaf received his own possession, and Denmark thus once more held the key to the Sound.

So far all had gone well for Queen Margaret. But from another direction, she incurred, by the further pursuit of her designs, a dangerous opposition. After uniting upon her own head the crowns of Denmark and Norway, she further intended to win for herself supremacy over Sweden; and by this she opened the door to lengthy and burdensome complications.

Since the year 1363, King Albert of the Mecklenburg ducal line had [as we have seen], reigned in Sweden. He had been raised to this eminence in the midst of the Danish Hanse feud, by the influence of the north German towns. This prince Margaret desired to push from his throne; which seemed to her the easier as Albert was little loved by the Swedes and, moreover, because the majority of the more distinguished nobility of his kingdom had declared themselves in her favour. In the year 1389, Margaret opened hostilities.

Not far from Falköping there was an encounter on February 24th, which ended most unhappily for Albert. In a swamp in which his horse had stuck, he was taken prisoner, and was brought thence in fetters to Lindholm. Immediately the whole country declared for Margaret; the chief ecclesiastical dignitaries came over to her side, and all the castles in the kingdom opened their gates to the victor.

THE CONSUMMATION OF THE UNION

Stockholm alone prepared itself for a valorous resistance. In this city, the Germans — drawn thither partly by the attractions of trade, partly in the train of King Albert — formed the majority of the population. For a long time past they had enjoyed extraordinary privileges, probably taking even at that time a very important position in municipal affairs, and they showed no inclination to abandon the cause of their princes and landowners without further reason. They shortly received very powerful foreign aid; when in 1391 Margaret decided to besiege the town, a universal sympathy was aroused throughout Mecklenburg for the oppressed inhabitants of Stockholm and for the fate of the unhappy king. Duke John, Albert's uncle, placed himself at the head of a squadron, to free his nephew from imprisonment. Numerous cruisers were fitted out to attack the Danes. The towns of Wismar and Rostock issued a proclamation, inviting all those "who at their own expense were desirous of buccaneering in Sweden, Denmark, and Norway, there to plunder, rob, or burn," to come forward and receive so-called "thieving" or pirating letters of marque; and declaring that Wismar and Rostock harbours were open to them, to receive their plunder and sell it according to their desires. At the same time, Duke John made an announcement that his harbour of Ribnitz would also be open as a refuge to these freebooters. Thus, from all parts, there assembled in Wismar and Rostock a crowd of adventurers who called themselves the Society of Victualling Brothers — a band of roystering pirates, who at first had no other purpose than to carry provisions to the inhabitants of Stockholm, but who soon after made common cause with the other Baltic pirates, took possession of Gotland, and thence continued their plundering expeditions on the sea and along the neighbouring coasts.

The active sympathy which the allied towns Rostock and Wismar showed in these circumstances, placed the Hansa in a curious position. On the one hand, the federation was unwilling to take up arms against Margaret, and was therefore obliged to condemn strongly the action of both towns; on the other, it knew very well that the freedom of King Albert, for which the Mecklenburgers busied themselves assiduously, was the only hope of peace in the

North. Meanwhile Stockholm languished under its third year of siege, nor was there any prospect of the Danes being able to force the town into capitulation. Moreover, the Victualling Brothers acted with such vehemence towards both friend and foe that even the German towns found themselves obliged for three years to give up their expeditions to Skåne, thus leaving the fishery stations on the Sound empty; and "herring became very dear."

At last, in 1394, the Hansa prepared to take decided steps, in order that peace might again reign in the North. To the consternation of the united Victuallers, who had just attacked Malmö and set it on fire, a municipal fleet appeared in the Sound and — Margaret herself having in the meantime opened the way to a treaty of peace — deputies from the Hansa went during Whitsuntide of the following year to Skåne, with the injunction to lay the utmost stress on the release of King Albert. The fact that this embassy was joined by two plenipotentiaries of the Teutonic order could only exercise a most favourable influence on the contemplated negotiations, for the grand master of the order stood in the friendliest relations not only with the Hansa, but also with Queen Margaret herself. Already in 1395 a treaty for an armed truce was signed on the feast of Corpus Christi, after which King Albert was given provisional freedom, and Stockholm was included in the Hansa. During the truce the regulation of other conditions of war was preserved. At the same time, the Hanse Towns engaged themselves, after the three years had elapsed, either to redeliver the king into Margaret's hands, or to pay a ransom fixed at 60,000 marks of fine silver, or to quit Stockholm finally. The treaty comprising all these conditions was to be concluded at Michaelmas, 1398.

The three years elapsed. Directly after he was set at liberty, Albert went to Mecklenburg. Here, as well as in Prussia, he in vain endeavoured to raise the necessary sum for his ransom. Since August 1st, 1395, there had been a powerful Hanse garrison in Stockholm, in readiness for the moment when either Queen Margaret or Albert should try to assume possession of the town. The insolence of the Baltic Victuallers was at length crushed since the Teutonic order had taken Gotland and scattered their bands.

Meantime Margaret had pursued her ends with untiring zeal. First, in order to secure the hereditary succession to Norway and Denmark in her house, the queen, now childless, sent for Eric, son of Duke Wratislaw of Stolpe in Pomerania, her own grand-nephew. By the advice of the council, she pronounced him heir to the united crowns of Denmark and Norway. A similar ceremony followed in Sweden: on the 11th of July, 1396, Margaret's foster-son, according to the native custom, was proclaimed future king on the Mora stone. After such happy results, the queen no longer hesitated to undertake the most ambitious of her schemes — the public proclamation of Norway, Denmark, and Sweden as a united kingdom. The main grounds upon which this political union was to rest were briefly as follows:

The three kingdoms were to be in future under one sovereign; in each of the three a council should take part in the government as before; should the sovereign die without issue, the councillors were empowered to elect a successor. In the event of one of the three states being entangled in a foreign war, the other two pledged themselves to assist. Each of the three was to keep its own laws and privileges; no feud between the three states would be lawful; treaties with foreign princes and towns would have a binding effect upon all three states.

These points were embodied in an act, and at Kalmar, in June of the year 1397, Eric was proclaimed king over Denmark, Norway, and Sweden.

The queen, on her birthday, some four weeks later, issued the document which was to seal the perpetual union of the three kingdoms.

While everything thus conspired to favour Margaret's plans, King Albert saw one hope after another disappear. The ransom could not be raised. Michaelmas, 1398, came ever nearer and nearer. The Hansa pressed him for a decision. At last the burgomaster of Stralsund was sent to interview the king and to bring back from him a definite statement of his intentions as to the Lindholm Treaty. As Albert still replied in an evasive fashion, the towns ceased to interest themselves in his behalf. Accordingly, Stockholm was evacuated and handed over to Margaret; and thus King Albert lost his kingdom.

The decided attitude which the Hansa had maintained throughout these negotiations, and which had not been without its effect in influencing the completion of the Scandinavian Union, was essentially instrumental in at once assuring the increase of friendly relations between the northern royal house and the German seaport towns.

THE HOLSTEIN WAR

Since 1409, Denmark and Holstein had maintained an almost uninterrupted feud. The duchy of Schleswig was the cause of this contention. As early as 1404, when Duke Gerhard of Holstein was engaged in warfare against the Ditmarshians, the crown of Denmark and the counts of Holstein were already contending for the duchy of Schleswig. Two years later, thanks to Margaret's discretion and foresight, a truce was arranged during which the dispute should have been adjusted. But her death, which followed in 1412, leaving the sole government of the kingdom's affairs in the hands of the passionate king Eric, closed the doors against all chance of a peaceable conclusion.

Only two years later, the Ditmarshians, close adherents of the Danish king, declared hostilities against young Duke Henry, Gerhard's eldest son. In 1415, Eric himself appeared at the head of a force — to which Sweden, according to the Treaty of Union, had added troops — and took possession of the entire duchy, with the exception of Schleswig itself, which was strongly fortified. At this crisis, urged by necessity, the Holsteiners seized upon a valuable expedient. They called to their aid the Victualling Brothers, who had long given up the Baltic and withdrawn to the western seas. Letters of marque to the Scandinavian Kingdom were issued, all harbours of Holstein were thrown open to the bold pirates, and in a short time the southern waters of the Baltic were swarming as in former days. It was thus possible for the Holsteiners to engage the enemy with great success both by sea and by land. In the summer of 1416, King Eric was compelled to return to Denmark, all his endeavours to snatch the town of Schleswig from the Holsteiners having been unavailing.[c]

During the campaigns of 1417 and 1418, he did not reduce a single fortress (he was too powerful to be openly met in the field), while he lost several, and had even the mortification to see the isle of Femern in the power of his enemies. In 1419, indeed, he recovered that island, and signalised his success by a horrible carnage; but this was his only advantage: reverse after reverse befell both his land and sea armaments. In 1423, he applied to the emperor, the lord paramount of the province, for a confirmation of the judicial sentence which his own chancellor had pronounced. In Sigismund he found one sufficiently disposed to favour him; and a final decision was given that the counts had forfeited all right to the duchy. In this decision they would not acquiesce; but the truce which followed enabled him to visit Jerusalem, by way of penance for the massacre which he had perpetrated in Femern. On his return, he found Schleswig and Gottorpch and the other fortresses still in the power of the counts. The imperial sentence, therefore, had been of no service; and for any tangible advantage, he must trust only to his own resources. With another large army, the equipment of which occasioned no little murmuring in all his kingdoms, especially in Sweden, he invested Schleswig and Gottorpch. But all his enterprises were destined to be unfortunate.

Scarcely had he opened his trenches, when he received from the Hanseatic League a declaration of war, in terms so absolute as to evince both their self-confidence and their contempt for his power. The blow, though it could scarcely have been unexpected, stunned him so much that he precipitately left the field. He foresaw that his own dominions would soon be invaded. That very year, he had the mortification to see Femern retaken; but, on the other hand, his enemies failed against Flensburg, and he had the good fortune to defeat them at sea, near the entrance of the Sound. Still they were not discouraged; they had evidently resolved on the reduction of Copenhagen — the possession of which enabled Eric to levy a tax on every vessel that passed through the Sound. That tax they felt to be obnoxious: it might be increased *ad libitum* or their vessels might even be excluded altogether from their lucrative traffic in Norway.

In 1428, Copenhagen was again invested by a powerful armament, which the league placed under the command of Count Gerhard of Holstein; and it would have fallen, but for the heroism of the queen Philippa, a daughter of Henry IV of England. She threw herself into it, and by her exhortations, no less than by her example, inspired the garrison with so much zeal that the assailants were at length compelled to retire. Elated by this success, while her husband was raising new supplies in Sweden, she determined to carry the war into the dominions of her enemies; and, with a fleet of seventy-five sail, she invested Stralsund. But on this occasion fortune was not propitious: her squadron was almost entirely destroyed in a long-contested action. In Eric's estimation, this disaster more than counterbalanced her successful defence of Copenhagen; and, without reflecting on his own martial reverses, which had been greater and more numerous than had befallen any general of his age, he yielded to his anger so far as to strike her. This brutality was not to be borne; and the high-spirited queen retired to Vadstena Convent, where she soon after ended her days. Her fate commanded the pity of the Northmen, who had reason to esteem her for her many virtues, especially for the success with which she had so frequently inclined her cruel and capricious husband to mercy.

After her death, new disasters awaited Eric. In 1430, one of his vessels, laden with specie, was captured; the following year, Flensburg capitulated to the count of Holstein; and in 1435, he was glad to make peace with both those nobles and the cities of the League, on such conditions as they pleased to dictate to him. During twenty-six years of war, he had gained nothing; on the contrary, he had lost several of his fortresses; and though these were restored, who was to repay him and his people for the losses which had been inflicted on their commerce — for the perpetual ravaging of their coasts — for the heavy ransom which had been paid for so many captives — for the waste of the national resources — for the dishonour of the Scandinavian arms?

THE UNION IS SHAKEN ; ERIC RESIGNS HIS CROWN

Internally, the administration of this monarch was no less disastrous. Three or four years before the peace of Vordingborg, many of his people murmured at his oppressive levies of money and troops — the more so, as they were levied only for dishonour. On every occasion, the Swedes, whose detestation of everything Danish was not less than it is at present, distinguished themselves by the loudness of their tone. In addition, they complained that the most lucrative and the most honourable posts were given to the Danes, while themselves were overlooked; that these civil functionaries were universally rapacious; and that the national commerce was ruined by the wanton measures of their king, whose wars had not even the pretext of Swedish good for their object.[d]

On Midsummer Day of 1433, the peasants of the Dalecarlian valleys, formerly the Swedish iron country, rose under the leadership of a miner, Engelbrecht Engelbrechtsson, against the tyrannous rule of their Danish governor. The complaints of the Swedes against the harshness of the foreign governors sent by King Eric into their country, were of long standing. The whole nation had found heavy the price it paid for the union with the Danish Empire; for the extortions of money and soldiery which Eric considered necessary to his campaign against Holstein seemed endless.

Indignant at this oppression, the Dalecarlians had already in 1432 made complaints through Engelbrechtsson to their king, but their position had not improved. The following year the insurrection broke out. Armed with steel bows and pikes, the Dalecarlians marched through the neighbouring country to storm the castles and drive away the king's bailiffs. Soon the entire provinces of Upland, Vermland, and Södermanland were in revolt. The Swedish council still tried, from dread of the terrors of anarchy, to support Eric; but the nation was no longer to be controlled. On August 16th, 1434, a letter of defiance was despatched from Vadstena to the Danish king. At the beginning of the following year, a council, called at Arboga, declared Engelbrecht Engelbrechtsson administrator of the country. Norway and the Hanse Towns received pressing invitations to make common cause with Sweden against Denmark. Eric's position was for the moment very grave. But his good fortune did not yet desert him. In order to throw a sop, in the first place, to the Hanse Towns, which in fact had already threatened to side with Sweden, he hastily concluded the peace of Vordingborg. Then he went to Stockholm, knowing well that he could still count upon the adherence of a not inconsiderable number of Swedish nobles in the council, who would decline to recognise the new order of things and the governorship of Engelbrechtsson. In October, 1435, Eric and the council were already in negotiation, with the result that the union between Denmark and Sweden was re-established, and the king reinstated, with few limitations, in his former position. Engelbrechtsson was now quickly discredited: he was believed to have been bought off by the concession of the fief of Örebro. The office of royal administrator, which had combined in one person the chief civil and military power, was abrogated, and by unanimous decision of king and council, the offices of a high bailiff and a marshal substituted. The first was given to an old friend of King Eric, Christer Nilsson Vasa. But for commander of both the sea and land forces they chose Charles Knutsson Bondé, at that time twenty-seven years of age — a scion of one of the richest aristocratic Swedish families, with a temperament so imbued with the ardent enthusiasm of youth, and so fired with personal ambition, that from that moment he knew no rest until time and his own exertions had raised him to the topmost pinnacle of power.

The king had left Stockholm in November, to return to Denmark. During the voyage, he was often forced by autumn storms and bad weather to land on the Swedish coast, and had then quietly permitted the crew of his ship to behave as, in war-time, during an invasion — to take by force from the inhabitants cattle for food, and other means of subsistence. This created a universal feeling of bitterness. Besides this, the king had appointed Danish bailiffs in Stockholm, Kalmar, and Nyköping, which caused the old complaints to resound through the land. Suddenly the popular excitement, which had been temporarily allayed, turned the scales and once more allegiance to the king was renounced. In Stockholm, thirty members of the council met to choose an administrator for the kingdom, and this time Charles Knutsson was elected to the post, by a majority of twenty-five votes to five. Thus young Bondé found himself thrust nearer and nearer the goal of his desires. For a time, it is true, he was obliged to share the government with the popular favourite, Engelbrecht Engelbrechtsson, who had, with some foresight, been elected joint governor, in order that his numerous admirers should have no cause for discontent. But this association, so irksome to Charles Knutsson, did not last long. On the 27th of April, 1436, Engelbrecht Engelbrechtsson was assassinated by a Swedish nobleman on an island in the Hjellmar Lake; and the administrator had now a free hand.

COSTUME OF SCANDINAVIAN KING
OF THE FIFTEENTH CENTURY

These events in Sweden made the deepest impression on King Eric, ageing as he now was. Too weak and undecided to venture upon a serious attempt to reinstate himself, he gradually lost all hold on the government and all interest in it. Finally, when dangerous outbreaks threatened among the Danish peasantry, he resigned his crowns and kingdoms, and in 1439 took ship for Gotland, never again to return to Denmark. He died in the year 1459, at the age of seventy-four, at Rügenwalde in Pomerania.

THE THREE COUNTRIES ACCEPT CHRISTOPHER (1442 A.D.)

Eric died childless, and immediately upon his deposition the Danish council met to choose a new prince. It was decided that Duke Christopher of Bavaria, a nephew of Eric, should be offered the government. Before the king's deposition, in 1439, Christopher had gone to Lübeck, in compliance with an invitation from the Danish council, which met there. Here the immediate future of Denmark had been discussed. King Eric's rule was declared detrimental to the kingdom. Christopher, in the first place elected to the post of administrator, or manager, only received in the following year the royal Danish crown.

Scarcely had the new king planted his foot firmly in Denmark before he began to covet the land on the farther side of the Sound, where Margaret's work, the Kalmar Union — although much shaken, particularly in Sweden, by the events of the last years — could with prompt assistance still be maintained. At Jönköping there had been, in 1439, a gathering of the Danish and Swedish delegates of the church, to assure Christopher of their allegiance and devotion to the Union. It soon became evident that the influence of the bishops and other church dignitaries was decisive in this matter, and their efforts resulted in Charles Knutsson's being persuaded to resign his office. It may well be that Charles had for a time cherished a vague hope of wearing the kingly crown himself. By the prophecy of a holy nun, whose words were carried from mouth to mouth among the people, he was designated as the future king. In the church at Vadstena a young child declared it saw a shining crown suspended over Charles' head. But a feeling of rectitude seems to have restrained him from stretching out his hand towards that dignity, since the will of the church outweighed the wishes of the laity. Accordingly, after Finland had been assured to him for his lifetime, and the island of Öland mortgaged to him, he resigned his office of administrator, and so left the way to the Swedish throne clear for the Danish king. On October 4th, 1440, the council elected Christopher king. Charles Knutsson remained for a while longer in Sweden, and then betook himself to Finland. He went, to be sure, but not forever. In Norway, where Eric's following was still very considerable, the difficulties were serious, and under better leadership it might well have become formidable. The pendulum, nevertheless, gradually swung round in that country too; and in 1442 Christopher was proclaimed king of Norway, at Opslo (Christiania).

After nearly fifty years of war and tumult the longed-for peace appeared likely once more to descend upon the northern seas. In the Scandinavian kingdom, calm and outward security reigned everywhere. Charles Knutsson lived far from the Swedish capital, in his self-elected and distinguished banishment at Viborg in Finland; and an insurrection which broke out among the peasantry in Zealand and Jutland, about 1444, was quickly suppressed.

Norway remained loyal to its king; and Christopher, proud of the title, had ever since 1442 signed himself King of Denmark, Sweden, and Norway, and Lord of Gotland and Wendland. The sea-robberies of the Victualling Brothers had been put down in 1434, by the exertions of Hamburg, Bremen, and Lübeck. The leaders of the antagonistic robber-bands were either put to flight or securely imprisoned. On the Swedish coast, feeble attempts at plunder by a few pirates were occasionally heard of. These pirates were sent by King Eric from his rocky castle of Visby on Gotland, to supplement his means of livelihood: to do lasting harm was no longer in his power. Industry and commerce received a new impetus, and fleets of merchant ships once more sailed peacefully back and forth on their accustomed voyages on the high seas.

SWEDEN AND DENMARK SEPARATE UNDER CHRISTOPHER'S SUCCESSOR, CHARLES KNUTSSON

This calm however was not of long duration. There were constantly marvellous reports of a great conspiracy of princes against the head of the Hanseatic federation, and of plans, which King Christopher was maturing in secret, against Lübeck and the other seaport towns, with a view to their ruin. It is certain that after the year 1441 there was a marked difference in the

king's behaviour to the Hansa. Whereas formerly he made use of its help
against the Dutch, he now ranged himself suddenly on the side of the latter,
gave them the most important privileges in trade, and in every way treated
them with unmistakeable partiality. All this was merely to put an end to
the renewed influence, threatening to become more powerful than ever, which
the Hansa exercised throughout the Scandinavian kingdom. As these means
were not successful, King Christopher hit upon another policy. An attack
upon Lübeck was prepared; the requisite funds had already been collected
in secret, and several Bavarian and other princes had been won over to the
plan, which was to be carried out in 1448. But at the commencement of this
year, Christopher died suddenly. "His death," wrote the Lübeck chronicler,
"defeated the wicked project of humiliating and destroying the Hanse
Towns."

But other consequences linked themselves to Christopher's death. The
continuance of the Scandinavian union was now again in question, and once
more dark clouds gathered from all sides over the northern heavens. Scarcely
four months had elapsed since Christopher's death, when Charles Knutsson
re-appeared in Stockholm. He considered that the moment had arrived when
the royal crown must fall to his share; and he was not mistaken. A council
hurriedly summoned, elected him to the throne by an overpowering majority;
and he was crowned in June of the same year, the separation of Sweden from
Denmark being announced at the same time.

Meanwhile, Christopher having left no heirs, a German prince was once
more called to the Danish throne — Count Christian of Oldenburg, a nephew
of Duke Adolf of Holstein. On the 28th of September, 1448, he was formally
acknowledged, and thus the foundation of the royal house still reigning in
Denmark was laid.[1]

UNDER CHRISTIAN THE THREE KINGDOMS ARE AGAIN UNITED

The question was now only whether Norway would henceforward be subject to one of the two kingdoms, or whether it would choose a sovereign for
itself. For the last contingency, a by no means inconsiderable party in the
north had already declared itself, at the same time alluding in unmistakeable
fashion to the deposed king Eric, whom it might possibly be desirable to
receive again as king. Meantime, another opinion quickly claimed attention,
according to which the welfare of the country would best be served by uniting
Norway with Sweden and acknowledging Charles Knutsson as the liege lord

[1] Descent of Christian I of Denmark :

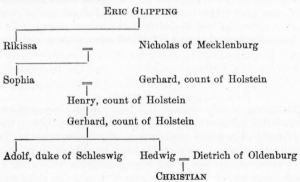

of both countries. This view finally prevailed, and before the end of that year (1449), the Norwegian crown was entrusted to the king of Sweden.

In the general uncertainty of the situation, such a settlement could not last. Soon a strong party sprang up in Norway for Christian of Denmark, which actually succeeded, in the following year, in declaring Charles' election null and void and handing over the crown to Christian. The young king received the news with delight; but a whole world of hope must have opened out for him when he learned, almost simultaneously, that in Sweden, too, the strength of Charles' position was declining. Without hesitation, he now raised the banner of the union, and prepared to reinstate the old Scandinavian federation, after the fashion of his predecessors, at the point of the sword.

The war now kindled between the two monarchs lasted, with slight interruptions, until the year 1457. Charles was at first stubbornly resolved against yielding, though the ground resounded more and more hollow beneath his feet and treachery and disloyalty surrounded him. At last he gave way. The hatred with which he was pursued by the archbishop Oxenstierna and the clergy sapped the last of his strength. He forsook his kingdom, and fled at night, on the 24th of February. A ship laden with gold and silver took him to Dantzic, where his safety was guaranteed, and where he remained seven years. Four months after Charles' departure, Christian received the royal crown in the cathedral at Upsala. The three kingdoms were thus once more united.

It was then exactly sixty years since the foundation of the Kalmar Union. In June, 1397, Eric, the first king of the union, was crowned; in June, 1457, the coronation feast of Christian was celebrated. What changes had there not been throughout Europe within this period! What disastrous wars the lust of power in Margaret's successor had forced on every country between Finmarken and the Eider! They were all fought for the sake of that scheme of union which sprang from the heroic mind of the young queen, but which, manipulated by her with wise deliberation, changed its character after the time when her foster son Eric seized upon it with his undisciplined zeal, and continued to change, until finally there was little left of it but its mere outer husk. The deeper feelings which should have desired coherence for reasons of state policy never awoke in the minds of the generality of the Scandinavian peoples; instead of the anticipated union, that unquiet party spirit ensued, which through its resultant — the constant change of those in power — as well as through the ebb and flow of public opinion, would have inoculated with poison the character of any nation, no matter how sound or healthy by nature.

These Scandinavian convulsions had scarcely exercised any influence over the neighbouring countries. The relations of England to Norway were of a purely commercial order, exclusive of political interests. At Novgorod, the old border quarrels still continued, which now and again gave an incentive to the Swedes for invading Russian territory — without any definite result, however. Finally, the Teutonic order had since the beginning of the fifteenth century been too busy with its own affairs to be able to take more than a very slight part in those of the far North.[c]

The capitulation which Christian I had signed on his election may afford us some idea of the limits within which, by the constitution, the royal authority was confined. Christian recognised the crown to be purely elective. Unless he had direct issue, none of his heirs could lay claim to any portion of his property, personal or real. He engaged never to call any foreign prince into Denmark, and never to pension one, without the express consent of the rigsraad, or council of the kingdom. Without that consent he was not to undertake any war, or make peace, or impose any tax, or confer the government of any fortress: nay, by the advice of that body he was to regulate his court. Other regulations of the same nature would have converted the government into what it was meant to be — a pure aristocracy, or rather oligarchy — had such compacts been of much avail. But they were always violated by the crown, for the plain reason that they were inconsistent with the existence of an executive.

The power thus arrogated by the rigsraad, of electing a sovereign without the consent of the nobles, prelates, and people — that is, without the inter-

ARISTOCRATS OF THE FIFTEENTH CENTURY

(After an old print)

vention of a diet — is not the least striking illustration of the progress made towards an oligarchy in Denmark. If there was one custom more ancient and more obligatory than another, it was this, that without the concurrence of deputies from all the orders of the state — the church, the nobles, the rural gentry, and even the peasantry (the municipal corporations were of more recent admission) — there could be no election. This custom, indeed, had existed in full vigour down to the Union of Kalmar. As a whole multitude could not leave the country, necessity demanded that the suffrage should be confided to a few deputies (never exceeding thirty), who were to meet other deputies from Sweden and Norway at Halmstad, or some other place, where all might conveniently assemble. The trust was soon claimed as a right; the precedent was appealed to when there was no concurrence of other states; and, unfortunately for the liberties of the people, the claim was not resisted when the circumstances which had led to the trust no longer existed. Thus, when Eric of Pomerania fled to the isle of Gotland, the rigsraad assumed the right of offering the crown to Christopher of Bavaria; nor do we read that the assumption was condemned by the rest of the nation. On the present occasion, when that assumption was so much more glaring, there was still the same silence. In subsequent elections, down to the reign of Frederick III — after the union had ceased to exist, and both Sweden and Denmark elected, as before, three separate rulers — the four orders of the state, indeed, were present by their deputies, but they were present as spectators merely; the rigsraad performed the real business of the election. A similar innovation had been introduced into all the countries, except Poland, where popular suffrage once existed. Thus, the great dignitaries of Germany — the seven or eight hereditary officers of the imperial household — had usurped the right of the nobles and freemen. Thus, also, in Spain, the immediate descendants of Pelayo, originally chosen by all the assembled warriors, were soon chosen by a few. In Denmark, the multitude present at an election had, perhaps, for ages, or at least prior to the reign of Christopher the Bavarian, done little more than approve the choice made by the leading nobles.

In 1457 the three northern crowns were again on the same brow; but the wearer soon found one of them too heavy for his ease. Christian VI made the most ample concessions to the Swedish clergy. In return, they were the chief means of instituting a process against Charles, whose possessions, on his non-appearance to the citation, were forfeited to the actual monarch. By revoking some of the grants which Charles had made to his creatures, Christian suddenly found himself in possession of ample revenues. The exiled prince endeavoured by alliances to open a way for his return; but the victor, too, could make allies, even in the regions where Charles had sought refuge — among the Livonian and Teutonic knights. It was not from foreign aid, but from the acts of Christian himself, and, above all, from the natural inconstancy of the Swedes, that the exile could hope for a change. Different circumstances tended to embroil the reigning king with the church. In the first place, he had a long and angry dispute with the pope respecting the presentation to the see of Trondhjem. The chapter, under his influence, elected one churchman; the pope nominated another; and, though the dispute was carried on for many years, the holy see triumphed. Next, Christian did not show to the papal legate, who was sent into the north to raise money by the sale of indulgences, the respect due to so confidential a messenger of the pontiff; on the contrary, he insisted on participating in the profits of the traffic, and to a certain extent attained his object. Again, he laid forcible hands on some money held by the Dominicans of Stockholm, on the pretext that it belonged to the fugitive Charles. Next, on very slight suspicion, he put some innocent men to the torture, on the charge of corresponding with the exile. He imposed taxes, apparently without the sanction of a diet; but had he obtained its sanction a hundred times, the collection would not have rendered him the less unpopular. Even the excellent police regulations which he published gave offence, and properly so, since they issued not from Stockholm, or any Swedish city where a diet was held, but from Copenhagen. But what most operated to his disadvantage, was his disputes with the very man who had raised him to the throne — the archbishop of Upsala. He went so far as to commit that princely churchman to a prison in Copenhagen. The clergy took fire at what they termed a bold invasion of their rights, and the pope menaced him with excommunication if he did not liberate his prisoner. He persisted, however, and with as much injustice as impolicy, refused to take sureties for the appearance of the prelate to answer any charge that might be urged against him.

Seeing that nothing was to be obtained from the justice of Christian, Ketil Carlsson, bishop of Linköping and nephew of the primate, published a manifesto in which he denounced the conduct of the king, who, as he had little difficulty in proving, had in some respects broken his compact with the Swedes. The bishop, therefore, released them from their oath of allegiance, and still further imitated his uncle's example by a recourse to arms. At the outset he was defeated and compelled to flee into the wilds of Dalecarlia; but being pursued thither by the royal troops, his knowledge of the localities enabled him to triumph in his turn, to follow the king to Stockholm, and besiege him there. As the sea was open, Christian, leaving a garrison in the citadel, returned to Copenhagen. By the victorious, or, as they called themselves, the national party, Charles Knutsson was recalled and restored to the throne, while the Danish garrison was so vigorously pressed as to be compelled to surrender.

THE LAST CONFLICTS OF CHRISTIAN'S REIGN

It was now that Christian perceived the error which he had committed, in quarrelling with the only man who could maintain him on the throne.

FIFTEENTH CENTURY ARCHERS

From this moment he determined to smother his resentments, and to act with policy. He therefore sought a reconciliation with his prisoner, the archbishop of Upsala, who, as the price of liberty, readily entered into his views, and preserved no angry feeling for the indignities which he had sustained. Retiring to Sweden, he declared openly against Charles, whom he charged with all the troubles of the country. Fortunately for his views, his nephew Ketil had already quarreled with the restored monarch, and was anxious to send him a second time into exile. The union of temporal with spiritual arms soon effected the object. Charles, frequently defeated, was compelled to renounce the Swedish crown; but in one respect he was more fortunate than on the former occasion — he received for his support the government of Finland, with the castle of Rosenberg for a residence.

The primate now became the real sovereign of the country, and he ruled it with a vigour that no king had attempted. This vigour was hateful to the

nobles, who could not bear a master: they began to murmur; but none was
bold enough to assail the formidable churchman, until Nils Boson Sture, one
of the leading magnates, ventured to arraign the conduct of the administrator.
To escape the vengeance which he had provoked, he withdrew to Viborg, of
which his friend Eric Axelsson, a member of the great family of Tott, was
governor. There the two concerted the means of humbling the man to whom
Christian had entirely abandoned the exercise of power. In the next diet,
held at Vadstena (1466), the adherents of both talked so freely that the primate, in alarm, sought the aid of Christian, who had quietly watched the
progress of events, in the hope of benefiting by the distraction of the hostile
parties. Deputies from the diet met those of the Danish king, and, as before,
a resolution was taken to maintain inviolate " the ancient and precious union
of Kalmar." No effort, however, was made to recall Christian, through the
opposition of another member of the Tott family, Ivar Axelsson, who, having quarreled with him, married a daughter of the exiled Charles, and threw
all the weight of his party into the national scale. Its great heads, the Stures
and the Axelssons, declared that they would not hear of a Danish connection;
that they would obey only Charles, or some administrator elected by the
voice of the diet. Through their opposition, the primate was compelled to
resign that dignity to Eric Axelsson. From this moment his influence was
at an end. He proceeded, indeed, to Copenhagen, and obtained troops; but
his operations proving disastrous, he retired to the isle of Öland, where he
shortly afterwards terminated his restless life. With him disappeared for a
time (in such a country nothing could be permanent) the influence of the
Danish party. Charles was invited by Axelsson to reascend the throne; and
the invitation was eagerly accepted by the sexagenarian, who proceeded, with
all the ardour of former years, to reconstruct the edifice of power which the
breath of a moment might overturn.

That Charles should long remain without rebellious subjects, was not to
be expected. Eric Nilsson, of the family of Oxenstierna, and Eric Carlsson,
of the family of Vasa, refused to acknowledge him, and joined the prelates
who were friendly to the Danish connection. After some fruitless attempts
at negotiation, both parties took the field. For some time the arms of Charles
were unfortunate, and no doubt was entertained that his rival would reascend
the throne; but in the chiefs of the Sture family he had generals so able, and
resources so ample, that the fortune of the war was changed. The Danish
troops were so signally defeated that any open attempt to seize the sovereignty would have been treated as wild. Recourse was therefore had to negotiation; but it failed, through the influence of the Stures, who, perceiving
how necessary they were to the reigning king, exercised a larger degree of
power than himself. The death of Charles, in 1470, did not diminish it. In
his last will, he left to Sten Sture the high post of administrator. The choice
of course, required confirmation by the diet; and some nobles, among whom
was Eric Carlsson, endeavoured to prevent it. But, though he placed himself at the head of a considerable body of Danish troops and of as many
natives as were favourable to the union, he could effect nothing against the
Stures, aided as they were by the Axelssons and by the new archbishop of
Upsala. Both Ivar and Eric Axelsson had recently married into the family
of the deceased king — the one a daughter, the other a sister — and this
alliance, coupled with the lucrative dignities which it brought them, will
explain their adherence to the national party. Eric Carlsson was defeated.
Equally fruitless were the efforts of Christian to attain by negotiation what
could not be attained by arms. In great wrath, he again betook himself to

the physical argument; but, though he had the advantage for a moment, his followers were so roughly treated before Stockholm (October, 1471) that he returned home with the full resolve no more to employ violent means to regain his sovereignty. From 1474 to 1477, he frequently negotiated with the senators; but the rulers of Sweden were too fond of power to resign it into his hands, or into the hands of any other king. In much vexation of spirit, he adopted the wise resolution of interfering no more in the affairs of that kingdom.

These everlasting disputes with Sweden were not the only bitterness which Christian was destined to swallow. He found rivals as troublesome as Charles Knutsson in his own family. Adolf, duke of Schleswig and count of Holstein, uncle of King Christian, died in 1459. As he left no issue and had no kinsmen — for with him the great family branch to which he belonged was extinct — the important question arose, Who shall inherit these fiefs? The question involved some great principles of feudal law. Schleswig, as a Danish fief, would indisputably have reverted to the crown had not the last instrument of investiture declared it hereditary and transmissible to heirs general, with the concurrence of the principal estates, however. In regard to Holstein, there were not wanting legists who declared that it was a masculine fief; that it could only follow the Salic law of inheritance; that Christian and his brothers, being sons of Hedwig, the sister of Adolf, therefore had no claim; and that the inheritance devolved on Otto, count of Shauenburg, who descended in a right line from the original counts of Holstein. There can be no doubt that, by the feudal law of Germany, this argument was valid; but that law had never been fully recognised in these provinces, the local constitution of which left much to the decision of the estates.

Otto was not slow to urge the claim. The best course, perhaps, would have been for Christian to enter into possession of the duchy, and either leave the countship to Otto for some equivalent, or purchase the claims of that prince to the latter province. But the matter, in itself sufficiently jarring, was complicated by two circumstances. In the first place, Christian himself, before his accession to the crown, had, to tranquillise the people of Schleswig, agreed that the province should never be united with Denmark. Next, the two states, which had so much influence in the choice of a ruler, believing that, from their proximity, union would be their best policy, agreed, in an assembly at Rendsburg, never to follow separate interests, but in all things to act as if they were component parts of the same political system. Whatever justice the claims of Otto might possess, he could not hope to succeed against so powerful a rival, still less could he indulge the vision of inheriting both provinces. Christian lost not a moment in urging his claim as the proximate heir of Adolf; and, with the view at once of flattering the estates, and of preventing the cause from being taken before the imperial tribunal, which he well knew would be adverse to him, he left the decision entirely to them. He did more: he consented, in the event of his election, to conditions which virtually rendered these provinces independent of any ruler. The result was no longer doubtful: in March, 1460, he was elected duke of Schleswig and count of Holstein.

Some of the conditions to which we have just alluded may surprise the reader. The king acknowledged that he had been elected duke of Schleswig and count of Holstein by the free choice of the estates, not as king of Denmark, but purely through the good will of the electors. He agreed that his descendants could only succeed in virtue of a similar election, and that the estates should forever enjoy the right of choosing their princes. He promised to levy no tax without the sanction of the estates, nor to compel any inhabitant to follow his banner beyond the confines of the two provinces. Whenever he should come into the country, he engaged to pay for whatever his suite might consume. He engaged to ratify whatever the grand bailiff of Schleswig and the marshal of Holstein, in concurrence with the senate of either province, might do during his absence. He exempted from custom dues the commodities which the clergy and nobles might require for their own use. These and other conditions he not only swore to observe, but, on the requisition of the estates, caused some of his most distinguished subjects to guarantee that observance.

Yet, with all these restrictions, there was some advantage in the possession of these provinces. They formed a natural bulwark, on the German side, to the Danish monarchy. An enemy advancing in that direction would be sure to be assailed by two warlike peoples, whose fortresses could not be reduced before aid was brought from the Danish provinces. Through them, a passage would always be open to the Danish troops, whenever they took the field against a southern enemy. For these reasons, Christian was extremely anxious to make this acquisition secure. He persuaded Count Otto to renounce all claim to the succession for a considerable sum of money, and for the possession of three bailiwicks in Holstein. This arrangement was approved by the emperor Sigismund. As his two brothers, Gerhard and Maurice, might also trouble him or his descendants, he prevailed on them to renounce their claim, in consideration of 40,000 florins, and of his ceding to them the domains which he inherited conjointly with them in the lordship of Oldenburg. Having received the investiture from the hands of the bishop of Lübeck — a see which had enjoyed that privilege about thirty years, in virtue of an imperial grant — he called on the city of Hamburg to do him homage as count of Holstein; and the call was promptly obeyed.

But these measures, secure as the monarch deemed them, contained the germs of future strife. First, his two brothers disagreed about the limits of their respective domains in Oldenburg and Delmenhorst. Victory declared for Gerhard; and the peace of 1463 gave the former territory to him and the latter to Maurice. When Maurice died, the guardianship of his infant son, and the administration of Delmenhorst, fell to Gerhard, who soon proved himself one of the most restless spirits of the age. His resources being thus augmented, he demanded that portion of the 40,000 florins which yet remained unpaid; and when, from the royal necessities, it could not promptly be paid, he seized some castles in Holstein. Christian was then embarrassed with the Swedish war; and to satisfy his importunate brother, he ceded to him, in 1467, the revenues of Schleswig and Holstein for four years, with the government of those provinces. Gerhard, therefore, assumed the title of administrator of both; but his sway was so rapacious, so tyrannical, so faithless to the interests of the sovereign, that the latter was compelled to seize his person, and to regain by force of arms the fortresses which had been seduced from their allegiance. In other respects Christian took no advantage of his brother, whom he paid in full, and released when sureties had been given that the latter would not again molest him, his allies, or his subjects. The prince, however, had not been long at liberty before he resumed his intrigues; and, in 1473, he entered Schleswig at the head of an armed force. But the appearance of the king sufficed to disperse his troops; some of the chief rebels were punished, but he himself contrived to escape. Placed under the ban of the empire, he offered his services to one of a kindred spirit, Charles the Bold, duke of Burgundy. On the fall of that prince, he served with honour in the wars between England and France, and ended his days in a manner characteristic of the age — on a pilgrimage to Compostella.

Christian himself was not, in this respect, above his age. Early in 1474, he undertook a pilgrimage to Rome, to procure absolution from a vow which he had made to visit the Holy Land. Assuming the black habit of pilgrimage, with cross and staff, and accompanied by some bishops, nobles, and knights, he proceeded on his journey, and was everywhere nobly entertained. The emperor of Germany, the archduke of Austria, the duke of Milan, and the pope, vied with each other in doing honour to the monarch of Scandinavia. This journey was not without its uses. In the first place, he had the good fortune to reconcile the duke of Milan with the emperor Frederick. From the latter monarch he obtained the cession, or rather the confirmation, of Ditmarsh (since it had been ceded to Denmark early in the thirteenth century, to Valdemar II by the emperor Frederick II), a region bordering on Holstein and Stormarn, and hitherto, from its inaccessible situation, enjoying perfect independence. If the gift itself was of no great value, since the people could not become his subjects until they were subdued, the ducal title which he received, with the honours and privileges of prince of the empire, were not to be despised. But the greatest boon was one for which two, at least, of his predecessors had applied in vain —permission from the pope to found a university in his dominions. The "mundane sciences," as they were termed, might have been taught without the papal sanction; but for theology, a formal bull was requisite. The archbishop of Lund was ordered to prepare the statutes; and the establishment was opened with great pomp in June, 1477. It was honoured with many important privileges, but was not well endowed before the reign of Christian III. Its benefits were soon apparent: Danish youths were no longer sent to Cologne, or Paris, or Bologna; and the influx of foreign students, from Iceland to north Germany, not only diffused money in the capital, but greatly refined the manners of the people.

Christian was not inattentive to foreign alliances. In 1456, he signed the first treaty with France. His object was to obtain support against the apprehended hostilities of England, the commerce of which both he and his predecessors were anxious to annihilate in the north of Europe. The alliance with France was so far useful that the interference of that power more than once saved him from hostilities. Thus, in regard to Scotland, the annual contribution of 100 marks which Alexander III had agreed to pay the kings of Norway for the possession of the Hebrides, had never been punctually sent. When Christian ascended the throne, he found the arrears considerable enough to justify negotiation on the subject. The Scottish king, James III, having neither the inclination nor the power to pay the arrears, war would have been inevitable but for the interference of the French king, who negotiated a marriage between James and Margaret, daughter of Christian. The dowry of the princess was to be 60,000 Rhenish florins, besides a total cancelling of the arrears. The position of the two monarchs was thenceforth changed, the Dane becoming the debtor of the Scot — 2,000 florins only were paid; and for the rest, the Orkney and Shetland isles were given in pledge. From that time (1469), both possessions remained with the Scottish crown.

This monarch died in 1481. By his queen, Dorothea, widow of his predecessor, Christopher III, he had issue — besides the princess Margaret, four sons, two of whom preceded him to the tomb. The third, Hans or John, was recognised as his successor while a child. In 1478, this prince had been married to Christina, daughter of Ernest, duke of Saxony. The fourth son,

Frederick, who was created duke of Schleswig and Holstein, succeeded Hans on the thrones of Denmark and Norway.

THE STORMY REIGN OF HANS

Hans ascended, without opposition, the throne of Denmark, but not those of Norway and Sweden, though by the estates of both kingdoms he had been solemnly recognised as the successor of his father. Two years elapsed before he could prevail on the Norwegian deputies to elect him. The grounds of this reluctance may be sought in the wish of the nobles and landowners to obtain for themselves as many new privileges as they could from a monarch eager to govern them, and still more in the intrigues of Sten Sture, the administrator of Sweden, who, not satisfied with the government of one country, aspired to that of Norway. When, by promises and bribes Hans did attain the crown, he obtained but little power. The conditions, or, as they were called, the capitulation, which he was compelled to sign, left the administration and the revenues of the country in the hands of the aristocracy.

In regard to Sweden, sixteen years of intrigues, of negotiation, and of secret or open hostilities, were necessary before he could secure the crown; and we shall soon perceive that, when he did obtain it, his possession of it was brief. Sten Sture had tasted the sweets of power, and he would not surrender them without compulsion. Such compulsion was long difficult, for though the church, or rather her dignitaries, were generally in favour of the Danish connection, there was a strong native party which detested everything Danish and everything foreign; and by its aid, no less than by his own talents, which were of a high order, he succeeded, during the long period we have mentioned, in baffling every effort of a great monarch to hurl him from his post. Not that several diets were not friendly to the claims of Hans; that of Kalmar, for instance (1483), elected him, but left to the next diet the confirmation of that election. When that diet met, Sture prevailed on it to insist on the restitution of Gotland, as a necessary preliminary. To this condition Hans was unable to consent; the Danish estates, indeed, would not have permitted it. At another time, the administrator, who had been induced to meet the king, insinuated that, if the isle of Öland were ceded, the Swedish deputies would desist from their views on Gotland, and confirm the election. The credulous king surrendered the island, but found that he was not one step nearer to the object of his ambition. In revenge of what he called the rebellion of the people, he sometimes instigated the Russians to lay waste Finland with fire and sword. By this nefarious policy, he hoped so to embarrass the administrator and the national party that they would be compelled to solicit his interference. In the meantime, his own party, consisting not merely of all who favoured the Union of Kalmar, but of the personal enemies of the administrator's family, endeavoured to place him on the throne. In 1494, the senate decreed that Sweden could no longer remain without a king; but this decree, through the address of Sture, had no effect.

Hans now lost all patience (1496), and prepared to support his claims by force of arms. The opportunity was, in another respect, favourable. The Russians had just desolated Finland; the Swedish generals sent to oppose them, being unprovided with adequate means, loudly condemned Sture, and from that moment passed over to the army of the Danish king. Even one of the administrator's family, Svante Sture, who had zealously supported his kinsman, followed to the same side. In 1497 the senate, being convoked at Stockholm, accused him of governing the state rather for his own advantage than for that of the country.   The charge, indeed, was baseless, since he was one of the best regents the nation had ever had; but it served the purpose of the members, who passed upon him a sentence of deposition.   To that sentence, however, he paid little regard.   On the contrary, in a public manifesto, he accused the senate of all the evils which the country had sustained, and declared that, as he had not received his authority from it, but from a general meeting of the estates, so to the estates only should he hold himself responsible for his acts.   In revenge, the senate invited the king to wrest the crown from the hands which withheld it.   With a powerful armament, Hans reduced Kalmar, where he received the homage of the greater part of that body.   At this time Sture was besieging the primate in Upsala; but hearing of the king's advance towards Stockholm, he hastened to that city.   Though his losses had been severe, he still found himself at the head of ten thousand men, with the assurance of a far greater reinforcement from Dalecarlia.   That reinforcement, however, was defeated by the Danes; a sortie from the citadel of Stockholm had no better success; and Sture, with all his courage, was at length compelled to submit.   Yet he obtained honourable terms.   He received, by way of fief, the two Bothnias and Finland, with some fortresses. At the coronation, which was celebrated at Upsala with much pomp and amidst much rejoicing, he was invested with the high dignity of grand master of the kingdom; while his kinsman, Svante Sture, was created marshal. In return, he swore unbounded fidelity to Hans; and, like the rest of Sweden, recognised Prince Christian, Hans' eldest son, who had already been recognised by Denmark and Norway, as heir to the Swedish crown.

The administration of Sten Sture had been peculiarly agreeable to the great body of the people, though distasteful to the clergy and the leading nobles. For this reason, Hans treated him, for some time, with marked attention; and to screen him from the vengeance of his enemies, among whom the primate was the most active, guaranteed him from all past responsibility by letters of abolition.   Yet, in spite of this instrument, the archbishop obtained the papal authority to proceed against him in the ecclesiastical tribunals; and to secure himself, he hastily withdrew into Finland.   The following year Hans returned to Sweden, and endeavoured by gifts and benefits to secure the attachment of all classes and individuals.   For a while he was, indeed, eminently popular. His queen was crowned with much splendour at Upsala; and with equal solemnity, the succession of his son Christian was confirmed.   But the futility of such acts has been apparent enough in the present chapter, and will be more apparent as the reader proceeds.

The popularity in question was as brief as it was sudden.   Conceiving that he had now less need of Sten Sture's support, and instigated by that nobleman's enemies, Christian resumed several of the grants which he had made or confirmed in his behalf.   The other quietly surrendered the governments of Åbo, Niflet, and some other domains; but he was not the less determined to wait his day of revenge — a day which the frequent absences of the king would necessarily hasten.   He well knew the fickleness of his countrymen; he knew that the great body of them were hostile to the Danish yoke, and that the discontented nobles would comprise all who were excluded from royal grants.   Two or three arbitrary acts on the part of the royal officers — one, the execution of a vassal belonging to him, without even the form of a trial — soon converted the loyalty of the people into indifference, or even dislike.   The king, too, was taught to distrust the noblest of his new subjects; and it was Swedes who thus instructed him.   His conduct naturally produced the same feeling on the other side, and that feeling was disposed to revive every rumour unfavourable to him. It was asserted, for instance, that he was still instigating the Russians to devastate Finland — a charge sufficiently absurd. That his suspicions of Swedish fidelity should hourly deepen, was to be expected. That people could never be loyal, even to its own princes; to a foreigner, belonging to a nation always detested, and not unfrequently giving reason for umbrage, it bore a sentiment more unfavourable than want of loyalty. Sten Sture was the man whom, above all others, Hans was led to suspect. He was told that his vassal was intriguing to supplant him; that he was in secret communication with the Dalecarlian peasantry, who were peculiarly hostile to foreign domination; and that he had prepared a strong body of those men, with the determination to intercept and perhaps to kill the monarch.

In this critical position, the king (1501) convoked the estates-general; expressed his unconsciousness of having injured any of his subjects, and his readiness, if he had done so, to make any compensation that arbiters, chosen by the diet itself, might adjudge; and finally accused Sten Sture of treason. The precipitate departure of that noble, without taking leave of the king, had given some colour to the charge — his subsequent conduct deepened it. When required by the deputies to appear and defend himself, though a royal safe-conduct and hostages for his security were sent to him, he appeared with a body of horse formidable enough to alarm the king. Relying on this force, he did not so much vindicate himself as become accuser in his turn. Hans heard his complaints with much coolness, and replied to them with great moderation — so great, indeed, as to command the approbation of the senators, and to draw from many of them new assurances of fidelity. That there was some hypocrisy in this demonstration, may be inferred from the ease with which Sture caused armed bodies of men to approach the capital. The king, more than ever convinced that his life or his liberty was in peril, shut himself up in the citadel, and refused to meet his too powerful vassal in any other place. The other was equally unwilling to trust himself into the royal hands. This mutual distrust, which deepened into hatred, was fatal to the dominion of Hans. By the native party, a confederation of senators and deputies was formed at Vadstena, and one of its avowed objects was to defend the liberties of the country against the tyranny of the Danish king. This meeting was attended by a powerful Norwegian chief, Knud Alfsson, whose connections and whose attachments were Swedish, and who readily undertook to secure for the party the co-operation of many leading nobles. It was also determined that a league should be formed with the Hanse Towns, or at least with Lübeck, which had been the open or secret enemy of Denmark. The appearance of things was so menacing, that Hans sailed privately for Copenhagen, leaving his queen Christina and about a thousand of his adherents to defend the citadel until his return.

Whatever the necessity may have been which dictated this precipitate departure, it was immediately followed by the entire subversion of Hans' authority. A new assembly of deputies and senators at Vadstena sent him not merely a formal renunciation of their allegiance, but a warlike defiance. Hostilities under the direction of Sten Sture showed that the act was not an empty one. Örebro was first reduced, and the Danish officers treated with great severity; Stockholm was next invested; and as the winter season had arrived, there was little hope of its relief, or of a protracted resistance. Christina, indeed, was soon forced to capitulate, but was not allowed to return to Copenhagen — the convent of Vadstena was selected by herself as the most eligible place of imprisonment. Three days after this event, she had the mortification of learning that a Danish armament had arrived before Stockholm, and that, hearing of her departure, it had promptly returned. Other fortresses were speedily reduced: at the end of the year (1501) Kalmar only on the continent, and Borkholm on the isle of Öland, held out for the Danes. Even the archbishop of Upsala was compelled to join the party of Sture, who was again invested with the high post of administrator. In revenge for the succour which Lübeck had sent to the Swedes, Hans ordered his seamen everywhere to seize the vessels of that city, proceeding with merchandise (arms, ammunition, provisions, etc.) to Stockholm; but the city had ships as well as he; and by these hostilities he gained no advantage, while he augmented the number of his enemies.

While these events were passing in Sweden, others, not less disastrous, agitated Norway. Knud Alfsson did not lose sight of the promise which he made to Sture, and success crowned his efforts. To oppose the rising insurrection, Hans sent the bishop of Roeskilde and one of his senators to Christiania, with instructions, the flagitious tenor of which may be too well inferred from the tragedy that ensued. Arriving off the coast, they proclaimed that they were empowered by their royal master to effect a reconciliation between the disaffected Norwegians and the crown. They consequently invited Knud on board, assured him of their pacific intentions, and sent him a safe-conduct. Unsuspicious of danger, he repaired to the vessel, and was deliberately killed in the midst of some high words which they probably raised for the occasion. This perfidious murder created a deep sensation throughout Norway, especially as not even the shadow of a chastisement was inflicted on its authors. It naturally hastened the effect which it was intended to destroy — the southern provinces immediately confederated with the Swedes. With much difficulty, Hans whose resources were exhausted, collected forces, partly from his nephew, the king of Scotland, and partly from his son-in-law, the elector of Brandenburg. ·These he placed under the command of his eldest son, Prince Christian, then about twenty years of age; and joined with him the bishop of Hammer, without whose sanction the prince was to undertake nothing of moment. But Christian was not of a temper to submit to restraint. Obstinate in all his purposes, and ferocious by disposition, he soon showed what history would have to record concerning his reign. Having defeated a party of insurgents near Christiania, and taken the leader prisoner, he put him to the torture. Whether, in the hope of saving himself, Herlof Hiddefad accused those who were not guilty — whether the accusations were wrung from him under his intolerable pain — or whether the conspiracy was as universally spread as he asserted — must always remain doubtful; but unfortunately, there is no doubt as to the use which Christian made of the information· thus obtained. Herlof was broken on the wheel, and those whom he had deluded were put to death under circumstances of great atrocity. A great portion of the Norwegian nobility is said — perhaps with much exaggeration — to have thus perished. When the bishop of Hammer remonstrated with the prince on this inhuman policy, he was placed under restraint, consigned to a dungeon, and used so ill that in a few years death put an end to his sufferings. These executions had the effect designed: they terrified the nobles and the people, who, seeing with what a stern master they had to deal, universally submitted.

From Norway, Christian proceeded into Sweden, where, by the same conduct, he hoped to secure the same success. He besieged two fortresses in Vestergötland, defeated a body of troops sent by the administrator to relieve them, took them by assault, and put the garrison to the sword. Negotiations were now renewed with both the Hanse Towns and the Swedes, but led merely to a short suspension of arms, and to the deliverance of Queen Christina after two years of detention.   One of the last acts of Sten Sture was to conduct her to the frontier.   He died suddenly — not without suspicion of poison (1503).   The loss of so able and so persevering a man afflicted the national party; but little time was lost in procuring him a successor in his kinsman Svante Sture, who had long exercised the office of marshal.   The first act of the new administrator was to besiege Kalmar and Borkholm, the only fortresses which held for the king.   Against the latter he failed; the former he reduced, but only to lose it again in a few weeks.   Enraged that the Swedish deputies did not, as the administrator had promised, meet his own to concert the terms of peace, Hans exercised more than his wonted severity against the Swedish officers whom he had made prisoners at Kalmar.   This severity did no service to his cause, and his next proceeding covered him equally with ridicule and contempt.   The pretext that all his Swedish subjects were rebels might have been admitted three centuries before, in France, or England, or Spain; but in Scandinavia, the crown of which even in the darkest ages, had been always elective, such a pretext, especially in the sixteenth century, was as ridiculous as it was insulting.   Yet the king proceeded to act upon it, and in a way more extraordinary than the pretension itself. He submitted the conduct of the Swedish senators — who, as the representatives of the aristocracy, the rural gentry, and even small landed proprietors, might almost be called the whole Swedish nation — to a judicial tribunal, composed entirely of such Danish and Norwegian senators as had followed him to Kalmar, that is, entirely of his own creatures.   The proceedings were gravely opened in presence of envoys from several European powers; the delinquents who had been cited to appear not answering to their names, judgment went by default — Svante Sture, Eric Johansson Vasa, Sten Christersson, Oxenstierna, the two Bielkes, and all the other senators who adhered to the administrator, were pronounced guilty of high treason, were deposed from their dignities, and their estates were confiscated.

Thus about half a hundred Danes and Norwegians ventured to sit in judgment on a great and independent nation.   The thing was wholly unparalleled; but, as it had a magnificent sound, it was less depised out of Sweden than might have been expected.   Hans valued it so much that he carried it before the emperor Maximilian, whose confirmation he besought.   That the emperor should be otherwise than gratified at this recognition of his superiority over the northern kingdoms — a doctrine which, from the Carlovingian times had always been a favourite one with the imperial legists — was not to be expected.   He readily heard the cause, confirmed the decision of his royal vassal, and menaced with the pains of treason all who should presume to aid or abet, with troops or money or merchandise, the twofold rebels of Sweden — rebels at once to their own immediate ruler, and to their lord paramount, the emperor.   This blow was particularly aimed at the Hanseatic League, especially Lübeck; and it was expected that the Swedes would offer no resistance to it: they would, no doubt, obey the imperial citation (for Maximilian had indulgence enough to fix a time when by submission they might appease their two mighty lords), and escape the severe penalties which were suspended over their heads.   When this decree was ridiculed, the next step was to put the Swedish senators under the ban of the empire — to confiscate all their substance; to deprive them of all civil rights, to place the very life of each at the mercy of anyone who thought it worth taking away.   Nay, even the pope threw the weight of his crosier into the scale unfavourable to the Swedes.

Because they would not receive as bishop of Linköping, the cardinal legate Jayme of Arborea, whom both he and the Danish monarch had presented to that see, but insisted on the choice of a countryman, Hemming Gadd, he threatened both Hemming and them with excommunication if they persisted in their opposition. But nothing could daunt the Swedes. They fought when they had money and stores; when they had neither, owing to the frequent inactivity of their Hanse allies (for the latter, true to their interests and caring for neither party in the abstract, were sometimes induced by some royal concession to stand aloof from the contest), they consented to negotiate, but whether with any sincere wish for peace may be doubted. Their object apparently was to gain time — especially when they found the people of the Hanse Towns ready to furnish them secretly with the sinews of war. When, as in 1509 and the two following years, Lübeck, and other towns of the league were openly at war with Denmark, they did not neglect so favourable an opportunity of annoying their implacable sovereign — if he could be called one, who held the title without even the shadow of the power. In general, the successes of both parties were nearly balanced: the confederates were superior in number of ships; but the genius of the Danish admiral, Severin Norby, compensated for this inferiority. After innumerable events which it would be equally tedious and uninteresting to enumerate, Lübeck and her allies, with all their resources, became tired of the war, and as the condition of peace, agreed to abandon the Swedes (1512).

The loss of so powerful an ally rendered the Swedes, as usual, disposed to negotiate. The death of Svante Sture, too, or rather the divisions to which the event gave rise, contributed to the same end. In the choice of a successor there was much animosity: one party declared for Eric Trolle, a senator nobly connected, but suspected of some partiality to the Danish succession; another for Sten Sture, son of the administrator of that name and generally known as Sten Sture the younger. The latter triumphed. As a matter of course, the former, more decided in the expression of his partiality, became the head of a league, of which the prelates, with the archbishop of Upsala at their head, were the most distinguished members. But no advantage accrued to Denmark beyond this, that the party favourable to the connection between the two countries arose from its despondency and was enabled to maintain something like an equality with the other.

The dispute with Sweden would probably have been more brief in its duration and more satisfactory in its conclusion, but for two other circumstances which equally distracted the king's attention, and of which one had the more disastrous termination. The recognition by Christian I of the right claimed by the estates of Schleswig and Holstein to elect their own dukes, could not fail to be the source of some trouble. On that monarch's death, they urged the claim, and showed unequivocally that they should prefer Frederick, the brother of Hans to Hans himself. Such a disregard of the primogenital law had never entered the minds of the Danish monarchs, who had always considered the succession to the two duchies as inseparable from that of the crown. Yet justice was so manifestly on the side of the estates that the king was placed in a situation of considerable embarrassment. On the one hand, he would never consent to the separation between the ducal and royal dignities; on the other, he was loth to risk a war with his southern subjects — especially when he reflected that they would be sure to have allies and that the aspect of affairs in Sweden was sufficiently gloomy. What added to his embarrassment was the fact that, by his father, Frederick had been invested with the ducal title, and had been designed as the successor — subject, of course, to the approval of the estates. This disposition of Christian had been created by his queen, who had more attachment for her second than for her eldest son. The same influence was now at work; and Hans was compelled to show more deference towards his mother's wishes than he liked. To secure his election, she hastened with the young prince to Kiel, where the diet was to be held. The king followed, to protest against the mediated choice. He was surprised no less than embarrassed, when his brother, at the instigation of his mother and tutors, demanded also a share in the government of Norway, which had been declared equally elective, and which might devolve on the second as well as on the eldest son. This latter claim, indeed, was for the present withdrawn; but Frederick would undoubtedly have been elected to the ducal throne had not the king hastily collected a strong body of troops and overawed the diet. This was a glaring violation of the right which Christian had so solemnly declared to be inherent in the estates; but what could abstract justice avail against brute force? The electors were glad to adopt a compromise, and to choose both brothers as their rulers.

For some years the regal power was exercised by the king. In 1483, he prevailed on the diet of Flensburg to vote him two florins for each plough. Whether any portion of this tax was directed to other purposes than the wants of the local government, is not very clear; for, though Hans redeemed many of the fortresses and domains on which his father had raised money, complaints were not wanting against the application of the proceeds. In conjunction with his brother, he received the homage of the Hamburgers — always a reluctant homage, and on the present occasion successfully withheld during five years. In a few years more, he found that Frederick would not be satisfied with merely a nominal share in the administration. In vain did he strive to send the obnoxious claimant into the cloister: the prince, indeed, dissembled for a time; but in 1490 he appeared with many supporters at a diet, and demanded a participation in the government. Hans was reluctantly compelled to sanction a division of the territories in dispute, so that each might govern his own portion without collision with the other. The only reservations were Ditmarsh, which had yet to be subdued and the sovereignty over Hamburg, which was of little value; these were to be held in common. Ample as were the possessions which Duke Frederick thus obtained, he was not satisfied. He next applied for an appanage, which, he contended, by the immemorial custom of Denmark, ought to be his; and he indicated three islands with their fortresses and dependencies. The rigsraad, however, and next the estates-general, refused to entertain the application. Hans did not openly interfere in the matter; but his influence, no doubt, induced both powers to reject the application.

THE CAMPAIGN IN DITMARSH (1500 A.D.)

The second disaster to which we have alluded was the signal defeat of the Danish troops by the wild and independent inhabitants of Ditmarsh. In the reign of the preceding monarch, we have recorded the grant of that country to the Danish crown by the emperor Frederick IV. From the commencement of his reign, Hans meditated its subjection; but his disputes with Norway, with Sweden, and the Hanse Towns, left him, during twenty years, no leisure for the enterprise. But no sooner was he recognised by Sweden (1499) than, in conjunction with his brother, he aspired to something more than a nominal sovereignty.

By the emperor Henry the Fowler, this region had been formed into a countship dependent on the dukes of Saxony. But, in the twelfth century, the archbishops of Bremen, profiting by the misfortunes of those mighty feudatories, had obtained the superiority over the fief. By Valdemar, bishop of Schleswig, this superiority was contested; and the misfortunes of that prelate threw the province into the hands of the Danish kings. Knud VI had left it to Valdemar II, who had been confirmed in it (1214) by the emperor Frederick II. But in about thirteen years (1227), the Danish monarch lost it in the disastrous battle of Bornhöved. From that period, the inhabitants, though nominally dependent on the see of Bremen, were in reality independent. In vain several counts of Holstein had endeavoured to subjugate them. Protected by the nature of their country—by their deep marshes, their scarcity of paths, and their sluices, by which the progress of an invading army might at any time be arrested — they had regarded with indifference the warlike preparations of their neighbours. The summons of Christian I, in virtue of the emperor Frederick's decree, to do him homage, they had heard unmoved. They were not, in the present instance, more favourable to the claim of Hans; and, in a general assembly of the people, they resolved to die sooner than sacrifice the independence which they had enjoyed for so many ages. Hans and his brother, who had claimed the sovereignty in common, expected this answer; and they collected troops with so much expedition, that they were soon ready for the field.

It was in February of the year 1500, that the two princes penetrated into that region. Why they should have marched at such a season, unless they calculated on a long frost, is not very clear; but perhaps they were indifferently aware of the obstacles they would encounter; and they certainly believed that no force could resist the formidable army (thirty thousand strong) which marched under their orders.[d]

A chronicler of the fifteenth century gives the following account of the expedition:[a]

The king and his brother, having made all their preparations, entered Ditmarsh in the beginning of February. Nearly six thousand of the numerous foot soldiers were said to be Rytheræ, who were mercenaries. Others who flocked from the towns and country of Jutland, Friesland, and Holstein, cannot be counted. Secure in the hope of victory, many came provided with the means of carrying away the money which they were going to take as booty, and with tokens to serve as receipts when the money was weighed out. Magnificent horsemen from Holstein, Jutland and all Denmark went thither, with that splendour of arms which is customarily prepared for great weddings, and they carried gold in their purses. Some came from the territories of Lüneburg and Brunswick. The invaders were persuaded that to such a force the Ditmarshians would yield forthwith, and that if it should come to a pitched battle the result would not be doubtful. Thus, with every advantage of time and place, on the 15th of February the princes marched a great army into the enemy's country and occupied the town of Meldorf. *Sauve qui peut.* The utmost ferocity was displayed towards persons of every estate, rank, and sex, so that they might be subdued the more quickly. The princes sent spies, one of whom, being taken, was forced to confess by what avenue the enemy would arrive. When they had learned this, the Ditmarshians dug, during the following night, an intrenchment in the muddy way by which the invaders were coming. There some thousand men lay in wait for them, and others in another place. It was therefore under the worst auguries that, in ignorance of the intrenchment the princes struck camp on the Monday which was February 17th, amidst loud acclamations. But the counsels of the captains of the guard (which came first, to the number of two thousand, with a still greater crowd of citizens and country people) prevailed. The cavalry followed, so sure of an easy victory that they even had carts in their train. They advanced, moreover, by a path whose narrow width was the cause of infinite disaster to the horsemen. No one thought there would be any danger when the foot guards had passed, and the whole affair was regarded as an easy matter. The mire and depth of the road, lined on each side by wide ditches, threw the riders into confusion as they advanced in a great crowd, hoping and expecting to pass over solid ground. The Ditmarshians, hidden by their rampart, now poured forth missiles at the advancing enemy, and not without effect. The foremost of the foot soldiers, however, placed their shields before them, and, throwing away their spears, crossed the ditches and stood presenting a solid front, but so close together that they could not fight. The day was cloudy, and rain, mingled with hail, and raging winds were fighting for them. But the earth dug from the numerous ditches prevented them from using their swords, or attacking.

The royal artillery was now brought up, but rain and wind prevented the discharge of the missiles. Some of the Ditmarshians rushed up to prevent the artillery from being fired, but were flung back. Meantime a fire was poured from the whole rampart, and the lines of the foot were broken. But when the Ditmarshians perceived they were surrounded by the enemy, they attacked though few in number — not more than three or four hundred — these thousands of men cooped up in the mire and cold in a narrow place. Springing across the ditches, they fought, few against many; twice repulsed, they returned twice, recovered from flight, and cut down their enemies — thus caught in a trap and deep in mire — and threw them down into the ditches. And now the sluices were opened, and the waters poured in, so that in the rushing floods the ditches could not be distinguished. The foot soldiers of the guard were the first to take to flight, in which, however, many fell. Then the Ditmarshians, gathering courage, inflicted deadly punishment on the remaining band, collected from the neighbouring towns and villages, and these were drowned in the waters, which came in a great flood. Finally they fell on the crowd of horsemen pressed together in that narrow spot and unable to move or flee. With the fallen infantry in front of them, pressed in the rear by the flying, and flanked on either side by the ditches, they stood motionless and pale in the presence of death. The Ditmarshians, thronging round them, flung lances and arrows from the side, first wounding the horses. These, when they felt the steel, went mad, flinging their riders and trampling on them. A dismal noise was heard, and a horrible vapour of rising sweat obscured the eyes. The princes themselves got away with many others, not knowing how they had escaped; for the rainy and foggy atmosphere, together with snow, wind, and the mist of perspiration, deprived everyone of sight. In order that none might get away, the Ditmarshians pressed the flying. Some are believed to have escaped through the crowd of corpses of the slain and drowned.

Incredible as it may seem, this slaughter is said to have occurred within the space of three hours. The greater number of dead, however, were unwounded, and it was said that most were drowned by the waters. No one knew exactly what took place. Each was terrified by his own danger, the fog, and the gathering night, and blinded by the smoke and the vapour exhaled from his own horse. Soon some of the Ditmarshians came up and stripped the fallen of their arms, clothes, belts, and purses, and those whom they found breathing they massacred. They robbed the dying of their very shirts. With such cruelty did they war against the slain. They buried some thousands of the foot soldiers, but this favour was denied to the horsemen. Amongst the latter were two counts of Aldenborgh, Adolphus and Otto, and many soldiers — Danes, Holsteiners, and levies without number. The very flower of the Holstein army perished, to the lamentation of their own people and the great regret of all. The number of slain is not given exactly. The Ditmarshians say, a great number, but others deny this, saying a few thousand. The cause of the disaster may be imputed to two things, namely, overconfidence in beginning the war, and the cruelties at Meldorf against all persons of either sex and all ages and ranks.[e]

The king, in great wrath, vowed to be revenged; but a new army was not easily raised, and he was glad to accept the mediation of the Hanse Towns, which concluded a treaty that left both parties exactly where it found them.

KING HANS AND HIS SONS

(From an old tomb)

The king preserved his claim, and the natives their independence.

The reign of Hans was, in other respects, troubled. During much of it, the northern seas were infested with pirates, not from the Hanse Towns merely, but from Russia, Scotland, England, and Holland. At length a treaty of commerce was concluded between the king of England (Henry VII) and Hans — the more easily as at that period (1489) the latter was dissatisfied with the Hanse Towns. It secured to the English the right of commerce in the north seas, subject to certain duties; it allowed them to have their commercial establishments in the seaports, and their own judges in all controversies between their own countrymen. It even allowed them to fish on the coast of Iceland; though the permission was to be renewed every seven years. Let us add that famine and the plague more than once visited the north during this monarch's life; and we may term it the reverse of a happy one.

The death of Hans was hastened by a fall from his horse (1513). In his last illness, he called Prince Christian to his bedside and gave him some advice, the tenor of which shows that he perfectly understood the character of his successor. The latter was exhorted to forsake low and dissolute company, to consult only men esteemed for their age and wisdom; to renounce great designs, which would end only in disappointment; to forswear violence, and trust to calm moderation; to employ natives in preference to foreigners; to win the love of all by a government of mildness. In general, Hans himself had so acted: he had been always popular in Denmark; he had preferred caution to rashness, the solid to the splendid. His wisdom, in this respect, was frequently evident. For instance, he carefully refrained from all interference between the emperors and the holy see. Again, when besought by his nephew James IV, king of Scotland, to join the latter in the war against England — a war so disastrous for the Scot — he exhorted his fiery kinsman to cultivate the blessings of peace.[d]

CHRISTIAN (II) THE TYRANT (1513–1523 A.D.)

Christian II, called in Sweden the Ungentle, and also the Tyrant, whose administration in Norway had already been stained with blood, and who now succeeded his father in that country as in Denmark, laid claim also to the Swedish throne, to which he was at once elected, and commenced negotiations whereby the truce concluded with Denmark was several times renewed. In 1516 the war broke out anew, produced by the intestine commotions which the new archbishop Gustavus Trolle excited. This prelate sprang from a family linked with the union interest by its large possessions in Denmark, and which for two generations back had been inimical to the Stures. An attempt had already been made

QUEEN CHRISTINA AND HER DAUGHTERS

(From an old tomb)

by one faction to set up his grandfather, Arvid Trolle, against Sten the Elder, while his father, Eric Trolle, had lost the government by the election of the younger Sture. This Gustavus Trolle was of a temper that never forgave a past wrong, real or fancied, although the administrator himself, to bring about a reconciliation, had promoted his election to the archbishopric.

Their animosities now led to open war, in consequence whereof Gustavus Trolle, after a Danish fleet had fruitlessly endeavoured to relieve him, was unanimously declared at the diet of Arboga to have forfeited his office, and his fortified castle of Stacket was demolished. Next year Christian himself accomplished a landing in the neighbourhood of Stockholm, but suffered a complete overthrow from Sten Sture. In this battle, fought at the Brennkirk, July 22nd, 1518, and celebrated in a popular ballad, the Swedish banner was borne by the young Gustavus Ericsson Vasa. Being afterwards sent as a hostage to the Danish fleet on the occasion of a personal interview which the king requested with the administrator, he was carried off prisoner to Denmark, contrary to the pledged faith of the former, along with Hemming Gadd and four other Swedish nobles. Thither Christian also returned, after he had so treacherously broken off the negotiations which he had himself commenced. By the papal command, an investigation was instituted into the charges which the deposed archbishop had brought against Sten, at the see of Rome. A spiritual court commenced its sittings in Denmark; the administrator with all his adherents was excommunicated, and the whole kingdom was placed under an interdict.

"The Swedes," says Olaus Petri (Olaf Peterson), "did not in the least regard this ban and interdict." Christian, however, procured the execution of the sentence to be committed to himself, and the whole of the year 1519 was spent in making preparations. New taxes were imposed; levies were made in various countries; and in the beginning of 1520, the Danish army broke into Sweden under their general Otte Krumpen, who caused the papal ban to be affixed to all the churches upon the march. Sten encountered the invaders on the ice of Lake Asunden, by Bogesund, in Vestergötland; he was wounded at the opening of the battle, and obliged to be carried out of the conflict, the issue of which was decided by this disaster. Being conveyed to Strengnäs, he soon received intelligence that the Danes, to whom a Swedish nobleman pointed out the way, had surrounded the intrenchment in the forest of Tived, had cut to pieces the troops stationed there, and were already on their march to Upland. Collecting the remains of his strength, he hastened to Stockholm, but died in his sledge upon the ice of Lake Mälar, February 3rd, 1520. By his death, all government in Sweden was dissolved; the magnates indeed held consultations, but no one had courage to command, or will to obey. The country-people gathered in the view of attempting a stand against the enemy, but from want of a leader were soon dispersed by the foreign soldiery, whose track was marked by homicide and conflagration, and who insolently boasted that they would not care although in Sweden it should rain peasants from heaven. The heroical Christina Gyllenstierna alone, widow of Sten, and the mother of four children still of tender age, did not lose heart; she continued to defend Stockholm, and refused to accede to the convention ratified with the Danish generals at a baronial diet convoked in Upsala, by which Christian was acknowledged king, on condition that he should govern conformably to the laws of Sweden and the Treaty of Kalmar, and not exact vengeance for what had passed.

These engagements were personally confirmed by the king upon arriving with his fleet before Stockholm, with the express addition, that the measures adopted against Gustavus Trolle, who was now restored to his office, should be forgotten and forgiven. The same promises were repeated in the king's letter to all the provinces, and being seconded by the efforts of the prelates and the nobility, completely disarmed the resistance still kept up by the people. These assurances were again renewed when Hemming Gadd, after a life spent in struggling against Danish domination, now appeared in his old age as its advocate, and by the weight of his influence at length induced Christina Gyllenstierna to surrender Stockholm, although against the wish of the burghers. When the king in the autumn returned to Sweden, and was crowned in Stockholm, he once more confirmed by oath and reception of the sacrament the securities he had given. But at this very moment Christian had resolved that the blood of the chief men of Sweden should be shed, although he himself "appeared friendly to all, and was very merry and pleasant in his demeanour, caressing some with hypocritical kisses, and others with embraces, clapping his hands, smiling, and displaying on all hands tokens of affection." The instigator of this resolution was Didrick Slaghök, formerly a barber, and a relative of Sigbrit, a Dutch huckster, who by the beauty of her daughter had gained an ascendancy over the king's mind, which she had tact enough to preserve during his whole reign.

The Carnage of Stockholm

On the third day of the solemnities which followed the coronation, the gates of the castle of Stockholm were unexpectedly barred, and the archbishop Gustavus Trolle came into the king's presence, to complain of the violences and injuries suffered by himself and the archiepiscopal see of Upsala, at the hands of the deceased administrator, for which he now demanded satisfaction. He was probably himself ignorant of the atrocities, for the perpetration of which he was to be used as an instrument. He is said, as we may conclude from a contemporary account, to have maintained that the question of punishment and compensation must be referred to Rome; but the king negatived his proposal, declaring that the matter should be adjudicated forthwith. As the prelate's charges were really directed again Sten Sture, his widow Christina Gyllenstierna stood up and appealed to the resolution of the estates, whereby Gustavus Trolle was unanimously declared to have forfeited his dignity, and which the principal spiritual and secular lords had subscribed under an express obligation to common responsibility. Such of these as were now present, and among them two bishops, were immediately seized and thrown into prison; the remainder were confined over night in the castle — the clergy in a separate chamber.*j*

CHRISTIAN II
(1481–1559)

The following morning, the 8th of November, at nine in the forenoon, several of the Swedish clergy, who had been shut up during the night, were called to the large hall, where they, together with Jöns Beldenack, Gustavus Trolle, the bishops, Hans Brask, and Otte Swinhufwud, were to form a spiritual court. Jöns Beldenack then put to them the question whether those who had conspired against the pope and the holy chair of Rome ought not to be considered heretics. Some of the priests were agreed with Christian, and answered "Yes." Others did not perceive what this was meant to conceal, and answered, "Yes." Others again, though they very well perceived the drift of the question, also answered, "Yes." The king was satisfied with the result, and pronounced the rest of the judgment himself — that the Swedish lords, having set themselves against the pope, were heretics according to the judgment of the court, and therefore should as heretics die.

The whole of that day the city gates were shut, so that none could get out. Early in the morning the trumpeters rode round the town, proclaiming that no citizen was to dare, for his life, to leave his house, till permission was again granted to do so. Large crowds of armed Danes were placed here and there on the chief squares; loaded cannon were drawn out on the Great square with their muzzles pointed towards the principal streets. The whole town was in a dread and solemn expectation. The castle gates were at last thrown open at noon; and a mighty body of armed soldiers first appeared, and placed themselves in two long lines, reaching from the castle to the town house. The imprisoned Swedish lords were led between them as far as the

Great square, where a strong guard of Danish soldiers closed around them. The people who had now regained permission to leave their houses, streamed in that direction, and with anguish and alarm beheld the frightful preparations. Sir Nils Lycke, the new knight, now appeared on the balcony of the town hall, and addressed his speech to the assembled multitude thus "Ye good men, are not to wonder at what ye here behold, for these men altogether were wicked heretics, disobedient to the holy father in Rome. They have laid powder under the castle to kill the king, who would notwithstanding have spared them; but Archbishop Gustavus Trolle has three times knelt before him and demanded justice."

Bishop Vincent, from the square below, now interrupted him, and called aloud that all this was lies and nonsense, but that God would yet punish Christian's cruelty and treachery. Sir Anders Karlsson and Anders Rut, two councillors of Stockholm, also loudly called on the other Swedes, begging and beseeching them in future not to permit themselves to be deceived by false promises, but one day to avenge this terrible treachery and tyranny. The Danish soldiers now made a great noise, so that their words could no longer be distinguished, and at the king's order (it is said, that from a window in the town hall he looked on during the whole proceedings) the execution began, and Klas Bille placed himself at hand to receive the golden chain and ring of every knight before he was beheaded. The prisoners then implored that they might at least be permitted first to confess and receive the holy sacrament. But even this was refused, and Bishop Matthias was led forth first. While he was kneeling with clasped and uplifted hands, his secretary Olaus Petri and the latter's brother rushed forward; but before they could reach the spot, their beloved master's head had fallen before one blow of the sword, and rolled towards them on the ground. Beside themselves with horror, they cried out that this was an inhuman action. "For these words they were immediately seized and dragged within the circle, and would certainly have been executed had not some German soldiers saved them."[1]

Bishop Vincent was next beheaded, and then came the senators' turn — Eric Lejonhufwud, Knut Kurk, Eric Johansson Vasa, father of Gustavus Vasa, Eric Ryning, Eric Gyllenstierna, Eskil Banér, Joachim Brahe, and thirteen nobles and knights of the senate. These were followed by the three burgomasters of the town, and thirteen of the town council, together with fifteen of the chief citizens, some of whom, without the slightest warning, were snatched out of their houses, and led to execution. A citizen named Lars Hansson was standing in tears beholding this terrible scene; the soldiers dragged him within their lines, and he was made to pay with his death for his compassion. At last the execution stopped for that day; the heads were set up on poles, with the exception of that of Bishop Matthias, to whom, in consideration of his great services to the king, this favour was shown that, instead of being impaled, it was laid between his feet. The dead bodies were left where they had fallen, to the horror of all. A violent rain came on, which yet more disfigured the pale remains, and redly dyed water ran everywhere from the Great square down into the streets, bearing a bloody witness to what had there taken place.

The second day, Friday the 9th, Christian remarked that many had hid-

---

[1] These two brothers had studied at the University of Wittenberg in Germany. Ewert Leuf, one of the German soldiers, had seen them there, and believing them to be Germans, represented to his comrades that, not being Swedes, they ought to be spared. This had its effect; the brothers escaped, and some years later afforded Gustavus Vasa signal assistance in the introduction of Lutheranism into Sweden.

[1520 A.D.]

den themselves whom he would willingly have murdered; he therefore made a proclamation that the inhabitants might now freely show themselves, for he did not intend to punish any more. Some were simple enough to permit this trick to deceive them, and imprudently showed themselves, on which the massacre recommenced. Six or eight were beheaded on the square; the gallows were continually full of dead bodies, and the servants of the deceased lords, who came to town ignorant of what had happened, were often pulled from their horses with so much haste, that they were hoisted on the gallows, booted and spurred, as they had come. The king's soldiers and satellites broke into the houses, murdering the men, violating the women, and plundering everywhere. They bore away as much as they could carry; and it seemed to them enough to leave the bare walls standing for the widows and fatherless children. The corpses remained this whole day and night still lying on the Great square; and with horror and loathing the people saw the dogs begin to tear the remains of so many noble and innocent men. As the air, was yet mild, a poisonous exhalation began to arise, which, it was feared would bring the plague; it was therefore determined that the bodies should be carried away before the break of the Sabbath morn. Jöns Beldenack, however, remembered that they, as heretics, could not be buried in form; but ought, properly, to be burnt, which was done. A huge pyre was erected in the southern suburb on the very spot where St. Catherine's church now stands, to which the pale and mangled corpses were carried by cartloads, and there burned to ashes.

Christian seemed to have given himself up to a sort of madness of rage and fury. He ordered that the body of Sten Sture the Younger should be torn from his grave in Riddarholm church; and it is said that in his frenzy he bit at the half-consumed remains. He also caused the remains of the young son of Lord Sten and Lady Christina, who had died during the siege, to be disinterred. He permitted the revengeful Gustavus Trolle to disentomb the remains of the reverend father Martin Jönsson, who had, while he was Sten Sture's secretary, highly offended the archbishop. These three bodies were carried to the great pyre on the Södermalm to be burnt with the rest, and the quarters of the town of St. Catherine's church, still bear the name of Sture, in memory of the dead.

Christian next called Christina Gyllenstierna to his presence. When she, in her sorrow and despair, presented herself before him, he bid her choose whether she would be burned, drowned, or buried alive. The noble lady fainted at his feet. The entreaties of the witnesses of this scene, her own tears and great riches, at last mollified the tyrant; but she was obliged to promise to recall her young son from Dantzic that he might be educated in Denmark. Her mother, the old Lady Sigrid Banér, who by a former marriage was grandmother of Gustavus Vasa, was shut up in a bag and thrown into the stream; but some of the people on the shore succeeded in saving her by promising Christian her great fortune — for this was the best way to soften him to mercy. Lady Sigrid was taken up; but she herself, her two daughters, Lady Christina and Lady Cecilia of Eka, two of Gustavus Vasa's sisters, together with many other noble and honourable women, were carried away as hostages to Copenhagen, and shut into the dreadful dungeon, called the Blue Tower. There Gustavus Vasa's mother and two sisters died, and many others, of hunger, thirst, and cold; and those who escaped with their lives had to thank Queen Isabella's mildness alone, who against her cruel husband's will, softened their captivity as much as lay in her power.

Further Atrocities

Not in Stockholm alone did the blood-thirsty monarch let the sword of the executioner massacre the Swedes: he commenced similar executions throughout the country. Such a king had taken care to place officers whom neither shame nor horror could withhold from the performance of such a command. Didrik Slaghök, who succeeded Vincent in his bishopric, and was likewise appointed governor of the castle of Stockholm, Jöns Beldenack who succeded Matthias in Strengnäs, Anders Perssons in Örebro, Jöran Matsson, and the young Sir Thomas in Finland, all possessed the king's greatest confidence in this matter, and never for an instant spent a thought on shedding Swedish blood. These persecutions were carried on in every province, and many of the Swedish nobles were despicable enough to betray each other to the Danes, seeking thus a hateful and contemptible revenge for private and often insignificant disputes.

Some days after the massacre in Stockholm, Christian received the news that his queen had borne him a daughter. The miserable flatterer Gregorius Holst prepared a great festivity. The citizens were invited to assemble for a magnificent repast in the town hall, to be followed by dancing and other amusements, in demonstration of their joy at the happy news. The entertainment was to take place at the expense of the burghers; and one may imagine with what satisfaction they paid their money, and their wives danced with their bloody oppressors. Christian then published a manifesto throughout the kingdom, in which he declared that, the Swedish lords whom he had beheaded having been heretics, their death alone was able to deliver the country from the pope's curse and excommunication, and that, as this had now taken place, he would be at liberty to rule the country according to its old laws. The government during his absence was to be superintended by Archbishop Gustavus Trolle and his father, Sir Eric Trolle.

Christian, still fearing a rebellion, renewed the old resolution of the council of Linköping, made in 1153, that no peasant should bear arms; and he even, in many places, had them taken from them by force. It was not a little humiliating and hard for the Swedes to see the Danes, proud and triumphant, rob them of their guns, bows, and swords. It is related that some, irritated beyond endurance, suffered the words to escape them, that iron and swords should not be wanting to punish the tyrant, as long as they were permitted to retain their feet to pursue, and their hands to revenge. To this the arrogant conquerors replied that a hand and foot might well be cut off from the Swedish peasant; he would be able, notwithstanding, with one hand and a wooden leg to steer his plough. This senseless report was spread, believed, and caused a general panic; for Christian's unnatural cruelty was such that the incredible became credible.

At last, in December, he prepared for his return; the wheel, the gallows, and bloody executioners marked his journey. In Nyköping he caused his own favourite, Klas Holst, to be hung. He passed Christmas in Linköping with Bishop Hans Brask, who betrayed to him two of Sture's most devoted friends, Sven Hök and Peter Smed — they were both quartered and exposed on the wheel. He laid hold of Sir Lindorm Ribbing in Jönköping, and beheaded him and his servants. Shortly after, seeing by chance Sir Lindorm's two little boys, the one eight and the other six years old, and fearing their revenge at a future period, he determined to make away with them both. The eldest boy was led out first and was beheaded. The younger looked at the streaming blood and the red stains on his brother's clothes,

[1520 A.D.]

without knowing what it meant; but when he was led out, he turned with childish innocence to the executioner, and said: "Dear man, don't stain my shirt like my brother's, for then mamma will whip me." The executioner, melted at these words, threw the sword from him, and said: "I would rather blood my own shirt than thine." But the tiger-hearted Christian, who had been an eye-witness of this heart-rending spectacle, was not to be touched by it. In a fury, he called for a more savage servant, who struck off the heads of the innocent child and the compassionate executioner. From this he proceeded to Nydala cloister, and continued the same course there. But enough has been already said of his madness and fury.

In this detestable assemblage of crimes, it is a consolation to find some noble-minded men who dared to breast the dangerous stream. When Suckot, the emperor Charles' legate, found that by all his exhortations he could not restrain Christian from the massacre in Stockholm, he left him suddenly, expressing his abhorrence of such a deed. Sir Otte Krumpen abandoned Christian immediately, and would no longer serve such a master. The Danish nobles detested and cursed their king's treachery; and Severin Norby openly protected the Swedish lords who took refuge with him — but these were not many. Death or dread had concealed many in the grave, and the poor remnant, in the inaccessible mountains. If they had by their selfishness, ambition, litigiousness, and stubbornness during previous ages prepared so many misfortunes for their native land, they had now themselves paid the bitterest penalty. But Christian, the means of punishment, we cannot contemplate in his dreadful progress without horror, from the moment he had determined on the impious and monstrous treachery we have related. Neither compassion nor the fear of God nor the advice of his friends, his own reason nor his own advantage, were in any way able to stem his fury. He had thrown himself, with firm determination, into the path of crime; blindly he rushed on in it, trampling justice, humanity, and virtue, boldly under his feet; and flung himself at last with greater haste into the deep destruction which already had long awaited the royal criminal.*g*

In these sanguinary proceedings, we may be surprised at the little deference which Christian showed to the church. Though her avowed servant, the minister of her vengeance, he did not hesitate to violate her long-established rights, whenever his own interests or caprice intervened. Of this disposition he afforded two signal proofs immediately after his return from Sweden; and he also showed how little dependence his most necessary creatures could place on the continuance of his favour. Early in 1520, he had forced the chapter of Lund to annul their election of an archbishop, and place one of his favourites on the vacant throne. In this violence, his design was to find a ready instrument for some purposes which he had in view. One of these was the restoration to the crown of the isle of Bornholm — the possession of which had long been a subject of dispute between the chapter and his predecessors. He demanded from the new primate the cession of the island. The position of the latter was one of difficulty. On the one hand, there was his oath to maintain at all risks the rights and privileges of his church; on the other, was the royal displeasure, which seldom spared its victims. In this emergency he obtained permission to resign his dignity and retire into a monastery; but he soon left his retreat, and hastened to Rome, to complain of the violence which he had sustained. The canons, thus left to Christian's influence, were terrified into the cession, and into the election of the notorious Didrik Slaghök now bishop of Skara, to the vacant dignity. In his administration of Sweden — of which he had been appointed one of the regents — this worthy had successfully imitated the violence of his master. The complaints which rose from every quarter against him were received by Christian at the moment of his return from a short visit to his brother-in-law, the emperor Charles; and their inefficacy was proved by the elevation of the obnoxious churchman to the supremacy of Denmark.

The arrival of a papal legate, whose mission was evidently to inquire into the Stockholm massacre, gave him at first some uneasiness; but he soon divined the character of the stranger, a Dominican friar, whose good opinion he gained by extravagant praises of the order, and by the most delicate personal attentions. Still, the complaints of the celebrated Johannes Magnus, canon of Linköping, then at the Roman court, and the fact that two bishops, besides other ecclesiastics, had been executed by his commands, were too grave even for the most reverend Dominican to overlook; and the king found it necessary to sacrifice the new primate of Denmark. The career of this wretch was now at its close: as he had not received his bulls of confirmation, he was bishop only in virtue of the royal nomination. His person, therefore, was not yet invested with the necessary episcopal sanctity; and he was delivered over to the secular arm, as the sole author of the massacre, and was burned to death in the public square of Copenhagen (1522). This holocaust was intended to propitiate the legate. The zeal with which the king destroyed everything Lutheran in his dominions (and many attempts at reformation had been made both by his father and himself) was a more acceptable offering. The piety of the good friar was gratified by the royal wish that all the monasteries of Denmark were subject to the rule of St. Dominic, and by the ardour with which he was aided in effecting the objects of his mission. The character of Christian was represented to the pope in the most favourable colours, and his absolution from all church censures recommended. But Adrian VI, who now ascended the papal throne, took a different view of the affair, and entrusted the legatine authority to Johannes Magnus, who was sent into Sweden to examine the matter de novo. The new functionary after a careful examination threw the blame on the king, and declared Gustavus Trolle incapable of holding the primacy of Sweden. Two years afterwards, the sentence was confirmed by Clement VII; but no step was taken to punish the royal criminal.

Gustavus Vasa

Before the termination of this affair, Sweden was the theatre of events which forever terminated the authority of Denmark over that kingdom. Though, by a royal decree, the peasantry were disarmed — though the fortresses were filled with garrisons devoted to the king, and all places of trust by his adherents — he had scarcely left the country, when the public mind began to recover its vigour, and to devise the means of his downfall. The instrument designed by Providence for this purpose was the captive Gustavus Vasa. Whether the patriotism of this noble equalled his ambition, or his thirst for revenge, may be doubted; but if his motives have been too highly esteemed, and his general character over-rated, there can be no dispute as to the good of which he was the cause — that he was the saviour of his country. That he had many faults, will be acknowledged by everybody out of Sweden, but this only proves that he was a man; and if great undertakings should devolve on the immaculate only, history would have none to record. His own wrongs sank the most deeply into the soul of the captive (he had not heard of his father's murder before he effected his escape); he was agitated by apprehension of the future, since under such a king he could scarcely hope to end his days in peace. To escape was his first resolve. But how elude the vigilance of his keepers? He feigned resignation to his lot, and so won the confidence of his noble guardian Eric Banér, that he was guarded with much less strictness; he was allowed to walk, and even to hunt, for hours together, in the vicinity of the fortress where he was confined.

One fine morning he assumed the disguise of a peasant, passed undiscovered through the gates, and proceeded with such diligence as to reach Flensburg the following day at noon. By entering into the service of a cattle-drover who was proceeding with a herd into Saxony, he escaped the notice of the men whom Banér had sent in pursuit of him; and he safely reached Lübeck. There he made himself known to the authorities, in the belief that they who had so recently assisted Christina, the widow of Sten Sture, would be ready to assist him. For some months, however, he was in great jeopardy: the republic knew its interests too well to quarrel openly with the king, who reclaimed the fugitive, with the most terrible menaces in case of a refusal. Banér, his gaoler, also appeared to demand him, and he had reasons to be apprehensive that he would be delivered into the hands of his enemies. Such, no doubt, would have been his fate, but for the juncture of favourable circumstances. In the first place, the doctrines of Luther were making great progress in Lübeck, and Gustavus embraced them— whether through conviction, or with the view of obtaining the support of the reformed party, can be known only to the Omniscient. In the next place, he had an engaging presence and much natural eloquence; and he had little difficulty in persuading

GUSTAVUS I, SWEDISH KING
(1496-1560)

some of the senators that to deliver him into the hands of an hereditary foe — one necessarily hostile to the prosperity of the city — would not only be the most foolish policy, but a deep stain on the hospitality of the place. Again, the union of Sweden and Denmark had never been approved by the people of Lübeck: it might, if consolidated, render the monarch too powerful a rival in commerce, and it would certainly destroy the opportunity, so long enjoyed, of profiting by the dissensions of the two kingdoms. Sweden, from apprehension of the Danish yoke, would always be the ally of the Hanse Towns, and especially of Lübeck. Interest, therefore, turned the scale; and the resolution was taken to provide the noble Swede with a vessel, and send him back to his own country.

In May, 1520, some months previous to the massacre of Stockholm, Gustavus landed at Kalmar. This place had not yet acknowledged the Danes; but it had little chance, and less desire, of resisting. His eloquence had no effect either on the garrison or the inhabitants; and in some apprehension for his personal safety, he precipitately left the place. As all the other fortresses were in the hands of the Danes, and as his departure from Lübeck was known both in Sweden and Denmark, and a price was put on his head, his motions could not fail to be attended with extreme danger. Proceeding through Småland and Östergötland, he was compelled frequently to change his disguise, to travel by night rather than by day, and to choose the least frequented paths.　At length he reached the house of his brother-in-law, the senator Brahe, where he found a hospitable reception but no encouragement for his ambitious designs.　Both his sister and the senator opposed them, and earnestly besought him to renounce an enterprise which would be followed by ruin.　The rural gentry to whom he addressed himself were not more favourable;　the peasantry were equally indifferent;　and he was advised by some to make his peace with Christian.　"Whoever is king," replied the people, "we must labour.　We have herring and salt under Christian, and we should have no more under any other ruler."

Finding these people too reasonable for his views, Gustavus, who was now informed of the massacre at Stockholm, and who had reason to fear lest the fate of his father should speedily be his own, hastened into Dalecarlia.　That region, as we have had frequent opportunities of remarking, had always been distinguished for the restless disposition of its inhabitants.　Isolated from the rest of the kingdom, and impassable in many places from its vast forests, deep marshes, and abrupt mountains, it had preserved an independence unknown to other provinces.　The poverty of the people, too, had offered no inducement to the rapacity of power;　and their strength, their courage, their love of freedom — the necessary results of their hardy life, their temperate habits, and their consciousness of strength — rendered them impatient of any attempt on the part of the government either to abridge their privileges, or to load them with new taxes.　This hardy race heard with anger of the dreadful scenes in the capital;　they detested the Danish yoke;　but then they had equal reason to detest the rapacity of their own nobles, which it required all their energy to resist.　Among them Gustavus might find a greater degree of security than anywhere else, but even there were men eager to deliver him into the hands of the Danes;　and to defeat treachery, he was frequently compelled to change alike his garments and his place of refuge.　On one occasion, while the master of the house in which he was entertained went to the nearest military station to reveal his name and designs, the wife, more compassionate, contrived the means of his escape.　Frequently, therefore, was he forced to bury himself in the deepest obscurity, and to trust to the most precarious means of support. It has been said that he worked in the mines as a common labourer;　that his rank was at length discovered by his embroidered collar;　that he was recognised by a neighbouring gentleman;　that he obtained a wonderful ascendency over the sons of the cavern, and by degrees prepared them to be his assistants in the subversion of the Danish yoke.　All this is romance, like a thousand other incidents, to which the imagination of poets, and of historians no less inventive than poets, has given rise.　That on one occasion he hired himself to thresh the corn of a farmer, seems to be true;　but this expedient was not adopted for securing a maintenance so much as for temporary safety.

After many wanderings, many disguises, many hair-breadth escapes from treachery, even more than from his Danish pursuers, Gustavus harangued a great multitude who had repaired to Mora for the celebration of the Christmas festivities.　The picture which he drew of ancient plenty under the government of their own princes, was chiefly drawn from imagination, since the "good old times" in which every mind is fond of dwelling, are fair only at a distance;　but it answered his purpose.　It made a deep impression on hearers who had little happiness in the present, and who, therefore, beheld it in the past.　When he spoke of the insults which Christian had heaped upon the national character — of his perfidiousness, bloodshed, and tyranny — of

[1521 A.D.]

the rapacity for which many of the Danish officers had distinguished themselves; and still more, when he spoke of the exactions, the insults, the wrongs
in store for them — that they were to be deprived of their dearest liberties, and
transformed into slaves, for the benefit of their Danish masters — he roused
his hearers to the highest pitch of indignation. Artfully alluding to their
strength, which, if concentrated, would be capable of effecting anything, he
offered to obtain for them the restoration of their ancient happiness, if they
would support him. His eloquence induced about two hundred to join him;
the rest would wait the course of events, and help him to the throne or scaffold, according to his success or failure. Of the handful who did join him,
more were actuated by hope of plunder than by love of freedom. But this
was a beginning, which was all that the adventurer wished. With this little
band, which was soon augmented by the idle and the industrious, the male-
factor and the patriot, he overran the more obnoxious districts, plundered or
destroyed the houses of all the Danish adherents, intercepted the local taxes,
massacred every enemy to Sweden, — that is, every friend to the Union of
Kalmar — and inspired with some alarm not merely the provincial governors, but the regents to whom Christian had confided the administration of
the kingdom. At the head of three thousand resolute followers, he now
prepared for higher achievements. He forced whole provinces to declare
for him; and, while organising a larger force, had the satisfaction of hearing
that one of his captains had defeated a body of Danish and Swedish troops,
sent by the regents to exterminate him. In another engagement he was less
fortunate, but as the number of his followers hourly increased — for when
was the standard of rebellion in any country erected in vain? — he was so far
from losing his confidence that, in a public manifesto, he declared Christian a
usurper whom he was resolved to punish.

His next exploit was the reduction of Vesterås, a town which, from its
position on the high road between Dalecarlia and Stockholm, was of the utmost
importance as a military station. The citadel refused to surrender; but it
was closely invested, while detachments were spared from the main body to
besiege four other fortresses, which were at length forced or persuaded to
capitulate. The next object of assault was Upsala, the archbishop of which,
as head of the regency, was peculiarly obnoxious to the patriots. The place,
incapable of a long defence, soon opened its gates; the canons were immediately expelled, were sharply upbraided for their attachment to a foreign yoke,
and required to take the oath of allegiance to the liberator. Trembling and
irresolute, they requested permission to consult their chief, then in Stockholm, and a short delay was granted them for that purpose. The indignant
primate insisted on being the bearer of his answer at the head of a select body
of troops; and he arrived within half a league of Upsala, at a moment when
Gustavus had weakened himself by allowing many of his followers to repair
to the harvest. Unable to resist, the latter was compelled to evacuate the
place. But this check was temporary; reinforcements were soon collected,
and before the archbishop could reach Stockholm on his return, he was
defeated by one of the liberator's captains. Elated by this success, Gustavus himself hastened to the capital, and invested it in form.

Christian Aids His Own Downfall

During these events, what was the conduct of Christian? He has been
accused of crimes equal in atrocity to those which he had perpetrated at
Stockholm. He informed Gustavus, we are told, that if the siege of Stock-

holm were not immediately raised, he would put to death the mother and sister of that noble, and with them all the Swedish ladies whom he held in captivity. The menace being disregarded, proceeds the story (which a hundred pens have repeated), all were drowned, and many of them were previously compelled to make the sacks in which they were cast into the river. The character of Christian need not be unnecessarily blackened, however, for it is dark enough. The mother and sister died of the plague; the other prisoners were restored by the successor of Christian.[1]

The garrison of Stockholm defended the place with great bravery; it even forced the assailants to encamp at a greater distance from the walls; and though, owing to the unprepared state of Denmark, supplies could not soon be expected, there was no prospect of an immediate reduction of the place. Gustavus, therefore, turned the siege into a blockade, and marched detachments into other quarters of the kingdom, both to increase the number of his adherents by compulsory levies, and to gain possession of such towns as had hitherto refused to acknowledge him. His followers were now so numerous, his hope of ultimate success so flattering, that in August, 1521, he convoked a general diet at Vadstena. Many of the nobles through jealousy of his ascendancy, some through attachment to the Union of Kalmar, refused to attend; but the greater part was present, and most of the towns were represented by their deputies. The assembly, indeed, was a numerous one, and animated by the best spirit. The speech of Gustavus had on this occasion less of his wonted exaggeration, more reason, more argument, more patriotism. It was heard with applause; he was justly hailed as the liberator of Sweden, and might easily have obtained the crown, had not good policy induced him to decline that which could not add to his power, but would be sure to disgust many of his supporters and alienate many of the oldest nobility. The titles of administrator and of captain-general, he willingly received; and at the same time he expressed his readiness to support, on some future occasion any candidate for the crown who might have a majority of suffrages. For this speech he has been much lauded; but its policy was at least equal to its magnanimity, for he well knew that the most powerful, the most successful of candidates — in other words, himself — must obtain the prize.

The cause of Gustavus, being thus rendered legitimate by the sanction of the people, could not fail to increase in prosperity. The most important fortresses opened their gates to him. Stockholm, indeed, still held out; but the garrison was mutinous for want of pay, and the primate Trolle, with one of his suffragans, hastily retired into Denmark, under the pretext of obtaining new supplies. Their reception by a monarch whom the intelligence of every day soured, was not the most grateful. But they had reason to congratulate themselves on their escape, when they learned that, in the irritation of his feelings, he had transmitted orders to the Danish governors to execute all the Swedes — especially the nobles — whom they could seize. Some obeyed the order; some, instead of becoming the instruments of another atrocious massacre, passed over to the service of Gustavus. There was at all times an infatuation in the conduct of this prince, indicative of his impending fall. While he exasperated everybody, he made no serious effort to avert the loss of a kingdom. His admiral Norby, however, fought nobly for him, and pre-

[1 Dunham's version of this incident is not accepted by the Swedish writers. Geijer *f* states that the mother and sister of Gustavus were thrown into dungeons, where they died either of plague or, as Gustavus complained, by violence. Fryxell *g* accepts the story that Christian sent letters to Gustavus threatening to drown the captive wives and daughters of the victims of the Stockholm massacre and to torture Gustavus' mother, and adds that the latter died of want and neglect.]

served the three keys of the realm: Stockholm, Kalmar, and Åbo. Had he himself done what his chancellor in Sweden advised him to do — sent an army through the Gothlands to the relief of Stockholm — a great portion of the kingdom would have returned to its obedience.

But Christian had other difficulties besides those of the Swedish rebellion, and his ruin was not to come from that quarter. Those difficulties, and still more his own conduct, were hastening the period of his domination in. Denmark itself. He offended his uncle Frederick, by obtaining from the emperor letters patent transferring the right of investing Schleswig and Holstein from the bishops of Lübeck to the kings of Denmark. Frederick, who had manifestly aspired to an independent sovereignty in those regions, was extremely dissatisfied with a change which must necessarily make them more dependent on the crown than they had lately been. Yet for this act the king is surely not to be blamed; it might injure an individual, but it was for the good of the people. The manner, however, in which he attempted to enforce homage from the duke, was in the highest degree censurable. At Kolding where he met that prince together with many Holstein nobles, he caused gibbets to be erected to terrify them into the act, but the brutal exhibition only exasperated them. Again, after the Swedish war, where troops of Schleswig and Holstein were employed, he dismissed them to their homes without pay, without even the horses which some of them had brought into the field. In the next place, he drew on himself the enmity of the people of Lübeck, not merely by his new commercial regulations, but by his seizure of the supplies destined for the insurgents of Sweden and Finland. That in both instances he was justifiable, will be readily admitted; yet policy should have taught him to manage a power that, by openly embracing the cause of Gustavus, must greatly increase the difficulties of his position. The war with that formidable republic was immediately disastrous. Copenhagen was insulted; Elsinore was plundered and burnt. In these hostilities he could no longer rely on the aid of his uncle, or the people of Holstein, whom he had offended beyond forgiveness, and who were in no way obliged to assist in any expedition beyond the bounds of their own territories.

But his greatest crime was held to be one which, in the eyes of posterity, does him the most honour: his constant efforts to restrain the power of the lord over the vassal, of the noble over the serf. No class in Europe urged pretensions so monstrous, or committed acts so tyrannical, as the territorial lords of that kingdom, especially those of Jutland. In the two codes which Christian compiled — the one chiefly ecclesiastical, the other chiefly civil — he abolished as impious and wicked the custom of selling human creatures like brute beasts; and he permitted serfs who were ill-treated, to flee and settle in other provinces. All the provinces of Denmark were not equally guilty; in some — Skåne for instance — the local customs were more favourable to that unfortunate class. Another law — that which abolished the right of plundering shipwrecked mariners — was dictated by a kindred feeling of humanity, not unmixed, perhaps, with some delight of annoying the aristocracy. Whatever his motive, the benefit (so far, at least, as the law could be put into operation) was the same; and for it Christian must be no less praised by history. The laws which procured him the enmity of the church do him no less honour. He passed one similar to the English Statute of Mortmain: future bequests were to be in money only. On every clergyman with a cure of souls, residence was to be compulsory. No bishop, when he travelled, was to have a greater suite than fourteen domestics, no archbishop, more than twenty. Against these ordinances churchmen declaimed with much anger: the king was depriving them of their manifest right to expend their revenues in whatever manner they pleased — to do what they would with their own. Nor were some, at least, of these holy personages less dissatisfied with the ordinance respecting shipwreck. The bishops of Borglum and Viborg, and the arch-bishop of Lund, openly exclaimed against it. All three, says a contemporary writer, were accustomed to send out their men to the coasts, to seize on all the property which the tempest threw on the shore, and to kill without pity any of the crew that ventured to resist spoliation.

As the crown itself had extensive domains on the Jutland coast, the conduct of the king in this case is the more to be praised. History has preserved the reply which he made to one of his officers who remonstrated with him on the loss that the royal revenues must sustain by such an edict: "I would rather have no revenues at all, than that the poor mariners should be so inhumanly treated." Equally striking was his reply to another bishop, who complained of the ordinance in question as subversive of the ancient customs of the realm. The king observed that he had no wish to alter any ancient customs, except such as were contrary to the divine law. "And how," demanded the other, "is the ancient custom in regard to shipwreck contrary to that law?" "It is contrary," was the reply, " to two express commandments: 'Thou shalt not steal,' 'Thou shalt do no murder.'" By the law of Christian the authorities of the district were compelled to assist shipwrecked mariners in the preservation of their merchandise; but this assistance was not to be gratuitous; it was to be paid for by the mariners.

Bloodthirsty as was the character, tyrannical as were many acts, of this monarch, it may be doubted whether these hastened his downfall half so much as the noble ordinances to which we have alluded. As by them the nobles and senators of Jutland were the most aggrieved, so they were the first to plot his deposition. Towards the close of 1522, the result of their secret association appeared in a solemn act, by which they forever renounced their allegiance to Christian and transferred it to Duke Frederick. The reasons which they adduced for this extraordinary proceeding were numerous, and no doubt, weighty. They could, indeed, scarcely exaggerate, when they dwelt on his tyranny; but, still, their own privileges, their own immunities, were evidently the only things of which they really felt the violation. The prelates had an additional reason for his deposition, in the favour which he had shown to the apostles of Lutheranism. Before this act could reach him, he had probably some notion of the real state of the province; he could not well, indeed, be ignorant of it. Yet he convoked, at Kallundborg in Zealand, the nobles of Jutland, whose opinion, he said, he wished to obtain respecting the pretensions of his uncle to a portion of Norway, and the war with Lübeck and Sweden. That he had another object — the extermination or the imprisonment of the leading nobles — is affirmed by a contemporary writer. Of this opinion were the intended victims themselves, since not one of them repaired to the place of assembly. They might suspect that their secret consultations, and their correspondence with Duke Frederick — who, though little exposed in these transactions, was, beyond doubt, the soul of the conspiracy — were known to the king; and they could scarcely hope for more favour than the nobles of Norway and Sweden had experienced at his hands. Their refusal to obey the royal summons hastened the catastrophe. The act which deposed him was ingeniously laid before him, while the one that called Frederick to the throne was forwarded to that prince. Jutland was soon in arms; the duke prepared an army to take possession of the crown; and Christian hastened to Kolding, to consult with the handful of nobles who still adhered to him.

[1522-1523 A.D.]

He was advised to try the effect of entreaties, promises, and engagements to do whatever his rigsraad should wish him to do; to exclaim against the injustice of condemning him unheard; and to request a meeting with the most discontented of the aristocracy. There was so much justice in the request that, had not his ruin been long determined, it must have been heard. After some delay, the only answer returned was, that the estates (the nobles and prelates, for no other class was requested, or would have been allowed, to give an opinion) had already judged him; that another king, whose presence was daily expected, had been chosen; that his own evil deeds were known to everybody; and that no other evidence was needed. Seeing the utter hopelessness of a reconciliation with that great province, Christian passed into Fünen, the estates of which acknowledged him; and from the people of Zealand he received even stronger assurances of support. Skane, too, through the influence of the primate (his own creature), was induced to declare for him. But probably none of these provinces had at this time much notion of the extent to which the conspiracy had been carried, for these acts were followed by no outward demonstration of assistance.

While Christian threw himself into Copenhagen, which he declared his resolution of defending, the Jutland rebels (for history cannot give them a more honourable name) were not inactive. They wrote to all the other provinces, using alike entreaties and menaces to procure their co-operation. They entered into a close league with Lübeck, which was still at war with Christian, and which readily agreed to furnish both money and troops towards the common cause. They urged the preparations of Duke Frederick, who required little stimulus on the occasion. A civil war seemed inevitable, when, to the surprise of the kingdom, Christian, collecting all the money, the jewels, and other precious effects he could, abandoned Copenhagen in company with the despised Sigbrit, the archbishop of Sweden, and others whom his misfortunes could not alienate from him. His object, according to his own account, was to solicit aid from his brother-in-law, the emperor Charles. His departure was the signal for a general defection. The fate of Christian was, henceforth, a melancholy one. A tempest, by which he lost most of his valuable effects, threw him on the coast of Norway. With difficulty his life was saved; nor was his subsequent escape to the Low Countries without danger. He was no longer to taste the sweets of royalty. An exile for some years from his throne and country, with limited means of support, without the respect of his old adherents or the fear of his enemies, he could not attempt, without rashness, to regain possession of the crown. Yet, as we shall perceive in the reign of his successor, that attempt he did make, and it had the result which might have been anticipated. It led to his close imprisonment for the remainder of his life — that is, for no less a period than twenty-seven years.

By his queen, Isabella of Austria, Christian had issue: (1) John, who was educated in the Low Countries, by the famous Cornelius Agrippa, and who did not discredit his tutor; (2) Dorothea, married to Frederick the elector palatine; (3) Christina, married, first, to Francesco Sforza, duke of Milan, and afterwards to Francis, duke of Lorraine. Besides these, there were two princes who died young.

FREDERICK I (1523–1533 A.D.)

No sooner did Frederick hear of his nephew's unexpected flight, than he hastened to Viborg, in Jutland, where he received the homage of the estates.

As his royalty was the work of the nobles of that important province, he endeavoured to secure their favour by the most lavish concessions to their order. In criminal matters he gave them the power of life and death, with confiscation of substance, over their vassals; and in civil actions that of deciding in cases where the fines amounted to 40 marks. "Never," observes the chancellor Hoitfeld, "did the Danish nobility obtain such advantages under former kings: from this period, it became equal, in power and rank, to the nobles of Schleswig and Holstein. Those of Norway and Sweden have no such powers; even in Germany, they are enjoyed only by the princes of the empire, and the counts and barons with territorial jurisdiction; so that our gentry, without titles or dignities, are in this respect on a par with those princes."

From these observations may be deduced the true cause of the revolution which we have just contemplated. The policy of Christian II was to diminish the overgrown privileges of the aristocracy; and in the same degree to elevate the peasantry and burgesses in the social scale. His expulsion was the effect of the ill-will engendered by that policy, and of the understanding between the nobles and Duke Frederick that the latter should not merely undo what his nephew had done, but confer on the privileged orders rights which they never yet had enjoyed. It is melancholy to see that the clergy were among the most eager in producing this odious revolution. Some of them had subsequently the honesty to confess their error. "I repent," wrote one of them to a canon of Roeskilde, "the share which I had in the last revolution; the new form of government has not been established as I could have wished it. Vain was the hope that some remedy was thereby devised for the evils of the state, and that the blessings of the change would soon be felt; there are now more heavy complaints of the prelates and nobles than there ever were of Christian II. It is the opinion of many that this prince was expelled rather for the advantage of the great, than for the welfare of the commonwealth. Would that they had moderated the exercise of their rights (if they can be called rights) over the peasants until tranquillity had been restored. Many are the people who think that the tyranny of one man would have been far preferable to that of so many oppressors, whose rapacity cannot possibly be satiated."

But criminal as were the grants of this prince, and much as the higher orders of the state were, in consequence, disposed to aid him, his accession was not without its difficulties. Though Fünen declared for him, Zealand and Skåne refused for some time to acknowledge him, and Copenhagen and Kallundborg avowed their resolution to resist him to the last. With a body of six thousand men, which he had assembled at Kolding, a reinforcement of two thousand more, and some vessels sent him by the regency of Lübeck, he landed in Zealand, and invested the capital. Though he obtained possession of Kallundborg — probably by the golden key — he could make no impression on Copenhagen. The fidelity of the garrison was strengthened by the report that Christian himself, with a large German force, would soon arrive to relieve them. That the exiled prince was using every effort to obtain assistance, was indeed true: but many were the disappointments which he had to endure. His brother-in-law the emperor was in Spain, and could only address menacing letters to the inhabitants of the three kingdoms. Henry VIII of England could spare neither money nor troops. The elector of Brandenburg, his kinsman, would try what could be effected by negotiation before he would sanction an appeal to arms, the issue of which, as he well knew, must be doubtful. In vain did the imperial chamber, in vain did the German univer-

XVI. Ignominious Entry of Peter Sunnanväder and Master Knud

into Stockholm (1526)

(*From the painting by C. G. Hellqvist, in the Metropolitan Museum of Art, New York*)

sities, declare for him; in vain were the authorities of Lübeck commanded not to take part with the rebels. The cause of Frederick grew stronger every day. He persuaded the estates, or rather the nobles, of Skåne, to follow the example of Jutland, by conferring on them the same privileges that he had conferred on the other nobles. Of all the towns in the province, one only held for Christian. Norway was next induced to declare for him; and in return he recognised the elective privilege of that kingdom as fully as it existed in Denmark or Sweden. He also engaged to procure from the Scottish crown the restoration of the Orkney and Shetland isles. His triumph, indeed, was considerably abated by the news that an army of twenty-six thousand Germans, commanded by the elector of Brandenburg, was preparing to invade the kingdom; but he was not discouraged. Leaving the siege of Copenhagen to his son Christian, he hastened to meet his rival, whose forces were soon dispersed for want of pay, and even of necessaries. Nothing now remained to resist the progress of Frederick. Early in 1524, Copenhagen capitulated; and the example was speedily followed by Malmö. The two kingdoms, therefore, of Denmark and Norway, with the exception of two provinces — Vigen, dependent on the latter, and Blekinge, on the former, both of which had during the recent troubles been seized by the Swedes — were now held by the new monarch. Still, Admiral Norby, who had been invested by Christian with the government of Gotland, and whose valour at sea had often been proved by the Swedes and Lübeckers, refused to submit; but less, as we shall soon perceive, through a principle of loyalty than from a wild ambition.

The transactions of Frederick with Sweden were seldom of an amicable character, though the circumstances of both kingdoms prevented an open collision. On the flight of Christian, Gustavus Vasa, as might have been foreseen, was raised to the throne. This circumstance, indeed, did not prevent Frederick from assuming at his coronation the vain title of king of Sweden, in virtue of the Union of Kalmar; and it probably inspired Gustavus with the resolution of maintaining his sway over the two provinces just mentioned. Gotland too was a subject of dispute. At the instance of Lübeck, which severely felt the piratical courses of Norby, Gustavus sent a body of men to reduce the island. The admiral, politic enough to discern the true sentiments of the two kings, submitted to Frederick, on the condition of his being recognised governor of the island. The Swede, unwilling to try the hazardous experiment of a war at a time when he was exposed, no less than his rival, to the wrath of the exiled Christian, who had the avowed support of the empire, withdrew from the contest. The same apprehension induced the Dane to conceal his dissatisfaction with the Swede. It led both to negotiate, where, in a different position, both would have recurred to hostilities. In 1524, it produced a personal interview and a conference between them. Gustavus restored Blekinge, which, though geographically included in Sweden, had always been subject to Denmark; but he retained Vigen until a congress of deputies should decide on this and other disputes between the two crowns. Gotland was provisionally to remain in the hands of the nation whose troops should, at a given period, be in possession of the fortress of Visborg. But, in regard to the last place, a third party had to be consulted — Admiral Norby, who, though nominally the vassal of Frederick, was attempting, as King Eric had done before him, to establish for himself an independent sovereignty in that island. Suddenly declaring for the exiled Christian, whose cause he valued no more than Frederick's, he invaded Skåne, which he speedily reduced. Nor will this success surprise us, when we observe that Frederick was at this critical juncture (1525) absent in Holstein, and that the peasants, universally oppressed through the fatal concession of the reigning king, flocked in great numbers to his standard. A letter of Christian, adroitly published, still further explains the secret of that success. It declared that whatever Norby did would be done by his authority. It promised freedom to his "poor people," whom "children of the devil so impiously treated." It asserted that the royal misfortunes were attributable only to his determination to resist the intolerable rapacity of men "who held a peasant in no higher estimation than a dog." These representations were admirably adapted for the purpose in view; and had Christian been advancing to aid them by the physical argument, they must have been resistless. Excited by natural, although reprehensible, feelings, the peasantry arose, assailed these tyrants, and, whenever victors, showed them little mercy.

The triumph was of short continuance. Frederick readily obtained aid from his allies, the Swedish king and Lübeck, who had suffered so much from the piracy of the admiral; a small army was sent into Skåne, and Norby was twice defeated — on the second occasion so completely, that he was glad to capitulate. In return for the government of a fortress and a considerable sum by way of indemnity, he surrendered Gotland to Frederick. But his disposition was too restless to allow him to remain at peace. War was his element; he had been nursed in it, and out of it he could not live. With vessels which he bought or built, he recommenced his piratical courses, on the ships of Denmark no less than on those of Sweden and Lübeck. It was now the interest of all the three powers to combine their forces for the destruction of this audacious outlaw. He was defeated, and compelled to seek refuge in Muscovy, where, through the influence of Gustavus, he was detained a prisoner until 1529. Charles V obtained his liberation; he entered the service of that prince, but soon fell, at the siege of Florence.

During these transactions, Christian was not idle. The victory [Pavia, 1525] which placed Francis I at the mercy of the emperor, seemed also to menace his speedy restoration. The belief was very generally entertained that Charles would arm in behalf of his brother-in-law. To avert this probable event, Frederick, who could be influenced only by his fears, and who had not one particle of generosity or of common feeling for his deposed kinsman, consented to negotiate. By certain arbitrators it was agreed that he should purchase a foreign lordship for Christian, or allow him a suitable pension. Nor was this all: in a subsequent negotiation, the Danish rigsraad proposed that, after Frederick's death, the crown should devolve on Prince John, the son of Christian; and that Frederick's own son should be content with the duchies of Schleswig and Holstein. Why this convention was not executed, we are not informed: probably Frederick devised means to annul it. This, at least, is certain, that both parties continued to make preparations — the one for attack, the other for defence. It was soon reported in the North that Ferdinand, king of the Romans and brother of the emperor, was preparing to assist the dethroned king more efficiently than by negotiation. Why such assistance had not been long given, will surprise no reader who is acquainted with the empire, in regard both to the war with France and to the progress of the Reformation. Both Gustavus and Frederick were known to be friendly to the opinions of Luther: both, therefore, were obnoxious to the universal Catholic party, which openly threatened an invasion in behalf of Christian, who, though perfectly indifferent to religion, had policy enough to declare himself the champion of the ancient faith. On the other hand, the reformed princes of Germany declared for the actual occupants of the Northern thrones. Had the Scandinavians themselves been uniform in their doctrines, they

[1529–1530 A.D.]

would have had little to apprehend from foreign enemies; but, though the Reformation had undoubtedly made considerable progress among them, especially in the large towns, the majority, perhaps, still adhered to the Romish communion. This was particularly the case in Norway, which, for that reason, was more favourable to Christian than to the reigning king.

So apprehensive was Frederick for the result that, in 1529, he sent his son into that kingdom, to obtain from the estates a recognition as successor to the crown. They refused to act, on the just ground that they had the elective right no less than Denmark; and that, as the two crowns were inseparable by the treaty of union, the sovereign elected by the one would naturally be chosen by the other. But their real motive was their attachment to Prince John — or, we should rather say, to the church of which John was considered the champion. They hoped, too, that the day was not far distant, when he or his father would arrive with a formidable armament to restore the ancient worship throughout the North. Frederick and Gustavus participated in the opinion; and, in 1530, they renewed another of the disputes which had so often agitated them. Vigen was restored to Norway; but the administration and the revenues were to remain six years longer in the hands of Gustavus, as a kind of indemnity for the renunciation of his pretensions. At the same time, both monarchs drew still closer the ties which connected them with the reformed princes of Germany.

Christian Reappears, and is Cast into Prison

The time was now come when Christian could again try the fortunes of war. Emboldened by a supply of money from the emperor; by another from Norway, with the promise of a general rise on his disembarkation in that kingdom; by numerous emigrants from all the three kingdoms; by the good wishes of the clergy and peasantry; by about ten thousand mercenary soldiers belonging to several nations; and by a fleet of about thirty sail which the merchants of the Low Countries hired to him, he left the ports of Holland late in October, and steered for Norway. Why he should venture to sea at such a tempestuous period of the year, can only be explained by that fatality which seemed to attend everything he undertook. On the coast of Friesland, a storm sank ten of his vessels; with the rest in a shattered condition, he reached Christiania.

His proclamations, however, had much effect: thousands, including senators and nobles, but especially the clergy and the rustics, flocked to his standard. Among these were the primate, two bishops, many priors, and a great number of the inferior clergy. Even towns declared for him; so that in a short time three fortified places only in the south of Norway — Aggershus, Bergenhus, and Bahus — held for Frederick. But these were by far the strongest towns in the kingdom. They were defended by valiant men, and the governors were actuated by the best spirit. At such a season of the year, there was little hope of reducing them; but Christian invested Aggershus, the key of Christiania, and suffered himself to be deluded by the promise of the governor that, if the place was not relieved within a given time, it should be surrendered to him. He might have known that Frederick would never suffer the fall of so important a place, but he seems to have relied, with something like infatuation, on the promises of men whose sole object was to gain time. That there was an understanding between Frederick and these functionaries not to spare assurances of any kind, so that he might be lulled into perfect security until the hour of action was past, is evident from the tenor of his negotiations with Gyllenstiern, the governor of Aggershus, from his otherwise unaccountable inactivity, and still more from the result. While treated with so much respect by that officer — while made to believe that relief could not arrive in time, that the stipulation was only to save the honour of the commandant, and that the place would infallibly and immediately be surrendered — while receiving the homage of the Norwegians, who acknowledged his son, Prince John, as his successor, and sent to Frederick a renunciation of their allegiance — he had the mortification to learn that one thousand chosen men, with stores and provisions of every kind, had thrown themselves into the fortress. Indignant at the deception which had been practised on him, he now invested the place with vigour — but in vain. He could make no impression on the massive bulwarks, and had even the grief to perceive that a formidable armament was approaching to raise the siege entirely.

The Danish fleet, increased by the vessels of Lübeck disembarked within sight of Christiania early in May (1532). At this moment Christian was making an unsuccessful attempt on the neighbouring provinces of Sweden, in the belief that the Roman Catholics generally, and all who wished for the restoration of the Kalmar Union, would either aid him, or at least offer no resistance to his progress. But the troops of Gustavus offered resistance enough. Having sustained a defeat, he was compelled to throw himself into Konghella, where, owing to the Danish and Swedish reinforcements daily received by his enemies, his position was soon a critical one. That he was betrayed into it by one of his faithless attendants — and he had many of the kind — was his own firm belief, and must be the belief of all impartial writers. But the conviction arose too late: if the traitor was punished, the evil could not be recalled. With much difficulty, indeed, Christian cut his way through the surprised enemies who environed the place, and threw himself into Christiania; but if this step delayed, it could not avert, his fate. That place was soon invested by new and more formidable armaments; his own vessels were burnt before his eyes, and he was thus cut off from all supplies; his provisions were alarmingly diminished; he had no longer money to satisfy his mercenaries; and it was evident that he must soon either fall with arms in his hands, or make terms with the besiegers — if, indeed, he could not escape in disguise. Perceiving the hopelessness of resistance, he made overtures of accommodation. What follows is not the brightest page of this dark history. Under the walls of Christiania, his deputies and the Danish chiefs met to agree on the terms of surrender. After some parley, it was manifest that they could not agree; and, in conformity with the entreaty of the latter, Christian himself repaired to the conference. There, with much affability of manner, with the greatest sincerity, with the noblest confidence in the honour of the chiefs, he requested them to name the course which they would have him adopt. They advised him to go to the court of his uncle, who, they assured him, would receive him with the utmost distinction, and even kindness; "they engaged, before God, on their faith, their honour, and their salvation, to provide for his safety, and that of one hundred persons in his suite;" to treat him with all possible respect; to let him negotiate with whomsoever he pleased, whether in Norway, or on his passage to Copenhagen, or during his sojourn in Denmark; to procure for his adherents a complete oblivion of the past; to use their influence to obtain for him the best terms from Frederick; and if the two kings should not agree, still the safe-conduct which they gave him should be equally binding, and he should be at liberty to go wherever he pleased.

After this clear and unequivocal engagement, Christian no longer hesitated to confide in the Danish chiefs. He received the safe-conduct; wrote a humble and even affecting letter to his uncle, whom he promised "thenceforward to obey as a son would his father"; and in July embarked for Copenhagen. He now discovered the extent of the treachery of which he was the victim. Frederick refused to sanction the convention. But so notorious a breach of faith required some colour of excuse, and he assembled his rigsraad, or rather, such members as he knew would abide by his resolution. The majority — for there was an honourable minority — were of opinion that the conditions and the safe-conduct should be disregarded, on the ground that they had been signed "against the intentions of the king." Gyllenstiern, the chief actor in the perfidy, was next examined; and he too advised the retention of Christian, on the plea that he (Christian) had violated the safe conduct, which was therefore null! The determination to imprison him, which was urged alike by the nobility and the deputies from Lübeck, was soon taken. All this time he remained on board the ship which had brought him from Norway, suspicious, indeed, of some knavery, but little apprehensive of the severe fate which awaited him. To his demand that he should be admitted into his uncle's presence, it was replied that the king was at Flensburg, and that the interview solicited would there take place. Towards that city the course of the vessel which carried him, and of some others, designed not to honour him but to secure his imprisonment, was immediately directed. From the sea he contemplated with a gleam of hope the towers of Flensburg, but that gleam soon vanished; the squadron passed along, and bore him to the strong fortress of Sonderburg, in the solitary isle of Alsen, within which he was speedily immured. The place was well chosen. It lay far from the route of the Swedish and Norwegian vessels, but within a short sail of Lübeck and Holstein, both of which had an interest in his safe detention. He had but one apartment, and that a dungeon the door of which was walled up. There was a small grated window in the wall, through which his scanty provisions were daily handed. During twelve long years he languished in that horrible abode, with a dwarf as his only companion. He was abandoned by the world, even by his imperial brother-in-law; and his existence was remembered only by the anxiety of the nobles of Holstein, Denmark, and Sweden to prevent his enlargement.

Two other circumstances concurred in the establishment of Frederick's throne. One was the submission of the Norwegians, who bent to the power which coerced them; the other was the death of Prince John, the son of Christian. There was now no rival to the pretensions of Prince Christian, the son of Frederick, who had already been acknowledged heir to the thrones of Denmark and Norway by the estates, or rather, by the rigsraad and nobles of both kingdoms.

Before we dismiss the reign of this monarch, we must advert more particularly to the religious state of the North. From the contiguity of Denmark to the Protestant states of Germany, the new opinions could not fail to be introduced into it immediately after their promulgation by Luther. The Scandinavians, too, had sense enough to perceive the monstrosity of the doctrines respecting indulgence, openly preached by the papal legate Arcemboldi. Rome claimed a right which God himself has not claimed — that of dispensing with the eternal obligations of religion and morality. But if reason has often led to the conversion of individuals, it has seldom influenced a nation, and still less that portion of it denominated the great. The majority of men do not reason: they are led by example; while those in authority are influenced by their interests. Christian looked on the Reformation with a favourable eye, because it gave the prince, in matters purely ecclesiastical, a voice which, since the days of Constantine, perhaps — certainly since those of the Carlovingian dynasty — no sovereign had enjoyed. It did more: it placed at his disposal the revenues of the church and many extensive domains, which, by the suppression of the monastic orders, reverted to the crown. These advantages, coupled with the diminished power of the bishops, who had often been the tyrants of the North, made him so much favour the Reformation as to send for missionaries to preach it openly.[d]

PONTOPPIDAN TELLS THE STORY OF THE REFORMATION IN DENMARK

Things had come to such a pass that it can justly be said that the government had become dual, and the archbishop a monarch of the church who scarcely gave precedence to the king. It may not be true, as is related, that a bishop on drinking the king's health said: "Our favour brings your favour;" but it is, nevertheless, certain that these lords had gone far toward gaining the ascendancy over the king.

How great the state and revenues of these prelates were, can be guessed from the fact that King Christian II, who with jealous eyes watched the increase of their power, gave orders that in future the archbishop was only to be accompanied by twenty horsemen when in the field, and the remaining bishops by only ten. Previously they had had a hundred. In the twelfth and thirteenth centuries they were real war heroes, who generally commanded the army of the kings at sea and on land. When they summoned their peasants and those of the capital, they could assemble a fair force of so called "choirmen," who fought with clubs, and even attacked royal castles. In the battle fought at Fodevig in 1135, under King Niels, six bishops and six hundred priests were killed. By wills and other presents for masses for the dead, these lords had gained so many noble lands that thirty-three fiefs were subservient to the episcopal see of Roeskilde; and, as can be seen from a writing of King Christopher I, a great many nobles were bound by allegiance to them alone, and not to the king. Only daily misfortune and weakness could therefore arise in the state. The luxury and terrible extravagance of the clergy of those times certainly could not have been greater.

Coarseness and Ignorance of the Clergy

Most of the bishops, abbots, prelates and priests were according to the literary standards of the period, to be counted among the unlettered. In the time of the Reformation there was not one who, at the conference at Copenhagen in 1530, could have been compared to Magister Hans Thausön and other Protestants who had studied at Wittenberg; but Doctor Stagefyer and other learned men were brought from Cologne as champions.

Those of the prelates who had studied were rarely theologians, but mostly *Juris* and *decret doctores* or *Licentiati*. They applied themselves to that which belonged to the maintenance of their state, supremacy, and advantage. They "disputed," with the ban, against the heretics and relied on the argument of the sword. Those who had scruples were told, "Eat, bird, what is placed before you, or die." It must also be remembered that theology and the Holy Scriptures were not allowed to be taught at the University of Copenhagen. One Dane appends to a document the statement: "As I cannot write myself, so and so has signed in my stead." Jerpager, in Orat. Jubil., assures us that a canon of Ribe, Nicolaus Ebbonis, was not able to sign his own name. Some studied in Paris and in Cologne on the Rhine, but these were few compared to those who learned a little bad Latin in the convents, or who had been only officials and servants of the bishops, and had then become preachers.

As they themselves had little light they could not impart much to others. Their sermons were full of absurd fables of miracles which were said to have taken place here and there; and these preachers concerned themselves only with private confession, veneration of the saints, etc. This is satisfactorily attested by the work of the papist Postil still kept in the libraries of curio lovers — written in the Danish language by Christen Pedersen, canon of Lund, and published in Paris shortly before the Reformation, namely in 1515. In this volume one finds a whole store of superstitious absurdities. It is worth while to introduce the following passage as a specimen of the old Danish credulity:

"We read that there was a jailer who, whenever he passed before the image of the Virgin Mary, honoured her with an Ave Maria, and commended himself to her care. Once when he was praying to the Virgin Mary, the judge ordered that he should come and hang a man. On the way, his enemies came and killed him. Now, there was in the town a pious priest, who had the habit of going round all the churches of the town at night. In the night he came to the churchyard of Our Lady where he found many people he had known in their lifetime. To one of them he said, 'How is it there are so many people here to-night?' He replied, 'The jailer of this place has been killed to-day, and devils have taken his soul, and say it belongs to them; on the other hand the Virgin Mary asserts it belongs to her. Now all the people are standing here to see the outcome of the affair. For the almighty God, a severe and just judge, is now to come from Heaven to disperse them by one word.' Then the priest thought to himself, 'I wish I could hide myself somewhere here, so as to listen to the sentence.' He therefore crept behind some timber. When he had thus hidden himself, he saw the all-powerful Judge descend, sitting on his judgment seat and accompanied by his devoted Mother, the Virgin Mary. Then came the devils, bringing with them the jailer's soul, which they had bound tightly. They asserted that, on account of the many evil deeds committed, it rightly fell to them. Then Mary replied that in the hour of his death the jailer had prayed to her, and commended his soul to her, and that therefore by right it was hers. When the Judge heard this he did not wish to anger his dearly loved Mother, neither did he desire to wrong the devil. He therefore commanded the soul again to enter the body, so as to atone for its sins, and ordered a notification sent to the pope that the universal prayers of the church should be offered up for the jailer. Someone asked who was to inform the pope. Then the Virgin Mary replied, 'Call the priest who has hidden himself.' When the latter came forth she gave him a beautiful rose saying, 'Take this to the pope, and tell him what thou hast heard and seen, and give him this rose as a proof.' As soon as the pope saw the rose he believed the priest and credited his mission, and he had the prayers said. Afterwards the soul was released and entered Heaven. May almighty God grant us all the joy of entering and abiding there. Amen!"

Wretched as was the standard of sermons, few priests had energy to preach at all. Many village churches belonged to the cathedral chapters; and therefore it was the duty of the canons, either themselves or through their deputies, to conduct divine service. But they neglected it at their leisure, yet nevertheless demanded their rents and tithes from the peasants, who uttered constant complaints. Once under King Christopher III they raised a rebellion, but found little redress.

The Odense Recess and its Results

In 1527, a free and public diet was held in the town of Odense on the festival of the Assumption. The bishops, prelates, knights, and lower estates appeared there to consider various matters. The principal question was that of religious disturbances, and the speech which the king then publicly made to the bishops redounds to his undying honour. The tenor thereof was that they should be mindful to keep the charge of their great pastoral office more heedfully than had been done heretofore; and should at least see to it that the pure and saving word of God should everywhere be expounded to the lay people in their churches — in place of which nothing had been heard up to this time save miracles, fables, lies, and foolish inventions of men. Although he had promised to maintain the doctrines of the church of Rome, yet they should not stretch his promise farther than to cover what was true and fundamental in the said doctrine, nor extend it to the palpable errors which might so easily creep in at divers times. What he had promised concerning the dignity of their order, he fully intended to abide by. But they themselves should consider no less what use they made of their greatness and power, and with what conscience they thought one day to give account of it to God, to whom both they and he owed fuller obedience than to the see of Rome. For the rest, since by this time the teaching of Luther had been so far disseminated in the country that they could not hope to stifle it without detriment to the common weal, and since they had heard that in other countries the said teaching had been adopted by whole kingdoms and provinces, and could therefore no longer pass for heresy, he, for his part, taking all these things into consideration, was determined to tolerate both religions within his kingdom, until at length, as all men hoped and expected, a general council of the whole Christian church should be held. That which was then decreed in the matter of religion he, in common with other Christians, would hold binding upon himself.

After many debates, and in spite of the opposition of the bishops, who obstructed it, so to speak, with hands and feet, the king, reinforced by the support of several members of the rigsraad, overcame all obstacles and obtained this much: that the subjoined constitution was made and confirmed by the *publica auctoritate*. It is the more remarkable because it laid the foundation of the liberty of the Danish church, and paved the way for a complete reformation.

Article 1. From this day forward every one of the clergy shall enjoy liberty in so far as no man shall be authorized to examine another's conscience, whether he be Lutheran or papist. Rather let every man take thought for his own soul. Article 2. The Lutheran confession in particular, which had hitherto had no full security nor safeguard [Danish *Leyde*], the king henceforth receives into equal protection and shelter as the papist. Article 3. The estate of matrimony, which for several hundred years hath been prohibited to the servants of the church, canons, monks, and clerics of all sorts, is now permitted; and every man is free to enter into the married state, or to remain in purity of life (*Reenlijvenhed*). Article 4. Henceforward bishops shall not go to Rome for the *pallium*, but shall receive confirmation from the king only, after they have been lawfully elected by the chapter, which retains its liberty in the matter.

Furthermore, another constitution was made concerning the jurisdiction of the clergy and their right or claim to fines, tithes, etc. The quarrel that was pending between the bishops and nobles on the question of forty-mark fines, was settled in such wise that fines due for murder and offences against the church, the peace of the church, and clerical persons, remained under the jurisdiction of the clergy.[h] In all other cases the crown was to levy the fines from its dependants according to law, and the nobles were to do the same from theirs. The tithes were confirmed to the clergy according to the statutes of King Christopher III and other kings, the king as well as the nobles undertaking to bestow them. Any man might make offerings for the souls of the departed as God put it in his heart to do, but voluntarily and without compulsion. Bishops, prelates, churches, and abbeys were to retain possession of the property they held, till such time as it should be taken from them by the law of the land. Priests, monks, and other clerical persons were not to be brought before the assizes or provincial courts, but left to the jurisdiction of their rightful judges the prelates, except in cases concerning certain localities with which the assize and provincial courts alone should be competent to deal.

Immediately after the diet of Odense, the character of the church and of religion in Denmark assumed a new and far more satisfactory aspect. The assurance of religious liberty and toleration aroused joy unspeakable in some thousand peculiarly timorous souls, but no small indignation among the bishops and their followers, who saw whither matters were tending, yet were powerless to interfere. The strength of truth was not on their side to enable them to hold the fort, and had it been otherwise, they would not have known how to avail themselves of it, for there were but few among them who had rightly perused God's word, or had laboured honestly at theology — as could be said of their opponents, especially of Hans Thausön, Jörgen Sadolin, and others, who had employed their time well at Wittenberg. On the other hand, "the fleshy arm and the strength of an horse," which had hitherto been the papists' strong support, began to corrupt, yea, to perish altogether, by the aforesaid constitution of Odense. When men would no longer be forced to believe and confess the faith, but sought to be convinced out of the Scriptures, their method of teaching was undone. Many a Nicodemus might now be seen creeping out of his corner, and coming over to the Protestant side. There were now almost as many Protestants as papists, and that not only in the towns, but in the villages and on the estates of the nobles. But many clave to the old superstition. The bishops were concerned only to save their order with the *sæcularibus* thereto appertaining. They almost abandoned the defence of their doctrines, and could only look on and see, not the lay people alone, but a goodly number of preachers turn against them. Whereby, alas! it is to be feared that much impurity mingled with men's motives, and some so-called priests were induced to change, rather by the liberty to marry than by heartfelt acceptance of the truth. Anthon Heinrich adduces more than one example of those who had long had their *foscaria* (who were called *Steelten*), and were now joined with them in matrimony, according no uncertain recognition to children they had already had. Nicol Helwaderus, who was secretly inclined to popery, casts ridicule upon them for this, saying in *Sylva Chron. Mar. Balth.*, "Then they began to look round upon the daughters of men (*Si te delectant formosæ membra puellæ, I, pete conjugium.*"

Some monks and nuns who had been thrust into the cloister in youth, and without due probation, began secretly to desert in certain places, and to take upon themselves a different manner of life. But there were not many such, since the proceeding was approved by few; and most monasteries remained in fair condition for a long while, save that a few mendicant friars in the towns, for lack of alms and for other causes, abandoned their monasteries, which were then turned to different uses. But the members of the

many endowed orders or those which lived *de propriis*, especially the Bene-
dictines, Bernardines, and Augustinians, abode by their former way of life.[h]

THE DEATH OF FREDERICK

Events soon showed that the decree of the estates of Odense was not to be
a barren one. Independent of the secularisation of ecclesiastical property,
occasioned alike by the desertion of the monastic orders and the forfeitures
exacted from clerical delinquents, no bishop was thenceforth elected without
the recommendation of the crown. His confirmation only had been stipulated, which was to act as a kind of veto on the choice of the chapter, if an
improper subject should be elected. But by this innovation — by an exercise of authority, which even the pope, in all the plenitude of his power, had
never claimed — the chapter had no longer a voice in the matter. Nor was
this all: such dignities were no longer to be gratuitous; they were to be
bought. Thus, in 1529, on the death of the bishop of Roeskilde, his successor, who was recommended — that is, nominated — by the crown, was
constrained to pay 6,000 florins to the king. Even this was not all: he also
engaged not to oppose the progress of the reformation, but to fill his diocese
with evangelical — that is, Lutheran — preachers; and, lest he should violate
the engagement, he was required to give security for its due performance.

The effect of such measures soon appeared. Holstein, Schleswig, Jutland,
and still more, the cities of Copenhagen and Malmö, were filled with Lutheran
missionaries, whose zeal and whose novelty of manner made a great sensation
wherever they appeared. In the cities, there was more education, more general intelligence, than in the rural districts; in them, the new doctrines were
more eagerly examined and more promptly adopted. We do not, however,
read of public disputations in this country, which were so common in Germany. In 1530, indeed, a great one was to be held at Copenhagen; but,
owing to some misunderstanding as to the conditions, it never took place.
Frederick took advantage of the circumstance to obtain from the estates a
confirmation of the decree that the professors of both religions should be
equally protected by the law. Yet this decree could not prevent occasional
disturbances. Sometimes the bishops found opportunities of persecuting;
sometimes the Protestants refused to tolerate what they termed the idolatry
of the mass, and became persecutors in their turn. In general, however, there
was much less tumult in Denmark than in most other countries. The bias of
the court was too evident to allow of the Lutheran professors' being materially hurt; and the latter, though vehement in their sermons, had too much
prudence needlessly to exasperate a yet powerful body, who might be assisted
at any moment by foreign intervention.

On the whole, then, the Reformation made great progress in Denmark,
and some in Norway, during this monarch's short reign. The ancient church
received a blow from which it could not afterwards recover. It might totter
for a while; it might for a while appear majestic, and even formidable, to all
who assailed it; but its ultimate ruin was inevitable. One of the king's last
acts was to receive the Confession of Augsburg, which, though he could not
enforce it on his Catholic subjects, he imposed on the Protestants.

Frederick died in 1533. His character has been much lauded by the
national historians, from the chancellor Hoitfeld down to our own day.
But a foreigner can see little to admire in it. Without genius, without generosity, without honour, without any other guiding principle than his own

interests, he has no one claim to our respect. By his queen, Anne of Brandenburg, he had issue — Christian III, his successor; and Dorothea, married to Albert, markgraf of Brandenburg and first duke of Prussia. These connections will account, in some degree, for his decided measures in regard to the Reformation. His second wife, daughter of Bogislaw, duke of Pomerania, was also a Protestant. By her he had (1) John, who inherited one-third of the duchies of Schleswig and Holstein, (2) Adolf, successor of the ducal branch of Gottorp, (3) Frederick, successively bishop of Schleswig and Hildesheim, and coadjutor of Bremen.

INTERREGNUM (1533-1534 A.D.)

The fifteen months which followed the death of Frederick were among the most momentous in the modern annals of Denmark. It might have been supposed that the captivity of Christian II, and the death of his son John, would have removed all obstacles to the accession of Christian, the eldest son of Frederick — especially as his brothers were yet in their infancy. But the bishops and the superior clergy were determined to exclude him — first, because they were angry with his father; and, next, because they knew his own attachment to the principles of the Reformation. Their influence over the other members of the rigsraad, who were few in number, connected with them by the ties of blood, and still adherents of Rome, will go far to explain the events which followed.

The rigsraad, as we have before observed, had by degrees usurped many of the attributes of the estates general; among them was the momentous one of a royal election. As usual, they met at Copenhagen, not so much to fix on the choice of a sovereign, as to consult with each other on the aspect of affairs, and to hold the reins of government until they could agree in the election of some prince. Their intention to exclude Christian was evident from their not inviting him to be present, and still more, from their receiving with coldness the envoys whom, without their invitation, he sent to protect his interests. He had even much difficulty in securing his election as administrator of Holstein until his brothers should reach maturity. He was thus in danger of losing, by the elective suffrage, all chance of authority in the estates held by his father. He saw, too, that in Denmark there was a party which, though adopting a policy distinct from that of the bishops, was no less hostile to him: this was the party favourable to the restoration of Christian II. He had, however, the satisfaction of perceiving that the majority of the nobles — those, at least, of Jutland, Fünen, and Skåne — were zealous for his election. Thus, there were three divisions in the state; and, though that of the bishops was numerically the smallest, yet, as representatives of the church, as leading members of the rigsraad, and invested with the actual administration, their preponderance was manifest.

This influence was strikingly displayed at the meeting of the estates general on the festival of St. John. In the discourse which the prelates delivered on the occasion, they condemned the " rash innovations" of the preceding reign, especially the abandonment of the cloister by the monks, the transfer of church property to the hands of laymen, the desecration of church buildings, the lamentable decline in voluntary offerings, and the contempt in which the holy sacrifice of the mass — the only foundation of religion — was held by a great portion of the kingdom. In conclusion, they loudly demanded the restoration of the old order of things. These complaints were heard with comparative indifference by many of the nobles, especially by those who had shared in the usurpations of the times; but a body equal in number, who had not touched the spoil, were either neuter or disposed to the bishops. Some management, therefore, was necessary — some concessions must be made, which it was intended to revoke whenever there should be a monarch ready to assist in the act. A decree was passed that bishops alone should have the power of conferring holy orders; that the tithe should be duly paid; and whoever should refuse it should have no protection from the civil power; that bequests to the church might be lawfully made and peacefully enjoyed; that the church should be supported in her actual rights and possessions. These concessions were openly opposed by two members of the rigsraad, but their opposition could avail little against the demands of one party and the timid policy of another.

The next proceeding of the rigsraad was to prepare for the election of a king. There was no intention in any quarter of excluding the Oldenburg family; but, respecting the individual, there was likely to be dissension enough. Opposed alike to Christian II, and Christian duke of Holstein, who divided the wishes of above three-fourths of the nation, the bishops declared for Prince John of Holstein, brother of the duke. The reasons which they advanced for the preference of the younger over the elder prince, were specious. Christian, they affirmed, being born while his father was merely a duke, had less claim to the crown than John, who, from his birth, was the son of a king. The former had received his early education in Holstein, a stranger to the habits, the manners, the feelings, the very language of the Danes; and had imbibed at the courts of his kinsmen, the German princes, a spirit that must necessarily be in many respects irreconcilable with the institutions of the North; while the latter was truly a Dane in birth, education, language, sentiment, and principle. But the true reason for this preference was carefully withheld by the noble ecclesiastics; and this was the tender youth of John, who was scarcely twelve years old, and who, in their hands, might be moulded to any shape. The majority exclaimed against the choice of a mere child at a time when the maturest judgment and the greatest firmness were necessary to guide the vessel of the state. At length, the contest assumed a character almost entirely religious; the Roman Catholics following the example of their spiritual heads, by declaring for John; the Protestants, with equal pertinacity, calling for the elder brother. The former, apprehensive lest violence should be done to their independence of choice by the unruly mob of Copenhagen, were anxious to gain time, by the very natural proposition, that the Norwegians, who were as deeply interested in the choice as themselves, should concur in the act. Here, too, was displayed the usual cunning of churchmen; for the majority of that people were hostile to the Reformation. As the season was too far advanced to allow the arrival of deputies from that kingdom before the winter, it was agreed that the election should be postponed until the following year. The interim each determined to employ in the manner best calculated to advance his own end.

Scarcely was this compromise effected, when the members of the rigsraad found themselves in an embarrassed position. From Duke Christian, who was too good a politician to menace them, they experienced only offers of mediation with their enemy, the governor of the Low Countries — a power that they had incensed alike by the imprisonment of Christian II and by the shackles which they had imposed on commerce. But from Lübeck, which had resolved, in active commercial spirit, to derive every advantage from the internal dissensions of a rival, they received a very different treatment. Wollenwever, the envoy of that regency, and one of the burgomasters, demanded for that all-engrossing republic the exclusion from the trade of the Baltic, of all other people, especially the English and the Dutch, to whom the Sound was to be rigorously closed. Considering the power of Lübeck, the head of the Hanseatic League, and the services which she had recently performed in behalf of northern independence, a refusal might provoke a dangerous enemy, and would certainly be construed into ingratitude. On the other hand, to exasperate the Low Countries and consequently the emperor and his allies, might be more dangerous, and would assuredly be more detrimental to the national interests. After much hesitation, a negative to the envoy's proposition was returned in terms of studied courtesy, and with many expressions of gratitude and goodwill. But these availed nothing. Foiled in his project of engrossing all the trade of the North, and of humbling the Dutch, who had become the most formidable rivals of Lübeck, Wollenwever determined on revenge. The bishops, who ruled the rigsraad, must first be overpowered; and this could be done only by contributing to the exaltation of the reformed party. By his artful representations of the danger to which the Protestant religion was exposed, and of the advantage which their respective communities must reap by an alliance with the Hanse Towns, he brought the two burgomasters of Copenhagen and Malmö — magistrates otherwise dissatisfied with the conduct of the bishops, and eager for revenge — completely within his influence. But the views of these allies were widely different: he aimed merely at perpetuating dissension, and profiting by it; they, at the termination of all dissension by the election of Prince Christian, and the consequent triumph of their own party. The conduct of the bishops, which daily became more arbitrary and more odious to the reformers, did, for the cause of the latter, more than intrigue or even arms could have effected. The two burgomasters forsook with disgust their seats in the rigsraad, and confined themselves to their magisterial duties. By so doing, they became popular in proportion to the unpopularity of the churchmen.

At length, seeing the archbishop of Lund and his suffragans openly enjoin silence on the reformed preachers, and menace with excommunication all who refused to return to the ancient church, they repaired to Duke Christian in Holstein, and exhorted him to place himself at the head of the Protestants, and seat himself on the vacant throne. Christian had the good sense to decline the dazzling offer, though he well knew that it would obtain the end proposed. He declared, that no one ought to be king of Denmark, who was not previously elected by the estates; and that he should not attempt to obtain by violence what ought to be conferred by the deliberate voice of the nation. This moderation was as much the result of good policy as of good feeling, since it would not fail to make a favourable impression on the electors. In other respects he cultivated their goodwill. He negotiated a union between the nobles of Denmark and of the two duchies, and advised a treaty of commerce between Denmark and the Low Countries. By this treaty, the Sound was opened to the Dutch vessels on payment of the usual dues. The Danish senate even entered into a defensive alliance with the queen regent of the Netherlands, and provided still farther for the security of the realm by a similar alliance with Sweden.

The alliance with the Netherlands was the more offensive to the people of Lübeck, as the two powers were then at war. Influenced by Wollenwever, the latter power bent its thoughts towards revenge — revenge on Denmark, which thus opposed its monopoly, its interests, its ambitious policy in every respect. In the attainment of so great an object, all minor ones must be disregarded: every jealousy of the Dutch was sacrificed to indignation against

the Danes; and a peace between the two commercial powers was soon negotiated. One of the conditions was that Holland might send as many vessels
as she pleased into the Baltic. For this entire change of policy we may easily
account. Lübeck now began to entertain the project of seizing for herself
the passage of the Sound, and consequently the dominion of the Baltic; then,
nothing could be so easy as to exclude Holland and all Europe from participation in the monopoly. The means for executing this magnificent project
must be an immediate war with Denmark. War, therefore, was resolved.
But who was to head the expedition? Lübeck had no citizen or vassal important or able enough to undertake such a trust. Choice was at length made
of a German count named Christopher, a member of the house of Oldenburg,
whose talents and whose ambition were well known. He was easily persuaded
to assume a command, which might possibly obtain him a sceptre, which
would certainly bring him riches, and probably avenge his imprisoned kinsman Christian II. The deliverance of that monarch was one of the pretexts
which would most justify the war in the eyes of Europe. He therefore
demanded the prisoner's enlargement from the duke of Holstein. When the
demand was refused, he did not repeat it to the Danish rigsraad, which might
have been frightened into compliance, but declared war against both Holstein
and Denmark (1534).

THE COUNT'S WAR

Christopher had raised 4,000 infantry in Germany; these, added to the
armaments which the Hanse Towns themselves furnished, made a respectable
force. With it he penetrated into Holstein, took several towns, plundered
them and the open country, and before he could be resisted by either the
duke or the Danes, returned with great plunder to Lübeck. There he obtained
large reinforcements; and then, with the burgomasters, sailed for Copenhagen. Within four leagues of that capital, he was joined by the burgomaster
of Malmö, who assured him of the good wishes of the inhabitants. He therefore with his ships blockaded the city, while with a land force he disembarked,
seized Roeskilde, forced the people to swear allegiance to Christian II, and
replaced the bishop by the famous Gustavus Trolle, whose life had been one
continued series of intrigues. That Copenhagen should offer no resistance to
the invaders, may seem extraordinary; but the majority of the inhabitants
were in favour of Christian II, and their leaders were certainly won over by
the agents of Lübeck. The count, after pillaging the two nearest towns, proceeded towards the capital, and summoned it to acknowledge the captive
monarch. The summons was obeyed by the city; and though the fortress
held out, it was soon compelled to capitulate. All Zealand was persuaded or
forced to do the same; Malmö opened its gates, and, with most of Skåne,
declared for Christian II. The bishops, the clergy, and such of the nobles as
were still hostile to that monarch, fled into Jutland, which would listen to no
proposal that involved his restoration. The isles south of Zealand submitted,
Fünen was blockaded, and Jutland menaced. In these successes, the conqueror — if he who declares himself the head of a large native party, and
triumphs by the aid of that party, may be called one — committed many
excesses. There was, at the best, little discipline among his mercenaries;
but he gave full run to their rapacity, by abandoning to them the domains of
all who were represented as unfavourable to his views. A worse evil was
the ferocity of the peasants, who, actuated by revenge against their feudal
oppressors, massacred all that were so unfortunate as to fall into their hands,
and delivered their dwellings to the flames.

Why, it may be asked, did Duke Christian not advance to the aid of the rigsraad and nobles? Two reasons may be assigned for this inactivity. The first and chief was that he was not solicited; and he knew too well the apprehensions entertained of him by the church, wantonly to obtrude the offer of his services. Besides, he was too discerning not to perceive that the progress of events was favourable to his hopes. He alone, of all the members of the Oldenburg family, was in a condition to measure arms with the invaders; and sooner or later his interference would scarcely fail to be solicited. But another reason is that he was, at this very moment, effecting a powerful diversion in favour of the kingdom by menacing Lübeck itself. That important city he invested by sea and land; and, though he could scarcely hope to reduce it, he effectually interrupted its commerce, and in other respects wasted its resources. The only consolation left — and this was no slight one — was that the arms of the regency were as successful in Denmark as they were disastrous at home.

The foresight of Duke Christian was soon justified by the event. The nobles of Jutland and Fünen began to exclaim against the obstinacy of the bishops, in excluding from the throne those who alone could save the rest of the kingdom. In a general meeting of the rigsraad at Ry, in the former province, the burgomaster of Copenhagen harangued the members with much force and much eloquence. He observed, that if the duke had been chosen, Skåne and Zealand, and the other islands would not now be in the power of Lübeck; that if the choice were not immediately made, the party of Christian II must triumph — and who present could wish for the restoration of a king always sanguinary, and rendered ferocious by exile and imprisonment? The secular members applauded the discourse, but the bishops still resisted, and would have continued to resist had not the nobles, who were outside the hall, suspected the truth, forced open the doors, rushed into the room, and exclaimed with a loud voice, that Duke Christian must be chosen. Terrified at this demonstration, the churchmen withdrew their opposition — with a protest, however, against the violence of the nobles, and on the express condition that Christian should recognise the privileges of the rigsraad and of the church. He was instantly proclaimed; deputies were sent to acquaint him with the event, at the camp before Lübeck; he hastened to meet other deputies and confirm the privileges of the rigsraad and nobles; and at Horsens, in Jutland, he received the homage of that province and Fünen. To the bishops and all ecclesiastics, he promised the continuance of their revenues, privileges, and immunities, whether they remained in the church, or embraced the Reformation; and he guaranteed to both communions perfect liberty of worship. How he kept these promises will appear in the sequel.

THE ACCESSION OF CHRISTIAN III (1534 A.D.)

No monarch ever ascended the throne in circumstances more difficult or more disheartening than those by which Christian III was surrounded. One half the kingdom held, the other half menaced, by a powerful enemy; the church, the peasantry, and most of the burgesses — constituting at least five sixths of the nation — unfriendly to his claim; the nobles themselves, his only supporters, discouraged; the empire and the Netherlands no less hostile to him than Lübeck — these conditions were surely enough to damp the enterprise of any thinking man. But Christian was in all the fire of youth; he had not experienced the chilling misfortunes of life; his ardour was unquenched; he relied on the sympathies and even the support of Sweden and the reformed princes of Germany; and he had at his command a body of martial nobles, whose interests, and even whose lives, were inseparably connected with his success. At the events of the war which followed — events complicated, uniform, and uninteresting — we can only glance.

Having prevailed on Gustavus of Sweden to make a diversion in his favour by the invasion of Skåne, Christian proceeded to attempt the deliverance of Fünen, which was now almost entirely in the hands of the count of Oldenburg. He succeeded but he had scarcely left the island to carry his arms elsewhere, when the count returned and again reduced it. That ambitious chief had other objects than the interest of the republic or that of Christian II, in whose name he had drawn the sword. Hearing of the new king's departure, he detached a part of his force into Jutland, the reduction of which would insure the submission of the whole kingdom. The attempt was an arduous one, since that province contained the most numerous, the most

CHRISTIAN III

warlike, and the most devoted portion of the Danish nobility. Yet Aalborg was taken; all Verdsyssel was occupied; devastation marked the track of the invaders, and terror preceded their march. The undisguised prayers of the peasantry for the success of men whom they hailed as their deliverers, alarmed the nobles and caused them to flee to the strong fortress of Renders. A stand was, indeed, made by the royal generals, but they were signally defeated. The moral effect of this victory was more valuable than the victory itself, since it induced the peasantry, whom fear had hitherto kept aloof, to take an active part in the war. Woe to the local tyrants on whom they laid their hands! Yet they could not perpetrate worse deeds than the invaders, or the nobles themselves, whenever the latter had the opportunity. Fortunately for Christian, Renders repelled its assailants and forced them to seek a refuge in Aalborg. Equally fortunate was the convention which, under the mediation of some reformed princes, he made with Lübeck. That republic, on the condition of his raising the siege and of respecting its territory, which was thenceforth to be neutral, engaged not to act against Holstein, which was to be equally neutral. But in regard to the war in Denmark, both parties were at liberty to push it as zealously as they wished. In accordance with this treaty, the king hastened with the troops which were thus rendered disposable to the succor of the Jutlanders, while the regency sent the defenders of Lübeck to prosecute the war in Denmark.

With the reinforcements thus obtained, the royal party laid siege to Aalborg, defended by Clement, one of the count's generals, with a considerable body of Danish peasantry. Brave as was the defence, the place was taken by assault, and every man put to the sword; two thousand rustics thus perished, while their leaders were reserved for more lingering and more painful deaths. No wonder that the people should retaliate when such horrible severity disgraced the royal army. What few rights the Jutland peasantry still held, were declared forfeited by their rebellion. During the winter which followed Christian made some overtures to the count, but they were rejected; and preparations were made for the resumption of the warfare in the spring. The count had men enough, but he wanted money to pay his German mercenaries, and this he could not obtain from the peasantry: he could only wring it from the nobles and the clergy; and in proportion to these demands upon them, were their secret aspirations for the triumph of Christian. The progress of the Swedish arms in service inspired them with new hope. Halmstad, Varberg, and Helsingborg, with the intervening region, were reduced. Malmö and Landskrona were invested; a fleet which Christian had obtained from his allies soon appeared off the coast of Fünen; and in a general action victory declared for the king. A new armament soon arrived from Lübeck headed by Albert duke of Mecklenburg, who had married a niece of Christian II. The count of Oldenburg complained bitterly of this supersession, which was most impolitic; and as he had a large body of devoted followers, he retained a share in the command. But this compromise was worse than the evil it was designed to remedy; the two chiefs were too jealous of each other ever cordially to co-operate. The necessary result was, that few trophies more were won by the invaders. Fünen was restored to the royal dominion. Zealand was next occupied, and Copenhagen invested. At the same time, detachments were spared from the royal army to commence the siege of other fortresses on the neighbouring islands, and to press those of Malmö and Landskrona, which still resisted.

Before the siege of Copenhagen, southern Norway had been induced to acknowledge Christian III. But the northern provinces, influenced by the clergy and the archbishop of Trondhjem, would listen to no terms of accommodation. Yet the adhesion of a part of that kingdom was a great advantage to the king, since it furnished him with vessels to press the siege of Copenhagen. Equally useful were those which he received from Sweden, independently of the inestimable benefit produced by the diversion of the Swedish troops in Skåne. Christian had the satisfaction to see the reconquest of Varberg, which the Lübeckers had recovered by stratagem. On this occasion, he stained his laurels by the execution of Meyer, burgomaster of Lübeck and governor of the fortress; and that, too, in opposition to the terms of the capitulation. On the rack, Meyer is said to have confessed that the republic had agreed to sell Denmark, or at least its chief fortresses, to Henry VIII of England. Henry, surely, who was no general, and whose army was in no high state of discipline, could not be so foolish as to offer money for what could never be his. Probably the whole is an invention of the Danish writers, to lessen the odium inseparable from this violation of the laws of Landskrona now capitulated; while Copenhagen and Malmö were pressed with renewed vigour. To relieve them, a new armament of eighteen vessels arrived from the Hanse Towns; and notwithstanding the opposition of the royal fleet, supplies were thrown into the former. The place, therefore, was in a condition to resist many months longer. On the other hand, early in the following year (1536), Cronenburg, the key of Copenhagen, was reduced, and some other fortresses on the islands; so that the capital in Zealand and the town in Skåne were the only places which now held for the Lübeck party. That republic was weary of the war; and after much negotiation, peace was finally made between the king and the regency. The latter retained their commercial advantages in the Baltic, and received Bornholm, which they were to hold fifty years as some indemnification for their heavy expenditure during the war. Faithful to their new engagement, they recalled their troops at Copenhagen and Malmö; but the latter, at the instance of the two generals, chose to remain, in the expectation of aid from the Netherlands. The only advantage, therefore, which the king derived from this treaty was an open sea, which the vessels of the republic had previously infested. This, however, was a great advantage, and it enabled his fleet to intercept the supplies sent from some towns in Pomerania for the besieged. His next success was the capitulation of Malmö.

But Copenhagen, without provisions, without hope, except from a doubtful reinforcement promised by the Netherlands, still held out. Famine at length appeared; horses, dogs, cats, and the vilest aliments were all consumed; and starvation seemed inevitable, unless the obstinate chiefs could be brought to capitulate. An evil scarcely less tolerable was the license of the soldiers, who went from house to house to seize any bread that might remain, to violate the women, and often to murder the fathers or husbands. Some died of hunger in the public streets, more in their beds; the survivors, pale, emaciated, scarcely able to walk across the floor of their own houses, awaited in despair the issue of this dreadful extremity. These privations were less felt by the soldiery than by the inhabitants; yet the soldiery found them intolerable, and were the first to make overtures of submission to the king. A capitulation was soon negotiated. The two chiefs were to be sent to their respective lordships, followed by all the Germans who chose to go; but they were to leave their artillery and stores of every kind. There were no conditions imposed on Albert; but the count of Oldenburg was obliged to swear never to re-enter Denmark, and never to make war on the king, his subjects, or his allies. All the citizens who wished were also at liberty to accompany the German mercenaries; but two leaders were excepted, Munter and Bogbinder, who were to remain in the kingdom. Yet even these were assured of pardon; and so were all the citizens who remained. Albert, the count, and many followers, embarked while Christian made his public entry into Copenhagen. The spectacle of the distress to which the citizens were reduced is said to have moved him; but if he had such compassionate feelings, they were sure to be absorbed by his thirst of vengeance on the originators of the late resistance. But he knew how to dissemble, and his entry was hailed with joy by the famished inhabitants [July, 1536].

THE DIET OF COPENHAGEN (1536 A.D.)

In the opinion of Christian and his Lutheran adherents, these originators were no other than the bishops, the destruction of whose order had been determined in the royal mind long before the fall of Copenhagen. Probably they were not ignorant of this hostile feeling towards them, when they so zealously resisted his election; but in that resistance they were justified alike by the constitution and their duty to the church. From the time they had acknowledged Christian, and received his engagement to protect them in their actual rights, they had taken no part in the war against him. What, indeed, could they expect, in the event of the former Christian's restoration, but a persecution more bitter than they had before experienced? Passively, but not without anxiety, they had watched the progress of events; and now that the king was master of all Denmark, they could only trust to the royal faith for their continued security. But that he cared very little for such engagements was evident from his treatment of Meyer and from his avowed intention of bringing to justice one whom in the recent capitulation he had solemnly agreed to pardon. This was Bogbinder, who, to escape the fate designed him, swallowed poison. But it was still more evident from his plot

[1536 A.D.]

against the bishops. His first step was to exclude them from the rigsraad; to interdict them from all authority in temporal concerns. But his thirst for revenge, and, still more, his avarice, were not to be thus satisfied. It was not difficult for him, a conqueror, to procure the sanction of the rigsraad to any proposal affecting churchmen, especially when they knew that they were to share in the spoil. Having privately assembled them, a resolution was put to abolish the temporal authority of the bishops, to confiscate their revenues for the use of the state, to destroy their jurisdiction in the church as well as in the state, and not to restore them if even a general council should decree their restoration, unless the king, the rigsraad, and the estates of the realm should see fit to revoke the present resolution. It was also agreed to adhere in future to the Protestant religion, to defend and advance its interests. An act embodying these resolutions was signed by each member, who promised to keep the secret.

At this very crisis, the archbishop of Lund and the bishop of Roeskilde arrived, with the intention of testifying their duty to the sovereign. Both were arrested, and committed to close custody. At the same time, in accordance with a preconcerted design, all the other bishops of the kingdom were seized — some by open force, some by perfidy. To justify this extraordinary step in the eyes of the nation, and of all Europe, Christian convoked the estates at Copenhagen — if those could be called estates where the clergy, one of the most important sections, were not present, because not summoned. From an elevated stage, on which the king and the members of the rigsraad appeared, he inveighed against the whole church, especially against the bishops: they had opposed by every species of violence the progress of the Reformation; they had persecuted the ministers of the gospel; they had promulgated statutes and decrees contrary to the national laws; they had been tyrants within their dioceses; they had resisted the election of the king; and were, in short, the source of all the troubles which the realm had suffered, or was suffering. Accusations so indefinite, so vague, so unsatisfactory in every legal sense, would have had no weight where the accusers were not the judges and predetermined to find a verdict of guilty. That verdict was given; it annihilated for ever the haughty domination of the clergy, and declared that the work of the Reformation must be completed by a total abolition of the Roman Catholic worship. It adjudged the vast revenues of the church to the wants of the state, to the support of the Protestant ministers, to the maintenance of the poor, to the foundation of hospitals, and to the sustentation of the university and the schools.

In virtue of the sentence, a public edict appointed reformed theologians called superintendants, one to each of the vacant dioceses (the name of bishop, however, was soon restored). It united for ever to the crown all the palaces, towns, fortresses, villages, estates, and revenues of every kind, that had hitherto belonged to the church. It allowed the monks and nuns either to leave the cloister, or to remain in it provided they agreed to lead an edifying life and hear the preaching of God's word. It divided the tithe into three equal portions, of which one went to the feudal superior of the parish, one to the crown, and one to the support of the resident minister. Some schools and hospitals were founded, and some lands were appropriated to the reward of such theologians as might distinguish themselves by their acquirements; but the great portion of church property in Denmark, as in some other countries, went neither to learning nor religion, neither to poverty nor sickness.[d] [To reorganise the church Christian summoned from Germany the learned Dr. Bugenhagen, of whom Pontoppidan gives the following account:]

Doctor Johann Bugenhagen, otherwise called Pomeranus, belonged to an old and noble family, although his father had held the office of alderman at Wollin in Pomerania, where he himself was born on June 24th, 1485. He pursued his academic studies at Greifswald, and in the 20th year of his age became rector of Treptow, having early given many proofs, not only of skill in languages, but of true piety and devotion; for he was ill content with the ancient and frigid system of outward worship, and insisted at every opportunity upon faith, love, and the true obedience of the heart. Nevertheless, he could not at first rid himself of a prejudice, derived from hearsay, against the doctrines of Luther; but in 1520, when the said teacher's book upon the Babylonian captivity was shown to him amidst a company of good friends, and his opinion demanded thereon, he said, after reading a few pages, that since Christ had suffered, many heretics had shamefully misled and distracted the church of God, but none so mischievously as Luther. But it was not long before the scales fell from the good man's eyes, and having read the whole book in solitude and maturely reflected upon it, he spoke to his friends and colleagues in a very different tone: "What need of many words? The whole world is blind and lies in outer darkness; Luther alone sees the truth." His friends agreed with him, but likewise fell with him under the displeasure of the bishop of Kammin, who expelled them from the town.

Under these circumstances Bugenhagen went to Wittenberg, where he found Karlstad in the full tide of iconoclasm, and opposed him in such acts of violence. He soon became intimately acquainted with Luther, who was returning from his Patmos, and likewise with Melanchthon, and, by the magistrate of that place, was first appointed regular town preacher (*Stadt-Prediger*) and, soon after, professor of Holy Writ. Both these offices he held so dear that he would never exchange them for the bishoprics which were several times offered to him. Meanwhile his reputation for great piety and profound erudition was so spread abroad that he was summoned to various places in the north of the empire, to draw up new systems of church organisation and to give good counsel and help in all that concerned the Reformation. When he was in Hamburg about this business, and while the Flensburg *colloquium* with Melchior Hoffman *in puncto S. cœnæ* was in prospect, he received his first call to Denmark. He was likewise present at the aforesaid *colloquium*, and there pleased Christian, the prince royal, who was also present, so well that when, in the year 1536, the latter ascended the throne to which his claim had been disputed, and resolved to depose the popish bishops and to introduce the Protestant form of church government, he summoned Bugenhagen to the country once more as a reformer of much experience. As it appears from his letters, he arrived at Copenhagen at the beginning of the so-called dogdays. Soon afterwards he had the honour of crowning the king and queen, ordaining seven superintendents, presiding in conjunction with Petrus Palladius, bishop of Zealand, at the First synod of Copenhagen — which was convoked from all the provinces to establish new church ordinances — and providing for the regulation of its *lectiones* at the University of Copenhagen.

At the beginning of the year 1539, he journeyed into Saxony for a short time, but speedily returned, in June, and was present at the ratification of the ecclesiastical ordinances at the diet of Odense. He then went to Copenhagen again, lectured at the university, and frequently preached at court upon the psalms of David. He remained there, engaged in such affairs, until the year 1542, and enjoyed great favour with the king; so much, indeed, that in the year 1541 the wealthy bishopric of Schleswig was offered to him. This he declined, saying, "Should I act thus, it might be said that we thrust the popish bishops from their sees to set ourselves in them." From which, among other things, his humility and moderation are clearly manifest. This man is said, by his mildness, frequently to have moderated the vehemence of Luther. In 1542 he returned to Wittenberg for the last time, and greatly extolled the love that had been displayed towards him in Denmark. During his stay in Denmark he wrote various things concerning the state of the church there to his colleagues at Wittenberg.

After his departure men would have been glad to see him return to Denmark for the fourth time and there abide till death. This the king asked him to do — in a letter dated Gottorp, *die trium Regum*, 1543 — in which he says, among other things: "Therefore we have thought upon you with favour, and have desired to request you, if it be in any way possible, to come hither again, since we should be glad to have such an old Pomeranian or Chaw-bacon, who might perhaps endure the air of this country better than another. We would take such care of him that he should have cause to be grateful to us."

But Bugenhagen was already a man of sixty, enfeebled by many labours and desired to end his days in his beloved Wittenberg — which he did on April 20th, 1558.[h]

NORWAY AND PROTESTANTISM

The bishops continued in prison for some time after the diet of Copenhagen; but at length, they were all liberated except one, on their engagement never to disturb the new order of things. That one was the bishop of Roeskilde, whom no entreaties, no threats, could induce to submit, and who therefore died in confinement. From this moment must be dated the entire ruin of the Romish church in Denmark. Liberty did not gain by the change. The reformed clergy had not influence enough to curb that wild and licentious power by which both thrones and altars, both freedom and religion, have been frequently swept away. The burgesses also were too insignificant *per se* to offer any resistance; and the peasantry were, as we have already stated, deprived of what little voice they had enjoyed in the general assemblies. No check, therefore, remained on the inevitable usurpations of the nobility.

The decree of the diet of Copenhagen is remarkable for two other points deserving of the reader's consideration. There was evidently a compromise between the crown and the nobles. (1) It was asserted that, as experience had proved the danger of leaving the throne vacant, the recurrence of such evils must be averted by the recognition of Duke Frederick, eldest son of the king, as successor to the throne. If he died before the father, then the next son should be the designated heir; and if all the sons died, the estates, during the life of the king, should be bound to name a successor, and that intended successor should assume the title of Prince of Denmark. Here was the legal establishment of the hereditary principle. The price which Christian paid for it was, first, a large participation, as we have just seen, in the titles, and, we may add, in the confiscated church lands. (2) But the other articles of the decree to which we have alluded will equally establish the fact of a compromise. The king confirmed to the nobles the power of life and death over their vassals; the infliction of fines up to forty marks; and "all other privileges, powers, and prerogatives which the king himself could exercise on his domains."

The conduct of this monarch towards Norway does not increase our respect for his memory. The southern provinces of that country had, as we have before related, acknowledged him; the northern, influenced by the archbishop of Trondhjem and the clergy, had refused to do so. Before the reduction of Copenhagen, yet when his ultimate triumph was inevitable, he despatched three members of the rigsraad to Norway, demanding not only his election by all the estates, but a subsidy for the continuance of the war. The former demand was received with coldness, the latter with indignation. In the north, the people called on the archbishop to prevent the election. To that call he, who was one of the most violent of men, instantly responded; and, as the head of the regency which had been established, arrested the bishop of Christiania, the bishop of Hammer, and another senator in the interests of Christian. He did more: he procured the condemnation of all the senators who had offered the crown to the "Danish tyrant." Some were put to death; some were imprisoned; and the popular mind throughout the realm — in the south no less than in the north — became hostile to his claims. But what dependence can be placed on such a basis? The victories of Christian inspired the Roman Catholics with fear, the Protestants with hope. That he would struggle for the crown, and struggle successfully, became by degrees the general opinion — so much so, that even the primate released the senators whom he had imprisoned and made overtures of submission. As usual, they were accepted by the royal officers, with a belief that they would not be ratified by the king. But whether ratified or not, one advantage would be gained — his immediate election. It was gained, and the royal perfidy was soon made apparent by the equipment of a fleet to seize the archbishop and other persons supposed to be unfriendly to the new king. Warned of the fate designed for him, the churchman fled to the Netherlands. His metropolis was seized; while another royal general marched on Christiania, which had also refused to acknowledge Christian. The bishop capitulated; so did all the southern towns which had not already submitted. What was the reward? At this very time, and immediately after the destruction of the Danish bishops and clergy, a royal decree forever destroyed the independence of Norway by declaring it to be an integral portion of the Danish monarchy, "just the same as Jutland, Fünen, Zealand, or Skåne." Nor was this a vain menace — it was immediately carried into effect. By degrees, too, the Roman Catholic religion was extirpated, and the Protestant faith established: nor was there any open opposition to the change. But in Iceland there was much resistance; and it required an armament to convince that sequestered people how necessary the Reformation was to their everlasting welfare.[d]

The state of the church in this island during the year 1540 has been described as half evangelist, particularly in the southern part, under Bishop Marten Enersön of Skálholt, an enthusiastic reformer, though still half popish. The northern part, the bishopric of Holum, was under Bishop Jon Arnesön, who, although he received, as the others had, the royal command to abstain from manifest superstitions and to reform his see, not only refused to comply, but also endeavoured in every possible way to contravene the activities of his fellow bishop. In this he was especially active in the year 1547, and caused Bishop Marten Enersön such distress by his knavish tricks that Enersön found himself necessitated to make the long sea-journey to Denmark in person, in order to lay before the king his own distress and the troubles of the church. When he had arrived in Kolding, he was given gracious audience by his majesty; he took the oath of fidelity and received thereupon a royal *protectorium* for his person and teachings, with the assurances of adequate help for the propagation of the Reformation throughout his fatherland.

[1551 A.D.]

His enemy, Bishop Jon Arnesön, received an imperative summons to present himself before the king. But for such a journey Arnesön had no inclination. Instead, he instituted a fresh rebellion, put himself at the head of three hundred men, attacked Bishop Marten and took him prisoner, deposed the royal judge who should have executed the king's commands and (by which one sees that he was in the matter of celibacy not papistically inclined) installed his own son in his place. Besides this, he was reported to have had the intention of placing himself and the whole island under the protection of the English. In Denmark there was much dismay at this news, and great bitterness was felt against the scoundrel. But for certain reasons this state of things was for a time endured, and the rebellious bishop was not only spared excommunication, but was pronounced exonerated by royal patent.

For the sake of sequence, we will here give a summary of this affair, although in actual time it belongs to the chronicle of 1551. For in that year it dawned upon the king that the time was ripe for crushing Jon Arnesön, and for leaving the Protestant faith an open path in Iceland. Therefore two ships were sent with the two knights, Axel Tuul and Christopher Trund-Trundsön, and five hundred soldiers, carrying with them a command dated from Flensburg on the Thursday after Low Sunday, to give the imprisoned Bishop Marten his liberty, and, should he be already dead, to ordain another evangelist teacher bishop; but especially to seize the persons of Jon Arnesön and his sons, and bring them prisoners to Flensburg; also again to put the inhabitants of the land to the oath of fidelity and duty. But before these ships and their passengers could arrive, as they did about Whitsuntide, their trouble was saved them by another person, Bishop Jon Arnesön's father-in-law, a man of wealth and consideration, David Gudmundarson. Jon Arnesön expected no good of this man, and dared not push his designs to fulfilment, or have himself, with the aid of the English, constituted king of the country, until he had put Gudmundarson out of the way — knowing him for a powerful man, devoted to the Protestant doctrines, and a loyal subject of the king.

To effect his purpose he gathered a force of five hundred soldiers, and took the field against Gudmundarson. The latter made all counter preparations with what haste he could, but could only muster three hundred armed men. With these he met his enemies boldly, but, before the attack, made a sensible speech to his faithless countrymen, representing to them how perfidious their conduct was, and how thankless in the end they might expect to find the service of the popish bishop. When by this means he had won some minds and persuaded them to return to their duty, he attacked the remainder with so much spirit that he soon overmastered them; and the often-mentioned bishop, together with two of his sons, fell prisoners to him, whereupon he had them all three beheaded, urged by the consideration that, if they were spared a new revolt to give them freedom would be instigated by the bishop's third son, who had escaped. When, after this event, help arrived from Denmark, the knights in authority made one Oluf Hultesön evangelist bishop and absolute head of the see of Holle, adding all necessary aids for the propagation of the Reformation of the church similar to those which ten years previously had been successfully carried out in the Skálholt see.[h]

The transactions of Christian III with Germany in themselves were of no great moment. His position, in regard both to the emperor and to the Roman Catholics, naturally threw him into the arms of the Protestant party; and he shared the fate of that party. He was fortunate enough to defeat all the attempts of the elector palatine, who had married a daughter of Christian II, on the crown. He was equally successful in humbling the Dutch, and in opposing all the designs of the emperor to undermine his authority The Peace of Speier (1543) reconciled him with Charles V as sovereign of the Netherlands, but not as emperor. By adhering to the league, he was necessarily the enemy of that monarch; but he exhibited no great zeal in the reformed cause, and he was generally reproached for the indifference with which he beheld the most deadly blows aimed at it by the opposite party. With Sweden he maintained pacific relations to the close of his life. Not that war was not often impending, but both he and his ally always contrived to adopt some compromise by which actual hostilities were averted.

THE DEATH OF CHRISTIAN III

Two other things must be recorded of Christian III. Towards the close of his life, he so far relaxed in his behaviour to Christian II as to transfer that unfortunate king to Kallundborg in Zealand, to enjoy more room, less restraint, better food, and more indulgence in every respect — as much, perhaps, as could be enjoyed consistently with the prisoner's safe custody. The other event relates to the injudicious partition of Holstein and Schleswig. In conformity with a pernicious usage, the king, considering that his brothers had a right to a share of the inheritance, reluctantly consented to invest two of them with extensive domains (his third brother, being a Romish ecclesiastic, had no share in the inheritance). This division, as we shall have too frequent occasion to record, was the source of the worst evils to the monarchy. Christian died in 1559.[d]

Pontoppidan's Estimate of Christian III

Christian III, under God the true reformer of the Danish church, was born at Gottorp on the 12th of August, 1504. In early youth he was sent by his father Frederick, at that time duke of Holstein, to his brother-in-law, the elector Joachim I of Brandenburg, to be educated at his court. Although the latter, who was his mother's brother, was zealously devoted to popery, Prince Christian had opportunities of gathering so much information concerning the religious quarrels then just arisen in Germany that his mind was early disinclined to popery and well disposed to the new doctrines proclaimed by Luther. Of this he gave proof early, when in the seventeenth year of his age he went with the aforesaid prince, his uncle, to the diet at Worms. There it came to pass that, in a church wherein the emperor Charles and many princes were assembled, a Franciscan monk inveighed vehemently against Luther and his heretical followers. The sermon ended, he knelt down to pray, and accidentally let the cord of his order wherewith he was girded slip through a chink in the pulpit. Prince Christian, who was seated just below the pulpit, delayed not to make the cord fast with a knot, so that the monk could not rise up again until he had summoned help. Whereupon he, noting the trick played on him, cried out: "My Lord Emperor, if even in your sovereign presence they do not refrain from such treatment of us poor monks, what will not be done in your absence?" When the emperor afterwards met our prince at dinner, and heard that it was he who had played the trick on the monk, he is reported to have laughed and said of him that it might be this was a token that he would give the monks more cause for annoyance in his day; which also came to pass in Reformation times. We may infer, from this and other proofs, that in his early years he was somewhat over-sprightly and almost of a flighty temperament; which may likewise be the reason why in the twenty-first year of his age he married Princess Dorothea of Lauenburg, who was at that time fifteen years old, in direct opposition to the will of his father, who at first looked upon the marriage with a very unfavourable eye. Until Christian ascended the throne, 1535, by the election of the Danish estates, he lived with her at the castle of Hadersleben, as governor of the two principalities.

But since this youthful precipitancy was but *vitium naturae*, not *animi*, the lapse of years and the grace of God, which wrought powerfully in his heart, changed and amended all this in such degree that Christian not only grew into a most admirable ruler well worthy of the purple, but also, as his name denoted, into a true Christian and a man after God's own heart, whereof so many evidences are extant that only a few of the most weighty can be cited. To his fear of God Arild Hvitfeld,[i] among others, bears witness in the words: "He led a devout life; no day passed on which he did not make his prayer to God on his knees, and have the Bible read to him in his chamber, and the psalms of David sung.

He was meek, charitable, and compassionate to such a degree that, when his notorious enemies Count Christopher of Oldenburg and Duke Albert of Mecklenburg were reduced to such straits in the protracted siege of Copenhagen, that they had nothing to eat and must have died of hunger, he sent certain refreshments and personal necessaries *expresse* for them into the town, and when they afterwards came humbly into his camp with white staves in their hands, he received them into favour as though they had never given him trouble. Blasphemers, murderers, and adulterers he did not readily pardon. But save in these cases he was loth that blood should be shed, and in punishments as in rewards he was a prudent ruler. He usually travelled through the country yearly, taking a few councillors with him, that in the principal towns of every province he might hear the complaints of those who were in distress, and remedy them as far as in him lay. With his neighbours he lived in peace and confidence, and after having successfully and valiantly put down the rebellion plotted in the interregnum, and the sanguinary civil wars, he would not hear of war any more, though he was frequently provoked to it. The great work on which, above all else, Christian's desires and inclinations were set, and for which Heaven had raised him up in these perilous times, was the very necessary task of reforming the radically corrupt system of the church and the schools of Denmark.

The death of this king, like his life, was admirable and worthy beyond the wont of men, hence I hold it good for edification to cite certain *specialia*. Though of his body he was well-grown, strong, and robust, he did not live as long as was expected, but only to the fifty-fourth year and fourth month of his age. An obstruction of the so-called "golden vein," from which he had suffered many times before, compelled him to take to his bed in the castle of Arnsburg at Kolding in December, 1558, and gave no uncertain warnings of the approach of death. But another herald is said to have warned him likewise; to wit, an angel or, as Selneccerus expresses it, a man in white garments, who appeared to the king eight days before his death, as he lay in bed, though (as he himself strongly asseverated) neither sleeping nor wandering in mind, and who, drawing near, thus addressed him: "On the coming New Year's Day thy sickness will end and be followed by eternal health!" Neither his chaplain in ordinary, Magister Paulus Noviomagus, nor his physician Cornelius ab Hamsfurth, could dissuade him from putting his trust in this glorious vision of consolation; but when New Year's Day, or the 1st of January, 1559, was come, he comforted his wife, blessed the royal children, bestowed gifts on his servants, begged forgiveness of all he had unwittingly offended, and exhorted his councillors that they should act according to their conscience, and loyally and honestly serve his son Frederick, who was then on his way from Malmö but had not yet arrived; that they should be vigilant in the maintenance of law and order, and should rather increase than diminish legacies bequeathed to churches, schools, and the poor. After that, to all men's amazement, he said, with cheerful voice and glad gestures, "Now I will sing, and you must sing with me, that it may be said that the king sang himself to the grave." Whereupon he himself started the hymn of praise taken from the 103rd psalm, "Praise the Lord, O my soul," etc., and when he came to the words, "As a father pitieth," his sanctified soul almost imperceptibly took flight. His inanimate body was at first buried in the church of St. Knud at Odense. His son afterwards had him borne to Roeskilde and buried under a very splendid marble mausoleum. Since I can find no epitaph upon this king, I will substitute for it the words of Reusner, quoted by Herr Lackmann: "His" (Christian III's) "royal capital was an eye of wisdom, a scale of justice, a seat of valour, a criterion of moderation, a pattern of honour, a well of kindness, an assembly of the liberal arts, a school of learning, a holy place for teachers of the church, a table for the poor, a refuge for the innocent; and he himself, a most godly Christian and indomitable prince. His motto was, *Mein Trost zu Gott allein, sonst andern kein* (My trust in God alone, and in no other).[h]

CHAPTER VIII

GUSTAVUS VASA TO CHARLES IX

[1523-1611 A.D.]

GUSTAVUS VASA ASCENDS THE THRONE (1523 A.D.)

The fall and flight of King Christian II cast the whole burden of the struggle against Sweden's ruler and the Wend states upon Severin Norby's shoulders. Norby as King Christian's governor ruled Gotland with the stronghold of Visborg and had command of the Baltic where he conducted his king's war against the Swedes and Lübeck. He took all the enemy's goods wherever he could find them, and he captured every ship he could, which went to and fro from the Wend Hanse cities and Dantzic to any of the parts of Sweden which were in the power of the kingdom's deliverer, and rich was the booty from that privateering, otherwise the war would soon have come to an end, as Norby could get no funds from King Christian.

At the time when Gustavus Vasa was chosen ruler in Vadstena there had been talk of placing him on the throne of Sweden. Then he declined the crown, but when the fresh insurrection betokened an irreconcilable breach with the other country it was necessary for Sweden to have a king. It was therefore natural and just that the diet in Strengnäs should choose the regent to be Sweden's king, and there could be no question of anyone but Gustavus. The 7th of June, 1523, was the ever-to-be-remembered day in the history of the North when the first king of the Vasa family ascended the throne.

Then the town of Kalmar was taken by Arvid Vestgöthe on the 27th of May; on the 7th of July the castle of Kalmar fell; and before the middle of June the city and castle of Stockholm also capitulated. On St. John's day, 1523, King Gustavus made his entry into his nearly deserted capital, and before the end of the year Finland was also taken from Norby's men. Even districts beyond Sweden's boundaries were conquered. If King Christian had not threatened the new ruler in Denmark and Severin Norby had not continued the war from Visborg with Sweden and Lübeck, the two new kings would soon have been at war with each other. However, Lübeck would not permit that: she wished to have peace between Sweden and Denmark, both as a condition for King Christian's expulsion, and for the freedom of the Baltic; and that could not be until Gotland had ceased to be the centre of a war which stopped one of the means of intercourse for their kingdom.

Lübeck regarded Gustavus' success and accession to the throne essentially as her own work, and she now wanted to be rewarded for her aid. The men of Lübeck meant to have in Gustavus a useful instrument for their plans, and to be in a position to keep him in dependence upon them. At the appointed diet at Strengnäs two of Lübeck's councillors demanded payment

OLOFSBORG FORTRESS, FINLAND

from the new king for Lübeck's outlay and great expenses. At that moment when the war in Sweden was still going on, and Gustavus had a considerable number of soldiers to satisfy in order to take over the government in that devastated land, he could naturally not produce a sum of over 69,000 marks, and the people of Lübeck would not consent to accept paper promises alone.

King Gustavus thus found himself obliged to consent to the proposed Strengnäs *Privilegium* of the 10th of June, 1523, which shows how the Hanse Towns would have treated the whole of the North if they had been able; because according to this *Privilegium* King Gustavus and his council had to give the sustenance of the whole of the Swedish people into their power. Nothing can show their self-interest plainer than these articles:

This agreement secured to Lübeck and Dantzic and their confederacy freedom from all taxes and other imposts everywhere in the kingdom. No foreigner of any land or nation was permitted to buy or sell in Stockholm, Kalmar, or any other place in the kingdom, except those of Lübeck and Dantzic and their confederacy and those whom the merchants of Lübeck should see fit to privilege. Neither should permission be granted to anybody else at any future time. Moreover no foreigners were allowed to be citizens either in Stockholm or Kalmar or to have permission to sail to other cities in the kingdom than those named.[b]

Though in possession of the object for which he had so long fought and so long intrigued, Gustavus refused to be immediately crowned. His pre-

[1523 A.D.]

text was that so long as Sweden was polluted by a hostile foot he would not consent to any public rejoicings: his real motive was to evade the oaths which he well knew the clergy would, on that occasion, impose upon him. His intrigues were now directed to the augmentation of the royal authority; and he obtained, from the gratitude or fear of the states, concessions which had been granted to none of his predecessors. The public voice called upon him to procure the liberation of the late administrator's widow and the other ladies who had lingered in captivity ever since the massacre of Stockholm, under the eyes, first of Christian and now of Frederick, his successor. He was for some time evidently averse to the return of the princess, since she had borne to Sten Sture two sons, who might trouble him at some future period. But he yielded to the popular voice, and indeed his own reason told him that he should have less to apprehend under the influence of a monarch who, though outwardly amicable, was secretly hostile to his elevation. He received them and their mother with much external respect; lodged them in his own palace; and to be secure against her being made the instrument of some enterprising, ambitious noble, married her to a man of bounded intellect, without courage, without weight in the state. Her eldest son too soon descended to the tomb; and the younger, being merely an infant, could not for many years cause him any uneasiness.

GUSTAVUS AND THE CLERGY

To abase the clergy, yet without appearing their enemy, was an object that no monarch whose dissimulation was less profound than that of Gustavus could have attained. Nothing indeed can equal the caution or the effectiveness of his measures. He began by nominating to the vacant sees such ecclesiastics as he knew were devoted to his will. He forced the chapter of Upsala to make another election, in lieu of Archbishop Trolle, who remained in Denmark occupied in preparing the restoration of Christian. That body had no right to venture on such a step; but violence induced them to cite the absent prelate to appear, and, on his non-appearance, to unite their suffrages in behalf of the royal candidate, Johannes Magnus, the celebrated historian of Sweden.

His next object was to encourage, underhand, the preaching of the Lutheran doctrines; and when the party was sufficiently strong to throw off the mask, seize the revenues of the dominant church and abolish her worship. When pressed by Lars Anderson [Laurentius Andreæ], a man of low birth but of great talents and greater ambition, whom he had elevated from a subordinate post to the dignity of chancellor, to submit to the ceremony of his coronation, he replied that he was well acquainted with the effect such a ceremony must have, but that he could not, in his actual circumstances, consent to its performance. He should, he added, never think himself a king — never be able to support the proper dignity of the office — until he were in possession of all the fortresses held by the bishops; until he had reunited to the crown all the church lands and revenues which his predecessors had alienated from it. He confessed, however, that he was afraid to venture on such a measure, knowing as he did the influence which the clergy exercised over their flocks.

Anderson, who was a Lutheran at heart, endeavoured to remove the royal scruples by reasoning in which there was much truth and some falsehood. The king needed not arguments, but aid, in the course which he had resolved to pursue; and he was overjoyed to find his chancellor as clearsighted as himself. Both agreed that the first and most necessary step, the foundation of all future proceedings, was to increase the number of Lutherans, without seeming to notice them. In accordance with their secret scheme, new doctors, new missionaries were brought from Germany; and those who were already in Sweden were privately informed by the chancellor that they might disseminate their opinions in the confidence that they would not be opposed by the monarch. Emboldened by this intimation, they preached with less secrecy. As they were superior in eloquence and knowledge to the established clergy, as they had that fervour which distinguishes the missionaries of a new creed, and which has more influence over mankind than either, their success was prodigious.

As the king witnessed the rapid advance of the new doctrines, he proceeded to assail the clergy in matters where he knew he should be supported by most Roman Catholic laymen. The jurisdiction of the bishop and his officials had, in all countries — in Sweden quite as much as anywhere else — encroached on that of the temporal judges. Fines and other penalties were exacted for offences which the canons, indeed, denounced, but which, in the best ages of Christianity, had never been amenable to any tribunal; so that the church could raise a fruitful harvest from the disorders of society (and most crimes of this nature were commutable by money), she cared little for either religion or morals. By degrees, Gustavus abolished this onerous jurisdiction; and, even in cases where no just complaint could be made against the ecclesiastical tribunals, he substituted for them those of the royal judges. The clergy were loud in their murmurs: to punish them he resorted to an expedient which none of his predecessors would have ventured to adopt — he billeted his troops on their domains during the long winters. To annoy the monks especially, whom he cordially hated, he assigned their houses to his cavalry, who dwelt in them as securely as in any hostel. Some of the more obnoxious monasteries were commanded to exhibit the charters by which they held their lands; and such as could not (during the civil troubles many had been lost or destroyed), were at once deprived of their possessions. All these were so many preparatory measures, designed to accustom the people to see the humiliation of the church, and to prepare them for the far greater innovations contemplated.

One of the most popular missionaries of the Reformation was Olaus or Olaf Petri, a divine of great zeal, great eloquence, considerable talent, and undaunted courage. To prove that the peculiar doctrines of the Catholic church were not to be found in the Scriptures, but were the inventions of men, he published, in the Swedish language, a translation of the New Testament. This was, in the main, a translation of Luther's German version; it contained the same bold license; and, as it was peculiarly adapted to the understanding of the vulgar, it made a profound impression on the national mind. Yet the Scriptures, however perverted by human error in their transfusion into other dialects, have always a captivating simplicity about them that finds its way to the heart. Thousands who had never before learned to read now applied themselves to the task, that they might be able to judge for themselves how far the new doctors were justified in forsaking the ancient church. In great alarm, the bishops called on the king to suppress the new version, to silence its advocates, and even to punish them as heretics. As he had hitherto shown no partiality for the Reformation; as he had listened to none of its apostles, but had constantly attended the established service, some hopes were entertained that he might be induced to arrest the progress of the missionaries. With much apparent indifference, he observed that he was ready to abandon Olaus, or any other doctor, that should be convicted of heresy; but he must hear before he would condemn. He had heard nothing against the morals of the preachers; and he was afraid that there was more acrimony among churchmen of all denominations, more contention for points trifling in themselves, than became the ministers of peace. The archbishop, who was the spokesman of the deputation, was both surprised and offended with the gentle language of the king. He engaged to prove, that some of Olaus' doctrines, so far from being idle and useless speculations, had a most pernicious tendency. The offer was accepted, and a day appointed for a public disputation at Upsala.

When that day arrived, the king, with a numerous court, with many of his nobles and dependents, repaired to the place of meeting. As the bishops were to be the judges of the controversy, they prudently refrained from taking any part in the debate; and they devolved the defence of the Catholic doctrines on a theologian named Gallus [or Galle]. Olaus was there, secure of the royal protection, and disposed to spare none of the abuses which had crept into the church. But such exhibitions have never been of much service; they may gratify partisans; they never carry conviction to the hearer. The two adversaries could not agree on their premises. Olaus would receive Scripture only in matters whether of faith or discipline; Gallus gave equal authority to tradition, to the decisions of synods and councils, to the sentiments of the ancient doctors. Whatever might be thought of the other points of dispute, most of the nobles present applauded Olaf when he demanded a scriptural warrant for the enjoyment of temporal principalities by the clergy. What resemblance was there between Peter the fisherman and his pretended vicar, the Roman pontiff? In what did the bishops of that age resemble the Apostle of the Gentiles? Did not the Gospel itself expressly and earnestly prohibit all ecclesiastics from seeking, or even holding the dignities and riches of the world? Here Gallus was vanquished. He was more successful when he began to assail the mistranslation, the wilful perversions of the new version of the Scriptures.

The king interposed by requesting the archbishop to make a new and more accurate translation. This, he observed, would be the most effectual way to convict Luther and Olaus of error, and would do much good in Sweden, where very few could read the Latin vulgate. For his own part, he should read an authorised, orthodox version with much pleasure; and the nobles, who were always intent on treading in his footsteps, made the same request. Unable to refuse, the archbishop gave the necessary directions, and within a short period the new translation appeared. This was just what the monarch wanted. To place two different versions before his subjects was to familiarize them with religious matters, to exercise their reason, and teach them to rely on their own judgment in the interpretation of God's Word. It may be doubted whether the authorised version did not occasion nearly as much injury to the church as that of Olaus. Little fit was the simple-minded prelate to deal with so astute, so sagacious a hypocrite as the Swedish king.

Olaus was not slow to publish the acts of this dispute, and to claim all the honour of victory. They were read with much interest. So rapid was the progress of the new missionaries that the houses of the greater part of the nobles were thrown open to them, and they were not merely allowed but invited to preach. It was now that Gustavus, overjoyed at the sensation which had been created, determined to commence his long-meditated career of spoliation. Assembling his senators at Stockholm, he besought them to put the realm into a defensive state — to repair the fortresses and to augment the military force.   In conformity with his views they replied that the public revenues were reduced to nothing, in consequence of the monopoly enjoyed by Lübeck; that the people were exhausted by their past efforts; that the only way to replenish the treasury was to pay the regency of Lübeck, and open the ports to the vessels of all nations which should pay the usual duties.   But, however necessary the discharge of the debt, where could the means be found for that purpose?   The chancellor came at once to the object of the government.   In his anxiety not to oppress his loving subjects the nobles, burghers, and rural inhabitants, the king proposed that two thirds of the tithe should, for a time at least, be applied to the support of the armaments required by the public weal: and as to the debt due to the regency of Lübeck, might it not be discharged by the superfluous church plate?   All present (for all had been gained) applauded this proof of paternal regard on the part of their monarch, and two decrees were passed — one that two thirds of the tithe should be apportioned in the way proposed; the other that the church bells, no less than the plate, should be seized in every province, every district, for the uses of the state.

The blow came on the church like a thunderbolt.   The primate flew to the court to remonstrate with the king on this plunder of the holy things. The latter listened with patience, and then proudly answered that the useless ornaments on which so much value was placed were surely better employed in the service of the state than in idle pomp; and that the tithes would be more useful in the same way than in supporting the dignity of worldly-minded bishops or a host of lazy friars.   This was the first time that Gustavus had clearly expressed himself on the subject of church temporalities; and his words sounded ominously in the ears of the primate.

That, notwithstanding the empire which Gustavus had obtained over the national mind, he should meet with no opposition when he attempted to urge such measures was impossible,   The clergy declaimed against him as a heretic and a usurper; and the peasants, influenced by them, were soon organised for an insurrection.   The approaching fair at Upsala was to be the rendezvous for the disaffected.   Aware of the design (for he had his spies everywhere), the king, with a body of cavalry, hastened to the place; remonstrated with them for their stupidity in opposing what was designed for their own advantage; and, when reasoning was ineffectual, commanded his soldiers to level their pieces.   Terrified by this unexpected demonstration, they knelt, implored his mercy, and were allowed to depart.

He was much more seriously embarrassed by the attempt of an impostor to pass as Nils Sture, son of the late administrator, who had died in the palace of the king near two years before.   His name was Hans; and he was a muleteer of Vestmanland.   He must, however, have been used to better society than the province yielded, or he would never have duped so many thousands, not merely of the peasantry but of the clergy, the burghers, and the rural gentry. But his career in Sweden was a brief one.   At the request of the monarch, the mother of the deceased prince wrote to the authorities of Dalecarlia, mentioned the time of her eldest son's death, appealed to all Stockholm as witness of his funeral, and concluded by observing that her second son was still in the royal palace, and treated with as much distinction as if he were the son of Gustavus.   Discredited and scorned, Hans now took refuge in Norway, and was supported for a time by the nobles and clergy of Trondhjem. On the complaint of the Swedish king, he was compelled to leave that country and seek a refuge at Rostock.   But even there he was pursued by his vindictive enemy, who menaced the magistrates of the city with the seizure of their vessels unless they surrendered the fugitives. They had the baseness to exceed his commands by putting the adventurer to death.

The monks and friars were the next objects of the royal displeasure. Foreign abbots were banished, and the brethren allowed to leave their monasteries only twice a year, and then for a short period. He then endeavoured to obtain the surrender of the fortresses held by the bishops. Two of the order — those whom he had nominated — showed no repugnance to the proposal; but the primate was inflexible. He had, he said, yielded enough, and he would now make a determined stand against every new demand. Fearing the influence of his virtues, the king determined to send him away under the pretext of an embassy to Poland. Landing at Dantzic, he repaired to Rome to solicit the aid of the pope; but the pope was more intent on the

TOMB OF KING CHARLES KNUTSSON IN STOCKHOLM

aggrandisement of his family than on the prosperity of religion in so barbarous a country as Sweden. Besides, the pontiff was in jeopardy from one of his own sons — the most Catholic king of Spain and most redoubtable emperor of Germany, whose army was about to sack the holy city. This was an occasion peculiarly favourable to the views of Gustavus, who proceeded more eagerly in what he called the work of reformation. If the bishops now refused to surrender the fortified towns and castles they should be reduced to obedience; and all grants made to the church since the time of King Knutsson were to be revoked. Assembling the estates-general at Vesterås, he secretly directed his officers to attend and demand the arrears of pay due to the army.[c]

THE DIET OF VESTERÅS (1527 A.D.)

Olaf Celsius,[d] the eighteenth century biographer of Gustavus, gives the following account of the diet: The opening of the diet was appointed for the 24th of June. The day before, the king gave a magnificent banquet to which the bishops were invited, as well as the gentlefolk among all ranks. When they went to the table, the priests, according to their usual custom, stepped forth to take the high places. At the moment when the king sat down, he commanded the council of the kingdom to sit next to him, and then the chief nobles were shown to places next to these; and therefore the bishops received their command to place themselves in proximity to the lesser ecclesiastics — where the burghers and peasants were ranged.

The bishops could not conceal their consternation at this clap of thunder. They who for a long time had been accustomed to be next to the king, and who always went above the council and also above the regent, now found themselves not only below the council of the kingdom but also below the knights. They did not know whether to go away or to sit down. The first would have been the better choice, but the fear of the anger of the king impelled them to take the seats to which they were shown. The king made himself quite merry at their expense, when he saw their indignation. For a long time they were silent and had nothing to offer, because they were so exasperated, until the king himself suggested that they should have an opportunity to come before the diet with their complaint. Then arose a great dispute about the rights of the clergy, and the bishops fought, in order to get at the mere truth, while the king, who now and then allowed his ardour to run away with him, had the intention of allowing them a hearing. The banquet and the contention

STRANGO CHURCH DOOR

were finally over, with this resolution — that in the future the bishops should content themselves with the rank which the king deigned to concede to them.

The estates assembled in the great hall of the cloister because the castle had not been repaired since the last storm. Everyone was all attention and on the alert for what was coming, looking beforehand to see what was to follow worthy of remark in the order of the day. Finally the archdeacon Lars Anderson, who filled the office of chancellor to the royal court arose; he was to make a speech in the name of the king. He gave a report of all that had happened during the seven years in which Gustavus had reigned, and also of the reasons which actuated him to receive the onerous burden which belonged to the richly honoured title of king, saying that the honours to which Gustavus was raised might be considered too great a responsibility, if the love which he bore the fatherland had not overtopped the annoyance which unceasing cares brought with them. Knowledge of his sincerity must spread far and wide; why should he be censured for punishing the conspirators? What else could he do under such circumstances? What course would be most advantageous and acceptable? Should he cast away the sceptre which was entrusted to him? Such a resolution he had already formed, but the council of the kingdom and the estates had hindered it. They had repented of their folly with tears, and entreated pardon; yet they had kept on in the same way with new acts of the same tenor. He demanded a freewill offering with the advice and consent of the estates. In reply they ranted about the expensive times, as though famine and plenty were in the hands of the king. There were indeed many establishments for housing sufficient corn and salt. The needs of the hungry were already quieted by his care. It must also be understood that while universal disquiet reigned in Europe, Sweden also, as well as other lands, would be disaffected and feel its share. They had no need with cunning and power to tear the sceptre from his hand. He would give it to them, although he had the power to show them his strength. What kind of a prop would it be to him, that he should care for it? On the contrary, he would be glad to dwell in retirement on the thought of their happiness under another master. They need fear from him neither trouble nor any violence. Yet he would first lay the common needs before them — those which concerned the whole body of the kingdom, without the supply of which no one could favourably esteem his government. For the first act the income of the crown must be increased, to meet the increase of the annual expenses. The maintenance of the court, the government, the fleet, relations with foreign powers, and other needs must be supplied, but the lesser income of the kingdom must be separate from that. The obedience of inferiors to their ruler must be given the first place. The nobility of the kingdom must be uplifted from its poverty to its former prestige. It would then appear as an ornament and a bulwark of the kingdom.

The castles and fortifications of the kingdom, the best and the most desirable of which the bishops had in their possession, must be improved and given up to the crown. The inward discontent, which for a long time had been the ruin of the noble houses and which had spread into other sections of the nation, must be wholly laid aside. The fatherland had recognised the divine teaching and it must be the thought of all to strive for one aim, to use one means — to obey the king.

These were the ill-assorted matters with which a Swedish ruler had to deal. His subjects must settle these points in order that he might not be wearied with the burden. This was the sole condition on which he would be their king.

When the chancellor had finished the address the king turned to the leader of the senate, Thure Jönsson, in order that he should reply in the name of the nobles. Immediately Thure Jönsson gave his oration in order publicly to show to the bishop of Linköping that priority belonged to him. The prelate spoke afterwards: "We of the religious world must recognise," he said, "that we are under obligations and bound by different oaths and to different masters, *viz.* to the pope and to the king of Sweden. To the first we have sworn an inviolable obedience, and never to allow any changes which would be detrimental to the rights of the clergy. For we possess this wealth, not as our own but as a fief of the church. And for its administration we must render a sharp account to the apostolic tribunal."

The king turned again to the senators. Jönsson replied immediately: "We are all with one mind in favour of what the bishop of Linköping has said, in whose well-composed speech everything has been expressed." "Good!"

answered the king. "It is also my conclusion. I renounce the kingdom and only demand my own again — my father's inheritance which I turned over to the good of the land. After that, I will journey out of the kingdom and I promise never to burden you with my company hereafter."

It almost seemed [he proceeded] as if the subjects thought that the king controlled the rain and storms as much as he did his kingdom, when they permitted themselves to blame the ruler for every evil with which the land was plagued. He said: "There is no devil in hell, much less a man, who would be able to rule it." With these words the king's countenance changed, the tears flowed from his eyes, and he went out. This occasioned an amazing and universal stillness. Then, little by little discussion began. The priests drew near to Brask while the nobility approached the leader of the senate. The burgher and peasant were without courage and almost without feeling.

The King is Besought to Assume the Administration

However, the burghers had grasped the right view of the whole thing and they were on the side of the king. On the following day the estates met again There was a high, wordy debate, without result, and conducted in great disorder. The first half of the day passed in such proceedings, without practical results or earnestness of effort. At length the leader of the burghers arose and took the floor. He entreated the nobility and the bishops by all that was sacred to weigh the importance of the thing — to study it with determination and energy, in order to reach a final conclusion. Many of the burghers began to shout: "The king brought peace, his rule was so cautious; and everyone must know that he was pre-eminently wise. How could any-one desert him?" But the Catholic priests stormed so much the more, in order to quell the sound with their murmurs and also audibly to express their displeasure. The speech of the burghers rang out with clear full tone: "If those in authority do not soon decide what is to be done, then the burghers will decide to give to the king all that he wishes. They have determined to follow the counsel of the king and they are sure to stand and persevere in their oath of allegiance to him. If any oppose and stir up discord, then at their own cost and for two years long they will hold, for the service of the king, all lake cities and especially chief cities." The peasants everywhere now said the same.

In his heart Brask pitied himself for being deceived by his colleagues; he could do nothing further, however, than pity himself. The nobility thought that the Catholic priests should be recalled and allowed to defend their teaching against opposition. The first question was whether the discussions should be in Latin or Swedish. Olaus Petri spoke for Swedish, in order that all might understand it; Gallus held out for the Latin because this thing could only be properly rendered in that language. So they argued — one for Swedish, and one for Latin. There was no end to the war till late in the evening, when Olaus Petri conquered, and the estates closed the day's proceedings. Several of the nobility, besides the common people, went immediately to the king in order on that day to take a firm oath of loyalty to him.

The assembly began on the third day with the same clamour as on the day previous. The Catholic priests had ever new grievances to state and their speeches were so filled with circumlocution that the day was spent fruitlessly. But the burgher and peasant showed their earnestness: "We are all of one mind," they said, "and by our deputies we have declared our loyal allegiance

GUSTAVUS VASA ENTERING STOCKHOLM

(Painted for THE HISTORIANS' HISTORY OF THE WORLD by Thure de Thulstrup)

to the king, and also our wish to follow his desire." One Mans Bryntesson went to the leader of the senate and whispered to him that he must restrain himself and defer his anger till another time. With that Jönsson allowed his vehemence to subside and declared himself ready for an accommodation. However, it was impossible for him to forbear to remark, "The king can be found another time; his highness can wait."

Now arose the question of how to conciliate the king. How it would be possible to bring him into the assembly? The chancellor Lars Anderson and Olaus Petri were chosen to bear the loyal request. They maintained that because a resolution had been passed which was conformable to the will of the king he would not be disinclined to resume the administration. The deputies declared to the king the repentance of his subjects and they heartily implored forgiveness. However, Gustavus listened to their prolonged address with coldness and hauteur, and after it was concluded he replied briefly: "I am tired of being your king." The deputies continued most urgent. They stamped their feet with vehemence, and struggled to emphasise their words with an accompaniment of tears; but there was no reply. This scene aroused great anguish in the assembly of the estates; and for the moment everything was in an uproar.

THE RECESS OF VESTERÅS (1527 A.D.)

After numberless deputations the king finally returned the answer that he would join them. This occasioned universal joy, and all awaited his return with eagerness. Gustavus allowed them to wait for three long days. On the fourth day, accompanied by the council of the kingdom, by the chief nobles, by the common people, also by the burghers and peasants, besides twelve of the bodyguard, who were newly clad in polished armour, he went to them. Only the priests were lacking in his following. On his arrival the estates went out to meet him. His form, speech, and bearing took on a double majesty for this occasion, and so impressed the common people with high thoughts of his person that the tone of their language could not be submissive and loyal enough to him. All entreated forgiveness and laid before him their requests.[d]

All his demands were conceded. The king's propositions were answered by each class for itself — by the nobility, the traders, the miners, and the peasants, although their deliberations appear to have been held in company. The statute which was the result of these, known under the title of the Recess of Vesteras, and dated on Midsummer's Day, 1527, was issued in the name of the council of state, whose seals were appended to it, with those of the nobility and of certain burghers and miners appointed on the part of the commonalty. The bishops, who from this time were no longer summoned to the council, briefly declared, in a special instrument, that they were content, how rich or poor soever his grace would have them to be. The act of the council on the Recess of Vesterås contains (1) a mutual engagement to withstand all attempts at revolt and to punish them, as also to defend the present government against all enemies, foreign and domestic; (2) a grant of power to the king, to take into his own hands the castles and strongholds of the bishops, and to fix their revenues as well as those of the prebends and canonries, to levy fines hitherto payable to the bishops, and to regulate the monasteries, in which there had for a long time been "woeful misgovernment"; (3) authority for the nobles to resume that part of their hereditary property which had been conveyed to churches and convents since the Inquisition (räjst) of

Charles Knutsson in 1454, if the heir-at-law could substantiate his birthright thereto, at the Thing, by the oaths of twelve men; (4) liberty for the preachers to proclaim the pure word of God, "but not" the barons add, "uncertain miracles, human inventions and fables, as hath been much used heretofore."

Respecting the new faith, on the other hand the burghers and miners declare that "inquiry might be made, but that the matter passed their understanding"; as do the peasants, since "it was hard to judge more deeply than understanding permitted." The answer of the latter betrays the affection they still, for the most part, bore to the clergy, with the exception of the mendicant friars or sack-monks, of whose conduct they complain. Of the bishops' castles they say that the king may take them in keeping, until the kingdom shall be more firmly settled; for the article respecting the revenues of the church, they believe they are unable to answer it, but commit this matter to the king and his council. In that supplement to the statute which is entitled the Ordinance of Vesterås, it is enacted that a register of all the rents of the bishops, cathedrals, and canons should be drawn up, and the king might direct what proportion of these should be reserved to the former owners, and how much paid over to him for the requirements of the crown; that ecclesiastical offices, not merely the higher but the inferior, should for the future be filled up only with the king's consent, so that the bishops might supply the vacant parishes with preachers, but subject to reviewal by the king, who might remove those whom he found to be unfit; that in secular matters priests should be amenable to the civil jurisdiction, and on their decease no part of their effects should devolve to the bishops; finally, that from that day the gospels should be read in all schools, "as beseems those which are truly Christian."

When these arrangements had been concerted, the king turned towards the prelates, and demanded from the bishop of Strengnäs the castle of Tynnelsö, which the latter declared himself ready to surrender. A similar answer was returned by the bishop of Skara in reference to that of Leckö; but when the king came to Bishop Brask and requested his castle of Munkeboda, silence and sighs were the only reply. Thure Jönsson begged for his old friend that the castle might be at least spared to him during his lifetime, but the king answered shortly, "No!" Eight lords of the council were obliged on the spot to become sureties for the bishop's obedience. Forty men of his bodyguard were taken from him to be entered among the royal forces, and they formed a portion of the troops, who were forthwith dispatched to take possession of the fortress with its artillery and appurtenances. At the same time the king sent various men of note as commissioners to the principal churches and monasteries throughout Sweden, to take into their keeping all documents concerning the estates and revenues of these foundations, and a declaratory letter of the council on the Recess and Ordinance of Vesterås was issued to all the provinces. Bishop Brask succeeded by a seeming submission in freeing himself from the securities he had been obliged to find; shortly afterwards, pretending a visitation to Gotland, he quitted the kingdom forever and joined the archbishop, who was likewise a fugitive in Dantzic.[e]

At the head of his cavalry, with the evangelical doctors in his train, Gustavus proceeded into the provinces, caused them everywhere to preach before him, and resumed the lands which had been granted to the church, before as well as after the time of Charles Knutsson. At one blow he took away two thirds of all her revenues: no fewer than sixteen thousand manors were thus placed at his disposal. The greater number he united to the crown;

but many also he gave to his nobles, to his officers, to his courtiers, to all whose co-operation was likely to be useful. But he touched not the lands or revenues of the churches, or even of the monasteries, which consented to embrace the Lutheran doctrines. This was the most effectual way of proselytising. The next in efficiency was the permission now allowed the ecclesiastics to marry and mix with the world. A great number, however, with the bishop of Linköping, retired into foreign countries; and many into Dalecarlia, with the hope of enjoying religious liberty and of organising a more successful resistance.

Gustavus was well prepared for the manifestation now visible in Dalecarlia and the western provinces. Through the influence of the ecclesiastics, a formidable band was ready to take the field. But, in the first instance, it was judged advisable to send him a deputation, praying him to undo what he had lately done. He answered them by fair promises until his forces were collected; then he hastened to them, seized such of their chiefs as had not time to escape, and made the multitude sue for pardon. The ancient church was overthrown. The king declared himself a Lutheran, nominated Lutherans to the vacant sees, and placed Lutherans in the parish churches.[c]

MARIA ELIZABETH, WIFE OF DUKE JOHAN OF ÖSTERGÖTLAND
(1596–1618)

THE SYNOD OF ÖREBRO (1529 A.D.)

The Lutherans had spread themselves over the entire kingdom; but the greater part of the common people, who occupied the land, still had Catholic teachers; for that reason there were everywhere traces of a medley of Lutheran and Catholic ceremonies. Gustavus wished to have a uniform worship throughout the kingdom. Finally, he summoned a general council to Örebro. He had doubtless often thought of convoking such an assembly, but the priests especially had zealously opposed it, and they had succeeded in hindering it until this time.

Finally the religious body met, in the beginning of the year 1529, at Örebro. Besides the bishops and priests, who were clothed with the highest authority, there were also assembled in opposition to them the foremost men of the kingdom. The chancellor, Lars Anderson, who was at the same time archdeacon of Upsala, presided over the assembly, in the name of the king. He exerted himself in every particular to put all Catholic ceremonies out of the way at once; made use of all kinds of expedients and many artifices in order to bring this about. He scarcely dared to mention the name of Luther in this connection, and still less could he acknowledge his teachings as the underlying motive of the thing in view. It was appropriate and fitting for the chancellor to declare that the sacred writings should be industriously read. However, most of those present were not inclined to concede that Luther's version should be universally introduced into the kingdom. The monks must be allowed instead to furnish the Latin version, generally used in the popish church, which is usually ascribed to the saintly father, St. Jerome. The number of the feast days must be limited; yet the Lutheran must suffer still, in order that the feasts of the patron saints of the kingdom and of the church might be kept.

Lars Anderson fully realized that at this time it would be simply impossible to tamper with and abrogate what it was perfectly evident would be publicly missed from the service of God; then he adopted the means of explaining things away: the holy water should be used, not for the reason that it washed away sins — because the blood of Christ alone could effect that — but as a mere remembrance of the baptismal vow. The pictures should remain in the churches, not for adoration and worship but as an ornament to the temple, and in order to direct the thoughts of the people to the glory of the saints. Palms should be waved — not as if any power could be derived from the act or anything effected by it, but as a remembrance of the honour which the people showed to Christ when he was on his way to Jerusalem. The priests were exhorted to instruct their hearers diligently in this particular, and to teach them to cherish no superstition which was connected with the usual ceremonial of the church. The final resolutions of this council were subscribed to by all who were present, and they were put under seal on Low Sunday, 1529.

As soon as Olaus Petri had returned to Stockholm from this council, he wrote a Swedish *Handbook of Evangelical Proofs*, wherein many popish ceremonies were omitted and several were retained. However, the priests found great difficulty in using this handbook among the women; as they were wholly unreconciled to the abolition of the prayers for the dead. Neither did they feel that their children were properly baptised unless salt were placed in the mouth during the ritual of baptism, and unless the horrible exorcisms were used to which they were accustomed. In order to avoid an uproar the king indicated to the priests that salt and exorcisms might be added to the service to pacify the people, who were indeed so strong and so imperative that they might better be conciliated in matters which, themselves, meant nothing and which contributed little to the confirmation of the faith.[d]

THE REVOLT OF THE VESTERGÖTLANDERS

Of all the insurrectionary movements in the time of King Gustavus, the revolt of the Vestergötlanders was the only one which was called into activity at the instigation, not only of the clergy, but of the nobility. Yet the lords sought to push forward the peasants — a proof sufficient that the barons were no longer so powerful as they had been. The energies of democracy in Sweden were never more vigorous than after the massacre of Stockholm had broken the strength of the magnates, and the diet of Vesterås, that of the bishops. Gustavus stood amidst a turbulent stream of popular force which had burst its bounds. This had first raised him to a throne which during twenty years it struggled to overturn. His accustomed mode of action, to follow the torrent when it was about to overpower him, until he should gain firm footing, was dictated to him by necessity; and it must be acknowledged that he well knew how to guide himself among the dangers of his position.

Letters of the king and his council were despatched to all the provinces, to the effect that he would gladly mend whatever might be wrong in his government; touching religion and the church, nothing had been determined without the assent of the council and the estates, nor should be hereafter. The Smålanders were, besides, wheedled with a pledge that two convents should be preserved; the clergy he engaged to exempt from entertaining the royal troops, if they would give their aid in appeasing the commons; to the Dalesmen he promised the remission of the tax they had so keenly contested; and to the miners, an acquittance from some of the demands of the crown. The abundance of the sovereign's good words seemed not to suffice; he begged that others too would employ the like. It was usual at this time when one province was in revolt to invoke the mediation of the rest, in reference to the ancient league by which they had been united. Thus the town of Stockholm now wrote to the Dalesmen, praying them to refrain from taking part in this insurrection. The Dalesmen and the miners on the other hand, although two years afterwards they were themselves ready for a new rising, addressed on this occasion a special letter of admonition to the factious Vestergötlanders and Smålanders; but the Östergötlanders, the neighbours of the latter, were in particular employed as mediators. Delegates from Upland and Östergötland, with the royal envoys, hastened to Vestergötland and Småland, bearing an offer of full pardon for the men of these territories, if they returned to their obedience. The result was that when Thure Jönsson convoked a meeting of the Vestergötlanders on Larfs heath, on April 17th, 1529, and harangued them from a great stone — on the expediency of electing another king, Magnus, bishop of Skara, and also assuring them that the pope would absolve them from their oaths, the yeomen made answer that "a change of lords seldom made matters better; therefore it seemed to them most advisable to hold fast to the fealty which they had sworn to king Gustavus." Thereupon both the Vestergötlanders and the Smålanders, who had informed the royal commissioners that they would be guided by the decision of their brethren, laid down their arms. In the writ of accommodation, pledges were given to them, that what had happened should be as a matter dead and forgotten, and that no heresy should be introduced into the kingdom; yet, the king added, the recess of Vesterås should be observed on every point. In this settlement the mediators are placed on a parallel with the authorities, for it is stated that "the good men of Upland and Östergötland likewise, who have interceded for the disturbers, shall have power to mulct of goods and life every man who, after this day, by word or deed shall stir up any disorders against the king." So this sedition was quelled. Jöran Thureson, the dean who had attempted to raise the Helsingers, was at last seized by them and delivered to the king, who was satisfied with dismissing him from his office. His father, the old high steward, with bishop Magnus, fled across the border to Denmark.

Seven barons, who all styled themselves councillors of state in Vestergötland, had plotted with the rebel leaders of Larfs heath, before the resolution of the yeomanry was known, to change the government of Sweden, and had renounced fealty and obedience to King Gustavus. Their letter was not sent; and assurances were afterwards given them by the priest, master Nils of Hwalstad, that all the documents by which their participation in the revolt might be proved should be committed to the flames. Deeming that the king did not know or would not see their guilt, they ventured to lay the whole blame of this transaction on Thure Jönsson and the bishop, and to offer themselves to the judgment of the council and the estates at the diet now convoked in Strengnäs. Here Gustavus vindicated himself at length from the accusations brought against him, and caused a defence of the Recess of Vesterås, composed by Lawrence Peterson, to be made public. On the trial, it was declared that the arraigned lords had forfeited all claim to be included in the warrant of peace granted by the king, or to obtain a pardon; the more so as, although thrice called upon by him to acknowledge their guilt and sue for grace, they had refused to comply. They were, therefore, in accordance with the tenor of their own letters now produced against them, condemned to death; and the sentence was executed on two of them. The pardon of a third was granted to the supplications of his mother, but he was obliged to pay a fine of 2,000 guilders (£158), and the rest of those who had borne a leading part in the revolt saw themselves under the necessity of afterwards purchasing the king's good will with money and costly presents.

THE DEBT TO LÜBECK

The debt to Lübeck was still unpaid. From an account adjusted in 1529 by the king's brother-in-law, the count of Hoya, with the authorities of the town, it is plain that the capital had not been diminished since the year 1523, notwithstanding the tax levied for its discharge, and this circumstance was one cause of the general discontent which prevailed. An agreement had now, indeed, been concluded, by which the privileges granted in 1523 were to be confined to Lübeck, the town consenting that the debt should be paid by instalments within four years; but even this arrangement rendered necessary the employment of extraordinary means. Imitating an example which had already been set in Denmark, a baronial diet held at Upsala in the early part of the year 1530 resolved that, from all the town churches of the kingdom, one bell should be taken towards the cancelling of this debt. The municipalities acceded to this measure, and in the following year the same requisition was extended to the rural churches, the bells being redeemable with money, at the option of the parishes. Agents specially commissioned by the council settled the conditions of arrangement with the commonalty of the various districts; engaging, on the king's part, that what was thus collected should be applied only to the object specified, and that the expenditure of the sum should be accounted for by persons thereto appointed. The tithes for the years were besides exacted, with all the money and plate still remaining in the church coffers that could be spared. In this way the debt to Lübeck was entirely paid off; but its discharge cost the king a new insurrection. The Dalecarlians once more rose; took back their bells, which they had already delivered up; and despatched letters throughout the kingdom, in which they invoked the remembrance of the ancient confederation, request-

TOCKMOCK'S CHAPEL

ing that twelve men of condition from every hundred might assemble in a general diet at Arboga, on St. Eric's day (the 18th of May), 1531, in order to deliberate, and to come to a decision upon certain affairs of the commons, which concerned the interests of all men, more especially respecting the dissensions in the Christian church. The peasants in Gestricland, in a part of Vestmanland, and in Nerike, likewise resumed possession of their bells. The king with difficulty appeased the discontent of the Uplanders; subsequently he employed their chiefs, with the magistrates of Stockholm, in a negotiation with the insurgents of Dalecarlia. At the head of the latter, in the present attempt, appeared men who had heretofore been the most faithful adherents of the king. The peasants of the Dales, said these, would not again allow themselves to be pinned in a ring, as once upon Tuna Heath: to come across the Dal-elf at Brunbäck without the Dalesmen's leave, was what no king or lord of the land had ever dared, and even Gustavus should not come into their country without safe-conduct, or with a greater following than they themselves should appoint; nor would they suffer any officers to live among them, other than such as they had themselves consented to receive, and as had been born among them. All this they alleged to be the old custom of their country, and they now kept armed guard upon the borders. When the king came to hear this, he said that it was now the time of the Dalesmen, but that his own time was coming; and to the astonishment of all, he nominated one of the principal insurgent leaders to be governor of the Dales.

GUSTAVUS DEFEATS CHRISTIAN IN NORWAY

This caution was rendered **necessary** by the perils which threatened from another quarter. Christian II, though dethroned, was ever busied with plans for recovering the kingdoms of which he had been master, and he had more than once, for this purpose, collected troops, which yet he never had succeeded in keeping together. Meanwhile the dwelling of Christian in the Netherlands, where he lived under the protection of the emperor, was a point of reunion for all the Swedish malcontents and exiles. Here resided the former archbishop, Gustavus Trolle, who had carried off with him the old records of the kingdom; here were gathered Thure Jönsson, bishop Magnus of Skara, and Jon Ericson, dean of Upsala, who held communication with bishop Hans Brask, now likewise a refugee. In the year 1530 they bound themselves, by a special covenant, to replace Christian "by the arms of their adherents" on the throne, and invoked the aid of the emperor, "to free Sweden, for the boot of Christendom, from a tyrant who cared neither for God nor men, for word, honour, nor repute." By the end of October, 1531, Christian put to sea with a fleet of twenty-five vessels, and though these were dispersed by a storm in which several were lost, he was himself fortunate enough to effect a landing in Norway at Opslo. The Northmen, who had long been disaffected from Danish rule, perceived in Christian the instrument by which they might regain independence. The fate of Christian was, however, soon decided. His ships were burned by the united squadrons of Denmark and Lübeck; and the unfortunate prince was incarcerated in the eastern tower of the castle of Sonderburg, in a vaulted chamber of which all the apertures were walled up, one little window excepted, through which his food was introduced. In this abode of horror, where a Norwegian dwarf was his only companion, King Christian lived seventeen years, the first twelve without any alleviation of his misery. His imprisonment lasted in all seven and twenty years, and was only terminated by death.

THE LAST RISING OF THE DALECARLIANS

Such being the event of Christian's invasion, Gustavus obtained time again to turn his thoughts to the Dalecarlians, in whose territory all was for the present tranquil. The Dalesmen, weary of moving about in arms among their forests, had made an offer to the king, at the end of the year 1531, to redeem their bells with a sum of 2,000 marks, and were the more gladdened by his promise of pardon, as they regarded it as a silent confirmation of their privileges. They celebrated with feasts, say the chronicles, the old liberty of the Dales. But the king, on the other hand, had determined forever to extinguish their claims to peculiar privileges above the other inhabitants of the kingdom; and he was, besides, moved anew to indignation when the miners set at naught his summons to defend the kingdom against the attack of Christian, and held communications with his runaway subjects. These mutinous excesses were ascribed more especially to "Magnus Nilson with his faction," who — the real instigator of the bell-sedition — was at that time the richest miner in the Kopparberg, and of whom it is popularly said that he shod his horses with silver. In the commencement of the year 1533 Gustavus cited his own retainers, with those of the nobility, to meet at Vesterås. No man knew against whom this armament was really directed, although rumour spoke of new complots by the factionaries of King Christian. The king's injunctions to his captains were, "Wheresoever ye see me advance, thither haste ye speedily after." The expedition took its way to the Dale country, whose inhabitants had lately sent representatives to Vesterås. These the king detained, and in their stead despatched proclamations to the Dalecarlians, purporting that "he well knew that little of what had happened could be imputed to the common people; he came only to hold an inquisition upon the guilty, whom it was meet they should cast out from among them." He invited them all to come to a conference at the Kopparberg.

The king arrived as soon as the letters, and the commonalty assembled — some with good will, others by constraint. As on the previous occasion, troops encompassed the assembly; first several lords of the council spoke to the people, afterwards the king himself. He asked the Dalesmen whether they remembered their promise made six years before, when he had pardoned the revolt then commenced, or they supposed they might play this game with him every year with impunity. This bout should be the last. He would suffer no province in his dominion to be hostile; for the future theirs should be either obedient, or so desolated that neither hound nor cock should be heard in it. He asked them where they would have that border which their king must not dare to overstep, and whether it became them as subjects thus to master their magistrates. What was the true reason why the Stures, although the rulers of the land, had never ventured to cross the stream at Brunbäck without the leave of the miners? To such insolence he, at least, would not submit. After this fashion, the king spoke to them long and sharply, and during that time the whole of the commonalty were upon their knees. He called upon them to deliver up the instigators of the last sedition, which was forthwith performed. Five of them were tried and executed upon the spot; the rest were carried prisoners to Stockholm, where, in the following year, three of them, pursuant to the judgment of the council and the town magistrates, were put to death — among them Anders Person of Rankhytta, in whose barn Gustavus had once threshed. The forfeited property of the offenders was restored to their wives and children. Thus ended the third and last rising of the Dalecarlians against King Gustavus.

LÜBECK'S LAST EFFORTS ARE SUBDUED

At this time Lübeck was calling up its last energies for the maintenance of its commercial power; for its citizens, who "wished to hold in their sole grasp the keys of the Baltic, looking only to their own advantage," had long seen with reluctance the Hollanders dividing with themselves the trade of the North. They had contributed to the overthrow of Christian II because he had favoured these rivals, but they had not reaped the fruits expected from his fall; and they ended by wishing to raise him from his prison to the throne. Gustavus had already, in 1526, formed a commercial treaty with the regent Margaret of the Netherlands, and although Christian had received support from that quarter in his last enterprise, the misunderstandings thereby created were eventually adjusted. Lübeck, on the other hand, demanded that Sweden and Denmark should declare war on the Hollanders, and in the mean time postpone the assertion of its own quarrel with them, in order to kindle a new one in the North. Marcus Meyer and Görgen Wollenwever, two bold demagogues, were the men who, having ejected the old council of Lübeck and usurped the government in the name of the populace, ruined the power of their native city by the attempt again to make and unmake kings. By the death of Frederick of Denmark, on the 3rd April, 1533, and the disputes which afterwards arose respecting the succession, their plans were advanced. To excite new troubles in Sweden they employed the name of young Svante Sture, a son of the last administrator, who had fallen into their hands. The generous youth refused to be the tool of their designs, for which they found a more willing instrument in the count John of Hoya, whom Christian reckoned one of the persons "introduced into the government by the towns." Gustavus had united him in marriage with his sister, placed him in his council, and bestowed upon him a considerable territory in Finland. Estrangement seems to have first arisen between the count and his sovereign from the computation of the Swedish debt made by the former at Lübeck in 1529, fixing the amount at 10,000 marks higher than Gustavus would acknowledge. The debt was afterwards discharged within the period agreed upon, but the Lübeckers maintained that from 8,000 to 10,000 marks of the same were still wanting, while Gustavus asserted that the Lübeck commissioners had omitted just so much from their accounts, and applied the money to their own use. The consequence was that the Lübeckers seized a ship belonging to the king, whereupon he laid an embargo on all Lübeck vessels in Swedish harbours, the bitter hatred of the townsmen to him finding vent in speeches, writings, overt acts of hostility, and at last also in clandestine designs against his life. The count of Hoya fled, with his wife and children, from Sweden, and was received at Lübeck with public demonstrations of rejoicing. Associating himself with the other Swedish exiles, he took part with Gustavus Trolle and Bernard of Melen in the war which now broke out.

In the year 1534 began the Count's Feud, so called because the possessors of power in Lübeck placed Count Christopher of Oldenburg at the head of their attack upon Denmark. This was the last blow struck for Christian II, whose cause Lübeck pretended to lead.

Lübeck saw itself reduced, in 1536, to conclude a peace with Denmark, which brought the war with Sweden also to an end. But the dissatisfaction of Gustavus that Denmark should have concluded a separate peace, and under conditions by which he deemed his interests to be prejudiced in several points, the difficulties which arose concerning the payment of the loan wherewith he had assisted Christian III, and various other disputes, afterwards well-nigh led to a rupture with Denmark. At length a good understanding was restored, and an alliance between the two kingdoms for twenty years contracted, at a personal interview of the sovereigns in Brömsebro. The Hanse Towns, on the other hand, after this unsuccessful attempt to restore their ancient influence in the North, never recovered their former privileges. In Lübeck, the party which had instigated the war was overturned. Among their plans was included a conspiracy against Gustavus: the king was to be assassinated, and Stockholm delivered to the Lübeckers. The plot was detected; and its authors, who were for the most part German burgesses, suffered (in 1536) the penalty of their crime.

THE ACT OF HEREDITARY SETTLEMENT

As early as the year 1526, when the council solicited the king to choose a consort, provision was made that, if God should grant him sons, one of them — and the eldest in preference — should be his successor, while lands and fiefs were to be settled on the others, as was beseeming for the children of a sovereign. Eric and John (the king's firstborn son by Margaret) were presented to the council convened at Orebro on the 4th of January, 1540, along with several of the chief nobles and prelates. The king drew his sword, and the assembled peers, touching the blade, took an oath, administered by him and confirmed by the reception of the sacrament, in which they acknowledged his sons as the legitimate heirs of the kingdom. Four years afterwards, at the diet of Vesterås, this act was further confirmed, and the succession to the throne settled, according to priority of birth, upon the male heirs of the sovereign, the estates recognising and doing solemn homage to Eric as crown prince. The act of Hereditary Settlement passed at Vesterås, and dated the 13th of January, 1544, was drawn up in the name of all estates by order of the nobles, who here styled themselves "members and props of the crown of Sweden." At the diet of Strengnäs, in 1547, the estates declared themselves likewise ready to acknowledge and maintain "the testamentary disposition which the king's majesty has made or may yet make for the princely heirs of his body." The statute for this purpose was framed by the clergy, although it is plain, from various records, that the other orders also gave their assent to it. Now, for the first time after the beginning of the Reformation, we find this estate — no longer represented by the bishops only, but also by pastors of churches, both in towns and rural parishes — again mentioned as present at the diet; a proof that the greater number, at least, were now Protestants. After the act of settlement had been passed, an order was made, "that the king's majesty might not daily be burdened and troubled with so many affairs," for the councillors of state to be in attendance upon him continually, two every month.

TROUBLES CONCERNING FINLAND

In 1554 the Russian war broke out on the borders of Finland. Gustavus had regarded this portion of his dominions with a paternal solicitude which was extended likewise to the more distant Laplanders. He forbade the oppressions practised by the trading peasants of Norrland and Finland upon this wild and defenceless race, and sought to disseminate Christianity among the Lapps by missionaries. By the labours of Michael Agricola, a Finn by birth and the pupil of Luther and Melanchthon, whom Gustavus appointed ordinary of Åbo, the Finlanders obtained the Bible, prayer-book, psalms, and the first books of instruction in their language. Their manners were still marked by much barbarity and lawlessness. The king was obliged, in 1551, to chastise the Tavastrians, who had surprised and burned the newly established settlements of the Swedes, already flourishing, in the forests of East Bothnia. Dark and extraordinary crimes are mentioned, and the remoteness of situation, tempting by the prospect of impunity, led to great outrages on the part of the possessors of fiefs and the royal bailiffs, as is shown by the king's letters to the Flemings, who then exercised great power in Finland. The peace subsisting with Russia since 1510 had been last confirmed in 1537; but the frontier was undefined, and in desolate Lapland it was unknown to either side. Yet disputes speedily arose which produced quarrels between the bailiffs respecting the collection of the crown dues, and at length mutual plundering, homicides, and burnings. As early as 1545, Gustavus, in a letter to Francis I, complains of an inroad of the Russians into Finland. This was returned with equal damage from the Swedish side, though without the king's orders, and brought on an open war, in which the grand master of the Livonian knights and the king of Poland promised their aid to Gustavus against the czar Ivan Vasilievitsch II. The king himself repaired to Finland in the following year, with a fleet and army. But mutual devastations, from which Finland suffered most, composed the whole occurrences of the war. The Russians laid fruitless siege to Viborg with a very large army, and carried off with them a crowd of captives. Their chronicles relate that a man was sold for ten copecks, and a maiden for fifteen. The war occasioned great outlay, and disease raged among the soldiery. These causes, coupled with the failure of the promised help from Livonia and Poland, led first to a cessation of arms, and thereafter to a peace, concluded at Moscow (April 2nd, 1557), for forty years. The disputed boundaries were to be determined by special commissioners.

Designs on Livonia from this side were soon to set the whole North in flames. The Russian giant was now beginning to struggle towards the sea, whence fresher air might stream upon his sluggish body. Gustavus kept aloof from the discords which were soon engendered. His sons, however, did not share his own caution, and his knowledge of their character filled him with apprehension. Heavy was the weight of care which accumulated upon his last years. He complained that his old friends had departed, and that he felt himself lonely in the world. He had lost, in 1551, his beloved consort Margaret Lejonhufvud, who had borne to him ten children: five sons and five daughters. He married again, after the lapse of a year, the young Catherine Stenbock.

In February, 1559, after the Russians had plundered the whole country to Riga, Ivan Vasilievitsch II was informed by his commanders that Livonia lay in ashes. Before this invasion, commenced in the year previous, fell the old but now shattered dominion of the sword-knights; and as aid was sought from Poland, the emperor, Denmark, and Sweden, the country was now about to become — as throughout a whole century it continued — the theatre for the settlement of their contending pretensions. He was already opening that series of wars beyond the Baltic in which Sweden was to be engaged; and it was not without good grounds that he who is justly styled the father of his country scrupled to enter on a path so full of uncertainty. All the sentiments recorded as having fallen from him in his last year show that he viewed with the profoundest anxiety the prospect of Sweden's future. The very expedient he adopted, to avoid setting her all to hazard in the dangerous hands of Eric, involved risks which undoubtedly did not escape his penetration. All around, clouds were darkening the political horizon. He had received information that another last attempt was about to be made on behalf of the family of his old enemy Christian; and, on the side of Denmark, under the new king Frederick II the chances of war seemed so imminent that Gustavus kept his army and fleet in readiness. Those who now invoked his assistance for Livonia, the granting of which would have provided a new war with Russia, were the same who deserted him in his former war with that country. He discerned only one Swedish interest at stake in the whole quarrel — that of setting bounds

A FEMALE SCHAMAN

to the augmentation of the Danish power in this quarter, after Reval had offered, in 1558, its submission to King Christian III — and beyond question this was his motive in binding himself to support the grand master of the order by a loan, obtaining that town as security; unless it was a mere pretext on the king's part to take the matter out of the management of his sons. For we know that John also, who had formed connections with Reval by giving shelter in Finland to the pirates of this town (the sea thieves of Reval, as Gustavus calls them), was negotiating with the grand master to furnish a loan upon the security of certain fortresses, and had made an engagement to this effect without his father's privity.

The king had observed, as he declared, that his son had some clandestine matter on his mind, and made him earnest representations on this subject. "Seeing thou well knowest that Finland is not a separate dominion from Sweden, but that both are counted as members of one body, it becomes thee to undertake nothing which concerns the whole kingdom, unless he who is the true head of Sweden, with the estates of the realm, be consulted thereupon, and it be approved and confirmed by him and them, as thy bounden duty points out, and Sweden's law requires." But John turned for counsel in this design, not to his father, but to Eric. The latter informed his brother, who was still busied with his embassy to London, that he had given orders to his secretary with Clas Christerson Horn to negotiate with the grand master for the delivery of the castles of Sonnenburg and Padis, for the sum of 50,000 dollars, of which 10,000 was to be raised in Finland. "And when the king our father hears that this matter has had a happy issue," he added, "and we hold the keys of the castles, doubt not that he will lay out the rest for us; or it can be procured in some other mode." He pledged himself to further the scheme, according to the engagement he had made, "even should it move the wrath of the king." Eric gave command for the immediate equipment of ships in Finland, which drew forth a letter from the old monarch, forbidding any obedience being given in matters of importance to "what Eric or our other children may order without our knowledge and sanction." Thus we see the sons united against the father on the very point which was to enkindle a deadly enmity between them.

THE DEATH OF THE KING

On June 16th Gustavus came to Stockholm, and informed the estates, by message, that he would meet them at the palace on the 25th of the month. On the appointed day he took his place in the hall of assemblage, accompanied by all his sons — King Eric, Duke John, Duke Magnus, and Duke Charles. The last, who was still a child, stood at his father's knee; the others on his left hand, each according to his age. The king having saluted the estates, they listened for the last time to the accents of that eloquence so well liked by the people. Upon the 14th of August, the very day of Eric's departure, Gustavus lay on his death-bed.

When his confessor began a long discourse of devotion, the king bade him cut it short, and instead of that bring him a medicine for a sick stomach and a brain that felt as if it were burning. He was heard to exclaim that he had busied himself too much with the cares of this world, but with all his wealth he could not buy himself physicians. Such of his bailiffs as were incarcerated for debts owed to himself, he now restored to freedom. His mood was capricious and changeable: now harsh and morose, so that his children trembled in his presence; now soft even to tears; at other times merry and jesting, especially at the endeavours of those who wished to prolong his life. When one asked him if he needed aught, his reply was, "The kingdom of Heaven, which thou canst not give me." He seemed not to place overmuch confidence even in his ghostly advisers; when the priest exhorted him to confess his sins, the king angrily broke out, "Shall I tell my sins to thee?" To the bystanders he declared that he forgave his enemies, and begged pardon of all for anything in which he had dealt unjustly with them, enjoining them to make known this to all. To his sons he said, "A man is but a man; when the play is out, we are all alike," and enjoined them to unity and steadfastness in their religion.

The consort of the dying king never quitted his side. During the first three weeks of his illness he spoke often, sometimes with wonderful energy, on temporal and spiritual affairs. The three following weeks he passed chiefly in silence and, as it seemed, with no great pain; he was often seen to raise his hands as in prayer. Having received the sacrament, made confession of his faith, and sworn his son to adhere firmly to it, he beckoned for writing materials, and inscribed these words, "Once confessed, so persist, or a hundred times repeated" — but his trembling hand had not the power to finish the sentence. The confessor continued his exhortations, till, as life was flying, Sten Ericson Lejonhufvud interrupted him by saying, "All that you talk is in vain, for our lord heareth no more." Thereupon the priest bent down to the ear of the dying man and said, "If thou believe in Jesus Christ, and hear my voice, give us some sign thereof." To the amazement of all, the king answered with a loud voice, "Yes!" This was his last breath, at eight of the clock in the morning, the 29th of September, 1560.^e

FRYXELL'S ESTIMATE OF KING GUSTAVUS

King Gustavus I was a tall and well-made man, somewhat above six feet high. He had a firm and full body without spot or blemish, strong arms, delicate legs, small and beautiful hands and feet. His hair of a light yellow, combed down and cut straight across his eye-brows; forehead of a middle height, with two perpendicular lines between the eyes, which were blue and piercing; his nose straight, and not long; red lips, and roses on his cheeks, even in his old age. His beard in younger years was brown and parted, a hand-breadth long, and cut straight across; in later years growing at will, till it at last reached his waist and became hoary like his hair. As his body was faultless in every respect, any dress that he wore became him. Fortune favoured him in all that he undertook: fishing, hunting, agriculture, cattle-breeding, mining, even to casting the dice, when he could be induced to take part in it — which, however, was very seldom.

As in his body, so in his soul was King Gustavus endowed with the most noble qualities. His memory was so strong that, having seen a person once, after the lapse of ten or twelve years he recognised him again at first sight. The road he had once travelled he could never mistake again; he knew the names of the villages; nay, even those of the peasants who lived there during his youthful excursions. As was his memory, such was his understanding. When he saw a painting, sculpture, or architecture he could immediately and acutely judge its merits and defects, though he had himself never received any instruction in these arts.

When there was a crowd of people at the Castle,[1] he spoke with each, and on the subjects which those he addressed best understood; all were familiar to him. No man in the kingdom was so well acquainted with it as himself; none knew as well as he did in what its deficiencies lay. For this reason, and because in the beginning he was entirely without well-informed and capable officers, he was obliged himself to compose every ordinance and decree which he enacted, and the kingdom was not a loser by it.

He was prudent in the highest degree. But once, when Gustavus Trolle was about to take him prisoner at Upsala, did he show himself careless or credulous. Otherwise he was so provident that he might rather be called suspicious. "Look well before you. Think well of all men; but most of yourself" — thus he exhorted the people; and it was thus true, as an old author says of him, "he calculated every step, and could stand firm as a mountain at each."

Firmness and perseverance in what he undertook were striking features in his character. Example sufficient of this we find in his long, vehement, but honestly conducted struggle with the power of popery. Most others would have wearied, or desired by a blow to decide the matter with violence. Gustavus let time and reflection work for him; though slowly, he went ever forwards. Seldom or never did he change his resolution; it was an adage of his which he often repeated: "Better say once and remain by it, than speak a hundred times."

He was a stern and serious gentleman, and well knew how to preserve his dignity. It was not advisable for any, whether high or low, to attempt to encroach upon it; in such circumstances he rebuffed peasants, bishops, or kings, with equal severity. He was just, but severe, with the men he had placed in civil charges; on which account many abandoned him. When any one laboured to show off his talents and capabilities in the hopes of ingratiating himself, or others commenced extolling such an one, the sharp-sighted king would answer: "He is but a dabbler with all his pound from our Lord."

---

[1] Or palace. The palace at Stockholm is still called the Castle.

Gustavus was careful of money; for, said he, "it costs the sweat and labour of the subjects." His court was very frugal. He generally lived at one or other of the royal estates, and consumed their produce. His children were kept strictly. Hams and butter were sent from the country for the supper of the princes at Upsala; the queen herself sewed their shirts, and it was considered a great present if ever one of the princesses got a blank riksthaler. Gustavus' love of money seduced him to several injustices, which, however, were not so striking in those days as now. He sometimes permitted parishes to remain without rectors, having them administered by vicars, and appropriated their returns to himself. He forbade the export of cattle to his subjects in general, buying them himself at a low price from the peasants, and selling them abroad with great profit. This last circumstance was one of the chief causes of the Dacke Feud.[1]

Several things of this kind which are less creditable to him are related; but the people overlooked them for the sake of his many virtues. They also knew that this money was not uselessly squandered. Herr Eskil's Hall, and the other vaulted chambers of the treasury, were full of good silver bullion at the king's death. When, however, pomp was required, he did not spare; but showed himself the equal of other kings. "The Lord's anointed," he said, "should be girded with splendour, that the commonalty may view him with reverence, and not imagine themselves to be the equals of majesty to the small profit of the land."

A pure and unaffected piety dwelt in his heart, and showed itself in his actions. Prayers were read morning and evening in his apartments; divine service he never neglected. He was better informed of the contents of the Bible and the catechism than most of the priests in his kingdom. Therefore Le Palm, his chief physician, wrote of him to Paris: "My king is a God's prince, who has scarcely his equal in spiritual and temporal measure. He is so experienced in the Scriptures that he can rectify his priests; and none understands the government of the kingdom like himself." During the Dacke Feud Gustavus wrote to the rebels as follows: "Ye can threaten us as much as ye will; ye can drive us from our royal throne; rob us of estate, wife, and children — ay, of life itself; but from that knowledge which we have attained of God's word, ye shall never part us, as long as our heart is whole and our blood is warm."

He was equally venerable in his domestic life. No vice stains his memory. He liked the society of handsome and agreeable women; but no mistress, no illegitimate child, not the slightest foible can be laid to his charge, though he was forty-one before he married for the first time. His marriage vows he kept inviolate. Gluttony, drunkenness, gambling, and idleness were what he could never endure in others, much less in himself.

As he in his younger years was of a cheerful temper, when business was done he kept a gay and lively court, though in all sobriety. Every afternoon at a certain hour the lords and ladies assembled in the great hall where the king's musicians made music for them while they danced. "For," said he, "youth shall not be clownish, but gallant to the ladies and to all." They were often out together, to walk or to hunt. Once a week a school for fencing

[1 The Dacke Feud was a formidable rebellion headed by Nils Dacke, a peasant, the chief seats of which were Småland and Öland. The rebels chiefly kept to the forest country, whence they plundered the wealthier landowners. They professed to have taken arms in order to restore the old form of worship and endeavoured, though unsuccessfully, to persuade Svante Sture, son of Sten Sture the younger, to become their leader and Gustavus' rival for the crown. The rebellion, which had begun in 1542, was finally suppressed in the summer of the following year.]

was open for the young nobles; tournaments were afterwards introduced, at which the victors received their rewards from the hands of the fairest ladies at court. They often entertained themselves with music, song as well as playing on stringed instruments, the latter especially, in which the king delighted. He made and himself played several instruments, of which the lute was his favourite. There was never an evening when he was alone that he did not occupy some hours with it.

He often travelled through the country, chiefly to great markets and other meetings, where he addressed the people; sometimes instructing them in matters of faith; sometimes regarding their house-keeping, agriculture, cattle-breeding, and so on. The peasants soon learned that the king's advice was good, and listened to him willingly; also on account of his extraordinary eloquence. His voice was strong, clear, expressive, and pleasant in sound. No king of Sweden has ever been or deserved to be more beloved by the common people than he was. Every peasant who possessed any fortune used to leave, by will, some silver to the king, so that at his death no inconsiderable store of bequeathed silver was found in the treasury; and in the unquiet years which followed the people used ever to speak with regret of "old King Gustaf" and his happy days.

Gustavus loved and protected learning. He was, however, supremely desirous of the instruction of the people, and sought by every means to get a sensible and well-informed peasantry. His own children received a careful education; so that they were amongst the most learned of their day. Like his children were their descendants, the whole Vasa dynasty as far as Christina; so that the royal house was the first, not only in pomp and bravery but likewise in science and knowledge, and in this last respect not in Sweden alone but in all Europe.

When the king grew older and his children were growing up, he used often after meals to sit before the fire, and conversing with them give them useful exhortations on many points. It was a royal school in its teacher, disciples, and doctrines. "Be steady in your faith; united amongst yourselves," said he. "If you fail in the first, you anger your Maker; if you neglect the second, you will fall a prey to man. Make war by compulsion — peace without compulsion; but should your neighbour threaten — strike. From my very childhood, and ever since, I have been at war; oftenest with my countrymen, sad to say! and I have grown grey in armour. Believe me, seek peace with all!"

When he saw them proud and vain-glorious of their royal birth and descent from Odin, he said: "One like another — when the play is out we are all equal." Another time: "Ye shall reflect on all things well, execute with speed, and remain by it, deferring nothing to the morrow. The resolves which are not carried at the right time into execution resemble clouds without rain in long drought. Let everything be done in its right time; time will then be sufficient for all — for the man in office, as for all others downwards; otherwise there will be provocation, hurry, and postponement in every part." Again he would say; "It is the fault of the rulers if the governed do not obey, for the law must be followed without partiality, and always. Let no one do what he pleases, but what he ought. No one in office is to be endured who is not frugal, useful, and industrious. The morning hour has gold in its mouth. Away with the idler; but honour and reward to the faithful labourer in the vineyard. Your men must live in discipline and the fear of the Lord, paying reverence to old age. He who does not may be expelled like the slanderers. Surround yourselves by answerable men of a pure life, for it will be believed

GUSTAVUS VASA ADDRESSING HIS LAST MEETING OF THE ESTATES (1560 A.D.)

of you as it is known of these." Of the nobility he said: "Virtue, sense, and manliness make the noble."

"The Swede," he would say again, "is often proud in the wrong season, and greedy to govern. They require a bold king with a manly mind; they cannot abide injustice, slavery, or a coward easily. They require a merry king, but a stern one; not one who looks through his fingers. In war they must fight — no parleying; they shame where little is done. Love therefore and honour this old kingdom whose inhabitants have been far and wide, and rebuked both east, south, and west. Encourage and found hospitals and schools, and your forces both on sea and land. Love and honour agriculture, mining, commerce, even books and the arts, and your subjects will willingly do so likewise: they will follow you. Therefore love yourselves, and keep your subjects to the pure word of God, prayers, and church-going; much depends upon these for the peace both of the soul and the country. Love your subjects; the right-minded among them will love you, and with them you will govern the rest. Thus have I done, dear children! I have, with God's grace, laboured on your fitting education. Remain such for the well-being of yourselves and others; and remember that the memory of a king ought not to die away with the sound of his funeral bells, but remain in the hearts of his people."

MANNERS AND CUSTOMS OF THE TIME IN SWEDEN

Frugality and simplicity in every-day life, extravagant pomp, often both tasteless and ridiculous on solemn occasions — such were the marks of the times. Many of our conveniences were wanting; glass was very rare, and instead of the wooden shutters once in use, fine net-work, linen, or parchment was now taken to supply their place. Hearths instead of stoves were used for a couple of hundred years longer. Carpets, very coarse with the poor, embroidered with gold and silk with the rich, covered the coarsely timbered walls. Thick benches were attached to them round the room, oaken in the houses of the rich. Before them stood long heavy tables equally thick; no chairs, but loose benches and small stools were moved about the room. Plates were scarce, and were never changed if the dishes were ever so many and so various; every guest had to bring his knife, fork, and spoon along with him. Clocks were so rare that when the grand duke of Muscovy at this time received one as a present from the king of Denmark, he thought it must be an enchanted animal sent for the ruin of himself and his kingdom; wherefore he returned it with the utmost despatch to Copenhagen.

Dinner was eaten at ten; supper at five; between nine and ten they went to bed, to rise the earlier in the morning. Wearing apparel was mostly woollen; linen was barely used next the skin. Holiday dresses were costly, but substantial; the same petticoat often served mother, daughter, and grand-daughter for festal occasions. The women had their hair combed back, and long tight-fitting gowns with stiff high ruffles; the men wore the Spanish dress. Their hair was in the beginning long, and the beard shaved; but this was soon changed, so that the clergy alone retained the long hair and smooth skin; the others adopted short hair and long beard. Wax-lights were only used in churches, tallow-candles by the richest and greatest, torches of dry wood by the people. The beds were broad, fastened to the wall, and few in number; the guests were laid several together, often with the host himself. This was the case even in the houses of princes. The roads were so bad that carriages could seldom be used; besides, the first coach was not introduced till the reign of John III. Most journeys took place on horseback, and when it rained the princesses were wrapped in wax-cloth cloaks. High titles were not in use. The king was called "his grace"; the princes *Junker* (young lord) the princesses *Fröken* (young lady). The nobles did not use their family but their fathers' names; for instance, instead of Thure Roos, or Lars Sparre, one wrote and said Thure Jönsson, Lars Siggesson, etc., or still shorter, Herr Thure, Herr Lars.

There was much of savage wildness and disorder yet amongst the people, partly a consequence of the times and of the long domestic broils. Club-law was more resorted to than the law of the land. Arms were in continual wear and exercise. According to an old custom the knights entered the bridal bed in full armour; but like the knights of old they were generally ignorant in the highest degree, especially the elder amongst them. Many of King Gustavus' officers and governors were unable to read, still less to write; they were obliged to keep a clerk on purpose to read and answer the king's letters. The Romish faith was done away with, but many of its superstitions remained, and that not alone among the people, but even the great ones of the land believed in witchcraft, fairies, elves, brownies, nixies, etc. The art of medicine consisted chiefly in prayers and exorcism.*f*

TAILOR OF VESTERGÖTLAND, SEVEN-
TEENTH CENTURY

ERIC XIV,[1] JOHN III, AND SIGISMUND

The second monarch of the Vasa dynasty exhibited, from the first, occasional aberrations of mind. In everything he was capricious, and peculiarly so in his courtships. Elizabeth of England, Mary of Scotland, the daughter of Philip, landgraf of Hesse, were pursued at the same time and with equal want of success. At length he took to his mistress a country girl, whom he saw standing in the market-place of Stockholm, and whom, in the last year of his reign, he married.

One of Eric's first acts was to create the hereditary titles of count and baron for certain families. He had the imprudence to interfere in the troubles of Livonia, which was always destined to be the theatre of contending powers. There was one party in favour of the Danes, another of the Russians, a third of the knights, and now a fourth power, Sweden, must be called in to increase the elements of strife. His arms had little success; but his demonstration drew on him the wrath of the czar, who embarrassed him both in Livonia and Finland. With his Danish wars we shall deal when we come to the reign of Frederick II.

But the greatest enemies of Eric were at home. From the first the design of dethroning him, or at least of obtaining a share in the administration, seems to have been indulged by his brother John, duke of Finland. That ambitious

---

[1] It would puzzle a Swedish antiquary to account for this numeral. If all the Erics of Denmark, Norway, and Sweden were added together they would amount to about the number. Such, as we shall have occasion to show, is also the case with the kings named Charles.

man, by marrying the daughter of Sigismund, king of Poland, and fortifying himself by other alliances, incurred the jealousy of Eric. Åbo, the capital of the duke's government, was taken by stratagem; and John, being conducted with his wife, his family, and his domestics to a Swedish dungeon, was tried for high treason, and condemned to death, unless the king should be graciously pleased to forgive him. That he was guilty cannot be denied, and Eric, who durst not venture on the experiment of executing him, sentenced him to perpetual imprisonment. If any faith is to be placed in the chronicles of the time, the king, who had frequent opportunities of learning that, even in captivity, his brother was to be feared, sometimes went to the dungeon to perform the task of executioner with his own hands. But on looking at the duke his heart smote him, and he begged pardon for the crime which he had intended to commit. In about four years, he consented, at the express instance of the estates, which beheld with dismay the existence of so much fraternal discord, to enlarge him on certain conditions, among which was the renunciation of the duchy which their father had left him. How this clemency was repaid will soon appear.

But the most disgraceful part of Eric's reign was his persecution of the Sture family, which had given administrators to Sweden. Nils, the representative of that house, was suspected, apparently with much injustice, of being an accomplice in the designs of Duke John. With Eric, suspicion was proof; but it was not so to the senate; and he could only exhibit his whimsical rage by making the nobleman ride through the streets of Stockholm with a crown of straw on his head, exposed to the derision of the lowest portion of the mob. The indignity was felt by the whole family; but it did not shake their loyalty, though it made them murmur. Baffled in this purpose, Eric now determined to sacrifice all the Stures. He was led to this atrocious project by an astrologer whom he maintained at his court, without whose advice he undertook nothing of moment, and who represented the obnoxious family as destined to occasion his downfall. By the intrigues of this worthy, charges were made against all of them; and forged documents were produced to confirm the charges. They were arrested and committed to close confinement; but, as the evidence was manifestly insufficient to ensure their condemnation, Eric adopted the summary way of removing them by assassination. With his own hand he stabbed Nils, who, in token of his loyalty, had presented him with his dagger. The deed was concealed; but the remorse of the king drove him frantic. He ran into the woods; he howled like a wild beast, and for some time eluded the search of his court. When discovered, his mistress alone had influence enough to bring him back to the palace. He now endeavoured to allay the pangs of conscience by heaping riches, honours, and favours of every kind on the kindred of the man whom he had so barbarously destroyed.

That the duke should be an inattentive spectator of these events was not in his character. It was his constant object to organise a conspiracy for the downfall of his brother; and he masked his proceedings with so much art that, though he was undoubtedly suspected, there was no evidence to criminate him. When the time for action was come, when he saw the public mind weaned from his brother, and knew that he could depend on the support of the chief nobles, he resolved not to delay a moment in executing his long-concerted scheme. He took advantage of the festivals given at Stockholm in honour of the king's marriage to seize the fortresses, three governors of which were in his interest.

The civil war now broke out. In the first action Eric triumphed; but the two dukes (for John was joined by his brother Charles) now overran several of the provinces, penetrated to Upsala, and finally invested the king in Stockholm. The place might long have held out, but little reliance was to be placed on the garrison, and still less on the citizens. They even informed him of their intention to surrender; and though he threw himself into the citadel, he was persuaded to capitulate. His life and liberty were to be secure on his abdicating the throne. But no sooner was he in the power of his enemies than they consigned him to a dungeon, where ill-usage was employed to hasten his end. But the vigour of his constitution enabled him to survive, until he was made to swallow poison by order of the usurper, after an imprisonment of ten years. For some time he applied himself to music; but even this indulgence was at length taken from him. He then devoted his time to literary occupation. He wrote a treatise on the military art, translated into Swedish the history of Johannes Magnus, and versified some of the Psalms. It is impossible not to feel the deepest commiseration for his fate.

JOHN III (1568-1592 A.D.)

No sooner did John make his triumphant entry into Stockholm than he was declared king by the senators assembled. Early in the following year his title was confirmed by a general meeting of the estates, which sentenced the unfortunate Eric to perpetual imprisonment, and deprived his children of the rights of succession. How came John to an influence so unbounded, yet so sudden, over the nobles of the kingdom? The answer must, doubtless, be sought in the senators whom he had bribed, in the hopes which a new reign always engenders, in the dislike borne to Eric by those who had suffered from his caprice, and in the powerful armed body of followers who were ready to assist him in any enterprise. Besides, in Sweden, as everywhere else, revolutions are, in general, the work of a minority: the bulk of the people regard them with comparative indifference. There was, however, one discontented noble, Duke Charles, to whom John had promised a share in the government. For some time the duke could obtain nothing; but an apprehension lest he should take part with the dethroned Eric led to his restoration to the provinces of Vermland, Södermanland, and Nerike, which, however, he was to hold with such restrictions on his authority as to render him merely a dependent functionary. The man who was behaving to one brother with so much brutality was not likely to be just towards another.

To the wars of John with Denmark we shall allude in relation to Danish history. Those with Russia were almost equally striking in themselves, though less so in their results. The scene of them was generally Livonia, sometimes Finland; and the advantage was ultimately with the czar. This, indeed, was the period when that barbarian power began to interfere in the general affairs of Europe. If its efforts were long isolated, they were bold enough to inspire its neighbours with alarm, since they indicated an ambition beyond all bounds, and a feeling which despised the ordinary maxims of justice. Fortunately for John, Russia was at war with the Tatars, who more than once poured their wild hordes over the empire; and he himself had an able general in Pont de la Gardie, a Frenchman who had entered his services, and to whom he was indebted for the only successes of his reign. The election, too, of his son Sigismund to the throne of Poland (1587) strengthened the eastern barrier against Russian aggression. Independently of his affection for a country over which he was one day to rule, Sigismund felt that he had as much need of Swedish help as Sweden had of his. Yet with all these advantages, in 1592, the last year of the Swedish monarch's reign, the preponderance of Russia in Ingermanland and Livonia was manifest. The blood and treasure of his reign were therefore wasted on objects which, though they might be obtained for a moment, could never be preserved.

More interesting than their indecisive however interminable hostilities were the disputes about religion. John had married Catherine, daughter of Sigismund II, king of Poland, and therefore a Roman Catholic. As her influence over her husband was great, she had little difficulty in prevailing on him to attempt many innovations in favour of her church. Her object was, doubtless, to favour its restoration to most of its ancient privileges; his was apparently confined to a union of the two churches, or, if that could not be obtained, simply to toleration and an equality of civil rights. How, considering the prejudices of the Swedes, he could hope to succeed in either view is not very clear. From the very first he encountered an opposition which forced him to look cautiously before him.

To some of his meditated designs he anticipated little resistance. The Lutheran clergy were no less fond of power than their predecessors; and they readily sanctioned maxims which elevated the church in the social scale, by rendering it less dependent on the state. And amongst them were some liberal men. They saw no harm in the colour of certain vestments, in the sign of the cross, in confession, or even in the mass — for did not Luther himself celebrate it to the last? Did he not believe in the real presence? The ceremonies of the church were purely arbitrary, and therefore indifferent: why, then, object to them? As the Romish church was the most ancient in Christendom, it had so far a fair claim to respect: many of its rites, and some of its tenets, might be the invention of later times; but still it possessed, however disguised, the essentials of Christianity. Thus reasoned many of the clergy, who at the king's request were induced to restore many observances of the fallen church. But a considerable number stoutly resisted every concession to anti-Christ; they condemned what they termed the lax spirit of their brethren, and declared that the Confession of Augsburg was worth all that had ever appeared before it. The nobles, who apprehended that if this spirit went on they might, in the end, be compelled to restore the lands which they had usurped from the church, were more sturdy in their resistance.

At their head was Duke Charles, who hoped that, by espousing their cause, he should win a support that might one day place him on the throne. At his instigation the diet gently remonstrated with the king on the course which he was pursuing; besought him not to favour popery; and hoped that Prince Sigismund would be placed exclusively under the care of reformed tutors. Sigismund, however, was too deeply imbued with his mother's spirit to admit any dictation on this subject: he refused to compromise his principles; and declared that he should prefer a crown in heaven to one on earth. But the opposition was, for this time, so strenuous, the intrigues of Duke Charles so manifest, that John was compelled to pause in his career, and even to profess for the Lutheran faith a respect which he did not feel. After a time, however, he recovered all his former zeal. He prepared a new liturgy, the very title of which sufficiently indicates its spirit — "Liturgy of the Swedish Church, conformable to the Catholic and Orthodox Church." Yet it was not agreeable to the pope, who considered it as bad as the Lutheran; while, by the more zealous reformers, it was execrated as a portion of anti-Christ.

Had John continued to act with moderation he might, indeed, have failed in his object, but he would have created no exasperation. But he became a persecutor of all the clergy who refused to adopt his ritual; and, what was worse, he became more of a Romanist as he advanced in years. The mission to Rome of Pont de la Gardie, to obtain the papal sanction of his liturgy, had been viewed with much displeasure by the people at large. The arrival, in 1578, of the Jesuit Possevin, in Sweden, ostensibly as the ambassador of the emperor but in reality as nuncio of Gregory XIII, was still more loudly condemned, especially by Duke Charles. A synod of the clergy subject to this prince assembled at Nyköping, and declared their adherence to the reformation. Still the king persevered; and in 1582 he prevailed on the greater part of the Swedish church to revise its liturgy, to declare all who refused guilty of schism, and to inhibit Duke Charles from continuing his opposition to measures which had been sanctioned alike by the church and the monarch.

But that ambitious prince was not to be restrained. Having connected himself by marriage with the count palatine of the Rhine, he formed a league with Holland, England, Navarre, and the reformed states of Germany — outwardly for the defence of their common faith, but really to dethrone his brother. Neither of these circumstances was hidden from the king, who again paused in his hazardous course. The death of his queen, and his marriage with a Lutheran lady, conspired to the same end — viz., increased moderation. But Duke Charles, who attributed it to hypocrisy, continued to harass him so much by intrigue, or open disobedience that he summoned him to answer for his conduct before the estates of Vadstena. Charles obeyed the citation; but it was at the head of a strong body of troops, with whom to overawe the assembly, that he encamped near the town. Civil war was averted through the interference of the nobles; but there was no harmony, since, in the following year (1588), he again prevailed on the clergy of his duchy to reject the new liturgy more decisively than before. To make head against open and secret hostility, John turned for aid to his son Sigismund, king of Poland; but the interview between the two monarchs had no other result than to make the duke more powerful by connecting him more closely with the Lutheran party. Harassed by continual cares, and by still greater apprehensions, the king now saw that his only hope of security lay in a cordial reconciliation with his brother. The price was a dear one — a share in the government of the kingdom; but it had been promised before the dethronement of Eric, and nothing less would have satisfied the other.

One of the last public acts of John was to demand vengeance on some nobles who, he asserted, had not only fomented the long misunderstanding between him and his brother, but had conspired against the royal family, and even intrigued with Russia. The justice of the accusation is not very clear; and as they were protected by the duke, he could not proceed with much severity against them. In 1592 he ended his agitated life — agitated by intrigues, disgraced by duplicity, and embittered by remorse for the murder of his elder brother.

Whether he was much attached to the Romish church may be doubted: probably he had a philosophical indifference for both churches; and in his advances towards the ancient one was actuated by the hope of making the Catholic powers of Europe his allies against the invincible hostility of Denmark, no less than by the affection which he bore to his first wife, a princess of that communion. It is certain that, after his union with his second wife, a Protestant, he exhibited less zeal for the cause than he had previously shown. Such, however, was his obstinacy of temper, that he would never wholly change, though he would modify, his policy. It is worthy of remark that his death was for some time concealed by his queen and some of the senators, even from Duke Charles, now regent of the kingdom during the absence of Sigismund, king of Poland, who rightfully succeeded to the Swedish crown. The object of this policy was soon shown by the robbery of the public treasury no less than of the palace: everything that could be carried away was shared between the queen and the nobles in her confidence.

SIGISMUND (1592-1604 A.D.)

That the reign of Sigismund would be nominal rather than real, and of short duration, might have been foreseen by the least prophetic. His absence in Poland, his religion, and, above all, the talents of his uncle, now grey in duplicity and intrigue, were insurmountable obstacles to his enjoyment of the regal power. One of the first acts of the regent was sufficiently indicative of his long-cherished design: he ordered the Swedish officers in Esthonia not to deliver up the fortresses to Poland, even if the king should command them to do so. In the same view he endeavoured secretly to detach the leading nobles from their allegiance to his nephew. To the multitude, and to all who had profited by the robbery of the church, he was agreeable, as the great champion of the Reformation. To show his zeal for its interests, though in reality he cared as little for it as he did for Romanism, he induced the synod of Upsala (1593) to abolish the liturgy which the late king had employed so much time to introduce. The ecclesiastics who had defended that liturgy were deposed. Another blow at the royal power of Sigismund was of a still heavier kind: it prohibited all appeals to him whenever he should not be in Sweden; and if he refused to confirm both decrees, he was not to be regarded as king of Sweden. That he should long remain ignorant of the intrigues directed to deprive him of one of his crowns was impossible; many, indeed, of the discontented nobles (and what governor was ever without them?), and many who preferred their loyalty to the seductive offers of the duke, either hastened to him in Poland, or communicated with him. He soon found that his return to Sweden was necessary, and he obtained, without much difficulty, the consent of the Polish diet for that purpose.

But he had the imprudence to select as his confidential adviser Malaspina, the papal nuncio, who was suspected — probably with much justice — of having obtained his consent, and even the promise of his assistance, in the restoration of the ancient church. And in the first diet which he convoked he had the still greater folly to propose the revocation of the decree made by the synod of Upsala — that which abolished the ritual introduced by his father. He insisted, too, that in every town there should be a Catholic church, where its votaries might worship in peace. The Lutheran ecclesiastics, sure of his uncle's support, now declaimed against him with vehemence. In the diet of Upsala, where he was crowned (1594), Charles appeared with an armed force, and compelled him to make some concessions to the popular voice; but in that of Stockholm, which was held immediately afterwards, he exasperated the Lutherans by the undisguised manner in which he attempted to promote the interests of the church. Disgusted with men whom he could neither persuade nor force to his will, and discouraged by the intrigues of his uncle, he listened to the cry of the Poles for his return, and left Sweden in the utmost confusion (July, 1594).

By the retreat of Sigismund, Charles was the regent, though some portion of his authority was divided with the senate, and he determined not to relax his labours until he had obtained the title with the authority of king. The birth of a son, who became famous in history as Gustavus Adolphus, confirmed him in his purpose.*c*

Astrology was at that epoch both fashionable and respected. In every court there was a mysterious man clothed in a robe sown with constellations, and wearing a pointed hat, and who spoke the tongues of Asia, living alone in the highest room of the castle tower, a stranger to earthly things, his eyes constantly fixed on the heavens. This man claimed the power to foretell, by following the march of the stars, the destinies of his fellow beings. His predictions were given, as is the case with all prophets, in ambiguous terms, lending themselves to double meaning and thus to some interpretation justified by the development of events. And so the whole cohort of ambitious men, and intriguing women besieged the door of his laboratory in crowds. Even those whose talents placed them at the head of affairs, came like the most ordinary minds, to lend an eager ear to the charlatans' lies — so difficult is it for man, however vast the extent of his intelligence, to shake off the yoke of prejudice.

The astrologer of the court of Stockholm had scarcely learned of the prince's birth, when he drew his horoscope and predicted, they say, that this prince would be king, that he would widely extend the limits of his kingdom, that he would die a violent death, and that his name would shine after him.

So far back as 1572 Tycho Brahe, had announced that the comet then appearing in the constellation Cassiopeia, presaged the birth, in Finland, of a prince who would confer a great benefit upon all those of the reformed religion.

This famous astrologer inhabited in 1594 his magnificent palace of Uranienborg on the island of Hven which he owed to the liberality of Frederick II. From this lone rock in the Sound his great voice resounded and found an echo from the whole world. On learning of the event which had caused such joy in Sweden, he declared to his numerous pupils, gathered from the ends of the earth to listen to his learned discourse, that the new-born child was really the great prince whose birth the comet had predicted twenty-two years before. When someone objected that the child had come into the world in Sweden, not in Finland, he replied that the duchess of Södermanland having spent some time in the latter province, the child was conceived there, and even if he was born on the other side of the Gulf of Bothnia, the prediction could be perfectly well applied to him. Chronicles further relate that Tycho Brahe, dowered with marvellous divinatory powers traced in a still famous lecture the future life of the man of genius whose coming he had announced. It would appear, however, that his predictions were much less understood in his lifetime than after his death, from the fact that the famous astrologer, after having incurred the disfavour of Christian IV, and being compelled to leave his native land, found at the court of the emperor Rudolf, devoted to alchemy and astrology, a generous hospitality, and kept to the day of his death the friendship of this prince. Is it likely, is it possible that the emperor, restless and suspicious to a degree, and knowing the jargon of this profession, would have granted so many favours and shown such good will to a man who had complaisantly prophesied the ruin of his house? It is certain that all that was said and done about the prince's birth has been exaggerated, but man likes to surround the cradles of genius with marvels and mysteries, and if Gustavus Adolphus had been an ordinary sovereign many details which have given place to all sorts of commentaries would have passed unnoticed.

Throughout Europe, but especially in the North, the Christmas and New Year festivals, which were celebrated together, were the signal for universal rejoicing. The duke of Södermanland was naturally pious, but his antagonistic position to Sigismund compelled him to give his piety an outward show that was perhaps a little too ostentatious, and history has accused him of making his religion serve his ambition. It is true that, to impress the people and make them more devoted to his son, he let it be understood that to the child's cradle was attached the fate of the nation, as had been the case with Moses' cradle. The ceremonies of the young prince's baptism were, to this end, mingled with the fêtes with which the nation celebrated the birth of its Redeemer, and gave these, indeed, a new éclat. We have already said that the child received the combined names of both grand-parents, Gustavus and Adolphus. Finally, to bind his destiny indissolubly to that of Protestantism, the duke of Södermanland founded, on the same day in his domain, and within the influence of his patronage, the celebrated University of Upsala whose devotion to the established church, and firmness in repelling the liturgy, have made it the victim of spoliations and persecutions without number. This clever and salutary measure was all the better received, since the Swedish clergy, justly alarmed at Sigismund's threatening projects, were not quite sure about the duke, whom they suspected of leaning towards Calvinism. In linking the famous school, whose professors bore the title of "Pillars of Protestantism," with the destiny of his son, was it not his purpose to establish beyond a doubt his intention to educate the boy in doctrines of the purest orthodoxy? It is thus that the people reasonably explained the duke's conduct.[h]

At any rate he was encouraged to renew a career of alternate duplicity and defiance, of which there is scarcely a parallel in the annals of princes. One of his first steps was to depose from their dignities all who were favourable either to Sigismund or to the Roman Catholic church. His next was to make peace with the czar, in direct opposition to the commands of the king. Emboldened by the obsequiousness of the senate, and by the attachment of the large towns, he convoked the estates at Söderköping, and caused a decree to be passed that the Confession of Augsburg should be the only rule of faith observed in Sweden; that all Romish priests should be banished in six weeks; that Swedes who had embraced the religion of Rome prior to the accession of Sigismund might remain in the country — but they should be excluded from all posts of honour or emolument, no less than from the exercise of their worship; and that all, in future, who should declare for the obnoxious opinions, or who should not conform both outwardly and inwardly to the established creed, should be banished forever. In temporal matters the proceedings of this diet were equally insulting to the king. No ordinance issued by him was to be obeyed, or even promulgated, until confirmed by the duke and senate. He was deprived of the power of deposing any Swede from office without the sanction of the senate. Nor could he appoint to any dignity or post: in every vacancy three names were to be sent to him, and he had the privilege of electing one of the number. In accordance with the ecclesiastical portion of these regulations, the priests, the monks, the nuns, and three fourths of the laity repaired to Germany, or to Poland, or to Finland.

That Sigismund should be incensed at these proceedings was natural; but he saw the necessity of temporising; and he sent messengers to detach the senators and nobles from the party of his uncle. In the first object of their mission they succeeded completely; in the second, partially. The means employed on this occasion are purely matter of conjecture. Probably they were not slow to perceive that a ruler at a distance was preferable to one at home; that if Sigismund retained the sovereignty, their own authority must necessarily be secure; while under the iron yoke of Charles they had nothing to expect beyond servitude. Nor was the same consideration lost on many of the people, who knew that, in affairs unconnected with religion, the sway of Sigismund was far milder than the regent's. Hence the authority of the latter declined, especially when the former conferred on the senate alone the administration of the realm. But that prince was not thus to be baffled in the great object of his ambition. He was still at the head of a strong party; and he had influence enough to prevail on the diet of Arboga (1597) to restore him. When the senators refused to ratify this act, he expelled them from the kingdom, or rather, to avoid a worse result, they exiled themselves. His next step was to gain possession of the royal fortresses, which he garrisoned with his own creatures, whom he enjoined to let no one enter, not even at the command of Sigismund. Yet all this while he pretended great zeal for the service of his liege lord, and threw all the blame of these measures on the senate, who, he asserted, were endeavouring to dethrone the dynasty of Vasa. By that mixture of cunning and violence in which he was so great an adept, he prevailed on the diet of Stockholm to ratify all that he had done, and to declare the absent senators traitors to their country.

Sigismund had still two or three fortified places in Finland; and when he heard that his uncle was besieging them, and was openly inculcating disobedience to all his mandates, he no longer hesitated to equip an armament for Sweden. He landed at Kalmar, and several provinces immediately declared for him. But he had not the degree of military talent necessary for one in his position, or perhaps he relied too much on the universality of the feeling manifested in his favour. In Linköping he suffered himself to be surprised by his active enemy: his guard was forced, his own person in danger. But to destroy him was not the object of the artful regent, who made overtures of peace — insisting, however, that five of the senators then with the king should be surrendered to him. To this hard condition Sigismund was compelled to accede, and to confirm Charles in the regency. All matters of dispute between the two and the fate of the imprisoned senators were to be decided by the estates — that is, by the creatures of Charles, who thus obtained every wish of his heart, without incurring the odium of wanton violence.

Sigismund, as was doubtless foreseen, protested, on his return to Poland, against the convention of Linköping; and, by so doing, enabled his uncle forever to throw off the mask which had been so long worn. Under his influence, the diet of Stockholm renounced its allegiance to the king, and offered the crown to Wladyslaw, son of Sigismund, on the impossible condition that, within a year, the young prince should repair to Sweden and be instructed in the Lutheran faith. If he refused to comply, then he, his father, and their descendants were to be forever excluded from the throne. To be prepared against the probable hostilities of his nephew, Charles entered into an offensive alliance against Poland with the czar, reduced more of the Finland fortresses, and put to death many adherents of the king. In the diet of Linköping (1600) he caused sentence to be pronounced and executed on the imprisoned senators, whose loyalty would have procured them favour with any other prince, and with any other people than the Swedes, who were now become the merest slaves of the usurper. The same obsequious assembly declared the throne vacant, and invested Charles with absolute power. Though he looked to the name as well as to the reality, he acted with consummate duplicity. In an assembly of the estates at Norrköping (1604), he proposed to resign the cares of government in favour of Prince John, a younger brother of Sigismund, and, consequently, his nephew. John, who had made his private arrangements with the regent, and been invested with the duchy of Östergötland, refused a gift which would have required a large army to retain it a single month, and proposed his uncle. The farce ended, as everybody saw it would end, by the election of Charles and by the designation of his son for his successor.

Thus ended the short and venial authority of Sigismund over Sweden. In his administration (if such it could be called), we see little to blame beyond his imprudent zeal on behalf of his co-religionists. Whether he hoped to obtain for them anything beyond mere toleration, is, notwithstanding the allegations of his enemies, exceedingly doubtful. But even in this object he was censurable enough, considering the progress which the Reformation had made in the kingdom. It was essentially Lutheran; and he had no right to disturb the unanimity of his people by the introduction of doctrines which they had long renounced, and to which they had vowed an unextinguishable hostility.

CHARLES IX [1] (1604–1611 A.D.)

The short reign of this prince was signalised by successive wars — first with the Poles, and then with the Danes. In Livonia his generals obtained some advantages; but they were lost as soon as won. Equally unsuccessful were his intrigues in Russia to procure the crown vacant by the death of Boris Godunor, for a prince of his own family. The Poles were nearer than he to the scene of ambition, and enabled to obtain more advantages — among others the election of

OLOFSBURG CASTLE, FINLAND

their prince Wladyslaw to the throne of the czars. But even they had little reason to congratulate themselves on this event; for Wladyslaw was soon expelled, and the barbarian sceptre transferred to the dynasty of Romanov. The Swedes had still less cause of triumph, in thus embarrassing themselves in wars of which the issue could not fail to be disastrous. A nearer enemy found them, during the rest of this reign, employment enough.[c]

[1] How the native historians of Sweden contrive to place eight sovereigns of this name before the present one, is curious enough. There are but two authentic rulers of the name, as kings of all Sweden; but in the Egyptian darkness prior to the tenth century, there is room for any number of any name. Probably the Goths and Svear, the two great branches of the paternal family, had petty chiefs after the German name; but we have conjecture only for their existence.

The Kalmar War

The northern part of the Scandinavian peninsula, as already noticed, had been peopled from the remotest times by nomadic tribes called Finns or Cwenas by the Norwegians and Lapps by the Swedes, from which their territory derived the name of Lapland. These aboriginal inhabitants retained their primitive manners, language, and religion, unaffected by the progress of Christianity in the North. No definite boundary separated the adjacent kingdoms of Sweden and Norway from the dreary wilderness occupied by their less civilised neighbours who subsisted by hunting and fishing. The progress of conquest had gradually pressed them nearer to the borders of the arctic circle, but still even under the Union of Kalmar their territorial limits remained undefined.

The tribes scattered along the coasts beyond the North Cape paid tribute to Norway as early as the reign of Harold Harfagr. The Laplanders round the gulf of Bothnia were subdued by associations of fur-traders, to whom the exclusive monopoly of their commerce and government was granted by Magnus Ladulås; and so far had these merchants abused their privileges and thrown off their dependence on the Swedish crown that they styled themselves "kings of the Lapps." Gustavus Vasa expelled these usurpers, and reduced the natives to the condition of tributaries. Charles IX after his accession assumed the title of "king of the Lapps of Norrland," and founded the new city Gothenburg (Göteborg), near the mouth of the Göta, to the inhabitants of which he granted the privilege of fishing on the northern coasts of Lapland.

These measures, added to the interruption of the Danish commerce with the ports in the gulf of Riga, awakened the jealousy of Christian IV of Denmark, who stationed a convoy in the Sound to protect all vessels navigating the Baltic, in which he claimed not merely freedom of mercantile intercourse but a right of dominion such as had been immemorially asserted by his royal predecessors. In vain did he remonstrate with the king and the senate against these encroachments upon the interests of his crown and the immunities of his people; Charles evaded all proposals for redress, and in 1611 commenced that sanguinary struggle between the two kingdoms usually called the war of Kalmar. Before taking the field, Christian despatched a herald-at-arms with a declaration of hostilities against Sweden, but Charles refused to admit him into his presence, and detained him as a prisoner; whilst his own messenger reached the enemy's camp, where he presented a counter declaration, repeating the arguments advanced in the Danish manifesto and endeavouring to throw the odium of the rupture upon his adversary.

The national land-forces of Denmark at this epoch consisted in the feudal militia, composed of the nobility and their vassals, the tenant of every crown fief being compelled to serve in person on horseback, and also to furnish a certain number of his serfs for the infantry, which was divided into regiments, or "banners," of six hundred men each, commanded by a captain, and subdivided into twelve companies, headed by as many lieutenants. These levies furnished an army of sixteen thousand native troops, and they were increased by four thousand mercenaries, consisting of German cavalry, with English and Scottish infantry. The defence of Norway was confided to the national militia. The whole naval force was divided into two squadrons, one of which was sent to cruise in the Kattegat, and the other to blockade Kalmar, the key of Sweden on the Baltic frontier.

Notwithstanding these formidable preparations, Christian laboured under certain obvious disadvantages; the Danish nobility grudged the pecuniary supplies; the nation had not heard the sound of war since the Treaty of Stettin in 1570; whilst the Swedes, on the other hand, had been constantly engaged in hostilities with Poland and Russia.

One division of the Danish army, under Steen Schestedt, grand-marshal of the kingdom, penetrated through Vestergötland to Jönköping; and the other, commanded by Christian in person, laid siege to Kalmar, which was soon obliged to capitulate, the king himself mounting the breech at the head of his troops. The garrison retreated into the citadel, but the town was given up to be plundered by the soldiery. Charles, and his son Gustavus Adolphus, who had surprised the principal military depot of the enemy, advanced by rapid marches to the relief of the place, whilst Admiral Gyldenstiern arrived with a superior naval force, and threw a considerable supply of men and provisions into the besieged citadel. Schestedt was recalled from Vestergötland, but the Swedes, determined to attack the Danish entrenchments before the arrival of this reinforcement, broke the enemy's lines, whilst the garrison made a sortie, set fire to the town, and penetrated to the royal camp.

On this occasion Christian signalised his personal courage, presence of mind, and other great military qualities, for which he was distinguished. After an obstinate combat, the assailants were driven back to their original position; and Schestedt, arriving in the midst of the battle, decided the fortune of the day. A short time afterwards the Swedes abandoned their camp in the night, and withdrew to Risby, in the expectation of receiving additional supplies. Their retreat compelled the surrender of the citadel, in which was found a vast store of bronze artillery, with other munitions of war.

LAPLANDER OF THE SIXTEENTH CENTURY

Exasperated by these misfortunes, the Swedish monarch sent a cartel to Christian, accusing him in the most bitter and reproachful terms of having broken the peace of Stettin, taken the city of Kalmar by treachery, and shed a profusion of innocent blood in an unjust cause. Every means of conciliation being exhausted, he offered to terminate the quarrel by single combat. "Come then," said he, after the old Gothic fashion, "into the open field with us, accompanied by two of your vassals, in full armour, and we will meet you sword in hand, without helm or harness, attended in the same manner. Herein if you fail we shall no longer consider you as an honourable king or a soldier." Christian answered this extraordinary letter in terms still more reproachful, declining to accept the challenge of "a paralytic dotard," whom he sarcastically counselled to remain by a warm fire with his nurse and physician, rather than expose himself to combat in the open field, with his younger and more robust competitor. This severe reply the king followed up by attacking the Swedes in their entrenchments at Risby; but after three days hard fighting, he was compelled to retreat, and set sail for Copenhagen, where he remained during the winter. Charles did not long survive these exertions, dying at Nyköping in 1611, worn out with fatigue of body and mind.[g] During this war the sixteen-year-old prince, afterwards distinguished as Gustavus (II) Adolphus, won his spurs. Commanding a separate division of the army, he accomplished the destruction of Christianopel, the principal arsenal of the Danes in Skånia, and reconquered Oland. These victories were perhaps the most notable achievements of the war.[a]

GEIJER ON CHARLES IX

One quality was ever pre-eminent in Charles, and in some measure it should mitigate our judgment of his blood-stained path: this was his inborn striving to reach across every limit, beyond every goal to set another. He struggled to win for himself a crown. At this point another would have halted; to him it was so far from being the greatest, the ultimate conquest, that he left it insecure. The strife ensuing, which from Sigismund's slowness and irresolution might, for some time longer, have been waged by words and manifestos, he straightway removed out of Sweden to Livonia, Poland, and Russia; nor did the outbreak of war with Denmark prevent him from mustering in his last gaze, as it were, the members of a future league against the papacy and the house of Habsburg; for we find that in his testament he especially recommends to his children friendship with the evangelical princes of Germany.

Thus in the soul of Charles, perchance more than in any of his contemporaries, laboured the burning future which burst forth in the Thirty Years' War; and not without significance was he wont to observe, laying his hand on the head of the young Gustavus Adolphus, "*Ille jaciet!*" (He will do it!) Such men verily there are, full of the hereafter, who, with or without their own will and intent, carry the nations onward at their side. Except his father, no man before him exercised so deep an influence on the Swedish people. More than a hundred years passed away, and a like personal influence was still reigning upon the throne of Sweden. The nation, hard to move save for immediate self-defence, was borne along, unwilling and yet admiring, repugnant yet loving; as by some potent impulsion, following her Gustavuses and Charleses to victory, fame, and to the verge of perdition. This is neither praise nor blame; but so it was. And as I write the history of the Swedish people, I feel convincingly that it is the history of their kings.[e]

CHAPTER IX

GUSTAVUS ADOLPHUS

[1611–1632 A.D.]

THE ACCESSION OF GUSTAVUS ADOLPHUS

The illustrious hero whom history has rendered immortal under the name of Gustavus Adolphus was a minor at the time of his father's death; but he had given such proofs of precocious wisdom and valour that the estates did not hesitate to suspend, in favour of a youth of eighteen, the fundamental law of the realm, by which the expiration of the king's minority was fixed at twenty-four years of age. The state of perplexity and confusion in which the affairs of the nation were found at his accession required all the talent and energy of which he was possessed. The campaign in Russia, under the conduct of De la Gardie, had been attended with brilliant success; but although that general had made strong efforts to have Charles Philip, second son of the late monarch, elected czar, in opposition to Wladyslaw of Poland, the negotiations for procuring him the imperial dignity had made little progress. Whilst Sweden was menaced with formidable enemies on every side, her only support at home consisted of weak friends, ill-paid armies, and empty treasuries, exhausted by a series of wars and revolutions. In this feeble condition, it was of the utmost importance to secure internal tranquillity; and, accordingly, the diet prevailed with Duke John to confirm his renunciation of all claim to the throne, and allow the young prince to take upon himself the sole administration of the government.

The first acts of Gustavus' reign impressed his subjects with a favourable opinion of that singular penetration and capacity for business which marked the whole of his extraordinary career. The celebrated Oxenstierna was made chancellor, and every post, civil and military, was filled with equal discrimination. To carry on the foreign wars in which he was engaged, he resumed all the crown-grants, and ordered an account of the produce of tithes and feudal lands to be delivered annually into the royal exchequer. The peace concluded with Denmark allowed him to devote his attention, for a short interval, to the study of civil affairs. He concluded a treaty of commerce with the Dutch, and established a society of trade at Stockholm, every subscriber to which advanced certain sums to the crown on being released for the space of three years from all taxes, duties, and imposts. To encourage agricultural industry, he absolved peasants and farmers from the obligation of supplying the government with horses and carriages. An edict was published to abridge the tediousness and expense of litigation, especially in affairs of regal judicature; and no measures were omitted that could improve the national institutions or ameliorate the condition of the people. Within three years after his accession, Gustavus assembled the estates at Helsingborg, to deliberate on the proceedings necessary to be adopted for the speedy adjustment of the dispute with Russia. The whole northern quarter of that great empire had expressed a desire to have a Swedish prince, in the hope of extending their commercial relations with the Baltic; but Charles Philip had no ambition to become the ruler of a nation of barbarians. The scheme, which for some years had been a favourite object at the court of Stockholm, was now finally and suddenly defeated (1613) by the election to the dignity of czar of Michael Feodorovitch, a native prince of the Romanov family, remotely connected with that of the Ruriks, and founder of a new dynasty, which has continued ever since to sway the sceptre of that immense empire.

GUSTAVUS ADOLPHUS
(1594–1632)

Determined to revenge this affront, Gustavus obtained the concurrence of the estates in a resolution to compel the Muscovites to refund the debt they had contracted under the late reign. Their haughty refusal led to immediate hostilities; the indignant monarch entered Ingermanland at the head of an army, took Kexholm by storm, and was laying siege to Pskov, when James I of England offered his mediation, and succeeded in restoring peace (1617), on condition of Russia's making payment of the loan and ceding the contested provinces of Ingermanland and Karelia to Sweden. Brief as was the duration of this war, it is memorable as the school where Gustavus learned the rudiments of that art which afterwards made him the admiration of Europe.[d]

THE POLISH WAR

It was impossible to get Sigismund, king of Poland, to agree to renounce his claims to the Swedish throne, and to recognise the reigning dynasty in that country. He continued to take the title of King of Sweden and to give Gustavus Adolphus that of Duke of Södermanland, Nerike and Vermland, the provinces which had formerly formed Charles IX's appanage. Sigismund also sought to incite trouble by introducing clandestinely ordinances and letters, signed by himself, and spies, into the realm, but he went no further. At the moment of Charles IX's death, Sigismund could at least have taken Esthonia while Sweden and the young king were occupied with threatening wars. He did not take the slightest advantage of the favourable opportunity, however, either because of his natural slowness, or because the Polish estates-general showed themselves little disposed to uphold him. The Polish and Swedish troops, face to face in Livonia, in small numbers and in bad condition, remained in complete inactivity, and truces continually succeeded one another. Thus the years passed from 1611 to 1617.

Gustavus Adolphus had had the good fortune in this interval to terminate his wars with Denmark and Russia, and was disposed to turn all his forces against Poland. Sweden, however, desired peace in this direction also, in order to put an end to the sacrifices demanded by a war which had lasted nearly sixty years. The young king himself felt the necessity for this. He proposed reasonable conditions to Sigismund, but the latter responded with such exorbitant demands as the renunciation by Gustavus Adolphus of his father's throne. These pretensions, on the part of a prince who could

AXEL OXENSTIERNA, CHANCELLOR OF SWEDEN

(1583-1654)

not even defend his own frontiers, aroused great anger in Sweden. The diet assembled at Orebro in 1617, and Gustavus Adolphus gave proof of his pacific intentions and of Sigismund's unjust claims, and caused to be read a letter from this prince, addressed to [the latter's half-brother] Duke John, and written with the intention of fomenting troubles in the kingdom. The estates-general, irritated by Sigismund's conduct, declared that, in spite of the great necessity there was for peace, they would grant the subsidies asked for to chastise "the insolent king of Poland." The war against that country recommenced with new vigour, and lasted twelve years. Its principal arena during the first eight years was Livonia and afterwards Polish Prussia, particularly in the vicinity of the lower Vistula. During 1617 and 1618 there was nothing but insignificant skirmishes, after which a truce was concluded, to last until 1621. By this time the negotiations for the marriage of Gustavus Adolphus with Maria Eleonore, sister of George William, elector of Brandenburg, were finished, and the kingdom had recovered some of its strength; so the war was renewed with spirit. From 1621 to 1625 there was fighting in Livonia and Courland. Gustavus Adolphus seized these two provinces, took Riga, a commercial city of great importance, made an excursion into Samogitia, and defeated the Poles in several encounters.

Again the question of peace was raised. The Lithuanians, dreading a Swedish invasion, were disposed to some sort of an arrangement; but the Poles proper allowed themselves to be influenced by Sigismund, and the negotiations came to nothing. Gustavus Adolphus then determined to act more vigorously, in order to inspire the Poles and their king with thoughts of peace. He transferred the seat of war to Prussia, to make the Poles realise what misery it could bring with it. His plan was to seize all the ports, to impede the enemy's trade, and turn all the customs revenue to his profit. Jakob de la Gardie and Gustaf Horn were charged with the defence of Livonia against the Lithuanians, and acquitted themselves with honour. On the 15th of June, 1626, Gustavus Adolphus landed not far from Pillau, and seized the same year Königsberg, Braunsberg, Elbing, Stuhm, Marienburg, Mewe, etc. He returned to Sweden for the winter, rejoined the army in the month of May, 1627, and again measured his strength with the Poles —first near Dantzic, and then in the vicinity of Dirschau. He would have obtained very great advantages, if wounds had not twice prevented him from giving his troops the inspiration of his presence. He returned again to his country for the winter, coming back to the army in 1628, and pushing his conquests as far as the Polish frontier. His light troops marched all around Warsaw, spreading universal terror. The king would perhaps have won more signal victories with the main body of his army, if he had not made it a principle in all his wars to keep as close to the shore as possible, in order always to be within reach of relief from Sweden. Gustavus Adolphus passed the following winter in his kingdom, and it was during this interval that Hermann Wrangel won the important victory of Gorzno. This series of defeats made the estates-general of Poland more and more disposed to peace; but Sigismund was not yet willing to renounce his claims, all the more as he expected the emperor's long-promised help. In fact, ten thousand auxiliary troops arrived from Germany in 1629. Gustavus Adolphus had also received fresh troops from Sweden. Bloody conflicts took place near Stuhm and Marienburg, but without decisive victories for one side or the other. At the same time, a pest broke out in both camps, which was more deadly for the Poles. Misunderstandings arose between the Poles and the Germans; and neither the former nor the latter seemed disposed to let themselves be killed in support of Sigismund's preposterous claims. This prince was, therefore, forced to arrange, in September, 1629, a six years' truce, afterwards prolonged to twenty-five years.

The superiority of the Swedish troops over the Polish became more apparent as the war lasted from year to year. The Polish troops maintained themselves with great difficulty in Prussia, whose inhabitants began also to show a particular personal attachment to Gustavus Adolphus. He was often received in the towns with the acclamation, "Our king has come!" Had it not been for his wounds and the rainy summer of 1628, it is most probable that all Prussia would have been conquered, as well as Livonia. It must not be forgotten, however, that the stubborn defence of Dantzic contributed much to save the country.[e]

SWEDEN AS A MILITARY MONARCHY

Sweden had enjoyed no peace since the days of Gustavus I. There had been fraternal war and civil war; two kings had been overthrown. Charles bequeathed to his son a blood-besprent throne — and war with all his neigh-bours. And if we cast our glance forwards — war, again war, without inter-mission, during long times to come! Through Gustavus Adolphus, the weight of the Swedish arms was to be felt over the world. It is a foreground lighted up by the flames of war. But the fame which may outstand the probing gaze of history must possess other claims to the homage of the afterworld than the splendour of arms alone.

We begin with what concerns most nearly the constitution itself. The greatest change in this respect was the hereditary monarchy, and the contest which it had called forth was scarcely yet fought out. This was carried on under circumstances which instructively show how, in politics, the word "liberty" is not always a sure indication of the presence of its real benefits. Who can doubt that in Sweden, during the union, this idea was represented by the insurgent peasants and the lawless power of the administrator, and that the magnates employed all the liberty known to the law of Sweden only to preserve for the union-kings the name, and for themselves the exercise, of power? Gustavus Vasa stamped legality on revolt, and suppressed it after-wards; but found himself, on the instant, directly opposed to that party which so long had used the cloak of the law for its own advantage. Thus was the foundation of royal power in Sweden, as everywhere, at the com-mencement of modern history, the work of stringent absolutism; and yet, who can deny that the unity and self-rule, thus established, was in the very deed the mainspring of freedom? With Charles' consolidation of his father's work, men in Sweden seemed to have ascertained the dangers of extremes clearly enough to return to a middle way; and the royal warranty (konunga-försäkran) of Gustavus Adolphus may be termed a new form of government, which aimed at confining power on all sides within the bounds of law.

This warranty was founded upon the king's oath introduced in the ancient law-book, but contains besides divers more exact definitions and limitations. The arbitrariness to which, under the foregoing reign, so much calamity was chargeable, now gave occasion to a more express confirmation of the prin-ciple sanctified by the law, that no one should be apprehended or condemned upon a mere allegation, or without knowing his accuser and being brought face to face with him before the judgment seat. The king was to ensure to all orders, especially that of the nobility, due respect, and to every office dignity and power, dismissing no man from office unless he should be law-fully adjudged culpable. The enactment in the Land's Law (Lands-lag) that, without consent of the people, neither a new law should be made nor a new tax imposed, was ratified anew with the addition that the assent of Duke John, of the council, and of the estates, should likewise be requisite thereto. Without this, neither war, peace, truce, nor alliance, could be made. The council was reinstated in its position of mediator between king and people, and the estates deprecated their being burdened with too frequent holding of diets. Hereby, in the great necessities of the crown, the right of the estates to tax themselves was brought into jeopardy, especially as the expres-sions of the king's oath respecting the taxes are very indefinite, namely, that "they shall not be imposed without the knowledge of the council and the consent of those to whom it belongeth." Thus was the power of the council augmented both from the side of the king and that of the people; and, in proof thereof, the provision of the old regal oath which forbids the king of Sweden to alienate or diminish the property of the crown, was omitted from the form of warranty pronounced by the young Gustavus Adolphus.

King John III declared, in 1573, that every nobleman who was more than seventeen years old, and unable to discharge his horse service, should, if he would retain his shield of nobility, at least serve for pay, since in the service of the crown he must be. Charles IV required that all sons of noblemen, when they had reached the lawful age — even those whose fathers had been beheaded or banished — should come to the weapon show and follow him to the war; wherefore we hear thenceforward of noble volunteers and "younkers of gentry" who served as common soldiers, even on foot and for pay. The nobility of Sweden included all having command, whether civil or military, and almost all the public servants of the realm in the secular departments. Hence, the nobles looked upon their claim to offices of state as their highest right. At the same time, theirs was properly a military order; for every noble was at least a common soldier, if nothing else, and thereto born. Charles had strengthened the influence of the army by summoning to the diets a number of officers as its representatives, a practice which continued long afterwards. Axel Oxenstierna mentions this as a custom peculiar to Sweden. The military, which sent deputies from among both the officers and the privates (though they had no votes), strengthened the nobility at the diets, where every nobleman who had come to lawful years was bound to give his attendance. Add hereto long and prosperous wars, and the military monarchy is complete. Such a military monarchy had Sweden now become; and under this aspect it was regarded by its greatest statesmen. The military spirit pervaded all. With such a spirit and a young hero wearing the crown, we may not wonder at that claim of pre-eminence, so nearly coinciding with reality, made by the nobility, or its assertion that the nobleman was immediately, the peasant only mediately, the subject of the realm — claims which, finally led to the formally expressed dogma of the nobility, that "it could not be out-voted at the diets by the other estates."

After the close of the Danish war, in January, 1613, Gustavus caused a declaration to be drawn up for the right understanding of the nobility's privileges, which he committed to the custody of John Skytte. Those of the nobility, the declaration ran, who neither themselves bore part in the Danish war, nor fulfilled their horse service, but slunk away, while the king himself lay afield against the enemies of the realm, should lose their baronial freedom, unless they had lawful excuse and by grace obtained a new confirmation. They were reminded that inheritable estates, as well as fiefs, were subject to the burden of horse service. It was noted as an abuse that the nobility released their peasants, not only within the free-mile round their mansions, but generally upon their lands held in fief from the crown, from portages, lodgment, and other works of succour *(hjelp);* that they built as many seats *(sätesgårdarna)* as they pleased, and claimed for them the same immunities as for their individual place of abode, thus also withdrawing a large number of persons from conscription; that, whereas the houses of the nobles in the towns were free from all civic burdens, they unlawfully, either themselves or by others, pursued civic callings, maintaining even in some cases tap-rooms and places of dissolute resort; that they had abused likewise their toll-free right for inland traffic and foreign commerce, as well on their own account as that of others; with much else to the same purpose.

A statute passed in Gustavus' second diet, of the year 1612, provided that all fiefs conferred at pleasure should be revoked till the investigation of the grounds of tenure was completed; "since, in a word, the largest portion of the income and rents of the realm is bestowed in fiefs." This statute remained on the whole without effect; and naturally enough, seeing that such infeudations, however great the inconveniences they entailed on both governors and subjects, constituted from of old the payment for the entire service of the state, and the remedy of the evil would thus have required a new regulation of stipends in every department. For this, the wars that had broken out left no time, and the confusion of the finances, no means. We see the king for the most part reduced to the necessity of giving with one hand what he had taken back with the other. Great merits and brilliant proofs of bravery called for rewards which he, least of all men, could refuse; and the conquests of the Russian and Polish wars supplied new channels for his generosity. The erection of the Swedish House of Barons *(Riddarhus)* took place in 1625. The king gave his assent to the petition of the nobility on this subject, in recompense for the readiness wherewith they had received the royal proposals, respecting the maintenance of a standing army, made to the estates at the diet of that year. At this point the horse service virtually ceased to be the ground of freedom of nobility, and the old contest regarding it became at least of smaller importance. Nobility, as completely hereditary, was separated from the other gentry, although left open to merit of every kind; but its destination mainly for warlike objects continued the same, and, hence, in Sweden a standing army and a permanent house of barons were contemporary institutions. What Gustavus, looking into the future, designed by the great dignities wherewith he surrounded his throne, what he purposed with the nobility of Sweden, is as uncertain as what he intended with Sweden itself. Everywhere we find the tracks of greatness, but no goal — scattered premises to a conclusion cut off by death. That he held control over his work (which without him became something entirely different in character), is certain. The officers of the army continued to be called to the diets. The statutes were passed in the name of the "council and estates, counts, free-barons, bishops, nobles, clergy, military commanders, burgesses, and common folk *(menige allmoge)*, of the realm of Sweden," but the military commanders, although not named in the ordinance for the House of Barons, were reckoned of the nobility.

With all this enhancement of the influence of the nobility, the king yet possessed, in respect to all the estates, the power, requisite to a ruler, of having the last word in deliberations and resolutions. The forms appointed for a Swedish diet of estates, in 1617, were little different from the oldest in which the king spoke to the country's army, and acclamation decided the adoption of the statute. Nor was the plan of representation by estates yet fully developed. This can properly be said only of the first estate, which outweighed the rest, much was yet indeterminate. The presence of all the nobles, unless hindered by years, sickness, or the public service, was, though required by law, hardly possible. From the clergy, were commonly summoned the bishop of every diocese, with a member of the chapter, and a minister from every hundred; from the burgesses, the burgomaster and one of the council or the commonalty in every town; of the yeomen, one or two from every hundred.

The old popular right of self-taxation had become more and more a subject for the arbitrary disposal of the governors. These relations suffered little change under the first kings of the Vasa family; especially as, according to the country's law, supply was not yet a question for the diet in the later sense, and the representation long continued to oscillate between provincial and general estates. The crown, with augumented power, naturally intervened; and thus we see that Gustavus I sometimes levied heavy taxes, with no reference except to the consent of the council. The numerous diets of Charles IX in part changed this relation, and at the diet of 1602 we observe that even the amount of a tax was fixed, although it was to be paid in wares. But this was not the rule.

Over the grave of Gustavus Adolphus it was said: "He received his kingdom with two empty hands, yet deprived no man of his own by violence; but what the necessities of the realm required, that did he let his people know on their days of free assemblage, that they might consider the matter, and give tribute to the crown according to its need." In comparison with earlier times, this judgment may be viewed as correct; and it belongs to the undying renown of this king that he, the greatest warrior of the Swedish throne, was, among all the rulers of his house, the least given to violence. Those who speak so much of the weight of taxes with which he loaded the country, should at least reflect that what under him was done by the law, was before him often done against law, and that arbitrariness, heretofore almost the rule, now appears the exception. No Swedish king before Gustavus Adolphus demanded and received greater sacrifices from the nobility. The hardest sacrifice was the abolition, by the diet of the year 1627, of all exemptions from conscription previously allowed. Complaints of the pressure of the public burdens were not unknown; and the new burdens were not introduced without disturbances. In 1620 representations were made that the contributions which heretofore were paid to the crown had occasioned discontent and must be reduced, seeing that the poor and indigent paid equally with the rich and prosperous, whereby many were impoverished and their farms made waste. Therefore the cattle and field tax, which was now levied, was paid according to every man's ability. But to ascertain each man's circumstances, ministers, bailiffs, and the six-men of the church in each parish, had to enrol the cattle and seed-corn of every yeoman; and it was soon found that this brought with it great inconvenience. The land tax and excise imposed restrictions hitherto unknown in Sweden, on the industry of the country. Barriers, with gates and toll-houses, were built at the outskirts of every town, and inspectors appointed; the same forms being observed at the market-places throughout the country. The most ordinary household business, brewing, baking, or killing, could no longer be pursued freely in the towns. All this caused at the outset great discontent. The rigour of the levies was most keenly felt during the long period of war. Provinces occasionally made contracts with the crown, to avoid these levies; but they did not generally cease until the days of Charles XI. The militia contracts then entered into with the provinces were made yet more burdensome by the frequent returns of the conscription under Charles XII.

The sufferings of Sweden in those times and during wars of such long continuance pass our conception. The resources of the country appear to have been little answerable to its great undertakings; and the inadequacy of the income is best shown by the extraordinary means to which the government was compelled to resort, especially to procure ready money, whereof was great want for carrying on the war; when the crown revenues were mostly paid in produce, or consisted in the performance of personal services. The extraordinary means were loans, sale and mortgage of the crown estates, and monopolies; and these enforced expedients of supply are to be reckoned among the most grievous measures of this reign. They multiplied what the Swede sees with impatience — middle powers in his relations with his rulers. All who possessed influence through property — as lenders, holders of land-fiefs, farmers, managers of profitable enterprises — became intermediate powers, on which the government, no less than the subject, was dependent.

On the other hand, no administration evoked more abundant energies;

in this respect the reign of Gustavus Adolphus forms an epoch for Sweden. This is apparent not less in reference to the industry and education of the people, than in the executive and legislative functions of the state. We quote the judgment of a foreigner upon the country and its inhabitants at this day. "This kingdom," observes William Usselinx of Sweden, "has many advantages above other countries in sea-ports, timber, victuals, the wages of labour, copper, iron, steel, pitch, tar, shot, and other munitions of war. The inhabitants of the country are a hardy folk, who can endure cold and heat; they are docile, active, quick. They are, besides, obedient to their rulers, and little bent to sedition and revolt, wherein they excel many other nations and peoples. They have the qualities, if they would but exert themselves, of expert seamen; for they have no defect of intelligence, dexterity, and courage; and if they had a little practice, they would easily become good ship-builders, the more so as almost all of them know how to handle the axe. In respect to various manufactures of fine linen, cloth, worsted, baize, bombazine, and others, there is little of this kind done in the country, partly because impulse and materials are wanting, and partly also because there are no means for exporting their wares. But of skill and shrewdness they have no want, for we find peasants able at all sorts of handiwork. They are carpenters, joiners, smiths; they bake, brew, weave, dye, make shoes and clothes, and the like, wherein they surpass all other nations of Europe, inasmuch as in other countries hardly anyone will attempt to put hands to any craft that he hath not learned. Their wives and daughters make many curi-

A COSTUME OF THE VALLEY OF AURE

ous devices in sewing, weaving, and other pleasant arts, whence it appeareth that they are very knowing and wise-minded. True it is that they cannot arrive at the perfection which is found in other countries, when a man ever remaineth in one trade and becomes inured to it by long time, man after man, from father to son. But it is not to be doubted that he who hath wit and memory to learn in haste, and thereafter himself to invent, would become perfect in his trade, if from his youth upward he practised one thing and kept himself faithful thereto. Some are of opinion that this nation is given to intemperance in eating and drinking, as also to sloth, and therefore will not apply themselves to any steady labour. But concerning this I pronounce no judgment."

Sweden for the first time, under this reign learned to know in what the rule of officials consists. In earlier times we see but the contest between the power of the magnates and the arbitrariness of the kings; it was the former of these which obtained the sanction of law in the Swedish Middle Age. The old order, or disorder, of administration was in the hands of a polycracy of feudatories. This barbarous method was gradually abandoned, but at first only by the employment of violent and illegal means, and substituted by what we may call the secretary government, directly dependent on the king. Under it, in the country, was created the office of bailiff, confided, as was the secretary government of the towns, out of mistrust of the council and lieutenants *(ståthållarna)*, to persons of mean condition, dependent on the king alone, and who, though often inculpated, were yet a necessary evil. Thus matters remained under the first princes of the house of Vasa, until Charles IX broke the old power of the lieutenants, those "kings in their districts," as he himself named them; and after him Gustavus Adolphus ventured to collect around his throne great but subordinate legal authorities. The tension which the kingdom felt in all its members required the reins of government to be tightly drawn. We discern a stricter unity of power in the highest place, with its inevitable condition: a greater division of labour in the administration, so far as the preponderant demands of military affairs allowed. These arrangements (afterwards developed by Axel Oxenstierna in the form of government of 1634) — a complete gradation of offices, with powers in several respects even impairing the old political rights of the people; the five high officers of state at the head of as many departments assisted by royal councillors appointed thereto, and standing boards or colleges now first brought into intimate connection with the prefectures — all belong to the period of Gustavus Adolphus.

The king's absence, occasioned by the wars, too often hindered his own watchfulness over the judicatory. The council of state was in fact the supreme tribunal. In a period so unsettled, so small an amount of litigation is not a little wonderful. Such a fact lays open to our glance the inner moral life of the people, and indicates at the same time that hidden fund of strength which must have existed somewhere in the country, to outlast exertions so great, distress and unquiet so trying. Such a fund lay in the public morals; and in this respect, as in others, the era of Gustavus Adolphus presents the true transition from the Middle Age of Sweden. The old blood-feuds disappeared before the power of law; but the ties of kindred still retained all their natural freshness and force, purged of violent excess, and operating only to beneficent ends. No one was desolate; for all might reckon upon home, kindred, and help in need. Much was borne, but borne in common, and Sweden was as one man. Nor was the condition of the people at the king's death by any means such as might be imagined after so many years of war. D'Ogier, who visited Sweden in the winter of 1634, in company with the French ambassador, Count D'Avaux, says in his journal, that he does not remember having seen in the whole country any one naked or in rags. Peasant lads and lasses sprang gladsomely about the sledges; and though he had free portage, the yeomen showed themselves not at all slow in forwarding him on his way — probably, he adds, because in other matters they are not heavily taxed. On a journey to the Copper Mount, he saw the people gathered at a church in the Dale country, and exclaims: "These country folk are neither ragged nor hungry, as with us." And yet they were people with whom it was no uncommon thing to mix bark in their bread. They felt no unhappiness. A great present, a great future, quickened the spirit of all.

This trust in the future Gustavus Adolphus himself showed in nothing more clearly than in his immortal institutes for general education. In the University of Upsala the dissensions among the teachers, especially between Messenius and John Rudbeck, with their factions among the students, continued under the first years of this reign. The mode in which the king restored order, as well as the wisdom and bounty which marked his care of the university, redound to his honour. Messenius and Rudbeck, both men as hot-

tempered as they were able, were removed, but to honourable and weighty charges; and the work of instruction continued to be a main object of the king's solicitude. In the year 1620 he proposed to the bishops the question as to the manner in which art and knowledge might be furthered in his dominions, taking notice that the university and schools were ill-conducted, so that there were few fit for the office of the ministry, and none at all for affairs of government. The magistrates of the towns were so ignorant that they could not write their names; the students were hindered by their poverty from making progress; and instruction at the university was impeded by too many holidays.

The teachers were ecclesiastics; and as the clergy did not understand matters belonging to government and civic life, they could not teach these branches. There was a yet greater want of competent persons to do the work of the country than there was of money to repay them. Therefore the bishops were commanded to state how many royal schools and seminaries were needful in the kingdom; what course of education was most desirable to be given there; how good teachers might be obtained, and one general method of instruction introduced; how the so-called parish-rounds *(sockne-gangar)*, by which the students

CATHEDRAL OF ÅBO

begged their sustenance in the hamlets, might be abolished, and in their stead a fixed contribution, to be collected by the ministers, established. They were to declare how many professors were required in the university; and as there was a want of learned men at home, from what places these should be invited: how the professors should be paid, since the manner now in use — by the church tithes — was ineffective, yielding more one year, another less; how the community of the students, the privileges of the university, and the rendering of accounts by the professors, might be arranged. Lastly, the king required their opinion respecting the hospitals; especially as the grievous infection of leprosy was beginning to spread, chiefly in Finland, and what the crown expended upon hospitals was embezzled, and the poor were treated worse than dogs.

The reply of the bishops is fantastical and silly. But the king put his own hand to the work, and to his individual liberality the University of Upsala owes its existence. The first *gymnasium* in Sweden was erected at

Vesterås in 1620, and enlarged in 1623 and 1627; the second at Strengnäs in 1626; the third at Linköping in 1628. The same year Finland, which had possessed the gymnasium of Viborg since 1618, obtained another at Åbo. Thus was this great king in the midst of his wars the founder of Sweden's system of education. No hopes are nobler or more elevating than those which Gustavus Adolphus opened up to a future generation by his institutes. They were not less important for their political than for their scientific results; for if Sweden, from this time, continually saw men rising by their knowledge and merits from the hut to the highest dignities of the state, it was the work of Gustavus Adolphus.*

GUSTAVUS ADOLPHUS AND THE THIRTY YEARS' WAR [1]

Within a very few years the king, seconded by his youthful chancellor, Oxenstierna, had established the best organised representative monarchy of his time in the country so lately distracted by civil war. *Lagerquist* (Laurel Bough), *Oernflycht* (Eagle's Flight), *Erenrot* (Root of Honour) — such were the proud names of the great families which, like the aristocracy of the whole Baltic coast, were loth to bow their stubborn neck to the yoke of the monarchy. This hard-handed aristocracy was won over to the service of the crown, with amazing readiness, by the alluring prospect of military glory and spoil; any nobleman who, in time of war, stayed at home, "*den kericht zu hüten*" (to look after the dustbin) forfeited the fief he held of the crown. Hence it was possible to impose the heavy burden of military service on the loyal peasantry too, and every year the clergy read out from their pulpits the names of the young men who were called upon to join the militia. The king directed the whole administration by means of five great central bureaux. He permitted freedom of debate to the four estates of the diet, but after the royal decision was once given he required unquestioning obedience, for "no martial laurels grow amidst these eternal brawls and wrangles." Thus, in firm reliance on his people, he undertook to end the three wars his father had bequeathed to him; and in the school of nineteen years of warfare he trained an army accustomed to conquer.

Against the Danes, he maintained his position with difficulty. Evading his most formidable foe, he turned his arms against the Muscovite, drove the Russian robbers from their haunts on the Baltic, subjugated Ingermanland, Karelia, and all the maritime provinces of the Gulf of Finland, and, hard by the site where St. Petersburg now stands, erected the column which proclaimed to the world that here Gustavus Adolphus had set the frontier of the kingdom. He next led his trusty vassals against Poland, where he met the legions of the Counter-Reformation for the first time. For all her pride of victory, he inflicted on Poland the first great defeat she had suffered for two hundred years; he conquered Livonia, secured the Protestant church in her precarious tenure, and gained a foothold in the harbours of Prussia. The guiding idea of his life stood more and more plainly revealed: the scheme of a Scandinavian empire, which should unite all the countries of the Baltic under the dominion of the blue and yellow flag. Gustavus Adolphus had gained all these successes without any interference on the part of the western powers, for as yet there was no state system. The tract of central Europe — that Germany which was destined at some future time to bind the east and west of Europe into an organic association of political entities — was prostrate

[1] For a full account of the Thirty Years' War, and the part taken in it by Gustavus Adolphus, the reader is referred to volume XIV, pages 339–368.]

and bleeding from a thousand wounds, torn asunder by furious party strife; and not until his triumphal march brought him close upon the German frontier was Gustavus Adolphus drawn into the whirlpool of the great German war. For thirty-three years Germany had lived as in a dream, under the protection of the Religious Peace of Augsburg — a fallacious peace, which brought about no genuine reconciliation, and left all the burning questions of the law of the empire unresolved. Wholly preoccupied with the dreary quarrels of Lutheran and Calvinistic theologians, the German Protestants had looked on idly while the Jesuits, careless of the Peace, brought large districts in the south and west of Germany once more under the sway of the church of Rome; and while the Dutch, to the north of the German river, took up the desperate struggle against the Habsburg empire, William of Orange uttering the warning cry: "If Germany remains an idle spectator of our tragedy, a war will presently be kindled on German soil which will swallow up all the wars that have gone before it." The most ghastly of all wars began — ghastly not only by reason of the hideous havoc it wrought, but by reason of its utter barrenness of thought — for while the empire was tossed distractedly between four parties, religious and political contentions grew tangled into an inextricable maze, and of the lofty passions of the early days of the Reformation little survived beyond the gloomy malevolence of sectarian hatred.

Austria and Spain, the two branches of the house of Habsburg, made common cause in the struggle with heresy; they allied themselves with Maximilian of Bavaria, the head of the Catholic League in Germany, with Italian princes, and with the crown of Poland. Almost the whole of Catholic Europe, with the sole exception of France, placed its mercenaries at the service of this imperial policy, which strode resolutely towards its goal, daring and favoured by fortune, commanding the admiration of even Gustavus Adolphus by its ruthless strength of will. "The emperor," he often said, "is a great statesman; he does what will serve his purpose." All the emperor's hereditary dominions, including even Bohemia, that ancient home of heresy, and the Protestant peasantry of Upper Austria, had been coerced into conformity with the Roman Catholic faith. South Germany was already subjugated, the elector palatine exiled from his lands and lieges; Spain held command of a series of strongholds along the Rhine, and was thus able to send her mercenaries safely from Milan through the Tyrol and Germany, to make war upon the Netherlands. The little armies of the partisans of Protestantism in the north were crushed, even the Danish duke of Holstein was driven back. The emperor's legions pressed forward to Jutland, as they had done in the days of the Ottos. His victorious banners, bearing the emblems of the Virgin Mary and the double eagle, floated on the shores of both the seas of Germany, and his commander-in-chief, the Czech Wallenstein, was at work on the project of a maritime empire — he was going to link the Baltic and the North Sea by a canal between Wismar and the Elbe, and establish a naval port of the empire in the bay of Jade (where Wilhelmshaven now stands) at the very doors of the rebel Dutch.

In the year 1629 the imperial policy uttered its last fiat. The edict of Restitution excluded Calvinists from toleration under the Peace of Augsburg, and directed that all religious institutions which had joined the Calvinistic church since the date of the Peace, all the old "immediate" bishoprics of the ancient *Germania Sacra* of the north — Magdeburg, Halberstadt, Bremen, Lübeck — as well as the provincial bishoprics of Meissen, Brandenburg, and countless others, should be delivered over to the Romish church. What a prospect! The peaceful development of two generations wiped out at a blow; the people of these whilom ecclesiastical territories, with their thorough-going Protestantism, once more under the sway of the crozier, while an arch-duke should make his entry into Mainz as Catholic archbishop! The success of such a project would have struck a blow at the very root of German Protestantism, in its ecclesiastical no less than its political aspect; and nothing would have been lacking for its utter annihilation but that the illustrious Protestant dynasties of the empire — the electors of Brandenburg and Hesse, the elector Palatine and the Askanian Anhalts (the Aschersleben line) — should forfeit their fiefs to the empire as rebels and heretics, like the dukes of Mecklenburg and Brunswick and many other Protestant princes, who had been driven into exile and seen their ancient hereditary dominions fall a prey to the arbitrary rule of imperialist commanders. Never had Germany been so near a condition of political unity. "We need no more princes or prince electors," was Wallenstein's threat. But unity so created, by Spanish priests of the Society of Jesus, by *condottieri* and hordes of mercenaries who had renounced their nationality, would have destroyed all intellectual liberty, would have gone far to annihilate the essence of the German *ego*. A cry of horror rose from the whole Protestant world. And yet, whence was rescue to be looked for? The only two Protestants who still wore the electoral hat — the electors of Brandenburg and Saxony — saw their dominions flooded with imperial troops; they were paralysed by the weakness of their own will and by their traditional loyalty to the emperor — a feeling honourable even when mistaken — paralysed by the insubordination of the provincial estates, which obstructed every serious attempt at military preparation. There was no help for it; the dissensions and inertia of the German Protestants had brought things to such a pass that nothing but foreign intervention could save them.

LENNART TORSTENSON, SWEDISH GENERAL

(1603–1651)

The king of Sweden had no alternative. He realised the vast co-ordination of European affairs; he had long vainly striven to induce the free Protestant powers of Northern Europe — England, the Netherlands, and Denmark — to league themselves together against the Habsburgs; and during his Polish campaign he had already met the imperial troops in one unsuccessful engagement. If the sway of the brutal imperial soldiery were to extend farther along the Baltic, it would not only shatter the great septentrional monarchy of his hopeful dreams, but would endanger the little throne of his own dominions; for there was no question but that Austria's allies, the Polish Vasas, would endeavour to make good their claims to the crown. "In the safety of our neighbours," he said to his loyal estates, "we must secure our own." And in glowing language, he, who had never learned to dissemble, added, "I will deliver our oppressed co-religionists from the papal yoke." His political and religious duty both pointed to the same goal; but in this, as in all epoch-making crises, the issue was determined by the obscure promptings of genius, by the mysterious presentiment of prodigious successes, and by the call of divine providence.*g*

Leipsic, Lützen, and the Death of Gustavus

Gustavus negotiated with France, England, and Holland, before he began his march. Charles I agreed to send the king of Sweden six thousand men. These troops were raised in the name of the marquis of Hamilton and supposed to be maintained by that nobleman, that the appearance of neutrality might be preserved.

The most necessary supply that Gustavus received was an annual subsidy, from Cardinal Richelieu, of twelve hundred thousand livres — a small sum in our days, but considerable at that time, especially in a country where the precious metals are still scarce. The treaty between France and Sweden was a masterpiece in politics. Gustavus agreed, in consideration of the stipulated subsidy to maintain in Germany an army of thirty-six thousand men; and bound himself to observe a strict neutrality towards the duke of Bavaria and all the princes of the Catholic league, on condition that they should not join the emperor against the Swedes, and to preserve the rights of the Romish church, wherever he should find it established. By these ingenious stipulations, which do so much honour to the genius of Richelieu, the Catholic princes were not only freed from all alarm on the score of religion, but furnished with a pretext for withholding their assistance from the emperor, as a step which would expose them to the arms of Sweden.

Gustavus had entered Pomerania when this treaty was concluded, and soon after made himself master of Frankfort-upon-the-Oder, Kolberg, and several other important places. The Protestant princes, however, were still backward in declaring themselves, lest they should be separately crushed by the imperial power, before the king of Sweden could march to their assistance. In order to put an end to this irresolution, Gustavus summoned the elector of Brandenburg to declare himself openly in three days; and on receiving an evasive answer, he marched directly to Berlin. This spirited conduct had the desired effect: the gates were thrown open, and Gustavus was received as a friend. He was soon after joined by the landgraf of Hesse and the elector of Saxony. Gustavus now marched towards Leipsic, where Tilly lay encamped. That experienced general advanced into the plain of Breitenfeld to meet his antagonist, at the head of thirty thousand veterans. The king of Sweden's army consisted of a nearly equal number of men; but the Saxon auxiliaries were raw and undisciplined, and fled at the first onset. Yet Gustavus, by his superior conduct and the superior valour of the Swedes, gained a complete victory over Tilly and the imperials. The consequences of the victory at Leipsic were great; nor did the conqueror fail to improve that success which he had so gloriously earned. He was instantly joined by all the members of the Evangelical union, determined at last to throw off the imperial bondage. The measures of the Catholic league were utterly disconcerted; and Gustavus made himself master of the whole country from the Elbe to the Rhine, comprehending a space of near one hundred leagues, full of fortified towns. The elector of Saxony, in the meantime, entered Bohemia, and took Prague. Tilly was killed in disputing with the Swedes the passage of the Lech. Gustavus soon after reduced Augsburg, and there re-established the Protestant religion. He next marched into Bavaria, where he found the gates of almost every city thrown open on his approach. When pressed to revenge on Munich the cruelties which Tilly had perpetrated at Magdeburg, to give up the city to pillage, and reduce the elector's magnificent palace to ashes, he replied: "No! let us not imitate the barbarity of the Goths our ancestors, who have rendered their memory detestable by abusing the rights of conquest, in doing violence to humanity, and destroying the precious monuments of art."

During these transactions, the renowned Wallenstein, who had been for a time in disgrace, but had been restored to the chief command with absolute powers soon after the defeat of Leipsic, had recovered Prague and the greater part of Bohemia. Gustavus offered him battle near Nuremberg; but the cautious veteran prudently declined the challenge, and the king of Sweden was repulsed in attempting to force his intrenchments. The action lasted for ten hours, during which every regiment in the Swedish army, not excepting the body of reserve, was led on to the attack. The king's person was in imminent danger, the Austrian cavalry sallying out furiously from their intrenchments on the right and left when the efforts of the Swedes began to slacken; and a masterly retreat alone saved him from a total overthrow. Gustavus afterwards attacked Wallenstein in the wide plain of Lützen, near Leipsic, where a great battle was fought and the Swedish monarch lost his life in the height of a complete victory, which was improved by Bernhard, duke of Saxe-Weimar, his lieutenant-general.

No prince, ancient or modern, seems to have possessed, in so eminent a degree as Gustavus, the united qualities of the hero, the statesman, and the commander — that intuitive genius which conceives, that wisdom which plans, and that combination of conduct and courage which gives success to an enterprise. Nor was the military progress of any prince ever equally rapid. under circumstances equally difficult, with an inferior force against warlike nations and disciplined troops conducted by able and experienced generals.[h]

AIMS AND CHARACTER OF GUSTAVUS ADOLPHUS

What was his aim? This, posterity has striven to learn; this, it has fancied it has discovered. From generation to generation the story has gone — gathering assurance as it went, and being handed on and on with fresh embellishments — that he came down upon the empire from the North to save and protect the Protestant religion; that he aimed at uniting Protestant Germany and being himself the Protestant emperor. But the tale we have told points to other aims than these. Long after the death of Gustavus Adolphus the royal chancellor said to Bengt Oxenstierna, "King Gustavus Adolphus wanted the Baltic coast; he aspired to be one day emperor of Scandinavia, and his empire was to embrace Sweden and Norway, Denmark as far as the Great Belt, and the Baltic provinces. With this end in view, he first concluded a peace with Denmark on the most favourable terms he could get, and then one with Russia respecting the Baltic coast. By means of lucrative duties he took the coast and river mouths away from the Poles. He then attacked the German emperor, and demanded Pomerania and Mecklenburg as a war indemnity from the Protestant princes, who were to receive Catholic provinces in exchange. Denmark was to be reduced to the territory beyond the Great Belt, and Norway was to be ours. By such means this great king aimed at founding an independent empire. But it was not true (as report says) that he wished to make himself emperor of Germany."

His contemporaries were full of admiration for his soldierly courage and his wisdom as a general. For a general he was, bold almost to foolhardiness. A dagger in his hand would arouse all the Northman, "the Goth," in him; then he showed that he belonged to the Vasa brood. How often did he not stake his life on a chance before he finally threw it away in a rash skirmish! From the very beginning of his reign his improvements and innovations in military arrangements were the constant subjects of his thoughts. The embassy to the Netherlands in 1615, which has furnished so many personal details about Gustavus Adolphus, gives a list of these. "Nine large new ships" are mentioned, as well as the militia brought up to the strength of forty thousand men; there is, besides, an account of a new arsenal of great cannon and weapons of every description. The young king had begged of their high mightinesses "that the controller monier" might come to him for a time in Holland, bringing with him engineers, artillerymen, gunners, and other such people. His admiration for the military spirit of the prince of Orange impelled him to this step—to complete his armament after the Orange pattern, and with the assistance of Orange workmen. And how often in his German wars did he take Orange for his example, not only in operations in the field, but more especially when he had a fortress to besiege. He showed the envoys a piece of ordnance he had invented, which he wished to try in their presence. It weighed only twenty pounds, and threw balls of the same weight. He told them he hoped to make it still lighter. Europe witnessed the rise of a warlike star in the North. Spinola had already said at the battle of Prague, "Gustavus Adolphus is the only Protestant sovereign whom one must be cautious not to offend." The only history which appeared of him during his life echoed the universal contemporary judgment: "There are few men to be found in Christendom at the present day whose experience in war equals his."

And this determined, rough, reserved, hard ruler — this *leo arcticus* — taller than the tallest of his countrymen, broad-shouldered, white-skinned and with the fairest of fair hair, slow in his movements, which in later years when he became rather too corpulent were somewhat unwieldy, loved soft music and songs of the simplest kind, and would often sit, lute in hand, lost in the dreams which its tones awakened. We like to compare him, separated from us by a distance of over two centuries, with those who are nearer our times; and who is not strangely moved by the remembrance of how the conqueror of Silesia dreamed in restful solitude over the soft-toned lute? Concentrated will, energy pursuing a great end, sought an instant's pause, while genius lulled them musically into the short slumber the pressure of the time allowed. Like an aurora borealis Gustavus appears—great, wonderful, luminous, and cold.[i]

Geijer's Estimate of Gustavus Adolphus

Gustavus Adolphus was taken away in his thirty-eighth year. Never has one man's death made a deeper impression throughout a whole quarter of the world. Wheresoever his name had been heard, a ray of hope for the oppressed had penetrated. Even the Greek, at its sound, dreamed of freedom; and prayers for the success of the Swedish monarch's arms were sent up at the Holy Sepulchre. What then must he not have been for the partners of his faith? We may conceive this; nay, rather, it is no longer possible to do so. The feelings with which the inhabitants of Augsburg, with streaming tears, crowded to the evangelical worship restored by Gustavus Adolphus; the feelings with which the people in Saxony, on bended knees, stretched out thankful hands to the hero, for the second time their saviour, are become strange to the world in which we live. In those days men felt their dangers, and knew how to requite their deliverer worthily. We speak of the people whose champion Gustavus Adolphus was by his cause as well as by his qualities. The agency of both extended far, and burst even the bonds of hate and prejudice; for he is perchance the only man (so great was the might of his virtue) whose image is reflected with truth, even in the portraiture of his enemies.

It is not only Axel Oxenstierna who has said of him, "He was a prince God-fearing in all his doings and transactions, even to the death." Lutheran theologians have wished in some sort to exalt him into a saint of their persuasion. If withal he had too much of Cæsar and Alexander (whom he admired), we must acknowledge, on the other hand, that he was better than his spiritual advisers, and far above his age in Christian tolerance. The manner in which the future juggled with his life-work, frustrating his designs and letting his plans die with him, belongs to the common lot of mankind, and may silently be added to the immeasurable sum of hopes unfulfilled. One is conscious of a higher power working through the whole life of Gustavus Adolphus. There was in him that boundless reach of view which with conquerors is inborn, and he accepted without amazement his own fortune. His profound belief in his own destiny is conspicuous in all the transactions of his life; and yet, though nothing hardens the heart so much as prosperity, Gustavus Adolphus was humble and meek. In his vocation he acknowledged guidance from on high. He was far from looking upon himself as indispensable, however; for his goal was placed far above his own personality. Therefore was he, like the high-hearted Roman, not niggardly of his great life. "God the almighty liveth," he said to Axel Oxenstierna when that statesman warned him, in Prussia, not so rashly to expose himself to death. More cheerful and heroic courage never walked on earth.

What, besides, did he purpose? A great monarchy, without doubt; for whose future props in Germany he counted upon the young Frederick William of Brandenburg, afterwards the great elector, and Bernhard of Weimar, intending for the one the hand of his daughter, for the other that of his niece. Probably even a Protestant empire was not foreign to his contemplations. For the rest, nothing was determined, even in his own breast. The sphere of his vision stretched far and wide; and it was his pleasure to hold in his hand the threads of many possibilities. Thus we see him entertain the proposal that he, after Sigismund's death, should himself be elected king of Poland, through the Polish dissidents. Thus we find him in alliance with the prince of Transylvania, the Crimean Tatars, and Russia, for the weakening of the Austrian interest as well in Poland as in Germany. Great designs were extinguished with his life on the battle-field of Lützen.*f*

CHAPTER X

CHRISTINA TO CHARLES XI

[1632–1697 A.D.]

THE PEACE OF WESTPHALIA (1648 A.D.)

CHRISTINA, who succeeded Gustavus (II) Adolphus on the throne of Sweden, was only six years of age when her father fell upon the plains of Lützen; and a council of regency, consisting of five great officers of state, at the head of whom was the chancellor Oxenstierna, was placed over the realm.

It was expected by the Catholic party that now, when the hero of the reformed cause was no more, and that the elector of Saxony, one of his best supports, was about to pass over to the imperials, the war in Germany would be a short one. They were wofully deceived. It raged with alternate glory and disaster down to the Peace of Westphalia, in 1648. Gustavus had trained in his school a host of generals who were fit for every emergency; and the statesmen whom he had instructed were in no respect inferior. Horn, Banér, Torstenson, and Wrangel, assisted by Duke Bernhard and the landgraf, gathered laurels in the field, which would not have disgraced even the coronet of Gustavus.

For most of these successes, indeed, Sweden was indebted to other causes than even the ability of her generals or the discipline of her brave veterans. The ablest generals of France were also contending with the Catholic powers of Europe. But these events belong to German or to European history, rather than to that of Sweden. We will not, therefore, detail them, but will pass at once to the celebrated treaty which restored peace to Europe. That treaty was most honourable to Sweden. Five millions of crowns were conceded to her, as some indemnification for the expenses of the war. She was confirmed in the possession of Bremen and Verden, which were secularised. She was allowed to retain Upper Pomerania, a part of the Lower, with Rügen, Wismar, and three votes in the German diet. This was a glorious result; yet it was less glorious than the war itself, which had raised Sweden from an obscure state to one of the first of European kingdoms — which had disciplined her troops, established her martial character, and rendered her formidable in the eyes of Europe. Before the conclusion of this war, Sweden increased the number of her enemies by a sudden irruption into Holstein. The circumstances and end of this new war we shall give in a future chapter. It, too, contributed as much to the triumph of Christina as to the disgrace of her royal neighbour.

THE ABDICATION OF CHRISTINA (1654 A.D.)

But the most remarkable event of Christina's reign is her voluntary abdication. Though fond of power, the cares which surrounded it and the duties which it involved were too much for her inclination. Affecting a peculiar love of retirement, a peculiar devotion to birds, to antiquities, to the fine arts, to criticism, and to philosophical reflection, she lamented a course of life which interfered with the attainment of her wishes, and expressed her intention to abdicate, long before she carried it into effect. Her vanity was delighted with the homage paid to her by literary men; she corresponded with all of any note, and invited several to her court; she pensioned such as she thought ready to extend her reputation; she purchased, at an immense price, the rarest editions of old books, and the choicest specimens of art. Her subjects were not well pleased with her prodigality; they condemned her tastes; they lamented her unchastity; and sensibly advised her to marry and attend more strictly to her duties as a sovereign. Against marriage, which would have subjected her caprice to restraints that she would have felt to be intolerable, she indignantly remonstrated, and declared that she would retire into private life. This resolution alarmed her people, who were proud of the glories that illustrated her reign, and who loved the daughter of their hero. Her ministers, especially Oxenstierna, remonstrated with her on a resolution which, if carried into effect, must, as they were well convinced, end in their fall from power. Under such a woman, they were the virtual sovereigns of Sweden; but her designated successor, Charles Gustavus (the son of the hero's sister by the count palatine), was a bold, active, enterprising prince, who would reign alone. Though she yielded for a time to the entreaties of her advisers, she never renounced her purpose; and in 1654 she announced it so energetically that all opposition was felt to be unavailing.

It was in the diet of Upsala, held in May, 1654, that Christina made this irrevocable annunciation. In the event of her successor's dying without issue, she wished the sceptre to devolve on the count de Tott, one of her paramours, and descended from a daughter of Eric XIV; but she met with little encouragement in such a project. In the following month, wishing to imitate the illustrious example of Charles V, she publicly resigned all the ensigns of her dignity into the hands of her cousin, whom she exhorted to a right fulfilment of the royal duties. For the gratification of her pleasures, she reserved to herself the revenues of ample domains. Her subsequent life was not like that of the renowned emperor.[b]

[1656 A.D.]

She had reserved to herself her own independence, an absolute authority over such of her subjects as should accompany her, and the revenues of Pomerania and Mecklenburg, with those of several Swedish provinces. Quitting the habit of her sex, and taking the words *Fata viam invenient* as a device, she left her kingdom, traversed Denmark and Germany, and established herself at Brussels. Here she remained for nearly a year, signalising her sojourn by the private renunciation of Lutheranism, which she afterwards solemnly and publicly abjured at Innsbruck. From Innsbruck she went to Italy. She entered Rome on horseback, was received, confirmed, and baptised Alexandra by Alexander VII, and was lodged in the Palazzo Farnese, where she surrounded herself with artists and amorists, with philosophers and mountebanks. In 1656, having quarrelled with some members of the college of cardinals, she made her first trip to France, where she had much success as a spectacle, called on the king at Compiègne, was lodged at Fontainebleau, and stayed for some time in Paris. She was most gracious with the men of letters and science, but she outraged all the women by her expressions of contempt for their sex and themselves (which called forth many illiberal remarks concerning her spare figure and humped shoulder), and declared that Ninon de l'Enclos was the only one of them worth her regard. She also attempted to instil a few of her own political theories into the bosom of Mazarin; but that subtle diplomatist resisted, and when in the following year, after a journey to Italy, she attempted to renew her visit, he found means to have her detained at Fontainebleau. It was here that, after writing to Cromwell, who would none

QUEEN CHRISTINA OF SWEDEN
(1626–1689)

of her, she caused her favourite Monaldeschi, in revenge for the betrayal of her secrets, to be put to death by the captain of her guard.[c] The French historian Catteau-Calleville gives the following account of this famous incident.[a]

CHRISTINA OF SWEDEN AND MONALDESCHI

Attached to the queen were Count Sentinelli, her captain of the guard and first chamberlain, and the marquis Monaldeschi, her grand equerry. There reigned great jealousy between these two Italians, both desirous of keeping Christina's favour. The princess, however, had been for some time suspicious of Monaldeschi's conduct, and having intercepted his correspondence found that he was betraying her interests and at the same time attempting to lay at another door the treason of which he was guilty. She feigned innocence in the matter and asked the marquis one day what punishment treason deserved. "Your majesty," he replied, "should have the traitor executed on the spot without mercy." "Good," said the queen, "remember these words; and for my part I tell you I shall never forgive him."

On the 6th of November she summoned to her, in the Galérie des Cerfs, Father Lebel, the Mathurin prior, and put into his hand a packet of papers sealed in three places and bearing no address, with the charge that he was to return it to her whenever she called for it and requesting him to make note of the day, hour, and place he had received it. Meanwhile Monaldeschi observed that several posts had passed without his receiving any letters; and becoming mistrustful took several steps which looked like preparations for flight. But the queen forestalled him, and on the 10th of November she called him into the Galérie des Cerfs. He arrived trembling, pale, and haggard. After some irrelevant remarks by the queen Father Lebel entered by a door which was immediately shut, while through another entrance came Sentinelli the captain of the guard, and two soldiers. The queen asked the prior for the packet she had committed to his care, took out the letters and papers which she showed and read to the marquis, asking him in a firm but passionate voice if he recognised them. The marquis denied they were anything but copies she had made herself. "You have, then," she asked him, "no knowledge of these letters and writings?" Leaving him to think for a minute, she produced the originals which she showed him, exclaiming, "O you traitor!" After several attempts to justify himself Monaldeschi threw himself for pardon at Christina's feet. At the same time the captain and his soldiers drew their swords. Monaldeschi came closer to the queen, who listened a few moments but soon told him his arrest had been ordered and requested the prior to prepare him for death.

She left the gallery and withdrew to an adjoining room. It appears, from Father Lebel's narrative, that Sentinelli himself interceded for the culprit, or at least he made a pretence of doing so. This proceeding producing no effect, the marquis implored the prior to intercede for him; and the latter did go to the queen, whom he found with calm and unruffled countenance. He threw himself at her feet, and in a voice choked with sobs begged her for the sake of Christ's sufferings to deign to show a little mercy. She represented to the good man how sorry she was not to be able to grant what he asked, pointing out the blackness of Monaldeschi's crime, and adding that so guilty a man had no forgiveness or mercy to hope for and that many who deserved less than this traitor had been broken on the wheel. Whereupon the prior, who has himself given an account of this whole circumstance, took the liberty of observing that she was in the palace of a great king and that she should give careful thought as to whether the king would approve of what she was about to do. This remark of the prior's instead of moving Christina, only wounded her pride. She replied that she had the right to dispense justice; that the king was not treating her as a prisoner and fugitive; that she was mistress of her own wishes and could punish her own officials for anything and at all times; that she was responsible for her conduct to God alone, and that this particular act of hers was not without precedent.

The prior argued that there was a difference, and that if princes had done such things they did them on their own territory and not elsewhere; but, fearing to irritate her, he continued: "It is for the honour and reputation which your majesty has acquired in this kingdom, and for the hope which the nation has conceived of mediation that I humbly beg of you to consider that your action, entirely just as it maybe from your majesty's standpoint, might be regarded by others as an act of hasty violence. May your majesty do rather a deed of generosity and mercy towards this man by delivering him to the justice of the king and letting him stand trial in due form." "What," the queen cried, "I, who have sovereign and absolute judicial power over those who serve me, be reduced to plead at law against a traitor of my household of whose treason I hold the proof in my hands!" "That is true, madam, but your majesty is an interested party." "No, no," she replied, "I will tell the king about it. Go back and look after his soul. I cannot in conscience do what you ask." The priest, noting the change of tone with which she uttered these last words, remarked that perhaps she would have given in if things had not gone so far.

The priest returned to the gallery and announced the confirmation of arrest to Monaldeschi, whom he confessed, but who, preserving still some hope, addressed himself to the queen's chaplain who had arrived during his confession. But all attempts were unavailing and Monaldeschi was put to death by the soldiers and the captain of the guard, his rival for the queen's favour. As he wore under his vestments a thick coat of mail, he received several blows before expiring, and the gallery was stained with his blood. Finally a dagger was plunged into his throat and he was dead. The prior was charged with the burial ceremonies. The queen sent a sum of money to the monastery and had masses said for the repose of the marquis's soul. He was buried with the usual ceremonial in the parish church of Avon.[d]

CHRISTINA DIES (1689 A.D.)

In 1658 Christina returned to Rome; and, the Swedish revenues coming slowly in, Alexander allowed her a pension. In 1660 Charles Gustavus died, and Christina returned to Sweden, to claim the throne she had quitted so lightly and regretted so bitterly. But the Swedes had lost their old reverence for the daughter of Gustavus; her new religion and her treatment of Monaldeschi had made them weary of her; and she was compelled to sign another and more binding deed of abdication, and once more to retreat to Rome. She reappeared in Sweden some six years afterwards; but the exercise of her faith was denied her, and she withdrew to Hamburg, where she begged in vain the empty crown of Poland, and whence she made for Rome once more. In that city she lived for some twenty years, quarrelling, intriguing, and collecting, corresponding with men of letters and founding academies, active in the Molinist controversy and in the cause of the Venetians besieged by the Turks, consumed by the desire of that political power which she had thrown away, and endeavouring to assert her vanished influence to the last. She died, with great composure, in 1689, and was buried, under a sonorous epitaph, in St. Peters.[c]

CATTEAU-CALLEVILLE'S CHARACTERISATION OF CHRISTINA

The "daughter of the great Gustavus" as she called herself, had a throne for a cradle; born and educated to reign she held the reins of government with glory for ten years. She had not yet attained the age of thirty, and the faculties of her mind were in their full vigour, when she abdicated her power, seeking rest, leisure, independence, and perhaps still more a fame that might belong to her alone. But this resolution, praised by some, was condemned by others who foresaw its consequences. Christina found herself out of that sphere in which birth, education, and the exercise of power had placed her.

The qualities, even, with which she had been endowed by nature, and which had shone upon the throne, were now a burden and became completely changed under the new circumstances in which she was placed. Her pride, her greatness of soul being constantly irritated by contradiction, she was led into suspicion, jealousy, and fits of passion. Her perspicacity, her discernment, having no occasion to apply themselves to the great interests which decide the fate of nations, descended often to petty intrigue and insignificant combinations. Her imagination, as extensive as it was lively, could no longer work upon matters of real importance and lost itself in a labyrinth of illusionary projects.

But if the picture of Christina's life after her abdication offers several less attractive features, it presents others which cannot fail to win our admiration. In the painful struggle which she was obliged to undertake against obstacles and difficulties, Christina proved more than once that superior souls are masters of destiny and rule over events. Until the last moments of her life, she gave the highest proofs of elevation of sentiment, of force of character, and strength of mind. She had a resource at her disposition which she knew how to profit by, and which no reverses and no disappointments could take from her — in the bosom of literature and art she found compensation and consolation. Surrounded with masterpieces of genius, and being able to appreciate them, she forgot the caprice of fortune which she no longer had the means to thwart, now that she had renounced supreme power. The homage which learned men of letters and artists paid her kept alive the passion for interesting occupation having for aim the extension of the sphere of knowledge and the exercise of the faculties of the mind, by the gift of greater energy and the opportunity for higher flights.

Christina, who, according to her own words, possessed nothing in Rome but herself, made herself beloved by some, feared by others, and esteemed by all. Gilbert Burnett, who during his sojourn at Rome had several audiences with her and who has given an account of his travels, represents the palace of the queen as the home of good manners and good taste. "Her conversation," he says, "and the great variety of topics with which she is familiar make her the most wonderful thing to see in Rome, among the rare things to be found there." Christina's generosity was shown on all occasions. Learned men and artists received proofs of it, and the unfortunate never solicited it in vain. The queen employed more than four hundred people in Rome, and the grief shown by the people at her death proves how much they were attached to her.[d]

The following description of this strange woman is one of those quoted by Arckenholtz in his memoirs of Christina:[a]

BIELFELT'S CHARACTERISATION OF CHRISTINA

I am going to draw the portrait of Christina. I have studied her long enough to flatter myself that I shall do it with truth, if it were not so difficult to keep from being carried away by affection for her.

Christina's youth showed the superiority of her mind and the greatness of her soul — a thousand talents were born with her and almost as many weaknesses. A certain trait of enthusiasm manifested itself very early in her manner and even in her words. Christina did not know how to be amiable, disdained to be so, or would be so only after her own manner. The girl was always a statesman. Everything that could put her above human nature aroused Christina's admiration. Her soul leaned always towards great things, but her imagination, over sensitive to strong impressions, made her sometimes take on the appearance of greatness for its own sake. Extraordinary in all things, she wished but to distinguish herself by great deeds, and did not deign sufficiently to take notice of small ones.

Learned men, who sometimes embellish the mind, but more often spoil it, had perhaps too much control over her in her youth. She loved science with passion, and cultivated it with a success quite remarkable for her station; for she wished to know and fathom all. Tireless in work, assiduous in business, carrying out her plans with more firmness than prudence, incapable of revoking a resolution once taken, she wished to govern entirely alone.

What pleasure for a young girl to rule by the strength of her genius a council composed of old men who joined presumption to the wisdom of experience! To her mind gentleness was a vice and cowardice a crime.

With the most lively taste for pleasure she always shunned marriage, because she feared to find in it that which would bring her under the control of another. Although she knew friendship and her heart was not incapable of tenderness, all her passions were subordinate to the love of glory. This passion, which does not always lead great souls to the best things but often to extremes, is the base on which her whole life rested. She gave up the throne through disgust, say some; for political reasons, say others, or through her licentious life if we must believe the libertines. For me, I think that the desire to do a unique action was the most powerful motive for her abdication. Alexander wished to conquer the whole world. Christina wanted to abdicate an empire. After treating Europe to this astonishing spectacle, she gave it another, less striking, it is true, but quite as extraordinary as the first, in renouncing the faith of her fathers. It was as much through coquetry as curiosity that she travelled in foreign countries.

In Sweden, under control of the law, she had known none, even when she no longer had the power of making them. Monaldeschi was sacrificed less to her glory than to the fierceness of her vengeance, or perhaps to the pleasure of commanding the highest act of authority in the palace of the prince who was most jealous of her power. Everywhere she thought and acted as a queen; she could not suffer her person to be less respected than her dignity and did not hesitate to use her power to make herself obeyed. Such reverses as try the pride of men were added to her own — she supported them with as much insensibility as she had scorn for the great powers. The prince who gathered the fruit of her abdication made her repent it — but what this repentance was we are left to guess. There were contrasts in her character and traits impossible to reconcile, as in the majority of heroes. The great are not gods but only great.[e]

REIGN AND WARS OF CHARLES (X) GUSTAVUS

Charles Gustavus, born at Stockholm, son of John Kasimir, duke of Zweibrücken, and the princess Catherine, eldest daughter of Charles IX, had no right to the crown, for though the daughters of a king might succeed to the throne in virtue of the resolution of the diet of Norköping, they and their children were excluded from the succession on their marriage. Nevertheless, at Christina's recommendation, this prince was elected successor to the throne by the estates in 1649. The whole of his reign, which was of brief duration, was disturbed by wars, which prevented him from turning his attention to the finances of the state. By a resolution of the diet of 1655 the recovery of the crown lands, which had been alienated since the death of Gustavus Adolphus, had been determined upon. But the character of Charles Gustavus and the circumstances in which he found himself turned his thoughts to other enterprises than the consideration of financial questions.

John Kasimir, the son and successor of Sigismund, refused to abandon his pretensions to the crown, and in order to compel him to do so Charles Gustavus invaded the dominions of his enemy with an armed force. The Polish troops, which consisted for the most part of vagabond hordes, offered him but a faint resistance. He was even proclaimed king of Poland by some of the nobles of that country, but as far as his principal object was concerned he had gained nothing. The victory won by the Swedes near Warsaw, after a three days' battle, brought matters no nearer to a decision. Such advantage as he gained by it was largely due to Frederick William [the Great], elector of Brandenburg, who was induced to ally himself with Charles Gustavus by the rapid progress of the Swedish arms. In virtue of a treaty concluded at Königsberg on the 7th of January, 1656, the elector recognised the duchy of Prussia as a fief of the Swedish crown and promised to pay that power 4,000 ducats on his investiture and to furnish one thousand foot and five hundred horse for its service. This treaty was altered in that same year by the Treaty of Labiau, by which Charles Gustavus bestowed the sovereignty of the duchy of Prussia upon Frederick William on condition that it should revert to Sweden in case of the extinction of the male line of the house of Brandenburg. But Russia having broken the treaty of peace she had concluded with Sweden, and Denmark having declared war against her at the same time, Frederick William hastened to make his peace with the court of Poland by the Treaty of Wehlau, concluded on September 19th, 1657, and received the sovereignty of Prussia at the hands of John Kasimir.

CHARLES X
(1622–1660)

Charles Gustavus then found himself in a very embarrassing position. The manifesto of the court of Copenhagen was dated June 1st, 1657, and though it was too much to hope that the Swedish troops could be withdrawn from Poland and marshalled to meet those of Denmark so early, yet on the 23rd of July the king at the head of his army appeared within the borders of Holstein, where success followed upon success so rapidly that, having taken Fredericia by storm on the 24th of October, he found himself master of the whole of Holstein, and of all Schleswig and Jutland, with the exception of Glückstadt, Krempe, and Rendsburg.[f] Charles' next enterprise may be given in the account of an eyewitness.[a]

Terlon's Narrative of Charles X Crossing the Little Belt (1658 A.D.)

Charles X determined to attack the island of Fünen, by taking advantage of the ice. As the severe cold which had lasted for several days seemed to offer him an opportunity, he decided to carry out his enterprise, provided the

[1658 A.D.]

ice was sufficiently strong to bear in safety his army and his artillery. He had sent Chief-Admiral Wrangel in advance, to assemble the troops and keep them ready to march. Arriving on the 8th of February on the shores of the Little Belt, he immediately made some squadrons cross with one hundred dragoons, to seize a small peninsula called Bogen, which stretches out midway into the Little Belt, between the towns of Assens and Middelfart, where the prince went this same day in a sledge, having done me the honour to take me with him.

But Admiral Wrangel learned from those whom the king of Sweden had sent to examine the ice, and to cross over to the island of Fünen in case it was strong enough, that it was too weak in the direction in which they were marching. This was indeed true, for he had seen perish before his eyes some of his mounted men. Moreover the Danes, who had come down to the shores of this island with artillery, fired incessantly to break and weaken the ice; and as the Swedish army, which was unsheltered, was very much inconvenienced by the cannon-balls sliding over the smooth surface, except in some spots where there were mounds of ice and snow, where meeting with resistance they dashed violently, he warned the king of Sweden, who thought it best to retire and to put the expedition off till the following day, hoping that the ice would be stronger.

In the meantime the prince made his army encamp along the shore of the Little Belt, and during the whole of the night sent out small parties of men in all directions, to sound the ice and to find out where they could cross most safely. He awaited their news with much impatience and anxiety, taking no rest all night; towards two o'clock in the morning he was informed by the return of his parties and by the report of divers peasants that it had frozen severely all night, and that they could cross on the ice without danger to the island of Fünen.

I was at that moment in his room and I saw him that same hour give the order for all his army to advance into the peninsula, which he had seized the preceding day; and to carry out his plan he gave orders for the fight, and commanded that the cavalry should lead their horses by the bridle, and should walk at some little distance from one another, that the cannon also should go at an equal distance so as not to break the ice by too great a weight, until they had passed beyond the current of the sea where it was weaker. He also commanded that the army should arrange itself in battle order when it had crossed, to advance against the enemy which was seen the whole length of the seashore. The king of Sweden crossed so far in a sledge, then he went on horseback, which also I saw as I was always near his person.

The king of Sweden would not advance too quickly, for fear lest the Danes, seeing all his army crossed onto the island, should gain the road which leads into Jutland and Holstein, on the side where the island faces these countries, and by the same road along which the king of Sweden had come into Fünen, having left all his army baggage there, so as to go more freely on this expedition. This would have been a great advantage to the Danes, if they had had sufficient foresight to take this resolution, which would have caused much harm to the Swedes; and they would have done better to take this resolve, seeing that they could not prevent the king of Sweden from becoming master of the island as he did.

The king of Sweden, perceiving that the Danish troops were giving way instead of charging him, made the left wing advance briskly, all the more when he was informed that Chief-Admiral Wrangel had repulsed the Danes whom he found before him, and made prisoner the colonel who commanded them, with all the officers. This compelled the prince to hasten his march to approach the island, where he learned that Colonel Jens, who commanded all the Danish troops in the absence of General Guldenleu who was very ill, had posted himself in an extremely advantageous place, being sheltered by hedges on one side and by the sea on the other.

Having at last pierced the hedges, he ordered the markgraf of Baden to begin the attack with three squadrons, which he did with such success that he at first overthrew four Danish squadrons; and Chief-Admiral Wrangel, who was on the right of the king of Sweden, charged also at the same time, repulsed and broke likewise all that resisted him. It is true that in one spot, the ice breaking, two companies, one from either side, sank in the sea and were drowned. The king of Sweden lost in this same spot the coach which he generally used, and my chaise met with the same ill luck. The king of Sweden, having seen this accident, had reason to fear that the same thing might happen to him and to all his army, of which he was at the head; but being a dauntless prince, although he well knew the danger in which he was, instead of deciding to turn in the direction of the land, which he could have done without danger, he left the opening of the sea, where his horsemen had perished, on his left, and advanced to meet the enemies who were on the sea at his right; and for fear lest the Danes should make use of this circumstance to take Admiral Wrangel in the rear, the king of Sweden sent Count Toot against them with a Swedish regiment, who in this battle did all that a brave cavalier and a good officer could do.

After all the Danish squadrons were broken, Admiral Wrangel went himself to the Danish infantry who were on the ice, and who were guarding the post where the artillery was stationed, crying out to them to lay down their arms. Colonel Jens recognised him, and not being in a position to resist, begged quarter and gave himself up; the admiral willingly granted quarter to him and to all who wished it; for he felt esteem and friendship for brave officers and for soldiers who showed courage. Moreover, he knew that arms are fickle, and that the bravest are not exempt from the misfortunes of war. Thus all the Danish troops were defeated or prisoners, and flight did not spare two hundred of them.

When the king of Sweden heard of the prisoners who had just been taken, he ordered Major-General Berner to advance with a few regiments against the five hundred cavalry which had just joined the troops the prince had defeated, and General Archamberg was also ordered to go towards Middelfart where six hundred cavalry were on the road for the same purpose. They carried out their orders so well that all the enemy's troops, Danes as well as Germans, surrendered and went over to the side of the Swedish officers. Colonel Jens owned that all the troops in the island of Fünen under his command amounted to more than three thousand horse, seven hundred German infantry, and fifteen hundred native militia. This battle made the king of Sweden complete master of the island of Fünen.

Before the king of Sweden arrived at Svendborg he detached several small bodies of men to try to pass into Zealand and to ascertain if the ice would bear his army. When he left the table in the evening, some horsemen came and assured him that the ice was so strong that all his army and his cannon could safely cross; and to give a positive proof that they had been into Zealand, they brought before the king of Sweden some peasants whom they had taken prisoners. Thereupon the prince said that he had certainly thought that, since the messenger who had brought him the letters of Chevalier Medoüé had been able to cross with his horse, he could also cross with his troops, but

[1658 A.D.]

that very probably he would not have thought of it except for that. On the report of these men the king of Sweden gave orders to sound to horse, and set out accompanied by all his troops.

The intense cold from which I had suffered all day had forced me to retire to my quarters, as much for the sake of warmth as to take some rest. I had scarcely done so when they came to tell me that the king of Sweden had started. I immediately got into my sledge to follow him. I can in truth say that there was something terrible in marching by night on this frozen sea, because the large number of horses which were with the king of Sweden had, while cutting out a road, melted the snow, so that there were more than two feet of water above the ice, and one was always in fear of finding the sea open in any spot. Several of the parties lost their way in the darkness of the night and unfortunately perished, because the ice was either too weak or too shaken along the road which they took. I did four leagues in this way, uncertain whether at every step I took my sledge would not sink into the sea. However, I was fortunate enough to rejoin the king of Sweden.*g*

The Peace of Roeskilde; the Renewal of War

The adventurous prince crossed the successive straits between the islands, and pushed on through the deep snowdrift to Kioge, about eighteen English miles from Copenhagen.[1] In this extremity, Frederick III of Denmark, whose patriotic ardour was not supported by the Danish nobility, was advised by the rigsraad to sue for peace, and even to purchase it at the sacrifice of losing part of his dominions. Though elated with his singularly good fortune, the conqueror agreed to treat under the mediation of the French and English ambassadors; and within ten days after the landing of the invaders in Zealand the preliminaries were arranged and signed at the small village of Hage-Testrup. By the terms of this convention, affirmed by a definitive treaty subsequently concluded at Roeskilde (1658), the Danish provinces beyond the Sound, Skåne, Halland, and Blekinge, were irrecoverably ceded to Sweden, to which they have ever since remained attached, as also the district of Trondhjem, the northern part of Norway, and the island of Bornholm. The ratification of the peace was followed by an interview between the two sovereigns at the royal palace of Frederiksborg, where his Danish majesty had provided an entertainment for the foreign ministers.

But the grasping ambition of Charles was far from being satiated with this triumph over a rival state; he had observed its weakness, and secretly meditated a renewal of the war. Leaving his army under the command of Wrangel, he crossed the Sound, took possession of his newly acquired territories, and convened the Swedish diet at Gothenburg, to deliberate respecting the schemes of national aggrandisement which he had in contemplation; among which was a plan for the partition of Poland, between himself, the czar, the elector of Brandenburg, and the house of Austria. But Denmark was the object to which his views were more immediately directed. Accordingly, in defiance of the recent treaty, he repaired to Holstein, and being joined by his fleet he once more invested Copenhagen, to the astonishment and consternation of the inhabitants. Frederick threw himself on the patriotism of his people, and adopted the most energetic measures for a vigorous

[1 In commemoration of this remarkable expedition, Charles caused a medal to be struck, with the legend on one side, " *Transitus gloriosus maris Baltici*, d. 7, February, 1658 "; and on the other, "*Natura hoc debuit uni*," in allusion to the rare occurrence of the sea being frozen at the passage of the Great Belt.]

resistance. The siege continued three months, during which Wrangel took possession of the strong fortress of Kronborg, the gallant commander being obliged to capitulate by the mutiny of his garrison. In October the long-expected succour from Holland, under Opdam, made its appearance in the Sound. Wrangel, who acted alternately as general and admiral, disputed the passage of the Dutch, and opened a fire from the castles on each side of the strait. The two hostile fleets came into immediate collision, and after an obstinate contest, memorable among the naval achievements of that age, the Swedish squadron was completely defeated and compelled to retire to Landskrona, where it was shortly afterwards blockaded by the enemy. Opdam pursued his course to Copenhagen roads, where he was received with transports of joy by the besieged, who anticipated instant relief. But their hopes were not immediately realised; the rigours of winter had set in, and the ice, whilst it rendered their floating defences almost useless, facilitated the approaches of the besiegers, who made an unsuccessful attempt to capture the city by storm.

During these proceedings, the Swedes were equally unfortunate in other quarters. They had been expelled from Holstein and Schleswig by the Poles and the troops of the elector of Brandenburg, then in alliance with Denmark. They were also driven from the island of Bornholm, and from the province of Trondhjem by an insurrection of Norwegian peasants. In the spring of 1659, an English fleet made its appearance in the Baltic, commanded by Admiral Montagu, whom the protector and the parliament had despatched to watch the motions of the Dutch and enforce an armed mediation between the belligerent powers. The negotiation proving unsuccessful, De Ruyter, who commanded a separate squadron under Opdam, attacked the enemy's fleet, for the purpose of compelling him to evacuate the Danish territory. A battle was fought near Odense, in which the Swedes, almost in sight of their king, were completely routed by the Dutch and the Danes. The fortress of Nyborg was next attacked, and compelled to surrender after a sharp engagement. Eleven regiments of cavalry, the best troops of Sweden, were made prisoners; and of seven thousand who began the action there escaped only the two generals, Saltzbach and Steinbock, with a slender retinue of domestics.

THE DEATH OF CHARLES X; THE TREATY OF COPENHAGEN

This fatal blow sunk deep into the heart of Charles Gustavus; he began to feel that fortune, the deity worshipped by military conquerors, had deserted his cause; but instead of listening to pacific overtures, he only affected to negotiate in order to gain time to concert a plan for the invasion of the southern part of Norway. With this view he once more crossed the Sound and convened the national diet at Gothenburg, that he might obtain the necessary supplies of men and money for the enterprise. But in the midst of these preparations he was seized with a fever, which was epidemic in the camp, and died on the 11th of February, 1660, on the same day and at the same hour when he had made the memorable attack on Copenhagen the preceding year. He expired in the arms of Oxenstierna, at the early age of thirty-six; having appointed guardians to the young prince, his son, who succeeded him under the title of Charles XI, with a regency nominated to govern the kingdom during his minority.

Charles Gustavus bears the character of a bold, warlike, undaunted, but rash monarch, whose ardour for military fame engaged him in the most unjust quarrels, and whose inventive genius, had he lived a few years longer, would probably have triumphed over all difficulties, and extorted honourable terms from the different nations with whom he was then at war. On his deathbed, he had earnestly advised the regency to make peace with all the enemies of Sweden; and these injunctions were eagerly fulfilled by the government, who saw in the depressed state of the kingdom sufficient necessity for the immediate cessation of hostilities. The celebrated Treaty of Oliva was concluded in April, 1660, by which the long and deadly feud between the Catholic and Protestant branches of the house of Vasa was extinguished. The late king had made a truce with the czar Alexis, and the Peace of Kardis put an end to the war with Russia. By the present treaty, John Kasimir of Poland finally renounced his shadowy claim to the Swedish crown, which had long before been repudiated by the nation. He ceded at the same time the provinces of Livonia, Esthonia, and the island of Ösel, which were confirmed to Sweden.

The peace with Denmark met with greater obstructions; but at length all differences were adjusted and the Treaty of Copenhagen was signed on the 10th of June, under the guarantee of the three mediating powers — France, England, and Holland. This pacification embraced the conditions of the late Treaty of Roeskilde, except that the district of Trondhjem and the island of Bornholm were restored to the Danes. The tranquillity of the North was thus established in a manner creditable to Sweden, considering the number and power of her enemies, the length of the war, and the distressing situation in which she was left by the sudden death of the late monarch.[h]

CHARLES XI (1660–1697 A.D.)

During eleven years there was nothing to disturb the clear horizon of the kingdom. The regency acted as mediator in the disputes which arose between the maritime powers. They exhibited, too, a disposition to join in the triple alliance for the defence of the Netherlands against France, and they even signed an engagement to that effect; but the gold of Louis XIV was more powerful than the representations of English or Dutch; and a subsidy of 200,000 golden crowns per annum induced them to enter into a close alliance with that monarch. Disastrous was this alliance to the interests of Sweden: it plunged her into a war with Holland, England, Brandenburg, and the emperor, that crippled her energies during the whole of the reign of Charles XI.

In 1672 the king entered on the duties of government. Faithful to his engagement with France, his first step was to send a small army into Brandenburg, less to annoy than to overawe the elector. In 1674, however, he formally declared war against that prince, and despatched Wrangel, one of the veterans who had gained so much celebrity in the Thirty Years' War, to reduce the country. The command was obeyed with a degree of success indicative of the spirit which the great Gustavus had left behind him. The strongest fortresses were taken by capitulation or by assault. But the same year saw the end of these triumphs. During the sickness of Wrangel, the Swedish forces were defeated in several skirmishes and in one general action, and forced to retreat into Mecklenburg. These events led to results still more disastrous: they prevented the accession of states which would otherwise have served as allies; and they encouraged others openly to declare themselves against a power whose German possessions were tempting enough to invite aggression. Denmark, Holland, Lüneburg, Münster joined Brandenburg, and put their troops in motion; and the Swedish possessions were simultaneously assailed on several points, from Bremen to the eastern confines of Pomerania.

Fortress after fortress — Wollin, Wolgast, Wismar, Domgarten, Usedom — was reduced. In 1676 Visby received a Danish garrison. A Swedish fleet was defeated by the combined Danes and Dutch near the isle of Bornholm. Helsingborg, Christianstad, Landskrona, fell before the king of Denmark; Wennersberg and Kristianopel were equally reduced. The result of a great battle near Lund, where Charles and Christian fought in person, was doubtful; both claimed the advantage; but as the latter returned to Copenhagen for new troops, while the former succeeded in the object of the campaign — viz., the relief of Malmö — history must record it to the Swedes. But a naval action near Landskrona was disastrous to them; and they had the mortification of hearing that all the fortresses in Pomerania were, one by one, in the power of the elector of Brandenburg. But Charles was not discouraged: in a second land battle with his rival of Denmark, in which both kings exhibited extraordinary valour, he had the glory of complete success. In Norway, however, and still more in Pomerania, fortune was against him. On the whole, though Sweden never showed more valour, more constancy, she was not a match for all her enemies; and except for the triumphs of France, her great ally, she must have suffered for her imprudence by an alarming dismemberment. To the honour of Louis, he did not forsake his northern friend. In the separate treaties which he concluded with Holland and the emperor, he stipulated for the integrity of the Swedish possessions, as they had been left by the Treaty of Westphalia. The opposition of Denmark to the restoration of the conquests which she had made over her neighbour was overcome by the armed interference of France. In Pomerania and Livonia, as in Bremen and Sweden, Charles recovered, through the fidelity of his ally, that which he had lost through his own imprudence — or rather through the imprudence of his ministers, before he had reached an age sufficiently mature to weigh the consequences of his measures. A separate and subsequent treaty with Denmark, negotiated through the influence of the French ambassador, was strengthened by the marriage of Charles with Ulrica Eleonora, daughter of Christian.

During his minority, Charles had been taught to believe that the regents had abused their trust, and the senate encroached on the just prerogatives of the crown. In the former belief there was probably much truth; the latter served as a pretext for attempting a change in the government. By the constitution (if, indeed, the term has any meaning) the authority of the Swedish kings was extremely limited. They could not make peace in war, they could not impose taxes, they could not originate a law, they could not form or renew a treaty of alliance, they could not try a noble delinquent, without the sanction of the senate or of the diet. But the personal character of the monarch had more influence than custom. If he was of a bold, enterprising character, he could do whatever he pleased; and if his efforts were triumphant, he was never called to account for his outrage on the freedom of the other bodies of the state. If they were unfortunate, he was doomed to the same humiliation as other limited monarchs — to acknowledge his fault, to promise a better government in future, and often to bribe the leading members of the opposition against him. The history of the country is, in reality, a continued struggle between the crown and the other arms of the state. Gustavus I had reigned with absolute authority; so had the second of that name; so had Charles X; while Eric XIV, Sigismund, and Christina had been forced often to bend before the voice of the diet.

Charles XI wished that authority to be recognised by the law itself, and to pass unquestioned by posterity. Under the pretext of taking into consideration the general state of the kingdom, of reforming abuses, and of regulating the amount of taxation to be borne by the different classes of society, he convoked (1680) a diet at Stockholm. That he might encounter the less opposition to the measures which he contemplated, he reverted to the same mode of violence as the most tyrannical of his predecessors — *viz.*, he quartered in the city and its vicinity some of the regiments most attached to his interests. With such means of intimidation, he obtained a decree that the military force of the realm, the only sure support of arbitrary power, should, though in time of peace, remain on the same footing as during the late wars. To meet this charge, he obtained the levy of a tax on the rural population, and certain public bodies.

These measures were only preparatory to others more important. The first was to curtail the authority of the senate, against whom the accusation had been made that they had abused their trust. A commission, entirely of the king's creatures, was formed, to inquire into the origin and extent of that authority, and whether, in its existing state, it was commensurate or not with the spirit of the constitution. The result was a report that the senate did not form an independent or intermediate branch of the state, between the king and the nobles or the burgesses; that it was simply a royal council, with which he ought to advise. This was a severe blow at a body which, whenever the crown was weak or embarrassed, had arrogated to itself functions truly regal; but it did not satisfy him. He declared, and the diet sanctioned the declaration, that he alone was the judge of what affairs ought and what affairs ought not to be laid before it. He therefore raised himself above its influence, and entirely independent of its advice.

But even this was not all. In consequence of these changes, a new official board was appointed, called the grand commission, whose right it was to inquire into all transactions of the ministry, and to punish the excesses and usurpations of the senators. A college of provision was also established for the purpose of ascertaining the amount of lands and lordships granted, sold, mortgaged, or exchanged by preceding kings, either in Sweden or Livonia, since the year 1609, together with all the royal palaces alienated since 1655. An offer was at the same time made on the part of the crown to reimburse the proprietors for such sums as they had originally paid for them. By this proceeding a considerable augmentation was made to the royal revenues, but it ruined vast numbers of the nobility. The clergy likewise evinced their willingness to contribute towards the necessities of the government by offering a fifth of their income to the king, provided they might pay it in kine or brass money.[b] The states were again convoked in 1681, contrary to the usual practice of their meeting, except on extraordinary occasions, only once in four years. This diet went further in their concessions than the preceding; declaring by statute that, although the sovereign was enjoined to govern his dominions according to the laws, this did not take from him the power to alter that constitution of his own authority, or to put the kingdom in such a situation as he might think most conducive to its interest and security. The authors of this decision, which rendered the monarch absolute, were the deputies of the burghers and peasants, who overlooked all consequences in their blind zeal to oppose the aristocracy, and bring them down to their own level.

Another blow was struck at this doomed order in 1686, by the extraordinary expedient which the government resorted to of liquidating the public debt by raising the nominal value of money without increasing its real worth. The effect of this single transaction was the ruin of thousands, as the state creditors lost by it above nine millions of crowns. These, with a variety of other new measures, so disgusted and irritated the nobility that they sent repeated petitions to court, insisting upon their ancient privileges being respected. Seeing no prospect of redress, they drew up a still stronger remonstrance, which was to be presented to the king by Captain Patkul, a gentleman of Livonia, and one of their deputies, who had already distinguished himself by his bold freedom of speech and his ardent attachment to liberty. The attempt was unsuccessful, and excited resentment instead of procuring relief. An accusation was drawn up against the whole of the remonstrants, all of whom were convicted of high treason; but the chief victim selected for ignominious punishment was Patkul, who was sentenced to have his right hand cut off, and to be deprived of his life, honours, and estates. The University of Leipsic formally declared their opinion that the condemnation was unjust; but neither he nor his colleagues could avail themselves of that decision; he contrived, however, to elude the vengeance of his enemies for a time, by abandoning his native country and taking refuge at the court of Poland.[b] The violence of parties having thus thrown down every barrier that could check the unlimited exercise of the royal prerogative, an act was at length passed, in 1693, by which the king was made absolute, the sole depository of the sovereign authority, and entitled to govern the realm according to his will and pleasure, without being responsible to any power on earth.[h]

The facility with which Charles thus obtained a legal confirmation of despotism will not much surprise us, if we attend to the condition of society in Sweden. According to Whitelock, the British ambassador at Stockholm during Christina's reign, not the peasants only but the burghers were so completely the slaves of the aristocracy that they durst not openly express any will of their own. Hence they were extending the royal authority, which was always a shield to them against the encroachments of the nobles.[b]

The concluding period of this monarch's reign was spent in endeavouring to establish the peace of Europe, and in regulating the political and commercial affairs of his own subjects. To his mediation was owing, in a great degree, the congress at Ryswick, which terminated the war between France on the one side, and Austria, Spain, Holland, and England on the other, but his pacific labours were suddenly arrested by a disorder which cut him off (April, 1697) at the early age of forty-two.[h]

CHAPTER XI

DENMARK AND NORWAY IN THE 16TH AND 17TH CENTURIES

[1559–1677 A.D.]

ACCESSION OF FREDERICK II (1559 A.D.)

WE turn back now to take up the story of Denmark and Norway where we left it in an earlier chapter, namely, at the time of the death of Christian III, in 1559.*a* It was a novel spectacle in Denmark to see a king ascend the throne without opposition, and an election reduced to a mere formality. Long before his father's death, Frederick had been acknowledged by the two kingdoms. There was no longer any hope to the disaffected in Christian II, as that monarch had paid the debt of nature a few days after Christian III; nor in the discontent of the Roman Catholics, since the number in twenty-three years had so greatly diminished (the result of the entire suppression of their worship) that there were few of the communion left, and in another generation there would not be one. There had long been peace at home and abroad; and so long had the national prosperity increased. The throne of Frederick, therefore, was fully established; and much good was augured from his reign, especially as he had been for some years accustomed, by his prudent father, to the duties of administration.

This monarch has been praised for moderation: he had, however, quite as much ambition. Scarcely had he grasped the sceptre before he resolved to attempt something which should give lustre to his name. Near sixty years had elapsed since the unfortunate invasion of Ditmarsh; and though, owing to the troubles of the times, no effort had been made to wipe out the stain of defeat from the national honour, the design had never been wholly

345

abandoned. Christian III, indeed, had recognised the independence of the country in the Treaty of Lübeck, 1536; but what monarch ever regarded treaties when he could obtain some advantage by breaking them? To this enterprise Frederick was more induced by his kinsmen of Holstein — *viz.*, his uncles Adolf and John the elder, and his brother John the younger — all with the ducal title, and all eager to extend their territory by the conquest of a country so conveniently situated, and, in some respects, so fertile as Ditmarsh. The Danish nobles were induced, without much difficulty, to engage in a war which might be considered foreign; and an army of twenty thousand men, under the chief command of John Rantzau, led by the king and the dukes in person, took the field, after the publication of an elaborate manifesto, in which a brave and noble people were stigmatised as rebels. A herald was sent, according to the usage of the times, with a declaration of war against them; and such was their indignation that he would have been torn to pieces but for the interference of their magistrates. Owing to the same influence, their reply was a moderate one. They had never, they observed, been subjects of the house of Holstein; and, if any of their people had committed acts of violence on their princely neighbours, they were ready to make such compensation as the laws might award: why, then, should justice be sought by violence, when it was peacefully offered? In vain did they appeal to the common principles of equity: their subjugation was resolved; and their only hope lay in their own right arms.

Unfortunately for the inhabitants, they allowed themselves to be deceived by the report of spies whom they should have distrusted; and, in the belief that Hammer would sustain the shock of the main army, they left a small garrison in Meldorf. (The three fortresses of Tilsburg, Hammer, and Meldorf were the great defence on the side of Holstein — the only side accessible to an army.) The latter fortress was vigorously assailed by the whole army; and was no less vigorously defended. The paucity of defenders was partly compensated by the courage of the women, of whom many appeared in armour, and fought no less valiantly than their husbands or fathers. But the contest was too unequal; the place was carried by assault; and the inhabitants, women and children, as well as men, were barbarously put to the sword. The indomitable valour of the men may be illustrated by the fact that, among the slain, scarcely any were found with less than three or four wounds. But if they were good soldiers, they were bad generals, since they lost Tilsburg by a blunder similar to that which had led to the fall of Meldorf. Their greatest misfortune, no doubt, was the want of defenders in sufficient number; another was that, the season being uncommonly dry, they could not, as they had intended, overflow the country by opening the sluices.

Heide, their capital, and their last bulwark, was next invested. The defence was a noble one; assault after assault was repelled; and, though the besiegers were nearly equal in valour, and vastly superior in numbers, the place would scarcely have been reduced had not Rantzau caused it to be set on fire. Many perished in the flames, many were slain by the sword of the enemy, and many, convinced that resistance was hopeless, escaped. To spare the remnant, the elders tendered their submission. All the males capable of bearing arms — now reduced to four thousand — were assembled in a large plain, and compelled to do homage to the princes of Holstein as "lords of Ditmarsh." It is some consolation to find that this brave, virtuous, and patriotic community suffered less by the loss of their liberty than might have been expected. Their isolated position still availed them, since it placed them beyond the reach of daily coercion by the myrmidons of government.

This success gave some *éclat* to the coronation of Frederick, which immediately followed. The capitulation did not much differ from those which had preceded it. He was not to admit any foreigner into the rigsraad, nor to imprison any gentleman, nor to undertake anything important, without the advice of his rigsraad; nor to ennoble anyone not belonging to the privileged classes. The article which declared the Danish monarchy elective was drawn up with more care, lest the claim of the eldest son after the father should be drawn into a precedent. The progress of events, however, was more powerful than the jealousy of the rigsraad; the royal authority was evidently gaining ground; for when Christian, the son of Frederick, reached his fourth year, the rigsraad first and the nobles afterward acknowledged him successor to the united crowns of Denmark and Norway. In regard to the latter kingdom, Frederick asked not for its suffrage: he relied on his father's decree, by which it had been declared an integral portion of the monarchy; and he received, at Copenhagen, the homage of the Norwegian deputies, just as if he had been at Trondhjem. Yet there was some inconsistency in this respect; for in 1582, when the election of the infant prince Christian was confirmed by the Norwegian nobles at Christiania, Frederick by letter thanked them for the act, and declared that it should not be drawn into a precedent injurious to the rights of the estates or the laws of the kingdom. The truth seems to be that, however zealously the Danish monarchs might endeavour to destroy the nationality of the country, they were often compelled to suspend their efforts, and treat it with something like respect.

THE SCANDINAVIAN SEVEN YEARS' WAR (1563–1570 A.D.)

The most prominent but by no means the most interesting feature of this monarch's reign was the war with Sweden. The position of the two countries to each other was naturally hostile. We have seen with how much difficulty those experienced rulers, Gustavus Vasa and Christian III, had curbed their desire for war. Their two successors were too young, too headstrong, too inexperienced to put equal constraint upon themselves. Both had reasons for complaint, which, though petty in the eyes of a wise prince, were great in those of a rash one. Frederick continued to use the arms of Sweden on his shield; he would not forego the pretensions which the Union of Kalmar afforded him to the crown of that country; and his anger was greater than the occasion required when he saw Eric, in revenge, assume the arms of Denmark. From this period, though the two kings signed a treaty of amity, they regarded each other with ill-feeling, which they still further embittered by a series of vexatious however trifling annoyances.

Frederick was the first to afford just ground for war. In 1563 he arrested three Swedish ambassadors, as they were proceeding to the court of Philip the Magnanimous, landgraf of Hesse, to bring the daughter of that prince to their royal master. The only cause for this rash act was a suspicion that one of the ambassadors was hostile to Denmark! Eric demanded satisfaction; but none was offered. Two other circumstances deepened the animosity, and rendered war inevitable. By some mistake, or rather by that national dislike which was more remarkable between Denmark and Sweden than even between the Scots and the English in the Middle Ages, a fleet which Eric had sent to Rostock, to bring away the princess of Hesse, was engaged by a Danish fleet. Which was the aggressor? This question cannot be satisfactorily decided: probably both were equally culpable. However this be, the Swedes were the victors.

The mortification of Frederick was extreme; but chance soon placed in his hands the means of irritating his rival more effectually than by the loss of a battle. Eric was a fickle man — in his courtships more than in any other thing. At the very time he was on the eve of celebrating his marriage with the daughter of the landgraf, he was soliciting the hand of two queens, Elizabeth of England and Mary of Scotland. A letter to the former sovereign was intercepted by a Danish officer, who immediately sent it to Frederick. Frederick with joyful malice forwarded it to Philip. Philip contumeliously dismissed the Swedish ambassadors, and bestowed his daughter without delay on Adolf of Holstein. The mediation of friendly powers could no longer obtain a moment's notice; war was declared by both monarchs, and preparations were immediately made for prosecuting it with vigour.

Assisted by the nobles of Holstein and Schleswig, and by the republic of Lübeck, which was indignant at the diminution of its commercial privileges by order of Eric, Frederick, at the head of twenty-five thousand men, landed in Halland, and invested Elfsborg, on the site of which the modern Gothenburg is founded. At the same time a considerable fleet, manned by about five thousand seamen, was ordered to co-operate. On his side, Eric invaded Skåne, leaving a fleet to struggle for the sceptre of the Baltic. The result of the campaign did not correspond with the preparations of either: a naval action was indecisive; and the rest of the season was spent in devastating some portions of the neighbouring provinces. The following year the Swedes had much success in Norway; they even penetrated to Trondhjem; but they lost their conquests with as much rapidity as they were gained.

In the same manner the conquests of Frederick in the south and west of Sweden were equally transient; while a great naval engagement, in which both fleets exhibited all their skill and all their bravery, was no less indecisive. So frequently to both parties was the advantage of one day counterbalanced by the defeat of the next that the whole war might be called a regular alternation of success and failure. What instruction, what entertainment would be afforded by the detail of such events? It must be sufficient to observe that both nations displayed great valour; that the kings and generals of both covered themselves with fame; but that the people, whose resources were exhausted by the conflict, sighed for peace. Hostilities were sometimes suspended by the internal disputes of the Swedes, many of whom were justly dissatisfied with their king, whose capriciousness sometimes assumed a character of insanity. We have seen that a conspiracy, headed by his eldest brother, who assumed the name of John III, hurled him from the throne (1568).

Why the Danish king should remain an almost passive spectator of these disturbances — why he neglected to profit by them, seeing that his aid would readily have been purchased by both parties in the state — has been the subject of much conjecture. Whether he was bribed to this inactivity, or duped by the successor of Eric; whether (a more probable supposition) he hoped to see both parties so weaken themselves by this civil strife, as to become in turn his victims; whether, finally, he could have effected much with an army which often clamoured for arrears of pay, and sometimes broke out into open insurrection — would be idle to inquire. Probably all these considerations, though not equally, contributed to the result. At length, after many ineffectual attempts at mediation by the Protestant states of Germany and by the French king, peace was concluded at Stettin in 1570. The chief articles were that both kings might continue to use the obnoxious heraldic bearings, so that the one would not found upon them any pretensions to the dominions of the other; that John should renounce all claim to Skåne, Halland, Gotland, and Blekinge, and restore his Norwegian conquests; that, in like manner, Frederick should restore his conquests, receiving, however, for Gothenburg and its territory (which he had for some time held) a considerable sum of money, payable in two instalments; that the limits of the two kingdoms should remain as they were in the time of Gustavus Vasa and Christian III. Thus a destructive war of seven years ended as most wars do end: both parties were impoverished by it, and both, in other respects, remained as they were at its commencement.

REBELLIOUS FIEFS

Frederick could not, any more than his predecessors, avoid some trouble in regard to Schleswig and Holstein. Three circumstances — the elective form of the government, the attachment of the nobles to their own inordinate privileges, and the partition of the states among the princes of Denmark, to be held by hereditary right — were the source of perpetual troubles. For these dissensions the princes themselves were most to blame. By making all their male children heirs to some portion of territory, by loading them with dowries to females, by lawsuits as to the succession in particular instances, and by constant efforts to render themselves independent of Denmark, they were always at variance, either among themselves or with the royal chief of the family. Much confusion, too, arose from the difference of constitution in the two duchies. Holstein was always a fief of the empire, and therefore subject to the imperial feudal law. Schleswig was a fief of the Danish crown. While the dukes of the former, therefore, did homage to the emperors, those of the latter owed no allegiance, except to the royal Dane. But, ever since the union of the duchies, Schleswig had claimed the same rights as the sister duchy; for the sway of the empire, or rather of the imperial diet, was infinitely preferable to that of the Danish kings. By solemn compact, indeed, the two duchies ought to have shared equal rights, and to have been equally administered. In both, the elective principle, the independence of the local noble, the non-obligation to military service beyond the confines of the territory, and the right of self-taxation were recognised; but unhappily compacts of this nature had seldom any good effect — they were violated by bribery or by open force. We repeatedly read of armed troops being brought into the neighbourhood to overawe the deliberations of a diet. But the means of such coercion were not always, or indeed generally, at hand; so that virtually there was more independence than might be inferred from the arbitrary nature of the royal pretensions.

Still there remained an everlasting apple of discord, the tendency of which it required all the influence of friendly mediators to counteract. In 1580 the elector of Saxony, the duke of Mecklenburg, and the landgraf of Hesse effected a sort of compromise between the rival parties. By it so much was conceded to the dukes that Schleswig was declared a hereditary fief — a principle for which they had vigorously contended, but which the Danish kings had always endeavoured to nullify. On the other hand, those dukes were to receive the investiture from those kings, their liege superiors; and, whenever the welfare of the kingdom required it, to transmit and maintain, at their own cost, a body of troops for its defence. In like manner, the king was to succour the duchy in case of need. As to the disputes between the co-heirs themselves, it was agreed that whenever one of them died the inheritance should not be seized by any of the rest, but that all the rest should nominate commissioners to administer the vacant domain, until all should have amicably and legally determined the matter among themselves. In such agreements, we may observe, no one thought of the rights which had been so frequently and so solemnly guaranteed to the states. New states were treated as if they had no rights — none of deliberation, none of election, none of self-government; they were regarded as in hereditary vassalage to the dukes and the crown. That they should voluntarily concur in so monstrous an assumption was not to be expected. If by physical force they were sometimes constrained to receive the two-fold yoke, they sometimes evaded it. In general, the history of these duchies is merely a history of usurpations of their undoubted rights by the crown and the local dukes.

Frederick had also to encounter some resistance from Hamburg. This city, as we have before observed, was feudally dependent on the rulers of Holstein, to whom it was compelled to do homage. The mere act would have been felt to be derogatory by so great and prosperous a community; but other vassalitic duties were exacted from it. To escape from these obligations, which it was at all times more disposed to resist than to discharge, it petitioned the emperor to elevate it from a feudal to an imperial city — viz., to a position in which it should be recognised as dependent on the emperor only. The privilege was generally purchased from two persons — from the immediate superior and from the emperor; but sometimes it was bestowed as a gratuitous mark of favour. On the present occasion, the dukes seem not to have been consulted; and the emperor was sufficiently disposed to comply with the prayer of the municipality. One at least of his predecessors (Sigismund) had expedited letters patent, conferring on it two or three of the most important privileges enjoyed by the imperial cities. In spite of the protest entered by the dukes, Ferdinand confirmed these privileges, but he proceeded no further.

Nor was the Danish monarch without some anxiety as to Livonia. In the course of this history, it has been shown that some of the Danish kings held the feudal superiority over a portion, at least, of that region and of its immediate vicinity; but that its distance from the seat of power, the restless character of the inhabitants, and, above all, the intrigues of the military order, which aspired to the undivided sovereignty, had induced them to relinquish so precarious, so costly a dependency. So long as they had only pagans to oppose, these knights, though not without difficulty, maintained their establishment in the country; but when they had the archbishop of Riga, and still more the Russian czar, for enemies, they were compelled to solicit the support of foreign princes.

They first applied to Gustavus Vasa; but he was too cautious to embark in so hazardous an enterprise. Their next recourse was to Christian III, who consented merely to purchase the isle of Ösel and the province of Vick for his second son, Magnus. The bargain, however, was not concluded during the lifetime of that monarch; and Frederick on his accession, had the choice either of completing it or of surrendering to his brother a portion of Holstein. He chose the former; and after some negotiation purchased the isle in question, and the diocese of Courland from the Teutonic knights. Their object in the sale was to secure the aid of Denmark against the czar, who, they well knew, would soon disturb the new duke in his possessions.

On the other hand, the dislike borne by the inhabitants, not merely to the Russians but to the military aristocracy, which had so long tyrannised over them, seemed to afford an excellent opening for the establishment of a new and not inconsiderable empire in the vast regions on the eastern coast of the

Baltic. Magnus was received with much joy. The bishop and chapter of
Revel, the governor of Sonnenburg, and other authorities, submitted to him.
But the armies of the czar soon compelled him to forsake the continent, and
seek refuge in the isle of Ösel. Deceived in his hope of a protector, Kettler,
the grand master of the Teutonic knights, sold his superiority over Livonia
to the king of Poland. The price was the duchy of Courland and Semgallen,
which he was to hold hereditarily from the Polish king. This arrangement
was a blow at the policy of Frederick, who was expected to arm in its defence.
But he remained indifferent to events which only concerned his brother.
Rend, menaced by the Russians, and despairing of aid from either of those
princes, besought that of Eric, the Swedish king. Eric obeyed the call,
raised the siege, and was acknowledged sovereign, not merely of that territory
but of the greater part of Esthonia. To preserve the isle of Ösel and the
small portion of Courland which still belonged to him, and for which he seems
to have done homage to the Polish king, Magnus made overtures of peace to
the czar, Ivan IV. Three years of tranquillity followed, which were employed by Magnus and his brother in spreading the reformed doctrines over
the new duchy.

But Magnus had not the stability of character to remain quiet. His
intrigues with Russia led to his recognition as king of Livonia by the czar,
who sent him troops to expel the Swedes, the Poles, and the Germans. Though
he was assisted also by his brother, he made no impression on the enemy;
and the pacification of Stettin soon deprived him of Frederick's support.
Add that he was unpopular with those whom he wished to subdue, and we
may account for the coolness which the czar began to show towards his royal
vassal. Nor was this the worst: coolness was succeeded by studied insult;
he was once imprisoned — his life was in danger, and he fled with precipitation
to the court of the Polish king, against whom he had hitherto been fighting.
As the vassal of that monarch, he held Ösel, with two Courland provinces,
until his death in 1583. Frederick now claimed the succession; so did the
king of Poland: but, through the mediation of the duke of Prussia, a compromise was effected, by which Frederick retained the island, but surrendered
the Courland domains to the Pole for 30,000 crowns. This was a wise arrangement: the latter could not long have been held by a power so distant and
with so small a military force as Denmark.[b]

THE LAST YEARS OF FREDERICK II

The remainder of Frederick's reign was devoted to the peaceful pursuits
of internal administration. His active zeal for the Protestant religion, though
doubtless sincere, was tarnished by bigotry and the intolerant maxims of the
age. The unity of the Lutheran doctrines was jealously guarded by civil
penalties; and one of the most learned professors in the University of Copenhagen, Hemmingius, was deposed for the imaginary offence of publishing in
Latin a treatise on the Eucharist, which was supposed to lean towards the
Calvinistic interpretation of that symbolical ordinance. The elector of
Saxony had caused to be established, in his own and several other states of
the empire, a "formulary of concord" (Konkordienformel), which he sent to
Frederick; but the latter rejected it with indignation, as an element of discord, and even prohibited the introduction and sale of all books in which its
tenets were explained or defended.

Denmark, like other Protestant countries, might have derived advantage
from the arts and industry of the persecuted subjects of the Netherlands, exiled

by their bigoted princes for the crime of religious non-conformity; but they were expelled from her inhospitable shores by an edict requiring all foreigners settled in the kingdom to subscribe to the articles of faith professed by the national church, otherwise to be banished the realm. The intolerance of Frederick in theological matters was in some measure redeemed by his bountiful patronage of learned men, and especially of Tycho Brahe, the first Danish philosopher whose fame had extended beyond the narrow confines of his native land.c

TYCHO BRAHE AT HVEN

King Frederick granted Tycho for life the free disposal and proprietorship of the island of Hven, situated three leagues from Copenhagen. The circumference of this fertile little island is about three leagues. Its principal building, which received the name of Uranienborg, was a veritable castle built on the central plateau of the island a quarter of a league from the sea. With the luxury of a great lord and the intelligence of a learned astronomer Tycho united to the formalities of a pompous existence all the conditions favourable to the study of astronomy. In apartments decorated with paintings and statues, ingenious inscriptions recalled the progress of the science of the heavens and the memory of the most famous astronomers.

TYCHO BRAHE
(1546–1601)

In this retreat Tycho, raising himself above the pleasures of the world and the troublesome tumult of the court, set out to acquire a new nobility, of a kind unknown to his illustrious ancestors, and to give their name more brilliance than any he had received from them. Around the castle soon sprang up workshops for construction and repair, a printing establishment for the publication of completed writings, and buildings of all sorts destined to receive numerous instruments whose delicate precision would have been deranged by the vibration of the castle floors. Finally chemical laboratories permitted, in accordance with the ideas of the age, the mingling of the study of the stars with that of the metals under their influence. About twenty young men chosen from the cleverest students of the Danish universities were employed in making observations and calculations. Real astronomical apprentices, they learned from seeing their master work; guided by the enthusiastic and communicative spirit of the chief, the little colony soon seemed to form but one family. Without jealousy as without personal ambition, these well-born young men, united by the same ties which bound them to science, preoccupied by the same problems, and interested in the same phenomena, inspired one another by mutual and cordial assistance.

The works of Tycho assure him a place among great scientists of all time, but it is especially on account of his patient application and incessant assiduity to the detail of each day's regular operations that astronomy is so indebted to him. His dearest ambition was the formulation of exact tables of the plan-

[ca. 1583 A.D.]

etary movements, and his entire life was one long preparation for this immense work, which he did not finish but of which he left us all the elements.

He brought the construction and knowledge of the use of instruments to a perfection unknown before his time, and these things still remain among his principal achievements, in spite of the immense progress of his successors. The first to realise the great importance of the circumstances under which measurements must be taken, he did not fear to have recourse to indirect determinations in seeking in calculation the data whose observation seemed to him very inaccurate.   For Ptolemy's and King Alfonso's armillary spheres he substituted the mural circle to determine directly the declination of the stars.   The imperfection of his time-keeping instruments did not permit him, it is true, to measure right ascensions directly; he had to obtain them by solution of the spherical triangle, and the resultant values, although far from exact, surpassed greatly in their precision all that had been obtained hitherto.

After thirteen years of constant labour pursued with indefatigable patience, the news of King Frederick's death came to disturb the little astronomical colony and to trouble its laborious and harmonious tranquillity.   The heir to the throne, the young Christian IV, had always shown towards Tycho an affectionate esteem; but, although keeping their official status, the inhabitants of Uranienborg, distressed by cruel anxieties, no longer possessed the spirit of freedom necessary to their work.   Tycho had preserved all the pride of his race, and in consecrating his life to science, he believed that he had not lessened its dignity and worth.   Although naturally cordial and full of courtesy, he knew, on occasions, how to remind the haughtiest nobles that the king's will made him all-powerful on his island and to return disdain with disdain.   He thus made many enemies.   Physicians never forgave the often good advice he gave the sick or the remedies he prepared and distributed generously, even outside the limits of his island.   These formidable enmities did not show immediately on the surface.   They confined themselves to mingling artfully truth with falsehood, to slowly prejudicing the king's mind by the vague expressions of an almost universal malevolence.   The little weaknesses of Tycho's pride were brought up, he was accused of affecting a complete independence and assuming an excessive and unlimited authority on his island.   His detractors enumerated the privileges and uninterrupted liberties of fifteen years; they totalled up the sums expended in satisfying a vain ostentation and useless curiosity; they insinuated that it was time to put an end to such waste and prodigality; they bitterly criticised Tycho's pomp and style, the splendour and arrangement of his buildings, the richness of their equipment, and the sumptuousness of his hospitable board.   After eight years of annoyance, public opinion declared against the astronomer and a commission was appointed to decide whether the establishment of Uranienborg, whose fame had attracted the attention of all Europe, had been of sufficient benefit to astronomy to justify the generosity of the late king.

Tycho, disdaining a useless fight, returned neither answer nor apology to his enemies.   The commission, completely ignorant of astronomy and incapable of understanding the results achieved at Uranienborg, was still less able to foresee their consequences.   They were declared unhesitatingly to be completely sterile and fruitless for the state.   Tycho was retired on a royal pension, which meant that he had to leave his island, where the necessary expenditure greatly surpassed the resources that now remained to him. Tycho, indifferent to his interests and almost careless as to his own affairs, had added, without taking any account, his own private wealth to the benefits supplied by the king, and had gradually sold his patrimony and merged the proceeds in the common fund. He was therefore threatened with utter ruin, but nevertheless remained full of dignity in his misfortune and wrapped himself in complete silence, making immediate preparations for departure. Protected by his renown and like a king driven into exile, he felt sure of finding somewhere an asylum and honourable hospitality. His misfortunes were moreover those of a great nobleman. He fitted out a vessel for himself and his belongings and embarking, with his wife, nine children, and a few devoted disciples, quitted forever the temple of astronomy where he was not to be permitted to end his days. He betook himself to his friend Count Rantzau, governor of Holstein, bringing with him his consolation and his glory — namely, the precious instruments and manuscripts accumulated during twenty-one years of assiduous observation and laborious calculation. The celebrity of Uranienborg attracted infrequent visitors for some years to the island of Hven, but the marks of its past greatness rapidly vanished. The buildings soon went to ruins, and their materials were taken away by the fishermen. And when in 1671 the Paris Academy of Sciences sent Picard to determine the latitude of Tycho's observatory, as Tycho himself had been sent to determine that of Frauenburg, there were no vestiges of the castle to be seen, and it was necessary to dig in the ground in order to discover the foundations.[d]

THE MINORITY OF CHRISTIAN IV

In following out the story of the great astronomer, we have anticipated our chronology. There remained, however, nothing further to record of Frederick II, beyond noting his death at Copenhagen in 1588. He was succeeded, as already mentioned, by a son who became famous as Christian IV, and whose relations with Tycho Brahe have just claimed our attention.[a] As Christian was only eleven years old on his accession, there was necessarily a regency. The office was claimed by the queen-mother, and by one of the king's uncles; but the senate excluded both, and resolved to elect a council of regency from its own body. Four of the number, including the grand marshal and the high admiral, were thus chosen; but they were not to undertake anything of importance without the concurrence of their sixteen colleagues (the number of senators was not fixed: it varied continually; but at the period before us it was twenty). They were, in fact, to exercise just the same degree of authority as the king himself would exercise when he reached his majority, *viz.* his twentieth year. All four were men of great experience and of acknowledged ability; and they exercised their trust in such a manner as to afford much satisfaction to the nation at large.

Minorities have generally been seasons of trouble; and if the present was not, the honour must be awarded to the able government of the regents. Many events occurred which would otherwise have disturbed the public tranquillity: (1) The nobles were the first to show their dissatisfaction. Offended at their exclusion from the administration by the rigsraad, they hoped to gain their object by complaints of grievances which had no real foundation. Not only was redress denied them, but they were rebuked for their notorious selfishness, in preferring their own interests to the well-being of the community. (2) Pirates were infesting the coasts of Jutland and Norway; but they were soon dispersed. (3) But the most formidable antagonists of the regency were the nobles of Schleswig and Holstein. Now was the time for reasserting their ancient rights of election — a right which the armies of Danish kings had overpowered. When required to put the king and his brothers in possession of the territories which belonged to them, they replied that they could not recognise those princes and dukes of Holstein without a legal election. The ministers of Denmark were compelled to acknowledge the right: they agreed that when the king reached his majority he should guarantee the same privilege, and confirm all their other privileges. If he did not, then the homage now required from the estates should be null and void, and a new election might be made. With this guarantee the estates were satisfied; and they elected both the king and his kinsmen as dukes of Holstein. In regard to Schleswig, which equally claimed the right of election, there was less difficulty. This duchy was held to be a movable fief of the crown; and the dukes, when elected, were bound to receive investiture from the crown. On the present occasion, it was not a little singular to see the king himself, as duke of Schleswig, receive by his representative the ensigns of his dignity from the hands of the regents. After this act, the representatives of the king received the homage of both duchies in the diet of Flensburg. (4) Norway had its complaints, which every order of the estates, nobles, clergy, burgesses, peasants laid before the regency. This obstacle was removed with equal address. A guarantee was given that these grievances should be examined, and, if possible, redressed. There was confidence in the promise, and homage was done to the young monarch by the estates assembled at Christiania. Nor was the promise a vain one: every real complaint was redressed by the Danish senate. The manner in which the Norwegians had been treated may be inferred from one fact — that of all the crown fiefs in that kingdom three only had been conferred on natives. Henceforth, the natives only were to be invested with them. Yet the regency was not wholly blameless in its conduct towards this country. It, or rather the rigsraad, imposed contributions without the consent of the estates, or of the Norwegian senate itself. (5) Sweden was more difficult to manage; but some conferences between deputies of the two nations prevented the outbreak of hostilities. (6) The encroachments of Russia and Sweden on Norwegian Lapland were resisted — by negotiation, indeed, but not the less effectually. Nor were these the only benefits conferred on Denmark by the regency: it encouraged the arts, commerce, literature, and every branch of national industry. In short, it made the kingdom happy at home and respected abroad.[b]

CHRISTIAN'S ACCESSION; THE KALMAR WAR

Christian IV assumed the government [the regency being terminated] in 1596. He was a monarch full of force and desire to do good, and possessed the qualities necessary to a prince who wishes to work successfully for his state. Norway, which had been so neglected under his predecessors, soon attracted the attention of the young king. From his very advent to the throne, he made one or more journeys annually to that country and continued them to an advanced age, even to the year before his death, without being deterred by the fatigues of the long sea trip.

During his numerous visits to Norway he worked, by judicial reform, by a rigorous maintenance of equity, and by a strict surveillance over the internal administration of the realm, to repair the mistakes of his predecessors. One of the most remarkable of these voyages was the one he made in 1599 with a fleet in which he himself served as captain. He sailed along the north coasts of Norway, rounded the North Cape, and went as far as the gulf of Kola, reconnoitring the shores, harbours, and mouths of rivers, and carefully exploring the northeast boundary of Norway and Sweden. The special purpose of this trying voyage, when he was once in danger of death, was the claim that Sweden had raised with regard to a part of Norwegian Finmarken. On another voyage he dismissed the government official Peter Grubbe, as he had previously dismissed Louis Monk, both of whom had been guilty of the most shameful injustice and exorbitant exactions. Between the years 1600 and 1604 all the judiciary officials *(Lagmænd)*, with the exception of two, met the same fate on account of their corrupt administration.

The desire long nourished by the king of improving Norwegian legislation was realised in 1604, when the new Norwegian code, which for the most part was drawn up by the chancellor of Norway, Hans Pedersen Basse, was promulgated. This code was followed in 1607 by the ecclesiastical regulations for Norway. In fact, throughout the country where the influence of the rigsraad and nobility was slight, the king had freer hands; but in Denmark he had, from the first year of his reign to fight the opposition of the nobility in all measures of public utility. In 1604 Christian called together at Horsens representatives of all the Jutland towns, to discuss with them as to what could be done to further the prosperity of the towns and the progress of commerce; but as soon as the Rigsraad and the Jutland nobles got wind of this dangerous affair they addressed to the king such earnest and pressing remonstrances that he was obliged to countermand the assembly.

The misunderstanding that had long smouldered between Christian IV and the Swedish king Charles IX finally kindled into open hostilities in the Kalmar War [(1611), which we have already described in an earlier chapter of the present book].

INTERNAL ADMINISTRATION (1613–1625 A.D.)

The fortunate issue of the Kalmar War was followed by the most prosperous period of Christian IV's reign, from 1613 to 1625, the date of his participation in the Thirty Years' War; and during this interval Christian displayed all the rare qualities which have accorded him so high a place among the kings of Denmark. Science, commerce, industry, legislation, and fortification — all were in the highest degree the object of his tireless energy.

In order to induce his own subjects to participate in the benefits of trade with Iceland which, up to now had been largely in the hands of foreigners such as the English and the members of the Hanseatic League, he founded the Iceland Company in 1602 to which the trade with Nordland and Finmarken was afterwards assigned. He also established a "drapers' company," from which all the servants of the court obtained their clothes; also "silkmen's" and "salters'" companies: the ships of the latter went to France and Spain after salt. Christian IV encouraged shipbuilders to construct large vessels for long sea voyages, and to arm with cannon not only for protection against the still numerous corsairs and pirates but for service, in case of necessity, in defence of the realm. These were the days when the Portuguese and the Dutch were rapidly growing rich in trade with the East Indies. The king, anxious that Denmark should share in this source of wealth, founded an East India Company in 1616.

It was for the sake of this trade that he sought to acquire some possessions in the East Indies and at the instigation of a Dutch adventurer named Boshouver sent (1618) a fleet to Ceylon in command of Admiral Ove Gjedde. The attempt on this island failed, but instead the town of Tranquebar on the Coromandel coast was captured; here the fortress of Dansborg was built, and a flourishing trade kept up for a long time. Christian IV tried very hard to get in communication with Greenland and recover the eastern colony (Öster-böigd), the route to which had long been forgotten. He sent out four voyages of discovery to the northern regions; the first two were under the command of Admiral Lindenov, the third of the Holstein navigator Richardson, and the fourth of Jens Munk (1619). This last expedition was a search for a passage by the north of America to Asia — a passage which all the maritime powers of Europe were actively looking for at that time, and which had a special importance for Christian IV, since he had acquired possessions in the East Indies and established commercial relations with those lands. Jens Munk did not succeed, but he immortalised his name on this voyage by his unshaken courage and the rare talents for navigation that he displayed. He reached 63 degrees north latitude and was then frozen in and compelled to winter on a desert island where the crew suffered so from the cold that two alone of his men survived with him. So desperate a situation did not discourage him, however. With his two companions he re-embarked in one of the two ships he had brought with him and reached Denmark in safety the following year. While these costly and perilous voyages did not attain their desired ends — the discovery of a northwest passage and the ancient eastern colony of Greenland — they were successful in discovering the western shores of that country where a Greenland company founded for that purpose began to send out ships for the whale fishery. Christian IV got more happy results from his other efforts in favour of Danish commerce, which became so flourishing in this prosperous

CHRISTIAN IV
(1577–1648)

period of his reign that several towns attained a high degree of wealth and the merchant fleets of Denmark were to be seen in the most distant seas.

In 1615 he established a standing army of five thousand men, the first Denmark had had since the abolition of the *thingmannalid*. The soldiers were recruited from the peasants of the crown and garrisoned in the towns, and they were constantly exercised in the use of arms under the direction of officers who had distinguished themselves in the Kalmar War. Their pay and equipment were furnished from the king's privy purse. In 1598 Christian had organised a complete burgher militia *(borgerväbning)* in the towns, where he also raised fifteen hundred boatswains *(baadsmänd)* who were drilled in all sorts of seamen's duties at the arsenal of Bremerholm (Copenhagen), and formed a permanent nucleus for the manning of the fleet. The "new huts" *(nyboder)* were built to lodge this permanent force and the School of Navigation was founded for their instruction.

Christian IV was likewise a most energetic legislator. Besides the Norwegian law (1604), and the ecclesiastical regulations for Norway (1607), he published the *Small Recess* in 1625; the *Law and Procedure of the Kingdom (Rigens Ret og Dele)* in 1621; the *Seignorial Laws (Birkeret)* in 1623; and in 1643, the *Grand Recess*, which included all the ordinances and laws issued since his accession in 1596. He did not limit himself to making laws, but looked after their execution as well.

CHRISTIAN IV AND THE THIRTY YEARS' WAR

For twelve years Christian IV had devoted himself to the labours of peace, when he was a second time compelled to take up arms. The Thirty Years War was then desolating Germany, and the Protestant princes, who were on the point of being crushed by the imperials, appealed in their distress to Christian IV, who was elected director of the "circle" of Lower Saxony and commander-in-chief of the army. His German allies had made brilliant promises to decide him to take their cause in hand, but at the crucial moment they failed to keep them; nor did Holland, France, and England, which had promised him large financial aid, fulfil their obligations. The consequence was that the king, in spite of his courage and strategic ability, conducted a disastrous campaign. The success he had in the beginning came to an end when he fell from his horse from the top of the ramparts of Hameln, an accident that incapacitated him from command for a long time. After a desperate and long-drawn-out struggle which lasted from eight in the morning to five in the afternoon, he was vanquished by the Bavarian general Tilly at the battle of Lutter-am-Barenberge (1626). This defeat placed Denmark at the enemy's mercy, and the following year, under Tilly and Wallenstein, they seized Holstein, Schleswig, and Jutland.

Wallenstein tried after this to make himself master of the Baltic and thus to complete the conquest of Denmark, but Christian IV defeated this plan with the aid of his fleet and prevented all attempts from that quarter. As he could expect no help from his allies, and as the situation of the kingdom was becoming more critical every day, and the rigsraad besides was pressing him by prayers and even threatening remonstrances to make peace, he finally, in 1629, resolved to conclude the Treaty of Lübeck. He promised to interfere no further in the affairs of Germany and gave up the dioceses of Bremen, Verden, and Schwerin, which he had previously acquired for his sons Frederick and Ulrik. The terms were comparatively favourable, but Denmark was left in a melancholy plight, all the resources of the state were dissipated, and half of the kingdom, Holstein, Schleswig, and Jutland, had been two years occupied by an enemy who had ravaged these countries to a frightful extent. A well-organized state, under such a king as Christian IV, would have recovered its forces, but Denmark was dominated by an egotistic and unpatriotic nobility, whose stubborn refusal to stand a share of the public expenditure brought to nothing all the king's attempts to restore the nation. So the situation became worse and worse; fourteen years later a still more ruinous war broke out, and still ten years later a third, which brought Denmark to the very brink of destruction. In this state of public distress it became evident that a new spirit was beginning to animate the people and that they were no longer willing to endure patiently the tyranny of the nobles.

Christian IV was constantly increasing the Sound dues, and he believed himself the more justified in doing this, since he fitted out annually and at great expense a considerable fleet for the protection of navigation in the Baltic during the general European war. This increase in the tariff, joined to the king's pretension of being master of that part of the North Sea which lies between Norway and Iceland, aroused much discontent and provoked many protests from all the maritime powers, especially the Dutch and the English. But all complaints remained without result while Denmark was flourishing and in possession of a formidable navy. When, however, the king, pressed for funds after the war with Germany, raised the Sound dues so that a ton of saltpetre, for example, had to pay 14 rix-dollars to the customs, in spite of the protests of the Dutch, that nation entered into a close alliance with Sweden and watched for an opportunity to get away from Denmark those provinces lying to the east of the Sound.

WAR WITH SWEDEN

Sweden was very sore against Denmark because Christian opposed her great schemes of conquest in Germany, and also because through his mediation an end had been put to the bloody Thirty Years' War in such a way that Sweden did not gain much advantage from it.

The able minister Oxenstierna determined to send against Denmark one of the Swedish armies then in Germany and thus compel the inopportune mediator to take part in the struggle — a well-arranged plan in view of the bad condition of Denmark, which was not at all prepared for war. Christian had long feared the hostile designs of Sweden and earnestly exhorted the nobility and the rigsraad to furnish him the means to put the kingdom in a state of adequate defence, but the rigsraad was as indifferent and lacking in foresight as the nobility were indisposed to make sacrifices for their country. When Torstenson made such ominous progress in Germany, in 1642, Christian renewed his insistence before the rigsraad and declared for his own part and that of his successors that he would not be responsible for what might happen; but the council refused to adopt measures for the security of the realm. And when the Swedish general made a sudden descent upon Holstein, in 1643, without war being declared, there was not the slightest preparation to resist the enemy. Duke Frederick betrayed Denmark a second time by making a separate peace with Torstenson, who in a short time occupied the whole Nordalbingian territory. At the same time another Swedish army invaded Skåne. Like the one in Jutland it had to be transported to the islands of the Belt by a Swedish-Dutch fleet, collected in order to complete the conquest of Denmark.

But Christian was watching over his kingdom; and, although sixty-seven years of age, he displayed in this hour of peril the same indefatigable zeal that marked the best years of his manhood. He rushed from one province to another, from the fleet to the army, and from land to sea, and wherever he was the enemy's efforts were unavailing. However, the squadron which was bringing the Swedish army to the islands put to sea, and appeared before the island of Femern. Christian with thirty ships went to meet the enemy's fleet of forty-six, and came upon them in the roadstead of Kolberg near Femern, where on the 1st of July, 1644, was fought a desperate battle, three times interrupted and recommenced. The aged king took the command himself in his ship *Trefoldighed (the Trinity)* which was exposed to the enemy's hottest fire and which for a time had to fight unsupported. The king had already received several wounds when a ball struck a timber of the ship with such force that the flying splinters killed or wounded a dozen men in the king's immediate vicinity and he himself lost his right eye and several teeth. The shock threw him unconscious to the deck, and the crew believing him dead uttered lamentable cries and began to lose courage. But the king, covered with blood, raised himself suddenly and exclaimed, "No! God has still spared me life and strength to fight for my country while each of you does his duty." He took up his position on the deck, standing with bandaged head, and his sword for support, and continued the fight until nightfall, when the enemy retired in a badly battered condition.

The Swedish fleet sought refuge in the gulf of Kiel, whither the king sent Admiral Peter Galt to blockade it, with strict orders not to let it escape. It managed nevertheless to get away, thanks to the unpardonable negligence of Peter Galt, who afterwards paid the capital penalty.

Denmark Humiliated

The Dutch and Swedish fleet, making together sixty-four ships, effected a junction and unexpectedly attacked a Danish fleet of but seventeen in the waters around Laaland. The Danish admiral Pros Mund and his men fought like heroes, but succumbed to the greatly superior force; the whole Danish fleet was annihilated, but the conquerors suffered such great losses that they were compelled to take to the shore. Denmark was now in the most critical condition; the western portions, Holstein, Schleswig, and Jutland, were in the hands of the enemy under Torstenson and Wrangel, who conducted themselves with extreme barbarity. In the eastern portions of Skåne, Halland, and Blekinge also, the Swedes had made great progress, while the Swedish-Dutch fleet held possession of the sea. Denmark's sole ally, the emperor of Germany, rendered no service, for the imperial general, Gallas, who was sent with an army into Holstein, did so little that he became the laughing-stock of his friends as well as of his enemies. Christian IV, therefore, was compelled in spite of himself to seek an arrangement, the terms of which could not be otherwise than unfavourable. But when he learned the excessive claims formulated by the Swedish negotiators, his courage and his anger rose afresh. He convoked the estates and asked if they would not rather fight than endure the enemy's ignominious exactions. The burgher and clerical orders gave an almost satisfactory reply, but the nobility counselled peace "whatever the conditions might be," and the rigsraad was of the same opinion.

The Peace of Brömsebro (1645 A.D.)

The king had consequently to bend to the laws of necessity, and, by the Peace of Brömsebro (1645) he exempted Sweden from all customs-duty in the Sound and the Belts, ceded her Herjeådalen, Jemtland, and the islands of Gotland and Ösel, and, as guarantee for exemption from customs duty, gave her Halland in pledge for thirty years, after which that province could be exchanged for another. The exemption produced a sensible deficit in the Sound dues which, from 300,000 rix dollars, fell to 80,000. This great diminution, however, came not only from the Swedish exemption but still more from the use that other nations made of their flag, an abuse it was impossible to prevent since the Swedes were exempt from the visitation at Elsinore. It must also be added that the dues were lowered for the Dutch; indeed, the very day the peace was signed at Brömsebro a treaty with Holland was concluded at Christianopel, by which a new tariff most advantageous for the latter state was adopted, a tariff which was afterward extended to the other maritime nations. The history of Denmark in the last three years of Christian IV's reign presents the melancholy picture of a ruined and exhausted country, and of a most meritorious king daily insulted and humiliated by an arrogant rigsraad and an ill-disposed nobility.

DEATH AND CHARACTER OF CHRISTIAN IV

Christian IV died in 1648 A.D. He was one of the most remarkable monarchs Denmark ever had. The failure of several of his enterprises should not tarnish his glory, for these checks were due either to unfortunate circumstances for which he was not responsible or to the perversity of the nobility, who preferred their own welfare to the public good. He was animated by a deep appreciation of his duties as a monarch and a lively affection for the people he had been called upon to govern. Few kings have been gifted with the tireless energy with which he attacked all the affairs of state, the least as well as the most important; and his task was facilitated not less by his strong and healthy constitution than by the very varied knowledge he acquired in his youth. He had an open character, affable to everyone, great or small; he was pious, just, personally brave in the highest degree, a good general, and a still abler admiral. His countrymen have daily before their eyes monuments to his artistic tastes, but his great virtues and his truly patriotic spirit have raised in every Dane's heart a still nobler monument which will be transmitted to the most distant generations.[e]

THE NOBLES IN CONFLICT WITH FREDERICK III

The transmission of the crown from father to son during so many reigns was beheld with much antipathy by the proud nobles of Denmark. They exclaimed that their liberties were in danger; that the royal power would soon become too strong for the other orders of the state. But what order had any influence besides themselves? The burghers were allowed none; the clergy, since the Reformation, had been in this respect a cipher; and as to the royal authority, so far from being augmented during the late reign, it had lamentably declined.

The truth is that the country was in the hands of an aristocracy which would have been glad to destroy the very name of king; but as this was too bold a step, considering the age at which Prince Frederick had arrived, his experience in public affairs, and the confidence reposed in him by the bulk of the people — especially by the burghers and the clergy — they determined to rule through a king — to make him merely their instrument for their exclusive aggrandisement. The four great officers of the crown *viz.,* Ulfeldt, the grand master, Sehested, the grand chancellor, Bilde, the grand marshal, and Gjedde, the grand admiral — were by the rigsraad, immediately invested with the regency. Ulfeldt was suspected (and his conduct at every period of his life confirms the suspicion) of aspiring to the crown himself, in right of his wife, the daughter of Christina Munk. The marriage of Christian IV with this lady was what the Germanic law terms a left-handed one. She was the wife but not the queen of Christian. But if she had belonged to the noblest house in Europe, Ulfeldt would not have succeeded in the object of his ambition. The bare suspicion of its existence hastened the election of Frederick.

We have had frequent opportunities of observing that the election was made by the rigsraad; that the nobles were merely required to confirm the choice; and that the burghers, though assembled, were mere spectators. The Catholic clergy had been in possession of some influence; but the reformed ministers had never exercised any. Now, however, the burghers first, and the clergy in imitation, when commanded rather than desired to approve the choice of the rigsraad, protested against their exclusion. They were summoned, observed their speaker, the rector of Copenhagen University, to deliberate with the other orders.   The members of the rigsraad were equally surprised and indignant at this unexpected encroachment on their time-honoured rights; the burghers were equally sturdy: and much angry alter-cation followed, which might have led to an open quarrel had not all parties been friendly to Frederick's election.   It is pleasing to behold this growing spirit of liberty in a body which, two centuries before, would have crouched to the earth before their feudal tyrants.   This was their first stand; and the precedent, as we shall soon perceive, was not forgotten.

But if the nobles were thus opposed, they had reason enough for triumph in the articles of capitulation which they had devised.   One of them took from the king the right of nominating members to the rigsraad.   When a member of that formidable body died, the nobles of the province in which he was born were to present a list of six or eight names to the rigsraad, which would select one of them without consulting the king.   By another, the crown had no longer the power to appoint the viceroy of Norway, or any of the four great officers we have mentioned.   By a third, he could not leave the realm without permission of the rigsraad.   By another, he could not, in the slightest degree, modify any decree of that body.   If, to these new restric-tions, we add those which had so long existed that he could not make peace or war, form a new or dissolve an old alliance; that he could not refuse to in-vest the nobles with the crown fiefs; that he had no voice in the rigsraad where "the general good was concerned," we shall perceive that not even the most limited president of a republic had so little authority as this crowned head.   All this was the result of the continued usurpations of the nobles, who trampled alike on king and people, on the clergy and the burghers.   But their domination was about to end.

Like his predecessors, Frederick looked with jealousy on Sweden, which, though governed by a woman (the famous Christina), was regarded as the most military power in Europe.   Like them, he looked for allies, especially when the Peace of Westphalia left that queen and her chancellor leisure for con-templating less distant exploits.   Fortunately for his views, Holland was equally jealous of Swedish supremacy in the Baltic; and though, in defiance of the treaty made by his father (a treaty, indeed, which Christian himself had disregarded), he exacted duties at the Sound, the republic did not quarrel with him.   On the contrary, she agreed to pay, in lieu of these duties, an annual pension for the free navigation of the straits.   He had no principle of conduct but his own interest.   Mild, yet full of duplicity, affable, yet calculating (the characteristics of the Oldenburg family), he strove to win the affection of the burghers and clergy, preparatory to the execution of the grand scheme which he seems to have formed from the beginning of his reign. He did not forget the opposition of Ulfeldt to his accession, or the additional trammels which that noble had been so instrumental in placing on the royal authority; and he planned the ruin of his enemy.   To detail the acts by which he effected his object would be useless.   We shall only observe that they were not of the most honourable kind.   Ulfeldt was treated with much contumely; and being unable to brook such humiliation, he fled first to Amsterdam, and next to Sweden, determined to strain every nerve for the ruin of his country.   By Christina he was favourably received — the presump-tion is that he felt secure of a home before he ventured to her capital.   She consoled him for the loss of his dignities and fiefs by royal gifts, and above all by her friendship.   With all her boasted qualities, Christina was but a woman; and she beheld with pleasure the noble person and the diversified talents of her guest. The other daughters of the late king, by Christina Munk, and their husbands, were treated with much severity. Frederick had determined on their humiliation, chiefly with the design of replenishing his coffers. Two were banished; two, in dread of greater evils, banished themselves. Ulfeldt and his wife, therefore, had to avenge their immediate connections no less than themselves. Yet their efforts could not draw the philosophic queen into war, which it was reserved for her successor, the famous Charles Gustavus, to commence; and even he did not arm until forced to do so by the Danish king.

With all his studied mildness, Frederick did not hesitate to commit an act of violence when his immediate interest was before him. At the persuasion, we are told, of the Dutch minister (a power then at war with England), he seized twenty-two English vessels, which had put into the port of Copenhagen, and sold them. Cromwell was not of a temper to bear this outrage; and he declared war against Denmark. But the Dutch were tired of hostilities; and he was induced, at length, to accept their overtures of peace, in return for their engaging to make full compensation for the flagitious act of which they had been the advisers, and for the engagement of Denmark to place English vessels passing the Sound on the same footing as those of Holland. Frederick, therefore, escaped the consequences of his rash act; but he had provoked the stout protector so much, and was so intent on aggrandising himself at the expense of Sweden, that he solicited his nobles to augment the force, both naval and military, of the realm. As well might he have spoken to the rocks. Their reply in the diet of Odense (1654) was a demand for new privileges. He was no longer, for instance, to ennoble burghers, except for some distinguished feat in battle.

The abdication of Christina, and the accession of Charles Gustavus to the throne of the Goths, inspired Frederick with new hope. Besides, the new king was evidently resolved to embarrass him by marrying into the house of Holstein-Gottorp — a house which had much to fear from that of Oldenburg, and which, therefore, looked to Sweden for protection. On his side, Charles was of too martial a temperament to remain long at peace. Fortunately for Denmark, he selected the Poles as his first antagonists; and for a time he pushed the war with great glory; but his victories exhausted him, and he was too far from his resources to recruit his army with the necessary expedition. This was the moment so long desired by Frederick: now, indeed, he might hope to win for Denmark more advantageous terms than had been granted by the last dishonourable peace. He and the rigsraad, therefore, without the slightest provocation, prepared for war, which, in 1657, was formally declared. This declaration was followed by the invasion of Bremen, which the treaty of Westphalia had left to Sweden. Little did Frederick know what an enemy he had thus wantonly provoked. Hastening through Brandenburg and Pomerania, Charles was in Holstein before the Danes knew that he had left Poland. Aided by his allies, Hamburg and Lübeck, always the enemies of Denmark, he succeeded, though with only a handful of troops, in subduing the whole province.[b] The further successes of Charles and the progress of the war down to his death, we have recounted in the preceding chapter.[a]

By the famous treaty of Roeskilde (1658) Charles received Skåne, Blekinge, Halland, Bornholm, Båhus, Jämtland, Trondhjem, with some domains in Bremen and Rügen; in other words, half the kingdom was quietly relinquished. Satisfaction was ensured to the duke of Holstein-Gottorp; Ulfeldt was restored to all his fiefs, and his wife to all her privileges; and some other obnoxious individuals were recalled. When Charles died, however, during the second war, Frederick, exulting in the death of his adversary, and hoping to gain everything by resistance, for some time refused to listen to any overtures of peace. It required the menaces of both England and Holland to make him negotiate. The treaty was signed in May, 1660. Halland, Blekinge, and Skåne were declared to be rightful possessions of Sweden; but Trondhjem and Bornholm were restored to Denmark. Ulfeldt was again included in the treaty, on the same conditions as before.[b]

THE DANISH REVOLUTION (1660–1730 A.D.)

In the two wars with Sweden, Charles X had reduced the kingdom of the Danes to the verge of ruin. The king, shamefully deserted by his nobles, had held his own solely through the valour of the citizens of Copenhagen and the aid of the Dutch sea power, and while the Swedes were besieging his capital, he and his high-spirited wife, Sophia Amelia, vied with one another in all the chivalrous virtues which inspire a sorely tried nation with devotion to its chiefs. The bond which received its baptism of fire in these days of storm and stress was henceforth indissoluble, nor could anything withstand the strength of it. It first manifested itself in the memorable diet of 1660.

The diet, which assembled at Copenhagen on the 8th of September, and consisted of deputies from the nobility, clergy, and municipalities — the peasantry not having been summoned — was briefly informed on the 11th of that month that "the king, in accord with the rigsraad, desired them to grant a fair general tax on consumable commodities." While the nobles took counsel together how they might evade this burden, as they did all others, as far as possible, the commons and the clergy held meetings with a view to concerted action in a project of far wider scope than any mere financial question. The leader of the commons was Hans Nansen, burgomaster of Copenhagen, the leader of the clergy, Hans Svane, superintendent of Zealand. The former was a worthy man of sixty-two, who had borne himself with such courage and heroism during the siege of Copenhagen by the Swedes that one day the king, meeting him upon the city wall, unbuckled his own sword and gave it to him in the sight of all the people; the latter, seven years younger, was a man of extraordinary eloquence, gifted with rare skill in employing by turns the unction of a priest, the frankness of a plain gentleman, and the subtlety of a trained diplomatist. Both were in secret communication with the court through Christoph Gabel, the king's clerk of the exchequer closet (*Kammerschreiber*) — a loyal and devoted servant who, in spite of the subordinate position he held, had rendered the most valuable services to his master, with no other ambition than that of doing his duty. He was on a journey in the year 1658, and happened to be at Hamburg when he received the tidings of Charles X's breach of the peace. Without pausing to reflect, or waiting for instructions, he hastened to the Hague, besieged the states-general with solicitations for succour, and in four weeks the fleet which came, under Admiral Opdam, to the aid of the hard-pressed city of Copenhagen, was ready to put to sea. In the year 1660, the man who wrought this deliverance was still in receipt of a salary about half as large as that of the king's barber.

The aforementioned trio co-operated in a political campaign which brought about without violence or the slightest infringement of public order, one of the greatest crises of the Danish history. "Denmark a hereditary monarchy!" was the watchword on which clergy and commons agreed, by the 8th of October, for the breaches they purposed to batter in the sovereignty of the great nobles. The rigsraad resisted their demand; the answer it returned on the 10th of that month was an absolute and unconditional refusal. The clergy and the commons then went in solemn procession to the king, who accorded a favourable reception to the document they submitted to him, while the intense excitement of the capital expressed the popular feeling in its favour and against the nobles so unmistakably that the latter promptly gave way, and on the 13th of October actually headed the procession in which all three estates went in state to proffer the hereditary crown to the king. A natural consequence of the abrogation of the right of election was the abolition of the conditions which had hitherto been imposed upon the elective monarch in the capitulation or deed of election, by the nobles, who had elected him. On the evening of October 14th, a committee of the three estates handed over to the king a deed, by which they released him from his oath, and in full confidence left it to his discretion to draw up such a recess (or compact) as he thought fittest to serve the common weal and the best interests of every estate. On the 16th the deed of capitulation was solemnly annulled, and on the 18th the estates came together, with great pomp and ceremony, to take the oath of allegiance, by which they publicly acknowledged the absolute power of the king to be no longer circumscribed by any oath or deed, and ratified it as the fundamental principle of the new constitutional law of Denmark.

Under date of the 24th of June, 1661, the king published a charter, by which, "of his royal grace and favour," he conceded a number of privileges to the nobles, clergy, and citizens, without reference to the distress of the peasantry. A more important step was the new organisation he introduced into the whole administrative system, to oust the aristocratic rigsraad entirely, and educate a bureaucracy from among the commons. He distributed the affairs of state amongst six colleges, each consisting of an equal number of nobles and commons. The State college carried on the business of the foreign office and protected the interests of the dynasty. It was supplemented by a college of the Treasury, for finance; a college of War, for the army; a college of the Admiralty, for the navy; and by the *Chancellerie*, which last-named institution discharged the whole of the home administration and some part of judicial, police, and ecclesiastical affairs. The college of Justice, in which the king presided, was the highest judicial tribunal and court of last instance. The presidents of the five other colleges, together with the king, constituted the privy council of state, which, on particularly important occasions, summoned the members of all the colleges to a "great royal aulic council"; and the resolutions then passed had to be submitted "to all the estates of the kingdom." Hence we see that, originally, the latter were by no means excluded from all participation in the government. The collegiate system of administration in Denmark subsisted, without substantial alteration, down to the year 1848; and its practical bearing on the authority of the monarchy and the welfare of the country was far more important than that of the theoretical maxims concerning the legitimate absolutism of the royal will, contained in the act of Succession of November 14th. One of the most admirable acts of this king — the compilation of a new statute-book, which he entrusted to a commission of distinguished scholars, in 1661 — was not completed until the year 1683, in the reign of his son Christian V (1670–1699). Immediately after his accession (1671), the latter, acting upon the advice of his gifted secretary, Peter Schumacher, afterwards Count Griffenfeld, created a new order of counts and barons, which owed its large privileges entirely to the king, and therefore acted as a counterpoise to the old nobility.

Of the thirty-one counts and barons of his creation, twenty were Germans and only eleven Danes. The order of the Dannebrog, instituted about the same time, was intended as a reward for those persons who specially distinguished themselves in the service of the monarchy. The crown of Denmark gained a considerable accession to the extent of its dominions by the acquisition of the counties of Oldenburg and Delmenhorst, in the year 1676.*f*

DOMESTIC CONDITIONS

Lord Molesworth,*g* who was sent to the Danish court in 1689, as envoy-extraordinary from William III of England, reproaches the people for their levity in sacrificing the rights of themselves and their posterity. With that bitter spirit of sarcasm which pervades his work, he compares them to "the Cappadocians of old, who could not make use of liberty if it were offered them, but would throw it away if they had it, and resume their chains." "The commons," he remarked, "have since experienced that the little finger of an absolute prince can be heavier than the loins of many nobles, the only comfort left them being to see their former oppressors in almost as miserable a condition as themselves; whilst all the citizens of Copenhagen have obtained by it, is the insignificant privilege of wearing swords; so that at this day not a cobbler or barber stirs abroad without a tilter at his side, let his purse be never so empty.

FREDERICK III

(1609–1670)

Although Frederick III did not abuse the arbitrary powers thus vested in him by this extraordinary revolution, the fatal effects of that measure soon manifested themselves by impoverishing the higher orders, without alleviating the burdens of the lower. The noble author already quoted informs us that, previous to the year 1660, the nobility lived in great splendour and affluence. Their country houses were magnificent, and their hospitality unbounded. They resided chiefly on their estates, spending most of their revenues among their neighbours and tenants, by whom they were regarded as so many princes. At the annual convocations of the diet, they met the sovereign with retinues as numerous and brilliant as his own, and frequently sat with him at the same table. Within thirty years afterwards, their castles and palaces had fallen to ruin; their lands scarcely paid the taxes imposed upon them, "which obliged them to grind the faces of the poor tenants to get an overplus for their own subsistence." Some of their estates were charged at more than the full value of the income, so that the proprietors willingly offered to surrender them to the crown, rather than to pay the enormous public burdens to which they were liable. Besides being oppressed by these exorbitant exactions, they were deprived of the usual resources arising from civil or military employments at court. The lucrative and honourable posts which they formerly held, were then filled by men of low birth and little education — these being always found the most obedient instruments for executing the purposes of an irresponsible monarch.

The effect of this grinding system was as injurious to trade and morals as it was destructive of wealth and independence. The merchant lodged his profits in foreign banks rather than to purchase property at home subject to unlimited taxation. The burgher chose to waste, in pleasure or idle parade, the fortune that might have become dangerous by gaining him the reputation of riches; while the peasant expended his last rix-dollar in brandy, to prevent its being seized by a rapacious landlord. In Zealand, this degraded class, at the time when Lord Molesworth resided in Denmark, were as absolute slaves as the negroes in the British colonies, with the difference that they were worse fed. They and their posterity were fixed to the soil where they were born — bought and sold with the estate like the wood or the cattle upon it, and estimated as part of the stock belonging to the proprietor. Those who showed a more diligent or inventive turn than the rest, who lived better, or had acquired substance by superior industry, "would probably be removed from a neat, pleasant, and commodious house, to a naked and uncomfortable habitation, that the landlord might increase his rent by letting the improved farm to another." The quartering and paying of the king's troops was another grievance to which the miserable peasantry were subjected. They were obliged also, at their own expense, and at all seasons of the year, to furnish horses and travelling wagons to the royal family, with their baggage and attendants, whenever they made a journey to any of their places or residences in the country. Such, in short, was the general poverty and depression in Denmark at that period, that the collectors of the poll-tax were forced, as Lord Molesworth states, to accept of old feather beds, brass and pewter pans, or household furniture, instead of money, from the once wealthy inhabitants of Kioge — a small town which had supplied Christian IV with the sum of 200,000 rix-dollars upon the brief notice of twenty-four hours.

It is recorded to the praise of Frederick III that, as long as he lived, his uncontrolled power was exercised with mildness and forbearance. Far from alienating the affections of the nobles, it rather more strongly engaged their attachment, by putting an end to those factious discontents of which their exclusive privileges had hitherto been the unhappy source. Nor did the people, under their greatest misfortunes, ever repine at the sacrifice they had made; conscious, as they were, that he had, by his valour, perseverance, and intrepidity, saved the kingdom and rescued it from the jaws of perdition, when it was in danger of becoming a province of Sweden.

FREDERICK III IS SUCCEEDED BY CHRISTIAN V

The remaining ten years of this monarch's reign were devoted to the redress of grievances among his subjects, the re-establishment of his finances, the encouragement of industry, and the extension of commerce. In 1663, he joined the triple alliance, which had been entered into by the courts of London, Stockholm, and Copenhagen in consequence of the approaching rupture between England and Holland. The conduct of the Dutch factories established in Guinea involved him in a dispute with the United Provinces about their respective settlements on that coast; but the affair terminated in a quadruple treaty with Denmark, the elector of Brandenburg, and the duke of Brunswick, from which the estates-general reaped the advantage that their East India fleet found a safe retreat in the harbour of Bergen, and by this means baffled all the attempts of the English admiral, Lord

Sandwich, who was despatched to the north seas to intercept them. A misunderstanding had arisen between the Danish court and the duke of Holstein, in consequence of the latter's having concluded a treaty of amity with Sweden. Frederick was preparing to enforce his arguments by arms, when he was carried off by an affection of the lungs, caused by the fatigues he had undergone during the siege of his capital.

The eldest son of Frederick III, who had already been declared his successor, assumed the government under the title of Christian V. Notwithstanding the prudent measures of his father, he found the kingdom involved in confusion, and public affairs in a condition that presaged a reign not more pacific than the last. Happily the altercations with the dukes of Holstein and Gottorp terminated without leading to an open rupture. By a treaty concluded at Rendsburg (1674), the latter prince formally renounced all claim to the advantages which he had extorted during the late war; and the union between the two houses was restored on the footing established by their ancestors. It was from the ascendency of Sweden, however, that the greatest danger was to be apprehended. Independently of the provinces she had wrested from Norway, her conquests in another quarter had greatly strengthened her frontier, by making the

St. Ave Church, near Bergen

Sound the boundary of her dominions on the side of Denmark. These and various other reasons impressed the young king with the necessity of putting himself in a condition to curb the ambition and resist the aggressions of that powerful monarchy. With this view, he caused the fortifications everywhere to be repaired, the cities to be put in a state of defence, and new fortresses to be erected in all places exposed to the inroads of those restless neighbours.

Sweden, although still under a regency, exercised considerable influence in European politics. She interposed in the war between England and Holland, and her mediation greatly contributed to the peace concluded at Breda. Charles XI was afterwards one of the members of the triple alliance the object of which was to secure the Netherlands against the encroachments of Louis XIV; though he was soon detached from that league by the intrigues of the latter monarch, in order to be a check upon the emperor. By attaching himself to France, he involved Sweden in a war with the elector of Brandenburg. Wrangel was despatched with a force of two thousand men; and notwithstanding the brave resistance of the inhabitants, the invaders reduced most of the towns and fortresses in that province. But their career of triumph was cut short by the appearance of the elector, who took the field in person, defeated the enemy in several engagements, and compelled them to evacuate the whole of their conquests. It was at this crisis that Denmark seized the opportunity to humble the might of her formidable rival.

At the same time the United Provinces (then at peace with England), the duke of Lüneburg, and the bishop of Münster all embraced the occasion of wreaking their vengeance on Sweden, whose rising power they had beheld with jealous apprehension. [The war lasted till 1679 when it was terminated] by a treaty, concluded at Fontainebleau (September 2nd, 1679), between the three crowns of France, Denmark, and Sweden. Charles, after a series of losses and defeats, extricated himself with honour from a quarrel begun in his childhood, and obstinately maintained since his accession to the throne, against a combination of the most formidable powers of Christendom. On the other hand, Christian, after prodigious exertions, in which his courage and his conduct were equally conspicuous, was forced, through an unhappy coincidence of events, to retire from the scene of action, deprived of every advantage and disappointed in all those views which had been the primary cause of his embarking in the quarrel. In addition to the Peace of Fontainebleau, a separate treaty of alliance, offensive and defensive, was executed at Lund by the ambassadors of Denmark and Sweden, in presence of the French minister. Finally, to cement this amicable connection still more closely, a matrimonial union was effected between his Swedish majesty and the Danish princess Ulrica Eleanora.

One or two events, however, threatened to disturb the tranquillity of the North. Under pretext of certain claims upon the city of Hamburg, Christian advanced with a numerous army, and made preparations for a regular siege; intrenchments were formed and batteries erected; but the remonstrances of France and the prompt interposition of the house of Brunswick had the effect of terminating the dispute without the effusion of blood.

THE DEATH OF CHRISTIAN V

Some trivial differences concerning mercantile matters occurred with France and Sweden; but, instead of generating hostilities, they led to the conclusion of fresh treaties and the establishment of a closer connection with these kingdoms. Finally, the long pending controversy respecting the affairs of the duchy of Holstein, of which his Danish majesty still claimed the sovereignty, was at length adjusted by the convention of Altona (June 20th, 1689), under the mediation of England and Brandenburg. By that compact a general amnesty was agreed upon, and a lasting union begun between the ducal and the royal court. Christian restored to the duke all the dominions and prerogatives which he enjoyed or could claim from the late treaties; and thus terminated a feud which for years had been the source of jealousies and contentions, and had proved to be the immediate cause of the recent war with Sweden.

During the remainder of his reign, the attention of this great monarch was chiefly occupied with the internal affairs of his dominions and the preservation of peace with the neighbouring states. He expired at the early age of fifty-four, on the 4th of September, 1699, bequeathing to posterity a reputation for wisdom, courage, and military talent which his countrymen, even in modern times, contemplate with feelings of pride and admiration.[c]

CHAPTER XII

SWEDEN IN THE 18TH CENTURY

[1697–1814 A.D.]

ON the death of his father [in 1697], Charles XII had nearly attained his fifteenth year, which, though it had been frequently the period of majority for the kings his predecessors, was not so for him. To gratify the ambition of his grandmother, who was at the head of the regency, eighteen was the age fixed by the will of the late king. Probably, his apparent indifference to public affairs, his addiction to field sports, to splendid apparel, and the ordinary amusements of youth, had some influence in this measure. But it was rendered abortive by the enterprise of the young prince himself, who in six months acquainted two of his companions with his resolution to seize the reins of government. The members of the regency were more anxious to propitiate his favour than that of an old woman; and their consent to the resolution was prompt. The queen was persuaded or forced to sanction the convocation of the estates; and the latter unanimously agreed that the testament of the late king should be set aside, and Charles invested with absolute power. He was crowned in the cathedral of Upsala, not by the hands of the archbishop, whom he would only permit to anoint him, but by his own. The stern manner in which he snatched the diadem from the prelate and placed it on his own head, was beheld with applause by the stupid spectators. Little did they know the miseries which they were preparing for themselves, by thus encouraging the evil tendencies of one who was doomed to bring greater woes on his country than any preceding monarch of Sweden.

When Charles ascended the throne he found the kingdom in a flourishing state. Internally, the continuance of peace had given an impulse to industry and commerce.   Externally, the possessions of Sweden were vast, and formed so many admirable marts for the disposal of her traffic.   The great provinces of Livonia, Karelia, and Ingermanland, the strong towns of Wismar and Viborg; the isles of Rügen and Ösel; the sees of Bremen and Verden, with the greater part of Pomerania, were, when added to Sweden and Finland, ample enough for anything short of that unmeasured ambition which thinks nothing gained so long as anything remains to be gained.   In all these possessions the king was confirmed, not merely by long occupancy and by former treaties, but by that of Ryswick, which he was instrumental in bringing to a conclusion.

Whatever might be the ambition of Charles, whatever the extent of the projects which he seems to have formed in his very youth, his is not the guilt of striking the first blow in the wars that so long desolated Europe.   His ruin was conspired at the same time, and, what is still worse, secretly conspired, by three monarchs to whom he had given no offence, and who, relying on his youthful inexperience, hoped to profit by the division of his spoil.   These were, Frederick IV of Denmark; Frederick Augustus, elector of Saxony and king of Poland; and the czar Peter the Great.   The first of these princes, treading in the steps of his father Christian V, resumed his designs on the dominions of the Swedish king's brother-in-law, the duke of Holstein-Gottorp, which he determined to incorporate with Denmark.   The object of the second was to regain Livonia.   Peter wanted Ingermanland, which, being seated on the eastern shore of the Baltic, might become an excellent emporium for the commodities of Europe and Asia, and a convenient channel of communication between them.

The preparations which the three unprincipled allies were making could not long be hidden from Charles.   His brother-in-law, indeed, soon arrived at Stockholm, to implore his aid.   While his councillors and people were aghast at the magnitude of the impending danger, he was calm.   To the surprise of everybody, he suddenly renounced all his amusements, adopted the plainest style of living, inured himself to the most severe exercises, and fared as hardly, as humbly, as the meanest soldier.   They were still more surprised when they heard him declare that as he would never undertake an unjust war, so he would not finish a just one without the destruction of his enemies; that he would fall on the first that took the field; and that, when he had vanquished him, he should, he hoped, strike a salutary terror into the rest. Dejection gave way to confidence.   Had not the great Gustavus, at an age almost equally green, not merely saved Sweden, but raised her to the highest pitch of glory?

BEGINNING OF THE GREAT NORTHERN WAR

As Sweden was assailed at the same time on three different points — in Livonia, by the Saxons, who invested Riga; in Schleswig, by the Danish king, who captured several fortresses, especially Gottorp; in Ingermanland, by the czar, who invested Narva — Charles had to select the enemy whom he would first attack.   He chose the nearest; and instead of making Holstein the theatre of the war, resolved at once to disembark his land forces in Zealand, and besiege Copenhagen, while his fleet invested it by sea.   The design was a magnificent one; and its apparent rashness was diminished by important circumstances — one of which was that, as guarantees of the last peace, which Frederick was thus flagitiously violating, England and Holland sent a fleet into the Baltic to act in concert with Charles.

In May, 1700, Charles embarked at Karlskrona, and soon joined the combined fleets of his allies at the mouth of the Sound. That of the Danes offered no resistance, but quietly retired under the batteries of Copenhagen. It was now for the first time that the Danes, and even the Swedes, were aware of the young monarch's design, which was to finish the war at a blow by storming the capital. Notwithstanding a galling fire, he landed, defeated the army drawn up to receive him, and took possession of the trenches. The arrival from Skåne of a powerful reinforcement, the construction of formidable batteries, and the measures evidently taken for a *coup de main* alarmed the inhabitants, who in the absence of their king were apprehensive that they should be unable to make a successful defence. In this emergency, they sent a deputation to Charles, beseeching him to spare the city. Whatever might be their apprehensions, he had his as to the result of so hazardous a step : he knew that one of his bravest predecessors had besieged the place nearly two years in vain; and though it was now much worse provided for a siege, still it might hold out till Frederick advanced to its relief. He therefore consented to spare the city on two conditions: that he should be paid 400,000 rix-dollars, and that his followers should be supplied with provisions at the ordinary market prices. But his object was almost as well attained as if he had taken the place. Frederick, with one enemy before him sufficient to restrain his efforts, with another under the walls of his capital, and with his fleet blockaded by that of three formidable powers, was compelled to sue for peace.

CHARLES XII OF SWEDEN
(1697–1718)

Under the mediation of France and England, negotiations were opened at Travenal, and speedily brought to a conclusion. Frederick not only acknowledged, in all their plenitude, the rights of the duke of Holstein and engaged no more to molest him, but paid a heavy sum by way of indemnification for the expenses of the men. Thus, in three short months, a mere youth triumphed over an experienced monarch, and obtained what veteran generals would have thought themselves fortunate in obtaining after years of successful warfare.

The second enemy against whom the youthful victor marched, the czar, was doomed to be as easily subdued as Frederick. Landing at Pernau, in the Gulf of Riga, Charles hastened to the relief of Narva, which was invested by a prodigious number of Russians.[b]

VICTORY OF CHARLES XII AT NARVA (1700)

The number of the troops destined to march to Narva under the leadership of Charles, did not amount to over thirteen thousand men. After the despatch of one thousand men, sent by the king to reconnoitre in the environs of Dorpat and Lake Peipus, and after a second reduction of the forces by four thousand of the men-at-arms, left behind for the protection of the country, there remained only five thousand infantry and thirty-three hundred cavalry, with thirty-seven cannon, to march against the Russians. The country offered only two positions which commanded the approach of the enemy; and these were accessible only to a limited number.

When Peter the Great received the sure news that Charles' intention was to risk everything in order to save Narva, and that the Swedish army was already mustered for that purpose, he put confidence less in the fortifications, and in the strength of the army which he commanded, than in the two narrow passes which he occupied, and which the king of Sweden could not avoid, in his march against the fortress. These were the already named defiles of Pyhajokki and Silameggi. Especially the first-named of these narrow passes, which covered four miles before the Russian camp, was so inaccessible that a small handful of brave soldiers could hold it against a whole army of invaders. It was formed by two steep heights, which were cut through by a brook; and the Russian outposts occupied the high bank on the east side. Lower down, this position was protected by woods; and the Russian cannon were spread through the copse which formed this bank of the river; the opposite side of the stream, being entirely open ground, could not offer the least protection to the approach of the enemy. The defence of this position was given by the czar to Sheremetiev. Six thousand selected troops, chiefly cavalry, and many cannon besides, formed the strength of Pyhajokki; but Sheremetiev committed so many blunders that he showed his utter incompetence in the art of war. Instead of simply destroying the bridge and awaiting, in his impregnable position on the eastern bank, the approach of the enemy, on the 27th of November he detached eight hundred of his cavalry to ride to the other side, in order to forage and to waste the enemy's country for half a mile.

At noon this detachment of troops was suddenly overtaken and surprised by the Swedish vanguard, and the Russians immediately fled back in disorder, leaving their knapsacks and booty to the Swedes. The latter followed in pursuit of the fugitives, and were only held back by the fire of the Russian artillery and infantry from the narrow pass. Hearing the thunder of the cannon, Charles himself hastened up, but the oncoming darkness made it impossible at once to storm the naturally strong position. That same evening, two Swedish cannon were turned on the Russians, and under the cover of the night, the latter left the heights of Pyhajokki to be occupied by the enemy. Horror impelled them forward in their flight. On the following afternoon they arrived at the Russian camp, and spread the news that Charles had marched through the pass with twenty thousand men, and was now advancing towards the camp. The tidings awakened alarm less on the part of the soldiers than on that of the czar and the higher officers of Russian birth. Their despair and their tears did not become soldiers in the moment of danger, and aroused the contempt of the mercenaries. Even behind the fortified camp, the czar did not dare to await the attack of the enemy; but gave the command to march to Pskov, in order to bring back a new army; as he foresaw that the eighty thousand men and one hundred and fifty cannon standing before Narva were insufficient to gain a victory over Charles XII, king of Sweden. The quickly spreading rumour of the czar's departure, and the half-formed suspicion of Charles's approach, could not do otherwise than work disadvantageously to the courage of the Russians.

While all this was passing in the Russian camp, the Swedes were commanded steadily to approach the heights and outposts of Pyhajokki. The day had scarcely dawned, however, when it was discovered that the Russians had abandoned their position, so the march went on without attack, and they hastened to take possession of the pass of Silameggi. In an enemy's country, barren of all nourishment for the men and the cattle, everything depended on Charles' marching swiftly, before the enemy could gain time to recover from their horror at the strength of the opposition which they had encountered. A march was therefore determined upon, to the forest of Lagena, which lay another half-mile away from Narva, and where, on the morning of the 29th day of November, Charles arrived with his weary soldiers, hoping here to attain his ardent desire of measuring himself with the enemy. The army was allowed to spend the remaining hours of this day in gaining strength for the bloody work of the one following.

After the departure of the czar, the greatest consternation and dismay reigned in the Russian camp. Against his will, the duke of Croy was made commander-in-chief of the Russian army in the coming struggle, and when from the heights of the camp he could see the Swedes preparing for the charge on the intrenchments, his mind was filled with gloomy forebodings. He took all precautionary measures for the following day, and did everything that it was possible for a farsighted commander to do. As far as the time allowed, Croy fortified the line of circumvallation, which was protected at all points by the flower of the Russian infantry. The rest of the troops he placed along the entrenchment, and outside it the cavalry, under Sheremetiev.

On the morning of the 30th of November the Swedes began their movement. As soon as the troops had marched out of the forest, the king placed them in two lines — the infantry in the centre, the cavalry on either flank. When the duke of Croy saw the Swedish host leave the borders of the wood he supposed that it was simply the advance guard of the forces of the enemy, which he believed to be still concealed in the wood. The previous rumour gave him this idea; and the impression confirmed Sheremetiev's information, which gave the strength of the Swedes as twenty thousand men. After a salute twice repeated, which in vain invited the Russians to battle, Charles determined to seek them behind the intrenchments. The command was given; and at two o'clock in the afternoon, with the shout: "God is with us!" from all the Swedish columns, the attack began. The right division was commanded to break over the intrenchments. The left was divided into two columns, which directed their march against one of the strongest works of the enemy. It was as if Heaven made common cause with the little army now going into such apparent danger. During the whole forenoon the weather had been fair; but at the moment when the Swedes began their movements the air darkened, a heavy snow-storm fell, and the wind blew into the faces of the Russians, so that the movements of the Swedes were not discerned by the enemy. Thus favoured by wind and weather, and unobserved, the Swedish columns appeared on the verge of the fosse, at the mouth of the enemy's cannon. The attack took place immediately, and with such ardour that scarcely a moment elapsed between the Russians' recognition of the danger, and the charge. Within a quarter of an hour, the Swedish infantry had penetrated within the intrenchments. The Russians were immediately thrown into disorder, and fled precipitately, no longer heeding the commands of their leaders. The right wing sought to reach the bank of the Narova, in order to cross the bridge; but the latter was not able to bear the great army of fugitives. It gave way, and in a moment the waters of the Narova were filled with the bodies of Russians.

When the fugitives saw the bridge destroyed, before them the deep river, and behind them the pursuing Swedes, who cut down all that dared to oppose them; they finally realised that their only hope lay in a brave resistance. The duke of Croy also arrived on the scene, and by word as well as by example encouraged the men to be steadfast. The battle surged on, until the combatants were hampered by the bodies of the slain. Charles commanded the infantry of the victorious right wing to make the decisive charge. But the day was already declining, and darkness began to brood over the scene of battle; so that the guard were confused and had a hand-to-hand encounter with the Dalecarlian regiment, and, in consequence, many brave soldiers found death at the hands of their comrades. The darkness increased yet more and more; the opposition of the Russians, behind their barricade of wagons, grew gradually weaker. Towards evening, in the midst of the tumult, the Russian hatred against the Germans broke forth in the wildest fury. In their blind rage, they attributed all their misfortunes to German counsel; and all the Germans among them, without regard to rank, were sacrificed to the national hatred. Even the commander, the duke of Croy, and the ambassador of the king of Saxony were obliged to save their lives by taking refuge with the enemy, to whom they yielded themselves prisoners. In the evening the victory was decided for the Swedes, but it was uncertain whether the struggle would be renewed on the following morning. The Swedes, who stood within the fortifications, had possession of the heights which controlled the whole scene of battle, but the Russians were more numerous. Charles prepared to renew the fight early the following day. However, when the German officers preferred captivity to Russian treatment, and left the latter to their own military experience, the Russian commanders did not regard themselves in any position to retrieve their fortunes and sought salvation in laying down their arms. One of the leaders, Prince Dolgoruki, therefore went to Charles, and the terms of capitulation were signed by all of the generals and chief officers.

In the meantime the right wing of the Swedes had won an easy victory. During the fight the enemy was driven in part to Joola, and partly to the bank of the stream. The Russian cavalry, which under the command of Sheremetiev was placed at the left of the enemy, abandoned their position at the first attack, without the least resistance, and in cowardly fashion threw themselves into the Narova, leaving the battlefield to the enemy and the struggle to the infantry. Many horses and riders were drowned, partly owing to the impetus of the stream and partly to the exhaustion of the horses. The general who commanded the infantry belonging to this division, was seriously wounded, and surrendered when he learned the mild terms of the capitulation which the other generals had signed. Thus victory was attained, and Charles, with his seven thousand soldiers, stood as conqueror of eighty thousand, master of the camp of the enemy, and deliverer of a sorely oppressed city. During the assault, he had always been where the battle was thickest. A spent musket ball lodged in his collar, and he sank in a swamp and lost his boots and sword. His men pulled him out again; but he was unbooted during the remainder of the battle. Charles' all-powerful minister, Count Piper, was not merely present at the storming of the fortifications, but he was actually the first to scale the intrenchment, and was always found in the thick of the battle.

It was not till the day following that the magnitude of the battle and the fruits of the victory were fully realised. Eighteen thousand of the enemy had been either killed in the fight or drowned in the Narova; the remainder were captured, except the cavalry, which had saved themselves by disgraceful flight. It was impossible for the conquerors to guard the prisoners; the watch was not strong enough, and there were not sufficient provisions. They were therefore allowed to defile before the king with bare heads, to lay down their arms, and hand over their colours to the conqueror. The disarmed Russians returned to their frontier, whence they would have to come forth at the command of their leaders, to form new regiments and to suffer new defeats. Sweden's loss was two thousand dead and wounded, but a great part of the latter were again in readiness for battle.

All of the Russian generals and leaders remained prisoners. They were, however, treated in so clement a manner by their young conqueror that they did not know whether to admire more his bravery in battle or his great magnanimity as a victorious prince. The duke of Croy, who had lost everything, received from him 1,000 ducats as a royal gift. Besides the above named, the trophies of war included a great medley of ammunition of all kinds, 145 bronze cannon, 100 colours, 20 standards, provisions, and forage. The results of this battle to Sweden cannot be overestimated; but the momentary greatness of the honour was followed by a succession of most disastrous consequences. Europe saw in it the destruction of an eighteen-year-old prince, whose entire crime was that of being heir to a powerful realm. Old jealousies again were roused and meddling intrigue, which, during Charles' career, attained full maturity and development. He even despised his opponents the more; because in them he saw the reason for his misfortunes.[c]

CONQUEST OF POLAND (1701–1706 A.D.)

The third enterprise of the victor — against the Polish king — was crowned with equal success. In vain did the Saxons dispute the passage of the Düna. Burning wet straw, to raise a smoke thick enough to intercept his army from the view of the enemy, he passed over, arranged his men in order of battle, forced the Saxon intrenchments, and soon not a man was to be seen before him. Mitau, the capital of Courland, surrendered immediately after this victory; other fortresses were taken by him or his generals; an army of twenty thousand Russians was expelled from the region; the Saxons retreated into Poland; and in a few short weeks the whole of Courland was in his hands.

Had Charles been satisfied with the glory he had thus obtained, and with the advantages which he might have wrested from the humbled Augustus,[1] he would have been worthy of all praise. But conquerors are not much distinguished for moderation. He had overthrown three great monarchs; what, therefore, could resist him? Instead of listening to the proposals of the king, he haughtily observed that he would treat only at Warsaw. He had formed the project of dethroning his enemy, as much through the Poles themselves as through his own followers. Marching towards that capital, he entered it with little opposition; Augustus, the foreign ambassadors, the papal nuncio, and the whole court fleeing with precipitation. But this king was not unworthy of struggling with his fate. He concentrated his troops, and with them advanced to meet the invaders. With a combined army of thirty-three thousand Poles and Saxons opposed to about half that number of Swedes, he was justified in the act. But, with all his valour, he lost the battle, many thousands of his men, all his artillery and baggage. The satisfaction of the victor was considerably alloyed by the fall of his brother-in-law, the duke of Holstein-Gottorp, the original cause of the war. But the indulgence of the

[1 That is Augustus II of Poland, called the Strong, who was also elector of Saxony as Frederick Augustus I.]

CHARLES XII AT THE BATTLE OF NARVA

(Painted for THE HISTORIANS' HISTORY OF THE WORLD by Thure de Thulstrup)

private affections was no feature of his character; and he rushed forwards to Cracow, which he took without loss, and from which he exacted a very heavy contribution. An accident which confined him for some time to his couch — the breaking of his leg — delayed the consummation of his great object. The interval was not lost by Augustus, who, aware that his downfall was resolved, diligently collected new forces, chiefly from his Saxon states.

On Poland he could place little dependence; few of the nobles attended any diet which he convoked; and the deliberations, whatever they might be, were generally cancelled by a diet held by the party intent on his dethronement — a party of which the primate was the soul, and the Swedish king the head. He had, however, hope in the mediation of the emperor, and still more in the aid of Peter the Great, who was glad of the opportunity afforded him of making Poland and Lithuania the theatre of the war. But the loss of the battle of Pultusk, in 1703, emboldened the enemies of the Polish king to labour more openly for his dethronement. Under the baneful influence of the cardinal-primate, a diet assembled at Warsaw early in 1704 declared that the republic alone could treat with foreigners — thus excluding Augustus from all participation in general affairs. The next month it went farther, by proclaiming the throne vacant. In vain did he strive to defend himself in the neighbourhood of Cracow; his troops were dispersed, and he himself was forced to cross the Vistula with precipitation. Charles now intimated that if the republic wished to escape dismemberment, it must proceed to a new election. That he did not himself claim the crown surprised alike his councillors, Poland, Sweden, and Europe; but he preferred the glory of giving away to that of retaining a kingdom. The prince whom he selected for the dignity was Stanislaus Leszcynski, a piast or native noble, who, notwithstanding the opposition of a party, was proclaimed by the diet in 1704.

That Augustus would tamely submit to his exclusion could not be expected by anyone that knew his Saxon resources, his alliance with the czar, and still more the strength of his party in Poland itself. With a body of nineteen thousand Muscovites, aided by such Poles as remained faithful to his cause, he took advantage of Charles' absence on the frontier to approach Warsaw, which submitted, but not until the new court and the heads of the hostile confederacy had time to flee. Fifteen hundred Swedes, with Count Horn, one of their best generals, were forced to surrender themselves prisoners of war. Having exacted a heavy contribution from Warsaw, and been joined by sixteen thousand Saxons, he took the field. But many of his detachments were defeated, and he himself compelled to retire into Saxony. In Livonia the Russians had for a time more success; they reduced several fortresses, including Dorpat and Narva; but these advantages were counterbalanced by subsequent losses. Even Peter, at the head of 120,000 Cossacks and Russians, effected nothing corresponding with his mighty preparations. Early in 1706, too, Schulenberg, general of the Saxon troops, was signally defeated by Rehnskjöld, one of the Swedish generals. The loss of the Saxons, in men, artillery, and baggage, was most severe, while that of the Swedes was inconsiderable. Nothing can better illustrate the reputation for invincibility which the victorious troops enjoyed, than the fact that at this very battle of Fraustadt seven thousand Saxons ran away without discharging their muskets. (This splendid success of his lieutenant afforded some degree of jealousy to Charles, who wished to engross the undivided attention of Europe.)

Lithuania was soon cleared of Prussians, Saxons, and Cossacks; and though the palatinate of Cracow held for Augustus, he could not maintain his position, but precipitately retired at the approach of the Swedes.

THE ZENITH OF CHARLES

Charles was not satisfied with expelling his royal enemy from Poland; he determined to attack him in Saxony itself. Leaving General Meyerfeld to defend Great Poland against the Russians, Cossacks, and Saxons, he passed through Silesia into the electorate. At his approach the Saxons retired; and he advanced, almost without opposition, to the very heart of the country. Here Augustus, in alarm, nominated plenipotentiaries to obtain peace on any conditions. A victory gained over Meyerfeld by the allies did no service to the elector; the conditions were only the harder for it. He was forced, not only to renounce all claim to the Polish crown, but to acknowledge his rival Stanislaus. He tried, at a personal interview, to dispose Charles in his favour; but he failed in his object, which, indeed, he durst not openly propose. [The interview took place at Altranstädt, where Charles had fixed his headquarters]. "Charles," says Voltaire, "was on this occasion in his usual homely garb — a coarse blue cloak with gilt brass buttons, leather gloves that reached to his elbow, and a coarse piece of black stuff tied round his neck in lieu of a cravat or military stock. The conversation turned on little beyond his huge jack boots, which he had worn constantly, he said, for six years, only taking them off when he lay down to sleep.

The behaviour of the Swedish hero, at this summit of human prosperity, was such as might have been expected from his character. However plain in his dress or manners, however austere to himself, his overbearing haughtiness was not the less evident. He despised the half-uttered menaces of the imperial diet, at his violation of the imperial soil by the invasion of Saxony. He even sought an occasion to quarrel with the emperor, and insisted, before he would be satisfied, on the surrender of fifteen hundred Muscovites who had taken refuge in Austria; on the recall of four hundred German officers in the armies of the czar; and on the restoration of the Lutherans in Silesia to their churches, to the free exercise of their worship, and to all their civil privileges. The two last demands were readily granted; but the emperor, afraid of embroiling himself with the czar, gave secret warning to his Russian guests, and thus enabled them to escape.

Voltaire has given us an interesting account of the interview which the celebrated Marlborough had with the warrior. The object of the artful Englishman was to learn whether any intention existed, on the part of the king, to support the declining fortunes of Louis XIV. The courtly dress, the finished elegance, of the duke surprised Charles, who could not readily conceive how any man, and especially such a man, could for a moment dream of such trifles. Probably he underrated his visitor on that very account. But under the foppish exterior was a soul almost equal to his own. The mere look of Charles when the czar was mentioned, convinced him that Russia, not the allies, was the next enemy that would be assailed. A map of that empire lay on the table; and it was evidently the daily study of the hero. Gigantic as the project might seem, of dethroning so great a monarch as Peter, it had been formed. Charles, flushed with his successive victories over four monarchs, with his gift of a kingdom, and with the humiliation even of the Austrian emperor, anticipated no bounds to his career. He had a much larger scope of ambition than the poet has ascribed to him —

"From Moscow's walls let Gothic banners fly,
And all be mine beneath the polar sky!"

He had vowed vengeance against the pope, who had dared to condemn the recent concession to the Silesian heretics. His Gothic ancestors, he observed, had been at Rome; and, from his smile, he manifestly intended that the Goths should be there again. One year, he believed, would suffice for the conquest of Russia; a few weeks, according to the same calculation, would be sufficient to dethrone the holy father. Turkey seems to have been his next meditated object of attack; and after it, Persia; for he sent engineers into those empires to draw maps of the roads and plans of the cities. Little did this wild visionary dream that his baseless empire was about to vanish forever.

THE EXECUTION OF COUNT PATKUL

The execution of Count Patkul was a rigid proof of the Swedish king's inflexibility. Patkul was a Livonian, who had been deputed by his countrymen to the court of Charles XI, to obtain some alleviation of the heavy burdens imposed on them. Finding his petition received with contempt, and even his life in danger, he had fled from Stockholm to the court of Peter. He had entered into the service of the czar, and so won the latter's confidence that he was nominated ambassador to the court of Saxony. At the mandate of Charles, he was given up to his arbitrary master. As a subject of Sweden, he would have been deserving of punishment for advising the czar and the elector to invade Livonia, but still more for bearing arms against his country. But, independently of the provocation which had driven him into the arms of Peter, surely his character as ambassador should have ensured his safety. Intoxicated by his success, Charles paid no regard to the applications in Patkul's favour, nor to the voice of international law, which places the representative of a sovereign on the same footing as the sovereign himself; and nothing short of the most cruel, the most barbarous, of deaths would satisfy the implacability of his temper.[b]

The action of Charles in this matter is justified by some writers, in particular by R. Nisbet Bain[g] in his biography of Charles XII, on the grounds that Patkul was undoubtedly a traitor and that his genius, exercised in the service of the enemies of his native sovereign, had constituted one of the most formidable dangers with which Charles had had to contend. Bain is also of opinion that the blame for the brutality of the punishment should be laid on the age, and not on the sovereign who ordered it — a decision with which all will not agree. King Oscar[h] speaks of Charles as in general opposed to torture. In Bardili's memoirs of the Swedish king's devoted admirer and companion-in-arms, the young prince Maximilian Emanuel of Würtemberg, there is an account of Patkul's execution, and also the text of a singular document, said to have been written by Patkul shortly before his death.[a]

Wide-spread interest was excited by an extraordinary sentence. The great minister and general, Patkul, was to be executed in a terrible manner at Kasimir [in Posen]. The decision was published in a document which stated that he had opposed the royal command, that his two accomplices had been pardoned and he also would have received the royal mercy but that he had not ceased to instigate war, and had finally served as a general in the said war. He was tried, and condemned to be broken on the wheel and also beheaded. The execution was to take place with the greatest secrecy, so that the court and the army might hear nothing of it until it was over; only the officers who watched him, and the priests who prepared him for death, were to know of it. Nevertheless many thousand spectators were present. Until he was within the ring and saw the wheel beside the block, he perhaps did not know the manner of his death. At the sight of it he cried out, with his eyes raised to heaven, "O my king, what is this that you do?" The execution of the sentence was pitiful in the extreme; as the executioner (an inexperienced Pole) did not know how to handle the instruments. He did the work clumsily, especially with the wheel. Therefore it happened that, after Patkul had been tortured on the wheel, and brought to the block to be beheaded, he was still alive. Soon after Saxony was invaded by King Charles, the master whom Patkul had first offended, and by whom his fate had now been decided. There exists a document containing his last words, signed by his name, which are given under the following title: *Speech for the Justification of Patkul Which Three Days before his Death was written by The Wanderer, In the Year When he was justly rewarded for Treason:*

"Do not wonder that a death's head speaks to you. If I were silent, even these walls and columns would speak. And if these were not heard, then others would publish my adventures; and one has pity for misdeeds, in listening to the last words of the condemned. As for that, no one can blame you or me for the telling; because death does away with all fear. And even from that, I do not hold myself back. Then know that I am John Reinhold Patkul, by birth a nobleman, and by it a joy to my parents, but now a cause for tears and disgrace. My birth brought much satisfaction, and no one then conceived that the day of my death would bring more pain than the day of birth. It did not cost my own mother so much when she brought me into the world, as it has cost the universal mother, earth; for she tried to hinder the performance of the last rites for her child. Ah well! so be it! It is a misfortune to escape what is inevitable. I was born in Livonia, in a country where the nobility of that time enjoyed perfect freedom. The blood of the heathen stained their shields: what it betokened, I do not know, and whether the fatal titles indicated future misfortune to their order and to their country, remains a mystery forever unsolved. They yielded that freedom to the crown of Poland, in those unfortunate wars wherein Sweden, Moscow, and Poland were ruined and finally my native country fell under the sceptre of Sweden.

"Many a man is blind with his seeing eyes, and deaf with his hearing ears. My example can confirm this. Although warned in many places, yet I withstood the edict of the king. I took the ground of my freedom, which was already forfeited, and of justice, which had been ostracised. By that attitude, I brought on myself the disfavour of the king and my disgraceful sentence. I fled to find a sun which could revivify me. I asked the protection of the czar: and for that, not only King Augustus, but also my own king, Charles XII, persecuted me in the most relentless manner. I assisted the intrigues in all the councils; I commanded armies. In short, I was an enemy to Sweden, and became a personage of great importance, in every respect, among the opposing parties. Then I sought repose in Saxony. The most distinguished members of the court were not unfriendly to me. Yet the blossom of my misfortunes already began to manifest itself: it commenced with the mandate to put me into prison. Why this happened may remain a secret. It was the first manifestation of a divine vengeance, which followed me on foot, and came in the form of the Swedish army. My infuriated king haggled for my person, as the only condition of peace.

"At that time I learned that we can trust in nothing more unstable and uncertain than men. As for me, two great potentates could not protect me. I learned that nothing avails, when God withdraws his protection. I was convinced that resistance is useless when the hour of fate has struck. Thus I was led, with doubts and fears, in bands and chains, by the Swedish army in their march to Poland, always hoping for an extension of favour. However, the king's thoughts were not my thoughts. Kasimir was the chosen place for the expiation of my crime. It takes place with horrors, on the 10th day of October, 1707. Witness here the pitiful execution, of which I will make a few words. You see here a body without a heart, a heart without any keeping. A nobleman without grave or tomb, a general without protection! An ambassador on the wheel! I must die in Poland, because I helped Poland to become a theatre of war. I must be made an example to others. The sole thing in which I trusted is this — it alone, I know, upheld my soul till the last blow of the executioner, and even at the very gates of death — that, conscious, stroke and agony could not wrest from me the thought: 'My sins were atoned on the cross.' Mark then, finally, that which I forgot: fear God; honour the king!"

Whether this execution was the forerunner of the great misfortunes which followed the king of Sweden and his realm — the just sentence of heaven, as many have thought — remains undetermined. These may appear either as a judgment, from a religious point of view, or rather as having some natural connection with Patkul's execution. As to the latter, it is not yet proved whether Charles sinned against heaven, or against the laws of the holy Roman Empire. Before the execution, the Swedish misfortunes had already begun; during the march from Saxony, wind and weather proved unfavourable; and, in one way and another, there were constant mishaps.[d]

Whether the execution of Count Patkul had or had not any direct bearing on Charles' fate, it stands as a dark landmark at the turning point of his career. Harbingers of coming disasters may have already appeared; but from the height of his triumph at Altranstädt he could look back on seven years of continual success. The almost boyish arrogance of Charles' demeanour at Altranstädt makes his sojourn there seem like a comic interlude after the first and grandest drama in the series which constitutes his biography. The next opens with that act of dubious justice, and culminates on the "dread" day of Pultowa.[a]

THE RUSSIAN CAMPAIGN OF 1707

It was in September of the year 1707 that Charles took leave of Saxony. His army, the destination of which could only be conjectured even by his generals, consisted of forty-three thousand men, the best troops in Europe. His generals the Levenhaupts had, in addition, twenty thousand men in Poland; while fifteen thousand, who expected to be considerably reinforced, were stationed in Finland. What might not he effect with nearly eighty thousand such soldiers as the Swedes, inured to hardships of every kind? The wealth which each soldier possessed was a new incentive to enterprise; each had, besides splendid accoutrements ornamented with silver and gold, about fifty crowns in his purse. All, therefore, marched with cheerfulness, though Russia was suspected to be the destined scene of attack.

Apprehensive of the storm, the czar had prepared for it. With sixty thousand men he had laid waste the eastern provinces of Poland, just before Charles left the plains of Saxony; and then hastily retired into Lithuania at the approach of the Swedish hero. That country was speedily evacuated. Every impediment which could be devised, was employed to arrest his progress. The country, vast, and in some places pathless, was laid waste; the bridges were broken down: barren deserts had next to be traversed; hunger and cold (the winter of 1708 was one of uncommon severity) had to be supported.

But in spite of every obstacle, Charles had reached the Beresina before any enemy appeared. On the opposite bank of that river, a host was drawn up to dispute the passage. But resistance was vain: the barrier was passed with facility; the town of Beresina was carried by assault; the passage of the river Wabis was better disputed, but with equal want of success; the Russians were driven onwards; and Mohilev, a fortress of some strength, fell into the power of the victors.[b]

Charles XII's Account of the Battle of Holowczyn

A letter has been preserved in which the Swedish king gives his own simple account of this affair:[a]

There is really nothing of special importance to write about, except, indeed, that during last winter, and also in the summer, the enemy was continually driven back. Owing to the bad weather and the horrible roads, the marching was very toilsome and extremely difficult during the entire summer. The enemy was rarely encountered on the way — only occasionally in crossing the rivers. At the river Beresina there was a small division of hostile Tartars and Cossacks, when the first regiment arrived. They went off during the night, however. At this river, it happened that the prince of Würtemberg, who is here, was wounded in the left side by a ball from the other bank of the river. The wound was at first thought to be mortal. It was found afterwards, however, that the ball had not inflicted a severe injury, and soon he was very much better.

Since that, the enemy have constantly returned to this river. Wherever there is a river, they have erected breastworks and batteries, but have always left them before anyone came up, until the Swedes reached Holowczyn. When the Swedes arrived there, early in the morning, the enemy had placed a small guard on this side of the stream, which, however, quickly retired, and destroyed the bridge behind it. The Swedish regiment pitched its camp on the side of the river on which it had come up; and so, for several days, the opponents were encamped opposite one another. After several days the regiment found a convenient place between the right and left wings of the enemy, at which the little stream can be easily crossed. The Swedish artillery was therefore immediately carried to the ford, placed in position, and turned on the cannon and breastworks of the enemy. As soon as day broke, our guns and those of the enemy began to respond to one another. At the same time, our men began to improvise a bridge over the little river, when the discovery was made that the water was not deeper than the girdle; so the bridge was not completed, but the soldiers marched through the stream, and ranged themselves in line on the opposite bank. The hostile infantry thereupon showed signs of yielding, and finally drew back into the wood. The Swedish infantry overtook them, and a fierce battle raged, the Swedes driving them a short distance into the wood. Meanwhile, the enemy's dragoons appeared, and proceeded to the place where their infantry had stood. At that moment, the Swedish cavalry hastened forward, waded through the stream, and made the attack. The enemy was forced to give way. The latter, however, made a stand several times, and each time were obliged to yield, until finally they were driven a mile to the rear, according to their own estimate. The enemy lost several small pieces, a couple of standards, and some drums.

Since that time, nothing of consequence has happened; but the enemy has retreated to the other side of the Dnieper. The Swedish regiments are in camp here, at Mohiler: part in the city, and the remainder several miles away in the environs. For several weeks the regiments have been perfectly quiet and inactive here; I hope, however, soon to shift the camp.*e*

The czar, afflicted at the devastation of his country, offered to negotiate. "I will treat at Moscow," was the haughty reply, which showed that the same fate was intended for Peter that had been inflicted on Augustus. "My brother Charles," observed the czar, "wishes to be thought an Alexander; but he will not find me a Darius." This was the termination of the invader's success. From the opposition of the Russian armies, from the want of provisions, from the impassable nature of the roads, and above all, from the severity of the cold, extraordinary even in that climate, he found that he could not reach Moscow during the present year.

But instead of returning into Poland, as he ought to have done, he suddenly determined to diverge into the Ukraine. Mazeppa, the Cossack chief, had promised to join him with a large army and abundant provisions. But might not a hundred obstacles prevent the junction? Was the czar likely to be asleep, and make no effort to prevent such a junction? In any case, a general of ordinary prudence would have waited for the arrival of Levenhaupt, who had orders to join him. But success had so intoxicated the monarch that he disregarded the most ordinary maxims of caution; and he plunged into the wild, vast, and cheerless region which lay between him and the Desna, the place of *rendezvous*. But on reaching the margin of that river, he saw on the opposite bank, not Mazeppa and the Cossacks, but a strong body of Russians, determined to oppose him. Yet the river was passed; the Russians retreated — less, perhaps, through fear than from a design to draw the invaders into the more difficult parts of the country. Mazeppa, indeed, soon appeared, but not with the eighty thousand men who had been promised, or with one tenth of that number, and with no provisions. Nor was this the worst. Levenhaupt, who had left Livonia with a fine army, arrived with a mere handful of worn-out troops. He had, indeed, reason to boast that he had fought his way through sixty thousand Russians, and that he had slain one half of that number in six different battles; but he had lost his artillery, his baggage, and two thirds of his followers, and he brought no material augmentation of force to his royal master. Unfortunately, the weather in the early part of 1709 was more severe than in the preceding months. The region, too, was more wild, more impracticable; and difficulties of every kind accumulated. The force of the Swedes was reduced by famine, by sickness, and by the swords of the enemy, to sixteen thousand men and scarcely thirty pieces of artillery. Yet, with this insignificant host, the rash king continued to advance. He reached Pultowa; but there his march ended.

This town, which was the military and, to a certain extent, the provision storehouse of the Russian army, Charles found, as he ought to have anticipated, defended by good fortifications and a garrison of many thousands. The place, indeed, was immediately invested, but not closely enough to prevent supplies from being thrown into it. Three unexpected disasters arrived within a short period of one another. One of the Swedish detachments which was to intercept the communication between Pultowa and the Russians, was driven back with great loss. The king himself, while exposing himself with his usual rashness to the fire of the besieged, was severely wounded in the heel, so as to render a litter necessary. Last and worst, Peter approached with seventy thousand men to raise the siege. Charles, indeed, had been recently joined by some thousands of Cossacks; but these were not Swedes: they had courage, but not discipline; and they were little acquainted with the branch of the military art which relates to the attack of strong places. He hoped, however, to triumph over the advancing legions and strike such a panic into the garrison as to force a capitulation. Leaving, therefore, eight thousand men before the place, he hastened with as many Swedes and about twenty thousand Cossacks[1] to annihilate the enemy.[b]

Our account of Pultowa is taken from one of the most important biographies of Charles XII, that of Knut Lundblad, who attributes the loss of the battle to the friction between Rehnskjöld and Levenhaupt, the Swedish commanders, and to the incapacity of the former, whom he accuses of culpable negligence and ignorance of the ground. In Lundblad's eyes, Charles is the hero of the fight; though a perusal of the narrative would rather result in our assigning that rôle to Levenhaupt.[a]

CHARLES DEFEATED AT PULTOWA (1709 A.D.)

On the evening before the battle, the king appeared before the troops, seated on a litter, his sword in his hand. He encouraged the soldiers and exhorted them not to dishonour their former bravery in the battle which was impending. This aspect of Charles, however, was entirely different from that of Charles on horseback, at the head of his troops; and it created an entirely new impression among the soldiers. After the round was ended, he allowed the litter to be set down in the open field; whereupon all the generals and chiefs in command lay in a circle around their wounded king, and the first hours of the night were spent there.

Immediately after midnight, however, each one went to his post. Already with the first advance towards the enemy, extreme disorder prevailed. Levenhaupt wished to wait until the dawn, that he might range his columns in due order, but he was not permitted to do so; and in consequence, when all the troops marched out simultaneously into the darkness, many battalions were thrown into disorder, for which Marshal Rehnskjöld [who had been deputed to the chief command] at once took occasion to upbraid Levenhaupt. The latter remedied the difficulty, or at least what he had occasioned. The cavalry on the right had little ground to stand upon, and their column had to be in line with the front of the squadron — which is a strong proof of Rehnskjöld's ignorance of the ground upon which all the manœuvres of the army were to be executed. The infantry marched forward in good order. In the Russian camp reigned perfect quiet; only solitary blows from the hammers of the carpenters who were working on the parapet, broke the stillness. But as soon as daylight appeared the Russians saw what was happening; the alarum was sounded, and they flew to arms. Their strength was estimated at fifty thousand men — the right division under the command of General Bauer, and the left wing under Prince Menshikov, while the centre was controlled by Sheremetiev, and was under the command of the czar. The artillery was in charge of General Bruce. The Swedish infantry was led by Count Levenhaupt, the cavalry by General Creutz. Pultowa lay to the right of the Swedes, and the village of Zukki on their left.

When the infantry arrived at the appointed place, the cavalry were still delayed, which appeared greatly to alarm Rehnskjöld; for the king, carried

[1 Rambaud[m] (*History of Russia*) speaks of Charles' army as consisting of twenty-nine thousand men, with four cannon, and reckons the czar's forces at sixty thousand, with seventy-two guns. The latest English biographer of Charles, R. Nisbet Bain,[g] estimates eighty thousand Russians against eighteen thousand Swedes.]

on a horse litter, was to follow. He therefore turned to Levenhaupt to hear what were his plans for the impending battle. The latter was accustomed to listen to severe criticism and upbraiding on every occasion; and therefore, to this question, he merely replied by expressing the hope that it would end well. The place chosen was most unfavourable for the movements of the cavalry, which formed the chief strength of the Swedish forces. Owing to lack of ammunition, the muskets were of no use as firearms, and for the same reason the field artillery had been left behind, with the baggage; so that they only had steel upon which to rely, while the enemy had thousands of firearms, which even at a distance wrought destruction and death. Levenhaupt received orders, however, to set the infantry in motion, and to march against the enemy's intrenchments the moment the cavalry arrived. The Swedes had to range themselves under the fire of the Russians and endure a severe trial of their courage; for the balls of the enemy made gaps in the scarcely formed ranks with impunity. Nevertheless, they went bravely at their bloody work; and within a few moments two of the most dangerous bastions had been seized by them. The Russians could not withstand the bold attack of their adversaries. They at once took to flight, and Menshikov, who made every effort to hold them back and keep them in line, had three horses killed under him. The Swedish cavalry, part of which arrived at the left of the bastions, while part forced their way through the latter, drove the enemy before them.

At this moment the battle appeared to be decided with everything lost for Russia. Her cavalry retreated farther and farther, and was on the point of fleeing in wild disorder. The successful result of Levenhaupt's attack was beyond question, when, at the decisive moment, the order arrived to stop further attack and also the pursuit of the enemy. This was due to a lack of a definite plan, and also to Rehnskjöld's inability to grasp the whole situation. The right division, quickly withdrawn by Levenhaupt, escaped the firing from the remaining parapet. They made a *détour*, and went to the right so that the left division could follow. The count wished to stand still until the other division could join him. But the field-marshal, Rehnskjöld, riding up, replied to Levenhaupt's suggestion, "No! No! we must give the enemy no time!" Levenhaupt advanced, hoping to win the Russian intrenchment; for he discovered, on near scrutiny, that it was not so well manned as he had supposed. But with a farther advance he unexpectedly encountered a sharp ravine, which he could not pass. He would not allow himself to be baffled by this obstacle; and therefore went somewhat to the left, and reached a place where he could effect a crossing. As soon as the Russians realised that the ravine could not stop the Swedes, they began to give way; but then, wholly unexpectedly, the command arrived that the advance was to be stopped.

This delay gave the enemy ample time to recover themselves, and the indecision which resulted from the first manoeuvres of the Swedes was entirely overcome. To this blunder were added a multitude of others, committed by commanders of separate divisions of the army. The paramount influence in the unfortunate outcome of the battle was undoubtedly General Roos' long delay at the bastions, by which he was cut off, and rendered entirely useless to the remainder of the infantry. Wrong commands were issued on all sides, and increased the disorder. After Levenhaupt had been prevented from making his attack on the enemy's intrenchment, he drew back farther and farther. In this critical and fateful moment, when strong action was absolutely necessary, only indecision and hesitation prevailed in the Swedish camp, in sharp contrast to the former order of things, when Charles himself was the leader. At once the enemy made use of this advantage, and drew up into line, in the order of battle. Meanwhile, during the increasing danger, Rehnskjöld as usual could not give a civil word to Levenhaupt. The latter now received the command to march against the enemy. For the third time, the superior force of the enemy was set upon from all sides; but the cavalry was drawn back and huddled together in a compressed heap.

The entire strength which Levenhaupt could muster for the attack consisted of twelve battalions, which, after the loss already sustained, scarcely numbered four thousand men. With these he had to fight the assembled array of the hostile infantry — twenty-two thousand men — which was divided into two sections and protected at intervals by properly distributed artillery. A reserve of ten thousand stood behind. The Russians did not wait for the attack of the Swedes, but began to advance against the little band of men who, at Levenhaupt's signal, went instantly like lambs to the sacrifice, with Levenhaupt at their head. Marching undismayed and without a shot, the guard under the leadership of the young hero Eric Gyllenstjerna, Levenhaupt's nephew, who lost his life on this occasion, went on with firm step. Notwithstanding the great preponderance of the enemy, the Swedes did not yield in the least, but once more made the enemy turn about, at the first shock of battle, leaving many cannon in the trench. But this first success of the Swedes was of short duration. Their line being weak and not protected by the cavalry, they were soon obliged to flee; and the left division was separated from the right, which forced its way victoriously under the leadership of Count Levenhaupt. As soon as the latter became aware of this misfortune, he hastened to repair it. He found the regiment of Östergötland in full retreat. Already the enemy had begun a manœuvre for the purpose of enclosing in a semicircle the entire left division, so that the only thought possible was of escape. Levenhaupt now wished to hasten back to the right division, which was in the fury of the attack; but it was no longer possible for him to reach them. He was compelled to lead the retreat of the left division; and flattered himself that, if they could reach the wood for which they were aiming, they would be able to rally again. But, even here, he was met by disordered troops of fleeing cavalry. "I opposed them," Levenhaupt said, "with sword in hand, and begged, and threatened with cuts and blows; but I could not force any of them to turn about."

With the hope of meeting new fugitives and forming them into a grand cavalry division, Levenhaupt went on, and soon encountered the bodyguard. He called out to the soldiers not to desert their king. The fugitives finally regained their courage, and the word went from mouth to mouth, "The king is here! We will stand firm"; whereupon cavalry and infantry both drew up in order. During the entire battle Charles' one care had been to keep in the midst of the tumult and continually encourage the soldiers to bravery and endurance. His litter was shattered to pieces. One horse fell under him, and he owed his life to a brave officer (Gjerta) who, although wounded himself, gave him his horse. Charles was riding with his bandaged leg on the pommel of the saddle, when Levenhaupt met him. "Are you alive Levenhaupt?" the king asked, "And what are you going to do?" "There is only one thing left to be done when so many men are gathered about us," the count replied; "and that is to reach, if possible, the train of artillery, where fresh troops are stationed under cover." Levenhaupt ordered the remaining infantry of the left division and the cavalry to make haste. With them, he surrounded the king's person, and ordered a retreat to the place where the artillery had been left, which was safely reached.

While these events were passing, the deserted right was involved in a bloody engagement. The commanders of most of the regiments found death, that day, on the battlefield. Rehnskjöld himself was taken, in the midst of his indecision and hesitation. The prince of Würtemberg and Generals Schlippenbach, Roos, Stackelberg, and Hamilton met a like fate. Count Piper went voluntarily to surrender to the Russians in Pultowa, that he might not fall into the hands of the fighting Cossacks and of the hordes of Kalmucks.

This complete picture of horror is relieved by certain touches of heroic courage. Charles himself in his litter, in the wild tumult of battle, offers an example without parallel in history. The "Little Prince" of Würtemberg, at the head of his fine regiment of cavalry, did wonders in bravery. In truth, however, no one brave individual can equal the intrepid Charles although a hundred others distinguished themselves on that unhappy day. Regiments which before the battle counted from forty to fifty officers, were reduced to scarcely fifteen or twenty; and those who fell for the most part sold their lives dearly. On the Russian side also, no effort was spared to bring the battle to a successful issue. Realising the great importance of the fight, the czar exerted all his powers in order to come off conqueror. Riding on a horse, the gift of the sultan, he sped along his line, challenging the soldiers and officers to fulfil their duty and acquit themselves like men. He flattered himself with the hope of taking Charles, and when the prince of Würtemberg rode forward, he took him for the king. "Shall I not see my brother Charles to-day?" he said impatiently. They believed him dead; and the czar was troubled at the news. This extraordinary battle offered but few trophies to the Russians, but its results were of much greater importance. As far as the loss of the battle was concerned, the whole blame was due to Rehnskjöld's obstinacy and incapacity,[1] and his delay in obtaining, before the battle, sufficient knowledge of the ground, and of the enemy's position and means of defence.[c]

On this fateful day, nine thousand fell, six thousand were made captive. Charles himself was saved with great difficulty. The horse which he so painfully mounted was shot under him; but five hundred of his most resolute followers put him in a calash, cut a way for him through ten regiments of the enemy, hastened with him to the Dnieper, and crossed it in a small boat. Others followed; and some had the good fortune to pass on rafts or boats, or by swimming; but the greater portion, pursued by Prince Menshikov, were compelled to surrender. Of the large and noble army which had left Poland, eighteen hundred only remained to accompany their king through the vast desert which lay between them and the Bog. The heat of the summer sun (it was now July) in this arid wilderness was more intolerable to them than the rigour of the preceding winter. Many — especially those on foot, who were by far the greater number — fainted, and became the captives of the pursuing Russians; many found a grave; and of the remnant which reached the margin of the Bog, a short distance from Ouchakov, few had the good fortune to pass over with the king. There were few boats in readiness; and about five hundred men were captured before his eyes by the active cavalry of the enemy. This last blow affected him more deeply than we should have expected from the inflexibility of his character, for he is said to have shed tears.

[1] Others have accused Charles himself of hampering the operations by issuing orders independently of Rehnskjöld, to whom he had delegated the command.]

CHARLES XII'S EXILE

The reception which the royal exile experienced from the Turks, whose hospitality he had claimed, was highly honourable to the character of that people. His establishment at Bender was such as became a prince. Though his followers were soon a thousand (numbers from Poland and Sweden joined him every week) they were liberally maintained by the sultan Ahmet III, who allowed him 500 crowns a day for his own household. But he had no intention to remain long in this peaceful retirement. His mind was still full of the gigantic projects which he had formed when he had quitted Saxony. To procure a Turkish army sufficient to defeat the Russians and restore him to Sweden, was his constant object. Vizir after vizir he flattered or assailed, according as they aided or opposed his views; and the seraglio, in which gold brought him creatures devoted to his will, became the scene of innumerable intrigues.

The czar, however, had more gold than Charles, and it was distributed with better effect. Hence, though aid was repeatedly promised him; though on one occasion a large Turkish army was actually put in motion to restore him, and might have destroyed the Russians opposed to them; the same resistless argument reduced their mighty preparations and still mightier promises to nothing. His obstinacy, his intrigues, his inflexible temper, rendered him at length so disagreeable to his hosts that he was invited to return home, with the offer of a large sum of money and a suitable escort. He received the money, but refused to move. He was then told that he would, if necessary, be removed by force; and his reply was that if such a message were again sent him, he would hang the bearer at the door of his house. Force therefore was employed; and was met by resistance of the most desperate, most extraordinary kind. The manner in which he defended his house against a host of janissaries with heavy artillery; their irruption into the interior; their immediate expulsion; the conflagration of the building; his attempt to cut his way through the dense ranks of the assailants; his entanglement by his spurs; his consequent fall to the earth; his immediate seizure by the janissaries, who conducted him in triumph to the tent of the seraskier, are acts which seem too whimsical for sober history, and which yet are undoubted facts, embellished as in some respects they may have been by the genius of the narrators. All of them are perfectly in character of the man. He had once more the delight of fighting; and though on a humble scale, " the battle of Bender," as he playfully termed it, gave him no less pleasure than his most brilliant deeds in the north of Europe. From Bender he was removed to Adrianople, and thence to Demotika, a small town about twelve miles from that city. In this last place, as we shall soon perceive, his abode was brief.

During the monarch's residence at Bender, the face of the North, as might have been expected, was entirely changed. Immediately after the battle of Pultowa, Augustus, after publishing an elaborate manifesto in which he represented his abdication as compulsory on both his people and himself, and therefore invalid, invaded Poland, and without much difficulty expelled Stanislaus from the kingdom. The czar, not satisfied with freeing his territories from hostile feet and sending the captive Swedes to spread civilisation among his Siberian subjects, seized Ingermanland, Livonia, and Finland. The king of Prussia and the duke of Mecklenburg laid claim to Pomerania; and with an army of nearly fifty thousand men, among whom where Danes and Russians, they invaded that extensive province. But there was still a

Swedish army there, about thirteen thousand strong; and with all their mighty preparations, they only for a time reduced two of the fortresses. But the Prussian king reduced Stade, the most important fortress of Bremen, and that which commanded the whole duchy. Frederick IV of Denmark was not the last to profit by the misfortunes of this hereditary enemy. Protesting against the treaties that had dismembered his kingdom, and claiming Bremen, Holstein, and Skåne, he invaded the last of these provinces, and took Helsingborg; but the Swedes, thinned as they had been by the loss of so many myriads of men, were not prostrated. At the head of twelve thousand militia and eight thousand regular troops, Stenbock, one of their generals, hastened to repel the invaders. Such was the spirit of these men that he succeeded in his object, and inflicted so heavy a blow on the Danes that Frederick was glad to transfer his hostilities elsewhere. From Skåne, Stenbock hastened into Pomerania, captured Rostock, and after a nobly contested action obtained a splendid victory over the combined Danes and Saxons, near Gadebusch in Mecklenburg. He next laid Altona in ashes, in revenge for the sale of one hundred thousand Pomeranians as slaves to the Turks. But in Holstein he found the termination of his success. Defeated near the banks of the Eider by a combined force of Russians, Danes, and Saxons, he threw himself into Tönning, where he was speedily invested and compelled to surrender at discretion. The defeat of the Swedish fleet by that of the czar was felt no less severely than the surrender of Stenbock. Both events led to the immediate conquest of all Pomerania (except Rügen and Stralsund), which the Prussian king determined to hold in sequestration until the next peace.

Such, then, was the melancholy situation of Sweden towards the close of the king's captivity. If Skåne had been successfully defended, Finland, Livonia, Bremen, Holstein, and Pomerania were in the hands of her enemies, while 150,000 of her bravest sons were prisoners in foreign lands. In this extremity, her only hope lay in negotiating a peace. A diet was, therefore, convoked by the regent Ulrica Eleonora, sister of Charles. After enacting that the standing army should be augmented to thirty thousand men, and that, to support the increased expenditure, every Swede should send his plate to be coined at the royal mint, there was much dispute in regard to the negotiations. Was the absent king, whose intractable temper was so well known, to be consulted respecting them? Was the regent, who durst attempt nothing that was likely to offend her brother, to ratify them? The senators at length decided that they alone would undertake the delicate and difficult task; and the princess immediately resigned her office. Nothing can be more characteristic of Charles than his indignation when he heard of the presumption of the senators, their usurpation of his royal powers. He declared that, if they continued to interfere in matters which did not concern them, he would make them know their proper level, by sending one of his jackboots, to which they should pay as much homage as to himself when present.

Yet even this trait of his character is not more remarkable than another, which was displayed while on his journey from Bender to the neighbourhood of Adrianople. Being informed that Stanislaus, the dethroned king of Poland, was also a fugitive in Turkey, and had reached Bender a few hours only after his departure from it, he showed neither surprise nor grief over the event — it was too common, too insignificant, a calamity for sympathy. But he eagerly sent a messenger to the prince, whom he assured of a speedy change of fortune, and whom he exhorted never to abdicate — never to make peace with Augustus the usurper. With such infatuation did this extraordinary man adhere to his ancient but now visionary dreams of ambition.

THE LOSS OF STRALSUND

The negotiations to which we have alluded were broken off by an unexpected event — the arrival of Charles at Stralsund. Seeing that hope of awing the Turkish government was at an end, he had left the empire; and in disguise, accompanied only by two officers, had travelled from Demotika to that Baltic port in five weeks. At his appearance, just before the break of day [22nd of November, 1714], the half-awakened governor was lost in surprise; but that sentiment soon yielded to joy, which was shared by the whole garrison and the whole population of the town. One of his first objects was to inspect the fortifications; the next was to transmit orders to all parts of his dominions for the renewal of the war. Such was the enthusiasm occasioned by his arrival that his armies were recruited at once. The peasants flocked to his standard in such numbers as to threaten a famine, from the scarcity of hands to cultivate the ground.

GEORG HEINRICH VON GÖRTZ, MINISTER OF
SWEDEN

(1668–1719)

To fortify himself by alliances, he married his sister to the prince of Hesse-Cassel; and he invoked the aid of France. But Louis XIV, humbled by disasters, could only promise to aid him by negotiation. How little it was likely to avail, may be estimated from the fact that five sovereigns — those of Denmark, Hanover, Prussia, Saxony, and Russia — prepared to crush him at every accessible point. If this monarch was thus restored to his dominions, he was not restored to his former power. Wismar and Usedom and Rügen were assailed and taken by the allies; and Stockholm itself was menaced by the Danish and Russian fleets. He now threw himself into Stralsund, which was speedily invested, but which, as it was strong, and defended by nine thousand men, was not likely to be soon reduced. Yet, though he fought with all his former valour, and was nobly imitated by his soldiers, the efforts of the besiegers, who were so much superior in number and so eager to conclude the war by taking him, made greater havoc with the works than could have been foreseen. In two months it was manifest to all that the place was no longer tenable; and he escaped at midnight in a small boat, which conveyed him to a Swedish vessel then cruising off the coast. No sooner was he known to be safe than the garrison capitulated [December, 1715]. From Karlskrona, where he passed the ensuing winter, he transmitted orders for the immediate recruiting of the army. They were obeyed without a murmur; and so also were those which he issued for the increase of the revenue. Though every species of extortion was adopted, and the people were ground to the very earth, they considered any extremity preferable to the invasion of their country, with its probable result, the loss of the national independence. By these measures, twenty-five thousand men were raised and equipped, and sent to join the king.

With this army it was expected that he would hasten to the succour of his German possessions; that he would drive George of Hanover from Bremen, or the Danes from Holstein, or the Prussians and Saxons from Pomerania, or the Russians from Livonia and Finland. Europe was surprised to see him [March, 1716] pass into Norway, the rocks and mountains of which seemed scarcely worth the trouble of conquest, compared with the fertility of his southern dominions. But there was little reason for the sentiment. What could he, with all his bravery, hope to effect at the head of twenty-five thousand men, when so many powers, with forces so vastly superior, were preparing to crush him the moment he set his foot on the German soil? The resolution was a wild one. But his doom was fixed. Though on his march to Christiania he defeated the Danes in several cities of little moment, reinforcements from Denmark enabled them to triumph in their turn; he lost all the advantages which he had won, and was compelled, with a great loss of men, to return into Sweden.

BARON GÖRTZ AND HIS PROJECTS

If Europe had been surprised at the irruption of Charles into Norway, it was still more surprised at the inactivity of the czar. The latter circumstance must be attributed to one of the most extraordinary projects which the annals of the world can produce. Charles had a favourite minister, the baron von Görtz, a man of great capacity, of great enterprise, and still greater ambition — one every way calculated to be the confidential adviser of such a king. Görtz saw that the only hope of security for Sweden lay in fomenting divisions amongst the allies banded for her destruction. He heard that Peter was dissatisfied with them, because they would not consent to his forming an establishment in northern Germany. The offer of Wismar, he believed, or the isle of Rügen, with the cession of Carelia, Ingermanland, and Livonia — provinces which were forever lost to Sweden — would make the czar enter into any scheme for the aggrandisement of his royal master.

Nor was he deceived in these expectations. On the conditions to which we have alluded, Peter readily agreed to the dethronement of Augustus and the restoration of Stanislaus; and, in revenge for the seizure of Bremen by George I, to assist the son of James II [since known to history as the Old Pretender] in ascending the throne of Great Britain. The Russians and Swedes were, accordingly, to appear once more in Poland, not as enemies, but as allies; to over-run Hanover; to march into Bremen; to free Pomerania; and then to make a hostile descent on the English coast. The Catholics of Ireland were known to be favourable to the design; the refugees in Holland promised to contribute all they could to its realisation. But no one entered more readily into the plan than Cardinal Alberoni, minister of Spain, whose mind was not less capacious, and was inconceivably more profound, than that of either Charles or his minister. This treaty will account, not only for the inactivity of the czar, but in a great degree for the preference given by the Swedish king to Norway, as the seat of war, over Germany. There would, he thought, be time enough to recover his German possessions, when his troops, joined to those of Russia, had placed the Polish crown on another brow.[b] In consequence of these intrigues, Count Gyllenborg, the Swedish ambassador at the court of London, was taken into custody [February 1717], as was Görtz in Holland. They were set at liberty, however, after an imprisonment of six months, and Görtz renewed his negotiations with the court of Russia. Peter proceeded cautiously; but conferences were, at last, appointed to be held in the island of Öland, and everything seemed to promise the conclusion of a treaty which would probably have changed the face of affairs in Europe, when an unexpected event, fortunately for the repose of mankind, rendered abortive all the labours of the baron von Görtz.*f*

Until these negotiations should be perfectly concluded, Charles led another army into Norway. Despatching one division into the interior of the kingdom, he with another laid siege to Frederikshald. The season was December, and the cold so extreme that the sentinels were sometimes found dead at their posts. But nothing could affect "the frame of adamant, the soul of fire," which distinguished above all other men the northern warrior.*b* In order to encourage his troops Charles exposed himself to all the rigour of the climate, as well as to the dangers of the siege; sleeping even in the open air, covered with his cloak only.*f*

Charles was even now only thirty-six. Nine inglorious years had succeeded the nine of victory, but the magnificent designs of Görtz seemed to open before him a third period of greatness, corresponding to the first. The recollection, also, of the difficulties amidst which he had entered on the arena of European complications might have encouraged him to hope for a revival of his fortunes. But he was to chronicle no further successes.*a*

DEATH OF CHARLES XII

On the first Sunday in Advent all work ceased during the divine service, which the king himself attended. He appeared somewhat troubled, but showed himself unusually friendly to all who approached him. During the morning he glanced over some papers which contained warnings of a conspiracy against his person. He gave them a fleeting attention, and their contents made an impression on his mind. After the service, however, he threw them into the fire, thus giving them up to eternal oblivion, and took instead Gustavus Adolphus' prayer-book and portrait, which he placed in his pocket. Then he went to his work, and betook himself to the trenches.

This time he did not, as formerly, remain in his hut, but went immediately deeper into the trenches. The besiegers were now exerting themselves to the utmost, and with the increasing danger of a decisive attack on the fortress, the commandant of the latter redoubled his vigilance. During this night, he not only hung out lanterns and torches, but a succession of balls of fire were thrown up from the fortress, which illuminated the entire expanse of the field. By this clear illumination the besiegers directed their attack, and a cannonade was kept up during the evening. The king remained in the trenches already prepared, and was within a short distance of the fortress and also within range of the balls. Here he walked up and down, and spoke with one and another; but towards nine o'clock he was found lying over the crown of the parapet, on the inner slope of the breastwork. A musket-ball had penetrated his right eye, and passed out again through his left temple. Even to this day the question is asked: Where did that ball come from? Was it sent by the enemy, or was it fired by a secret assassin? Is it possible that it came from the fortress or from one of its out-works? In relation to the circumstances of this unfortunate event, we have but little information. At the moment of the deed, and immediately after, nothing could be seen or discovered to justify the suspicion, and give the proof, that a crime had been perpetrated. Thus it will forever remain a mystery which,

BODY OF CHARLES XII CARRIED BY HIS SOLDIERS

(Painted for The Historians' History of the World by Thure de Thulstrup)

as the flight of time gives quiet for reflection and after-thought, is still unsolved. In fact, the high officers in command in the immediate environment of the king did not desire a closer investigation and inquiry into the manner of death of their common lord. And neither Adjutant-General Von Kaubler — the first to exclaim, "Lord Jesus! the king is shot!" nor General Schwerin, who was immediately summoned to the spot, and the first to touch the lifeless body of the king, had knowledge of the event. The latter's expression of deep sorrow convinced the bystanders of the sad reality of what had occurred. Neither they nor he uttered one word, for future ages, of what they saw and heard during that fatal night, between the 11th and 12th of December, 1718. Their silence does not exculpate them, and it may be possible that the restraints which the circumstances enjoined upon them are the positive proof of their guilt.

Among the separate versions given by eye-witnesses of the events of that night, we possess one which was given by [the French officer] Colonel Maigret, and another by Karlberg, at that time lieutenant of the fortification. In a letter written from Paris in the year 1723, Maigret says, "In order to observe the progress of the work, during the approach and firing of the enemy, the king climbed so high up the inner scarp of the breastwork that half of his body was exposed, while he (the commander) was so far below that his head reached only to the top of the king's boot. Fearing a mishap, he sought a pretext to force the king to descend, but at that moment a cannon ball tore off more than half of the king's left ear, and went out again close to the right. The ball was as large as a pigeon's egg. After that the king never stirred or made a sound. His feet slipped from under him, and he remained lying on the breastwork. The adjutant-general Von Kaubler called out, 'The king is wounded!' but he (the colonel in command) immediately conjectured that the king was dead." In order to remove any doubt as to whether the shot came from the king's own people, or from the fortress, Maigret adds, at the end of the letter, "It was a musket from which the ball came that killed the king, but one much too large for any man, however strong, to handle." This is certainly something of a variation from the earlier version which was given of the case by Maigret. The conversation between him and the king, just before the event, is mentioned by many authors, and must have been reported by the colonel himself. According to this version, when the king intimated that the works appeared to be taking more time than usual, he protested that within eight days the fortress would be in the power of the king. When, several moments later, the king went away, and ascended the breastwork, Maigret is reported to have said, "This is not the right place for the king, where the balls are falling so thick." At the remark of some officers standing by that to remind him of his personal risk was the surest way to arouse the king to defy the danger, Maigret turned, intending to make a pretext of requesting the king to take a view of some new works, to remove him from his dangerous position. But before he could accomplish this, a ball whizzed by and the king called out, "That has safely hit your man!"

The report of Lieutenant Karlberg is, in substance, as follows: At four in the afternoon, the king went into the trenches. Something was wrong; for the men who should have been there were not in their places, for which reason he sent to fetch them back, and finally despatched the lieutenant [on this mission], with the words: "Go, and see what they are conspiring." But, nevertheless, the men kept him waiting. When they finally appeared, Karlberg received the order to hasten the filling of the gabions. He had scarcely taken six or eight steps, when he saw the king lying on the inner slope of the breastwork, to which he had mounted: he lay on his left side, his mantle half covering him. His left hand supported the chin, and the head was upright, over the crown of the breastwork. His gaze was turned somewhat towards the fortress. Below the king stood from eight to ten officers, of whom Karlberg was one. How long the king lay there, Karlberg did not know. He had not been there many minutes, however, when from without, on the left side, the king was shot in the head; and afterwards not the least movement was observed, but that the hand which had supported the head fell down, and the head slowly sank into the mantle. Not the least tremor was observed in the body, which remained immovable where it lay. Because of the depth of the intrenchment, no one could determine whence the shot came — whether from very near or far. The adjutant-general Von Kaubler was the first to announce the calamity at the moment when the head of the king sank down, by exclaiming, "Lord Jesus! the king is shot!" With these words, he touched Karlberg on the shoulder, and requested him to seek General Schwerin, who also came immediately. Karlberg now hastened to call the watch to bring the bier at once, to fetch away an officer who had fallen. While he was giving this order, Lieutenant-Colonel Count Posse came towards him with the question, "Is the king shot?" Karlberg, much alarmed at the unexpected question, denied it, and mentioned an officer of the fortification. Not half an hour had yet elapsed since the fatal event, and was it already known? The remaining part of the narrative relates to the removal of the royal body to the headquarters in Tistedal, under the escort of Lieutenant Karlberg. It also seems strange that, besides this, he was commanded to announce the death of the king to Prince Frederick, who was three-quarters of a mile in the rear. Why was not the adjutant-general called upon to do it? The prince received the message of death while sitting at the table with many officers. It was whispered to him, and afterwards passed from mouth to mouth, but not a word of regret or grief was heard. It was as though everything had been concerted, and had been known beforehand.[c]

ESTIMATES OF CHARLES XII

Lovers of the romantic may be disposed to add the circumstances of the death of Charles XII to the number of great historical mysteries. The story that the king was assassinated has been accepted without comment in the continuation of Geijer's history of the Swedes. King Oscar,[h] however, dismisses it as a baseless slander, and Bain[g] speaks of it as having been finally disposed of by Paludan-Müller.[i] The disgust of the Swedes at the continuance of the long foreign wars which had already involved so much suffering and ruin to them and their country was sufficiently natural, and doubtless sufficiently notorious to give colour to the idea that some bold and desperate spirits had resolved to end all with the life of the man whose ambition, though it might not have been the original cause of these evils, now seemed the great obstacle to the peace of Europe. But whether this enterprise was undertaken and executed, or undertaken and forestalled by accident, or whether no conspiracy at all existed, the circumstances attending the death of Charles are striking enough as an example of the irony of fate. The fall of the mighty conqueror before whom all Europe had quaked was "destined to a barren strand, a petty fortress, and a dubious hand." The death of the great general, if not the work of an unknown assassin, was due to a senseless refusal to take ordinary precautions.[a]

King Oscar on Charles XII

In contemplating Charles XII at the head of his "brave blue boys," it is his own unconquerable and heroic courage, as first among his warriors, that chiefly rivets the attention. His great qualities as a general are too often overlooked. Nevertheless, they were so distinguished, that a Frederick the Great, a Napoleon I, and other renowned commanders and military writers, have not hesitated to set them forth as examples. No Swede has met adversity with more indomitable firmness than Charles XII. None has been so indifferent to success; so little allured by the blandishments of fortune; so little dazzled by glory. These qualities, at times displayed to excess and often productive of mischief, must yet be admired. They were based essentially on religious principles. The uprightness of his character was rarely, if ever, untrue to itself. Charges of cruelty, however, have not been wanting; but they have generally come from quarters by no means unprejudiced, and remain unsubstantiated. On the other hand, it is known that he forbade the employment of torture, even when it was counselled by the highest officials of the kingdom.[h]

Rambaud's View of Charles XII

The adversary of Peter the Great was an admirable knight-errant rather than a sovereign. The absolute power of which he became possessed at an early age left without counterpoise his fiery temper and obstinate character — his "iron head," as the Turks said at Bender. Voltaire observes that he carried all his virtues to such an excess that they became as dangerous as the opposite vices. His dominant virtue and vice was a passion for glory. Glory, and glory alone, was to him the end of war. He appears not to have understood that it was possible to acquire it by practising the arts of peace. Up to the moment when the news of the coalition of Poland, Denmark, and Russia revealed to him his military vocation, he seemed the most insignificant of all the European princes. His conduct appeared to be regulated, not by the political principles current in the eighteenth century, but by some strange and archaic view of honour.[m]

Bain's Characterisation of Charles XII

[Charles'] personal habits were simple in the extreme. Nobody would ever have taken him for a king, from his dress. He would not tolerate even the most insignificant ornament, and wore invariably a dark blue coat with a high collar, yellow vest and trousers, large elkskin gauntlets, a broad unembroidered belt of buffalo hide, and huge, heavily spurred riding boots that reached above the knee, with an ordinary cavalry mantle thrown over the whole. His food was of the simplest kind. His manners were austere, but never rude. Nevertheless, Charles was far from being the stern and saturnine young hero he is commonly supposed to have been. On the contrary, he had inherited from his father a strong sense of humour, which constantly asserted itself in all sorts of ways; even in the most anxious and terrible times, he was always rather gay than grave. For his soldiers, Charles had a particular care. They always fared as well, and often better, than he did himself, and he frequently stinted himself to add to their comforts. There are also innumerable instances of his kindness to individuals. On the other hand, it is quite true that he exacted the most absolute obedience, the most complete self-surrender from his soldiers and his servants, and had no regard whatever for the sufferings of a foe who threatened to be obstinate. No one, however, could be more generous to the vanquished. Charles' valour, modesty, self-restraint, and piety were certainly his dominant qualities.

But it would be a great mistake to imagine that Charles XII was nothing but a mere warrior, or even a mere hero. Intellectually he was very highly gifted, and had many of the qualities of a great ruler. He had a quick comprehension, great acuteness, and a really marvellous memory, especially for figures.*g*

Crichton and Wheaton on Charles XII

At the time of his death, Charles was little more than thirty-six years of age — one-half of which time had been spent amidst the turmoil of arms or wasted in foreign exile. The instinctive traits of his character were few, but strongly marked. War was his ruling passion; and in him the world beheld the rare spectacle of a conqueror bent on subduing kingdoms for the mere gratification of giving them to others, and without any apparent wish to enlarge his own dominions. The glory of his exploits dazzled all Europe; but it was the passing splendour of a meteor; and not a vestige of his greatness survives, except the memory of his renown and the names of the places immortalised by his battles. All the actions of this prince, even those of his private life, appear to have sprung from a misdirected ambition; blind to consequences, he pursued his infatuated career, until his extravagance ruined Sweden and gave his enemies that ascendency which it had been the sole object of his reign to prevent.*l*

THE FATE OF VON GÖRTZ

The death of Charles was considered a signal for a general cessation of war. The prince of Hesse, who commanded under the king, immediately raised the siege of Frederikshald, and led back the Swedes to their own country. Nor did the Danes attempt to molest them on their march.

The first act of the senate of Sweden, after being informed of the fate of their sovereign, was to order the baron von Görtz to be arrested; and a new crime was invented for his destruction. He was accused of having "slanderously misrepresented the nation to the king." He had, at least, encouraged the king in his ambitious projects, which had brought the nation to the verge of ruin. He had invented a number of oppressive taxes in order to support those projects; and, when every other resource failed, he had advised his master to give to copper money the value of silver — an expedient productive of more misery than all the former. In resentment of these injuries, Görtz, though found guilty of no legal crime, was condemned to lose his head, and was executed at the foot of the common gallows.*f*

CHANGE IN THE CONSTITUTION

Scarcely was the dreaded Charles dead, when Sweden, aroused as though out of a long sleep, beheld the wounds inflicted upon her by despotism, and sought means by which she could forever make sure that there should be no return of such cruelties. Fortunately, Charles, who had never married, left no heirs; consequently, the council of state, after appointing a successor, could restrict his powers according to their inclination. Their choice fell upon Charles' younger sister, Ulrica Eleonora, wife of the hereditary prince Frederick of Hesse-Cassel. She had before renounced all claim to the throne and the detested sovereign power, by signing on the 23rd of January, 1720, a new constitution, the like of which neither Aristotle nor Montesquieu, nor any other political philosopher, had ever constructed or suggested; wherein the name of monarchy was retained simply as an antique decoration, but under the appearance of democracy, all the monarch's power was, in reality, in thraldom to the most detestable aristocracy.

According to this form of government, the highest (sovereign) power was to lie with the council of state, which was to consist of four divisions: nobility, clergy, citizens, and peasants. To the council of state, assembled in the diet, all incidental improvements and applications of the new form of government were to be referred; also the further restrictions of monarchial power if deemed advisable, the entire jurisdiction, the fixing of duties, the arrangement of the coinage, the right of declaring war, etc. The council should select those who were to be entrusted with the education of the royal children, and these persons were to be retained or replaced in their office as that body thought fit; its consent had also to be obtained before the monarch could cross the boundaries of the kingdom. Every three years the diet was to assemble, and the different classes were expected to attend, even if not especially summoned. The king possessed the executive power; but only with and within the council of the kingdom, which was to consist of sixteen persons chosen from the hereditary nobility of Sweden, who were to advise the king, unasked, what the law of the kingdom was, and who were independent of him and of all courts of justice, subject only to the council of state, and obliged to give an account of themselves only on the occasions when this was assembled. In the council of the kingdom the king had two votes and, in cases of equal voting, the usual right of a president; but in no case was his right of judging to be exercised without, and still less against, the council of the kingdom. When a decision was arrived at by the majority of the council of the kingdom, the king had to sign; or, failing this, the council was authorized to have the king's name cut on a stamp, which should be printed at the conclusion of a deed, and which should have equal value with the king's written signature.

In order, moreover, that this servant of the diet and president of the council of the kingdom called king, should, at least in the insignificant frippery of outside pomp, have something in common with the European sovereigns, the following rights were assigned to him, which were his exclusive property: (1) personal inviolability; (2) free rights of jurisdiction over his personal court and court servants; (3) the right, at his coronation, to create barons and counts, knights and commanders of the royal orders. To this new constitution, of which we have here only given the main outlines, a terrible clause was appended, which declared whoso should dare to scheme, or undertake, or even contemplate aught against it, should be punished as for high treason.

Thus manifold and oppressive were the conditions which attended Ulrica Eleonora's accession to the Swedish throne. In the following year (1720), with consent of the assembly, she resigned the crown to her husband, Frederick I, who had to submit to the same conditions.*j*

THE PEACE OF NYSTAD

The most urgent duty of Ulrica on her accession was to obtain peace; but this object could not be accomplished without many painful sacrifices. To

George I of Great Britain, as elector of Hanover, she ceded Bremen and Verden, in return for 1,000,000 crowns and the co-operation of a fleet in the Baltic. This reinforcement was of the highest advantage to her cause, since it enabled her to obtain more favourable terms from her other enemies. Prussia she disarmed by the cession of Stettin, Usedom, Wollin, and that part of Pomerania which lies between the Oder and the Peene. Denmark was propitiated by a gift of 600,000 dollars, and even induced to restore Rügen, Stralsund, Wismar, with Pomerania north of the Peene.

LINNÆUS
(1707-1778)

The czar had still to be pacified. His demands were large and vehement; and when they were refused, he ravaged the Swedish coast and burned some of the villages. The menaces of England, however, and the interposition of other powers interested in procuring something like a balance in the North, compelled him to negotiate. By the Treaty of Nystad, he consented to restore Finland, and to pay 2,000,000 crowns, in return for the cession of Ingermanland, Karelia, and Esthonia, Viborg with its territory, and the islands of Ösel and Dagö. He also agreed that the Swedish merchants should immediately export, duty free, from Reval or Riga, or any other port on the Baltic, corn to the value of 50,000 roubles. But to Sweden the most advantageous part of this treaty was the exchange of prisoners, of whom 150,000 groaned in the dominions of the czar.

REIGN OF FREDERICK I (1720-1751 A.D.)

The administration of Frederick I was one of great prudence. To reform abuses, to render his mines more productive, to encourage trade, to improve the laws, to place the kingdom in a better state of defence, were his constant objects. Yet he bore, with much secret dissatisfaction, the restrictions which had been placed on the royal authority. In his foreign relations, Frederick steadily looked to his interests. On the death of his father, in 1730, he succeeded to the principality of Hesse-Cassel, and therefore came into closer contact with the empire. This, however, was an evil to Sweden, which, from its isolated position and the circumscription of its territories south of the Baltic, could have little interest in European matters. The sovereign of the petty German state was generally more visible than the monarch of Denmark. The enemy which he watched with the most distrust was Russia.

[1 Carolus Linnæus (Karl von Linné) among the greatest of naturalists, was born at Råshult, Sweden, and is famous as the founder of systematic botany.]

He allied himself with Turkey, with Poland, with any power which dreaded the ambition of the autocrat. If Finland had been ceded, the act had been an ungracious one; and the location of Russian troops towards the frontier rendered necessary the transmission of Swedish armies into that province. Sometimes, too, the gold of Russia had its influence over the very senators of Frederick. Incensed at a conspiracy in which some officers of the administration were deeply implicated, the diet of 1741 declared war against Russia. *b* The Swedes wanted to repair the disasters of the Treaty of Nystad by recovering the numerous provinces they had lost through it. To achieve this end, the moment could not have been better chosen, for the Russians were then waging a bitter war with Turkey. Besides this, an officer named Sinclair, who was serving in the Swedish army, had been killed in Silesia by a detachment of Russian troops while returning from a mission of the government to Constantinople and Warsaw. It is true that he was charged with negotiating an alliance with Poland and Turkey against Russia; but his murder none the less was a flagrant violation of the law of nations.

France recognised these three reasons as valid, and found the majority in the estates well disposed to undertake a war which, thanks to the favourable circumstances, ought to restore to Sweden all that she had lost. According to the Constitution of 1720, it was to the estates that the right of declaring war belonged, but the estates were divided in opinion, and lost precious time in declamations and intrigue, so that by the time they decided to send an advance army of six thousand men into Finland, under the command of Baron Buddenbrock, Russia had already made peace with the sultan. War was then useless so far as the interests of Sweden and France were concerned, and preparations were suspended. The moment had passed; but a new occasion soon arose. The empress Anna had just died, and Russia seemed absorbed by the events following upon her death. France, which was looking for some powerful diversion, undertook to prevent the Russians from taking part in the war, which was about to ensue, for the succession of the emperor Charles VI, and employed all its influence with the Swedish estates to obtain a prompt expedition against Russia. Anarchy was reigning in the estates. The party of the caps opposed a strong resistance to that of the hats on the subject of the war; and the hats, who were in the majority, accused their opponents of high treason, while they voted the question to be submitted to a committee whose members were to be chosen from among their own party. As might have been expected, the committee pronounced for war, but the favourable moment had again passed, and by the time war was declared (August 4th, 1741) the Russians had made all their preparations.

This they proved well by beginning hostilities themselves. Their generals, Lacy and Keith, entered Finland, and placed themselves in front of the Swedish army commanded by Count Levenhaupt and Baron Buddenbrock. The meeting of the two armies took place at Willmanstrand on the 3rd of September, 1741; and after a terrible struggle the Swedes were put to flight. This cruel defeat utterly prostrated Sweden, which did not doubt that the Russians would follow up their victory. The victorious army was already advancing, when a revolution broke out in the palace at St. Petersburg. The empress Anna had designated the young prince Ivan, her nephew and son of Anton Ulrich of Brunswick, as her successor. Ivan was only three months old when the empress died, and was then proclaimed czar under the regency of Biron. But near to the throne stood Elizabeth Petrovna, daughter of Peter the Great, and everyone felt that a prince of tender years was the last thing wanted at that time upon the Russian throne. Elizabeth soon found herself supported by a powerful party, and Prince Ivan was shut up in a fortress. Elizabeth, having obtained possession of the government, wished to secure herself in it, and entered into negotiations with the Swedes, to whom she offered a truce. This was a fine occasion for the estates to repair the harm they had done to Sweden. Perhaps, with the exercise of some tact, they might have obtained not only a long truce, but even an honourable peace. They got neither the one nor the other, however, and this because they imagined that Russia was going to be forced to make peace, through the course of internal events, and would be only too glad to have it at any price. Their claims were so absurdly exaggerated that the Russian army again entered Finland. The Swedes, driven back to Helsingfors and entirely surrounded by Russians, laid down their arms on the 20th of August, 1742.

The news of this event filled Stockholm with stupor and fright; the estates had not realised the mistake they had made until they saw its effects. Sweden's position was becoming more and more precarious. She was now entirely at the mercy of her enemy and did not know what new concessions she might be obliged to make. Would she not have to cede the whole of Finland, and thus lose a third of her possessions? Most fortunately for Sweden, grave complications à propos of the future successor to King Frederick now arose, and distracted Russia from her projects of revenge by drawing attention to a danger of great gravity. Denmark, foreseeing the approaching end of King Frederick, and that he would leave no heir, had put forward her own prince royal [as a candidate], and incited a revolt in Dalecarlia, the aim of which was the re-establishment of the Union of Kalmar. The Dalecarlian peasants took up arms, and set out for Stockholm, which they besieged; but the senate and the estates energetically opposed the adoption of the Danish prince as heir to Frederick I, and the peasants were repulsed.

Elizabeth, who had been particularly frightened by the project of the re-establishment of the union of Sweden and Denmark, now intervened, and let it be understood that if she were consulted on the choice of Frederick's successor, the conditions might be less hard for Sweden. Counsel was taken at Stockholm, and it was decided to defer to the wish expressed by the czarina, as being infinitely better than the loss of Finland. Russia had always favoured the claims of the dukes of Holstein. There was, as a matter of fact, a son of the duke of Holstein-Gottorp and Anna Petrovna, eldest daughter of Peter the Great. This was Karl Peter Ulrich, who afterwards ruled over Russia as Peter III. But Elizabeth, his aunt, had just made him grand duke of Russia, and it was on the morrow of the day when he had been thus chosen to be her successor, that Swedish ambassadors arrived to offer him their crown. It was therefore necessary to fall back upon another prince of the house of Holstein; Adolphus Frederick, a distant descendant of Charles IX. Adolphus Frederick was therefore proclaimed successor to Frederick, and the empress at once sent emissaries to Åbo, where a treaty of peace, sufficiently favourable to Sweden, was signed in 1743. Elizabeth demanded in the treaty only a part of Finland, the province of Kymmenegard, and the fortresses of Nyslott, Fredrikshamn, and Willmanstrand. It seems a curious thing that Russia should by that treaty have guaranteed the constitution of 1720. This was a further proof that the form of government introduced into Sweden after the occurrence at Frederikshald could only weaken and lower Russia's rival.

After the Peace of Åbo, the senate found nothing better to do than to condemn to death the two generals Buddenbrock and Levenhaupt, who had faithfully executed its own stupid orders. Their heads were cut off as though they had been traitors.[k]

REIGN OF ADOLPHUS FREDERICK (1751–1771 A.D.)

Frederick died in 1751, and as he left no children, Adolphus Frederick, duke of Holstein-Gottorp, was elected as his successor — a good prince, but far from possessing the energy or grasp of mind which could turn to account a form of government in which only an overpowering supremacy of mind could have accomplished anything really effective. Before he mounted the Swedish throne, Adolphus Frederick had, in 1744, wedded Ulrica Louisa, the sister of Frederick II, king of Prussia; and from this union sprang three sons, Gustavus, Charles, and Frederick Adolphus.

Before his coronation, the state-council had fettered King Adolphus Frederick, by making him sign a document wherein he swore eternal enmity to absolute sovereignty, with the addition that, as soon as he had signed this oath, the members of the state council were immediately released from their vows of allegiance to him; and all who might contemplate working for the reintroduction of sovereignty were to be punished as the abhorred enemies and betrayers of him and their country. Whoever desired any secular or ecclesiastical office in the kingdom must first bind himself by an oath against absolutism; and, moreover, the power possessed by members of the diet did not confer authority to increase at their will the power of the reigning monarch, but merely the ability sensibly to restrict it.

The inevitable in such a form of government had already happened. As early as 1726, during the reign of his predecessor, King Frederick I, the diet had split into two parties. At the head of one faction stood Count Arvid Horn, whose supporters were called the "caps." The other party was led by Count Charles Gyllenborg, and went by the name of the "hats." The caps felt, and said, that Sweden absolutely needed a period of peace and strict economy. Accordingly, they desired peace with Russia, Prussia, and Denmark. The hats, on the contrary, were of opinion that Sweden must reconquer the noblest pearls in its crown, Livonia and Finland; Russia was Sweden's natural enemy, and so was Russia's best ally, France. In their earliest strife the caps were inclined towards the court, and supported by it; afterwards, the caps were more in sympathy with the republicans, and the hats with the court party.

These two factions now hated, caballed against, and persecuted one another — now in open enmity, now in secret intrigue — as bitterly and incessantly as did ever the Guelfs and the Ghibellines in the Middle Ages in Italy, or the democrats and the aristocrats in France. Nothing, to give a special instance, has equalled the tricks whereby, in the distribution of state offices, each party sought to weaken the other, and so make its own power supreme. The Swedish nobility was, for the most part, not rich enough to be able to live independently of office, and too proud to support itself by honest trade. It naturally happened, therefore, that for one office there were many candidates. Each of the unsuccessful ones loudly protested against the injustice exercised. He might confidently expect that the whole of the party at that moment inferior in power would join him in decrying the oppression he denounced; and that they eventually should get the upper hand would assuredly be to his advantage.*j*

Such was the state of affairs at home, and in addition, Sweden, contrary to her best interests as well as to the whole system of her politics, joined the confederacy formed by Russia, Poland, Austria, and France, against the king of Prussia, whose rising greatness the court of Vienna had contemplated with envy and alarm. While Bohemia, Saxony, and Silesia were the theatre of operations between the contending armies, twenty thousand Swedes had marched into Pomerania, under pretence of guaranteeing the Treaty of Westphalia, and with the hope of recovering their former possessions in that country. As the Prussians were occupied in other quarters, and defeating the Austrians and French in successive engagements, the northern invaders took the towns of Demmin and Anklam, reduced the islands of Usedom and Wollin, and laid the whole district under contribution, as the garrison of Stettin, consisting of ten thousand men, could not leave that important fortress in order to check their devastations. The important victory which Frederick of Prussia gained at Leuthen (December 5, 1757), and the retreat of the Russians, who were compelled to return home for want of provisions, enabled General Schwald to conduct thirty thousand Prussians into Pomerania, where he soon obliged the Swedes to abandon the greater part of their conquests and retire under the cannon of Stralsund. Anklam, Demmin, and other towns were recovered; the Russian magazines in Poland were destroyed; yet no advances towards peace were made by either the court of Stockholm or that of St. Petersburg.

At length the protracted storm was happily dissipated by the death of the empress Elizabeth and the accession of her nephew Peter III to the throne — events which created a total revolution both in the councils and the administration of the Russian government. The new czar was a profound admirer of the great Frederick, and he took an early opportunity of making pacific overtures to that sovereign. A suspension of arms was signed between the two monarchs, which was followed by a treaty of peace, concluded at St. Petersburg May 5th, 1762. By this convention, Peter surrendered all the conquests made in Prussia and Pomerania during the war; he renounced the alliance he had contracted against Frederick; and agreed to assist him with a body of troops in Silesia. Sweden, which had experienced nothing but defeats and repulses from armies greatly inferior to her own, followed the example of Russia in consenting to a truce with his Prussian majesty, which prepared the way for the treaty of amity signed at Hamburg on May 22nd of that year, between the two kingdoms.[l]

Meanwhile in Sweden the two parties, the hats and caps, alternately rose and sank. In the diet which sat from 1765 to 1767 — that is, three years, instead of the legal three months — the caps had the predominance. Wishing to make their triumph more public, during this diet they gave the Swedish nation freedom of the press and of thought — the best gift that can be given to mankind; but which has often proved dangerous to the giver. Protocols, reports, memoranda, leaflets of all kinds, with and without names, were now incessantly distributed in the provinces. Although of various kinds and tendencies, all were alike in the intention to discover the want of skill or the danger of the measures adopted by the victorious party; and it will be easily understood that therein all good which that party did was represented in a concave glass, and all mistakes magnified. By this means the discontent was spread so universally, and grew to such a height, that King Adolphus Frederick was advised to use it to his own advantage. Already in June, 1756, a previous conspiracy in favour of the court had sought, by an attempted revolution, to increase the power of the crown; but it was discovered prematurely, and the authors, who were unable to escape, atoned for it with their lives. The blood of Horn, and of others with equally great names, flowed on the scaffold at Stockholm. Made still more timid by this tragedy, Adolphus Frederick, who by nature was placid rather than bold, had patiently acquiesced in his fate. However, on the one side stood his wife, the sister

[1776 A.D.]

of Frederick the Great, whose high spirit was only too much wrought upon by circumstances, and on the other, a son born for greatness, Gustavus — to whose mind, at sight of the scorn with which his father was treated, the thought, "So they will treat you in the future," penetrated like a lightning flash.*j*

Foreign Interference in Sweden

It had been the constant policy of France to maintain her superiority in the councils of Stockholm, in opposition to Russia and England; and for several years the Swedish court might be called a battle-field on which these foreign powers contended for the mastery; not by shedding blood, but in trying, by secret intrigues and various means of corruption, to countermine each other's projects. According as these clandestine schemes succeeded, the hat or the cap party alternately prevailed; the king, either from want of firmness or motives of expediency, adhering sometimes to the one and sometimes to the other.

It was the preponderance of French agency that had hurried Sweden into the late unfortunate war, in which she was exposed not only to defeats, but to an oppressive load of expenses, estimated at £3,500,000, which the paltry subsidies of her ally contributed but little to reduce. Of the annual grants promised by France, a large sum remained due; and it was by threatening to withhold payment of these arrears that she contrived so long to maintain her ascendency in the Swedish diet. At length it was officially announced

GUSTAVUS III
(1746–1792)

that, if the court of Versailles did not speedily execute its engagements, a British minister would be received at Stockholm. During the Seven Years' War, no envoy from that country had been admitted, in consequence of the league with Prussia; but now Sir John Goodricke was despatched in that capacity, and through his co-operation with the Russian ambassador the caps became the triumphant party. The effect of this change was the conclusion of a new treaty of amity and commerce (1776) between these three states respectively, in which it was stipulated that the subjects of each should enjoy in their several kingdoms, ports, and havens, all the reciprocal advantages and immunities granted to the most favoured nations. France, after ten years of intrigue and a vast sacrifice of blood and treasure, thus beheld her primary object thwarted, and the political supremacy for which she had struggled, monopolised by her enemies. But neither the loss of her influence, nor the new combination of power against her, could eradicate her desire of dominating over Sweden.

The duke de Choiseul, then minister for foreign affairs, was determined to reassert her ascendency at all hazards. Having failed in one project, he invented another, and sought to govern under the name of Frederick Adolphus. The scheme was at once daring and ingenious, embracing the bold design of rendering the king absolute, and restoring to the crown all the prerogatives it had lost. Louis XV had endeavoured to implicate the Swedes in the war between Russia and the Porte; but as the sovereign was entirely dependent on the estates, which were then swayed by the party adverse to the interests of France, it became necessary to attempt a change in the constitution. The prospect of augmented power, and the influence of the queen, prevailed with his majesty to favour the enterprise of the French minister. The duke de Choiseul so far carried his point as to obtain the predominance in the diet of the hat or royalist party; but the more difficult task still remained: to procure the sanction of the diet to any proposal for subverting the constitution, particularly as the suggestion of such an alteration in that assembly was declared to be high treason.

As a last effort, the partisans of France made a secret proposal that force should be used to subvert the constitution of Sweden; but the moderation of Adolphus Frederick would not allow him to countenance that experiment. This obstacle, however, was speedily removed by the death of that excellent prince (February 12th, 1771), and the completion of the scheme begun under the father was accomplished by the bold and artful policy of the son.

GUSTAVUS III AND THE REVOLUTION OF 1772

Gustavus III, who next ascended the throne, was then in France, having undertaken a journey to that country with a view to obtain the performance of her pecuniary engagements. The acquisition of the regal dignity gave an unexpected success to the negotiation. A promise was obtained from the French court to pay Sweden 1,500,000 livres annually, and to furnish the means of supporting the French party at the ensuing diet. Count Scheffer, who had been despatched to Paris to communicate the intelligence of his late majesty's death, had the address, by representing to Louis XV the deplorable situation to which the finances of the kingdom were reduced by the withholding of payment of the subsidies so long due, to procure an order for immediately liquidating a considerable portion of the arrears.[l]

King Gustavus III made his entry into Stockholm on May 30th, 1771, amidst the acclamations of his people. After the reign of two German mock-kings, he was the first monarch who was a native of the country and a Swede at heart, and who spoke to his Swedish subjects in their mother tongue. He was, moreover, condescending and eloquent as no sovereign of that country had been within the memory of living man.

The diet assembled on the 13th of June. "It is the proud ambition of my life," thus the king addressed the estates, "to be the first citizen of a free nation. Not in pomp, nor in absolute power, but in concord and love, does the happiness of a people consist." But the diet did as all its predecessors had done. A scandalous quarrel between the hats, who ruled the nobility, and the caps, who dominated the other three estates, surged to and fro through eight months of tumult and clamour — a spectacle enacted as if by command, to exhibit once more to the whole world the hideous disorder of a commonwealth corroded through and through by the spirit of faction, and which was turned to account by skilful pens to prophesy through the press that Sweden would share the fate of Poland, unless she had timely recourse to the saving standard of monarchy. At the beginning of 1772, a Stockholm paper which had a wide circulation proclaimed: "It is time for us to think of the morrow. We are menaced by the fate of Poland, but we may find a Gustavus Adolphus even yet. What is to blame for the unhappy fate of Poland? The mutability of the law, the perpetual abasement of the power of the crown, with its inevitable consequence, the intermeddling of powerful neighbours in home affairs. Sweden is safe from such a doom as long as we do not prove false to our king and country; we have an ancient country to defend, and a great king to save. Fellow citizens! If the memory of Gustavus Adolphus still lives in your hearts, oh turn to his grave! From his ashes a voice goes forth that cries to each one of you, 'The hour is come at last!'"

After eight months of offensive brawling, the estates had at length got the new act of security into shape; and the king was to be crowned on May

STATE COACH OF GUSTAVUS III

29th, after it was signed. But while the caps were revelling in the proud consciousness of victory over the hats, the king was laying the mine which was to blow them all up. With his brothers, Princes Charles and Frederick Adolphus, and some enterprising officers of the army, among whom Colonel Sprengporten and Captain Hellichius were conspicuous, he had concerted the plan which was put into execution on August 12th, 1772, when the last-named officer paraded the three hundred men who formed the garrison of the fortress of Christianstad in Skåne, and read out a manifesto repudiating allegiance to the "so-called estates of the kingdom" because they had trodden law and justice underfoot, and had given the nation over to misery and famine, and the king's majesty to shame and dishonour. "The way is open, brave Swedes!" — such were the concluding words of the proclamation — "so long as our king and country do not receive their due, each one of us will rather die than lay down his arms. Come to us, convince yourselves of the sincerity of our intentions, and then make common cause with us." According to a preconcerted arrangement, the first person to get wind of this insurrection was Prince Charles, who was at Karlskrona, and who promptly collected five regiments to save the king from a pretended conspiracy, which was supposed to be impending over him and the constitution.

While the secret committee at Stockholm was endeavouring to quell the tumult by issuing tardy orders, the king played the *ingénu* with frigid composure, drew embroidery patterns for ladies of the court, went to the opera on the evening of the 18th of August, and afterward held a brilliant reception at the palace, jested and trifled, like the most simple-minded of mortals. On the morning of the 19th, he mounted his horse, rode to the armoury, collected the guards who were preparing to take their turn on duty, and led them in person to the palace. In the guard-room he made an affecting speech to the officers of the troops just coming on duty, and those about to go off, and concluded by asking them whether they were willing to support the enterprise he had taken in hand, for the good of his country and the deliverance of himself and all good Swedes from further oppression at home and abroad, and to take an oath to that effect to his majesty the king alone. All but two of his hearers took the oath; the king tied a white handkerchief round his left arm, and the officers followed his example. Orders were immediately issued for surrounding the hall of the council of state with a guard, which should allow no one in or out. The king then paraded the assembled troops, repeated what he had already said to the officers: the men hailed it with applause, and cried, "God save Gustavus III!"

As it had been in front of the palace, so it was in the city when the king rode through the streets, his drawn sword in his hand, bowing graciously to right and left; troops and citizens alike greeted him with a storm of cheers. The secret committee dispersed in haste; the council of state never stirred; while the king distributed powder and shot among the soldiers, and posted cannon in front of the palace, on the bridges, and at the city gates, with gunners beside them with lighted matches in their hands. All the administrative colleges and the admiralty had done homage already, when the king received, first, the new oath of fealty from the whole body of magistrates, in the guild hall, and, then, at noon, the congratulations of the foreign ambassadors, whom he had invited to dinner at the palace. In a couple of hours, and without shedding a single drop of blood, he had overthrown a government of hireling ranters and craven praters who did not venture to oppose him by so much as a word; and on the 20th he assembled all the citizens of Stockholm, in order that he might take the royal oath of fidelity to his people, and receive the oath of allegiance from them. The final act of the revolution followed next day, when the king received the estates in the assembly hall of the diet, round which the grenadiers and cannon were ranged on every side, and after administering a sharp rebuke to the spirit of faction by which Sweden had hitherto been distracted and disgraced, caused a new constitution, consisting of fifty-seven articles, to be read — a constitution that bore not the slightest resemblance to that of 1720, which he had sworn to respect, but nevertheless accorded well with his promise to establish no form of despotism. For, in substance, the new fundamental law of the state, which the estates accepted without debate and with touching unanimity, established a monarchy limited by wise laws imposed by itself.

The main provisions of the new constitution were as follows: (1) The estates of the kingdom to subsist as before; no new laws to be made nor old laws repealed without their concurrence (Art. 40); but the king alone to determine when and where the diet shall assemble (Art. 38); the estates to concern themselves solely with the matters submitted to them by the king (Art. 49); and no diet to last longer than three months (Art. 46). (2) The king to appoint the councillors of state, who are responsible to him alone; the councillors to advise him in matters in which he shall confer with them (Art. 4); but to have no more than a consultative voice, and the decision to rest with the king alone (Art. 8). (3) The king to have the prerogative of concluding armistices, peace, and offensive and defensive alliances (Art. 6); likewise the right of waging a defensive war on his own absolute authority (Art. 45); an offensive war, only with the consent of the estates (Art. 48). (4) The existing taxes to remain in force until new ones have been agreed upon (Art. 46); in the event of war, the king to be at liberty to take any measures conducive to the good of the state, particularly in the matter of levying taxes. (5) The supreme command of the forces by land and sea to pertain to the king alone.

At six-and-twenty the nephew of Frederick the Great had given proof of an unusual combination of prudence and energy, and those who had held no methods beneath them in their attacks on the king and his party, could not fairly complain of his duplicity and breach of faith. The factions had raged together, using the dungeon, the rack, and the headsman's axe against all who would have put an end to the heinous corruption of the body politic by strengthening the monarchy; the monarch who broke their dominion needed only to show his weapons, only to draw his sword, and the cowardice that waits upon an evil conscience did the rest. A couple of arrests of a few hours duration was the whole extent of the force required for the victory of the 19th of August.[n]

In a few years Gustavus is said to have repented of his liberality in regard to the constitution. That his powers were more limited than he intended is probably true; but they were larger than pleased such people as were in the interest of the Russian empress. He always looked with anxiety towards the east. In 1777, he paid a formal visit to Catherine II, whose intentions respecting him he was desirous to fathom; but she was impenetrable; and though he was magnificently entertained, and, in return, acceded to the armed neutrality, there was no good-will between them. She ever regretted the decline of her influence over a kingdom which she had been accustomed to regard in the light of a province; the other, aware of the sentiment and apprehensive of future intrigues, could not assume a cordiality which he did not feel.[b]

Gustavus, as Schlosser[q] says, had at last introduced law and order into Sweden; but otherwise he did more for court festivals, masked balls, theatres, architectural structures, and a French genre of literature, on which enormous sums were wasted, than for the benefit of the people, and he even imposed greater restrictions on the press than those existing under the oligarchy he had overturned. In the middle of the 18th century, the Swedish masons had discovered that the English masonry, which had found its way in among them, was too simple and humble; and they longed for greater splendour and pomp, secrets and elaborations. The fantastic king endeavoured to supply these supposed needs by working out a new Swedish system, made up from the genuine masonry and what was understood by the term "Rosicrucianism," but in particular from the system of Clermont; and in this creation the writings and teachings of the mystic Swedenborg may not have been without their effect.[p]

From the year 1777 Gustavus entered on a path which Catherine II must have been pleased to see him tread; and she therefore did everything in her power to encourage him in his folly. He strove to imitate her splendour, without being possessed of her means, and wished, like her, to become a patron and protector of the fine arts. In reference to the empress of Russia, indeed, Gustavus III of Sweden played no very honourable part. He condescended to accept her presents, and received her acts of politeness with gratitude, and afterwards wished to play the hero and measure his strength with hers.

If we ascribe ever so much of the reproaches thrown upon the king to intrigues and to the calumnies of that portion of the high nobility which was humbled in 1772, still his extravagance on his journeys and in fêtes and balls, operas and plays, jousting and ostentation, with the arts and artists, was proof enough that the proceeds of his hateful brandy monopoly, which his extravagance had impelled him to make in 1775, would not long suffice to meet those deficiencies which his waste and extravagance had caused in the finances of the kingdom. *q*

RUSSIAN WARS OF GUSTAVUS III

The treaties which Sweden formed with the Porte, though chiefly designed for commercial objects, also gave umbrage to the empress, who wished to engross the wealth, no less than the power, of the North. When, in 1787, the sultan declared war against her, Gustavus did the same, without consulting the diet. That war was not agreeable to the nation, still less to that portion of it in the interests of Russia — the nobles and leading burghers who were pensioned by Catherine. Even the moderate of all parties were dissatisfied with the power thus claimed by the king; but the armaments sailed. While the land forces reduced several fortresses in Russian Finland, a fleet of twenty sail, under the duke of Södermanland, the king's brother, appeared off Kronstadt, and threw St. Petersburg itself into consternation. The reduction of Fredrikshamn, which may be called one of the outworks of the Russian capital, was the great object of Gustavus; but to his inexpressible mortifica-

EMMANUEL SWEDENBORG, SWEDISH
PHILOSOPHER

(1688–1772)

tion, many of his officers refused to march any farther, alleging as the reason that, by the Swedish constitution, they could not join in a war which the nation had not sanctioned. In vain did he remonstrate; in vain arrest the officers, and send them to be tried at Stockholm: their example influenced the rest, and he was compelled to suspend his operations. His disquietude was increased by the hostilities of the Danes, who, at the call of the empress their ally, invaded Sweden, penetrated into Vestergötland, and laid siege to Gothenburg. The result might have been more serious had not England, Holland, and Prussia, ever intent on the balance of European power, forced the two kings of Denmark and Sweden to sign a truce.

That Gustavus should be incensed with this failure of his hopes was natural; and he determined to set at rest the dispute as to his right of making peace or war, by wresting from the estates its formal recognition. The measures which he submitted were embodied in the Act of Security, and included some other declarations which he wished to be made. By the three inferior orders the act was sanctioned; but the nobles withheld their consent. He then contended that, as the bill was not legislative but merely declaratory, and had been received by three-fourths of the orders, it would have the force of law if signed by the president, without the consent of the nobles. The president concurred in this view of the case, and signed it.

With his increased prerogatives, or rather, with their amplified declaration, Gustavus now hoped to push the war against Russia with new vigour. In the first campaign, the fortune of the war was nearly balanced, both in Finland and on the deep. In the next, the advantage was manifestly on the side of Sweden. In one naval action he captured or destroyed forty-two vessels of the enemy. Both parties, being deserted by their allies, inclined for peace; and it was concluded in 1790, in the camp near the bank of the Kymmene. They restored their conquests and their prisoners, so that things remained exactly as they were before the war. In two years Russia and Turkey agreed to articles of pacification. That portentous event, the French Revolution, made all Europe hasten towards a reconciliation, that the progress of the new power might be watched and resisted.

From the first appearance of that change, the chivalry of Gustavus induced him to propose some magnificent design for the benefit of the French royal family. He was also anxious for the general interest of thrones; and he was easily persuaded to become the head of a European coalition against principles and measures which struck at the root of all security. With a large army of Swedes and Russians, he was to land in Normandy and march at once on Paris: on the south, France was to be invaded by the Spaniards; while, in the east, the Austrians, the Sardinians, and other allies were to be equally active. These combined operations were to be directed by Gustavus who, in conjunction with the emperor Leopold, was adopting the most effectual measures for success, when Leopold paid the debt of nature, in less than a month after the signature of the treaty. In a fortnight more, the king himself was assassinated at a ball.

TRAGIC END OF GUSTAVUS III

The author of the deed, Anckarström, was traced, arrested, tried, and executed; but he had accomplices who did not suffer the extreme penalty, and of whom some were nominally punished. This circumstance, coupled with the little zeal shown for his memory by his brother, the duke of Södermanland (regent during the minority of his son, Gustavus IV), and with other events, caused the Swedes themselves to believe that the nearest of his kinsmen were privy to the deed; that the Jacobins of Paris had no participation in it; and that the discontented nobles were equally innocent of it. It may be, however, that all these parties were, more or less, implicated in it; and that the duke, seeing the agitation of men's minds, placed himself at the head of the movement, though he directed its operations unseen.

Connected with this tragedy are some facts given by Laing in his *Tour in Sweden:* "The assassin Anckarström appears to have had no injuries to avenge, to have been no political or religious fanatic, no madman, but simply a cold-blooded murderer, who had miscalculated the political position or wishes of those who would gain by his crime, and the circumstances on which he had relied for his escape and their protection and secret favour. He shot the king at a masquerade in the Opera House, about midnight, on the 16th of March, 1792." In a recent Swedish publication the following anecdote is given, which points out the direction public suspicion has taken: When the king felt himself wounded, his first care was to send his confidential page

De Besche to communicate the event to his brother, the duke of Södermanland; probably, says the writer, to ascertain how deeply wounded the fraternal heart would be by the tidings. The duke's court establishment had
supped and retired at an early hour, as usual, and his chamberlain, who slept
in the anteroom, wished to prevent De Besche from going into the duke's
sleeping apartments, as his royal highness had long before retired to rest.
De Besche, having the king's orders, persisted in going in, and found the
duke, not undressed and in bed, but arrayed in his full state uniform as high
admiral — his blue riband on, his sword and feathered hat in readiness on a
stool beside him — with wax candles lighted on the tables and sitting on a

ADOLF FREDERICK MUNCK, FRIEND OF
GUSTAVUS III OF SWEDEN

(1749-1831)

sofa, awaiting, as the writer expresses
it, the calls of providence. Such suspicions are often adopted, because they
solve circumstances not otherwise ex-
plicable, and because the situation and
character of the individual admit the
possibility or probability of his guilt.
The king had long been married without issue, and his brother was considered heir to the crown. The birth of
Gustavus' son, on the 1st of November,
1778, put an end to prospects reckoned
upon as a certainty. The peculiarity
of this position might give rise to the
suspicion; and the subsequent actions
of the duke furnishing nothing to refute
and something to confirm it, the demoralised state, also, of the Swedish
court rendering nothing evil incredible,
the suspicion still attaches to this personage.

He was regent during his nephew's
minority, and one act of his government marks his character. His late
brother's personal friend, a general
Armfeld, was condemned, while absent, for treason; and the countess Mag-
dalena Rudensköld — a young lady of great beauty, the daughter of an old
friend of his father, brought up at the court of his own sister, and who it was
known had rejected his licentious addresses — was condemned as an accomplice in the treason of her friend or lover, General Armfeld, and punished, by
the duke's special command, with the pillory and imprisonment for life in the
common house of correction. The young king, on coming of age, restored the
parties to their honours and estates. Suspicion can scarcely injure such a
character. Many small circumstances during the minority and subsequent
seventeen years of Gustavus IV's reign indicate the will of this uncle, if a safe
and unsuspected way could be found, to seize the crown. During the regency
inquiries were secretly made of the physicians, it is stated, with regard to the
mental capacity and faculties of the young king; as Gustavus displayed in
infancy much of that singularity of character which marked his future life.
Absurd reports were also industriously circulated that he was not the offspring of the late king, but of an adulterous *amour* of the queen with a Colonel
Munk, to whom he bore a resemblance. It was even whispered that the duke

[1792 A.D.]

of Södermanland had incontrovertible proofs of the facts in his hands, but from motives of delicacy did not produce them, and rather renounced the right to the crown than unveil the family dishonour. English travellers of repute, such as Wraxall, have not scrupled to adopt and circulate this tale, evidently got up to serve a court intrigue. Subsequent events sufficiently proved that the duke of Södermanland had no such delicacy or consideration for his family honour in his character. On this subject we will not decide. Let the reader draw his own inference.

The character of Gustavus was not without greatness. On his death-bed (he lingered twelve days), he evidently attributed the deed to a political conspiracy; begged that the authors might not be punished; and expressed a hope, that now, when he was about to leave all sublunary things, there would be a reconciliation of parties. Heroic, enterprising, a great patron of literature, science, and the arts, he would have been idolised, but for his selfish ambition and the mixture of duplicity and violence with which he restored arbitrary power.[b]

CHAPTER XIII

DENMARK IN THE EIGHTEENTH AND NINETEENTH CENTURIES

WE have seen that in 1699 the reigning king of Denmark, Frederick IV, was tempted by the youth of Charles XII of Sweden to invade the dominions of his ally the duke of Holstein. Frederick was little aware of the spirit of his opponent. We have seen how Charles, determined to strike at once at his enemy's capital, lost no time in crossing the narrow sea between Sweden and Denmark, and in investing the city of Copenhagen; how the inhabitants in alarm appealed to the humanity of the young monarch; and that the result was the speedy conclusion of peace, with the payment of a sum of money to the Swedes. Taught by this lesson, the Danish government remained neutral in the following years, when the course of events led Charles and his army into Poland and Saxony. After the defeat of Charles at the battle of Pultowa, in the year 1709, and his subsequent flight into Turkey, the king of Denmark eagerly embraced the opportunity of renewing hostilities with Sweden, and invaded both Holstein in the south and the province of Skåne to the north.

Skåne was badly provided with troops, but it had officers trained in one of the best military schools of the age, and a peasantry full of national antipathy to the Danes. The result was a spirited attack on the invading army, followed by its defeat and precipitate flight into Denmark. The war was then carried on with alternate success in different parts — in Pomerania, in Holstein, and in Norway; until at last the military career of Charles XII came unexpectedly to a close, in the end of 1718. Some time afterwards negotiations were opened between Sweden and Denmark, under the mediation of England, and ended in 1720 in a definitive treaty of peace, concluded at Stockholm. It was then that Sweden lost all the advantages gained since the Peace of Westphalia, and that George I of England as elector of Han-

412

over, Prussia, and Peter the Great shared with Denmark the spoil of Sweden. From that time no danger threatened Denmark from the side of its neighbour, though the cessation of the rivalry was more perceptible in the decline of Sweden than in the progress of Denmark. The Danish government had now ample experience of the sacrifices attendant on war, and of the expediency, to a state of such limited power, of avoiding political collisions. It consequently adopted a peace policy, to which it has almost ever since endeavoured to adhere.[b]

A narrow-minded and gloomy puritanism held Christian VI (1730–1746) aloof from his people, who never reposed confidence in him; while the extravagant tastes of his queen, Sophia Magdalena, threw the finances of the kingdom into disorder, and a militia law, enacted in 1733, rendered the lot of the peasantry even more melancholy than it had hitherto been under the constant oppression of aristocratic rule. Nevertheless, his reign was not wholly unmeritorious. Among the services it rendered to the country, we may mention the revival of the University of Copenhagen, which had lapsed into utter decay; the reform of the higher schools, and the establishment of national and city schools; the institution of a bank of issue, exchange, and loan; a fire insurance society, and a general widows' insurance fund; the introduction of factories and manufactures; the promotion of trade; and, more especially, an extremely active solicitude for the efficiency of the navy, which was doubled by Count Danneskjold Samsoe and Admiral Suhm (father of the historian), and raised to thirty ships of the line and sixteen frigates.

Under the jovial and amiable King Frederick V (1746–1766), a complete transformation took place. The court flung aside its monkish garb, and gave the people in town and country liberty to sing and dance and indulge in the old traditional popular sports, which had been prohibited in the previous reign. The Copenhagen theatre restored to the stage the comedies in which Ludvig Holberg, Denmark's first national poet (1684–1754), had held up the mirror to his fellow countrymen. Count Johann Hartwig Ernst von Bernstorff, an admirable minister, established friendly relations with Sweden, steered his country prudently through the perils and temptations of the Seven Years' War, and had the good fortune to escape, by the sudden dethronement of Peter III, the war with Russia which would otherwise have been inevitable. This minister looked upon the fostering of national industries as his peculiar task, and actually stimulated them to a certain degree of artificial prosperity, by prohibiting the importation of one hundred and fifty kinds of merchandise. More beneficial results accrued from a commercial policy which opened the Mediterranean to the Danish flag, hitherto excluded from those waters, by means of commercial treaties with Algiers, Morocco, Tunis, Tripoli, Genoa, Naples, and the sultan. An East India company carried on a very profitable trade with the East Indies, while the West Indian trade began to flourish only after the monopoly of the company which exploited the sugar plantations in Santa Cruz had been abolished. The king brilliantly distinguished himself as a Mæcenas of learning and the fine arts, taking not Bernstorff alone, but Count Moltke and Eric Pontoppidan, the learned vice-chancellor of the University of Copenhagen, into council in the matter. From Germany he brought the pulpit-orator Johann Andreas Cramer, and his friend the poet Klopstock, the naturalists Oeder and Kratzenstein, the pedagogue Basedow, and the historian Johann Heinrich Schlegel. Karsten Niebuhr, the father of the historian, made his famous travels in Egypt and Arabia at the expense of the Danish government. The academy for the sons of noblemen at Sorö, which had been closed since 1665, was again opened by the help of a munificent donation from the poet Holberg, and became the scene of the labours of a large body of distinguished Danish scholars. A society of the fine arts came into being at Copenhagen, a Norwegian scientific society at Trondhjem. The king founded the Frederick hospital at Copenhagen, and Oeder laid out a botanic garden in the vicinity of the town. In his House of Education the king had two hundred and sixty boys, the sons of poor parents, brought up and taught, free of charge, between the ages of five and sixteen.

From the economic magazine which Pontoppidan was allowed to edit free of censorship, from 1757 to 1764, went forth the impulse to that intellectual

FREDERICK V
(1723-1766)

movement which never rested till, towards the end of the century, it had completed the work of emancipating the peasantry, to which even Frederick V lent no direct aid by statutory reforms. Thus the Danish monarchy, which had been absolute *de jure* for more than a hundred years, had only exerted its absolute authority within strictly defined limits, and had by no means adequately fulfilled its most sacred duty, the protection of the weak and wrongfully oppressed. Open conflict between the monarchy and the aristocracy was avoided by a tacit compromise of which eight hundred thousand peasant serfs were the victims — slaves, as a competent Danish judge says of this period, whose lot was to be born to suffer without guilt, to labour without reward, to roll the stone of Sisyphus, to draw water in the vessel of the Danaides, and to endure the thirst of Tantalus. And yet the experiments made by certain magnanimous noblemen of German descent, in the emancipation of their own serfs, had been crowned with such brilliant success that every thinking landowner ought to have followed their example for the sake of his own interest. Conspicuous among these few was Count Hans von Rantzau, who, in 1739, abolished serfdom and villein service on his magnificent state of Ascheberg, on the banks of the Lake of Ploen; converted his peasantry into a hereditary tenantry; and in the year 1766 was able to demonstrate — as the result of twenty-seven years' experience — that the peasants had thereby become well-to-do, industrious, and well-conducted members of society, while, in spite of all his outlay on new houses, draught cattle, etc., he himself drew a far larger income than before.

Enthusiasm for peasant emancipation, in theory, had already become the fashion in enlightened circles by the time that, after a long illness, Frederick V died (January 14th, 1766), and was succeeded by his son Christian VII, who was then seventeen years of age, and one of the most singular beings ever fated to wear a crown. Endowed with striking beauty of feature, great physical strength and mental vivacity, he early became a favourite with those who hold that felicitous inspirations betoken intellectual maturity, that eloquent conversation in, it may be, one or two foreign languages argues a basis of solid learning, and who take certain courtly graces as evidence of thorough good breeding.   But, even when he was twelve years old, the best of his tutors, Reverdil of Waatland, noted an uncanny contrariety of temper in him: variable as an April day, he alternated between wild spirits and profound moroseness, vehement desire and indolent weakness of will.   Vain to foppery, as *quasi*-geniuses are apt to be, he desired to shine in every possible sphere; but his ambition aimed no higher than that of an actor who is sure of applause.   As crown prince, it was his greatest grief that he would one day be king: a vague presentiment warned him that a king must work, and work of every kind was abhorrent to him.   When Christian actually became king, Reverdil indulged in the illusion which he has recorded in the words, " I was pleased to observe how my seventeen-year-old pupil consoled himself for the misfortune of being king, by hopes of the good he could do."   Christian VII, however, did nothing that duty required of him, and everything that was unworthy of a king.

In the hope of diverting him from the undignified courses to which he had abandoned himself in the company of worthless associates, the ministers, who still retained the offices they had held under his father, married him to Caroline Matilda, sister of George III of England, a lovely and sprightly princess, fifteen years of age, who bestowed her hand upon him on the 8th of November, 1766.   The marriage brought about no reformation, and the follies the king perpetrated day and night suggested to the ministers the idea of improving his mind by foreign travel.   He started on his tour in May, 1768,

JOHANN FRIEDRICH STRUENSEE

(1737-1772)

accompanied by his bosom friend, Count Holck; but after recklessly spending a vast amount of money in London and Paris, he came back in January, 1769, as sick in body and mind as when he went.

THE ADMINISTRATION OF STRUENSEE

Christian, however, brought with him a young physician-in-ordinary, Johann Friedrich Struensee by name, whose acquaintance he had made at Altona.   To the amazement of the whole court, this man effected an immediate change in the situation.   The king and queen became a united couple; the former was all at once as gentle and yielding as he had been harsh and intractable; while the latter overcame the aversion with which misery had inspired her, governed her husband, and gave her heart to the man who had taught her to love him, that through her he might rule the king and the country.

Equally indispensable to them both, Struensee was appointed the king's reader and the queen's private secretary, in the spring of 1770.   He lived in the palace, and followed the royal pair like their shadow on every excursion they made; the queen had no pleasure nor life apart from him, and abandoned herself to her passion as freely as though no cloud could ever dim the smiling heaven of her first love.   On the pleasure tour which the inseparable trio made in Holstein in the summer of 1770, she seemed absolutely intoxicated — she had often forgotten that she was a queen, but now she forgot that she was a woman.   She appeared in public in male attire; she was perpetually to be seen at the side of her beloved Struensee, on horseback or afoot; and, in the autumn of the same year, the latter suddenly dropped the part of a favoured courtier to grasp the helm of the state.   By an order of the 13th of September, the worthy minister Bernstorff was dismissed with the utmost suddenness; and on the following day an edict was published, which was nothing less than the announcement of a complete breach with previous usage and precedent.   The royal edict of September 14th, 1770, abolished the censorship of the press, and granted it unrestricted freedom — an unexampled proceeding, which was received in Denmark with blank amazement and greeted with a veritable chorus of acclamation by Liberals everywhere.   Voltaire celebrated it in a poetical letter to his majesty the king of Denmark. On the 24th of September, the press edict was followed by the repeal of the oppressive tax upon salt, and this in its turn by the abolition of the so-called "third holy days" at Christmas, Easter, and Whitsuntide, and of six other church festivals.   On the same day, a strict regulation was issued to check the abuses practised in connection with reversions of offices by the appointment of unfit persons; on the 10th of November, the administrative colleges were admonished to confine themselves to exhaustice preliminary deliberations, and to leave the ultimate decision in all affairs to the king; and on the 31st of December, the duty of observing laconic brevity and unreserved candour in the proposals and arguments brought under discussion was enjoined upon them.   A more decisive blow was aimed at the existing system by the abolition (December 27th) of the privy council, which was superseded by government by the king's cabinet.   On the same day, a whole series of impediments to marriage, some of them insurmountable and some only to be set aside by money payments, were simply abrogated.   Thus, the latter half of the memorable year of 1770 ended with a quantity of profitable innovations, such as no Danish government had ever bestowed upon the country in so short a space of time.

The original author of all these measures was Struensee, whom the king followed blindly.   He was a man who saw, with the unbiassed vision of a foreigner, all the rotten places in the state of Denmark, and could make the saving incision in the right spot with the steady hand of a practised surgeon.   He was not a creative genius: his ideas were neither comprehensive nor particularly novel; in everything that he wrote and did we recognise, now the type of Prussian absolutism, now the school of French enlightenment and the educational wisdom of Rousseau.   His method, too, suffers from grievous defects.   We must not blame the reformer of thirty-three too severely for the heedless haste with which he often acted; his power was wholly based on the love of the weak wife of an utterly worthless king, and he had need of haste to work while it was yet day.   Far worse faults were: his obvious lack of any homogeneous plan; the unnecessary way in which he provoked the susceptibilities of the Danes, even in matters in which no harm could have been done by considering them; and the fact that, at the height of his power, he did all he could to put weapons in the hands of his enemies, and nothing to protect himself against a sudden reverse.   In such matters as the reform of

[1771 A.D.]

old abuses, the invention of simple and workable methods, the utilisation of the best material at his command, the thoughtful consideration of points which invariably elude the notice of an unreasoning bureaucracy, and the superintendence of all those things which a paternal monarchy, in the best sense of the word, regards as falling within the sphere of its duty, Struensee displayed an acuteness of judgment and a reforming energy such as Denmark had never known, and for which the country owes him a debt of gratitude to this day. He could not have taken the vigorous line he took with such intrepidity, except by the help of the careless optimism which manifested itself in all his actions: but this very optimism blinded him to perils of his own making, and thus sealed his doom.

The next year, 1771, besides witnessing the dismissal of a number of court and government officials, brought forth a salutary regulation of the forced service of the peasants, limiting it to a certain number of days; the better enforcement of the liability of aristocratic debtors; the elevation of the Danish and German court of chancery (Justizkanzlei) to the rank of college, with an admirable staff; a municipal organisation for Copenhagen, with Count Holstein as chief president; considerable economies at court, due to the abolition of useless posts and the reduction or confiscation of pensions; a reform of the public finances by the erection of a college of finance, which Oeder, the botanist, regulated and reduced to a uniform system, and which was fortunate in securing the valuable services of Councillor of Justice (Justizrath) Karl August Struensee, the minister's elder brother; the institution of a Superior and a Municipal Court of Justice at Copenhagen, which introduced into the administration of justice in the capital a uniformity and promptitude which had long been sadly lacking; the founding of a foundling hospital; the repeal of all the penalties hitherto attached to the parentage of illegitimate children and the laws prohibiting marriage between persons guilty of adultery; the numbering of houses in Copenhagen; arrangements for the cleaning and lighting of streets, etc. Struensee had brought about all these reforms, partly on his own initiative and partly at the suggestion of his confidential agents, without himself assuming any rank higher than that of master of requests. On the 14th of July, 1771, however, he proceeded to have himself appointed minister of the privy cabinet, with authority to draw up orders in council, without the royal signature, which should have equal validity with those issued under the king's own hand — a privilege which no Danish minister had up to that time enjoyed, and one which was incompatible with the old act of Succession of 1665. A week later Struensee and his friend Enevold Brandt, the king's chamberlain, who had acted as the king's attendant during his minority, were raised to the rank of counts.

If we except the introduction of the lottery system, hitherto unknown in Denmark, we must upon consideration unreservedly allow that the new financial administration was the bright side of Struensee's rule; but, though it freed the country from debt and rid it of parasites, it raised up a host of enemies for its author. Numbers of officers of the court and government had lost place and preferment, salaries and pensions; hundreds of artisans had been deprived of work and wages by the abolition of state factories. He had now only to fall out with the army, to find himself defenceless against the indignation of the patrician families of Copenhagen, who were mortified by the new municipal organisation; against the fanaticism of the Lutheran zealots, who called down the vengeance of heaven on him for a free thinker and libertine; and against the profound grudge which the nobles bore the foreign upstart who had eclipsed and affronted them. A government which did not even take the trouble to publish Danish translations of edicts drawn up in German — a government of which the head laughingly avowed that he had no time to learn the Danish language — seemed in their eyes un-Danish and no better than foreign domination.

THE FALL OF STRUENSEE

When a government that is hated ceases to be feared, it is lost. For Struensee, the fatal moment came on the 24th of December, when the royal guards replied to an order of the king, directing that they should be disbanded and distributed among other regiments, by an armed mutiny, which ended, after scenes of gross public misdemeanour, in the dismissal of the men to their homes, by the terrified count, with bag and baggage and a bounty of three rix-dollars a piece. Nothing but armed intervention could have quelled the storm which broke forth against Struensee in the free press, and which an admonitory edict of the 7th of October had proved powerless to keep in check. The dismissal of the guards consequently meant nothing less than the disarmament of the court.

A conspiracy was promptly formed, with the queen-mother Juliana Maria, the crown prince Frederick, and his private secretary, the theologian Otto Guldberg, at its head; its executive instruments being Lieutenant-General Count Rantzau-Ascheberg, Commissary-General for War Beringskjold, Major-General von Eickstedt, and Colonel Köller — that is to say, the chiefs of that very armed force with which despotism can by no means do everything, and without which it can do nothing whatever. In the night between the 16th and 17th of January, 1772, Köller and Eickstedt were on guard at the castle, the former with the Falster regiment of infantry, the latter with the Zealand dragoons. A great masked ball had been held at Christianborg castle that evening; it was over by about two o'clock. At four the conspirators made their first move. The king was roused from his bed, and forced to sign orders for the arrest of the queen, Struensee, Brandt, and thirteen of their adherents. All the arrests were effected within a few hours; the populace welcomed the news with acclamation; the king rewarded, with orders, honours, and presents of money, the faithful servants who had saved the country; and the free press overwhelmed with a flood of invective the "monster" who, with his accomplices, now lay in fetters under lock and key.

At the trial, which was opened on the 20th of February by a special commission of inquiry, Struensee from the beginning manifested all the symptoms of utter breakdown. He confirmed the depositions which brought so heavy an indictment against his relations with the queen that silence or denial was hardly possible, by confessions which betrayed shocking meanness of spirit. How far above the wretched man did the unhappy queen tower, when, receiving in her prison at Kronborg the news of Struensee's confession, she declared with unexampled self-command that she took all the blame upon herself, for she had been the temptress! On April 28th, 1772, Struensee and Brandt were publicly beheaded; and Caroline Matilda, divorced by the king, was banished to Celle, where her short life came to an end on May 10th, 1775.

The new administration, of which Guldberg was the moving spirit, hastened to restore, as far as restoration was possible, everything that Struensee, to the great profit of the country, had abolished; and for the space of twelve years displayed the utmost zeal in refraining from anything that bore the remotest resemblance to reform. Not until the 14th of April, 1784, when the seventeen-year-old crown prince Frederick took the bold step of himself assuming the reins of government in the place of his imbecile father, dismissed Guldberg, and appointed Count Andreas Bernstorff, nephew of Count Johann Hartwig Bernstorff, to the head of the ministry, did Denmark rejoice in a government worthy and capable of wiping out the old score against the monarchy and of effecting the emancipation of the peasantry in all the dominions of the Danish crown. The abolition of the peasants' link with the soil and of villein service, the relief of the burdens on trade and corn and cattle, the conversion of the peasantry into free men and landed proprietors, first in Denmark proper and then in Schleswig and Holstein, was the work of a commission appointed by Count Bernstorff, of which Count Christian Reventlow was the most active member. Its edicts of the years 1787 and 1788 bear the same significance in the history of the agricultural population of Denmark as the resolutions of August 4th, 1789, bear in that of France, and the edicts of October 9th, 1807, and July 27th, 1808, in that of Prussia.c

DENMARK AND THE FRENCH REVOLUTION

A short time after [the war of 1788 between Russia and Sweden, in which Denmark was forced to take part as Russia's ally,] the French Revolution broke out, and soon had all Europe aflame. Denmark alone preserved a prudent neutrality under the wise direction of Andreas Peter Bernstorff, and did not let herself be moved by the brilliant promises of the other powers and their importunate requests to take part in the coalition against the French Republic, represented as the common enemy of Europe. This prudent and firm policy bore the most happy results.

ANDREAS PETER COUNT VON BERNSTORFF,
DANISH MINISTER

(1735-1797)

While blood was flowing in rivers over Europe, whole countries were scourged, and commerce, industry, and art were at a standstill, Denmark attained a high degree of prosperity and internal strength; and the government had the time and means to introduce many salutary reforms into the social structure, particularly in the direction of agrarian economy, which put the state in a position to support the great calamities that overtook her later on.

In these years of peace, when all the other maritime powers were implicated in the general war, Denmark's commerce reached an unparalleled height and development. England — who, thanks to her powerful navy, was in a position to protect her merchant marine — North America and Denmark shared the commerce of the world. There were agents in Copenhagen who had relations with every trading nation. Trade with the East Indies and China was so brisk that there were imported annually into Copenhagen commodities worth 5,000,000 rix-dollars; while business with the West Indies and the carrying of trade to the Mediterranean were equally lucrative. Commerce on the latter sea underwent a short interruption in 1797, when the bey of Tripoli took it upon himself to insult the Danish flag; but the

intrepid Steen Bille, after a fight between three Danish ships and seven
Tripolitan vessels, forced the bey to sue for peace, and secured the safety
of Danish commerce within his waters. Yet Denmark did not enjoy this
commercial prosperity and other advantages of peace, without undergoing
attacks and insults on the part of the belligerent powers. The French Republic acted in a notably arbitrary manner, which was surpassed only by proud
and powerful England. It took all the consummate tact of a Bernstorff,
whom even his own enemies could not refuse to admire, to keep peace, without
buying it at the price of the nation's dignity, or abandoning the political
policy she had still been able to adhere to. An important measure taken by
Bernstorff to secure the safety of Northern commerce, was the alliance between
Denmark and Sweden, which was concluded in 1794 and which undertook
to establish a common patrol within Northern waters, in order to protect
the Danish, Norwegian, and Swedish merchant marine against attacks by
the belligerent navies. But the able minister died in 1797; and his passing
drew tears from a whole nation which realised its irreparable loss.

It is doubtful, however, whether his wisdom could have dispelled the
threatening storm; for the time had come when the laws of nations were
trampled underfoot, and the most powerful states of Europe tried to surpass
each other in violence and injustice. During the wars of the Revolution,
England kept encroaching further and further upon the commercial liberty
of neutral nations, seeking especially to give a broad and hitherto-unheard-of
interpretation to the idea of contraband, which, if rigorously applied, would
have almost entirely destroyed Denmark's trade. In fact, while up to this
time it had been understood that by contraband of war were meant small-
arms, powder, cannon, and ammunition, England now tried to include in this
category meat, flour, and corn, challenging Denmark's right to bring these
commodities into France and other belligerent countries. France, in turn,
took similar steps with regard to neutral ships carrying on trade with England
and her colonies. Over this many difficulties arose, which the skilful negotiations of Andreas Peter von Bernstorff seemed to settle amicably. After
the minister's death, however, began the practice of convoying merchant
fleets with war vessels — a thing which Bernstorff had particularly abstained
from, in order to avoid collisions with England. The consequence was that
the latter country refused to recognise the right of war ships to protect commerce, and began hostilities by attacking and capturing the Danish frigate
Freia, which sought to prevent English cruisers from visiting a merchant
fleet to which it was acting as convoy (July 25th, 1800). To avoid other
hostilities for the moment, Denmark came to an agreement (August 29th,
1800) by which the Freia was restored to her, but she was obliged to refrain
from sending out escorts to merchant ships until the question at issue should
be settled by negotiation.

A short time after this, Russia, Sweden, and Prussia concluded a treaty
of armed neutrality, similar to one already arranged in 1780; and Denmark
was invited to join the alliance. Before the agreement with England, such
overtures would have been heartily welcomed by the Danish government,
which had on several former occasions proposed to Russia and Sweden a
league for the protection of the neutral flag. But just at this moment these
proposals were somewhat embarrassing; and it was only after long hesitation that the Danish government yielded to the threatening schemes of the
capricious czar Paul. It subscribed to the treaty, with certain reservations,
however, in order not to violate the agreement with England. But these
did not keep the latter from hostilities; two days before Denmark entered

[1801 A.D.]

into the neutral alliance (January 16th, 1801), England put an embargo on all Danish ships within English ports, and issued orders for the occupation of the Danish West Indies (January 14th, 1801).

The War with England

An English squadron of fifty-one ships, among which were twenty ships of the line, entered the Sound, under command of Admirals Parker and Nelson, in the month of March; and, although exposed to a raking fire from the fortress of Kronborg, it succeeded in passing the batteries uninjured, because it hugged the Swedish shore, where no preparations had been made to repulse the enemy. The reason of this neglect was the mutual distrust of the Danish and Swedish governments. The crown prince Frederick would have taken it in bad part if fortifications had been built on the Swedish shore of the Sound; and people would have said that Gustavus IV had his eye on a part of the customs of that waterway.

When the British fleet came in sight of Copenhagen, it separated into two divisions, of which one, under Nelson, pushed farther south, to attack the southern line of Danish fortifications; the other, under Parker, cruised between the island of Hven and the battery of the Three Crowns (*Tre Kroner*). Nelson's fleet was composed of twelve ships of the line, seven frigates, and nineteen smaller vessels, with twelve hundred cannon and a crew of about nine thousand men. The southern line of Danish defence — the only one they had to fight with — consisted of seven large low-decked ships, some smaller ones, a few prams, and two small frigates; the whole fitted with 620 guns, and a crew of scarcely five thousand men. The superiority of force was decidedly in favour of the enemy; and it consisted not only in the greater number of ships and guns, but also in that the British vessels were all under sail, while the Danish flotilla, with the exception of four small ships, was stationary. On Holy Thursday, the 2nd of April, 1801, at ten in the morning, a fierce battle began, which lasted with extreme fury for five or six hours. The Danish sailors fought with their hereditary bravery and, under the command of Olfert Fischer, upheld their former naval glory against Nelson, the favoured of victory, and his overwhelming force. The admiral's ship was badly damaged; and in the end could use but few of her guns. On the other side, Olfert Fischer, who was on board the *Dannebrog*, left that vessel when she caught fire in the midst of the battle, and transferred his flag to the *Holstein;* and afterwards, when the latter ship was riddled with shell and made useless, the Danish commander, although wounded, betook himself to the Tre Kroner battery, where he continued to direct the fight. The crew of the *Dannebrog*, commanded by Braun and afterwards by Lemming, continued to fight although the vessel was in flames; and it was not until a third of the men had been either killed or wounded, and all her guns, with the exception of three, put out of action, that the blazing ship was abandoned to the enemy. Among the low-deck ships, the *Prævestenen* especially distinguished herself. The brave Lassen defended her against two ships of the line, a frigate, and a brig, until she was reduced to a mere skeleton and had only two guns that could be served. Risbrich, on the deck of the *Wagrie*, fought none the less bravely against almost equally disproportionate forces. The young Villemoes, who commanded a floating battery in which he placed himself very close to the English admiral's ship, and fired several shots which hit her on the water-line, won Nelson's admiration, and immortalised himself in the memory of his countrymen.

When the battle had lasted for three hours, Admiral Parker gave Nelson the signal to retreat; but the latter took no notice of the order, and continued to fight for some hours. Meantime the southern line of defence was for the most part destroyed, while that on the north had scarcely suffered, and the majority of the English fleet was in a deplorable condition. Most of the vessels had lost their sails and yards, and the masts were so riddled with projectiles that they threatened at any moment to fall into the sea; besides, in the narrow strait with which the enemy were not familiar several of their ships had gone aground. Three of their most powerful ships of the line had drifted in front of the Tre Kroner, and one even stranded just opposite the battery, whose guns opened a deadly fire upon her. In these circumstances, Nelson sent a letter ashore saying that, if the Danes continued to fire, he would be compelled to burn the Danish ships which he had in his power, without even saving the crews. Whilst his messenger was executing his mission, the English admiral held a council of war to decide whether this was an opportune moment to attack with his least damaged ships the northern line of defence, which had not yet taken part in the action. But his officers were unanimously of the opinion that this would be impossible, and that the best thing to do was to retire; they must take advantage of the favourable wind then blowing to get out of the dangerous passage, where they were every moment in danger of going aground. After receiving Nelson's letter, the crown prince, who had not been well informed as to the details of the battle, sent an envoy under flag of truce, with full powers to conclude a preliminary armistice and pave the way for future negotiations.

Thus closed this sanguinary affair, so glorious for Denmark. Nelson rendered justice to the bravery of the Danes; and when he came on shore to conduct negotiations in person, he declared that, among the one hundred and five sanguinary battles in which he had taken part, that of Copenhagen was the bloodiest and fiercest. The Danes lost 1035 killed and wounded; the English, according to their own statement 1200; but there is no doubt that this figure should be much higher, since they admitted having lost 220 men on a single ship. The negotiations ended in a truce of fourteen weeks, during which Denmark agreed to take no active part in the armed neutrality. The czar Paul having been assassinated on March 25th, 1801, affairs took a new turn; for his son and successor, Alexander, abandoned the neutral league, and concluded a peace with England, to which Denmark also acceded.

Peace is Followed by a Second War

Danish commerce soon recovered from the blow which the war with England had dealt it. Trade with the East and West Indies flourished as in former days, and there was annually imported from North America merchandise to the value of 8,000,000 rix-dollars. As a consequence of the war with France and her allies, English commerce was considerably reduced, and neutral Denmark was the highway through which a large part of Europe was provided with colonial products. For this reason, navigation in the Sound and in the Eider canal was extraordinarily active during these years of war. About twelve thousand ships passed annually through the Sound, and about three thousand through the canal. But during this entire period the state had to support heavy burdens on account of the continental hostilities at the Danish frontier, which subjected it to great expense in keeping a body of troops in Holstein. At the dissolution of the German Empire, in

[1806-1807 A.D.]

1806, Holstein was relieved of its vassal duties to the emperor, and by patent of September 9th, 1806, was declared an inseparable part of the Danish monarchy.

Since 1720, with a few short intervals in 1780 and 1801, Denmark had enjoyed a peace which, especially in latter years, had had the most happy influence over the progress of the state and its internal development. This fortunate situation came to an end in 1807, when a series of calamities, mostly unforeseen and undeserved, fell upon Denmark and brought her to the verge of ruin. The Danish government had sought to maintain neutrality as long as possible; but in the midst of the violent struggle which was shaking all Europe, Denmark's geographical position made it impossible to remain neutral, and as she hesitated to pronounce for either of the parties, she was finally brought violently into the *mêlée*. Napoleon wished to shut all the continental ports to the English; and to attain this end, it was agreed between him and the emperor Alexander of Russia, in certain secret articles of the Treaty of Tilsit (July 9th, 1807), that Denmark should be asked to declare war against England if the latter power would not come to reasonable terms of peace with France. However, before overtures in this direction could be made to Denmark either by Russia or France, England opened hostilities by capturing some Danish ships and sending to the Sound a fleet of fifty-four vessels, including twenty-three ships of the line, and five hundred transports, under the command of Admiral Gambier. The latter demanded that the Danish fleet should be surrendered to him, "because" (he said) "the British government had been informed that it was about to be ceded to France for use against England." In case of refusal, he threatened to have recourse to force.

The Danish government had been several times, and from different sources, warned of England's meditated step; but by a singular blindness the minister of foreign affairs, Christian Bernstorff, had refused to take any note of the warnings; and, in consequence, no provision for defence had been made. The feelings of the citizens of Copenhagen and the few soldiers stationed in the city were, however, loyal; and they rose to enthusiasm when the popular prince Frederick arrived in hot haste from Holstein, on the 11th of August. They were sure that he would share the perils of the citizens and their common fate. But their hope was soon cruelly destroyed; at the end of one day the prince left for Holstein, to bring back, it was said, the troops stationed there — which was impossible, since the English had control of the sea and intercepted all marine communication. It was not thus that King Frederick III had defended Copenhagen, in 1658. The departure of the crown prince made a bad impression; and all the other members of the royal family likewise abandoned, one by one, a capital which seemed doomed to destruction. While these events were very discouraging, yet the citizens were ready to do all in their power. When the revolting demand of the English had been deliberately rejected, the latter landed, without resistance, at Vedbek, about 10 miles north of the capital, on the 10th of August, 1807. The corps which landed was commanded by General Cathcart. Little by little, reinforcements from north Germany brought it up to thirty thousand men. The militia, under Castenskjöld and Oxholm, tried to resist it near Kjöge; but these troops, inexperienced and ill-armed, without enough powder even for the few antiquated cannon they brought with them, could not stand up against the trained soldiers under Arthur Wellesley (Wellington). While several sections fought bravely, disorder soon seized upon the ranks of the militia, and the English scattered them with little difficulty, by a violent cavalry charge and a terrible fire from their numerous artillery. From the city itself several sorties were made, in which the citizen corps of light infantry guards, under F. C. Holstein, won glory and sanguinary laurels. The students maintained their old time reputation, and the gunners also fought with distinction in several encounters along the shore.

The city had been surrounded on the 18th of August; and, on the 2nd of September, began a terrible bombardment, which lasted three days. More than three hundred private houses, to say nothing of a large number of public buildings (including the magnificent church of Our Lady, with its high belfry), were reduced to ashes, and several hundred men killed or maimed. A continuation of the bombardment would have transformed the city into a mass of ruins, and it would have been impossible to repel the attack the English were preparing. The commander-in-chief, the aged General Peymann, therefore decided to sign a capitulation (September 7th, 1807), by the terms of which the fleet was turned over to the English, and the citadel of Frederickshavn was to be occupied by them for six weeks while the ships were being fitted out. The resistance having been entirely creditable considering the forces and existing circumstances, there was nothing dishonourable about the surrender. No help could be expected, since the English ships were cruising in the Little Belt and prevented the crossing of the Danish army from Holstein to Zealand. A messenger from the crown prince, with orders to burn the fleet rather than surrender it to the enemy, was unfortunately taken prisoner by the English. The rich booty which the latter took away consisted of eighteen ships of the line, seventeen frigates, thirty-five small vessels and gunboats, with the great stores of every kind of supplies contained in the naval arsenal. The little island was completely pillaged; and the enemy destroyed what they could not carry off. They mutilated and overturned several warships then on the stocks.

General Peymann, commander-in-chief, Generals Bielefeldt and Gedde, and other prominent officers were dragged before a council of war, and condemned to severe punishment — Peymann and Bielefeldt to loss of life, honour, and wealth; Gedde to death — for the crime of surrendering a city which their superiors had neglected to provide with sufficient means of defence. By these trials and judgments the government seems to have wished to cover its own capital crimes, as well as its lack of prudence and ordinary precautions. The condemned men were, however, soon pardoned.

Napoleon Forces Denmark's Hand (1807 A.D.)

After this high-handed proceeding, the English government dared to offer Denmark a choice between an alliance with England, or the maintenance of her former neutrality, or war; in the last-named alternative, it threatened to work for the separation of Norway and the union of the latter with Sweden. This was the first time such a plan, realised seven years later, was mentioned. The proposition for an alliance which England was making to Denmark was a fresh insult, a cruel derision. The indignation which animated the people and government of Denmark did not permit them to give ear, for one minute, to this proposition, although the prospect of the restitution of the stolen fleet at the close of the war was held out to them as the price of an alliance.

But a union with England would be a declaration of war upon France; and it would have been little different with a treaty of peace. Several historians have thought that Denmark should have accepted peace; for, with the advantage of a fortunate neutrality, she could have prevented not only the great reverses and internal misfortunes of the seven years' war she was obliged to carry on when she had been half-disarmed, but also the loss of Norway, the fatal result of the struggle. It may, however, always be objected that Denmark was not free to act differently; for when the English fleet set sail for the Sound, Napoleon had said, "If Denmark does not declare war against England, she will have to reckon with me;" and he held on the Danish frontier an army ready to execute his orders. There is no reason to believe that he would have changed his resolution after the carrying off of the Danish fleet, or that he would have allowed Denmark to make peace with England. For, in truth, it would have resulted from this that commercial relations would have been re-established between the two nations, and that neutral Denmark would have been the means of placing Great Britain in communication with the countries round the Baltic. Now, Napoleon's principal aim at this period was to destroy the power and wealth of his rival, by shutting her out from all trade with the Continent. He did not permit any nation to remain neutral in this struggle; and still less would he have allowed a state situated as Denmark was to hold peaceful relations with his mortal enemy, the only one of his adversaries he had not yet been able to vanquish. The manner in which he treated Denmark shows, indeed, that such would have been the case.

FREDERICK VI, KING OF DENMARK
(1768-1839)

Napoleon's powerful will was at that time law for all the Continental powers of Europe, and Denmark could not avoid their common fate. In any event she could not remain neutral. The crown prince decided, therefore, to continue hostilities with Great Britain, and conclude a close alliance with the French Empire, but not until he had seen his capital destroyed, his navy taken from him, and several hundred vessels of his merchant marine captured. Under these circumstances Denmark declared war against England, November 4th, 1807. England's attack excited indignation, not only in Denmark but in every European people for whom the law of nations was not a meaningless word; even among the English themselves, in Parliament as well as out of it, the actions of the ministry were the subject of lively and bitter criticism. The emperor Alexander of Russia loudly expressed his disapprobation, and declared that he would break off all relations with England until she had repaired the wrong done to Denmark. Yet this sentiment of justice did not prevent him, a few years later, from leaguing with England and Sweden to sever Norway from Denmark. In the year following the rupture with England, a new enemy came forward against Denmark. This was King Gustavus IV of Sweden, moved by violent hatred of his neighbour in the west. Although he was scarcely in a state to defend himself in his own kingdom, he was stretching forth his hand for the crown of Norway. His hostile sentiments and his relations with England justified a rupture which became inevitable after Denmark's alliance with Napoleon. As Napoleon was embroiled with Sweden, the Danish government declared war on that power,

February 29th, 1808.   A few days later, March 13th, Christian VII died at
Rendsburg, leaving the kingdom in a critical condition.   His successor was
his son, who took the title of Frederick VI.   Denmark was now at war with
two countries; and, having no navy, she was not in a condition to inflict
much injury on her most dangerous enemy, England.   Her policy was allied
with that of Napoleon, who looked out for his own interests and did not consider those of Denmark.   The finances were beginning to fall into confusion;
internal activity was paralysed, and commerce almost extinct; six hundred
merchant ships, worth 18,000,000 rix-dollars, had been captured by the English during Denmark's period of neutrality, and almost as many more since
war with Great Britain had been declared.

Under pretence of aiding Denmark against Sweden and undertaking
an invasion of Skåne in company with the Danish troops, a French army of
thirty-three thousand men, under Bernadotte, prince of Pontecorvo, entered
the Jutland peninsula in the beginning of 1808.   A considerable portion of
these (14,000) consisted of Spanish troops, commanded by the marquis de la
Romana; the rest were French and Dutch.   Great preparations were made
for landing in Skåne; for instance, several hundred transports had been
collected in the spring, in the Great Belt and the Sound, and had been kept
there a long time, to the great injury of commerce and of the provisioning of
Norway, which was badly in need of corn.   While Bernadotte was dragging
the affair out at great length, a new difficulty arose by England's taking
occasion to send warships to the Belt and the Sound.   Little by little it
became apparent that Napoleon never had any intention of invading Skåne;
and even if this project had been carried out, there is good reason to believe
that it would not have been with the idea of helping Denmark and procuring
her advantage, but only as a diversion in favour of the Russians, who, with
Napoleon's connivance, had at this moment attacked Sweden, and were
trying to take Finland from her.   In occupying Nordalbingia and Fünen,
the Emperor seems to have had especially in view the quartering of his troops
in a fertile country and making sure of Denmark, whom he always suspected
of trying to deal in an underhanded manner with England.   The foreign
auxiliaries spread themselves over Holstein, Schleswig, and a portion of Jutland, and behaved like masters of the country; they even furnished a part
of the garrisons at the fortresses of Rendsburg and Glückstadt.

Good feeling did not always rule between the various elements composing the army.   The Spanish soldiers had been taken from their native
land against their will, and sent into the far north to fight in a cause to which
they were alien and indifferent.   They were, consequently, extremely discontented, and fraternised badly with the French.   To get rid of the Spaniards, a large number were transported to Fünen, and several regiments to
Zealand.   Napoleon had dethroned the king of Spain and put his own brother
Joseph in his place; but now the Spanish nation rose up in its entirety against
the ruler who had been imposed upon them. . At the news of this event the
Spaniards quartered in Denmark passed from irritation to open revolt; the
majority refused to take the oath to the new monarch, or did it with reservations that could not be admitted; in several places riotous scenes occurred.
The marquis de la Romana, who shared the sentiments of his soldiers, resolved
to make an attempt to relieve them of the foreign yoke, and put himself in
communication with the English ships cruising near Fünen and Langeland,
which were perfectly willing to take the Spaniards on board.   A large number
of these embarked from the island of Langeland; others surprised and occupied
Nyborg, from which place they boarded the British vessels (August 9th, 1808).

Those who were in North Jutland hastened to Aarhus, and taking possession of the ships in the harbour, sailed after their compatriots. Those, on the contrary, who were in the more southern parts of Jutland, and the two regiments stationed in Zealand, were disarmed and made prisoners.

Bernadotte remained in the Northern peninsula for a long time after these events, and it was not until the spring of the following year (1809), after having spent more than a year in Denmark, that he entirely withdrew his troops, of which Napoleon had need elsewhere. The army had been a plague and a heavy burden upon the inhabitants. It had consumed the resources of the state by the extraordinary expenditure required for its maintenance, and its presence had not been of the slightest benefit to Denmark.

The Loss of Norway

Since the English had control of the sea, communication with Norway was becoming extremely difficult; and it was judged best to hand over the government of that country to a commission sitting at Christiania. In 1806 its president, Prince Christian Augustus of Augustenburg, became also the commandant-general of Norway. While the enemy's privateers and cruisers ploughed the Kattegat and the North sea, Denmark had the greatest difficulty in sending corn to Norway; and that country was now threatened with famine and high prices. The Danish government took extraordinary measures to prevent these evils, and if it did not succeed entirely, it was not because it had not made sacrifices. After the rupture with

WOMAN OF FINLAND IN HOLIDAY COSTUME

Sweden, hostilities began on the Norwegian frontier. A Swedish corps, the army of the west, crossed the frontier, but the able commander of the Norwegian troops, Prince Christian Augustus, repelled the enemy in several glorious combats. Hostilities ceased before the close of the year 1808.

Denmark continued, in desperation and at the price of enormous sacrifices, the war with Great Britain; but as a consequence of the loss of her navy she could deal no hard blows to her hated enemy, whose fleets covered the whole of the northern seas. The few warships which, not being at Copenhagen in 1807, had escaped coming into the possession of the English were, one by one, overtaken and destroyed by them. In the nation's distress patriotism rose to its highest point. The burghers rivalled each other in noble sacrifices of property and money, and by this means a fleet of galiots was built in a short time with which the Danish navy faced its proud enemy. In truth, Denmark had nothing but gunboats, except the indomitable courage of the Danish sailors, which was never b·tter exhibited than in this unequal contest, counterbalanced the country's weakness, and made the enemy undergo many sensible losses in the course of the war. Many British ships, brigs, and cutters had to lower their flag before the Danish and Norwegian gunboats. England's commerce in the northern seas was also continually harassed by bold privateers, sailing from Danish and Norwegian ports. But in spite of all their efforts, the Danes could not prevent the English from establishing themselves on the island of Anholt, in the middle of the Kattegat (1809), which was a great hindrance to international commerce. An attempt made in 1811 to retake the island met a disastrous ending, with great loss of life.

This state of things was prolonged until 1812; for six years Denmark had defended herself with great difficulty against Great Britain, her sole enemy. But soon she had many others, and was carried into the great whirlpool of European war. John Bernadotte, or Charles John, as he was afterwards called, [had been elected heir to the throne of Sweden, in 1810,] and had taken up the plan already conceived by Gustavus III, which consisted in seizing Norway from Denmark and uniting it with Sweden — a policy the success of which would have contributed immensely to the popularity of the new dynasty. The ex-marshal of France could not count on the support of Napoleon, with whom he now held somewhat strained relations, because

A WOMAN OF FINLAND IN WINTER COSTUME

since his election he had not been willing to follow the imperial policy, which was contrary to Sweden's interests. At this time the latter country, at Napoleon's demand, had declared war upon Great Britain. But this was a mere feint, for to Napoleon's great indignation trade between the two nations was kept up as in times of the most profound peace. French troops were already occupying Swedish Pomerania, and to complete the rupture nothing but a declaration of war was needed.

Another perspective, however, now unfolded itself, and was favourable to the views of Charles John. Relations between France and Russia were becoming more and more unfriendly, and the latter country was expecting at any moment to see her frontiers crossed by the immense army the French

[1812 A.D.]

emperor was collecting.   In view of the terrible struggle which would then take place, it was necessary for Russia to protect herself on the side of Sweden, her old enemy, who, it might be supposed, would not neglect so favourable an opportunity.   The amputation of so important a member as Finland had left a still open wound, and the Swedish army had an experienced leader in the heir presumptive to the crown.   The czar therefore began negotiations for an alliance with Sweden, and Charles John entered willingly into a union which permitted him to satisfy his hatred for Napoleon, and to realize a long-cherished project.   The price of this co-operation was not to be Finland, but Norway.   On April 5th, 1812, a treaty was signed at St. Petersburg, by which Sweden promised her support to the czar, who in return pledged himself to make Denmark surrender Norway to Sweden, if possible amicably, and in return for compensation in German territory; if not, by force.   The alliance was confirmed in a personal interview between Charles John and the emperor Alexander at Åbo in Finland, in August, 1812, at the very time when the grand army was marching into the heart of Russia.

FINLAND PEASANT

It is to this strange complicity of two hereditary enemies, coming to terms to despoil a weak neighbour, that the separation of Norway and Denmark is due.   It must be noted, moreover, that both Sweden and Russia were entirely at peace with Denmark. The czar Alexander, who five years before had publicly expressed his horror of England's treatment of the Danes, now in his turn made himself guilty of no less odious a violation of the law of nations.   Although Great Britain was already at war with Denmark, it was not until the following year (March 3rd, 1813) that she agreed, in spite of herself and after many hesitations, to the conditions which Charles John imposed in return for his participation in the war against Napoleon.

Frederick VI was informed of Charles John's projects towards the close of 1812, and was enabled by negotiations and a change of policy to stave off the immediate danger.   It was the more necessary to take this course of action, since, after the defeat of France in Russia, there was little or no hope of assistance from her.   The king sent word to Napoleon that circumstances imposed on him the pressing necessity of separating his cause from that of the empire and of seeking to come to terms with England and the other powers which were threatening Denmark. Napoleon recognised that the king's representations were well founded, and left him free to act as the interests of his realm demanded — an extraordinary piece of moderation on the emperor's part, which, however, would have been much more praiseworthy in the days of his prosperity than in the decline of his power. Frederick VI now began negotiations with Russia and England, offered to enter the league against Napoleon, and sent special plenipotentiaries to Alexander and the English government to appeal to their sense of equity.

Renewal of the Alliance between Denmark and the French Empire

Repelled by both England and Russia, Frederick turned once more to Napoleon, who received him with kindness and in such a manner that the alliance between Denmark and the French Empire was renewed. About ten thousand Danes, under the leadership of Prince Frederick of Hesse, the king's brother-in-law, joined the French army of north Germany, commanded by Marshal Davout, Prince of Eckmühl. A prince of royal blood, Christian Frederick, son of the crown prince Frederick, was sent to Norway. The situation was a difficult one for the young Christian Frederick, but his sympathetic personality won him the people's love and made his task easier. If it had been a matter for the Norwegians only, the danger would not have been so great, for they were still devotedly attached to their ancient union with Denmark, and had no desire to contract a new one with Sweden. There were only a few malcontents; at whose head was Count Herman Wedel, who plotted a crime and entered into relations with his sovereign's enemy.

For a moment fortune appeared to smile on Denmark. Napoleon seemed to have recovered his former vigour; he defeated his enemies in several battles, and in the beginning of 1813 assumed an energetic and threatening attitude, which gave Denmark the hope of a successful solution of her difficulties. The Danish army, under Frederick of Hesse, operating in concert with Davout, entered Mecklenburg in August, and fought with success until some reverses overtaking the French in Eastern Germany forced it to fall back to Lauenburg, where, throughout the autumn of 1813, it sustained the honour of the Danish arms in a series of skirmishes with the Germans and Russians, under Walmoden and Tettenborn. But finally fortune completely abandoned Napoleon. The loss of the great battle of Leipsic and the defection of his allies compelled him to evacuate Germany. Marshal Davout was thus compelled to shut himself up in the fortified city of Hamburg, and to cut himself off from the Danish contingent, which had nothing left to do but to retire before the great masses of troops that poured upon it from all sides. The brave French general Lallemand stayed with the Danish army, and Davout kept with him the Jutland dragoons, commanded by Colonels Engelsted and Bonnichsen. By their courage and exploits in this short campaign, this body of cavalry won a brilliant reputation. Charles John, who had taken an important part in the success of the allies against Napoleon, now commenced to look after his own interests. Abandoning the pursuit of the French army, at the end of November he deviated from Hanover towards the Danish frontier; it was in Holstein that he was to conquer Norway. He had twenty-five thousand men under his orders; but Walmoden's German troops and Tettenborn's Russian corps having effected a junction with him, the combined army reached a total of fifty thousand men, which could easily be augmented, if necessary, by the divisions encamped in the vicinity.

It was this force that the little Danish army, reduced to nine thousand men, was called upon to resist. Charles John marched across eastern Holstein, through Lübeck and Segeberg; Walmoden, through the middle of the duchy, by way of Oldesloe and Neumünster; and Tettenborn, across the western portion, towards the Eider. In their retreat, the Danish troops had a first encounter with those of Walmoden near the village of Boden, in the outskirts of Oldesloe; but a short time after (December 7th) a more serious struggle took place at Bornhöved. The advance of the Swedish army, composed of twelve squadrons of hussars under General Sköldebrand, had let pass without molestation the Danish rear-guard, under General Lallemand, on the moors of Segeberg; but when the greater part of this body of troops had entered the narrow pass, nearly a mile in length, which is crossed by the road to the south of Bornhöved, the Swedes charged upon it with great fury, captured two cannon placed before the entrance to the pass, pushed into it, fought their way through the Danes, and advanced as far as Bornhöved.

But here they found superior forces and had to beat a retreat. It was now necessary to get through the narrow way again, and to pass through the shot and shell of the Danes, who occupied both sides of the defile. The Swedish losses were considerable; from their own report, they left behind several hundred dead and wounded.

The Battle of Sehested (1813 A.D.)

The Danish army continued its march to the north, and reassembled in the neighbourhood of Kiel to prepare to cross the Eider canal, which it did on the 9th of December. But the situation soon became critical. Walmoden advanced to the Eider, and took possession of the crossing of Kluvensiek, opposite Sehested; a division of his army, under General Dörnberg, crossed the Eider, and marched in the direction of Egernfjörd. General Tettenborn had crossed the Eider at Frederiksstad, and his Cossacks galloped towards the city of Schleswig. The Swedes, finally, were on the march to form a junction with Walmoden. The Danish army was turned, its line of retreat towards the south cut off, and communication with the fortress of Rendsburg intercepted.

Under these circumstances, Frederick of Hesse resolved to open up, cost what it might, the road to Rendsburg; for there alone his troops would find protection, and so could the rest of the Danish army if the latter took the field, as might be expected. The only way by which he could reach Rendsburg lay through Sehested, and a lively battle took place for the possession of this town. It began at ten o'clock in the morning of the 10th of December, and lasted the whole day. The Danes drove the enemy from the position he held north of Sehested, and made themselves masters of the town after several hours of fierce fighting. But the Swedes rallied at the southern gate of the village, which they took after reinforcements had come up. They did not keep it long: Prince Frederick gave the order of attack to three squadrons of dragoons from Fünen; and they dashed madly into the town, causing havoc among the battalion that occupied it, seized several cannon, and took 250 prisoners. The fate of the battle seemed to be decided; but when the dragoons, in their progress, encountered fresh troops, and had to retire with loss, Walmoden thought the moment had come for a fresh attack, and decided to try to tempt fortune to his side. A furious fight broke out anew to the south of Sehested; and after a bloody *mêlée*, in which a whole squadron of Mecklenburg chasseurs at the front of the attacking line was cut to pieces, the enemy was finally repulsed, and retreated towards the Eider. To clear them entirely from the northern bank of the river, a fresh charge was made by the two squadrons called Holsteiners, but exclusively composed of Jutlanders from the neighbourhoods of Kolding and Hadersleben. They routed all the enemy's infantry which they met; but as their courage knew no bounds, and, in their zeal, they ventured too far, like the cavalry of Fünen, they met with considerable losses. Walmoden, despairing of obtaining a better result, crossed the Eider at Kluvensiek between four and five in the afternoon, and encamped on the south bank of the river.

The road was now free for the Danish army, which continued its march to Rendsburg without molestation. The Danish loss amounted to about three hundred killed and wounded; the enemy admitted a loss of from four to five hundred dead and wounded, and about 650 prisoners. The battle of Sehested was a fine feat of arms, and gave much prestige to the Danish army, but it fell far short of satisfying the patriotism of the Danish people. In seeing a single corps fight with such bravery, they might well ask, What might not a whole army do?

The Peace of Kiel (1814 A.D.)

The army, however, remained motionless, like a chained lion. Nothing was done; Frederick VI was abandoned by everyone; and he did not find in himself the confidence, strength, and decision demanded at this critical moment. After the fight at Sehested, an armistice was concluded and negotiations begun, which ended in an unfavourable peace. Shortly before the signing of the treaty, a new misfortune was added to the others. General Chernikov, commanding the well-provisioned fortress of Glückstadt, surrendered it unnecessarily to the enemy, after a short and feeble resistance. By the Peace of Kiel (January 14th, 1814), Norway was ceded to Sweden, which gave a sort of indemnity to Denmark by resigning to her Swedish Pomerania and the island of Rügen, later exchanged with Prussia for Lauenburg and a sum of money. Iceland, the Faroe islands and Greenland remained to Denmark. The same day and at the same place, a peace was concluded with England, which obtained the island of Helgoland. Denmark further undertook to take part in the war against Napoleon, and to provide to that end a contingent of ten thousand men. The former relations with Russia, Prussia, and Spain were re-established a short time after, by different treaties.[d]

The Norwegians, however, were not inclined to submit tamely and at once to absorption into Sweden. They rallied round the Danish king's nephew and heir presumptive, Prince Christian Frederick, afterwards Christian VIII, and elected him their king, while at the same time the national assembly voted a new constitution for Norway. A comparison of this with the Danish constitution of 1849 has been drawn up by Jenssen-Tusch, the biographer of Christian VIII.[a]

THE NORWEGIAN CONSTITUTION OF 1814 AND THE DANISH CONSTITUTION OF 1849

The Norwegian fundamental law, dated from Eidsvold, May 17th, 1814, states in its first paragraph that "the kingdom of Norway is a free, independent, and indivisible realm. The form of its government is an absolute and hereditary monarchy." The Danish fundamental law, dated from the castle of Christiansborg, June 5th, 1849, likewise states in its first paragraph, "The form of government is a limited monarchy; the sovereignty is heredi-

[1814 A.D.]

tary." The Norwegian constitution declares the Protestant *(evangelisch-lutherisch*, the united Calvinist and Lutheran bodies) religion to be the established religion of the country; enjoins on those subjects who profess it the duty of educating their children in its tenets; and excludes Jesuits, monastic orders, and Jews from the kingdom. The Danish constitution, on the other hand, states that the Protestant *(evangelisch-lutherisch)* church is the national church of Denmark, and as such is supported by the state; while paragraph 7 grants complete liberty in matters of faith and worship.

In the second paragraph, which treats of the executive power, the king and the royal family, the Norwegian constitution runs: "The executive power is in the hands of the king;" and the Danish fundamental law contains a statement to the same effect. In like manner, the paragraphs dealing with the king's majority and the responsibility of his ministers are almost identical in substance. But while, according to the Norwegian fundamental law, the succession passes in direct line through heirs-male only, so that only an heir-male can inherit from a male progenitor, the Danish constitution abides by the provisions of the *Königsgcsetz* (King's Law) of November 14th, 1665, paragraphs 27-40, which establish lineal succession through the male and female line (agnates and cognates). Should there be no heir to the throne, the king of Norway may propose a successor to the storthing, which is at liberty to accept or reject him. The Danish fundamental law, on the contrary, states that under such circumstances it is for the diet to choose an heir to the throne and determine the future succession. The case, however, could occur only on the supposition that both the male and the female lines were extinct. By the Norwegian fundamental law, the king comes of age on the attainment of his twentieth year, while that of Denmark fixes his majority at eighteen. By the *Königsgesetz*, he is qualified to assume the reins of absolute government on entering his fourteenth year. The tenor of the oath taken by the king of Norway on his accession, is that he will govern the kingdom in accordance with the constitution and the laws of the country; the king of Denmark's oath is limited to the promise to maintain the fundamental law of the kingdom. Both fundamental laws agree in requiring the king's oath to be taken before the assembled storthing in Norway and before the united diet in Denmark.

The coronation and anointing of the king of Norway take place in the cathedral of Trondhjem, the ceremonial being decided upon by the king himself. The Danish fundamental law contains no such provision; hence the ceremony must be regarded as non-essential. The king of Norway is obliged to reside within the boundaries of his kingdom, nor may he be out of the country for more than six months without the sanction of the storthing, on pain of forfeiting his personal right to the crown. On this point, again, the Danish constitution has no provision except that if the king, by reason of absence or ill-health, shall find it necessary to nominate a regent, he shall convoke the diet and submit to it a bill to that effect. According to the constitution of Eidsvold, the king of Norway may not assume the crown or government of any other country, unless with the assent of two-thirds of the storthing. This answers to the provision of the Danish fundamental law: "Without the sanction of the diet the king cannot be ruler over other countries than those pertaining to the Danish monarchy." The king of Norway must profess, and always have professed the tenets of Protestantism, and must be ready to defend and protect them. In the Danish constitution, on the other hand, the phrase is merely: "The king must be a member of the Protestant church." By the Norwegian constitution the king is enjoined to have the oversight over public worship and religious assemblies, and to see to it that teachers adhere to the rules prescribed for religious instruction. There is no such provision in the Danish fundamental law, which, on this subject, says concisely, "The national church is regulated by law."

The king of Norway can issue regulations dealing with commerce, trade, and police, but such regulations must not be contrary to the constitution and the laws passed by the storthing, and remain in force provisionally only, until such time as they shall have received the sanction of the next storthing. The Danish fundamental law, on the other hand, contains a provision that under circumstances of peculiar urgency, and when the diet is not sitting, the king may issue provisional laws, provided they are not contrary to the fundamental law, and that every such law must be submitted to the next diet for ratification. "The king levies the taxes and duties imposed by the storthing," says the Norwegian fundamental law; that of Denmark contains no such definition, but in general terms assigns the executive power wholly to the king. "The king sees to it that the state property and royalties are used and administered in such wise as is prescribed by the storthing and conducive to the common weal," so runs the law of Norway; while that of Denmark prescribes that no demesne pertaining to the state shall be alienated except by a decree of the diet. According to the Norwegian constitution, the king in council has the prerogative of pardoning criminals after sentence has been pronounced by the Supreme Court, and on the advice of the same. The condemned person is free to choose whether he will accept the king's pardon or undergo the sentence awarded by the court. In actions brought before the Supreme Court by the odelsthing (one division of the national assembly), the king cannot exercise the prerogative of mercy except by remitting a capital sentence. With regard to such cases the Danish fundamental law merely says, "The king can pardon and grant amnesties; he can exempt ministers from the penalties imposed upon them only by consent of the folkething."

In accordance with the fundamental law of Norway, the king selects and appoints all civil, ecclesiastical, and military officers, after consultation with the council of state; and they are required to take the oath of allegiance to the constitution and the king. Princes of the blood royal are incapable of holding civil office. The king, after consulting with the council of state, may dismiss any member of the said council, or any person holding an appointment in the office of the said council, or any ambassador, consul, superior official either civil or ecclesiastic, regimental or divisional commander, commandant of a fortress or naval officer in command of a man-of-war, without the formality of a trial. Other officials the king can only suspend, after which they must immediately be brought to trial; but they may not be deprived of their office except by sentence of the court, nor transferred to another without their own consent. All these cases the Danish fundamental law covers by the statement: "Appointments to all offices are in the king's hands to the same extent as heretofore." This general statement, however, points back to a legal ordinance by which the signature of a responsible minister must be added to that of the king in the case of each appointment. As a rule the king of Denmark can dismiss the officials he has appointed; but there is a proviso that judges are not to be deprived of their offices without trial, or transferred elsewhere against their will, and exceptions in the case of other classes are to be determined by law. It is a curious fact that the fundamental law of the kingdom of Denmark contains no provision whereby officials are required to take the oath to the constitution and vow loyalty and obedience to the king.

[1814 A.D.]

According to the Norwegian constitution, the king can, at his good pleasure, bestow orders as a reward for distinguished service, but no title except such as is inseparable from office. Nor can he grant personal or mixed hereditary privileges to any person. This last provision corresponds to the article in the Danish constitution whereby all privileges appurtenant to lineage, title, or rank are abrogated, and whereby no fiefs, family estates, or entail may be established for the future, while those which already exist are gradually to pass over into free tenure; but the Danish law says not a word of orders and rewards for service rendered to the state. The provisions with regard to the civil list are practically the same in both fundamental laws, but by a clause subjoined to that of Denmark, the civil list may not be burdened with debt. The Norwegian constitution gives the king a free hand in the appointment and dismissal of his court officers and servants. The king has supreme command over the forces by land and sea, but they may not be transferred to the service of a foreign power without the consent of the storthing, nor may foreign troops be admitted into the country, except as auxiliaries in case of hostile invasion. The king likewise has absolute power to muster troops, to declare war and conclude peace, to enter into and dissolve alliances, and to send and receive ambassadors. The provisions of the Danish constitution are similar to these, except with regard to foreign troops, and it contains the addition that the king cannot cede any portion of the country to a foreign power, or dispose of the public revenue, or subject the country to burdensome obligations, without the consent of the diet.

The provisions respecting the king's competence to take despotic measures against subjects are alike in both fundamental laws, which is also the case in the matter of the constitution of the council of state and ministerial responsibility. Some provisions of the Norwegian constitution concerning princes and princesses of the blood royal are adopted from the Danish *Königsgesetz* (King's Law) of 1665, to which the Danish fundamental law likewise refers in conclusion. According to both constitutions, a regency or government by a guardian, with the co-operation of the storthing or diet, may be instituted; but the Norwegian constitution makes special mention of the members of the royal family; while that of Denmark permits the diet to appoint a regent. In default of any heir to the throne, the storthing may found a new dynasty, while in Denmark, under similar circumstances, the diet chooses a king and determines the succession. The Norwegian fundamental law also contains a series of provisions on the subject of the education of a king under age, by the queen-mother and certain men selected by the storthing; of which nothing is said in the Danish fundamental law.

The third section of the Norwegian constitution, headed, "Of Civil Rights and the Legislative Authority," states that the Norwegian nation exercises legislative authority by means of its storthing, which consists of two Things, the ladthing and the odelsthing, that meet together under certain circumstances in a storthing session. The Danish Parliament likewise consists of two chambers: the folkething and the landsthing. When they meet together, as they do under certain circumstances, and form a single assembly, the two chambers constitute the united diet, while the Norwegian Things remain two distinct bodies. The Eidsvold constitution admits of only one election for the whole storthing; the Danish fundamental law institutes a two-fold election, each chamber being elected separately. Only such Norwegian citizens are qualified to vote as have attained their twenty-fifth year, have been five years domiciled in the country, and hold or have held public office, or such as have possessed or managed registered property in land for more than five years, or are freemen of a city, or possess houses or land in ports or places of lading to the value of 300 *rchsbkthlon*. By the Danish fundamental law, on the other hand, every man in the country who is thirty years of age, and of unimpeachable reputation, is entitled to vote for both Things, provided he possesses the rights of a native. Hence, in the kingdom of Denmark no census is taken to decide electoral qualifications; and on this point again its fundamental law is far more liberal and democratic than that of Norway.

In sparsely populated Norway, one elector is nominated by every fifty persons qualified to vote. From amongst themselves or the other qualified voters, these electors choose one-fourth of their own number to sit in the storthing; any number of electors from three to six sending one member; any number from seven to ten, two members; from eleven to fourteen, three members; and from fifteen to eighteen, four members; which last is the largest number of deputies any one town can send to the storthing. If a town has less than one hundred and fifty inhabitants, it elects in conjunction with the next town. In every country parish the qualified voters among the inhabitants choose electors in proportion to their numbers, one for every hundred, two for any number between one and two hundred, three for any number between two and three hundred, and so on. The electors proceed, like the others, to elect one-tenth of their own number, either from among themselves or from the qualified voters of their administrative district, to take their seats in the storthing; any number from five to fourteen electing one; from fifteen to twenty-four, two; from twenty-five to thirty-four, three; and of thirty-five and over, four, as the largest number of deputies that can be sent by any one electoral district. The storthing has the power of making alterations in these electoral regulations, so as to arrange for the representation of town and country in the proportion of one to two, and to keep the total number of deputies in the storthing above seventy-five and below one hundred. In Norway, no man can be a popular representative who has not passed his thirtieth year and been ten years domiciled in the country.

In Denmark this mode of election is employed only for the first chamber or landsthing, and the provisions of the Danish fundamental law are consequently more democratic in this respect than the constitution of Norway. The number of deputies to the second chamber or folkething in Denmark is approximately one to every fourteen thousand of the population (the constitution of Eidsvold sets it at about one to every ten thousand). The votes are taken by circles, the extent of which is determined by the election law. Each circle chooses one candidate out of those who present themselves for election. The only qualification necessary for election to the folkething is that the candidate shall have attained the age of twenty-five; for the landsthing, he must be forty years of age, and must have fulfilled the conditions necessary for qualification as a voter, though no limitation is imposed in respect of length of residence in the electoral circle. No man is eligible for election to the Danish landsthing unless he has paid to the state 200 *rchsbkthlon* in direct taxes during the preceding year, or can prove that he enjoys an annual income of 1,200 *rchsbkthlon;* while the Norwegian constitution requires no property qualification in a candidate. On the other hand, by the fundamental law of the latter country, neither members nor subordinate officials of state, nor court officers, nor pensioners are eligible for election; a restriction which does not exist in Denmark, where officials accept or refuse nomination as deputies to the diet without reference to the government.

According to the constitution of Eidsvold, the popular representatives thus elected constitute the storthing of the kingdom of Norway and the diet of Denmark, which last-named body consists of the folkething and landsthing. The Norwegian storthing is held every three years at Christiania, the capital of the country; the Danish diet annually, wherever the seat of government happens to be. The storthing elects one-fourth of its own members to form the lagthing; the remaining three-fourths constitute the odelsthing. Thus, in Norway the whole storthing is the original body, by the division of which the two Things come into being; while in Denmark, on the contrary, the folkething and the landsthing constitute the original body, and the united diet is the product of the coalition of the two Things. The storthing and the diet are both legislative and deliberative assemblies. In Norway, every legislative proposal must first be moved in the odelsthing, either by a member of that body or by the government through a member of the council of state. If the odelsthing accepts the proposal it is sent on to the lagthing, which either assents to or rejects it; and, in the latter case, sends it back to the odelsthing with an explanation of its motives in so doing. The odelsthing deliberates upon these observations, and then either passes over from the original motion to the order of the day, or sends it back to the lagthing for fresh consideration, with or without alteration. If a motion has been twice submitted to the lagthing by the odelsthing and twice rejected, the two chambers meet in a session of the storthing, and the final decision is given by a majority of two-thirds. An interval of three days, at least, must elapse between any two of the above named transactions.

When a legislative proposal of this kind, brought into the odelsthing and approved by the lagthing or the assembled storthing, has been voted on and passed in the manner described, it is submitted to the king or his representative by a deputation from both chambers of the storthing, with a request for his assent. If he approves of the proposal, he appends his signature to it, thus giving it the force of law. If he does not approve it, he sends the draught back to the odelsthing, with the remark that he does not think it expedient at this time to sanction the resolution of the storthing; after which the proposal cannot again be made and submitted to the king by the same storthing. If the next lawfully elected storthing again brings forward the same law, the king can again prevent its promulgation by refusing his assent. But if a third lawfully elected storthing submits the same proposal to the king, after it has again been deliberated upon by both chambers, and again requests his assent to a law which, upon mature consideration, they think for the public advantage, the proposal acquires legal validity even if the royal assent is not given before the end of the session. A law thus adopted by the storthing is drawn up in a different form from those which have received the royal assent. The Danish fundamental law, on the other hand, concedes to both Things the right of moving and discussing legislative proposals; but no final decision can be taken upon any proposal until it has been under deliberation three times in each Thing. There is, however, an essential difference between the two fundamental laws in the fact that the veto of the king of Norway is suspensive only, while that of the king of Denmark is absolute. It cannot, therefore, be denied that upon this point the constitution of Norway is more democratic than that of Denmark, though the latter more vigorously champions the rights of the people. Hence, the legislative authority in Denmark pertains neither to the diet nor to the king alone (not even in exceptional cases to the latter, as it does in Norway), but to the two conjointly.

With respect to the judicature, and especially to the Supreme Court, the provisions of the two fundamental laws are almost identical. By the constitution of Eidsvold the defendant can challenge as many as one-third of the members of the court, without giving any reason, so long as he does not reduce the number below fifteen. The constitution of Christiansborg contains no such provision. The fifth and last section of the Norwegian fundamental law bears the superscription " General provisions." It provides, among other things, that offices of state in Norway shall be occupied by none but Norwegian subjects who profess the Protestant religion, have taken the oath to the constitution, sworn fealty to the king, and are able to speak the language of the country. The Danish constitution is more liberal, for it briefly lays down the principle that no man shall forfeit his claim to the full enjoyment of all civil and political rights on account of his religion, and here again there is no mention of any oath to be taken by holders of office. The Norwegian constitution contains various other precepts of general application respecting the administration of justice, among which is the singular provision that no dues may be levied by the state upon the fees paid to constables. The sixth and eighth sections of the Danish fundamental law treat of the administration of justice on principles of natural law which are to be brought into use by fresh legislation, and lays down the special rule that the courts must be competent to settle all questions beyond the scope of magisterial authority.

The freedom of the press is guaranteed by both fundamental laws. The Norwegian constitution lays down the principle that no new and permanent restrictions may in future be anywhere imposed upon trade; while the Danish fundamental law states that all restrictions upon admittance to the freedom and equal rights of industry, which are not based upon considerations of public advantage, are for the future abrogated by law. Thus, the former extends protection to that which already exists; while the latter refers the question to the wide principle of interpretation: what may or may not be regarded as conducive to the public weal. The fundamental law of Norway permits inquisition in criminal cases; that of Denmark runs: " The home is inviolable; where no exception is by law established, domiciliary visits and the seizure and examination of letters and other papers may not take place till after the verdict of the court." Both fundamental laws agree in recognising the inviolability of property and in providing for full compensation where the interests of the state or the common weal require an owner to resign possession. The Norwegian constitution ordains that udal rights and the right of inheritance in landed property shall not be abrogated, but that the details of the conditions under which these privileges shall continue to exist, for the greater advantage of the state and the good of the rural population, shall be determined by the next duly elected storthing or the next after that; and that in future it shall not be lawful to institute counties, baronies, ancestral seats, nor entailed estates. The Danish constitution contains a corresponding provision to the effect that the manner in which the fiefs, ancestral seats, and entailed estates, then existing, shall pass over into free tenure shall be regulated in detail by law, and that no new possessions of this king shall be acquired, while all privileges pertaining to descent, rank, or title shall be abolished. Both fundamental laws enunciate the principle of universal obligation to military service, but the diet of Denmark was slower to admit of the provision of a substitute.

The purpose of the 110th and last paragraph of the Norwegian constitution is that the provisions of the constitution here set down shall become the fundamental law of the kingdom, so soon as they shall have received the assent of the diet. Should future experience go to prove that any part of them require alteration, a proposal to that effect shall be submitted to a duly elected storthing, and be made public through the press. But it shall be reserved for the next duly elected storthing to decide whether the proposed alteration shall be made. Such a proposal, however, may never be subversive of the principles of the fundamental law, but must merely aim at a modification of particular provisions not affecting the spirit of the law; and two-thirds of the members of the storthing must vote in its favour. The hundredth and concluding paragraph of the Danish fundamental law likewise assumes the possibility that alterations may be necessary; but they cannot be made as easily as in Norway. Proposals of this nature must first be moved in a duly elected diet. If this and the next duly elected assembly accept the proposal without alteration and it receives the royal assent, both Things are dissolved, and fresh elections take place both to the folkething and the landsthing. If the proposed alteration is accepted by the new diet in ordinary or extraordinary session and sanctioned by the king, it thereby acquires the force of a fundamental law.

The constitution of Eidsvold is signed by the deputies of the kingdom, and sealed by each of them; and this draught of a constitution which had been accepted by the diet is thereby raised to the rank of a fundamental law. The constitution of Christiansborg, on the other hand, is signed by the king and his ministers for the time being, and the royal seal is appended to it.*g*

The failure of Norway's efforts to preserve her independence of her eastern neighbour will be more fully described in our next chapter: the constitution of Eidsvold survived the union with Sweden, and the separate rights of Norway continued to be stoutly maintained. For Denmark the great problem was now that of her relations with the duchies of Schleswig and Holstein, a question which became a matter of agitation to all Europe.*a*

THE FIRST SCHLESWIG-HOLSTEIN WAR

After the restoration of peace in 1815, the estates of the duchy of Holstein, never so cordially blended with Denmark as those of Schleswig, began to show their discontent with the continued non-convocation of their own assemblies, despite the assurances of Frederick VI. The preparation of a new constitution for the whole kingdom was the main pretext by which the court evaded the claims of the petitioners, who met, however, with no better success from the German diet, before which they brought their complaints in 1822.

After the stirring year of 1830, the movements in the duchies, soon to degenerate into a mutual animosity between the Danish and the German population, became more general. The scheme of the court to meet their demands by the establishment of separate deliberative assemblies for each of the provinces failed to satisfy the Holsteiners, who continually urged the revival of their long-neglected local laws and privileges. Nor were matters changed at the accession in 1839 of Christian VIII [the quondam king of Norway], a prince noted for his popular sympathies and liberal principles. The feeling of national animosity was greatly increased by the issue of certain orders for Schleswig, which tended to encourage the culture of the Danish language to the prejudice of the German. The elements of a revolution, being thus in readiness, only waited for some impulse to break forth into action.*b*

In 1846, King Christian VIII of Denmark thought the propitious moment had come for announcing, by a so-called "open letter," that, on the extinction of the royal line, the union of Schleswig-Holstein with Denmark would continue to be maintained.   Contrary to all expectation, the opposition to this arbitrary proceeding was not confined to the two duchies, but found vigorous support in all parts of Germany.   Men everywhere began to remember that the hardy race which had chosen king Christian I of Denmark to be its duke, in 1460, had entered into union with the neighbouring kingdom only on condition that the duchies should retain their independence, and should remain in undivided conjunction for all time *(ewig tosamende ungedeelt)*. Experts pointed out that the conjunction of the duchies, which had found expression in a common administration, had not been impaired by the fact that Holstein had become a member of the German Confederation, together with Lauenburg, which had been ceded by Prussia in 1815.   The song composed by M. F. Chemnitz, first sung at the musical festival *(Sängerfest)* at Schleswig, and now adopted by an indomitable race as its song of defiance, winged its way to every corner of the common fatherland, and was presently sung all over Germany.

The growing resistance of the Schleswig Holsteiners was greeted with no less unanimous applause.   The emphatic repudiation which the estates of the duchies returned to the declaration of King Frederick VII, who had succeeded his father Christian VIII, on the 20th of January, 1848, to the effect that Schleswig-Holstein was to be incorporated with Denmark, met with general approval, as did the formation of a separate government, by which they proceeded to reply to that declaration.   Prussia and the German Confederation declared that they regarded Schleswig and Holstein as independent and intimately allied states, in which only the male line was entitled to succeed. To give point to this declaration, the Prussian general Wrangel crossed the frontier in concert with the troops of the Confederation, and on the 23rd of April inflicted so decisive a defeat upon the enemy that in a few days they evacuated the duchy as far as Alsen.   He then carried the war into Jutland, beyond the Konge Aa, to indemnify Germany for the injury Denmark had inflicted upon her by the seizure of large numbers of merchant vessels.   His operations for that year were only brought to a close by the armistice of Malmö.   In spite of these defeats, however, Denmark was not yet vanquished.   Trusting to the support of foreign powers and to dissensions in Germany itself, she terminated the armistice in the spring of 1849, and set on foot a simultaneous attack on the German troops, from Jutland, Alsen and Eckernförde.   The Danes achieved some successes at the first two points, but on the 5th of April suffered a defeat at Eckernförde, than which history records few more memorable.   The two proudest ships of the Danish fleet, the Christian VIII, a ship of the line of eighty-four guns, and the Gefion, a frigate of forty-six guns, under cover of which the transports had run into harbour to land their troops, were not merely vigorously repulsed by two insignificant shore batteries mustering only ten guns between them, but were compelled to surrender.   However great a part may have been played in this disaster by a singular concatenation of untoward circumstances, the credit of it is chiefly due to the resolution of the heroic men who took up the struggle and carried it through to the end.

In the other theatres of war the Danes did not hold their ground against the steady advance of the Germans.   On the 13th of April, the Confederate troops stormed the entrenchments at Düppel, and on the 16th of May, General Bonin, the leader of the forces of Schleswig-Holstein, proceeded to besiege Fredericia.   There the tide of fortune turned.   On the 5th of July, the enemy's army made a night sortie, broke through the attenuated line of besiegers, and inflicted severe loss upon them. Before the injury could be avenged, Prussia confounded all hopes by the peace which she concluded in her own name and that of the Confederation. She abandoned the duchies. They still strove to maintain their rights by their own sword, but the defeat of Idstedt, not far from Schleswig (July 25th), put an end to their resistance; the country lay defenceless at the conqueror's feet. But the worst was still to come. The very power which two years before had nerved it for the struggle helped to disarm those who refused even then to despair of the ultimate victory of their rightful cause. And policy, while it imposed its stern laws on the stubborn race in the present, robbed it of its hope for the future, by settling the succession question. By the London Protocol (May 8th, 1852), Russia, Austria, Prussia, England, France, and Sweden resolved to maintain the existing frontiers of the Danish dominions, and to recognise Prince Christian of Glücksburg as the rightful successor of the childless king Frederick VII, compounding with the duke of Augustenburg for passing over his prior claim. The plenipotentiaries ignored the fact that, to make this arrangement valid, the consent of the parties principally concerned, the estates of Schleswig-Holstein, was necessary and also that, in the case of Holstein, they could not dispense with the consent of the German Confederation; and yet this very neglect bore in it the seeds of fresh complications. The German great powers were guilty of an additional error; for, relying on Denmark's assurance that she did not contemplate the incorporation of Schleswig with the kingdom, they rested satisfied with the royal proclamation of January 28th, 1852, which promised absolute political equality to German and Danish subjects and separate government departments for the kingdom and provinces.

CHRISTIAN IX

The authorities at Copenhagen cherished no serious intention of fulfilling this last condition. The party of so-called Eider Danes, who desired to see Schleswig completely severed from Holstein and finally incorporated with Denmark, soon gained the upper hand; and the government yielded to their wishes. The alterations they introduced into the constitution, and the administrative measures they adopted, provoked such vehement opposition on the part of the estates of the duchies and the German Confederation that even the non-German great powers advised them to give way, but in vain. A royal proclamation of March 30th, 1863, declared that the fulfilment of the promise of January 28th, 1852, was impracticable, and decreed the separation of Holstein and Lauenburg from the coalition, that is to say, the severance of the duchies. This proceeding naturally called forth tremendous excitement there, and loud protests were raised at public meetings against such a breach of the law. The Danish government replied by arbitrary measures: German officials were dismissed on frivolous pretexts and superseded by Danes, the use of the German language in churches and schools was restricted, and even prohibited in districts unquestionably German. Even German travellers on whose passports the words Schleswig and Holstein were united by a hyphen, had to suffer much annoyance at the hands of the police. The hopes of the Eider Danes seemed to have been fulfilled: the duchy of Schleswig was transformed into "South Jutland."

In vain did the leading powers of Germany and the German Confederation enter formal protests, in vain did they threaten to put the execution of the league in force. The Danish government, trusting to English and Swedish support, submitted to the rigsraad the draught of a new constitution for Denmark and Schleswig, which was intended finally to consummate the separation of Holstein and the incorporation of Schleswig.[1] At the same time they asked for special grants for reinforcing the army and fleet. It was an audacious step, well adapted to exhaust the patience of the most long-suffering of nations. The Germans were sensitive to the blow, and laments for the violence their kinsmen suffered were mingled with the rejoicings with which they celebrated the fiftieth anniversary of the victory of Leipsic.

On the 13th of November, the fatal constitution was accepted, with the provision that it should take effect from January 1st, 1864. It lacked nothing but the royal signature to give it the force of law. Then a sudden event took place, fraught with momentous consequences. King Frederick VII died, on the 15th of November, after a short illness, and was succeeded by Prince Christian of Glücksburg, under the title of Christian IX.[e]

THE DANISH CONSTITUTION

At the same time that Denmark was undergoing insurrection as well as a hard struggle with Germany, a great work of peace — her liberal constitution — was being formed. Frederick VII had promised on March 22nd, 1848, to share his power with the nation, and had faithfully kept his word. On the 23rd of October the constituent assembly met for the first time at Copenhagen. Its members had been chosen under an electoral law which took no account of wealth or property; but a few members chosen by the king took their seats alongside of those elected by universal suffrage. The March ministry had laid aside the project of a fundamental law for the Danish monarchy — a scheme to which the November ministry, coming into power a short time after, gave its adherence. After lengthy debates, in the course of which several articles underwent modification, the constitution was adopted by the assembly, and received the king's approval, June 5th, 1849. Its application extended to Schleswig; and the right of consent was reserved to this duchy, which had been prevented by the war from taking part in the labours of the constituent assembly.

The principal articles of this fundamental law, which afterwards received various modifications, concerned elections to the landsthing; the legislative power and the right to impose taxes were vested in the *rigsdag* (parliament) and the king conjointly; the voting of all laws, in the rigsdag; and no contribution could be imposed, modified, or abolished save by a law. The ministers were to be held responsible for the acts of the government, for which they could be called to account and judged before the supreme court

[1 Allen [d] says that there was no question of incorporating Schleswig with Denmark, because the separate constitution of Schleswig was to continue to operate. He speaks of the new constitution as intended to provide for the management of such matters as concerned both Denmark and Schleswig.]

[1863 A.D.]

(*Rigsret*). The rigsdag was to meet once a year, and to be composed of the folkething (chamber of the people) and the landsthing (chamber of the landed proprietors). The right to elect and to be elected to the folkething belonged to everyone within certain natural limitations — the candidate elected must, for example, be of a certain age, of irreproachable morality, etc., but it mattered little as to his social status and fortune. The right of suffrage for the landsthing was also submitted to the same conditions; but it could not be exercised directly — there were two steps. To be eligible to this second chamber, one must, besides complying with the general conditions, possess an annual net income of at least 1200 rix-dollars (£140), or have paid to the state or the commune during the year past 200 rix-dollars (£23), in direct taxes. The members of the folkething were to be elected for three years; those of the landsthing, for eight.

Officials elected to the rigsdag were not obliged to obtain permission from the government to take their seats.

Among other important articles whose object was to guarantee civil and personal liberty, the independence and impartiality of the magistracy, and the general equality of citizens in regard to public rights and burdens, must be mentioned complete liberty of conscience, the right to form religious societies and hold public worship, on condition that nothing should be done or taught to offend public morality and order; and, besides these, freedom of association, of meeting, of the press under its legal responsibility, and the permanent abolition of the censorship. Personal liberty was guaranteed by the obligation to bring every arrested person before a judge within twenty-four hours; and the magistrate had to decide at once whether the accused was to be kept under arrest, or set at liberty. Every man

QUEEN LOUISE
(1817–1898)

in condition to bear arms was obliged to contribute in person to his country's defence. Judges could not be dismissed without trial, or removed without their consent. The administration of justice was to be entirely separated from the executive authority, and the judiciary privileges attached to certain properties were to be abolished by law. Publicity and oral procedure were to be introduced, as far as possible, into the courts. Criminal and political cases were to be submitted to juries. Such were the fundamental points of the new constitution with which Denmark was provided, and through which her society was in future to be governed, directed and developed.[d]

When the question came up of a common constitution for the kingdom and the duchies, an attempt was made to give it an autocratic form, but this failed. According to the constitution of 1855, the assembly, intended to deliberate on the affairs common to the kingdom and the duchies, was to be known as the *rigsraad* (council of the kingdom) and to consist of eighty members, of which thirty were to be chosen by direct and thirty by indirect election, while the remaining twenty were to be appointed by the king. It was to have a deliberative voice in all common affairs of legislation and taxation.

The constitution of 1863 made some changes.[a] The new rigsraad or parliament was to consist of two chambers; the folkething, with 130 members (one hundred and one for the kingdom and twenty-nine for Schleswig), who were to be elected directly by the nation according to the rule in force for the electorate and eligibility to the rigsdag of the kingdom; and the landsthing, with eighty-three members, of which eighteen were to be designated by the king, whilst the rest were to be chosen by direct election. Other important steps in a liberal direction were the rights accorded to the rigsraad concerning the initiative for the proposition of laws, amendments in the details, interpellations, etc.[d]

CHRISTIAN IX AND THE SECOND SCHLESWIG-HOLSTEIN WAR

Christian IX was a younger brother of the reigning duke of Glücksburg, the representative of the Beck line of the house of Oldenburg. The founder of this Beck line was Augustus Philip, whose father, Alexander, was the son of John the Young, a younger son of Christian III. The house of Augustenburg descended from Ernest Gunther, a son of Alexander older than Augustus Philip; and the duke of Augustenburg was therefore the representative of an older line than that of Glücksburg. But the wife of the prince of Glücksburg was the Princess Louise of Hesse, whose mother was a sister of Christian VIII, and in whom the claims of her family to the Danish throne had been vested with their consent. It was on Christian of Glücksburg and the male heirs of him and Louise of Hesse that the London Protocol had settled the succession to the Danish throne; and this arrangement had been finally recognised by the Danish parliament, in June 1853, though not till after a severe struggle, while the duke of Augustenburg had been induced to resign his claim — a resignation in which his son and the other members of his family did not, however, acquiesce.[a]

Three days after the death of Frederick VII, the new fundamental law for the kingdom of Schleswig was sanctioned. But in Germany an event had already occurred, which set the smouldering fire ablaze: from the castle of Dolzig in Silesia, the son of the old duke Christian of Augustenburg, the self-styled "crown prince" Frederick of Augustenburg, had notified the people of Schleswig-Holstein, by a manifesto dated the 16th of November, that, being the concessionary of his father's claims to the duchies, and having become duke by the extinction in the person of Frederick VII of the royal male line of Frederick III, he assumed the title of Frederick VIII. On the same day, the envoy of Baden at the Frankfort diet notified the duke's accession. Throughout Germany there arose a national agitation still greater than that of 1848; it was said that the moment had come for the Germans to deliver their oppressed brothers from the yoke of tyranny. In all the great towns, as Stuttgart, Dresden, Munich, Darmstadt, and Berlin, the governments were overwhelmed with addresses, petitions, and interpellations, requesting them to succour the duchies. The same disposition was manifested in the duchies themselves, where a number of officials refused to take the oath of fidelity to the new king, whilst some of the deputies to the estates of Holstein loudly claimed the protection of the diet of the German Confederation. As the latter had not signed the London Protocol, it had no scruple in denying its validity; and on the suggestion of Count von Beust, the minister of Saxony, it refused to receive into its midst the envoy of Christian IX, and resolved to allow the seat of the representative of Holstein to remain vacant for the time being.

Neither Prussia nor Austria, however, would follow in the wake of the diet; both were signatories of the London **Protocol,** and both had motives for maintaining it. Meantime, though the question of the succession held no direct connection with the constitutional question, the courts of Berlin and Vienna now succeeded in making the confederation diet adopt the resolution to proceed to the occupation of the duchies, without prejudice to the constitutional question (December 7th). It was to no purpose that the Danish government had offered (November 14th) to grant to the representatives of Holstein full authority in matters of finance, and had annulled (December 4th) the proclamation of the 30th of March, 1863. The most violent agitation animated the German people against the Prussian government, because it had betrayed the cause of the Augustenburgs. A numerous assembly of members of the legislative bodies of Germany pronounced in favour of the pretender, and appointed a committee to direct the movement. This agitation was not without its influence on the petty princes of Germany, and the king of Bavaria himself recognised the duke of Augustenburg; but Count Bismarck was unmoved, and supported with imperturbable calm the storm raised in the Prussian chamber of deputies. In consequence of the resolution taken by the confederation diet, Russia, England, and France put pressure on the court of Copenhagen, to induce it to abrogate the fundamental law of the 18th of November, the latter having been qualified by Prussia, in a despatch written two days before the death of Frederick VII, as the stumbling block to a pacific solution; but this abrogation would not have had the effect of suspending the occupation. Under this pressure the Danish government decided to evacuate Holstein; and, consequently, the troops of the Confederation, composed of twelve thousand Saxons and Hanoverians, under General Hake, encountered no obstacles when they crossed the frontier on the 23rd of December. Wherever they passed the pretender was proclaimed duke.

On the 1st of January, 1864, the fundamental law was put in force. On the 11th of January, Prussia and Austria laid before the diet a proposition to the effect that Denmark should be called upon to abrogate the constitution of the 18th of November, 1863, so far as Schleswig was concerned; and that, in case of refusal, that duchy should be occupied in order to compel the court of Copenhagen to fulfil its pretended obligations of 1851 and 1852. When, however, the majority of the diet, which shared the prejudices of the whole German people, and saw in this motion a betrayal of the rights of the pretender, had rejected this plan (January 14th), the two powers resolved to assume the direction of the affair without delay, in spite of the protests of the majority; and, on the 16th of January, they addressed an ultimatum to Denmark, calling upon her to abrogate the fundamental law, so far as Schleswig was concerned, within twenty-four hours. It was in vain that the Danish ministry declared itself ready to convoke the rigsraad for the purpose of proposing to it to effect this abrogation within six weeks; that it entered into the views of England concerning a congress of representatives of the powers signatory of the London Protocol, to whom should be joined a plenipotentiary of the German diet. The decisive moment had arrived; the whole question now was whether Denmark would be left isolated in the struggle. No assistance was to be expected from Russia. The project of the emperor Napoleon of submitting the question in debate to a general congress had shortly before been defeated by the opposition of England, and the emperor had not openly repelled the prince of Augustenburg, who had appealed to him; whilst the French minister for foreign affairs, Drouyn de Lhuys, declared in general terms that the emperor was inclined to support the principle of nationalities. England, as before, wrote notes upon notes, but that was all. The greatest disappointment, however, was the conduct of Sweden and Norway.

The relations between the Scandinavian states had never been so friendly as under the reign of Frederick VII. Numerous pamphlets had even propagated the idea of a more intimate union between the peoples of the North, but for the partisans of the complex state Scandinavianism was an abomination; and in February, 1857, in a despatch addressed to the Danish envoys at London, St. Petersburg, Paris, and Stockholm, the Swedish minister for foreign affairs had anathematised the Scandinavian idea as incapable of a practical realisation, so long as it was found expedient to adhere to the principle of the integrity of the Danish monarchy in its present extent. This arbitrary act of the minister troubled not a little the good understanding between the two countries, the more so as King Oscar had proposed to Frederick VII an alliance between Sweden and Norway, and Denmark "to the Eider," including Schleswig. In May, 1862, Sweden and Norway had expressed readiness to act in concert with the non-German powers; but she urged on the court of Copenhagen, with increasing insistence, the separation of Holstein. The proclamation of the 30th of March, 1863, was a rapid advance in this direction, and King Charles XV proposed to Frederick VII a defensive alliance between their states (July, 1863); but the death of Frederick VII led the government of Sweden and Norway to withdraw its offers. Nevertheless, in both Sweden and Norway the nation manifested in various ways its sympathy for Denmark.

On the 19th of January, 1864, Prussia and Austria notified the German diet that they proposed to occupy Holstein, where they believed they would encounter no opposition from the troops of the Confederation, and on the same day Prussian couriers announced that Prussian troops would be quartered at Hamburg. The two great powers did as they had said. On January 21st Prussian troops entered Holstein, and the next day were followed by the Austrians, the troops of the Confederation making no show of resistance. The Prussians were commanded by King William's nephew, Prince Frederick Charles, who had taken part in the war in the same countries six years before; the Austrian leader was Gablenz; and the chief command of the combined armies, which numbered about seventy thousand men, was in the hands of Field-Marshal Wrangel, who had distinguished himself in the first Prussian campaign in the peninsula of Jutland (April–August, 1848). To these forces Denmark could oppose little more than thirty-five thousand men, under Lieutenant-General Meza, who had occupied the position of the Dannevirke, which had been so strongly fortified during recent years that many regarded it as impregnable, provided it were defended by sufficient troops. On the 31st of January, a Prussian major sent by Wrangel summoned the Danish commander to evacuate the duchy of Schleswig; and, on the latter's refusal Prince Frederick Charles attempted an assault against the intrenchments of Missunde, at the extreme left of the Danes. He had intended to cross the Schlei at this point, but Lieutenant-General Gerlach victoriously repelled the attack after six hours of fighting. On the 3rd of that month, the Austrians succeeded better when, after a combat at Jagel and Oberselk, they took by assault the Kongshöei, and arrived at the foot of the Dannevirke. It was then resolved that, whilst the Austrians attacked the front of the position, the Prussians should make a turning movement by Arnis and Kappel, to the east of Missunde.

Meantime, at the Danish headquarters it was decided, in a council of war, to evacuate the position of the Dannevirke; the execution of this measure began at a late hour of the evening, without due warning having been conveyed to the government. In a dark winter night the Danish army operated in despair its painful retreat, which the biting cold, the frost, and hunger and thirst rendered still more difficult. The Danish nation was struck to the earth by the news of this movement to the rear. The government deprived Meza of his command, which was given provisionally to Lieutenant-General Lüttichau, who was in his turn soon replaced by General Gerlach.

The Lines of Düppel

As soon as the allies got wind of the evacuation of the Dannevirke, they set to work to pursue the Danish army; but, as the latter had a considerable start, it was only at Sankelmark, to the south of Flensburg, that its rear guard, under Colonel Max Müller, was caught up by the advance guard of the Austrians. The encounter which followed was extremely sanguinary. Meantime, the main body of the Danish army, consisting of three divisions, occupied without obstacle its other principal position, the lines of Düppel (Dybbel) on the peninsula of Sundewitt, while the fourth division, under Hegermann-Lindencrone continued its retreat towards the north of the peninsula. Whereever the allies passed they assumed the rôle of masters; the Danish officials were expelled, often with brutality; the fortifications of the Dannevirke were rased; the column at Skamlingsbanke, where innumerable national *fêtes* had been celebrated in honour of the dawn of liberty, was destroyed by a mine; German once more became the language of the schools and the administration, for everything that recalled the Danish dominion was to be effaced.

Whilst the Austrians and a division of the Prussian guard advanced northwards, the main body of the Prussian army turned on Düppel and invested the Danish position. But it was not till the 17th of March, after the arrival of the siege train, that the Prussians succeeded in gaining possession of Rageböl, Düppel, and Arnbjerg. They then opened a heavy fire on the enemy's fortifications and gradually approached them. The Danes responded as well as they could to the fire of the besiegers; but the earthworks could not resist the ravages of the projectiles, and it soon became impossible to defend them. Although the Danes endured with admirable fortitude the perils and privations of the siege, the issue of the affair could not be doubtful. On the morning of the 18th of April, the Prussians made the assault. The first six works at once fell into the power of the assailants; it was the same with the second line, where General Duplat, who fell there gloriously, arrested for some time the progress of the enemy; but soon the Danes were compelled to retire behind the fortified *tête de pont*. A fierce artillery duel resulted in the capture of this intrenchment also, though the victors were unable to cut off the retreat of the Danish army and prevent it from regaining the island of Alsen. The losses of the vanquished rose to 4,846 killed, wounded, and prisoners, including 108 officers; those of the Prussians were 1,184 men, of whom 70 were officers. Meantime, Jutland had also fallen into the power of the allies. As early as the eighteenth of February, they had crossed the Konge Aa, which forms the boundary between North Jutland and South Jutland or Schleswig; but for the time being the Austrians, who were not anxious to prolong hostilities, remained motionless near Kolding. It was not till the Prussian general Von Manteuffel had smoothed away all difficulties at Vienna that operations were resumed. After a savage fight, the

Danes were compelled to evacuate Veile, and Fredericia was invested the same day. General Hegermann-Lindencrone had retired to the island of Mors in the Limfjord. On the 28th of April, the Danish government ordered the evacuation of the fortress of Fredericia; and the allies thus became masters of the peninsula of Jutland as far as the Limfjord.

While these events were passing diplomacy had given matters a new turn. England had worked energetically to assemble a conference of the states signatory of the Treaty of London; and, after many difficulties, it had been agreed that the plenipotentiaries of those powers should enter into negotiations, though on no defined basis and without the interruption of hostilities. The conference was to open on the 12th of April, but the German courts delayed the arrangements until the taking of Düppel had rendered their position more favourable; it was not till the 25th that the session was opened. On the 9th of May, an armistice for one month was concluded which was afterwards extended to June 25th. On that day the conference closed, having accomplished nothing, and hostilities were resumed. On the 9th of May, the day on which it had been agreed at the London conference that the armistice should be concluded, a Danish squadron, consisting of the frigates *Niels Juel* and *Jutland* and of the corvette *Heimdal* had sustained an honourable struggle against the Austrian frigates *Schwarzenberg* and *Radetzky*, which were escorted by an Austrian steam corvette with two Prussian gunboats and a Prussian bark. But the fight could exercise no influence on the general course of events; and the Danish fleet was reduced to playing a merely accessory part in a war carried on chiefly by land.

The impotence of the navy was deplorably manifest when the decisive moment arrived. During the night between the 28th and the 29th of June, the Prussians, under Herwarth von Bittenfeld, crossed the Alsen Sound, the Danes making no serious resistance; and next day the island, feebly defended by General Steimann, was in the power of the Germans, with a loss of 3200 men for the Danes. The peninsula of Vendsyssel, north of the Limfjord, was evacuated soon after, and German officers pitched their tents as far north as the Skaw (July 14th). Finally, the islands in the North Sea belonging to Jutland were likewise occupied by the enemy (July 19th).

THE SEVERANCE OF THE DUCHIES

The force of the resistance was broken. The court of Copenhagen entered into negotiations, and by the 4th of August the preliminaries of peace were signed at Vienna; the final treaty was concluded on the 30th of October. Denmark surrendered to Prussia and Austria the duchies of Schleswig, Holstein, and Lauenburg, and undertook to recognise as valid the dispositions which those two powers might make relative to their conquests. The portions of Jutland enclosed in the territory of Schleswig were also ceded to that duchy, but in return Denmark might incorporate the island of Ærö and some portions of Schleswig territory enclosed in that of Denmark; no war indemnity was to be paid; the duchies assumed a share of the common debts.

Thus, the present moment paid dearly for the political errors of the past and the absence of a national policy with regard to Schleswig; one of the oldest monarchies of Europe had been humiliated and dismembered, while none held out a hand to sustain her. The indifference of the powers which had guaranteed Denmark in the possession of Schleswig gave a melancholy idea of the nature of political morality.[d] The gainer by the war was not the insignificant Augustenburg claimant, whose resistance to the demands of

Bismarck soon ended in his abandonment by that too powerful friend. Austria, who continued to support his cause, was herself soon involved in a disastrous war with Prussia, which ended in the Treaty of Prague, whereby she abandoned the duchies to her conqueror. Clause 5 in that treaty did indeed provide for the restoration to Denmark of the northern portion of Schleswig, if such an arrangement were desired by the inhabitants of that district, where there was a large Danish population; but this clause was subsequently abrogated.[a]

The loss of Schleswig necessitated a revision of the Danish constitution; and a bill to that effect was brought forward by the government, in December, 1864. This was, in the main, a revision of the fundamental law of 1849; but there were several new and important articles, as for example, concerning the composition of the landsthing; the restriction of the suffrage to those who had had in recent years a net revenue of 2,000 rix-dollars ($1165, £233), or had paid 200 rix-dollars in direct taxes; the submission of the budget to a committee composed of members of the two assemblies, equal in numbers and enjoying the same rights, in case the chambers should be unable to agree on financial questions; the convocation of the rigsdag every two years and, in consequence, the vote of the budget for a biennial period.[d] This project did not meet with universal approval, but at last, in 1866, after long disputes, it finally became law.[a]

RECENT HISTORY OF DENMARK

The recent political history of Denmark offers very little of general interest. The country has not been engaged in the political struggles of Europe, and has been left in peace.

The most noticeable feature in the internal history of Denmark is the constitutional struggle which has been going on for many years between successive governments and the Left party, which commands an overwhelming majority in the folkething. No practical questions of great importance have been at the bottom of this disagreement, save that of the fortification of Copenhagen. The government considered this necessary, because without it the capital was exposed to a *coup de main* at any time, while the Left opposed it as a piece of aggressive militarism, which would be unnecessary if Denmark only proclaimed her neutrality in any war that might arise. For this reason the majority of the folkething refused to sanction the outlay; but the government — considering that the danger was real, and that the neutrality of a state cannot be secured by her own declaration, but depends on the good-will of her neighbours, which cannot be guaranteed — nevertheless carried out the work by means of a huge accumulated surplus. In the course of this conflict, the majority in the folkething even went the length of refusing supplies altogether; but under the premiership of M. Estrup the government nevertheless collected the revenue and sought its justification in the approval of the landsthing, whose political power, according to the charter, is in every respect equal to that of the folkething. This procedure met with no serious resistance in the country. The election in the spring of 1901 resulted in the return to the folkething of seventy-six members of the reform party of the Left, sixteen members of the moderate Left, fourteen social democrats, and only eight members of the Right, the party which had held the reins of power for so many years.

Professor Deuntzer, one of the law professors in the University of Copenhagen, became the head of a government composed of prominent men, drawn from the different sections of his own side of the folkething, and including among their number a simple peasant as minister of agriculture. The most prominent articles in the policy of the new government were a reform of the customs, a readjustment of the system of taxation, a reform of the judicial procedure, a reform of primary education, and a reduction in the expenditure for military purposes.*j*

In 1902 the question of the sale of the Danish West Indies to the United States being on the *tapis* and the sale being apparently on the verge of completion after years of delay, the results of a new election seemed to promise the ratification of the treaty concerning it. But the event proved otherwise; the landsthing refused the ratification and those islands still remain in possession of the little kingdom whose power has been established there since the seventeenth century, though the material advantage she derives from them is somewhat problematical.

Professor Deuntzer's government was sustained in the elections of 1903, but in January, 1905, a cabinet disagreement occurred over the question of national defense, and Jens Christian Christensen, who had previously been minister of public instruction, undertook the formation of a ministry. The new premier announced a program which included universal manhood suffrage in communal elections, the settlement of the national defense on the basis of the neutrality of the state, and a rearranging of the districts for elections to the folkething.

A year later, on the 29th of January, 1906, King Christian IX died after a long reign of forty-two years. His death excited universal regret among his subjects; and since one of his sons-in-law was king of England, one of his sons king of Greece, and grandsons the rulers of Norway and of Russia, while others of his descendants were connected with yet other ruling families, it threw most of the European courts into mourning. The crown prince quietly succeeded to the vacant throne under title of Frederick VIII.*a*

CHAPTER XIV

SWEDEN AND NORWAY IN THE NINETEENTH CENTURY

In the wars consequent on the French Revolution, the duke of Söder-manland, regent of Sweden, took no part. By a treaty which he entered into with Frederick prince regent of Denmark (1790), sixteen vessels were equipped to defend the entrance of the Baltic against the ships of the belligerent powers. Russia was indignant at this exclusion; she tried to hurl the duke of Södermanland from power by flattering the vanity of Gustavus IV. That young prince, who attained his majority in 1796, was tempted by the offer of Alexandrina Paulovna, grand-daughter of Catherine II; but the difference of religion was an obstacle which could neither be surmounted nor removed. Sweden, reformed Lutheran Sweden, would not allow the princess the exercise of her own worship. Yet, by marrying the princess Frederica of Baden, sister to the wife of the grand-duke Alexander, Gustavus, who had little strength of intellect, was merged into the sphere of Russian influence.

For some years after his accession, the Swedish monarch was satisfied with condemning the encroaching ambition of France. His alliance with Alexander led him more deeply into the political views of that emperor. Like the other, he protested against the murder of the duke d'Enghien and the assumption of the imperial dignity by Napoleon. As duke of Pomerania, too, he inveighed in the Germanic diet against the usurper. In revenge, Bonaparte, who affected to despise him, caricatured him in the *Moniteur*. He was reproached with having deserted his allies the Danes at the battle of Copenhagen, and was ridiculed for his imitation of Charles XII, of whom he had inherited only the jack-boots and the rashness. To these insults he was more sensitive than became a wise man. He ordered the minister of "Monsieur Napoleon Bonaparte" to leave Sweden, and prohibited all intercourse, public or private, between the two countries. Hence he joined with eagerness the coalition formed by Pitt (1805). Subsequently he agreed that Hanoverian troops should be located in Pomerania, and that Swedish regiments should serve in the pay of England.   The folly of Prussia, then the slave of Bonaparte, prevented the execution of these conditions, but could not prevent Gustavus from placing himself at the head of his armies, and proceeding to expel Bernadotte from Hanover.   He arrived too late: the confederacy which had been formed was dissolved by the victories of Napoleon, who after the battle of Austerlitz dictated terms of peace to the emperor Francis.   Hanover was evacuated by the allies, and the Continent left to the victor.

Though Russia and Prussia, like Denmark, were banded with the great enemy of European independence, Gustavus would listen to no overtures of conciliation.   Among the most tempting of them was the offer of Norway; but he preferred his honour and his principles to every advantage.   He cannot, however, be exculpated from the charge of extreme rashness in venturing to withstand, single-handed, the colossal power of his enemy.   Arriving in Pomerania, he assailed Marshal Brune; but being vanquished, he was forced to retire under the cannon of Stralsund.   Leaving that fortress, he had the mortification to see it invested and taken.   Rügen and all the islands on the Pomeranian coast were equally reduced.

In these transactions Gustavus had expected English co-operation, but it was delayed until it was too late to be of any service in Pomerania.   Now when the Danish islands were occupied by the French and Spanish forces, he had a right to urge it.   But the danger was averted by the war with Austria, and by the escape of the Spanish troops under the marquis de la Romana. Denmark, however, at the instigation of Napoleon, declared war against Gustavus [February, 1808]

LOSS OF FINLAND (1808 A.D.)

The situation of Gustavus at this time was one of peculiar embarrassment. He was menaced by Russia, now the tool of Napoleon, with hostilities if he did not co-operate with her and Denmark in declaring the Baltic *mare clausum* and by Prussia, the slave of that emperor, war was declared against him. With Denmark, Prussia, France, and Russia against him, he looked to England for aid.   A subsidy of £100,000 monthly emboldened him to resist. The war soon raged.   Finland was occupied by the Russians and immediately declared an integral portion of Russia.   The Swedish armies were defeated everywhere.   The arrival from England of Sir John Moore with eleven thousand men might have been of some little advantage to Gustavus had he not insisted on the command of these auxiliaries, and by other demands so offended the general that he returned, without striking a blow, to England. Hence all his subsequent attempts to expel the enemy from Finland were unavailing.   Nor was the war more fortunate in Norway, which the Swedish troops had invaded, and from which they were soon expelled with much loss. He was unfortunate, too, on the deep; and was even advised to make peace with both France and Denmark.   But he declared that he would never treat with the French usurper, or with any ally of that usurper.[b]

In many respects Gustavus resembled the best of his progenitors.   His private life was unimpeachable, and his zeal for the social and domestic improvement of his people unwearied.   His devoted patriotism and inflexible honour were manifested in the resolute perseverance with which he alone, of all the continental sovereigns, rejected the offers and defied the power of the French conqueror.   But there was in his constitution that family disease which had displayed itself in the eccentricities of Christina and the military

[1808–1809 A.D.]

madness of Charles XII. His unreasonable obstinacy, his capricious sallies of passion, his conduct towards Sir John Moore, and his whole system of policy in the Finnish and Norwegian campaigns, were all symptoms of that mental derangement which rendered it necessary for the interests of the kingdom to put an end to his reign. Besides these causes, others existed, arising purely from incidental circumstances. The machinery of government was ill compacted, and this defect became doubly mischievous when the helm of administration was guided by the hand of a prince who knew not how to regulate his own conduct. The long struggle between the crown and the aristocracy had left a rankling spirit, which even the blood of Gustavus III had not satiated. The discontent of the nobles was inflamed by the haughtiness of the king, who exacted the strictest etiquette at court, and was never approached except with the most ceremonious respect. Towards the close of 1808, he is said to have proposed rigorous measures for punishing the disaffected, but the threat, if really made, was in vain, as he had not the power of carrying it into effect. Many among the higher classes were imbued with that baneful attachment to the language and manners of France which had contributed so fatally to the overthrow of the continental thrones; and this treasonable spirit both Denmark and Russia openly abetted by the unworthy means which they adopted to corrupt the loyalty of the Swedish people.c

General Akrell, in his Memoirs, writes of Gustavus as follows: "The imprudent policy of Gustavus IV, his foolhardy obstinacy in face of overwhelming odds, and his blind, fanatical belief in supernatural aid, had ended by bringing upon his country the calamity which had long been foreseen. At the beginning of March, in the year 1808, news came that the Russians had crossed the frontier of Finland at several points. The meagre force which was all the Swedes could muster in haste had been repulsed, and after the Finnish army had received orders to retreat, the whole country lay open to the enemy." Thus the year 1808 opened upon gloomy and alarming prospects. Sweden could send no succour, and Finland and its brave defenders were therefore left to their fate. The universal indignation aroused among the people of Sweden by this abandonment was increased by the traitorous surrender of the fortress of Sweaborg to the enemy. Denmark's declaration of war against Sweden was followed by an attack in the rear, from the direction of Norway. In Sweden, on the other hand, dejection, mistakes, and lack of method were the order of the day, and from the war department issued orders, counter-orders, and disorders.

The year 1809 opened under circumstances from which Sweden had good cause to apprehend absolute annihilation and disintegration, unless some efficacious remedy were promptly discovered. Finland was already lost, Åland occupied by the Russians; the remnants of the gallant Finnish army had capitulated, the winter was so exceptionally severe that troops could cross the ice at Åland and Quarken; a flying squadron of Russians appeared at Grislehamn, another paid a visit to Umeå. The unhappy Swedish militia had perished by hundreds from neglect and insufficiency of clothing; a pestilential sickness was raging among the survivors at home; all the hospitals were filled to overflowing, while the treasuries and depôts stood empty, and a grant in aid (kronsteuer) of five millions was about to be imposed upon the whole country. In every department of defence, error and confusion came to light; the temper of the nation was sullen and menacing; the king met danger by defiance, obstinately repelling all reasonable remonstrances and relying upon the supernatural succour which, as a chosen instrument of the divine will, he expected speedily to receive.

DEPOSITION OF GUSTAVUS (IV) ADOLPHUS (1809)

The prompt dethronement of the king now began to be generally spoken of, without the slightest pretence of secrecy, as the only means of saving the country. A conspiracy was soon set on foot by determined men, who purposed to arrest him on his way to the town from the castle of Haga, where he resided. The plan was generally known several days before that fixed for its accomplishment, the sovereign alone remained in ignorance. In spite of this fact, and although the enterprise was attended with no real danger, the whole scheme was frustrated by the indecision of one of the conspirators at the very moment when they were assembled in Becker's Tavern, in Nortullsgatan (North Toll street) at Stockholm, for the purpose of putting it into effect. Meanwhile, the western army had started under the command of Lieutenant-Colonel Adlersparre, and was now marching on Stockholm to bring about a change of government. The king, at length apprised of the matter, resolved to go to the towns of southern Sweden, under the escort of the second Pomeranian regiment, which was in garrison at Stockholm, and to take with him such ready money as was lying at the bank. Thus civil war was imminent, but was fortunately averted by General Adlercreutz's bold resolution to arrest the king on the 13th of March, the very day of his meditated flight.

"The rumour of extraordinary proceedings in the capital soon spread to Karlberg" (where Akrell was engaged as instructor at the military academy). "Suspecting what was in the air, I went at once to the city, accompanied by Wallin (afterwards archbishop), who was at that time assistant-master in theology at the academy; but at the toll office we were refused entrance into the city by a guard of the town militia stationed there. In answer to a question from me, the sentry confessed that the muskets of the guard were not loaded with balls, so that it would have been easy for us to jump over the turnpike gate and go on; but Wallin would not hear of such a proceeding, and we were therefore obliged to get into the town another way. On my arrival at the castle I met General Adlercreutz, commander-in-chief at the time, in the *Trabantensaal* (halberdier's hall); and he gave me orders to stay, and to undertake the office of keeping guard over the king, who was under arrest, in concert with a few other officers who had already collected there. This unexpected and absolutely illegal command had to be obeyed. The officers mounted guard, two at a time; and when the watches were apportioned, Lieutenant Gripenwald of the Finnish guards fell to my lot as companion. Our very first period on duty was signalised by gruff questions on the part of Gustavus Adolphus and rude unseemly answers from Gripenwald, and ended in behaviour and expressions which plainly showed that the former was not merely dull-witted, but suffered from actual mental aberration.

"The king was to be removed to Drottningholm later in the evening. The carriages had already driven up to the castle hill and been ranged in order, when it became known that large crowds had collected round the castle hill and the hill where the church stood. Instead of dispersing them by means of the military, General Adlercreutz very sensibly gave orders that two officers should try to induce the mob to break up, by kindly words and suitable expostulations. Captain Lagerheim of the cavalry and I were detailed for this duty. Lagerheim was admirably qualified for the task; my appointment was less happy, as I did not possess his ready tongue and easy knack of persuasion. I addressed myself to various well-dressed persons of the so-called upper class, told them that it was true that the king was under restraint, but that he was treated with all due respect, and was to be removed to Drottningholm under a strong escort; I reminded them of the mischief that might ensue if the people there assembled placed obstacles in the way of his removal, etc., and begged them by suitable admonitions to induce the crowd to disperse. This they very soon did; and a short time after, when the procession was to start, not a creature was visible in the vicinity of the castle or in the streets. The silence and tranquillity that prevailed in the city, where people were fully aware of what had happened that morning, bore eloquent testimony to the temper of the lower classes. No patrol marched through the streets, no extraordinary measure of precaution was perceptible, only the ordinary fire-watches (Brandwachen) proclaimed to us, as we drove by, that the hour of midnight was past.

" At the castle of Drottningholm, the state bedchamber was assigned to the use of Gustavus Adolphus, and there he was guarded day and night by relays of two officers apiece. A squadron of cuirassiers and a battalion of the king's own regiment kept guard before the castle. General Silversparre was the chief in command. Differences of opinion prevailed among the officers who had to be on guard in the king's chamber, as to the behaviour to be observed towards him; the general opinion being that they ought to treat him with the respectful attention due to the great position he had held, and to his present misfortunes. A few, among whom was Lieutenant Gripenwald, did not share this view. Gripenwald declared that the king had forfeited every claim to respect, and that he intended to treat him accordingly. Unfortunately, the king's stiff manners and want of tact furnished Gripenwald with abundant opportunities for uncivil behaviour. The position in which this placed the other officers was all the more painful because the noble prisoner never conversed upon any but the most trivial, dull, and even tiresome subjects; sometimes indulging in scornful looks and gestures, and sometimes responding to the officers' observations with a stupid, clumsy condescension, rendered more awkward still by his unconquerable suspiciousness of temper and his dread of an attempt on his life."[d]

CHARLES XIII AND THE NEW CONSTITUTION

Meantime the duke of Södermanland, who was no stranger to the intrigues against his sovereign, was invested with the title of administrator until the meeting of the diet, on the 1st of May. The people expected that this revolution would at once put an end to the war; but neither the czar nor the Danish king would treat with an insecure government. Hostilities therefore continued; the isle of Åland was taken, and Sweden itself was invaded from the north; but the regent obtained an armistice. The diet met at the appointed time; an act of abdication, signed by Gustavus, was produced; and a double decree was passed — first, that having broken his compact with the people, the throne was vacant; and secondly, that his posterity, born and unborn, should forever remain excluded from it.[1] The duke of Södermanland was raised to the throne as Charles XIII; and a new constitution, restoring the power of the monarch, was drawn up.[b]

The throne was pronounced to be hereditary, with limitation to the male issue; the sovereign was required to profess the Lutheran religion, and to conduct the ordinary administration of business with the assistance of a

[1] The dethroned king retired to Switzerland with his family, and died at St. Gallen in 1837. He left a son known as the prince of Vasa and two daughters. The prince of Vasa's only child was a daughter.]

state council, to be appointed by him, and responsible for their advice. The members, who must be native Swedes and of the established faith, were to consist of nine individuals: the two ministers for judicial and foreign affairs, the chancellor of the court, and six councillors, one-half of whom, at least, must be civil officers. The four secretaries of state were to sit in council whenever any case belonging to their respective departments should be under consideration; all matters, except the foreign and diplomatic relations, were to be submitted to the deliberation of the king and his legal advisers, of whom three, at least, were required to be present (that number being necessary to constitute a council for the transaction of business); but he was not obliged to adopt their suggestions, and might by virtue of his prerogative decide in opposition to their votes or opinions. In the event of his decision being repugnant to the laws of the realm, the assessors were bound to remonstrate, and to record their protest; otherwise they should be deemed guilty of counselling and abetting him in his unconstitutional proceedings, as he was not held responsible for any act of his own. Before declaring war or concluding treaties, he was expected to state his motives to the council and hear the sentiments which it was their duty to express. Of the army and navy he was to have the supreme command, and the ultimate determination in all matters relating to both services, assisted by the ministers of state for these departments. Civil and military employments were placed at his disposal, as also the appointment of archbishops and bishops; but he could not remove a judge from office, except for just cause and on proof of criminality. He was not allowed to deprive any subject of life, liberty, or property, without a legal process; nor could he arraign religious opinions, unless the profession or dissemination of them should appear to be injurious to the public. The supreme court of justice was composed of six nobles and six commoners, whose continuance in office depended solely on their upright conduct; the king had a double voice, and might pardon criminals and mitigate or commute punishments.

The deputies of the estates were to be freely elected, and to enjoy liberty of speech during their deliberations. The diet was to assemble in the capital every fifth year; and the session was not to continue above three months, unless urgent business should demand an extension of that period. It was part of their duty to nominate a committee for superintending the freedom of the press and inquiring into the conduct of the ministers and council. No taxes could be imposed without their sanction; nor had the sovereign the privilege of negotiating a loan, or altering the currency, or alienating any part of the Swedish territory. Several changes and reforms of minor importance were at the same time effected. A decree of Gustavus, prohibiting the entrance of any Jews into his dominions, was revoked; and the fashion of wearing a white scarf round the left arm, which, since the revolution of 1772, had continued as a badge to distinguish the king's friends, was abolished. A pension was also granted to the deposed monarch and his family, after the amount of his private property had been ascertained; and to obtain credit for economy, his successor gave up to the disposal of the estates most of the royal palaces, with their gardens, parks, and dependencies. He likewise dismissed the household of the late sovereign, contenting himself with the same establishment as when he was duke of Södermanland.*c*

Thus Charles, who readily sanctioned the new constitution, obtained the object which he had so long pursued. As he had no issue, the succession had yet to be settled; the choice of the diet fell on Christian Augustus of Holstein Augustenburg, a prince connected by birth with the dynasty of Vasa, and by marriage with the royal family of Denmark. This revolution did not lead to peace. Alexander of Russia, with his usual haughtiness, would not grant it without the cession of Finland, which Bonaparte had guaranteed to him, and of the isle of Åland. The north of Sweden was again ravaged by his troops, and the generals of Charles were, as before, beaten. In one or two isolated cities the natives had the advantage; but their best defence lay in the nature of the country, where provisions could not be obtained, and in the activity of the English cruisers, which intercepted the supplies destined for the Russian army. Still, peace was indispensable; and in September of the same year, it was concluded at Fredrikshamn, on conditions deeply humiliating to Sweden. Finland was surrendered, so was the isle of Aland, so was East Bothnia, so was West Bothnia, down to Torneå; and all these were declared an integral portion of the empire. Sweden then acceded to the continental system, and closed her ports to British shipping. She was, however, after much difficulty, permitted to import salt and colonial produce from England. Thus she lost one-third of her population, one-fourth of her territory, and her best fortresses; while internally every province was exhausted.

Before the conclusion of the year, a treaty of peace was also signed between Sweden and Denmark. Both kingdoms remained in the same position to each other as before the war. The opening of the ensuing year was signalised by a treaty with France which virtually rendered Sweden a province of that empire.[b]

SWEDEN AND THE CONTINENTAL SYSTEM

Excluded from Holland and thwarted upon the North Sea, English commerce, under a neutral flag, was carried on and flourished on the Baltic. While the enemy continued his northerly movement by sea, Napoleon followed him on the shores in order to close issues with him. In July, Napoleon ordered Denmark, Prussia, and Mecklenburg not to receive any ships laden with colonial articles. Shortly afterwards, by the decrees of August 5th and September 10th, 1810, which he forced all the German states to adopt, he put upon these commodities the enormous duty of fifty per cent. In principle, this tax was only applicable to merchandise captured on the high seas, all other being absolutely excluded; but, in point of fact, it might be applied to articles admitted through tolerance, provided the stigmata of their origin were not too clearly shown.

When he believed himself to have enclosed the North Sea and the German Baltic with a continuous line of circumvallation, he perceived an almost imperceptible fissure which would allow English products to get through, and decrease the whole efficiency of the scheme. Between Prussia and the duchies of Mecklenburg a small piece of shore line, a narrow band of territory — a fraction of Pomerania — still belonged to the Swedes. This was all that remained of their vast possessions in Germany, a fragment or, rather, a souvenir of the empire created by the great Gustavus Adolphus. When Napoleon had granted them peace, on January 6th, 1810, he had restored them Pomerania, on condition that they would declare war on England and bind themselves to all the necessaries for the blockade. In spite of this positive agreement, Pomerania with the port of Stralsund remained open to colonial products; here they found protection, were collected together, and distributed throughout neighbouring countries. Moreover, Sweden proper kept up direct relations with the enemy, and lent him precious aid. For if the Scandinavian peninsula, poor and sparsely populated, did not offer any considerable market to the prohibited articles, she collected them in her ports, particularly in that of Gothenburg, where they were accumulated and stored up, awaiting a propitious occasion to seek German soil. A contraband was organised, and found here a point of support and facilities for activity. In the Baltic Gothenburg rendered the English the same services as did Helgoland in the North Sea, but in an infinitely greater degree.

It was this vast storehouse, with its branches in Germany and Pomerania, that Napoleon now wished to close, and Sweden took a prominent place in his thoughts. Only, by Sweden's side stood Russia; if he established his authority too openly at Stockholm he would adjoin, on the extreme north, the empire which he already touched with the duchy of Warsaw; and by creating a second point of contact, he would redouble the opportunities for quarrels and discord. In the month of May, Napoleon addressed to the Stockholm government a peremptory and threatening note, demanding at the same time the declaration of war with England, the extradition of a certain number of French refugees, and the sequestration of all the colonial merchandise stored in Pomerania. By failing to acquiesce in these demands within five days, Sweden was to lose all the benefits of the treaty, and expose herself to a rupture and its consequences.

By instinct and tradition Sweden inclined to France. She felt the advantage of adhering to her old ally and Napoleon's protection seemed indispensable in order to resist Russia, established henceforth just across from her capital, and to renew her political existence. But the first necessity of a people, even before providing for the security and dignity of the state, is to meet its daily needs. Now a rupture with England would render Sweden literally without the necessaries of life. Trade with the ports of the United Kingdom had become one of the normal and essential functions of her life. This means alone enabled the Scandinavians to turn the riches of their soil into money; to exploit their forests and mines by opening a permanent outlet for their timber, iron, and steel. In exchange for these products, England furnished her northern creditors with a quantity of articles necessary to their existence — commodities of the highest importance, as salt, for example, which Sweden did not possess or know how to manufacture. A complete suspension of these relations would have submitted her to intolerable privation. Between Napoleon, who could crush her or at least deliver her over to the Russian, and England, who possessed the means of starving her, she found herself reduced to ruse and subterfuge, making the former promises which she constantly eluded in favour of the latter.

THE QUESTION OF THE SUCCESSION

To the agonies of the situation were added the difficulties and danger of the morrow of a revolution. In the interior, passions were not yet quieted down; they remained active and irreconcilable, and nothing appeared strong enough to thwart or master them. King Charles XIII was old, infirm, and without posterity. The queen was unpopular and despised, and suspected of the worst intrigues. The elder branch of the Vasas formed a party by themselves; the leaders of the nobility were accused of connivance with Russia and denounced by the hatred of a turbulent demagogy, which coloured its subversive tendencies with an exalted patriotism.

In the midst of this confusion and danger, Sweden sought desperately for means to recover herself, or at least to bolster up her tottering destinies, and conceived the great idea of creating a new dynasty, in order to give herself a race of kings which should succeed the younger branch of the Vasas on the death of Charles XIII. This would be to graft a new limb on the dying trunk. On June 14th, 1809, the estates had chosen Charles of Augustenburg, brother-in-law of the king of Denmark, as heir to the crown, but at this moment, as if adversity were eager to strike the unhappy people, an unexpected thunderbolt fell upon Sweden. On the 28th of May, 1810, during a review, the prince of Augustenburg was suddenly stricken with illness, fell from his horse, and died on the spot. This catastrophe, too sudden to be attributed in the popular grief to natural causes, put Sweden's future again in suspense and delivered her over to every uncertainty. It was now necessary to proceed to the election of a new prince royal, and convoke a diet, which meant the re-opening of scenes of competition and disorder. In the midst of this confusion, the government perceived that providence had pointed out a means of shortening and simplifying the crisis. The prince they mourned had a brother, and by calling this young man to replace him, thus limiting themselves to the substitution of a member of the same family, they would cut short the conflicting intrigues beginning to work on all sides.

On the 2nd of June, while the cabinet was subscribing in principle to all the demands of a French note, the king wrote the emperor a pitiful letter; he dwelt upon the misfortunes which were crowding on his old age, indicated his preferences, made allusions to the second prince of Augustenburg, and asked Napoleon, in sufficiently explicit terms, to accept this candidate and give him the investiture. Before receiving this letter, Napoleon had learned of the death of the prince royal. The choice of a successor concerned him little as to the person himself; his purpose was simply to build up in Sweden a power strong enough to impose the rupture with England upon the nation, and strong enough, also, not to come under the influence and guidance of Russia. His idea all along was to bring it—a friend of France, without being an enemy of Russia, and already master of Norway—into close connection with Denmark, and then create around the Baltic a group of powers, a sort of Scandinavian federation. Had not the hour now come to take a decisive step—not only to establish the most intimate relations between the two governments, but to unite their crowns? This could be done by calling to the succession, instead of a Danish prince, the king of Denmark himself. When Napoleon for the first time passed the possible candidates in review, there was a slight inclination in favour of this *dénouement;* or, at least, this seems to be indicated in an article that appeared under date of June 17th, in the official *Journal de l'Empire.* The attention of the Swedes is there called to the king of Denmark in a few lines sufficiently clear to justify this opinion.

The candidature submitted to the emperor in Charles XIII's letter did not materially differ from that which in the first place had his preference; it tended in less direct fashion to the same end. Without preparing the union of the two crowns, it made a tie between Sweden and Denmark; and it had the advantage of being more acceptable to Russia, whom the prospect of complete fusion between the Scandinavian states would probably have alarmed. Napoleon accepted with good grace the choice of the prince of Augustenburg. He did not pronounce his adhesion to it in formal terms, having made it a principle not to meddle directly in the Swedish affair, but he inserted in his reply to the king the following words: "I have received your majesty's letter of June 2nd. I take a sincere share in all your anxieties, and I am troubled by the predicament into which this new circumstance puts you. I have had some satisfaction in seeing by your letter that providence has

spared you your strength. The project of binding more closely the ties of
Sweden and Denmark seems to have special advantage for your country."

French diplomacy was charged with furnishing the commentary to these
vague words. Since the peace, France had retained at Stockholm only a
simple *chargé d'affaires*, and if the emperor had already appointed Baron
Alquier his minister at the capital, he had ordered him to remain in Paris
until Sweden had fulfilled all the conditions in the matter of the blockade.
On the 24th of June, he sent M. Alquier the order to set out the following
day and immediately join his post.

The Election of Bernadotte

The next day (the 25th of June) the letter was sent off, and Alquier hastily
made preparations to depart. Everything seemed disposed towards action
in favour of the prince of Augustenburg; and the emperor would doubtless
have been greatly astonished to learn that, at that very hour, in the heart of
Paris at the house of a marshal, brother-in-law to King Joseph, a very different
scheme was being hatched, unknown to him. A few days before, a young
Swedish officer, Lieutenant Moerner, had arrived in Paris. He came without
a commission from his government; he did not represent any party, but only
a clique — a circle of friends who had given him orders to create a prince
royal for Sweden. A few military men and some professors at the University
of Upsala, eagerly desiring the regeneration of their country, and passionate
admirers of France and her army, had conceived the idea of feeding Sweden
from this source of warlike virtue and heroism; and they set about to seek,
from among the marshals in the imperial staff, the heir to the crown and the
future king.

Among the marshals, their choice very naturally fell upon the only one
whom Sweden knew other than by reputation. During the campaign of 1807,
Bernadotte, prince of Pontecorvo, had had to fight the Swedes in Pomerania;
and he had shown himself towards them a courteous enemy and a generous
conqueror. Later, in 1808, charged with operating a descent upon Skåne,
while Russia attacked Finland, he took advantage of the indefinite terms of
his instructions, to respect Swedish territory. He preferred to be lenient
towards old allies to vanquishing them at their own expense; and his course
of action, which gave great displeasure at St. Petersburg, was the foundation
of his popularity in Sweden. This is what Moerner and his friends had
principally in mind; and the young lieutenant, with the daring confidence of
his years, had offered to sound the ground at Paris, propose new destinies to
the marshal, solicit the adherence of the French government, and win over
Bernadotte and Napoleon.

At Paris Moerner began with an obscure friend, a geographer named
Latapie, provided with a modest berth in the ministry of foreign affairs.
Moerner and Latapie, after having taken up and gone over together the list
of marshals, were convinced that Bernadotte, who shared in Napoleon's
prestige, without passing for a blind servitor of his policy, was the only one
in the whole list who possessed the necessary qualities. The most difficult
thing was to make France believe in the reality and importance of a plan
which had as yet taken shape only in a few minds "filled with military enthusiasm." The scheme which did not exist in Sweden, it was necessary to
develop in France. Moerner won over to his idea the consul of his country,
M. Signeul, and after him the count of Wrede, a man of great name and
distinguished bearing, who had been sent by his government to congratulate

[1810 A.D.]

the emperor on his marriage. It was Wrede who was charged to inform Bernadotte and make the first overtures. This he did on the 25th of June. Bernadotte asked nothing better than to be a reigning monarch, but at first he affected the disinterestedness which is proper and customary in such circumstances, and then let himself be convinced that he was indispensable to the welfare of Sweden. A few hours later, he was with the emperor, declaring that a powerful party was clamouring for him, and begging permission to present himself to the suffrage of the diet.

The emperor listened at first with some incredulity, and could scarcely take this unexpected candidacy seriously. But when the Swedes in Paris brought it to his attention through various persons who surrounded him, and to whom the scheme had been mentioned, he gave the matter more respectful consideration. There was a new element in the whole matter which now arose. Would it suit him next to crush the movement peremptorily, or to make use of it? Napoleon had known Bernadotte too long to rely upon his character and fidelity. He prized his military talents, without ever having liked him. In him Napoleon had never found, at any time, that impulse from the heart, that passionate devotion, which he recognised and appreciated in his other marshals. He credited him with an underlying thought for self which had showed itself on many occasions, a reasoning and intractable mind, and a stubborn temperament — everything, in fact, which he included under the generic term "Jacobinism." After showering wealth and favours upon Bernadotte, without drawing him any nearer, Napoleon had been compelled to reprimand the marshal more than once; and, in fact, since Wagram he had been in a kind of semi-disgrace, which did not at all lessen the marshal's smothered rancour. It was therefore quite possible that the latter would not be a docile agent of the imperial will; and Napoleon placed so little confidence in him that he thought for a moment of proposing another French candidate, Prince Eugène, to the Swedes who were asking Bernadotte of him. But as Eugène refused, and was not willing to change his religion — an indispensable condition in order to reign at Stockholm — it was necessary to fall back on the prince of Pontecorvo, who did not exhibit the slightest scruples on this subject.

In Sweden, during the same period, the government was far from taking the marshal's candidacy seriously, although the idea had begun to work its way among the lower classes and the army; and it seemed little more disturbed at hearing this candidacy distinguished from the others as the emperor's choice; but its impatience grew under the pressure of more urgent alarms. At Stockholm the instincts of disorder and anarchy in the people had just broken out into flame. On June 20th the body of the crown prince was brought back to the capital. During the passage of the convoy, Count Fersen,[1] grand marshal of the kingdom, upon whom all sorts of iniquitous suspicions were fastened, was dragged from the procession and massacred by a mob of frenzied people. It was demagogy which now came upon the scene, with its accompaniment of violence and crime. Terrified by the spectacle, Charles XIII and his council turned the more anxiously to Napoleon, and looked to him as their saviour — to him who could with one word calm the excited passions, reunite divided opinions under any name whatever, and renew the moral unity of the nation. In their anguish they addressed themselves to the only Frenchman they had near them, the humble secretary of

[1] This nobleman had served with distinction as a volunteer in the American war, and he was known at the court of Louis XVI for his gallantries and the favourable notice which he received from Marie Antoinette.c

[1810 A. D.]

legation who was acting chargé d'affaires, M. Désaugiers, by name, who found himself importuned with visits, pressed with questions, and begged to speak only a word, which would be received as a command. Sweden threw herself at Napoleon's feet and asked to know his intentions, that she might conform to them, and only begged the right to obey.

"Let the emperor give us one of his kings, and Sweden will be saved," said the king's first aide-de-camp, M. de Suremain, to Désaugiers; and he

AXEL VON FERSEN, MARSHAL OF SWEDEN
(1755-1810)

would not believe that the latter did not possess the secrets of the French court. It was only too true, however, for Champagny, the French minister for foreign affairs, in order the better to serve the emperor's negative intentions, had thought it well to break off all correspondence with Désaugiers and leave him isolated and like an exile at his distant post. Astonished and humiliated by this silence, Désaugiers strove like everybody else to discover, to divine the reason which was now nothing but a great riddle; and, in default of any precise information, was reduced to examining and interpreting the lightest symptoms, questioning the slightest rumours, and seeking in the gazettes for the opinions of his government. At the moment, the article of June 17th in the *Journal de l'Empire* came under his eyes. It will be remembered that this article, the echo of an early, immature consideration of the subject, was expressed in terms sympathetic to the king of Denmark. This vague indication was in accord with the personal preferences of the chargé d'affaires, and encouraged by the language of the official paper, he thought to act in concert with his court by following the bent of his own aspirations.

Entreated by all the Swedes who surrounded him to speak some word, to take some action, he did not have the wisdom to refuse, but loosened his tongue. Twice, on the 4th and 5th of July, he made his declaration in favour of the king of Denmark and the union of the two crowns, by presenting this measure as a means of offence and defence against Russia. It would have been difficult for Désaugiers, in thus permitting himself to indulge his own opinion, to have gone more completely in opposition to the emperor's actual intentions. Above all things, Napoleon wished to keep, at least in appearance, on good terms with Russia; and it was to this end that he refrained from supporting Bernadotte. To repair as far as possible the effect produced by Désaugier's statements, the emperor at last despatched Alquier. But if he were to leave Paris at once, the minister could not arrive in Sweden before the end of August; that is to say, after the election, which was appointed to take place in the first fortnight of the month. Therefore he would play no rôle in it, which pleased his master; but he was charged to say and to repeat that, whatever the outcome was, the emperor would have preferred most the prince of Augustenburg, who was the neutral and, above all the colourless candidate. The object of this retrospective, and consequently essentially disinterested statement was to release the French from any responsibility to Russia, without in any way influencing a result already determined.

The diet assembled the 25th of July in the city of Örebro. At this moment the royal government was more perplexed and more out of reckoning than ever. The words of M. Desaugiers had not removed doubts, for Charles XIII received at the same time the letter of the 24th of June, in which the emperor seemed to pronounce in favour of the late prince's brother. In the presence of these contradictory signs — for, on the other hand, Napoleon had omitted giving Bernadotte the least sign of sympathy — the Stockholm cabinet judged itself authorized to follow its first inspiration, and work for the success of the Augustenburg candidate; and to accomplish this end, it trod devious paths and employed the subtlest of strategy. The election of the candidate recommended by the court seemed assured, the desired *dénouement* predetermined and accomplished when, at the eleventh hour, a rumour arose, spread, and blazed up, like a train of powder: it was on everyone's lips that Napoleon had spoken; that he desired, that he was determined to have Bernadotte; and that he had made this known to the electors of Sweden. This report was untrue, and the deed of an impostor. At the time when a few Swedes had fixed upon the candidacy of the prince of Pontecorvo, a Frenchman named Fournier had taken an active part in their manœuvres. He had formerly been a merchant in Gothenburg, and had even filled the office of vice-consul, but had to give up his post as the result of some unfortunate speculations in which he had sunk his wealth and much of his reputation. Having been unsuccessful in trade, he sought a means of recruiting his fortune in politics. Bernadotte's election seemed to him an affair worth supporting, and he entered into it heart and soul. Skilful and insinuating, he wormed his way into the ministry of foreign affairs, and even laid siege to the door of the ministerial chamber.

After some little time, Fournier succeeded in persuading Champagny that France would find it to her advantage to have someone on the look-out in the Swedish city where the diet was to be held, and obtained permission to betake himself to Örebro in the rôle of a spectator, charged solely with seeing, listening, and notifying Paris of the incidents of the struggle. In order to facilitate his introduction into Sweden and the accomplishment of his mission, Champagny furnished him with a paper, known as a diplomatic passport, and even stretched his complaisance to the point of signing it himself. Thus armed, Fournier set out at once, not without having taken, on the other hand, commissions and instructions from Bernadotte. In truth, it was not long before Champagny realized his imprudence, and feared that he had placed in the hand of an unsafe man a weapon it would not be impossible to make bad use of. As quickly as possible he wrote to the French Legation at Stockholm, in order to release himself from all responsibility with regard to the dismissed vice-consul. Unfortunately, the precaution was taken too late. While the letter of disavowal was pursuing him, Fournier, well in advance, landed in Sweden, and reached Örebro the 11th of August, some days before the date of the election. He had scarcely arrived before he turned round and boldly altered his course. A simple emissary of the marshal and observer for the minister, he posed as the spokesman of France. His language was this: the French government desired the success of the prince of Pontecorvo, and as the high interests France had at stake did not permit her to express this wish openly, it had been necessary to resort to modest intermediary, to bring it to the knowledge of the diet. In support of these words, Fournier presented his passport, showed the ministerial handwriting, and used it to establish confidence in the Swedes. He had also brought other things — a letter written by the marshal, and a portrait representing "Bernadotte's young son playing with his father's sword." With these various objects of propaganda he knew how to play a wonderful part. In one night he made a hundred copies of the letter; his lodgings were transformed into a work room, putting forth at every moment brochures, pictures, patriotic songs, and popular dialogues, which flooded the town and circulated among the members of the diet. Pamphlets, distributed in profusion, appealed to the national passions and hates, endeavouring to represent the success of the French hero as a moral defeat for Russia and the beginning of revenge. At the same time, the four orders of the diet — nobles, clergy, burghers, and peasants — were successively taken in hand; yielding to appropriate arguments, each class of the nation came to believe that Bernadotte cherished for it a particular predilection and would accomplish its happiness. Above all, the thought that Napoleon was showing himself behind his representative, that he had broken the silence and made known his intentions, stimulated devotion, discouraged resistance, and silenced all opposition. In forty-eight hours, with a promptness scarcely credible, the current was formed, grew, threw itself along, and carried everything before it.

HAPSAL CASTLE, ESTLAND

The old king alone resisted. He was not resigned to accepting an heir, a parvenu of the sword, whom Napoleon had not even placed on the first steps of the throne by the gift of one of the states at his disposal. The ministry, feeling the necessity of yielding to the torrent, deputed M. de Suremain to the king, to reason with the latter and make him give way. Suremain found him exhausted by a night of insomnia, wearing the imprint of his distress on his features. "I know no longer whom to choose," he said. "I had decided on the prince of Augustenburg. He is my cousin and a brother of the late prince. But now that cannot be; even you have spoken against it. Now they come with their Bernadotte. They say the emperor wants him. His chargé d'affaires acts differently. It is enough to drive me mad. If the Emperor wishes me to accept a French general it would be better for him to

[1810 A.D.]

say so than to leave me to guess it.   Haven't you told me that he doesn't like Bernadotte?"

"Yes, sire, that was so well known that last winter during my visit to Paris I was advised to see very little of him."

"What do you think of him?   Gustave Moerner praises him to the skies."

"It is impossible for me to judge the essential qualities of a man with whom I have had only social relations.   He is a handsome man, very polished, and expresses himself with great facility.   His whole bearing is truly distinguished."

"Nothing that reeks of the Revolution?"

"I noticed nothing.   He has a good reputation in France; he is not judged by the amount of his thievings."

"Even if he should have all the necessary qualifications, have you thought of the absurdity of taking a French corporal for the heir of my throne."

"Sire, I agree with you, and the idea shocks me as much as it does you. But we must think of the danger there will be of being forced to do it."

"Do you think they can force me to it?"

"Sire, think of the unhappy state of the kingdom, and of your own age."

"He questioned me for a long time about the prince of Pontecorvo," adds Suremain in his account, "on his origin, his son, and his wife.   I told him all I had learned.   When we parted he said with emotion, 'I fear there is nothing for me to do but to swallow the pill.   God alone knows how all this will end.'"

Five days after this conversation, the ministerial council, furnished with royal authority, officially presented Bernadotte; and on the 21st of August the four orders elected him, fully persuaded that they were obeying an order from the Tuileries, and were voting for the emperor's candidate.   Thus compromised and thwarted by a series of stupidities and intrigues, Napoleon suffered the penalty of a policy which was purposely obscure and veiled, and which always systematically neglected to declare itself.   A word from him in the beginning would have prevented everything; Désaugiers's blunder, Fournier's impudent envoy, and the decisive manœuvres of this "messenger magician."   Instead of stopping Bernadotte's budding enterprise with one decisive word, Napoleon had preferred to let it develop and take its chance; he thought to get profit from it, both by forbidding it and by refraining from taking any part in it.   But nobody believed in that surprising abnegation, in that effacement of a will which Europe was accustomed to look for, and find everywhere, and feel perpetually active.   As the emperor had not spoken everyone assumed the right to speak for him; finally his name, audaciously usurped, brought about the election.[e]

BERNADOTTE AS CROWN PRINCE

If Napoleon expected to find a mere instrument in the new crown prince [henceforth known as Charles John], he was soon miserably disappointed. The latter had duties and interests irreconcilable with such a state of vassalage.   For some time the outward forms of amity were observed; and when invested with the chief cares of government through the infirmities of Charles XIII, he grew more cautious, more eager to profit by the course of events.   He would not offend Bonaparte; and therefore he embraced the continental system, and even declared war against England.   But he adopted no serious measures to the prejudice of this country; and what he did was the result of fear rather than of enmity.

By degrees, he ventured to remonstrate against the mandates of the emperor, and in some instances to return a decided negative.   In revenge, Napoleon urged his privateers to seize Swedish vessels wherever they could be found.   The injury thus effected was incalculable, and it produced some energetic representations from the crown prince.   But they led to no result. The seizure of Pomerania and Rügen by the French broke the last remaining bond which united him with his native country.   From this moment, Charles John turned towards the English, whose vessels he freely admitted into his ports, and with whom he signed a treaty of peace.   He also cultivated the friendship of Alexander, then menaced by the most formidable power Europe had seen since the days of Charlemagne.[b]   The treaties with Great Britain and Russia provided for the cession of Norway to Sweden as a consolation for the recent loss of Finland to Russia; and as the country thus coolly assigned to Bernadotte's kingdom was the property of Denmark, the latter power was to receive compensation in Pomerania.   The island of Guadaloupe was also ceded to Sweden by Great Britain, and large subsidies promised. It is said that in these transactions the crown prince of Sweden did not always allow his personal advantage to be thrust into the background in favour of that of his adopted country.   In Ahnfelt's narratives of the Scandinavian court and state the crown prince is represented as playing a decidedly ignoble rôle.[a]

An inquiry into the benefits that accrued to Sweden from the sale of Pomerania and Guadaloupe [in 1815] lies outside the scope of this record; let it suffice to say that Charles John took more than an equal share, and stipulated, moreover, for a large annual sum, which the Bank of Sweden was required by the estates to place at the disposal of his dynasty in perpetuity.   If to this sum we add the notorious rouble fund (*Rubelfonds*) and the old *Passevolanskasse* deposited with the college of War — which may reasonably be regarded as a reserve fund for Charles John's private ends, since he kept it under lock and key, by his resolute refusal to give the auditors of the estates of the kingdom access to it — we must own that the adopted son of Charles XIII knew how to get paid for the honour he had done Sweden in accepting the succession to the throne.   At this point it may be well to say a few words concerning the manner in which the above-mentioned rouble fund came into being.   In the summer of 1812, the emperor Alexander's situation was so desperate that almost his only chance of saving his dominions, and maintaining the sovereignty of Russia in Europe, was to pave the way for an alliance with Sweden, and to associate himself with Charles John, then crown prince, at any price.   This was the motive of the ill-starred interview between the two at Åbo.   It is asserted, and not without good reason, that in the Russian deliberations which preceded the interview, it was decided that Alexander should begin by making a money payment the basis of negotiation, and, if necessary, should proceed to offer the restoration of Finland and Åland, and, it may be, the possession of Norway.

Alexander himself was far too skilled a diplomatist not to have given his minister at Stockholm instruction to make the study of the new heir-apparent his first object, after Charles John had arrived in Sweden, and while a rupture between France and Russia appeared imminent; and more especially after the latter had gained the absolute ascendency over the cabinet which he already enjoyed over the army.   And, in truth, the task could have been confided to no better man than that adroit and practised diplomatist, General van Suchtelen the elder [a Dutchman who had entered the Russian service].   The Russian diplomatist held good cards in his hand: Charles John's envy and hatred of Napoleon were already a matter of historical certainty; his bombastic speeches and proclamations were the sure indication of a character steeped in self-love and ambition; and lastly, it is not likely that his domestic economy had escaped Van Suchtelen's practised observation.   We are therefore tolerably well justified in assuming that, even before the interview at Åbo, Alexander knew with whom he had to do, and was in a position to frame the lines on which to negotiate with the heir-apparent. The interview itself was a snare laid for Charles John's vanity.   When they met, Alexander and the crown prince locked themselves into a private apartment together.   The most distinguished members of Alexander's suite were in waiting in the adjoining room, as well as a few gentlemen who had accompanied the crown prince.   The Russians had gathered together in a group near the room in which the conference was held, to await the result.   While they were talking together, the door opened, and Alexander came out alone, turned straight to the group of Russians, and with evident self-satisfaction exclaimed, "He will take the money!"   This was the rouble fund.[d]

During Napoleon's expedition to Russia, Charles John kept in check the French troops in the north of Germany.   The following year he declared war against France, and in return for the guarantee by Great Britain of the annexation of Norway to Sweden, agreed to take the field with a large force against the common foe of Europe.   Landing at Stralsund, he took command of a combined army of ninety thousand men, and thence proceeded to Berlin, where he fixed his head quarters.[b]

SWEDEN IN THE WAR OF LIBERATION

In this memorable campaign, none of the allied generals bore a more distinguished part than the crown prince of Sweden, by whom the plan of operations is said to have been originally sketched.   Detachments of the allies had already driven the invaders from Hamburg, Lübeck, and Lauenburg, from the duchy of Mecklenburg and Swedish Pomerania; but the Danes and the French, under Davout, occupied the two first-named cities (May 30th, 1813), which were subjected to the horrors of pillage and devastation.   Numerous engagements during the summer months had taken place in Saxony, the chief theatre of the war, from which Napoleon had suffered so severely that he was obliged to solicit a truce.   An armistice was concluded (June 4th) at Poischwitz, and this interval the confederated sovereigns employed in contracting new engagements with foreign courts, and arranging those treaties of alliance and pecuniary subsidies with Britain and Austria, which constituted the sixth grand coalition against France, and ultimately led to the restoration of the Bourbons.

Hostilities were resumed (August 10th), when the cities and plains of Poland, Saxony, Bohemia, Bavaria, and Silesia were once more deluged with the blood of contending nations.   In this sanguinary strife, victory declared unequivocally for the allies; and on various occasions they owed their success to the prudent dispositions of the crown prince of Sweden.   The plan of the campaign, as arranged in a conference held at Trachenberg, was to allure Bonaparte from his asylum at Dresden, and draw him into a situation more accessible to the combined operations of his antagonists.   In this scheme they succeeded entirely to their wishes; and Leipsic, which had so often witnessed the triumphs of civil and religious liberty under its walls, was again destined to see the freedom of oppressed Europe vindicated and restored on its classic soil; where nearly half a million of combatants were assembled exhibiting a strange diversity of nations and tongues, unparalleled in history since the expeditions of Xerxes and Attila.[c]

However useful the talents of Bernadotte may have been to the allies they entertained doubts of his good faith.   He is said to have cherished a design of replacing Napoleon on the French throne, for which reason he refrained from striking decisive blows at the power of France.   The small rôle played by the Swedish troops in the great battle of Leipsic is thus described by one of their own officers.[a]

A Swedish Narrative of the Battle of the Nations (1813 A.D.)

The emperor Napoleon's attempt to prevent the junction of the north German army with that of Silesia having been frustrated by the retrograde movement beyond the Saal, he collected all his forces in the neighbourhood of Leipsic, there to await the attack of the allies.   He did not wait in vain. On the 16th of October, he was hotly engaged with the Bohemian army to the south of Leipsic and with the Silesian army to the north, but without decisive results in either case, though the latter force, under General Blücher, gained some advantage.   On the 17th a few skirmishes took place to the north of the town, considerable reinforcements were brought up, and all the necessary preparations made for the general conflict, the great battle of the nations, which was to be fought next day by more than half a million men.

The allied armies advanced in massed columns, early on the morning of the 18th, overpowered the advanced posts of the enemy, and took up their position in such order as to surround the enemy with an unbroken concentric curve, more than two miles in length.   About 8 o'clock the Bohemian army opened the cannonade, which spread along the whole line; at noon the highest pitch of horror was reached in every part of the vast battle-field, over which between thirteen and fourteen hundred throats of fire breathed death and destruction from all directions.   One by one, the lines of fire were pushed forward; and it was evident that the united armies were advancing concentrically, and that victory, though dearly bought, would fall to the allies. But there were many fierce struggles to come: the enemy's positions were everywhere stubbornly defended; villages were taken and retaken; nor did even darkness set a truce to the conflict — the men fought on by the light and amidst the flames of burning villages.   As usual, the Swedish army had no share in the glory and danger of that memorable day; it was only held in reserve, together with a Russian corps of ten thousand men.   But for all that, a portion of the Swedish artillery, which was posted on the right wing to support General Luageron's army corps, found an opportunity of distinguishing itself — in consequence, it must be owned, of a colossal blunder on the part of its commander, General Cardell.

The inaction imposed upon the Swedish army aroused discontent and displeasure in the ranks, and was a real grief to General Adlercreutz, who longed for at least one chance of showing what could be done with it.   In the absence of any such opportunity, he kept perpetually hurrying to the points where the fight was fiercest and the firing hottest, thus exposing his person and his staff with the express object, as he repeatedly said, of "showing the Swedish uniform under fire."   An opportunity for so doing presently arose in the storming of Paunsdorf, with which the north German army began its attack.   The expulsion of the enemy from Sellerhausen and the taking of Schönefeld decided the victory on the right wing, and ended the day's bloody work at this point of the fighting line.   Next morning it was evident that the enemy had abandoned the field of battle and withdrawn to Leipsic, leaving strong detachments in the villages about the town to cover its retreat.   These villages had consequently to be taken before the town could be attempted.

While the Silesian and Bohemian armies were making an assault on the northern and southern sides of the town, Swedish and Prussian columns, under the command of General Adlercreutz, stormed the eastern portion, known as the *Grimmaische Thor* (Grimmai gate).   The storming parties met with desperate resistance at all points, but this did not suffice to check the advance of the attacking columns of the allies, nor prevent the reduction of the town.   By midday Leipsic was completely in their power.   The Swedish troops had suffered a loss of about 150 killed and 100 wounded — a considerable number in proportion to the force engaged, for barely 1,200 men of the Swedish army had been under fire.   I myself was among the wounded, and was obliged to qu't the field just at the decisive and eagerly desired moment when General Adlercreutz came up with fresh troops.[d]

UNION OF SWEDEN AND NORWAY (1814 A.D.)

After the battle of Leipsic Charles John displayed much activity.   He blockaded Hamburg; and by the Peace of Kiel, concluded in January, 1814, he forced Denmark to give up Norway.   He then entered France, but soon returned, and devoted his energies to the conquest of Norway.[f]

The rupture of the ties which for several centuries had made two peoples brothers, evoked lively grief in Denmark, which was shared by the great majority of the Norwegian people.   If at different periods complaints and discords, comparatively rare, had arisen, they were now completely forgotten; the one thought was of the services which the two nations had mutually rendered one another, of their common historic memories, of the fidelity with which they had remained side by side in good and evil ways, of the intimacy established during a long union which had, so to speak, fused the two peoples together.   Through the violence and injustice of foreign nations they were now separated; and Norway, treated as a domain or as booty, became the prey of the successful conqueror.   But such treatment aroused every feeling of the Norwegian people.   Prince Christian Frederick [afterwards Christian VIII of Denmark], who had won the nation's love while the king's representative in Norway, and who returned this affection, became the leader round whom all who wanted independence and liberty for Norway gathered.   He consulted with several important personages, and took up the reins of government, rejecting on Norway's part the dispositions of the Peace of Kiel, and proclaiming the country's independence.   An elective assembly was convoked at Eidsvold on April 10th, 1814, to deliberate on the fate of Norway, and provide her with a constitution [the details of which we gave in the last chapter].   This constitution, constructed on new liberal ideas, was voted by the national assembly of Eidsvold on the 17th of May, and the same day Christian Frederick was elected king of Norway.

But it was now necessary to maintain the country's independence by force of arms; for Charles John hurried back to Sweden with all haste, and set out for the Norwegian frontier, to carry out forcibly the conditions of the Peace of Kiel with an army of thirty thousand men, trained and hardened by recent campaigns.   England and Russia had promised help in this enterprise, while English and Swedish ships blockaded the ports and coast of Norway. It was difficult, and almost impossible, to resist such aggression.   The people were, in truth, brave and determined, but badly trained in arms; and Norway lacked money, provisions, war supplies and, more than all, a capable general — for, while Christian Frederick was dowered with fine qualities, he was no strategist. There was no help to be expected; Denmark was powerless, and Frederick VI, pushed by the other governments, found himself in the painful position of having to reprimand and threaten Christian Frederick. Hostilities began on the 26th of July. Success alternated with reverses for the few weeks the war lasted, but it was not difficult to foresee the final result. Fortunately, Charles John was disposed towards moderation; he realized that the new union would be badly cemented with blood, and sought to win over the Norwegian people by considerate treatment. He proposed an armistice and conditions by which no one would lose anything, unless it were Christian Frederick, who would have to give up his newly acquired crown. The truce was signed at Moss, August 14th, 1814, and at the same time and place an agreement was reached in which Charles John, in the name of the king of Sweden, recognised the constitution voted at Eidsvold, to which nothing was to be added but modifications necessary to the union with Sweden, and these only with the consent of the storthing (grand assembly). Christian Frederick undertook to resign before a storthing convoked for that purpose. This was done, and on the 10th of October he laid down his crown and power before the assembly. He deserves the kind remembrance and gratitude of the Norwegian people, who owe to him principally the ease with which they passed from the old to the new order of things. It was under him that were founded at the same time their independence and liberty; and this work, once accomplished, was not easily destroyed. Who knows what would have happened if Norway had not had in him a leader at this criticial moment? His presence prevented the discord, indecision, and disorder which would so easily have been generated in such circumstances, and which would doubtless have suggested, and partly justified, other sentiments in Charles John.g

At 10 o'clock in the morning of the 13th of October, 1814, the Swedish commissioners appeared in the storthing. They handed the president their credentials and the proposal for a Norwegian constitution with their signatures appended. In principle and in all essential points this constitution was identical with that of the 17th of May, and only contained such alterations as were considered necessary in view of the new relations between Norway and Sweden. The President promised to inform the commissioners of the resolution at which the storthing should arrive after mature consideration; and they thereupon withdrew. On the 14th, the storthing resumed its deliberations. A committee was appointed to inquire into the internal condition of the country, and another to treat with the Swedish commissioners on points of detail in the terms of union. National antipathy to the union was by no means extinct, and found vent most freely among the representatives of the remoter provinces, who were least well acquainted with the true state of the kingdom. From several districts the storthing received offers of voluntary contributions in money and kind, which were placed at the regent's disposal, to help to maintain the independence of the country. These offers were manifest proofs of the zeal of the givers for what they thought their country's good; and they were all the more worthy of respect because the sacrifices they entailed must have been made out of the poverty of persons who certainly did not suffer from superfluity; but considerable as they might appear in proportion to the circumstances of the givers, they were wholly inadequate to fill the great chasm opened by the lack of every kind of necessary. It is not known how or where they were used. The storthing also received information that a volunteer corps of chasseurs had been formed at Trondhjem, to contribute to the defence of the country, and that its regulations were already drawn up. Several demonstrations of this kind went to show that the union with Sweden was by no means universally desired.

The committee appointed to examine the internal condition of the country presented an exhaustive report, the tenor of which was anything but an encouragement to prosecute the war. On the 19th of October, Etatsrath Treschow came forward, and submitted the following proposal to the consideration of the storthing: "Tomorrow the period of armistice will be at an end. No decisive resolution has yet been arrived at concerning the principal subject under deliberation in this assembly; no step of any importance has been taken to effect a *rapprochement* with Sweden or to accept any of her proposals. If no such resolution is taken, it is probable that within a week the war will have broken out more destructively than ever, and whether with great hopes of a happy issue for our cause, I leave it to the storthing to infer from a consideration of that knowledge of the resources and feeling of the nation as a whole — though not of the opinion that prevails in certain districts — which it has gathered, partly in time past, and partly from the investigations of the select committee as to the state of the country and the army. The result of these investigations, together with the considerations concerning the relations of Norway to Sweden, as well as to other European powers, which I have put forward now and at previous times, lead me to submit the following proposal to the storthing: (1) Whereas King Christian Frederick has resigned the government into the hands of the people, absolved the people of Norway from the oath of allegiance sworn to his majesty, and abdicated, for himself and his descendants, all rights to the crown of this country; and whereas Norway, according to its fundamental law, must always be governed by a king, another king shall and must be chosen in place of him and his descendants, as speedily as possible; (2) the Norwegian storthing declares a union with Sweden, in conformity with the first paragraph of the proposals made by the Swedish commissioners, to be for the advantage of both kingdoms and, in view of external conditions and the safety and independence of both, necessary to be concluded upon this basis. (3) Whereas Charles XIII, king of Sweden, by the ratification of the assembly of the estates of the kingdom at Eidsvold and the fundamental law therein enacted, and by the declaration that he will propose only such alterations as are manifestly necessary for union with Sweden, in the proposal made to this storthing by his accredited commissioners, and in the statements and explanations by them given, has not only furnished convincing proofs of his respect for the honour, liberties, and rights of the Norwegian nation, but also manifested his inclination to accede to our demands and give ear to our representations, his aforesaid majesty King Charles XIII is hereby elected king of Norway. (4) Until this proposal has been debated and put to the vote, no other proposal hitherto submitted or hereafter to be submitted shall be considered by the storthing. (5) Memoranda upon the second and third points of the proposal shall be made orally and entered in the protocol. (6) The election must be unconditional, for whereas very diverse opinions may prevail concerning the conditions under which the union should take place, unanimity would be unattainable by any other means; and the committee appointed for the purpose shall conclude the examination of the numerous proposals submitted concerning the matter, at such time as is convenient in view of the date at which the resolution must be taken; the danger of precipitancy being greater now than hereafter, since after the election of the king the storthing will be allowed sufficient time for mature consideration of any alteration proposed in the fundamental law."

On the 20th of October, the storthing resumed its deliberations, and the proposal of Treschow, quoted above, was made the subject of debate. The principal question at issue was the second article of the proposal: union with Sweden. Several of the representatives made lengthy speeches, the net result of which was in the main in favour of union. Every representative then voted *viva voce*, and the votes were added to the protocol. Seventy-two were in favour of union, and five against it. The five dissentients deposed that they gave their votes in conformity with the express desire of their constituents, a declaration which implied that they were not actuated by their personal convictions in so doing. Thus the most knotty question was solved, and it only remained to elect the king. By forty-seven votes against thirty, it was decided to postpone the election until an agreement should have been arrived at, respecting the alterations in the fundamental law. The deliberations were resumed and concluded on the 4th of November, and on the same day Charles XIII, king of Sweden, was unanimously elected king of Norway.[h]

The union was more fully defined by the act of Union, which was accepted by the national assemblies of both countries in the following year. In the preamble to the act it is clearly stated that the union between the two peoples was accomplished "not by force of arms, but by free conviction"; and the Swedish foreign minister declared to the European powers, on behalf of Sweden, that the treaty of Kiel had been abandoned, and that it was not to this treaty, but to the confidence of the Norwegian people in the Swedish, that the latter owed the union with Norway. The constitution framed at Eidsvold was retained, and forms the *Grundlov*, or fundamental law of the kingdom. It is generally acknowledged to be the freest and most democratic constitution of all monarchical states. The union thus concluded between the two countries was really an offensive and defensive alliance under a common king, each country retaining its own government, parliament, army, navy, customs. The relations between the two countries may be more clearly understood when it is realised that a Norwegian is a foreigner in Sweden, and a Swede in Norway; and that consequently a Norwegian can hold no official appointment in Sweden, and *vice versa*. In Sweden the people received only an imperfect and erroneous insight into the nature of the union, and for a long time believed it to be an achievement of the Swedish arms; while to the leading men of the country, who knew the terms of the union better, it was a great disappointment. They had hoped to make Norway a province of Sweden, and now they had entered into a union in which both countries were equally independent. During the first fifteen years, the king was represented in Norway by a Swedish viceroy, while the government was, of course, composed only of Norwegians, selected from various parties in the country. Count Wedel Jarlsberg was the first to be entrusted with the important office of head of the Norwegian government, while several of Prince Christian Frederick's councillors of state were retained, or replaced by others holding their political views. The Swedish count von Essen was appointed the first viceroy of Norway, and was succeeded two years afterwards by his countryman Count von Mörner, over both of whom Count Wedel exercised considerable influence.

During the first years of the union, the condition of Norway was in many respects most unprosperous. The country suffered from poverty and depression of trade, and the finances were in a deplorable condition. The first storthing was chiefly occupied with financial and other practical measures.

In order to improve the finances of the country, a bank of Norway was founded, and the army was reduced to one half, as the defence of the country was not considered to be of great importance now that the union had been concluded.   The paid-up capital of the bank was procured by the assessment of an extraordinary tax; and this, together with the growing discontent among the peasantry, brought about a rising in Hedemarken and the neighbouring districts, the object of which was to dissolve the storthing and to obtain a reduction in the taxation.   It was also rumoured that the organizers of this agitation intended establishing an absolute government, and many therefore imagined they saw the machinations of the royal power behind the rising; while, on the other hand, the king himself believed he had to deal with Danish intrigues.   The rising, however, soon subsided, and the bountiful harvest of 1819 brought more prosperous times to the peasantry.

Meanwhile, however, the financial position of the country had nearly endangered its independence.   The settlement with Denmark with regard to Norway's share of the national debt common to both, which had so long been deferred, and could not be evaded, had assumed threatening proportions.   In the interest of Denmark, the allied powers asked for a speedy settlement; and in order to escape their collective intervention, Charles John, who had now succeeded to the throne of Sweden, and Norway, on the death (February 5th, 1818) of the old king Charles XIII, accepted England's mediation, and was enabled in September, 1819, to conclude a convention with Denmark according to which Norway was held liable for only 3,000,000 specie dollars (nearly £700,000).   But the Norwegians considered that this was still too much, and the attitude of the storthing in 1821 had nearly occasioned a fresh interference of the powers.   The storthing, however, yielded at last, and agreed to raise a loan and pay the amount stipulated in the convention.

NORWAY UNDER CHARLES (XIV) JOHN

Although this matter now seemed to be in a fair way of being settled, the king evidently had his doubts as to whether the Norwegians really intended to fulfil their obligations.   As his relations with the storthing had already become strained, and as he was occupied at that time with plans which, it is now known, meant nothing less than a *coup d'état* in connection with the revision of the Norweigan constitution, he decided to adopt military preparations; and in July, 1821, he collected a force of three thousand Swedish and three thousand Norwegian troops in the neighbourhood of Christiania — ostensibly for the mere purpose of holding some manœuvres, but his object was undoubtedly to impress the storthing with his authority, and to frighten it into submission.   In a circular note (June 1st) to the European powers, signed by the Swedish foreign minister Engström (but it is not difficult to recognize the hand of the king as the real author); the minister complained bitterly of the treatment the king had met with at the hands of the storthing, and represented the Norwegians in anything but a favourable light to the powers, the intention being to obtain their sympathy for any attempt that might be made to revise the Norwegian constitution, as, for example, by the substitution of an absolute for a suspensive veto, by conferring upon the king the right to dissolve the storthing and to elect its presidents — in short, to adapt the Norwegian constitution to the liking of his less democratic Swedish subjects.

About this time another important question had to be finally settled by the storthing, which the king was anxious to oppose at all costs.   The storthings of 1815 and 1818 had already passed a bill for the abolition of nobility, but the king had on both occasions refused his sanction. The Norwegians maintained that the country was too poor consistently to keep up an aristocracy, and that the few counts and barons still to be found in Norway were all Danish and of very recent origin, while the really true and ancient nobility of the country were the Norwegian peasants, descendants of the old jarls and chieftains, who had no desire for titular distinction. According to the constitution, any bill which has been passed by three successively elected storthings (elections are held every third year) becomes law without the king's sanction. When the third reading of the bill came on, the king did everything in his power to obstruct it, but in spite of his opposition the bill was eventually carried and became law. These conflicts with the king had increased the strained relations which for some time had existed between him and the storthing; but after the question of the debt to Denmark had been settled, and the king had formally sanctioned the bill for the abolition of nobility, a more conciliatory feeling set in.

In 1822 Count Wedel Jarlsberg retired from the government. He had become unpopular through his financial policy, and was also at issue with the king on vital matters. In 1821, he had been impeached before the Rigsret (the supreme court of the realm) for having caused the state considerable losses. J. Collett was appointed as his successor to the post of minister of finance.

Royal Proposals for Constitutional Revision

The king had by this time apparently abandoned his plan of a *coup d'état*, for in the following August he submitted to the storthing several proposals for fundamental changes in the constitution, all of which aimed at removing what was at variance with a monarchical form of government. The changes, in fact, were the same as he had suggested in his circular note to the powers, and which he knew would be hailed with approval by his Swedish subjects. It may seem strange that the king, favoured as he was by circumstances, took the constitutional course, when he might easily have gained his end by a *coup d'état;* but although Charles John was a man of courage on the battlefield, he seems to have been wanting in *courage civil*, and he doubtless feared that a *coup d'état* might result in unpleasant and humiliating consequences for himself. At the same time he knew that the great powers looked upon him with distrustful eyes, and that even in Sweden there were powerful enemies working against him.

When the storthing met again, in 1824, the royal proposals for the constitutional changes came on for discussion. The storthing adopted a friendly attitude towards the king personally, without, however, showing itself subservient; but the assembly unanimously rejected not only the king's proposals, but also several others by private members for changes in the constitution. The king submitted his proposals again in the following session of the storthing, and again later on; but they were always unanimously rejected. In 1830, they were discussed for the last time, with the same result. The king's insistence was viewed by the people as a sign of absolutist tendencies, and naturally excited fresh alarm. They felt they would have to be on their guard against all attempts at encroachment and at amalgamation between Norway and Sweden. In the eyes of the people the members of the opposition in the storthing were the true champions of the rights and the independence which they had gained in 1814.

For several years the Norwegians had been celebrating the 17th of May as their day of independence, it being the anniversary of the adoption of the constitution of 1814; but as the tension between the Norwegians and the king increased, the latter began to look upon the celebration in the light of a demonstration directed against himself; and when Collett, the minister of finance, was impeached before the supreme court of the realm for having made certain payments without the sanction of the storthing, he also considered this as an attack upon himself and his royal prerogatives in general. His irritation knew no bounds, and although Collett was acquitted by the supreme court, the king, in order to express his irritation with the storthing and the action they had taken against one of his ministers, dissolved the national assembly with every sign of displeasure. The Swedish viceroy at the time, Count Sandels, had tried to convince him that his prejudice against the celebration of the 17th of May was groundless, and for some years the king had made no objection to the celebration. In 1827 it was, however, celebrated in a very marked manner, and later in the same year there was a demonstration against a company of Swedish actors who had been performing a foolish political piece called *The Union*. This being privately reported to the king, and represented to him in as bad a light as possible, he thought that Count Sandels, who had not considered it worth while to report the occurrence, was not fitted for his post, and had him replaced by Count Platen, an upright but narrow-minded statesman, who was looked upon as a mouth-piece of the prevailing opinion in Sweden, where the people considered themselves defrauded of the real union they had hoped for.

Count Platen's first act was to issue a proclamation warning the people against celebrating the day of independence; and in April, 1828, the king against the advice of his ministers, summoned an extraordinary storthing, in consequence of the judgment of the supreme court and the uncertain basis upon which that judgment seemed to place his royal prerogatives; his intention being to wrest from the storthing the supremacy it had gained in 1827. He also intended to take steps to prevent the celebration of the 17th of May, and, in order to give due emphasis to his proposals, he assembled a force of two thousand Norwegian soldiers in the neighbourhood of the capital. The king arrived in Christiania soon after the opening of the extraordinary storthing. He did not succeed, however, in his attempt to make any constitutional changes; but the storthing met the king's wishes with regard to the celebration of the 17th of May by deciding not to continue it, and the people all over the country quietly acquiesced.

The " Battle of the Market-place "

This was all that resulted from the king's great efforts on this occasion; but even this little triumph did not last long. The following year trouble broke out again. The students had decided to celebrate the 17th of May with a festive gathering, which, however, passed off quietly. But it was known that the authorities had made extraordinary preparations, and large masses of the people paraded the streets, out of curiosity, singing and shouting, and gathered finally in the market-place. There was no rioting or disturbance, but the Riot Act was read, and the police and the military eventually dispersed the people, and drove them to their homes with sword and musket.

This episode has become known as the "Battle of the Market-place," and did much to increase the general ill-feeling against Count Platen, who, it has since been proved, was no friend of Norway, having actually advised the king to try a *coup d'état*. His health eventually broke down from disappointment and vexation at the indignities and abuse heaped upon him. He died in Christiania at the end of the year, and owing to the state of public feeling his post was not filled by a Swede, but remained vacant for several years, the presidency of the Norwegian government in the meantime being taken by Collett, its oldest member. From this time the day of independence has been celebrated every year with increasing enthusiasm.

Increased Political Power of the Peasantry

By the July Revolution the political situation in Europe became completely changed, and the lessons derived from that great movement reached also to Norway. A new generation had grown up, which was more familiar with the forms of political freedom, and also bolder in adopting them. The representatives of the peasantry, for whom the constitution had paved the way to become the ruling element in political life, were also beginning to distinguish themselves in the national assembly, where they now had taken up an independent position against the representatives of the official classes, who in 1814 and afterwards had played the leading and most influential part in politics. This party was now under the leadership of the able and gifted Ole Ueland, who remained a member of every storthing from 1833 to 1869. The storthing of 1833 was the first of the so-called "peasant storthings." Hitherto the peasantry had never been represented by more than twenty members, but the elections in 1833 brought their number up to forty-five — nearly half of the total representation.

The attention of this new party was especially directed to the finances of the country, in the administration of which they demanded the strictest economy. They often went too far in their zeal, and thereby incurred considerable ridicule and even the contempt of the officials and well-to-do classes, who began to regard the new party with distrustful and hostile feelings. About this time the peasant party found a champion in the youthful poet Henrik Wergeland, who threw himself heart and soul into the political questions of the day, and soon became one of the leaders of the "Young Norway" party. He was a republican in politics, and the most zealous upholder of the national independence of Norway, and of her full equality with Sweden in the union. He soon became as much detested by the so-called "party of intelligence" — the official and well-to-do classes — as was the party he had joined. In addition to the political struggles of the day, a literary conflict now began, which lasted for many years, and which in violence and intensity has scarcely ever been equalled in the history of the country. A strong opposition to Wergeland and the peasant party was formed by the upper classes, under the leadership of another rising poet and writer, Johan Sebastian Welhaven, and other talented men, who wished to retain the literary and linguistic relationship with Denmark; while Wergeland and his party wished to make the separation from Denmark as complete as possible, and in every way to encourage the growth of the national characteristics and feeling among the people. Wergeland had therefore welcomed with joy the increase of the peasant party: he considered the peasantry the real descendants of the old Northmen — the kernel of the nation in fact — and, with the prophetic foresight of the poet, saw the important part they would play in the future political and intellectual life of the country. He devoted much of his time, by writing and other means, to promote the education of the people; but although he was most popular with the working and poorer classes, he was not able to form any political party around him, and at the time of his death he stood almost isolated. He died in 1845, and his opponents now became the leaders in the field of literature, and carried on the work of national reconstruction in a more restrained and quiet manner. The peasant party still continued to exist, but restricted itself principally to the assertion of local interests and the maintenance of strict economy in the budget.

The violent agitation that began in 1830 died away, and, after Wergeland's death, the political life of the country assumed a more quiet and harmonious aspect. The tension between the king and the legislature, however, still continued, and reached its height during the session of 1836, when all the royal proposals for changes in the constitution were laid aside, without even passing through committee, and when various other steps towards upholding the independence of the country were taken. The king, in his displeasure, decided to dissolve the storthing; but before it dispersed it proceeded to impeach Lövenskiold, one of the ministers, before the supreme court of the realm, for having advised the king to dissolve the storthing. He was eventually sentenced to pay a fine of 10,000 kroner (about £550), but he retained his post. Collett, another minister who had greatly displeased the king by his conduct, was dismissed; but unity in the Government was brought about by the appointment of Count Wedel Jarlsberg as viceroy of Norway. From this time the relations between the king and the Norwegian people began to improve, whereas in Sweden he was in his later years not a little disliked.

The National Flag Question

When the king's anger had subsided, he summoned the storthing to an extraordinary session, when several important bills were passed. Towards the close of the session, an address to the king was agreed to, in which the storthing urged that steps should be taken to place Norway in political respects upon an equal footing with Sweden, especially in the conduct of diplomatic affairs with foreign countries. The same address contained a petition for the use of the national or merchant flag in all waters. According to the constitution, Norway was to have her own merchant flag, and in 1821, the storthing had passed a resolution that the flag should be scarlet, divided into four by a blue cross with white borders. The king, however, refused his sanction to the resolution, but gave permission to use the flag in waters nearer home; but beyond Cape Finisterre the naval flag, which was really the Swedish flag, with a white cross on a red ground in the upper square, had to be carried. In reply to the storthing's address the king, in 1838, conceded the right to all merchant ships to carry the national flag in all waters. This was hailed with great rejoicings all over the country; but the question of the national flag for general use had yet to be settled, and later on gave rise to long and violent strife before it was finally settled in accordance with the wishes of the people.

With regard to the question raised in the address of the storthing about the conduct of diplomatic affairs, and other matters concerning the equality of Norway in the union, the king, in 1839, appointed a committee of four Norwegians and four Swedes, who were to consider and report upon the questions thus raised. In 1835 a royal decree had ordained that when the Swedish minister of foreign affairs transacted business which concerned the two countries, or Norway only, the Norwegian minister in attendance upon the king at Stockholm should be present; but the storthing, in its address, declared that it only considered this resolution to be a preparatory step towards a more complete and satisfactory arrangement of this important matter.

During the sitting of this first "union committee," as it was called, the question of a complete revision of the act of union was raised by the division of the Norwegian government in attendance upon the king at Stockholm, but the proposal was not accepted by the Norwegian home government. The powers of the committee were, however, extended to consider a comprehensive revision of the Act of Union, with the limitation that the fundamental conditions of the union must in no way be interfered with. But before the committee had finished their report, the king died (March 8th, 1844), and was succeeded by his son Oscar I.

CHARLES JOHN SUCCEEDED BY OSCAR I

According to the constitution, the Norwegian kings must be crowned in Trondhjem cathedral, but the bishop of Trondhjem was in doubt whether the queen, who was a Catholic, could be crowned; and after the question had become the subject of public discussion, the king decided to forego the coronation both of himself and his queen. The new king soon showed his desire to meet the wishes of the Norwegian people. Thus he decided that, in all documents concerning the internal government of the country, Norway should stand first where reference was made to the king as sovereign of the two kingdoms. After having received the report of the committee concerning the flag question, he resolved (June 20th, 1844) that Norway and Sweden should each carry its own national flag as the naval flag, with the mark of union in the upper corner; and it was also decided that the merchant flag of the two kingdoms should bear the same mark of union, and that only ships sailing under these flags could claim the protection of the state. The union committee did eventually present a report, in which it was proposed that the two countries should have a foreign minister in common, which the Norwegian government gave their opinion upon, but which the Swedish government rejected.

The financial and material conditions of the country had now considerably improved; and King Oscar's reign was marked by the carrying out of important legislative work and reforms, especially in local government, of which Norway now possesses one of the most perfect systems. New roads were planned and built all over the country, the first railway was built, steamship routes along the coast were established, lighthouses were erected, and trade and shipping made great progress. The king's reign was not disturbed by any serious conflicts between the two countries, and the relations between the government and the storthing were of a harmonious character, both working for the internal development of the country. No change took place in the ministry under the presidency of the viceroy Lövenskiold upon King Oscar's accession to the throne; but, on the death or retirement of some of its members, the vacant places were filled by younger and talented men, among whom was Frederik Stang, who in 1845 took over the newly established ministry of the interior. During the Schleswig-Holstein rebellion (1848–50) and the Crimean war, King Oscar succeeded in maintaining the neutrality of Norway and Sweden, by which Norwegian shipping especially benefited. The abolition of the English Navigation Acts (repealed in the year 1850) was of great importance to Norway, and opened up a great future for its merchant fleet.

Relations with Russia

In 1826, a treaty had been concluded with Russia, by which the frontier between that country and the adjoining strip of Norwegian territory in the Polar region was definitely delimited; but in spite of this treaty, Russia, in 1851, demanded that the Russian Lapps on the Norwegian frontier should have the right to fish on the Norwegian coast, and have a portion of the coast on the Varanger Fjord allotted to them to settle upon. The Norwegian government refused to accede to the Russian demands, and serious complications might have ensued if the attention of Russia had not been turned in another direction. While his father had looked to Russia for support, King Oscar was more inclined to secure the western powers as his allies, and during the Crimean war (1855) he concluded a treaty with England and France, according to which these countries promised their assistance in the event of any fresh attempts at encroachment on Norwegian or Swedish territory by Russia. In consequence of this treaty, the relations between Norway and Sweden and Russia became somewhat strained; but after the peace of Paris (1856) and the accession of Alexander II, whose government was in favour of a peaceful policy, the Russian ambassador at Stockholm succeeded in bringing about more friendly relations.

In 1855 two commissions, consisting of an equal number of Norwegians and Swedes, were appointed. One of these was to consider a new bill for regulating the commercial relations between the two countries, which was to take the place of an older one of 1827; while the other commission was to prepare a bill for the execution, in either country, of judicial judgments delivered in the other. The reports of these commissions were laid before and passed by the Swedish riksdag; but when they came before the Norwegian storthing, they were rejected as unsuitable for Norway, a decision which caused great irritation in Sweden.

CHARLES XV

Owing to the king's ill-health, his son, Crown Prince Charles, was appointed regent in 1857, and two years later, when King Oscar died, he succeeded to the thrones of the two countries as Charles XV. He was a gifted, genial, and noble personality, and won the hearts of all who came into contact with him. He was also of an artistic nature, and devoted himself to painting, poetry, and music. He had desired to inaugurate his reign by giving the Norwegians a proof of his willingness to acknowledge the claims of Norway but he did not live to see his wishes in this respect carried out. According to the constitution, the king had the power to appoint a viceroy for Norway, who might be either a Norwegian or a Swede. Since 1829 no Swede had held the post, and since 1859 no appointment of a viceroy had been made, the general hope being that the office would be abolished altogether. But the paragraph in the constitution still existed, and the Norwegians naturally wished to have this stamp of "provinciality" obliterated.

A proposal for the abolishment of the office of viceroy was laid before the storthing in 1859, and passed by it. The king, whose sympathies on this question were known, had been appealed to, and had privately promised that he would sanction the proposed change in the constitution; but as soon as the resolution of the storthing became known in Sweden, a violent outcry arose both in the Swedish press and the Swedish estates. The latter adopted a resolution declaring that the paragraph relating to the office of viceroy was a necessary condition of the union between the two countries, and could not be altered without the consent of the Swedish executive. Under the pressure that was brought to bear upon the king in Sweden, he eventually refused to sanction the resolution of the storthing; but he added that he shared the views of his Norwegian counsellors, and would, when "the convenient moment" came, himself propose the abolition of the office of viceroy. This was but a poor consolation for the Norwegian people, who well knew that it was the dominant feeling in Sweden against the equality of Norway in the union which had come out triumphantly on this occasion. When the storthing received the news of the refusal, it adopted an address to the king (April 1860), which stated that no Norwegian who had any regard for his country and his own honour would take any share in the revision of the act of Union on any other basis than that of the complete equality of the two kingdoms in the union.

Swedish Proposals for Revision of Act of Union

In the following year, the Swedish government again pressed the demands of the Swedish estates for a revision of the Act of Union, which this time included the establishment of a union or common parliament for the two countries, on the basis that, according to the population, there should be two Swedish members to every Norwegian. The proposal was sent to the Norwegian government, which did not seem at all disposed to entertain it; but some dissensions arose with regard to the form in which their reply was to be laid before the king. The more obstinate members of the ministry resigned, and others, of a more pliable nature, were appointed under the presidency of Frederik Stang, who had already been minister of the interior from 1845 to 1856. The reconstructed government was, however, in accord with the retiring one, that no proposal for the revision of the act of Union could then be entertained, as the attitude of Sweden towards the claims of the Norwegians for equality in the union seemed to be the same as in 1859 and 1860, and the question was in consequence to be allowed to rest for the time being. The king, however, advocated the desirability of a revision, but insisted that this would have to be based upon the full equality of both countries.

In 1863 the storthing assented to the appointment by the king of a union committee — the second time that such a committee had been called upon to consider this vexatious question. It was not until 1867 that the report of the committee was made public, but it could not come on for discussion in the storthing till the latter met again, in 1871. During this period the differences between the two countries were somewhat thrust into the background by the Danish complications in 1863–64, which threatened to draw the two kingdoms into war. King Charles was himself in favour of a defensive alliance with Denmark; but the Norwegian storthing would consent to this only if an alliance could also be effected with two, or at least one, of the western powers. Under the circumstances, the king felt himself obliged to withdraw from the proposed alliance with Denmark, as none of the western powers showed any sign of assisting the Danes, although they had guaranteed the indivisibility of Denmark.

Foundation of the Norwegian National Party

In 1869, the storthing passed a resolution by which its sessions, from 1871, were made annual instead of triennial according to the constitution of

1814. The first important question which the first yearly storthing, in 1871, had to consider was once more the proposed revision of the act of Union. The Norwegians had persistently maintained that, in any discussion on this question, the basis for the negotiations should be: (1) the full equality of the two kingdoms; and (2) no extension of the bonds of the union beyond the line originally defined in the act of 1815; but the draft of the new act contained terms in which the supremacy of Sweden was presupposed, and which introduced important extensions of the bonds of the union. Strangely enough, the report of the union committee was adopted by the new Stang ministry, and even supported by some of the most influential newspapers and in several of the leading circles of the Norwegian community. The reactionary tendencies which were hidden under the plausible garb of "Scandinavianism," reasserted themselves, and the official classes saw in this new union a safeguard against the growing liberal and democratic movements in the country.

Under these circumstances the "lawyers' party," under the leadership of Johan Sverdrup, who was to play such a prominent part in Norwegian politics, and the "peasant party," led by Sören Jaabœk, a gifted peasant proprietor, who was also destined to become a prominent figure in the political history of the country, formed an intimate alliance, with the object of guarding against any encroachment upon the liberty and independence which the country had secured by the constitution of 1814. This was the foundation of the great national party, which became known as the *Venstre* (the left), and which before long became powerful enough to exert the most decisive influence upon the political affairs of the country. When, therefore, the proposed revision of the Act of Union eventually came before the storthing of 1871, it was rejected by an overwhelming majority; and this contentious question, which, since 1859, from time to time had assumed a most threatening aspect, may now be said to have been finally shelved and disposed of. The position which the government had taken up on this question helped to open the eyes of the Norwegians to some defects in the constitution, which had proved obstacles to the development and strengthening of the parliamentary system, of which the constitution had laid the foundation; and to the desirability of a harmonious co-operation between the executive and legislative powers of the country, in order that the smaller state might more effectively assert its rights and position in the union, in opposition to the greater, which seemed ever intent upon assuming the *rôle* of the predominant partner in the union. And this gave rise to the great question of the admittance of the ministers to seats in the national assembly, which came to a crisis in the 'eighties.

In 1872, a private bill came before the storthing, proposing that the ministers should be admitted to the storthing and take part in its proceedings. After a number of stormy debates, the bill was successfully carried under the leadership of Johan Sverdrup, by a large majority (80 against 29); but the government, evidently jealous of the growing powers and influence of the new liberal party in the storthing, advised the king to refuse his sanction to the bill, although the government party itself had several times in the preceding half-century introduced a similar bill for admitting the ministers to the storthing; but at that time the opposition had looked with suspicion on the presence of the ministers in the national assembly, lest their superior skill in debate and political experience should turn the scale too readily in favour of government measures. Now, on the contrary, the opposition had gained more experience and confidence in its own strength, and no doubt found that the legislative work could be better carried on if the ministers were present to explain and defend their views; but the government saw in the proposed reform the threatened introduction of full parliamentary government, by which the ministry could not remain in office unless supported by a majority in the storthing. The king's refusal created great dissatisfaction and irritation, both in the storthing and throughout the country. The relations between the government and the majority in the storthing were already considerably strained, and in the refusal the storthing only saw another ill-timed assertion of governmental authority. Before the storthing separated, the liberals carried a vote of censure against the government; but the king declared that the ministers enjoyed his confidence, and that he would uphold his right to appoint and keep what ministers he pleased, and took no further notice of the vote. However, two of the ministers, who had advised the ratification of the bill, resigned. Numerous public meetings were held all over the country in support of the proposed reform, fully approving of the step the storthing had taken by proposing the vote of want of confidence. Among the speakers was Johan Sverdrup, who had now become the acknowledged leader of the liberal party, and who was hailed with great enthusiasm as the champion of the proposed reform.

KING OSCAR II
(1829-)

This was the political situation when King Charles died (September 18th, 1872). He was succeeded by his brother, who ascended the throne as Oscar II. In the following year this monarch gave his sanction to the bill for the abolition of the office of viceroy, which the storthing had again passed; and the president of the ministry was afterwards recognised as the prime minister and head of the government in Christiania. Frederik Stang, who was the president of the ministry at the time, was the first to fill this office. In the same year Norway celebrated its existence for a thousand years as a kingdom with great festivities.

PROPOSALS BY THE STORTHING FOR FULL POPULAR CONTROL

In 1874 the government, in order to show the people that they to some extent were willing to meet their wishes with regard to the great question before the country, laid before the storthing a royal proposition for the admittance of the ministers to the national assembly. But this was to be accompanied by certain other constitutional changes, such as giving the king the right of dissolving the storthing at his pleasure, and providing fixed pensions for ex-ministers, which they held up as a guarantee against the majority of the assembly's misusing its new power. The liberal party, in the meantime, received more and more support all over the country for their proposal and for full parliamentary government. Johan Sverdrup well summed up their policy in the following curt sentence: "All power must be gathered in this hall." The bill which the government brought in was unanimously rejected by the storthing, the conservatives also voting against it, as they considered the guarantees insufficient. The same year, and again in 1877, the storthing passed the bill for admitting the ministers to the national assembly, but in a somewhat different form from that of 1872. On both occasions the king refused his sanction to the bill.

The storthing then resorted to the procedure provided by the constitution to carry out the people's will. In 1880 the bill was passed for the third time, and, on this occasion, by the overwhelming majority of 93 out of 113. Three storthings after three successive elections had now carried the bill, without the adoption of any divergent resolution in the period between the first and third reading, and according to the constitution, the bill would then become law with or without the king's sanction. It was, however, generally expected that the king and his government would at length comply with the wishes of the people; but the king on this occasion also refused to sanction the bill, declaring at the same time that his right to the absolute veto was "above all doubt." A feeling of disappointment and irritation pervaded the whole country, and many even of the conservatives, both in and out of the storthing, deeply regretted the king's decision. Johan Sverdrup, the leader of the liberal party and president of the storthing, brought, however, the question to a prompt issue, by proposing to the storthing that the bill, which had been passed three times, should now be declared to be the law of the land without the king's sanction. This proposal was carried by a large majority on the 9th of June, 1880, but the king and his ministers in reply

SOPHIA, QUEEN OF SWEDEN
(1836–)

firmly declared that they would not recognise the validity of the resolution.

From this moment the struggle may be said to have centred itself upon the existence or non-existence of an absolute veto on the part of the crown. The king requested the faculty of law at the Christiania University to give its opinion on the question at issue; and, with one dissentient, the learned doctors upheld the king's right to the absolute veto in questions concerning amendments of the constitution, although they could not find that it was expressly stated in the fundamental law of the country. The ministry also advised the king to claim a veto in questions of supply, which still further increased the ill-feeling in the country against the government; and the conflict in consequence grew more and more violent. In the midst of the struggle between the king and the storthing, the prime minister, Frederik Stang, resigned, and Christian August Selmer became his successor; and this, together with the appointment of another member to the ministry, K. H. Schweigaard, plainly indicated that the conflict with the storthing was to be continued. In June, 1882, the king arrived in Christiania to dissolve the storthing, and on this occasion delivered a speech from the throne, in which he openly censured the representatives of the people for their attitude in legislative work and on the question of the absolute veto, the speech creating considerable surprise throughout the country.   Great preparations were now made by both parties for the impending elections, and public meetings were held during the recess all over the country.   Johan Sverdrup and Björnstjerne Björnson, the popular poet and dramatist, were the principal speakers, and called upon the people to support the storthing in upholding the resolution of the 9th of June, and to rouse themselves to a sense of their political rights. The elections resulted in a great victory for the liberal party, which returned stronger than ever to the storthing, the liberals now numbering eighty-three and the conservatives only thirty-one.   The ministry, however, showed no sign of yielding or resigning their offices; and when the new storthing met in February, 1883, the odelsthing (the lower division of the national assembly) decided upon having the question finally settled by impeaching the whole of the ministry before the rigsret, or the supreme court of the realm — the last constitutional means by which the storthing could obtain the dismissal of the ministry, which for years had continued to govern without the confidence or support of the national assembly.   The jurisdiction of the rigsret is limited to the trial of offences against the state, and there is no appeal against its decisions.   The charges against the ministers were of having acted contrary to the interests of the country, by advising the king to refuse his sanction — first, to the amendment of the law for admitting the ministers to the storthing; secondly, to a bill involving a question of supply; and thirdly, to a bill by which the storthing could appoint additional directors on the state railways.

The trial of the eleven ministers of the Selmer cabinet began in May, 1883, and lasted over ten months.   In the end, the rigsret sentenced the prime minister and seven of his ministers to be deprived of their offices, while three, who had either recommended the king to sanction the bill for admitting the ministers to the storthing, or had entered the cabinet at a later date, were heavily fined.   The excitement in the country, already considerable before the verdict had been given, rose to feverish anxiety in expectation of what the king would do.   The conservative organs of the country openly advised the king to disregard the judgment of the supreme court, while party feeling everywhere ran high.   Rumours of all kinds were afloat, and it was generally believed that the king would attempt a *coup d'état*.   Many of the conservative party in Sweden also encouraged the king to set the judgment aside; and it was even hinted that he might depend upon the Swedish army to assist him in carrying out his policy in Norway.   Fortunately, the king did not follow this advice, and after some hesitation, he issued (March 11th) an order in council, announcing that the judgment of the supreme court would be carried into effect; and Selmer was then called upon to resign his position as prime minister.   The king, however, in his declaration upheld the constitutional prerogative of the crown, which, he maintained, was not impaired by the judgment of the rigsret.   The conservatives were much disappointed with the king's course of action, but consoled themselves by forcing upon the king the urgent necessity of appointing a new conservative ministry, which would carry on the policy of the late cabinet.   The following month the king, regardless of the large liberal majority in the storthing, asked Schweigaard, one of the late ministers whose punishment consisted in a fine, to form a ministry, and the so-called "April ministry" was then appointed.   It tried to adopt the policy of its predecessors in a moderate form, but it met with such opposition from the very first that it sent in its resignation in the following month. Professor Broch, a former minister, next attempted to form a ministry, but without success, and the king was at last compelled to appoint a ministry in accordance with the majority in the storthing. In June, 1883, Johan Sverdrup was asked to form a ministry. He selected for his ministers leading men on the liberal side in the storthing, and the first liberal ministry that Norway had was at length appointed. The storthing, in order to satisfy the king, passed a new resolution admitting the ministers to the national assembly, which then received the formal sanction of the king.

During the following years, a series of important reforms were carried through. Thus, in 1887, the jury system in criminal matters was introduced into the country after violent opposition from the conservatives. A bill intended to give parishioners greater influence in church matters, and introduced by Jakob Sverdrup, the minister of education and a nephew of the prime minister, met, however, with strong opposition, and was eventually rejected by the storthing, the result being a break-up of the ministry and a disorganization of the Liberal party. In June, 1889, the Sverdrup ministry resigned, and a conservative one was formed by Emil Stang, the leader of the conservatives in the storthing; and during the next two years the storthing passed various useful measures; but the ministry was eventually wrecked on the rock of the great national question which about this time came to the front — that of Norway's share in the transaction of diplomatic affairs.

THE QUESTION OF DIPLOMATIC REPRESENTATION

At the time of the union, in 1814, nothing had been settled as to how diplomatic affairs were to be conducted, but in 1835 a resolution was issued, that when the Swedish foreign minister was transacting diplomatic matters with the king which concerned both countries, or Norway only, the Norwegian minister of state in attendance upon the king at Stockholm should be present. This arrangement has not always proved satisfactory to the Norwegians, especially as the Swedish foreign minister cannot be held responsible to the Norwegian government or parliament; but in the meanwhile this state of affairs has been allowed to drift on, and gradually the Swedish foreign minister has come to be looked upon as the foreign minister for Norway also. But this is not sanctioned by any paragraph in the constitution or the Act of Union, neither has it been confirmed by any act of the storthing; and the Norwegians maintain that Norway has not enjoyed equal rights in the union and equal share in the transaction of diplomatic affairs with Sweden, as, according to the Act of Union, it had a right to demand.

By a change in the Swedish constitution, in 1885, the ministerial council, in which diplomatic matters are discussed, came to consist of the Swedish foreign minister and two other members of the cabinet on behalf of Sweden, and of the Norwegian minister at Stockholm on behalf of Norway. The king, wishing to remedy this disparity, proposed that the composition of the council should be determined by an additional paragraph in the Act of Union. The representatives of the Norwegian government in Stockholm proposed that three members of the cabinet of each country should constitute the ministerial council, to which the Swedish government were willing to agree, but on the assumption that the minister of foreign affairs should continue to be a Swede as before, which the Norwegians, of course, would not accept. The matter was, in consequence, shelved and remained in abeyance for some time, but continued to be discussed in the press and at public meetings. At the king's instigation, the negotiations with the Swedish government were resumed at the beginning of 1891; and the Stang ministry succeeded in coming to an agreement with the Swedish government that a measure should be introduced, by which the Norwegians would practically obtain what the storthing of 1886 had asked for, while the question of the nationality of the minister of foreign affairs was left for settlement in the near future. The Swedish riksdag, however, rejected the proposal, while the Norwegian storthing insisted upon "Norway's right, as an independent kingdom, to full equality in the union, and therewith her right to watch over her foreign affairs in a constitutional manner."

The Stang ministry then resigned; and a liberal ministry, with Steen, the recognized leader of the liberal party after Sverdrup's withdrawal from politics, as prime minister, was appointed. In the same year, the provision in the constitution empowering the king to instal the crown prince as regent in Norway was repealed, and the resolution was sanctioned by the king. The new ministry had placed the question of a separate minister of foreign affairs for Norway prominently in their programme, but little progress was made during the next few years. Another and more important question for the country, as far as its shipping and commerce are concerned, now came to the front. The storthing had, in 1891, appointed a committee to inquire into the practicability of establishing a separate Norwegian consular service, instead of the existing combination with Sweden, with which the Norwegians maintain they have had reason to be dissatisfied. In 1892, the storthing, acting upon the committee's report, determined to establish a consular service in accordance with a plan prepared by the department of the interior. The king, no doubt influenced and supported by public opinion in Sweden, which was against the proposed separation of the consular services, refused his sanction; and the Norwegian government, in consequence, sent in their resignation, whereupon a complete deadlock ensued. This was terminated by a compromise to the effect that the ministry would return to office, on the understanding that the question be postponed by common consent. The following year the storthing again passed a resolution, calling upon the Norwegian government to proceed with the necessary measures for establishing the proposed consular service for Norway, but the king again refused to take any action in the matter. Upon this, the liberal ministry resigned (May, 1893), and the king appointed a conservative government, with E. Stang as its chief. Thus matters went on till the end of 1894, when the triennial elections took place, with the result that the majority of the electors declared in favour of national independence on the great question then before the country — that of separate consuls for Norway, and eventually of a separate responsible minister of foreign affairs for the country.

The ministry did not at once resign, but waited till the king arrived in Christiania to open the storthing (January, 1895). The king would not accept their resignation there and then, but kept the country for over four months without a responsible government, during which time the crisis had become more acute than ever. A coalition ministry was at last formed, with Professor Hagerup as prime minister. A new committee, consisting of an equal number of Norwegians and Swedes, was appointed to consider the question of separate diplomatic representation; but after sitting for over two years, the committee separated without being able to come to any agreement, having, like the two previous "union committees," proved the impossibility of the two countries coming to an understanding on this important question. While the committee was sitting, the disputes concerning the political relations between the two countries were allowed to lie in abeyance.

The elections in 1897 proved again a great victory for the liberal party (seventy-nine liberals *versus* thirty-five conservatives), and in February, 1898, the Hagerup ministry was replaced by a liberal, once more under the premiership of Steen. Soon afterwards the bill for the general adoption of the national or "pure" flag, as it was called, was carried for the third time, and became law without the king's sanction. By this act the device or mark of union in the upper corner of the flag was abolished, but is still retained on men-of-war and fortifications. In 1898, universal political suffrage for men was passed by a large majority (seventy-five *versus* thirty-six), while the proposal to include women received the support of only thirty-three votes. In 1901, universal municipal suffrage was given both to men and women; to the latter, however, with certain limitations. In January, 1902, a committee was appointed to consider the consular question, and it was hoped that at last it would be settled. In April, 1902, Steen the prime minister resigned, and retired into private life. He was succeeded by Otto Albert Blehr.[i]

RECENT HISTORY OF SWEDEN

For Norway's sister kingdom the nineteenth century has been one of material progress and social reform. In 1845, the criminal law was revised, and the establishment of a network of railways at the same time taken in hand; in 1859, permission to acquire land was conceded to the Jews; 1863 saw the establishment of free trade. The problem of political reform and a modification of the Swedish constitution in a popular direction was long found to present insuperable obstacles. At last, in 1866, Charles XV granted a constitution (modified 1894), according to which the executive power was vested in the king, acting by the advice of his responsible ministers, while the legislative body was to consist of two chambers — the lower elected by the people according to a property qualification, the upper, by the provincial assemblies and certain municipalities. The upper chamber was to be chosen for nine years, while the election to the lower chamber was for three only. The members of the lower chamber received allowances.

As regards foreign policy, Sweden has not played a great *rôle* in the affairs of Europe. During the Schleswig-Holstein troubles her sympathies were with Denmark, and in 1848 she sent troops to Fünen, while the armistice of Malmö, concluded the same year, was effected by her mediation. Subsequently, however, she remained an inactive spectator of the struggle, to the great disappointment of the Danes, who had calculated on her aid. In 1855, whilst the Crimean war was in progress, Sweden, provoked by Russian encroachment on her fisheries, concluded a defensive alliance with Great Britain and France, and obtained a satisfactory adjustment of her difficulties with the Muscovite power by the Treaty of Paris of 1856.[a]

The economic condition of Sweden, owing to the progress in material prosperity which had taken place in the country as the result of the Franco-German war, was at the accession of Oscar II to the throne, on the 18th of September, 1872, fairly satisfactory. Politically, however, the outlook was not so favourable. In their results, the reforms inaugurated during the preceding reign did not answer expectations. Within three years of the introduction of the new electoral laws, De Geer's ministry had forfeited much of its former popularity, and had been forced to resign. In the vital matter of national defence no common understanding had been arrived at, and during the conflicts which had raged round this question, the two chambers had come into frequent collision, and paralysed the action of the government.

The peasant proprietors, who, under the name of the *landtmanna* party,[1] formed a compact majority in the second chamber, pursued a consistent policy of class interests in the matter of the taxes and burdens that had, as they urged, so long oppressed the Swedish peasantry; and consequently, when a bill was introduced for superseding the old system of army organisation by general compulsory service, they demanded, as a condition of its acceptance, that the military burdens should be more evenly distributed in the country, and that the land taxes, which they regarded as a burden under which they had wrongfully groaned for centuries, should be abolished. In these circumstances, the landtmanna party in the riksdag, who desired the lightening of the military burden, joined those who desired the abolition of landlordism, and formed a compact and predominant majority in the second chamber, while the burgher and liberal parties were reduced to an impotent "intelligence" minority. This majority in the lower chamber was at once attacked by another compact majority in the upper, who on their side maintained that the hated land taxes were only a kind of rent-charge on land, were incidental to it, and in no way weighed upon the owners, and, moreover, that their abolition would be quite unwarrantable, as they were one of the surest sources of revenue to the state. On the other hand, the first chamber refused to listen to any abolition of the old military system, so long as the defence of the country had not been placed upon a secure basis by the adoption of general compulsory military service. The government stood midway between these conflicting majorities in the chambers, unable to find support in either.

Such was the state of affairs when Oscar II, surrounded by his late brother's advisers, began his reign. One of his first cares was to increase the strength of his navy; but in consequence of the continued antagonism of the political parties, he was unable to effect much. In the first riksdag, however, the so-called "compromise," which afterwards played so important a part in Swedish political life, came into existence. It originated in the small "Skåne" party in the upper house, and was devised to establish a *modus vivendi* between the conflicting parties, *i.e.*, the champions of national defence, and those who demanded a lightening of the burdens of taxation. The king himself perceived in the compromise a means of solving the conflicting questions, and warmly approved it. He persuaded his ministers to constitute a special inquiry into the proposed abolition of land taxes, and, in the address with which he opened the riksdag of 1875, laid particular stress upon the necessity of giving attention to the settlement of these two burning questions; and in 1880 again came forward with a new proposal for increasing the number of years of service with the militia. This motion having been rejected, De Geer resigned, and was succeeded by Count Arvid Posse. The new prime minister endeavoured to solve the question of defence in accordance with the views of the landtmanna party. Three parliamentary committees had prepared schemes for a remission of the land taxes, for a new system of taxation, for a reorganisation of the army based on a *stammtrupp* (regular army), by the enlistment of hired soldiers, and for naval reforms. In this last connection, the most suitable types of vessels for coast defence and for offence were determined upon. But Count Posse, deserted by his own party over the army bill, resigned, and was succeeded on the 16th of

---

[1] The Swedish landtmanna party was formed in 1867. It consisted mostly of the larger and smaller peasant proprietors, who at the time of the old *ständers riksdag* were always opposed to the nobility and the clergy. The object of the party was to bring about a fusion between the representatives of the large landed proprietors and the regular peasant proprietors; to support the interests of landed proprietors in general against those of the town representatives; and to resist crown interference in the administration of local affairs.

May, 1884, by Oscar Themptauder, who had been minister of finance in the previous cabinet. The new premier succeeded in persuading the riksdag to pass a bill, increasing the period of service with the colours in the army to six years, and that in the militia to forty-two days, and as a set-off, a remission of thirty per cent. on the land taxes.

Protectionist Movement

Influenced by the economic reaction which took place in 1879, in consequence of the state of affairs in Germany, where Prince Bismarck had introduced the protectionist system, a protectionist party had been formed, which tried to gain adherents in the riksdag. It is true that, in the riksdag of 1882, the commercial treaty with France was renewed; but since 1885 the protectionist party was prepared to begin the combat, and a duty on corn, which had been proposed in the riksdag of the same year, was rejected by only a slight majority. During the period of the unusually low price of corn of 1886, which greatly affected the Swedish farmers, protection gained ground to such an extent that its final triumph was considered as certain within a short time. During the riksdag of the same year, however, the premier Themptauder emphatically declared himself against the protectionist party, and while the parties in the second chamber were equal in number, the proposed tax on corn was rejected in the first chamber. In the riksdag of 1887 there was a majority for protection in the second chamber, and in the first the majority against the tax was so small that the tax on corn would have triumphed in a combined meeting of the two chambers. The government, availing itself of its formal right not to dissolve the chamber in which it had the support of a majority, therefore dissolved only the second chamber (March, 1887).

The new riksdag assembled in May with a free-trade majority in the second chamber, but nothing in connection with the great question of customs was settled. In the meantime, the powerful majority in the second chamber split into two groups — the new landtmanna party, which approved protection in the interests of agricultural classes; and a somewhat smaller group, the old landtmanna party, which favoured free trade. The victory of the free traders was not, however, destined to be of long duration, as the protectionists obtained a majority in both chambers in the next riksdag (1888). To the first chamber, protectionists were almost exclusively elected; and in the second, all the twenty-two members for Stockholm were disqualified, owing to the fact that one of their number had not paid his taxes a few years previously, which prevented his being eligible. Instead, then, of twenty-two free-traders, representing the majority of the Stockholm electors, twenty-two protectionists, representing the minority, were elected; and Stockholm was thus represented in the riksdag by the choice of a minority in the capital. This singular way of electing members for the principal city in the kingdom could not fail further to irritate the parties. One result of the Stockholm election came at a convenient time for the Themptauder ministry. The financial affairs of the country were found to be in a most unsatisfactory state. In spite of reduced expenses, a highly estimated revenue, and the contemplated raising of taxes, there was a deficit, for the payment or discharge of which the government would be obliged to demand supplementary supplies. The Themptauder ministry resigned. The king retained, however, for a time several members of the ministry; but it was difficult to find a premier who would be able, during the transition from one system to another, to command sufficient authority to control the parties.　At last Baron Gillis Bildt, who, while Swedish ambassador in Berlin, had witnessed the introduction by Prince Bismarck of the agrarian protectionist system in Germany, accepted the premiership, and it was under his auspices that the two chambers imposed a series of duties on necessaries of life.

The new taxes, together with an increase of the excise duty on spirits, soon brought a surplus into the state coffers.　At a council of state (October 12th, 1888) the king declared his wishes as to the way in which this surplus should be used.　He desired that it should be applied to a fund for insurance and old-age pensions for workmen and old people; to the lightening of the municipal taxes by state contributions to the schools and workhouses; to the abolition of the land taxes and of the obligation of keeping a horse and man for military service; and, lastly, to the improvement of the shipping trade. The riksdag, however, decided to devote it to other objects, such as the payment of the deficit in the budget, the building of railways and augmentation of their material, as well as to improvements in the defences of the country. Baron Bildt resigned as soon as the new system seemed settled, making room for Baron Gustav Akerhjelm.　The latter, however, also soon resigned, and was succeeded on July 10th, 1891, by Erik Gustav Bostrom, a landed proprietor.　The protectionist system gained in favour on the expiry of the commercial treaty with France in 1892, as it could now be extended to articles of industry.　The elections of 1890, when the metropolis returned free traders and liberals to the second chamber, certainly effected a change in the latter, as the representatives of the towns and the old landtmanna party united, and established a free-trade majority in the chamber; but, in the combined meetings of the two chambers, the compact protectionist majority in the first chamber turned the scale.　The customs duties were, however, altered several times in accordance with market prices and ruling circumstances.　Thus in 1892, when the import duty on unground corn was reduced from 2s. 10d. to 1s. 5d., and that on ground corn from 4s. 9d. to 2s. 10d., for 100 kilogrammes, the same duties were also retained for the following year.　They were also retained for 1894, at the request of the government, which desired to keep faith with their promise that, while the new organisation of the army was going on, no increase of duties on the necessaries of life should take place.　This measure caused much dissatisfaction, and gave rise to a strong agrarian movement, in consequence of which the government, in the beginning of 1895, before the assembling of the riksdag, made use of its right of raising the two duties on corn just referred to, to 3s. 7d. and 7s. 2d., which were afterwards somewhat reduced as far as seed corn for sowing purposes was concerned.

The question of customs duties now settled, that of national defence was taken up afresh; and in the following year the government produced a complete scheme for the abolition of the land tax in the course of ten years, in exchange for a compensation of ninety days' drill for those liable to military service, proposed to retain the old military system of the country and to strengthen the defences of Norrland; and the government bill for a reorganisation of the army was accepted by the riksdag in an extraordinary session. But it was soon perceived that the new plan was unsatisfactory, and required recasting, upon which the minister of war, Baron Rappe, resigned, and was succeeded by Colonel von Crustebjorn, who immediately set to work to prepare a complete reorganisation of the army, with an increase of the time of active service on the lines of general compulsory service.　The riksdag of 1900, in addition to grants for the fortifications at Boden, in the province of Norrbotten, on the Russian border, and other military objects, voted a considerable grant for an experimental mobilisation, which fully exposed the defects and faults of the old system.   In the riksdag of 1901, E. G. Bostrom resigned, and was succeeded by Admiral F. W. von Otter, who introduced a new bill for the army reorganisation, the most important item of which was the increase of the period of training to 365 days.   The cost in connection with the new scheme was expected to amount to 22,000,000 kronor.   The riksdag, however, did not accept the new plan in its full extent.   The time of drilling was reduced to 240 days for the infantry, to 300 days for the navy, while for the cavalry and artillery the time fixed was 365 days.   The plan, thus modified, was then accepted by the government.

Franchise Reform

After the elections in 1890, the alliance already mentioned between the old landtmanna party and the representatives of the towns had the result that the liberals in the second chamber, to whom the representatives of the towns mostly belonged, were now in a position to decide the policy which the two united parties should follow.   In order to prevent this, it was proposed to readjust the number of the members of the riksdag.   The question was only settled in 1894, when a bill was passed fixing the number of the members of the riksdag in the first chamber at 150, and in the second at 230, of which 150 should represent the country districts and 80 the towns.   The question of protection being now considered settled, there was no longer any reason for the continued separation of the two landtmanna parties, who, at the beginning of the riksdag of 1895, combined and became once more a compact majority in the second chamber, as they had been up to the riksdag of May, 1887.

The influence of the country representatives was thus re-established in the second chamber; but now the demands for the extension of the franchise came more and more to the front, and the premier Bostrom at last felt bound to do something to meet these demands.   He accordingly introduced in the riksdag of 1896 a very moderate bill for the extension of the franchise, which was, nevertheless, rejected by both chambers, all similar proposals by private members meeting the same fate.   When, at last, the bill for the reorganisation of the army, together with a considerably increased taxation, was accepted by the riksdag of 1901, it was generally acknowledged that, in return for the increased taxation, it would only be just to extend the right of taking part in the political life and the legislative work of the country to those of the population who hitherto had been excluded from it.   The government eventually laid a proposal for the extension of the franchise before the riksdag of 1902, the chief feature of which was that the elector should be twenty-five years of age, and that married men over forty years should be entitled to two votes.   The riksdag, however, finally agreed to a proposal by Bishop Billing, a member of the first chamber, that an address should be presented to the king, asking for a full inquiry into the question of extending the franchise for the election of members to the second chamber.

In 1897, the riksdag had received among its members the first socialistic representative, in the person of R. H. Brauting, the leader of the Swedish social democrats.   The socialists, who had formerly confined their activity to questions affecting the working classes and their wages, took, however, in 1902 an active part in the agitation for the extension of the franchise.   Processions of many thousands of workmen were organised, in Stockholm and in other towns of the kingdom, just before the riksdag began the discussion on the above-mentioned bill of the government; and when the bill was introduced in the chambers, a general and well-organised strike took place, and continued during the three days the debate on the bill lasted. As this strike was of an exclusively political kind, and was intended to put pressure on the chambers, it was generally disapproved, and failed in its object. The prime minister, Admiral von Otter, resigned shortly after the end of the session, and was succeeded by Boström the ex-premier, who at the request of the king again assumed office.

During King Oscar's reign many important social reforms have been carried out by the legislature. The statistics show in a very striking manner how the country has developed in all directions. In the riksdag of 1884 a new patent law was adopted, the age at which women should be held to attain their majority was fixed at twenty-one years, and the barbarous prison punishment of "bread and water" abolished. In order to meet the cost of the new army organisation, the riksdag of 1902 increased the revenue by progressive taxation, but only for one year. Bills for the improvement of the social conditions of the people and in the interests of the working classes have also been passed. During the five years 1884–1889, a committee was occupied with the question of workmen's insurance, and thrice the government made proposals for its settlement; on the last occasion adopting the principle of invalidity as a common basis for insurance against accidents, illness, or old age. The riksdag, however, delayed coming to a decision, and contented itself by earmarking money for an insurance fund. At last the riksdag of 1901 accepted a bill for insurance against accidents which also extended to agricultural labourers, in connection with the establishment of a state institution for insurance. The bill for protection against accidents, as well as for the limitation of working hours for women and children, was passed, together with one for the appointment of special factory inspectors.

The so-called "Nobel gift" has given Sweden an important *rôle* in the history of culture which is quite unique. Alfred Nobel, a civil engineer, in 1896 left the whole of his immense property, amounting to over £1,750,000 to a fund, the yearly income of which was to be divided among those who, in the course of the current year, had rendered the greatest service to mankind in various branches of science, in literature, and in the cause of peace. The prizes for 1901 were distributed as follows: Professor Röntgen (natural philosophy), Professor Van't Hoff (chemistry), Professor Behriz (medicine), and Sully Prudhomme (literature). These prizes were adjudged by the Swedish Academy; while the prize for services rendered in the cause of peace is, in accordance with the testator's will, left in the hands of the Norwegian storthing to distribute. The prize for 1901 was divided between Henri Dunant, the founder of the Red Cross, and Frederic Passy, the secretary of the peace congresses [that for 1905 was awarded to Baroness Bertha von Sutner, author of the novel *Die Waffen Nieder* and editor of the organ of the International Peace Bureau at Bern]. Each prize amounts to about £8,300, and will be distributed yearly.

When, in 1897, King Oscar celebrated his jubilee of twenty-five years as king, the exhibition which had been organised in Stockholm offered a convincing proof of the progress the country had made in every direction, while the thousands of provincial visitors who flocked to the metropolis took the opportunity to attest their respect and loyalty to the king and the royal family. The amount collected all over the country on the occasion of the jubilee as a gift to the king, amounting to £140,000, was, according to his majesty's wishes, applied to the building of sanatoria for sufferers from consumption.*j*

THE DISSOLUTION OF THE UNION

But the king's popularity was not sufficient to prevent a great misfortune. Throughout his reign the relations between the two states which composed his dominions had frequently been precarious. One of the chief causes of dissension was the desire of Norway for full equality with Sweden in the management of foreign affairs. In 1899 the Norwegian storthing for the third time passed a bill for a national or "pure" flag, and King Oscar eventually sanctioned it. Under the management of Lagerheim, the new Swedish minister of foreign affairs, there was a temporary lull in the contest, but after a time the Norwegian radicals began to press their demands for a separate consular system and a ministry of foreign affairs more vigourously than ever. Negotiations on the subject continued for a long time, and the Swedish government and king at length agreed to allow separate consuls for Norway, provided these should be subordinate to the minister of foreign affairs in the Swedish cabinet. This was unsatisfactory to Norway, and on May 18th, 1905, the Norwegian storthing passed a bill for the establishment of a separate consular service to be placed under the direction of a Norwegian government department. When the king vetoed this measure, the storthing empowered the Norwegian ministry to exercise the powers hitherto vested in the king, and pronounced the dissolution of the union, but at the same time issued an address to the king disclaiming animosity to the royal house and asking that a prince of that house might be allowed to accept the Norwegian throne. A plebiscite taken on the question of the dissolution resulted in a vote of 368,200 for, and only 184 against it. The Swedish government and king protested vigourously against this secession, and for some time an armed conflict between the two countries appeared possible. More peaceful councils, however, prevailed, and on August 31st, delegates from both countries met at Karlstadt, where on the 23d of September a complete agreement for a separation was reached. This agreement was ratified by the legislatures of both countries, and Sweden passed an act dissolving the union and recognising Norwegian independence.

The question of what form of government Norway should adopt was an open one. King Oscar refused to allow one of his family to accept the Norwegian throne, and in Norway many persons favoured setting up a republic. Ultimately a monarchy was established and the kingship was offered to Prince Charles of Denmark, a grandson of King Christian IX, and a son-in-law of King Edward VII of England. The prince accepted the offer, and took the title of Haakon VII. He made his formal entry into Christiania on the 25th of November, 1905, and was enthusiastically received by the people.

The revolution produced some political changes in Sweden also. The Boström ministry had taken the view that the union could not be abrogated by the act of one country alone, and decided not to recognise the Norwegian provisional government, but to enter into negotiations with the storthing for a resumption of the union. As the riksdag did not sustain this policy, the ministry resigned, and Herr Lundeberg formed a coalition ministry which carried through the negotiations for a dissolution. After the Karlstadt Conference new elections were held for the second chamber. The king desired the Lundeberg ministry to retain office, but owing to dissensions it ultimately resigned, and in November Karl Staaf formed a liberal ministry, the first in the history of Sweden.*a*

BRIEF REFERENCE–LIST OF AUTHORITIES BY CHAPTERS

[The letter *a* is reserved for Editorial Matter]

CHAPTER I. THE LEGENDARY PERIOD OF SCANDINAVIAN HISTORY

b S. LAGERBRING. — *c* JOHANNES MAGNUS, *Historia de Gothorum Sveorumque Regibus.* — *d* O. RUDBECK, *Atlantica.* — *e* O. MONTELIUS, *Ueber die Einwanderungen unserer Vorfahren in dem Norden* (from the Swedish). — *f* SNORRE STURLESON, *Heimskringla* (Laing's translation, *Chronicle of the Kings of Norway*). — *g* SAXO GRAMMATICUS, *Historia Danica.* — *h* CORNELIUS TACITUS, *Germania.* — *i* ALFRED THE GREAT, *Periplus Otheri, ut et Uulfstani,* in Langebek's *Scriptores Rerum Danicarum.* — *j* H. WHEATON, *History of the Northmen.* — *k* S. A. DUNHAM, *History of Scandinavia (Cabinet Cyclopædia).* — *l* THE SAXON CHRONICLE. — *m* ADAM OF BREMEN, *Historia ecclesiastica.* — *n* F. C. K. H. MÜNTER, *Kirchengeschichte von Dänemark und Norwegen.* — *o* THE YOUNGER EDDA. — *p* THE ELDER EDDA. — *q* Translator's notes to S. Laing's translation of SNORRE's *Heimskringla.*

CHAPTER II. THE AGE OF THE VIKINGS

b SNORRE STURLESON, *Heimskringla* (translated by S. Laing). — *c* HERVARAR SAGA. — *d* A. CRICHTON and H. WHEATON, *Scandinavia, Ancient and Modern.* — *e* P. C. SINDING, *History of Scandinavia.* — *f* S. LAING, *Residence in Norway.* — *g* C. F. ALLEN, *Histoire de Danemark.* — *h* S. LAING, *Introduction to* SNORRE's *Heimskringla.* — *i* H. WHEATON, *History of the Northmen.* — *j* B. THORPE, *Northern Mythology.* — *k* Translator's notes to S. Laing's translation of SNORRE's *Heimskringla.* — *l* C. F. ALLEN (from Beauvois' French), *Haandbog i Fädrelandets Historie.*

CHAPTER III. NORWAY TO THE UNION OF KALMAR (1050–1397 A.D.)

b ADAM OF BREMEN, *Historia ecclesiastica.* — *c* S. A. DUNHAM, *History of Scandinavia.*

CHAPTER IV. ICELAND (874–1275 A.D.)

b EYRBYGGJA SAGA (abstract by Sir Walter Scott in MALLET's *Northern Antiquities*). — *c* H. WHEATON, *History of the Northmen.*

CHAPTER V. DENMARK TO THE UNION OF KALMAR (1050–1397 A.D.)

b S. A. DUNHAM, *History of Denmark, Sweden, and Norway.* — *c* SNORRE STURLESON, *Heimskringla.* — *d* ADAM OF BREMEN, *Historia ecclesiastica.* — *e* C. F. ALLEN, *Histoire de Danemark.* — *f* P. H. MALLET, *Histoire de Danemark.* — *g* ARNOLD OF LÜBECK, *Chronicle,* in *Monumenta Germaniæ historica.* — *h* D. SCHÄFER, *Die Hansestädte und König Waldemar von Dänemark.*

CHAPTER VI. SWEDEN TO THE UNION OF KALMAR (TO 1397 A.D.)

b S. A. DUNHAM, *Denmark, Sweden, and Norway* (in Lardner's *Cabinet Cyclopædia.*) — *c* ABBÉ FLEURY, *L'Histoire ecclésiastique.* — *d* F. HAMMERICH, *Den hellige Birgitta og Kirken i norden.* — *e* G. BINDER, *Die heilige Birgitta von Schweden.*

494

CHAPTER VII. THE UNION OF KALMAR (1397–1523 A.D.)

b O. DALIN, *Geschichte des Reiches Schwedens.* — *c* K. VON SCHLÖZER, *Verfall und Untergang der Hansa und des deutschen Ordens in den Ostsee-Ländern.* — *d* S. A. DUNHAM, *History of Denmark, Sweden, and Norway.* — *e* O. PETRI, *Chronica Regum Danorum* (in *Scriptores-Rerum Danicarum Medii Ævi*). — *f* E. G. GEIJER, *History of the Swedes.* — *g* A. FRYXELL, *History of Sweden.* — *h* E. PONTOPPIDAN, *Kurtzgefasste Reformations-Historie der dänischen Kirche.* — *i* A. HVITFELDT, *Danmarks Riges Kronike.*

CHAPTER VIII. GUSTAVUS VASA TO CHARLES IX (1523–1611 A.D.)

b K. P. P. PALUDAN-MÜLLER, *De förste Konger af den oldenborgske Slægt.* — *c* S. A. DUNHAM, *Denmark, Sweden, and Norway.* — *d* O. CELSIUS, *Geschichte Königs Gustaf des Ersten.* — *e* E. G. GEIJER, *History of the Swedes.* — *f* A. FRYXELL, *History of Sweden.* — *g* A. CRICHTON AND H. WHEATON, *Scandinavia, Ancient and Modern.* — *h* A. DE FLAUX, *Histoire de la Suède sous les princes de la maison de Vasa.*

CHAPTER IX. GUSTAVUS ADOLPHUS (1594–1632 A.D.)

b A. DE FLAUX, *Histoire de la Suède sous les princes de la maison de Vasa.* — *c* C. L. VON BUCH, *Reise durch Norwegen und Lappland.* — *d* A. CRICHTON AND H. WHEATON, *Scandinavia, Ancient and Modern.* — *e* A. FRYXELL, *Histoire de Gustaf II. Adolf.* — *f* E. G. GEIJER, *History of the Swedes.* — *g* H. VON TREITSCHKE, *Gustaf Adolf und Deutschlands Freiheit.* — *h* HISTORY OF MODERN EUROPE IN LETTERS FROM A NOBLEMAN TO HIS SON. — *i* G. DROYSEN, *Gustav Adolf.*

CHAPTER X. CHRISTINA TO CHARLES XI (1632–1697 A.D.)

b S. A. DUNHAM, *Denmark, Sweden, and Norway.* — *c* ENCYCLOPÆDIA BRITANNICA, article on Christina of Sweden. — *d* J. P. W. CATTEAU-CALLEVILLE, *Histoire de Christine, Reine de Suède.* — *e* J. ARCKENHOLTZ, *Mémoires de Christine, reine de Suède.* — *f* S. LAGERBRING, *Abrégé de l'histoire de Suède.* — *g* H. DE TERLON, *Mémoires.* — *h* A. CRICHTON AND H. WHEATON, *Scandinavia, Ancient and Modern.*

CHAPTER XI. DENMARK AND NORWAY, SIXTEENTH AND SEVENTEENTH CENTURIES (1523–1677 A.D.)

b S. A. DUNHAM, *Denmark, Sweden, and Norway.* — *c* A. CRICHTON AND H. WHEATON, *Scandinavia.* — *d* J. BERTRAND, *Les fondateurs de l'Astronomie moderne.* — *e* C. F. ALLEN, *Histoire de Danemark.* — *f* W. ONCKEN, *Das Zeitalter Friedrichs des Grossen.* — *g* LORD MOLESWORTH, *An Account of Denmark as it was in the year 1692.*

CHAPTER XII. SWEDEN IN THE EIGHTEENTH CENTURY

b S. A. DUNHAM, *Denmark, Sweden, and Norway.* — *c* K. LUNDBLAD, *Geschichte Karls des Zwölften.* — *d* J. W. BARDILI, *Des weyland durchlauchtigen Printzen Maximilian Emanuel Hertzogs in Würtemberg Reisen.* — *e* CHARLES XII, *Die eigenhändige Briefe König Karls XII.* — *f* HISTORY OF MODERN EUROPE IN LETTERS FROM A NOBLEMAN TO HIS SON. — *g* R. N. BAIN, *Charles XII and the Collapse of the Swedish Empire* (Heroes of the Nations). — *h* OSCAR II, King of Sweden and Norway, *Charles XII.* — *i* K. P. P. PALUDAN-MÜLLER, *Er Kong Carl XII falden ved Svigmord.* — *j* E. L. POSSELT, *Geschichte Gustafs III.* — *k* E. DE BEAUMONT-VASSY, *Les Suédois depuis Charles XII.* — *l* A. CRICHTON AND H. WHEATON, *Scandinavia, Ancient and Modern.* — *m* A. RAMBAUD, *History of Russia from the Earliest Times to 1882.* — *n* W. ONCKEN, *Das Zeitalter Friedrichs des Grossen.* — *o* S. LAING, *Tour in Sweden.* — *p* O. HENNE-AM-RHYN, *Kultergeschichte der neuern Zeit.* — *q* F. C. SCHLOSSER, *History of the Eighteenth Century.*

CHAPTER XIII. DENMARK IN THE EIGHTEENTH AND NINETEENTH CENTURIES

b E. W. GOSSE, article on Denmark in the *Encyclopædia Britannica.* — *c* W. ONCKEN, *Das Zeitalter Friedrichs des Grossen.* — *d* C. F. ALLEN, *Histoire de Danemark.* — *e* K. BLASENDORFF, *Der deutsch-dänische Krieg von 1864.* — *f* C. A. GOSCH, article "Denmark" in the new volumes of the *Encyclopædia Britannica.* — *g* G. F. VON JENSSEN-TUSCH, *Zur Lebens und Regierungsgeschichte Christians VIII.*

CHAPTER XIV.   NORWAY AND SWEDEN IN THE 19TH CENTURY

[b] S. A. DUNHAM, *Denmark, Sweden, and Norway.* — [c] A. CRICHTON AND H. WHEATON, *Scandinavia, Ancient and Modern.* — [d] A. AHNFELT, *Skandinavische Hof- und Staatsgeschichten des neunzehnten Jahrhunderts.* — [e] A. VANDAL, *Napoléon et Alexandre Ier.* — [f] J. SIME, article on History of Sweden in *Encyclopædia Britannica.* — [g] C. F. ALLEN, *Histoire de Danemark.* — [h] G. P. BLOM, *Geschichte der Staatsveränderung Norwegens im Jahre 1814.* — [i] H. L. BRÆKSTED, article on the recent history of Norway in the new volumes of the *Encyclopædia Britannica.* — [j] O. H. DUMRATH, article on the recent history of Sweden in the new volumes of the *Encyclopædia Britannica.*

A GENERAL BIBLIOGRAPHY OF SCANDINAVIAN HISTORY

BASED ON THE WORKS QUOTED, CITED, OR CONSULTED IN THE PREPARATION OF THE PRESENT HISTORY; WITH CRITICAL AND BIBLIOGRAPHICAL NOTES

A. A., Tour in Zealand, 1802. — **Adam of Bremen,** Historia Ecclesiastica, in Monumenta Germaniæ. — **Adlerfeldt,** G., Histoire militaire de Charles XII, Paris, 1741, 3 vols., English translation, London, 1740. — **Ahlquist,** A. G., Konung Erik XIV, Stockholm, 1879. — **Ahnfelt,** A., Skandinavische Hof- und Staatsgeschichten des 19 Jahrhunderts. — **Alberg,** A., Charles XII, London, 1883. — **Alembert,** J. le Rond d', Mémoires et réflexions sur Christine reine de Suède, 1767, Paris, 1805 ; English translation, Glasgow, 1765. — **Alfred the Great,** Periplus Otheri, ut et Uulfstani, in Langebek's Scriptores Rerum Danicarum. — **Allen,** C. F., Haandbog i Fädrelandets Historie, Copenhagen, 1840, 1880 ; German translation, Handbuch der Geschichte des Vaterlandes, Leipsic, 1849 ; French translation, Histoire de Danemark, Copenhagen, 1878, 2 vols. ; Det danske Sprogs Historie i Slesvig, Copenhagen, 1857–1858, 2 vols. ; De tre nordiske Rigers Historie under Hans, Christiern den Anden, Frederik den Förste, Gustav Vasa, Grevefejden 1497–1536, Copenhagen, 1864–1872, 5 vols.

The Danish historian, *Carl Ferdinand Allen*, was born at Copenhagen in 1811 and studied at the university there. He spent three years (1845–1848) in investigating the archives in Holland, England, France, Italy, and Germany, and then returning to Denmark became, in 1851, a lecturer at the Copenhagen University, and in 1862 professor of history and northern archæology. His principal work, *De tre nordiske Rigers Historie 1497–1536*, is regarded as one of the masterpieces of Scandinavian history. His *Haandbog* was written in 1836 for a prize which the Society for Posterity (*Selskabet for Efterslaegten*) had offered to the author of the best history of Denmark, giving special attention to the internal development of the state. Allen's work was successful, but was revised according to the suggestion of the society, before publication. The French edition contains a copious bibliography. The views expressed by Allen in his publications on the ethnography and languages of Schleswig, which appeared during the agitated period preceding the annexation of Schleswig-Holstein to Germany in 1864–1866, excited vehement refutations from German writers.

Anderson, R. B., Norse mythology, Chicago, London, 1875. — **Anon.,** Characters and anecdotes of the court of Sweden, London, 1790, 2 vols. ; Memoirs of an Unfortunate Queen (Caroline Matilda, wife of Christian VII of Denmark), London, 1776 ; Noten zur Beleuchtung der augenblichen Thatsachen in dem *Memoir* of Bunsen, Copenhagen, 1848 ; Politisches Vermächtniss des Königs von Schweden Karl Johann, Altona, Leipsic, 1845 ; The History of Gustavus Vasa, London, 1852. — **Arckenholtz,** J., Mémoires de Christine, reine de Suède, Amsterdam, Leipsic, 1751–1760. — **Arnold of Lübeck,** Chronicle, in Monumenta Germaniæ Historica, Hanover, 1829 ff. — **Avaux,** Comte d' ; see Mesmes.

Baden, G. L., Danmarks Riges Historie, Copenhagen, 1829–1832, 5 vols. —**Bain,** F. W., Christina, Queen of Sweden, London, 1889, 2 vols. — **Bain,** R. N.. Charles XII and the Collapse of Swedish Empire (Heroes of the Nations), New York, London, 1895 ; Gustavus III and his Contemporaries, London, 1894, 2 vols. — **Baird,** R., Visit to Northern Europe, New York, 1841. — **Bardili,** J. W., Des weyland durchlauchtigen Printzen Maximilian Emanuels Reisen und Campagnen [under Charles XII], 1730, Frankfort, Leipsic, 1739. — **Barfod,** P. F., Fortaellinger af Fædrelandets Historie, 4th edition, Copenhagen, 1874 ; Danmarks Historie fra 1319–1670, Copenhagen, 1885–1893, 4 vols. ; den dansk-tyske krig 1864, 1890–1892, 2 vols. — **Baring-Gouid,** S., Iceland, its Scenes and Sagas, London, 1873. — **Baumgartner,** A., Island und die Färöer. Nordische Fahrten, Freiburg in Breisgau, 1889. — **Beaumont-Vassy,** E. de, Les Suédois depuis Charles XII, Paris, 1841.

Édouard Ferdinand de la Bonninière, viscount de *Beaumont-Vassy* (1816–1875), was the author of various novels and of histories on French and European subjects, the last named at any rate of no great merit. To the work on the Swedes, however, for which he collected material during a mission to Sweden, a considerable value has been assigned.

Bernadotte, see Charles XIV John. — **Bernhardi,** Th. von, Der Streit um die Elbherzogtümer, Tageblätter aus dem Jahre 1863–1864, Leipsic, 1895. — **Bertrand,** J. L. F., Les Fondateurs de l'Astronomie moderne ; Tycho Brahe, Paris, 1865. — **Beskow,** B. von, Om Gustaf den tredje såsom Konung och menniska (in Handlingar of the Swedish Academy), 1860–1869, 5 vols. ; French translation, Gustave III, jugé comme roi, Stockholm, 1868.

The reputation of *Bernhard von Beskow* rests chiefly on his historical dramas. The work on Gustavus III, cited above, is prized rather for its literary merit than its historic faithfulness.

Björlin, G., Der Krieg in Norwegen 1814, Stuttgart, 1895. — **Binder,** G., Die heilige Birgitta von Schweden und ihr Klosterorden, Leipsic, 1891. — **Blangstrug,** Christian VII og Caroline Mathilde, Copenhagen, 1890. — **Blasendorff,** K., Der deutsch-danische Krieg von 1864, Frankfort, 1889. — **Blom,** G. P., Geschichte des Staatsveränderung Norwegens im Jahre 1814, Leipsic, 1858. — **Bolten,** J. A., Ditmarsische Geschichte, Flensburg, Leipsic, 1781–1788, 4 vols. — **Bourne,** C. E., The Life of Gustavus Adolphus, London, 1883. — **Boyesen,** H. H., History of Norway, London, 1886.

Hjalmar Hjörth Boyesen (1848–1895) was a Norwegian by birth who emigrated to the United States in 1869. From 1882 to 1895 he was German professor at Columbia College, New York. He is chiefly known by his t!es on Norwegian subjects.

Bræksted, H. S., article on history of Norway in the new volumes of the *Encyclopædia Britannica.* — **Brewster,** Sir David, Martyrs of Science: Tycho Brahe, London, 1874. — **Bring,** see Lagerbring. — **Brown,** J., Memoirs of the Sovereigns of Denmark, 1766–1818, London, 1895, 2 vols. — **Browning,** O., Charles XII of Sweden, London, 1899. — **Buch,** C. L. von, Reise durch Norwegen und Lappland, Berlin, 1810, 2 vols. — **Bunsen,** C. K. J., Memoir on the constitutional rights of the duchies of Schleswig and Holstein, London, 1848. — **Butler,** C. M., The Reformation in Sweden, New York, 1883.

Carlsen, J., H. **Olrik,** and C. N. **Starcke,** Le Danemark, Copenhagen, 1900. — **Carlson,** E., Die eigenhändigen Briefe Konig Karls XII, 1894. — **Carlson,** F. F., Sveriges Historia under Konungarne af Pfalziska huset, Stockholm, 1855–1885, German version (in A. H. L. Heeren and Ukert's Geschichte der Europäischen Staaten), Geschichte Schwedens, in continuation of Geijer, Gotha, 1855–1887.

Fredrik Ferdinand Carlson was born in Upland in 1811 and educated at Upsala, where he took his degree in 1833, and where, after travels in Denmark, Germany, Italy, and France, he became professor of history in 1835. He was subsequently appointed tutor to the sons of Oscar I (afterwards Charles XV and Oscar II) and in 1849 became professor of history at Upsala. He was minister of public worship, 1863–1870 and 1875–1878. From 1850 to 1863 he represented the University of Upsala in the lower house of parliament, and in 1865 was member for the Academy of Sciences. In 1873 he took his seat in the upper house. His History in continuation of Geijer is the chief of numerous writings completed in the course of his life, which terminated in 1887.

Carlyle, T., Early Kings of Norway, London, New York, 1875. — **Catteau-Calleville,** J. P. W., Histoire de Christine, Reine de Suède, Paris, 1815, 2 vols. — **Celsius,** O., Konung Gustaf I Historia, Stockholm, 1746–1753, 1792, 2 vols., German translation, Geschichte Königs Gustaf des Ersten, Copenhagen, Leipsic, 1749 ; Konung Erik XIV Historia, Stockholm, 1774, German translation, Geschichte Eriks XIV, Flensburg, 1777, French translation, Histoire d'Eric XIV, Paris, 1777, 2 vols.

Olaf Celsius, bishop of Lund and a member of the Swedish Academy, was the son of the botanist of the same name, from whom he is sometimes distinguished by the epithet of "the younger." He was born in 1716, and died in 1794. In 1747 he became professor of history at the University of Upsala. His historical researches were not confined to the field of Swedish history, though it was here that he won most distinction. The works mentioned above are praised as evidences of careful investigation, and are remarkable for the picturesque presentation of the subject. Their author was the forerunner of the critical historians, but in his other writings still clung to the ancient legends they have discarded. A work on the history of the Swedish church (Svea rikes Kyrkohistoria, Stockholm, 1767) was the earliest attempt of its kind, but only one volume was finished. Celsius was the founder of the first literary periodical in Sweden, which was entitled *Tidningar om de Lärdes arbeten,* and whose first number appeared in 1742.   A tragedy from his pen, entitled *Ingeborg*, appeared anonymously in 1739, and he was also the author of various poems described as lacking in imagination.

Chalybæus, R., Geschichte Dithmarschens bis zur Eroberung des Landes im Jahre 1559, Kiel, 1888. — **Chapman**, B., Gustavus Adolphus, London, 1856. — **Charles XII, King of Sweden**, Die eigenhändige Briefe König Karls XII, Berlin, 1894. — **Charles XIV, John, King of Sweden and Norway**, Correspondance de Bernadotte avec Napoléon de 1810–1814, Paris, 1819. — **Charles, Prince of Hesse-Cassel**, Mémoires de mon temps, Copenhagen, 1861. — **Chemnitz**, B. P. **von**, Der koniglich schwedische in Teutschland geführte Krieg, Part I in German and Latin, Stettin, 1648; Part II, German, Stockholm, 1653; portion of Part III and Part IV, Stockholm, 1855.

This work of *Bogislav Philipp von Chemnitz* is a valuable source for the history of the Thirty Years' War down to the year 1636, and also contains an account of the campaigns conducted by the Swedish general Lennart Torstenson between 1641 and 1646.   Chemnitz was a German from Stettin who, after spending some time as a soldier in the service of the Dutch, passed to that of Sweden under Queen Christina, and was subsequently appointed by her councillor and historiographer.   A pamphlet signed Hippolytus a Lapide, and entitled *De ratione status in imperio nostro Romano-Germanico*, was attributed to him and contained a furious attack on the house of Austria.   Chemnitz died in Sweden in 1678.

Christiani, W. E., Geschichte der Herzogthümer Schleswig und Holstein, Flensburg, Leipsic, 1775–1779, 4 vols.; Geschichte der Herzogthümer Schleswig und Holstein unter dem Oldenburgischen Hause (1460–1588), Kiel, 1781, 2 vols., continuation by D. G. Hegewisch (1588–1694), Kiel, 1802, 2 vols. — **Conybeare**, C. A. V., The Place of Iceland in the History of European Institutions, Oxford, London, 1877. — **Corner**, J., History of Denmark, Sweden, and Norway, in Historical Library, London, 1841. — **Coupé de Saint-Donat**, A. A. D. M., Mémoires pour servir à l'histoire de Charles XIV, Paris, 1820. — **Coxe**, W., Memoirs of John, Duke of Marlborough, London, 1817–1819, 3 vols. — **Crichton**, A., and H. **Wheaton**, Scandinavia, Ancient and Modern, Edinburgh, 1838, 2 vols. — **Cronholm**, A., Skånes politiska historia, 1847–1851, 2 vols.; Sveriges historia under Gustaf II Adolphs regering, 1857–1872, 2 vols. — **Cronholm**, N. N., A History of Sweden, Chicago, 1902, 2 vols.

Dahlmann, F. C., Geschichte von Dänemark, Hamburg, 1840–1843, vols. 1–3, continuation by Schäfer, Gotha, 1893.

Friedrich Christoph Dahlmann was a distinguished statesman as well as historian. Though a German by birth, he attended the university at Copenhagen besides that of Halle, and in 1811 established himself at the former as a teacher of philology.   In 1812 he became history professor at Kiel.   As secretary of the permanent delegation of the prelates and nobles of Schleswig-Holstein he set himself in opposition to the Danish government, and finding this attitude hampered his career accepted a professorship of political science at Göttingen ; but his active participation in Hanoverian politics eventually led to his banishment from that kingdom, and in 1842 he became professor of history and political science at Bonn.   At the revolution of 1848 he was one of those appointed to draw up a constitution for Germany, and the result was mainly his work.   After the failure of all attempts to bring about a unification of Germany at that time, Dahlmann abandoned politics altogether.   He died in 1860.   Besides the valuable history of Denmark, Dahlmann produced several important historical works relating to other countries and also edited Neocorus' *Chronicle of Ditmarsh.*

Dalin, O. von, Svea Rikes Historia, Stockholm, 1747–1762, 3 vols.; German translation, Geschichte des Reiches Schwedens, Rostock, 1756–1763, 2 vols.

It was as a poet and a writer in *belles-lettres* that *Olof von Dalin* (1708–1763) attained distinction.   As the founder of the *Svenska Argus*, modelled on Addison's *Spectator*, which constituted a wholly new departure and appeared in 1733, Dalin attained enormous popularity.   A work on criticism, an epic on Swedish liberty, and numerous satires and serious poems are among his writings.   The *Svea Rikes Historia* was undertaken at the request of the Swedish diet, and takes a high place in the historical literature of Sweden ; it is not without pretensions to be regarded as in some degree a critical history.

Den dansk-tydske Krig i Aarene 1848–1850, edited by the Danish general staff, Copenhagen, 1868–1887. — **De Flaux**, A., Histoire de la Suède sous les princes de la maison de Vasa. — **Dirckinck-Holmfeld**, C. L., Danmark, Slesvig og Holsteen, Copenhagen, 1844. — **Droysen**, G., Gustav Adolf, Leipsic, 1869–1870, 2 vols.; Schriftstücke von Gustav Adolf, Stockholm, 1877. — **Droysen**, J. G., and K. **Samwer**, Die Herzogthümer Schleswig-Holstein und das Königreich Dänemark, Hamburg, 1850. — **Du Chaillu**, P. B., The Land of the Midnight Sun, London, 1881, 2 vols. ; The Viking Age, London, 1889, 2 vols. — **Dunham**, S. A., Denmark, Sweden, and Norway, London, 1839, 3 vols.

Edda, The Elder, translated by B. Thorpe, London, 1866. — **Edda,** The Younger, Copenhagen, 1848, 2 vols. — **Ekendahl**, D. G. von, Geschichte des Schwedischen Volks und Reichs, Leipsic, 1827–1828. — **Erslev**, C., Dronning Margrete, 1887.

Christian Erslev, a Dane and professor of history at the University of Copenhagen, was born in 1852.   His work is distinguished by the critical ability displayed.   *Dronning Margrete* presents the Kalmar Union in a new light.

Falckenskjöld, S. O., Mémoires de M. de Falckenskjöld à l'époque du ministère et du catastrophe du comte de Struensée, Paris, 1826. — **Fant**, E. M., E. G. **Geijer**, and J. H. **Schröder**, Scriptores rerum Suecicarum medii ævi, Stockholm, 1818–1828, 2 vols. — **Fleury**, C. Abbé, L'Histoire ecclésiastique, Paris, 1691–1711, 20 vols. — **Fryxell**, A., Berättelser ur svenska historien, Stockholm, 1823–1879, 46 vols.; English translation of vols. 1–3, History of Sweden to 1569, London, 1844, 2 vols.; German translation of the portion on Gustavus Adolphus, Leipsic, 1842–1843, 1852, 2 vols.; German translation of the section on Gustavus Vasa, Neustadt on the Orla, 1831; German translation of the section on Charles XII, Brunswick, 1861, 4 vols.

The long life of *Anders Fryxell*, a native of Dalsland, extended from 1795 to 1881. During fifty-six years of this period his great work *Berättelser ur Svenska historien*, or Stories from Swedish History, continued to appear, and was completed with the forty-sixth volume. Only the first three are included in the English translation with its somewhat misleading title, *The History of Sweden*. The work has attained an enormous popularity, and has been praised both for its vivid presentation and for its accuracy in detail, though it is hardly worthy to rank with modern critical histories. The author's original scheme was for a popular work intended to awaken the interest of the masses of the Swedish people in the history of their own country. The idea of investigating the original sources only came to him afterwards. Fryxell had been ordained in 1820, took his degree of *Magister Philosophiæ* at Upsala in 1821, and received the title of professor in 1833. In 1834 he settled at Sunne, of which he became pastor. In 1847 he received a dispensation from his bishop, exempting him from ecclesiastical duties in order that he might devote himself wholly to historical labours. His writings include a Swedish grammar, *Svensk Språklara*, which became the ordinary text-book in Swedish schools, and a work on Swedish literature not highly valued.

Gaimard, P., Voyage en Islande et au Groenland pendant les années 1835 et 1836 (including Histoire de l'Islande by X. Marmier), Paris, 1839–1843, 7 vols. — **Geffroy**, M. A., Histoire des États scandinaves, 1851 ; Lettres inédites de Charles XII (Text and French translation), 1852 ; Gustave III et la cour de France, 1867, 2 vols. — **Geijer**, E. G., Svenska Folkets Historia, Örebro, 1832–1836, 3 vols. ; German translation in A. H. L. Heeren and Ukert's Geschichte der europäischen Staaten, Hamburg, 1832–1836, 3 vols.; French translation, Histoire de Suède, Brussels, 1845; English translation, History of the Swedes, London, 1845 : Teckning af Sveriges tillstånd och af de fornämste handlande personer under tiden från Karl XII's död till Gustaf III's anträde af regjeringen, Stockholm, 1838 ; Konung Carl XIV Johans historia, German translation, Stockholm, 1844 ; Konung Gustaf III's efterlemnade Papper, Upsala, 1843–1845, 3 vols., German translation, Gustavus III, nachgelassene Schriften, Hamburg, 1843–1846, 3 vols.; Samlade skrifter (collected works), Stockholm, 1849–1855, 1873–1875.

Erik Gustaf Geijer, born in Vermland in 1783, died at Stockholm in 1847, is counted the greatest of Sweden's historians. His versatile genius also won him distinction as a poet and musical composer, and some of his poems have become household words. The opinions advanced in the philosophical introduction to his edition of Thorild's works led to a prosecution (1820), which however ended in his exoneration. In 1838 he started a periodical, the *Literaturbladet*, to which he contributed a series of essays on the poor laws, when the liberal views he expressed formed a striking contrast to the conservative opinions hitherto supported by him. It was at Upsala that Geijer was educated, and he became lecturer there in 1810. After an interval during which he held a post in the public record office at Stockholm, where he founded the " Gothic Society " and contributed essays and some of his principal poems to the society's organ, *Iduna*, he returned to Upsala as assistant professor of history (1815), and then became professor in ordinary (1817). Elected to the Swedish Academy in 1824, he published a volume of *Svea Rikes Häfder*, a work on Swedish antiquities. But he abandoned it for the *Svenska Folkets Historia*, his best known work, which also remains unfinished. He had previously (1818–1825), in conjunction with Schröder, prepared a continuation of Fant's *Scriptores Suecicarum medii ævi*. All his historical work is based on extensive researches, and exhibits a critical spirit (then a new thing in Swedish history) as well as a mastery of literary style.

Gfrörer, A. F., Gustav Adolph, König von Schweden, Stuttgart, 1835–1837, 1863, 2 vols. — **Giessing**, H. P., Zur Regierungsgeschichte Friedrichs VI, Kiel, 1851–1852 ; Lebens- und Regierungsgeschichte Christians VIII, Altona, 1852–1853. — **Gosch**, C. C. A., Denmark and Germany since 1815, London, 1862 ; article on "Denmark" in the new volumes of the *Encyclopædia Britannica*. — **Gosse**, E. W., articles on "Denmark" and "Norway" in the *Encyclopædia Britannica*. — **Granberg**, P. A., Kalmare Unionens Historia, Stockholm, 1807–1811.

Halem, G. A., Geschichte des Herzogthums Oldenburg, Oldenburg, 1794–1796, 3 vols. — **Hammerich**, P. F. A., Den hellige Birgitta og Kirken i Norden, Copenhagen, 1863. — **Handelmann**, G. H., Die letzten Zeiten hansischer Übermacht im skandinavischen Norden, Kiel, 1853 ; Die dänische Reunionspolitik um die Zeit des Siebenjährigen Krieges, in Forschungen zur deutschen Geschichte, vols. 5 and 10, Göttingen, 1866, 1870 ; Geschichte von Schleswig-Holstein, Kiel, 1874.

Gottfried Heinrich Handelmann (1827–1891) was a native of Altona and from 1866 conservator of the Schleswig-Holstein Museum of Antiquities and professor of history at Kiel. He had previously been one of the leaders of the anti-Danish party in Schleswig-Holstein. Besides the works cited, which enjoy a high reputation, he wrote three others on American history and several books on the archæology of Schleswig-Holstein.

Haumant, E., La guerre du Nord et la paix d'Oliva, Paris, 1893. — **Headley,** J. T., Napoleon and his Marshals, New York, 1846, 2 vols. — **Headley,** P. C., The Island of Fire, or, A Thousand Years of the Old Northman's Home: 874–1874, Boston, 1875. — **Hegewisch,** D. G., Continuation of W. E. Christiani's Geschichte der Herzogthümer Schleswig und Holstein unter dem Oldenburgischen Hause, Kiel, 1802, 2 vols. — **Hellfried,** C. F. von, Politisk Overskuelse af Englands Overfald paa Danmark, Copenhagen, 1808; English translation, Outline of a Political Survey of the English Attack on Denmark 1807, London, 1809. — **Henne-am-Rhyn,** O., Kulturgeschichte der neuern Zeit, Liepsic, 1870, 3 vols. — **Hervarar Saga,** in Scripta Historica Islandorum de gestis veterum Borealium, Copenhagen, 1828–1832. — **Hildebrand,** H. O., Svenska folket under hednatiden, 2nd edition, 1872, German translation, Das heidnische Zeitalter in Schweden, Hamburg, 1873; Sveriges medeltid, Stockholm, 1879.

Hans Olof Hildebrand (1842–1890), a Swedish writer on the history of civilisation, was educated at Upsala and became antiquary of the kingdom in 1879. His numerous writings include works on archæology relating to various parts of Europe, and he was one of the founders of the Swedish geographical and archæological society.

Holberg, L., Danmarks Riges-Historie, Copenhagen, 1753–1754, 1856, 3 vols.; Berömmelige Mænds og Heltes sommenlignede Historier, Copenhagen, 1739, 1864–1865, 2 vols.; Heltinders eller navnkundige Damers sammenlignede Historier, Copenhagen, 1745, 1861.

Ludvig Holberg, Baron Holberg, the creator of the Danish comic drama and indeed of Danish literature generally, is esteemed the greatest of the writers in that language. Born at Bergen (Norway) in 1684 and educated at Copenhagen, he endured many vicissitudes in his youth and much poverty, in spite of which he collected sufficient means to extend his travels to Holland, Germany, France, Belgium, and England. In 1720 he became professor of rhetoric and in 1730 professor of history and geology at Copenhagen. His satirical epic, *Peder Paars,* his earliest publication, is one of the great Danish classics, and the numerous comic plays he produced in the new Danish national theatre, of which he was director, were translated into several languages. His writings cover the whole field of the knowledge of his day. Holberg's history of Denmark is still regarded as a masterpiece, though of course written before the methods of critical investigation had been applied to the ancient period of Swedish history. Holberg was ennobled in 1747 and died in 1754.

Holm, P. E., Danmark-Norges udenrigske Historie 1791–1807, 1875, 2 vols.; Danmark-Norges indre Historie 1660–1720, 1885–1886, 2 vols. — **Horn,** F. W., and J. **Anderson,** History of the Literature of the Scandinavian North, Chicago, 1884. — **Höst,** J. K., Struensee og hans Ministerium, Copenhagen, 1824, 3 vols.; German translation, Der Graf Struensee und sein Ministerium, Copenhagen, 1826. — **Hvitfeldt,** A., Danmarks Riges Kronike, Copenhagen, 1597–1604, 10 vols., 1650–1652, 2 vols.

This chronicle was composed by *Arild Hvitfeldt,* a Danish writer (born in 1549 and died in 1609), who was imperial chancellor. It is highly esteemed and forms one of the principal sources of Danish history.

Jenssen-Tusch, Die Verschwörung gegen die Königin Karoline Mathilde und die Grafen Struensee und Brandt, Leipsic, 1864. — **Jœrgensen,** A. D., Voldemar Sejr, Copenhagen, 1879. — **Johannes Magnus,** Historia de Gothorum Sveorumque Regibus, 1554.

Keary, C. F., The Vikings in Western Christendom, New York, 1891; Norway and the Norwegians, London, 1892. — **Keilhau,** B. M., and others, Gaea norvegica (German), Christiania, 1838–1850, 3 vols. — **Keyser,** J. R., Norges Histoire (to 1340), Christiania, 1866; continuation by Rygh, to 1387, 1870; Den norske Kirkes Historie under Katholocismen, Christiania, 1856–1858, 2 vols. — **Kjellgren,** Danmarks Historia, Stockholm, 1862. — **Kobbe,** P. von, Schleswigholsteinsche Geschichte 1694–1808, Altona, 1834; Geschichte und Landesbeschreibung des Herzogthums, Lauenburg, Altona, 1836–1837, 3 vols. — **Kraft,** J., Topographisk-statistisk Beskrivelse over Kongeriget Norge, Christiania, 1820–1835, 6 parts; in Historisk-topographisk Haandbog over Kongeriget Norge, Christiania, 1845–1848. — **Krag,** N., Christians III Historie, Copenhagen, 1776–1779, 3 vols. — **Küster,** J., see Neocorus.

Lacombe, F., Histoire de Christine 1762, English translation, London, 1776, 1890. — **Lagerbring,** S., Svea rikes historia, Stockholm, 1769–1783; French, Abrégé de l'histoire de Suède, Paris, 1788.

Sven Bring, called *Lagerbring* after 1769, when he was ennobled, was a Swede and professor of history at the University of Lund. His *Svea rikes historia* marks a stage in the development of critical history, but is defective in literary form. Lagerbring was born in 1707 and died in 1787.

Laing, S., Journal of a Residence in Norway, London, 1836. — **Larsen,** J. E., J. J. A. **Worsaae,** C. F. **Allen,** and others, Antislesvig-helsteenske Fragmenter, Copenhagen, 1848–1851, 16 books; German version, Anti-schleswig-holsteinische Fragmente, Copenhagen, 1848–1851.

A series of memoirs published for the consistory of Copenhagen University in refutation of the claims of the Schleswig-Holsteiners. — **Le Royer de Prade,** Histoire de Gustave-Adolphe, dit le Grand, 1686 ; English translation, London, 1689. — **Lloyd,** L., Peasant Life in Sweden, London, 1870. — **Lund,** T. F., Historiske Skitser efter utrykte Kilder, 1876 ; Danmarks og Norges Historie i Slutningem af det 16. Aarhundrede, 1879–1891, 14 vols. ; German translation, Das tägliche Leben in Skandinavien während des 16. Jahrhunderts, Copenhagen, 1882.

Troels Frederik Lund, born 1840, is the first of a school of historians belonging to the last two decades of the nineteenth century. It was as a government official of his native country, Denmark, that his attention was attracted to the secret archives of the kingdom, and he began the researches which resulted in writings that do not deal with political events, but aim at reconstructing pictures of the daily life and mental and moral position of average people in past times.

Lundblad, K., Konung Carls XII historia, Stockholm, 1825–1829, 2 vols.; German translation, Hamburg, 1835–1840, 2 vols.

Maccoll, L. M., Story of Iceland, London, 1887. — **Magnus,** J., Historia de Gothorum Sveorumque Regibus, Rome, 1554. — **Mallet,** P. H., Introduction à l'histoire de Danemark, Copenhagen, 1755–1756; English translation as Northern Antiquities, 1770, London, 1847, in Bohn's Antiquarian Library ; Histoire de Danemark, Copenhagen, 1758–1777, Geneva, 1788, 9 vols.

Paul Henri Mallet, a Swiss of Geneva, born 1730, was appointed professor of *belles-lettres* in the Academy of Copenhagen, 1752. After the publication of the *Introduction* he was appointed tutor to the prince of Denmark. In 1760 he returned to teach history in Geneva, and afterwards travelled in Italy and England. On the outbreak of the French Revolution he quitted Switzerland, but returned in 1801 and died there in 1807. Mallet's *Introduction*, or *Northern Antiquities*, is a work of great research, though superseded by modern discoveries. It contained the first French translation of the Prose Edda which was reproduced in Bishop Percy's English translation (Northern Antiquities) of 1770. The English edition of 1847 contains a revised translation of the Edda.

Marmier, X., Histoire de l'Islande, in P. Gaimard's Voyage en Islande, Paris, 1839–1843. Histoire de la Littérature in Danemark et en Suède, Paris, 1839. — **Maurer,** K., Die Entstehung des isländischen Staates und seiner Verfassung, Munich, 1852; Die Bekehrung des norwegischen Stammes zum Christenthum, Munich, 1855–1856, 2 vols. ; Island von seiner ersten Entdeckung bis zum Untergange des Freistaates, Munich, 1874 ; Zur politischen Geschichte Islands, Leipsic, 1880.

Konrad Maurer, a modern German authority on the history of Iceland, was born at Frankenthal, in the Rhenish Palatinate, in 1823, and from 1847 to 1893 was professor of northern law at Munich. In 1876 he was invited to Christiania to deliver lectures on ancient Norwegian law.

Maximilian, Emanuel, Prince of Würtemberg, Reisen und Campagnen durch Teutschland, in Polen, Lithauen, Roth und Weiss Reussland, Frankfort, Leipsic, 1739. — **Mellin,** G. H., Stockholm and its Environs (from the Swedish), Stockholm, 1841. — **Meredith,** W. A., Memorials of Charles (XIV) John, King of Sweden, 1829. — **Mesmes,** J. A., Count d'Avaux, Négociations de M. le comte d'Avaux, ambassadeur extraordinaire à la cour de Suède, 1693, 1697, 1698, Utrecht, 1882–1883. — **Meursius** (J. van Meurs), Historia Danica, Amsterdam, 1638; Florence, 1746.

Johannes Meursius, or *Jan van Meurs,* was a Dutchman, born near the Hague in 1579. He became professor of Greek at Leyden and historiographer to the states of Holland. His connection with the family of Barneveld having involved him in trouble with the Dutch government, he accepted a professorship of history at Sorö, where he took up his residence in 1625. He became historiographer to the king of Denmark and died in 1639. His Danish history is written in Latin and is a compilation, offering useful materials.

Michell, T., History of the Scotch Expedition to Norway, 1612, London, 1886. — **Middleton,** J. N., article on Sculpture in the *Encyclopædia Britannica.* — **Mill,** H. R., article on Geography in the new volumes of the *Encyclopædia Britannica.* — **Molbech,** C., Fortällinger af den danske Historie, Copenhagen, 1837–1838, 2 vols. — **Molesworth,** Lord, an account of Denmark in the year 1692, London, 1694. — **Monteith,** General W., Narrative of the Conquest of Finland by the Russians, 1808–1809, London, 1854. — **Montelius,** O. (with others), Sveriges Historia 1875 ; Om Lifvet i Sverige under Hednatiden, 2d edition 1878, German translation, Die Kultur Schwedens in vorchristlicher Zeit, Berlin, 1885, English translation, London, 1888 ; Uber die Einwanderungen unserer Vorfahren in dem Norden (German translation by J. Nestorf), 1884.

Oskar Montelius, a Swedish antiquarian born in 1843 and since 1888 professor of the Swedish State Museum of History, was commissioned to arrange the collections of that institution. His numerous writings on ancient civilisation have been translated into various languages.

Mosheim, J. L. von, Institutiones historiæ ecclesiasticæ, Helmstedt, 1755; English translation, Institutes of Ecclesiastical History, London, 1850, 4 vols., Boston 1892. — **Müller,** P. E., Sagabibliothek, Copenhagen, 1816–1819, 3 vols.; German translation, Berlin, 1816, Frankfort on the Main, 1832. — **Munch, P. A.**, Det norske Folks Historie (to 1387), Christiania, 1851–1863, 8 vols.; German translation of vols. 1–4, Lübeck, 1853–1854, 2 vols.

Peder Andreas Munch, the chief historian of whom Norway has to boast, was distinguished as philologist and archæologist. He was born at Christiania in 1810 and educated at the university there, becoming professor of history in 1841. In conjunction with J. R. Keyser he edited the ancient Norwegian laws and also originated a system of Icelandic orthography. He died in Rome in 1863.

Münter, B., Bekehrungsgeschichte des Grafen von Struensee, Copenhagen, 1773. — **Münter, F. C. K. H.**, Kirchengeschichte von Dänemark und Norwegen, Leipsic, 1823–1833, 3 vols.

Neocorus (Johann Küster), Chronik von Ditmarschen in sächsischen Sprache (edited by F. C. Dahlmann), Kiel, 1827, 2 vols. — **Nervo, J. B. R. G.**, Gustave III., roi de Suède, et Anckarstroem, 1746–1792, Paris, 1876. — **Nicoll, J.**, An Historical and Descriptive Account of Iceland, Greenland, and Faroe Islands, Edinburgh, 1844. — **Nielsen, Y.**, Norges Historie efter 1814, Christiania, 1882–1892, 3 vols. — **Nilsson, S.**, Skandinaviska Nordens Urinvånare, Christiania, 1838–1843, 1866–1872; English translation by Sir J. Lubbock, Primitive Inhabitants of Scandinavia, London, 1868.

Oncken, W., Das Zeitalter Friedrichs des Grossen, Berlin, 1880–1882, 2 vols. **Oscar II, King of Sweden**, Carl XII ; English translation, London, 1879. — **Otte, E. C.**, Scandinavian History, London, 1874. — **Öttinger, E. M.**, Geschichte des dänischen Hofes von Christian II bis Friedrich VII, Hamburg, 1857–1859, 8 vols.

Paludan-Müller, K. P. P., De förste Konger af den oldenborgske Slægt, 1874 ; Er Kong Carl XII, falden ved Svigmord. — **Peringskiöld, J. Peringer de**, Monumenta Sueo-Gothica, Stockholm, 1710–1719. — **Petersen, N. M.**, Danmarks Historie i Hedenold, Copenhagen, 1834–1838, 1854. — **Petri, O.**, Sver crönika (chronica Regum Danorum), in Scriptores Rerum Danicarum Medii Ævi, Upsala, 1818. — **Pontoppidan, E.**, Kurtzgefaste Reformations-Historie der dänischen Kirche, Lübeck, 1734 ; Annales ecclesiæ Daniæ, or, Kirchen-historie des Reichs Dänemark, Copenhagen, 1741–1752, 4 vols.

Erik Pontoppidan, born 1698, died 1764, was bishop of Bergen and afterwards chancellor of Copenhagen University. His history of the reformation of the Danish church contains many curious details and furnishes entertaining reading.

Posselt, E. L., Geschichte Gustafs III, Carlsrühe, 1792, Strasburg, 1793. — **Pufendorf, S. von**, De rebus Suecicis (1630–1654), Utrecht, 1686; English translation, The Complete History of Sweden, translated and continued to 1701, London, 1702 ; De rebus a Carolo Gustavo Sueciæ rege gestis, Nuremberg, 1696, 2 vols.

The fame of *Samuel Pufendorf*, born 1632, was acquired by his writings on natural and civil law, in which he attacked the German governments, and which created a great stir both on account of the novelty of the principles advanced and their political tendencies. Pufendorf's connection with Sweden began in 1658, when he was tutor in the family of the Swedish ambassador at Copenhagen, and was imprisoned with the rest of the ambassador's suite on the occasion of the invasion of Denmark by Charles (X) Gustavus. In 1670 Pufendorf gave up the chair of the law of nature and nations, which in 1661 had been created for him at Heidelberg, and transferred his activity to the university which the Swedish government had just established at Lund, and in 1677 he became royal historiographer of Sweden. In the succeeding years he wrote his works on Swedish history, but in 1688 he exchanged his office for that of historiographer to the elector of Brandenburg, and it was at Berlin that he died in 1694.

Rambaud, A., Histoire de la Russie, Paris, 1878. — **Repp, T. G.**, A Historical Treatise on Trial by Jury in Scandinavia, Edinburgh, London, 1832. — **Rink, H. J.**, Om Grönlands Inland (No. 9. Fra Videnskabens Verden, 1875); English translation as Danish Greenland, London, 1877. — **Robinson, J.**, Account of Sweden, 1717. — **Rudbeck, O.**, Atlantica, Upsala, 1679–1702, 3 vols.

Sarauw, C. F. K., Die Feldzüge Karls XII, Leipsic, 1880. — **Sarrans**, Histoire de Bernadotte, Charles XIV Jean, Paris, 1845, 2 vols.— **Sars, E.**, Udsigt over den norske Historie Christiania, 1871–1891, 4 parts.— **Saxo Grammaticus**, Historia Danica, edited by K. Pedersen, Paris, 1514, P. E. Müller and Velschow, Copenhagen, 1839–1858; A. Holder's edition, Strasburg, 1886; English translation by O. Elton (Books 1–2), London, 1894.

Saxo Grammaticus or *Longus* is the oldest of Danish chroniclers. He lived in the end of the twelfth and beginning of the thirteenth century, and was apparently secretary to Archbishop Absalon, for whom he wrote, and whose statements are the authority for much of the portion dealing with the events of the writer's own day. This part, giving the narrative of the age of Valdemar the Great and the wars with the Wends, is the only part that is authentic, and forms the chief and very valuable source for the history of that period. The earlier sections, ascending to remote antiquity, are based almost wholly on poems and oral tradition, and incorporate many wonderful and picturesque legends, including that of Hamlet, or Amleth.

Saxon Chronicle, edited by B. Thorpe (in Rolls Series), London, 1861, 2 vols. — **Schäfer,** D., Die Hansestädte und König Waldemar (IV), Jena, 1879 ; continuation of Dahlmann's Geschichte von Dänemark, Gotha, 1893. — **Schefer,** C., Bernadotte Roi, 1899. — **Schiern,** Bidrag tel Oplysning af Katastrophen den 17 Januar, 1772, Copenhagen, 1871. — **Schlegel,** J. H., Geschichte der Könige von Dänemark aus dem oldenburgischen Stamm, Copenhagen, Leipsic, 1777, 2 vols. — **Schlosser,** F. C., Geschichte des 18. und 19. Jahrhunderts bis zum Sturze des französisch Kaiserreichs, Frankfort, 1836–1850, 6 vols. — **Schlözer,** K. von, Verfall und untergang der Hansa und des deutschen Ordens in den Ostseeländern, Berlin, 1853. — **Schmidt,** F., Schweden unter Karl XIV Johann, Heidelberg, 1842. — **Schöning,** G., Norges Riges Historie (to 995), Sorö, 1771, 4 vols. — **Schouw,** J. F., Stimmen aus Dänemark über die Schleswigschen Verhältnisse (a collection of memoirs translated from the Danish weekly review, *Dansk Ugeskrift*), Copenhagen, 1843. — **Schweitzer,** Ph., Island ; Land und Leute, Geschichte, Litteratur und Sprache, Leipsic, 1885. — **Scott,** C. H., The Danes and the Swedes, London, 1856. — **Sheridan,** C. F., History of the Late Revolution in Sweden, London, 1778. — **Sidgwick,** C., Story of Norway, in Historical Handbooks, London, 1885. — **Sime,** J., article on history of Sweden in the *Encyclopædia Britannica.* — **Sinding,** P. C., History of Scandinavia, New York, 1858. — **Slange,** N., Kong Christiern IV, Historie, Copenhagen, 1794; German translation, Christian IV, Hanover, 1864. — **Snorre Sturleson,** Heimskringla, or, Noregs-konunga sögur, Stockholm, 1697, Christiania, 1868, Copenhagen, 1893 ; English translation by S. Laing, Heimskringla, or Chronicle of the Kings of Norway, London, 1844, 1889.

The history of the great Icelandic writer *Snorre* (*Snorri* or *Snorro*) *Sturleson* (or *Sturluson*) is typical of his day. Born in 1179, he was brought up by Jon Loptsson, a powerful chief, and also a man of great learning, and soon won renown as a poet. Snorre's marriage with the daughter of a wealthy priest raised him to affluence, and he acquired political distinction, attaining to the office of *lögs ögumayr* or lawman, i.e. president of the Icelandic legislative assembly. In 1218 he was summoned to Norway by King Hakon the Old, and was the means of averting a Norwegian invasion of Iceland. But he afterwards quarrelled with Hakon, then joined in a revolt against him, and it was at the king's instigation that in 1241 Snorre was murdered by his own sons-in-law at his house of Reykjaholt. The Heimskringla, so named from the first words of a defective manuscript, *Kringla heimsins* (*orbis terrarum*), is a series of biographies of Norwegian kings down to Sverri (1177), and is written with a good deal of critical discrimination and great power of picturesque narrative. The extant manuscripts have been much abbreviated by transcribers, with the exception of the saga of St. Olaf. Laing's English version follows a Danish manuscript. The *Younger* or *Prose Edda* also bears Snorre's name as the *Snorra-Edda.* It contains the *Gylfaginning*, the most valued source of Scandinavian mythology, but probably the arrangement only is due to Snorre.

Sörensen, C. Th., Den anden Slesvigske Krig, 1883, 3 vols. — **Sörensen,** S., Norway (Nations of the World), New York, 1901. — **Spittler,** L. T. von, Geschichte der dänischen Revolution 1660, Berlin, 1796. — **Steenstrup,** J., Normannerne, Copenhagen, 1876–1882, 4 vols.

A work of the first rank. The author, *Johannes Steenstrup*, an energetic investigator of antiquity, was born in 1844 and in 1877 became professor of the science of northern antiquities at the University of Copenhagen.

Stevens, J. L., History of Gustavus Adolphus, London, 1885. — **Storm,** A. V., Pages of Early Danish History from the Runic Monuments of Sleswick and Jutland, London, 1901. — **Storm,** G., Kritiske Bidrag til Vikingetiden's Historie, Christiania, 1878 ; Monumenta historica Norwegiæ, Christiania, 1880. — **Strinnholm,** A. M., Svenska folkets historia under kunungarna af Wassaätten [to 1544], Stockholm, 1819–1824, 3 vols.; Svenska folkets historia från äldsta till närvarande tider [to 1319], 1834–1854, 5 vols. — **Strodtmann,** A., Das geistige Leben in Dänemark, Berlin, 1873. — **Strombeck,** F. C. von, Memorabilien aus dem Leben und der Regierung des Königs Karl XIV, Brunswick, 1842. — **Suhm,** P. F., Historie af Danmark fra de äldste Tider til Aar 1400, Copenhagen, 1782–1828, 14 vols.; German translation, Leipsic, 1803–1804. — **Svenskt Diplomatarium,** Stockholm, 1819–1878, 9 vols.

Tacitus, C., Germania, Venice, 1470; London, 1882. — **Terlon,** H. de, Mémoires, Paris, 1681, 2 vols.

These memoirs contain an account of the expedition of Charles (X) Gustavus across the ice for the invasion of Denmark. The writer was himself present with the troops.

Theoderich the Monk, Historia de regibus vetustis norvagicis, in Storm's Monumenta historica Norwegiæ. — **Thorpe,** B., Northern Mythology, London, 1851, 3 vols. — **Thorsoe,** Den danske Stats politiske Historie 1800–1864, 1873–1889, 4 vols. — **Thrige,** Danmarks Historie i vort Aarhundrede, 1889, 2 vols. — **Torfäus,** Th., Historia rerum norwegicarum, Copenhagen, 1711 ; Historia rerum Orcadensium, 1715.

Thormodr Torfæus or *Torfason,* an Icelander by birth, became royal historiographer of Denmark under Christian V and Frederick IV. He was well versed in northern antiquities according to the knowledge of his day, and wrote a number of works in Latin.

Touchard-Lafosse, G., Histoire de Charles XIV, Paris, 1838. — **Treitschke,** H. von, Gustaf Adolf und Deutschlands Freiheit. — **Trench,** R. C., Gustavus Adolphus in Germany, London, 1872, 1886. — **Turgenson,** C., Land of the Vikings, London, 1885.

Usinger, R., Deutsch-dänische Geschichte 1189–1227, Berlin, 1863.

Vaupell, Kampen for Sonderjylland 1848–1850, Copenhagen, 1863–1867, 3 vols. — **Vertot,** R. **Aubert de,** Histoire des Révolutions de Suède, Paris, 1695; English translation, London, 1729. — **Voltaire,** F. M. **Arouet de,** Histoire de Charles XII, Paris, 1731; in Œuvres, 1877–1885 ; English translation, London, 1807, New York, 1901.
This work is valued more for its literary merit than for its historic accuracy.

Waitz, G., Schleswig-Holsteins Geschichte, Göttingen, 1851–1854 ; Urkunden und Akten-stücke zur Geschichte der Herzogtümer Schleswig und Holstein, Kiel, 1863 ; Kurze Schleswig-holsteinsche Landesgeschichte, Kiel, 1864.
Georg Waitz (1813–1886), an eminent German historian, was a native of the duchy of Schleswig and took an active part in politics, his sympathies being in favour of the annexation of Schleswig to Germany. He was coadjutor of Pertz in editing the great *Monumenta Germaniœ Historica,* in 1842 was appointed professor of history at Kiel, and in 1847 at Göttingen. In 1848 he represented the revolted duchies at Berlin and then was delegate for Kiel at the Frankfort assembly. In 1875 he became chief editor of the *Monumenta Germaniœ Historica.* As an historian he is careful and sound, but does not possess an attractive style.

Watson, P. B., The Swedish Revolution under Gustavus Vasa, London, 1889. — **Weidling,** Schwedisch Geschichte im Zeitalter der Reformation, Gotha, 1882. — **Weitmeyer,** H., Denmark, London, 1891. — **Wheaton,** H., History of the Northmen, 1831. — **Whitelock,** B., A journal of the Swedish embassy in the years 1653 and 1654, London, 1855. — **Wittich,** K., Struensee, Leipsic, 1879. — **Wittman,** P., Kurzer Abriss des Schwedischen Geschichte, Breslau, 1896. — **Worsaae,** J. J. A., Danmarks Oldtid oplyst vnd Oldsager og Gravhoie, Copenhagen, 1843, English translation, Denmark's Old Time illustrated by Old Things, London, 1849; Minder om de Danske og Nordmaendene i England, Skotland og Irland, Copenhagen, 1851, English translation, An account of the Danes and Norwegians in England, Scotland, and Ireland, London, 1852.
Jens Jacob Asmussen Worsaae (1821–1885), the eminent Danish archæologist, was inspector of the monuments of antiquity throughout Denmark and subsequently director of the Museum of Antiquities. His account of the Danes and Norwegians in England, Scotland, and Ireland was the fruit of travels in those countries between 1846 and 1851.

Wraxall, F. C. L., Visit to the Seat of War in the North, London, 1854 ; Life and Times of Caroline Matilda, Queen of Denmark and Norway, London, 1864, 3 vols.

A CHRONOLOGICAL SUMMARY OF THE HISTORY OF SCANDINAVIA

DENMARK

B.C. 350 Pytheas, supposedly a Greek, travels in the far North, and returns to write remarkable accounts of a land which he calls Thule. Little further is heard of the land or its people until the fierce "Cimbri" drift south to be repulsed by the Romans.

101 Defeat of the Cimbri at Verona.

100 Migration of **Odin** and his followers, the Svear. He founds the empire of the Svear, and from one of his sons descend the Ynglings, who long hold sway over Sweden and Norway. Another son, **Skiold,**

4 founds the Danish monarchy; but it cannot be said to have even a semblance of unity until the time

A.D. 35 of **Dan Mykillati,** the sixth in descent from Skiold. His son, **Frode the Peaceful,** is the reigning monarch at the beginning of the Christian era.

623 **Ivar Vidfadme** conquers Sweden and joins it to Denmark. His grandson, **Harold Hildetand,** inherits both kingdoms. **Sigurd Ring,** his nephew, kills him in battle, and the throne falls to **Ragnar Lodbrok.**

794 Death of Ragnar; **Sigurd** (Sivard) succeeds to a least part of Denmark.

803 Death of Sigurd and succession of **Harde Knud,** his son. Another son, **Eric I,** seems to have ruled over some part of Denmark. **Eric II** follows, his reign overlapping that of **Gorm the Old,**

883 who violently opposes the spread of Christianity. He subdues all the petty kings and
935 abdicates.

941 Gorm dies and his son **Harold (II) Bluetooth** succeeds. He is compelled by the emperor to accept Christianity.

991 **Sweyn Splitbeard** succeeds. The invasion of England marks his reign. Massacre of the Danes, and Sweyn's terrible retribution. He becomes king of England and dies soon after—supposedly by assassination.

1014 **Canute** (Canute the Great) is proclaimed by the Danes. Before his death he divides his states (consisting of Denmark, England, Norway, and part of Sweden) among his sons. The government of Denmark devolves

1035 upon **Harthacnut.** He makes a compact with Magnus of Norway, by which, upon the death of Harthacnut,

1044 **Magnus the Good** becomes joint king of Denmark and Norway. His claim is disputed by Svend Estridsen, a son of Ulf Jarl and Estrida, sister to Canute the Great. Magnus dies during the war and

1047 **Sven Estridsen** obtains the throne. He is the patron of Adam of Bremen.

1076 **Harold Hejn,** his son, succeeds. After a short reign he dies

1080 and his brother, **Knud the Saint,** is called to the throne. He is killed in a rebellion,

1086 and his brother, **Olaf the Hungry,** is recalled from exile to rule over Denmark. Upon his death

1095 another brother, **Eric Eiegod,** succeeds. He undertakes a pilgrimage to the Holy Land, and dies at Cyprus.

1103 **Niels,** his brother, is elected king by the people, setting aside a son of Eric. He is killed,

1134 and is succeeded by **Eric Emun,** who puts to death his brother and seven of his brother's sons. After a short but cruel reign he is murdered.

1137 The people's choice falls upon a nephew of the dead king, **Eric the Lamb.** His reign, feeble and inglorious, is followed by civil strife. Three pretenders to the throne appear,

1147 of whom two, **Knud V** and **Svend,** unite to oust the other. The Wends meantime ravage the borderlands, even penetrating into the interior. Valdemar, son of Knud Lavard (the Lord), marches against the two kings, and a fierce struggle ensues,

1157 from which **Valdemar (I) the Great** emerges triumphant, and a period of glory and prosperity begins in Denmark. He defends his frontiers against the Wends, and wins the affection of his people and the respect of other nations. After his death

1182 **Knud VI,** his son, succeeds. The emperor Frederick Barbarossa, infuriated by repeated failures to reduce Denmark to vassalage, incites the bishop Valdemar, natural son of Canute the Great, and Sverri, king of Norway, against Canute. He triumphs over all his enemies, mainly by aid of the military experience of his brother, who upon his death without issue

1202 succeeds him as **Valdemar (II) the Victorious.** He makes brilliant conquests in the north of Germany.

1210 He conquers a large part of Prussia and forces the inhabitants to accept Christianity.

1219 He conducts the celebrated expedition into Esthonia, which he utterly subdues. Denmark has now reached a height of power undreamed of since Canute the Great. But disaster waits in the person of Henry of Schwerin, who captures the king while he is reposing in the woods after the chase, and keeps him prisoner for three years, during which utter confusion reigns in Denmark and the newly subdued countries; when

1225 he is released, after signing an extortionate treaty, he finds a deplorable state of affairs, which he spends his remaining years in straightening out, until his death in

1241 He commits the fatal error of dividing his kingdom among his sons; so that the heir, **Eric Plovpenning,** succeeds to a curtailed dominion. A quarrel is the inevitable outcome. Eric is foully murdered by his brother,

1250 and the fratricide **Abel** comes to the throne, for a brief two years, when

1252 he loses his life in an expedition against the Frisians. His sons are set aside, and his brother, **Christopher I,** is called to the throne, to the great future detriment of Danish entirety. His reign is occupied with fierce religious strife, and he is poisoned

1259 by a provost of the chapter, Arnfest. His son, **Eric Glipping,** being but ten years old, the situation is mastered by the prudence and self-possession of Margaret, the queen-mother. Strife at home and abroad bring neither glory nor advantage to Eric, and

1286 he falls a victim to a conspiracy. His son, **Eric Menved,** falls heir to the struggle between church and state; his brother Christopher heads a rebellion against him; and the nobility join the clergy in keeping up civil strife.

1319 Eric dies childless, and the kingdom reverts to his brother, **Christopher II,** in spite of Eric's warnings to the people. He robs his subjects right and left, and

1326 they depose him and elect Valdemar, duke of Schleswig (South Jutland), to the kingship. He divides up the kingdom among his partisans.

1330 The exiled king seizes the opportunity to regain his kingdom. He is humiliated and defeated in all his undertakings, and dies,

1332 leaving Denmark to suffer all the sorrows of a kingless kingdom during eight unhappy years —divided up among a dozen petty princes, quarrelling each with the rest over his share in her dismemberment. Valdemar, the youngest son of Christopher II, watches the progress of events from his retreat in Germany, where he is sought out by a number of distinguished Danes, who beg him to come to the rescue. He is crowned as **Valdemar (III) Atterdag** (the Restorer)

1340 and during years of anxiety, labor, combat, and peril he toils for the reunion of Denmark. His greatest hindrance is the ill-will of his own people, who resent his war expenditures. Revolt ensues.

1350 The Black Death ravages the country.

1360 Valdemar concludes a peace with his foreign enemies, and also, at the diet of Kallundborg, comes to an understanding with his subjects, which endures only until

1368 when the malcontents unite with foreign foes and expel Valdemar, who is permitted to return only upon signing

1372 the treaty dictated by the Hanseatic League.

1375 Sudden death of Valdemar and accession of his grandson **Olaf,** son of King Hakon of Norway and Margaret of Denmark. Upon the death of Hakon

1380 Olaf becomes king of Norway, fusing the two countries in a union which continues for centuries.

1387 He dies, leaving his mother **Margaret** to deal with Albert of Mecklenburg, whom she conquers.

1397 Margaret unites Sweden with Denmark and Norway by the "Kalmar Union."

1412 Upon her death her grand-nephew, **Eric of Pomerania,** succeeds.

1439 Revolt of Sweden under Eric's incompetent rule. He is deposed and

1440 his nephew, **Christopher of Bavaria,** is elected.

1448 Death of Christopher. Denmark elects **Christian (I)** of Oldenburg and withdraws from the Union. Christian proves himself an improvident and imprudent monarch, and the country loses nothing by his death,

1481 and the accession of his son, **Hans,** who keeps up the struggle with Sweden.

1500 He proceeds against the Ditmarshians, who defeat him miserably. Hans dies

1513 after a long and remarkable reign. **Christian II,** his son, succeeds, and accomplishes the end for which his father laboured in vain—the conquest of Sweden ; which by his cruelty he loses again. Hated at home and despised abroad, he is deposed

1522 and his uncle, **Frederick I,** is elected in his stead. He is harassed by the deposed king, and finally captures and imprisons him.

1533 Death of Frederick. Interregnum.

1534 Frederick's son, **Christian III,** is elected, but meets with much opposition. Upon his recognised establishment

1536 he sets about the introduction of the Reformation. This enterprise accomplished, he dies in

1559 His son succeeds as **Frederick II.** He reduces the Ditmarshians to submission.

1563 Beginning of the Seven Years' War, which ends

1570 with the Peace of Stettin, a treaty extremely advantageous to Denmark. Tycho Brahe, André Vedel, and the celebrated financier Peter Oxe are among the stars that illumine this reign, only to be extinguished by ignorance and persecution in that which follows.

1588 Death of Frederick. The ambitious Rigsraad overrules the queen-mother Sophie's claim to the regency, and appoints four of its members guardians of the state during the minority of **Christian IV.** He constructs a splendid fleet, which does service under his personal direction

1611 in the war of Kalmar with Sweden. In this war a body of Scottish auxiliaries for the Swedes, under Colonel Sinclair, perishes at Gudbrandsdal.

1613 Peace with Sweden concluded, and a period of peace and progress follows, till

1625 Christian is dragged into the Thirty Years' War, with disastrous results ; deserted by his allies, beaten by his enemies, he is forced to sign

1629 the Treaty of Lübeck. His efforts to repair the exhausted finances and to relieve the serious public distress are met with indifference by a corrupt and unpatriotic nobility. Popular indignation finds expression in the diatribes of the Dybvads, father and son, condemned to imprisonment and confiscation for their audacity. The perversity of the aristocracy neutralises the generous efforts of the king. They refuse his entreaties for war supplies, and the outbreak of the Swedish war

1643 finds Denmark totally unprepared. After desperate efforts to save a cause foredoomed to failure by the amazing indifference of the nobles, the valiant Christian is constrained to sign

1645 the Peace of Brömsebro. He dies in the beginning of

1648 and several months ensue during which the throne is vacant, before the Rigsraad agree upon the succession of the late king's son as **Frederick III.** His attempts to raise the country out of the abyss of ruin and despair are no more successful than were those of his father, and the war into which she is forced

1657 finds Denmark with neither fleet nor army, nor yet money to provide them. Her most vindictive enemy is the traitor Korfits Ulfeldt, by whose machinations is concluded

1658 the ruinous Peace of Roeskilde, which, however, fails to satisfy the ravenous appetite of Charles X of Sweden. He prepares to obliterate the identity of Denmark ; but having counted without the courage invoked by a desperate situation, the determination of the king, and the interference of Holland, he is subjected

1659 to a crushing defeat before Copenhagen, and another near Nyborg in the same year.

1660 England, Holland, and France oblige the combatants to sign the Treaty of Copenhagen. The long-pent-up popular bitterness finally forces the Rigsraad to important concessions. The king is proclaimed a hereditary monarch with absolute sovereignty. Ulfeldt, suspected in Sweden of double treachery, flees to Denmark, where he is accused of traitorous relations with Holland ; he is tried and

1663 condemned to death, but escapes and dies in misery the following year.

1667 A war with England threatens, but is settled by the Peace of Breda.

1670 Death of the king. His son, **Christian V,** mounts the throne without signing the capitulation. His vanity leads him to extend fresh privileges to an already too arrogant aristocracy, and later to create a "high nobility," which, drawn mainly from German sources, casts the old order into the shade.

1675 War with Sweden declared. The Treaty of Rendsburg signed by the duke of Gottorp, which he breaks at the first opportunity. Wismar taken by the Danes; but fortune deserts them and they lose ground at every step.

1676 The blame of these evil fortunes falls upon Griffenfeldt, who is arrested and condemned to life imprisonment. This wise head removed, matters go from bad to worse, and

1679 the Danes are forced to conclude the disadvantageous Peace of Fontainebleau with France and that of Lund with Sweden, and to remit to the duke of Gottorp all possessions ceded by him in the Treaty of Rendsburg.

1699 Death of the weak and dissolute king. **Frederick IV** inherits with his realm his father's quarrel with the duke of Gottorp.

1709 Frederick gathers an army and sets out to reconquer the provinces of Skåne from Sweden.

1712 The Danes suffer a bloody defeat at Gadebusch.

1713 Signal successes for the Danes in Schleswig ; and at sea they are not less fortunate. The admiral Tordenskjold graces this epoch. Upon the death of Charles XII

1718 the new Swedish government negotiates for peace, which is concluded

1720 at Frederiksborg with happy and honourable results for Denmark.

1721 Schleswig annexed to Denmark, becoming a source of anxiety and constant dispute for the latter.

1730 Death of Frederick. **Christian VI** inherits an extended territory and an exchequer refilled by his father's economies. By his exaggerated religious zeal and his severities toward the rural population he renders himself extremely unpopular. Peace with other nations is preserved at the sword's point during his reign. Commerce, art, science, and navigation flourish.

1744 Denmark is forced to take over Greenland, to prevent the extinction of the trade of that island.

1746 At his death Christian is both mourned for his virtues and execrated for his deficiencies. His son **Frederick V** is on the contrary universally beloved. He lifts the pall spread over the country by his father's gloomy piety. Amicable relations with Sweden are established. The sudden death of the Russian czar, Peter III, averts a war with that country. Industry and the arts and sciences continue to develop. The great blot on the bright picture is the condition of the finances, wretchedly administered ; the nobility, too, are accorded dangerous privileges, and the misery of the rural classes obtains but momentary alleviation.

1766 Succession of **Christian VII** upon the death of his father.

1767 Schleswig and part of Holstein amicably ceded to the Danes by the Gottorp line in exchange for Oldenburg and Delmenhorst.

1770 Struensee, the king's favourite and prime minister, rises to an almost unprecedented authority. His innovations excite the animosity of a sober and thrifty race. He attempts to maintain his position by force, which leads to an armed resistance. He is taken by the people

1772 and condemned to a shameful death. Ove Guldberg assumes the direction of affairs.

1778 Bernstorff concludes negotiations for an armed neutrality between Denmark and Russia ; Russia withdraws, and a storm threatens, but is averted

1780 by the treaty of July, signed by all the neutral powers and respected by the belligerents. Another treaty concluded by Bernstorff a few days previously with England is considered by Russia so detrimental to her own interests that Guldberg finds it necessary to dismiss that official. East Indian commerce increases, but so does the public debt ; and the misery of the peasants augments from year to year.

1784 The king formally dismisses Guldberg, and the crown prince assumes the reins of government, since Christian remains incompetent until his death. The crown prince does much towards the amelioration of the condition of the rural classes ; he also occupies himself with affairs in Schleswig-Holstein ; he reinstates Andreas Bernstorff, minister of foreign affairs.

1788 By her alliance with Russia Denmark is forced on her behalf into a war with Sweden, to which England and Prussia put a peremptory stop. During the French Revolution Bernstorff maintains for Denmark a prudent neutrality, obtaining for her an interval of signal prosperity.

1797 Death of Bernstorff, a clash with England follows. Denmark joins the new "armed neutrality" and England declares war. The English under Parker and Nelson win in resulting naval encounter. Alexander succeeds at this time to the throne of Russia with an entirely different policy from that of his predecessor, and peace is concluded between the three countries. Quiet reigns until

1807 when Napoleon forces Denmark into a new war with England. The English under Wellington take Copenhagen. The Danish fleet is surrendered to the enemy. Sweden, with an eye to Norway, takes part in the struggle.

1808 Death of the figure-head king ; the crown prince becomes **Frederick VI.**

1809 The Treaty of Jönköping signed by Denmark and Sweden. Shortly afterwards Charles John of Sweden reopens the campaign.

1813 Battle of Sehested. The campaign ends in

1814 with the Peace of Kiel, by which Denmark loses Norway. Peace with England is concluded the same year.

1839 Death of Frederick VI. after a long and disastrous reign ; succession of **Christian VIII,** who is scarcely established on the throne before an endless struggle begins over the constitution. The affairs of Schleswig-Holstein become more hopelessly entangled. Ill feeling increases, and a violent rupture is averted

1848 only by the death of the king. **Frederick VII** takes up the burden. He begins by drawing up the new constitution long refused by his father ; but its terms are far from satisfactory to the people. Holstein revolts. Its improvised army is beaten with great slaughter at Bov. The king of Prussia sends an army to the aid of the insurrectionists, and the Danes are beaten before the city of Schleswig ; victorious at Sundewitt, but suffer naval disasters.

1849 Battle of Fredericia won by the Danes, followed by the armistice of Berlin.

1850 Reopening of hostilities. Battles of Helligbæk and Idstedt. Siege of Friedrichstadt. Treaty of London regulates the Danish succession.

1851 An Austrian army occupies Holstein with a view to keeping down insurrection.

1852 Manifest of the 28th of January. Charles Moltke becomes minister of Schleswig and Reventlow-Criminil of Holstein. The state of Danish politics rouses German opposition. None of the Danish propositions proves favorable to the estates of Schleswig and Holstein. The diet of Frankfort interferes and

1861 refuses to sanction the letters-patent of 1859 or the budget of 1861–1862. The situation becomes more and more critical. The storm is on the point of breaking when a truce is called by the death

1863 of Frederick VII. By virtue of the Treaty of London, Prince Christian of Glücksburg succeeds as **Christian IX.** The duke of Augustenburg disputes his claim. A number of the German princes uphold Frederick of Augustenburg ; all Germany feels the effects of the agitation. Pressed by Russia, England, and France, the Danish government decides to evacuate Holstein. The minister Hall gives in his resignation.

1864 Denmark is deserted by the government of Sweden and Norway. Prussia and Austria occupy Holstein. They invade Jutland. At the conference of London convoked by England the Germans refuse to consider any proposed adjustment, and hostilities recommence. The Danes keep up a losing struggle, until by the Treaty of Vienna they are obliged to give up Schleswig-Holstein to Prussia and Austria, who immediately fall out with each other.

1866 The Treaty of Prague obliges the emperor of Austria to cede to the king of Prussia all right over Schleswig-Holstein.

1870 With the outbreak of the Franco-Prussian War Denmark begins to hope for the restoration of Schleswig-Holstein ; but these hopes come to naught. At home she is occupied with constitutional struggles, between the king and the *Landsthing* on the one side, and the *Folkething* on the other ; which are not brought to any satisfactory conclusion till

1901 when by the defeat of the conservatives the king is brought to consent to a change of policy and of system.

1906 Death of Christian IX and accession of **Frederick VIII.**

NORWAY

It is with Halfdan the Black that the authentic history of Norway begins. But long before his time the terrible Vikings were known and dreaded by their southern neighbours : "*A furore Normannorum libera nos, Domine,*" prayed the pious Frenchman ; and in England a day of each week was set apart for prayer for aid against the dreaded Northmen. The Ynglings were their rulers, one of whom, Olaf Trætelia (the "woodchopper "), was driven from Sweden by Ivar Vidfadme.

630 **Olaf Trætelia** founds Vermland. Is succeeded

640 by his son **Halfdan Huitbein.** His son **Eystein,** a pirate, is killed

840 in one of his expeditions and his infant son, **Halfdan the Black,** succeeds. After a turbulent career he is drowned,

860 and his son, **Harold (I) Harfagr** (the "fair-haired") succeeds. He unites the petty tribes into one kingdom by conquering their chiefs and making them his vassals.

885 The army of Vikings under Rolf Ganger invades France ; Charles the Simple cedes Rolf Ganger the province afterwards known as Normandy, gives him his daughter in marriage, and has him baptised under the name of Robert. His descendants are the powerful earls of Normandy.

930 Upon the death of Harold, Eric Blodæxe, his son, slays several of his brothers. The people banish him

935 and call to the throne his brother **Hakon (I) the Good,** son of Harold I. He has been educated in England. He is killed in battle

961 by Eric's sons, of whom the eldest, **Harold (II) Graafeld,** succeeds to the throne. He is killed, and **Harold of Denmark** becomes king over Norway ; he appoints

970 **Hakon,** son of Jarl Sigurd of Trondhjem, actual ruler, in conjunction with **Harold Gränske.** The latter is murdered by Sigfrida, but a posthumous son is born to his wife. Hakon is murdered by a slave.

984 Greenland discovered by Eric the Red.

995 **Olaf I,** son of Tryggve, a southern king, grandson of Harold the Fair-haired, establishes himself on the throne. He is killed

1000 in battle with **Eric,** the exiled son of Hakon Jarl, who occupies the throne in conjunction with his brother **Svend.** After their death

1015 **Olaf (II) the Saint,** posthumous son of Harold Gränske, succeeds. The discontented make advances to Canute of Denmark and war results. Olaf is obliged to flee. He returns to the fray and is killed in battle.

1028 **Canute** subdues Norway. He places his son

1030 **Svend** on the throne. His yoke is so heavy for the Norwegians that they drive him out and establish

1035 **Magnus the Good,** son of Olaf II, on the throne.

1042 On death of Harthacnut, Magnus claims the throne of Denmark. Svend Estridsen disputes his claim and joins with Harold Hardrada to oust Magnus from all his dominions. Meantime the king dies, leaving Denmark to Svend and Norway to

1047 **Harold Hardrada.** He is killed in battle with the English. He is succeeded by his son

1067 **Olaf Kyrre** (the "quiet"), who after a series of battles settles the feud with King Svend of Denmark by marrying his daughter. The remainder of his reign is peaceful and prosperous.

1093 Death of Olaf and succession of his son **Magnus Barfod** (the "barefoot"), a vigorous and ambitious ruler. He conquers the isle of Man, but is killed in battle in Ireland. His three sons, **Sigurd Jorsalafari, Eystein,** and **Olaf** are proclaimed joint rulers ; Olaf dies

1103 shortly after.

1122 Eystein dies suddenly, and Sigurd is sole king. The year before his death a young man comes to Norway from Iceland, declaring himself a son of Magnus Barfod. Sigurd accepts him as his brother, and after his death

1130 the kingdom is divided between his son, **Magnus the Blind,** and the son of Magnus Barfod, **Harold Gilchrist** or **Gille.** There is scant harmony between them ; they finally open hostilities, resulting

1134 in the battle of Fyrileif. Magnus is victor, and shows great magnanimity towards his enemy, which Harold requites by capturing him and putting out his eyes. Magnus ends his days in the cloister. Harold enjoys his kingship for about six years, when

1136 another son of Magnus Barfod appears, murders Harold, and aspires to the kingship ; but the indignant Norwegians will have none of him and proclaim Harold's illegitimate son **Sigurd Mund.** His claim is disputed by the followers of Inge, the infant heir.

1155 Sigurd is slain in his house. Another son of Harold, **Eystein,** snatches the reins of government, but is murdered by his remaining brother's followers

1157 and **Inge** is acknowledged. A large part of the people, dissatisfied with this result, go to war in the interests of Sigurd's son Hakon. Hakon is victorious and Inge

1161 is killed. **Hakon Herdabred** takes possession of the whole country. Erling Skakke, a powerful chief, collects a following and proclaims his son Magnus king. With the help of the Danish king he succeeds in defeating Hakon.

1162 Hakon being killed, **Magnus** is proclaimed king. He is the first king to be crowned in Norway.

1177 Sverri, a natural son of King Sigurd Mund, lays claim to the crown, and collects a following. Long-continued hostilities result, ending

1184 in the battle of Fimreite, in which Magnus is killed. **Sverri Sigurdsson** establishes himself on the throne. He has constantly recurring rebellions to repress, and after a tumultuous reign he expires,

1202 leaving his son **Hakon IV** on the throne. His reign is brief ; in

1204 he dies, supposedly of poison, without issue, and his nephew **Guthrum Sigurdsson** is elected king. He dies suddenly, evidences pointing to poison. The people elect **Inge Bardsson,** a son of King Sverri's sister.

1217 Upon Inge's death a young son of Hakon IV is proclaimed as **Hakon V,** afterwards called **The Old.**

1261 Greenland is annexed to Norway.

1262 Iceland acknowledges itself a dependency of Norway.

1263 Death of Hakon. His son **Magnus Lagabætr** (the "law mender") is crowned at the age of six.

1280 He dies, and his son **Eric Præstehader** (the "priest hater") succeeds. He begins a war with Denmark which at his death

1299 is not ended and which with the crown is inherited by his brother **Hakon (V) Magnusson.**

1309 Peace of Copenhagen, which ends the war with Denmark.

1319 Death of Hakon and succession of his grandson, **Magnus Ericsson Smek** (the "fondling"). Magnus is proclaimed king of Sweden and the two kingdoms are for the first time united under one rule.

1350 The Norwegians become discontented under the union, and upon their demand for a separate king Magnus gives over the government of Norway to his son **Hakon.** Hakon sets up a claim to Sweden also, but is defeated, and

1380 dies, leaving Norway to his son **Olaf the Young,** already crowned king of Denmark. Under him the two kingdoms are united, Olaf's mother Margaret acting as regent.

1387 Olaf dies at the early age of seventeen. **Margaret** becomes queen of Denmark, Norway, and afterwards also of Sweden.

1397 The queen causes her nephew, **Eric of Pomerania,** to be crowned king of the three countries, and

1412 dies, leaving the government to his feeble administration. First Denmark, then Sweden, finally Norway, rebel and depose the king, who retires to Pomerania.

1442 The three countries accept **Christopher of Bavaria.** He attempts restriction of privileges of the Hanse towns, but

1448 death interrupts his plans. The Swedes elect Charles Knutsson for their king, while Denmark and Norway are united under **Christian I.**

1481 Death of Christian, and his son **Hans** becomes king over the two countries.

1497 Hans invades Sweden and has himself proclaimed king at Stockholm. The Swedes expel him.

1506 Hans sends his son Christian as his viceroy to Norway.

1513 Death of Hans ; beginning of the cruel reign of **Christian (II) the Tyrant.** His great aim is the throne of Sweden, which

1520 he finally attains ; he celebrates his coronation by the notorious Carnage of Stockholm. The Swedes rebel and Christian flees to Holland.

1524 **Frederick I,** his uncle, is proclaimed king.

1531 Christian lands with a force in Norway, is taken prisoner by Frederick and shut up in a dungeon, where he dies in 1559.

1533 Death of Frederick. Quarrels over the succession follow, resulting

1534 in the election of the late king's son as **Christian III.**

1536 The Danes recognise Christian III. The Reformation is established. The king resides during his entire reign in Denmark, where he dies,

1559 being succeeded by **Frederick II,** his eldest son.

1563 Beginning of the Northern Seven Years' War. Norway suffers greatly under the rule of the dissolute king, who, residing in Denmark, leaves Norway a prey to unscrupulous Danish officials. Her condition improves when, upon his death,

1588 his son **Christian IV** succeeds to the two kingdoms. He studies the interests of the Norwegians.

1611 War with Sweden.

1613 Peace concluded at Knæröd.

1625 Christian takes part in the Thirty Years' War, from which, after several defeats, he is by the Peace of Lübeck

1629 obliged to withdraw.

1643 Outbreak of another Swedish war.

1644 Battle of Kolberger Heide.

1645 Peace of Brömsebro.

1648 Death of Christian. **Frederick III** follows. The struggle with Sweden continues, and is only ended

1660 by the peace signed at Copenhagen.

1670 Death of the king. His son **Christian V** succeeds. He reopens hostilities with Sweden, with but indifferent success. Louis XIV of France interferes and the peace proposed by him is concluded

1679 at Lund.

1699 Death of Christian. **Frederick IV** inherits the two thrones. He allies himself

1709 with Russia and Poland against Sweden. Frederick is victorious.

1718 The Swedish king is killed and

1720 peace is concluded at Frederiksborg castle by the king's sister.

1730 Death of the king, and his son **Christian VI** embarks on an extravagant and ruinous career; Norway is reduced to a pitiable condition, hordes among her population dying of starvation.

1746 **Frederick V** becomes king upon the death of his father ; he dies in his forty-third year

1766 from dissipation and over-indulgence, and his seventeen-year-old son **Christian VII** succeeds. He is even more dissolute than his father, and eventually becomes insane. The government is conducted by one after another of the more or less unscrupulous advisers of the wretched monarch, until

1784 the crown prince Frederick becomes regent.

1807 War with England breaks out as a result of the Napoleonic schemes.

1808 Death of the insane king ; the crown prince becomes **Frederick VI,** with an empty treasury, a lamentable fleet, a starvation-racked dominion, and a war with England on his hands. Sweden chooses this moment to attack her unhappy neighbours. She gains but indifferent advantage till her new crown prince, Charles John (Bernadotte), opens a systematic campaign, ending

1814 by the cession of Norway to Sweden by the Peace of Kiel, after a four-hundred-years' union with Denmark. The king yields peaceably, but Prince **Christian Frederick,** his nephew and heir presumptive, incites the Norwegians to resistance and they elect him king. The allied powers join Sweden against Norway. The Norwegian king is forced to abdicate. He retires to Denmark, whose throne (1839) he later assumes. Norway and Sweden are formally united under **Charles XIII.**

SWEDEN

Upon the death of **Odin** his son **Njörd** succeeds as lord over all the provincial kings. His son **Frey-Yngve** founds the dynasty of the Ynglings, who continue to rule over Sweden until six hundred years after Christ, as follows :

B.C. 100 **Fiolner,** son of Yngve, succeeds. He visits his friend, King Frode of Denmark, and during a nocturnal wandering after the festivities he falls into a tank of mead and is drowned. His son **Svegdir** succeeds ; he likewise falls a victim to drunken indiscretion.

A.D. 1 **Vanland,** his son, succeeds. He disappears, and his son **Visbur** becomes ruler over the Swedes. He is murdered by his two elder sons, who are driven away by the Swedes, and the succession falls to his third son,

100 **Domald.** Famine marks his reign, and the Swedes offer him to the gods as a sacrifice, and appoint his son **Domar** as their ruler. Upon his death,

200 **Dyggve,** his son, succeeds. **Dag** follows, famed for his wisdom. **Agne,** his son, a great warrior, subdues the Finns. He carries off the daughter of their king, whom he marries, and who upon their wedding night hangs him to a tree.

300 **Alrek** and **Eric** become joint rulers, but kill each other ; and Alrek's two sons, **Yngve** and **Alf,** follow. They likewise kill each other, and Alf's son, **Hugleik,** is elected king. **Hake,** a sea-king, conquers him and rules over his dominions for three years, but

400 is killed by **Jorunder** and **Eric,** sons of Yngve, who are followed by Jorunder's son, **Aun the Old.** His son **Egill** succeeds ; he is gored to death while hunting, and

500 **Ottar,** his son, succeeds ; his son **Adils** follows, but is killed by accident, and **Eystein,** his son, becomes king. He is murdered by **Salve,** a sea-king, who rules for a while, but is finally killed by the Swedes, who call **Yngvar,** son of Eystein, to the throne.

600 **Braut-Onund** follows. **Ingiald,** his son, succeeds upon his death. He is called Illrada (the "the ill-ruler").

620 He is burned to death, and his son, **Olaf Trætelia** (the "wood-chopper"), the last of the line, is driven into exile

623 by **Ivar Vidfadme,** king of Denmark, who annexes Sweden to his realm. Upon his death he is succeeded by **Harold Hildetand,** his grandson.

740 Battle of Bravella, when Harold is killed, and the two kingdoms go to **Sigurd Ring,** who commits suicide ; and **Ragnar Lodbrok** becomes king of the Swedes and Goths. Upon the death of Ragnar

794 the throne of Sweden falls to his son **Björn (I) Ironside,** the founder of a new dynasty.

800 Death of Björn and succession of **Eric Björnson.**

815 **Emund** succeeds, followed by

829 **Eric Emundson** and

885 **Björn Ericson.**

935 **Eric (I) the Victorious,** son of Björn, succeeds.

983 Battle of Fyrisval. Death of Eric and succession of his infant son,

993 **Olaf the Lap King.** He abdicates in favour of his son, who upon his death

1024 becomes sole ruler under the title of **Anund Jacob.** He dies,

1050 and his brother **Edmund Slemme** succeeds ; upon his death in

1060 **Stenkil,** his son-in-law, is elected by the provinces in unison. He wars with Harold Hardrada of Norway. Dying, he is succeeded in

1066 by his son **Inge I,** during whose minority Hakon is recognised as regent during thirteen years. He is succeeded by

1112 **Inge II** and **Philip.** The latter's reign is short. Inge is poisoned in

1125 He is the last of the Stenkils on the male side. A period of confusion and civil strife follows, during which the provinces elect their own kings.

1130 **Swerker I,** who has married the widow of Inge II, is generally accepted as king. He is murdered,

1155 and **Eric the Saint,** brother-in-law of Inge II, is elected. He firmly establishes Christianity in Sweden

1157 He directs a crusade against the Finns. He dies in battle

1160 against Prince Magnus of Denmark, and is succeeded by **Charles,** son of Swerker. Knud, son of Eric the Saint, soon lays claim to the kingdom. He goes to war with Charles. The latter is killed in battle near Visingsö,

1167 and **Knud** is recognised by all the Swedes. He dies, and his sons are set aside in favour of

1195 **Swerker II,** son-in-law of Jarl Birger Brosa. Knud's sons dispute his claim on the field of battle, and he is killed

1210 near Gestibren. **Eric,** son of Knud, is crowned. He dies suddenly, leaving an infant son, whom the nobles set aside to elect

1216 **John I,** son of Swerker II. John dying suddenly in
1222 **Eric Læspe** (the "lisper"), son of the former King Eric, is elected to the succession.
     With the death of Eric died also the royal line of Saint Eric. The powerful lords
     therefore elected a son of Birger Jarl,
1250 **Valdemar,** to found a new dynasty. Valdemar is dethroned
1279 by his brother **Magnus Ladu-laas.** He leaves three sons, the eldest of whom, **Birger,**
     succeeds him.
1290 His brothers, dukes Eric and Valdemar, wage war against him ; but in
1318 they die in prison. Their exasperated friends execute the young son of King Birger,
     and in
1319 elect Duke Eric's three-year-old son, **Magnus Smek,** to the double throne of Norway and
     Sweden. Broken-hearted,
1321 King Birger dies. Albert of Mecklenburg, the king's brother-in-law, stirs up civil strife,
     and, deposing
1363 the king, gives the crown to his own son, **Albert of Mecklenburg.** The Swedes, dissat-
     isfied, call Margaret of Norway and Denmark to their aid. She defeats Albert
1389 near Falköping. Sweden, Norway, and Denmark are united under **Margaret.**
1396 Margaret secures the election of Eric of Pomerania as her successor.
1397 She obtains the passage of the act called the Kalmar Union.
1412 Death of Margaret. **Eric of Pomerania** sole ruler over the North.
1439 Eric formally dethroned on account of misrule, and the council elects
1440 **Christopher of Bavaria** (Eric's nephew) sovereign.
1448 Death of Christopher. The estates elect **Charles Knutsson** to succeed him. The Danes
     elect Christian of Oldenburg for their king. Thus, after sixty years of union, Sweden
     and Denmark become separate kingdoms.
1450 Norway separates from Sweden, electing Christian for its king. King Charles elects his
     friend and relative, **Sten Sture the Elder,** to succeed upon his death, which occurs
1470 King Hans of Denmark marches against Stockholm, which he takes; he compels the
     Swedes to recognize him as king. The Swedes stir up a rebellion and drive the Danes
     out of the country; but on his return
1503 Sten Sture dies suddenly. **Svante Sture,** one of the late king's generals, is elected ad-
     ministrator, under protest from Hans of Denmark, and a prolonged struggle follows.
1512 He dies in the midst of it, and his son, **Sten Sture the Younger,** succeeds him. Hans
     dies the following year, but Sten Sture finds another foe in the person of Gustavus
     Trolle, bishop of Upsala.
1516 The bishop connives with Christian II of Denmark to bring an army into Sweden. Thrice
     repulsed by Sten Sture, upon the administrator's death in battle
1520 the Swedish government is dissolved, and **Christian II** succeeds in being crowned king of
     Sweden. His barbarities infuriate the people, who expel him and elect
1523 **Gustavus Vasa** for their king.
1525 Insurrection of the Dalecarlians.
1544 Act of Hereditary Settlement passed.
1560 Death of Gustavus. He is succeeded by his eldest son, **Eric XIV.**
1567 Eric becomes insane. He is confined and
1577 is poisoned. His brother John is proclaimed king under title of **John III.**
1592 Death of John ; succession of his son, **Sigismund,** king of Poland. He attempts to govern
     Sweden from Poland, but the Swedes are discontented and support Charles, brother of
     the late king. Civil war results, Sigismund's army is defeated, and Duke Charles is
     declared king
1600 as **Charles IX.** Wars with Russia and Denmark continue.
1611 Charles dies suddenly. He is followed by his son, **Gustavus (II) Adolphus.** Danish,
     Russian, and Polish wars rack the country.
1632 Battle of Lützen and death of the king. Axel Oxenstierna assumes the governing power
     during the minority of **Christina,** daughter of the dead king, and carries on the Danish
     wars.
1644 Christina attains her majority.
1648 Treaty of Westphalia.
1654 Christina's extravagance renders her unpopular. She abdicates in favour of **Charles (X)
     Gustavus,** her first cousin. He conducts the Polish and the Russian wars.
1657 Denmark declares war.
1658 Peace of Roeskilde, which Charles breaks to invade Denmark. He is preparing to invade
     Norway,
1660 when he dies of a fever. **Charles XI,** his son, being but four years of age, the queen-
     mother Hedvig Eleonora is appointed regent. Party strife is rampant, foreign compli-
     cations break out, the financial situation becomes desperate.
1672 The king is declared of age. Holland declares war.
1675 Charles takes command of the army. The Danes make inroads into Sweden.
1676 Battle of Lund.
1696-7 Failure of crops and consequent wide-spread famine.

1697 Death of Charles. Great conflagration at Stockholm. Accession of **Charles XII.**
1699 Frederick IV king of Denmark, Augustus of Saxony king of Poland, and Peter the Great of Russia conspire to ruin the young king of Sweden.
1700 Charles sets out on his first campaign. He defeats the Danes, who sue for peace. He marches against the Russians, defeating them in the battle of Narva.
1701 Beginning of the Polish War.. Swedes successful before Riga.
1702 Charles enters Warsaw. Cracow surrenders.
1703 Swedes victorious at Pultusk. Charles remains inactive in Poland for two years, after which
1705 he concludes peace with her.
1708 He decides to march upon Russia, and joins Mazeppa, prince of the Ukraine, against the czar.
1709 Battle of Pultowa, in which the Swedes are put to rout and Charles narrowly escapes with his life. The whole army is destroyed and its generals are made prisoners. Charles plots with the Turks to revenge himself on Russia, while the Danes ravage Sweden. Stenbock obtains a victory over them. Riga, Reval, Viborg, and Kexholm are taken by Russia. Charles in Turkey is negotiating to bring about war between that country and Russia, in which
1711 he is finally successful. The sultan sends two hundred thousand men under the grand vizir to invade Russia. Peter sets out with eighty thousand for the Turkish frontiers. After some skirmishing a peace is concluded by the machinations of Catherine between Russia and Turkey, in which no mention is made of Charles XII. The Turks turn against him, burn him out of his quarters, and take him prisoner. Stenbock at home is captured by the Danes.
1714 Charles returns to Sweden and prepares for war with Norway and Denmark.
1718 While watching the erection of his fortifications before Frederikshald he is shot through the head; with his death Sweden loses her prestige. Two pretenders to the throne appear, the dead king's nephew and his sister Ulrica Eleonore, married to Prince Frederick of Hesse.
1719 The estates, meeting in Riksdag, elect **Ulrica Eleonore** queen of Sweden. A new constitution is adopted. All the enemies of Sweden flock to her undoing, but she is saved by an alliance with the English, who help to drive back the Russians beyond the Baltic.
1720 Ulrica abdicates in favour of her husband, and **Frederick** is crowned in the presence of the Riksdag. Peace concluded with Denmark and Russia.
1727 Sweden enters the Hanoverian Alliance. Arvid Horn assumes the reins of government, and commerce and manufacture enjoy a rapid development.
1734 Quarrels and intrigues between the Hats and Caps result in war with Russia, which ends
1742 with the disgraceful capitulation of Helsingfors. Adolphus Frederick, prince bishop of Lübeck, and Frederick, crown prince of Denmark, dispute the Swedish succession. The result is the triumph of **Adolphus Frederick,** who upon the death of the king
1751 is elected to the throne.
1753 The Gregorian calendar is adopted. The king and the council fail to agree.
1756 Conspiracy of counts Brahe and Horn, who are beheaded. The Seven Years' War begins.
1762 Peace concluded with Prussia. Hat and Cap quarrels keep politics in a continual tumult.
1771 Death of the king; accession of **Gustavus III.** He endeavours to settle the strife between the two political parties, but in vain; and he consents to a plan which
1772 results in a revolution whose consequences are arrest of the dangerous members of the contending factions and unity and harmony in the government.
1780 Sweden, Russia, and Denmark form an armed neutrality for the protection of navigation.
1783 Sweden concludes a treaty with the United States. The king's popularity begins to wane.
1786 He calls together the estates in Riksdag, and their dissatisfaction and opposition are openly manifested.
1788 Gustavus opens a campaign against Russia, in which he is unsupported by the estates. A second revolution results.
1789 Having re-established his authority by violent measures, Gustavus recommences the war.
1790 Battle of Viborg and peace with Russia.
1792 Assassination of the king at a masked ball. Prince Charles, brother of the dead king, is by his testament appointed guardian of the young **Gustavus (IV) Adolphus.**
1800 The young king is crowned. He revives the armed neutrality of 1780. England proceeds against Denmark and compels her withdrawal from the alliance; Russia also yields to her demands, and Sweden is obliged to follow suit.
1805 Gustavus joins the enemies of Napoleon.
1808 Sweden is attacked by Russia and Denmark.
1809 The king dethroned and banished. Prince Charles, uncle of the dethroned king, is persuaded to assume the government, under title of **Charles XIII.** Peace plans are projected, by which Sweden loses Finland to Russia.
1810 Marshal Bernadotte elected crown prince under name of "Charles John." Napoleon, failing to precipitate hostilities between Sweden and England, invades

1812 Swedish Pomerania. The crown prince forms a new coalition against Napoleon, who in response invades Russia.
1813 Battle of Leipsic. Charles John proceeds against Denmark.
1814 Peace agreed upon between Denmark and Sweden (Treaty of Kiel), by which Norway is ceded to Sweden, while Denmark receives Swedish Pomerania. Norway, rebelling against this arrangement, elects as her king Prince Christian Frederick. After a sharp struggle the Norwegians yield, and elect Charles XIII of Sweden king of Norway.

SWEDEN AND NORWAY UNDER ONE KING

1815 The "Riksact" passed.
1818 Death of the king; accession of **Charles (XIV) John.** Discontent against the government is encouraged by Count von Schwerin, and
1823 an opposition party is organised.
1834 Serious outbreak of cholera.
1835 Sentence of Magnus Jacob Cruserstolpe creates riots in Stockholm. Dissatisfaction with the king's policy increases.
1840 The Riksdag hint at dethronement; but the discontent subsides, and
1844 he is removed by death, and succeeded by his son **Oscar I.** He sets out with a remarkably liberal policy, but grows gradually more and more conservative.
1857 The king's health breaks down, and the government is vested in his son Charles.
1859 Death of Oscar. **Charles XV** is king.
1860 Failure of crops and consequent famine, resulting in the emigration of hundreds of thousands to America.
1867 Formation of the Landtmanna party.
1872 Death of the king. His brother succeeds as **Oscar II.**
1882 Commercial treaty with France renewed.
1888 The Riksdag devotes the surplus funds to the payment of the deficit in the budget and to transportation improvement; and
1895 the political parties join issue and occupy themselves with franchise reform.
1900 The Riksdag takes up the question of the national defences.
1905 Norway withdraws from the Union and chooses a grandson of the king of Denmark as her sovereign. He takes the title of **Haakon VII.**

GREENLAND

986 Eric the Red, exiled from Iceland, discovers and settles Greenland. Other colonists follow, and a considerable foreign trade is established. The government is independent and republican until
1261 when Hakon, king of Norway, induces the Greenlanders to render him allegiance. Foreign dominion, the plague, and barbarian invasion combine to effect their undoing, and
1585 the Eskimos are the sole inhabitants.
1721 Hans Egede lands and devotes himself to the Christianisation and civilisation of the people.
1733 Small-pox nearly depopulates the island.
1744 Denmark takes over the trade of Greenland, hitherto a private monopoly.
1894 A new trading and missionary station is established at Angmagsalik: but trade has rather diminished than increased of late years, and the colony is a source of expenditure for Denmark. Population is also on the decrease. Exploration has been active and persistent in this region, and there remains unmapped but a very small portion of the coast.

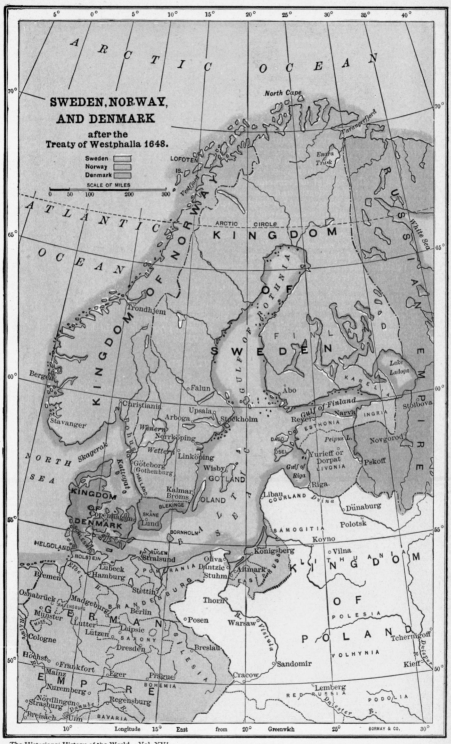

SWEDEN, NORWAY, AND DENMARK

after the
Treaty of Westphalia 1648.

Sweden
Norway
Denmark

SCALE OF MILES
0 50 100 200 300

PART XX

THE HISTORY OF SWITZERLAND

BASED CHIEFLY UPON THE FOLLOWING AUTHORITIES

W. A. B. COOLIDGE, A. DAGUET, C. DÄNDLIKER, J. DIERAUER, J. K. L.
GIESELER, MAGUENOT, G. O. MONTELIUS, J. VON MÜLLER, W. OECHSLI,
R. VON RADEGG, E. RECLUS, J. STRICKLER, A. VIEUSSEUX, J. VITO-
DURANUS, J. VULLIEMIN, J. WILSON

WITH ADDITIONAL CITATIONS FROM

W. COXE, E. A. FREEMAN, V. GROSS, F. GUICCIARDINI, A. HUBER, F.
KELLER, G. MEYER VON KNONAU, J. LUBBOCK, A. MORIN, W. MÜLLER,
R. MUNRO, A. RILLIET, M. STETTLER, STRABO, T. STUDER, F. TROYON,
P. VERRI, R. VIRCHOW, R. WEISS, J. H. D. ZSCHOKKE

CHAPTER I

SWITZERLAND TO THE FOUNDING OF THE CONFEDERATION

[Earliest times to 1289 A.D.]

THE ASPECT OF THE COUNTRY

THE land of which the history lies before us has been said to fight the battles of its inhabitants, and by the very structure of the ground to screen them from subjection, as well as to preclude them from conquest. Its main features still remain the same as Strabo[b] has described them. "Through the whole extent of the Alpine chains," says that exact geographer, "there are hilly platforms capable of cultivation; there are also highly cultivated valleys: yet the greater part of the hill country, especially in its highest recesses, is unfruitful, on account of the snow and of the severity of the climate."

No other division of our quarter of the globe presents a panorama so astonishing; no other exhibits so surprising a diversity of landscapes, ever interesting, and ever new in their features. Nowhere else do such extremes meet as in Switzerland — where external Alpine snows are fringed by green and luxuriant pastures; where enormous icebergs rise above valleys breathing aromatic scents, and blest with an Italian spring; and where the temperatures of each zone alternately reign within two or three leagues. East and west, from the lofty central point of the St. Gotthard, the Alps extend, in the form of a mighty crescent, embracing the north of Italy, and on every side environed by tremendous clefts and caverns, which ensnare the incautious traveller with a veil of greyish snow. Here is the dread birthplace of the glacier and the avalanche; but hence, too, streams well forth in the genial warmth of nature to supply romantic lakes, and spread fertility over the face of the soil. Four principal rivers flow through Switzerland: the Rhine, the

Rhone, the Ticino or Tessin, and the Inn. All of them originate in the high line of the Alps, and indicate by their course the main declivities of the country. The northern slope is watered by the Reuss and the Aare, which meet in the Rhine; the southern by the Ticino, the north-eastern by the Inn, and the south-western by the Rhone.[c] Switzerland was inhabited in the dawn of human existence in Europe. Men of the ice-age and the rude cave-dwellers have left traces of themselves; but it is from a much later period that we first get evidence of a people that had begun to progress toward civilisation. This

CASTLE OF CHILLON

was the race that inhabited the *Pfahlbauten*, or lake-dwellings. The discovery and investigation of these structures gave a new outlook upon the early history of man.[a]

THE LAKE-DWELLERS

During the winter of 1853–1854, a remarkable depression was observed in the level of the Lake of Zurich: the retreat of the waters laid bare a wide surface, of which the inhabitants of the shores took advantage to construct dykes far in advance of the ancient water line, and thus acquired extensive tracts which had been hitherto submerged. Near the hamlet of Obermeilen, the labourers occupied in the work of embankment discovered, under a bed of mud of half a decimetre in depth, some piles, bits of charcoal, stones blackened by fire, bones, and various utensils which indicated the existence of an ancient village. Having been informed of this interesting discovery,

Ferdinand Keller,[d] of Zurich, hastened to investigate the relics just discovered, and soon after announced to the scientific world the result of his researches. This formed the starting-point of incessant explorations. The larger cities of Switzerland and the homes of many learned individuals offer, to the inspection of the curious, archæological museums comprising thousands of ancient relics. From the aquatic village of Concise alone, which is situated in the lake of Neuchâtel, about twenty-five thousand objects have been obtained.

It is easy to conceive the principal reason which determined the ancient tribes of Helvetia to erect their constructions on the shallows of lakes. Before the Roman epoch, the valleys of the Alps were covered with immense forests, through which roamed the bear, the wolf, the boar, the urus, and other formidable animals; while man, since war must from time to time have raged between the scattered tribes, was still more to be dreaded than wild beasts. The first care of each group of families, therefore, was to secure its safety against an unforeseen attack, by establishing itself in some place defended by natural obstacles. Those who inhabited countries strewn with lakes, like Switzerland and Savoy, abandoned the dry land, and built their huts in the midst of the waters, at some distance from the shore. Here they found the surest means of guarding against sudden attack, with the advantage of being able to transport themselves at pleasure in their canoes to every point of the coast, their rude structures serving at the same time as stations for fishing. Perhaps, also, in choosing the surface of the lakes as a sojourn, they obeyed an irresistible attraction which all .res every infant colony towards the water. At all the epochs of history, and in all parts of the world, the requirements of defence and the facilities of fi hing, joined with the natural charm of beauty in the sheets of water, have determined many tribes of men to build their habitations, whether of boughs or of reeds, above the surface of the waves.

It would be easy, even if all the structures of this kind existing in different parts of the world furnished no medium of comparison, to rebuild in thought, by help of the numerous relics found at the bottom of lakes, the lacustrian cottages of ancient Helvetia. A mere glance of the eye through the transparent water enables us to perceive piles in parallel rows, or planted, it may be, without order. The charred beams which are seen between the posts recall the platform once solidly constructed at a height of some feet above the waves. The interlaced boughs, the fragments of clay hardened by fire, evidently belonged to circular walls,[1] and the conic roofs are represented by some layers or beds of reeds, straw, and bark. The stones of the fire-places have fallen just below the place which they formerly occupied. The vessels of clay, the heaps of leaves and of moss which served as beds of repose, the arms, the trophies of the chase, the large stag horns and skulls of wild bulls, which adorned the walls, all these different objects, mingled together in the mud, are nothing else but ancient furniture of the inhabitants. By the side of the piles we can still distinguish remains of the hollowed trunks of trees which served for canoes, and a range of posts indicates the pristine existence of a bridge which was laid from the threshold of the lacustrian dwelling to the neighbouring shore. We are enabled to determine from the number of piles what were the dimensions of the largest aquatic cities, composed gener-

[1 It appears from the discovery of a hut at Schussenried, Würtemberg, that the lake-dwellings, in some instances at least, were rectangular in shape, measuring about ten by seven meters. This, however, does not preclude the supposition that some of them were of circular form, as is indicated by pieces of their walls.]

ally of two or three hundred cabins.[1]   Athwart an interval of thirty or forty centuries, we can conceive how picturesque an effect must have been produced by this agglomeration of small huts closely compacted together in the midst of the waters.   The shore was uninhabited; a few domestic animals alone fed in the grassy clearings; great trees spread their masses of verdure over all the slopes; and a deep stillness brooded in the forest.   Upon the waters, on the contrary, all was movement and clamour; the smoke curled above the roofs; the populace bustled upon the platforms; the canoes passed and repassed from one group of dwellings to another, and from the village to the shore; in the distance floated the boats which served for fishing or for war.   The water seemed then the real domain of man.

From the first of their discoveries, the Swiss archæologists decided that the lacustrian habitations did not all date from one and the same epoch.   The state of the objects found at the bottom of the lakes has led them to divide the first cycle of our history into three ages: that of Stone, that of Bronze, and that of Iron.[2]

The Stone Age

It is in German Switzerland chiefly that the traces of settlements belonging to the age of Stone have been recognised.   Western Switzerland likewise possessed important lacustrian cities, among others that of Concise, near the southern extremity of Lake Neuchâtel; but the lakes of Zurich and of Constance appear to have been the most active centres of population.   It was there that the pile-work of Obermeilen was erected, the discovery of which, as we have said, was the starting point of all that has been since effected. Thanks to the relics obtained at that point, and on the shores of the lakes of Constance, Pfäffikon, Sempach, Wauwyl, and Moosseedorf, we can at this day sketch in broad lines the manner of life of the lacustrian populations, and give some general but uncertain indications with regard to their history.

Early Improvements of the Lake-Dwellers

One of the most surprising considerations suggested by the view of the remains of these primitive constructions is the vast amount of labor accomplished by men who had at their disposal no other implements than flint stones and the brands of their fires.   There was an abundance of trees, tall and straight, growing in the forest; but, to fell and trim them, it was necessary to employ alternately the sharpened stone and the flame.   Afterwards, by the same means, the end of the log was to be reduced to a point, that it might penetrate easily into the soil to a depth of several feet.   The hewing of the trunks of trees, which were to serve for floors and esplanades, and which were cleft with wedges of stone, in order to form a sort of plank, demanded still more labour than the preparation of piles.   What time and pains must have been expended when it was requisite to level a trunk of oak, from ten to fifteen metres long, and to shape it into a canoe!   Some villages, of which we still see the remains, were reared on more than forty thousand piles.   It was the work, no doubt, of several successive generations, but for each of these generations an incessant labour is not the less implied.

[1 A lacustrian settlement near Morges has been found to extend over 60,000 square meters, and one at Robenhausen, in the lake of Pfäffikon, contained more than 100,000 piles, covering 13,000 square meters.   About 250 sites of lake-dwellers' villages have been discovered.]

[2 This division had been made by archæologists before the discovery of the lake-dwellings, but its correctness received striking confirmation from the study of these remains.]

The lacustrians had no instruments at their command but those of stone and of bone. The fabrication and the repairing of these instruments must have required inexhaustible patience, for the stone must be cut with stone, and it is with difficulty that we can conceive how these unwearied artisans succeeded in giving a finish to points and blades of silex. They attacked the hardest substances, and worked even in rock crystal. "The hatchet," says M. Troyon,[e] "played the greatest part in the primitive industry." This instrument is found by hundreds on the sites of the ancient villages. Not only was it the weapon of hunting and of war; it served also for various domestic uses, and probably never quitted the hand or belt of the owner. The blade of the Swiss hatchet, most frequently hewn from a block of serpentine, is much smaller than that of the hatchets used in Scandinavia during the age of Stone, and is of an average measure of from four to six centimetres only. The mode in which the handle was attached to these sharpened stones varied considerably: some were adjusted, by means of ligatures or mortises, at the end of curved sticks, and others were made fast to handles of deer's horn. It was as the national weapon that it most exercised the imagination of the workman and artist. Each warrior modified it according to his personal taste, and perhaps ornamented it with feathers and fringes, like the Indian. Other arms, of less importance than the hatchet, were arrows of flint or of bone, fixed at the ends of long reeds; they resembled those discovered in France, in England, and on the banks of the Mississippi; but in general they are not so long as those of Scandinavia. It is very probable that the sling was in use.

Among the instruments of labour manufactured by the lacustrian people of the age of Stone, may be cited blades of silex, edged or toothed, which served as knives or saws; hammers, anvils; awls of bone or of deer's horn, paring-knives, and needles, which were destined, no doubt, for cutting or sewing leather or skins. The fragments of pottery which occur are formed of a coarse clay, the paste of which is intermingled with small grains of quartz. These vessels betray the infancy of the art, and very seldom present traces of ornamentation. Some of quite a fine paste have a smooth surface, and are coloured black by means of graphite. At Wangen, on the borders of the Lake of Constance, and at Robenhausen, on the lake of Pfäffikon, mats of hemp and of flax, and even real cloth, have been discovered, as well as small baskets in all respects like those of ancient Egyptian tombs. The lacustrians manufactured likewise cords and cables from textile fabrics and the bark of various trees. Vain, like all savages, they bestowed great pains on their corporeal beauty, and sought to enhance it by numerous artifices: they tucked up their hair with pins of bone; decorated their fingers with rings, and their wrists with heavy bracelets; and loaded their shoulders with collars formed of balls of deer's horn mingled with beads of stone; on their breasts they wore the teeth of bears, doubtless to endue them with the force of the wild beasts, and preserve them from mischances. The pierced nuts now scattered in the mud were, no doubt, toys with which, as rattles, the mothers amused their little nurselings.

Occupations of the Lake-Dwellers

Other discoveries have been made, which show that agriculture was somewhat advanced among the lacustrian tribes of this first period. Doubtless hunting and fishing supplied the greater part of their food, as is indicated by the very situation of their houses, in the midst of the waters, and by the bones, partly devoured, of the urus, the bison, the deer, the elk, the roe, the chamois, and birds of the woods, which are found in the beds of turf or mud of their ancient habitations.   Wild fruits also furnished a portion of their aliment, as there have been found, amongst the remnants of their fare, pine and beech nuts, walnuts, and seeds of the raspberry; but at the same time they reared herds of beeves, sheep, goats, and swine, and were accustomed to employ the dog as a substitute in the care of their domestic animals.   They manufactured a kind of cheese in vessels pierced with holes; cultivated the apple, pear, and plum tree, and stored away their fruit for the winter.   They sowed barley and different sorts of grain of excellent quality.   Among the ruins of a lacustrian village, on the Lake of Constance, M. Löhle discovered an ancient storehouse, containing about a hundred measures of barley and wheat, both shelled and in the ear.   He found likewise a portion of real bread, which had been preserved by its carbonisation, and consisted of crushed grains, to which the bran still adhered.

The possession of the cereals, those humble plants which constitute the most important acquisition of the human race, would, of itself, suffice to prove that the nameless tribes of the age of Stone might lay claim to a long period of past progress.   The careful exploration of lacustrian villages has shown that their inhabitants also practiced on a large scale what we call " division of labor."   Certain localities, in fact, such as the Moosseedorf, Obermeilen, and Concise, present so great a provision of implements, some finished and others simply rough-hewn, that we cannot help recognising those settlements as real places of manufacture.   They were the industrial cities of that era, and each of them exercised a peculiar specialty, which employed a considerable system of exchanges between the different centres of production.   There must have existed an unimportant commerce with distant countries, for there have been found on the lacustrian sites a great number of substances foreign to Switzerland.   The rocks of the neighbouring mountains, the horns of deer and bones of wild animals might have served, it is true, for the fabrication of almost all the implements; but the projectile arms, made of silex, could have come only from Gaul or Germany.   By exchange from one hand to another, the lacustrians received coral from the tribes of the Mediterranean, purchased yellow amber from the dwellers on the Baltic, and imported the valuable nephrite from the countries of the east.

If their agricultural knowledge, their industry, and their extended commerce were of a nature to raise in the scale of races these primitive tribes, whom we should have been tempted at first to consider but little developed, their religion — that is to say, the highest expression of their genius — bore also good testimony in their favour.   Like the Celts, the lacustrians seem to have adored the divinity in open nature, on the summits of the hills, in the mysterious shade of the woods, on the bosom of the waves, or more especially, at the foot of the erratic blocks, which they doubtless regarded as stones fallen from heaven.

Articles made of metal were not absolutely unknown to the lacustrians at the close of the first age, as is shown by some relics found at Obermeilen and Concise; but the perfection as well as the rarity of the objects discovered, evince that they came from abroad, either in the way of exchange or through the chances of war.   It would be absurd to suppose that those primitive tribes had proceeded fully prepared to the fabrication of bronze, without having previously availed themselves of copper and tin.   The phenomenon of an alloy of the two metals can be explained only by the arrival of a new people, bringing with them a new civilisation.   In Hindostan, in

Central Asia, in America, the age of Copper succeeded slowly and gradually to the age of Stone; the age of Bronze, in turn, replaced by degrees the age of Copper; but in Helvetia, as well as in all western Europe, this latter period is not represented — the bronze abruptly follows the Stone.[1] The cause of this is that two races had come into collision. The end of the first age must have been marked by terrible events. In almost all the lacustrian villages, the verge of the two epochs is sharply indicated by the burning of dwellings and the massacre of the people. The intruders, probably of the Celtic stock, wielded axes of metal; and by the virtue of the superiority of their arms, must have had their own way with the poor natives.

The Bronze Age

It would seem that the lacustrian population of eastern Switzerland suffered most from the conquest. The greater part of the pile-work settlements of that region were completely abandoned, and since that epoch their remains have been buried beneath the waters. The aquatic villages of western Switzerland also show distinct traces of conflagration. Some, such as the celebrated Steinberg (mountain of stones), situated in the Lake of Bienne, were reconstructed on the same site; others, after their destruction, were rebuilt at a greater distance from the shore, so as to be beyond the reach of incendiary projectiles; in fine, numerous groups of habitations were reared on the shallows, till then unoccupied, of the lakes of Geneva, Neuchâtel, Bienne, and Morat. At the commencement of the age of Bronze, the lacustrian population of the country seems to have removed in a mass to escape the vicinity of the enemy, who had seized upon the whole of eastern Helvetia.

Withdrawn into the territory which forms the present French Switzerland, the lacustrians were fortunate enough to repress all invasions and at the same time to appropriate all the industrial secrets which their conquerors had brought with them. Thanks to this contact with a more civilised race, a new era of prosperity seems to have opened for them, and the census of the lacustrian population largely increased.[2] The villages of the age of Bronze much surpass in number those of the preceding period; and in the fens of the Thiele, between the lakes of Bienne and Neuchâtel, the piles are found in such quantity as to have given rise to an actual trade in wood. The wear and waste, more or less complete, of the piles suffice in general to indicate whether the villages whose sites have been recognised pertained to the age of Bronze or that of Stone. Almost all the piles of the more ancient epoch have been wasted away by the waters, to the very surface of the ground, while those of the second period still project to the extent of one or even two metres. In general, the lacustrian constructions underwent no change of form, doubtless because the customs of the people had remained the same. As to the choice of sites, there is apparent, in the second age as well as the first, a rare sagacity. The points of the shore opposite the places colonised by these old lacustrian tribes have, for the most part, not ceased to be occupied even to our own day

[1 More recently, copper implements, mixed with those of stone, have been found in suffi-cient numbers to induce some archæologists to set up a Copper or Transition period between the ages of Stone and Bronze. Other investigators, namely V. Gross,ᶠ consider these finds as de-noting merely the latest portion of the Stone Age. These discoveries have done much to destroy the theory of an invasion at the end of the Stone Age and the sudden introduction of a new civilisation with the coming in of bronze.]

[2 By measuring the dimensions of fifty-one aquatic settlements of the age of Stone, dis-covered in 1860, M. Troyonᵉ computes that the total population of the lakes amounted to 31,875 persons. By an analogous calculation, 68 villages of western Switzerland, constructed during the age of Bronze, would have contained a population of 42,500 inhabitants.]

by cities or important villages. The city of Zurich covers a lacustrian set-tlement of the age of Stone; during the age of Bronze a village on piles might have been on the site of the present city of Geneva.

Once in the possession of metal, industry attained a great superiority over that of the preceding period, but a resemblance subsists in the form and nature of its product. The axe continued to be the faithful comrade of the warrior, and the artist employed all his skill in decorating it. To this weapon new instruments of death were added — the sword of bronze and the mace of stone — but arrows had become very rare, which proves that, instead of engag-ing in combat at a distance, like their fathers, the natives were accustomed to march straight up to the enemy, and fight face to face. Among the indus-trial remains of that age we also find knives, reaping-hooks, stones for grind-ing and sharpening, needles, pins, weaver's shuttles, fish-hooks, quoits, toys, ear-drops, ornaments in rock, crystal, pieces of amber, necklaces of glass and of jet. The pottery resembles that of the age of Stone, and is composed of an analogous paste, generally mixed with small silicious pebbles. Yet the art of the potter had made incontestable progress: the variety of forms is greater and the ornaments more numerous. All the settlements of any importance had their manufactory of earthenware, as is proved by the specimens which have been disfigured in baking, and rejected as unmarketable. [Upon the site of a lake-village at Corcelles, on the lake of Neuchâtel, have been found pieces of clay vessels which have at the bottom small cavities, evidently caused by the artist's pressing his finger tips into the clay. So perfectly have these been preserved that Prof. F. A. Forel has been able to determine even the arrangement of the tiny ridges on the skin marking the distribution of the nerve terminals in the ancient lake-dweller. He found them practically the same as in individuals of our own day.]

There were special manufactories for instruments of bronze; for a fine mould for hatchets has been discovered at Morges, and real foundries at Echallens, in the canton of Vaud, and at Dovaine, near Thonon. Moreover, a bar of tin which was taken from among the piles of Estavayer proves that bronze was not imported from abroad in a state of alloyage. The people of Helvetia knew how to procure raw metals, and those valleys of the Alps, which even during the age of Stone had been the centre of commerce, on the one side with the Baltic and on the other with the Mediterranean, now exchanged their products with the islands of the Cassiterides.[1] Agriculture developed itself simultaneously with commerce, and it was probably to the progress made in the production of alimentary commodities that the popula-tion owed its marked increase. The breeding of domestic animals equally augmented in importance, and the horse, scarcely represented in the age of Stone, now appeared in numbers. The advances of the lacustrian colonies appear not to have modified their religion.

The Iron Age

The duration of the lacustrian settlements of the age of Bronze was very long, to judge from the thickness of the beds of remains, and from the great difference of the waste which appears in the piles planted at different epochs on the same site; but the destruction of these settlements was as violent as that of the aquatic habitations of the preceding age, for what remains of them under the surface of the waters incontestably bears traces of pillage and con-

[1 The Tin Islands.   Sometimes identified with the Scilly Islands.]

flagration.   A new people, armed with blades of iron, invaded the vast undulated plain which stretches between the base of the Alps and that of the Jura; and after a war of more or less duration, finished by possessing themselves of the wooden fortresses in which the lacustrians had taken refuge. The catastrophe was nearly final.   The lacustrian villages of Steinberg and Graseren, in the lake of Bienne, and of La Tène, in the lake of Neuchâtel, were the only important localities in which the primitive population could seek a refuge.   The people disappeared, and history has not even recorded their ruin.   The lacustrian villages, which had been during the course of so many centuries the residence of a powerful race, were replaced by miserable huts, where the families of fishermen, suspended above the waves, sought a meagre existence.   Some remains of rude pottery dating from the Roman epoch, show that these aquatic abodes were still inhabited at the commencement of our era.

The invaders are known — they could be no others than the Helvetians of Gaul or southern Germany.

PROBABLE ORIGIN OF THE LAKE-DWELLERS

What were these aborigines, whom archæology has, as it were, resuscitated, by an examination of the remains found in the mud of the lakes?   Were they of Finnish, Sicilian, Iberian, or Pelasgic origin?   Should we seek their native country on the table-land of Iran, or on the soil of western Europe itself? One thing only seems certain: that they were men of small size, more remarkable for their agility than their strength.   Their narrow bracelets could encircle only delicate arms; their swords, with short handles, could not have been grasped by the large hands of the Gauls, and necessitated a certain skill in fencing — in viewing them one might say that they had been wielded by agile warriors, like the Basque soldiers.   Nothing, however, as yet authorises the learned to give a definite answer.   Here we have tribes, who reveal to us their intimate life, their domestic habits, and who make a mystery of their name.   Their productions have been collected in our museums, we have been able even to draw up their statistics in an approximative manner; but they pass before us in history like apparitions, and we know not how to connect them with any of the races which precede or which follow them.[g]

The most recent investigations as to the age of the lake-dwellings have fixed their chronology somewhat more definitely.   Gustaf Oscar Montelius,[h] the most eminent authority on the dates of these early ages, announced, in 1899, certain conclusions, as to their chronology, based upon a comparison of finds in the lake-dwellings with similar objects of known date, found in Italy and at Troy, and believed by him to be contemporaneous.   He adopted an arrangement into four ages which had become quite generally accepted by scientists.   The term "Transition period" is used to denote the time when among the objects of stone appear a few of copper.   Upon the conclusions of Dr. Montelius may be based a chronology, which, expressed in general terms, is as follows: (1) Stone Age before 3000 B.C.; (2) Transition period 3000 to 2000 B.C.; (3) Bronze Age 2000 to 1000 B.C.; (4) Iron Age 1000 to 100 B.C.

The chief matters for controversy that still remain are concerned with the nature of the change from one characteristic period to another, and with the identity of the peoples inhabiting the lake-villages in the different periods. In contradiction to Troyon's[e] views, the original investigator, Dr. Ferdinand Keller,[d] upheld a theory which was endorsed by Sir John Lubbock[i] (now

Lord Avebury), who thus sums it up: "The primitive population did not differ, either in disposition, mode of life, or industry, from that which was acquainted with the use of bronze; and all the phenomena of the lake-villages, from their commencement to their conclusion, indicate clearly a gradual and peaceable development. The number of instances in which lake-villages have been destroyed by fire has been, he [Doctor Keller] considers, exaggerated. It must, I think, be confessed that the arguments used by Troyon do not justify us in believing with him that the introduction of bronze was accompanied by an entire change of population." It should be noted, however, that Troyon's theory does not call for "an entire change of population," but merely the driving of the original population of the Stone Age into the western part of Switzerland by the invaders.

Troyon's theories, on the other hand, have received strong support. Studer,[j] who came to Troyon's conclusion that, with the introduction of bronze, a new race came in, based it upon the fact that in the Bronze Age two types of skulls were found, dolichocephalic and brachycephalic, whereas in the pure Stone Age appears only one type, the brachycephalic. Rudolf Virchow,[k] the great German anthropologist, on practically the same basis, put forth the opinion that during the Bronze Age a new people did indeed join the original lake-dwellers, but by degrees, not as one great immigration subverting the previous order of things. This view Munro[l] thinks is "greatly strengthened by collateral circumstances. No violent disturbance of the previous conditions of life is anywhere to be detected." Munro,[l] moreover, upholds Troyon's conception of the entrance upon the scene of the people of the Iron Age. "With the introduction of iron into general use in Switzerland," he says, "we have a new people, who conquered and subjugated the lake-dwellers, and gave the death-blow to their systems of lake-villages. The owners of these La Tène [Iron Age] weapons in Switzerland were the Helvetians, of Roman fame, who, according to Cæsar, were a branch of the great Celtic family. Who these Celts were, is a question which still puzzles historians, philologists, and archæologists."

We now come to the question still in dispute among archæologists and ethnologists, as to who were the original lake-men of the Stone Age. Doctor Keller[d] believed that these were Celts — a view which Munro[l] opposes. "They were part of the first neolithic inhabitants," says Munro, "who entered the country by the regions surrounding the Black Sea and the shore of the Mediterranean, and spread westward, along the Danube and its tributaries, till they reached the great central lakes. Here they founded that remarkable system of lake-villages whose ruins and relics are now disinterred, as it were, from another or forgotten world."

Professor Virchow[k] well sums up the whole matter, and emphasises a point brought out by Troyon.[e] He says of these ancient peoples of Switzerland: "Nothing in the physical characteristics of this race warrants the assumption of an inferiority of their bodily structure. On the contrary, the splendid skulls of Auvernier may be exhibited with honor among the skulls of the highly civilised nations of to-day. By their capacity, their form, and the details of their construction, they rank equal with the best skulls of the Aryan race. The solution of the problem whether a single people ran through this entire course of development, from the Stone Age to the characteristic Iron Age, will yet require much work; but the fact that in the same spot, or at any rate within one and the same district, such great changes in civilisation were accomplished, will forever assure the lake-dwellings a conspicuous place in the esteem of men."[a]

CONFLICTS WITH ROME: THE HELVETIANS

The condition of the tracts between the Rhine, the Rhone, and the Jura, remains involved in almost entire obscurity till the appearance of the Helvetians, a race of Gallic Celts, whom some unknown accident had guided from the borders of the Rhine and the Main to those of the lake of Geneva. The toilsome cultivation of these regions, while it left but little time for martial enterprise, conduced with the pure mountain breezes to form a stout and hardy people, which divided itself into four districts, then, as in later ages, connected with each other by the feeble bonds of a federal union.

It is probable that the Gallo-Celtic inhabitants of these regions, bordering

CHÂTEAU VUFFLENS, ON THE LAKE OF GENEVA
(Ninth century)

so closely upon Italy, took part in the great inroads of the Gauls on that country. But their first ascertained military enterprise was conducted in alliance with the Cimbri and Teutones, who roamed from unknown regions in the east and the north, extended their conquests and ravages along the banks of the Rhine, and even struck the already powerful Roman commonwealth with terror. Whether few or many Helvetian tribes accompanied that expedition, is a point which cannot now be determined. What is evident, however, is that each of these tribes had full liberty of waging wars and allying itself with foreigners. Thus, the Tigurini, for example, marched with the Cimbri nearly to the mouths of the Rhone. But when a Roman army, under the consul Lucius Cassius, threatened their rear, they suddenly wheeled round, apprehensive of being cut off from their homes; and led by their young general Diviko, completely defeated the Romans [at Aginnum, now Agen, on the Garonne, 107 b.c.]. The consul and his lieutenant Piso were left dead on the field. The conquerors only permitted the retreat of the survivors after they had given hostages and marched under the yoke.[1]

[1 A clan of the Helvetians, the Toygeni, was annihilated, 102 b.c., by the Roman armies under Marius in the defeat of the Cimbri at Aquae Sextiae; and a Helvetian clan, the Tigurini, alone escaped the slaughter of the barbarian invaders by Marius and Catullus at Vercelli, 101 b.c.]

Long after Diviko's excursion with the northern marauders, recollections of the fat pastures and rich domains of Gaul, of which a glimpse had been caught in the course of that excursion, furnished all who had, and many who had not, shared the adventure, with a theme for the most highly coloured description. There the vine and olive ripened under a warmer heaven, and the winter's snows were all but unknown. The effect of these reminiscences was enhanced by the accounts brought by travellers from the left bank of the Rhine, which produced their natural workings on a rude and simple people — a people highly irritable, daring, and self-confident — with whom prudent deliberation passed for cowardice, and in whom successful excursions had encouraged the propensity to predatory warfare. Their pastoral habits adapted them for any wandering enterprise; those distinctions of rank which are described as having existed among them marked out a military order. A leader of this class stood forth among the Helvetians in the person of Orgetorix, a man of rank and ambition. In peace he could not gratify his appetite for absolute power, and therefore built his hopes upon warfare. Having secretly gained a number of adherents, he came forward in a public assembly, and artfully persuaded the people to quit their rocky fastnesses, which barely furnished food for themselves and their cattle, and to march with him into the fair and fruitful territories of Gaul, where little resistance was to be feared from the effeminate inhabitants. It was resolved that they should break up and emigrate after the lapse of three years, with their wives and families, cattle and possessions. The interval was to be used in making the needful preparations. Before the year of the expedition had arrived, however, the despotic designs of Orgetorix were discovered; and he was reduced to lay violent hands on himself, in order to escape death at the stake.[1]

The resolution of the Helvetians must have been based on deep conviction, since it suffered no alteration from so ominous an outset. That retreat might henceforth cease to be thought of, they burned their habitations and even their corn, reserving only three months' provisions. Moreover, they succeeded in persuading several neighbouring tribes to burn their towns and villages in like manner, and accompany them. Three hundred and sixty-eight thousand souls, of whom ninety-two thousand were able-bodied warriors, are computed to have marched out on this Gallic expedition. The Roman province of Gaul was, at the point of time before us, under the government of Julius Cæsar — already no less eminent as a military leader than he became, a few years afterwards, as a statesman. Without granting the passage desired by the Helvetians through his province, he found means to put them off, to gain time and collect reinforcements. He followed, with his army, their march through the lands of the Sequani and Ædui (inhabitants of the territory afterwards the Franche-Comté and duchy of Burgundy), alleging as his reasons the danger caused to the province under his charge by the descent of so warlike and enterprising a people, and the petitions for aid addressed to him by the Ædui, who were annoyed by the Helvetian inroad. In fact, however, any and every pretext for intervening in the affairs of Gaul was welcome to him. He made no demonstration of hostility till the main invading body had already crossed the Araris (Saône), when, falling on the Tigurini, who alone had remained on the left bank, he cut most of them to pieces, and dispersed the rest.

Notwithstanding this unlooked-for catastrophe, the Helvetians did not yet renounce the main scope of their enterprise, and made overtures to treat

[1 Whether Orgetorix died by murder or suicide is uncertain.]

with Cæsar. Old Diviko, who did not forget in recent defeat his former superiority, was commissioned for this purpose. No treaty could be brought to a conclusion; and Cæsar followed the march of the invaders a fortnight longer. At length, after a desperate and long-sustained conflict (58 B.C.) in the neighbourhood of Bibracte (Autun), the superiority of the Roman arms and discipline decided the day against the stubborn courage of the Helvetians. Their strength and spirit now completely broken, they submitted. The terms imposed by Cæsar on the vanquished invaders were: to return into their desolated country, and rebuild their wilfully ruined habitations. For their immediate provision, he supplied grain through the Allobroges (inhabitants of the territory extending from Geneva to Grenoble, and from Vienne on the Rhone to the Alps in Savoy); and promised for the future that they should live under their own laws, under the specious denomination of allies of the Roman people. In order, however, to watch and overawe these new allies, a fortress was built at Noviodunum (Nyon), near the lake of Geneva. Several other garrisons were stationed throughout the country. The Rhætians [inhabiting the Grisons] only, screened by their lakes and icebergs, might for a moment yet esteem themselves invincible, and form leagues with the natural allies of their tribe, who were scattered along the course of the Inn, throughout the vales of the present Tyrol, and in the plains later included in the circle of Swabia. They pursued a wild and reckless mode of life: plundered travellers, or broke suddenly forth in numerous hordes through their mountain passes, and fell by surprise on the neighbouring towns of Italy.

Even during Cæsar's Gallic proconsulate, there are traces of the Roman arms being turned against the Rhætians; and so soon as Augustus had firmly secured his dominion over the empire, he endeavoured to confine within more narrow bounds, on the southward, a people whose incursions had by this time become formidable even to the plains of upper Italy. Soon afterwards he sent against the Rhætians his two step-sons — Drusus from Italy, Tiberius through Gaul and by the Lake of Constance. Only after an obstinate struggle, renewed with repeated efforts, were these vigorous asserters of their country's independence compelled to bow beneath the universal empire of Rome (15 B.C.). A number of their youth were afterwards embodied in the legions, and the subject land was occupied by permanent encampments.

THE ROMAN OCCUPATION

We have seen that the Helvetians were at first flattered by the Romans with the title of allies — a title of precarious value at any time, and which in the present case seems only to have been given till the land should be secured in subjection. This is rendered still more evident by the circumstance that an equestrian colony, even in Cæsar's time, had been founded at Noviodunum (Colonia Julia Equestris). Under Augustus, Munatius Plancus founded the Colonia Augusta Rauracorum; and the settlement at Vindonissa (Windisch) cannot be of much later date. The franchises conceded to these settlements, the grants of land and subsidies which (in order to encourage such establishments, and build them up as outworks of the Roman dominion) were conferred upon the Roman soldiers and colonists who chose them for a permanent residence, prove nothing with regard to the general welfare of the country and the condition of its primitive inhabitants. They, indeed, retained in part their simple forms of polity, which soon, however, became merged in the central administration; and even so early as the reign of Augustus, heavy poll and land taxes, hitherto unknown, were introduced in these regions.

When the weaker come in collision with the stronger, one precipitate step may easily plunge them into ruin. This was experienced by the Helvetians, on the occasion of the murder of the emperor Galba (69 A.D.) — an event of which the tidings either did not immediately reach them, or found them disinclined to acknowledge Vitellius, the candidate for the purple against Otho. This prevalent indisposition or ignorance was not at all corrected by the conduct of the twenty-first legion (surnamed *rapax*) at Vindonissa, which, with a rapacity suiting its surname, seized the pay set apart by the Helvetians for the garrison of the castle. The latter retaliated by intercepting letters between the German and Pannonian armies, and by arresting a centurion with a company of soldiers. Their general, Cæcina, who was marching from the Rhine with his unbridled bands to meet Otho in Italy, sacked and destroyed the bathing-place (now Baden) on the Limmat, which had grown during long peace to the importance of a municipal town. He called out reinforcements from Rhætia, to fall upon the rear of the native insurgents. These, without practice in arms, discipline, or tactics, were, in fact, without any of the conditions of success, and found themselves attacked by mountaineers like themselves — Rhætians. Assailed in flank by the legions under Cæcina, in rear by the cohorts coming up from Rhætia, as well as by the disciplined youth of Rhætia itself, they suffered a severe defeat. Borne down by the Thracian cohort, pursued and tracked to every retreat by the light German and Rhætian troops, many thousands were left dead upon the field, or made prisoners and afterwards sold for slaves.

When the news of the lost battle reached Aventicum,[1] amazement and distress prevailed. The ambassadors, who were instantly sent to appease the wrath of the conqueror, were received and addressed with harshness by Cæcina. He demanded, first of all, the execution of the principal man in the nation, Julius Alpinus. He referred the people for mercy to the emperor, who alone had power to mitigate their well-deserved chastisement.[c] A story, to which Byron gave poetic setting in Childe Harold, to the effect that Julia Alpinula, a daughter of Alpinus, pleaded in vain at the feet of Cæcina for her father's life, has been shown to rest upon the falsification of an inscription.[a] The Helvetian envoys made their appearance before Vitellius, anxious yet scarce hoping, to avert the last extremities. Audience at length being given, the infuriated soldiers brandished weapons of death before their eyes, and demanded loudly the total extirpation of a race which had laid presumptuous hands on Roman warriors. Vitellius himself knitted his heavy brows, and muttered menaces. The spokesman of the Helvetians, Claudius Cossus, stood pale as death before him, made no attempt to excuse the facts, but only depicted in the liveliest hues the misery of his country, threw himself at the emperor's feet, and begged so irresistibly that all hearts were affected, and the soldiers themselves took part in supplicating mercy for Helvetia. Thus that country was preserved by one man; but instead of being, as hitherto, entitled the ally of Rome, it was degraded into union with the province of Gaul.

It, however, remains doubtful whether, even at this period, when the whole land was nominally subject to the Romans, a certain measure of freedom, in its wooded and rocky recesses at least, might not still have continued to exist compatibly with a nominal allegiance, perhaps even with the payment of a tribute. The remains of Roman settlements, extending from the Albis to the Bernese Oberland, lead to the inference that a connected line of

[[1] Now Avenches. This place, the chief city of the Helvetians, flourished greatly under the Romans. It is here that the principal remains of the Roman civilization in Switzerland are to be found.]

garrisons was kept up for security towards the interior of the country. Roman coins, etc., have been found in the interior, and even in the higher parts of the mountains. Roman habiliments, manners, and usages became diffused throughout the country, along with their attendant effeminacy, luxury, and moral corruption. The Latin language gradually encroached upon and in some measure superseded that of the country. Even in things of common use and in agriculture, many Latin names, which have not been adopted into the formed and matured dialects of Germany, are to be met with at the present day in Switzerland. All genuine nationality was extinguished, and the very name of Helvetia disappeared. The inhabitants became mere subjects.

The government of Nerva, Trajan, Adrian, and the two Antonines, in almost its whole duration, may be reckoned among such blessings as providence but sparingly vouchsafes to mankind. Human industry penetrated the fastnesses of the mountains. The Alpine cows became an article of commerce; for though the breed was small and poor in flesh, it was capable of enduring labour, and afforded abundance of milk: the Alpine cheeses gained at that early period the renown which they retain to this day. Experiments were undertaken in agriculture; and the Falernian hills were rivalled by the vineyards of Rhætia. The Helvetians paid peculiar veneration to the god of wine; and preserved his gifts, not as yet in wine cellars, but in wine casks. They worshipped also the sun, by the name of Belin, the invincible god; and his sister Isis, the moon; the sylphs, their guardian angels; and the shadowy powers, the *dii manes*. But the period must soon terminate in which individual qualities softened the workings of pure despotism and military dominion. The inseparable consequences of boundless prodigality and consequent rapacity, on the part of the rulers, had made government a mere unpunished system of plunder. Admission to the rights of Roman citizenship, which under Caracalla became easier than ever, had the effect of introducing Roman citizens into all situations hitherto filled by natives. Thus the latter came at length to be governed by functionaries, who acted upon interests wholly distinct from theirs — a grievance which rose to its highest pitch in the reign of Diocletian, who conferred upon the higher class of officers powers of proceeding summarily, without calling assessors.

Christianity, during this period, spread by degrees throughout Helvetia. The original announcement of the new faith has been ascribed by the legends to a certain Beatus, so early as the first century; in the third century, to Lucius, a Rhætian; at the close of the fourth, to the members of the so-called Theban legion. In like manner, the signatures of bishops or presbyters of churches in the Valais, at Geneva, Coire, Aventicum, and elsewhere, are handed down to us, bearing date from the fourth century. These, however, are of extremely doubtful genuineness. What is better made out, is that a church existed at the close of that century in the Valais. During the fifth, others were established in the rest of the above-mentioned places.

THE GERMANIC INVASIONS; FRANKISH RULERS

Meanwhile the Roman power sank lower and lower. Not the misused people only, but many men of rank and power, encouraged foreign, in order to get rid of domestic, enemies. Under the perpetual minority of the imbecile Arcadius and Honorius, the empire, already more than once dissevered, became permanently parted into eastern and western. Precisely at this epoch of exhaustion, more numerous swarms of semi-barbarous nomad nations set themselves in motion than at any former period; the roughest and remotest of which drove the others forwards on the now defenceless frontiers of the empire.[1] While from the east the Goths fell upon Italy, while the Vandals and the Suevi attacked Spain, the Burgundians marched on the upper Rhine, from the Oder and the Vistula. (409 A.D.) Imperial Rome, too feeble to repel them, granted them, according to former examples, the possession of the larger part of the lands which they had devastated; thus purchasing their alliance against enemies yet more formidable.

The Burgundians fixed their residence (443 A.D.) on both sides of the Jura, on the lake of Geneva, in the Valais, on the banks of the Rhone and the Saône. They had adopted Christianity on their reception as Roman allies — a title which, by this time, had completely changed its import; and, instead of future subjugation, augured future mastery. They combined with large and vigorous outward proportions a character less rude than that of some northern nations. In the quality of peaceable guests and new allies of the empire, they spared the still remaining towns and other Roman monuments, and permitted the former owners to retain their established laws and customs; appropriating, however, to themselves, a third of the slaves, two thirds of the cultivated lands, and one half of the forests, gardens, and farm buildings. Much obscurity, during this period, rests on the history of those regions which are now German Switzerland. It is not exactly known how far the first Burgundian Empire extended itself over the plain of the Aare. Eastward of that stream, and over a great part of Germany, the land was overrun by the Alamanni. These new-comers, embittered towards whatever bore the name of Roman, destroyed the still remaining fragments of fortresses and cities, which, in common with all German tribes, they utterly detested. They did not treat the inhabitants with cruelty, but reduced them to a state of complete servitude. All Roman landed property they seized without exception, and only allowed the tenants to remain there in the situation of bondmen, and on the condition of paying them dues. This barbarian torrent overwhelmed the public monuments and symbols of Christianity. Whatever yet remained of the old culture disappeared, or, at all events, concealed itself.

Towards the close of the fifth century, another German race, or rather confederacy of tribes, obtained ascendency. These were the Franks, a sturdy stem of heathen, whose power was established in Gaul by their leader Chlodwig (Clovis, Louis). This chief engaged in hostilities against the Alamanni. The hostile nations met in deadly conflict (496 A.D.). The fall of their prince decided the Alamanni to surrender, and transfer their allegiance to the victorious king of the Franks; and Clovis marched along with them into their territories. Here, however, hostility towards the Franks and their new gods induced many to refuse him obedience. It was not until nine years after his victory that the body of the tribe was brought to submission. Clovis resolved to extirpate a population so unmanageable. While he raged thus furiously against the Alamanni, his brother-in-law Theodoric, king of the Ostrogoths, wrote to remind him that mercy and moderation better became a monarch than vengeance. As Clovis turned a deaf ear to this wise and benevolent counsel, many of the conquered Alamanni finally threw themselves into the arms of their intercessor. Thus Rhætia became added to the dominions of the Ostrogoths; and at length, in the year 500 A.D.,

[1 The Alamanni, about 260 A.D., over-ran Switzerland, and laid Aventicum in ashes.]

south-western or Roman Switzerland belonged to the Burgundians, northern or German Switzerland was shared between the Franks, the Alamanni, and the wilderness — Rhætia was possessed by the Ostrogoths. These partitions, however, were destined to have no long duration. The first Burgundian Empire owed its final dissolution 534 A.D., in a great degree to the family feuds and vices of its princes. The empire of the Ostrogoths verged to its fall about the same period. Five successive kings incurred successive losses in war and land. Dietbert, king of the Franks, took advantage of their weakness (536 A.D.) to recover the possession of Rhætia. Thenceforward the Franks held exclusive rule over the whole extent of Rhætia and Helvetia.

From this period is derivable, in a general way, without aiming at impossible exactness, the distinction of the French and German languages in Switzerland. So far as the dominions of the Alamanni, and since their subjection those of the German Franks, extended, the present Swiss dialect of German took its rise from the original roots of that language. In the lands about the lakes of Geneva and Neuchâtel, where the power of the Burgundians was established, the Gallo-Roman popular dialect kept its ground, from which were formed the several Romance dialects; from these, again, the Provençal; and at last the modern French. More obscure in their origin, however obvious in their existence, are some characteristic varieties in the divisions of the race itself; for notwithstanding all the mixtures which have hitherto taken place, and all local exceptions, a marked dissimilarity exists between them. The more rounded contours of the western inhabitants are distinguishable at once from the strong features of the eastern. The latter may conjecturally be traced to the Alamanni, while the former are more probably inherited from a Frankish stem.

The Frank kings of the family of Merovæus were the third exclusive rulers of Helvetia. As no fixed laws of succession existed, the country belonged, under their government, now to one head of the whole Frank dominions, now to several princes, amongst whom those dominions were divided, and who were no less divided by disputes among themselves. In the year 613 A.D., Clotaire II succeeded in uniting the whole empire of the Franks, after long internal wars and scenes of violence had taken place. Prosperity was gradually restored to the wasted lands of Gaul and of Helvetia. On the demise of Clotaire in 628 A.D., his son Dagobert ascended the throne. What the father had begun, the son successfully continued; and administered his realm with vigour, wisdom, and justice. In these times Helvetia, which in earlier days had counted twelve towns, four hundred villages, and above 350,000 inhabitants, lay in great part waste and desolate, covered over with morasses and forests. Here and there a cluster of rude tenements might be met with, around a farm, a fortress, or a monastery. The revival of a country is difficult after long disasters; especially when its natural site and qualities are unfavourable to the rapid growth and bloom of civilisation. The recovery of Helvetia, therefore, could only advance slowly. It commenced, however, under Clotaire and Dagobert. Villages and towns arose in many places; and their rise was often favoured by religious foundations. Those of St. Gall, Disentis, Zurich, Lucerne, and Romain Motier may be traced to the times of which we have been treating. The bishops — who, like their clergy, very generally lived in wedlock — were elected by the latter and by the people, and afterwards confirmed by the king.

Soon after the time of King Dagobert, the Merovingian dynasty began to verge towards ruin. They gave over the government altogether into the hands of their prime functionary, the mayor of the palace (*major domûs*);

who was also commander-in-chief of the army. In the year 751 A.D., two centuries and a half since the erection of the Merovingian dynasty by Clovis, Childeric III was deposed from the throne by the assembly of the people at Soissons, thrust aside into a convent, and succeeded on the throne by the mayor of his palace, Pepin the Little, who founded the new Carlovingian dynasty.

The Carlovingian dynasty, founded by Pepin, received its name from his son Charles; who not only excelled his father in greatness, but exalted himself high above the mass of his contemporaries. Pepin, with consent of his nobles, had, in 768 A.D., divided his kingdom between his sons, Charlemagne and Carlomann; and the early death of the latter did not leave the former free from the suspicion of having hastened it by poison. Charlemagne, shortly after his accession, put an end to the Lombard kingdom in upper Italy. He was crowned at Rome as emperor, by the pope, in the year 800.

Helvetia had her share of the provisions made by Charlemagne, with a wisdom far beyond his age, for the popular instruction. Among the schools which he established or reformed was that of Zurich,[1] where the grateful recollection of his bounty was preserved by an annual celebration. He also introduced vine-cultivation into Helvetia; and peopled several districts by transporting thither the conquered Saxons. He occasionally made some stay at Zurich, and enriched the cathedral church with his donations. We read, moreover, that men from the Thurgau served in his campaigns, whose strength and spirit attracted general notice.

Many common-lands were divided, and converted into arable. In the Valais, and even in the neighbourhood of Zurich, vines were cultivated. The inhabitants, formerly scattered, now collected themselves into farms and villages, in which commonly stood a baronial tower or mansion. Every village had a special jurisdiction, under its *vogt*, or bailiff. The whole district assisted in the trial of important cases. The general assembly, which was held in the open air, was joined by every one who possessed seven feet of land before and behind him. The elders took the first place; the count stated the case; and every man gave judgment on it, as God had given him understanding. After the case had been thus debated, the judges, properly so called, stepped into the circle — that is to say, into the middle of a ring formed by the rest of the meeting — and that which they declared was received for doom. The monastery of St. Gall, already wealthy and powerful, distinguished itself for science and for discipline. It was not, indeed, an age of native learning; nor had St. Gall much to boast of in the shape of intellectual productions of its inmates or tenantry. Here, however, the books of the fathers and ancient historians were read and copied; and many a Latin work, now extensively diffused, might have been lost to the modern world but for the toils of these obscure monks, inhabiting a corner of the Thurgau.*c*

GERMAN AND BURGUNDIAN HELVETIA

In the division of Charlemagne's empire, the Helvetia of the Alamanni — German Helvetia — fell to the share of Ludwig the German, and afterwards continued attached to that part of the German empire called the duchy of Swabia. Burgundian Helvetia was dependent sometimes on the kingdom of Italy, and sometimes on France until after the death of Louis le Bègue in 879, when the monarchy fell into confusion. The kingdom raised by Boson

[1 The Institute of Canons and the Karolinum claimed to have been founded by him.]

[888-937 A.D.]

[Arles, or Cisjurane Burgundy] was parcelled into three. Rudolf count of western Helvetia, son of Conrad count of Paris, and related to the Carlovingian dynasty, assembled at St. Maurice, in the Valais, several lords and bishops, who crowned him (888) as King Rudolf I of Upper Burgundy. He was acknowledged in western Helvetia, and in the country west of the Jura, as far as the river Saône. Rudolf, after sustaining a war against the emperor Arnulf, who came into Helvetia with an army of Germans, was induced to repair to Regensburg (Ratisbon), where a general diet was held, in which the affairs of France and Burgundy were regulated. Upper or Little Burgundy was acknowledged as an independent kingdom (890). Rudolf, after reigning twenty-four years, was succeeded by his son Rudolf II.

Meantime German Helvetia, ever since the abolition of the ducal dignity by Pepin, was governed by *missi cameræ* [imperial commissioners], who resided in Swabia. Two brothers, Erchanger and Berthold, who were entrusted with this office, became jealous of Solomon, bishop of Constance and abbot of St. Gall, and lord of several other convents and domains. He had been a favourite of Arnulf and of Louis IV, the last emperor of the Carlovingian race, who granted him lands from the imperial domains. The two brothers took Solomon prisoner, but the bishop's reputation stood so high that the country rose in his favour; he was released, and the two commissioners, being arraigned for sacrilege before a court of Swabian nobles, were condemned to death and executed. Burkhardt count of Thurgau was the principal instigator of this severe sentence. Soon after, Burkhardt himself was made, by the emperor Conrad, with the consent of the nobles of the province (917), duke of Alamannia, called also duke of Swabia, which government included German Helvetia.

Burkhardt quarrelled with Rudolf II of Burgundy about the frontier district of Aargau; but peace was re-established between them, and Rudolf married Burkhardt's daughter.[1] The river Reuss seems to have marked the limits between the two states. Rudolf was then called into Italy by a party of lords of that country. Hugo count of Provence, who had expelled Boson's grandson from his little kingdom of Arles, started as rival to Rudolf for the crown of Italy. Rudolf called to his assistance Burkhardt, his father-in-law; the old warrior came, but, being over-confident in his contempt for his Italian enemies, he was killed near Milan. Rudolf then returned to his own dominions, which the emperor Henry I enlarged by part of German Helvetia, detached from the dukedom of Alamannia; and for this Rudolf did homage to the empire.*m* As a result of the Italian campaign Rudolf gave up his pretensions to Italy, and received in exchange from Hugo, Provence (930). By the addition of this country (the old Arles or Cisjurane Burgundy) to Rudolf's possessions (Upper or Transjurane Burgundy) the earlier kingdom of Burgundy was reunited, and the Burgundian power raised to a height that it had not reached before. Switzerland, as an important part of this realm, partook of its greatness.*a* Hugo of Provence died soon afterwards, and the Burgundians of both parties were finally expelled from Italy. It appears that the Italians had conceived great aversion to the whole nation, on account of their excessive eating and drinking, and because the Burgundian voices sounded too rude for Italian ears.

After the death of Rudolf II, in 937, Otto I, emperor of Germany, came into Burgundy and took away Conrad, Rudolf's son, who was still a minor, in

[1 This was Bertha, afterwards famous as "good Queen Bertha." As a marriage portion, she brought to Burgundy her lands in Upper Aargau, thus enlarging the kingdom by a considerable part of Switzerland.]

order to have him brought up under his own eyes.*m* During the absence of
Conrad, Bertha, the good queen Bertha, governed the kingdom. Who has
not heard of the humble gracious queen who, mounted on her palfrey, a
spindle in her hand, went from castle to castle, from monastery to monastery,
from farm-yard to farm-yard, doing everywhere deeds of piety and charity?
One day the queen of Payerne — for that was her name in the traditions of
Burgundy — met in the fields near Orbe a young peasant woman who was
spinning while she watched her flock. Bertha, well pleased, gave a valuable
present to the girl. On the morrow the ladies of her train all appeared
before her, each with a distaff in her hand. But the queen smiled at sight
of them. " Ladies," she said, " the young peasant, like Jacob, came first,
and she has carried away my blessing." The rule of Queen Bertha and her
husband Rudolf II was distinguished by the laying of foundations for numerous pious and useful institutions, and the building of churches, monasteries, bridges, roads, castles, and hostelries.*p* Conrad, having become of
age, was restored by Otto to his dominions; and the emperor married Conrad's sister, Adelaide queen of Italy. In Conrad's reign another irruption took
place of the Hungri or Madjars, called by some Turci, who had some years
before overrun Italy and Rhætia; they afterwards penetrated into Western
Helvetia. Conrad defeated the Madjars, as well as some bands of Saracens
who had found their way to the valleys of Jura, by opposing the barbarians
to each other and deluding each party with the expectation of his assistance
against the other. While the wandering hostile hordes were fast engaged in
combat, Conrad fell upon both and destroyed them. After this he reigned
long and in peace.*m*

SWITZERLAND TORN BY DISSENSIONS IN THE EMPIRE

Helvetia hoped in vain to enjoy repose beneath the wide-extended wing of
the German Empire. The obstinate, protracted, and destructive strife which
raged between the emperor and the pope, engendered the most violent disorders even in its mountain recesses. On the demise of Henry III, in 1056,
the imperial crown descended on the head of his son Henry IV. Under his
reign, the discord between emperors and popes broke out into open warfare,
which raged through nearly half a century, and at a later period blazed out
anew. Hildebrand ascended the papal throne, as Gregory VII (1073). Having contrived to obtain the emperor's assent to his nomination, though the
election had already taken place without his concurrence, Gregory at once
set to work in the accomplishment of his schemes against the secular power.

Helvetia, at this period, offered no agreeable aspect. Its first and most
powerful prince, Duke Rudolf of Swabia, along with Berthold of Zähringen,
duke of Carinthia, and many other princes, had revolted from the emperor.
The country was divided betwixt the parties: Rudolf was ascendant in
Swabia; the emperor, in Burgundian Helvetia. Through the excommunication launched against Henry, Gregory freed from their oaths of allegiance
all the imperial vassals and subjects. Henry's friends became discouraged;
and events took such a turn that the princes at length threatened to give
effect to the papal sentence if Henry did not clear himself from it within the
term of a year. In this situation the emperor had no resource left but to
creep with his wife and children into Italy, in the depth of winter, amidst
unheard-of difficulties and dangers, without money, without escort, through
the mountain passes occupied by Rudolf and the rest of his enemies. On his
arrival he was hailed with loud acclamations by his Lombard vassals; and

nothing but want of spirit could have induced him to implore remission of the sentence, at the price of the hardest conditions and the deepest humiliations. With rage and revenge in his heart, he returned to Germany. Here he found Duke Rudolf of Swabia enthroned as anti-Cæsar. But he found, too, a strong party of adherents in the free towns, in the clergy, who were mostly averse to Gregory's innovations, and amongst all who felt indignation over the dishonour done to the German name, and sympathy for their deeply humbled emperor. Now began a war of extermination, by which even a large portion of Helvetia was depopulated. The fortune of war declared itself in favour of Henry. In a decisive battle at Merseburg, in 1080, Rudolf was mortally wounded; and his hand, which had been cut off in the combat, being shown him, he is said to have repentantly exclaimed, "That is the hand which I pledged in swearing fealty to the emperor!" His fall was regarded as a judgment of God, and Henry's adherents gained the ascendency.

After the fall of Rudolf of Swabia, the anti-Cæsar, at Merseburg, his vacant dukedom was bestowed by the victorious Henry IV on his son-in-law Frederick of Hohenstaufen. Rudolf's son, Count Berthold of Rheinfelden, contested in a long war the possession of his father's domain with its new owner. Berthold died in the year 1090, by which event the rights of the count of Rheinfelden were transmitted to his brother-in-law, Berthold II of Zähringen. The nobles in Ulm recognised the new duke immediately, and tendered him the oath of allegiance. Frederick of Hohenstaufen prepared for a renewal of the war with fresh vigour; but Berthold well knew that the land was tired out by protracted vexations, and he himself preferred a moderate fortune to the doubtful issue of warfare. He therefore appeared in the presence of the emperor at the diet of Mainz, in 1097, and there surrendered the ducal office and dignity into Frederick's hands, terminating by this submission the four-and-twenty years' hostility maintained by his house against Henry IV. As a recompense for this renunciation, Henry shared the sometime duchy of Swabia or Alamannia between the two candidates; so that Swabia, properly so called, was allotted to Frederick, while Helvetia was conferred upon Berthold, almost in its present extent.[1] This arrangement finally separated Swabia from Helvetia, and extinguished the very name of Alamannia. Thus the land was tranquillised, and thus the beneficent power of the princes of Zähringen was established in Helvetia. They found the land in a far from happy condition. Long and furious warfare had engendered insecurity, immorality, distress, and disorder. On the other hand, foundations, pious and useful for the times, increased in number, and promoted culture, physical and moral. The towns, too, acquired more and more importance: on the whole, the accession of the dynasty of Zähringen seemed to announce an era of more general well-being.

In the year 1152, Berthold IV stood at the head of the house of Zähringen. He had numerous dependants, but even more numerous enemies who envied his preponderant power. In order to keep these within bounds, and to strengthen himself against the nobles of Burgundy, Berthold walled in many existing hamlets, or built new towns, and gave them extraordinary privileges. In these the love of freedom, of tranquillity, or of profit, collected together a multitude of persons, who naturally adhered with steady fidelity to the duke, by whom their new position had been given and was secured to them. On the other hand, the duke intruded no one as a citizen, nor prevented any from

[1 Berthold received the office of imperial warden over the town, chapter, and district of Zurich, with the title of duke. The Zähringens later became imperial rectors of Burgundy, Conrad III of that house, in 1127, being granted this dignity by the emperor Henry V.]

changing their places of residence at pleasure; so that free and bondsmen vied with each other in pressing into the towns. The latter became free when their masters did not claim them within the term of one year, and prove their vassalage by the oath of seven witnesses. The burghers imposed taxes on themselves. They were obliged to march no farther in the wars of the duke than so that they might still sleep at home the same night. Every burgher must possess a house, as pledge of his allegiance. In good or evil fortune they stood each for all, and all for each. Thus simple were the laws and customs observed by the rising class of burghers.

These laws and regulations, indeed, were calculated, not for the general good of a state, but for a single town, and for those who belonged to it. This apparent selfishness may be pardoned, if we recollect the necessities and circumstances of the period. At the time when towns were founded, nothing like patriotism, far less zeal for the general rights of humanity, could exist. The burgher who was heartily attached to his town, and the knight who cherished love for his prince and cultivated the virtues of his order, were regarded as fulfilling their whole duty. For in those times the burgher viewed his town in the light of his fatherland, and the citizen knew no state but the court of his prince. A closer bond between the individual parts of a commonwealth, the sacrifice of private to public interests, respect for the rights of others — in a word, a general love of country — was the product of a more advanced age. Besides, the nobles and clergy strove with their whole strength to keep down the growing power of the citizens. This imposed on them the most vigilant regard to their own interests and the most complete union among themselves, so that the well-being of others could not be taken into account.

SWISS CASTLE

Berthold V followed the example of his father in laying the foundations of towns; for the dukes of Zähringen governed on a plan grounded upon, or rather prescribed by, the circumstances of the times. They found their power menaced by the nobility, and were therefore obliged to seek its humiliation. All the nobles of Burgundy revolted from the government of Berthold V, so that he was forced to live in a state of open warfare with his subjects. The duke twice defeated the insurgents.c

THE FOUNDING OF BERN (1191)

The spirit of the time of city-building is revived for us in the story of the founding of Bern — the city that grew to be the most important of them all

— as it was set down from the contemporary chronicles in the *Annales* of Michael Stettler,[n] published at Bern in 1626. It reads as follows:[a]

Berthold V, the most excellent of his race, accompanied the emperor Frederick to Syria and, as he liked not the war — called the Holy — he betook himself back from Tyre to Europe, overcame the Burgundians, and dwelt much in Little Burgundy, especially in Burgdorf, which in several old letters he calls his capital. He served the empire honourably as rector of Burgundy, ruled with might, loved justice, and so disciplined the lords of the lands subject to him that they feared him, and that subjects of the realm had to humble themselves and bow down before his power, as before one who held, next to the imperial dignity, the highest rank in German lands. The glorious duke Berthold's brave reign, his high honours and great power, at last became irksome and displeasing to certain of the lords; so much the more, because they felt that their hearts could not fashion the means whereby to repress and destroy this princely race that had risen to such a height. On the other hand, there were among the nobility of Burgundy and the Oechtland those who were well disposed towards the honourable duke; so that, out of his own impulse and at the urging of his close friends, he held steadily the purpose to build a city able to defend itself, for the checking of his haughty and defiant enemies and for the protection of his true-hearted subjects. There could not be found in these lands a more comfortable spot, according to the reports of his people, of his masters of the hunt, who upon his command had viewed all suitable places, than at a narrow place, where he had already a good castle called Nydeck. This was a peninsula nearly surrounded by the Aare. Because of its being by nature well fortified and having at hand the much needed wood for building, it was hoped that a most desirable site had been chanced upon. [This was imperial soil, a fact that from the first brought Bern into direct relation to the German Empire.]

When now the noble duke, full of great deeds, had determined to accomplish his purpose, he appointed an excellent nobleman, of the family of Bubenberg master-builder and executor of the work. Amid all this happy and praiseworthy work of building, Duke Berthold was minded to witness a merry hunting in the oak forest wherein the city was to be built. When it befell that the first wild beast that came forth to the hunters was a bear, which they, according to their wishes, slew and brought to their dear lord, he took it for a good omen, and resolved to call the new city, after the bear (bär), Bern — hoping that, as the bear is among all European four-footed beasts the strongest, the most courageous, and the most staunch, likewise the city of Bern might triumph over others that might, within or around her forests and boundaries, act wantonly toward her, and that she might bring the unseemly lot to fear and obedience. This name of Bern, moreover, fits very well the first three letters of Berthold, so that it may be supposed Bern received its name not only from the bear, but also from Berthold its founder. Much of the wood needed for building was cut upon the site itself. Not only many of the country-folk went willingly into the city, but Duke Berthold, that he might defend it from hostile onslaught by means of courageous, strong-fisted men, himself settled within it, and with him two powerful, renowned families, namely, the Müntzers of Zurich and the Müntzers of Fribourg in the Breisgau. Thereupon the lords and the nobility opposed to him became the more embittered against his power and princely happiness; yea, so that they spared not innocent youth, but secretly had poisoned his two young sons, the only hope for the preservation of his illustrious race. They were buried at Solothurn, in the choir of the church of St. Urs. Afterwards when this choir in the course of rebuilding was moved, their bones, together with those of their mother, were found there wrapped in decaying black velvet bearing certain insignia.

In the year 1218, Berthold of Zähringen, greatly renowned, exchanged the temporal for the eternal life. Before his death he gave the city of Bern, which was very dear to him, to the emperor Henry VI and into the protection of the Roman Empire. From him the city received its first liberties. The burghers of Bern bewept with hot tears this their illustrious and benevolent ruler, as a true father of his established children, an introducer of liberties, worthy of praise and fame, a planter of peace and unity, and a right, honest and true lord. Frederick the Roman king, the son of Henry VI, remembering the kindness of his imperial father toward this new city, granted it many royal liberties and rights (1218).[n]

THE FREE CITIES AND THE EMPIRE

Upon the extinction of the race of Zähringen, which had united a large portion of Switzerland under one rule, the rectorate of Burgundy reverted to the German Emperor and became extinct. Thus, many towns and dynasties were rendered immediately dependent on the empire. The towns thereby obtained the much coveted degree of independence known as imperial freedom *(Reichsfreiheit)*. Chief among those to profit by this advance toward freedom, gaining the proud title of free imperial cities *(freie Reichsstädte)*, were Zurich, Bern, and Solothurn. Other portions of Switzerland already held similar privileges. The imperial cities now began to loom large in power and wealth. Freedom in individual localities made strides that proved significant in the future progress of Swiss nationality. On the other hand, a number of lay possessions (among which were those of the counts of Savoy, Geneva, Gruyeres, Neuchâtel, Lenzburg, Habsburg, Rapperschwyl, and Toggenburg) and spiritual properties (as, for instance, those of the bishops of Geneva, Sion, Lausanne, Bâle, Constance, Coire; of the abbots of St. Gall, Einsiedeln, and Muri) had acquired considerable independence and power. The large estates of the extinct house of Zähringen fell to the already powerful counts of Kyburg, and their possessions came later into the hands of their relatives the Habsburgs.[a]

In 1273, Rudolf of Habsburg was, by universal consent, elected emperor, and the archbishop of Cologne proclaimed on the occasion that Rudolf was "wise, just, and beloved of God and man." After leading a wild and irregular life in his youth, Rudolf had later fully retrieved his character. He was, in general, a favourite with the towns, who, amidst the troubles of the interregnum, had felt thankful for the countenance and protection of so powerful a chief. Zurich had chosen him to command its militia, on being threatened by his neighbour Ulrich, baron of Regensburg. Rudolf defeated the baron, and obliged him to seek forgiveness of the citizens. He was not, however, on such friendly terms with the people of Bâle. The misunderstanding originated in some disputes he had with the bishop of that city; and an affray which occurred soon after widened the rupture. During the carnival of 1273, a number of knights and other young noblemen, the friends and dependents of Rudolf, repaired to Bâle to enjoy the festivities of that merry season. Some of them behaved rudely to the burghers' ladies, the husbands and fathers of whom rose against the insolent intruders, and killed several of them. The count of Habsburg, on receiving the dismal news, collected troops and marched against the city. While he was besieging the place, the news arrived of his election to the imperial throne. On hearing this, the citizens of Bâle came out of their walls, with every mark of respect for the new emperor, and invited him to enter their city with his troops. The past was easily forgotten: Rudolf assured the citizens of Bâle of his friendship, and they swore allegiance to him.

It was a time of wonder and rejoicing in Helvetia; the magistrates of the towns, the nobles, great and small, all repaired to Brugg, in Aargau, to congratulate the emperor. Their countryman, the valiant Rudolf, had been raised to the first throne of Europe. Rudolf, on his part, notwithstanding his elevation, the multifarious cares it brought on him, and the distance to which it removed him from his country, retained to the end of his life an affectionate regard for his brethren, the people of his native valleys. He granted Zurich a solemn pledge that that city should never be alienated from the empire. This was an important privilege in those times, when the emperors often gave away to the nobles, for pecuniary or other considerations, lands and towns belonging to the empire, as if they had been their private domain, by which means the inhabitants lost their immunities and privileges. He secured to Zurich, Schaffhausen, and Soleure the right of having their judges and avoyers taken from among themselves, and of being governed by their own municipal laws; and he bestowed on another town (Lucerne) similar franchises. These he also extended to Bienne, Aarau, Winterthur, Laupen, Diesenhoffen, and other secondary places; he moreover protected Lausanne and Fribourg against the encroachments of the counts of Savoy, asserting in that part of the country the imperial authority, under which he restored to their liberties all those who had been free before. He raised the bishop of Lausanne and the abbot of Einsiedeln to the rank of princes of the empire. He was liberal, but just and impartial, as well towards the towns as towards the nobles. On their part, the towns and the country at large showed their sense of gratitude to him by abundant supplies of men and money, in the exigencies in which he was often placed.

The city of Bern formed, unfortunately for both parties, the only exception to this good understanding. That city had acquired great importance in western Helvetia; it stood constantly in arms against the neighbouring nobles. Its fidelity to the empire having excited numerous enemies, it was compelled, during the interregnum, to place itself under the protection of Philip count of Savoy, and to make alliances with Soleure, Fribourg, and other towns.

Disputes, which were then of frequent occurrence among neighbours, brought the count of Kyburg [cousin to Rudolf] to besiege Bern, but his attempt was vain. Rudolf himself, in 1288, threatened the city, under pretence of protecting the Jews, whom the Bernese had driven away; but he retired without accomplishing anything. The same year, the Bernese defeated the baron of Weissenburg, took his castle of Wimmis, and destroyed that of Jagdberg, taking the knight of Blankenburg prisoner, who was afterwards received as a citizen of Bern. The following year Albert, son of Rudolf, known by the name of Albert of Austria, endeavoured to take Bern by surprise; but being discovered, he was himself attacked by the citizens; and after a severe engagement, in which many of the burghers fell, though their banner was saved by a desperate effort of valour, Albert, struck with regard for the bravery of the Bernese, made peace with them.[m]

CHAPTER II

THE RISE OF THE SWISS CONFEDERATION

[1291–1402 A.D.]

It is specially needful to bear in mind, first, that, till the last years of the thirteenth century, not even the germ of modern Switzerland had appeared on the map of Europe; secondly, that the Confederation did not formally become an independent power till the seventeenth century; lastly, that, though the Swiss name had been in common use for ages, it did not become the formal style of the Confederation till the nineteenth century. It is no less needful to root out the notion that the Swiss of the original cantons in any way represent the Helvetii of Cæsar. The points to be borne in mind are: that the Swiss Confederation is simply one of many German leagues, which was more lasting and became more closely united than other German leagues; that it gradually split off from the German kingdom; that in the course of this process the league and its members obtained a large body of Italian and Burgundian allies and subjects; lastly, that these allies and subjects have in modern times been joined into one federal body with the original German confederates.—FREEMAN.[c]

NATURE AND MAN IN THE WALDSTÄTTE

At the foot and towards the centre of the Alps, which form a sort of natural wall between Germany and Italy, there lies on the northern side a deep-sunk lake, cut up into several basins, upon which open out three valleys, separated from one another by this sheet of water or by lofty and steep mountains. Watered by torrential rivers or by insignificant streamlets, divided at increasing heights into ever-narrowing valleys, shut in by steep inclines — above which mount, even to the region of snow, meadows, forests, and rocks — these valleys afford but little space for the cultivation of the soil, and are even in this respect unequally favoured.

The herds are here the principal source of wealth: one finds more shepherds than mechanics and labourers. Cattle-raising, dairying, the chase, and fishery furnish the natural resources of these harsh and picturesque regions. They cannot be inhabited except by robust peoples, content with little, having simple and rude habits, for everyone must be sufficient to himself, and in need count on nothing but his own strength. Incessantly in combat with nature, to which they must look for everything they hope for and everything they fear, the inhabitants of these secluded places contract in this struggle a sort of jealous love for all the possessions which they

[853 A.D.]

are obliged unceasingly to defend. That which they have snatched from floods, avalanches, storms, and abysses, in boldly risking their lives, they do not intend to see menaced or lessened by the encroachments of a neighbour or by the demands of a master. If necessary, they will make war on men as well as on the elements. In this combat against nature they feel, on the one hand, that everything depends on their own efforts and their perseverance — which renders them self-confident — and that, on the other hand, everything depends on a supreme divine will — which renders them patient and religious. As life in the open air of the Alps and in the fields fortifies their bodies, so the uniformity of their habits gives to their character a sort of moral serenity which preserves, and hands down from generation to generation, sentiments and tastes whose long duration is their strength. The simplicity and the small amount of variety of their way of living favour the spirit of equality among them, while the small number of new ideas put into circulation in their midst preserves them, longer than other people, from the love of innovations.

Reduced from of old, for all means of communication with the world, to the mountain paths or the difficult navigation of a stormy lake, this sort of seclusion has naturally drawn them close together among themselves. From this spirit of association and of mutual aid, which they possess in a high degree, accompanied as it is by isolation of the individual — a natural result of the pastoral life — there develops in each one of them a courageous independence. It is thus, by the configuration of the land as well as by the habits of the people, that these little valleys seem to have been providentially destined to become, in the centre of Europe, the cradle and one of the fortresses of liberty.*d*

ORIGINS OF THE SWISS CONFEDERATION

In various city communities, but above all, among the apparently insignificant peasant associations on the Lake of Lucerne (Lake of the Four Forest Cantons), the Habsburg rule had from the beginning met with peculiar difficulties, which set barriers to its perfect sway. There, in the secluded Alpine valleys, a vigorous tree had risen, which was spreading its branches ever farther, to afford a refuge for popular freedom against the demands of princely power.

Frequently it has been emphasised in historical delineations that nature favoured the development of unique political organisations in the centre of the Switzerland of to-day. For centuries, every district touching upon the Lake of Lucerne was a separate little world, in which the conditions of public and private right shaped themselves in peculiar fashion. All three lands — the valley of Uri, bounded by mighty mountains of rock; the fields of Schwyz, spreading out at the foot of the Mythen; and the irregularly branching tracts of Unterwalden — were, on the other hand, drawn together into closer relations by the lake with its numerous indentations. Moreover, by means of its western connecting arm they were directed, for communication with the outside world, towards neighbouring Lucerne and the level plains lying further down. Thus the valleys of the original Switzerland, walled round by the High and Middle Alps, were formed into a federative nucleus, to which, gradually, new members in the open country joined themselves. It is impossible to determine with exactness the time in which the districts of central Switzerland, remote as they were from the great routes of travel of the earlier Middle Ages, were first peopled by their Alamannian inhabitants.

Uri

Uri first emerges into the light of history. Ludwig the German, July 21, 853, gave to the Fraumünster abbey at Zurich, in addition to other royal estates, the little land of Uri, *pagellus Uroniœ*. We find, in the thirteenth century, other owners of land in the valley. It is, moreover, beyond doubt that considerable land — especially in the Schächenthal, which branches off toward the east — was the personal property of·freemen, and that these free farmers, together with the dependents of the abbey *(Gotteshausleute)*, of Fraumünster, who were enjoying a mild rule, essentially determined the later fortunes of Uri.

Uri was a part of the Zurichgau, which, since the second half of the ninth century, had been separated from the Thurgau. The people of Fraumünster, because of the immunity that the chapter enjoyed by grant of the emperor, were subject to the imperial bailiwick of Zurich. The jurisdiction of the imperial bailiff probably extended not only to those belonging to the abbey, but also to all inhabitants of the valley, however they might differ in station; so that, at the time of the Zähringens, the inhabitants of the district appeared in their relation to the bailiff and the empire as a unit, having a common set of laws. Still more significant, however, was the circumstance that the population of Uri, from the mouth of the Reuss to the height of Schöllenen, constituted — according to the customs of the old Alamannian settlers — an association of the mark *(Markgenossenschaft)*, which from time to time met in common assembly to settle questions concerning the use of the forest and pasture composing the *Almend*, or common land. Thus there gradually came to be a "community of the people of Uri," and the sense of unity was kept alive among the members of the markgenossenschaft. It was, moreover, difficult to prevent them from taking under consideration, in addition to the transactions strictly concerning the common holdings, matters of a general nature. These peasants found in their economic freedom the germ of a movement toward a freer political activity.

The dukes of Zähringen, in accordance with their known dynastic intentions, were in a good way to convert their official relations [as representatives of the empire] with the abbey of Zurich and its dependencies into full territorial jurisdiction, when with the death of Berthold V, in 1218, everything received a different aspect and direction. King Frederick II dissolved the imperial bailiwick of Zurich, and among other things, expressly reclaimed for the empire the stewardship of the chapter of Fraumünster — an event which had a decisive significance for the possessions of the chapter. In Uri, the abbey retained only its landed property and revenues, whereas the sovereignty and judicial rights probably at once went over to the counts of Habsburg, who, since the extinction of the Lenzburgers, had entered upon the government of the landgrafschaft in the southern part of the Zurichgau. The Gotteshausleute of Uri thereby virtually lost their immunity, and the whole valley was threatened with the danger — made the more imminent by the weakening of the imperial authority — of becoming a hereditary possession of this race of rulers of the Aargau, then already vigorously extending its power on all sides. Just then King Henry, the son of Frederick II, prompted by some cause which cannot now be determined with certainty — probably the influence of former subjects of the abbey, the freemen, and the remaining landowners — declared in a document, made out at Hagenau, May 26th, 1231, that he took "his faithful, all the men of the valley of Uri (*"homines in Valle Uraniae"*) out of the possession of Count

Rudolf I of Habsburg, and brought them directly and inalienably under the rule of the empire. By virtue of this letter, Uri was from this time on an immediate dependency of the empire. Ordinarily, the lord of the empire dealt directly with a "minister" or *Ammann* (high bailiff), who was chosen from among the people of the country. By the side of the old markgenossenschaft arose a form of political association *(Gemeinschaft)* which, as was in the nature of things and common to the individualizing endeavors of all dependencies of the empire at that time, rapidly took a direction towards independence. The community, under its ammann, levied common taxes for the needs of the country, and since the year 1243 bore its own seal, which carried as emblem a steer's head with a nose-ring. In the year 1291 we meet with the title *Landammann* for that of ammann.

When Rudolf was made king, he recognised without hesitation, in indubitable and hearty terms, the immediate dependence of the people of Uri on the empire. In a charter dated January 8th, 1274, he assured his "loyal, excellent people" that under no circumstances would he pledge them or in any way alienate them, since he regarded them as special wards of the empire. What had been done in 1231 received new force with this new instrument, and in the sequel the imperial freedom of the people of Uri was never seriously disputed.

Schwyz

In Schwyz circumstances shaped themselves in quite a different manner, up to the time of King Rudolf of Habsburg. The old nucleus of the land of Schwyz included originally only the neighbourhood of the hamlet of Schwyz with the Muota Valley. Here, too, non-resident chapters and lay principalities held landed property with unfree tenants. Various estates belonged to the monasteries of Kappel, Muri, Schänis, Engelberg, and Einsiedeln. Two larger farms were the property of the counts of Lenzburg, and came finally, apparently by inheritance, into the hands of the Habsburgs. By far the most important part of the land, however, was held by free peasants, who were subject to no kind of territorial jurisdiction. These formed the deciding element of the population. The free peasants, as well as the dependents of the spiritual and lay rulers, were in Schwyz also bound together as a markgenossenschaft, by their common interest as owners of land in the almend; and this unity of their economic interests prepared the future equable union of the various classes of the people.

The land was subject to the judicial authority of the counts of the Zurichgau — *i.e.*, to the end of the twelfth century, to the Lenzburgers — and to them, as bailiffs, the Schwyzers had to pay a considerable tax. Thus, the same persons here, on the one hand, held territorial rights, while, on the other, they represented by their office the authority of the empire. In the twelfth century, the counts of Lenzburg twice appeared in their capacity as land-owners before the imperial court, to bring suit on behalf of their associates of the common mark against the abbot of Einsiedeln. For from early times, at least from the days of King Henry II, dated the obstinate quarrel of the Schwyzers with the monks, concerning the use of forest-covered boundary lands by the sources of the Alp and the Sihl, to which both neighbours by means of continual clearing had gradually advanced. King Henry V (1114) and King Conrad III (1144) decided in favour of the monastery; and the Lenzburgers, with their associates, had to pay a fine and damages. But the Schwyzers seem to have cared little for such awards, and without regarding natural boundaries, apparently continued always to keep an eye to the free extension of their almend toward the north and northeast.

When the power of the Lenzburgers had come to an end, their territorial rights in the landgrafschaft fell to the house of Habsburg. Rudolf I, in 1217, in his position as count, or as he designated himself, "by true inheritance rightful bailiff and protector of the people of Schwyz," pronounced a judgment in the newly re-opened quarrel between Schwyz and Einsiedeln. The decision was somewhat more favourable for the Schwyzers than the previous awards.

CASTLE OF LAUSANNE (1840)

(Founded in the thirteenth century)

Accordingly, there must have been at that time a good understanding between the free peasants and the Habsburgs. When, after the death of Count Rudolf, fifteen years later, his two sons divided the paternal possessions, the younger, Rudolf II — the founder of the Laufenburg line — came into the rights of the landgrafschaft of the valley at the southern foot of the Mythen. From this time on, the relationship of the Schwyzers to the holders of the sovereign power became troubled, so that the country people hit upon the thought of following the example of their neighbours in Uri, and completely withdrawing themselves from the rule of Habsburg. The uncertain attitude which Count Rudolf assumed toward his imperial master when, in 1239, the latter was excommunicated, gave them the desired occasion for a bold step. They sent messengers and letters across the Alps to the emperor, who was besieging Faenza — perhaps also sent him a company of men — and declared that they of their own free will desired to be under the government of the realm itself, and to come under the sheltering wings of the empire as free men, who otherwise owed no allegiance.

Frederick granted the wish of "the united men of the valley of Schwyz" ("Universis hominibus vallis in Swites"), by means of a letter issued in December, 1240. This, the oldest charter of freedom of the Waldstätte, extant in the original, is still preserved, like a priceless gem, in the public archives of Schwyz. The emperor took them under his special protection, and gave them the assurance that at no time should they be alienated or withdrawn from the authority of the empire. We must not, however, rate the significance of this document too highly. For, at bottom, the emperor did not employ a binding form, and was careful not to express explicitly the exemption of the

valley of Schwyz from the landgrafschaft. He found, moreover, the less
cause to give definite form to the new arrangement of immediate jurisdiction
by the empire by means of a bailiff, as Count Rudolf, in the succeeding years,
beginning with 1242, again openly took the emperor's part. Thus the charter
remained at first ineffective for the Schwyzers. When, relying upon the charter, they rose in revolt, they failed to obtain aid from the emperor. They
were obliged again to swear allegiance to Count Rudolf, and to bind themselves thereafter to remain quietly under his rule, and to hold neither to the
emperor Frederick nor to any other ruler in opposition to Rudolf.

Soon thereafter began the general world-moving struggle between empire
and papacy. Its traces may be followed even to the shores of the Lake of
Lucerne. When Count Rudolf II of Habsburg, after the formal pronunciation of the papal anathema and the deposal of Frederick II at the council of
Lyons (1245), went over into the papal camp, the Schwyzers took up arms
against the ruler they had but just acknowledged. They formed alliances
with the people of Unterwalden and the citizens of Lucerne; the first league
of confederates of which we have knowledge falls into these years.[1]

Strife must have raged violently for a time in the valleys; and if tradition
— particularly for its story of the good archer Tell — had fixed upon these
events, it would not have been so easy to gainsay it. Count Rudolf, in the
midst of the contest, received an order from Pope Innocent IV, in which the
provost of Ölenberg, in Sundgau, was directed to set a term for the rebellious
people of Schwyz and Sarnen in which to renounce Frederick, to unite with
the church and dutifully to acknowledge the rule of the count. If this did
not have any effect, he was to declare them and the people of Lucerne —
probably acting in common with them — under sentence of excommunication,
and subject them to the penalty of the interdict. Concerning the course of
the struggle all information is wanting. The change of personnel, however,
which occurred in the years 1249 and 1250, by the deaths of Count Rudolf
II and the emperor Frederick, prevented in any case the continuation of the
revolution in Schwyz and the communities allied with her. The Ghibelline
league on the borders of the Lake of Lucerne fell apart; the sons of Rudolf
again attained to a free exercise of their power, probably in Schwyz as well
as in Unterwalden. The attempt at insurrection had totally failed, and there
could be the less hope, at this time, of a realisation of the endeavours of Schwyz
to secure freedom as the rights of the Habsburgs, in this period of decline in
the power of the empire, were continually taking firmer root.

These were the years of the rise of Count Rudolf III — the nephew of
Rudolf II and the representative of the elder line of the house of Habsburg —
when, favoured by fortunate happenings of all sorts, he knew with a character-
istic wariness how to enlarge his lands as well as his powers of jurisdiction.
When, in 1273, the personal estates of his cousin Eberhard von Habsburg-
Laufenburg, located in the Waldstätte, came into his possession by purchase,
the rights of jurisdiction as landgraf, which the house of Habsburg claimed in
Schwyz, probably went over to him. With the elevation of Rudolf to the
German imperial throne things took an unexpected turn for the Schwyzers.
To be sure, they could not dare to believe that the new king would confirm
their charter of freedom, as it was directed against Habsburg, and at least
questionable as to its essential rightfulness and formal binding power. They
were affected, on the other hand, by the declaration that he would not
recognise the grants of Frederick II, dating from a time when he was under

[1 The document itself is lacking. The proofs of the existence of the league have been
put together by Segesser.]

sentence of excommunication. At the same time, their situation did not prove itself so unfavourable as might have been feared from the well-known dynastic policy of Rudolf. For, however effectively the Habsburgers observed the interests of their house in all directions, it cannot be said that they worked systematically toward restricting the rights of the free peasant communities. In regard to the execution of justice, Rudolf granted the Schwyzers notable concessions. He gave them the assurance that they would have to appear before no judges except himself, his sons, or the judge of the valley; and, in a letter dated February 19th, 1291, he granted them the privilege that no serf should be permitted to act as judge over them.

It was under this generally mild rule that the inborn impulse toward independent action again came to the front in Schwyz, and that the local government — if that term may be used of this early period — had an opportunity to develop into more definite form. Of the old quarrel with the monastery of Einsiedeln we, indeed, hear nothing in this period. On the other hand, a new feud arose with the convent founded in 1262 at Steinen. It is during this very quarrel with the nuns of Steinen, in 1275, that the Schwyzers first appear as a community (*universitas*). Six years later, they had their own seal, which by its inscription gave expression to their political unity.

We find at first two judges (*Ammänner*), then four, whom Rudolf appointed out of the leading families, and in the selection of whom, it appears he took into consideration the four component elements of the country — the community of the free people, the two independent principalities, and Steinen which recently had become an element. At the end of Rudolf's reign these officials were replaced by a single landammann, as representative of the royal Habsburg rule. Thus the king himself, probably in the interests of an easier administration, prepared the complete unity of the country. He could not foresee that, in this strengthening of the communal foundation in the valley of Schwyz, he was creating for the people a new and strong support.

Unterwalden

The development of public affairs in Unterwalden had been less uniform than in Uri and in Schwyz. This first named district — which, indeed, did not receive its name as a whole till the fourteenth century — exceedingly fertile in its lower portions, was divided by nature into two parts; the basins of the Sarner and the Engelberger Aa: Obwalden and Nidwalden. The property rights here, which since the times of the Carlovingians had been much sought after, received value because of the adaptation of the land to cattle-raising and Alpine dairying, as well as to agriculture. They were held in the thirteenth century by the Habsburgs, by the lower nobility, by the religious houses of Engelberg, Murbach, Lucerne, Muri, Münster in Aargau, and by numerous farmers, personally free, and living scattered in the valleys. The many widely extended landholding houses here made the uniting of the free portions of the population much more difficult than was the case in the other two Waldstätte. The administration of the landgrafschaft, as in Schwyz, was in the hands of the house of Habsburg — that is, after the death of Rudolf I, the younger line of Habsburg-Laufenburg — until, in 1273, upon the occasion of the purchase already noted, it went to Rudolf the king. To the Habsburgs, too, had fallen the wardenship of the religious houses. Only the Benedictine monastery of Engelberg preserved during the following centuries an independent position.

Already in the middle of the thirteenth century, when the Ghibelline movement had extended to the valleys about the Lake of Lucerne, the free people of Unterwalden seem to have constituted themselves a community, which, either from the beginning or later seems to have united in itself also those of the people in the neighbourhood of Sarnen who cherished similar ambitions. So far as we are able to determine, however, this community still lacked the royal privileges which its neighbours had already won for themselves.

THE EVERLASTING LEAGUE (1291 A.D.)

Such were the circumstances existing in the three lands toward the close of the reign of Rudolf. In Unterwalden, but weak germs of a growth toward freedom had been developed. Uri enjoyed the secure position of a territory exempted from the power of the counts, and directly dependent on the empire. The Schwyzers, indeed, lacked the formal acknowledgment of their imperial freedom, which had been promised half a century earlier, or the hope of which, at least, had been given them. But, as a matter of fact, they stood in direct communication with the head of the German Empire; their community had a uniform organisation, and had won weighty privileges with reference to the administration of justice. With prudent employment of external events, they now aimed to establish the permanence of these gains and, if possible, to increase them. From the Schwyzers, who at all time evinced a keen eye for the political changes in the German Empire, doubtless came the impulse for an enduring union of the communities about the Lake of Lucerne.

Hardly had news of the death of King Rudolf spread in the Waldstätte, when the country people *(Landleute)*, in view of the uncertain conditions which now arose, made common cause. Only seventeen days after the death of the king, that is, on August 1st, 1291, "the men of the valley of Uri, the association of the valley of Schwyz, and the community of the men of the forest of the lower valley"(*i.e.* Unterwalden), in view of the difficult times and for the purpose of a better defence of their interests, made an everlasting league (ewigen Bund). The three lands promised in good faith to stand by one another, with help, counsel, and favour, with body and possessions, to their full power, inside and outside of the valleys, against all hostile attacks and insults. To this they swore, renewing, as they expressed themselves, the *Antiqua Confœderatio* confirmed by oath. They added the reservation that everyone, according to his rank, should serve and obey his lord, in a proper manner. They affirmed, however, by common council and unanimous consent, that they would accept no judge in their valleys who had bought his office, or who was not an inhabitant or a native of the valleys. But if there should arise a dispute among the confederates the more sensible among them should come together and settle the quarrel according to their judgment; and if one side should then be unwilling to acquiesce in the decision, the remaining confederates should give aid to the other party to the dispute.

The three communities, moreover, included in the covenant provisions for the punishment of various crimes and common regulations as to the preservation of order in the country. "These regulations for the common welfare and safety," they concluded, "shall with God's help endure forever, and in evidence of this determination, there has been prepared, at the wish of those herein afore-mentioned, a document strengthened with the seals of the communities and valleys herein named." The venerable covenant — the oldest document of the Swiss Confederation — is still preserved in Schwyz.*e*

The Earliest League

Quite recently, Prof. H. Bresslau has brought to light fresh facts bearing upon the earliest league of the forest districts, which had been placed by most historians in the period 1245–1250.[a] His essay shows most conclusively, by a careful examination of surviving documents, that the *Antiqua Confœderatio* mentioned in the League of 1291 cannot possibly refer to the events of 1245 *et seq.*, for the simple reason that at that time Uri, Schwyz, and Unterwalden took different sides in the great strife between pope and emperor — Schwyz and Obwalden supporting the emperor, while Uri and Nidwalden stood by the pope. It is further shown that the *Antiqua Confœderatio* was not formed against the Habsburgs, but was simply an ordinary agreement to preserve peace and quiet in that particular district, having probably been made during the interregnum in the empire (1254–1273); and that it is possible in the existing text of the League of 1291 to distinguish the main features of the old league, as well as the additions made in 1291.[f]

SWISS COSTUME

(Fifteenth century)

THE WALDSTÄTTE UNDER ALBERT OF AUSTRIA

The first permanent alliance became the basis of the Confederation. This was not a revolutionary step, for it was not directed against the emperor and the empire. Like other contemporaneous leagues this one had no other object than to secure to the confederates, by means of their own united efforts, the protection which the imperial power could not give them. In this instance the members of the league were not, as was the case in Italy and Germany, wealthy cities, but simple rustics, who recognised clearly their political interests, and had the courage to defend them. The league was made "forever," and it has maintained itself without a break. While the leagues of the cities were dissolved in the course of time, the Swiss Confederation strengthened itself against danger, and acquired an irresistible power, before which went down the house of Habsburg and all its proud nobility vanishing as the stars vanish at sunrise.

Convinced that their strongest support was to be found in a union with their fellows, the Waldstätte joined the League of Zurich against Habsburg. The house of Habsburg had acquired through Rudolf the arch-duchy of

[1292–1298 A.D.]

Austria, which from that time on became the main support of Habsburg's power. The head of the house of Austria-Habsburg was at that time Albert, the son of Rudolf. When Adolf of Nassau was elected anti-king, all the enemies of Habsburg embraced his cause, and war broke out. But the men of Zurich, who had marched against the Austrian town of Winterthur, were completely defeated (April, 1292); their city was besieged by Albert, and forced to surrender.*g* Old chronicles relate that the defeat was caused by a ruse of the Austrian leader, who approached the men of Zurich under the banner of their allies, as though bringing aid, and then suddenly fell upon them; and that Albert was finally induced to make peace by seeing in the market place of the city, as he approached, large bands of warriors in armour. The warriors were women and girls accoutred as men.*a* The league against Habsburg was thus for the time being dissolved, and Lucerne and the Waldstätte were also compelled to give up the struggle. But liberty was not vanquished. The rural community of Schwyz protested against the injustice which exempted the convents from taxation. King Adolf confirmed to Uri and Schwyz their imperial liberties. In the west, the Austrian cause received a check by the victory of the Bernese at Dornbühl, in 1298. When, however, King Albert had defeated his rival, and remained sole ruler, he did not recognise the franchises of the Waldstätte and of Bern; but set himself to reestablish the Austrian power in eastern and central Switzerland by means of the Habsburg-Austrian management. The Habsburgs were once more menacing the independence of the Waldstätte when Albert was assassinated, in 1308, at Brugg, by a discontented noble — his nephew, John of Austria.*g*

In the last half-century, the writing of Swiss history has undergone a revolution with reference to the treatment of events having to do with the origin of the Confederation. We have now reached the period to which the older historians assigned the familiar story of William Tell, "the friend of freedom," the oath on the Rütli, and the expulsion of the Austrian bailiffs. The following is the narrative of the great Swiss historian, Johann von Müller, which won for these events general acceptance as authentic history.*a*

The Tradition of the Bailiffs

The death of Adolf in battle (1298) caused fear to spread throughout the mountains among all those who had held to King Adolf's party. Representatives of the Waldstätte sadly and thoughtfully returned home from Strasburg, where the king had replied to their request to have their liberties confirmed, by saying that "he intended soon to propose to them a change in their condition." Albert desired to unite all the dominions of his house. The limitations of the royal prerogative in Germany and the country communities in Austria and Styria incited him to dislike the liberties of the people as obstructions to his power.

Thus he came to send to the Waldstätte the lords Von Ochsenstein and Von Lichtenberg, with a message to the effect that they would do well for themselves and their descendants if they would put themselves under the perpetual shelter of the royal house; that the king would like to have them as his dear children; and that, having heard what brave men they were he would like to lead them to victory, and make them wealthy with booty and knighthood and feudal estates. To this the nobles and free men and all the people of the Waldstätte replied that they loved the condition of their forefathers, and wished to remain therein. They prayed the king to confirm it, as his father had done. Thereupon they sent Werner, Freiherr von Attinghausen — who, like his forefathers, was Landammann of the men of Uri — to the royal court to ask for confirmation of their liberties and for a bailiff with power over life and death. But the king, who was carrying on war against the electors, was ill to speak to. The affairs of the imperial bailiwick he turned over to the officials, whom he had on his private estates at Rotenburg and Lucerne. In order that their obedience to Austrian officials might not become a fixed duty, the people now sent again to the king to ask for an imperial bailiff. King Albert gave them Herrmann Gessler von Brunek and Beringer von Landenberg (Beringer had shown overbearing manners even at court). He gave the Waldstätte bailiffs whom they must of necessity hate; especially when these, because of poverty or greed, and emboldened by the king's evident displeasure, followed the usual oppressive ways of such magistrates. These imperial bailiffs, because they had no castle of their own, or because they were ordered by the king to do so, decided to live in the Waldstätte: Landenberg, in Unterwalden near Sarnen, while Gessler built a *Zwinghof* (manor of coercion) near Altorf in Uri.

In accordance with its conservative customs, there are among such a people many families of ancient repute that remain long in the management of communal affairs. In Schwyz, Werner Stauffacher was much respected, as his father, Rudolf, had been an honoured leader of the people, and as he himself was a farmer rich in land and well-intentioned. In such men the country people put their trust; they know them; they have known their fathers and their untarnished ancient loyalty. The people live in many hamlets, of which the houses for the most part, as among the old Germans, stand alone on meadows, on lovely hills, and by springs. They have certain implanted principles handed down from the old days; if strangers object to them, they become suspicious, and hold the more strongly to the teaching of their fathers. They hate everything that is new, for, in the monotonous life of the shepherds, every day is like the same day of preceding and succeeding years. They are sparing of speech, but remember a thing always. In their lonely huts they have much leisure for quiet thought. They exchange ideas when, on holidays, the people come down from the mountains to meet together in church. The observers of the rustic will find to this day, in Schwyz, a people proud of freedom; in the land of Unterwalden, a pious old-fashioned folk; and also in Uri, a very true-hearted people, full of the sentiment of confederacy.

When the imperial bailiffs punished every delinquent with exceeding long imprisonment, in dark towers and at a distance from the country, and when the duties upon imports into the neighbouring hereditary lands of Austria were raised, and export often was entirely forbidden, the country people sent to the king. When the younker of Wolfenschiessen, in Unterwalden, so departed from the convictions of his nearest relatives that he became the king's castellan (*Burgvogt*) at Rozberg, honest men feared yet greater treason to the country from the indiscretion of ambitious youth. All the people of the Confederation — who in orderly times were of a just and quiet mind, who were accustomed, without fear or much vexation or trouble, to live their days by their cattle in contented cheerfulness, and habituated from of old to find favour and esteem with the emperors — grew sad of heart. Despite excessive punishments, there had so far existed an appearance of justice; to explain the taxes, it was believed that necessity alone was forcing the king to extortionate measures. Faith was still rife that he cherished the people of the

Confederation, and thought highly of them.   But, because undeserving people who are thrust into unaccustomed prominence always show insolence
towards those who are not much inferior, there was, in the words and manners
of the bailiffs, an offensive boasting of their power and a haughty contempt
for the people.   They called the old honourable families "peasant nobility."
As Gessler was riding through Steinen, past Stauffacher's house, and saw
that it was built of well-hewn wood, according to the style of a rich farmer,
with many windows, painted with names and mottoes, roomy and gleaming,
he said, in the presence of Stauffacher, "Is it to be borne that peasants should
live so finely?"   When Landenberg fined a man in the Melchthal, in Unterwalden, a pair of good oxen, his servant remarked, "The peasants probably
can draw the plough themselves."

At Schwanau, on the Lake of Lowerz, in Schwyz, there lived a burgvogt
who seduced the daughter of a man of Art.   The burgvogt was slain by the
brothers of the girl.   One morning, as Wolfenschiess [burgvogt at Rozberg]
came forth from Engelberg, he saw upon a flowery meadow a beautiful woman.
When he had, by questioning her, discovered that her husband, Conrad von
Baumgarten, was away from home, he ordered that a bath be prepared for
him, and tried many acts whereby her honour was imperilled.   At last,
under the pretence of going to divest herself of her clothes, she sought her
husband, by whom Wolfenschiess was killed.   Before Baumgarten was discovered, or the killing of the burgvogt could be avenged, Margareta Herlobig,
the wife of Stauffacher, was thinking with disquiet how this violent man
[Gessler] envied her her house.   She talked it over with her husband, and
persuaded him to provide against the threatening disaster.   Werner Stauffacher crossed the lake to the land of Uri, to his friend Walther Fürst of Attinghausen, a rich farmer.   With the latter he found secreted a young man of
courage and good sense, who was said by Walther to be from Melchthal in
Unterwalden.   His name was Erni (Arnold) von der Halden, and he was related
to his host.   For some trifling act of Erni's, Landenberg had fined him a
yoke of fine oxen; and his father had much lamented the loss.   Then the
bailiffs' servant had said that, if the peasants would eat bread, they might
draw the plough themselves.   This had made Erni's blood boil, and he had
broken one of the servant's fingers with his stick — which was the cause of
his hiding here.   In the mean time, the bailiff had had the eyes of Erni's
father put out.

In talking of this, the three men voiced their common grief that justice
was being more and more trodden under foot; and Walther testified that
the much experienced master of Attinghausen had said that the innovations
were becoming unbearable.   They well believed that resistance would bring
cruel revenge upon the Waldstätte, but they were one in the sentiment that it
were better to endure death than an unjust yoke.   With these thoughts,
they decided that each should sound his friends and relatives.

The Oath on the Rütli

That they might see one another in safety, they picked out the Rütli, a
grassy mead upon a height in a lonely region near the Lake of Lucerne, not
far from the boundary between Unterwalden and Uri (on the spot where the
Mythenstein stands solitary).   There they often took counsel together, in
the stillness of night, concerning the liberation of the people, and brought
news to one another as to how they progressed in preparing for this deed.
Thither came Fürst and Erni von der Halden of Melchthal by lonely paths;

Stauffacher in his boat; and from Unterwalden, the son of Stauffacher's sister, the squire of Rudenz. From various hamlets, they brought friends to the Rütli. There, without fear, one entrusted to another his thoughts. The more dangerous the deed, the more firmly were their hearts bound together.

On the night of Wednesday before St. Martin's-Day, 1307, Fürst, Von der Halden, and Stauffacher each brought to this spot ten honourable men of his land, men who had honestly opened their hearts to all three of them. When these three-and-thirty stout-hearted men, full of the consciousness of their inherited freedom and everlasting bond of brotherhood, and united by the dangers of the times, were gathered on the Rütli, they feared neither King Albert nor the might of Austria. In this night they gave one another their hands, and made a pledge to the effect that in these matters none of them would undertake anything upon his own judgment; none would forsake the others, they would in this friendship live and die; each would, upon common counsel, so uphold the innocent people of his own valley in their ancient rights that all the Confederate people forever might have the benefit of this friendship; they would not alienate from the counts of Habsburg the smallest part of all their estates, their rights, or their own people; the bailiffs, their retinue, their servants and soldiery, should not lose a drop of blood; but the freedom which they had received from their forefathers they would preserve and hand down to their descendants.

When all were firmly resolved upon this, and each looked at his friend with a resolute countenance and held him fast with a loyal hand-clasp, knowing that upon their good or ill fortune would probably depend the fate of all those that were to come after them, Walther Fürst, Werner Stauffacher, and Erni von der Halden of Melchthal raised their hands toward heaven, and took an oath in the name of God — God who has brought forth emperors and peasants from the same stem, and gifted all with inalienable human rights — manfully to preserve this freedom together. When the thirty heard this, each of them also raised his hand and took the oath in the name of God and the saints. As to the manner of fulfilling their purpose, all were united. Then each went to his cottage, kept quiet, and looked after the wintering of his cattle.

William Tell

It now happened that the bailiff Herrmann Gessler was shot dead by William Tell — a man from Uri, of the hamlet Bürglen — the son-in-law of Walther Fürst. He was one of those bound by the oath. The bailiff, because of a tyrant's natural suspicions, or because of a warning of disturbances to come, undertook to discover those who bore his rule the least patiently. A hat was to represent the dignity of the duke, and the friends of freedom were to be forced to offer obeisance to that though they would not obey the ruler himself.

A youth, Tell, a friend of freedom, scorned to bow before the meaningless symbol, the hat; and as a result he was compelled to shoot an apple from the head of his son. After this feat, the feeling that God was with him took possession of Tell; and he confessed that had he failed in the enterprise, he would have avenged his son. The bailiff, fearing Tell's relatives and friends, did not dare to keep him prisoner in Uri for this, but carried him across the Lake of Lucerne (thus violating the rights of the people, which forbade imprisonment outside of the country). When they had got just beyond the Rütli, the Föhn,[1] with its peculiar force, suddenly broke forth from the gorges

[1 A storm of the Alps.]

of the Gotthard. The narrow lake tossed its angry waves high; the depth roared, and the mountains reverberated with the clamour. In this great danger of death, Gessler, filled with proper apprehension, ordered that the fetters be removed from William Tell, a strong and mighty man, whom he knew to be an excellent oarsman. They rowed in fear past the dreaded rocky cliffs, and came as far as the Axenberg, to the right as one is leaving Uri. At this spot, Tell grasped his cross-bow and, leaping, gained a flat rock, whence he climbed the mountain side. The boat rebounded from the shore. Tell fled through the land of Schwyz. The bailiff, too, escaped the storm; but when he had landed near Küssnacht, he fell in a pass, shot down by the arrows of Tell. Herrmann Gessler met this end before the hour determined upon for the liberation of the country, by the righteous anger of a free man.

In the first hour of the year 1308 a youth from Unterwalden, of the number of those who had sworn to undertake the liberation of the Waldstätte, was by a domestic in the castle of Rozberg drawn up with a rope to her room. In the ditch of the castle twenty friends of the lad were waiting, and were drawn up by him with this rope over the wall. The young men took the commander of the place, his people, and four knights prisoners, took possession of the gate, and remained quiet. Early in the day, when the bailiff Landenberg, in Sarnen, was going down from the castle to mass, he was met by twenty men from Unterwalden with calves, goats, lambs, chickens, and rabbits, for a New Year's gift, in accordance with ancient custom in the mountains and the neighbouring lands. The bailiff, pleased by the presents, let the peasants bring them into the castle. When the twenty were within the gate, one of them blew his horn; and upon this signal each of them took from his bosom an iron, and stuck it upon his long pointed stick. From the alder-bushes thirty of their fellows ran, through the water, to the castle, and together they took the inmates prisoners. Then they made a signal, whereupon the whole country of Unterwalden came together from all the hamlets, in a united movement for the preservation of liberty. From alp to alp travelled the signals agreed upon. Then the men of the Uri took the Zwinghof. Then Stauffacher and all the people of Schwyz met at the Lake of Lowerz. There they soon got possession of the castle of Schwanau. Upon the Lake of Lucerne the hastening messengers met one another, bringing their good tidings.

On this day, when the blind father in Melchthal was again glad of his life, and the wife in Alzellen was happy over the home-coming of her husband; when Walther Fürst openly honoured his son-in-law, and, in Steinen, Stauffacher's wife kept open house for all who were with him on the Rütli and at Lowerz, not a drop of blood was shed, and no lord was robbed of a single right, in the first moment of the feeling of freedom regained, after the castles had been broken. When Landenberg, fleeing from the church through the fields, from Sarmen toward Alpnach, was overtaken, he was compelled, like the others from the castles, to take a solemn oath that he would not again come into the Waldstätte. He returned to the king. The Swiss people, on the following Sunday, met together, and confirmed by oath the ancient Everlasting League.[k]

Critical Survey of the Tradition

A literature has sprung up out of the controversy over the authenticity of the preceding narrative. The following sketch represents in brief the conception of the whole matter which is general among historians of the present day.[a]

The remembrance of the glorious events of the liberation lived during centuries in the memory of the people, and, for want of chroniclers, was handed down from generation to generation.   In this way, facts were misrepresented, and little by little, the course of events was reported rather as the people imagined it to have been than according to the true nature of things.   By degrees it was forgotten that Swiss freedom was a gradual development, rising by successive stages upon the groundwork of the primitive legal condition of the Swiss people — just as the cities had acquired, step by step, their rights and franchises.   The various revolts against the house of Habsburg (1245–1273 and 1291–1315) were fused in the recollections of the people into a single sudden revolution; and, in order to justify this revolution, it was referred to a time when the character of the struggle was that of a defence of sacred rights against an impious despotism. The imagination of the people then demanded particular episodes, suited to each of the events of that struggle, and found them in the local legends. All similar accounts, gathered up at home or abroad — whatever still remained of the most distantly related recollections— were fastened on to the exploits properly belonging to the struggle for freedom.   Thus the quarrels of the peasants with the lords of Küssnacht and the assassination of one of them were joined to events that had occurred in the Waldstätte.   The story of Tell's shooting of the apple from his son's head is to be found in Spanish,

A Swiss Mountain Shrine

Norwegian, English, and Indo-Germanic legends. It goes back to times much more remote than that of the *Song of Tell*, of 1474.   Legend does not trouble itself about dates, and mixes events remote and of different ages, just as the poem of the Nibelungen puts into the same scene Attila and Theodoric, and combines in a single story popular tales whose origins are widely different. The historians of the fifteenth century (Justinger, 1420; Hämmerlin, 1450; the *Chronicle of the White Book*, of Obwalden [Sarnen], in 1470; the *Chronicle of Lucerne*, by Melchior Russ, 1482; Etterlin of Lucerne, in 1507) have embellished the facts, and have added to them unauthentic information; several of

[1308 A.D.]

them, indeed, have not hesitated to change the documents in order to prove the truth of their narratives. Nevertheless, there remained differences among the traditions, and even contradictory versions. The narratives are not even in accord among themselves, either as to the dates of the events or as to their causes and the persons who played a *rôle* in them. While some of them (Hämmerlin is among these) grant a general rising, provoked by the tyranny of the bailiffs, others attribute the deliverance of the Swiss solely to the action of Tell (the *Song of Tell*, in 1474, and the *Chronicle* of Russ); or, again, they represent Tell as one of the three confederates (*Drama of Uri*, in 1511).

The historian Ægidius Tschudi,[1] of Glarus (1505–1572), endeavoured to do away with all these differences. Obedient to an ardent patriotism, he wished, by a brilliant and thrilling composition, to set the glory of the Confederation in a bright light. He treated the history of the foundation of the league with perfect freedom, like an epic poem, a romance, or as G. Meyer von Kronau says, "like a historical painting, whose heroic figures the painter groups in such a way as to obtain the desired effect." He placed the insurrection in the period that seemed to him most suitable (in 1307 and 1308, immediately before the death of Albert), and has given the dates to a day, although even the most ancient authors had not determined them. He has added new names (among others the Christian name of Herrmann and the designation "of Bruneck" to Gessler's name; Walther Fürst, Beringer von Landenberg; Conrad Baumgarten, Arnold an der Halden, Wolfenschiess, etc.). He sought to reconcile the contradictions of the first chroniclers, and has well arranged all the effects of his dramatic subjects. Thus were produced little by little the stirring recitals of the taking of the oath on the Rütli, of the expulsion of the bailiffs, and the story of Tell, of Gessler, and of Stauffacher, which Johann von Muller, by his *History of Switzerland*, and Schiller, by his beautiful drama *Wilhelm Tell*, have rendered so popular that they are still the common property of all the world.

But when J. Eutych Kopp, professor at Lucerne, in 1835 published the documents bearing on the birth of the Confederation, the inaccuracies of those narratives were plainly seen. It was thus proved that the enfranchisement took place little by little, by the securing and confirmation of imperial charters, that the Everlasting League was formed in 1291, that the Gesslers and the Landenbergers never had anything to do with the Waldstätte, etc. These documents show, above all, that the destruction of the strongholds of the vassals of Habsburg could have occurred only in the middle of the thirteenth century (1247–1252). The most ancient accounts (Justinger), moreover, agree with this.

It appears, at any rate, from the documents, that tradition has faithfully preserved certain isolated recollections, and that it has accurately outlined the *rôle* played by the family of Stauffacher as landammann of Schwyz and by Werner of Attinghausen as the head of Uri. Since Kopp, historians no longer confine themselves to denying the traditions, but go on to explain their origin (as Vischer and Meyer von Kronau) and to disentangle truth from error.*g*

Evidence for the Tradition; Its Significance

The last word, apparently, has not yet been said concerning the authenticity of the traditional narrative of the struggle of the people of the Waldstätte against the Austrian bailiffs. Thus, for instance, a recent paper of

[1 " The Plutarch and the Herodotus of Swiss history." — RILLIET.]

Dr. Th. von Liebenau holds out some promise of rehabilitation as history to certain portions of the so-called legendary account.*a* Doctor Liebenau has shown that, in 1283, the emperor Rudolf of Habsburg gave the right of receiving the tolls for escort over the St. Gotthard Pass to his sons, the dukes of Austria. The levying of these tolls gave rise to various disputes between the men of Uri and the bailiffs of the dukes of Austria; and by 1319 (if not already in 1309) the claim to levy them was silently given up. But these facts show (what could not hitherto be proved), that at the time where legend places the rising of Uri, Tell's exploit, etc., the dukes of Austria really had disputes with Uri.*f*

Ever wider will spread the circles of those who have become accustomed to the conception that the story of the origin of the Confederation, in its old customary form, is internally devoid of support as a means to the understanding of historic facts, as it contradicts truth, and is therefore no longer to be included in the history of the country. The Tell episode they will completely shut out, and in regard to the rest — the tradition of the league of the Rütli — they will have to admit that it is now no longer possible to extract from it its historic kernel, the recollection of events occurring about 1247. But they will console themselves with the thought that not all these beautiful legends are to be cast aside, as the idle invention of the learned, as has been proposed in recent times; but that, on the contrary, in them has been preserved a priceless memento of the plastic tradition, of the poetic activities of several generations of the Swiss people.

But incomparably greater will be their gratification on realizing that, instead of legends, attractive, to be sure, yet having their beginnings veiled in mist, history has provided them a picture of the founders of the Swiss Confederation — a picture as beautiful as ever a people could desire of the originators of its government. Unshaken steadfastness in persevering towards the aim once selected, courage that suffered no abatement in spite of numerous disappointments, clear understanding of the necessary unification of the elements of political life — until then unequally distributed — wisdom that chose an alternation in the use of prudent moderation and active resoluteness: these are the characteristics that brought into unity the country people of Uri, Schwyz, and Unterwalden. The existence of these things is taught us by the original documents, on which is built up the earliest history of the Swiss leagues. Such a gain for history undoubtedly much outweighs the too great emphasis laid upon the solitary whirring of a death-dealing bow-string.*l*

HENRY VII AND THE FOREST DISTRICTS

We have spoken of the murder, on May 1st, 1308, of King Albert by his nephew, John of Austria, and fellow-conspirators. After an interregnum of seven months Count Henry of Luxemburg was elected Albert's successor. Although the latter, directly after his election and again after his coronation, had promised the dukes of Austria to grant them all the feudal rights which they or their ancestors had possessed under the kings Rudolf, Adolf, and Albert, and to protect them against all attacks; he nevertheless assumed a hostile attitude toward the dukes, probably incited thereto by the archbishop Peter of Mainz, the most irreconcilable enemy of Austria. Almost a whole year had passed since his accession, before he visited the lands of the upper Rhine and the lake of Geneva; and he still delayed to grant their *enfeoffment* and pronounce the ban of the law against the murderers of their father and king.

[1309–1311 A.D.]

The inhabitants of the forest districts, who never lost sight of the general relations of the empire, endeavoured to utilize for themselves this disposition of the king, and sent ambassadors to him at Constance. With open contempt for the solemn promise repeatedly given by him to the dukes, Henry VII, on June 3rd, 1309, confirmed to the inhabitants of Uri and also of Schwyz the charter of freedom given by Frederick II and King Adolf in 1240 and 1297, thus acknowledging them immediate states of the empire. He went even further than this, and as if Unterwalden had always been in the same position as Uri and Schwyz, he treated it, too, as an immediate state of the empire. At the same time the king granted to all three countries, though on conditions, the privilege of not being liable to be brought before any secular court outside their own valleys, with the exception of the king's supreme court. The king appointed as governor and guardian Count Werner of Homburg, who, however, was recalled before a year had expired. After this, no special governor was appointed for the forest districts, and they were probably subject to the governor of the countries south of the Rhine, Count Rudolf of Habsburg Laufenburg, and afterwards Eberhard of Bürglen. The inhabitants of Schwyz had, for the third time, reached the goal they had striven for with such admirable perseverance during two generations, and had a better prospect than ever of maintaining their connection with the empire; the people of Uri, though probably not without anxiety about their political freedom when the Habsburgs should be in a position to establish their sovereignty all around, had been firm allies of Schwyz for many years; the inhabitants of Unterwalden, who until now perhaps had not stood in close connection with the people of Schwyz, and had not signed the league with Zurich in 1291, were forced, in their own interest, to unite themselves closely with the other valley states, as then they could expect help from the king against Austria should the need arise.

However justifiable were the complaints of the dukes at the infringement of their rights — for the king had destroyed their power not only in Schwyz, but also in Unterwalden — they were not in a position at the time even to dream of restoring their prestige by force of arms. Occupied with bringing the king's murderers to justice, they were glad not to be attacked by the inhabitants of the forest districts and their governor, Werner of Homburg. Even when they had become completely reconciled with the king, and had avenged in blood the murder of their king and father, they employed no violent measures against the valleys, but sought to be reinstated in their rights by the king himself. By their faithful service, and particularly by the brilliant bravery of Duke Leopold — who accompanied the king to Rome, and distinguished himself in the dangerous rising of the Milanese against the Germans, on the 12th of February, 1311 — their relations with Henry VII became much more friendly. At last Leopold was able, in the camp before Brescia, on the 15th of June, to petition the king to reinstate him and his brothers in the possession of the property and rights which were their due in Alsace, and in the valleys of Schwyz and Uri. The king who, as he explained, was not fully acquainted with the rights which he and the empire had there, appointed the noble Eberhard of Bürglen to make a full inquiry into the matter, while Leopold made Count Frederick of Loggenburg his representative. The king promised, after official examination, to restore to the dukes all the goods and rights which they and their ancestors from time immemorial had held by hereditary right, and in the quiet possession of which King Rudolf had been count, and King Albert duke, by virtue of inheritance or purchase.

The hopes of the dukes to recover possession of their lands and rights by lawful means, without recourse to arms, were not fulfilled, however. Henry was too much engaged in Italian affairs, and was in too great need of men there, to think of allowing Eberhard of Bürglen to return home in order to examine into the legal rights and relations of the forest districts. The Austrian dukes, therefore, applied to Henry's son, King John of Bohemia — the imperial administrator in Germany — who promised them, on the 25th of July, 1312, to try to induce the emperor to fulfil the promises made before Brescia, by Candlemas, the next year; and, in default of this, to take proceedings himself, as imperial administrator, for their fulfilment. At the same time, he promised to assist them with two hundred men should they find that any command of his was disobeyed in Swabia.

But, before the matter had proceeded any farther on this path, fraught with danger to the freedom of the forest districts, death carried off the emperor, on August 24th, 1313, and the condition of things was essentially changed.[m]

THE ATTACK ON THE ABBEY OF EINSIEDELN

At the time of the election to the German throne, in 1314, the Schwyzers found the time favourable for renewing their old-time quarrel with the great abbey of Einsiedeln, of which Frederick the Handsome of Habsburg was the hereditary "advocate" or patron. A midnight raid made on the abbey by the Schwyzers, January 6th, 1314, had serious consequences. Rudolf von Radegg,[n] "the school-master" — a monk of the abbey and himself a captive of the mountaineers — gives us a vivid though probably much prejudiced picture of the Schwyzers of that day, in an account of the affair in his curious Latin poem *Capella Eremitana*.

"There is a nation that is no nation," he begins, "men who cannot be called men, but wild beasts. This nation inhabits a valley called Schwyz, and is hardened in evil unto damnation, for God himself has given it up. It is perverse, bad — worse, worst. It is spared in order that it may hereafter suffer heaped-up ills. It carries on wild wars — ever thirsty for blood — turns from the good, and cherishes all that is bad. It abuses the people, and does much harm to the brothers of the abbey. It has torn from the brothers by force of arms many a lucrative piece of land belonging to this house of God. But the abbot, although not warlike, has yet withstood them. He summons them, then excommunicates them, and hurls at them the lightning of his curse. Finally he interdicts them; but no judgment, no interdict, terrifie ᵗhem so that they give that which they have stolen in tithes to the Lorᵈ Thus, the abbot trusts in his right, and they in their weapᵒⁿ

ᵢevers are celebrating the feast of Epiphany, and are praying to the Lᵒᵣᵈ for enduring peace. These people, however, scorn the holy day; they are busy plotting evil deeds. The sun goes down, but the other heavenly orbs are shining. At midnight, these people approach us and occupy the ways leading to the house. The warder in the tower strikes his bell, and this sound tells the sheep that the wolves are at hand. The whole swarm quickly surrounds the building, in order that none of us may flee away. Slumber leaves us — fear penetrates us to the marrow and shakes our limbs — our bones tremble — our souls are thrilled, and we shudder — none knows where he is, or what to do. With tottering steps, stunned by fear, we run from the chambers. Meanwhile, the wolf breaks into the sheep-fold. Great crowds press towards us and storm the house. They demand no keys to the chambers, cells, and sleeping rooms, but tear open the doors without keys. No lock, no door, is strong enough to withstand them; no bolt avails. A loud and crashing din is heard: they open the chests and closets — they search through our secret possessions. Our books, clothing, and beds they take away, as well as other things that are useful. They scatter everything we have collected which is of the slightest use, and break things under their feet.

"With great beams and axes they dare to splinter the doors of the holy temple. They drag away tapestries, carpets and sacred garments. They take the gilded cabinets of relics, studded with jewels, and the candlesticks. They rob the temple of all adornment. They tear the doors of the holy altar from the hinges; the bones of the saints that had been put to rest in peace, and which all the faithful reverence, they dare to touch with their sinful hands, and to tear from their rest; they scatter the relics in the aisles. With burning torches, the mob presses into the tower that has received us in our flight. The monks in the tower are made captive, and the invaders ransack the building from cellar to roof. Pulling fugitive, trembling monks out of dark corners, and laughing at their terrors, they drag them to the village. Arrived there, the prisoners are brought before the landammann, and are jeered at by the women. 'Zounds,' the latter say, 'these are they whose fine quibbles unjustly make us guilty and take away our food from us. Let them now find out themselves how hunger like ours feels, so that just punishment may fall upon the guilty.'"

After eleven weeks of captivity, the monks were released. This good fortune they owed to letters from the friends of the abbey, the counts of Toggenburg and Habsburg. These missives were couched in remarkably humble terms, considering the relations of those concerned. A special assembly of the *Landsgemeinde* took action upon them, March 2nd, 1314. A semblance of reconciliation, however, failed to remove the cause of friction. The abbot had the mountaineers excommunicated, and Frederick placed them under the ban of the empire.

Meanwhile, the dispute for the German throne was again in progress. The people of the Waldstätte opposed Rudolf, the Habsburg candidate, and sided with Louis, the choice of the majority of the electors. At their request he at once removed the ban. Determined to reduce the Waldstätte mountaineers to submission, Duke Leopold of Austria, brother of Rudolf, prepared to invade the country with arms. How he fared is best told in the words of a contemporary, who was in part an eye-witness — the chronicler Joannes Vitoduranus (John of Winterthur) — with which we proceed:[a]

A CONTEMPORARY ACCOUNT OF THE BATTLE OF MORGARTEN

At this time — in the year of our Lord 1315 — the peasants who dwelt in the valleys called Schwyz, and were walled in on all sides by mountains reaching nearly to the skies, trusting in their strong mountain bulwarks, refused the obedience, the taxes, and accustomed services which they owed to Duke Leopold, and armed to resist him. This the duke would not let pass. In great anger he collected, about St. Martin's day, from his subject towns and such other neighbouring ones as gave him aid, an army — about twenty thousand fighting men, 'twas said — to battle against those mountaineers that had risen against him, and to plunder and subjugate them. In the army. Duke Leopold had the strongest, most select, most battle-seasoned, and most fearless knighthood. The men of his army, single of soul, then came together in the purpose of thoroughly subduing and humbling these peasants, who were surrounded with mountains instead of walls. So assured were they of their victory and of capturing, robbing, and plundering that land that they carried with them ropes and cables by means of which to lead away their booty in large and small cattle.

When the Schwyzers heard of this, they fell into great fear, and fortified all the weaker places of the land where there might possibly be an approach, with walls and ditches and in other ways, as best they could; and they commended themselves to God with prayers, fastings, and processions, and occupied the mountain heights. The whole people cried with great earnestness to the Lord, calling upon Him that He might not permit their cattle to be given up for booty; their women, for distribution among the enemy; their villages, to destruction; and their honour and virtue, to suffer stain. And, on account of their refractoriness, they sought with all their power for mercy and peace through the count of Toggenburg — an excellent man, who offered himself as intermediary between the parties. Though he strove long and faithfully to further the interests of both sides, he accomplished nothing with Duke Leopold; because, altogether too incensed and flaming with too great a rage, the latter would not accept the humble conditions proposed to him through the count of Toggenburg, but wished only to crush the Schwyzers and to annihilate them, together with their possessions.

When the Schwyzers heard this, they were seized with fear and trembling. They therefore took up their weapons of war, and stationed themselves in those places where there was a narrow pass and where the way led between cliffs; and there they waited day and night. Now, Duke Leopold with his warriors sought to make an entrance into the land by a pass between a mountain and a lake called the lake of Ägeri, but was prevented by the steepness and height of the mountains. Nearly all the noble horsemen, burning with eagerness and in the hope of adventure to come had placed themselves in the front ranks; yet they had not the ability, nor was it possible, to ride up the mountains for the foot soldiers could hardly gain a firm foothold there. The Schwyzers, however, knew beforehand, by warning from the count of Toggenburg, that they would be attacked on that side, and knew the checks and obstacles that the enemy would meet with because of the difficulty of access to their country. They therefore charge, valorous and strong of heart, from their hiding places down upon their enemies, and catch them like fish enclosed in the net, cutting them to pieces with no resistance. They had, indeed, on their feet climbing irons, by means of which they could easily walk on the steepest mountain side, and keep their footing; whereas the enemy, and the horses of the enemy, could in no way find a foothold. The Schwyzers, moreover, had in their hands certain terrible instruments of death — halberds, with which they cut through the most strongly armed opponent, and hacked him in pieces. There was no battle, but, because of the reasons cited, only a butchering of Duke Leopold's men — like that of a herd driven to the shambles — by these mountain people. They spared none, nor did they trouble themselves to take any prisoners, but struck dead every one, without distinction. Those, however, who were not killed by them, were drowned in the lake, through which they sought to escape the hands of the Schwyzers, hoping that they might be able to swim across. Some of the foot soldiers, indeed, when they heard how cruelly their fighters were struck down by the Schwyzers, threw themselves, bereft of their senses by the fear of so terrible a death, into the lake, and preferred drowning themselves in the depths of the waters to falling into the hands of enemies so dreadful.

It is reported that, in this slaughter, fifteen hundred men fell by the edge of the sword, besides those who were drowned in the lake. Because of the knighthood that was lost there, the knighthood of the surrounding lands was for a long time but thinly scattered; for almost all who were knights, or others of the nobility accustomed to arms from their youth up, perished. Those, however, who had taken other roads for the conquest of the country escaped the blood-thirsty enemy; for, when they heard that the others had been cut down so terribly by the foe, they forsook everything and fled to save their lives. Out of every city, castle, and little town, several men were killed. And, therefore, everywhere the voice of joy and of mirth was silenced, and only the sound of weeping and lamentation was heard. Out of the little town of Winterthur, however, none were lost — except a single burgher, who had separated himself from the others, and, to his harm, joined the nobles — the others all returned home with sound bodies and all their belongings safe. Among these came also Duke Leopold, who seemed half dead with overmastering grief. This did I see with my own eyes; for I, — at that time a school boy — with no little joy, ran out before the gate with other and older school boys to greet my father.

It was for good cause, indeed, that the countenance of Duke Leopold appeared sad and troubled; for he had lost almost the entire heart and flower of his army. This happened while his brother Frederick was in Austria, in the year of our Lord 1315, seventeen days from the calends of December [15th November], on the day of St. Otmar [16th November]. When the battle was over, the Schwyzers stripped the slain and the drowned of their weapons, robbed them also of their other possessions, and enriched themselves with arms and money, deciding to make that day, because of the God-given victory, a yearly feast and holiday, forever.[o]

THE THREE STATES ARE FURTHER STRENGTHENED

This great victory of the Confederates had decisive consequences. Not only did it deliver the three states from Austrian domination, but it also strengthened the old alliance. Drawn together more closely by the common danger, the three states renewed the League of 1291, at Brunnen, December 9th, 1315. The unity of the confederate lands was again solemnly affirmed; no individual land was to accept a master or undertake negotiations or treaties, except by the consent of all; whoever should attack or betray any one of the states should be outlawed and incur the enmity of all. The following year, Louis confirmed the charters of the Waldstätte.

In 1310, Austria made a truce with the Waldstätte, which, while it assured her of her rents from her landed properties, annulled all her rights of sovereignty. In spite of the rude shock which the battle of Morgarten had given to the power of Austria, she could not resist the temptation to round off her domains into one compact principality, by the full possession of the Waldstätte. In 1313, she had brought into subjection the Kyburgs and their landgrafschaft of Burgundy, and, in the west, was seeking military forces and support to begin a new war. But the Burgundian towns of Fribourg, Bern, Solothurn, Morat, and Bienne united against the duke. Leopold determined to subdue them by force, and besieged (Solothurn) in 1318.[g] The old chronicles quaintly relate the story of a deed of knightly generosity that was done there. We give the version of one of the earliest of these accounts:[a]

In the year 1318, the duke of Austria had a great war with the people of Solothurn. He besieged the town with a large force, and lay in camp there ten weeks. Above the town of Solothurn, the enemy also made a bridge over the Aare, so that they might hem in the town on all sides. Now, the people of Bern had sent them four hundred men, who behaved very bravely, and destroyed the enemy's works, their throwing machines, and their shelters. Then a great rain poured over the land in floods; and the enemy were afraid that the mighty water would break their bridge and carry it away. A great many of them therefore went to look after the bridge, and to make it heavier, so that the water should not carry it away. Now, while there were many of them on the bridge, the mighty water came with such a rush that it broke down the bridge, and the enemy fell into the water and clung fast to trees and pieces of wood wherever they could. Nobody could help them, and they were driven towards the town bridge. The people in Solothurn saw what was happening to their enemies, and they commanded all their soldiers to do them no hurt, either in body or in goods; and they at once got large boats and helped their enemies to escape, and sent them back to the duke. When the duke saw that he could do nothing, he was persuaded to depart, and went against Bern.*p*

Thus failed the designs formed against the Waldstätte. These, on the other hand, improved the opportunity to strengthen their defences, allying themselves with others who shared their sentiments, while the house of Austria was occupied with other conflicts and suffered reverses in other countries. The common danger brought closer to them the Burgundian cities, especially Bern and Thun. They made a particular effort to gain over the neighbour whose hostile policy had been most troublesome to them, and whose friendship was an urgent necessity. This neighbour was Lucerne, the town which, already at the time of the first rising against Habsburg, in 1250, had formed an alliance with them. Their commercial relations and neighbouring position rendered their interests the same. Menaced by Austria also, Lucerne was the more disposed to renew its alliance with the Waldstätte.*g*

The city of Lucerne, which, since 1291, had become subject to the dukes of Austria, felt all the inconvenience of being in a state of war with its immediate neighbours of the Waldstätte. The great thoroughfare to Italy through the St. Gotthard was now stopped, and the trade of Lucerne suffered materially from the obstruction; its fairs were deserted, its lands exposed to the incursions of the Swiss and Bernese, and its burghers obliged to be under arms night and day for the defence of their walls. Yet the duke of Austria, instead of endeavouring to make some compensation to the people for these hardships, aggravated their distress by imposing fresh duties on them to carry on the war. At last the burghers of Lucerne, weary of these undeserved calamities, made a truce with their Swiss neighbours without consulting the duke. Although the noblemen in the town and neighbourhood were still in their hearts attached to the Austrian power, the citizens for their own safety concluded, in 1332, a perpetual alliance with the Waldstätte, and were admitted as a fourth canton into their confederation, on the same terms as the others. It was stipulated that in case any difference should arise between the first three cantons, Lucerne should side with the majority.

Frederick of Austria had died in 1330, and by his death peace was restored to the empire. But his successor, the duke Albert II, was not of a temper to give up tamely the possessions of his house in Helvetia. The nobles of Aargau armed in his name against Lucerne, and surrounded the town; but the citizens, reinforced by their new allies of Schwyz, defeated them. The Austrian party attempted next to gain possession of the town by a conspiracy. The nobles who were in Lucerne agreed to sally out in the night, and, after surprising the leaders of the popular party in their beds, to open the gates to the baron of Rotenburg. The conspirators assembled in arms on the borders of the lake, in a subterraneous vault under the hall of the corporation of tailors. A boy accidentally overheard their conversation, but he was perceived, seized, and would have been put to death but for the interference of some, more humane than the rest, who made him swear solemnly not to reveal to any living person what he had heard. The youth was then released, and went to the butchers' hall, where some men were still loitering, drinking and playing; he placed himself facing the stove, with his back to the company, and there told in a loud soliloquy all he had heard and seen, and the oath he had been obliged to take. The others listened attentively, then rushed out and awoke their townsmen.[1] They seized the conspirators, sent to Unterwalden for assistance, exiled the nobles who were still in the magistracy, and formed a council of three hundred citizens to administer the affairs of the canton.[q]

The treaty between Austria and the confederates had lasted about six years, when Louis summoned the Schwyzers, in 1323 to aid in the war of the empire against Austria.[2] In this, as in its former contests, the latter power was unsuccessful; and Duke Leopold's life is supposed to have been shortened by disappointment. In 1326, the armistice with Switzerland was renewed by his brother and successor, Duke Albert. In the same year the forest districts which adhered with remarkable loyalty to the emperor, followed him in an expedition to Italy. Excommunicated on that account in 1328, they knew, as they had known before, how to reduce to nothing the force of that so much dreaded sentence, by setting before their priests the alternative of doing their duty, or of leaving the country. Against such determined resolution, Pope John XXII felt himself powerless, and said of the clergy who chose to remain in the country that their conduct was unrighteous, but prudent. Notwithstanding all the feuds and disturbances which crowded upon each other during so short a time, prosperity made progress in the land. Towns and convents vied with each other in diffusing cultivation, even throughout the wildest mountainous regions. Considerable commercial intercourse was also maintained with Italy, Germany, France, and Flanders. Zurich and St. Gall possessed linen and silk manufactures; the pasture lands produced hides, wool, cheese, and butter; in Bern and Fribourg, cloth-making and dyeing establishments flourished; the western districts traded in iron, horses, hawks, and horned cattle; Geneva, in southern fruits and spices. The trade in gold was prohibited, and that of silver restricted.

Religion still appeared in all its primitive simplicity. Wealthy knights still knew no better method of perpetuating their memory in the land than through the medium of bequests for the foundation of cloisters. The respect in which the monks were held, however, already began to decline, by reason of their flagrant violations of the rules of their order, in spite of frequent attempts at reformation of their discipline. Accordingly, no fault was found with the conduct of the forest districts, which, when under excommunication, as we have seen, in 1328, left their priests free to perform divine service or

[1 The story of this conspiracy is regarded as legendary by most historians, so far as its details are concerned. The date is variously given as 1343 and 1332.]

[2 The forest states at this time also entered into alliance with Bern and Thun for the same purpose.]

quit the country. No fault was found with the clergy for accepting the former alternative. Again, it was heard without disapprobation that the men of Bâle had seized on a distinguished papal legate, who had dared to affix to the walls of their church the bull of excommunication against the emperor Louis, and had drowned the legate in the Rhine.

Such violent acts were perfectly in the spirit of the times. The people of Zurich cared so little for the bulls of the pope that, in 1331, they drove the clergy out of their town for obeying them, and for eighteen years there was no divine service in Zurich, except such as was rendered by the barefooted friars. The whole population often resisted ecclesiastical ordinances, when they ran against their old traditional adages, and detected with instinctive sagacity whatever was indifferent or useless in them. Such was in those times the state of Switzerland, which contained sufficient elements of those great changes which we shall presently see effected in its polity.*r*

BERN

The proud imperial city of Bern had hitherto been attached to the emperor Louis, having, in 1323, joined him and the forest districts against Austria. Louis, however, became reconciled to the Austrian nobles; and Bern, taking advantage of the fact that he had been placed under the papal ban, refused to acknowledge him. The growing power of this town, moreover, had placed her at odds with all the surrounding nobility, and had aroused the envy of Fribourg, her neighbour to the west. A league was formed against Bern by King Louis, the counts of Gruyères, Kyburg, Nidau, and Neuchâtel, and the dukes of Austria and Fribourg. A great council was held at Nidau, and the total destruction of Bern was determined upon.

The story of the ensuing struggle of Bern against Fribourg and the nobles is best told in the words of the old chronicles. The account we give, known as the *Conflictus Laupensis*, was written by an anonymous contemporary citizen of Bern. Its manner recalls the battle narratives of the Old Testament. It is evident that the Bernese are the chosen people.*a*

The Siege of Bern, by a Contemporary (1339–1340 A.D.)

When the Bernese saw how the count of Aarberg favoured Count Gerhard of Valentgin, they determined to avenge all the evil deeds done to them by Count Gerhard. So they went out armed, after sunset on holy Whit-Sunday of the year 1339, marched the night through, and besieged the count of Aarberg with their soldiers and machines, but could not overcome him. Then the Fribourgers and all the counts arose fearlessly and openly to the assistance of the count of Valentgin and the count of Aarberg; and collected all their own people and every helper whom they could get, with engines, shelters, wagons, and horses, and encamped as an enemy round the royal town and fortress of Laupen [1] on the eve of St. Barnabas Day (June 10th) in the same year.

In this siege were the Fribourgers with all their troops; the count of Neuenburg with his, and many picked knights whom he had brought with him out of Burgundy; the count of Nidau with his people and 140 helmets, strong, noble knights, proved warriors, whom he had sought out and chosen in Alsace and Swabia ; the count of Gruyères, Gerhard of Valentgin, Count

[1 A possession of Bern toward Fribourg, and the key to Bern's defence.]

[1339-1340 A.D.]

John, the only son of the duke Louis of Savoy, master of Vaud, and the count of Montenach, each one with troops. But Lord Eberhard, count of Kyburg, did not come with his men-at-arms to the siege, but attacked Bern from the other side, particularly from the east, with robbery, murder, and fire. The bailiffs of the duchy of Austria had united the troops which they had in Aargau, and were preparing to join in the siege. Now these all lay encamped twelve days with their men before the fortress and town of Laupen, strutting and riding about in mighty numbers and in all kinds of grand and costly garments. There were, it is generally said, sixteen thousand armed footmen and one thousand knights, or helmets, in steel armour. There was abundance of wine and pleasure, plenty of other things too, and very great insolence of every sort. All the enemies of the Bernese had sworn together a fierce oath to rase to the ground the town and fortress of Laupen without mercy or compassion, and to put all the inhabitants to the shameful death of hanging — for which purpose ropes and cords were ready to hand; and to destroy utterly the town of Bern itself.

At that time in Bern the chief avoyer or magistrate was the knight Lord John of Bubenberg the elder. Lord Antony of Blankenburg, knight, was governor for the Bernese in Laupen. But the real chief man and ruler there was Lord John of Bubenberg, knight, the younger; with Master Burkhard, the architect; and Master Peter of Kranzingen. And a banner of Bern was in Laupen, which was carried by Rudolf von Muleren and six hundred men, who had been chosen out of Bern and also out of those who belonged to Laupen and of those who had taken refuge in the town. The lay priest of Bern, Brother Theobald, like a faithful father and guardian of souls, had openly and lovingly instructed those under him in the church, and had encouraged and exhorted them to stand fast in their obedience, as true sons of holy church, to the apostolic chair and the Roman church, and rather to suffer death and the loss of their worldly goods from the aforementioned enemies than to go against the apostolic commands and the sentence given against the aforesaid Lord Louis, who gave himself out for the Roman emperor. The Bernese, therefore, so faithfully and obediently instructed and exhorted by their lay priest, that they might escape evil and remain true sons of holy church, were ready to endure any misfortune which the enemy might bring on them, either in life or goods, because they placed their firm trust in the help of heaven. And after they had assembled a thousand armed men out of the four forest cantons, particularly out of Schwyz, Uri, and Unterwalden, and some from Hasli, and the young noblemen of Weinenburg, the Bernese turned out in the presence of Johann von Weissenburg, all armed and with banners, which from the highest to the lowest were marked with the sign of the holy cross in white cloth, and they came to Laupen to free from death the six hundred men who were shut up and besieged in the castle and the town. With the Bernese went out also the good pastor, who was willing to give his life for his sheep, the aforementioned Brother Theobald, the lay priest of Bern, of the order of the German brotherhood.

When the Bernese saw that a great number of the enemy were over against them, they all gathered together in one body and placed themselves on a little hill, and formed themselves into the shape of a small wedge. But they did not dare to attack the enemy. The latter left their tents and prepared themselves for battle, the red glow rose up from the tents which were set on fire; the new knights mocked at them by throwing their swords into the air; suddenly they came rushing toward them. About two thousand Bernese men saw this and turned with fright to flee away into the forest, so to escape the strong hand of the enemy. Amongst these were a few without weapons, but many of them were strong and armed, and had been thought to be brave fighters. The rest of the Bernese, however, who did not see this flight — they might perhaps be about three thousand men — stood fast together and awaited the enemy. On one side the men from the four cantons were fiercely surrounded by the enemy's knights; on the other the Bernese were attacked by the Fribourgers and other foot soldiers. But the Bernese, like Samson, so to speak, broke the fetters of every danger, received the fierce onslaught of the Fribourgers and took from them all their banners, and slew their standard-bearers and many others, and put to miserable flight all the rest of the infantry, every one. And turning to help those surrounded by the knights, they forthwith slew all the latter or put them to flight. The number of the slain, it is commonly said, was fifteen hundred men; amongst them were many knights and noblemen. The others escaped by flight and the men of Bern took twenty-seven standards and eight crowned helmets as booty from the slain.

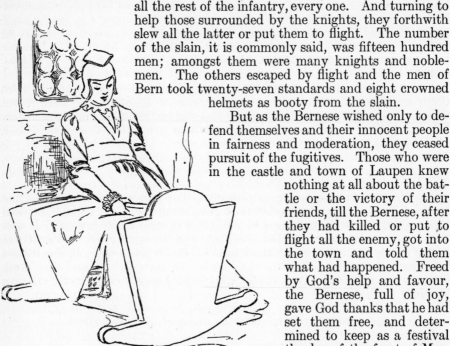

SWISS NURSE-MAID IN THE MIDDLE AGES

But as the Bernese wished only to defend themselves and their innocent people in fairness and moderation, they ceased pursuit of the fugitives. Those who were in the castle and town of Laupen knew nothing at all about the battle or the victory of their friends, till the Bernese, after they had killed or put to flight all the enemy, got into the town and told them what had happened. Freed by God's help and favour, the Bernese, full of joy, gave God thanks that he had set them free, and determined to keep as a festival the day of the feast of Martyrs, on the vigil of which this had happened, and in the future to give on that day great alms to the poor. On the other side the Fribourgers and their helpers, the enemies of Bern, full of rage at their shame and loss, thirsted for revenge on the Bernese, and till the next Easter (April 10th, 1340) they laid waste with all their might the district round Bern with fire and sword and killed without mercy all whom they took unawares. And the most noble dukes of Austria and their bailiffs assisted the Fribourgers. So the Bernese, abandoned by all men, were fought against on all sides and could not get victuals or provisions, especially wine or milk, without going to the town and castle of Spiesz with armed men and banners and carrying home the food.

After the Bernese had done many things to their enemies they turned out armed in the holy week after Palm Sunday, and went to the town of the count of Kyburg which is called Hutuwyl. And the chief magistrate, Lord John of Bubenberg, with his standard bearers and the other Bernese knights, hurried in front of the rest who were on foot; and before those who were on foot arrived, the knights who had ridden stormed the town, set fire to it, plundered and burned it to the ground; those who were defending it being killed or taken prisoners.

On the Tuesday in the week after Easter, April 24th, 1340, the Bernese went out alone with their standards and troops, and attacked Fribourg. And the Fribourgers coming out against them turned and fled at the sight of the Bernese. And the Bernese pursued them in their flight to the town gate; and on that day there fell of the Fribourgers seven hundred men, who were drowned in the river in their flight from the weapons of the Bernese. In that victory the leader of the Bernese, and their most faithful helper, was the knight, Lord Rudolf of Erlach, who, like a most powerful lion, was never afraid of the attack of any wild beast. On the next Thursday following, they again attacked Fribourg, plundered that part of the town called Galteren, as well as all houses as far as the town bridge, setting fire to them. The Bernese became famous amongst their enemies for such great earthly success, so that it was said on all sides that God was openly on the side of the Bernese and fought for them, and it seemed that God was a citizen in Bern. At last the enemies and adversaries of Bern were so wearied and broken with their many defeats and disgraces, and the Bernese so bowed down with their many troubles and worries that all enemies and adversaries returned to peace and unity.*p*

Significance of the Battle of Laupen

As McCrackan well points out, "A particular importance attaches to this battle of Laupen from the fact that it gave an opportunity for the Bernese to co-operate with their friends of the forest states against Austria. It was the first occasion on which the east and west of what is now Switzerland joined hands against a common enemy." The companionship of the battlefield was followed by a renewal of an earlier alliance of Bern and the forest districts and formed the prelude to the later entrance of Bern into the growing league.*a*

THE ACQUISITION OF ZURICH, GLARUS, ZUG, AND BERN

The city of Zurich began about this time to be distracted by internal dissensions, which continued for years and brought that republic to the verge of ruin. The council was composed of four nobles and eight of the most influential burghers, who at the expiration of four months chose their own successors. Power and office were, therefore, in the hands of a few families, who were not responsible to their fellow citizens for their public conduct, or for their employment of the public moneys. The citizens murmured, but submitted, until at last one of the members of the council itself took their part and became their leader. Rudolf Braun was a man of great talents, but ambitious. He won to his side some of the other members, who supported the demand of the citizens that the council should produce the accounts of the public expenditure. But the majority of the members endeavoured by procrastination to avoid complying with this claim. At last the people, under Braun's directions, assembled in crowds round the town house, and the obnoxious councillors left the hall, and afterwards the town, in alarm.

Braun, supported by his friends and invested with discretionary powers, formed a new government; he divided the traders and artisans into tribes or guilds, and separated them from the gentry and nobles, who together formed one class. One half of the council consisted of the heads of the guilds, and the other of members of the nobility, and each was to be renewed every six months. Braun was named burgomaster for life, with extensive powers. No alteration was made, however, in the relations of the town with the empire, to which it continued to own allegiance. The people sanctioned this new constitution in 1336. The heads of the trades, having seats in the council, used their newly acquired power each for the interest of his respective craft,[1] by excluding all foreign competition, and preventing the country people from manufacturing goods. Another great object which they had in view was to secure for the town the monopoly of the transit trade between Italy and Germany. The runaway councillors were banished forever, with their adherents, and fines were levied on their property. But the exiles found refuge in the castles of the neighbouring nobility, and were especially supported by the count of Rapperschwyl, who was possessed of the Marches, the valley of Gasterenthal, and of several other districts. From his castle the discontented emigrants made frequent incursions into the lands of their countrymen. The people of Zurich, on their side, allied themselves with the count of Toggenburg, who was in continual war with the lord of Rapperschwyl concerning a disputed inheritance, when, after several engagements, the latter was killed, with many of his men, near Gronau.

Years passed, during which time, former feuds being partly forgotten, several of the exiles obtained leave to return to Zurich. These, in concert with the rest of the emigrants, as well as with the neighbouring nobles, formed a conspiracy to get rid of Braun and his friends. Many of the conspirators came into the town under various pretexts, others were waiting outside for their friends to open the gates for them. A baker's boy overheard part of the plot in a house where the conspirators assembled. Braun was informed of it in the night; he put on his armour in haste and ran to the town-house, calling the citizens to arms. The conspirators, in a body, endeavoured to effect a retreat out of the town, but Braun, at the head of the citizens, met them in the market-place, and an obstinate engagement ensued, in which most of the conspirators were either killed or taken prisoners. The captives were beheaded or broken on the wheel, together with several citizens of their party. Braun then marched against Rapperschwyl, took the castle by storm, drove all the inhabitants out of the town, and then burned it and rased it to the ground. The counts John of Habsburg and Ulrich of Bonstetten, being taken prisoners, were kept as hostages. These events occurred in 1350.

The duke of Austria strongly resented the conduct of the Zurichers towards Rapperschwyl, the lord of which town was his relative, and he threatened the citizens with his vengeance. The nobility around rose also to avenge the humiliation inflicted on their own body. The people of Zurich, seeing the storm gathering, applied to the Swiss, and Zurich was received into their confederation as a fifth canton in 1351. But in consideration of the wealth and importance of the city of Zurich, the others yielded to it the first place in order of rank. This prerogative, however, gave Zurich no superiority over the rest, but merely constituted it as a central point where all the affairs which concerned the whole confederation were transacted; its deputies had also for a time the precedency in the general diets.

[In the league of Zurich was first outlined a federal circle within which the confederates should render aid. It was an area of considerable extent, including all the roads and passes of importance. The principle of arbitra-

[1 The chief manufactures of Zurich consisted then of silks, linen, and leather.]

[1351–1352 A.D.]

tion, of such prominence to this day in Swiss statesmanship, was adopted for the settling of internal dissensions.]

Albert, duke of Austria, repaired to Brugg in Aargau in the month of August, 1351, and there he assembled his forces. He formally demanded of the Zurichers that they should rebuild the town and castle of Rapperschwyl at their own expense, and restore the Marches, of which they had taken possession. Upon their refusal to comply with these conditions, he laid siege to Zurich with a considerable force. The Waldstätte ran to arms for the assistance of their new confederate. The duke of Austria, on his side, summoned the people of Glarus for their contingent. The latter refused, saying that they were "under the protection of the empire, and subject to the abbey of Seckingen, and bound to take up arms for the defence of these, but not for the private wars of the dukes of Austria." The duke, however, in his quality of *vogt* or warden of the abbey, understood the matter otherwise. Besides, he wished to occupy the country of Glarus, in order to check the people of Schwyz on that side and prevent them from sending succour to Zurich. But the Schwyzers, anxious to secure their own frontiers, were beforehand with him; they occupied the country of Glarus in November of the same year, 1351, without striking a blow, and Glarus [June 4th, 1352] was received into the Swiss confederation, of which it formed the sixth canton.

The cavalry of Duke Albert was stationed in the country of Baden, whence it made incursions into the lands of Zurich. The citizens, having resolved to attack the enemy, advanced on Christmas Day [1351], to the number of thirteen hundred men, towards Baden, whose suburbs they destroyed, together with the baths, the Austrians having retired into the town. But the Zurichers were intercepted in their retreat near Mellingen by four thousand of the enemy, whom they bravely attacked; and, being joined by the contingents from the banks of the lake, they obliged the Austrians to retire, after the loss of six hundred or seven hundred men. The Zurichers had captured at Baden a number of mares, which they drove towards the enemy's horses, and thus threw them into disorder — a stratagem which mainly contributed to the defeat of the Austrians.

Next year Walter de Stadion made an incursion into the territory of Glarus, but was defeated and killed near Nafels [1352]. The people of Glarus pursued their advantages, and laid siege to the town of Zug, a hereditary possession of the duke of Austria. Deputies from Zug repaired to Königsfeld, where Duke Albert was quietly enjoying the sports of the chase, whilst a war in which he had wantonly engaged was desolating the territories of his own subjects. The deputies, who came to implore his assistance, found him engaged with his falconer: he would hardly listen to their urgent requests for assistance, and told them peevishly that they might, if they chose, give themselves up to the Swiss. When this answer was reported to the people of Zug, they immediately followed the duke's advice, and were readily received, in 1352 [June 27th], into the Swiss confederacy, of which they formed the seventh canton.

The duke of Austria arose at last from his apathy, and a second time laid siege to Zurich, in the month of July; but seeing no better chance of success than before, he listened to the proposals of the Markgraf of Brandenburg, who negotiated a truce.

[The terms of the Peace of Brandenburg, as this was called, were somewhat unfavourable to the league. Glarus and Zug were compelled again to admit the sovereignty of Austria.]

The republic of Bern, which had of late greatly extended its dominions both by arms and by purchases, having some differences with its subjects of the Oberhasli, the cantons offered their mediation, and in 1352 a diet was held at Lucerne for that purpose. On this occasion the first three cantons proposed that Bern should enter into the Swiss alliance. The Bernese, grateful for the assistance the Swiss had afforded them at the battle of Laupen, readily accepted the offer. Bern was thus received into the confederation [March 6th, 1353], of which it formed the eighth canton. This important accession imparted to the Swiss Confederacy a reputation for power and stability which it had not till then enjoyed. It also led to the settlement of a general system of polity among the Swiss, which, while keeping inviolate the independent sovereignty of each canton, provided for cases where a diversity of interests might lead to a rupture. This last and most difficult object was obtained by constituting the deputies from each state into a diet or representative council of the whole Helvetic body, to whom the neighbouring princes might accredit their ministers, and before whom all important affairs concerning the general welfare of the country might be discussed and concluded.

The eight cantons — Schwyz, Uri, Unterwalden, Lucerne, Zurich, Glarus, Zug, and Bern — constituted for more than a century the whole federative republic of the Swiss, and even after the accession of other cantons they retained, together with the title of the "eight old cantons," a superiority over the younger members of the league. During that period they made considerable conquests, which were distributed among themselves according to the decrees of the diets.

The Peace of Brandenburg which Duke Albert had made with the Swiss was not of long duration. He soon pretended that the stipulation which secured to him his rights in the cantons of Glarus and Zug meant the annihilation of their alliance with the Swiss. The affair was brought before the emperor Charles IV, who, after some vacillation, finding that the Swiss would not hear of any infraction of their confederation, took the part of the duke of Austria. The Austrians renewed hostilities in July, 1354, by laying siege, for the third time, to Zurich. The emperor joined them with the troops of the empire, as well as those of Solothurn, Schaffhausen, and several other imperial cities. The combined army amounted to more than forty thousand men. The garrison of Zurich, reinforced by contingents from the other cantons, held out for several weeks against their numerous enemies; at last they hoisted on one of the towers their great banner, which consisted of the arms of Zurich surmounted by the imperial eagle; this reminded the contingents of the free towns that they were waging war against one of their own body. The Zurichers also secretly made representations to the emperor, who, naturally jealous of the power of the house of Austria, and weary of a war from which he could expect no advantage, at length withdrew his troops; and Duke Albert, weakened by this defection, raised the siege.*g*

Terms of peace similar to those of the Peace of Brandenburg were agreed upon July 24th, 1355, at Regensburg. In 1360 the confederates again opposed Austria. The emperor Charles IV formally recognised the confederation in 1361 as a lawful union for the preservation of the public peace (*Landfriedensverbindung*). The men of Schwyz by a bold stroke in 1364 gained possession of the town and lands of Zug, and in 1368, Zug, by the consent of Austria at the Peace of Thorberg, became permanently a member of the league. This district, originally composed of the town and the land of Zug, had been formed into one community and now formed a transition link between the civic and the rural members of the league.*a*

THE GUGLER WAR

The whole of Switzerland enjoyed tranquillity until, in 1375, an army of strangers, French and Englishmen, after ravaging Alsace and the borders of the Rhine, invaded the country on the banks of the Aare, and, carrying fire and sword, advanced along the Limmat as far as Wettingen. This unexpected irruption, which recalled to mind the former incursions of the northern tribes, was led by Enguerrand de Coucy, a French nobleman, who had inherited, through his mother, a grand-daughter of the emperor Albert, several towns and castles in Alsace and Aargau, of which, however, he had never obtained possession. Leopold of Austria, Enguerrand's cousin, refused to deliver up to him his mother's portion, and Enguerrand, who had married Isabella, princess of England, availing himself of the peace between that country and France, came with a large army of adventurers, chiefly English, to regain his inheritance by force of arms.

The invaders, dividing their forces, advanced with a strong party towards Bern. One of their principal leaders, a Welshman, erroneously styled by the chroniclers "duke of Wales," encamped at Frauenbrunnen, on the road to that city. Having met little or no opposition so far, the English were reposing in security, when in the night of the 26th and 27th of December the Bernese surprised their camp. They found little resistance except in the convent, where the principal officers were lodged, and where they fought singly in the corridors and cells. The English were thrown into confusion and dispersed in the darkness, with the loss of eight hundred men. Others of their bands met with similar reverses in various parts of the country. The lord of Coucy, who had his headquarters at the abbey of St. Urban, seeing this, and finding that he could not maintain discipline in his motley army, or procure provisions in a country which he had ravaged, began his retreat, and returned to Alsace, which he completely devastated. This expedition was called by the Swiss the Gugler War from the pointed kind of helmet which the English wore, and which in German is called Gugelhut.*q*

NEW BATTLES AND NEW VICTORIES

As the towns grew in power and importance the strength and wealth of the nobility in western Switzerland had decreased. To recuperate his dwindling fortune Count Rudolf of Kyburg in 1382 prepared to capture Solothurn by a sudden night attack, but his plot was discovered and the attempt failed. The Bernese hastened to the assistance of their old allies; the confederates also lent aid, and their joint forces laid siege to Burgdorf. They were unable to take the place, however, because the Austrians came to its aid, treacherously violating an agreement to remain neutral. The Kyburgs were the losers in the end, being forced to sell Burgdorf and Thun to Bern; they, moreover, bound themselves not to make war in the future except with permission of Bern and Solothurn. Bern, thus steadily pursuing her policy of extending her territory by conquest or purchase, now ruled over all the territories of the upper and middle Aare.

Quarrels with Austria were soon renewed. In 1385 Zurich, Bern, Solothurn, Lucerne, and Zug joined the great union of south German cities for protection against the nobles. The forest districts of all the members of the league alone held back. Duke Leopold of Austria seized the opportunity of apparent disunion to refuse the demands of Lucerne for the abolition of the payment of custom duties to the Austrian bailiff at Rotenburg. Lucerne held that she had the right of free traffic. Her citizens stopped paying tolls, attacked the custom house at Rotenburg, and granted co-burghership to the inhabitants of the neighbouring town of Sempach, which was discontented with Austrian rule.[a]

Nothing remained but for Leopold to convoke his vassals and subjects. He united them at those places where, seventy-one years before, the army had marched out against Morgarten. The Swiss also took measures of defence. Zurich prepared for a fresh siege. Berne, while condemning the unreflecting violence of the Lucernaise, held herself ready for anything. She would rather have seen the confederates make common cause with the German towns, who, to gain time for concerting a plan of war, sought an armistice. But neither were these towns long in dividing and joining Leopold, leaving the confederates entirely alone and at issue with Austria.

Already hostilities had begun at certain points. The Glaronaise, taking up the quarrel of the Swiss, destroyed some castles in their neighbourhood. Zurich, which expected to be the first attacked, had received a federal garrison within her walls (1386). But Leopold's plan was not that of the confederates. Leaving five thousand men, destined to keep Zurich in alarm, at Brugg, he advanced (July 1st, 1386) at the head of four thousand horse and a well armed infantry. After some days had passed, the army, skirting the eastern bank and the green lake of Sempach, marched on Lucerne. It was harvest time, and reapers were putting the sickle to the corn. At this moment, on the morning of July 9th, the Swiss appeared, coming out of a wood which traversed the route leading to Lucerne by Rotenburg. The duke hastened to range his army for battle, but as the country did not lend itself to cavalry movements, he ordered the horsemen to dismount. Formed in a large and deep square, with serried ranks and set lances they marched on the enemy, leaving the infantry behind because they would not divide the honour of punishing the peasants. Presenting to the Swiss a forest of sharp steel they attacked with so much impetuosity that sixty men were killed and the magistrate Gundoldingen was wounded, before they had lost a single man themselves.

But soon the scene changed. All accounts of this battle mention the sudden change, but ascribe different reasons. The Austrian narratives blame the extreme heat, the weight of the nobles' arms, and the treason of the mounted gentlemen-at-arms, who, remaining inactive witnesses of the battle, were said to have set the example of flight. The Austrians acknowledge the defeat, but give an imperfect account of it. The Swiss version completes the story and gives a more natural explanation of the event. When all was going as badly as possible, it says, and the long lances of the cavaliers were slaughtering the foremost ranks, without allowing the Swiss halberds to reach the enemy, this is what a pious and faithful confederate did — he seized as many lances as he could and bent them under his weight, so that his companions, advancing through the breach, broke the order of the nobles' ranks. It was then that counts, cavaliers, and servitors fell pell-mell together; even Leopold himself, whose ardour his men had vainly tried to restrain, also fell dead in the melée.

And that is all of the battle of Sempach. More ancient chronicles relate it in a still simpler manner. The Swiss wrote little, contenting themselves at first with saying that it pleased the all-powerful God to give them victory, and that they were in sore straits when they gained the field. Even the more explicit narratives, in relating how the victory was won, do not name the hero, the noblest embodiment of that love of country which allowed the

[1388 A.D.]

Swiss to conquer powerful neighbours. Very tardily a popular song made famous the name of Arnold von Winkelried.

Large booty, of gold and silver and rich standards, was found on the field. The confederates lost 116 men, the Austrians nearly 700. After having, according to custom, passed three days on the place which saw them victorious, the conquerors with outspread banners sought the road to their own homes. Swift as the wind travelled the news of this victory, till the disgrace the nobility had suffered was known beyond the limits of the empire.

After Sempach the war spread. Wishing to pursue their advantages, the Swiss extended their forces in various directions, ravaging the enemy's country. Bern, seeing war inevitable, took up arms. Twenty-four villages were, according to the conqueror's expression, "blown sky high." Bern exacted homage from the towns of Thorberg, Unterséen, and the upper Simmen Thal. Then she turned her forces against Fribourg, where the Austrian party again ruled. Time after time the Bernese tried to seize Fribourg and the Fribourgese to surprise Bern. [The Bernese finally took possession of the dominions of Fribourg and Austria in the Bernese Oberland and in Seeland].

THE BATTLE OF NÄFELS AND SUBSEQUENT PEACE

Elsewhere war had also pursued its course. The Glaronaise, believing their independence assured by the victory of Sempach, had constituted themselves a free people, and had, with confederate aid, taken Wesen by assault. The Austrians, however, thanks to agents they had in that place, had no trouble in regaining possession (February, 1388). Soon after, they presented themselves to the number of about six thousand men on the borders of the Glarus country, ordering submission.

This was in winter. Accumulated snow on the Alps separated the Swiss from their allies. Reduced to their own small number, they nevertheless ranged themselves behind an intrenchment constructed from one mountain to another in the environs of Näfels. Mattis am Buhl commanded them. When on the 9th of April he saw the Austrian army on the march, he sent orders for every member of the confederation to sound the alarm, while, by a vigorous resistance, he gave the people time to assemble. The moment came when he saw himself constrained to yield to numbers. The Austrian army was spreading in wave after wave on every side, seizing the flocks, burning Näfels, and seeking booty. Am Buhl led his little group to the side of a mountain (an der Rauti) so that they could not be surrounded. There, passing through the enemy by detachments of twenty, thirty, or sixty men, came contingents from the valley. The women and children fled into the Alps, leading the cattle. Thirty auxiliaries of Schwyz succeeded in passing the mountains.

The Austrians, in their turn, re-formed. They were ranged in battle when the Glaronaise rained on them showers of stones, wounding both men and horses and throwing the ranks into confusion. Then, agile as usual, they fell on their enemies, throwing them off their horses and covering them with wounds. Ten times they had to retire, yet ten times returned. The eleventh onslaught was decisive; for, seized this time with panic, the Austrians fled, and being hotly pursued perished in great numbers either in the plain or in the waters of the Linth. [Seventeen hundred Austrians are said to have perished.] The battle of Näfels is still celebrated every year on the first Thursday in April.

During the days which followed the battle of Näfels, contingents of confederates arrived one after the other, to learn from the Glaronaise how they had helped themselves. All together they meant to march on Wesen, when they learned that the enemy had forestalled them and destroyed this town with their own hands. Then was formed a plan for profiting by these circumstances to seize Rapperschwyl, but the resistance of the inhabitants constrained them to go away after three weeks. They returned to their homes fighting on the way and pillaging and seizing booty on the enemy's territories. These were the final hostilities. After a year's warfare the country showed towns and villages reduced to ashes, stores destroyed, premature harvests hastily reaped. Famine followed in the train of high prices. Taking in the situation, seeing their treasure exhausted, their armies dispersed, as well as fiefs lost, Argovia and Thurgovia in danger, the dukes and Leopold's son laid down their arms. A seven years' peace was concluded [April, 1389]. The Swiss kept their conquests.[s]

THE CONFEDERATE RELATIONS STRENGTHENED

Glarus was at this time definitely acknowledged a member of the league.[a]

No further members were admitted till 1481, after the Burgundian war. But, in order thoroughly to understand the nature of the league, it must be remembered that, while each of the five new members was allied with the original nucleus — the three forest districts — these five were not directly allied to one another; Lucerne was allied with Zurich and Zug; Zurich with Lucerne, Zug, and Glarus; Glarus with Zurich; Zug with Lucerne and Zurich; Bern with no one except the three original members.[f]

The defeats of Sempach and Näfels gave to the Austrian power in Switzerland a blow from which it never recovered. The feudal nobility, the vassals of Austria, had lost in those fights their bravest leaders; and the dukes of Austria, occupied with others matters, neglected the affairs of Switzerland. The feudatories, finding themselves unsupported, made the best terms they could with the cantons; some of them, being in want of money, sold or mortgaged their estates and jurisdictions to the wealthy towns of Zurich, Bern, or Solothurn; others entered into co-burgherships with them, engaging to assist them in their wars. In a few years more than forty lordships belonging to the dukes of Austria, or to vassals of that house, came into possession of the Swiss confederates, especially of Bern and Zurich.

In 1393 Leopold, duke of Austria, and son of the Leopold who was killed at Sempach, came to Baden on the Limmat, and thence he endeavoured to sow dissension among the Swiss, with whom, however, he was at peace at the time. He succeeded in bribing Rudolf Schön, burgomaster of Zurich, and some of the other councillors of state, or members of the executive, who agreed to conclude a treaty offensive and defensive between Zurich and Austria, one of the conditions of which was that Zurich should not support the other cantons in the possession of the territories they had seized during the last war. A draft of the treaty was made out and sent to Leopold for his sanction. All this was done by the burgomaster without consulting the great or legislative council of Zurich.

Meantime the other cantons, having heard of the negotiation, became alarmed, and sent deputies to Zurich to remonstrate against a transaction which they denounced as a treason against the federal alliance which bound Zurich to the rest of the Swiss. The Swiss deputies insisted upon the question being referred to the great council; and appealed to the citizens whom they met in the streets. These angrily and clamorously demanded the convocation of the great council. The magistrates were obliged to comply, and the great council, being assembled, summoned a meeting of the commune, or general assembly of the citizens. These impeached the magistrates, and ordered them for trial before the "council of two hundred," or great council, which pronounced that the alliance with Austria was illegal, and condemned Rudolf Schön, and seventeen other individuals concerned in it, to banishment. After this the council and burghers together adopted several resolutions, to the effect that in future the burgomaster and councillors of state and tribunes should be renewed every six months and that the councillors should be chosen from among all classes of citizens without exclusion. Duke Leopold, being thus baffled in his scheme of detaching Zurich from the confederation, and unwilling to recommence hostilities, entered into a fresh treaty with the Swiss in 1394, renewing the former truce for twenty years longer, and regulating the question of their recent acquisitions. It was after the death of Duke Leopold, and during the disputed successions and weak administration of the dukes Albert IV and Albert V, that Austria lost her remaining influence in Helvetia.*q*

The treaty of 1394 was prolonged in 1412 for fifty years. The hundred years' struggle of the Swiss League to throw off all political dependence on the Habsburgs was thus finally crowned with success. The confederation as a whole was relieved from the overlordship of the Habsburgs, to whom, however, all their rights and dues as landed proprietors were expressly reserved. Thus the distinction always made by the confederates between the Habsburgs as rulers and as land owners was once more upheld; and though that powerful family entertained hopes of recovering its former rights, so that technically the treaties of 1389, 1394, and 1412 were but truces, it finally and forever renounced all its feudal rights and privileges within the confederacy of the "everlasting compact" of 1424.*a*

THE PFAFFENBRIEF AND THE SEMPACHER BRIEF

The course of events compelled the confederates to strengthen and regulate their political relations by the adoption of principles binding upon all. When the provost of the cathedral of Zurich, after becoming guilty of an attempt on the life of Peter von Gundolding [mayor of Lucerne], had refused to appear before the civil tribunal, the majority of the confederates adopted the principle that the clergy should be subject to the authority of the state. This was done in the decree of September 7th, 1370, known as the Pfaffenbrief.

On the 10th of July, 1393, the eight confederates adopted a common military ordinance, the Sempacher Brief (Letter of Sempach). By this they forbade all individual enterprises, pillage, violation of sacred places, and violence to women and defenceless girls. This is the only example of a regulation of military discipline in the interest of humanity during feudal times and affords good evidence of the noble principles which actuated the league and the lofty aims towards which it strove.

These two documents were confirmed by oath every five years, like all other treaties. It is plain from all these facts that the confederates did not have from the beginning a preconceived design and did not make their gains in the full consciousness of a chosen mission. They strove rather to realise step by step whatever circumstances rendered possible. This lack of aim was, it is true, a tax upon energy or enthusiasm for internal progress; and served as a deterrent from decisive actions. And yet, when the conduct of the confederation is contrasted with the disorderly movements of the lower classes in France, England, etc., we praise the moderation that preserved the confederation from all violent reaction and permitted it to continue tranquilly its onward march.*g*

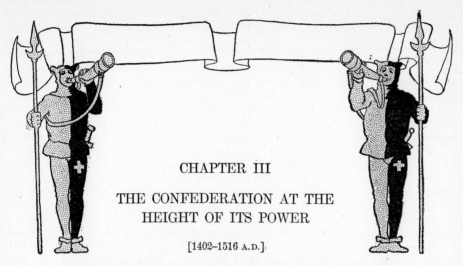

CHAPTER III

THE CONFEDERATION AT THE
HEIGHT OF ITS POWER

[1402–1516 A.D.]

The great victory at Sempach not merely vastly increased the fame of the Everlasting League, but also enabled it to extend both its influence and its territory. The fifteenth century is the period when both the league and its several members took the aggressive, and the expansion of their power and lands cannot be better seen than by comparing the state of things at the beginning and at the end of this century. — W. A. B. COOLIDGE.[b]

THE EMANCIPATION OF APPENZELL

ABOUT the beginning of the fifteenth century, misunderstandings arose between the mountaineers of Appenzell and their lord, the abbot of St. Gall. The agents of the abbot encroached on the privileges of the people, and levied taxes in a harsh and oppressive manner: one of them, the bailiff of Schwendi, exacted a duty on the cheese and butter which were carried to market, and he kept two fierce mastiffs to fly at anyone who attempted to pass the toll-house without having paid the duty. The bailiff of the town of Appenzell had the right of *catel* or "chattel," in virtue of which the best garment of every man who died became his perquisite. He one day caused the grave of a man lately buried to be reopened, in order to seize the clothes in which the children of the deceased had dressed their parent.

These and many other vexations, joined to the example of their neighbours the Swiss, led the Appenzellers to think of emancipating themselves from the abbot's rule. On a fixed day they rose, surprised the castles, and drove the bailiffs away. The abbot Cuno of Staufen, having no means of suppressing the revolt, applied to the imperial towns of Swabia, who were his allies, and who sent messengers into Appenzell. The mountaineers said they were ready to pay the abbot his lawful dues as before, provided he chose his bailiffs among a certain number of honest men whom they would propose to him. The imperial towns, however, rejected the proposal, and insisted that the former bailiffs of the abbot should be reinstated, and these, through malice and revenge, treated the people worse than before. The Appenzellers then turned to the town of St. Gall, which, having grown around the abbey, and being in some measure dependent on it, yet enjoyed imperial franchises and immunities, and was allied to other imperial towns. Its

581

position between Germany and Italy rendered it a place of considerable trade, which the industry of its inhabitants had increased by the establishment of manufactures. The people of St. Gall had also their grievances against the abbot; they listened readily to their neighbours of Appenzell, and formed an alliance with them [1401] for the purpose of defending their respective privileges. The abbot, incensed at this, redoubled his severity against the Appenzellers, and appealed again to the league of the imperial towns of Swabia, which decided that the alliance between St. Gall and Appenzell must be dissolved, but that the abbot should choose his bailiffs from among the natives of the latter country. St. Gall submitted to this decision.

The Appenzellers, perceiving that the nobility of the imperial towns preferred the friendship of a prince abbot to the interests of a race of humble mountaineers, addressed themselves to their brethren of the Swiss cantons, expecting more sympathy from that quarter. Schwyz and Glarus alone answered the call; the former entered into a co-burghership with the people of Appenzell [1402], and Glarus, without stipulating any act of alliance, proclaimed that all those among the citizens who chose to serve in the cause of Appenzell were free so to do. All the inhabitants of Appenzell attended in their respective rhodes,[1] and they all swore to each other, and to the landammann of the village of Appenzell, to remain firmly united for the defence of their common rights. On hearing this, the imperial towns, urged again by the abbot, collected a considerable force, both horse and foot, and sent it to St. Gall, where the abbot reviewed and entertained them. Thence they proceeded towards Trogen, a village of Appenzell, the cavalry in full armour, followed by five thousand infantry.

On the 15th of May, 1403, they entered the hollow pass of Speicher. The men of Appenzell, informed by their scouts of the approach of the enemy, had left their wives and children, and after receiving the blessings of their aged parents they posted themselves, to the number of two thousand, on the summit of the mountain; eighty of them advanced to the cliffs which overhang the hollow way, while three hundred men of Schwyz and two hundred of Glarus placed themselves in the wood on each side of the road. The enemy's cavalry boldly ascended the mountain. The eighty Appenzellers began the attack with their slings, whilst the men of Glarus and of Schwyz rushed upon the flanks of the column. The cavalry, pressed in a narrow way, spurred their horses to gain the plain on the summit of the hill, when they perceived the whole force of Appenzell advancing to meet them. At this sight the leaders of the column ordered a retreat, in order to regain the open country below. The dismal word "Retire!" sounded along the files of the long column: the infantry in the rear thought all was lost, and began to disband — the people of Appenzell, Schwyz, and Glarus fell from every side on the cavalry cooped up in the hollow way. Six hundred cavaliers lost their lives; the rest spurred their horses through the ranks of their own infantry; the rout became general, and the discomfited troops reached St. Gall in the greatest confusion.

The imperial towns, disheartened by this defeat and having lost many of their most distinguished warriors, forsook the cause of the abbot and made their peace with Appenzell. The abbot, deeming himself not safe in St. Gall, retired to Wyl. The Appenzellers, being masters of the country, attacked and destroyed his castles, and ravaged his domains. The abbot and the gentry, his vassals, implored the assistance of Frederick duke of

[1 Rhodes, from *Rotte*, troop or band, means the communes or hundreds into which Appenzell is divided. This denomination continues to the present day.]

Austria, who, after some hesitation, assembled a force in the Tyrol, which he divided into two columns; the stronger advanced on the 17th of June, 1405, from Alstetten, in the Rheinthal, by the mountain called Am Stoss, on the borders of Appenzell. The count Rudolf of Werdenberg, who had been deprived by the dukes of Austria of his possessions in the Rheinthal, offered his services to the Appenzellers, and, throwing aside his knightly armour, assumed their mountain costume. He was unanimously entrusted with the defence of the country.

The Appenzellers had posted themselves on the mountain, from whence they threw down enormous stones and trunks of trees on the advancing column. The day was rainy, so that the slope upon which the Appenzellers were posted, and which was covered with short grass, was extremely slippery. The Austrians had scarcely reached the middle of the ascent when Rudolf gave his men the signal to advance. The Appenzellers were barefooted, and they rushed safely down the hill upon the enemy, whose ranks were thrown into disorder and whose bowstrings were rendered unserviceable by the rain. The Austrians, however, fought desperately man to man with sword and spear. On a sudden they perceived on the hills a fresh body of Appenzellers, which threatened to cut off their retreat. A general panic then seized them: it was no longer a fight, but a slaughter; and the streams of rain flowing down the sides of the hill were reddened with the blood of the invaders. The combat and the pursuit lasted six hours, after which the Appenzellers returned to the field of battle, and there, falling on their knees, they returned thanks to the Almighty for the deliverance of their country. The troop whose appearance had decided the flight of the Austrians was composed of the women of Appenzell, in shepherds' frocks, who had come to share the dangers of their husbands and their brothers!

Duke Frederick, who had advanced with another body of troops from Arbon, and vainly besieged the town of St. Gall, attempted to penetrate into Appenzell from another side, but was also repulsed and obliged to retire into the Tyrol. The Appenzellers now formed an alliance with St. Gall, conquered the Rheinthal, and advanced into the Tyrol, whilst another body assisted their allies of Schwyz in conquering the valley of Wäggis and the Lower March, which have ever since formed part of the latter canton. The war of Appenzell lasted five years, during which the shepherds of that country, whose name was hardly known before made themselves formidable, extending their incursions to Bregenz and Landeck on the Inn, and in Thurgau as far as Weinfelden. They took by force more than sixty castles, and destroyed thirty. They also entered the town of Wyl, and made the abbot of St. Gall prisoner. It was in vain that they were excommunicated by the bishop of Constance, and put by the emperor under the ban, in 1406; they disregarded both. Their too enterprising spirit, however, received a check under the walls of Bregenz, whence they were driven back. At last in 1408, the emperor Robert, who had come to Constance, negotiated a peace, by which the abbot of St. Gall gave up his seigniorial rights over Appenzell, retaining, however, certain revenues. The Appenzellers restored the Rheinthal to the house of Austria. They contracted [November 24, 1411; St. Gall in 1412] an alliance with the Swiss cantons, Bern excepted. The Swiss, in this alliance, showed some mistrust of the newly awakened ambition of the mountaineers of Appenzell, for they stipulated that the latter should not engage in any war without the consent of the confederates, and that in all cases the expenses of the war should be defrayed by Appenzell alone.

THE CONQUEST OF THE AARGAU

In 1415, the famous council of Constance began. No less than three popes, John XXIII, Gregory, and Benedict, contended for the see of Rome, to the scandal and distraction of the Christian world. The emperor Sigismund determined to put an end to this deplorable schism, and for this object the council was mainly convoked. But the emperor's disposition was false and rapacious. The duke Frederick of Austria favoured John XXIII, a prelate of a worldly, profligate character, and protected and abetted him even after the council had deposed him, as well as the two other pretenders to the papacy, and elected in their place Martin V. For this Frederick was excommunicated by the council, whilst Sigismund, jealous of the power of the house of Austria, and covetous of its vast domains, put him under the ban of the empire, and invited all the imperial vassals and towns to make war against him. The same invitation was addressed to the Swiss cantons.

The Swiss refused at first, with the exception of Bern, ever ready to seize a favourable opportunity to aggrandize itself. The old forest cantons hesitated; they had lately renewed their truce with the duke of Austria for fifty years longer, and although the bishops, in council assembled, absolved them from their engagements, and the emperor promised them the permanent possession of all the conquests they should make on Frederick, they for some time withstood the temptation, saying that a breach of faith could never be justified by either church or empire. But Zurich, more covetous and less scrupulous than the rest, having followed the example of Bern, the other cantons, threatened on one hand and tempted on the other, also declared war against Austria in April, 1415. The canton of Uri and the brave shepherds of Appenzell formed the only honourable exceptions; they remained faithful to their truce with Frederick, and took no part either in the war or in the spoil. Bern, joined by Solothurn and Bienne, entered the Aargau. This fine province was the cradle of the house of Habsburg; it extends from the Aare to the Limmat, and northward to the Rhine, and was divided between towns enjoying franchises under the protection of the dukes of Austria and several lords vassals of the duke. Hearing of Frederick's interdict, and of the movements of the cantons, they assembled a diet at Sursee. The towns were for remaining neutral in the approaching struggle, and forming a close alliance among all the districts of Aargau for the defence of their liberties, with leave to treat with the Swiss confederates in case of necessity, and to join them as a distinct canton, as Glarus and Zug had done. But the nobles did not accede to the compact; they preferred having the duke as their master to placing themselves on a level with the burghers. This was the cause of the misfortunes of Aargau, and of its state of subjection, which lasted till the end of the eighteenth century.

The towns then resolved to place themselves under the protection of the confederates in order to secure their freedom, but it was too late. As the assembly broke up, and the deputies were returning to their homes, they espied on the hills the banners and the troops of the cantons, who had hostilely entered the country. The town of Zofingen was the first attacked, and was obliged to renounce its allegiance to Austria, and swear fidelity to Bern. The same happened to Aarburg, Aarau, Brugg, Lenzburg, and others. In a few weeks the Bernese had conquered the greater part of Aargau, the rapidity of their movements preventing any effectual resistance. Lucerne on its side took Sursee, Meienburg, and other places, as far as the Bernese line of conquests. The Zurichers, having crossed Mount Albis, occupied the bailiwick of Knonau, Dietikon, and the banks of Limmat towards Baden. The forces of the confederates united between the Limmat and the Reuss, and conquered in common, in the name of the seven cantons (that of Uri being excepted), Mellingen, Bremgarten, and the country of Baden. The strong castle of Baden held out for some time longer for Austria, but the artillery of the Bernese having battered down part of the walls, the garrison surrendered and the castle was burned.

The confederates then divided their spoils. Bern, Zurich, and Lucerne kept each its conquests with the same rights as the house of Austria had exercised over those districts, and the country conquered in common was formed into bailiwicks under the authority of the united cantons, who sent by turn bailiffs every second year to govern them. Bern, which had already obtained the lion's share, did not participate in the common bailiwicks. Thus the Swiss republicans began to have extensive subject districts, over which they ruled as sovereigns. The practice was afterwards widely extended: it became an abundant source of discontent and civil war, and was at last the main cause of the overthrow of the old Swiss Confederation.

Whilst the house of Austria was thus stripped of its ancestral possessions in Helvetia, Duke Frederick made his submission to the emperor Sigismund, and, having given up Pope John, became reconciled with the church. This re-establishment of peace was signified to the Swiss cantons, with the injunction that they should restore their conquests to the duke. Uri again lifted up its voice for the cause of honesty, but its scruples were laughed at by the other cantons, who were determined to hold fast their prize, and they propitiated the cupidity of Sigismund by a sum of 10,000 golden florins. By a treaty concluded in 1418 between the emperor and the duke of Austria, the duke renounced all his rights over the Aargau, and the counties of Lenzburg and Baden, and the other bailiwicks. Such was the end of the war called the war of Constance, the first in which the Swiss acted on the offensive without having received provocation.

FIRST ADVANCE SOUTH OF THE ALPS; THE VALAIS

About this period the Swiss cantons first carried their arms across the Alps into the valleys of Italy. The cantons of Uri and Unterwalden had grounds of complaint against the officers of the duke of Milan, who had annoyed some of their countrymen and seized their cattle. The duke refused to give them satisfaction. They crossed the St. Gotthard, took possession of the valley of Leventina or Livinen,[1] and then, with the full consent of the inhabitants, they occupied the valley of Oscella or Ossola. The duke Visconti engaged the duke of Savoy to reconquer the latter. The troops of Savoy crossed the Valais, and, penetrating by the Simplon to Domo d'Ossola, drove the Swiss garrison away. The cantons of Uri and Unterwalden next purchased of the baron of Mesocco, a Rhætian nobleman, the town and valley of Bellinzona as far as Lake Maggiore. The duke of Milan sent a large force under the command of Pergola, one of the ablest condottiere of his time, to prevent the Swiss from keeping possession of their purchase.

The two armies met at Arbedo near Bellinzona, and an obstinate combat ensued, which lasted the whole day. The landammann of Uri, the standard bearer of the same canton, and the ammann of Zug, Peter Kolin, were among

[1 The Vallis Lepontina of the Romans. The Ticino, descending from the St. Gotthard, waters the valley in its course to the Lago Maggiore.]

the killed. The son of Kolin seized the banner dyed with his father's blood, again waved it at the head of the men of Uri, and although he too perished the banner was saved. Swiss bravery, however, could not triumph over the steady discipline of the veteran troops of Italy. Weakened by the loss they had sustained, the Swiss mournfully recrossed the St. Gotthard, leaving a garrison, however, in the Val Leventina. The battle of Arbedo was fought in June, 1422, and Bellinzona was soon after given up to the duke of Milan by a treaty.

These Italian broils were the cause of a popular insurrection in the Valais. The lord of Raron, captain-general of that country, had allied himself to the duke of Savoy, whom he had assisted in his expedition against the Swiss at Domo d'Ossola. The cantons, resenting this, excited the people of the Valais against the lord of Raron, whose ambition had already offended his countrymen. An old custom prevailed among the people of that country; when they wanted to obtain from their lords redress of their grievances, they hoisted in the market-place an enormous club, one end of which was rudely carved into something resembling a human face, bearing an expression of woe and crowned with thorns; this was called *La Mazze*, and was meant to represent oppressed justice. A man stood behind it, and the people came one after the other to ask of the Mazze what made it so sad? Was it such or such a lord, mentioning several, that had grieved it? The Mazze remained motionless. But when the lord of Raron came to be mentioned, the Mazze made an inclination of the head. Then the man lifted up the Mazze and carried it from village to village, the people following it, and increasing at every step; and it was proclaimed that the Mazze was going to demand satisfaction of the lord of Raron, of his nephew the bishop of Sion, and their adherents. The baron, seeing the whole country risen against him, escaped to Savoy; and the people destroyed his castle near Siders, as well as that of the bishop.

Having obtained no assistance from the duke of Savoy, the lord of Raron repaired to Bern, whose co-burgher he was. Bern espoused his cause, the forest cantons took part with the Valaisans. A diet, assembled at Zurich, decided that the property of the baron should be returned to him first, and that, on the other hand, he should do justice to the people. But the people were not satisfied with this decision, and hostilities commenced between them and Bern. The Bernese, joined by Fribourg and Solothurn, sent an army of thirteen thousand men over the Sanetsch Alps into the Valais.

The forest cantons offered their mediation in vain; and the Valaisans, having refused to accede to any terms with Raron and Bern, were left to their own resources. They fought desperately, and repulsed the Bernese. At length fresh proposals of peace were made, and the Valaisans agreed to restore Raron's domains, to pay 10,000 florins as a compensation for the damage they had done him, an equal sum to Bern for the expenses of the war, and 4,000 florins to the chapter of Sion. This was in 1420; but the lord of Raron died at a distance from his country, and his family losing all their influence, the Valaisans continued, ever after, to govern themselves according to their own municipal constitution. The upper, or German Valais was divided into six *dixains* or hundreds, and the town of Sion formed a seventh. Each sent deputies to the general assembly of the country, at which the bishop of Sion presided. The lower Valais was afterwards wrested, by the upper Valaisans, from the duke of Savoy, and was governed by them as a subject district. The Valais entered also into alliances with various Swiss cantons, and particularly with Bern.

LEAGUES OF THE GRISONS

Another country, more extensive and populous than the Valais, effected its emancipation about the same time. This was the highlands of Rhætia, with their sixty valleys, where the Rhine and the Inn have their sources, a wild secluded region, surrounded and intersected on all sides by the highest Alps. The house of Habsburg, or of Austria, had no pretensions over the country. Its numerous nobles had become independent, holding directly of the empire; indeed the bishop of Coire, who had great possessions in the country, was a prince of the empire. A century had now elapsed since the Swiss cantons had achieved their independence, and their neighbours of the Rhætian valleys still groaned under the oppressions of their petty lords, far more overbearing and capricious than the Austrian rulers had been in Helvetia. Perched up in their castles, built on lofty cliffs, they sallied thence like birds of prey, scaring the poor shepherds and cultivators below, and extorting from them the produce of the soil, insulting the chastity of their daughters, and disposing of the liberty and lives of their sons. The chronicles of Rhætia record many instances of rapacity and barbarity perpetrated in those remote valleys, which have never been surpassed in the most corrupt countries by the most depraved tyrants. We read of a baron of Vatz, who used to starve his prisoners in his dungeons, and listen with complacency to their moans from his banqueting hall, and who, to try an experiment on the process of digestion, had three of his servants ripped open some hours after dinner. In another place, we find the chatelain of Guardovall sending deliberately to demand, for his private pleasures, the young and beautiful daughter of Adam of Camogask, one of his tenants — an outrage, however, which led to the revolt and emancipation of the fine valley of Engadina. We are told of the governor of Fardun driving his wild colts among the ripe crops of the farmer Chaldar, whom he cast in chains into a subterranean dungeon for pursuing and killing the destructive animals.

The nobles were often at variance with each other. Hartmann, bishop of Coire, unable to defend the scattered domains of his see, authorized his vassals to form alliances with the neighbouring communes and lordships; accordingly, in 1396, his subjects of the valleys of Domleschg, Avers, Oberhalbstein, and Bergun entered into a treaty, offensive and defensive, with the powerful counts of Werdenberg, lords of Schams and Obervatz. This was the first origin of one of the three leagues or federations of Rhætia, afterwards called the League Caddea, (Casa Dei) or of the house of God, from its being under the bishop's jurisdiction. The increase of strength thus derived by the prelate excited the jealousy of the nobles of the upper Rhine, who formed likewise, in 1400, an alliance with their neighbours of the free canton of Glarus. But they did not grant any franchise to their vassals as the bishop had done, and this made the people more impatient of their servitude. They had no justice to expect from the courts, nor protection on the high roads, nor security for their persons or properties. Several of the elders among the peasants of the country formed a secret association for the purpose of devising a remedy for the evils with which the country was afflicted. They assembled at night time in a wood near the village of Trons, between the abbey of Disentis and the town of Ilanz. There they framed certain resolutions, which they communicated to the trustiest among their respective neighbours. On a fixed day all the communes of upper Rhætia sent deputies to their respective lords, demanding a solemn compact, by which the rights of all, high and low, should be defined and guaranteed, and justice and security rendered inviolable.

The barons were taken unawares; they had few soldiers on whom they could depend. The abbot of Disentis, a prudent and pious man, who himself belonged to an ancient native family, received the deputies kindly, and acceded readily to their demands. The two barons of Razuns followed his example. Count Ulric of Saxe, one of the most powerful feudatories of the Alps, did the same, as well as old Count Hugo of Werdenberg, brother to the defender of Appenzell. Henry of Werdenberg-Sargans, lord of Schams, whose father had been defeated at Näfels by the people of Glarus, alone rejected with scorn the deputies of the communes. In May, 1424, the abbot and all the lords of upper Rhætia joined the deputies of the various valleys, and of the towns of Ilanz and Tusis, in an open field outside of the village of Trons, and there forming a circle round a gigantic maple tree, all of them standing, nobles, magistrates, deputies, and elders swore, in the name of the holy Trinity, a perpetual alliance for the maintenance of justice, and the security of everyone, without, however, infringing on the rights of any. The articles of the league which, to this day, rules that country, were then stipulated. This was called the Grey League, from the colour of the smocks which the deputies wore. By degrees it gave its name to the whole country, which was called Grisons, *Graubünden*, and that of Rhætia became obliterated. Such was the glorious covenant of Trons, one of the few events of its kind which can be recorded with unmixed satisfaction.

The baron of Werdenberg-Sargans, who had alone stood aloof in that day of joy from his countrymen, soon lost his domains. The cruelty of his own agents hastened the crisis. His chatelain of Fardun, after having imprisoned Chaldar, as above mentioned, released him upon the payment of a large ransom, by the united exertions of the prisoner's friends. Chaldar had returned to his cottage; one day when he had just sat down to dinner, with his numerous family round a table, in the midst of which stood a large bowl of boiling porridge, the dreaded chatelain suddenly entered the room. All rose respectfully to receive him, when he, looking surlily at them, approached the table, and spat in the mess which was to supply their humble repast. He then insultingly told Chaldar to begin his meal. The mountaineer could refrain no longer: He rushed upon the chatelain, and seizing him by the neck, "Wretch!" he cried, "thou alone shalt taste of the dinner thou hast contaminated." He then plunged the chatelain's head into the scalding liquid, and held it there until life was extinct. Chaldar, leaving the deformed body stretched on the floor, rushed out to alarm the country around, telling them what he had done and the provocation he had received. The people, already ripe for revolt, rose to a man and attacked the castle, which they took and demolished; and the valley of Schams and the Rheinwald were free, and joined the Grey League which was able to protect them against any further attempts of Werdenberg.

The Engadine, one of the finest and largest valleys in all Helvetia, is watered throughout its length, about sixty miles, by the river Inn, an affluent of the Danube, and is separated on one side from Italy and on the other from the rest of the Grisons by two lofty ridges of the Rhætian Alps. The inhabitants speak the *ladin*, a dialect of the romansch language, greatly resembling the Italian. After the emancipation of the neighbouring valleys, the people of Engadine aspired to the same liberty as their brethren of the Grisons League. The brutal insult offered to Theresa of Camogask, which has been noticed above, decided the explosion. Her father, with assumed composure, told the emissary of the tyrant that he would himself bring his daughter to the castle next morning in a more becoming attire than she was in at present.

Meantime he collected his friends and exhorted them to follow the example of their neighbours. Next morning he led forth his daughter in her best clothes, and, followed by several young men, proceeded to the castle, near which another party had posted themselves in ambuscade. The chatelain came out of the gate, and, seizing the maid from her father's arms, he rudely kissed her lips. At the same moment the father's dagger pierced his heart, and he fell lifeless to the ground. The men of Engadine rushed into the castle, overpowered the guard, and destroyed the walls. The independence of Engadine was proclaimed, and that fine valley joined the Caddea League.

Some time after, the count Frederick of Toggenburg having died without issue, his numerous vassals at Davos, Maienfeld, and other parts of eastern Rhætia, on the borders of the Tyrol, assembled and proposed to form a league similar to the other two for their common protection, during the troubles which broke out about the disputed succession of Toggenburg. "As soon as the legitimate heir shall be acknowledged," they said, "we will restore him his inheritance, but our league shall remain for the security of all. None of our countrymen shall be arraigned before foreign judges, no commune shall form an alliance without the consent of all." In 1436 they swore fidelity to the league, which was called of the Ten Jurisdictions. Thus were formed the three leagues of the Grisons, which have ever since maintained their independence and their municipal liberties. Most of the valleys gradually redeemed the dues they owed to their lords, but by mutual consent and without violence. In 1450 a union, called the Black League, formed of many noblemen who disliked the enfranchisement of the communes, endeavoured to reduce the communes to subjection, but it was defeated, and many of the nobles lost their lives in a conflict in the valley of Schams.

Alliance of the Three Leagues

The three leagues now proposed for their mutual support a solemn alliance among themselves, embracing all the Rhætian valleys. Each commune sent deputies, in 1471, to the village of Vazerol, which stands nearly in the centre of the country, and there a perpetual defensive alliance was sworn to between the leagues, and general diets were appointed to be held by turns in each of the three leagues to deliberate on the interests of the whole. If differences should arise between two of the leagues, the third was to be umpire, and the decisions of two leagues should be obligatory on the third. But in their internal affairs each league, and even each commune, governed itself according to its own laws and customs, held its own meetings, and elected its own magistrates; several communes together formed a jurisdiction, having its courts of civil and criminal justice, and a landamma was elected for a time by the majority of voices; several jurisdictions formed a league, having its annual diet; and the three leagues together formed the confederation of the Grisons. Their government, like that of the Valais, contained a mixture of pure democratic and representative forms, suited to an extensive but mountainous country, where each valley forms a little world of itself, being secluded from the rest by ice and snows during great part of the year. It was not till 1497, during the war called of Swabia, that the Grisons contracted a perpetual alliance with the Swiss cantons, which they maintained ever after, forming an important accession to Switzerland, and protecting its eastern frontiers on the side of the Tyrol, and of the other dominions of the house of Austria.

THE OLD ZURICH WAR

The death of the last count of Toggenburg, in 1436, became a source of fatal dissensions among the Swiss. Zurich pretended to the inheritance, because the count had been a freeman of that city. But he was also a burgher of the canton of Schwyz. His widow sided with Zurich, but those subjects of the count who inhabited Uznach, Lichtensteg, and other districts of Toggenburg, between the Lake of Wallenstadt and the river Thur, sent deputies to their neighbours of Schwyz, and requested to be admitted among its citizens, saying that such had been their master's wish before his death; and in fact he had himself expressed this intention before the deputies of Schwyz and several other witnesses. The cantons of Schwyz and Glarus admitted the inhabitants as co-burghers, and took possession of Toggen and of the Upper March, of which the count had given them the reversion by a former treaty. Zurich prepared to oppose these arrangements by arms, and seized upon several other districts. The other cantons interfered, and prevented the explosion for a time, but in 1440 the war broke out between Schwyz and Glarus on one side and Zurich on the other. One condition of the Swiss Confederacy was that any canton having disputes with another, and refusing to submit to the direction of arbiters chosen according to the prescribed forms, should be constrained by force. Zurich was in this predicament, having refused to abide by the decisions of the umpires, and she drew upon herself the forces of all the other cantons. Uri and Unterwalden, Lucerne, Bern, and Zug all sent their contingents, and Zurich was threatened with an immediate attack, when, perceiving the danger, it submitted to what is called the *jus Helveticum*, or public law of the confederation. Arbiters were appointed from the five mediating cantons, whose decision was that Zurich should restore all it had taken out of the Toggenburg estates, while Schwyz and Glarus were to retain their conquests.

Stüssi, burgomaster of Zurich, a bold ambitious man, thinking solely on revenge, forgot the sacred ties of his country with the Swiss cantons, and sought the alliance of the hereditary enemy of their common country, Frederick III of Austria. This prince had been elected emperor of Germany, and he aimed at reconquering the Aargau, and the other domains which his house had lost in Switzerland. An alliance offensive and defensive between Zurich and Austria was concluded at Vienna in 1442. Frederick soon after repaired to Zurich, when the citizens swore fidelity to the empire, and tearing from their sleeves the white cross, the badge of the Swiss in all their wars, assumed the red cross of Austria. The confederates were indignant at this conduct; Zurich had broken the federal pact, and in 1443 war was declared by all the cantons against the perjured republic. The confederates defeated the Zurichers and Austrians in several battles, and took or destroyed many towns and villages.

At last they advanced against Zurich in the month of July. The Zurichers came out of the city, and crossing the bridge on the river Sihl, under their walls met the Swiss, led by Ital Reding of Schwyz, a man brave and resolute even to ferocity. A desperate battle was fought in the fields near the Sihl, close to the ramparts of Zurich. At last the Zurichers gave way, and recrossed in disorder the bridge to re-enter their town. The old burgomaster Stüssi alone stood on the bridge, with his battle-axe in hand, trying to stop the flight; but a citizen of Zurich, exclaiming that he was "the main cause of all this mischief!" ran him through with his spear. Stüssi fell in his heavy armour, and friends and foes passed over his body on their way to the gate.

Some of the confederates had entered the town, but a Zuricher had the presence of mind to lower the portcullis, and thus saved the city from the horrors of a storming. The confederates set fire to the suburb, committed the greatest devastations in the country around; they brutally cut open the body of the burgomaster Stüssi, pulled out his heart, and then threw the mangled remains into the river. The night was spent by the confederates in drinking and carousing among the bodies of the dying and the dead. Such were the brutalizing effects of civil war, and so much altered were the Swiss since the days of Morgarten and of Sempach!

Next year the castle of Greifensee was taken by storm after an obstinate resistance. Ital Reding, who led the confederates, ordered the commander and the whole garrison to be beheaded by the public executioner. In vain Holzach of Menzingen implored the Swiss not to offend their God, not to stain the honour of the confederation, "by so inhuman an act." "*Down with them!*" was the answer of the ferocious soldiers; head after head fell to the number of sixty and the work of blood was completed by the light of torches.

In the following summer, 1444, the confederates, to the number of twenty thousand, laid siege to Zurich. The emperor Frederick and his cousin Sigismund of Austria, being engaged in distant wars, strove to raise up another enemy against the Swiss. They wrote to Charles VII, king of France, to whose daughter Sigismund was betrothed, and who, having just concluded a truce with England, was not sorry to employ abroad the mercenary companies of partisans which proved very troublesome guests in time of peace. These companies were composed of soldiers of fortune of all nations, accustomed to a life of violence and plunder, and impatient of any restraint. An old chronicler calls them *filii Belial*, sons of the Devil. They were better known by the name of Armagnacs, being the remains of the faction of that name which had figured in the civil wars of France. The king collected them and sent them first into Alsace, and then against Bâle, under the command of the dauphin Louis, afterwards Louis XI of France. They desolated the countries on the left of the Rhine, sparing neither friends nor foes, and at last, on the 23rd of August, they appeared under the walls of Bâle to the number of thirty thousand men, chiefly cavalry.

The citizens of Bâle sent one of their councillors in great haste to request the assistance of the Swiss against this formidable irruption. The Swiss detached twelve hundred[1] men of Bern, Solothurn, and the forest cantons from their camp before Farnsburg, which place they were then besieging. On the 26th of August this little band met the advance guard of the Armagnacs at Brattelen, and drove them back beyond the river Birs. The main body of the enemy was posted on the left bank of the river. The Swiss, seeing the bridge of Sankt Jakob well guarded, threw themselves into the stream and forded it, notwithstanding the fire of the French artillery. Having reached the opposite bank, they cut their way through the numerous ranks of the Armagnacs, with the intention of reaching Bâle. The inhabitants of that city, seeing from the summit of their towers the efforts of this band of heroes, made a sortie to join them; but a body of eight thousand horse, whom the dauphin had placed on that side, drove them back into the city. The Swiss were divided: a body of them, surrounded in the plain by forces ten times their number, were all slain, after making dreadful havoc among their enemies: they fell in their ranks close to each other. Another party of five

[1 Some historians say fifteen hundred, but the calculation of the dead and wounded found on the field of battle seems to correspond with the lesser number.]

hundred threw themselves into the hospital and chapel of Sankt Jakob. The gardens of the hospital were surrounded by high walls; there this handful of Swiss, hemmed in by a whole army, stood, determined to sell their lives dearly. Three times they repelled the attack, twice they sallied out like lions against the close ranks of their enemies; at last the walls were battered down by cannon, and the French cavaliers, having dismounted, entered the breach; yet the Swiss still opposed a desperate resistance. The hospital and the chapel took fire, and the surviving confederates were smothered among the ruins. Out of twelve hundred Swiss who fought on that day ten alone escaped by flight, and these were shunned and driven away with scorn in every part of Switzerland, for not having shared the fate of their comrades.

The fight lasted ten hours. Thousands of men and horses of the Armagnacs strewed the field of battle. The dauphin was dismayed at the sight of his own loss; and, hearing that the whole confederate army was moving against him from the camp before Zurich, he thought it prudent not to attempt to proceed any further, after witnessing such a specimen of Swiss intrepidity. Æneas Silvius Piccolomini, afterwards Pope Pius II, who happened to be at Bâle at the time, mentions in his epistles several circumstances of that memorable combat. He says the Swiss, having emptied their quivers, snatched out of their wounds the arrows of their enemies, and shot them back. Burkhard Monch, a nobleman bitterly hostile to the Swiss, who served in the ranks of the dauphin, as he was walking in the evening among the bodies of the dead Swiss, and, observing the streams of blood which drenched the ground, exclaimed, "Now am I bathing among roses." Arnold Schilk of Uri, who was lying near, wounded, overheard him, and picking up a large stone flung it with such force at the inhuman boaster that he fell dead to the ground.

Two days after the battle, the dauphin granted a safe conduct to the citizens of Bâle, that they might bury the dead and carry away the wounded: 1,158 Swiss were found dead, and 32 wounded. The dauphin withdrew his army, and signed a peace with the cantons and with Bâle in the following October. Struck with admiration at the bravery of the Swiss, he even sought their alliance, and this was the origin of the long friendship and connection between the French kings and the Helvetic body.

The war against Zurich and its allies continued the whole of the following year; several parties of Austrian troops were defeated by the Swiss, who took the town of Rheinfelden. At length, in 1446, several of the German electors and the bishop of Bâle interposed, and a peace was concluded [1450] on these conditions: that Zurich should renounce its alliance with Austria, and return again to that of the Swiss cantons; that the conquered districts should be restored on both sides, with the exception of Pfeffikon and Wolran, which remained to Schwyz. The Toggenburg, the cause of all this war, was left in the possession of the lord of Raron, a relative of the late count, and both he and his subjects remained co-burghers of the cantons of Schwyz and Glarus. The alliance of Bâle with the cantons was confirmed. This unnatural war cost the Zurichers more than a million of florins.

But the differences between the cantons and Austria were not yet settled. The vassals and partisans of the latter power in Switzerland continued to make incursions on the lands of the confederates. They pillaged Rheinfelden; they surprised Brugg by night, and slaughtered its inhabitants, or carried them away and obliged them to pay a high ransom; Aarau was partly burned. John, lord of Falkenstein, distinguished himself in this predatory warfare. On the other hand, the Swiss burned many of their castles. The town of Fribourg remained faithful to the house of Austria, although now become quite isolated in the midst of hostile states. But the dukes of Austria did not reward the fidelity of its citizens; on the contrary they burdened them with fresh taxes, and its governors acted in an arbitrary manner by deposing the avoyers and council. This conduct alienated the hearts of the Fribourgers.

About the same time the duke of Savoy claimed payment of 200,000 florins, due to him by the city. The duke of Austria, despairing of retaining possession of Fribourg, ordered its governor, Halwyl, to quit the town, which he did after taking possession, by a stratagem, of the best part of the burghers' plate. The citizens, preferring the domination of Savoy to that of Bern, which had long had views upon their country, submitted to the former power in 1452, and swore fidelity to the duke of Savoy, who guaranteed to them their ancient privileges.

THE PEACE OF WALDSHUT (1468 A.D.)

The only possessions remaining now to the house of Austria in Switzerland were the county of Rapperschwyl, the town of Winterthur, and the landgrafschaft of Thurgau; and these were lost soon after. Rapperschwyl gave itself voluntarily to the three forest cantons and that of Glarus. Duke Sigismund of Austria, upon this, treated the four cantons as enemies. But Sigismund himself, happening to have disputes with the pope, was excommunicated, and the pope called upon the Swiss to seize on his domains. The confederates were not slow in obeying the call. In 1460 they entered the fine province of Thurgau, which extends from the frontiers of Zurich to the Lake of Constance, and consists of gentle hills and plains, fruitful in corn, flax, and wine, and watered by the river Thur. They encountered no opposition; the town of Diessenhofen alone defended its allegiance to Austria, but was obliged to capitulate, retaining its privileges as a little republic, under the protection of the cantons. All the rest of Thurgau was taken possession of as a conquered country, the cantons assuming the rights which the house of Austria had till then exercised over it (as they had done with the Aargau about half a century before). Each of the eight old cantons by turns appointed the bailiff, who resided at Frauenfeld, and who was changed every two years. This order of things continued till the end of the eighteenth century. In 1467 Duke Sigismund mortgaged Wintherthur, his last remaining possession, to the citizens of Zurich, to whom it was finally given up ten years after. And here was the end of the power of the house of Habsburg in Helvetia. When in the following century Charles V was raised to the thrones of Germany, Spain, Italy and "the Indies," the house of Austria had lost every acre of its old patrimonial estates; the castle of Habsburg itself having passed into the hands of strangers.

Mülhausen, an imperial town in Alsace, finding itself annoyed by the neighbouring nobility, contracted an alliance with the Swiss cantons, which it maintained for centuries after. This, however, led to a fresh quarrel with Sigismund. The banks of the Rhine, from Schaffhausen to Bâle, were again the scene of a desultory though destructive warfare, in which, however, the Austrians were worsted.[c] The confederates laid siege to Waldshut. The garrison made a stubborn resistance, but in August, 1468, hostilities were ended by the Peace of Waldshut. Sigismund surrendered to the confederates his rights over the Thurgau and promised to pay 10,000 gulden damages by June 24th, 1469, giving as security Waldshut and the Black Forest.[a]

THE BURGUNDIAN WAR

Sigismund was not in a state to fulfil the engagements he had entered into with the Swiss. The penury of his finances made him lend an ear to those gentlemen who, in their hatred against the confederates, did not fear to see once more the key to their country in the hands of France. They determined to offer to his brother-in-law, King Louis XI, Alsace, Sundgau, and the two Rhine banks as pledge for a considerable loan. But the maxims of Louis were those followed in imitation of Italian tyrants, by the princes of his time — maxims which Machiavelli exposed later, leaving them his name. Everything in France was making for the downfall of feudalism and the creation of a united monarchy. The king did not forcibly demand what he could obtain by trickery, and he awaited from his enemies' mistakes what others sought from the issues of war. Thus he guarded himself from losing the friendship of the Swiss by accepting the offers of Sigismund. It was to his powerful and redoubtable vassal, Duke Charles of Burgundy, that he addressed the archduke.

Eleven years younger than the king, Charles expected from his riches and his army that which Louis sought from politics. Taking Alexander and Cæsar as models, he conceived vast plans which he embraced with great enthusiasm, though he gave little thought to making them clear. The pope, who, since the taking of Constantinople by the Turks in 1453, had preached a new crusade, called "the great duke of the west" to lead it. It is well known that Charles, already more powerful than his suzerain, dreamed of founding a kingdom of Burgundy, which should stretch from the Mediterranean and the sources of the Rhine to the mouth of this river. When, then, Sigismund offered him five provinces in mortgage for a loan of 50,000 florins; when he made known to him the prospective marriage between Maximilian, only son of the emperor, and Mary, the Burgundian heiress, and Charles learned that the only thing asked in exchange was support in a struggle against the Swiss, he saw in the offer a mark of distinguished good fortune. He hastened to give up the necessary sums, more considerable than those asked at first, and to receive homage from the mortgaged countries (1469).

He charged with the administration of these countries one Peter von Hagenbach, a low born and conceited parvenu, who was avaricious and vulgar in manner, and who succeeded in making his master's rule detested and in uniting in a common hatred nobles, bishops, free towns, the new subjects of Burgundy and the Swiss leagues. However, Charles laid his ambitious designs before the emperor. The two monarchs met at Treves on the 29th of September, 1473. One might almost have thought Charles was the emperor, and the aged Frederick of Austria his humble vassal! Seeking equally to deceive each other, one urged the marriage of his son with Mary of Burgundy, and the other, who dreaded above all things having a son-in-law, only wanted to obtain, without giving anything for it, the title of King of the Romans. The throne was all ready: the sceptre and crown were exposed to public view, when the emperor made off without taking leave, playing with hopes that he had allowed Charles to conceive (1473).

The duke's anger was extreme. His approach spread alarm in Alsace. The inhabitants fled; peasants shut themselves up in the towns, and these towns shut their gates. Arrived at Ensisheim, Charles convoked there the nobility of the country. Nicholas von Sharnachthal and Peter von Wabern presented themselves in the name of Bern. Kneeling, they complained among other things of the ill treatment that Mülhausen, a Swiss ally, had had to endure from Hagenbach. "I am about to set forth," responded the duke; "follow me to Dijon." They did so, but after long waiting left Dijon without any answer.

However, the king of France did not neglect to profit from the alarm spread by the duke of Burgundy. He knew the keen desire of the Habsburgs to recover their patrimony, and did not ignore the fact that Frederick III had even recently put the confederates under ban of the empire. Nevertheless, he conceived the project of reconciling the Swiss with the house of Austria, and uniting them in a common alliance against the prince named by his contemporaries Charles the Bold, known in history as Charles the Rash. Everywhere he found obstacles in his path.

Since the eyes of the confederates had turned towards France, Bern had become the scene of negotiations with that country; and she had left the direction of them to her most eminent political and military leaders. But debate had arisen between these men of the old or new nobility and the townsfolk. As the nobility, in order to become Bernese citizens, had been obliged to abandon many privileges irreconcilable with the new notions of a state, but had preserved nevertheless certain justiciary rights, they were called Lord Laws (Twingherrn). Time came when also these rights were opposed by ideas hostile to feudalism. A butcher named Kistler had constituted himself at Bern the organ of the new tendencies. In 1470 at the annual election for the head of the republic, Nicholas von Diessbach obtained fifteen votes, Adrian von Bubenberg twenty, Rigoltingen thirty, Scharnachthal forty, and eighty were given to Kistler. The gentlemen withdrew to their castles, while the new head of the republic let his zeal as reformer run its course. He took note of the luxury of high-born ladies and proscribed their long trains, their high heeled shoes. They braved his proscription and proudly retired to their own lands.

Strife would have been engendered if the lords, united to the country people by a habit of living together in peace and war, had not had the wisdom to hinder the peasants from assembling or waging an unequal fight against the town. They knew how to wait to see what time and amicable intervention from the confederates would do. And, indeed, a large deputation from the cantons was not slow in going to Bern, urged by the necessity of establishing concord in those difficult times. The lords consented that the town should hold the jurisdiction demanded. Left free to invest themselves as they pleased, the deputation returned from Bern amidst universal jubilation. Kistler, who had not been useless to his fellow citizens, remained in their midst as a magistrate worth listening to. From this time the republic, fresh from triumphing over intestine dissensions, could give all its attention to the serious events happening abroad.

The Everlasting Compact (1474 A.D.)

Two men in Switzerland directed and served the politics of Louis XI. These were the advocate Nicholas von Diessbach, and, in the eastern cantons, the Lucernaise, Jost de Silinen, provost of Münster and for some time administrator of the bishopric of Grenoble. Coming from a family enriched by commerce and ennobled by the acquisition of imperial fiefs, Diessbach had been royal page and chamberlain. At Bern he was the distributor of royal largesse and the leader of a French party. When the Fribourg advocate, Raoul de Wuippens, and Adrian von Bubenberg, who had lived at the Burgundian court and fought for the duke at Montlhéry, reminded him of the good relations the Swiss had always held with their neighbours from beyond the Jura — when they made clear what had been imprudent on the part of the confederates in overthrowing a barrier which still separated them from a powerful monarchy, Diessbach contented himself with answering that those who were useful were always estimated at their right value. Already, in the course of the year 1470, he had obtained the conclusion of a treaty, by which France and the confederates mutually engaged not to support one another against the duke of Burgundy. But Louis wanted more: the agreement was defensive, and he sought the offensive.

To arrive thereat, Silinen urged on the one hand that the archduke Sigismund should redeem the mortgaged countries for the duke of Burgundy; while on the other hand he knew how to prevail upon the confederates to allow the king to direct the terms of their reconciliation with the Habsburgs. All took place concurrently. The house of Austria and the cantons agreed to a perpetual peace, the Everlasting Compact (March 30th, 1474). The confederates remained in full possession of that which they had acquired. The parties promised each other good neighbourship and mutual succour. Immediately upon the signature of the treaty the principal Alsatian towns arose and allied themselves with the Swiss. They made up without difficulty the sum necessary for the redemption of the province, deposited it at Bâle, and invited the duke to receive it. Hagenbach, who during a popular insurrection at this time had fallen into the enemy's hands, was imprisoned, judged by a tribunal, and put to death. Aided by the Swiss, the duke retook possession of his lands.

The Treaty of Lucerne; Battles and Skirmishes

While these events were in progress, Charles, who had fought against the German Empire, was obstinately besieging Neuss, a fortress of the archbishopric of Cologne (June, 1474 to March, 1475). He had to confide to Italian condottieri the task of reducing Alsace and the neighbouring county of Ferret (August, 1474). But on the news that these "Lombards," as the condottieri were called, were putting all to fire and sword, the confederates rose and united at Lucerne, where the royal envoys urged them, under an appearance of cordiality, to show themselves "friends to friends, inimical to enemies." A treaty was signed, in which the king was promised, in case of war against Burgundy, six thousand men at a pay of $4\frac{1}{2}$ florins a month. The king on his side engaged to pay each canton 2,000 francs yearly, and 20,000 francs every three years to the confederates, if he could not, in case of war against Burgundy, help them with arms. Neither party was to conclude peace without the other. A secret convention dealt with the sums, still more considerable, that the king engaged to pay to the principal cantons and their most influential magistrates.

The treaty concluded, an army of twenty thousand men, composed of divers contingents from the cantons and their allies, Swabian horse-soldiers sent from friends and from the towns of the league on the Rhine, laid siege to Héricourt, a fortress of the Franche-Comté, the property of Marshal Thiebault of Burgundy. The marshal, succoured by the count of Romont, Baron de Vaud, tried to raise the siege. They fought valiantly, but could not resist the impetuosity of the Swiss, their long halberds, and double-handled swords. The rout was complete (November 13th, 1474). Héricourt surrendered. The Swiss returned home laden with spoil.

Diessbach did not intend his army to remain long inactive. From the first months of 1475 expeditions went forth from various points in the Franche-Comté. At Neuchâtel a new house, that of the Hochberg counts, had succeeded that of the Fribourg counts, and relied on Bern. Rudolf everywhere exercised his *rôle* of mediator. His men had fought in the Swiss ranks at Héricourt, but his son served Charles the Bold; he himself had gone to Neuss to try to bring Charles and the emperor together and reconcile them with the Swiss. Diessbach reminded him of his duties towards Bern in letting a troop of adventurers ravage his lands.

A more considerable army corps crossed the Jura to surprise Pontarlier and ravage it with fire. The Bernese found themselves under the walls of this city in the presence of Louis de Châlons, lord of Château Guyon, who possessed on this side of the Jura, Granson, Orbe, and Echallens; at Héricourt they had to fight against Count Jacques de Romont, their fellow citizen, who held an appanage comprising the greater part of the Vaud country. They also thought to comprise in their offensive operations all the countries along their way as far as the Jura. They surprised Granson, seized the castle of Orbe which was heroically defended, reduced that of Jougne, and did not retire until they had made themselves masters of all the fortresses situated in the mountain passes.

A fresh expedition was directed on the county of Montbeliard. The Blamont fort, defended by walls eighteen feet thick, dominated all this country and important routes. It was during this siege that Nicholas von Diessbach, wounded by a kick from his horse, then seized with an epidemic which was decimating the troops, died while still young, at Parrentruy. He was not to see the end of a war he had started. He had opened a glorious career to his party, but had also given it an example of venality and bound it with chains from which it took long centuries to free itself. Scharnachthal replaced him before Blamont. Town, castle, all were ruined from base to turret amidst wild cries. His partisans ravaged the land as far as the gates of Besançon.

Bern and Fribourg Open a Campaign in the Vaud (1475 A.D.)

Bern had not yet declared war against the house of Savoy. This house, her ancient ally, was very different from what she had been. Since Felix V had, in 1449, abdicated the pontifical power, in the church of the Lausanne Franciscans, so doing to enter into the solitudes of Ripaille, and had renounced all his high authority, keeping only the titles of Bishop of Geneva and Cardinal Coadjutor in Switzerland and Savoy, the star of his family had waned. The change of the title of count into that of duke was far from being for the house a sign of aggrandisement. To a century and a half of glory there was to succeed as long a time of trouble and misfortune. There was an interrupted series of weak princes, minorities, regencies; and meanwhile the sceptre was found in hands too weak to bear it, nobles disputed for power, and the country was a prey to factions. Finally the hour came when the Swiss and the duke of Burgundy decided their quarrel on the fields of Romande Helvetia.

Yolande of France, sister of Louis XI, governed the Savoy counties in the name of Philibert I, her son, then a minor. She wanted to preserve the neutrality; yet hatred of her brother, and the hope she cherished of seeing the young prince of Savoy marry the heiress of Charles the Bold, inclined her to the side of Burgundy. Around her worked the young princes' uncles, of whom one, Philip of Bresse, was wholly French, whilst the two others, the bishop of Geneva and the count of Romont, adhered to Charles.   The nobility of the country had embraced the same cause.   The Gingins, high-minded according to their crest, served the duke with devotion.   Torrent of the house of Compois, who had made use of the troubles to form a kind of satrap government in Aigle, welcomed on their way the Italian condottieri that Duke Sforza of Milan had sold to the duke of Burgundy, while at the same time he pressed Louis XI to make war on this prince.   Bern felt herself justified in carrying fire and sword into the Vaud country, and in asking the allies of Neuchâtel, Solothurn, and Fribourg to join their armies to hers.

She first addressed herself to Fribourg.   For a long time two parties had been at issue in Fribourg.   The one, Savoyard, the other, faithful to Austria. Abandoned by the archdukes, the Austrian party ended by succumbing, and the Fribourgers in 1452 floated on their towers the white cross of Savoy. Soon after they had renewed their alliance with Bern she urged them to enter on a campaign with her without waiting for the confederates to come and take part in the conquest of the Vaud counties.   Thus Bernese and Fribourgers were the first to set out (October, 1475).

They sacked Vully, and received the submission of Morat and Payerne.   Contingents from many cantons had joined with them and the army, ten thousand strong, spread over the country like a torrent.   Three hundred men of Nyon threw themselves into Estavayer — their courage was useless.   All was "chopped up and skinned."   They came to the pillage by sea and land.   A hundred chariots carried to Fribourg the fabrics in which Estavayer did great trade.   Eleven soldiers of the garrison were hidden in a redoubt.   Discovered, they were handed over to the Bern executioner; bound together with ropes, they were to be drowned in the lake.   But the rope broke, and the Swiss soldiery, disappointed of the expected sight, killed the unfortunate men with their pikes and ended by killing the executioner for his awkwardness.

Yverdun had never been attacked without making honourable resistance.   She had prepared to defend herself well, when the count of Valentgin obtained permission for the garrison to march beyond the walls with the insignia of war; while for the town he secured the maintenance of its liberties.   The castle of Clees only yielded after several vigorous assaults.   At Greifensee those of her defenders who survived were condemned to be beheaded.   But as the Swiss had killed the Bern executioner, they

SWISS SOLDIER

(Fifteenth century)

offered pardon to that one of the prisoners who would take his place.   A German, valet to Pierre de Cossonay, commander of the place, undertook the office, and the captives fell beneath his axe, Pierre de Cossonay the last.

The castles of Jougne and Sainte-Croix had the same fate as that of Clees. Those of Montagney, Champvans, and La Sarra, vigorously defended by their lords, were reduced to ashes.   The army, increased daily by reinforcements, drew near Lausanne and Geneva.   Its leader, Peter von Wabern, had orders to take nothing from churches.   But the true episcopal towns had, nevertheless, to pay ransom. Lausanne, which had amicable relations with Bern, paid 2,000 florins, and Geneva 28,000; the parishes of Lavaux paid 5,000 florins.

The Alliance of Bern and Upper Valais (1473 A.D.)

The war had begun at the foot of the Alps. The Valais were, at this time, governed by a bishop as firm in his actions as he was skilful in managing popular favour. German by birth, and born in the tithing of Conches, Walther von Supersax maintained himself among the patriots of Upper Valais, without bending to their democracy. It was not until a long time after he had forbidden them to renew their alliance with the Alpine cantons, their neighbours, that he lent himself, in 1473, to a renewal of this alliance. Two years after, when he saw the Burgundian war beginning, and a chance of recovering the patrimony of Saint-Thesdule, usurped from the church by the house of Savoy, he allied himself with Bern and did not delay marching on Lower Valais. Pierre and Amédée de Gingins, at the head of eight thousand men, threw him back on Sion. But as the two armies were at close quarters under the walls of this city, three thousand Bernese, descended from Sanetsch, took the Savoyards on the flank, and forced them to retire in great disorder. The conquerors then overran all Lower Valais. At the same time there came down from Simmenthal and Haute Grunyère mountaineers always ready to work havoc on the plains. They destroyed the castle of Aigle, and the town submitted to Bern and became her subject.

Emperor and King Desert the Confederation

Charles, however, had continued the siege of Neuss; the emperor having finally advanced upon this place at the head of German contingents, the two princes found themselves face to face. As neither one nor the other desired war, but an understanding, an agreement was made without difficulty (June 4th, 1475). For the hope of obtaining for his son the hand of the Burgundian heiress, the emperor sacrificed the French alliance and broke his pledge with the Swiss and Archduke Sigismund. Louis XI hastened, on his side, to conclude a long treaty with Charles; he granted him free passage to march against the Swiss (September 13th, 1475). Thenceforth free in his movements, Charles came to an understanding with the archduke, conquered Lorraine, whence came the heritor of Duke René, and made ready from the first days of 1476 to cross the Jura.

Charles, in conquering Lorraine saw his star for the last time in ascendancy. It was not that his army was less splendid, his artillery less numerous — his court, transported into camp, was still the most magnificent in the West; but, being no longer able to rely on the affection of subjects whom he had wearied, he saw himself compelled to put his chief confidence in the foreigners who served him, in the Italians and their leader, Campobasso, who might betray him. And as he showed himself more and more incapable of supporting contradiction, the fidelity of those made proud by fortune was no longer secure.

The Swiss garrisons had evacuated Jougne, Orbe, Yverdun, to retire on Granson, on the borders of Lake Neuchâtel. It was round this spot that Charles made his army encamp — an army thirty thousand strong. Granson resisted fifteen days and was taken only by treason. Its defenders were induced to believe that Fribourg was burned, that Bern had submitted, that all resistance was useless; but that nevertheless, touched by their bravery, the duke would grant them life. When, under the influence of this false news, they had come to the Burgundian camp, some were hung on the nearest trees and the others drowned in the lake (February 28th, 1476).

Charles had a strong encampment beyond the Arnon, but his intention was not to receive the enemy there but to march on Bern, skirting the base of the Jura. Already he had sent on a reconnoitring party as far as the castle of Vaumarcus, where he had left five hundred men. Before him stretched an undulating plain. Still farther, Mount Aubert descended abruptly towards the water. The route passed by it. A difficult road, the Voie d'Estraz, wound along its flank. It was on this road that the first encounter took place.

The Battle of Granson

The confederates advanced from Neuchâtel, to the number of twenty thousand—the Bernese under Scharnachthal and Halwyl, the Waldstätte under Rudolf Reding, the Lucernese commanded by their old commander Hasfourter, and the Zurichers by Goeldli. As both sides were impatient to meet, the Schwyzers had got ahead of their brothers in arms, and on the morning of March 2nd found themselves suddenly face to face with the Burgundian advance guard. Promptly rejoined by Bern, Solothurn and Fribourg, they made them retreat until, coming out of a wood, the sun having dispelled the mists, they saw advancing in battle array all the duke of Burgundy's forces. At this sight they stuck their pikes and banners into the ground, kneeling asked help of the God of battles, and prepared for the fight.

The duke also hastened to place his men. He posted his artillery on the right, on the plateau which dominates the village of Corcelles, ranged his infantry behind them, and charged his gendarmerie, under Louis de Château Guyon, to follow a hidden winding in the Jura so as to fall on the flanks of the Swiss. But the artillery was posted too high; the gendarmerie were broken on the long lances of the confederates, and lost their leader in the melée. On his side, Charles, at the head of his infantry, met with invincible resistance. Sometimes the Swiss opened their ranks to let bows and culverins hurl projectiles on the enemy, but immediately they closed again, presenting a formidable hedge of pikes. Charles essayed a retrograde movement, to draw them into the plain; but just as his commands were being executed a new army appeared. These were the Swiss of the Waldstätte, who came on making wood and plain re-echo to the sound of their Alpine trumpets of the bull of Uri, the cow of Unterwalden, sounds known well enough to the Austrians, and which the Burgundians also were to learn that day in their turn. Fear took possession of them; they were panic stricken, and they fled in every direction. "The leaguers," says the Neuchâtel chronicler, Hugues de Pierre, "cut up these fine gallants on every hand. So thoroughly and completely were these poor Burgundians discomfited that they were as smoke before a strong wind."

However, the pursuit was short. After thanks were rendered to the God of battles, the army hastened towards the camp where pillage had already begun. Some endeavour was made to inspire order in the sharing of the immense booty, but the leaders themselves hardly knew the riches of those conquered. The duke's big diamond, which had not its equal in the world, passed through many hands, beginning with those of the curé of Montagney, who bought it for a crown, and arrived eventually in those of Pope Jules II, who paid 20,000 ducats for it as an ornament in his papal tiara. Draperies of silk and velvet, rich embroideries, cloth of gold and damask, Flanders lace, Arras carpets were cut up as if they were ordinary cloth and shared by the army. The duke's seal, his collar of the Golden Fleece, his splendid sword fell into the hands of men "gross and bucolic," says Paradin, "who knew not how to profit by them." Forty artillery pieces, eight hundred bows, and three hundred barrels of powder were distributed among the cantons and their allies. The duke's treasure was equally divided. It was so considerable that the division was made without counting or weighing, simply by measuring out hatfuls.

The garrison of Vaumarcus succeeded in escaping by passing the mountains; that of Granson surrendered unconditionally. Those who composed it were either thrown from the walls, hung, or drowned. Then the conquerors, carrying spoil, set out for their cantons, whilst Charles, who had suffered less a defeat than a rout, and who had not lost a thousand men, thought only of renewing the campaign with a stronger force.

Charles Renews the Campaign

Lausanne was chosen as his centre of action (March 15th). The duchess of Savoy installed herself near him. Romont retook possession of the Vaud country. The army re-formed on the Jorat plateau, the "plain of wolves." Three thousand hired English passed for being the best in the army; four thousand Italians, recruited from the papal states, tried to cross the St. Bernard, but, repulsed by men of the Valais, only arrived in camp after a long détour in the Savoyard Alps. But Charles had to yield to bodily fatigue and severe anxiety. Fever seized him, he became delirious, and it was only after some weeks' illness that the unfortunate monarch came to himself, and still pale, with the traces of death on his face, rallied his troops and retook command (May 27th, 1476).

He had hoped the Swiss would come to meet him in the Vaud country, where the land was more favourable. But the army which had conquered at Granson was dispersed, and now occupied on their farms; these Alpine mountaineers, who knew nothing of a Romande Helvetia or the natural limits of the Jura, had renounced all warlike preoccupations at Bern. The confederates were hardly prepared for a campaign when the enemy came on afresh. Bern gave them rendezvous on the right bank of the Saane (Sarine), three leagues from Morat, where an advance guard was posted. She sent there Adrian von Bubenberg with fifteen hundred men. Bubenberg, it is true, passed for a Burgundian, but under these circumstances the private person gave place to the citizen. He asserted that he knew how to defend Morat. Soon after, Charles came on at the head of thirty-four thousand men (June 9th), and covered all the country with his army, a country formed of wooded hills which fell away from around Morat, towards a rather deep lake. Three vigorous assaults were successively repulsed.

On the 22nd of June the confederates crossed the Saane. Burgomaster Herter of Strasburg brought them German contingents, and René of Lorraine three hundred gentlemen attached to his fortunes. One could reckon on thirty thousand foot and four thousand horse. It would be difficult to say who commanded them. It was really the genius of the confederation which allowed them to act each according to his strength in a common plan.

Still, it was to the burgomaster of Strasburg and the Zurich Waldmann that the principal direction of the combat was entrusted. Halwyl marched in advance at the head of the men of the Waldstätte and the Oberland. René was on his flank with a corps of pikemen, bowmen, and culveriners. Herter and Waldmann took places in the main body, and the commissioner Hertenstein, of Lucerne, in the rearguard. There were a thousand rencounters.

The Battle of Morat (1476 A.D.)

All the morning the duke had awaited a battle, which the confederates did not hurry to begin. They made a good show by capering about and deceived the impatience of their men, but were really awaiting the middle of the day to fatigue their enemies. The sky was dark with driving rain. But when, towards mid-day, the sun appeared — "Know, my men," said Halwyl, waving his sword, "that God sends us his sun. Think of your wives and children. Would you abandon to the Welsch those whom you love?" A chapel was afterwards built in the village of Cressier in the place where his troops said their prayers and whence, always restraining their ardour, he led them on to the enemy.

The duke began to collect his troops, tired of long waiting, and had hardly time to place them in battle order. He had intrenched his camp by a quick-set hedge and a ditch, ranging his artillery in front and his cavalry on their flank. The artillery did wonders. They bore entire ranks before them. But Halwyl, getting behind the hedge, fell from above on the Burgundian flank. Then, animated with fresh ardour, the confederates leaped into the ditches, trod the hedge under foot, and by the force of their sinewy arms bore their cannon beyond the ditch, forcing back the artillery on the main body.

Charles was there in person. He had round him Orange, Hugues de Château Guyon, Somerset and his English, his bravest soldiers and his best captains. On his left, on the shores of the lake, was the Burgundian bastard, and hidden beyond Morat the count de Romont, who might be dangerous. But the Swiss had deceived Romont by a false attack; and Bubenberg having sufficiently occupied the left wing by a sortie, the principal efforts of the confederates were directed on the main army, where Charles fought like a lion. He had just seen Somerset fall at his side; fifteen hundred gentlemen-at-arms strewed the ground around him — yet still he fought. But when Hertenstein, with the Swiss rearguard, having scaled the heights, threatened to fall on his remaining host, despair seized him. Giving rein to his horse he mournfully fled, and trotting day and night did not stop until he had reached the Lake of Geneva.

His troops had not awaited the moment of his flight to disperse like the wind. As this time there was no lack of cavalry, the pursuit was hot and bloody. From Morat to Avenches it was simply a battle. No prisoners were made, they were all killed. "Morat cruelty" was long afterwards a popular phrase. Fifteen thousand dead were counted. Driven back on the lake, the cuirassiers and the Italians of the Burgundian bastard, who had tried to rejoin the count of Romont by following the banks covered with reeds, had become entangled in a marsh. Romont alone succeeded in escaping with his Savoyards. The conquerors had lost three thousand men. The dead were buried in a vast ditch. Four years afterwards the bones were exhumed to make an ossuary, a tribute to the valour of a people who had fought for their hearths and the destruction of Charles of Burgundy.

The Vaud is again Invaded; the Congress of Fribourg

The battle of Morat was followed by a new invasion of the Vaud country. Already the mountaineers of Upper Simmenthal and Gressenay, having descended to the plain, had destroyed the Tour de Beilz and Vevey. Twelve thousand Bernese and Fribourgers had in their turn spread over the towns and country, not killing but pillaging. At Lausanne, finishing the work of the count of Gruyères, who had gone ahead and put the town under contribution, they sacked indifferently churches, convents, and private lands, only stopping at the gates of Geneva and at the voice of Louis XI. The Swiss had beaten his powerful rival, but he did not wish the Romande country to become their prey. He demanded a suspension of arms and a congress to meet to decide the conditions of peace.

The Congress assembled at Fribourg on the 25th of July. The heroes of Morat, as first magistrates in their cantons, met with the ambassadors of France, Austria, and Savoy. The confederates differed in their point of view. The Bernese coveted domination, others repose from hostilities. Bern demanded, for war expenses, the counties of Vaud, Geneva, and Le Chablais; but the mediators ordered otherwise. They exacted the restitution of the Vaud country under condition of an indemnity of 50,000 florins mortgaged on the country. They recognised the house of Savoy as debtor towards the Fribourgers for a sum of 25,000 florins, as balance of that which they had engaged to pay when they detached themselves from Austria to lean on Fribourg. Geneva had to give guarantee for the ransom which had been imposed on her in the preceding war. The Valaisans restored the Chablais and kept the Lower Valais, the gate of their country. The Bern canton was enlarged. Bern and Fribourg remained in possession of Morat, Granson, Orbe, and Echallens. The two towns agreed to govern these little towns in common, and to send them a bailiff who should remain five years in charge, and who, if he were a Bernese, should take orders from Fribourg; if a Fribourger, from Bern. Finally Fribourg was recognised as independent, and floated the eagle of the empire.

Soon afterwards an embassy, composed, like the diet of Fribourg, of men who had commanded at Morat, went to King Louis XI at his residence in Plessis-les-Tours (October). The king gave them hearty welcome, and pronounced his intention of using for the future the Swiss as his own personal guard and the guard of the French sceptre. He made the captains detail their victories and did not suffer them to go until they were loaded with largesse for the cantons and presents for themselves. The richest gifts were for Adrian von Bubenberg, whom the king wished to win over. He did not neglect to recommend to the envoys that Charles the Bold should be crushed.

The Battle of Nancy; the Treaty of Peace

The unhappy prince, too proud to show his grief openly, had retired to the Château de la Rivière, near Pontarlier, where he remained solitary, shut up in his gloomy sorrow. His subjects had ceased to respect his orders. However, at the news that René had conquered Lorraine, and entered Nancy, he roused himself, succeeded in getting together six thousand soldiers, and laid siege to this place. René, on his side, hastened to ask help from the cantons. He wanted six thousand men. Enthusiasm yielded him eight thousand. The cold was excessive, yet the men marched as if to a fête.

The meeting took place on the 5th of January, 1477, not far from Nancy. There was a desperate resistance and a bloody defeat. Among the slain was found the almost unrecognisable corpse of Charles of Burgundy — "*Jamais plus n'est rentré chez lui*" runs the old war-song.

Then Louis deemed his cause won. The Swiss had earned the victory; his privilege it was to gather the fruit of their exploits. He occupied a part of Burgundy, while at the same time seeking to divide the confederates, whose intervention he feared. The time was an important one. A modern world was awakening. The contest had involved the test of monarchy *versus* republic; public opinion was profoundly shaken by the victories of the Swiss. The two tendencies, monarchical and republican, had everywhere their representatives. In Italy, Venice, Genoa, and Florence were in ferment. Milan had just tried, unsuccessfully it is true, to found an Ambrosian republic. Among the countries lately subject to the duke of Burgundy the Netherlands, tyrannically ruled by the prince, indulged hopes of enfranchisement. This was also the case of the Franche-Comté. Bern, also, would have liked the cantons to cross the Jura, and to add to Switzerland a province that furnished salt and wheat. The people of Franche-Comté even went beyond this, demanding to be received in a perpetual alliance, even as subjects. Straitened though they were, they offered to buy Swiss aid at the price of 150,000 florins. But the king showed a willingness to give much more.

Under these circumstances the confederates sent an embassy to Louis XI, composed of Bubenberg, Waldmann, and Imhof. Of the three, Bubenberg alone showed himself faithful to his country. He served her in France as he had done at Morat. His colleagues in their turn also returned, but with heads held high, honoured with rich presents, bound by secret bonds, and rallying the fears of the Bern commissioner. These were, nevertheless, the ones listened to by the confederates. The king offered them, as the price of their pretentions to Upper Burgundy, 200,000 florins cash and 150,000 florins to be raised on the revenue of the province. They agreed to this offer; but they seem never to have received the indemnity — at least we find mention of it in the treaty of peace they concluded January, 1478, with the heritors of Duke Charles, Mary, and her husband Maximilian of Austria, as being still due.

During these negotiations, war had continued in Bourgogne. The Swiss mercenaries had not ceased to shed their blood — some for the king's cause, some for that of Franche-Comté. They had even lost in the ungrateful struggles many more than in the course of the Burgundian war. Swiss had fought against Swiss, but as the king paid most, the greater part had joined his banner and aided him to conquer the province. It is known that Franche-Comté remained at heart Burgundian, and did not definitely become part of the French kingdom until two centuries later.

THE BATTLE OF GIORNICO (1478 A.D.)

The ruin of Charles the Bold had not so much changed the Swiss boundaries as it had prepared the day when she might attain her natural limits. Outside she had drawn nearer to France by frontier cantons and acquired the Netherlands and Upper Bourgogne from the house of Austria, who thenceforth surrounded the confederation on three sides. She had also brought France and Austria, thenceforward rivals, into contact. In adding to the greatness of their neighbours the Swiss had worked to their own weakening.

Yet their renown they kept, and were to keep some time yet — the renown of being the unconquerable nation whose arms would assure victory to those who sought for help. Three battles, three names known far and wide, Granson, Morat, and Nancy, would guard their frontiers for three centuries, and keep them from the danger of a serious invasion.

More than ever their mediation was called for. Fifteen times in two years they were taken as arbitrators in quarrels. Their principle was to refrain from seeking alliance, and to accept or reject, according to their usefulness, those offered. But they nevertheless found themselves led into alliances with most of the western states, sometimes in the interests of commerce, sometimes in those of their mercenaries, often in those of their cupidity.

SWISS WARRIOR

(Fifteenth century)

Matthias of Hungary had recourse to them, less in the hope of obtaining an army at such a great distance than in that of enrolling volunteers there and hindering the emperor from attacking his kingdom while he himself fought against the Turks. Pope Sixtus IV was then learning in Italy what sacerdotal power united to the enterprising spirit of a prince could do. The Burgundian War had made him acquainted with the Swiss, and he neglected no means to win them over to his projects. Knowing them religious to superstition, he began by offering them the means of relieving themselves from the weight of sins committed in the course of bloody wars. It would be necessary, he said, only to confess to obtain absolution. Then he sent them a red silk banner, symbol of the blood they were to shed for the liberty of the church; and as the holy see was then at war with the duchy of Milan it offered them its rights over this duchy[1] and invited them to conquer it. The confederates at first refused; they had just renewed a capitulation with the Milanese, who had made them buy it dearly, and had obtained of Leventina the abandonment of the canton of Uri, on the condition of an annual payment of four hawks and a crossbow. Uri was, nevertheless, the first to allow herself to be attracted to the holy see, and when she could find only one pretext, war broke out between Milan and Switzerland on the subject of a chestnut grove (November 15th, 1478).

It was winter when the men of Uri floated their banner, calling all confederates to arms. Immediately ten thousand men under Waldmann and Bubenberg crossed the St. Gotthard. From the money they had just given him for the remission of their sins, Sixtus paid them subsidies. But the confederates were not all animated by the same spirit. A lady, Bona of Savoy, governed the duchy, in the name of her young son Galeazzo. She offered to renew the capitulation with the Swiss, with new concessions and 22,000 florins, as the price of peace. Bern also, who condemned the rise to arms, had

[¹ More accurately, the cession of the valleys of Bellinzona, Locarno, and Lugano.]

sent three commissioners with an army charged with a pacific mission. These mediators had just obtained quick and sure success when the landammann Beroldingen of Uri appeared brusquely, repulsed the enemy's advance guard, and advanced on Bellinzona with such impetuosity that he took one wall by assault and made a breach in another. This, too, would probably have been taken if discord had not reigned in the camp. Some accused the mediators of treason and demanded an assault. Others wished to spare a town in which the Swiss had commercial interests. While the irritation gained ground, heavy snow fell on the Alps. This was the pretext seized on for return. The army regained its firesides, accusing its leaders of having an understanding with the enemy. Only six hundred men, under Troguer of Uri, remained at the entry of the Leventina in the fortified village of Giornico, charged with the militia of the country and their captain, Stanga, to defend the entrance to the valley.

This feeble garrison was not long in being attacked by the Milanese. Fifty thousand men advanced, followed by a numerous cavalry and powerful artillery. On the mountain peaks nature reigned in her fiercest and sternest aspect; at the foot the sun reminded one of Italy. But the season was cold, the night icy. Stanga advised diverting the waves of the Ticius on to the road and fields, providing the armed men with grappling hooks, and letting them engage one another on the ice which covered the slopes and the plain. When they had with great trouble got near, Swiss and Levantines rolled enormous stones on them; then, made firmer by grappling hooks, they broke on their adversaries whose courage was cowed. The Italians hastily retreated, continually pursued. Their cannon were taken and turned against them. Terror seized their hearts. A young Lucernese, Frischans Theilig, fought in such a way as to merit equally with Stanga the honours of the day. Fifteen hundred Italians had reddened the snow with blood. Cannon and magnificent horses were taken back to Giornico. The Milan regency hurried to invoke aid from the king of France, and to submit to the Swiss exigencies. Peace was bought at 100,000 ducats; 24,000 florins were paid for war expenses, and 1500 to satisfy divers pretensions. The feudal tribute of Uri was reduced to a candle of three pounds. The terror of the Swiss name spread through all Italy.*d*

CONSEQUENCES OF THE BURGUNDIAN WARS

Having become arbitrators in European struggles and guardians of victory, the confederates preserved the glorious role of Morat till Marignan; that is, from the time of their greatest victory until that of their greatest defeat (1476–1515). The half-century that elapsed between these two memorable days is the most brilliant period of their history. But this exterior glory was too dearly bought by the ever-increasing progress of demoralisation and the decline in the customs and institutions of the old Switzerland.

The Burgundian war contributed greatly to this result. Before this time corruption had touched only the leading men and a small proportion of the nation. The gold from Granson, measured by the hatful amongst the soldiers, corrupted the masses. These same people, who had been so economical. so industrious, so upright, so faithful to the law, showed themselves after the Burgundian war corrupt, dissolute, perjured, selfish, and at the same time both unmanageable and servile. The history of the time is filled with incidents of license and violence. Robberies increased in an incredible manner; so much so that the diet of Baden commanded the robbers to be hung (1480).

In the next few months, more than fifteen hundred capital executions followed this mandate in the midst of a population that, according to a chronicler of the time, numbered but fifty-four thousand men capable of carrying arms.

To these scenes of disorder attaches the escapade of the companions of the *Bande vom tollen Leben* (Band of the Mad Life). The year in which took place the battle of Nancy [1477 A.D.] an unruly assembly of young people of the Waldstätte gathered at the carnival of Zug. There, amidst drinking and foolish mirth, they decided to despoil Geneva and Savoy, and forthwith two thousand or more men started to march across the territory of Bern, which place hastened to close its gates. Fribourg, however, was forced to open hers and to receive these unwelcome guests (February 26th, 1477). Several days later, with the Schwyz chiefs at their head, the famous youths penetrated into the Savoyard country. The people of the *folle vie* had put on their banners a pig and a thistle — dignified symbols of a dishonourable undertaking! To free herself from this invasion, the duchess of Savoy was obliged to pawn her jewels and Geneva was forced to give the men drinks and to pay each of them two florins. The armed seizure was by no means a simple revel. The rumour spread through the Waldstätte that "Messieurs Bern and Fribourg had pocketed the money of Savoy," and that the people of these countries thought it just that they receive their share. The expedition had not been made without the connivance of certain members of the diet, who were jealous of these cities.[e]

THE CANTONS AND THE CITIES (1481 A.D.)

When Fribourg had recovered independence by redeeming its seigniorial rights from the dukes of Savoy (1477), she showed a desire to be associated with the Confederation, but the democratic cantons repulsed her demand. It had been the same with Solothurn. However, these two towns had incontestable rights to reckon up. The Solothurnese, present on the battle-field of Sempach, had thenceforth taken part in all the confederate wars. The Fribourgers had fought with distinction at Héricourt, Morat, Granson, and Nancy.

The confederate towns of Bern, Zurich, and Lucerne were irritated by the refusal. They did not feel the importance of primitive cantons, as they had done in the early days of the confederation. Proud of their own power, they unwillingly submitted to having in the diets a voice only equal to that of these small republics. Ostensibly, it was in the name of justice that they demanded the admission of their faithful allies, but in reality they coveted for themselves the preponderance which the early states had enjoyed until then. They aspired also to the obtaining, not only in conquest but in pillage of every kind, of a share proportionate to the number of troops they had set on foot.

For the towns, an access of property, while augmenting their own importance, was in no way inconvenient, by reason of the facility with which the form of their governments permitted them to administer large tributary states. On their side, the earliest confederation cantons feared to lose the influence which a redivision of votes would bring them in the diets, where they had four votes, Glarus being also a canton governed by a *Landsgemeinde*, while the towns only counted three. Zug, whose headquarters was a town, had a democratic organisation, and made the balance incline in their favour. They also doubted the support which Fribourg and Solothurn could give to the pretentions of three towns for this repartition of conquest, although the acquisition of tributary states had for them more inconveniences than advantages. In reality, if a few families found in the office of bailiff a source of riches, the people themselves saw with displeasure the inequalities resulting therefrom. But it was necessary to them that the other cantons should not become unduly large, and reduce them to an insignificant rôle. Moreover, after having ceded for a minimum sum to Bern and Fribourg the share of the conquest made at the expense of the seigniorial vassals of the duke of Burgundy and the house of Savoy, they then refused the people of Franche-Comté the favour of becoming confederate subjects. As to the unequal sharing of conquests and booty, made and taken in common, there was no question. The democratic cantons had furnished help to the towns far more frequently than it had been claimed. Drawn by this political ambition into foreign wars of independence, an equal share of the benefits which they procured was only just compensation for their sacrifices. Guided by these motives, the democratic cantons shut their eyes to the services rendered by their allies, and quite lost sight of the consolidation of the federal edifice; so much so that, seduced by the example of the towns, they sacrificed principle to the vain ambition of possessing subjects.

With the intention of attaching Solothurn and Fribourg to the communal fatherland, and fortifying themselves against incursions of disordered bands from the small cantons, Zurich, Bern, and Lucerne formed a perpetual civic league (1477), in which they promised aid and succour on all occasions. This departure was highly disapproved of by the oldest cantons: they considered it a movement against themselves. At different intervals they sent deputations to the towns to engage them to desist; but in vain. The towns answered that this alliance did not affect preceding ones. However, in contracting this one without the consent of the Waldstätte, Lucerne had violated an article of contract with the Waldstätte, and these wanted, in virtue of federal right, to exclude them from the civic league.

THE PLOT OF AM STALDEN

While this was going on, a man of some standing in Obwalden, Peter am Stalden, was suddenly arrested at Lucerne (1481) charged with plotting against that town. He acknowledged his guilt, but attributed the plot to two men of his canton — Bürgler von Lungern, late landammann of the place, and his brother-in-law, Künegger. Lucerne was to have been surprised on St. Leger's night on the Unterwalden side; the chief magistrates and citizens were to have been put to death, the walls and towers rased; it was planned to substitute the constitution of the early cantons for that existent. The citizens of Obwalden, with a view to seducing them, had promised them the office of landammann in democratised Lucerne. The magistrates openly took precautions, and reinforced the night guard — measures which the people of Unterwalden only laughed at. The two inculpated citizens pretended that the prisoner was a barefaced liar. This latter maintained what he had said by offering to repeat it before them, and did so effectively in full council before an Unterwalden deputation. The citizens of this canton did not think it seemly to let their former chief magistrate, an esteemed citizen, appear at Lucerne to be confronted with Am Stalden, whom they considered an impostor. They demurred because such a suspicion had been expressed against them, and because they had been thought capable of such a criminal act. The real truth of this affair had always remained a mystery, but these reports circulating in the confederation considerably augmented misunderstandings between the towns and the democratic cantons.

The Compact of Stanz (1481 A.D.)

To put an end to the growing irritation, the deputies met at Stanz. Not only did they fail, however, to come to any understanding, but the debates were so violent and the recriminations so bitter that recourse to arms seemed the only possible issue, until the pious hermit, Nicholas von Flühe, appeared. He had come on the appeal of Heinrich am Grund, a native of Lucerne and now vicar at Stanz — thereby in charge of the two cantons most opposed to one another. Although retired from the world, Von Flühe — this man who succeeded in soothing disputes which seemed purely political — was not a stranger to managing public affairs, and had formerly borne arms for his country. Although a citizen of Obwalden, his religious character rendered him indifferent to party feeling. Accustomed to think of God and holy things, he was high-minded and of rare firmness. It is not known positively if the pious hermit came personally to Stanz, or remained in his cell at Ranft and charged Am Grund to carry his peace message; but it is certain that his ascendency led the deputies back to pacific feeling, and disposed them to come to some arrangement.

The irritation was so violent as to paralyse deliberations and all measures conducive to the restoration of harmony. To restore men to right judgment, to consider the confederation as a work of God, to bring liberty to the people of these valleys, to have all momentous questions discussed on the old plan, and to reanimate the first motives which the confederates had obeyed — this was the purpose of Von Flühe. He sought to make them feel that, whether towns or cantons, they belonged to one family. They should, he thought, be brought to see that if federal fidelity was violated when one member of the confederation broke the laws of alliances, it was not less so when so strict an interpretation was put on the laws that other members of the confederation were deprived of power to provide the necessaries of existence, and their development was thereby arrested. Finally, he reminded them that obedience must be strengthened, not weakened, at an epoch when violence was rife and when intestine war would lead the confederation to ruin.

This basis established, Nicholas von Flühe made known his propositions. They bore only on essential points, and, in the first place, on the relations between Solothurn and Fribourg with the cantons. His words carried the assembly away. The articles of the Compact of Stanz are not altogether his. His was the moving spirit, but the details were the work of deputies. Those of Zug and Glarus had already made many efforts to maintain peace, and had discussed matters at great length. When concord regarding basic principles was established, an hour sufficed for an understanding on minor points. The legislation concerned all the perpetual allies, present and future, of isolated cantonments, and included the assurance of protection to each canton against all violence, and against any attempt on the part of a fellow state to subvert the pillars of regular government or to promote revolt; the punishment of authors of such attempts; the prohibition of gatherings of the people, secret meetings, and unauthorised petitions; the keeping of subjects in obedience; the sharing among the combatants of booty taken in war, and the equal sharing of conquests among the states — such were the things decided on in the Stanz Compact. The preceding decrees were confirmed.

Complete independence was assured to the cantons in the management of their interior affairs. Plots against Lucerne and the incursions of disorderly bands who, setting out from their small cantons, had lately spread alarm in western Switzerland, doubtless contributed to the introductions of these guarantees into the federal right. The consolidation of constituted powers against assemblies and illegal popular gatherings showed the hand of men accustomed to take the helm of affairs. By them was accomplished that maintenance of public order which the emperors had sought in vain for over a century to introduce into Germany, and which was only realised under Maximilian (1495).

Later on, the principles laid down in the Stanz Compact were abused as arresting the popular development and fettering liberty. The prohibition of illegal assemblies was very suitable to cantons with local parliaments, in which the entire people were assembled regularly; and these assemblies were a too subversive element in the towns where all the powers were exercised by delegation. One might say as much of the collective petitions, which were only popular assemblies disguised. But to prohibit all measures having for their object the modification of governmental organisations was to destroy national development. The democratic cantons had adopted, or did adopt later, a form assuring to each citizen the right of making known beforehand, and discussing in the local parliament, all projects having for their object the modification of the constitution, or which concerned public affairs. But no petition of this kind could be presented collectively. This legislation procured for the country the benefit of all measures useful in dispelling subversive influences.

If the states guaranteed their confederates against the devices of their own leaders, they were, however, not to interfere in another canton, except on demand from its government. It seems as if Waldmann, to whom the insertion of this clause in the Compact of Stanz is perhaps due, foresaw the fatal influence that the spontaneous intervention of the confederates would have after the Zurich troubles in 1489, and from which resulted the fall and death of this illustrious citizen. The help which the cantons offered for the maintenance of order had no oppression in view. The ancient alliances mentioned the maintenance of rights and liberties for the lordships and villages, without admitting that these governments and the rebels were always on the same footing. But, order once established, the wrongs of the parties were discussed. Later, when the powers had become almost absolute, a forced interpretation was given to these texts and they were employed to subjugate the populations.

The measures adopted for the sharing of war, pillage, and conquests were conformed to the Sempach Decree, and the principle of legality between the states was recognised. When the principle of proportional shares had been solemnly abandoned, the democratic states became more favourable to the aggregation of new states, and consented to the incorporation of Solothurn and Fribourg. Zurich, Bern, and Lucerne renounced their exclusive civic league with these two towns. It was replaced by a perpetual alliance with all the cantons, dated the same day as the Act of Pacification. This double event was hailed with transports of joy in all Switzerland./

HANS WALDMANN

The transient restoration of concord could not restore the primitive moral habits of the people. Rapacity and ostentation flourished in the towns, corruption in all seats of civic authority, immorality and idleness in the people. Young men often marched in troops of hundreds and of thousands, headed by bands of music, over the Rhine and over the Alps, to follow royal standards in quest of booty or a grave. Nor was there any lack of fuel for their ardour. In one year, on the side of Italy, four wars were raging. Internal strife and uproar soon recommenced. The noble lords and priests of Zurich, who hated Waldmann the burgomaster, because he sought to impose bounds on their arrogance, inflamed the town and country people against him by their discourses.

Hans Waldmann was the son of a peasant of Zug, and had come to Zurich first in the humble character of a tanner; he had distinguished himself at Morat and at Nancy, and had at last attained to eminence by sheer force of courage and intellect. But it was now whispered against him that he favoured Milan and Austria; and the Zurichers accused him of abuse of power through pride and passion. The burgomaster gave himself no concern about secret murmurs; and woe to those who dared to speak or act against him openly. When Theilig of Lucerne, the hero of Giornico, who had offended him, came into Zurich, bringing bales of cloth for sale, the burgomaster caused him to be taken into custody and beheaded, though his native town made urgent solicitations for the life of her illustrious citizen.

Such tyranny, notwithstanding his great qualities, brought universal hatred and at length ruin on Waldmann. His enemies took advantage of the tumults of the peasantry, and a revolt of the rural communes on the Lake of Zurich. The country people advanced in arms up to the walls of the town, complaining of the injustice of the laws and of other grievances. Delegates from the other cantons offered their mediation, and at length a proclamation was agreed upon by the council, that the complaints of the communes should be investigated and satisfaction given to the people. But Waldmann, who thought fit to regard the honour of the town as being compromised by such a declaration, caused the town clerk to alter parts of the wording, as if the country people had only alleged supposed grievances, and only obtained thus much by their humble supplications — that those grievances should be looked into on the first fit opportunity.

As soon as the falsification of this document became known, a new revolt took place against the town, which, moreover, was disturbed in its interior. The burgomaster no longer went out without armour, and usually slept at the town hall. Authority is tottering when it protects itself by any other panoply than the popular attachment. The burgomaster Waldmann was arrested amid tumult, put to the torture, and finally decapitated, on the 6th of April, 1489.

On the day of his death, the subjects and authorities of Zurich presented themselves as parties before the bar of the confederacy, who brought about a permanent agreement between them. It was enjoined upon the peasantry, in the first place, to be faithful and obedient to the great council of Zurich. On the other hand, the privilege was granted them of bringing their commodities to what market they pleased, of exporting them wherever they chose, of exercising arts and trades in the villages, planting vines and purchasing lands at pleasure, electing a sub-vogt in the lake-district, etc. If at any time the town attempted to exercise a lawless power on their subjects in the rural communes, the latter should send delegates to the diet of the confederacy, that justice might be done to their complaints. This instrument was signed on the 9th of May, 1489, for the seven cantons of the confederacy, by their delegates.*g*

THE SWABIAN WAR

Maximilian succeeded in 1495, by the death of his father, Frederick III, to the imperial throne. After his elevation, he convoked a general diet, and

established at Worms a court styled the imperial chamber, before which all
the civil affairs of the empire were to be laid, and which was to be supported
by contributions from all the members of the empire.   A subsidy of the hundredth penny was also ordered to be raised, for the sake of defraying the
expenses of the war against the Turks.   Maximilian communicated these
ordinances to the Swiss diet assembled at Zurich in 1496, and ordered the
cantons, as members of the empire, to conform to it.   The emperor required
them likewise to join the great Swabian League, of which he made himself
the head, and which had been formed in order to settle intestine differences,
and commanded them to furnish him a contingent of troops.   The Swiss, in
all their wars against the dukes of Austria and the emperor of the same family, had never renounced their allegiance to the German Empire, however ill
defined and problematic that allegiance had become.   Most of the cantons
replied to Maximilian's ambassadors that their alliance with France did not
allow them to enter into any engagement which might militate against the
interests of that power, and that the Swiss, having achieved their independence,
hoped to be left undisturbed in possession of it.

The town of St. Gall was put under the ban of the empire.   Maximilian,
having inherited, by the death of his cousin Sigismund, in 1497, the dominions
of Austria, applied to the cantons for the renewal of the "hereditary union,"
and demanded likewise that the Swiss would not favour the views of Louis
XII of France upon the Milanese.   The cantons, in reply, insisted, as a preliminary step, on the redress of the grievances of their allies, and especially
of St. Gall, before they listened to further proposals.   Maximilian said to the
Swiss deputies, who had attended him at Innsbruck in the Tyrol, "You are
rebels to the empire, and will oblige me at last to pay you a visit in person,
sword in hand."   Naught dismayed at this threat, the deputies replied that
"they humbly begged his imperial majesty would abstain from such a visit,
as the Swiss were rude-fashioned men who had not yet learned the respect
due to crowned heads."

Hostilities broke out first on the side of the Grisons.   The Austrian regency
in the Tyrol regarded with ill will those newly risen commonwealths on its
frontiers, and some border feuds between the two countries kindled the
flame.   The Tyrolese made an attempt to surprise the convent of Münsterthal
in January, 1499, but were repulsed by the inhabitants.   The Grisons upon
this demanded assistance from the cantons.   Meantime the troops of the
Swabian League, on their side, took Maienfeld by force, in the month of February, and put the Grisons garrison to the sword.   But the Swiss, having
joined their allies [defeated the Austrians at Triesen], retook Maienfeld and
the strong pass of Luziensteig, the key of the Grisons country.   The troops
of Bern, Fribourg, Solothurn, Zurich, and Schaffhausen entered the field
against the Swabian League, and formed a fortified camp at Schwaderloch, in
a forest near the imperial town of Constance.   But the principal scene of
action was on the upper Rhine towards Bregenz, where ten thousand Germans
were encamped; these the Swiss and the Grisons attacked and put to flight
with great loss [at Hardor Fussach].

Louis XII of France was not slow in turning to his advantage this quarrel
of the Swiss with his rival Maximilian, who thwarted his views on the side
of Italy.   Louis sent ambassadors to Zurich, and concluded with the Swiss
an alliance defensive and offensive, in which the amount of pensions and
subsidies to be paid by France was stipulated.   The cantons were deficient
in artillery, and the king promised to supply them.

Meanwhile the war was carried on with unabated vigour on the upper thine. The Swabians and Tyrolese had intrenched themselves in a strong position at Frastenz, near the river Ill, from which they made incursions across the Rhine into the land of the abbot of St. Gall, and other allies of the Swiss. The confederates, having collected their forces, drove back the enemy, and crossing the Rhine in their turn, determined to force the German camp, under the command of Henry Wolleb of Uri. They dislodged the enemy from their redoubts, and notwithstanding a formidable fire of artillery, which the Swiss avoided by lying down at each discharge, they stormed the intrench-ments sword in hand, and completely routed the Germans [April 20th], taking possession of the camp and of all it contained, including many pieces of artillery. The Swabians lost more than four thousand men in this affair. The emperor Maximilian was at that time engaged in the Netherlands, warring with Count Egmont about the possession of Gelderland. The Swabian League, alarmed at the successes of the Swiss, applied to him for assistance. He made a truce with Egmont, and arrived in April at Fribourg in Brisgau with six thousand men. Thence he issued a manifesto against the Swiss, in which he upbraided them in the strongest terms, calling them rebels to the empire. He concluded by inviting all the members of the empire to join their forces, in order to destroy these " rebel boors."

The Swiss meantime pursued the war from their camp at Schwaderloch; they defeated eight thousand Swabians [April 11th] who had entered Thurgau; they then crossed the Rhine, devastated the Kletgau, and took the town of Thungen, sparing the garrison nothing but their lives, and making them file off in their shirts through their camp, each soldier bearing a white wand in his hand. The noblemen they kept prisoners for the sake of ransom. They also took several castles, in one of which was the baron of Roseneck, an inveterate enemy of the Swiss, who was consequently excepted by them from the capitulation by which the garrison had their lives granted to them, together with whatever they could carry on their persons. The baron's lady, abandon-ing all her valuables, came out bearing her husband on her shoulders; and so touched were the Swiss by this ingenious trait of affection, that they not only gave the baron his liberty, but allowed his wife to take away whatever belonged to her.

The frontiers of the Grisons continued to be the principal theatre of the war. Fifteen thousand Tyrolese, and other German troops, from their posi-tion of the Malserhaid [on the Calven], annoyed the Grisons, who, to the number of eight thousand, commanded by one Fontana, [May 22nd] resolved to attack their intrenchments. Fontana mounted the first; being wounded in the abdomen, he supported with his left hand his protruding intestines, and defended himself with the right, until his friends joined him. With his dying breath he encouraged them to drive the enemy before them, and at last, exhausted, he fell into the ditch below. The intrenchments were carried by the men of the Engadine and the Austrians were driven away with the loss of five thousand men.

Maximilian himself repaired to Feldkirch in the Tyrol, where he assembled his troops to strike a decisive blow on the Grisons. He detached two thousand men, who penetrated into the Engadine, and burned several villages; but the desperate resistance of the inhabitants and the want of provisions obliged them to retire. The desolation was complete in those border countries; and the provinces of Maximilian had their full share of the work of destruction committed by the soldiers and partisans on both sides. Birkheimer, one of Maximilian's commanders, relates that in crossing the Tyrol he found the country utterly devastated and forsaken by the inhabitants; he mentions, in his account of that war, that he saw two women driving before them a troop of four hundred children, like a flock of sheep, and that as soon as this crowd entered a green field, he saw them fall upon the grass, snatch it up by handfuls, and devour it, to satisfy the cravings of hunger.

The count of Fürstenberg, with fourteen thousand foot and two thousand horse, advanced to the castle of Dornach, which was defended by the men of Soleure. At this news Bern sent three thousand men under D'Erlach; and Zurich and other cantons sent also their contingents. A reinforcement came up, consisting of the men of Luzern and Zug. The Germans began to lose ground, and in trying to retire across the river Birs their retreat became a decided flight. Night prevented the confederates from pursuing them, but the count Fürstenberg, with three thousand of his men, lost their lives in the battle. Next morning, July 23rd, the troops of the Waldstätte also joined their allies, and the whole Swiss army marched upon Bâle; but seeing nothing more of the enemy, the confederates, according to their custom, separated and returned to their respective homes.

Practical Freedom from the Empire

In eight months Maximilian, by his own wanton aggression and obstinacy, had lost more than twenty thousand men, while hundreds of towns, villages and castles had been reduced to ashes on both sides; and he was now induced to listen to proposals of mediation which were made to him by Louis XII himself, as well as the duke of Milan. After some negotiations, and some vacillations on the part of the emperor, peace was concluded at Bâle in September, 1499, by which Maximilian yielded to the Swiss the high judicial power in Thurgau, and fully acknowledged their unconditional independence as a nation. The differences between the Tyrol and the Grisons were left to an amicable adjustment between the parties concerned. The Swabian war was the last the Swiss had to sustain for their independence. From that time, and for three centuries after, neither Austria nor the German empire, nor any other monarchy, made any attempts or put forth any pretensions against the liberties of the Swiss cantons, which assumed their station as an independent power in Europe.[1]

THE CONFEDERATION OF THIRTEEN STATES (1513 A.D.)

The towns of Bâle and Schaffhausen, in consideration of their attachment to their Swiss confederates, were received in 1501 as two additional cantons. The bishop of Bâle and the chapter, who were not favourable to the Swiss, had lost all their influence in that city, which by degrees made itself completely independent of them; and lastly Appenzell, another ally of the Swiss, became also one of the confederation in 1513, and completed the number of thirteen cantons, which constituted the Helvetic body till 1798: namely, Zurich, Schwyz, Uri, and Unterwalden, the three Waldstätte or forest cantons, Lucerne, Glarus, Zug, Bern, Fribourg, Solothurn, Bâle, Schaffhausen, and Appenzell. All of these were essentially German, both in their language and habits. Some districts belonging to Fribourg and Bern spoke Romance or French dialects; and the great bulk of the Pays de Vaud, which is essentially Burgundian or French in language and habits, was afterwards incorporated with Bern.

[1] The Peace of Bâle secured Switzerland practical independence of the empire, but it was not until the Peace of Westphalia in 1648 that this was formally proclaimed.]

The allies of the Swiss at the beginning of the sixteenth century were of two sorts — the *socii* and the *confœderati*. The first, which consisted of the abbot of St. Gall, the city of the same name, and the towns of Mülhausen and of Bienne, sent deputies to the federal diets, and, without being cantons, were considered as parts of the Helvetic body. The *confœderati* were either, like the Grisons and the Valais, allied to all the cantons, or only to some of them, which last was the case with the republic of Geneva and the county of Neuchâtel. They did not send deputies to the diets, but were entitled to assistance in case of foreign attack. Several of these associates and confederates had also their subjects, as well as the cantons themselves.

The abbot of St. Gall was sovereign of a fine district extending from the river Thur to the Lake of Constance, and including several little towns, such as Roschach, Wyl, etc.; he was also prince of the county of Toggenburg, as far as Glarus and Schwyz, and he had the lower jurisdiction over the Rheinthal. The abbot's palace — or rather castle, it being surrounded with walls and ditches — stood in the middle of the town, which had grown up around the abbey, but had become at an early period independent of it, whilst the jurisdiction of the abbot was maintained over the surrounding country and to within a mile or two of the city gates. This singular state of things gave rise to frequent altercations, and it happened at times that the abbot was blockaded within the precincts of his abbey by the citizens of St. Gall, whilst his dependents in the country coming to his relief beleaguered the city.

Geneva and its bishop were under the protection of the German Empire, and they also contracted an alliance in 1438 with the cantons of Bern and Fribourg in order to protect themselves against the dukes of Savoy, who having become masters of the surrounding country by cession from the counts of the Geneva, were attempting to establish their authority also within the city. The bishops continued to exercise a partial jurisdiction in concert with the citizens, till the Reformation.

The district of Neuchâtel had its counts, who were vassals of the empire and co-burghers of Bern, till about the end of the fifteenth century, when the last count, Philip, died, leaving only one daughter named Jane, who married Louis d'Orléans, duke of Longueville. This prince, having taken part against the Swiss in their Italian wars, was deprived of his possession of Neuchâtel in 1512 by the cantons of Bern, Fribourg, Solothurn, and Lucerne, who sent bailiffs to administer the affairs of the county in the name of the confederates. However, in 1529, through the mediation of France, Neuchâtel was restored to Jane, upon condition that the treaties with the four cantons should continue in force. Jane was the first to take the title Princess Sovereign of Neuchâtel. She died in 1543, and her son Francis, duke of Longueville, succeeded to the principality, to which the county of Valentgin was united in the course of the same century. The town of Neuchâtel enjoyed peculiar privileges and franchises; it had its own treaties of alliance with the four above-mentioned cantons, and was included in the neutrality of Switzerland. Of the Grisons and the Valais we have spoken already. These were the confederates of the Swiss cantons. The prince bishop of Bâle, after having lost all authority over the city and canton of that name, entered into a partial alliance with some of the cantons for his great territories in the valleys of the Jura, as we shall have occasion to notice hereafter.

Thus it was that, two hundred years after the first declaration of independence by the Waldstätte, the confederation of the thirteen Swiss cantons, their allies and subjects, had become possessed of the whole country of Helvetia and Rhætia, having for boundaries the Jura to the west, and Lake Leman (the Lake of Geneva) and the Pennine Alps to the south, the farther chain of the Rhætian Alps and the Rhine dividing it from Tyrol on the east, and the Lake of Constance and the course of the Rhine from Schaffhausen[1] to Bâle marking its boundaries towards the north. These limits, which appear marked by nature's hand, Switzerland has ever since maintained, with the addition of some valleys on the Italian side of the Alps which were the subject of early contention with the dukes of Milan.

CONQUESTS IN ITALY

The cession of the valleys of Bellinzona, Locarno, and Lugano was promised to the forest cantons by Louis XII, when duke of Orléans, during the reign of his predecessor Charles VIII, if they assisted him in the conquest of the Milanese. The Swiss had done so;[2] the French, with their assistance, had become possessed of Milan, and the cantons now demanded the fulfilment of the compact on the part of Louis. But the French king, instead of acquiescing in their demand concerning Locarno and Lugano, claimed of them the restitution of Bellinzona, of which they were already in possession, the inhabitants having voluntarily put themselves under their protection. The blunt mountaineers answered that they were determined to keep Bellinzona, and that if his majesty did not choose to ratify the cession, they would appeal to God and their stout halberds. And they kept their word.

After several fruitless negotiations the forest cantons took up arms in 1503, demanding of their confederates their contingents as stipulated by treaties. The other cantons, after vainly endeavouring to avoid a rupture with France, felt themselves bound to send their troops; and an army of fifteen thousand men was collected, which, crossing the Alps, occupied in a few days the whole country around the Lago Maggiore. Louis XII, in his quality of duke of Milan, offered to make peace by giving up to the three cantons Bellinzona and some other districts in perpetuity. The treaty was signed on the 10th of April, 1503. But the Swiss had become mercenary in their engagements with foreign powers. A few years afterwards Pope Julius II, the declared enemy of the French in Italy, having, by means of Matthew Schinner, bishop of Sion, formed an alliance with the cantons, obtained from them a force of six thousand men, nominally for the defence of the papal states, but in reality for the purpose of attacking the French in Lombardy. In spite of the opposition of the French generals, the Swiss, in 1511, forced their way by Varese to the very gates of Milan, which was thrown into the greatest alarm by their sudden appearance; when all at

[1 The little canton of Schaffhausen, and the town itself, are on the right or Swabian side of the Rhine, and consequently beyond the line stated. A very small portion of the canton of Bâle is also on the same side.]

[2 When Ludovico Sforza reconquered for a short time the duchy of Milan, in the beginning of the year 1500, he had sixteen thousand Swiss in his pay. The French had nearly as many in their army. While the two forces stood in front of each other at Novara, the Swiss diet sent orders to the Swiss of both parties, forbidding them to fight. But the French envoy, Brissy, bribed the courier who was entrusted with the order for the Swiss in the French camp, and he tarried several days on the road. The other courier having arrived at the quarters of the Swiss in the duke's pay, they obeyed the orders. The French commanders meantime attacked Novara, which Sforza was unable to defend, as his Swiss had forsaken him, and he was taken prisoner with all his adherents. This has been represented by Guicciardini and other historians as treachery on the part of the Swiss, but the manuscript correspondence of Morone has revealed the truth.[h]]

once, owing to a misunderstanding among the confederates, their camp broke up and they retraced their steps homewards.

The year following the Swiss openly espoused the cause of the emperor and the pope against France. Julius sent them the banners of the holy see, and bestowed on them the title Defenders of the Church. They entered Italy by way of the Grisons and Trent, and, uniting with the Venetians, drove the French before them, and conquered the Milanese in the name of the Holy League, for so pope Julius had called his crusade against the French. Differences, however, broke out among the conquerors, concerning the disposal of the duchy of Milan. The Swiss, who had a garrison in the duchy, and the pope insisted that it should be restored to Maximilian Sforza, son of Ludovico, whom the French had deposed and imprisoned. The Venetians, on their part, wished to keep Brescia, and Crema with the whole country as far as the river Adda; and the emperor put forth his own pretensions. All these powers, as well as the king of France, Ferdinand of Spain, and Henry of England, sent ambassadors to the Swiss diet, which was held at Baden. The cantons were now courted, and bribes were offered to them by almost every court of Europe. But they stood firm in holding the duchy of Milan for Maximilian Sforza, and the emperor was ultimately obliged to accede to the treaty which was concluded at Baden in 1512. By this treaty Sforza engaged to pay the cantons 40,000 ducats annually, besides 200,000 ducats for the expenses of the war, and to give up to them in perpetuity Locarno, Lugano, and Valle Maggia; the Swiss, on their side, guaranteeing to him the possession of the Milanese. The cantons then appointed deputies to instal Maximilian Sforza as duke of Milan.

On the 31st of December, 1512, Sforza made his public entrance into Milan, and received the keys of the city from the ammann Schwarzmaurer of Zug, to whom he expressed his deep gratitude towards the Swiss for all their good services on his behalf. Thus we find the Swiss mountaineers, the "rebel boors" as Maximilian had styled them a few years before, bestowing the crown of one of the finest states of Italy against the will of that emperor. The Grisons, whose troops formed part of the Swiss army, took possession for their pains of the fine district of Valtellina and the counties of Chiavenna and Bormio on the south side of the Rhætian Alps, which had formed part of the Milanese, and they kept and governed them as subject bailiwicks till Bonaparte's conquests in Italy in 1796.

In 1513 the Swiss defended their Milanese ally Sforza against a new army of France, at the battle of Novara, in which they lost two thousand men and killed more than ten thousand of the enemy. Guicciardini, the Italian historian, describes their bravery on this occasion as surpassing all that we read of the Greeks and Romans. At the same time, in order to make a diversion against France, and at the instigation of the ever-intriguing and restless Maximilian, a Swiss army of sixteen thousand men, paid by that emperor and commanded by Jacques de Watteville of Bern, joined to an equal number of imperial troops, entered Burgundy, and laid siege to Dijon, which was defended by the French commander, La Trimouille. This officer, doubting of his ability to hold out, treated with the Swiss generals without having authority from his master to that effect: he stipulated in the king's name that France should renounce her pretensions to Milan, and that she should pay the Swiss 600,000 crowns within a fixed time, on condition that the Swiss would leave Burgundy and return home; and for the due performance of these stipulations four persons of rank were named to be delivered to the cantons as hostages. This being done, the Swiss departed, without having consulted with the emperor their ally, alleging as a reason that the emperor had not made the payments he had promised them.

Louis XII disapproved of La Trimouille's conduct, and would not listen to any renunciation of the duchy of Milan, to which he was still pertinaciously attached, notwithstanding all his reverses. But Guicciardini,[i] who relates the above facts, does not notice the dishonest conduct of the French general with regard to the hostages. It had been agreed that, beside La Trimouille's own nephew, the sieur de Mézière, four of the principal inhabitants of Dijon, whose names were mentioned, should be given over to the Swiss. La Trimouille substituted in their place four persons of the lowest condition and under false names. This conduct was keenly felt by the Swiss, who, whatever may have been their love of money, were still observant of the faith of treaties. Blame was attached to their own generals, but the public indignation rose chiefly against France, and the ancient sympathy of the Swiss with that nation was turned into hatred. The flight of De Mézière, who broke his parole at Zurich next year, added to these angry feelings. The Swiss, as a measure of reprisal, arrested the president of Grenoble, who was at Geneva, and treated him severely. They then resolved to invade France again, and in 1514 sent deputies to King Henry VIII of England to propose an alliance for that purpose. Henry dispatched in return two envoys to Switzerland; but he suddenly concluded the negotiations on learning that the king of Spain had concluded a treaty of peace with France.

The Swiss at Marignano (1515 A.D.)

Leo X, who had succeeded the warlike Julius in the papal see, adopted a system of politics different from that of his predecessor. He inclined to peace with France, and offered his mediation between that country and the Swiss. In the midst of these negotiations Louis XII died, in January, 1515; and Francis I, who succeeded him, assumed the title of duke of Milan, together with that of king of France. In notifying to the cantons his accession to the throne, he requested the renewal of their friendship. The Swiss replied that, if his majesty would ratify the Treaty of Dijon, concluded under his predecessor, he might rely upon their friendship; but otherwise they could not listen to any proposals on his part. Francis made great preparations for war, and the emperor and the duke of Milan on their side strengthened their alliance with the cantons. The king of Spain also agreed that, should the French invade Italy, he would enter France on the side of the Pyrenees; he, however, did not keep his word, and the defence of the duchy of Milan was ultimately left to Swiss intrepidity alone. Hearing that a French army under Trivulzio, an Italian himself, and a commander of great abilities, had assembled at Lyons, the cantons sent no less than forty thousand men into Lombardy, who occupied the passes of Mont Cenis and Mont Genèvre. But Trivulzio entered Italy by another pass, which leads by the Col d'Argentière into the plains of Saluzzo, and which the Swiss had neglected as impracticable.

The Swiss fell back upon Novara, and, finding themselves unassisted and alone, they were actually marching out of that town on their return to their country, when the subsidy of money promised by the pope reached them. This timely arrival decided the troops of Zurich, Bâle, Schaffhausen, Appenzell, the forest cantons, and Grisons to turn again towards Milan by the way of Galera. But the contingents of Bern, Fribourg, and Solothurn continued their retreat towards Domo d'Ossola, at the foot of the Alps.

This separation of the Swiss was occasioned by the intrigues of Francis I among the cantons, with whom he had never ceased to negotiate. The Swiss troops at Galera, expecting to be attacked every day by the French, who had taken possession of Milan, solicited their countrymen to join them, and they were supported in their expostulations by Watteville, who commanded the Bernese, but in vain. The latter, having heard from their country that negotiations were far advanced, disbanded themselves; and of seven thousand Bernese who were at Domo d'Ossola there remained together no more than one thousand.

At last the troops of the other cantons who were at Galera, with the exception of the Waldstätte and Glarus, agreed to a peace with France, on the 8th of September, 1515, and took the road towards the Alps. The men of the forest cantons refused to ratify the treaty, and those of Zurich and Zug, persuaded by Schinner, the cardinal of Sion, following their example, their united bands, not more than ten thousand strong, boldly took the road to Milan. Trivulzio, on hearing of their approach, abandoned that city, and took up a position at Marignano, in order to prevent their junction with the pope's troops. The position of the little Swiss army was singularly critical. They had before them more than forty thousand soldiers of France, headed by the king in person, with whom several of the cantons had just concluded peace. But they were joined by a number of volunteers, among whom was a Winkelried, from Unterwalden, who left the ranks of the retreating army in order to assist their gallant countrymen in the hour of danger.

The Swiss began the attack late in the afternoon; the French camp was fortified by a double intrenchment, and defended by numerous artillery. On the report of the battle having begun, all the Swiss that were still lingering at Milan ran out without waiting for orders and joined in the attack. The Swiss forced their way into the intrenchments and seized part of the French artillery. Francis himself charged them at the head of his cavalry, and the combat continued with the greatest obstinacy till four hours after dark. At last the two armies separated through fatigue; the French retired to their camp, and the Swiss lay on the field of battle. The next morning, September 15th, 1515, the fight was renewed; but D'Alviani, who was bringing up the Venetian auxiliary forces, arrived in the midst of the battle, and took the Swiss in their rear. This circumstance obliged them to sound a retreat, which they effected in the best order to Milan, carrying away their cannon and their wounded in the midst of their column; and so astounded were the French by their intrepidity, that there was no one, either horseman or foot, who dared to pursue them. Trivulzio himself used to call this a "battle of giants." The number of Swiss engaged in the battle was about eighteen thousand, of which six thousand were killed, with many officers, especially from Zurich and the forest cantons. The loss of the French was equally great. After this the Swiss took the road towards the Alps, and the whole duchy of Milan submitted to Francis I.

The Perpetual Peace (1516 A.D.)

In the following year (1516), the king of France having agreed to give up to the Swiss the Italian bailiwicks, which had been the first origin of the war, a treaty of peace was concluded in November, at Fribourg, between France and all the cantons. This was called the Perpetual Peace. The principal conditions were that the bailiwicks of Bellinzona, Locarno, Lugano, and Valle Maggia were to remain subject to the Swiss, on condition that the privileges and liberties granted to these districts by the dukes of Milan should be maintained. The Valtellina and county of Chiavenna were likewise to remain in possession of the Grisons. The allies of the Swiss were included in the Perpetual Peace with France. Each of the cantons, as well as the Grisons and the Valais, were to receive a pension of 2000 francs a year. The king was besides to pay 400,000 crowns for the expenses of the Dijon war, and 300,000 for those of the war of Italy. The Swiss merchants and other citizens were allowed free ingress and egress through the French territories, with the privileges they had enjoyed under the preceding reigns. In case of either of the contracting parties being engaged in war, the other was not to give assistance or passage over its territories to the enemy's forces; and lastly, all differences that might arise between the Swiss and the French were to be referred to arbitrators. This treaty served as the basis of all subsequent treaties with France during the course of nearly three centuries.

In the subsequent wars of Francis I in Italy, Swiss auxiliary troops fought in his ranks in several actions, especially at the battle of Pavia, in 1525, in which the king was made prisoner and the Swiss lost no less than seven thousand men. Such repeated and heavy losses gave them at last a distaste for those disastrous Italian wars, where they could gain nothing but a barren reputation for mercenary valour.[c]

THE ALLIANCE WITH FRANCE (1521 A.D.)

Francis I, in spite of the victory of Marignano, judged it better to buy peace of the Swiss for considerable sums and a cession of territory. But, on the other hand, he had ensured the absence of his enemies' armies and had everywhere guaranteed his French and Italian frontiers where they were in contact with confederation territory. Annual pensions were again paid to the majority of the cantons and their allies to assure their good will.

However, the inconveniences of pensions, the distribution of moneys and enrolments were felt so much by the Swiss government that Zurich and Schwyz made great efforts to put an end to them. A convention was held at Bern at the end of the Italian disasters to forbid pensions and presents from foreign monarchs; and at Bern, even, the government, recoiling before a sedition, temporarily renounced them. But habit was too strongly engrained; cupidity was allowed to stand before the country's dearest interests. Thus when, in spite of their decision, the governments saw bands of volunteers depart enrolled by French agents or on Austria's behalf, they were but reaping the sad yet inevitable consequences of that turpitude of which they had set the example and to which they had accustomed the nation.

Schinner, banished from Valais, was no longer there to aid the efforts of Maximilian and England by his influence. The confederation, drawn away by a torrent of private ambition and yielding to the influence of the gold scattered so profusely by France, concluded a new treaty with Francis I, which was to last during the king's life and three years after his death (1521).

This treaty granted power to enrol not less than six thousand and not more than sixteen thousand men, on condition they served on land only. If the confederates were attacked, the king was to furnish at his expense two hundred lances, twelve cannon, six small, six large, and pay 25,000 gold crowns every three months as subsidy, whether he himself was or was not engaged in warfare. If they preferred, they could, in place of the two hundred lances, receive 2,000 gold crowns every three months. The king allowed them the provisioning of his states with salt. No one of the parties was to

[1521 A.D.]

conclude a peace without notifying the other and procuring him the means of taking part in it. Each was to drive from his territories the adversaries of the other. During the term of the alliance the king engaged to pay a surplus pension to the cantons and their allies. The ordinary reserves were mentioned, but with this difference — that their effect was suspended if one of the persons or powers reserved attacked the allied party. This treaty had for object the protection of countries situated on either side the mountains — the French and the Milanese. It concluded the majority of the Swiss allies, the abbey and town of St. Gall, the Grisons, Valais, Mülhausen, Rottweil, and Bienne.

Thus the confederates, salaried by France, compromised their relations with other states in her favour, renouncing their independent position and submitting more and more to the influence of this powerful neighbour. They consented to play simply a secondary rôle in European politics. Zurich would not accept this humble position. Schwyz, Bâle, and Schaffhausen hesitated a long time. The Swiss, drawn by Charles VIII into the Italian wars as allied troops, had then acted as a sovereign power. In the Swabian war the confederation had gloriously maintained its independence against the empire. During the Italian wars she wanted to exercise a protectorate over the southern countries, and Lombardy in particular, and to extend her influence beyond them. For some time the fate of the duchy of Milan was in the hands of the confederation: thus it acted and was treated as a great power. But at the end of reverses which its arms experienced in Lombardy it renounced the striking rôle to which it had aspired while feeling its martial strength.

SWISS WARRIOR

(Sixteenth century)

THE FOREIGN RELATIONS OF SWITZERLAND

Recalled to her natural destinies, Switzerland thenceforth did not share in the agitations or conflicts of general politics. Though strong enough to maintain her independence, she felt not enough so to dominate other countries; she was not organised for conquests. From that time she gave herself up to a full enjoyment of her liberty, and served as a refuge in the midst of the general European unrest. However, as she had only instinctively retired, and not as the result of any decision, foreign powers continued for some time to attribute to her an importance she no longer had. One sees Francis I and Charles V soliciting her help to gain the imperial throne. Little by little her position was better understood, and she knew how to maintain her neutrality during the Thirty Years' War.

But while renouncing an active rôle, Switzerland opened up for her children the career of foreign service. It was a natural ending to the old-fashioned wars amongst the populations, who only thus took an indirect part in the events of this epoch. This portion of the national history presents lights and

shades. The mercenary regiments for centuries upheld the military reputation of the country and Helvetian honour. If they combated for causes
foreign to them they were not servants dependent on a master's caprices,
but remained Swiss although serving other kings. The brightness of their
glory reflects on their country and raises its military reputation.

It was imperative that the confederation should occupy itself less actively
with foreign interests and give all its attention to itself. There was strong
irritation against those western towns whose troops, by brusquely quitting
the army, had paved a way for the disaster of Marignano. The fears inspired
by this state of opinion led Solothurn, Bern, and Fribourg to unite more
closely in a civic league. In each canton there was the same distrust among
the citizens, the same disorganisation in public institutions.

However, certain positive ameliorations had been accomplished. As to
the Italian subjects, placed under the power of the eleven cantons by the
treaty of peace with Francis I, they were governed by a bailiff named in turn
by each of the states and ruled for two years. This functionary swore to
observe the statutes and received homage from the councils and communes.
Eleven deputies went to receive the annual accounts at Lugano, then at
Locarno, then alternately at Mendrisio and Valle Maggia. To administer
death sentences the countries named judges to whom the bailiff gave adjuncts.
The secretary was taken from one of the eleven cantons and generally named
for life. On this functionary rested the practice of jurisdiction and delivery
of business. The bailiff received part of the taxes; the executions and the
confiscations went to the cantons. The country, moreover, paid them a
moderate contribution. The ordinary administration belonged to the communal councils.

In the interval which had elapsed between the Perpetual Peace and the new
agreement with the French, the thirteen cantons had admitted in their perpetual alliance the imperial town of Rottweil, situated in Swabia (1519), on
the same conditions as the town of St. Gall. But these bonds were tacitly
and by common accord broken at the Thirty Years' War, because the confederation, in abstaining from taking part, could not offer its new ally a
sufficiently strong protection. Thenceforth the Rottweil deputies ceased
attending the diets. On their side the three Grisons leagues had formed
a perpetual alliance with the house of Austria similar to the hereditary
alliance.*f*

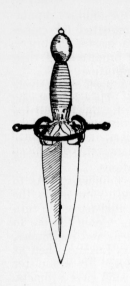

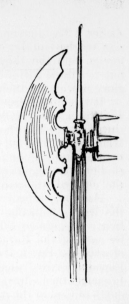

CHAPTER IV

THE 16TH AND 17TH CENTURIES

[1519–1715 A.D.]

WHILST the Italian wars between Austria and France employed the arms of the Swiss youth away from their own country, a most important change was silently taking place at home. This was no other than the great religious reform of the sixteenth century. In Switzerland the corruption of the clergy at the beginning of the sixteenth century seems to have been even more general and barefaced than in other countries of Europe. There was a grossness in it which was characteristic of a rude, uninformed, and still imperfectly civilised people. Remonstrances had been several times made by various cantons on the increasing licentiousness of the churchmen. As early as August, 1477, the Bernese had complained to Benedict de Montferrand, bishop of Lausanne, that they saw with grief the clergy of their country given up to libertinism. But little redress could be expected from that quarter, for we find repeatedly the burghers of Lausanne complaining still more bitterly of their own bishop, and more especially of Sebastian de Montfaucon, who filled the see in the early part of the sixteenth century, and "whose servants beat and killed the citizens in affrays, and the bishops protected them openly and by force from the hands of justice."

The young men returning from the Italian wars brought back with them habits of dissipation and profligacy not favourable to religious veneration. But even the friars laboured as it were to throw discredit on religious ceremonies and practices. A disclosure of monkish imposture had been made at Bern some years before, arising out of an ancient jealousy between the two rival orders of the Dominicans and the Franciscans. The former, to obtain a triumph over the Franciscans, resorted to pretended miracles: they worked

623

on the weak fancy of a poor tailor called Jetzler, who had entered the Dominican convent of Bern as a lay brother, and made him believe that several saints, and the Virgin herself, whom a friar personated, appeared to him. Crowds flocked to the Dominican convent to see Jetzler, the favourite of heaven, who exhibited on the palms of his hands and on his feet the stigmata, or marks in imitation of our Saviour's wounds, which the Franciscans boasted that St. Francis alone had ever borne. Jetzler's marks, it appears, were produced by corrosives. The whole was an impious piece of jugglery, but the friars relied too much on Jetzler's credulity: they were discovered — Jetzler confessed all; Pope Julius sent a legate to examine the friars, and the council of Bern having taken cognisance of the matter, four friars were condemned and burned to death. This occurred in 1507.

Another subject of great scandal and mischief was the manner in which livings in Switzerland were bestowed upon foreign adventurers, chiefly Italians, who publicly bought them at Rome, or received them from the favourite retainers of the papal court. The Swiss cantons, in 1520, made remonstrances to Pucci, the pope's legate, about this scandalous abuse; and they issued an order banishing all "courtisans" (the name they gave to the clerical intruders on livings) as "wicked, ignorant persons, who had nothing of the spirit of God in them," and threatening, if found again within their territory, to drown them in sacks. But the immediate cause of the schism with Rome was, in Switzerland as well as in Germany, Leo X's famous bull for the sale of indulgences in 1517.[b]

ZWINGLI INVEIGHS AGAINST ECCLESIASTICAL ABUSES

The brightest spot in Switzerland was Bâle. Amongst other divines strongly attached to ancient learning, Thomas Wyttenbach of Biel, taught at the university of this place, to which he was called in 1505, and Wolfgang Fabricius Capito, a native of Alsace, was an instructor from 1512 to 1520. They opened to their hearers many clear views of isolated doctrines. But Erasmus especially, who settled at Bâle in 1516, gathered round him a circle of enthusiastic admirers of ancient learning and refined views in religion. To this circle Huldreich (Ulrich) Zwingli united himself; he was born on the 1st of January, 1484, at Wildhaus in the county of Toggenburg, and was educated at the universities of Vienna and Bâle; at the latter place he received from Wyttenbach his first incitement to the study of divinity. From 1506, when he was elected by the community of Glarus to be their pastor, he devoted himself to a zealous study of the Latin classics and fathers of the church. He inveighed as an eloquent preacher against the corrupt morals of his day; in 1510 he pursued the same course in satirical and allegorical writings. Nevertheless he was still quite devoted to the pope; he received from him a pension as an influential preacher, and regarded the support which the Swiss rendered to the pope as a dutiful protection of the holy see. But afterwards he began to see into many of the errors and abuses of the church.

When, in the year 1518, a trafficker in indulgences, the Franciscan Bernardin Samson, made his appearance in Switzerland, and surpassed all his co-workers in effrontery, then Zwingli, as well as many others, raised his voice against this abuse. Many private expressions of his may have contributed to the opinion which soon prevailed in Zurich that he was a Lutheran at heart. The monks first attacked him; then several canons of his cathedral complained that he denied the divine right of tithes, and in the exercise of his spiritual office did not keep sufficiently in view the increase of the

[1522–1523 A.D.]

revenue of the chapter; his adversaries could not as yet accuse him of heresy. In order to avoid quarrels, the council charged all their clergy to hold forth the doctrine of the holy Scripture only.

Zwingli resigned his pension from Rome in 1520, and declared that he would not be hindered by anything from preaching the gospel. He was first entangled in controversy in 1522. He had designated the rule of fasting as a human ordinance; several townsmen broke the rule and were called to answer for so doing. The clergy, when questioned by the council, under the direction of Zwingli, censured the arbitrary transgression, but persisted in the statement that the rule was a human ordinance. The bishop of Constance accordingly sent a commission to Zurich to command the observance of the ceremonies (April, 1522). However, the council took Zwingli's part, and demanded more satisfactory directions from the bishop. In May, 1522, the bishop of Constance issued a pastoral to warn his flock against innovations, and the diet of Lucerne forbade all preaching likely to cause disquiet. Zwingli defended the free preaching of the Gospel.

As the celibacy of the clergy had led to the grossest abuses in Switzerland, Zwingli and his friends prayed above all things for the abolition of this human ordinance. However, no answer was given; on the contrary, the diet and the bishop began to persecute several of the clergy who had made themselves too conspicuous. The most disgraceful calumnies with regard to Zwingli were disseminated in the neighbouring cantons; in the three monasteries of Zurich, the resorts of the professors of the old faith, sermons were preached against him incessantly. Now that the efforts of the council to restore peace remained without success, it yielded to Zwingli's wish to encounter publicly these calumnies and attacks, and fixed a religious conference betwixt the two parties for the 29th of January, 1523, in which they were to produce their doctrines, and support them by holy Scripture alone.

For the same political reasons for which the pope had overlooked other arbitrary acts of the Swiss in church matters, he took no notice of these great movements. Zurich was the only canton which steadfastly refused the league with France, and still in 1521 granted soldiers to the pope; whilst the rest of the cantons supported France, and treated the papal legate in Switzerland with hostility. Adrian accordingly overlooked what scarcely could be overlooked any longer; and at the very time in which this conference, no less in its form than in the results to be expected from it, was threatening the existing constitution of the church, he sent Zwingli a flattering letter, to induce him to employ his influence to retain the powerful canton on the pope's side.

For the disputation to be held on the 29th of January, 1523, Zwingli had comprised in sixty-seven articles the doctrines he had preached; and so defended them on that day against the vicar-general Faber, that the council charged him to persevere in his course, and all their preachers to hold forth the pure Gospel as he did. By this disputation, by the interpretation of his articles which was soon after (in July) published by Zwingli, and by the preaching of Zwingli and his friend Leo Judae (Léon Juda), who came to Zurich in the beginning of 1523 as lay-priest at St. Peter's, men's minds were more and more won over to the Reformation; and many wished to see it brought into actual existence. For them it was not enough that the council allowed nuns to leave their convents (June 17th), that several of the clergy married without restraint, that a German baptismal service was introduced in the city (August 10th), and that the cathedral chapter at its own request received a new and suitable constitution (September 19th). They wished to feel sure that all that was idolatrous in the divine service was abolished, especially images and masses, and accordingly they soon began on their own authority to demolish images and the paraphernalia of superstition. These events made an evil impression on most of the remaining confederates. They were in part frightened at the prospect of a schism in the church, in part they concluded from certain exaggerated rumours that all civic order was overthrown at Zurich, and dreaded the force of the example. Proclamations were issued against all innovations in the church.

All excess of zeal, whether displayed in behalf of the old or the new religion, was held in check; and every outbreak or arbitrary demonstration was chastised. On the other hand concession was gradually made to the desire for reform; in December the shrined pictures in the churches were allowed to be closed up, and every priest was left free to celebrate mass or not as he chose. In 1524 a more thorough reform of the church was begun with the abolition of images. One after another all the objects and usages of superstition quickly disappeared; the monasteries were suppressed, and changed into schools and almshouses.

ULRICH ZWINGLI

(1484–1531)

Beyond the canton of Zurich the reformation was at this time in actual existence only in Appenzell and the town of Mülhausen. The free inhabitants of Appenzell, to whom, since the year 1522, Walter Klarer, pastor at Hundweil, had preached the Gospel, after a violent struggle granted to every parish the right of judging for itself (1524). Out of the eight parishes of the canton, six at once came over to the Reformation, and began to model their church constitution without suffering themselves to be withheld by any considerations. Mülhausen was won over to the Reformation by Ulrich von Hutten, and reconstituted its form of worship accordingly as early as 1523. Still a party of adherents to the ancient order, who relied upon the confederates for support, imposed upon the council the necessity for prudence.

The government endeavoured to maintain their influence by holding an intermediate position betwixt the parties. The preaching of the gospel was freely conceded, but every attack upon church usage and all controversy were forbidden and punished with severe penalties.c

RELIGIOUS QUARRELS AND RELIGIOUS LEAGUES

Zwingli, not content with attacking the church, censured also the civil power, reproaching his fellow countrymen with their inconsistency in considering it "a sin to eat the flesh of animals during Lent, whilst they thought it lawful to sell human flesh to foreign princes." Upon hearing of this and other similar attacks, the deputies of the cantons assembled at Bern ordered his arrest. The great council, or legislative assembly of Zurich, however, protected him, and in that same year (1523) convoked all the clergymen of the town and country, and forbade them, under penalties, to preach any doctrines which were not clearly grounded on holy writ; at the same time they condemned images and image worship. In the following year the service of the mass was formally abolished.

These decisions were communicated to all the cantons and to the bishops of Switzerland. Most of the cantons, and especially the three Waldstätte, made strong remonstrances against the new doctrines, as much perhaps from political as from religious motives; for the evangelical preachers condemned the practice of enlisting in foreign wars, which was very prevalent and popular in the mountain districts. Deputies from the cantons repaired to Zurich; and while they promised that they would reform clerical abuses, they exhorted the Zurichers to abstain from further innovations, under pain of being expelled from the confederacy. But the great council of Zurich replied that it was "better to obey God than man," and the work of reformation proceeded. They abolished processions, fastings, and pilgrimages; they buried the relics; removed the images, reduced the number of festivals, and established a new liturgy. The convents were suppressed, their inmates released from their vows and allowed to marry; the buildings being devoted to hospitals or schools, and their revenues applied to the support of the new establishment and to that of the clergy. The chapter of Zurich willingly gave up its rights and property to the state,[1] and its twenty-four canons became professors, preachers, or tutors, and had an allowance secured to them for life. Zurich became the first reformed canton in Switzerland. The cities of St. Gall and of Mülhausen soon followed the example, and the canton of Schaffhausen, and somewhat later that of Bâle, did the like. Bern hesitated, its councils were divided, and anomalous enactments followed each other. Endeavouring to avoid an open schism with Rome, its magistrates curtailed the authority and revenues of the clergy, and seemed disposed to allow both parties to follow their respective doctrines in peace, and thus save the country from civil war. They gave permission to the nuns of Königsfeld to leave their convent and enter the marriage state. Marriages of nuns and of churchmen took place likewise in several other cantons, and gave occasion to the sarcasms of the Catholic party.

Conferences were opened again in the town of Baden, in the year 1526, between the theologians of the two parties. The Catholics had sent for a celebrated doctor of divinity from Ingolstadt, named Johann von Eck, and he was supported by two capuchins well versed in the scholastic subtleties of those times. Zwingli was offered a safe conduct, to which, however, he did not trust. Eck had been heard to say that "with heretics there were no better arguments than fire and sword," besides, about that time an evangelical preacher had been burned at Lindau, and another had been drowned at Fribourg in the Brisgau. Œcolampadius, Berthold Haller, and other evangelicals repaired nevertheless to Baden. The disputations lasted eighteen days; during which vituperation and recriminations were resorted to oftener than argument.

The Catholic cantons, Schwyz, Uri, Unterwalden, Zug, Lucerne, and Fribourg, became, however, after this conference, strengthened in their hostility to the evangelical doctrines, and they issued decrees of proscription against its professors in all places subject to them. In the territories of the cantons themselves this course was comparatively easy, as the new doctrines had not made much progress there, but the case was different in the bailiwicks which were held by the Catholics cantons in common with those which had either like Zurich embraced the evangelical doctrines or like Bern wished to enforce

[1 The revenues thus acquired Zwingli devoted to the use of a school (the Carolinum) intended to increase knowledge of the humanities.]

toleration and avoid measures of persecution. Accordingly, the bailiwicks of Aargau, Thurgau, Rheinthal, Sargans, and Baden became a wide field of discord and violence. Several monasteries were attacked and plundered. The unfortunate people of the bailiwicks were distracted between the two parties, who preponderated according as the landvogt, or governor, was from a Catholic or a reformed canton. The county of Baden at first adopted the Reformation, and the famous convent of Wettingen on the Limmat was converted into a school. But afterwards Baden returned to Catholicism. In Thurgau, on the contrary, the Catholic cantons began by forbidding the reading of the Bible, but the reformed religion afterwards gained the ascendancy.

In the midst of the increasing discord, a new firebrand was thrown by another set of fanatics. These sectarians were commonly called Wiedertäufer, *i.e.* anabaptists, because they rebaptised adults. They spread into Switzerland. Two men of Zurich became their chiefs. The dissolute, the turbulent, the bankrupts in character joined them. They renounced every form of worship, they assembled in great multitudes in the fields or forests, they threw off all allegiance to the laws or magistrates. Some of their bands had their wives in common. The cantons, both Catholic and reformed, tried persuasion and mild correction, but to no purpose; capital punishment was resorted to against the most outrageous of the leaders, but they went to the scaffold with the zeal of martyrs. At last Bern assembled six thousand men to put down the bands which were infesting its territory, and were living in a state of open rebellion. Fribourg and Solothurn joined their contingents. Zurich took similar measures, and by degrees the sect fell into disrepute, and at last became harmless and unnoticed. The Catholics, however, did not fail to throw the blame of these lamentable excesses on the new doctrines, as being, at least, the indirect cause of all the mischief.

The council of Bern, which had long proceeded on religious questions with a caution bordering on irresolution, came at length to a determination. In 1528 it announced the opening of a new and final conference, in order to throw all possible light on the pending controversy. Six cantons, namely the three Waldstätte, Lucerne, Zug, and Fribourg, declined sending any deputies. A great number of clergymen, and men of learning, came from various parts of Switzerland and the neighbouring countries. Zwingli himself came with an escort. It was altogether a solemn assembly, the most important that had yet met in Switzerland on this great controversy.

The council of Bern, considering the result as decidedly in favour of reformation, decreed the abolition of mass in the capital. They assembled the citizens of every condition, and requested their oath that they would support the government in what they were going to do for the good of the state. They then addressed to all the subjects of the canton a general edict of reformation. Bern became the steadiest pillar of reformation in Switzerland. At the same time they prohibited for the future receiving pensions from foreign states, or enlisting in foreign services, so far as this could be done without infringing the treaties already existing with France and other powers; and in fact the following year Bern rejected the urgent request of the king of France to extend the capitulation to a further contingent of troops. This good resolve, however, was only kept while the religious fervour lasted which had dictated it. In November, 1528, the five Catholic cantons [1] and the Valais formed a league for the defence of the Catholic faith, which was called the

---

[1] The Waldstätte, Lucerne, and Zug.

[1529 A.D.]

"league of the Valais." The canton of Fribourg joined the league afterwards, and, what was worse, the hereditary enemy of Switzerland, Ferdinand of Austria, king of Hungary, was admitted the following year [February, 1529] into the alliance [*Christliche Vereininung*, Christian Alliance].

Zurich and Bern formed a particular alliance between themselves, which they called evangelical co-burghership [*Evangelisches Burgrecht*], to which the towns of Bienne, St. Gall, Mülhausen, and Constance acceded. The objects were, their mutual defence and the protection of their subjects of the common bailiwicks who would embrace the reformed doctrines, leaving to the rest full liberty of conscience, and observing in every other matter which did not concern religion the obligations which bound them to the other cantons of the confederation. This treaty was concluded at Bern on the 3rd of March, 1529. The five remaining cantons were divided. At Bâle the people fought in the streets, the burghers against their Catholic magistrates; they destroyed the images, and at last drove the Catholic clergy out of the city. The service was ordered to be read in German. Most of the nobles, remaining attached to the old faith, were excluded forever from the senate. The famous Erasmus, a man of quiet, studious habits, left Bâle amidst all these tumults; but he returned soon after, and passed the remainder of his life in that city, although he never would openly abjure the doctrines of Rome. Nicholas Diessbach, coadjutor of the late bishop, and upon whom that rich see devolved, refused the preferment. Bâle, as well as Schaffhausen, was ranked from that time among the reformed cantons. In the canton of Appenzell the reformed doctrines gained ground, chiefly in the external Roden or districts, while the interior and more secluded parts remained attached to Catholicism; and a separation followed, by which each of the two districts formed a separate state, although still representing together but one canton of the confederation.

SWISS ECCLESIASTIC

(Middle Ages)

The Reformation spread early among the Grisons, but did not produce at first any serious troubles. Both parties availed themselves of the opportunity to reduce the power of the church; the feudal rights of the bishop of Coire and of the abbeys were suppressed, the corvées abolished. In this both Catholic and Protestant agreed, and, without quarrelling about theological controversies, they turned them to the account of political liberty. The town of Bienne was one of the first reformed, through the agency of its citizen Wyttenbach. That of Mülhausen, an ally of the cantons, though without the borders of Switzerland, also embraced the Reformation.

The most strenuous champions of Catholicism were from the first the five old cantons, namely the three Waldstätte, Lucerne, and Zug. There reformation made no inroads, or if it did at first at Lucerne it was soon effectually checked by severe measures. These five cantons had frequent disputes with Zurich and Bern about the common bailiwicks; a new subject of discord arose concerning the country of Hasli and Oberland. Serious causes of irritation occurred, especially in Thurgau, Gaster, and Toggenburg. Zurich demanded the free exercise of religion for the people of those districts, among whom the doctrines of the Reformation had widely spread. Jacob Keyser, a minister from the canton of Zurich, as he was one day going to preach as usual at the parish of Oberkirch, in the bailiwick of Gaster, which was subject to the two cantons of Schwyz and Glarus, was seized by four armed men and taken to Schwyz. After seven days' trial, he was sentenced to be burned. In vain Glarus remonstrated, in vain Zurich protested — the unhappy Keyser was burned publicly at Schwyz at the end of May, 1529. Several traders from Zurich, who had gone to Schwyz on business, were beaten, pelted with stones, and obliged to escape. The Zurichers, on their side, seized the landammann Wehrli of Unterwalden, on his return from Thurgau, where he had, in his capacity of bailiff, persecuted the new doctrines; and although he wore his cloak with the colours of Unterwalden, in token of his office, he was publicly executed at Zurich.

THE FIRST RELIGIOUS PEACE; SECTARIANISM

All these and other grievances produced at last an open rupture. Zurich declared war by a manifesto against the five Catholic cantons, and claimed the assistance of Bern. The latter put in motion a body of ten thousand men. St. Gall, Mülhausen, Bienne sent also their contingents to the evangelical cause. These allied troops advanced by Kappel towards Schwyz. The five cantons marched to Baar to meet them; and thus twenty-four thousand Swiss stood opposite to each other, ready to fight. John Œbly, the landammann of Glarus, who had already saved his own canton from civil war, hastened to the field between the combatants, and interfered with humane zeal in the name of his own and the other neutral cantons. Bern appointed a conference to take place at Aarau; and a suspension of hostilities having been immediately proclaimed, the soldiers of both armies were seen mingling on friendly terms like brethren.

Peace was concluded on the 26th of June, 1529. This was the first religious peace between the Swiss, and it served as a precedent for subsequent treaties. The articles of the peace were seventeen in number. The principal ones were that the Catholic cantons should renounce their league with Ferdinand of Austria; that no endeavours should be made to induce the five Catholic cantons or their subjects to embrace the reformed religion; with regard to the common bailiwicks, every parish should decide by plurality of votes whether they would have mass or not, and abstain or not from meat on fast-days, and their decision should be the rule in force as long as the inhabitants continued of the same mind; that those parishes which had already abolished the mass and the images should be left undisturbed. The principle of the whole treaty was perfect toleration. None of the cantons were to hold together partial diets, except for private and particular business; and the old Compact of Stanz, agreed to in 1481, was sworn to again as the national compact of the whole Swiss federation.

This peace was favourable to the evangelicals, inasmuch as it protected the spreading of their doctrines through conviction, but not by violent means. The Catholic cantons were reluctantly obliged to sign it, because they found themselves forsaken by Austria and by the pope. These two powers were then at variance, since Charles V's army had stormed and pillaged Rome in 1527. On the other side, the Turks, under Sultan Solyman, had overrun Hungary and besieged Vienna, giving full employment to Ferdinand, who, as well as his brother the emperor, deemed it necessary to conciliate the Protestant princes of Germany. Thus these Turkish and Italian wars proved indirectly the means of sheltering the growth of reformation both in Germany and Switzerland.

Meantime a dispute had arisen between the Swiss evangelicals and the great German reformer, Luther, on the subject of the eucharist. The landgraf of Hesse invited Luther and Zwingli to meet at Marburg, in 1529, in order to come to an understanding on the point in controversy. The two parties had several conferences, but each remained convinced of its own opinion. The landgraf prevailed on them to shake hands at parting; but Luther said publicly afterwards, " We have, by so doing, given the Zwinglians a token of Christian charity, but not a title to our brotherhood."

In the year 1530 the reformed religion made great progress in western Switzerland. Farel, a native of Dauphiné, a man of zealous temper, who had been driven out of France by persecution, was the evangelical preacher in all that part of the country where French is spoken. At Neuchâtel the people burned the images, upset the altars, and, in spite of the opposition of the authorities, demanded that the question of religion should be decided in a general assembly by the majority of votes. The burghers, having assembled on the 4th of November, decided that mass should be no longer performed in the town, that images should be removed, and that other Catholic observances should be abolished. Farel proceeded next to the valleys of the Jura, which were under the lordship of the bishop of Bâle. The Val St. Imier embraced the Reformation; but in the neighbouring valley or provostship of Münster great disturbances arose. On arriving at Münster, Farel found the minds of the people disposed to listen to him. They at once broke the images and prevented the service of the mass.

Zwingli published his confession of faith, which differed from that of Augsburg, especially on the subject of the real presence, which he totally denied. This confession, which was called "evangelical," was also taken to the emperor by the deputies of three cantons, Bern, Zurich, and Bâle, who had meantime entered into an alliance with the landgraf of Hesse and the city of Strasburg to defend each other against anyone who should molest them concerning their religion. It is a remarkable fact that Francis I at that time asked to be received into the alliance, but his offer was declined.

On the 19th of November, 1530, Charles V published an edict enjoining all subjects of the empire to live according to the regulations of the Roman church, until a general council should be assembled; and threatening those who should not conform to this order. It was then that the German reformed states assembled at Schmalkalden, in December, and entered into a resolution to defend each other mutually, and to repel force by force. This was called the Smalkaldic League. They also protested, with the elector of Saxony at their head, against the election of Ferdinand, Charles' brother, as king of the Romans, by which Charles, who was occupied with the affairs of Spain and Italy, meant to transfer to his brother the imperial authority.

The reformed cantons were invited to join the Smalkaldic League at the instance of the landgraf of Hesse, who saw the urgency of the Protestants' strengthening themselves by all means within their reach; but the elector of Saxony imposed as a condition that they should all sign the Confession of

Augsburg. This the Swiss reformers refused to do. The Swiss evangelicals continued separate from the German Protestants, or Lutherans. In a great synod held at Bern in 1532 the articles of the Helvetic Confession of Faith were finally established and proclaimed.

The five Catholic cantons, dissatisfied with the spreading of the reformed doctrines in consequence of the liberty of conscience granted by the religious peace of 1529, and emboldened by the appearance of affairs in Germany, sought an opportunity for a fresh quarrel. The reformed cantons, and Zurich especially, were not long before they furnished them with a plausible one. Zurich and the reformed part of Glarus had been promoting the reformation in the territories of the abbot of St. Gall with a violence of zeal that made them overlook the dictates of justice and the faith due to existing treaties. On the death of the abbot, in March, 1529, the four cantons, protectors of the abbey, Zurich and Glarus on one side, and Lucerne and Schwyz on the other, disagreed about the election of his successor. The abbey was completely secularised by force. The other cantons, and even Bern, disapproved of this arbitrary proceeding, which was an infraction not only of the rights of the abbey but also of those of the other co-protectors. At a general diet held at Baden in January, 1531, the five Catholic cantons remonstrated strongly. Zurich, on its part, assumed a very high tone, and demanded that the Catholic cantons should allow the Scriptures to be freely read amongst them. At this diet the evangelical cantons objected to the test of plurality of votes in the diets being conclusive in matters of religion, for the Catholic cantons, being many and small, were always sure of a majority against the reformed ones, who were few though large. This was a grave question, thus first broached, for it affected the very constitution of the confederation.

SECOND WAR OF KAPPEL

Zurich, in order to force the Catholic cantons to submit to its dictation, forbade all commerce with them, and even prevented the supply of necessary articles of provisions, such as salt, which the people of the Waldstätte used to receive through Zurich. Zwingli opposed, as became a minister of the Gospel, this uncharitable interdict, and he even preached against its principle on Whitsunday, 1531. The inhabitants of the five cantons were furious. They considered themselves, and not without reason, unkindly treated. "The sword alone can unloose the knot," was the cry in the Waldstätte. In September manifestoes appeared on either side. Zurich, which had shown in this business, as it had done in others, an intemperate and overbearing spirit, asked Bern and the other reformed cantons for the assistance stipulated by the so-called evangelical co-burghership of March, 1529. Bern, although wishing for peace, could not refuse the appeal; it raised a body of eight thousand men.

DEFEATS OF KAPPEL AND ZUGERBERG; PEACE OF KAPPEL

The few Catholic cantons, strengthened by a body of Valaisans, assembled their troops at Zug; and the duke of Savoy and the pope sent them some Italian auxiliaries. The Zurichers divided their forces into small detachments, one of which, six hundred strong, took up a position at Kappel, on the road to Zug. But, as the Catholics threatened that position, they collected in haste a body of two thousand men to reinforce it, and Zwingli was ordered by the magistrates to accompany the soldiers, as it was known that his pres-

ULRICH ZWINGLI, 1484–1531 A.D.

(From the painting by Holbein the Younger, in the Uffizi Gallery, Florence)

ence would tend greatly to encourage them, and as it was also customary for a minister to attend whenever the great banner of the city was unfurled. Zwingli obeyed, though with gloomy forebodings of the result of the strife, which he told his friends would be the death of him, and of many other honest citizens. He was observed to pray fervently during the whole march. While this reinforcement was moving from Zurich, the Catholic troops, eight thousand strong, marched out of Zug on the morning of the 11th of October, to attack the detachment at Kappel. The Zurichers who were posted there, being joined by people from the country, amounted to about twelve hundred men.

The attack began by a cannonade, which lasted from twelve to three in the afternoon, when the reinforcement of two thousand men from Zurich appeared in sight, but in a state of great confusion, the troops having been hurried on their march by repeated messages, and having left a number of stragglers behind. The day was waning fast, and it seemed at one time as if the Catholics would defer the attack to the following morning. But a veteran warrior from Unterwalde, by name Tauch, advised an immediate assault on the Zurichers before the reinforcement had time to put themselves in order. This advice was followed, and he led the attack. The Zurichers, besides their great inferiority in numbers, were taken by surprise; their artillerymen had abandoned their duty, and their pieces were not served. Their leader Lavater and Zwingli himself encouraged the men, the latter crying out to them that their cause was good, and that God could still save them. They fought bravely, but without order. The main body of the Catholics, having rushed in upon them, broke through as far as the banner, which the Zurichers defended desperately for a time; at last the rout became general. Zwingli had fallen in the thickest of the fight. The Catholics pursued their enemies for some distance, after which they returned to the field of battle, when they knelt down, according to the old Swiss custom, and thanked heaven, the Virgin, and all the celestial host, for having given them the victory. They then went about asking the wounded if they would confess or invoke the saints, and those who refused they despatched with their pikes. Some, however, there were among the Catholics who had more humanity than the rest, and who took the wounded to their tents and nursed them.

Next day the body of Zwingli was recognised among the slain. The Catholics instituted a court-martial over the senseless corpse, and condemned it to be broken in four by the common executioner, and then burned to ashes, and the ashes mixed with rubbish and scattered to the winds. Such was the end of Ulrich Zwingli, the great reformer of Switzerland, a man single-hearted, pious, and disinterested; who, although warm and zealous in his cause, was as free as the times allowed from any violence or fanaticism, and still more from inhumanity towards his antagonists.

The defeat of Kappel threw Zurich into consternation.[1] Altogether nearly one hundred burgesses, including twenty-six councillors and fifteen clergymen, and about one thousand men had fallen; four standards and eighteen cannon were lost. The disorder of the remaining troops, and their murmurs, gave fresh life to a party which still existed at Zurich, opposed to the Reformation. Nevertheless the national spirit of the people came to their aid; and the inhabitants of the country districts remained faithful in this emergency. Mount Albis was covered with fresh troops, and messengers were despatched to Bern to urge the advance of its contingent. The Bernese,

[1 This defeat of the evangelicals ushered in the counter Reformation or Catholic reaction in Switzerland.]

four thousand strong, were joined by volunteers from Bâle, Schaffhausen, Solothurn, Neuchâtel, and even from Lausanne and Geneva. This army, after passing Bremgarten, followed the course of the river Reuss, and plundered on their way the convent of Muri. They then entered the canton of Zug and took Baar three days after the battle of Kappel. The Catholics, to the number of ten thousand, were posted on the Zugerberg, a hill which overlooks the town of Zug. But the Bernese and their allies instead of attacking their enemies with all their force, amused themselves marauding over the country. While many of them were thus dispersed in the villages, Hug, son of the avoyer of Lucerne, surprised them in the middle of the night of the 24th of October, killed a great many, and drove many more down the precipices, where they perished. The main body of the Bernese remained inactive, fearing to strike their own friends. The loss on their side was about one thousand.

This second defeat was fatal to the cause of the evangelicals. The people of Glarus and of Toggenburg detached themselves from the alliance, and considered as to the means of making a separate peace. Ten thousand men from the Grisons, who were on their march to protect the canton of Zurich, halted, and then returned home. The people of Zurich called loudly for peace. Luckily, the Catholic cantons were no less desirous of it: they felt severely the scarcity of provisions, arising from the interruption of communications; and many moderate men on both sides deplored this war between fellow countrymen. In these circumstances, the neutral cantons, as well as the envoys of France and Savoy, interfered to bring about a peace. The demands of the Catholics were at first moderate; but the greatest difficulty was that of the common bailiwicks, the reformed cantons wishing them to have full liberty of conscience, whilst the Catholic ones earnestly maintained that "they could not in conscience allow their subjects a liberty which must prove detrimental to their salvation, and would be a temptation and a snare unto their souls."

Meantime the magistrates of Zurich, being urged by the people and threatened by the Catholic troops, concluded in haste a separate peace, which was signed at Baar on the 20th of November, 1531. The first article was as follows: "We, the people of Zurich, promise to leave unmolested, as we ought, our faithful and beloved confederates of the five cantons, their allies of the Valais, and all their adherents, now and forever, in their ancient, true, and undoubted Christian faith, without importuning them by any disputations, and renouncing all evil intrigue or artifice. We, the five Catholic cantons, promise to leave on our part our confederates of Zurich and their adherents in the peaceful exercise of their religion." The Zurichers were to renounce the so-called Christian League, and to pay the expenses of the war.

The Bernese, being left alone, soon after subscribed to similar conditions. The common bailiwicks were thus left at the mercy of the Catholics, although the latter promised not to molest those of the inhabitants who had already embraced the reformed religion. But covert means were not wanting to suppress the reformed doctrines. The images were re-established everywhere, the evangelical ministers were expelled from many places. The abbey of Wettingen was restored to its monks. The abbot of St. Gall re-entered his abbey in triumph, and the town of St. Gall lost its purchase, and was obliged to pay 10,000 florins. The Toggenburgers were again placed under the dominion of the abbot, but they preserved their liberty of conscience. Bern likewise maintained with firmness the same privilege for those inhabitants of Aargau who had embraced the Reformation.

At Solothurn fresh troubles broke out; the Catholics were on the point of firing on the assembled evangelicals, when the old avoyer, Nicholas von Wenger, stepped before the loaded cannon, crying out, "If you want the blood of your countrymen, take mine first." This noble act, and the aspect of the venerable magistrate, checked the fury of the people, and no blood was spilt; but the reformed families were obliged to leave the canton. Solothurn, as well as Fribourg, joined henceforth the five old cantons, so that the Catholic cantons became seven, while the reformed ones remained four, namely Bern, Zurich, Schaffhausen, and Bâle; and this line of demarcation has continued ever since. Glarus and Appenzell alone remained mixed. The Treaty of Kappel, however, insured internal peace to the Swiss cantons for more than a century after.

THE PROGRESS OF LIBERTY IN GENEVA

We now turn to the affairs of western Switzerland. It was only in the sixteenth century that Geneva and Vaud became connected with the Swiss Confederation, of which they now constitute an essential part. Until that epoch, Geneva had been governed by its sovereign bishop, who was a prince of the German Empire. The bishop was elected by the chapter, conjointly with the burghers; he had no armed force at his disposal, and his authority was very limited. The counts of Geneva, *Comites Genevensium*, being feudal lords of the empire over the province of which Geneva was the chief town, administered justice; but their authority in the city was limited by that of the bishop, who had his own courts of justice, and whose jurisdiction was independent of that of the counts. Placed between these two powers, the burghers contrived to extend their privileges. The powerful house of Savoy, however, aspired to extend its power over the city.

Charles III, duke of Savoy, who at the beginning of the sixteenth century succeeded the good Philibert, showed himself especially disposed to encroach on the liberties of Geneva, and was favoured in his views by the bishop, Pierre de la Baume, a weak unprincipled man, who seemed willing to abdicate his temporal rights in favour of Charles. The citizens became alarmed, and turned their eyes towards the Swiss cantons for protection. One of the former bishops had, in 1478, concluded a treaty of alliance for himself and the citizens with Bern and Fribourg. Berthelier, a citizen of Geneva, who was exiled on account of some affray with the bishop's authorities, and had retired to Fribourg, of which city he was also a burgher, proposed to the latter canton to renew their alliance with Geneva. The treaty of alliance and co-burghership with Fribourg was concluded in 1519. Berthelier returned to Geneva. The city was now divided into two parties: the more numerous, who were for independence and the alliance with Fribourg, styled themselves *Eidgenossen*, "bound by oath," in imitation of the Swiss confederates; and they gave their antagonists, who were devoted to the house of Savoy, the appellation of mamelukes. The word *Eidgenossen*, disfigured by a French pronunciation, was transformed into that of *Huguenots*, and was afterwards applied generally to the French evangelicals or Calvinists. But Huguenots meant originally the republican party at Geneva.

The duke of Savoy, incensed at the news of the alliance, marched with ten thousand men against Geneva. The syndics being unable to resist, the gates were opened, the troops entered, and lived at free quarters upon the inhabitants. Berthelier was executed, and other acts of vengeance were perpetrated. The canton of Fribourg, being apprised of this, marched troops into the duke's territories of the Pays de Vaud; whereupon the duke issued a general amnesty, and withdrew his army from the city, having first obliged the latter to rescind its alliance with Fribourg: but he continued, in concert with the bishop, to persecute the Huguenots, under various pretences. In 1525 the Huguenots became bolder, and talked of renewing the alliance with Bern and Fribourg. A treaty was concluded in February, 1526, by which the two cantons engaged "to defend Geneva against all attacks on their persons, properties, liberties, privileges, jurisdictions, and ancient usages." Geneva took a similar engagement towards the cantons; with this difference, however — that its citizens were to pay for all assistance afforded to them, but were to furnish aid to Bern and Fribourg, when required, at their own expense. This was a general condition in all the treaties of alliance between the Swiss cantons and their weaker neighbours. But as Geneva was more likely to be in want of assistance than Bern and Fribourg, the Genevans thought themselves fortunate in concluding the treaty.

The duke exerted himself strenuously to dissolve this alliance; but the cantons stood firm, and at last signified to him that, if he did not desist from annoying Geneva, they would rescind their own treaties with Savoy. From that moment the mamelukes lost all influence in the town, and they at last emigrated. Being summoned by the magistrates to return and give an account of their conduct, they were, on their non-compliance, declared outlaws, and their property was confiscated. They then joined the Savoyard nobles in the neighbourhood, and formed with them an offensive league against Geneva. They took the name of "knights of the Spoon," on account of their having boasted that they would hew down the citizens, and cut them into small pieces, so as to be able to eat them with their spoons, and they wore, accordingly, as a badge of their confraternity, a spoon. They ravaged the estates of the citizens outside the town, burned the suburbs, killed those of the inhabitants they fell in with, and blockaded the place in order to starve it. It was during this most calamitous period that the Genevans showed an energy and perseverance worthy of the highest praise — resisting all the intrigues of the duke and of the fickle-minded bishop, who still remained within the city, as well as the open attacks of their enemies from outside, and holding fast by the treaty with the cantons, as their only anchor of safety. At this time also the doctrines of the Reformation began to spread rapidly amongst them. The flagrant immorality of the clergy contributed to this. Bonnivard, prior of St. Victor, was one of the first to preach in favour of a reformation in religion. But here again a new difficulty arose. Fribourg, one of the two allied cantons, wrote that if the Genevans abandoned their old faith it would renounce their alliance. The magistrates, therefore, were cautious not to encourage the spreading of the new doctrines.

Geneva meantime was reduced to the greatest extremities by the Savoyard nobles and the knights of the Spoon; the citizens could not venture outside the walls, no provisions were allowed to come in, and they suffered the severest privations. At last, after repeated but useless negotiations, Bern and Fribourg resolved, in 1530, to take the field, and relieve their ally. A Bernese army of seven thousand men, under John d'Erlach, joined by two thousand men from Fribourg, five hundred of Solothurn, and three thousand volunteers from other parts, with eighteen pieces of cannon, entered the Pays de Vaud, which they crossed without opposition, although they committed serious depredations on the subjects of the duke, and arrived at Geneva on the 10th of October, having on their march taken and destroyed the castles of the knights of the Spoon. The other cantons and

[1533–1534 a.d.]

the Valais now sent deputies to mediate a peace, and the Treaty of St. Julien was the result. The duke engaged, among other things, that if he should be the first to attack the Genevans again he should forfeit the Pays de Vaud to Bern and Fribourg. The Swiss army left Geneva, after having been paid by the inhabitants, who with great difficulty raised the sum required. The prior Bonnivard,[1] whom the duke had kidnapped and confined in the dungeons of Chillon, was to be released. The duke was to defray the expenses of the war, and pay an indemnity to Geneva; and, on the other hand, he was to appoint a *vidomne* in the latter city, to administer justice. The duke appointed this officer, but neglected to perform the other conditions of the treaty.

The preaching of the Reformation had formed two new parties in the city. The majority of the people and some of the magistrates were favourable to it; but the clergy and most of the councillors and of the wealthy citizens were for remaining Catholic. Farel, who had come to Geneva, was driven away, but some of his disciples continued to preach. In 1533 the animosity between the two parties had reached the greatest height. Conspiracies, seditions, murders were the melancholy consequences. Relative was against relative, brother against brother, father against son. The magistrates endeavoured to enforce mutual toleration. Farel returned, and held forth against the Catholics. Fribourg now demanded that Farel should be punished for preaching against its religion, and threatened to withdraw itself from the alliance. Bern insisted on the public preaching of the Gospel; and the council being obliged to accede, Farel preached in the church of the Franciscan convent, and made numerous proselytes. Then it was that the deputies of Fribourg declared, in presence of the council of Geneva, on the 23rd of April, 1534, that the alliance on their part was at an end, and they publicly tore the seals from off the treaty, which they had brought with them.

SWISS SCHOLAR

(Sixteenth century)

Bern remained now the only ally of Geneva, and its influence became paramount. The reformers, thus emboldened, kept no measures; they overturned the altars, and destroyed the images. Many Catholic families emigrated. The bishop, who had retired to Gex, excommunicated the town. The sovereign council of Geneva then declared that the bishop's authority was at an end and his see vacant. The canons retired to Annecy, whither the see of Geneva was finally transferred. On the 10th of August, 1534, the great council forbade the mass till further orders. Another edict enjoined that God should be worshipped according to the Gospel, and it forbade every act of papal idolatry. The Catholic party in the town dwindled to nothing; but the nobles of Savoy and the bishop blockaded Geneva, and annoyed the citizens. Bern remonstrated repeatedly for more than a twelvemonth, but without effect. The duke, who was engaged in war with France, pleaded his inability to restrain his turbulent Savoyard nobles; but he had certainly

[1 A famous historian of the time, and the subject of Byron's poem, *The Prisoner of Chillon*.]

given repeated proofs of his insincerity concerning the stipulations of the Treaty of St. Julien. He still held Bonnivard in prison at Chillon.

On the other hand, Bern was probably not sorry to have an opportunity of seizing the Pays de Vaud. Being assured of the general sympathy of the people, and of their co-operation, the great council of Bern formally declared war against the duke of Savoy, in consequence of his breach of the Treaty of St. Julien, and of the state of intolerable oppression in which he held the city of Geneva, on account of its religion. The Bernese army, seven thousand strong, marched in January, 1536, by Morat; and as they proceeded they received the submission of most of the towns in the Pays de Vaud, except Yverdun. In eleven days the Bernese entered Geneva, where they were hailed as deliverers. The duke was at the same time attacked by the French, who conquered all Savoy and the greater part of Piedmont; so that he was stripped at the same time of all his dominions. The Valaisans, on their side, by an agreement with Bern, took for themselves all that part of the Chablais which extends along the southern shore of the Lake of Geneva, as far west as the river Drance.

The Bernese now unexpectedly demanded of the Genevans the surrender of all the rights and revenues which the duke and the bishop held over the city. The Genevans, surprised at this demand, calmly but firmly refused. The Bernese councils desisted from their unjust demand. In August, 1536, a treaty was concluded between the free town of Geneva and the canton of Bern. The co-burghership was renewed for twenty-five years, at the expiration of which it was converted into a perpetual alliance. Geneva retained all the lands of the bishop, chapter, and convents, and of the priory of St. Victor, the Bernese reserving to themselves an appellate jurisdiction over those lands in all cases in which formerly appeal lay to the dukes of Savoy. The city and its territory were declared free from all jurisdictions of the neighbouring lordships. Thus Geneva became a really independent republic, and the evangelical religion was solemnly established there. The effects of these changes were soon perceived in the revival of activity, industry, and trade. A number of foreigners from France, Italy, and Savoy, came to reside within the walls of Geneva, bringing their property with them, for the sake of enjoying peace and liberty of conscience.

The Bernese had reduced the whole Pays de Vaud into subjection. Lausanne had not been visited by them, that city forming a separate sovereignty, and being still governed by its bishop, who was a prince of the empire. The citizens boldly opened the gates to Bern, which took possession of all the lands and jurisdictions of the bishop, extending over Lausanne, Avenches, Lucens, and Pully. The whole Pays de Vaud was divided into eight bailiwicks, a bailiff from Bern being appointed to each. The people in general were pleased with the change, except the nobility, who lost their influence by passing under the dominion of a republic. They were besides attached to Catholicism. Many of them even refused the offer of having themselves inscribed and admitted among the Patricians of Bern.

A religious disputation took place at Lausanne, in which Farel took the lead; it lasted seven days, but the Catholic clergy of Lausanne declined to take part in it. After its conclusion, the Bernese proclaimed all over the country the abolition of the mass and of images, and reformed clergymen were appointed to the various parishes. The castle of Chillon was the last place that surrendered. In the dungeons below the level of the lake was found Bonnivard, who had been confined there for six years. Although Fribourg had borne no share in the expedition, yet Bern willingly allowed her to take possession of several districts of the conquered country, such as Romont, Rue, and Estavayer, which were contiguous to her own territory. Some years afterwards the two cantons purchased the rights of the counts of Gruyères, the last remaining of the old feudal nobility of Helvetia. Bern had now doubled its territory, and it became by far the most extensive and powerful of the Swiss cantons.

The Reformation spread to the Italian side of the Alps, in the bailiwicks or districts subject to the Swiss confederates. After many vexations and disturbances, and in spite of the protests of the reformed cantons, an order was issued by the Catholic cantons, sentencing all the evangelical converts at Locarno to be banished their country with their families. The sentence was carried into execution in March, 1555. Most of them found an asylum at Zurich, where the families of Orell and Muralt, with a slight change in their names, became naturalized, and continue to this day. Several of these Italian exiles were silk-weavers and dyers, and they carried to Zurich those branches of industry from their Italian land.

CALVIN AT GENEVA

In 1536 John Calvin was obliged to make his escape from Italy, where his doctrines had attracted the attention of the clergy and the court of Rome, and he made his way into Switzerland by an unfrequented path over the Col de Ferret. Passing through Geneva he saw Farel, who earnestly invited him to fix his residence in that city and to assist him in the great work of reformation. Calvin, though at first unwilling, was persuaded, and he was appointed the same year professor of theology. He was then only twenty-seven years of age. Both he and Farel went further in their innovations than the Swiss reformers. This made them many enemies, and drew upon them the disapprobation of the evangelical synod then sitting at Lausanne for the purpose of regulating the discipline of the reformed church. As Calvin and Farel, however, would not submit to the decision of the synod, they were ordered by the magistrates to leave Geneva in 1538, and Calvin went to Strasburg, where he established a French evangelical church. Soon after, however, a deputation came from Geneva to invite him to return, as his presence was found necessary to enforce order and religion. Farel had, meantime, settled at Neuchâtel, where he remained till his death.

Calvin, on his return to Geneva, in 1541, perceiving the necessity of having a moral censorship, in order to restrain the utter licentiousness which threatened the very existence of the community, proposed to establish a consistory, to act as *censor morum*, composed of the pastors or parish incumbents, two members of the council of state or executive, two members of the council of two hundred, one of the syndics, and a secretary. This and other regulations proposed by Calvin concerning church government and discipline were approved by the general council of all the citizens, and received the form of law in November, 1541. The consistory assembled every Thursday, and Calvin, who always attended the sittings, may be said to have been its presiding spirit. It had very extensive and almost inquisitorial powers; it took cognisance of immoralities, of blasphemy and profanation, and other offences against religion. The punishments were fine, imprisonment, and in some cases death. This institution of the consistory continues to exist though considerably modified. Calvin also assumed the task of collecting and revising the old laws and edicts, so as to form a body of civil law for the republic, which was approved of in 1543 by the council general. At the same time he was not unmindful of the cultivation of the mind, and he proposed and effected the establishment of a public college, called academy, for teaching the arts and sciences, in which he himself lectured three times a week on theology, and which soon acquired and has ever since maintained a high character among the schools of learning in Europe, and has been a nursery of clergymen and divines to the reformed churches of France and other countries.

The influence of Calvin's searching and austere mind remained impressed on the manners and habits of the Genevans for ages after his death, and the stamp is not yet altogether obliterated. He was intolerant according to the temper of his age, but he was conscientious in his intolerance. The execution of Michael Servetus is the act from which Calvin's memory has suffered most. Servetus was a Spanish physician, a man of a wild, fantastic mind, who had adopted the tenets of the Samosatenians against Trinity, denying the eternity and divinity of the Son. He held forth his doctrines in various places, and finally came to Geneva, where Calvin now reigned paramount. He was tried and sentenced to the stake, as an obdurate heretic, although it appears that Calvin voted for a milder mode of death. He was, however, burned alive.

SWISS GENTLEMAN

(Sixteenth century)

Geneva owes much to Calvin. He consolidated both its religious and municipal institutions. He died on the 27th of May, 1564, at the age of fifty-five, worn out by study and application. He was buried without pomp or epitaph, as he had himself directed, in the common burying ground of Pleinpalais, and his funeral was attended by almost the entire population. He left the care of his flock to his friend and disciple, Théodore de Bèze.[b]

The effects of the Reformation made themselves manifest in all the relations of private and public life. General attention was directed to the internal wants and welfare of the country; and the rising generation acquired taste for the arts of peace, and for the sciences by which the mind is most enlarged and elevated. The study of the ancients and of history had been revived by theological inquiries. If enlistments still continued to take place for foreign services, yet the venality of rulers and their subjects had ceased to be so prevalent as formerly. Improvements were made in agriculture, commerce, and manufactures; and the reception given to fugitive co-religionists introduced or furthered several branches of industry. Almshouses and hospitals were instituted or improved. Strict regulations were made against prodigality, gambling, and usury; and rigid limits were set to public amusements.

Under the name of ecclesiastical discipline the clergy in Geneva and the canton of Bern assumed a very extensive jurisdiction. The clergy possessed important weight and influence with the people; and when they interfered in word or in writing with the constituted authorities, their dicta were in general received as decisive. Their intervention, as might be expected, was not in all cases free from polemical passions or sacerdotal arrogance; but it oftener took an aspect of beneficence, particularly when the secular authorities neglected their duties. The better part of the clergy themselves never lost sight of the evils engendered by an unlimited domination of their order.

The independence of the cantons and the difference of their forms of polity necessarily occasioned variations in their church discipline. These were taken advantage of by the enemies of reform to reproach its friends with the want of a sure foundation for their faith. The subsequent evangelical leaders, harassed by the virulent attacks of their opponents, imagined the production of explicit confessions to be requisite for their justification. The four evangelical cantons, Zurich, Bern, Bâle, and Schaffhausen, and the three allied towns, St. Gall, Mülhausen, and Bienne, agreed upon a common form of confession, to be laid before the general assembly of the church when convoked by the emperor. In the same year (1566) Geneva also issued a confession, composed by Farel. Finally, on the 1st of March, 1566, the so called Helvetic confession was promulgated at Zurich.

The reformed cantons made frequent but for the most part ineffectual intercessions for their oppressed co-religionists in France and Savoy. Numerous refugees from these countries found protection and support in Switzerland. Geneva became a city of refuge for persecuted Italians, and Zurich for the English, who fled from the tyranny of Queen Mary. The church of Rome, unable to withstand any longer the demands for reformation, even of Catholics themselves, had at last consented to open a council at Trent. The reception of its decisions by the Catholic cantons occasioned the reformed ones to be regarded by them more than ever as renegades and reprobates, while it served to increase the suspicions and imbitterment of the latter. All sentiments of patriotism yielded to religious hatred, which constantly found new food for itself.

In former times the confederates had always maintained a jealous vigilance with regard to the pope, considered as a foreign power, and with regard to the clerical order in general, as instruments of that power. But now, the zeal of polemics, and the prevalent ideas of the duty of submissiveness to the spiritual authority, placed a part of the Helvetic body entirely at the command of their ecclesiastical superiors; and by consequence attached them to that line of foreign policy most conformable to clerical interests.

At this epoch, Cardinal Carlo Borromeo exercised a distinguished influence in spiritual and political matters. Elevated at the age of three-and-twenty to the bishopric of Milan and the dignity of cardinal, he felt an early vocation to the office of reformer of the Catholic clergy and church discipline; but his mind was so thoroughly imbued with the spirit of a dominant priesthood that even the heads of the Catholic cantons were compelled to resist his proceedings. He powerfully contributed towards putting in execution the decrees of the Council of Trent; he established at Milan a college for the bringing up of Swiss youth to the clerical profession; he induced the pope to keep a permanent nuncio in the Catholic cantons. His establishment of Jesuits at Lucerne was still more momentous in its influence on the public mind and on education; while the effect produced by the Jesuits on the upper classes was rivalled by that which the order of Capuchins exercised over the lower.

The first permanent nuncio, the bishop of Vercelli, a *protégé* of the cardinal

Borromeo, brought about, in 1579, a league between the bishop of Bâle and the seven Catholic cantons. This may be regarded as a sort of Catholic counterpart to the evangelical co-burghership of Bern and Zurich. The contracting parties promised each other aid in the affairs of religion, etc. The seven cantons engaged to retain in the Catholic faith such subjects of the bishop as had not yet abandoned it, and to use their endeavours in re-converting those who had apostatised. In 1586, the so-called Borromean or "golden league" was sworn to by the seven Catholic cantons, the provisions of which were similar to those of the foregoing one, with the addition of the following clause: that, in case of individual members manifesting any inclination to desert the faith, the others should compel them to abide by it, and visit the promoters of defection with condign punishment.

A ludicrous example of the length to which distrust of Rome was carried by the Protestant party was afforded by the controversy excited on the occasion of the reform of the Julian calendar. Pope Gregory XIII commenced his reform of the calendar by striking off ten days from the year 1582. The Catholic cantons adopted this arrangement, after Unterwalden had offered some objections to it. The Protestants, on the other hand, conceived an apprehension lest the reception of a calendar decreed by the pope, and named after him, might pave the way for future papal encroachments; and lest their compliance might wear the appearance of deference to a papal mandate. The Catholic cantons not only adopted the Gregorian calendar, but enjoined its observance on the free bailiwicks, and instructed the vogts to punish recusants.

Irritated by this mode of proceeding, Zurich turned the affair into a question of religion: the greatest ferment, however, was in the Thurgau. The two religious parties had now not only different feast days, but confusion took place on market days, and other civil arrangements. After the waste of much discussion on the matter at successive diets, the neutral cantons, in concert with the French ambassador, finally concluded an arrangement by which the regulation of the calendar was committed to each canton within the bounds of its own territory.[d]

RELATIONS WITH SAVOY; THE ESCALADE (1602 A.D.)

In October, 1564, Bern, by a peace concluded at Lausanne, restored to Emanuel Philibert, duke of Savoy, the Chablais and the county of Gex, on condition that he should allow the free exercise of the reformed religion in those districts. The duke, on his side, made a formal cession to Bern and Fribourg of his rights in the Pays de Vaud, and this cession was confirmed in 1617 by Duke Charles Emanuel. Emanuel Philibert maintained the article of the treaty concerning religion until his death, but his successor, Charles Emanuel, disregarding his father's promise, drove away, in 1598, the reformed clergy from the Chablais, and abolished the Reformation by force. He also resumed a system of annoyance and intrigue against Geneva, and he encouraged several conspiracies, for the purpose of recovering possession of that city.

At length, in 1602, he made a bold attempt to take the town by surprise. Under pretence of watching the movements of the French on his frontiers, he assembled a body of troops near its walls, and in the night between the 11th and 12th of December (old style), scaling ladders having been prepared for the purpose, a party of two hundred of the duke's soldiers silently mounted the walls at one o'clock in the morning, while the rest waited outside for a signal to force the gate. They had been promised the plunder of the city, but Geneva was providentially spared the horrors that would have followed their success. A sentry hearing noise in the ditch gave the alarm, the citizens ran to arms and barricaded the streets, the guard at the gate let down the portcullis, and fired a cannon which enfiladed the ditch and swept away the ladders. The troops outside, seeing the attack had failed, began a retreat while those that were in the town, being assailed on every side by the citizens, were either killed or thrown into the ditches. Thirteen were made prisoners and hanged next day as midnight assassins. Théodore de Bèze, who, owing to his great age, had discontinued preaching, mounted the pulpit next morning and began singing the 124th psalm, in gratitude to the Almighty who had snatched his countrymen from the jaws of destruction. The anniversary of the Escalade has been ever since religiously kept at Geneva. The canton of Bern strongly resented this treacherous attack upon its ally, but the neutral cantons interfered, and a new treaty was at length concluded in July, 1603, by which the duke of Savoy engaged not to raise any fortress or assemble troops within sixteen miles of the city. From that time the republic neva was left in the undisturbed enjoyment of its independence; and, s Bern, Zurich contracted with it a perpetual alliance.

DISORDERS IN THE GRISONS

In the early part of the seventeenth century, the country of the Grisons came involved in war with the courts of Spain and of Austria, in consequence of a revolt which broke out in the Valtellina, and was a source of great and lasting calamities to both countries. The origin of the disturbances in the Valtellina was of a remote date. The people of that valley (which had become subject to the Grisons a century before) were Catholic, while the majority of their Grisons masters had embraced the reformed communion. The government of the Grisons, stimulated by some of the more zealous evangelical clergymen, interfered in a certain measure with the consciences of their subjects. On the other hand, the conduct of the agents of Rome excited the suspicions of the Grisons.

Pope Pius V, a strenuous defender of the prerogatives of his church, endeavoured to recover certain tithes and other revenues in the Valtellina, which had been given up by the Grisons to lay impropriators. He commissioned for this purpose John Planta, baron of Räzuns, and his son Conrad, who was a canon of the cathedral of Coire, to whom, in 1572, he issued a bull, conferring on them the management of all church lands and revenues in the Valtellina and in the adjoining county of Chiavenna, "which were then held by improper persons," meaning thereby several Protestants, and among others the Salis, a powerful Grisons family, and ancient rivals of the Plantas. The Salis appealed to the diet of the Grisons, who decided that the grant by the pope to the Plantas was illegal. The baron of Razuns, not having paid sufficient deference to this decision, was imprisoned, tortured, and put to death. His son escaped, and soon after [1574], through the mediation of the Swiss cantons, public tranquillity was restored, at least in appearance.

In the beginning of the following century the duke of Fuentes, the Spanish governor of Milan, raised, at the northern extremity of the Lake of Como, a fort which commanded the only carriage-road leading into the Valtellina. Spain had long been ambitious of possessing that fine valley, through which lay the only direct communication between Lombardy and the Tyrol, and other Austrian territories; for as the two branches of the house of Austria were allied by policy as well as by blood, it was their interest to have some road by which they could receive or send speedy assistance to each other. On the other hand, the republic of Venice, which was then the only independent power in Italy, and whose territories lay between Austria and Spanish Lombardy, was essentially interested in maintaining the Grisons in possession of Valtellina, which bordered on her two provinces of Bergamo and Brescia, and through which she could obtain recruits from Switzerland, her natural ally against any encroachments from Spain and Austria. In 1603, Venice made a treaty with the Grisons leagues for the purpose of having free passage through the territory of the latter. This excited the jealousy of the duke of Fuentes, and the Grisons, in order to keep on good terms with the Spanish governor, and to continue to receive the usual supplies of corn and other provisions from Lombardy, granted likewise free passage to the Spanish soldiers through the Valtellina.

In 1615, the alliance between Venice and the Grisons expired. The Venetian senate sent an agent to renew it, who, in order to overcome obstacles raised by the Spanish and Austrian agents, found means to in the Protestants both religious and political suspicions of their Ca subjects of Valtellina. A great synod of the Protestant ministers assen and the Venetian alliance was urged with expressions of violent ranco against Spain and its supposed partisans in the Valtellina and the Grisons. The Protestant communes rose in arms against those who were suspected of being favourable to Spain; some persons were killed, and many more were fined and banished, and among these were the two brothers Planta and the bishop of Coire himself. This happened in 1618. The violent leaders of the Protestants gave orders for the arrest of Nicholas Rusca, the archpriest of Sondrio, the head of the Catholic clergy of Valtellina, a man much respected for his pious and moral conduct, but who had opposed the efforts of the Protestants to make converts among his flock. Rusca was taken into the Grisons country, and tried before a summary tribunal on the charges of treasonable correspondence with the Spaniards, and of resistance to the edicts of the government. The old man denied the first charge, of which he appears, in fact, to have been innocent; and with regard to the second, he said he had only opposed, though not by seditious means, those innovations which were detrimental to the Catholic faith and contrary to the religious privileges of Valtellina. He was put to the torture, and he died in consequence in his prison after a few days. His body was burned by the public executioner.

These cruelties exasperated the people of Valtellina, as well as the partisans of the Plantas among the Grisons. The emigrants of that party assembled at Milan and in the Tyrol; they corresponded with the discontented in Valtellina, and aimed at overturning the government of their own country. A wealthy native of Valtellina, named Robustelli, put himself at the head of the conspiracy, which was to shake off the sovereignty of the Grisons. The duke of Feria, governor of Milan, secretly encouraged the conspirators, and gave them money. At break of day on the 19th of July, 1620, the day fixed for the breaking out of the revolt, Robustelli and his companions, with a number of armed men, entered Tirano, one of the largest villages of Valtellina, and having rung the bells as a signal, they began to massacre the Protestants, whether Grisons or their own countrymen. At the first alarm, both the Catholic and the Protestant inhabitants who were unacquainted with the conspiracy arose from their beds, thinking that some party of outlaws were come to commit depredations, as had before happened.

The Grisons governor, John Cappoli, suspecting the same thing, ordered the town-house bell to be rung to summon the people to arms. But as these came out of their houses, the conspirators, who were in waiting, fell upon the Protestants; while the Catholics, being apprised of the true cause of the tumult, and excited by the leaders of the insurrection, joined in the massacre, and having broken open the place where the arms were deposited, proceeded to the well-known dwellings of the Protestants. These strove to defend themselves, but in vain; they were hunted out and barbarously killed, five alone escaping. Several of them who had run out of the town were attacked by the peasants of the neighbourhood, who showed them no mercy. Some women were also murdered. The governor was shot, and the Protestant preacher's head was cut off and stuck on his own pulpit. The houses were plundered, although the conspirators had solemnly agreed to respect the property of the victims, for the sake of their wives and children: but those who did not refrain from murder were not likely to be restrained from robbery.

At Sondrio, the chief town of Valtellina, the insurrection broke out in the same manner. The governor, however, had time to make a show of defence, which enabled him to obtain a safeguard for himself and his family; but all the rest of the Protestants were butchered without mercy, except two natives of the place, a man and a woman, who had become Protestants, and who were sent to the Inquisition at Milan. The man abjured again, and so saved his life; the woman, more firm of purpose, refused to retract, and was burned alive. At Teglio, a small village, the assassins came just as the Protestants were attending service in their church. The church was surrounded by armed men; the people within endeavoured to defend the entrance, but the assailants climbed to the windows, and fired on the congregation. Men, women, and children here fell victims promiscuously. The door was then forced open, and the women being pushed out the men were all killed, with their pastor. Some had taken shelter in the belfry, but in vain; their tormentors lighted a fire underneath, and burned them.

The whole valley fell into the power of the insurgents. The victims of this catastrophe have been stated as amounting to 350; probably they exceeded that number. The fugitives were hunted after, shot at, stoned to death, or thrown into the river Adda.

At the first news of this sanguinary revolt the Grisons loudly expressed their indignation. Two of the leagues, Caddee and the Ten Jurisdictions, sent two thousand men, under one of the Salis, to march against Valtellina; but the Grey League, in which the Catholics were most numerous, held back from the rest. A body of five hundred Spaniards entered the county of Chiavenna, in consequence of which the Grisons thought prudent to evacuate Valtellina, and repass the mountains to their own country. An order came from Madrid by which Valtellina was placed under the royal protection of Spain, and Spanish garrisons were sent to Morbegno and Tirano.

The cantons of Bern and Zurich, being applied to by the Grisons for assistance against their revolted subjects, sent a considerable body of men, who entered Bormio and marched upon Tirano, committing many acts of cruel retaliation on their way. Two thousand Spanish veterans defended Tirano. The troops of each canton fought separately; those of Bern hurried forward to the attack, without waiting for their allies of Zurich, and were defeated with the loss of their commander. The Zurichers came up next, but the Spaniards waited for them within the walls of the town, and after seven hours of fruitless attack the Swiss were obliged to retire with great loss; and, being harassed by the peasants, few of them succeeded in recrossing the Alps. The people of Valtellina, elated with their success, set about establishing a regency, of which Robustelli was appointed president.

The ministers of France did not behold with indifference the Spanish power stretching itself over Valtellina, and threatening, in conjunction with Austria, the independence of the Grisons. The Venetian senate was likewise deeply interested in preventing the increase of Spanish dominion in Italy. The duke of Savoy saw things in the same light. And, as it happened, Pope Paul V, the great supporter of the Valtellina insurgents, having died in January, 1621, his successor, Gregory XV, a man of moderate sentiments, felt as an Italian prince a jealous suspicion of the aggrandisement of Spain, and also openly disapproved of the barbarous transactions of the Valtellina insurrection. All these sovereigns remonstrated strongly with the king of Spain against the occupation of Valtellina; and insisted on some conciliatory arrangement by which the rights of the Grisons over the valley should be acknowledged with proper security for the religion and privileges of their subjects.

The duke of Feria, on the other hand, not wishing to lose the fruit of all his intrigues, endeavoured to bring about an arrangement with the Grisons under his own superintendence, before the ministers at Madrid should come to an understanding. He succeeded in persuading the Grey League, where the Catholics were most numerous, to send agents to Milan, and the Plantas favoured his scheme. The negotiations turned in favour of Spain and of the Catholic party in the Grisons. Valtellina was to remain for eight years garrisoned by Spaniards; the executive authority was to be restored to the Grisons, but no Protestant was to settle in the valley; full amnesty was given for the past, and the Catholic religion was prescribed as the only religion in Valtellina.

The other two leagues, however, would not listen to these conditions, and they came to an open rupture with the Grey League. One of the chief Protestant leaders, George Jenatsch, once a clergyman and now a soldier, assembled his countrymen of the Ten Jurisdictions, entered the valleys of the Grey League, drove away from it the auxiliaries sent by the Catholic cantons, and obliged its representatives to renounce their treaty with Milan. Jenatsch having surprised, in the castle of Rietberg, Pompey Planta, one of the two emigrant brothers attached to the Spanish party, and whom he looked upon as a traitor to his country, clove his head with a battle-axe.

Meantime the conferences at Madrid were proceeding, though slowly. Philip III died, but by his will recommended his son to settle the Italian question according to the advice of the pope, and for the peace of Europe. In April, 1621, a treaty was concluded at Madrid, by which the Valtellina was to be evacuated by the Spaniards, and the Grisons were to be reinstated in their possession of it; a full amnesty for the past and security for the future were to be given to the natives, under the guarantee of the French king, the Swiss cantons, and the pope. But these conditions pleased neither the Grisons nor the people of Valtellina. The Grisons again took up arms and entered the county of Bormio, but the Spaniards advancing upon them on one side and the Austrians from the Tyrol on the other, they withdrew again in confusion.

Upon this the duke of Feria took possession of Chiavenna, and the Austrian general, Baldiron, entered the league of the Ten Jurisdictions, and on the plea of former claims took possession of it, as well as of Lower Engadine, or valley of the Inn, in the name of Austria. The inhabitants were obliged, under pain of death, to give up their arms, and to swear fidelity to Austria. The other two leagues were also overrun by the Austrians, who placed a garrison at Coire, the bishop of which town, availing himself of the terror of foreign arms, put forth his former pretensions to sovereignty, and assumed the exercise of almost despotic authority. A forced treaty was entered into in January, 1622, by the two leagues, the other being considered as extinct, in which they gave up forever their sovereignty over the Valtellina and Bormio; they acknowledged the incorporation of the Ten Jurisdictions, the Lower Engadine and the Münsterthal, with the Austrian dominions; and they submitted to the passage of Spanish troops through their own territories. The independence of the Grisons was in fact annihilated. Such were the consequences of their harsh and imprudent treatment of the people of Valtellina and of their obstinate rejection of the conditions of Madrid.

The Grisons Recover Independence

The overbearing conduct of the Austrians was, however, the cause of the restoration of Grisons independence. In that part of the country which they now considered their own, it having been incorporated with the Austrian dominions, Baldiron's soldiers oppressed the inhabitants with the greatest insolence, interfered with their property, obliged them to carry heavy loads, and treated them more like beasts of burden than like men. A swarm of Capuchins spread over the valleys to convert the peasants to Catholicism. All the reformed clergy were driven away, seventy-five evangelical churches were left without pastors, and the people were compelled by blows to attend the Catholic service.

This last act of tyranny roused them to resistance. The robust and spirited inhabitants of the fine valley called Prätigau, disarmed as they were, hied to the mountain forests, made themselves spears and clubs, and on Palm Sunday, 1622, they issued out with loud shouts, surprised the Austrian detachments, cut them to pieces or made them prisoners, and drove away the main body as far as Maienfeld. They then invested Coire, where Baldiron himself was. The rest of the country followed their example, the mountaineers from Appenzell joined them, and Baldiron was obliged to demand a truce to withdraw from the country. Rudolf von Salis was named general of the patriots. But Baldiron came again into the Prätigau the next summer with ten thousand men, eager for vengeance. The people fought with the fury of despair in the valleys, in the villages, in the mountains. It is recorded that in the last fight thirty brave men threw themselves, armed with clubs only, into the enemy's ranks, and fell one after the other upon heaps of soldiers whom they had slain. The succour from Coire came too late. The whole country of Prätigau was already in flames, and the population almost entirely destroyed.

The Grisons leagues sent envoys to the archduke of Austria at Lindau, but they had to submit to hard conditions. The league of the Ten Jurisdictions was declared to belong to Austria, and free passage was to be allowed through the whole Grisons country to the Austrians and Spaniards. The king of France, Louis XIII, who was jealous of the Austrian power, had already interfered by negotiations, in concert with the duke of Savoy and the senate of Venice, to prevent the permanent occupation by Spain and Austria of the important passes of the Grisons and the Valtellina. At last, in 1624, he sent a force under the count de Cœuvres into the Grisons country. Bern and Zurich not only gave a free passage but added their contingents. All the exiled Grisons, under Rudolf von Salis and Jenatsch, led the van. As they reached the frontier of their country a general rising took place, and the Austrian garrisons and governors were driven away. The following year Chiavenna and the Valtellina were reconquered from the Spaniards. The treaty concluded at Monçon, in Aragon, between France and Spain, in 1626, settled for a time the affairs of the Grisons, though not to the full satisfaction of the latter, who still clung pertinaciously to their rights of sovereignty over the Italian valleys. The Valtellina, Chiavenna, and Bormio were to pay an annual tribute to the leagues, but they had the right of governing themselves. Some troops in the service of the pope garrisoned the towns of Valtellina *pro tempore;* and Robustelli remained at the head of the regency of the valley.

In 1628 the disputes about the duchy of Mantua brought the French again into Italy. The Austrian armies sent to oppose them entered suddenly the country of the Grisons, by the pass of Luciensteig, took Coire [1629], and again occupied the Ten Jurisdictions and the Engadine. Although this time there was no slaughter of the inhabitants, yet vexations of every sort were heaped on them. Famine followed, and a pestilence brought by the German troops, probably from the frontiers of Turkey, devastated the unfortunate Rhætian valleys; twelve thousand people died of the latter scourge. Luckily for the Grisons the successes of Gustavus Adolphus in Germany induced the emperor to conclude with France the Treaty of Cherasco, in 1630, by which he engaged to withdraw his troops from the Grisons. The duke of Rohan then came to Coire as ambassador from France and brought with him some troops, who assisted the Grisons in fortifying their passes towards the Tyrol.

In 1635, war having broken out again between France and the emperor, Rohan, at the head of a Grisons force, crossed the Alps, and after some sharp fighting, reconquered Valtellina, Chiavenna, and Bormio from the Austrians and Spaniards united. But the court of France now imperiously required that the Italian valleys should be governed according to the Treaty of Monçon. The French envoy Lanier, an overbearing man, assumed the tone of a master at Coire, and talked of the Grisons as rebels. The Grisons chiefs said among themselves, "Austria takes and France lies; let us trust no foreign power, but seek help only from our own arms."

In February, 1636, several of the principal men of the leagues assembled at Coire and swore to risk their all to deliver their country from all foreign domination. Colonel Jenatsch was of the number, and he with great secrecy negotiated a treaty at Innsbruck with the archduke of Austria, nephew to the emperor Ferdinand II, by which the former relations of friendship between the two countries were restored, and Austria promised to co-operate in driving the French out of the Grisons. Jenatsch armed his countrymen secretly; but the duke of Rohan, nevertheless, suspecting something, reinforced his posts on the banks of the Rhine and of the Landquart. On a sudden Jenatsch, with six battalions of his countrymen, appeared before the French intrenchments, while at the same time a body of Austrians showed itself at Lindau, threatening the rear of the French, who, fearful of being surrounded [1637], agreed to withdraw, which they did to the number of about five thousand; and this time the deliverance was complete, for no foreigners remained in the Grisons country. The Grisons were left in possession of the Italian valleys, to which they granted a full amnesty, besides acknowledging the Catholic religion as that of the country.

Spain made a perpetual peace with the Grisons at Milan in September 1639, on the above conditions, and Austria, too, renewed its former treaties with the leagues at Feldkirch, in August, 1641, preserving its seigniorial rights and fees in the Engadine and the Ten Jurisdictions: these, however, were

[1602–1608 A.D.]

bought off ten years after by the payment of 75,000 florins. Thus Austria ceased to have any jurisdiction in the Grisons territory excepting the baronies of Räzuns and Tarasp.

The brave Colonel Jenatsch, two years after he had freed his country, was murdered in January, 1639, while at a party of officers at Coire. Conspirators entered the hall in disguise, and pressing round him, as if in sport, murdered him in the middle of the festival. Rudolf Planta, being accused by public rumour of having thus avenged the murder of his brother Pompey, withdrew to his estates in the Engadine, where he died some time after.

Meantime the Thirty Years' War was proceeding in Germany. With the result of that war the Swiss were deeply concerned, for had the house of Austria, assisted by its relatives of Spain, succeeded in laying the German confederation at its feet, the Swiss cantons would not have been left long in the enjoyment of their civil and religious liberties. The conduct of the Austrians towards the Grisons, the allies of the Helvetic League, sufficiently showed what the cantons themselves had to expect. The termination, however, of that great contest by the Peace of Westphalia eventually put the seal to the independence of Switzerland.[b]

SWITZERLAND IN THE THIRTY YEARS' WAR

In the sixteenth century the house of Habsburg fought for the ancient church and the mediæval unity of all Christian people, in order first of all to gain political predominance but in the end undivided sway. The successors of Philip II renewed the struggles that had distinguished the reign of that monarch. Their mighty enemy the king of France again sought to double his strength by alliance. He obtained the services of the Swiss through an advantageous treaty [1602] and many proofs of friendliness; he encouraged the reformed states of the empire in the formation of the "evangelical union" (May, 1608) which was backed by himself; he was on good terms with England and the emancipated Netherlands. In Italy the fear of the boundless ambition of the Habsburgs brought him much support (such as that of Savoy, Venice, etc.). Under the guise of a great liberator and peace-maker Henry now dreamed of making France the sovereign of the whole of Europe. Such a design threatened to involve Switzerland in the vicissitudes of external and internal wars and in difficult relations with the other great powers.

SWISS GUARD

Through the renewal of a league with the Catholic districts of the confederation [1602] Spain weakened betimes the French influence; therefore France in a particular compact claimed the assurance that Switzerland would allow no passage to the enemy's troops. The open partisanship for Spain of the five [Catholic] districts might have excited the reformed towns to enter the German "union"; but they refused all invitations to join the allied princes. They also evaded an alliance with Sweden; but Zurich and Bern consented to a defensive alliance with the markgraf George Frederick of Baden-Durlach, a member of the union (August 19th, 1612, for twelve years): for the most part the evangelical districts (*Orten*) kept up a friendly correspondence with the united imperial states about their political condition.

Meantime the sudden death of Henry IV thwarted the expectations of his supporters and allies. Spain now exploited the universal fluctuations in political circumstances in order to establish her power. The duke of Savoy (Charles Emanuel) again joined the Spanish court, and counting upon the latter's assistance he fitted out an expedition against Geneva and the Vaud (1610-1611); but the watchfulness of the Bernese prevented his gaining a decisive battle. When his claims to the principality of Montferrat caused him to quarrel with the Habsburgs, he made friends with Venice, which was on the point of an alliance with the Swiss, and sought help from the enemies of Spain. In honour of the Protestant powers, he began negotiations with Bern as to an alliance which was brought about by English mediation (June 23rd, 1617), after Savoy had formally renounced all pretensions to Vaud.

From the ecclesiastical differences of the German Empire finally arose a war lasting many years [known as the Thirty Years' War], which affected the confederation in various ways. The evangelical towns had repeatedly been in fear of a united attack by the Catholic "districts" and the Habsburg supremacy, and they therefore made preparations for their defence; they proposed a common evangelical *defensionale* (military organization), but did not succeed in carrying through this scheme, because Bâle refused to co-operate, in order not to excite opponents. At the time of nearer danger, the reformed states made inquiries as to the disposition of the Catholic districts, who each time promised to provide their federal contingent. When the emperor after the victory over Denmark (1625-1627) carried an army into Germany, which, as its leader threatened, was to "bring the rebellious Swiss into order" get back the old Habsburg possessions and repress the reformed church, the Catholic districts felt moved as confederates to make declarations by oath and to conclude certain treaties. This attitude pacified the evangelicals.

Preparations were unanimously made for the protection of the common bailiwicks. A commission took in hand the numbering and collecting of those capable of bearing arms: it inspected the arsenals, fortresses, and passes on the frontiers; provided for good guards and quick assembling of troops; and the provincial governors received extended powers. As Austria imperiously claimed the free use of the Alpine passes, the Swiss diet resolved to hold their first contingent of troops in readiness for defence against foreign powers, and to equip the rest of the men without delay; the proposal of the confederate *defensionale* was seriously considered.

The proclamation of the Edict of Restitution at this time also disgusted the evangelical towns (March 6th, 1629). The ecclesiastical princes (Bâle, Constance, St. Gall, etc.) demanded the immediate restitution of the churches, property, and lordship which had been lost for a century, and, as they were openly supported by the emperor, the reformers had fresh reason for establishing a strict defensive alliance. Confidently relying on foreign assistance, the five districts meantime defended with all their power the claims of the prince abbot and the bishop of Constance; on the other side Zurich held firm to the prescriptive authority of her "divorce court" and the rights of the reformed congregations. The bitter feeling rose to such a pitch that only danger from the outside could prevent a civil war.

The Baden Compromise; Struggles concerning Neutrality of Soil

By the victories of the Swedish king Gustavus Adolphus (1630-1632) Austria was driven into a corner. She proposed without result an alliance with the confederation. The evangelical towns declared themselves neutral; but as the five districts continually violated this neutrality by giving the Spanish troops leave to pass through them, Gustavus Adolphus at last threatened to carry the war into Switzerland (April, 1632). This declaration had the effect of restricting at once the privilege of marching through neutral territory, and of inducing the Catholics to seek a reconciliation with Zurich. A court of equity did away with the quarrel about "restitution" through the Compromise of Baden (September 7th, 1632), the acceptance of which was brought about by the French ambassador (Rohan).

Scarcely had the religious parties made up their quarrel and resolved on unanimous action when internal peace was again disturbed by the "attack in the defiles." A number of Bernese intended for the protection of Mülhausen, who were marching along the usual road through the territory of Solothurn were stopped at a narrow pass near Balsthal, in order that inquiries might be made as to whether they were on their way to join the Swedes. The government called all the people to arms, but finally, on the indignant explanation of Bern, granted freedom of passage (September 20th). Scarcely had the Bernese set forward on their journey when the governors Roll and Brumer fell upon them, in order to crush the "heretics." Fifteen men were killed, the rest wounded and plundered. The government of Solothurn, deceived by false reports, refused to give the compensation demanded. Thereupon Bern stopped supplies and prepared to obtain satisfaction by violence. Solothurn gave warning of the matter to the confederation; part of the diet decided to defend the guilty to the utmost; the independent districts, however, forced them to bring the offenders under the law and to pacify Bern by an example of strict justice. Roll was banished for ten, Brumer for six years, their property confiscated; and three peasants, as chief participators, were executed.

Still more seriously was peace endangered by an invasion of the Swedish army (September, 1633). General Horn forced a passage through Stein [canton of Zurich] and marched over Swiss territory to besiege the town of Constance. Enraged at this violation of declared neutral ground, the five districts demanded restitution from Zurich. As the latter made restitution, though with complaints, she was suspected of having made a secret treaty with Sweden. Three thousand men from the Catholic territories marched into the district of St. Gall to protect the abbot. In the meantime the Swedes decamped, after unsuccessfully bombarding Constance, and returned to Germany. But the mistrust of the Catholics could only be allayed by a sacrifice. As a citizen of Zurich, the military commandant of Thurgau, Kilian Kesselring, fell under the suspicion of having secretly hindered the assembling of the militia. He was taken prisoner and put on the rack. As he firmly maintained his innocence, he was taken into Schwyz, where he was kept seventy weeks in strict confinement. It was only with great effort that Zurich and Bern, whose interference was supported by the independent districts and the French court, could procure his discharge, on the payment by himself of a heavy fine. Zurich compensated him by giving him a lucrative appointment.

These proceedings embittered the public mind to such an extent that the negotiations for a *defensionale* remained in abeyance for three years. The five districts renewed their alliance with Spain (March, 1634), and again agreed to open their roads to the Spanish army and in case of necessity to help to protect Upper Burgundy. Whilst Bâle, Schaffhausen, and Zurich sought to protect their territory and to preserve the neutrality of the Swiss soil, both religious parties participated openly in the victories and defeats of their co-religionists. Many volunteers and mercenaries joined the armies in Germany. On the other hand thousands exchanged their cruelly devastated homes for the peaceful districts of Switzerland.

Bâle found herself in the most difficult position. As a frontier town filled to overflowing with refugees, and a close neighbour of the Austrian forest towns, around which the imperial and the Swedish troops fought with rapid alternations of success, she could only maintain her free position by dint of indefatigable watchfulness, by extraordinary sacrifices and opportune compliance towards an oppressive superiority. In the spring of 1633 the Swedes took possession of the forest towns and Upper Alsace. Bâle was obliged to open her gates to an imperial army of thirty thousand men, in order to spare herself irreconcilable hostility. Rheinfeld and Breifach were conquered by Austria. At the same time the inhabitants of Bâle had to bear with the ill will of the Swedes and to defend themselves against wandering guerrilla troops. When the former had the upper hand they went through the territory belonging to the town without asking for permission, and defiantly obtained the grant of a free passage through her gates. Shortly afterwards the imperial troops requited this favour shown to the enemy with barbarous deeds of violence, which were at last, in October, revenged by a bold sortie.

The Defensionale (1647 A.D.)

To these misfortunes were added an oppressive rise in prices, the plundering of the country by unbridled mercenaries and robber bands, the breaking-out of a ravaging sickness (Lazarus fever), and the growing burden of the foreign beggars. The burghers found a slight compensation for these sacrifices in the advantageous trade in the booty of the marching army, which could not be repressed by the authorities in spite of commands and punishments.

When the district of Freigraf, Alsace, and the bishopric of Bâle were garrisoned by the French — by whom Bâle and Solothurn were endangered — all the thirteen districts reunited for the uniform defence of the frontiers. New proposals for an energetic organisation of defence cropped up. The confederation cautiously sought now to pacify all the powers by a strict neutrality; and yet Bâle could not hinder Duke Bernard of Weimar from breaking into Frickthal through her territory [1636]. The long negotiations about the protection of Freigraf demanded by Spain had no result; even the Catholic districts were not inclined to it. An attempt was made to protect Constance by a fortress. Zurich also began to build extensive earthworks. The reformed towns took foreign war-experts into their service; but they could not agree about effectual preparations for the defence of Bâle and Schaffhausen.

Both religious parties meantime became more and more convinced that they had the worst to expect from outside; and yet a new plan for a regulated guarding of the frontier was not carried out, and once again the confederation, torn with disputes about confessions of faith (about Utwyl and Lustorf), was to be brought to its senses by a threatening danger. The approach of a

[1647-1653 A.D.]

French army under Turenne, of a Swedish one under Wrangel [1647], the attack on Bregenz, the siege of Linden caused them to garrison the eastern border from Sargau to Baden, to appoint a council of war, "and to combine the long matured plans for a common defence of the country, so that they might serve as a workable basis for a lasting organisation." [This was the long-considered *defensionale*, drawn up in 1647, finally adopted in 1668.]

The Swiss Independence Proclamation (1648 A.D.)

During this period negotiations for peace were undertaken in Münster and Osnabruck. The reformed districts resolved to let the confederation be represented by an envoy, and the mayor of Bâle was chosen. He was to free his town from a tiresome lawsuit with the imperial chamber and was to bring into recognition the complete independence of the Swiss League. The interposition of the French and Swedish envoys forced the emperor to lend an ear to the modest ambassador and to undertake an inquiry into the point of law in dispute. In order to break down the stiff-necked resistance of the states of the empire, the claims of the Swiss were at last recognised by the former as their own; the reformed confederation was therefore included in the general peace, and the emperor granted their request. But it was not till a year later that the great proclamation of peace was signed in which the independence of Switzerland was recognised and assured.[e]

THE PEASANTS' WAR (1653 A.D.)

The re-establishment of peace with Germany was a cause for profound uneasiness among the country people of Switzerland. This uneasiness, joined to several other reasons for discontent which the populations were nourishing against their governments, provoked that intestine struggle called the Peasants' War.

In the canton towns the peasants had to complain of the ever-increasing restrictions on their ancient rights and the tyranny of the governments and their bailiffs. In the sixteenth and seventeenth centuries a transformation was taking place in the government of the towns. In the beginning the magistrates were elected by the burgher class who, when united in general assembly, had besides the right of dealing with important affairs of the community. As time went on those families which had most frequently furnished functionaries to the republic evinced a tendency to separate themselves from the rest of the citizens and form a distinct class. In the town the government changed from democracies to aristocracies. Thus at Bern, Fribourg, Solothurn, and Lucerne, in the seventeenth century, a certain number of families of the higher classes already possessed the privilege of having sole access to office. The townsfolk were not only excluded, but saw their ancient political rights taken away. Thence arose an ever-increasing discontent.

The country people were loaded with burdens. Feudal rights still weighed upon them. Besides the tithe and quit rent there were all kinds of taxes to pay to the bailiffs, and these latter did not fail to inflict fines for the smallest offence. One of the consequences of the Thirty Years' War was to aggravate the people's condition already miserable enough. To meet the expenses contracted by the obligation of having to furnish the frontier troops on the German side, the government had recourse to war taxes, to import and export duties, to wine *(Ungeld, Ohmgeld)*, salt, cattle dues, etc.

During the war a number of rich Germans had sought shelter in Switzer-

[1653 A.D.]

land. Thence had resulted an augmentation of value in land and buildings.
The price of provisions had gone up considerably. Unfortunately, the country people took advantage of this increase in their incomes to live well — even
luxuriously — acquiring wasteful habits difficult to get rid of. When, the
Peace of Westphalia being concluded, the foreigners returned home, property
reverted to its original value and the price of everything went down one half.
Thence arose deep discontent, which became greater when several thousand
mercenaries who had served in Germany and France, and lost while in camp
all working habits, returned to the cantons.

An arbitrary measure taken by several governments caused revolt to burst
out. Switzerland was flooded with false and debased coinage. Bern, Lucerne,
Fribourg, and Solothurn considerably lowered the price of this money. This
augmented the disorder which already reigned in the monetary system, and
filled up the cup of misery for the poor. The peasants rose, incapable of supporting the yoke laid upon them by the town aristocracy.

The Revolt of Entlebuch

The signal for revolt was given by Entlebuch. The inhabitants of this
valley had become subject to Lucerne after the Sempach War, and had retained
important franchises. To defend these they had already revolted six times.
When the Lucerne government, following the example of Bern and Fribourg,
had fixed a tax on cattle, salt, hunting and fishing, and finally had determined
on debasing the currency (December, 1652), the Entlebuchers passed from
complaint to revolt. They sent delegates to headquarters to expose their
wrongs. But these obtained no hearing; a councillor, Krebsinger, threatened
them, saying: "With regard to the Entlebuchers we have long and fruitlessly
tried gentle and kind measures. They are turbulent and irrational beings
who will never return to reason until we have sent four or five hundred bullet-
proof Italians against them."

This suggestion, carried back to the mountaineers by their principal
deputy, Jean Emmenegger, gave rise to great irritation. A king's officer from
headquarters who came to claim the payment of some debts was seized and
bound by the "three Tells,"[1] Stadelmann, Unternacher, and Hintervoli; then
conducted to the frontier amidst the jeers of the people. On the 26th of
January, 1653, all the parishioners of Entlebuch, the vicars leading, went in
procession to the church of Heiligenkreuz near the village of Hasle on a
mountain which dominated all the country. There the Entlebuchers swore
mutually to maintain their rights against all.

On their renewed refusal to send deputies to Lucerne, the government
delegated to them the chief magistrate Dulliker and some councillors. At
the Schüpfheim parliament, whereat fourteen hundred armed mountaineers
assisted, the offers made by the magistrate were rejected and ever-increasing
exigencies formulated. Dulliker reminded them that magistrates held authority from God. "Yes, yes," cried the giant Krummenacher; "you come from
God when you are just, but from the devil when you are not." The delegation had to return without having gained anything.

The revolt spread rapidly in the rest of the canton, where the same causes
of discontent existed. Five bailiwicks alone remained faithful to the government. On the 20th of February an assembly of delegates from ten bailiwicks took place at Wolhusen, where a pact of alliance (Bundesbrief), pre-

[[1]They dressed in the traditional costumes of the heroes of the Rütli, symbolising the
spirit of that time.]

pared by Emmenegger, was signed. Peasants of Bern and Solothurn took part in this assembly, and, when they returned home, sowed seeds of revolt. The Lucerne government feared the *bourgeoisie* of the large towns almost as much as the peasants. On hearing of these events they requested the intervention of the Catholic cantons. These succeeded after much trouble in getting a compromise accepted by both sides (March 18th).

Now everything seemed over. But, on the contrary, the fight was just beginning. The Bernese who were at Wolhusen had brought back the text of the alliance the Lucerne peasants had made and provoked much stir in Emmenthal and upper Aargau. Insurrection rapidly spread in Bern, Solothurn, Aargau, and Bâle.

The diet sitting at Baden, for its part, decreed a levy of thirteen thousand men and issued a threatening proclamation to the insurgents. These measures and a few concessions quieted the rising for awhile, but it began again almost immediately. Not having any confidence in promises from the Lucerne government, the Entlebuchers refused them obedience. Their emissaries succeeded in relighting insurrection in the Bern, Solothurn, and Bâle countries. On the 23rd of April, in an assembly of delegates held at Sumiswald, a rich peasant, Nicholas Leuenberger, of Schönholz, of the Ruderswyl commune, was, in spite of himself, proclaimed head (Obmann) of the Peasants' League, whose pact of alliance was solemnly sworn to.

Nicholas Leuenberger, a man of heart and good sense, lacked the activity, energy, and decision necessary to direct the movement. The peasants lost time in fresh popular assemblies at Hutwyl and Langenthal, thus giving the diet and the aristocratic governments of Lucerne, Bâle, Bern, and Zurich all time necessary to prepare means of resistance.

The diet ordered a levy of twenty-five thousand men, divided into three corps; the first, under Conrad Werdmüller, of Zurich, was to go into the free bailiwicks and lower Aargau; the second, commanded by Zweier von Evebach, of Uri, was to occupy the Lucerne country; while a third, under Sigismund von Erlach, of Bern, was commissioned to repress the revolt in Emmenthal and upper Aargau.

When these measures of the diet came to be known in the country, Leuenberger, the "peasant king," sounded an alarm for a general rising. More than thirty thousand insurgents took up arms. At the head of twenty thousand men, Leuenberger bore down upon Bern. The government saw itself obliged to negotiate and come to an arrangement [Peace of Murifeld, May 24th].

The Defeat at Wohlenschwyl (1653 A.D.)

During this time, the peasants of Aargau and Lucerne, commanded by an old and intrepid soldier of Lucerne, Christian Schybi, of Escholzmatt, had gone on in front of Conrad Werdmüller, who was advancing on Aargau with nine thousand eastern Swiss. Leuenberger came up to join with Schybi. The insurgents, in number about twenty thousand, but badly armed and directed, attacked Werdmüller near Wohlenschwyl and fought heroically until the evening (June 3rd).

The next day, gained over by conciliatory words from the Zurich burgomaster Waser, the peasants of Aargau laid down arms, under a promise that their wrongs should be examined by arbitrators in conformity to federal right. Schybi, full of blind rage, returned into the Lucerne canton with his men. Leuenberger, discouraged and heart-broken, retired to Langenthal.

General Zweier von Evebach, who with troops from the small cantons was in garrison at Lucerne, attacked Schybi near the bridge of Gislikon (June 4th, 5th). After a resistance worthy of the old confederates, the peasants dispersed. In the Bern canton, Sigismund von Erlach, at the head of eight or nine thousand men, the greater part from Vaud and Neuchâtel, entered upper Aargau, which he gave up to pillage. Leuenberger managed to unite five thousand Emmenthal peasants and fought fiercely near Herzogenbuchsee (June 8th). The country folk, after a desperate defence, were put to flight. At the same time the Solothurn and Bâle insurgents laid down their arms.

Cowardly in danger, cruel after victory, were the aristocratic governments of Bern, Lucerne, and Bâle. The chiefs of the federal army constituted themselves a criminal tribune at Zofingen. Solothurn, where the peasants had only taken a feeble part in the revolt, was forced to deliver up eighteen men to the tribunal. Among the number was found the under-bailiff Adam Zeltner, who, against his own wishes, had been drawn into the revolt. When a decision had to be given as to his fate seven judges voted for decapitation, seven against it. Werdmüller, called upon to give the presidential vote, pronounced for death, being deaf to the prayers of Zeltner's wife and six children. Schybi underwent the cruellest tortures with courage and died on the scaffold. Leuenberger, who had retired and occupied himself with his own affairs, was given up by a traitor and led to Bern, a wooden sword at his side and a straw scarf round his body. After two months of durance in prison, he who in power had given proof of such extreme moderation was decapitated and his body quartered (September).

Governmental vengeance was wreaked on several hundred individuals. The number of executions was forty-eight. Many of the insurgents were mutilated, thrashed, thrown into dungeons, condemned to fines, or confiscation of goods with exile. Zurich, whose population had not joined in the fray, demanded from the confederates 40,000 florins for war expenses. Bern very reluctantly paid a share; the greater part was imposed on Solothurn, which was accused of encouraging or at least tolerating the insurgents. In revenge, the government of Solothurn signed a private alliance with France (1654). Such were the immediate results of the Peasants' War.

Triumphant, the aristocratic governments of Bern, Lucerne, Bâle, Fribourg, Solothurn, and even Zurich made rapid progress towards oligarchy — that is, not an entire ascendancy of the higher classes, but of a small number of privileged families. The people, crushed beneath the yoke, had, until the French Revolution, a fate as little enviable as that of subjects under despotic monarchs around Switzerland.*f*

THE BATTLE OF VILLMERGEN

Scarcely was the peasant insurrection well disposed of, when a new dispute broke out among the cantons of the confederacy. This was a fresh manifestation of that unchristian hatred which prevailed between Protestants and Catholics. The clergy on both sides, instead of extinguishing the flame of discord, blew it up by their preaching.

There never were wanting occasions of dispute among the governments, especially in the common or free bailiwicks, where each contended exclusively for its own creed and its own jurisdiction; and none reposed confidence any longer in their colleagues, as none would believe anything but evil of the rest. The Catholics would not believe that Bern and Zurich built fortifications and entered into alliances with Holland and with England for nothing.

The Protestants complained of the Catholics, for confirming the Borromean League [1655], renewing their alliance with Savoy and the bishop of Bâle, and keeping up relations of close amity with the court of Spain.

It happened that six families of Art, in the canton of Schwyz, were obliged to fly for holding the evangelical persuasion, as their lives were hardly safe in their native village. They presented themselves with tears and prayers before the council of Zurich, and only begged that the free transport of their property might be procured for them. Upon this the council of Zurich addressed pressing intercessions to Schwyz in behalf of these persecuted people; but Schwyz refused to listen to their overtures, and demanded the surrender of the persons of the refugees. When upon this the reformed cantons appealed to the rights of the confederacy, Schwyz replied: "Within our own land we owe no account to any one, except to God and to ourselves." Moreover they confiscated the goods of the emigrants, threw their relatives (as they also were of the Protestant persuasion) into prison, put some of them to the torture, and condemned others to death.

Zurich now [1656] took up arms, as all admonition and mediation from the neutral cantons at diets had been useless. With equal celerity, Schwyz and the Catholic cantons were in the field. Zurich, supported by Bâle, Mülhausen, and Schaffhausen, marched troops towards the Rhine, occupied the Thurgau, and besieged Rapperschwyl. But the Catholics had already occupied Rapperschwyl and the Albais, as well as Bremgarten, Mellingen, and Baden, and the Brünig, on the side of Bern. The Bernese sent detachments to the defence of Fribourg, Solothurn, and Unterwalden, and marched to Lenzburg with forty banners to the succour of the Zurichers.

There was, however, nothing like discipline in the ranks of the reformers. They sacked and burned wherever they came, pillaged the monastery of Rheinau, plundered villages and churches, and drove off the cattle. So little order was preserved by the Bernese that they encamped in the district of Villmergen, without troubling themselves at all about the enemy; sent out no scouts; and were not even provided with sufficient ammunition. And although some men of the Aargau had descried the enemy by the village of Wohlen, and gave the alarm to the Bernese, yet no attention was paid to them, as some young men of Bern had ridden out to reconnoitre and reported that all was safe.

More than four thousand men of Lucerne, in effect, lay in ambush on the heights of Wohlen. From a ridge in the hollow way, where they were covered up to the waist, they suddenly opened a fire on the Bernese lines. These fell into such a panic and confusion that they could hardly be formed in order of battle. As powder and ball were deficient, they discharged only two rounds from their field pieces; the rout was general. Ten fresh squadrons, indeed, came to their aid; but those wheeled about and took to flight along with the rest. The general of Lucerne had in his pocket during the action a letter from his government containing an order not to fight, as a peaceable arrangement was in progress: but he put it up unopened, as he could guess at the contents, and pursued the flying Bernese, of whom a vast number were cut to pieces. They lost about eight hundred men, and eleven pieces of heavy artillery. A strong body of Bernese troops were posted in the neighbourhood and saw the flight of their countrymen towards Lenzburg, but did not leave their position, not having orders.

Such was the fatal battle of Villmergen. The victors lay encamped, exulting, three days on the field of battle; they then marched homewards, loaded with plunder. A few weeks afterwards an armistice and finally a peace were concluded. The pacification restored things to their previous situation. In matters of religion, and with regard to freedom of transit for goods between one canton and another, each canton retained the power of acting in its own domain at its own pleasure. Peace was now restored without the spirit of peace. Both sides were exhausted; but the damage done reciprocally remained without compensation, and the minds of both parties were embittered more than ever. It lacked but a slight impulse to occasion a renewal of warfare.

An officer of Lucerne, who had levied troops for the service of Spain, marched them through the Thurgau, and led them, with drawn sabres, into the Protestant church of Rapperschwyl. Thence a woman pursued them with curses and horrible cries to Wigoldingen, where the population were speedily up in arms against the Spanish soldiers, five of whom were slain, some wounded and others taken prisoners. This event [1664] called up the reformed and Catholic cantons in arms. Troops were levied; the five Catholic cantons immediately occupied Kaiserstuhl, Mellingen, and Bremgarten. Much debate and negotiation followed. The Catholic cantons were not to be pacified save by blood. Two men of Wigoldingen were sentenced to death by the majority of the cantons, which exercised sovereignty over the Thurgau, notwithstanding Zurich's urgent solicitations for their pardon. The commune of Wigoldingen being sentenced to pay the whole expenses of the lengthened dispute, collections were made in aid of that object in all the churches of Zurich.

Similar disputes were very frequent in these times; and persecutions on account of faith were practised without mercy. Thus sorrow and distress were introduced into many households. Contagious sickness next was added to all the other sources of misery, which carried off numbers, especially in Bâle and in the Aargau.

SECOND VILLMERGEN WAR

Many of the Swiss, though called free, were poor subjects, possessed of fewer rights than the subjects of kings; nay, force and fraud were often used without scruple to extirpate, little by little, the few franchises of the people, that the power of their lords might luxuriate without limits. The people had a special experience of this in the district of Toggenburg. In former times, through the favour of the old counts of Toggenburg, the communes had enjoyed important privileges in this district — participation in the appointment of the higher and lower courts of justice, and in general assemblies called to consult upon the military and civil administration. No landvogt, moreover, could be imposed on them but by election from amongst the native inhabitants.

But the abbots of St. Gall having purchased of the barons of Raron the jurisdiction over the land which the latter had acquired by inheritance from the old counts of Toggenburg, the new possessors aimed in their turn at privileges which, far from having purchased, they had formally acknowledged to belong to the people. And in like manner as the people of Toggenburg had set up, for the protection of their freedom, a common-law jurisdiction with the cantons of Schwyz and Glarus, so, in 1649, the abbot also established a defensive league with the same cantons, for the maintenance of his territorial rights. As his abbacy was connected with the confederacy, and he himself bore the title Prince of the Holy Roman Empire, he always knew how to take advantage of his two fold title. He opposed himself to the emperor, when it suited him, in his quality of confederate; to the confederates as prince of the empire and delegate of imperial majesty; and thus he made his double character stand him in good stead.

He now began to speak of the freedom of Toggenburg in ambiguous terms, and went so far as to call the people his vassals, in order to accustom them to become such. At last he attacked their franchises openly, and much debate took place before the diets of the confederacy. These, however, seconded his pretensions. The people were prohibited from holding assemblies; and the war administration of the country fell, in 1654, entirely into the abbot's hands.

At length, the abbot Leodegar considered himself absolute lord in the land; he commanded the people to make and to maintain at their own cost a new highway, and when the delegates of the people dared to remonstrate that this would be a burden more oppressive than had formerly been the feudal service from which they had already bought themselves free, he condemned them to a heavy fine, to public recantation, and he declared them disarmed and dishonoured. The oppressed Toggenburgers now brought their complaints before Schwyz and Glarus. Glarus took the distress of the poor peasantry to heart, as also did Schwyz [1702], although the Toggenburgers professed the reformed faith. "And even though they were Turks and heathens," cried the Schwyzers in the general assembly, "they are nevertheless our countrymen and confederates, and we should help them to assert their rights." This incensed the abbot, who appealed to all the cantons on behalf of his confederate rights.

Now came diet upon diet, from year to year. Many were well-inclined towards the Toggenburgers, on account of their reformed and oppressed faith; many hostile to the abbot, for having shortly before closed a defensive alliance with Austria [1702], and for appearing to regard the county of Toggenburg as a fief held of the emperor and the empire. At length the old religious hatred threw in its venom; for so soon as Schwyz and the other Catholic cantons perceived that Zurich and Bern afforded assistance to the Toggenburgers chiefly on the ground of their common faith, and encouraged them to stand fast for their old rights, Schwyz [1707] became better inclined to the abbot of St. Gall. This, however, did not deter Zurich and Bern from their purpose, nor the citizens of Toggenburg from the exercise of their franchises. The imperial envoy now stepped in with a missive from his court, of which the purport was that the emperor would settle the affair, as the county of Toggenburg had indubitably, from time immemorial, been a fief of the empire; but Zurich and Bern replied that Toggenburg lay within the Swiss frontier, and that the abbot of St. Gall had long acknowledged them as arbitrators. Moreover, the ambassadors of Holland and the kings of England and Prussia encouraged the men of Zurich and Bern in resistance to the emperor.

THE TOGGENBURG WAR

The matter of dispute became more and more indefinite, and tumult and violence now arose in Toggenburg itself. The abbot adhered stiffly to the maintenance of his usurped power. The Toggenburgers refused obedience, and drove away his functionaries; whereupon the abbot posted troops on all the bridges, roads, and passes in the district of St. Gall. Bailiff Dürler, in Lucerne, the most zealous friend of the abbot, called the Catholic cantons out, to keep in check the rebels of Toggenburg. On the other hand, the mayor of Bern, Willading, exhorted the reformed cantons to appeal without delay to the sword, for the old rights of the people of Toggenburg and the safety of the Protestant church.

So soon as the men of Toggenburg saw that Zurich and Bern stood on their side, and that General Bodmer was on his march from Zurich to their aid, with a force of nearly three thousand men, they proclaimed war for the maintenance of their rights against the abbot. Rabholz, an eminent member of the government of Zurich, became their leader. The abbot's cloisters and castles were besieged, and the troops of Zurich ravaged the whole district of St. Gall without the slightest restraint of order or discipline.

Now also Lucerne, Uri, Schwyz, Unterwalden, and Zug took up arms, advanced on Toggenburg, and occupied the county of Baden. The nuncio gave them 26,000 thalers out of the papal treasury; and in Rome prayers were offered up to the saints for their success. Consecrated bullets and amulets were distributed by the priests to the soldiers. Bern, on her part, raised 10,000 crowns from her own treasury, and brought five thousand men into the field. A Bernese force advanced against the Stilli, crossed the Aare, and joined the forces of Zurich at Würelingen these, at the same time, had taken possession of the whole Thurgau.

Under these circumstances, Glarus and Solothurn remained neutral, as likewise did the bishop of Constance. Bâle and Fribourg lamented this civil contest between Swiss and Swiss, and once more exhorted both sides to an amicable agreement; but the admonition came too late. The abbot of St. Gall transported his valuables to Lindau, betook himself to Rossbach, and applied to the town of St. Gall and to the territory of Appenzell and Glarus for assistance; but they promised him nothing further than their neutrality. The emperor, on the other hand, summoned the circle of Swabia, as far as Presburg, in Hungary, to the assistance of the abbot.

Meanwhile, the brave Rabholz had marched into the old abbey-lands; the banners of Bern and Zurich went victoriously through the whole Thurgau, as far as the town of St. Gall: they there placed a garrison in the abbey, and at Rossbach. The panic-stricken abbot had already taken refuge for himself and his valuables at Augsburg. The Toggenburgers, now that their cause was victorious, condemned to death those of the abbot's people who had acted the part of betrayers towards them; they threw off the abbot's dominion altogether, as well as the connection with Schwyz and Glarus, and proposed to the people of Gaster, Utznach, and others to found a free and independent state, like the cantons of the confederacy; and they planned a new constitution, which they brought before the diet at Aarau. But such language displeased the leaders of Bern and Zurich, as they would rather have had the Toggenburgers for subjects than for fellow confederates: even Rabholz, the zealous champion of the Toggenburg cause, declined to second the wishes of the people, although they offered him large sums of money to do so.

Meanwhile infinite wrath and discord prevailed in the Catholic cantons. Some were for peace, others for war. The French and Austrian ambassadors promised assistance; the pope sent money; Fribourg and Solothurn espoused their cause with the Valais, and the whole Catholic portion of the bailiwicks. But those reformed districts, on the other hand, which had hitherto remained quiet, threatened to take up arms; and all of that persuasion in the common bailiwicks actually did take up arms in support of Zurich and Bern. Thus, at this time, nearly 150,000 Swiss stood arrayed for mortal conflict with each other: at no former period had the confederacy taken the field in equal force against a foreign enemy. And so it happened that one sword kept another in the scabbard.

The Peace of Aarau; the Trückli-Bund

While the envoys of the confederacy sat at Aarau and treated of peace, the land-vogt and knight, Ackermann of Unterwalden, marched with five thousand men upon the bridge of Sins, where the forces of Bern lay in their encampment. The priest of Sins, on a previous understanding with Ackermann, had given a banquet to the leaders of the Bernese, in order to lull their vigilance. They were thus taken by surprise, so that they saved themselves with difficulty. Many of the Bernese were slain. Their leader, Meunier, who, with two hundred men, defended himself valiantly, first in the churchyard and then in the church, was obliged at last to give up himself and his men as prisoners: they would infallibly have been cut down without mercy, had not Ackermann, with generous boldness, curbed those bloodthirsty men. The Schwyzers had moreover pressed forward, in the direction of Hütten and Bellenschanz, towards the Lake of Zurich. There, however, they came upon Hans Wertmüller, the vigilant commander of Zurich. Seven hours long the Schwyzers fought — they lost two hundred men; but they were finally compelled to yield to the Zurichers. Among their slain were found consecrated tickets, with numbers, and crosses, and assurances of victory.

Ackermann drew Catholic reinforcements around him from all quarters. His troops were above twelve thousand strong. He marched with vigour through the land by Muri to Wohlen and Villmergen, where the Bernese stood with eight thousand men. Here, in the same region where the Bernese once before had suffered a bloody defeat from the Catholic cantons, in 1656, the turf was again to be reddened with Swiss blood shed by Swiss hands. It was the 25th of July, 1712. The Bernese had taken position near Meiengrün. The thunder of artillery opened the conflict. Six long hours the struggle was protracted. At length the Bernese brought confusion and panic among the champions of the Catholic cantons, broke their ranks and put them to flight. The plain was strewn with the corpses of above two thousand Catholics.

The Toggenburgers having now gained possession of Utznach and Gaster, the town of Rapperschwyl being surrendered to the Zurichers, and the conquerors having pressed from all sides into the Catholic territory, their antagonists at length became intimidated and begged for peace. Already had the cantons of Lucerne and Uri subscribed to the terms of peace at the diet in Aarau; but the peasantry of the former canton, incited by the papal nuncio, as well as by their own priests and monks, would not hear of peace, but had marched against the town to force the government into hostilities, and thence against the Bernese at Villmergen. Here they had rushed on merited destruction.

The general peace of the country was at length concluded at Aarau, on terms of course advantageous to the victors. The five Catholic cantons were not only compelled to cede their rights over Baden, Rapperschwyl, and the lower bailiwicks in favour of Zurich and Bern, but, besides, to take these two preponderant cantons into partnership of dominion over the Thurgau and the Rheinthal, where both religious parties thenceforward exercised equal rights. Glarus remained exclusively in the possession of Bern and Zurich.

The humbled abbot Leodegar of St. Gall would not, however, accept the terms of pacification; and consequently remained, to the day of his death, in obstinate exile. Meanwhile the troops of Bern and Zurich occupied his lands. But when the new abbot, Joseph, in 1718, accepted the above-mentioned terms of peace in Rossbach, his lands were restored, and the Toggen-burgers placed once more in subjection to him; but with augmented rights and franchises, under the guarantee of Bern and Zurich. The pope and his nuncio alone persisted in rejecting the Peace of Aarau, declaring it altogether null and void.

This, however, troubled the reconciled confederates but little: and when the people in some districts of the canton of Lucerne were incited by the clergy against the government, a garrison from Entlebuch was taken into the town, a tax on monasteries demanded of the pope towards covering war expenses, and at the same time the recall of the nuncio Caracciolli was insisted on, who was denounced as the principal promoter of all the mischief. The bitter effects of this war were long felt by the Catholic cantons, which, in carrying it on, had incurred immense expenses. Schwyz imposed on every household a tax of five thalers. Lucerne was compelled to use force in collecting her imposts. Uri could pacify her subjects in the Valle Leventina only by conceding extensive franchises, and by designating them thenceforwards as "well-beloved and faithful countrymen." [d]

With these successes Zurich and Bern at the head of the reformed party gained predominance in the confederation. Since the battle of Kappel in 1531 this had belonged to the Catholic members. These planned revenge. The aged Louis XIV in 1715 concluded an alliance with the five Catholic states and the Valais by which he undertook to have the lands lost in the recent war returned to them. The pact was kept secret and the document itself was concealed in a small iron box, bearing the seals of France and of those Swiss states which were party to the bargain. This mysterious alliance excited considerable alarm among the Protestant states. "For many years," says Daguet,[g] "they thought of the Trückli-Bund (the league of the box) as a sword of Damocles suspended over their heads; and this anxiety, far from rendering them more tolerant toward the Catholics, only embittered all hearts and poisoned them with hate."[a]

BRIEF REFERENCE-LIST OF AUTHORITIES BY CHAPTERS

[The letter *a* is reserved for Editorial Matter]

CHAPTER I. SWITZERLAND TO THE FOUNDING OF THE CONFEDERATION (earliest times to 1291 A.D.)

b STRABO, *Geographica.* — *c* JOHN WILSON, *History of Switzerland,* in the *Cabinet Cyclopœdia.* — *d* FERDINAND KELLER, *Pfahlbauten.* — *e* FREDERIC TROYON, *Habitations lacustres.* — *f* VICTOR GROSS, *Les Proto-helvétes.* — *g* ELISÉE RECLUS, *The Lacustrian Cities of Switzerland,* in *Smithsonian Report* for 1861. — *h* G. O. MONTELIUS, *Die Chronologie der Pfahlbauten,* in *Mittheilungen der Anthropologischen Gesellschaft in Wien. Vol. XXX.* — *i* JOHN LUBBOCK, *Prehistoric Times.* — *j* T. STUDER, *Pfahlbau Bevölkerung,* in *Zeitschrift für Ethnologie,* 1885. — *k* RUDOLF VIRCHOW, in letter prefixed to V. Gross, *Les Proto-helvétes.* — *l* ROBERT MUNRO, *The Lake Dwellings of Europe.* — *m* A. VIEUSSEUX, *The History of Switzerland.* — *n* MICHAEL STETTLER, *Annales.* — *o* JOHANN VON MÜLLER, *Geschichte der Schweizerischen Eidgenossenschaft.* — *p* ALEXANDRE DAGUET, *Histoire de la Confédération suisse.*

CHAPTER II. THE RISE OF THE SWISS CONFEDERATION (1288–1402 A.D.)

c E. A. FREEMAN, *The Historical Geography of Europe.* — *d* A. RILLIET, *Les Origines de la Confédération suisse.* — *e* J. DIERAUER, *Geschichte der Schweizerischen Eidgenossenschaft.* — *f* W. A. B. COOLIDGE, *History of Switzerland,* in the *Encyclopædia Britannica.* — *g* K. DÄNDLIKER, *Histoire du Peuple suisse.* — *k* J. VON MÜLLER, *Geschichte der Schweizerischen Eidgenossenschaft.* — *l* G. MEYER VON KNONAU, *Die Sage von der Befreiung der Waldstätte,* in *Schweizer Oeffentliche Vorträge.* — *m* A. HUBER, *Die Waldstätte, Uri, Schweiz, Unterwalden, etc.* — *n* R. VON RADEGG, *Capella Eremitana.* — *o* JOHN OF WINTERTHUR, *Chronikon Vitodurani,* in W. Oechsli's *Anfänge der Schweizerischen Eidgenossenschaft.* — *p* W. OECHSLI, *Quellenbuch zur Schweizer Geschichte.* — *q* A. VIEUSSEUX, *The History of Switzerland.* — *r* J. WILSON, *History of Switzerland.* — *s* J. VULLIEMIN, *Histoire de la Confédération suisse.*

CHAPTER III. THE CONFEDERATION AT THE HEIGHT OF ITS POWER (1402–1516 A.D.)

b W. A. B. COOLIDGE, *History of Switzerland,* in the *Encyclopædia Britannica.* — *c* A. VIEUSSEUX, *The History of Switzerland.* — *d* J. VULLIEMIN, *Histoire de la Confédération suisse.* — *e* A. DAGUET, *Histoire de la Confédération suisse.* — *f* A. MORIN, *Précis de l'Histoire.* — *g* J. WILSON, *History of Switzerland.* — *h* P. VERRI, *Storia di Milano.* — *i* F. GUICCIARDINI, *Historia di Milano.*

CHAPTER IV. THE SIXTEENTH AND SEVENTEENTH CENTURIES

b A. VIEUSSEUX, *The History of Switzerland.* — *c* J. K. L. GIESELER, *Compendium of Ecclesiastical History.* — *d* J. WILSON, *History of Switzerland.* — *e* J. STRICKLER, *Grundriss der Schweizer-Geschichte.* — *f* MAGUENOT, *Abrégé de l'Histoire de la Suisse.* — *g* A. DAGUET, *Histoire de la Confédération suisse.*

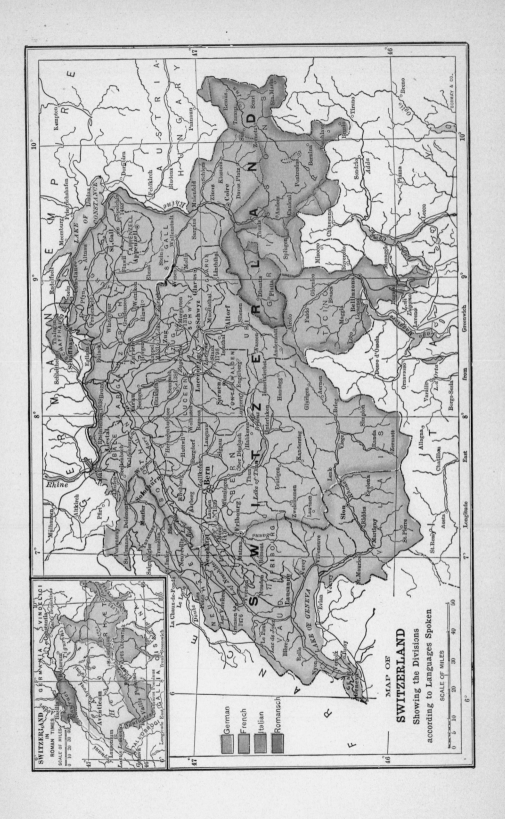

MAP OF
SWITZERLAND
Showing the Divisions
according to Languages Spoken

SCALE OF MILES

German
French
Italian
Romansch

SWITZERLAND
IN
ROMAN TIMES

77